THE CAMBRIDGE HISTORY
OF CHINA

General Editors

DENIS TWITCHETT and JOHN K. FAIRBANK

Volume 5

Part One: The Sung Dynasty and Its Precursors, 907–1279

Work on this volume was partially supported by the National Endowment for the Humanities, Grant RZ-20535-00, and by a grant from the Chiang Ching-Kuo Foundation for International Scholarly Exchange (USA).

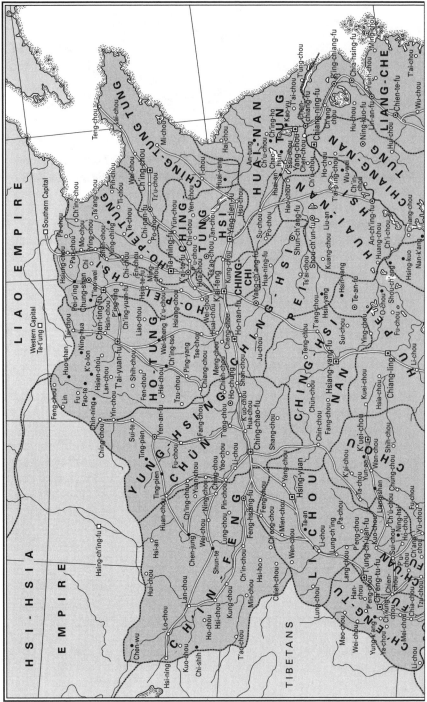

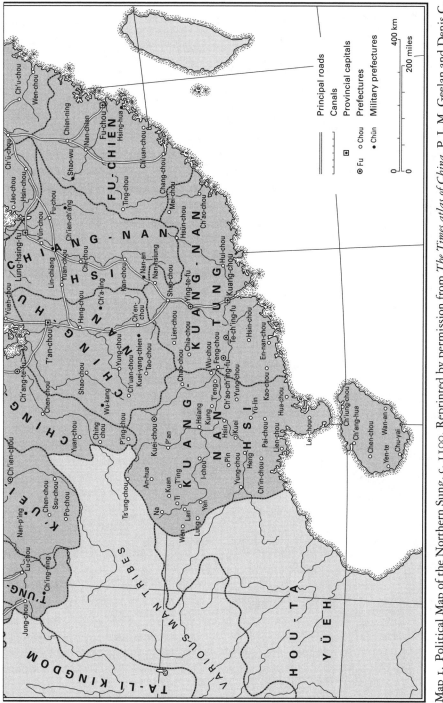

Map 1. Political Map of the Northern Sung, c. 1100. Reprinted by permission from *The Times atlas of China*, P. J. M. Geelan and Denis C. Twitchett, eds. (London: Times Books, 1974).

THE CAMBRIDGE HISTORY OF CHINA

Volume 5
Part One: The Sung Dynasty and Its
Precursors, 907–1279

edited by

DENIS TWITCHETT and PAUL JAKOV SMITH

CAMBRIDGE
UNIVERSITY PRESS

CAMBRIDGE UNIVERSITY PRESS
Cambridge, New York, Melbourne, Madrid, Cape Town, Singapore, São Paulo, Delhi

Cambridge University Press
32 Avenue of the Americas, New York, NY 10013-2473, USA

www.cambridge.org
Information on this title: www.cambridge.org/9780521812481

© Cambridge University Press 2009

First published 2009

Printed in the United States of America

A catalog record for this publication is available from the British Library.

Library of Congress Cataloging in Publication Data
(Revised for volume 5, part 1)
Main entry under title:
The Cambridge history of China.
Bibliography: v. 5, pt. 1, p.
Includes indexes.
1. China – History.   I. Twitchett, Denis Crispin.   II. Fairbank, John King, 1907–
DS735.C3145   951'.03
76-29852

ISBN 978-0-521-81248-1 hardback

In memory of Denis Crispin Twitchett (1925–2006)
Mentor, friend, and inspiration

PREFACE

This volume has been long in the making, many of its authors freshly minted Ph.D.s when recruited by Denis Twitchett in the late 1980s. Since that time sinology in general and the field of Sung history in particular have undergone several significant changes: *pinyin* has become the most widely used form of romanization; authoritative versions of key Sung texts have been made widely accessible online and through the electronic edition of the *Ssu-k'u ch'üan-shu*; and a punctuated, annotated version of the writings of most Sung authors has been issued in the 360-volume *Ch'üan Sung wen*. But the writing of the chapters in this volume predates those changes, which has influenced the conventions we have followed.

With respect to romanization, we continue *The Cambridge history of China* practice of rendering most Chinese terms and proper names (the names of persons, places, official titles, bibliographic entries, and so on) in the Wade-Giles system. Following the example of previously published volumes, we use familiar (pre-*pinyin*) forms for the names of modern provinces (yielding Kiangsi rather than Chiang-hsi or Fukien rather than Fu-chien) and principal cities (such as Peking, not Pei-ching, and Canton rather than Kuang-tung). Otherwise, all place names are in Wade-Giles, according to the standard set in Hope Wright, compiler, *Geographical names in Sung China: An alphabetical list* (Paris: École Pratique des Haute Études, 1956). For both place names and personal names, numbers are used to differentiate between homonyms, such as Chief Councilor Chang Chün and his subordinate General Chang Chün2, or the prefectures of Ho-chou (in Sung Kuang-nan East circuit, modern Kwangsi province) and Ho-chou2 (in Sung Hsi-ho circuit, modern Kansu province). We have sought to ensure that all places mentioned in the text can be found on one of the volume's many maps, but for fuller coverage readers should consult T'an Ch'i-hsiang, compiler, *Chung-kuo li-shih ti-t'u chi*, volume 6: *Sung-Liao-Chin shih-ch'i* (Shanghai: Ti-t'u ch'u-pan, 1982).

Because our authors prepared these chapters prior to the widespread avail-ability of standardized editions or online and electronic text databases and in varying sinological environments, multiple versions of the same work may be cited between chapters and occasionally within the same chapter. Variant editions are all listed in the Bibliography. Translations of terms and official titles are consistent across chapters, with occasional deference to contextual differences. In all matters of translation, romanization, and geographic nomenclature, we aim for a high degree of consistency between this and the companion Volume 5, Part 2. These two volumes, in conjunction with Volume 6 (*Alien regimes and border states, 907–1368*), provide a thorough survey of the history of China and its neighboring states from the tenth through the fourteenth centuries.

CONTENTS

TABLES AND FIGURES

TABLES

FIGURES

MAPS

ACKNOWLEDGMENTS

Of the many debts that have been incurred in the evolution of this volume thanks must first be paid to our contributors. They labored long and hard to produce what were, in many cases, the first English-language narratives of their assigned periods, and it is through no fault of theirs that it has taken so long to get their efforts into print. They, and their department chairs and personnel committees, have shown exceptional forbearance.

Everyone associated with this volume is indebted to the late Denis C. Twitchett, the visionary scholar, mentor, and friend who brought us all together and whose guiding hand has shaped *The Cambridge history of China.* As Denis's coeditor from 2001 to his death in 2006, I was a privileged beneficiary of his profound scholarship and the boundless warmth and generosity of his spirit. Although this would be a stronger work had Denis still been here to give it one final inspection, we hope he would be pleased that it is finally out, and dedicate it to him as a token of our deep esteem.

Many others have helped to bring Volume 5, Part 1, to completion. In working through the various chapters it was always a delight to come across comments and suggestions by the late James T. C. Liu (1919–93), the preeminent Sung historian, who like Denis was friend and mentor to many of us involved in this project. Ralph Meyer, long-time project manager for *The Cambridge history of China,* brought preliminary order to the chapters and to the union glossary and bibliography until his retirement in 2002, when he was ably succeeded by Michael Reeve. John Chaffee and Willard Peterson, editors respectively of Volume 5, Part 2, and Volume 9, Parts 1 and 2, took time from their own volumes to offer valuable advice and assistance on this one. Many of the maps in this volume were initially drafted using Geographic Information System datasets created by the late Robert M. Hartwell (1932–96) and made available to the scholarly community by the China Historical GIS Project at Harvard University; I am grateful to Peter K. Bol and Merrick Lex Berman of Harvard and to the Academic Computing Center of Haverford College for their help with this invaluable resource.

The East Asian Studies Program at Princeton University, directed during the relevant years by Martin C. Collcutt and Benjamin A. Elman, has generously supported *The Cambridge history of China* project in numerous direct and indirect ways. The Project has been privileged to receive financial support from the National Endowment for the Humanities and from the Chiang Ching-Kuo Foundation for International Scholarly Exchange. We are grateful to these institutions for their financial support and the scholarly recognition it implies.

Paul Jakov Smith
2007

ABBREVIATIONS

CPPM	*Tzu-chih t'ung-chien ch'ang-pien chi-shih pen-mo*
CWTS	*Chiu Wu-tai shih*
CYYL	*Chien-yen i-lai hsi-nien yao-lu*
HCP	*Hsü tzu-chih t'ung-chien ch'ang-pien*
HTC	*Hsü tzu-chih t'ung-chien*
SHY	*Sung hui-yao*
SS	*Sung shih*
TCTC	*Tzu-chih t'ung-chien*

Table 1. *Sung Weights and Measures*

Length
  1 *li*   = 1/3 of a mile

Weight
  1 *liang*   = approx. 1.3 ounces
  1 *chin* (catty) = 16 *liang*, approx. 1.3 pounds

Volume
  1 *sheng*   = approx. .86 quart
  1 *tou*   = 10 *sheng*, approx. 2 gallons
  1 *shih* (*tan*) = 100 *sheng*, approx. 2.7 bushels, or 21.5 gallons

Area
  1 *mou* (*mu*) = approx. 1/7 of an acre
  1 *ch'ing*   = 100 *mou*, approx. 14 acres

Currency
  1 *min* (*kuan*) = a unit of account nominally worth 1,000 cash

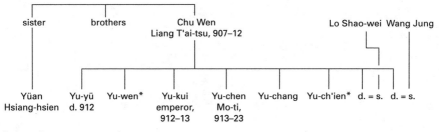

Figure 1. Genealogy of the Later Liang ruling house.

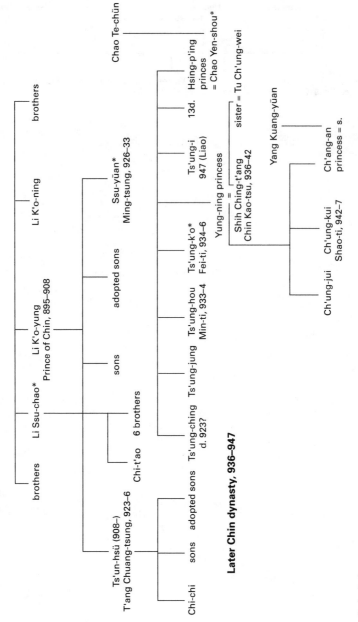

Figure 2. Genealogy of the Later T'ang and Chin ruling houses.

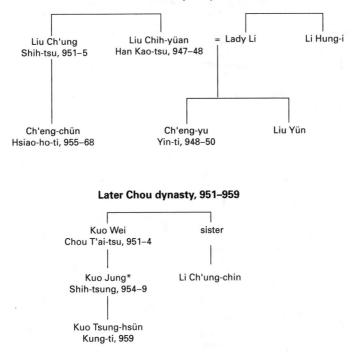

Later Han dynasty, 947–950

Liu Ch'ung
Shih-tsu, 951–5

Liu Chih-yüan
Han Kao-tsu, 947–48 = Lady Li

Li Hung-i

Ch'eng-chün
Hsiao-ho-ti, 955–68

Ch'eng-yu
Yin-ti, 948–50

Liu Yün

Later Chou dynasty, 951–959

Kuo Wei
Chou T'ai-tsu, 951–4

sister

Kuo Jung*
Shih-tsung, 954–9

Li Ch'ung-chin

Kuo Tsung-hsün
Kung-ti, 959

*adopted

Figure 3. Genealogy of the Later Han and Later Chou ruling houses.

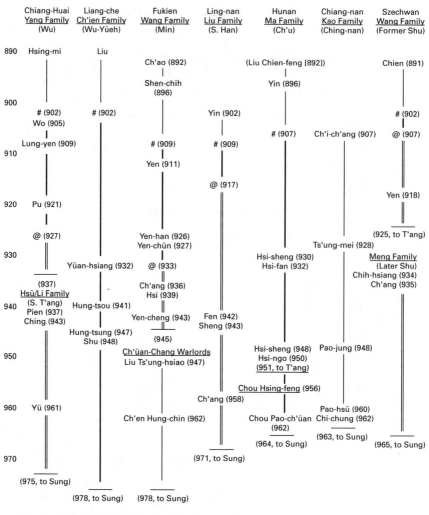

Figure 4. Rulers of the Southern Kingdoms.

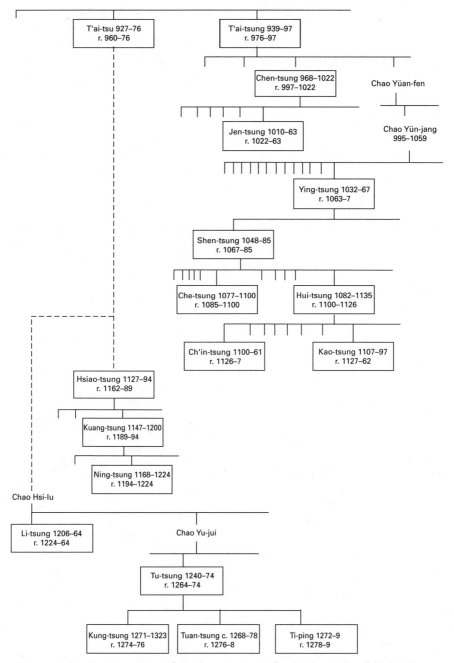

Figure 5. Outline genealogy of the Sung imperial family. *Source:* For full details see Arthur C. Moule, *The rulers of China, 221 B.C.–A.D. 1949: Chronological tables,* with an introductory section on the earlier rulers c. 2100–249 B.C. by W. Perceval Yetts (New York, 1957); James M. Hargett, "A chronology of the reigns and reign-periods of the Song dynasty (960–1279)," *Bulletin of Sung-Yüan Studies* 19 (1987), pp. 26–34; and John W. Chaffee, *Branches of heaven: A history of the imperial clan of Sung China* (Cambridge, Mass., 1999).

Table 2. *Sung Emperors and their Reign Periods*

Name	Dates	Temple Name	Reigned	Reign Periods	Dates
Northern Sung					
Chao K'uang-yin	927–976	T'ai-tsu	960-976	Chien-lung	960–963
				Ch'ien-te	963–968
				K'ai-pao	968–976
Chao K'uang-I	939–997	T'ai-tsung	976–997	T'ai-p'ing hsing-kuo	976–984
				Yung-hsi	984–987
				Tuan-kung	988–989
				Ch'un-hua	990–994
				Chih-tao	955–997
Chao Heng	968–1022	Chen-tsung	997–1022	Hsien-p'ing	998–1003
				Ching-te	1004–1007
				Ta-chung hsiang-fu	1008–1016
				T'ien-hsi	1017–1021
				Ch'ien-hsing	1022
Chao Chen	1010–1063	Jen-tsung	1022–1063	T'ien-sheng	1023–1032
				Ming-tao	1032–1033
				Ching-yu	1034–1038
				Pao-yüan	1038–1040
				K'ang-ting	1040–1041
				Ch'ing-li	1041–1048
				Huang-yu	1049–1054
				Chih-ho	1054–1056
				Chia-yu	1056–1063
Chao Shu	1032–1067	Ying-tsung	1063–1067	Chih–p'ing	1064–1067
Chao Hsü	1048–1085	Shen–tsung	1067–1085	Hsi-ning	1068–1077
				Yüan-feng	1078–1085
Chao Hsü2	1077–1100	Che-tsung	1085–1100	Yüan-yu	1086–1094
				Shao-sheng	1094–1098
				Yüan-fu	1098–1100
Chao chi	1082–1135	Hui-tsung	1100–1126	Chien-chung ching-kuo	1101
				Ch'ung-ning	1102–1106
				Ta-kuan	1107–1110
				Cheng-ho	1111–1118
				Ch'ung-ho	1118–1119
				Hsüan-ho	1119–1125
Chao Huan	1100–1161	Ch'in-tsung	1126–1127	Ching-k'ang	1126–1127
Southern Sung					
Chao Kou	1107–1187	Kao-tsung	1127–1162	Chien-yen	1127–1130
				Shao-hsing	1131–1162
Chao Shen	1127–1194	Hsiao-tsung	1162–1189	Lung-hsing	1163–1164
				Ch'ien-tao	1165–1173
				Ch'un-hsi	1174–1189

Name	Dates	Temple Name	Reigned	Reign Periods	Dates
Chao Tun	1147–1200	Kuang-tsung	1189–1194	Shao-hsi	1190–1194
Chao K'uo	1168–1224	Ning-tsung	1194–1224	Ch'ing-yüan	1195–1200
				Chia-t'ai	1201–1204
				K'ai-hsi	1205–1207
				Chia-ting	1208–1224
Chao Yün	1205–1264	Li-tsung	1224–1264	Pao-ch'ing	1225–1227
				Shao-ting	1228–1233
				Tuan-p'ing	1234–1236
				Chia-hsi	1237–1240
				Ch'un-yu	1241–1252
				Pao-yu	1253–1256
				K'ai-ch'ing	1259
				Ching-ting	1260–1264
Chao Ch'i	1240–1274	Tu–tsung	1264–1274	Hsien-ch'un	1265–1274
Chao Hsien	1271–1323	Kung-tsung	1274–1276	Te-yu	1275–1276
Chao Shih	c. 1268–1278	Tuan-tsung	1276–1278	Ching-yen	1276–1278
Chao Ping	1272–1279	Ti-ping	1278–1279	Hsiang–hsing	1278–1279

Note: Table 2 follows the conventional approach that treats the Chinese lunar year and the Western solar year as essentially coterminous, thus preserving the traditional count of years in each reign period. For a convenient reference see *Chung-kuo li-shih nien-tai chien-piao* (Peking, 1973), pp. 135–56. Reign periods were sometimes changed mid-year, to respond to or to influence significant events. For a translation of the Sung reign-period names, along with a conversion of their inaugural dates to the Western calendar by day, month, and year, see James M. Hargett, "A chronology of the reigns and reign-periods to the Song dynasty (960–1279)," *Bulletin of Sung-Yüan Studies* 19 (1987), pp. 26–34. Emperors are referred to throughout this volume by their temple names (e.g., T'ai-tsu, Kao-tsung, and so on), although these were conferred posthumously. The filiation of the Sung emperors is thoroughly documented in John W. Chaffee, *Branches of heaven: A history of the imperial clan of Sung China* (Cambridge, Mass., 1999).

INTRODUCTION: THE SUNG DYNASTY AND ITS PRECURSORS, 907–1279

Paul Jakov Smith

INTRODUCTION

We present here the first of two volumes on the Sung dynasty (960–1279) and its Five Dynasties (907–60) and Ten Kingdoms (c. 907–79) predecessors. Whereas our companion volume (Volume 5, Part 2) takes a thematic approach to Sung institutional, social, economic, and cultural history, our task here is to present the political history of China from the fall of the T'ang dynasty in 907 to the Mongol conquest of the Southern Sung in 1279. Because our focus is on political events as seen from the perspective of the Sung court, we recommend that this volume be read in conjunction with *The Cambridge history of China*, volume 6: *Alien regimes and border states, 907–1368*, which covers the same period and many of the same events from the vantage point of the non-Chinese regimes and border states that had so momentous an impact on China in this multistate era of the tenth through the thirteenth centuries.[1] This overview will offer a brief introduction to the intersection of political trends and Sino-steppe encounters during the Five Dynasties and Northern and Southern Sung that are portrayed in the chapters to follow.

COMING OUT OF THE T'ANG: STATE BUILDING IN NORTH AND SOUTH

The collapse of T'ang power in the final decades of the ninth century unleashed massive forces of rebellion, warlordism, and territorial fragmentation, giving way to what traditional narratives depict as a half century of political division and social turmoil before the reestablishment of unity and order by Chao K'uang-yin and his new dynasty, the Sung (960–1279). The social turmoil was powerful enough to sweep away the underpinnings of the old T'ang aristocracy and usher in new social and political elites. But as the first two chapters of

---

[1] Herbert Franke and Denis C. Twitchett, eds., *The Cambridge history of China*, volume 6: *Alien regimes and border states, 907–1368* (New York, 1994).

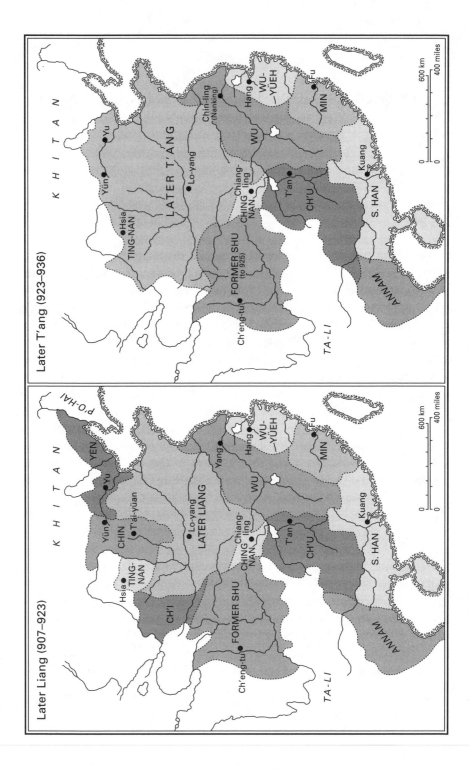

Later Liang (907–923)

Later T'ang (923–936)

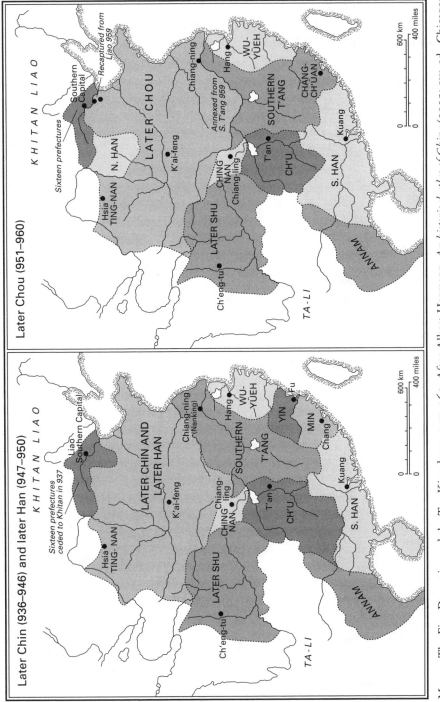

Later Chin (936–946) and later Han (947–950)

K H I T A N   L I A O

Sixteen prefectures
ceded to Khitan in 937

Liao
Southern Capital

Hsia
TING-NAN

LATER CHIN AND
LATER HAN

K'ai-feng

Ch'eng-tu

LATER SHU

CHING
NAN

Chiang-
ling

Chiang-ning
('Nanking')

Hang

WU–YÜEH

SOUTHERN
T'ANG

T'an

CH'U

YIN

MIN

Chang

Fu

Kuang

S. HAN

ANNAM

TA-LI

600 km
400 miles
0

Later Chou (951–960)

K H I T A N   L I A O

Sixteen prefectures

Southern
Capital

Recaptured from
Liao 959

Hsia
TING-NAN

N. HAN

LATER CHOU

K'ai-feng

Chiang-ning

Annexed from
S. T'ang 959

Hang

WU-
YÜEH

CHING
NAN

Chiang-ling

LATER SHU

Ch'eng-tu

T'an

CH'U

SOUTHERN
T'ANG

CHANG-
CH'UAN

Kuang

S. HAN

ANNAM

TA-LI

600 km
400 miles
0

Map 2. The Five Dynasties and the Ten Kingdoms, 907–960. After Albert Hermann, *An historical atlas of China* (1935; rev. ed., Chicago: Aldine Publishing Company, 1966), p. 33.

this volume demonstrate, the picture of chaos and political disorder that has long dominated our understanding of the transitional epoch separating T'ang and Sung must now yield to a view of the Five Dynasties in the north and nine kingdoms in the south as an era of robust state building that laid the foundation for unification under the Sung.

The political trajectory over time and across space during the first half of the tenth century is depicted in Table 3 and Map 2. In terms of territorial expansion, the successive regimes of north China consolidated their control along a north-south axis encompassing all of north China and the Central Plains from the Yellow River south to the Huai and Han rivers, and west along the corridor formed by the Wei River valley and the north face of the Ch'in-ling range. Sovereignty over north China was by no means complete during this period: the T'o-pa-ruled military governorship of Ting-nan, in the southern Ordos region of the future Hsi Hsia domain, remained beyond effective Five Dynasties' dominion; the Sha-t'o stronghold centered on T'ai-yüan (in Sung Ho-tung circuit, or modern Shansi) slipped the noose of central control in 951; and – most momentously for later events – the Sixteen Prefectures comprising the 300-mile barrier between the Central Plains and the steppe were ceded by the Sha-t'o state of Later Chin to the Khitan in 937. But the overall trend was toward the deepening of territorial control, culminating under the fifth, Later Chou, dynasty with the recapture of two of the Sixteen Prefectures (Mo-chou and Ying-chou) in the north and the annexation of the plains between the Huai and Yangtze rivers (the region known as Chiang-Huai) from the Southern T'ang.

The process of territorial consolidation in the north was propelled by the increasingly effective assertion of centralized political authority. Volume 3 of this series documents the devolution of T'ang political power to the military governors (*chieh-tu shih*) and increasingly autonomous generals (many of Sha-t'o descent) in north China.[2] It was these generals, military governors, and regional warlords (like Huang Ch'ao's lieutenant and Later Liang founder Chu Wen) who competed with one another for mastery over the north, and who sought to recreate their own image of the defunct T'ang order that they had helped to destroy. Thus the chief challenge facing the successive would-be dynasts was how to recentralize power from other members of their own kind – in particular, the military governors – while rebuilding the apparatus of the centralized, bureaucratic state.

---

[2] See especially Robert Somers, "The end of T'ang," in *The Cambridge history of China*, volume 3: *Sui and T'ang China, 589–906, part 1*, ed. Denis C. Twitchett (Cambridge, 1979), pp. 682–789. See also Herbert Franke and Denis C. Twitchett, "Introduction," in *The Cambridge history of China*, volume 6: *Alien regimes and border states, 907–1368*, ed. Herbert Franke and Denis C. Twitchett (New York, 1994), p. 10.

The process of recentralization began with the very first Five Dynasties ruler, when the Liang founder Chu Wen began to systematically replace T'ang-era military governors with personally appointed prefects loyal to Chu alone. Although Chu Wen was never able to neutralize the animosity of the major military governors who were deeply opposed to his imperial aspirations and ruthless approach to governance, the four succeeding regimes (three Sha-t'o and one Han Chinese) were able to build on his momentum to impose ever-greater centralizing pressure on the military governors. By midcentury the Later Chou rulers Kuo Wei and his adopted son Ch'ai Jung had begun to win the war of attrition against the once-autonomous military governors. In this, they were assisted by the reemergence of civil officials operating through a regular bureaucracy. But they were also helped by Ch'ai Jung's recentralization of military authority through a series of reforms that transformed the two most potent armies – the Metropolitan and Palace Commands – from unpredictable power brokers to reliable agents of centralized imperial power, finally relieving the Later Chou rulers from dependence on the allegiance of the military governors.[3] Naomi Standen shows that as a consequence of these long-term efforts to reestablish the authority of the state in north China "power had unequivocally moved to the center" by the time the head of the Palace Command, Chao K'uang-yin, deposed his Later Chou masters.

Meanwhile, throughout this half century of ostensible fragmentation a parallel process of state building was taking place in the south. Whereas northern state builders came out of the class of military governors with roots in the T'ang political order, southern rulers emerged out of outlaw elements unleashed by the massive social dislocation and demographic upheavals produced by the rebellions that helped topple the T'ang. In chapter 2, Hugh Clark describes how outlaw adventurers rose to the top of local military confederations and then flowed opportunistically with the shifting migrant tides to assume power in troubled regions far from their original homes, where through a balance of protective and predatory activities they created alliances with the resident elites. As T'ang political authority was seized by Chu Wen and his Later Liang regime in the north, the most powerful military entrepreneurs carved out independent states in the physiographic cores of south China: Wu-Yüeh in the Yangtze delta; Min in the river valleys of Fukien; Wu (followed by its successor state of Southern T'ang) in the elongated valley formed by the lower Yangtze River, P'o-yang Lake, and the Kan River; Southern Han, in the Pearl River lands of Kuang-nan East and Kuang-nan West (modern Kwangtung and Kwangsi), traditionally dubbed Ling-nan; Ch'u, encompassing the Hsiang and

[3] The most important overview of this process is Edmund H. Worthy, Jr., "The founding of Sung China, 950–1000: Integrative changes in military and political institutions" (diss., Princeton University, 1976).

Table 3. *Chronology of the Five Dynasties and Ten Kingdoms*

Regime	Dates	Founder and Origins	Capital and Core Domain
Five Dynasties			
Later Liang	907–923	Chu Wen (852?–912). One-time lieutenant in Huang Ch'ao's rebellion who amasses sufficient military might to capture the T'ang court in 903, murder the last adult T'ang emperor (Chao-tsung, r. 888–904) in 904, then depose Chao-tsung's son and proclaim his own dynasty in 907.	K'ai-feng. North and Central China (Hopei, Shantung, and Honan) south to the Huai and Yangtse rivers, but Shansi and the Peking region beyond Liang control.
Later T'ang	923–936	Li Ts'un-hsü (885–926). Son of Li K'e-yung (856–908), a Shatuo Turk named military governor (and in 895 Prince of Chin) by the T'ang court who, with Khitan help, resists Chu Wen's military advances. Ts'un-hsü carries on struggle against Later Liang, which he destroys in 923.	Loyang. From core region in Shansi, Later T'ang expands well beyond Later Liang borders to control most of intramural north China south to the Huai and Han rivers; neither it nor the succeeding regimes establish effective control over the Ting-nan military governorship centered on Hsia-chou, south of the Ordos.
Later Chin	936–946	Shih Ching-t'ang (892–942). Shatuo Turk and son-in-law of last Later T'ang ruler Li Ssu-yüan.	K'ai-feng. Controls all of Later T'ang territory except for the Sixteen Prefectures spanning Yu-chou (renamed Yen-ching by the Khitan, modern Peking) to Yün-chou (modern Ta-t'ung), which Shih cedes to the Khitan in 937. This strategic barrier protecting north China from the steppe, later termed "The Sixteen Prefectures of Yen-Yün," becomes the chief object of irredentist passions during the Northern Sung.
Later Han	947–950	Liu Chih-yüan (895–948). Shatuo Turk and military governor of the Shansi region centered on T'ai-yüan who takes advantage of the Liao emperor's death following a punitive invasion of Later Chin to establish his own reign.	K'ai-feng. Same as Later Chin.

Later Chou	951–960	Kuo Wei (904–954). Chinese, son of a local T'ang military leader, becomes high military official under Later Han, takes advantage of a military coup to proclaim himself emperor of the Chou. Succeeded by adopted son Kuo (originally Ch'ai) Jung (921–959), who governs effectively with the help of senior military commander Chao K'uang-yin, the Sung founder.	K'ai-feng. Kuo Jung initiates campaign of territorial expansion, culminating in 959 with the capture of two of the Sixteen Prefectures (Ying-chou and Mo-chou) from the Liao and annexation of the Chiang-Huai plains between the Yangtze and Huai rivers from the Southern T'ang. But the Kuo rulers unable to dislodge the Shansi state of Northern Han.

Ten Kingdoms

Wu	902–937	Yang Hsing-mi (b. 851). Lu-chou (mod. Ho-fei, Anhwei) peasant turned bandit chieftain; named military governor by T'ang in 892, then Prince of Wu in 902. Wu rule usurped from within by Southern T'ang, 937.	Yang-chou, then Chin-ling (mod. Nanking). Controlled major portions of the lower Yangtze and Kan River valleys (Huai-nan East and West Chiang-nan East and West circuits during the Sung, modern Anhwei and Kiangsi provinces).
Former Shu	907–925	Wang Chien (c. 848–918). Butcher, salt smuggler, and outlaw leader in Hsü-chou–Ts'ai-chou region (Sung Ching-hsi North, modern Honan), joins T'ang forces against Huang Ch'ao, named military governor of Western Szechwan in 891, assumes title of emperor in 907. Region invaded by Later T'ang in 925.	Ch'eng-tu. Controlled all of the Szechwan basin, the upper Han River valley, and the corridors between Szechwan and northwest China (Sung Ch'in-feng Circuit, modern Shensi and Kansu).
Wu-Yüeh	907–978	Ch'ien Liu (d. 932). Emerges in late 870s as lieutenant to Eight Battalion militia leader Tung Ch'ang in the Yangtze delta region of Liang-che (modern Chekiang). Consolidates power in Hang-chou before turning on Tung Ch'ang in 896 in the name of the waning T'ang court, which names him Prince of Yüeh in 902, then Prince of Wu in 904.	Hang-chou. Controlled rich Yangtze delta and coastal regions of Liang-che circuit (modern Chekiang province).

(*continued*)

Table 3 *(continued)*

Regime	Dates	Founder and Origins	Capital and Core Domain
Min	909–945	Wang Shen-chih. One of three brothers in control of Fukien by 890s; outmaneuvers his elder brother to assume civil and military authority in the northern region centered on Fu-chou in 898, then title of Prince of Min in 909. Interfamily strife impedes political unification of the region, which is largely divided up by Southern T'ang and Wu-Yüeh by 945.	Fu-chou. Mirroring divisions in the Wang family, political control fractured along physiographic subregions of Fukien centered around Fu-chou in the north, the Chien-chou state of Yin (proclaimed in 943) in the northwest, and Ch'üan-chou and the coastal prefectures in the south. Chien-chou/Yin is taken by the Southern T'ang in 945 and Fu-chou/Min absorbed by Wu-Yüeh in 946, leaving only the Ch'üan-chou (or Ching-yüan) region – under control of the warlord Liu Ts'ung-hsiao – to maintain its independence until submitting to Sung rule in 978.
Southern Han	917–971	Liu Yin. In 894 inherits the positions of his father Liu Ch'ien, a hereditary tribal chieftain in the region west of Canton that allied itself with T'ang against Huang Ch'ao. In 902 is rewarded for service to the T'ang court with appointment as commandant of Canton, then named military governor of Canton in 905. In 917 succeeded by brother Liu Yen, who establishes the state as Great Yüeh in 917, then Southern Han in 919.	Kuang-chou (Canton). Controlled the region of modern Kuang-tung and Kuang-hsi (Sung Kuang-nan East and Kuang-nan West) traditionally designated as Ling-nan; asserted unenforceable claims to continue T'ang control over the Red River valley of Annam (modern Vietnam).
Ching-nan (or Nan-p'ing)	924–963	Kao Chi-ch'ang. Appointed regional military governor of Chiang-ling by Later Liang founder Chu Wen in 907, then assumes title of King of Nan-p'ing in 924, just after Later Liang's fall. Survives through diplomatic links to successive Five Dynasties.	Chiang-ling (Ching-chou, modern Sha-shih, Hupei). Controlled the three prefectures just within and east of the Yangtze River gorges, including sites of the two modern cities of I-ch'ang and Sha-shih, as well as the southern bank of the Han River around Ching-men-chün (modern Ching-men-shih).

Ch'u	927–963	Ma Yin. Bandit chieftain and adventurer from the same area of Honan as Wang Chien, uses his military prowess to occupy a power vacuum in Hunan in 892, leading to control of all of Hunan by 899. Named Prince of Ch'u 907; state of Ch'u confirmed by Later T'ang in 927. Internal quarrels allow Southern T'ang to capture the ruling Ma family in 951, but Hunanese forces drive the occupiers out in 952 and restore order (under Chou Hsing-feng) in 956. The restored Hunanese state persists until it and Ching-nan are absorbed by the Sung in 963.	T'an-chou (Ch'ang-sha). Controlled the region of modern Hunan (Sung circuits of Ching-hu North and South), including the Hsiang and Yüan River valleys and Tung-t'ing Lake.
Later Shu (Former Shu successor state)	934–965	Meng Chih-hsiang (874–934). Commands Later T'ang invasion of Szechwan and remains as military governor until proclaiming his own state of Later Shu in 934. Succeeded the next year by his son Meng Ch'ang.	Ch'eng-tu. Same as Former Shu.
Southern T'ang (Wu successor state)	937–975	Li Pien (a.k.a. Hsü Chih-kao). Raised as stepson of Yang Hsing-mi, whose state of Wu he usurps in the name of a T'ang restoration in 937. Subordinated by Sung in 961, and fully annexed in 975.	Nanking. Under second ruler Li Ching (r. 943–961) Southern T'ang expands beyond Wu boundaries to absorb Fukienese state of Min c. 945 and Hunanese state of Ch'u in 951, but loses Chiang-Huai region to Later Chou in 959.
Northern Han	951–979	Liu Min (a.k.a. Ch'ung). Brother of Liu Chih-yüan, founds Northern Han as a regional military regime in the wake of Later Han's collapse. Liao client state; resists Sung advances until 979.	T'ai-yüan. Built around the Liu family's military power base in Shansi. The only northern polity among the traditionally designated "Ten Kingdoms."

Note: Table 3 is based on F. W. Mote, *Imperial China, 900–1800* (Cambridge, Mass., 1999), pp. 12–16, supplemented by chapters 1 and 2 in this volume.

Yüan river valleys and their Tung-t'ing Lake drainage basin; and the successor states of Former and Later Shu, occupying the Szechwan Basin and the
mountain passes through the Ta-pa and Ch'in-ling mountains bisected by the
upper reaches of the Han River valley. The sole exception to these region-sized
states – the tiny kingdom of Ching-nan (or Nan-p'ing) – occupied a 170-
mile stretch of the Yangtze River from the eastern portal of the Three Gorges
(Kuei-chou, modern Hupei, Tzu-kuei county) downriver past Chiang-ling fu
(modern Hupei, Sha-shih), which it held at the sufferance of its more powerful
neighbors rather than through its own military might.

    Despite their outcast origins, the rulers of south China underwent a process
of political maturation that paralleled the evolution of their northern neighbors. Clark documents a shift from military prowess to political effectiveness
as the chief measure of prestige and governance, as once-itinerant bandit chieftains formed stable demilitarized regimes based on political acumen, alliances
with local elites, and the support of refugee literati in search of security and
employment. In fact, state building in the regionalized south was even more
robust than in the wartorn north. For (as both chapters 2 and 3 show) the
greater stability of the south enabled the new regimes to initiate agrarian
projects – especially water control – that enhanced agricultural productivity,
and to sponsor internal, interregional, and international trade over land and
by sea. Thus while the successive northern regimes had to focus on the crucial
political problem of wresting power from other military governors, fending off
each other, and developing workable approaches to the increasingly powerful
Khitan, the southern kingdoms were free to develop sophisticated ways of taxing and even facilitating the growth of the increasingly buoyant commercial
economy. And just like their northern counterparts, the rulers of the southern
kingdoms reintroduced bureaucratic governance into their regions, deploying
a mix of local and refugee literatus lineages as local circumstances allowed.

    From a spatial perspective, natural physiographic barriers kept political
boundaries in the south relatively stable. Only one of the southern kingdoms –
the Fukienese state of Min – permanently disappeared during this era, as
discord in the ruling Wang family opened the mountainous region around
Chien-chou to annexation by Southern T'ang and the coastal plains centered
on Fu-chou to absorption by Wu-Yüeh. Similarly, only one of the southern
states – the Southern T'ang – harbored imperial aspirations, openly rejecting
the legitimacy of the northern dynasties in order to promote its own ambitions
to reunify the empire in the name of the T'ang. For a short time in 951
Southern T'ang claimed control (as Clark shows) of over thirty prefectures
on a north-south axis from the Huai River to Ling-nan, and on an east-west
axis from the Wu-i Mountains of Fukien to western Hunan. But soon after
reaching this territorial peak its expansionist momentum was halted and then,

in 958, resoundingly reversed, as the Later Chou forcibly annexed the fourteen Southern T'ang prefectures north of the Yangtze River and obliged its rulers to accept subordinate status. A unification of China was indeed afoot, but as usual it came from the northern rather than the southern direction.

FOUNDING AND CONSOLIDATION OF THE SUNG, 960–1000

Chapters 1 and 3 detail the critical contributions made by the Later Chou rulers Kuo Wei (r. 951–4) and Ch'ai Jung (r. 954–9) toward strengthening bureaucratic governance, centralizing military power, and articulating and enacting a coherent strategy (conquering the south before the north) of territorial reunification. These measures were all crucial to the success of Chao K'uang-yin (927–76) as the founder of the Sung. Both Chao K'uang-yin (or Sung T'ai-tsu, r. 960–76) and the dynastic consolidator, his brother and successor Chao K'uang-i (or Sung T'ai-tsung, r. 976–97), emerged from what Edmund Worthy calls the "militocracy" of the tenth century, for their father, who had served in the imperial army of each successive northern dynasty except the first, helped the family make the transition from undistinguished civil officials in the late T'ang to established members of the Five Dynasties military elite.[4] But Chao K'uang-yin was not only a talented soldier who rapidly ascended to the position of commander of the palace army under Ch'ai Jung, he was also a keen observer of Chou bureaucratic reforms and a direct participant in Chou policies of military centralization and territorial expansion. As Lau Nap-yin and Huang K'uang-chung describe in chapter 3, Chao distinguished himself in battle against the joint Khitan–Northern Han invasion of Kao-p'ing (Tsechou, Ho-tung circuit, or modern Shansi) in 954, and then helped overhaul the Palace Command in the military reforms that followed that battle. He fought with distinction again in the expansionist campaigns against Later Shu in 955 and Southern T'ang a year later; and by 959, when Ch'ai Jung's death put a child on the throne, Chao had earned the intense personal loyalty of a reinvigorated imperial army and its confident military commanders. It thus came as no surprise when a reported invasion by Khitan and Northern Han forces in 960 provided an opportunity for Chao's troops to proclaim their thirty-four-year-old commander as emperor. It is possible to imagine the new Sung dynasty (named after the eponymous prefecture southeast of K'ai-feng where Chao K'uang-yin had served in the increasingly vestigial post

---

[4] For a discussion of militocracy and the transition from militocratic to bureaucratic absolutism under T'ai-tsung, see Worthy, "The founding of Sung China," pp. 295–316; John W. Chaffee traces the history of the Chao lineage in chapter 2 of John W. Chaffee, *Branches of heaven: A history of the imperial Clan of Sung China* (Cambridge, Mass., 1999).

of military governor) becoming just another placeholder in the succession of short-lived northern dynasties. But the social turmoil and political fragmentation generated by the collapse of the T'ang had gradually but inexorably given way to civic order and political stability in both north and south, and by midcentury the two most powerful states in north and south China had begun to look beyond their immediate problems to contemplate the possibilities of unification. By the time Chao K'uang-yin assumed the throne of the sixth northern dynasty since the fall of the T'ang the original 96 prefectures inherited by the Later Chou had swelled to 118, including 4 prefectures from Later Shu, 14 from Southern T'ang, and 2 of the coveted Sixteen Prefectures from the Khitan Liao. Unification had become a realistic ambition, and as a central player in the Later Chou campaigns of centralization and reunification Chao K'uang-yin was in an ideal position to capture the great prize. The Sung founder's approach to state building continued the measures practiced by his Five Dynasties predecessors, especially his own mentor Ch'ai Jung. Although T'ai-tsu was very much a military man, he is best known for subordinating the military to bureaucratic control.[5] Within a year of assuming the throne, T'ai-tsu famously employed the occasion of a private drinking party to persuade his generals to exchange their posts for comfortable sinecures as military governors. As Lau and Huang show, by peacefully demobilizing his general staff, T'ai-tsu severed the personalized links between commanders and their troops that had made "praetorian coups" – such as the one that brought T'ai-tsu to power – so common in the post-T'ang era.[6] At the same time he subjected the command hierarchy to more centralized surveillance and control, by vesting paramount responsibility for military administration in a civilian office, the Bureau of Military Affairs (*Shu-mi yüan*). T'ai-tsu's choice of centralized control over military autonomy – often described by the phrase "emphasizing the civil and deemphasizing the military" (*ch'ung-wen ch'ing-wu*) – is sometimes indicted as a source of the Sung's putative military weakness.[7] But Lau and Huang conclude that his personal assertion of widespread military authority "created a new image for his government as a whole, characterized by centralized and absolute authority. This distinguished him from his predecessors and former military colleagues as a real emperor, not an all-powerful warlord, and his state as a new-born empire." T'ai-tsu built on his prestige as absolute military commander to extend bureaucratic control well beyond what his Chou

[5] For a discussion of this militocracy and the transition from militocratic to bureaucratic absolutism under T'ai-tsu's brother and successor, T'ai-tsung, see Worthy, "The founding of Sung China," pp. 295–316.

[6] "Praetorian coup" is used in John R. Labadie, "Rulers and soldiers: Perception and management of the military in Northern Sung China (960–1060)" (diss., University of Washington, 1981), p. 35.

[7] Labadie, "Rulers and soldiers," pp. 229–32, disputes the notion of Sung military weakness.

mentors could achieve. Not only was T'ai-tsu able to neutralize the power-brokering role of the great generals, but he and his successor, T'ai-tsung, finally eradicated the military governors as a ruling elite. After more than a decade of slow co-optation, in 977 T'ai-tsung conclusively dismantled the territorial jurisdictions of the remaining eighteen military governors and replaced them with civilian officials under direct control of the capital. Thus the era of the T'ang military governors was finally terminated by its last incumbents, the Sung founders it had brought to power, and the position of *chieh-tu shih* turned into a purely titular office conferred primarily on aboriginal chieftains.[8]

In other areas of civil administration T'ai-tsu adapted T'ang and Five Dynasties precedents to recreate a network of county, prefectural, and circuit officials that implanted imperial authority throughout the empire through a growing bureaucratic apparatus. To staff these offices, T'ai-tsu (and to a lesser extent T'ai-tsung) employed men associated with or descended from the military governments of the Five Dynasties era, men of a social class very much like their own.[9] But to supplement his supply of officials T'ai-tsu also revived the system of civil service examinations. Although (as Lau and Huang point out) T'ai-tsu recruited no more than four hundred and fifty officials through the examination system, T'ai-tsung intensified the examination process to certify over five thousand officials in his twenty-one-year reign. As the chapters in this and our companion volume confirm, the examination system burgeoned to become a defining feature of Sung (and indeed all of mid- and late-imperial) political, intellectual, and cultural life.[10] At the same time, it gave rise to a new, literocentric political elite that however much it may have benefited from local prestige and the ownership of land was nonetheless defined – by itself and by others – through its mastery of learning and its prowess in the examination halls. Individually, the members of this new social class (who typically designated themselves by the old terms of *shih* [literati] or *shih-ta-fu* [literatus-official]) possessed little of the independent wealth or hereditary official status of their T'ang aristocratic predecessors. In this sense, they posed less of a challenge to the absolutist inclinations of some Sung emperors and (later in the dynasty) their chief councilors.[11] Yet while they never challenged

---

[8] Worthy, "The founding of Sung China," pp. 272–9.

[9] It is this group that Robert M. Hartwell calls the "founding elite." See Robert M. Hartwell, "Demographic, political, and social transformations of China, 750–1550," *Harvard Journal of Asiatic Studies* 42 No. 2 (1982), pp. 405–8.

[10] For complete studies of the Sung examination system in English, see John W. Chaffee, *The thorny gates of learning in Sung China: A social history of examinations* (Cambridge, 1985), and Thomas H. C. Lee, *Government education and examinations in Sung China* (New York, 1985).

[11] The issues of imperial and or ministerial absolutism are recurring motifs in this volume. No later emperors (with the possible exception of Sung Hsiao-tsung, r. 1162–89) ruled with the personalized authority of the founders T'ai-tsu and T'ai-tsung. On the powers of the early Sung emperors, see Liu Ching-chen,

the political prerogatives of the throne, the new exam-based literocracy came
to dominate Chinese cultural institutions for the next nine hundred years, as
they "[captured] hauteur from aristocrats, . . . sustained it against merchants,
and . . . grew as much as the monarchs in self-esteem and substance."[12]

Political consolidation paved the way for the founders to continue the process of territorial unification that had been initiated by the Later Chou. T'ai-
tsu launched the first reunification campaign in 963 with a swift conquest of
Ching-nan and Ch'u, gaining possession of the middle Yangtze region. This
was followed in 965 by a successful campaign against the upper Yangtze kingdom of Later Shu, although the conquest was so brutal and rapacious that the
resulting wave of rebellions rocked Szechwan for another four decades. Before
his death in 976, T'ai-tsu subjugated Southern Han (in 970–1) and Southern
T'ang (in 975). The remaining southern state of Wu-Yüeh and the Fukienese
military outpost of Chang-Ch'üan capitulated to T'ai-tsung in 978, completing the new dynasty's consolidation of its rule in south China. But in the north,
T'ai-tsu's attempt to topple the Northern Han in 969 was foiled by the armies
of the Sha-t'o regime's patron, the Khitan Liao. In 979, T'ai-tsung launched a
second invasion of Northern Han that Liao forces were unable to repel, bringing the breakaway region of Ho-tung (modern Shansi) back under centralized
control for the first time since 951. But this was as far as the Sung would get
in restoring control over north China. Flush with victory over the Northern
Han, T'ai-tsung pressed his troops on toward the Sixteen Prefectures, where
they were decimated by Liao forces near Yu-chou (modern Peking). T'ai-tsung
launched a second massive invasion of the Sixteen Prefectures in 986, but once
again Liao cavalry and their commanders overwhelmed Sung forces. The Sung
were never to regain the Yen-Yün region, for Sung state building came up
against a parallel process of state formation on the steppe that was to shape
events in China and Inner Asia for the next three centuries.

Pei Sung ch'ien-ch'i huang-ti ho t'a-men ti ch'üan-li (Taipei, 1996); on the increasing authority of the chief
councilors over the course of the dynasty, see Lin T'ien-wei, "Sung-tai ch'üan-hsiang hsing-ch'eng chih
fen-hsi," in *Sung-shih yen-chiu chi: Ti pa chi*, ed. Sung-shih tso-t'an-hui (Taipei, 1976), pp. 141–70. The
tension between monarchy and bureaucracy is captured in Anthony W. Sariti, "Monarchy, bureaucracy,
and absolutism in the political thought of Ssu-ma Kuang," *Journal of Asian Studies* 32 No. 1 (1972),
pp. 53–76. Rudolf Vierhaus traces the rise of the concept of absolutism, which was used to describe a
kind of monarchy in seventeenth- and eighteenth-century Europe characterized by "the concentration of
state power on a monarch who is not encumbered by other persons or institutions, and who can enforce
his or her sovereignty with the instruments of legislation, administration, taxation, and a standing army,
and who is also final arbiter of the courts." Rudolf Vierhaus, "Absolutism, history of," in *International
encyclopedia of the social and behavioral sciences*, ed. Neil J. Smelser and Paul B. Baltes (Amsterdam, 2001),
vol. 1, pp. 5–9.

[12] Joseph R. Levenson, *Confucian China and its modern fate* (Berkeley, 1965), vol. 2, p. 64. Literatus influence
on Chinese cultural institutions is a theme in many of the chapters in *The Song-Yuan-Ming transition in
Chinese history*, ed. Paul Jakov Smith and Richard von Glahn (Cambridge, Mass., 2003).

A CYCLE OF STATE BUILDING ON THE STEPPE, TENTH
TO THIRTEENTH CENTURIES

Overviews of Inner Asian state formation by Nicola Di Cosmo and Frederick W. Mote suggest the magnitude of the challenge that confronted the Sung from the steppe.[13] Over the long term, Inner Asian state formation was often precipitated by economic, social, or political crises that stimulated the militarization of pastoral societies. According to Di Cosmo, crisis could create social dislocation within tribes that provided the opportunity for a charismatic leader to rise to a position of supratribal ruler or khan. This disruption of traditional, semiegalitarian political relations was characterized by "a replacement of the clan nobility with a much more powerful, hieratic, and autocratic form of authority where collegial decisions were restricted to a small group of people." Political authority was in turn supported by the increased militarization of society into permanent fighting units placed under the direct control of the khan or royal clan.[14] But this conjoining of permanent militarization and political centralization within an aristocratic class required far greater economic resources than pastoral society could provide, stimulating the demand for invasions of wealthier sedentary regions to secure predictable supplies of external resources. For Di Cosmo, the development of forms of "state appropriation" of economic resources evolved over time: "Cast in a historical perspective, inner Asian state formations . . . display a gradual but sure tendency to form more and more sophisticated means of access to external resources." Moreover, this incremental growth in the ability of Inner Asian states to secure revenues external to their productive bases "was coeval with the emergence of the state apparatus and provided the basis for its survival, for foreign relations, for the projection of force beyond its political and territorial boundaries, and for the domination of different ethnic, linguistic, and economic communities."[15]

---

[13] Nicola Di Cosmo models Inner Asian state building over the imperial era in his "State formation and periodization in Inner Asian history," *Journal of World History* 10 No. 1 (1999), pp. 1–40; Frederick W. Mote surveys the formation of individual frontier states and empires in the mid-imperial era in Frederick W. Mote, *Imperial China: 900–1800* (Cambridge, Mass., 1999), chapters 2–4, 8–12, and 16–20. See also Franke and Twitchett, "Introduction," *The Cambridge history of China*, volume 6.

[14] Di Cosmo, "State formation and periodization," pp. 21–3.

[15] Di Cosmo, "State formation and periodization," p. 27. Because the process of Inner Asian state formation was fully reversible, with steppe states running the risk of dissolving and returning to a nonstate condition, Di Cosmo eschews an explicitly evolutionary formulation. This caveat notwithstanding, the developmental trajectory that he depicts, characterized by increasing sophistication based on explicit borrowing (what Mote, *Imperial China*, p. 226, likens to technology transfers) over the long duration from the Hsiung-nü to the Ch'ing, approximates an evolutionary path.

In Di Cosmo's formulation, then, the secular development of technologies of resource appropriation serves as a marker of Inner Asian state formation.[16] And the most intensive period of development and elaboration in the forms of Inner Asian resource appropriation occurred between the tenth and fourteenth centuries, when powerful steppe empires bordered and then eradicated the Sung. During the first millennium of the imperial era, Inner Asian states slowly progressed from a dependence on tribute during Han times to a combination of tribute and the systematic control of intercontinental and border trade during the Sui and T'ang. But the pace of change accelerated in the early tenth century, when the Khitan Liao (variously dated as 916 or 947 to 1125) pioneered a new form of governance that Mote describes as dual administration, and that Di Cosmo deems the beginning of the era of the "dual-administration empires" of the Liao, Chin, and early Mongol period (907–1259).[17] The institution of dual administration grafted an alien system of civil governance over the conquered farming families along the Chinese and Korean borders to a native Khitan state that administered all military and tribal matters and collected tribute from subordinate peoples like the Jurchen.[18] Dual administration did not displace the collection of tribute from the Sung, for the Khitan Liao used war or the threat of war to institutionalize tribute into a system of "indemnified peace" with the Sung that later proved equally profitable for the Tangut Hsi Hsia (1038–1227) and the Jurchen Chin (1115–1234).[19] But by developing increasingly effective techniques of dual administration, the Liao were able to supplement trade and tribute with an increasing proportion of revenues from the direct taxation of sedentary peoples, which helped finance the successful occupation and defense of the state of Po-hai and the Sixteen Prefectures of north China. These techniques of dual administration were in turn adopted by the Jurchen at the very beginning of their ascent to statehood under A-ku-ta (r. 1115–23) and employed in their governance of the sedentary domains conquered from the Liao in 1125 and the Sung in 1127.[20] The combination of

[16] Di Cosmo, "State formation and periodization," pp. 30–7, periodizes the stages of Inner Asian state formation as follows: tribute empires (209 B.C.E.–551 C.E.), trade-tribute empires (551–907), dual-administration empires (907–1259), and direct-taxation empires (1260–1796).

[17] Mote, *Imperial China*, pp. 39–40, 72–5; Di Cosmo, "State formation and periodization," pp. 32–4. Although neither Mote nor Di Cosmo (both published in 1999) refers to the other, they depict the phenomenon of dual administration and the process of political evolution through adaptation and emulation in similar terms.

[18] Mote, *Imperial China*, pp. 39–40.

[19] Mote, *Imperial China*, p. 71. As Mote puts it, "The Inner Asian states learned to threaten war, demand territory, or require other concessions, and the [Sung] learned to resist most of those demands by paying ever higher indemnities."

[20] Di Cosmo, "State formation and periodization," p. 33.

Chinese and steppe methods of governance pioneered by the Khitan evolved into what Mote describes as a technology of statecraft that was augmented by the Jurchen and the Tanguts throughout the twelfth century, adding to the store of universal governing techniques that the Mongols would draw on in their sweep through China and Eurasia in the thirteenth century.[21] As Di Cosmo argues, the Mongol Yüan (1271–1368) took the process of Inner Asian state formation one step further, by circumventing tribute (though not trade) as a source of revenue and extracting their resources from the conquered territories through a system of direct taxation. But Di Cosmo, like Mote, stresses the evolutionary trajectory by which the Yüan emerged as the first of the direct-taxation empires: "The completion of the conquest of China under Khubilai is the best example of the confidence achieved by the Mongols to summon a wide array of political resources derived from the storehouses of inner Asian, central Asian, northern Chinese (Liao and [Chin]), and Chinese political traditions."[22]

The rapid evolution of Inner Asian statecraft in the tenth to thirteenth centuries allowed states on the northern frontier to support formidable armies that offset agrarian China's advantages in wealth and numbers, thereby blocking Sung from assuming a position of supremacy at the center of a China-dominated world order and relegating it to a position of equal participant in a multistate East Asian system.[23] Even the Tangut Hsi Hsia, a tribute-trade empire (to follow Di Cosmo's formulation) occupying the largely unproductive lands of the Ordos bend and the Kansu Corridor, was able to match the Sung in military power and confront it as a de facto diplomatic equal, as the chapters in this volume show. Map 3 depicts how evolving Inner Asian states expanded ever farther south of the Great Wall frontier that traditionally divided sedentary China from the steppe, seizing north China in 1127, encircling south China by the 1260s, and finally absorbing all of China into the vast Eurasian empire of the Mongol Yüan in 1279. The pages that follow will briefly highlight the impact of steppe expansion and Sino-steppe relations on the tempo of Sung dynastic events and the shape of Sung political culture.

---

[21] Mote, *Imperial China*, p. 226.

[22] Di Cosmo, "State formation and periodization," p. 34. For Di Cosmo, the peak of the direct-taxation model was attained by the Ch'ing, which "achieved a level of social and political integration between conquerors and conquered far higher than that of earlier inner Asian polities." Di Cosmo, "State formation and periodization," p. 36. For a similar argument, see Paul Jakov Smith, "Introduction: Problematizing the Song-Yuan-Ming Transition," in *The Song-Yuan-Ming transition in Chinese history*, ed. Paul Jakov Smith and Richard von Glahn (Cambridge, Mass., 2003), pp. 30–4.

[23] This theme recurs throughout the essays in Morris Rossabi, ed., *China among equals: The Middle Kingdom and its neighbors, 10th–14th centuries* (Berkeley, Calif., 1983).

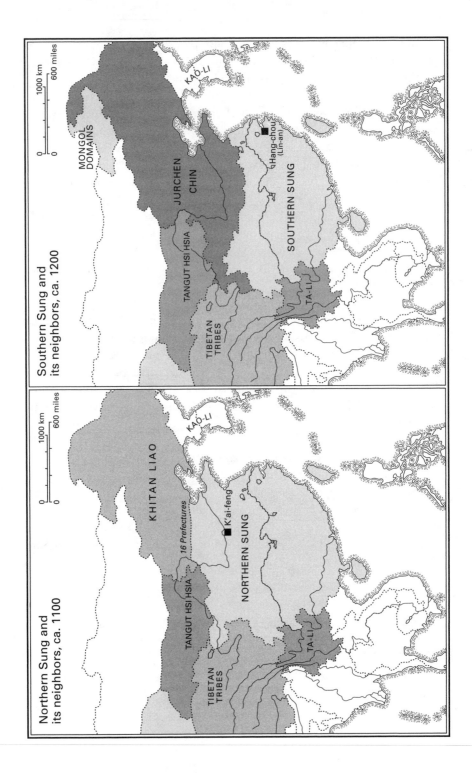

Northern Sung and its neighbors, ca. 1100

KHITAN LIAO

KAO-LI

TANGUT HSI HSIA

16 Prefectures

K'ai-feng

NORTHERN SUNG

TIBETAN TRIBES

TA-LI

1000 km

600 miles

Southern Sung and its neighbors, ca. 1200

MONGOL DOMAINS

KAO-LI

JURCHEN CHIN

TANGUT HSI HSIA

TIBETAN TRIBES

Hang-chou (Lin-an)

SOUTHERN SUNG

TA-LI

1000 km

600 miles

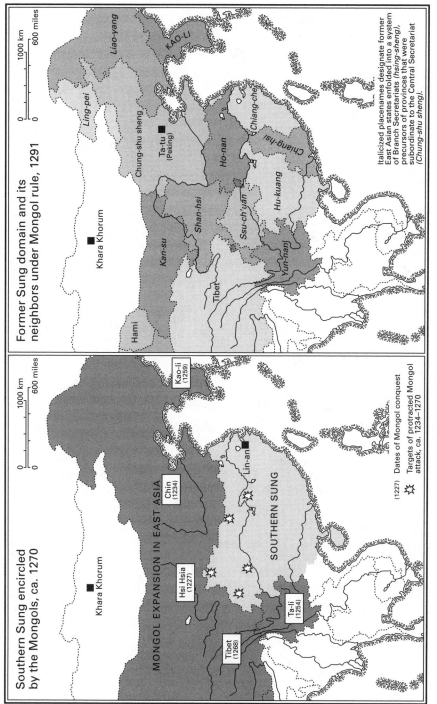

Southern Sung encircled by the Mongols, ca. 1270

0   1000 km
0   600 miles

Khara Khorum

MONGOL EXPANSION IN EAST ASIA

Chin (1234)

Hsi Hsia (1227)

Tibet (1268)

Kao-li (1259)

Lin-an

Ta-li (1254)

SOUTHERN SUNG

(1227)   Dates of Mongol conquest
✸   Targets of protracted Mongol attack, ca. 1234–1270

Former Sung domain and its neighbors under Mongol rule, 1291

0   1000 km
0   600 miles

Ling-pei

Liao-yang

KAO-LI

Khara Khorum

Chung-shu sheng

Ta-tu (Peking)

Hami

Kan-su

Shan-hsi

Ho-nan

(Chiang-che)

Tibet

Ssu-ch'uan

Hu-kuang

Chiang-hsi

Yun-nan

Italicized placenames designate former East Asian states enfolded into a system of Branch Secretariats *(hsing-sheng)*, precursors of provinces that were subordinate to the Central Secretariat *(Chung-shu sheng)*.

Map 3. The Sung domain and its neighbors, c. 1100–1291.

SINO-STEPPE RELATIONS AND THE SHAPE OF DYNASTIC EVENTS

Geopolitical equilibrium in the post-Shan-yüan era, 1005–1067

Sung policy makers formally acknowledged the irreversibility of a new multistate system regulated by treaties and the establishment of regular diplomatic
intercourse when they approved the Treaty of Shan-yüan in 1005. As a result of
T'ai-tsung's failure to dislodge the Sixteen Yen-Yün Prefectures from Khitan
control, advisors to his son and successor, Sung Chen-tsung (r. 997–1022),
instituted an extensive project of defensive construction centered on the fortification of frontier cities and the creation of a network of cavalry-blocking
waterways that diminished Liao military superiority and dashed Khitan hopes
of reestablishing a buffer zone between themselves and the Sung.[24] In response,
the Liao launched a massive invasion of China's Central Plains in 1004, hoping
to use war to achieve an advantageous peace that would bring Sung irredentist
attacks to an end. Although Khitan forces approached to within one hundred
miles of K'ai-feng, their own losses were considerable, and both sides soon
came to appreciate the advantages of a negotiated and dependable settlement.
The ensuing Shan-yüan Treaty of 1005, in which the Sung agreed to make
annual payments to the Liao and to repudiate claims to the Yen-Yün region,
constituted a recognition by the Sung court that the territorial, ritual, and
financial costs of diplomatic parity and a purchased peace were far less onerous
than the social and political costs of mobilizing the country for protracted irredentist war. The diplomatic equilibrium that accompanied Sung suspension
of its irredentist aspirations ushered in a concomitant period of political stability that spanned the remaining seventeen years of Chen-tsung's life as well
as the reigns of his son Sung Jen-tsung (r. 1022–63) and Jen-tsung's cousin
Sung Ying-tsung (r. 1063–7). The Shan-yüan settlement coincided with the
transition from battle-hardened dynastic founders to court-nurtured successors, precipitating a shift in political power from an absolutist throne to an
increasingly complex and self-confident bureaucracy.[25] The bureaucracy itself
was of course by no means homogeneous: it was staffed by men from different

---

[24] In addition to chapter 3 in this volume, see Lau Nap-yin, "Waging war for peace? The peace accord
between the Song and the Liao in AD 1005," in *Warfare in Chinese history*, ed. Hans J. van de Ven (Leiden,
2000), pp. 180–221.

[25] The most important study in English of this post-Shan-yüan evolution of the Northern Sung state is
still Edward A. Kracke, Jr., *Civil service in early Sung China, 960–1067; with particular emphasis on the
development of controlled sponsorship to foster administrative responsibility* (Cambridge, Mass., 1953). Winston
Lo offers a longer perspective, tracing the evolution of the Sung civil (and military) service over the
course of the entire dynasty, in Lo Wen (Winston W. Lo), *An introduction to the civil service of Sung China:
With emphasis on its personnel administration* (Honolulu, 1987).

parts of the empire, with potentially conflicting political views, interests, and affiliations; and it drew on a pool of examination graduates that grew faster than the number of available government posts, even as entry into government became the most prized avenue of social mobility. Irreconcilable policy differences and intense competition for office would eventually fracture the solidarity of the bureaucratic elite under the weight of factionalism and the concentration of power in increasingly hegemonic ministerial regimes. But in the decades following the Shan-yüan settlement the *shih-ta-fu* elite was still relatively cohesive and the still-evolving bureaucratic apparatus relatively robust. As a result, the arbitrary exercise of state power was restrained by the constitutional division of authority over civil affairs (under the Secretariat-Chancellery), military matters (under the Bureau of Military Affairs), and economic administration (under the Finance Commission). Furthermore, an institutionally embedded system of checks and balances prevented a single chief councilor from dominating the Council of State and subjected all the state councilors to independent oversight by a fully developed system of policy critics (*chien-kuan*) and censors (*yü-shih*).[26] At the same time, governance was characterized by a relatively conciliar approach to decision making, exemplified most graphically by the reliance on broadly staffed interagency ad hoc committees to advise the emperor on important policy issues.[27]

But the equilibrium sustained by the Shan-yüan settlement was by no means unassailable and could be shaken by any combination of internal or external shocks. Internally, there was always the threat of a domestic challenge to frontier stability, for the consensus on accommodation was pragmatic rather than principled, offered grudgingly rather than with enthusiasm. Moreover, the very "civilism" of the Sung state marginalized some individuals and groups who might benefit more from war than from peace, inclining them to acquiesce in if not agitate for frontier expansion. Externally, equilibrium could be jolted by the demise of a stabilizing ruler or state, or particularly by the entry of a vigorous new player on the steppe. Such was the case in the second decade of Jen-tsung's reign, when the Tangut ruler Li Yüan-hao (1004–48) proclaimed himself emperor of the Great Hsia empire in 1038. As Michael McGrath describes in Chapter 4, in the years following the Shan-yüan Treaty the Tangut domain had expanded from a handful of towns inside the Yellow River loop to an extensive cavalry empire that controlled the Ordos region and

---

[26] Chapter 3 of Kracke, *Civil service in early Sung China*. On the structure and political role of Sung remonstrance and censorial offices, see Chia Yü-ying, *Sung-tai chien-ch'a chih-tu* (K'ai-feng, 1996) pp. 155–212.

[27] On this important element of eleventh-century policy making, see Robert M. Hartwell, "Financial expertise, examinations, and the formation of economic policy in northern Sung China," *Journal of Asian Studies* 30 No. 2 (1971), pp. 281–314, especially p. 293.

the Kansu Corridor, and thus the most important trade routes linking Inner Asia and the Sung.[28] Sung reluctance to extend diplomatic recognition to the Hsi Hsia emperor instigated a four-year war (1038–42) that highlighted Sung deficiencies in strategic planning, tactical execution, and troop battle fitness. Ultimately, Sung military inadequacies were offset by its vast size and incalculably greater wealth, but even so the court was forced in the treaty of 1044 to purchase from Li Yüan-hao the same kind of indemnified peace with which it placated the Liao. Moreover, Sung incompetence in this first Sino-Tangut war exacerbated growing concerns about Sung governance and bureaucratic morale, catalyzing the Ch'ing-li reform movement of 1043–5 that heralded (as McGrath explains it) the political coming of age of the exam-dependent political elite.

Although the Ch'ing-li reforms succumbed to the abrupt withdrawal of imperial support, the problems of military impotence, bureaucratic demoralization, and growing Tangut power continued to fester. These potential threats to the post-Shan-yüan equilibrium converged again in the mid-1060s, as Ying-tsung's premature death brought his young son Sung Shen-tsung (r. 1067–85) to the throne. Internationally, Li Yüan-hao's son Li Liang-tso (r. 1048–68) was inspired by the deterioration of Tibetan rule in the Kansu-Tsinghai Highlands to launch expeditionary forces against Tibetan political centers, sinified frontier tribes, and even Sung commanderies throughout the northwestern borderlands.[29] Domestically, the very primacy of the examination-based civil service put indirect pressure on frontier stability by producing a surfeit of potential officials. The numbers of men with ranked civil service status more than doubled through the reigns of Chen-tsung, Jen-tsung, and Ying-tsung, from some ten thousand to around twenty-four thousand men. By Ying-tsung's death this glut of officials had begun to demoralize the entire civil service, with far more candidates than the system could absorb clamoring for posts, sponsors, and promotion from junior to senior status. In a sociocultural environment dominated by the state, the career aspirations of these supernumerary officials were best served by expansion in the scope of government activity in either the domestic or foreign arenas.

Even more direct pressure came from a group increasingly marginalized by the mid-Sung civil service: the hereditary military families who comprised

---

[28] The growth of the Hsi Hsia state is mapped in Ruth W. Dunnell, "The Hsi Hsia," in *The Cambridge history of China*, volume 6: *Alien regimes and border states, 907–1368*, ed. Herbert Franke and Denis C. Twitchett (New York, 1994), p. 171.

[29] The following paragraphs draw on Paul Jakov Smith, "Irredentism as political capital: The New Policies and the annexation of Tibetan domains in Hehuang (the Qinghai-Gansu highlands) under Shenzong and his sons, 1068–1108," in *Emperor Huizong and late Northern Song China: The politics of culture and the culture of politics*, ed. Patricia B. Ebrey and Maggie Bickford (Cambridge, Mass., 2006), pp. 78–130.

the core of the Sung general command. For in the half century following the Shan-yüan Treaty the Chen-tsung and Jen-tsung courts had systematically excluded the military's contribution to strategic decision making, replaced regular troops and effective generals with local militia, and transferred military authority and even outright field command from the generals to such top-ranking civilian officials (and Ch'ing-li reform leaders) as Fan Chung-yen (989–1052) and Han Ch'i (1008–75). Although the general staff was not dismantled, it was transformed into a bureaucratized and subordinate appendage of the civilian-dominated state.[30]

In mid-1067 Tangut incursions supplied the pretext for one military man to take frontier matters into his own hands, when the frontier commander Ch'ung O took it upon himself to kidnap a prominent Tanguts general and wall the Hsi Hsia town of Sui-chou (renamed Sui-te chün), just across the hotly contested northern border of greater Shan-hsi circuit.[31] Civilian courtiers like the influential Ssu-ma Kuang (1019–86), imbued with the worldview of the Shan-yüan settlement, demanded that Sui-te be returned to the Tanguts and urged the newly enthroned Shen-tsung to honor the policy of his predecessors by treating their Tangut treaty partner with respect and assuming a posture of compliance to reestablish diplomatic entente. In the past, such sober-minded exhortations had sufficed to bring frontier adventurism to an end. But the flame of irredentist longing burned far more brightly in Shen-tsung's heart than it had for Chen-tsung, Jen-tsung, or Ying-tsung, and he ascended the throne determined to "destroy the Hsia Nation and then personally lead the campaign to subjugate the Great Liao."[32] Fanned as they were by imperial passion, irredentism and frontier adventure emerged during Shen-tsung's reign

---

[30] Labadie, "Rulers and soldiers," p. 199, chapters 2 and 4.

[31] Greater Shan-hsi circuit denotes the administrative region encircled by (going clockwise) the Tangut-held regions of the Ordos, the eastern loop of the Yellow River, the Ch'in-ling Mountains, and the frontier zone east of the T'ao River. The circuit was formally established as one of the fifteen civil circuits of the Sung in 997; in 1041 it was subdivided into the four military circuits of Ch'in-feng, Ching-yüan, Huan-ch'ing, and Fu-yen. In 1072 the civil administration of Shan-hsi was divided between Yung-hsing-chün in the east and Ch'in-feng circuit in the west, with a fiscal and judicial intendant appointed for each. At the same time the military administration of Shan-hsi was divided into six military subdivisions – Yung-hsing, Fu-yen, and Huan-ch'ing in the east, and Ch'in-feng, Ching-yüan, and Hsi-ho (the easternmost sector of the Tibetan domains in Ho-huang) in the west – with a military affairs commission (ching-lüeh-ssu) and pacification commission (an-fu-ssu) designated for each. The maps for this volume follow the cartographic convention of dividing greater Shan-hsi into the two circuits of Ch'in-feng and Yung-hsing-chün even before the split in 1072, without attempting to outline the six military subcircuits. On this point, see the "Compiling Principles" section of the sixth volume (Sung Liao Chin shih ch'i) of Chung-kuo li-shih ti-t'u chi, ed. T'an Ch'i-hsiang (Shanghai, 1982). On the evolving territorial administration of Shan-hsi during the Northern Sung, see Michael Charles McGrath, "Military and regional administration in Northern Sung China (960–1126)" (diss., Princeton University, 1982).

[32] Shao Po-wen, Shao-shih wen-chien lu (1151; Peking, 1983) 3, p. 26.

as a potent form of political capital that swept a new constellation of men –
including generals, eunuchs, and hawkish bureaucrats – into power. Moreover,
the political capital generated in Shen-tsung's reign yielded interest for the
next half century, as Shen-tsung's own sons Sung Che-tsung (r. 1085–1100)
and Sung Hui-tsung (r. 1100–26) dedicated themselves to completing their
father's dream, fired by the zeal of what they and their public spokesmen
glorified as virtually a second dynastic founding.

Irredentism and state activism under Shen-tsung and his sons, 1067–1127

Disturbed by the new emperor's self-image as an activist (*yu-wei*), expansionist sovereign, his elder statesmen cautioned Shen-tsung to forgo talk of war,
practice fiscal restraint, and rectify his own heart while leaving governance to
the bureaucracy. Only the forty-six-year-old Wang An-shih (1021–86), whose
unease over impending political and cultural crisis had exploded to the surface
in his "Myriad word memorial" of 1058, emboldened his sovereign to believe
that "the time for doing great deeds is right now." But even Wang argued
that the emperor's irredentist aspirations must be deferred until political, economic, cultural, and military institutions were thoroughly revamped and the
empire made "prosperous and strong" (*fu-ch'iang*). As the chapters by Smith on
Shen-tsung and Levine on Che-tsung and Hui-tsung illustrate, the resulting
New Policies (*hsin-fa*) – the epitome of state activism in the imperial era –
came to characterize the reigns of Shen-tsung and his sons, and to dominate
the agendas of the chief councilors who catered to and in turn manipulated
their emperors' ambitions.

From an institutional perspective, the New Policies reflected Wang An-
shih's vision that the bureaucracy could be expanded and fine-tuned to intervene in and reshape every aspect of the social, cultural, and (most especially
for Wang) economic landscape. But Wang's original goal of enriching the
state without overtaxing the people by creating new wealth through state-
managed economic redistribution was soon transformed under the pressure of
Shen-tsung's expansionist dream into a hydra-headed bureaucratic apparatus
dedicated to extracting revenue for reformist projects and the emperor's war
chest.

Politically, the New Policies were abetted by the emperor's willingness to
abandon the system of bureaucratic checks and balances brought to maturity in the post-Shan-yüan decades, just as he was eager to repudiate the
Shan-yüan settlement itself. Persuaded by Wang that the only way to augment imperial authority was to unyieldingly support the reforms, Shen-tsung
allowed Wang to dominate the Council of State, control remonstrance offices,
create new reform-specific agencies that bypassed existing offices, and pack

the bureaucracy with his followers – young men with demonstrated expertise in finance and bureaucratic enterprises but low standing in the civil service whom more established literati denounced as "mean and petty men." This newly mobilized cadre of reformers and their sons and brothers would, with the exception of the eight-year antireform regency during Che-tsung's minority (1085–94), come to control the government throughout the reigns of Shen-tsung and his sons.

Such drastic changes in the political landscape were certain to generate a significant backlash, and from the very start of Wang's tenure in 1069 a growing circle of officials inveighed against his abuse of ministerial authority and the predatory intrusiveness of his New Policies. In Jen-tsung's reign similar opposition had led to abrupt suspension of imperial support for the Ch'ing-li reforms, but Shen-tsung's commitment was not so easily shaken. Driven by the potency of his irredentist dream, Shen-tsung acceded to Wang An-shih's insistence that dissent against the reforms be suppressed by purging opponents of the activist agenda, punishing antireform censors, closing the "roads of remonstrance" (yen-lu), and granting key reform cadre in the field immunity from censorial impeachment.

Except for brief interruptions, dissent against the New Policies remained silenced for the duration of Shen-tsung's reign, especially under the prodding of Ts'ai Ch'üeh, Wang An-shih's successor as reform commandant from 1077 to Shen-tsung's death in 1085. With the enthronement of Shen-tsung's eight-year-old son, power passed to a coalition of men headed by Ssu-ma Kuang and the dowager empress Hsüan-jen who were determined to abolish the hated New Policies and reverse the irredentist adventurism that spawned them. But despite the transfer of power to prudent, conservative men, political culture had been too thoroughly transformed by the heated partisanship of Shen-tsung's reign to permit a return to the relative collegiality of the post-Shan-yüan decades, for factional strife during the New Policies era had propagated the equivalent of a party system, with the victorious party claiming all the political spoils. Thus while Wang An-shih's erstwhile foes moved to reverse his policies, they enthusiastically emulated Wang's political techniques of capturing the Council of State and monopolizing the Censorate and the Remonstrance offices.

In particular, the Yüan-yu partisans (Yüan-yu tang), so named for the restoration reign period (1086–94), suppressed opponents with a counterpurge of New Policies adherents more sweeping than anything in the dynasty to that point, despite warnings from within their own ranks that perpetuating factional strife could only come back to haunt them. And indeed it did. On assuming personal rule in 1094, Che-tsung declared fealty to his father's achievements by proclaiming the new reign period of Shao-sheng (Continuing Sagacity), while his lieutenants denounced the antireform regency as a profound mistake and eliminated its supporters from office. As Levine demonstrates in chapter 6, "Late Northern Sung politics entered its most virulent and divisive stage during the personal rule of Che-tsung," when the casualty count of factionalism would rise exponentially.

Factional strife and its belligerent discourse reached a peak between 1102 and 1104, when the new emperor Hui-tsung authorized his chief councilor Ts'ai Ching (1047–1126) to proscribe all members of the "Yüan-yu party" – whether dead or alive – and extirpate their political and literary legacies. Although an ominous comet frightened Hui-tsung into rescinding the blacklist in 1106, opponents of the revived, more heatedly revanchist reform agenda remained effectively silenced by Ts'ai Ching's license to smother policy dissent. Indeed, as Hui-tsung asserted in 1108, it was Ts'ai Ching's suppression of policy opponents that enabled the emperor to fulfill his father's goal of annexing the Tibetan domains centered on Ch'ing-t'ang (modern Hsi-ning, Tsinghai province), intended to be the first step in Shen-tsung's war with the Tangut:

Previously my Divine Ancestor began plans for military success by delineating the western frontier. Although at that time not even [Hsi-chou2] had been recovered he established a unified circuit in order to bring all [the constituent regions] under a common name and to show that this great and sacred design must be brought to success . . . In bringing this plan to fulfillment [We have] relied on my Chief Councilor [Ts'ai Ching]. If he had not banished the doubting multitudes then how could [We] have fully realized [Our] forbear's ambition to spread Our majesty among the caitiffs beyond the borders?[33]

Through the reigns of Shen-tsung and his sons, then, irredentist ambition and imperial support for the chief councilors and statist policies that could help bring that ambition to pass had irreversibly undermined the constitutional division of authority that checked the arbitrary exercise of state power. The Sung political system from the New Policies through the end of the Southern Sung saw a growing consolidation of executive authority in the inner court, comprised above all by the sovereign and his chief councilors, especially Wang An-shih (in power from 1069–76), Chang Tun (1094–1100), and Ts'ai Ching (1102–19) in the Northern Sung, and Ch'in Kuei (1128–55), Han T'o-chou (1194–1207), Shih Mi-yüan (1208–33), and Chia Ssu-tao (1259–75) after the dynastic move south.[34] At the same time purges, suppressions,

---

[33] Smith, "Irredentism as political capital," citing Yang Chung-liang, *Tzu-chih t'ung-chien ch'ang-pien chi-shih pen-mo* 140, p. 13b.

[34] The historian Lin T'ien-wei measures the growing power of the chief councilors over the course of the Sung dynasty by the number of man-years the originally dual positions of "right" and "left" chief councilors were occupied by a single (and hence preeminent) incumbent. By that measure, 22 percent of the Northern Sung's chief councilors served alone, for a total of 63 of the era's 167 years or 37 percent of the time. During the Southern Sung, by contrast, 36 percent of the chief councilors served alone for

and irreconcilable policy differences had fractured the tenuous and inherently unstable solidarity of the bureaucratic elite, pitting insiders and outsiders against one another and eventually driving a wedge between the inner court and the ministerial political machines that dominated it, and the bureaucracy as a whole.

But what of the revanchist dream that underpinned the New Policies? In order to mobilize the nation for war, Shen-tsung and Wang An-shih promoted an intensive project of military strengthening that included revitalization of the officer corps through reforms in the command structure, establishment of a national military institute, revival of the national arsenal, creation of a reliable system of procuring horses for the cavalry, and the institution of mandatory military drill and review for virtually all members of the new mutual security (*pao-chia*) system in north China. In addition, both Shen-tsung and Wang An-shih chose to delegate autonomous authority to their generals in the field. With this they reversed a century-old policy of military centralization, setting off a countertrend that reached its peak around 1115 when Hui-tsung promoted the eunuch general T'ung Kuan (1054–1126) to the position of generalissimo of Shan-hsi, Ho-tung, and Ho-pei circuits and concurrent head of the Bureau of Military Affairs, thereby granting one man supreme control over the entire Northern Sung military apparatus.[35]

Sung military reforms yielded their most impressive results in extended campaigns against the weak frontiers of northeastern Tibet (the Ch'ing-t'ang region) and southwestern Szechwan, where Sung forces showed that with adequate time and massive resources they could dislodge indigenous populations from their native settlements, fend off their guerilla defenders, and buy off their chieftains with emoluments and titles. Victory against scattered tribal forces meant little when it came to doing battle with the far more sophisticated armies of the Tangut Hsi Hsia, however, against whom Sung forces under Shen-tsung and his sons never gained more than a stalemate when they were not thoroughly humiliated. Yet by Hui-tsung's reign so many men had ridden to power on the banner of Shen-tsung's irredentist mission that every victory, real or imagined, was an occasion for promotions and solemn celebrations. And so, when in 1118 defectors from the north reported that Jurchen invaders had created havoc on the Khitan frontier, Hui-tsung and his court defied anxious critics to make a pact with the Jurchen to help them topple the Liao in return

---

63 percent of the era's 149 years. See Lin, "Sung-tai ch'üan-hsiang hsing-ch'eng chih fen-hsi," pp. 141–70. For discussions in English, see Liu Tzu-chien (James T. C. Liu), *China turning inward: Intellectual-political changes in the early twelfth century* (Cambridge, Mass., 1988), pp. 81–104, and Gung Wei Ai, "Prevalence of powerful chief ministers in Southern Sung China, 1127–1279 A.D.," *Chinese Culture* 40 No. 2 (1999), pp. 103–14.

35 Smith, "Irredentism as political capital."

for recovery of the Sixteen Yen-Yün Prefectures. But in 1122, after four years of
negotiating over Yen-Yün as Jurchen armies devoured the Liao domain, T'ung
Kuan's expeditionary army was routed and humiliated by the putatively impo-
tent Khitan troops. After the Jurchen forces overthrew the last Liao remnants
in 1125 they turned their sights on the Sung, whose panic-stricken emperor
abdicated to his son Sung Ch'in-tsung. But with neither the trained corps
needed to conduct effective diplomacy nor the military discipline and reserves
of political capital required to mount an effective defense, the Sung left itself
open to a Jurchen blitz through north China "as if it were undefended," belying
the half century of war mobilization and military reform. In the first month
of 1127 K'ai-feng fell to the Jurchen, who marched both emperors and their
royal entourage to exile in the alien north. Shen-tsung's irredentist dream
had backfired, adding all of north China to the category of *terra irredenta* and
placing the survival of the dynasty in doubt.

Survival, recovery, and autocracy, 1127–c. 1260

Over the long term, the conquest of north China by the Jurchen ignited political, social, and intellectual changes whose ramifications extended beyond the
Southern Sung (as the surviving dynasty would be called) into the Yüan, Ming,
and even the Ch'ing. Perhaps most crucially, the loss of north China signaled
for many the failure of state activism, and shattered the identity of interest
between the state and the *shih-ta-fu* elite that had already been strained by
factional warfare under Shen-tsung and his sons. To anticipate a theme developed more fully in our companion volume, with the massive flight of Sung
subjects and officials to the south the bureaucratic elite of the eleventh century was absorbed into a much wider stratum of local lineages who viewed
government service as just one option in an array of mobility strategies, and
the family and local community as a more appropriate focus of institutional
reform than the centralized bureaucratic state. In concert with this change in
orientation, thinkers like Chu Hsi (1130–1200) who were associated with the
Learning of the Way (*Tao-hsüeh*, or Neo-Confucianism) articulated a new conception of the links between politics, community, and moral transformation
that gradually emerged as the ideological underpinning for an increasingly
self-conscious local gentry well into the sixteenth and seventeenth centuries.
In spatial terms, the eventual relocation of the new, embattled emperor Sung
Kao-tsung (r. 1127–62) and his court to the "temporary capital" (*hsing-tsai*)
of Hang-chou (renamed Lin-an) in 1132 superimposed the political center of
the dynasty over its economic core and helped transform the lower Yangtze
region (or Chiang-nan) – the only region during the Sung, Yüan, and Ming
eras to be spared the most extreme depredations of war – into China's social,

economic, and cultural heartland from the twelfth through roughly the six-teenth centuries.[36]

In the short term, however, the Jurchen conquest of north China unleashed explosive forces of political and social chaos that threatened to topple the dynasty, as Tao Jing-shen details in chapter 8.[37] From the moment the Jurchen Chin officially deposed the Chao clan in the second month of 1127, it fell to Ch'in-tsung's brother (then Prince K'ang) and a small coterie of loyal partisans to restore the dynasty in a south China that was itself roiled by rebellion, warlordism, and army mutinies and defections. As late as 1130, after Kao-tsung had been forced (in 1129) to temporarily abdicate the throne by a rebellious commander of the Imperial Bodyguard and then driven out of Hang-chou by a Chin invasion of the lower Yangtze region, the fledgling restoration seemed very close to collapsing.

As it happened, Southern Sung fortunes began to turn around later that very year, the same time that the Jurchen created the proxy state of Ch'i (1130–7) to provide a buffer between the Chin and Sung regimes. Gradually the Southern Sung court succeeded in co-opting the warlords who had come to dominate society along the Han, Huai, and Yangtze rivers, taking advantage of their neutralization to reorganize riverine defenses in the east and (as Tao explains) institute significant military reforms in the mountainous west. Yet survival required Kao-tsung to incur political risks, by delegating military authority to some thirty-nine military governors – many of them former warlords – to help secure order along the new frontier. In 1135 control over these strategic areas was consolidated under the "four great generals" (including Yüeh Fei) of the restoration era, each of whom was put in charge of an extensive garrison command (*tu-t'ung ssu*). Although it was these generals and their minions who were most responsible for quelling internal rebellion and mounting an effective defense against the Chin, their authority and de facto autonomy became increasingly worrisome to Kao-tsung and his courtiers, who sought opportunities to recentralize military control in the hands of the court. Such opportunities came with increasing frequency from the mid-1130s on, as order returned to south China, the Sung and Chin courts tired of war, and the death of the captive emperor, Hui-tsung, in 1135 and return of his coffin in 1137 made war less of a filial imperative. In 1137 the Jurchen abolished their proxy state of Ch'i, bringing the Chin and Southern Sung face to face along the Huai and Han river frontier. A year later, Kao-tsung, whom Tao Jing-shen depicts as

---

[36] These themes are addressed in Smith and von Glahn, *The Song-Yuan-Ming transition in Chinese history*.

[37] The most comprehensive study of the Southern Sung restoration is Teraji Jun, *Nan-Sō shoki seijishi kenkyū* (Hiroshima, 1988), translated into Chinese as *Nan Sung ch'u-ch'i cheng-chih-shih yen-chiu*, trans. Liu Ching-chen and Li Chin-yun (Taipei, 1995).

overcoming his earlier revanchist inclinations to favor instead the Shan-yüan approach to foreign relations through rapprochement, publicly proclaimed his willingness to humble himself in pursuit of peace with the Chin.[38]

Kao-tsung's declaration of intent by no means settled the issue of peace, and impassioned officials, inflamed by a sense of national humiliation at the loss of the Central Plains heartland, continued to oppose what they saw as appeasement in the most robust public policy debate since the abdicating Hui-tsung lifted the ban on remonstrance in 1125.[39] At the same time, Sung generals headed by Yüeh Fei showed surprising strength in fending off Jurchen forays and launching their own sorties as far north as Lo-yang and K'ai-feng. But following ten tumultuous years on an embattled throne Kao-tsung was eager to recapture the equilibrium of the post-Shan-yüan decades, as Tao Jing-shen explains, by seeking external security through peace with the Chin and internal security through control over the military. Both objectives Kao-tsung entrusted to his chief councilor Ch'in Kuei, whose task it now became to use on behalf of rapprochement the same political tactics that Wang An-shih, Ts'ai Ch'üeh, Chang Tun, and Ts'ai Ching had wielded on behalf of war: centralization of power, suppression of debate, and political intimidation. In the military sphere, Ch'in Kuei took advantage of the peace treaty concluded with the Chin in 1141 to strip the great garrison commanders of their positions and then to execute their one member – Yüeh Fei – whose irredentist zeal and military prowess could most easily undo the peace plan. In the political domain, Ch'in Kuei unleashed official censors and private informers against critics of the peace treaty in a fifteen-year campaign of innuendo, repression, and literary censorship, all under the same monarchical authorization on behalf of rapprochement that Hui-tsung had given Ts'ai Ching on behalf of war – that is, the authority to "smash all who differ."[40]

Although the 1141 treaty required the Sung to acknowledge ritual submission and pay annual tribute to the Chin, the peace it secured ushered in an era of remarkable economic and cultural development. That peace was founded

---

[38] Hsü Meng-hsin, *San-ch'ao pei-meng hui-pien* (1196; Taipei, 1962), 188, pp. 7b–8a.

[39] Hsü, *San-ch'ao pei-meng hui-pien* 25, pp. 91a–10b. The *San-ch'ao* compilation is the best source on the debates over war and peace during both the fall of the Northern Sung and the Southern Sung restoration. Hoyt Tillman provides an example of the passions inflamed by the loss of north China in his "Proto-nationalism in twelfth-century China? The case of Ch'en Liang," *Harvard Journal of Asiatic Studies* 39 No. 2 (1979), pp. 403–28.

[40] Cited in Charles Hartman, "The making of a villain: Ch'in Kuei and Tao-hsüeh," *Harvard Journal of Asiatic Studies* 58 No. 1 (1998), p. 89. As background to his study of biographical manipulation, Hartman provides a concise account of Ch'in Kuei's campaign of political suppression. For further studies, see Gung Wei Ai, "The usurpation of power by Ch'in Kuei through the censorial organ (1138–1155 A.D.)," *Chinese Culture* 15 No. 3 (1974), pp. 25–42; and especially chapters 9 to 13 of Teraji, *Nan Sung ch'u-ch'i cheng-chih-shih yen-chiu*, pp. 285–385.

on a balance of lethal force that gave the advantage to defense over attack; thus while Sung and Chin went to war three times in the next half century – instigated by Prince Hai-ling of the Chin in 1161 and by the Sung in 1163 and 1206 – in each case the outcome was disastrous for the aggressor. Indeterminate though war may have been from a strategic perspective, decisions about war nonetheless continued to serve as a vehicle for emperors and their chief advisors to consolidate power at the expense of the policy-making, administrative, and censorial agencies of the regular bureaucracy, thereby exacerbating the autocratic distance between the inner court and the civil service.

In the case of Kao-tsung's adopted son and successor Hsiao-tsung, political centralization assumed many of the classic attributes of autocratic rule by a monarch unencumbered by other persons or institutions. For as Gong Wei Ai describes in chapter 9, Hsiao-tsung not only bypassed the line bureaucracy but even his chief ministers to personally assume decision-making authority over an increasingly wide range of affairs. Hsiao-tsung took personal control of his government as early as 1163, after court vacillation over war policy induced him to brush aside his two chief councilors, his Council of State, and his Bureau of Military Affairs to secretly order his commanding general to attack the Chin. Nor did the disastrous conclusion of that campaign impel Hsiao-tsung to relinquish the reins of state over the next two decades, prompting outspoken representatives of bureaucratic professionalism such as Chu Hsi to decry the emperor's arrogation of civil service powers and the enfeeblement of his Council of State.

Monarchical autocracy gave way again to ministerial domination when Hsiao-tsung abdicated the throne to his son Kuang-tsung (r. 1189–94), an act that deprived the Southern Sung of its last effective emperor. In his three chapters covering the last century of the dynasty, Richard Davis portrays Kuang-tsung's reign as the beginning of a protracted era of political paralysis that weakened the Southern Sung from the inside even as it was beset by the rise of the Mongols from without. Moreover, the onset of an era of weak emperors did nothing to reconstitute the relatively conciliar, professionalized governance that had evolved under the passive rule of Chen-tsung and Jen-tsung of the Northern Sung. For the vacuum created by imperial withdrawal was quickly filled by palace favorites and powerful chief ministers, two of whom – Han T'o-chou (1151–1207) and Chia Ssu-tao (1213–75) – were themselves products of the inner palace quarters rather than the civil service career track.

Han T'o-chou epitomized the palace favorite, as Davis shows, rising to prominence on the skirts of such prominent palace women as Kao-tsung's wife and Han's own aunt, the dowager empress Wu. Yet when Kuang-tsung's unfilial conduct unleashed the fury of *Tao-hsüeh* partisans inside the court and out, it was only with Han T'o-chou's help that the state councilor and

imperial clansman Chao Ju-yü persuaded the reprobate emperor to abdicate
the throne to *his* son Sung Ning-tsung (r. 1194–1224). Fully expecting to
be rewarded for his help in engineering a smooth succession, Han instead
found himself boxed out of power by the same *Tao-hsüeh* statesmen he thought
he had helped, whose continued moralizing not only polarized the political
atmosphere but enraged the new emperor as well. Utilizing his position as
a palace insider, Han capitalized on Ning-tsung's aversion to the *Tao-hsüeh*
alliance to gain the emperor's trust and then, in 1194, win imperial designation
as special councilor. From this position Han drew on the repertoire of tactics
honed by Ts'ai Ching and Ch'in Kuei to keep the professional bureaucracy and
its *Tao-hsüeh* spokesmen at bay: Han incited his handpicked cadre of censors to
hound officials, issued special palace orders to circumvent the bureaucracy and
fire foes, and most famously, from 1195 to 1199, enacted an outright ban on
the *Tao-hsüeh* movement for its dissemination of "spurious learning." When all
this failed to silence his critics Han played his trump card – a war against the
Chin drummed up in an effort to co-opt his *Tao-hsüeh* detractors by catering to
their revanchist yearnings. But like Prince Hai-ling's war of 1161 and Hsiao-
tsung's campaign of 1163, the K'ai-hsi war of 1206–7 backfired: prominent
irredentist leaders withheld their support, the hereditary commander of Sung
forces in northern Szechwan rebelled, Chin troops humiliated Sung armies
all along the Sino-Jurchen frontier, and Han T'o-chou lost his head to court-
sponsored assassins.

The K'ai-hsi war marked the end of active Sung attempts to shape its relations with the steppe: for the next half century or so, events along the frontier
were decided and paced by the Mongols, whose extraordinary rise caught the
entire Eurasian world off-guard. But the end of the K'ai-hsi war also marked
what Davis describes as a new phase in Southern Sung politics, as *Tao-hsüeh*
moralism and Han T'o-chou's political intolerance and adventurism gave way
to moderation and compromise under the new, long-serving chief councilor,
Shih Mi-yüan (1164–1233, served 1208–33). Seen from the perspective of
the dynasty as a whole, restraints on political discourse were looser in the
last seven decades of the Sung than at any time since the New Policies. As
the son of a former chief councilor and a civil servant of impeccable credentials, Shih Mi-yüan repaid the support of his fellow literati with what Davis
portrays as a genuine commitment to intellectual pluralism and an abiding
respect for the *Tao-hsüeh* school, which enjoyed increasing imperial patronage
if no greater political influence from this time on. Moreover, Shih's tolerance
of public criticism, which became increasingly strident after students of the
Imperial University emerged as a potent political force, survived his death
in 1233; with the exception of a fruitless ban issued in 1158, the post–Han
T'o-chou era never witnessed the same proscriptions or blanket suppression

of debate over issues of war and peace that characterized Sung political culture from the 1070s to 1207. This absence of purges and bans by no means heralded a return to the broad-based governance of the early eleventh century, but simply a greater willingness on the part of the governing regime to manipulate, patronize, and co-opt rather than muzzle its critics. Shih Mi-yüan came under escalating attacks by *Tao-hsüeh* partisans for what they viewed as his humiliating military concessions to a deteriorating Chin regime and for his usurpation of monarchical authority – in short, his ministerial autocracy. But even so, Shih chose to frustrate rather than silence his detractors, all the while monopolizing the ear of his two emperors (Ning-tsung and Li-tsung [r. 1224–64]) and expanding his network of political power.[41]

Political stagnation and the fall of the Southern Sung

Shih Mi-yüan's political machine survived until 1251, when the death of his last close associate created a political vacuum that was filled largely by eunuchs and consorts until a new palace favorite, Chia Ssu-tao (1213–75), was named chief councilor in 1259. But by that time the Mongols had conquered the countries surrounding Sung, including Hsi Hsia (1227), Chin (1234), Ta-li (1254), and Korea (1259), with Tibet soon to fall (1268), and had laid waste to Szechwan and the cities along the Han and middle Yangtze rivers.

Despite Chia Ssu-tao's reputation as the dynasty's "last bad minister," Davis shows (in Chapter 12) that Chia's administration did everything possible to defend against the final Mongol assaults, but by then the Mongol military machine was simply too formidable for the decimated and poorly commanded Sung forces. Davis rightly highlights the Mongol's military superiority over the Southern Sung, but his own chapters, in conjunction with the work of steppe historians like Nicola Di Cosmo cited earlier, suggest that the Mongols owed their conquest of China as much to political as to military factors. For even as the Mongol capacity to synthesize a wide array of institutional resources from steppe polities and north China reenforced and amplified their military power with political innovation, the Sung political system had begun to atrophy.

In the realm of financial administration, for example, the centralization of executive authority in the hands of the emperor, chief councilors, and their minions was offset by the irreversible hemorrhaging of fiscal authority to regional agencies. According to Robert M. Hartwell, despite continued complaints by

---

[41] For one example of Shih Mi-yüan's ability to neutralize his critics, see Liu Tzu-chien (James T. C. Liu), "Wei Liao-weng's thwarted statecraft," in *Ordering the world: Approaches to state and society in Sung dynasty China*, ed. Robert P. Hymes and Conrad Schirokauer (Berkeley, Calif., 1993), pp. 336–48.

functionaries of the central government, regional fiscal agencies "supervised the accounts for nearly sixty percent of total government income and possibly more than seventy-three percent of expenditures" in the late twelfth century, giving them the power to retain the bulk of state fiscal receipts in the provinces. As a result, although total government revenues were approximately the same in the late eleventh and late twelfth centuries when north China is discounted, the Southern Sung court had weaker control over the empire's economic resources than its late Northern Sung predecessor had had, at a time of even greater national peril.[42]

With respect to frontier policy, a century and a half of arbitrary governance had undermined the court's ability to reach broad-based, well-considered decisions about issues of war and peace, paralyzing the Sung policy-making apparatus at the very moment that the dynasty confronted its greatest threat. As Charles Peterson shows (and Davis's chapters confirm), Sung frontier policy in the first decade after the K'ai-hsi war was timid and indecisive, with the court too fearful of provoking even a deteriorating Chin regime into war to give support to anti-Jurchen rebels in Shantung or even to undertake military preparations of its own, despite the urgent pleas of Chen Te-hsiu (1178–1235) and like-minded *Tao-hsüeh* revanchists.[43] From 1217 to 1224 Sung forces fared well against a series of attacks launched by Jurchen armies made desperate by Mongol assaults farther north; but the court's ambivalence toward the Shantung rebels eventually pushed the most powerful of them, Li Ch'üan, into the hands of the Mongols in 1226, quite possibly depriving the Sung of "a golden opportunity to strengthen its position in the northeast and even to lay the basis for the occupation of parts of Honan, Kiangsu, and Shantung."[44] The Sung had no direct contact with the Mongols until 1221, but even then fears about the disastrous Yen-Yün collaboration with the Jurchen a century earlier kept them shy of further entanglements.[45] These fears turned out to be prophetic, for in 1234 – the year after Shih Mi-yüan's death – Li-tsung launched an ill-considered preemptive campaign in Honan to wrest Lo-yang and K'ai-feng from the Mongols despite the warnings of even such fervent irredentists as Chen Te-hsiu.[46] Just as Chen and his cohort predicted, the Honan region and

---

[42] See Robert M. Hartwell, "The imperial treasuries: Finance and power in Song China," *Bulletin of Sung-Yüan Studies* 20 (1988), pp. 72–91.

[43] Charles A. Peterson, "First Sung reactions to the Mongol invasion of the North, 1211–17," in *Crisis and prosperity in Sung China*, ed. John W. Haeger (Tucson, Ariz., 1975), pp. 215–52.

[44] Charles A. Peterson, "Old illusions and new realities: Sung foreign policy, 1217–1234," in *China among equals: The Middle Kingdom and its neighbors, 10th–14th centuries*, ed. Morris Rossabi (Berkeley, Calif., 1983), p. 231.

[45] Peterson, "Old illusions and new realities," pp. 218–31.

[46] Peterson, "Old illusions and new realities," pp. 218–31. Peterson summarizes the views of Chen and his allies on pp. 227–8.

its cities were reduced to a useless and unprovisionable wasteland; the Sung military lacked the information, leadership, training, and supplies to mount an offensive campaign; and the Mongols responded to the unilateral provocation with harsh and lethal reprisals. Two years later the Mongols unleashed a massive campaign against Szechwan that by the end of 1236 had razed all but four of the region's fifty-eight prefectural capitals, initiating a long but inexorable process of conquest that Sung policy makers were helpless to arrest.

Finally, the Sung dynasty lost the support of its literatus elite just as it faced its greatest peril. Elite separation from the state was in part a result of the growing surplus of qualified candidates for the civil service, which impelled the eleventh-century oligarchy of exam-based bureaucratic lineages to supplement officeholding with an alternative mobility strategy based on the accumulation of wealth and property and the strengthening of family, community, and employment ties at the local level. This emergent localism, which for Robert Hartwell and Robert Hymes constitutes the most salient transformation of Southern Sung society, "served to widen and to emphasize a gap between elite interests and state interests at the local level, and to confirm and strengthen the independence of elite status and social position from the efforts of the state to certify, to validate, and so to control it."[47] But this demographically driven process of social differentiation was transformed into a more pointed estrangement by the factional warfare of the late eleventh century and the arbitrary governance of the Southern Sung, which frustrated and alienated those officials who, in addition to their stress on local initiatives, continued to take the ideals of professional bureaucratic service to heart. The most impassioned heralds of that estrangement were the leaders of the *Tao-hsüeh* movement, who collectively articulated a critique of absolutist rule whether monarchical or ministerial and outlined the limits of literati loyalty to an ethically compromised government.[48] As the breach between the state and the literati hardened, *Tao-hsüeh* learning came to provide a sense of group identity "that some [*shih*] believed could provide moral and social guidance in their roles as the elite of a local society relative to which they could be

---

[47] Robert P. Hymes, *Statesmen and gentlemen: The elite of Fu-chou, Chiang-hsi, in Northern and Southern Sung* (Cambridge, 1986), p. 212. See also Hartwell, "Demographic, political, and social transformations of China."

[48] For an example of Wei Liao-weng's critique of Shih Mi-yüan's absolutist rule and call for a return to constitutionally divided government, see Liu, "Wei Liao-weng's thwarted statecraft," pp. 344–5; for Chu Hsi's refusal to serve in a government so politically degraded that it would constitute "an insult to my person," see Conrad Schirokauer, "Chu Hsi's political career: A study in ambivalence," in *Confucian personalities*, ed. Arthur F. Wright and Denis C. Twitchett (Stanford, Calif., 1962), p. 170.

powerful, and . . . moral and political justification for their autonomy from a government relative to which they felt powerless."[49]

Although the political elite was by no means induced to rebel against the Sung, their alienation cost the imperiled dynasty both gentry and official support at its moment of greatest danger. While Davis (in chapter 12) highlights the small but devoted circle of loyalists who stood by to the end and died with the last Sung emperors – for their story is rich in drama and pathos – he describes as well the larger picture of political capitulation, as civilian and military officials relinquished southern cities to the Mongols without a fight, capital officials absconded in droves, and the once-firebrand university students fled for their lives. Moreover, once the Mongols consolidated their control over the Southern Sung domain, former Sung officials and landlords quickly accommodated themselves to Mongol rule in return for government protection of their property rights and local posts for themselves and their children. Even self-described Sung loyalists were induced to abandon the pretense of eremitic withdrawal by a combination of financial necessity, family interest, and a conviction that cooperation with the evolving Yüan state was the only way to reestablish local order and security.[50] Furthermore, no group was more closely connected with this accommodation to Mongol rule than the followers of the once staunchly irredentist *Tao-hsüeh* movement. For with the collapse of the Southern Sung dynasty that they had long critiqued, prominent *Tao-hsüeh* thinkers swiftly moved to put their imprint on the Yüan state by influencing its social, institutional, and legal policies. At the same time, their lower-level adherents fanned out into the provinces to found private academies and staff lineage schools that disseminated Neo-Confucian learning throughout the local elites of south China.[51]

In the end, then, the fall of the Southern Sung highlighted two intersecting trends. In the realm of Sino-steppe relations, an evolving cycle of Inner Asian state formation that was well under way at the founding of the Sung provided

---

[49] Peter K. Bol, "Neo-Confucianism and local society, twelfth to sixteenth century: A case study," in *The Song-Yuan-Ming transition in Chinese history*, ed. Paul Jakov Smith and Richard von Glahn (Cambridge, Mass., 2003), p. 245.

[50] On the adjustment of Sung elites to Mongol rule, see Jennifer W. Jay, *A change in dynasties: Loyalism in thirteenth-century China* (Bellingham, Wash., 1991); and Paul J. Smith, "Fear of gynarchy in an age of chaos: Kong Qi's reflections on life in south China under Mongol rule," *Journal of Economic and Social History of the Orient* 41 No. 1 (1998), pp. 1–95.

[51] These issues, the subject of a growing bibliography, are addressed in the chapters by Bettine Birge, "Women and Confucianism from Song to Ming: The institutionalization of patrilineality," pp. 212–40; John W. Dardess, "Did the Mongols matter? Territory, power, and the intelligentsia in China from the Northern Song to the early Ming," pp. 111–34; and Peter K. Bol, "Neo-Confucianism and local society, twelfth to sixteenth century," in *The Song-Yuan-Ming transition in Chinese history*, ed. Paul Jakov Smith and Richard von Glahn (Cambridge, Mass., 2003).

one steppe polity – the Mongols – with a repertoire of organizational means to draw on as it finally conquered all of China and integrated it into a vast Eurasian empire. But the fall of the Sung dynasty by no means meant the destruction of elite Sung society or culture. For by the twelfth century, state formation on the steppe was matched by a concomitant process of class formation within China. As a result, the literocentric sociopolitical elite had gained autonomy from the Sung state that had conceived it, facilitating its swift adaptation to life under steppe rule and ensuring its continued ability to flourish and to shape Chinese culture well into the late imperial era.

CHAPTER 1

THE FIVE DYNASTIES

Naomi Standen

INTRODUCTION

By the early tenth century, political control in the T'ang empire had been divided among regional governors, commanders, and warlords for some hundred and fifty years. This division of political power resulted chiefly from the effects of the momentous rebellions (755–63) of An Lu-shan and his followers, in which the capitals at Lo-yang and Ch'ang-an were seized, and the T'ang emperor driven into exile. By 907 the remnants of T'ang control of the central Yellow River valley had been extinguished.[1] Over the next fifty-three years, control of this region, from Ch'ang-an to K'ai-feng, would be seized and relinquished by several successive claimants, each trying, and for the most part failing, to construct a sustainable base of power – the Later Liang, the Later T'ang, the Later Chin, the Later Han, and the Later Chou.[2] During this time, known as the Five Dynasties period, regions outside the Yellow River valley that were once part of the T'ang empire were under administrative control of different sets of claimants also trying to legitimize and strengthen their rule.

In this period of social instability and near constant warfare, allegiances among regional commanders drove political events forward. In this chapter I examine the campaigns and allegiances, internal and external, that framed political events in the central Yellow River valley – the great center of power in the T'ang dynasty – and discuss how the development of allegiance strategies increased a ruler's ability to administer troops and resources, culminating fifty years later in a military force strong enough to conquer much of the southern

---

[1] The best introductions to these events are the last four chapters of Denis C. Twitchett, ed., *The Cambridge history of China*, volume 3: *Sui and T'ang China, 589–906, part 1* (Cambridge, 1979), and the references cited therein.

[2] The founders of each of these dynasties used the name of a previous dynasty as a way of linking their dynasty to lineages, regions, and successes of the past. Although these states did not, as a rule, refer to themselves using the prefixes Later, Northern, Southern, etc., it is a long-standing historiographic practice that helps to distinguish one dynasty from another.

territory once held by the T'ang. This increased capacity, although developed in the Five Dynasties, would coalesce around the Sung dynastic line after 960.

FIGHTING FOR ALLEGIANCES

An Lu-shan was one of ten military governors (*chieh-tu shih*) appointed by the T'ang to large frontier commands ideal for defending or expanding the empire's borders – and for overthrowing the dynasty. Restoration of the T'ang dynasty after the An Lu-shan rebellions relied heavily on extending the military governor system from the frontiers to the interior by appointing loyalists to new governorships created in the heartland of the empire, and at the same time winning over rebel governors by granting regional commands to those who surrendered. All of these governors enjoyed greater or lesser autonomy, and although the T'ang emperors T'ang Te-tsung (779–805), T'ang Hsien-tsung (805–20), and T'ang Mu-tsung (820–4) recovered the ability to appoint governors to all but the ex-rebel provinces in the region of Ho-pei in the northeast, the governors – court appointed or otherwise – chose and changed sides to prevent any one leader (including the emperor) from becoming powerful enough to threaten the status quo. The former rebel provinces sent no taxes to the court, and imperial attempts to claw the same returns from fewer people produced widespread banditry from the 830s on, exacerbated by a spate of severe natural disasters. Some bandit gangs developed into insurrectionary armies, one of which, led by the failed examination candidate Huang Ch'ao, seized the capital Ch'ang-an in 880, forcing the emperor to take refuge in Szechwan. Governors were unwilling to get involved on either side unless it was to their advantage, so the court eventually sought help from Li K'o-yung, a Sha-t'o Turkic leader whose father was a T'ang prefect. In 883 Li, leading a mixed steppe and provincial army, defeated Huang Ch'ao near Ch'ang-an, and was rewarded with the governorship of Ho-tung (roughly modern Shansi province).

Although the T'ang dynasty was again restored to its capitals, the emperor and his court now had no effective power, for they lacked the means to coerce obedience. Coercion required either control of resources or military strength, and both were held by the autonomous governors and their armies. The first ten military governors in the early eighth century had held appointments giving them full civil and military authority over at least one prefecture, as well as fiscal and supervisory rights over several others.[3] Already a provincial governor

---

[3] What follows draws upon David Graff, *Medieval Chinese warfare, 300–900* (London, 2002), pp. 211, 229–31, 243, as well as on Charles A. Peterson, "The autonomy of the northeastern provinces in the period following the An Lu-shan rebellion" (diss., University of Washington, 1966); Wang Gungwu, *The structure*

in effect, each commanded all military forces in his region, consisting of long-service professionals who were mostly volunteers. After An Lu-shan's rebellion the whole empire was divided into provinces (*tao*) that became an intermediate tier of local administration between the prefectures and the capital. They controlled both military and civil affairs. By the second restoration in 883 there were some fifty governors heading smaller provinces, some as small as two prefectures.[4] After the first restoration several ex-rebel provinces in the northeast had become hereditary regimes where the governors appointed all their own provincial and prefectural officials, brought the prefectural militias under provincial control, sent no taxes to court, and dominated county-level administration by creating parallel organizations in which the governors' own people performed the same functions as the court-appointed magistrates. These governors were independent but for their demand that the T'ang court formally confirm their positions. Yet most remained loyal to the T'ang until Huang Ch'ao's rebellion, when armies replaced many governors and prefects with their own choices. From then on the T'ang court received even fewer taxes and lost its ability to appoint administrators and prefects, while governors became warlords and fought among themselves over the dismembered carcass of the empire. Out of this chaotic environment emerged the nine kingdoms of the

---

of power in north China during the Five Dynasties (Kuala Lumpur, 1963); and Edmund H. Worthy, Jr., "The founding of Sung China, 950–1000: Integrative changes in military and political institutions" (diss., Princeton University, 1976), especially pp. 265–71. This work follows the Japanese pioneers, notably the four-part study by Hino Kaisaburō: "Tōdai hanchin no bakko to chinshō (ichi)," *Tōyō gakuhō* 26 No. 4 (1939), pp. 1–37; "Tōdai hanchin no bakko to chinshō (ni)," *Tōyō gakuhō* 27 No. 1 (1939), pp. 1–62; "Tōdai hanchin no bakko to chinshō (san)," *Tōyō gakuhō* 27 No. 2 (1940), pp. 1–60; and "Tōdai hanchin no bakko to chinshō (shi)," *Tōyō gakuhō* 27 No. 3 (1940), pp. 1–40; and, for the Five Dynasties, Hino's "Godai chinshō kō," *Tōyō gakuhō* 25 (1938), pp. 54–85, and Sudō Yoshiyuki's, "Godai setsudoshi no shihai taisei," *Shigaku zasshi* 61 (1952), pp. 289–329, 521–39. See also Han Kuo-p'an, "T'ang-mo Wu-tai ti fan-chen ko-chü," in *Sui T'ang Wu-tai shih lun-chi*, Han Kuo-p'an (1958; Peking, 1979), pp. 308–20; and Ou-yang Hsiu, *Historical records of the Five Dynasties*, trans. Richard L. Davis (New York, 2004).

[4] Owing to the fluidity of events in the last twenty years of the Tang dynasty and the beginning of the Five Dynasties period, these regimes inherited a confusing range of local offices and institutional nomenclature. In the early T'ang the central government had dealt directly with the prefectures (*chou*, renamed *chün* briefly under the emperor T'ang Hsüan-tsung). After the An Lu-shan rebellion the province (*tao*) became a higher level of authority. These larger administrative units contained a number of contiguous prefectures under the overriding authority of a military governor (*chieh-tu shih*) in most of the north China region, or of a civil governor (*kuan-ch'a shih*) in most of the south. These provinces varied widely in their degree of autonomy and their military strength. For a summary of this situation see Denis C. Twitchett, "Varied patterns of provincial autonomy in the T'ang dynasty," in *Essays on T'ang society: The interplay of social, political and economic forces*, ed. John Curtis Perry and Bardwell L. Smith (Leiden, 1976), pp. 90–109. As the military strength of the *chieh-tu shih* increased, and the control of the central government declined, provinces became increasingly autonomous, and by the 890s *chieh-tu shih* were the effective rulers of their districts.

south (discussed in the next chapter), and the five dynastic houses of the north that were to be founded and destroyed in swift succession.[5]

The second, third, and fourth of these regimes were established by Sha-t'o Turkic leaders, and scholars have paid much attention to the cultural differences between the leaders of these regimes and the rulers of apparently Chinese origin, with some even regarding these three dynasties as a period of foreign rule.[6] While an awareness of cultural differences is certainly visible in the sources, it is more striking that these differences are so rarely invoked and even more rarely governed people's actions.[7] It is more helpful to see the region of north China in the late ninth century as a frontier region in which groups of varied cultural backgrounds interacted according to considerations of power that were independent of culture. This northern region was part of the borderland between the T'ang empire and the steppe, but it also contained

[5] There is no general study of the Five Dynasties in any European language. Wang's *Structure of power* and Worthy's "The founding of Sung China" deal chiefly with institutions and the locus of power, while Peter Lorge's, "War and the creation of the Northern Song" (diss., University of Pennsylvania, 1996) addresses military issues and relations with the Liao. Wang's account stops in 947, and the story is picked up by Worthy and Lorge. In Chinese, see Lü Ssu-mien, *Sui T'ang Wu-tai shih* (1959; Shanghai, 1984), and T'ao Mao-ping, *Wu-tai shih-lüeh* (Peking, 1985). For a basic chronology for all provinces, see Kurihara Masuo, *Godai Sōsho hanchin nenpyō* (Tokyo, 1988). For a typology of the fifteen transitions between one ruler and the next, see Chang Ch'i-fan, "Wu-tai cheng-ch'üan ti-shan chih k'ao-ch'a – chien-p'ing Chou Shih-tsung ti cheng chün," *Hua-nan shih-fan ta-hsüeh hsüeh-pao: She-hui k'o-hsüeh pan* 1 (1985), pp. 22–30. On the broader context for the period, see Robert M. Hartwell, "Demographic, political, and social transformations of China, 750–1550," *Harvard Journal of Asiatic Studies* 42 No. 2 (1982), pp. 365–442. The historiography of the late T'ang, Five Dynasties, and Sung periods is complex. The dynastic histories themselves reflect the changing approaches to and control of the dynastic records. During this time the dynastic histories ceased to be called *shu* (documents) and took on the new label of *shih* (histories). Also, contending versions of the major dynastic records were compiled, in particular the *Chiu T'ang shu* (The old {version of the} T'ang documents) and the *Chiu Wu-tai shih* (The old {version of the} history of the Five Dynasties), completed in 945 and 974 respectively. They were superseded as standard dynastic histories during the Sung dynasty by Ou-yang Hsiu's *T'ang shu*, called *Hsin T'ang shu* (The new {version of the} T'ang documents), and *Wu-tai shih-chi*, called *Hsin Wu-tai shih-chi* (The new {version of the} history of the Five Dynasties), completed in 1060 and 1073. After Ou-yang Hsiu's versions became prominent, the text of the *Chiu Wu-tai shih* suffered from lack of attention. Having lost its status as an official history in 1206, no copies of the *Chiu Wu-tai shih* seem to have existed by the mid-fifteenth century. Three hundred years later, in 1775, Shao Chin-han (1743–96) and other Ch'ing scholars reconstituted the work from sections of the *Yung-lo ta-tien* and other sources. Although their reconstruction was incomplete, the *Chiu Wu-tai shih* gives a fuller and more faithful rendering of the earlier Five Dynasty documents than does the *Wu-tai shih-chi*, despite Shao Chin-han having to work under conditions that were sensitive to the ruling Ch'ing dynasty's own historiographical links with the Khitan rulers discussed in the *Wu-tai shih-chi*. See the entries on these histories in Yves Hervouet, ed., *A Sung bibliography (Bibliographie des Sung)* (Hong Kong, 1978), pp. 61–3, and Wang Gungwu, "The *Chiu Wu-tai shih* and history-writing during the Five Dynasties," *Asia Major*, new series, 6 No. 1 (1958), pp. 1–22.

[6] The clearest example of this approach remains Wolfram Eberhard, *Conquerors and rulers: Social forces in medieval China*, 2nd ed. (Leiden, 1965).

[7] See Naomi Standen, *Unbounded loyalty: Frontier crossings in Liao China* (Honolulu, 2007).

a network of internal borders between provinces.[8] In the years following the second restoration of 883, local leaders of all cultural stripes, from governors to bandits, fought each other for survival or expansion, and by 895 the number of regimes was greatly reduced. There was greatest scope for ambition in the regions surrounding the two capitals and the Yellow River valley, dominated by the three governors of Feng-hsiang (west of Ch'ang-an), T'ai-yüan (in modern Shansi province), and Pien-chou (modern K'ai-feng, in Honan province).

Those who controlled Feng-hsiang also controlled the western part of the Kuan-chung region "within the passes," the eastern part of which also included Ch'ang-an. The Feng-hsiang provinces were strategic, if not very productive, since although they did not include the capital province itself, they covered its western approaches from the Szechwan region. Since 887 the governor of Feng-hsiang had been Li Mao-chen, a former imperial general. Li had supported the emperor until 893, when an attempt to transfer Li to another post turned him into the court's most dangerous enemy. After Li's armies threatened Ch'ang-an and he forced the execution of three eunuchs and a chief minister, the fifteen or more prefectures of Feng-hsiang were lost to the imperial camp. In 895, Li acquired three more prefectures in Ho-hsi (modern Kansu) and appointed his own governor from among his officers without reference to the court.[9]

T'ai-yüan was the seat of Ho-tung, lying east of the great northern bend of the Yellow River and west of the T'ai-hang Mountains, which form the eastern border of modern Shansi. Ho-tung's natural topography made it an almost impregnable and highly strategic location. A combination of agriculture and pastureland also made it largely self-sufficient. It was well placed to dominate the east-west stretch of the Yellow River valley. Ho-tung had been granted to Li K'o-yung as his reward for recovering Ch'ang-an from Huang Ch'ao's rebels. He and his father already held other T'ang posts in the region, and by 895 Li had extended his direct control as far north as today's Ta-t'ung, east into two prefectures of the southern Ho-pei region, and south almost as far as the Yellow River. After years of alternately supporting and fighting with the court, in 895 he prevented the deposition of the emperor T'ang Chao-tsung (888–904) by the three Kuan-chung governors led by Li Mao-chen.

---

[8] Listed and mapped by Robert Somers, "The end of the T'ang," in *The Cambridge history of China*, volume 3: *Sui and T'ang China, 589–906, part 1*, ed. Denis C. Twitchett (Cambridge, 1979), pp. 764–5. The following summary is drawn chiefly from Somers's chapter and from Wang's *Structure of power*, chapters 2–3, pp. 7–84. The main earlier materials are in Liu Hsü et al., eds., *Chiu T'ang-shu* (945; Peking, 1975) 19 *hsia*–20 *hsia*, pp. 689–814; Hsüeh Chü-cheng et al., eds., *Chiu Wu-tai shih* [hereafter *CWTS*] (974; Peking, 1976) 1–2, pp. 1–43, 25–6, 331–64; and Ssu-ma Kuang, *Tzu-chih t'ung-chien* [hereafter *TCTC*] (1086; Peking, 1956) 255–60, pp. 8287–8482.

[9] For Li's biography, see *CWTS* 132, pp. 1737–40.

He received as his reward the title of Prince of Chin, three million strings of cash to pay his army, and the most beautiful woman in the palace service, together with the right to bestow noble titles and make appointments to office in his own districts.[10]

Between the Huai and Yellow rivers lay the densely citied region of Honan, divided into about a dozen tiny provinces. By 895 the central provinces, including Lo-yang, were controlled by the governor of Pien-chou, while two other provinces in the east were under siege by his armies and would fall in 897. This governor, Chu Wen (or Chu Ch'üan-chung), was from a family of teachers, but had joined Huang Ch'ao and by 882 was Huang's commander in T'ung-chou, guarding the eastern approach to Ch'ang-an. In that year Chu defected to the T'ang side with his prefecture, greatly easing Li K'o-yung's advance to Ch'ang-an. Thereafter Chu was regarded as the chief defender of the dynasty and received the Pien-chou governorship as his reward, giving him control of the transportation and storage of grain for both capitals. His first regional rival was Ch'in Tsung-ch'üan, who was based in Ts'ai-chou (in modern Honan) and was the last of Huang Ch'ao's followers. Chu's survival remained in the balance until he destroyed Ch'in in 888.[11] After this his main enemy was Li K'o-yung of Ho-tung, whom Chu Wen had tried to assassinate in 884. Their rivalry was to last two generations.

Several governors located farther from the capitals kept out of the struggle to control the court, focusing instead on regional expansion or survival. Huai-nan was a wealthy region south of the Huai River and north of the Yangtze. Here Yang Hsing-mi fought his way to dominance by 895, but he was continually threatened by his northern neighbor, Chu Wen. In Szechwan, beyond the Ch'in-ling ranges in the mountains south of Feng-hsiang, Wang Chien had ruthlessly bludgeoned his way to control of the region by 893.[12] These territories would become two of the nine Southern Kingdoms.

The region of Ho-pei, in the northeast, had been home to effectively independent governors since the rebellion of An Lu-shan, and by 895 four remained. The most important of their provinces was Yu-chou, formerly prosperous, with its capital at what is now Peking. In 894 the governor was overthrown by his brother, and a garrison commander called Liu Jen-kung took a loyalist stance and removed the usurper with active military backing from Li K'o-yung of Ho-tung. Li's sponsorship ensured that in 895 – the year Li saved the emperor from deposition – Liu Jen-kung was confirmed as the new governor of Yu-chou.

---

[10] The last of these appointments is reported in 908: *TCTC* 266, p. 8696.
[11] For Ch'in's biography, see Liu et al., *Chiu T'ang-shu* 200 *hsia*, pp. 5398–9.
[12] On Yang, see *CWTS* 134, pp. 1779–82; for Wang's biography, see *CWTS* 136, pp. 1815–19; and see the next chapter of this volume.

Rather than join in the tussle for supreme power, Liu pursued a regional objective, conducting a relationship of mutual raiding with the nomadic peoples to his north, chiefly the Khitan (*Ch'i-tan*).[13] Southwest of Yu-chou had once been the province of Ch'eng-te, now divided into I–Ting, with two prefectures, and Chen-chou with four. Sandwiched between Ho-tung and Yu-chou, their governors (Wang Ch'u-ts'un and Wang Jung) were concerned only with survival.[14] The last Ho-pei province was Wei–Po, comprising six rich prefectures – known for their silk production – that looked south across the Yellow River to Chu Wen's Honan. The capital at Wei-chou (at the southeastern tip of Ho-pei) was the base of a professional army that had become autonomous after An Lu-shan's rebellion and was notorious for choosing its own governors, most recently in 888. Accordingly, Wei–Po governors had only limited authority.[15]

The ability of armies to choose their own leaders highlights the importance of assent in the politics of this period. The major governors of the late T'ang relied heavily on their military strength for their positions, but that military strength included numerous separate units, most of which were, of necessity, not controlled by the governor himself. Prefects, generals, and even relatively junior officers, in regular contact with the forces they led, could build a personal following that gave them disproportionate influence over events, for with so many potential masters to choose from, even a relatively junior leader could play a significant role in politics by switching his allegiance. In this way, military advantage not only could be lost, but it could be turned against its original possessor. While leaders certainly tried to exercise the tightest control they could – preferably by appointing all their own subordinates – this could not guarantee that those so controlled would not change sides.

Accordingly, the chief concern of any leader, at any level, was how to secure the allegiance of his followers. Legitimate title of some kind was necessary – leaders always wanted their posts confirmed by the highest available

---

[13] For Liu's biography, see *CWTS* 135, pp. 1799–1803, 1806. On the history of independent Yu-chou, see Matsui Shūichi, "Roryō hanchin kō," *Shigaku zasshi* 68 (1959), pp. 1397–1432, and on the independent provinces of the Ho-pei region, see Peterson, "Autonomy of the northeastern provinces." On raiding relationships, see Naomi Standen, "Raiding and frontier society in the Five Dynasties," in *Political frontiers, ethnic boundaries, and human geographies in Chinese history*, ed. Donald J. Wyatt and Nicola Di Cosmo (London, 2005), pp. 160–91.

[14] See Wang Ch'u-ts'un's biography in Liu et al., *Chiu T'ang-shu* 182, pp. 4699–4701; and Wang Jung's in *CWTS* 54, pp. 725–31. Where provinces encompass two equally important prefectures, such as I and Ting or Wei and Po, the en-dash is used (e.g., I–Ting, Wei–Po) to designate the region.

[15] The full story of the professional army of the Wei–Po region is told in Mao Han-kuang, "T'ang-mo Wu-tai cheng-chih she-hui chih yen-chiu – Wei–Po erh-pai-nien shih-lun," *Li-shih yü-yen yen-chiu-so chi-k'an* 50 (1979), pp. 301–60. For the period down to the Later Liang, see also Hori Toshikazu, "Gi–Haku Tenyū gun no rekishi – Tō Godai bujin seiryoku no ichi keitai," *Rekishi kyōiku* 6 No. 6 (1958), pp. 65–72.

authority – but title was in itself no guarantee of allegiance from subordinates. Generosity in the form of plunder, rewards, and appointments was much more effective, as was entrusting people with important tasks or positions. Trust involved a risk of betrayal, but a leader unwilling to take that risk ran the alternative danger of implying a lack of faith in his own leadership. Successful military activity was necessary since it most readily provided the material benefits and opportunities for bestowing trust, and also demonstrated that the leader had Heaven's favor. Leaders also tried to bind their key followers with marriage alliances and by adopting them as their sons. At the heart of all these methods were personal relationships between individuals. In the late T'ang these were the chief methods used to win and maintain the allegiances essential for power, but they were not the only ones available. As the Five Dynasties unfolded, other methods came to the fore.[16]

Regional control through military expansion: Chu Wen's rise to dominance, c. 895–907

While some governors may have had considerable political control in the late T'ang, the emperor still retained the authority deriving from his claim to the Mandate of Heaven, however much this claim had been challenged.[17] The major governors had all received at least their initial posts from the emperor and usually sought formal confirmation of their gains. There was no need for them to threaten the existence of the dynasty, and indeed, much to be lost by so doing. The great rebels had twice overthrown the T'ang dynasty with dramatic swiftness, having won enough of a following to overwhelm the immediate opposition, but neither had been able to sustain their new dynasty beyond the short term. Emerging from Huang Ch'ao's defeat, the most ambitious governors were careful to build their strength slowly, nurturing personal relationships and rewarding their followers with

---

[16] Allegiance is to be distinguished from loyalty as understood by writers of the Sung and later, who emphasized undying adherence to a single master. Yuri Pines, "Friends or foes: Changing concepts of ruler-minister relations and the notion of loyalty in pre-imperial China," *Monumenta Serica* 50 (2002), pp. 35–74, is suggestive of the Five Dynasties situation too. On the topic of allegiance I have benefited from discussions with Scott Ashley, Bob Moore, Yuri Pines, and Denis Twitchett. There is much concern among historians of early-medieval Europe with issues related to allegiance, but as yet no comprehensive discussion. Starting points include R. H. C. Davis, *King Stephen, 1135–1154* (London, 1967); Heinrich Fichtenau, *Living in the tenth century: Mentalities and social orders*, trans. Patrick J. Geary (Chicago, 1991); Karl Leyser, *Rule and conflict in an early medieval society* (Oxford, 1979); and Eleanor Searle, *Predatory kingship and the creation of Norman power* (Berkeley, Calif., 1988).

[17] One response to this challenge to authority is discussed by Franciscus Verellen, "A forgotten T'ang restoration: The Taoist dispensation after Huang Ch'ao," *Asia Major*, 3rd series, 7 No. 1 (1994), pp. 107–53.

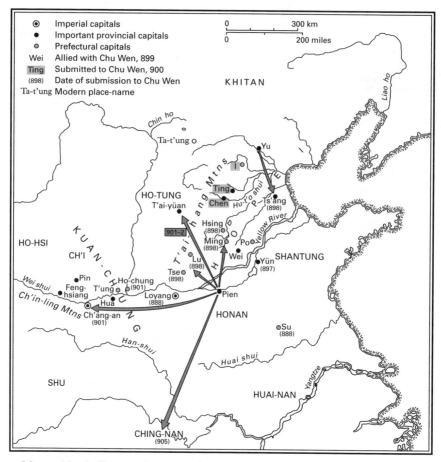

Map 4. North China, c. 895–905, showing Chu Wen's expansion out of Honan.

the fruits of success, and were concerned not with overthrowing the dynasty but with controlling the court, usually by assuming the role of the emperor's protector.[18]

In 896, Chu Wen of Pien-chou attacked two independent governors in the eastern region of Honan. The governors subsequently each asked Li K'o-yung for help. Li's army had to cross through Wei–Po, whose leaders in turn sought help from Chu Wen.[19] Li Mao-chen of Feng-hsiang, who had tried to install a

---

[18] The following paragraphs draw from Wang, *Structure of power*, chapters 2–3, pp. 7–84; and Somers, "End of the T'ang," pp. 777–84. The basic primary materials for late T'ang events are in Liu et al., *Chiu T'ang-shu* 20 shang–hsia, pp. 752–812; *CWTS* 1–2, pp. 15–42; *TCTC* 260–5, pp. 8462–8665.

[19] Li K'o-yung's own records say that his general received permission to cross Wei–Po but that relations broke down after pasturage was damaged. *CWTS* 26, pp. 353–4.

new T'ang emperor only the year before, again marched on Ch'ang-an while his two main rivals, Li K'o-yung and Chu Wen, were fighting each other. Emperor Chao-tsung was compelled to take refuge in the tiny province of Hua-chou located on the southern banks of the Wei River about sixty miles east of modern Hsi-an. When the Hua-chou governor, Han Chien, killed the imperial princes, Li Mao-chen and Li K'o-yung were unhappy that such a minor governor had seized such an important role, and their fears for the emperor's safety led the two Lis to join up to force the emperor's return to Ch'ang-an in 898.[20] Meanwhile, Chu Wen had gained two prefectures in southern Ho-pei from Li K'o-yung, as well as Tse-chou and Lu-chou (modern Ch'ang-chih, Shansi) in southern Ho-tung. The last two prefectures were located on major routes leading to both the capitals. Control of this strategic position won Chu Wen an alliance with Emperor Chao-tsung and his chief minister Ts'ui Yin, who wanted to be rid of the overmighty eunuchs who controlled the imperial armies and kept an eye on court-appointed governors.[21] The eunuchs were supported by Li Mao-chen and his Kuan-chung allies, but with Chu Wen's backing Ts'ui Yin was now able to remove the two chief eunuchs. This so imperiled the remaining eunuchs that in desperation they deposed Chao-tsung and offered the throne to Chu. He refused, and backed the restoration of the emperor in 901, after which his dominance of the court was unchallenged.

By the end of 901, Chu Wen also had by far the strongest regional position of all the governors. Liu Jen-kung of Yu-chou had pushed south into Ts'ang-chou in 898 and resisted Chu Wen's retaliatory siege until it was abandoned in 900, but in that same year the governors of I–Ting and Chen-chou offered their submissions to Chu, giving him allies who threatened the hearts of both Ho-tung and Yu-chou. The Wei–Po governor, Lo Hung-hsin, had died in 898 and was succeeded by his son Lo Shao-wei, who proved himself one of Chu Wen's staunchest allies after Chu helped him ward off an attack by Liu Jen-kung in 899.[22] Chu had already pushed into western Honan, and in 901 he took most of Kuan-chung, including full control of Ch'ang-an. In 899, Li K'o-yung had recovered the strategic Ho-tung prefectures of Tse-chou and Lu-chou, but now he lost them again, along with Ho-chung (on the Yellow River at the southwest tip of Shansi). Chu used Tse-chou and Lu-chou as a springboard for two sieges of T'ai-yüan in 901–2, and although the city held out, Li K'o-yung's fortunes were at such a low ebb that he unsuccessfully

[20] For Han Chien's biography, see *CWTS* 15, pp. 203–6.

[21] Ts'ui Yin's biography is in Ou-yang Hsiu, *Hsin T'ang shu* (1060; Peking, 1975) 223 *hsia*, pp. 6355–8. See Somers, "End of the T'ang," pp. 766–80; Wang, *Structure of power*, pp. 9–10, 13, for discussion of eunuchs and how the power they held was resented at court and in the provinces.

[22] Lo's biography is in *CWTS* 14, pp. 187–92.

sought peace and then withdrew from the fray, leaving Chu Wen unopposed to complete his conquest of Honan during 903.[23]

Chu now had the allegiance of every governor from Ch'ang-an to the tip of Shantung, and of two prefectures in southern Ho-tung and another two in southern Ho-pei. He had the friendship or submission of all the independent Ho-pei area governors except Liu Jen-kung, and another ally had just taken over the Ching-nan region on the middle reaches of the Yangtze River in what is now central Hupei. Chu was now the strongest of the governors, and next he tried to consolidate his control over the court.

That quest was hastened in 903, when Chu Wen installed his troops to guard the emperor and ordered that all the eunuchs be killed both at court and in the provinces.[24] Chu took day-to-day control of the emperor, which enabled him to end the maneuvering against him by his erstwhile ally, Chief Minister Ts'ui Yin, and to have Ts'ui and his cohorts demoted, replaced, and murdered. The new chief ministers that Chu selected could not stop him from moving Emperor Chao-tsung from Ch'ang-an to Lo-yang, deeper inside Chu's area of control. Ch'ang-an was plundered and left desolate. During the move Chu gained formal control of the emperor's own forces, the Six Imperial Armies. Most of these troops had already been dispersed, and Chu now had the last two hundred killed and surreptitiously replaced with his own people. The emperor was now isolated amid household servants all chosen by Chu.

With the eunuchs dead, most of the eunuch-dominated palace commissions that ran the emperor's personal administration had ceased functioning, and Chu now appointed his own followers to fill the nine commissions that remained. Li Mao-chen of Feng-hsiang, Wang Chien based in Szechwan, and others, including Li K'o-yung of Ho-tung, Liu Jen-kung of Yu-chou, and Yang Hsing-mi of Huai-nan, shelved their differences and planned to bring Chu to heel. The emperor had appealed to these governors for help, but when Chu marched west from Pien-chou to face them down, he arranged for Chao-tsung to be murdered during the campaign, leaving the throne to a twelve-year-old boy, T'ang Ai-ti (904–7). Chu next had Chao-tsung's other sons killed, and he allowed his right-hand man, Li Chen, to procure the demotion, banishment, or voluntary withdrawal of most of the remaining nobles and gentry in the bureaucracy, who were subsequently murdered or ordered to commit suicide.[25] All that remained was for Chu to take the throne formally, but this proved to be easier said than done.

[23] *TCTC* 262, pp. 8549–50. Li's letter to Chu is reproduced in *CWTS* 60, pp. 802–4.

[24] On the significance of this, see Wang, *Structure of power*, p. 87.

[25] For Li Chen's biography, see *CWTS* 18, pp. 251–3. The numbers of nobles and gentry had been greatly reduced by mass executions in 881–2 and 886–7. Wang, *Structure of power*, p. 98.

In taking over the court Chu had begun by installing his own troops and ended by replacing almost all the ministers, indiscriminately killing anyone who appeared to stand in his way. But this was just an extension of his earlier methods in the provinces, chief of which were straightforward military conquest and territorial domination. Chu worked at the prefectural level, installing his own military officers in every surrendered district unless it was politically infeasible, chipping away at a province until he forced the governor's submission. By 901 he had conquered eleven provinces and twenty-eight prefectures, and had appointed his own people to all but three. This method was slow, but it was intended to be thorough; Chu meant to keep what he had gained and not repeat the failure of his former leader, Huang Ch'ao. Although Chu was willing to place a degree of trust in those he had appointed to run his conquered districts, he bolstered their allegiance by the use of force. Resistance always brought a military response; so, for instance, when Su-chou2 in northwest Anhwei,[26] captured in 888, rebelled against Chu in 890, Chu went in person to supervise its recapture. And when Li K'o-yung captured Tse-chou and Lu-chou in 899, Chu's response was to march on T'ai-yüan. The key to this style of rulership was obviously Chu's armies, and especially the provincial units of Pien-chou that he turned into his personal force. Chu kept a tight grip on his main army, scattering his personal military retainers or *pu-ch'ü* through every unit, tattooing his soldiers, and enforcing a disciplinary code that included executing all the soldiers in a unit whose officer was killed. Most important, he reduced the powers of his senior generals after an episode in which Chu Chen, a trusted commander, gained sufficient strength to challenge Chu Wen and consequently was executed. Although Chu Wen relaxed his disciplinary approach slightly after he became emperor, he limited the responsibilities of his generals for the rest of his life.[27]

Chu's preference was to exercise absolute control over his conquests through violent coercion, but with his own senior followers he also used methods that solicited rather than enforced support. He used familial bonds but was highly selective in doing so. He did not employ large numbers of his blood relatives

---

[26] Where two prefectures are romanized the same way, they are differentiated here and on the accompanying maps 4–9 by number, as in Yün (in modern Shan-tung province) and Yün2 (in modern Shansi province).

[27] Wang, *Structure of power*, pp. 64–7; various sources including *TCTC* 266, p. 8687. On Chu Chen, see *CWTS* 1, pp. 7, 9; 19, pp. 259–61; *TCTC* 257, p. 8365; 258, p. 8389. On the personal armies of Five Dynasties governors, see Sudō Yoshiyuki, "Godai setsudoshi no gagun ni kansuru ichi kōsatsu — bukyoku to no kanren ni oite," *Tōyō Bunka Kenkyūjo kiyō* 2 (1951), pp. 3–72, and on Chu Wen's army in particular, see Hori Toshikazu, "Shu Zenchū no chōshito," in *Wada Hakushi koki kinen Tōyōshi ronsō: Shōwa 35-nen 11-gatsu*, ed. Wada Hakushi Koki Kinen Tōyōshi Ronsō Hensan Iinkai (Tokyo, 1961), pp. 819–31. On the development of the imperial armies during the Five Dynasties period, see Chang Ch'i-fan, *Wu-tai chin-chün ch'u-t'an* (Hang-chou, 1993).

and created only a handful of adopted sons.[28] Chu made a number of marriage
alliances, notably with his allies in Wei–Po and Chen-chou, and in 887 he
even made a "fraternal" alliance with the Yün-chou governor, Chu Hsüan,
who was said to be of the same Chu clan. But Chu Wen had most faith in the
personal loyalty of two groups of military retainers, those who either had stayed
with him when he transferred his allegiance from Huang Ch'ao to the T'ang
dynasty or had remained with Huang Ch'ao but subsequently surrendered to
Chu.[29] He gave these people command of his armies, senior administrative
posts, and governorships. Trust like this, and its attendant material rewards,
reinforced personal loyalties and offered the promise to his other officers that
they too would receive prefectures or even provinces of their own, with all
the perquisites that such postings brought with them. Constant campaigning
also gave the rank and file many opportunities to enrich themselves through
plunder and to lord it over the general populace, making Chu Wen a good
general to follow.

These methods worked while Chu's organization was small enough for him
to run with his most trusted followers, and his territory small enough to
dominate with his most reliable troops. But after 901 Chu's area of control
became so large that it was harder to replace those who surrendered with his
own men; greater expansion meant greater risk of overextending the military
forces needed to support all of his handpicked officials. Chu thus began to
leave in place the officials of conquered regions. But such a compromise could
be dangerous. For example, Chu left Yang Ch'ung-pen of Pin-chou in place
in Kuan-chung but kept Yang's family hostage. However, because Chu slept
with Yang's wife, when she was returned to Yang in 904 he promptly rejected
Chu's lordship.[30]

There was a limit to how far Chu could impose his will on those who
balked at it. In 905, for example, the governor of Ching-nan, Chao K'uang-
ning, sought peace with his neighbors, Yang Hsing-mi of Huai-nan and Wang
Chien based in Szechwan, and made a marriage alliance with Wang. Chu Wen
feared losing his influence over Ching-nan, and so sent in his armies. Chao
K'uang-ning fled to Huai-nan, leaving Chu to install his own governors in the

---

[28] On adoptive sons in the Five Dynasties period, see Kurihara Masuo, "Tō-Godai no kafushiteki ketsugō
no seikaku," *Shigaku zasshi* 62 No. 6 (1953), pp. 1–30, and his "Tōmatsu Godai no kafushiteki ketsugō
ni okeru seimei to nenrei," *Tōyō gakuhō* 38 No. 4 (1956), pp. 61–88.

[29] Wang, *Structure of power*, pp. 50, 58 for tables of Chu's oldest followers (a subject given close scrutiny in
Sudō, "Godai setsudoshi no gagun," pp. 13–19); see also p. 60 for discussion of Chu Hsüan of Yün-chou,
whose biography is in Liu et al., *Chiu T'ang-shu* 182, pp. 4717–18; *CWTS* 13, pp. 169–71.

[30] Wang, *Structure of power*, p. 79; *TCTC* 264, p. 8626. Biography in *CWTS* 13, pp. 181–2. On hostages,
see Yang Lien-sheng, "Hostages in Chinese history," in *Studies in Chinese institutional history*, ed. Yang
Lien-sheng (Cambridge, Mass., 1961), pp. 43–57.

two Ching-nan provinces. Against advice, Chu tried to follow up his victory in Ching-nan by marching on two prefectures in Huai-nan, but when they would not surrender Chu was forced into a costly retreat.[31] Here Chu Wen, unwisely acting on his desire to transform allies into subordinates, had reached the limits of his southern expansion. By now, however, his chief concern was to complete his takeover by becoming emperor.

Following the Ching-nan campaign Chu was made marshal of the various circuits, with command of all provincial military forces. This was a key step in a gradual buildup to the emperor's abdication, planned by one of Chu's close advisors, Chiang Hsüan-hui, and the ambitious T'ang chief minister Liu Ts'an, to provide a legitimate pretext for Chu to take the throne for himself. The next stage was for Chu to be enfeoffed as prince of a "great state" comprising the twenty-one provinces to which he appointed officials, and to receive the Nine Gifts, a traditional harbinger of an impending change of dynasty. Only then should Chu accept the abdication of the emperor. But Chu was enraged by Liu Ts'an's gradualist strategy (he eventually executed him) and repeatedly declined the princedom, the Nine Gifts, and even Ai-ti's statement of his intention to abdicate.[32] He wanted the throne itself and nothing less, but having rejected the gradualist approach he still needed to find a suitable moment.

In the end, it was the limits on Chu Wen's authority that provided the final impetus. In 906, Chu had finally responded to the requests from his staunch ally, Lo Shao-wei of Wei–Po, to act against the autonomous regional army that had installed Lo's father as governor but had continued to control the province. After an officer in the regional army mutinied, one of Chu's generals infiltrated a thousand troops into the army's base at Wei-chou, surprising the Wei–Po soldiers in the night and slaughtering some eight thousand, together with their families. But this sneak attack provoked a general uprising against Chu by various army units across Wei–Po, which was strengthened by support from the Ts'ang-chou governor and his father, Liu Jen-kung of Yu-chou. Chu Wen marched on Ts'ang-chou, but in response Liu Jen-kung persuaded Li K'o-yung of Ho-tung to join him in an attack on Lu-chou designed to draw Chu's forces back south. Chu's ability to control the Ho-pei region now depended upon the continued allegiance of Lu-chou's governor. This prefecture was so strategically important that Chu had entrusted it to Ting Hui, one of Chu's earliest supporters and the first commander of the Pien-chou armies

---

[31] *CWTS* 2, pp. 37–8; *TCTC* 265, pp. 8643–50.
[32] *CWTS* 2, pp. 38–9; *TCTC* 265, pp. 8648–53. The biography of Chiang Hsüan-hui is in Ou-yang, *Hsin T'ang shu* 223 *hsia*, pp. 6360–1. Liu Ts'an's biography is in Liu et al., *Chiu T'ang-shu* 179, pp. 4669–71. On the Nine Gifts, see Howard J. Wechsler, *Offerings of jade and silk: Ritual and symbol in the legitimation of the T'ang dynasty* (New Haven, Conn., 1985), pp. 34, and 91–101 to compare the formalities of the T'ang dynastic foundation.

a quarter century earlier. But, according to Ting's biography, Ting had wept copiously over the death of Emperor Chao-tsung, and at the end of 906 he offered his prefecture to Li K'o-yung, allowing Li to advance to just 120 miles north of Lo-yang. In an attempt to recover control of the situation, Chu Wen was forced to abandon his attack on Ts'ang-chou and was spurred finally to accept Ai-ti's abdication.[33] Chu Wen (Liang T'ai-tsu, 907–12) declared his own dynasty, the Later Liang, and instituted a new reign era in the fourth month of 907.

The Later Liang regime and the opposition, c. 907–915

Since Chu had already been ruling as if he were emperor for some time, his taking the throne was largely a formality, and he did not even bother to go to Lo-yang. He received the letter of abdication at his home base of Pien-chou and began holding court there even before the officials arrived from Lo-yang with the ritual equipment for the accession ceremony. Pien-chou was renamed K'ai-feng and designated the Eastern Capital, Lo-yang became the Western Capital, and Ch'ang-an was demoted to a mere province. The governors appointed by Chu sent gifts to show their acceptance of the new ruler, and, following convention, Chu gave out titles and reappointed all the central officials (whom he had himself appointed) to their previous posts.[34]

Chu Wen had come to the throne as a result of his unquestioned military superiority, but ironically, the immediate military circumstances of his accession undercut its legitimacy. Military conquest of the previous regime was the best legitimator for a new dynasty,[35] but Chu had founded the Later Liang at a military anticlimax rather than as a triumphant general. Since the T'ang's military forces were negligible and Chu had been adopted as the dynasty's protector, clear-cut conquest of the old by the new would have been awkward. Yet without an unequivocal military victory to demonstrate that he was fulfilling the will of Heaven, Chu's claim to the throne rested on his control of the capitals, the T'ang emperor's abdication in his favor, and above all on the continuing allegiance of governors who had the troops and resources to defy him. The historical sources reflect the concern about the importance of legitimacy. Ssu-ma Kuang cites criticism from Chu's older brother, Chu Ch'üan-yü: "How can you destroy overnight the T'ang house's three-century rule and set

---

[33] Wang, *Structure of power*, pp. 83–4. *CWTS* 2–3, pp. 39–45; 26, p. 360; *TCTC* 265–6, pp. 8656–69. Ting Hui's biography is at *CWTS* 59, pp. 789–90. On the importance of the Wei–Po element in this event, see Mao, "T'ang-mo Wu-tai cheng-chih she-hui chih yen-chiu," pp. 320–1.

[34] *CWTS* 3, pp. 46–53; *TCTC* 266, pp. 8672–80.

[35] On the importance of accession by conquest of arms, see Wechsler, *Offerings of jade and silk*, pp. 80–2, 96–7.

yourself up as emperor?"[36] Although this admonition did not stop Chu Wen, his annals are especially noted for their extensive use of supernatural portents to support the Later Liang claim to be fulfilling the will of Heaven.[37] The annals are also at pains to provide detailed accounts of loyal heroes devoting themselves to the Later Liang cause in the face of overwhelming odds, such as two governors who died fighting the Huai-nan forces on the southern border.[38] Heavenly signs and examples of undying loyalty had to compensate for the unambiguous signal that violent conquest would have provided.

Chu's overthrow of the T'ang dynasty meant that the other independent governors were confronted with the prospect that one of their number was overtly claiming supremacy over the rest, and several of them objected to this. Li K'o-yung of Ho-tung, Li Mao-chen of Feng-hsiang, Yang Hsing-mi of Huai-nan, and Wang Chien based in Szechwan all continued to use one or other of the T'ang reign eras, refusing to accept the new dynasty; Wang Chien even suggested that each make himself emperor locally until the T'ang could be restored. Li K'o-yung rejected this idea, but in Feng-hsiang only military weakness prevented Li Mao-chen from declaring himself emperor, although he adopted all the trappings associated with the imperial title. Wang Chien, however, followed his own suggestion and declared himself emperor of Former Shu without any intention of seeking control of the Central Plains.[39] With the notable exception of Li K'o-yung, most of the other princes abandoned the principle of a single emperor, and over time additional local emperors appeared in Southern Han (915), Huai-nan (927), and Min (933).[40]

The opposition of the major governors to the founding of the Later Liang meant more warfare: the only way Chu Wen could maintain his claim to be the legitimate successor to the T'ang dynasty was to fight for the allegiances that were his sole source of practical authority. Even as he ascended the throne, Chu Wen remained preoccupied with putting down the various mutineers in Wei–Po. This entailed painstaking military operations against several army strongholds within Wei–Po, as well as the vital task of recovering Lu-chou from Li K'o-yung. Possession of Lu-chou was crucial to both sides, and all was nearly lost for the Ho-tung forces when Li K'o-yung died in 908. The succession of Li's son, Li Ts'un-hsü, was almost prevented by Ts'un-hsü's adopted uncle Li K'o-ning, who planned to take Ho-tung's nine prefectures over to the Later Liang

[36] TCTC 266, p. 8673.

[37] Yao Ying-t'ing, "Lun T'ang Sung chih-chi ti t'ien-ming yü fan-tien-ming ssu-hsiang," in Sung-shih yen-chiu lun-wen-chi: 1982 nien nien-hui pien-k'an, ed. Teng Kuang-ming and Li Chia-chü (Cheng-chou, 1984), pp. 370–84.

[38] CWTS 3, pp. 55–6.

[39] TCTC 266, pp. 8675, 8685; CWTS 26, p. 360.

[40] See the discussion in chapter 2 of this volume.

and to send Li K'o-yung's widow and Li Ts'un-hsü to Chu Wen at Pien-chou. When the plot was discovered, Lu-chou's commander, Li Ssu-chao, refused to surrender even when Ts'un-hs'ü ordered him to. Chu Wen responded to Lu-chou's continuing resistance by cashiering his own commander and executing numerous officers and troops, which may well have helped the Ho-tung armies to win a major victory and relieve Lu-chou that summer. This success was to mark a revival of the Ho-tung regime's fortunes and may have prompted Chu Wen's enemies to work together more closely, for the Feng-hsiang leader Li Mao-chen now joined Li Ts'un-hsü (claiming the restorationist mantle) and Wang Chien of the Former Shu for a counterattack on Ch'ang-an. But when a Later Liang expeditionary army defeated the Feng-hsiang forces the others withdrew, and by 909 Chu Wen had gained the submission – sometimes voluntary – of four of Li Mao-chen's prefectures in Kuan-chung (what would become eastern Shensi), though not without the loss of two key followers who had been alienated by Chu Wen's suspicions that they were disloyal.[41]

In the spring of 910 rebellion again presented opportunities in the war between Chu Wen and the restorationists. The army at Hsia-chou in Ting-nan, north of Feng-hsiang and bordering Ho-tung, mutinied and killed their governor, only to have officers loyal to Chu Wen quell the mutiny and install the governor's distant cousin, Li Jen-fu, who was quickly confirmed in office by the Later Liang court. That autumn, Li Mao-chen organized a joint attack on Hsia-chou with Li K'o-yung, but Li Jen-fu sent for help and the allied armies withdrew in the face of Later Liang reinforcements.[42] Individual choices of allegiance were again significant, for it was chiefly Li Jen-fu's decision to stay loyal to Chu Wen that prevented the expansion of Chu's enemies. Li's display of allegiance also reinforced Chu Wen's claims to imperial authority more cheaply and effectively than had the fighting over Kuan-chung.

At the other end of the Later Liang realm, the continuing allegiance of Ma Yin, whom Chu Wen had made Prince of Ch'u (in modern Hunan), had also extended Chu's authority for a while, but in 908 the Later Liang governor of Ching-nan clashed with the Ch'u prince, who was victorious wherever he turned.[43] In Huai-nan the Yang family extended its control over the whole of the Kiangsi region by mid-909, seriously compromising Later Liang claims to the region. Worst of all, in the Later Liang province of Hsiang-chou (northern Hupei), the recall of the governor and veteran general Yang Shih-hou to fight in the planned Lu-chou campaign in 909 led Hsiang-chou and another prefecture

[41] *TCTC* 266–7, pp. 8681–8709; *CWTS* 3–4, pp. 362–70. For biographies of Li K'o-ning and Li Ssu-chao, see *CWTS* 50, 685–7; 52, 701–6, respectively.
[42] *TCTC* 267, pp. 8721, 8725–6; *CWTS* 5, pp. 84–6. Li Jen-fu's biography is in *CWTS* 132, pp. 1746–7.
[43] *TCTC* 266, p. 8674; 267, p. 8704.

to defect to the Former Shu. This rebellion took two months to put down and may have encouraged Emperor Wang Chien of the Former Shu to proclaim his independence by establishing his own calendar.[44] Overall, Chu Wen's position in the south was getting worse, although in the north he was able to neutralize a threat from the independent region of Yu-chou (modern Peking).[45]

In cataloging this opposition to Chu Wen, it is right to recall that within Chu's own realm, most of his governors stayed loyal.[46] Yet the rebellions clearly showed that Chu could never take the governors' allegiance for granted, and he worked to limit their autonomy. His favored method, predating his accession, was to make direct appointments at the prefectural level, thereby reducing the governor's access to resources while increasing his own. But building up prefects meant more personal allegiances to be maintained, although the fragmentation of the military threat to his regime seems to have compensated for the increased burden of so many allegiances. Chu Wen also followed the T'ang dynasty policy of dividing provinces, again to more firmly control access to resources. He created seven new governorships in the three years to 910. Two of these resulted from divisions of the rebel provinces of Fu-chou4 and T'ung-chou, which had each contained only two prefectures, making four provinces controlling just a single prefecture each.[47] Wherever possible, potentially dangerous provincial armies were also divided. The two thousand troops forming the personal army of Feng Hsing-hsi, governor of Hsü-chou2, south of K'ai-feng, had once been followers of Ch'in Tsung-ch'üan, Chu's main rival after the death of Huang Ch'ao. As such, they posed a threat to the regime, but after Feng died in 910, his army was split up and distributed to other units to avert that risk. This was thanks to barely veiled threats regarding the consequences of resistance, illustrating the continuing importance of Chu's military supremacy even within his own realm. Except where the risks were too great, coercion remained Chu Wen's favored method of control.

Nevertheless, Chu Wen remained essentially one ruler among many, reliant like the others on the uncertain allegiances of his governors. But there was one important difference between him and his neighbors: when he formally became emperor, he gained full access to the machinery of the central bureaucracy in the capitals. Chu clearly appreciated the increase, at least in theory, in his administrative reach, executive capacity, and access to resources, but he treated the administrative system, like the rest of his realm, as an extension of

[44] *TCTC* 267, pp. 8714–17.

[45] *TCTC* 266, pp. 8671–2, 8683–7; 267, pp. 8706–16, 8720; *CWTS* 4, pp. 59, 62, 70–1; 5, p. 81; T'o-t'o et al., eds., *Liao shih* (1344; Peking, 1974) 1, pp. 3–4.

[46] Wang, *Structure of power*, p. 124, cites twelve governors as loyal and five other governors as potential or actual threats, not counting members of Chu's family.

[47] Wang, *Structure of power*, pp. 130–3, 123–4.

his provincial organization. Conscious of the challenges that could arise from among the bureaucrats, by 907 he had already removed most of the late-T'ang officials and installed members of his own retinue in the palace commissions in place of the eunuchs slaughtered in 903. The palace commissioners ran the emperor's personal administration, but now Chu also gave them many of the administrative duties normally performed by regular bureaucrats. He thus bypassed the bureaucracy while reproducing institutionally the close relationships he enjoyed with his followers.

As a governor, Chu had been accustomed to ruling directly over both civil and military affairs, with the everyday assistance of his chief provincial administrator Ching Hsiang (an unsuccessful *chin-shih* candidate) and Ching's wife. So that Ching Hsiang could retain his access to Chu now that Chu resided in the inner palace – officially limited to women and eunuchs – Ching was given an indefinite appointment as head of the Ch'ung-cheng Hall. This office took on all the duties of the Bureau of Military Affairs (*Shu-mi yüan*), a palace commission abolished at Chu's behest in 905 because of its association with eunuch power. Ching thus was required to provide advice and discuss policy, and he controlled all communications between the emperor and his ministers until Chu's murder in 912; but because Ching also continued to exercise executive authority at court as he had in Chu's regional administration, the powers of the Bureau of Military Affairs began to expand, leaving the chief ministers with little to do and hence with little influence in affairs.[48] Chu's provincial followers also largely filled the Court of Palace Attendants (*Hsüan-hui yüan*), whose members worked outside the inner palace performing most of the functions of their eunuch predecessors but also taking over administrative, diplomatic, and sometimes military tasks from regular bureaucrats at all levels. The Later Liang court thus shows an almost complete transplantation of provincial personnel into the central administration. The most effective way to gain influence at the Later Liang court was to be a palace commissioner.[49]

---

[48] Ching Hsiang's biography is in *CWTS* 18, pp. 246–50. On the significance of his wife, see Wang, *Structure of power*, p. 90 n. 10. The duties of the Bureau of Military Affairs are described in *TCTC* 266, p. 8674, and a large secondary literature exists, including a useful discussion of the bureau's origins and powers in Worthy, "The founding of Sung China," pp. 212–21, as well as Saeki Tomi, "Godai ni okeru sūmitsushi ni tsuite," *Shisō* 46 (1989), pp. 1–19; Su Chi-lang, "Wu-tai ti shu-mi-yüan," *Shih-huo yüeh-k'an* 10 Nos. 1–2 (1980), pp. 3–19; Tu Wen-yü, "Lun Wu-tai shu-mi-shih," *Chung-kuo shih yen-chiu* 1 (1988), pp. 63–73.

[49] Wang, *Structure of power*, pp. 89–96, including an important distinction between the politics of military officials and inner officials, p. 101; Worthy, "The founding of Sung China," pp. 220–4. Comprehensive treatment of the general point is in Sudō, "Godai setsudoshi no gagun." For a detailed study of the palace commissioners and their role in running the army, see Chao Yü-yüeh, *T'ang Sung pien-ko-ch'i chün-cheng chih-tu shih yen-chiu (1) – san-pan kuan-chih chih yen-pien* (Taipei, 1993).

Chu Wen removed responsibility for financial affairs from central bureau-cratic control and gave it over to a palace commission. The transition was not easy at first, and there were no fewer than four commissioners (one of them was even a bureaucrat) before Li Chen took over in 910. It seems that until then Chu Wen and Ching Hsiang handled the finances directly.[50] We know little about Chu Wen's early finances, but it appears that provincial resources (together with local raiding and extortion) had funded Chu's personal provin-cial armies and administration, and now state resources were used to fund Chu's personal imperial armies and administration.[51] Chu had always taken these matters seriously, so that Chu's governors had long been appointed for their administrative rather than their military abilities. This practice paid off, for by 909 court expenses had been reduced sufficiently for officials to be paid their full salaries.[52] At the same time, unofficial methods of raising revenues also continued, notably those involving Lo Shao-wei of Wei–Po. From 900 and apparently until his death in 909, Lo tapped his wealthy province to pay many of Chu's campaign and imperial armies, and even offered to build three hundred ships to transport grain to Lo-yang.[53]

Formal accession as emperor brought not only control of the administrative apparatus but also possibilities for symbolic legitimation and demonstrations of the virtue that an emperor was expected to possess. Although the destruc-tion of Later Liang records by the next dynasty means we must be cautious about what remains to us, the surviving materials suggest that Chu paid lit-tle attention to such matters.[54] We have already seen his indifference to the conventions of abdication and dynastic foundation, and he was willing to fol-low the custom of reemploying all his predecessor's ministers only because they were already people he had chosen himself. His approach to the impe-rial administration was little short of revolutionary, and although there was symbolic value in promulgating a law code, as Chu did in 910, he retained nothing of the T'ang code, of which all copies were to be destroyed.[55] Paying full salaries to his officials can be interpreted as a manifestation of imperial virtue, but it seems likely that Chu viewed this as an entirely practical mat-ter, and one that would reward his own followers more than it benefited the

[50] Wang, *Structure of power*, pp. 96–7.

[51] Ku Chi-kuang, "Fan-lun T'ang-mo Wu-tai ti ssu-chün ho ch'in-chün, i-erh," *Li-shih yen-chiu* 2 (1984), pp. 26–7.

[52] Wang, *Structure of power*, p. 120 (administrative abilities); *TCTC* (1956) 267, p. 8707 (salaries).

[53] Wang, *Structure of power*, pp. 73–5; *CWTS* (1976) 14, pp. 188–91.

[54] Wang, "*The Chiu Wu-tai shih*," pp. 1–22.

[55] *TCTC* 267, p. 8730; 272, p. 8908; *CWTS* 4, p. 67. On the social consequences of this period, at least some of which can be laid at Chu Wen's door, there is a large literature in various languages. David G. Johnson, "The last years of a great clan: The Li family of Chao Chün in late T'ang and early Sung," *Harvard Journal of Asiatic Studies* 37 No. 1 (1977), pp. 5–102, is a useful introduction.

few remaining T'ang appointees. His authority rested on the allegiance of his personal following, and Chu made little effort to extend his appeal beyond them.

By contrast, Li Ts'un-hsü, Chu's rival from 908 and founder of the successor dynasty of the Later T'ang, has much fuller records and seems to have been greatly concerned to present himself as a ruler possessed of imperial virtue; and although he readily deployed coercive means in his home base of Ho-tung, he also worked to build a broad base of support. Unlike his father, Li K'o-yung, who seems to have ignored advice to promote good government, Li Ts'un-hsü commanded that all districts "seek out talent [for official service], dismiss the greedy and cruel, reduce taxes, comfort the orphaned and destitute, clear up false accusations and abuses, imprison thieves and robbers," and generally bring order to the region. After the successful defense of Lu-chou against Later Liang in 908, the new governor, Li Ssu-chao, further advised Li Ts'un-hsü to encourage mulberry farming (and thus silk production), reduce taxes, and delay punishments – policies that helped restore Lu-chou to its presiege state.[56] These carefully recorded displays of virtuous rulership were calculated to appeal to those who had doubts about Chu Wen's claim to the throne, not just among governors, prefects, and officers but also at the grass-roots level that would be most affected by any improvement in governance.

Li Ts'un-hsü further encouraged allegiance in his retinue by adopting several key individuals, but he continued to rely on a handful of the many officers adopted by Li K'o-yung and his brothers, who were Ts'un-hsü's adopted brothers or cousins but a generation older than he. Although one such adopted relative had tried to prevent his accession and another would eventually unseat him, many of the others served him well, chiefly as generals in the central armies.[57] Here Li Ts'un-hsü retained his father's military organization but improved training and discipline, which in turn boosted morale.[58] The military successes of these troops provided the plunder and provincial postings that helped to bind Li's officers and men to their leader. Overall, Li Ts'un-hsü, starting from a relatively weak base, was much less coercive in his approach than his rival Chu Wen and much more concerned to win a following by demonstrating his own worth than to compel one by sheer force.

---

[56] *TCTC* 266, pp. 8696–7. See also Tsang Jung, "Lun Wu-tai ch'u-ch'i ti Pien-Chin cheng-heng," *Shih-hsüeh yüeh-k'an* 3 (1984), pp. 34–40, who assumes that this recovery happens from 901–2.

[57] Wang, *Structure of power*, p. 135; Kurihara, "Tōmatsu Godai no kafushiteki ketsugō ni okeru seimei to nenrei," pp. 75–6; Kurihara, "Tō-Godai no kafushiteki ketsugō no seikaku," p. 4; Ou-yang Hsiu, *Hsin Wu-tai shih* (1073; Peking, 1974), 24, pp. 385–96 ("I-erh" biographies); in *TCTC* 266, p. 8690, Hu San-hsing's note suggests that Li K'o-yung had over one hundred such adoptees.

[58] *TCTC* 266, p. 8696.

Chu Wen's accession as emperor did nothing to stop the incessant warfare, but now the focus shifted to Ho-pei and its independent governors. In 910, Chu Wen prepared for a new push against Lu-chou in the autumn, and he also felt confident enough to seek a strategic showdown with Wang Jung of Chen-chou in central Ho-pei, aiming to directly control the province. Since his defeat in 900, Wang Jung had maintained his allegiance to Chu Wen. Chu had married a daughter to one of Wang's sons and Wang had made regular tribute payments.[59] Despite this history, a suspiciously convenient report suggested that Wang was now in contact with Li Ts'un-hsü, giving Chu an excuse to occupy Wang's two easternmost prefectures. Chu's aggression not only pushed Wang Jung to seek help from both Li Ts'un-hsü and the Yu-chou leader Liu Shou-kuang but also encouraged Wang's northern neighbor, Wang Ch'u-chih of I–Ting, to seek his own agreement with Li Ts'un-hsü. The two Wangs signaled their rejection of their allegiance to Chu Wen by resuming use of the T'ang dynasty calendar.[60] Chu's opportunism had succeeded in driving two faithful Later Liang allies into the camp of his greatest enemy, depriving him of friends in the northeast, where he was most vulnerable, and creating a larger alliance against him.

Liu Shou-kuang, nominally subordinate to Chu Wen but rightly regarded as unreliable, was invited to join the new northern alliance. At first he remained aloof, but when he heard of a heavy Later Liang defeat at the hands of a Ho-tung army at Po-hsiang (near Chao-chou in the south of Wang Jung's province), he sent emissaries to Wang Jung and Wang Ch'u-chih offering himself as leader of an alliance against Chu Wen. Since this was clearly a challenge to Li Ts'un-hsü's leadership of the existing alliance, both governors declined, and Wang Jung informed Li Ts'un-hsü of Liu's proposal. Although Li dismissed Liu's military strength, Yu-chou's strategic importance required that Liu be dealt with right away.[61]

Honored as Prince of Yen by Chu Wen in 909, in 911 Liu Shou-kuang asked Wang Jung and Wang Ch'u-chih to call him Shang Fu, a reference to the councilor traditionally considered the right-hand man of King Wen of Chou (r. 11th c. B.C.E.). The two Wangs, Li Ts'un-hsü, and three Ho-tung governors humored Liu Shou-kuang, and in addition called him director of the Department of State Affairs in reference to T'ang T'ai-tsung (r. 626–49), who had held this post before becoming emperor. When Liu offered to pacify Ho-tung and Wang Jung's province of Chao (based at Chen-chou) for

[59] CWTS 26, p. 357; 54, pp. 727–8; TCTC 262, p. 8534.
[60] TCTC 267, pp. 8728–9; CWTS 6, p. 92; 27, p. 371.
[61] TCTC 267, pp. 8734–9; CWTS 27, pp. 372–5; 135, pp. 1803–4. See also Hu San-hsing's commentary in the TCTC, which suggests that Li Ts'un-hsü took the initiative in acting against Liu Shou-kuang.

Chu Wen in return for being made commander in chief in Ho-pei, Chu also played along by giving him the title of Ho-pei investigation commissioner, a position that had not been used since An Lu-shan's rebellion. Frustrated that all his titles still did not permit him to perform the imperial sacrifices, Liu next demanded the investiture rite appropriate for an emperor, and in the eighth month declared his own reign era and established the Great Yen dynasty.[62]

Chu Wen had been preparing against an attack by the northern allies, but they now became preoccupied with Liu Shou-kuang, whose invasion of Wang Ch'u-chih's province of I–Ting was the signal for thirty thousand Ho-tung troops to sweep through to beneath the walls of Yu-chou in the first month of 912, where, according to the Liao records, they were soon joined by a Khitan force under A-pao-chi himself. Liu Shou-kuang, desperate, turned to Chu Wen, who was prepared to overlook the declaration of the Great Yen dynasty if it meant he could prosecute his quarrel with Li Ts'un-hsü and extend his own authority. He therefore attacked Wang Jung's province of Chao to assist Liu.[63] The war seems to have been marked by greater than usual ruthlessness. Liu Shou-kuang conducted a registration of his population in which even the literary classes were tattooed as soldiers, and Chu Wen is said to have slaughtered all the inhabitants of the first town he took, regardless of age or infirmity, so that "flowing blood filled the city."[64] By contrast, our sources highlight the cunning and bravery of a Ho-tung scouting force sent to help Chao-chou, but in fact they too resorted to brutality when they cut the arms off some of their Later Liang captives and sent them back to Chu Wen's camp with a message that convinced Chu that the main Ho-tung army had arrived. Accordingly, he withdrew southward, and when he found out he had been fooled his shame reportedly worsened his health. Shortly afterward, the Yen border outpost at Wa-ch'iao Pass surrendered to a Ho-tung attack, along with the neighboring prefecture of Mo-chou, opening up routes into Honan and the Yellow River plain. As if this were not dangerous enough for Chu, there followed a mutiny in Liu Shou-kuang's subordinate province of Ts'ang-chou in which one Chang Wan-chin killed the governor – Liu's son – and offered his submission to both Chu Wen and Li Ts'un-hsü. Li sent a messenger to "comfort" Chang, and Chu Wen, refusing to lose such a strategic foothold at such a difficult moment, confirmed Chang as governor without even protesting the murder of his ally's son.[65]

---

[62] *TCTC* 268, pp. 8742–5; *CWTS* 27, pp. 375–6; 135, pp. 1804–5.
[63] *TCTC* 268, pp. 8749–51; *CWTS* 28, pp. 379–80; T'o-t'o et al., *Liao shih* 1, p. 5.
[64] *TCTC* 268, pp. 8752–3.
[65] *TCTC* 268, pp. 8753–4; *CWTS* 28, p. 380.

Chu's help was ultimately of little assistance to Liu Shou-kuang, whose generals, officials, and population had been fleeing his side since he had disregarded the warning of an administrator, Feng Tao, that it was folly to attack Ho-tung. Some, like Feng, submitted to Li Ts'un-hsü; others to A-pao-chi of the Khitan. Forces from Ho-tung under General Chou Te-wei received the surrender of Liu Shou-kuang's subordinates one by one until in the spring of 913 they enclosed Yu-chou city from the north, then marched north and south accepting more submissions. When a final appeal for Khitan help went unanswered, it was only a matter of time, and Yu-chou city fell after a half-year siege. In early 914, Liu Shou-kuang and his father, Liu Jen-kung, were both executed, and Chou Te-wei became governor of Yu-chou.[66] With this conquest, the area under the control of or allied with the Li family in Ho-tung was now roughly the same size as the Later Liang's.

Chu Wen did not live to see this setback to his ambitions. He was seriously ill, and in the summer of 912 his oldest son died and an adopted son, Chu Yu-wen, became Chu Wen's favorite to succeed him, with the position of regent of the Eastern Capital. The following month, however, the emperor was murdered and the throne usurped by his second son, Chu Yu-kuei, who had Yu-wen killed too.[67] Chu Wen had lived by the sword, and now he died by it too. But Chu Yu-kuei was unable to win the allegiances he needed, and in early 913 he was murdered in a coup that brought his brother Chu Yu-chen (Liang Mo-ti, 913–23) to the throne.[68] This took place in the context of an ongoing war between the Later Liang and Ho-tung. During the many months of upheavals at court and in the south the Later Liang regime was protected from Ho-tung attack only by Li Ts'un-hsü's preoccupation with the conquest of Yen. Although Li gladly rewarded a Later Liang general who killed his prefect and brought Hsi-chou, on Liang's northwestern border, over to Ho-tung allegiance, Li did not take advantage of the access to the Yellow River during the brief submission of Ho-chung, nor did he follow up the victory won defending Ho-chung against Chu Yu-kuei. Distracted by the succession crisis, Later Liang rulers left Liu Shou-kuang of Yu-chou to his fate until Chu Yu-chen acceded, just as the final siege of Yu-chou began in 913.[69]

---

[66] *TCTC* 268–9, pp. 8747–81; *CWTS* 8, p. 118; 28, pp. 380–4; 56, pp. 752–3; 135, pp. 1805–6; T'o-t'o et al., *Liao shih* 1, p. 6.

[67] *TCTC* 268, pp. 8755–60. Chu Yu-kuei never received a temple name and has no annals. For what little survives of his biography, see *CWTS* 12, p. 165. Chang Ch'i-fan emphasizes that the forces led by Chu Yu-kui consisted mostly of the Liang palace armies; see Chang, "Wu-tai cheng-ch'üan ti-shan chih k'ao-ch'a," p. 25.

[68] *TCTC* 268, pp. 8761–8 (in which Yu-kuei commits suicide); *CWTS* 8, pp. 113–15 (where he is killed); 22, p. 297; 59, pp. 797–8; 63, pp. 845–6.

[69] *TCTC* 268–9, pp. 8764, 8772–84; *CWTS* 8, pp. 116–19.

War for supremacy, c. 915–926

The conquest of Yu-chou had given Li Ts'un-hsü effective control of all of Ho-pei except the southernmost provinces of Ts'ang-chou and Wei–Po, whose allegiance Chu Yu-chen badly needed to keep. In the spring of 915, the death of the Wei–Po governor, Yang Shih-hou, provided an opportunity for Li and Chu to expand their authority. Yang Shih-hou had seized control of Wei–Po in 912 and destroyed his predecessor's personal army, creating his own professional force and fostering the loyalty of his troops by indulging their rapacious behavior. Chu Yu-chen was constrained by his debt to Yang for his help in bringing Chu to the throne, but as soon as Yang died Chu moved to weaken Wei–Po by cutting off three prefectures to make a new province. This challenge to Wei–Po's autonomy prompted Yang's army to mutiny and to force one of the new governors, Ho Te-lun, to ask for Li Ts'un-hsü's help. When Li arrived at Wei-chou in person with a relief force, he offered the mutineers not an alliance, but the leadership they needed to survive. Presenting himself as the savior of the ordinary people of Wei–Po against the excesses of Yang's army, Li executed the rebel ringleaders. His firmness won him the allegiance of the troops, and Ho Te-lun offered him the governorship.[70] Almost without bloodshed, Li Ts'un-hsü had increased his military strength and gained access to Wei–Po's economic productivity at Chu Yu-chen's expense. Winning over an army offered far more benefits than fighting it.

At this point in the narrative historical sources shift their attention primarily to Li Ts'un-hsü, thanks to the efforts of successor dynasties to eliminate their predecessors from the record altogether.[71] This change of focus gives the impression that from now on Li's conquest of the Later Liang in 923 was a foregone conclusion, but even a moderately careful reading indicates that a great deal of uncertainty remained. By 915, Li had secured control of Wei-chou but he had to win the rest of the region prefecture by prefecture in his continuing war with the Later Liang. The struggle for authority involved an inglorious combination of localized attrition and the competition for individual allegiances. For example, Li captured Te-chou in Ts'ang-chou province and Shan-chou on the Yellow River, but at Pei-chou in northern Wei–Po the prefect, Chang Yüan-te, persisted in his allegiance to the Later Liang and disrupted Li Ts'un-hsü's supply route from his allies in Chen-chou and Ting-chou. As Li tried to isolate Pei-chou, his own base of T'ai-yüan came under attack from Later Liang troops. Pei-chou held out, but Later Liang control there

---

[70] *TCTC* 269, pp. 8786–90; *CWTS* 8, pp. 120–2; 21, pp. 293–4; 22, pp. 297–8; 28, pp. 384–5; Mao, "T'ang-mo Wu-tai cheng-chih she-hui chih yen-chiu," pp. 330–4.
[71] Wang, "*The Chiu Wu-tai shih*," pp. 8–10.

Map 5. North China, c. 911–916, showing Li Ts'un-hsü's conquest of Hopei.

was destabilized when a Ho-tung general offered protection to eight counties against the predations of Chang Yüan-te's troops, and then defeated in battle a much larger Liang army under Liu Hsün. Li gained many prefectures by abandonment and surrender, and Later Liang resistance was further undermined by an imperial army that mutinied, pillaged K'ai-feng, and attacked the palace. In the ninth month of 916, Li received the submission of Ts'ang-chou, and when Pei-chou was finally starved into submission after a year's siege, Li was master of the Ho-pei region save for the last Later Liang stronghold at Li-yang, downstream from Wei-chou2 (near Hsin-hsiang in northern Honan), giving him extensive access to the Yellow River.[72]

---

[72] See *TCTC* 269, pp. 8789–8806; *CWTS* 8, pp. 123–7; 23, pp. 310–12; 28, pp. 385–9; Ou-yang, *Hsin Wu-tai shih* 33, pp. 356–7.

While Li Ts'un-hsü was occupied with these successes, the Khitan leader A-pao-chi plundered Ho-tung, but withdrew as soon as he heard that a relief force was on its way. This was one of many Khitan raids in northern China between 902 and A-pao-chi's death in 926, all aimed at seizing goods and people. While his southern neighbors struggled for control of the northern Chinese districts that would give them access to people and resources, A-pao-chi restricted his expansionist ambitions to the conquest of Po-hai (Parhae) in 926 and sought only to plunder rather than to rule the Central Plains.[73] Victorious in the Ho-pei region, Li Ts'un-hsü saw the advantages of an alliance with the Khitan. A-pao-chi had risked a breach with the Later Liang by declaring himself emperor (Liao T'ai-tsu, 916–26) early in 916 and adopting his own calendar. Formal relations had continued between the Khitan and the Later Liang, but a more specific agreement between A-pao-chi and Li Ts'un-hsü is suggested by Li's sending his aunt and uncle as hostages to the new Liao court.[74]

Whatever the agreement, it did not prevent conflict, centered once again on Yu-chou. In 917, Li Ts'un-hsü's brother, the governor of Hsin-chou in northern Yu-chou, was killed by a general who then led his army over to A-pao-chi. A-pao-chi appointed the general to take command of Yu-chou, and he besieged the city and its Ho-tung governor Chou Te-wei for over two hundred days until a kind of peace was achieved.[75] In this instance, A-pao-chi supported localized ambitions in return for allegiance. As was the case further south, the general gained legitimation of his local position, but by offering his allegiance he also reinforced A-pao-chi's claim to superior authority.

The war between the Later Liang and the Ho-tung regime was now focused on the Yellow River, Chu Yu-chen's last line of defense. Although the Liao siege of Yu-chou lasted until the autumn of 917, Li Ts'un-hsü was able to maintain continuous southward pressure, thanks to the increasing usefulness of Ho-tung to the autonomous rulers south of the river. In 916, Li had allied with the state of Wu to attack the Later Liang and made a peace agreement with the rulers of Ch'u in Hunan. Southern allies allowed Li Ts'un-hsü to strike at the Later Liang's rear without crossing the Yellow River and to strengthen his bridgehead by capturing four forts on its southern bank. As Li launched a southern offensive in 918–19, the governor of Yen-chou in western Shantung, Chang Wan-chin, transferred his allegiance to Li. Nevertheless, Li's foothold south of the river remained precarious, and the Later Liang were

---

[73] On the significance of these raids, see Standen, "Raiding and frontier society."

[74] T'o-t'o et al., *Liao shih* 1, pp. 10–11; *TCTC* 269, pp. 8808–10. The Khitan regime used different designations at different times. For convenience it will hereafter be referred to as the "Liao."

[75] *TCTC* 269–70, pp. 8811–19; *CWTS* 28, pp. 389–90; 56, pp. 753–4; 137, pp. 1828–9; T'o-t'o et al., *Liao shih* 1, pp. 11–12.

able to maintain a year-long siege of Yen-chou while retaining significant armies in the field. They avoided battle until late in 918, when Li seized upon infighting between the Later Liang commanders to march on K'ai-feng with one hundred thousand troops. Substantial losses on Li's side led to a stalemate that was broken by a change of allegiance by Chu Yu-ch'ien, who governed Ho-chung where the Yellow River bends north. Across the river was T'ung-chou, forming a Ho-tung salient into Later Liang territory, and in 920 Chu Yu-ch'ien seized the city and installed his own son as governor. Since this appointment challenged Chu Yu-chen's imperial prerogative, Yu-chen refused to confirm it, and Yu-ch'ien turned to Li Ts'un-hsü for assistance as he had done once before. Li was happy to confirm the son's governorship since this brought T'ung-chou back to Ho-tung allegiance and also gained him the active allegiance of Ho-chung, which Li K'o-yung had lost to Chu Wen some twenty years before.[76]

Following his success in Ho-chung, Li seized an unplanned opportunity to turn his attention to Wang Jung's princedom of Chao, whose capital of Chen-chou now lay in the middle of Li's expanding regime. After a series of engagements in which the Liao were involved, the death of his adopted uncle Li Ssu-chao, and the defiance of his cousins, Li Ts'un-hsü finally made Chen-chou his own in 922.[77] As at Wei–Po, Li Ts'un-hsü became governor himself, apparently at the request of the people. This doubtless bolstered his claims to the Mandate of Heaven, and he divided the province while he had the chance.[78] North of the Yellow River, I–Ting was the last remaining holdout against Li's direct authority, and Li was finally free to concentrate all his resources on the war with the Later Liang.

Like Chu Wen, Li Ts'un-hsü did not rush to claim the throne, but in striking contrast to Chu, Li paid increasing attention to the symbolic legitimation of his position. In 913, before the besieged walls of Yu-chou, he had declared himself a T'ang dynasty restorationist, and immediately after the city fell his allies in Chao and I–Ting persuaded him to accept the title of director of the Department of State Affairs (which they had also bestowed on Liu Shou-kuang of Yu-chou). Li then set up a Branch Department of State Affairs as an imperial administration-in-waiting and began to appoint staff.[79] In 921, ostensibly acceding to pleas by the Former Shu and Wu rulers and his own generals and governors, he ordered imperial insignia made for himself before

[76] *TCTC* 269, pp. 8803, 8807–8; 270, pp. 8821–4, 8830–49; 271, pp. 8850–8; *CWTS* 9, pp. 135–9; 10, pp. 143–4; 13, p. 183; 28–9, pp. 391–7; 56, pp. 756–7; 63, pp. 846–7.

[77] *TCTC* 271, pp. 8859–75; *CWTS* 10, p. 146; 29, pp. 397–400; 52, pp. 705–7; 54, pp. 730–2; 62, p. 831; 137, pp. 1829–30; T'o-t'o et al., *Liao shih* 2, p. 17.

[78] *TCTC* 271, pp. 8876–7; *CWTS* 10, p. 149; 29, pp. 401–2; 62, p. 831.

[79] *TCTC* 268, p. 8777; 269, p. 8782.

receiving the original T'ang dynasty insignia from a monk who claimed he had been keeping them safe since Huang Ch'ao's sack of Ch'ang-an forty years before. When the long-serving eunuch Chang Ch'eng-yeh remonstrated at this breach of the Li family's pledge of loyalty to the T'ang dynasty, Li Ts'un-hsü replied that it was not his will, but the people's.[80] His intention was, after all, to restore the T'ang dynasty, and although we must be suitably skeptical about his explanations, we must also remember that the Mandate of Heaven was an important concept to him and his peers. In early 923, Li selected chief ministers and established the "hundred ministers," an act of state building that the ambitious Wu-Yüeh ruler Ch'ien Liu was also pursuing in the south.[81] In the fourth month of 923, Li Ts'un-hsü assumed the title of emperor (T'ang Chuang-tsung, r. 923–6) at his forward base of Wei-chou. He proclaimed a T'ang restoration regime, known as the Later T'ang, complete with a new reign era, and established Eastern, Western, and Northern capitals at Wei-chou, T'ai-yüan, and Chen-chou respectively. Li's empire contained thirteen provinces and fifty prefectures, but Honan remained beyond his grasp while the governors there maintained their allegiances to Chu Yu-chen.[82] The war was not yet over.

Yün-chou (in western Shantung), lying between the two bridgeheads of the Later T'ang on the Yellow River at Te-sheng and Yang-liu, was the first of the Later Liang strongholds to fall, but Chu Yu-chen immediately dispatched a relief force. Outside observers remained unsure of the ultimate outcome, for when Li Ts'un-hsü sought to ally himself with Hsü Wen of Wu, Hsü declined, fearing the consequences should Li Ts'un-hsü's armies be defeated. Chu Yu-chen's new commander in chief, Wang Yen-chang, then seized Te-sheng and pressed downriver to besiege Yang-liu, inflicting heavy losses. Pressure on the Later T'ang in the Yellow River basin was relieved only when court rivalries brought about Wang's brief recall to K'ai-feng. Farther north, Tse-chou fell to Later Liang troops just before Li Ts'un-hsü's belated relief force arrived; at the same time, the Later Liang troops halted the Later T'ang advance by the drastic measure of breaching the banks of the Yellow River at Hua-chou2 and flooding four prefectures. The Later Liang now had two armies in the field and plans to recover Yün-chou, while the Later T'ang leadership heard proposals for abandoning their southernmost conquests and withdrawing north of the Yellow River to regroup before recommencing hostilities. Li, however, felt he had nothing to lose by pressing toward whatever conclusion fate should decree. In the tenth month, he dramatically bid his family farewell before defeating Wang Yen-chang's army in a brief encounter near Yün-chou. Captured, Wang

[80] *TCTC* 271, p. 8862; *CWTS* 72, pp. 952–3.
[81] *TCTC* 272, pp. 8879–80; *CWTS* 29, p. 402; 133, p. 1768.
[82] *TCTC* 272, pp. 8880–3; *CWTS* 29, pp. 402–4; 52, pp. 707–8.

Yen-chang refused to enter the service of the Later T'ang and was eventually executed. Li declared that Wang's capture was a sign of Heaven's favor and marched swiftly on K'ai-feng – defended by just four thousand troops – unhindered by the second Later Liang army commanded by Tuan Ning. Chu Yu-chen persuaded a general to kill him, and the city's commander opened the gates to the conquerors. When Tuan Ning surrendered, Later Liang military resistance effectively ended.[83]

The establishment of the Later T'ang, 923–926

Unlike Chu Wen, Li Ts'un-hsü had seized the capital in the conventional military manner and the massed Later Liang officials had offered their submission to his rule. This ritual confirmed Li's earlier claims to the Mandate of Heaven and highlighted the renewed importance of the imperial center. In the last years of the T'ang dynasty, contenders for power had struggled to be puppet masters over the court, with the capitals becoming merely collateral goals. With the foundation of the Later Liang there had been a shift to an out-and-out struggle for primacy among equals, in which possession of the capital itself – with its population registers and organized army of bureaucrats – became the prime target. For even though many areas remained beyond the effective reach of the capital bureaucracy, within this system lay resources greater than any dreamed of by a regional governor. The Later Liang had used their control of this machinery to reassert central rule over their provinces, and Li Ts'un-hsü was the beneficiary: once he had taken the capital, all of Honan was his too. The Later Liang governors – numbering over fifty – all sent tribute and were kept on in their commands. Whereas Chu Wen had met widespread resistance from his peers to his accession, Li Ts'un-hsü enjoyed immediate recognition from all the neighboring powers except the Former Shu. The Li family's long-standing ally, Li Mao-chen of Feng-hsiang, sent congratulations followed by tribute and submission as a Later T'ang subject. When Li Mao-chen died in 924, two of his sons were allowed to succeed to Feng-hsiang's two provinces and became adopted sons of Li Ts'un-hsü, ending Feng-hsiang's independence. There was dissent, but nothing unmanageable. The Lu-chou branch of Li's family – Li Ssu-chao's sons – had been dissatisfied for some time, but Li Ts'un-hsü executed several plotters, and easily quelled a mutiny. Kao Chi-hsing (formerly Kao Chi-ch'ang) of Ching-nan resented his treatment at court and prepared to rebel, but thought better of it, and a few months later he accepted the title of Prince of Nan-p'ing.[84]

---

[83] *TCTC* 272, pp. 8884–900; *CWTS* 10, pp. 150–2; 21, pp. 291–3; 29–30, pp. 404–12; 73, p. 963.

[84] *TCTC* 272, pp. 8901–10; 273, pp. 8917–19; *CWTS* 132, pp. 1740–3; 133, pp. 1751–2. Kao changed his name while he was at court.

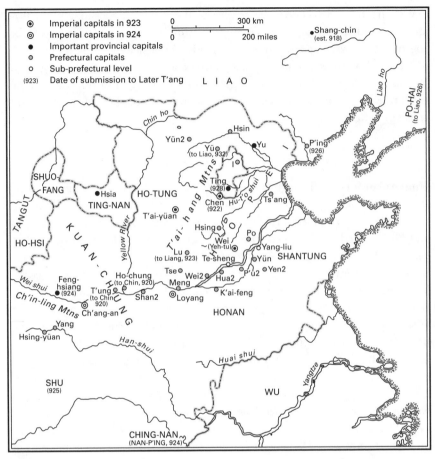

Map 6. North China under the Later T'ang, c. 926.

Li Ts'un-hsü demonstrated a desire, which others seemed to share, to restore
T'ang traditions. He returned Lo-yang and Ch'ang-an to their status as capitals
and demoted K'ai-feng. His legal officials strove to abolish Chu Wen's law code
of 910 and restore the laws of the T'ang dynasty.[85] The symbolic effectiveness
of such measures was such that Li was even compared to the emperor Han
Kuang-wu-ti, who had restored the Han dynasty in A.D. 25, but in practical
matters Li ended up retaining many of the changes made by the Later Liang
rulers. Li abolished the Ch'ung-cheng Hall and reestablished the Bureau of
Military Affairs, but the two offices had the same functions, and authority
remained in the hands of palace commissioners rather than returning to the

---

[85] Although Chu Wen had ordered all copies destroyed, one apparently survived in a provincial storehouse
and the T'ang laws were restored on the basis of that copy. *TCTC* 272, p. 8908.

regular bureaucracy. Li demoted or removed Later Liang personnel throughout the capital administration. Restorationists displaced some – but not all –
Later Liang bureaucrats, and most of the Later Liang palace commissioners and
attendants were replaced by eunuchs, who again developed political influence
incommensurate with their official rank and positions. Li is notorious for his
use of imperial favorites in his administration, but in fact the most important offices, as in the Later Liang, usually went to trusted retainers who had
already proven themselves at the regional court – and were entitled to expect
the rewards of success. Li's highly competent chief provincial administrator,
Kuo Ch'ung-t'ao, headed the Bureau of Military Affairs. Kuo is credited with
wielding immense power throughout Li's short reign, even though Kuo shared
his post with a leading eunuch and bureaucrat assistants had to guide Kuo
through court protocols. When Li gave Kuo the additional post of chief minister, Kuo initiated the process of taking the Bureau of Military Affairs out
of the palace service and converting it into an office of the regular bureaucracy, but the posts exercising the most authority did not necessarily carry
the highest ranks. Kuo Ch'ung-t'ao appointed three successive commissioners
for state revenue (*tsu-yung shih*) during 923–4, but the real work was done by
their assistant, K'ung Ch'ien, who had joined Li Ts'un-hsü's service in Wei-
chou and was finally promoted to commissioner himself. The Commission for
State Revenue had to provide for Li Ts'un-hsü's persistent overspending on his
armies, an outsized staff, and his many favorites. K'ung's ruthlessly exploitative methods earned him the epithet of "thief minister" among the people, as
well as the complaints of his ministerial colleagues.[86]

Apparently wishing to restore aristocrats to a leading role, Li Ts'un-hsü
chose most of his chief ministers from the best families. Kuo Ch'ung-t'ao
also favored pedigree over service in making appointments; but the chief
ministers seem to have remained largely on the sidelines, and there was no
obvious recovery of aristocratic influence at court. Kuo had pretensions to
aristocratic status himself and falsely claimed descent from the eighth-century
T'ang loyalist general Kuo Tzu-i.[87] Yet he also instigated an investigation into
the misuse of the certificates issued to those eligible for higher office – most
of whom were aristocrats – that led to the dismissal of at least three-quarters
of the certificate holders and the destruction of their certificates. Displaced
by Chu Wen, the aristocracy was now dishonored as well, and this must have
contributed to the drastic fall in the number of people (of all backgrounds) able

---

[86] For this and the following paragraph, see Wang, *Structure of power*, pp. 106–14 and Worthy, "The founding
of Sung China," pp. 225–7. The biography of Kuo Ch'ung-t'ao is in *CWTS* 57, pp. 763–73; K'ung
Ch'ien's is in *CWTS* 73, pp. 963–5.

[87] Johnson, "The last years," p. 57.

or willing to serve, for in 925 there were apparently only sixty appointments to fill two thousand vacancies. The return of the eunuchs notwithstanding, Li Ts'un-hsü probably did more to consolidate Chu Wen's revolutionary changes to the institutions and social composition of the bureaucracy than to undo them.

Li Ts'un-hsü also adopted a mixture of methods to strengthen his hold over his governors and their military forces. He appears to have undertaken a military reorganization, combining the officers from his own armies and the armies of the Later Liang into a single body in which mutual rivalries were calculated to counterbalance each other. Li retained significant forces at the capital and kept them under his personal control until early 924, while sections of the reorganized armies, with eunuchs as supervisors, were sent to all provinces. This followed the T'ang system, which Li had revived in Ho-tung and Ho-pei in 908, except that whereas T'ang army supervisors had been ineffective because the court controlled no significant military forces of its own, Li Ts'un-hsü's supervisors were backed by powerful armies. Their strong presence made it feasible to play off the governors against each other. At first the Later Liang governors were all kept on to minimize the risk of resistance to Li's rule, and were only gradually replaced with Li's own followers. Those governors whom Li had appointed in Ho-tung and Ho-pei before 923 were mostly the adopted sons of his father and his uncles and, having won him the throne, now posed the biggest potential threat to his position. During the fighting the governors had served as generals in Li's armies, leaving provincial administration to their subordinates, and after the conquest Li kept them with him in the capital for significant periods. The northern governors, separated from their provincial armies, would find it hard to sustain their military following, but their forces might still be used against uprisings in Honan. The Honan governors, entrusted with imperial forces in the central region, might in their turn be enlisted against trouble north of the Yellow River. Li also continued Later Liang efforts to strengthen the prefects, reducing the governors' privileges with a number of edicts in 924. Governors could now make fewer recommendations to office, and although they could nominate more of their own staff, so could the prefects. Meanwhile, K'ung Ch'ien, at the Commission for State Revenue, continued the Later Liang practice of controlling prefectures directly, even after governors' complaints had elicited an edict ordering him to stop.[88]

In external matters, ongoing localized Khitan raids prompted the appointment of a new Yu-chou governor in 925, but these were just a minor irritant;

---

[88] Wang, *Structure of power*, pp. 115–16, 134–40.

Li's chief concern lay with expansion into Former Shu territory.[89] In 924 the Shu emperor, Wang Yen (who had succeeded his father in 918 as emperor), fearing an attack from Later T'ang troops, garrisoned his strategic places but was compelled to accept a treaty disbanding or transferring these forces. The following summer (925), Later T'ang troops began acquiring warhorses for a major campaign, and while Wang Yen was on a progress around his territory, Li Ts'un-hsü assembled a combined force of provincial troops under his heir apparent Li Chi-chi, gave Kuo Ch'ung-t'ao full military responsibility, and ordered the invasion of Szechwan. The Later T'ang armies had such quick success that Wang Yen refused to believe the news until he saw defeated troops returning from surrendered prefectures. When he finally responded it was too late. Prefectures fell by the dozen, with only one pitched battle in the campaign. In the end, a Former Shu general, Wang Tsung-pi, took control of the regime and surrendered. The conquest had taken just seventy days and gave Li Ts'un-hsü sixty-four prefectures, thirty thousand troops, plus "ten million measures" of assorted goods.[90] He had acquired the means that should have allowed him to increase his income and continue granting his followers the rewards they expected.

This triumph was offset by the intrigues against Kuo Ch'ung-t'ao that led to his murder. A faithful servant of Li's from the early days, Kuo's dominance of the Later T'ang administration had made him many enemies. Objecting to the revived influence of the eunuchs, he continually warned Li Ts'un-hsü against them, and allied himself with a concubine (and later empress on Kuo's recommendation) to limit and counterbalance their access to Li. Objecting to the power of the eunuchs made Kuo popular with provincial leaders, but he also tried to limit the authority of generals such as Li Ssu-yüan, whom he denied command of the expeditionary army sent to conquer the Former Shu. After the fall of the Former Shu, eunuch messengers from court were horrified that Kuo received "gifts" from the Former Shu ruling classes at the expense of his nominal commander (and the heir apparent), Li Chi-chi. When Kuo – who had retained his court posts throughout the campaign – became a candidate for the governorship over the Former Shu territory, the eunuchs intimated not only that Kuo was about to claim the region for himself but also that the heir apparent was in danger. Li Ts'un-hsü tried to check the facts and resolved to test Kuo's intentions by ordering him home, but the empress acted faster, and on her orders Kuo was killed in Li Chi-chi's own quarters. Thus passed a minister who exemplified the new breed brought to court by

[89] *TCTC* 273, p. 8930; *CWTS* 32, p. 445.
[90] *TCTC* 273–4, pp. 8934–46; *CWTS* 33, pp. 454–60; 51, pp. 691–2; 136, pp. 1820–2; Ou-yang, *Hsin Wu-tai shih* 63, p. 794.

governors-turned-emperors. Kuo's antipathy to the eunuchs endeared him to the regular bureaucracy, who produced a remarkably sympathetic picture of someone whose illiteracy would normally have won him only their contempt.[91] His death has been blamed on the eunuchs and Kuo's own excessive powers, but it may also suggest a more general revival of court intrigue that seems to have been largely absent from Chu Wen's hands-on world of retinue organization. Such court intrigue was hard to avoid when the central institutions restricted the information reaching the emperor. This was a penalty for commanding an imperial regime.

On the positive side, the victory over the Former Shu prompted A-pao-chi, the Liao leader, to seek peace and secure the Liao southern frontier while he attacked his eastern neighbor, Po-hai.[92] This left Li Ts'un-hsü free to deal with a rash of mutinies early in 926, prompted by the murder of Kuo Ch'ung-t'ao but exacerbated by the governors' increasing resentment of court efforts to restrict their authority in their provinces. The first uprising involved part of the Wei–Po army, returning home to Wei-chou from a stint of garrison duty in Yu-chou. These troops killed their commander and selected a new leader, Chao Tsai-li, who led them to occupy and pillage their own city, and to hold it against a pacification force. Four days later, Li Shao-ch'en, a general in the campaign against the Former Shu, claimed large areas of the western half of Former Shu territory and marched on Ch'eng-tu. Although he had been denied a governorship of Former Shu territory by Kuo Ch'ung-t'ao, Li Shao-ch'en still claimed to be acting in response to Kuo's murder. At the end of the same week, in Hsing-chou, a prefecture north of Wei–Po, a general with only four hundred troops declared himself governor. And in the capital, a commander in Li Ts'un-hsü's bodyguard mutinied in reaction to Kuo Ch'ung-t'ao's murder. An expeditionary army was sent to quell the rebel army at Wei-chou, but this failed and a wave of further mutinies spread from Ts'ang-chou far upstream along the Yellow River. The provincial rebellions were accompanied by the murder of the local eunuch army supervisors.[93]

The Hsing-chou rebels and Li Shao-ch'en in Szechwan were swiftly dealt with, but Chao Tsai-li's mutineers in Wei-chou held out. Li Ts'un-hsü no longer trusted any of his generals and wanted to take over the campaign himself, but he was persuaded instead to send the Chen-chou governor Li Ssu-yüan, who was one of Li K'o-yung's adopted sons and an experienced general, as well as the subject of hostile rumors fed to Li Ts'un-hsü by his palace favorites. Li Ssu-yüan marched with what was probably a large part of Li Ts'un-hsü's

[91] *TCTC* 273, p. 8916; 274, pp. 8947–55; *CWTS* 57, pp. 771–2. On the possible overstatement of Kuo's role, see Wang, *Structure of power*, p. 110; and Worthy, "The founding of Sung China," p. 227.

[92] *TCTC* 274, p. 8956.

[93] *TCTC* 274, pp. 8955–64; *CWTS* 74, pp. 967–70; 90, pp. 1177–8.

capital armies and some provincial forces, but when he reached Wei-chou in the third month of 926 a mutiny spread quickly through the ranks, apparently in protest at Li Ts'un-hsü's order that the defending rebels – the same forces who had surrendered to Li in 915 and fought well for him since – should all be killed. It is unclear exactly what happened next, but it is claimed that Li Ssu-yüan's army wanted to make him emperor of the Ho-pei region while leaving Li Ts'un-hsü in control of Honan. When Li Ssu-yüan declined, the mutineers in his army apparently handed him over to Chao Tsai-li and the mutineers inside Wei-chou, who are said to have submitted to him. Li Ssu-yüan began to gather his own following of soldiers from his expeditionary force – now scattered – and raided the imperial grazing grounds for horses. Li Shao-jung, the punitive commander at Wei-chou whom Li Ssu-yüan was supposed to be replacing, neither joined Li nor resisted him, but when Li marched toward Lo-yang to "explain himself" at court, Li Shao-jung reported this as an act of rebellion and prevented Li Ssu-yüan's letters from reaching the capital. With reconciliation now impossible and a growing army demanding clear leadership, Li Ssu-yüan dispatched an advance force to K'ai-feng to gauge what support he might find south of the Yellow River, while in his province of Chen-chou his followers mobilized his provincial army to march south and were quickly joined by other northern governors. Li Ts'un-hsü planned to defend the river crossing at Meng-chou just north of Lo-yang, but his troops had been underpaid for some time and angrily rejected the additional payments he now offered them. Meanwhile, Li Ssu-yüan rewarded his troops with silk taken from boats captured on the Yellow River. Li Ts'un-hsü now headed east in person while the K'ai-feng city governor declared that he would submit to whomever reached him first. Li Ssu-yüan's advance guard won the race, and Li Ts'un-hsü returned to Lo-yang amid reports of one provincial defection after another to Li Ssu-yüan. When Li Ts'un-hsü reached Lo-yang, an officer in the capital armies mutinied and killed the emperor. Uncontrolled looting followed after Li's empress set fire to one of the palace buildings and fled. Li Ssu-yüan's arrival restored order, and the chief councilor, Tou-lu Ko, led Li Ts'un-hsü's officials to offer Li Ssu-yüan the throne. Li Ts'un-hsü's designated heir, Li Chi-chi, at first planned to occupy Feng-hsiang with the expeditionary army used to conquer the Former Shu, but then killed himself instead, leaving the army to the care of the bureaucrat-general Jen Huan, who decided to submit to Li Ssu-yüan. After that, what little opposition remained in the provinces was handled swiftly and locally.[94]

In stark contrast to Chu Wen and Li Ts'un-hsü, Li Ssu-yüan won his throne in 926 through consent rather than conquest. Momentum had built up so quickly behind Li Ssu-yüan that he overthrew Li Ts'un-hsü in the space of a

[94] *TCTC* 274–5, pp. 8960–82; *CWTS* 34, pp. 469–78; 70, pp. 926–7; 74, pp. 971–2; Wang, *Structure of power*, pp. 150–1.

few weeks, with scarcely a blow struck, and was able to take over the empire
more or less intact. It seems likely that nobody was more surprised by this
than Li Ssu-yüan himself. Although Li had seized the capital by military force,
he had not – in contrast to his predecessors – come to power by defeating all
his rivals on the battlefield. Instead, he had won his throne by providing a
convincing alternative to a ruler who had alienated his followers. Li Ts'un-hsü
had been at his best at the head of a conquering army, and so long as his
conquests supplied a constant stream of rewards for generals (who were also
governors), soldiers, and administrators, he had no difficulty in maintaining a
following. But once he became emperor, Li Ts'un-hsü was expected to delegate
tasks that he would sometimes have preferred to do himself and, immured in
the inner palace, he was denied the opportunity to exercise personal leadership
over his followers. His increasing mistrustfulness created resentment among
loyal governors who had once enjoyed Li's confidence as field commanders and
now chafed at being kept in the capital. Their displeasure was only aggravated
when Li copied Later Liang efforts and sought to impose closer control over
his provinces, but offered nothing in compensation. Li was so extravagant that
even the huge profits from the conquest of the Former Shu were gone by the
time Li Ssu-yüan marched on K'ai-feng, leaving Li Ts'un-hsü unable to pay
his imperial armies, let alone reward his close followers, who were alienated
accordingly. Without the solid backing of the imperial armies, Li Ts'un-hsü
was vulnerable to his governors and their forces. Li Ssu-yüan's appeal lay in
offering a remedy as one governor and general among his peers, rather than as
someone who might threaten the autonomy the governors so much desired.

As the last survivor of the generals adopted as sons by Li K'o-yung, Li Ssu-
yüan's background was impeccable, but he was not an outstanding commander
and his home province of Chen-chou was small. Thrown back on his own
provincial resources, he was never likely to pose a serious threat to his fellow
governors, and they probably calculated that his dependence on their support
would act as a check on how much he could use the imperial institutions to
undermine their authority. For governors whose ideal emperor was an open-
handed figurehead, Li Ssu-yüan was the perfect choice of leader.

ALLEGIANCE AND ALLIANCE

Winning allegiance, 926–936

Li Ssu-yüan's first task was to formalize his position as emperor, but because he
was Li K'o-yung's adopted son and not actually of his bloodline, there was some
controversy over whether he should establish a new dynasty or continue the
Later T'ang restoration. The precedent of T'ang dynasty practice won the day,

and Li Ssu-yüan's accession ceremony followed the ritual for a son succeeding his father. Hence Li (T'ang Ming-tsung, 926–33) changed the reign era but did not establish a new calendar.[95]

Li Ssu-yüan had come to the throne by winning over the leaders of armies, and he knew that to retain his position he needed military forces of his own. Accordingly, one of his first actions was to transform the palace armies into a powerful personal army that incorporated all other imperial units. Upon Li's accession the palace forces consisted of the Six Imperial Armies and the Imperial Bodyguard (*shih-wei ch'in-chün*) – commonly referred to collectively as the Imperial Guard – stationed in various places in and around the capital. Li quickly incorporated the remaining imperial armies into these two palace forces by removing the imperial army commanders. Li Ts'un-hsü's favorite, Chu Shou-yin, led units stationed in the capital; he was posted to K'ai-feng and then attacked and killed. Jen Huan, commander of the expeditionary army sent to conquer the Former Shu, was made a chief minister. Under Li Ssu-yüan the enlarged Six Imperial Armies and Imperial Bodyguard were sometimes merged at the command level by appointing a single general to be the commander of one army and the assistant commander of the other, but one person never held sole command of both armies. Supreme military command was always divided between one of Li's sons and one of his closest retainers.[96] This Imperial Guard – now comprising all imperial forces – gave Li Ssu-yüan the power to quell dissent without having to rely on the allegiance of his governors or expeditionary generals. Later emperors, however, would find that the benefit of a personal army with its own palace-appointed commanders simply displaced the question of allegiance from the provinces to the palace.

With his Imperial Guard at his back it was much easier for Li to freely appoint his own men to the twelve governorships that lay vacant on his accession. Moreover, during his first year on the throne two edicts limited governors' and prefects' rights of nomination, ordered counties and garrison towns to refuse provincial demands for extra taxes, and decreed that provincial staff appointed by a governor should follow him to a new posting rather than be left in his old province to preserve his influence there and thus extend his authority. By 928, Li was appointing governors to all but nine provinces as well as claiming the right to choose his governors' senior administrators. By 930 all but four of the governors had been installed by Li, but thereafter his

---

[95] *TCTC* 275, pp. 8982–3. On the significance of this event, see Wechsler, *Offerings of jade and silk*, pp. 86, 101–6.

[96] See Wang, *Structure of power*, pp. 158–9; and Worthy, "The founding of Sung China," pp. 107–25. Worthy gives the clearest exposition of these developments from the T'ang dynasty onward, with references to the extensive secondary literature.

authority in the provinces seems to have become less effective, and his earlier decrees were not always heeded.[97]

Overall, Li Ssu-yüan gained a tremendous advantage from not trying to unite northern China but merely to exert his authority over it. His general approach to rulership was to avoid armed confrontation and focus his efforts on persuading his governors and people that their interests lay in accepting his rule. The sources carefully record that in 927 Li conducted a ceremony dedicated to Turkic gods, but this made him unusual among Five Dynasties leaders of Sha-t'o origin, and overall he did little that would have been alien to a leader claiming a culturally Chinese background. Li Ssu-yüan seems to have adopted as many sons as the Chinese Chu Wen and the Sha-t'o Li Ts'un-hsü, but – probably because he had at least fifteen daughters – Ssu-yüan also made extensive use of marriage relations, and as we shall see, the families of his sons-in-law (Chinese and Sha-t'o) sometimes gained considerable power as a result of his favor.[98]

As ruler of a greatly enlarged state, however, Li needed to cultivate his appeal wider than kinship politics allowed. Accordingly, he followed the lead provided by Li Ts'un-hsü when he was still governor in Ho-tung and combined these methods of retinue leadership with those of a claimant to the Mandate of Heaven. This meant practicing good governance and thereby keeping order in the world, but good governance was in the eye of beholder, and since the governors' opinions counted most, some of Li's first actions were clearly intended to please them. He dismissed Li Ts'un-hsü's supernumerary postholders and ordered the execution of the group the governors hated most – the former head of the Commission for State Revenue, K'ung Ch'ien, and the eunuch army supervisors – decreeing that the supervisors would not be used again and that central finance officials must not interfere in provincial affairs.

But Li Ssu-yüan also had to reward his own followers, and like Chu Wen, he removed the eunuchs from the palace commissions and replaced them with his own retainers, who were often transferred directly from their provincial positions into the equivalent palace commissions. Li's junior retainers performed the same varied tasks that Chu's retainers had in the Later Liang and, as the sons and relatives of governors and generals, also served as a surety for their families' allegiance. Li's chief provincial administrator, An Ch'ung-hui, headed the Bureau of Military Affairs with wide-ranging powers similar to

---

[97] Wang, *Structure of power*, pp. 178–85, including notes on sources. Most of the documents are at *CWTS* 37, pp. 507–9; 39, p. 538; 42, p. 581.

[98] On his adoptions, see Kurihara, "Tō-Godai no kafushiteki ketsugō no seikaku," and Kurihara, "Tōmatsu Godai no kafushiteki ketsugō ni okeru seimei to nenrei." On the significance of Li's Turkish heritage, see the two-part article by Okazaki Seirō, "Kō-Tō no Minsō ni kyūshū (jō)," *Tōyōshi kenkyū* 9 No. 4 (1945), pp. 50–62, and "Kō-Tō no Minsō ni kyūshū (ge)," *Tōyōshi kenkyū* 10 No. 2 (1948), pp. 29–40.

Kuo Ch'ung-t'ao's, and like him was given concurrent appointment as a chief minister. Also like Kuo, An was only semiliterate, so Li Ssu-yüan (who himself could not read) created an office of Tuan-ming Academicians to assist him. But Li Ssu-yüan also maintained some continuity in government appointments by keeping on some of Li Ts'un-hsü's palace commissioners and bureaucrats, including Feng Tao, who was promoted to chief minister. By now most bureaucrats had begun their careers in a provincial administration, yet under Li Ssu-yüan, as they had under Li Ts'un-hsü, they remained on the sidelines in terms of political influence, although they could make important administrative contributions.[99]

Li Ssu-yüan boosted his appeal to the wider populace through practical measures demanding administrative skills in the central offices. State finances needed particularly urgent attention, and Li almost immediately abolished the additional land taxes introduced by his predecessors and attempted to reduce the cost of supplying the military and running the administration. He banned excessive favor-seeking gift giving from his officials and greatly limited the frequency of "tribute" from the provinces, explicitly prohibiting the exploitation of commoners for this purpose. Li then unified the three central financial offices (responsible for the salt and iron monopolies, population registers, and the budget) and appointed the experienced bureaucrat Jen Huan as chief minister with responsibility for running the new Finance Commission (San-ssu); according to the sources, "within a year the state coffers were abundantly filled, both civil and military populations were adequate, and the rules of the court were basically established."[100] Jen Huan was soon replaced by a finance expert from Li Ssu-yüan's retinue, Chang Yen-lang, who continued to improve the financial administration, writing off two million strings in unpaid taxes in 927, and replacing the (unenforceable) state monopoly on alcohol production with a general increase in the autumn taxes. Li Ssu-yüan tried to ban the circulation of iron and tin coins from Ch'u, and to end the overpriced horse trade with the Tangut. To avoid dependence on the Tangut for his horse supply Li established state pastures in Ho-tung in 927, although the horses reared on them proved inadequate in both numbers and quality. In 931 the acreage and fermentation taxes and the iron monopoly were abolished. Commoners were allowed to make their own iron implements and, as with the earlier abolition of the alcohol monopoly, their land taxes were increased to

---

[99] Wang, *Structure of power*, pp. 152–5, 180; Worthy, "The founding of Sung China," pp. 227–8. On Feng Tao's survival through successive administrations, see Wang Gungwu, "Feng Tao: An essay on Confucian loyalty," in *Confucian personalities*, ed. Arthur F. Wright and Denis C. Twitchett (Stanford, Calif., 1962), pp. 123–45; for a full biography of Feng Tao, see Tonami Mamoru, *Fū Dō* (Tokyo, 1966).

[100] *TCTC* 275, pp. 8983–4; *CWTS* 67, pp. 895–6. See also Wolfram Eberhard, "Remarks on the bureaucracy in north China during the tenth century" *Oriens* 4 (1951), pp. 280–99.

offset the revenue shortfall. The land taxes were themselves equalized shortly afterward, although local implementation of these changes depended on how autonomous the prefects were from their governors. While it was recognized that such technical tasks demanded literacy, the level of education was low, since a law of 928 declared that candidates only needed to know ten chapters of the Confucian Classics to pass the examinations.[101]

Demonstrating that he possessed the qualities of rulership won Li Ssu-yüan goodwill that made it easier for him to assert his authority over his realm, but he proved unable to exercise similar control at court. Even as Li was respectfully burying Li Ts'un-hsü's ashes, rivalries and intrigue arose at the center of the regime. The most powerful minister at court, An Ch'ung-hui, resented Jen Huan's power, and the men clashed over issues such as the appointment of senior ministers and the correct office for disbursing salaries. The latter issue resulted in a furious dispute in 927 between the two ministers in front of the emperor, an unprecedented breach of protocol. Jen Huan was asked to retire, and before the year was out An Ch'ung-hui had arranged his execution. But An went too far when he alienated Consort Wang and the eunuch Meng Han-ch'iung, and in 930 he and his wife were killed in his provincial residence and the murder justified by accusations of collaboration with the Szechwan region governors and the Wu-Yüeh ruler.[102] As with Kuo Ch'ung-t'ao, the sources are sympathetic – An Ch'ung-hui was overthrown by a classic alliance between a woman and a eunuch, after all – balancing An's easily offended nature against his unrelenting concern to prevent waste of state resources. An's passing put an end to the Later T'ang's initial focus on good rulership, since his successors tended to place their own concerns before any wider good.

Li Ssu-yüan's authority was also challenged from outside the court. Although he received the formal allegiance of all the provinces conquered by Li Ts'un-hsü, there remained definite limitations on the reach and sustainability of effective Later T'ang authority. Li Ssu-yüan could demonstrate his strength with a military campaign and appoint most of his own governors, but he could not necessarily impose his authority in a manner that would last. Districts often regarded as "border provinces" of the Later T'ang retained a high degree of autonomy due in part to their own wealth and strategic advantages, but often due to the ready availability of support from their neighbors. This support could be reversed at any time.

---

[101] *TCTC* 276, pp. 9021 (alcohol taxes), 9028 (coins); 275, pp. 9002–3, and 278, p. 9090 (horses); 277, pp. 9059, 9061 (land taxes); *CWTS* 39, p. 543 (examinations); 42, pp. 578, 581 (alcohol regulations), 583–4 (iron); 69, pp. 919–21 (Chang Yen-lang).
[102] *TCTC* 277, pp. 9045–6, 9055–60; *CWTS* 72, pp. 955–6. Worthy compares his end to Kuo Ch'ung-t'ao's, "The founding of Sung China," p. 228.

The first challenge to Later T'ang authority came from the governors in the Szechwan region, Meng Chih-hsiang and Tung Chang, whose rivalry is detailed in the next chapter. Fearing Li's intentions toward the enormous wealth of the Szechwan region, Meng Chih-hsiang sought to free himself of court control, wooing his population and enlarging his army units, and then in 927 executing a Later T'ang official sent to oversee his military affairs. Hoping to keep the Szechwan region divided, Li initially backed Tung Chang. The two Szechwan governors allied briefly in 930–1, but when they fell out again Tung proved no match for Meng, and in 932 Li Ssu-yüan conceded to Meng – now controlling all of Szechwan – the right to appoint his own provincial staff, from governors downward. When Li Ssu-yüan died the next year in 933, Meng Chih-hsiang proclaimed himself emperor of Later Shu.[103]

Li had more success in the south, where in 927–8 he was able to call on Ma Yin, whom Li designated "King of Ch'u," to use his naval forces to prevent Kao Chi-hsing of Ching-nan from abandoning his fealty to Later T'ang in favor of an alliance with Wu.[104] A similar situation occurred in 928 in the north, where Li Ssu-yüan successfully quelled an effort by Wang Tu, the long-time governor of Ting-chou, to organize Ho-pei governors and Liao allies against the extension of Later T'ang administrative authority.[105]

Li Ssu-yüan's success in Ting-chou was one of several that helped him to consolidate his authority in the regions beyond his own borders. In Shuo-fang (in modern Ningsia), the death of the Tangut prince in 929 prompted a local mutiny, and his successor turned to the Later T'ang. An Ch'ung-hui appointed one of Li's favorites to the governorship, who wiped out two Tibetan groups who dared to attack, and dealt with the mutineers. Li's agent had "greatly restored the majesty" of the Later T'ang, and thereafter Shuo-fang accepted court appointees. The reputation of the Later T'ang rose further when an expedition against Tangut raiders in the northwest captured twenty-seven hundred Tanguts and destroyed nineteen "tribes." Although Tangut raids continued, Later T'ang success may have encouraged the leadership in Liang-chou (in present-day Kansu), far beyond Li's authority, to seek Later T'ang confirmation of their new governor in 933. The Liang-chou region was caught between the ambitions of the Liao, the Tibetans, the Tangut, and the Uighur in western Kansu, and allegiance to Li Ssu-yüan may have offered it the best chance of preserving some autonomy.[106]

[103] *TCTC* 276–7 passim; 278, pp. 9074–7, 9102. Biographies at *CWTS* 136, pp. 1822–3; 62, pp. 831–4.

[104] *TCTC* 275–7, pp. 8979–9053, 9073; *CWTS* 133, pp. 1751–2; 134, pp. 1783–4.

[105] *TCTC* (1956) 276, pp. 9017–27; *CWTS* 39, pp. 537–41; 40, p. 548; 54, pp. 733–4; 137, p. 1832; T'o-t'o et al., *Liao shih* 3, pp. 28–9.

[106] Ruth W. Dunnell, "The Hsi Hsia," in *The Cambridge history of China*, volume 6: *Alien regimes and border states, 907–1368*, ed. Herbert Franke and Denis C. Twitchett (New York, 1994), pp. 164–5; *TCTC*

The allegiance of far-flung places improved Li's standing in relation to his independent neighbors, of whom the most important was now the Liao state. According to the *Tzu-chih t'ung-chien*, the Khitan emperor A-pao-chi sought advantage from Li Ts'un-hsü's death by demanding territory under threat of invasion. However, A-pao-chi's death in 926 produced several months of internal tension at the Liao court over the succession until A-pao-chi's son, Te-kuang (Liao T'ai-tsung, 926–47), secured the throne.[107] In such a personalized system, neither major power was in a position to exploit the other's situation, but it was an ideal opportunity for lesser leaders. That winter the governor in Fu-chien briefly seceded from Later T'ang overlordship, while on the northern frontier Lu Wen-chin, the governor of Liao, who controlled P'ing-chou, killed his Khitan general and returned to Later T'ang allegiance with an army of twenty thousand, claiming to miss his homeland.[108]

Te-kuang, the new Liao ruler, was at least Li Ssu-yüan's peer: a ruler whose confirmations of position legitimized regional leaders in conflict with their neighbors or superiors. Like regimes in the Central Plains, the Liao employed the diplomatic protocols established in the previous T'ang dynasty. Relations between Liao and Later T'ang now settled into the routine of audiences and gift exchanges (with the occasional delicate negotiation), and regular local plundering raids across both sides of the border.[109] In 930 A-pao-chi's eldest son, Pei, arrived in Later T'ang territory from the sea with forty retainers. As former heir apparent, he had found it politic to flee the dangers of his brother's court.[110] His arrival boosted Li Ssu-yüan's prestige, but over the next few years fear of Liao strength and unknown intentions grew at all levels of leadership in the Central Plains, encouraged by increasing centralization and a misunderstanding of pastoralist practices. Parts of northern China were used as

(1956) 276, pp. 9033–5; 277, pp. 9064–5; 278, pp. 9074, 9082. On relations between the Sha-t'o-led dynasties and their neighbors, see Wolfram Eberhard, "Die Beziehungender Staaten der T'o-pa und der Sha-t'o zum Ausland," *Annales de l'Université d'Ankara* 2 (1948), pp. 141–213.

[107] *TCTC* 275, pp. 8989–90. See Yao Ts'ung-wu, "A-pao-chi yü Hou T'ang shih-ch'en Yao K'un hui-chien t'an-hua chi-lu," *Wen-shih-che hsüeh-pao* 5 (1953), pp. 91–112; and Denis C. Twitchett and Klaus-Peter Tietze, "The Liao," in *The Cambridge history of China*, volume 6: *Alien regimes and border states, 907–1368*, ed. Herbert Franke and Denis C. Twitchett (New York, 1994), pp. 66–7. Te-kuang's approach was very different from his father's; see Naomi Standen, "What nomads want: Raids, invasions, and the Liao conquest of 947," in *Mongols, Turks, and others: Eurasian nomads and the sedentary world*, ed. Reuven Amitai and Michal Biran (Leiden, 2005), pp. 129–74.

[108] *TCTC* 275, pp. 8994, 8997; *CWTS* 37, p. 511; T'o-t'o et al., *Liao shih* 2, p. 23. Ten years before, Lu Wen-chin, the P'ing-chou governor, had taken the province as well as his army into Khitan service. The Khitan recovered P'ing-chou in 928.

[109] For discussion, see Standen, "Raiding and frontier society." The delicate negotiation stemmed from the Khitan request for the return of their generals captured in the 928 Ting-chou campaigns.

[110] *TCTC* 277, pp. 9052–3; *CWTS* 41, p. 571; T'o-t'o et al., *Liao shih* 3, p. 32; biography in T'o-t'o et al., *Liao shih* 72, pp. 1209–11.

stops in seasonal migrations, and although the movement of people and animals was not a hostile action, it could look ominous to Later T'ang military patrols, especially when it was accompanied by raids for plunder. These activities had been a lesser concern when the Later Liang were the main enemy and the Liao state was newly founded, but the consolidation of Liao and Central Plains states now made controlling pastoralist activity a higher priority. Breaches of the frontier, however customary or innocuous, threatened Li Ssu-yüan's claims to legitimacy by throwing doubt on his ability to police his borders. Raids in Yu-chou were stopped by its governor's defensive measures, but this maneuver simply pushed the raiders westward into Yün-chou2 (modern Ta-t'ung). At court there were fears of a major attack, and late in 932 Li Ssu-yüan's trusted retainer Shih Ching-t'ang became governor of Ho-tung and assumed overall military command in four other frontier provinces.[111]

Fears of the Liao were confirmed by a report of siege equipment being built near Yün-chou2, but the real dangers were suggested when a frontier prefect with a grudge against Shih Ching-t'ang apparently took his district of Yü-chou (between Yu-chou and Yün-chou2) over to the Khitan.[112] Te-kuang's capacity to be an alternative source of legitimacy for Later T'ang provincial leaders threatened the cohesion of the Later T'ang far more than any external military threat, and accordingly this threat lay behind many responses to events. Early in 933, the governor at Hsia-chou died and the army installed his son, Li I-ch'ao, as successor. The Later T'ang court, knowing the father had contacted Te-kuang, feared a joint attack and tried to transfer Li I-ch'ao, providing his replacement with an "escort" of fifty thousand troops. Li rebelled, but he was confirmed in Ting-nan after a siege was deemed too costly. When he died in 935, the Later T'ang leadership did not contest his brother's succession. The irony was that the Liao had in fact refused Li I-ch'ao's father any help.[113] Expending such effort to contest an appointment wasted lives and money, and worse for the court, damaged its prestige by highlighting its inability to impose its will. Dangers imagined out of imprecise understanding had a nasty habit of becoming all too real.

At this point in 933, the greatest threat to Li Ssu-yüan came from inside the realm. With Li seriously ill, his close advisors faced a challenge from Li's ambitious oldest son, Ts'ung-jung. Ts'ung-jung was proposed as heir apparent but successfully resisted for fear that confinement to the heir's palace would remove him from his command of the Six Imperial Armies. As senior ministers fled the capital, Li Ts'ung-jung was appeased, but the next time he attended

[111] TCTC 278, pp. 9076, 9079–80; CWTS 43, pp. 592, 596; 98, p. 1309.
[112] CWTS 43, p. 596; TCTC 278, p. 9080.
[113] TCTC 278, pp. 9082–5, 9090; 279, pp. 9127–8; CWTS 44, pp. 603–5; 47, p. 644; 132, pp. 1747–9.

on his father he marched a thousand troops into the capital, whereupon he was killed as a rebel by the commander of the Imperial Bodyguard, K'ang I-ch'eng. Ts'ung-jung's brother Li Ts'ung-hou was summoned from his province of Wei-chou and became de facto heir apparent. Li Ssu-yüan died shortly afterward, earning praise from later writers who characterized him as a good ruler in a difficult time.[114] Li had come to the throne as an experienced general and leader at the age of sixty, and although we might attribute the good harvests and relative peace of his short reign to fortunate timing, contemporaries took them to indicate his virtue as a ruler.

Li Ts'ung-hou (T'ang Min-ti, 933–4) acceded without incident late in 933, but his reign lasted only five months. He seems to have been well inten-tioned; he ordered instruction for himself in the lessons on rulership to be gleaned from T'ang T'ai-tsung's reign (r. 626–49), but he was not yet twenty years old and his short reign was dominated by Meng Han-ch'iung and Chu Hung-chao. Their priorities seem to have been to attack their enemies, real or potential, leaving them little time to address matters of wider import. Li Ts'ung-hou barely had time to make his initial distribution of posts and titles before Meng Chih-hsiang, observing Li's youth and weakness, declared him-self independent emperor of Later Shu, rightly calculating that there would be little response. With hindsight, the most significant act of the reign was to entrust the Six Imperial Armies and Imperial Bodyguard to the sole com-mand of K'ang I-ch'eng. This rewarded K'ang for his loyalty to Li Ssu-yüan, which had effectively brought Li Ts'ung-hou to the throne, but it departed from Ssu-yüan's practice of dividing the command. Since Li Ts'ung-hou was too young to have either the sons or personal retainers whom his father had employed in this job, reliance on K'ang must have seemed entirely reasonable. Six months later the Six Imperial Armies were formally incorporated into the Imperial Bodyguard, effectively placing the military power of the empire in the hands of a single general.[115]

The next major act of the reign was a general reshuffling of governors organized by Chu Hung-chao in 934, partly with the intention of bringing back to court Meng Han-ch'iung, who had taken over Li Ts'ung-hou's former province of Wei-chou. Rather than proper imperial commands, the orders were contained in letters issued by the Bureau of Military Affairs, which drew attention to the dominance exercised by retainer officials and increased the governors' resentment toward them. Still, most governors accepted their transfers, with the exception of Ts'ung-hou's adopted brother Li Ts'ung-k'o,

[114] *TCTC* 278, pp. 9087–95; *CWTS* 44, pp. 605–10; 66, pp. 876–7, 879–80.
[115] *TCTC* 278, pp. 9097–8, 9102, 9099; Wang, *Structure of power*, p. 160; Worthy, "The founding of Sung China," pp. 125–6.

the governor of Feng-hsiang. An earlier run-in with An Ch'ung-hui had left him isolated at court, and now Meng Han-ch'iung placed Li Ts'ung-k'o among his chief enemies. The prospect of attending court to accept his new posting was unwelcome to Li Ts'ung-k'o, but he lacked the troops to make a stand. He issued a call to arms to his neighboring governors and prefects, offering handsome payments and seeking their help "to explain the wickedness of those surrounding the emperor," but he received only one positive response. Very soon a section of the Imperial Guard joined up with several provincial forces at Feng-hsiang, but when one of the commanders forced his troops to assault the walls at swordpoint they mutinied and soon the whole expeditionary army had submitted to Li Ts'ung-k'o. K'ang I-ch'eng now marched west with the greater part of the Imperial Guard while Li headed east, enlarging his army at K'ang's expense as the punitive forces deserted and joined the rebel army. Near Shan-chou2 (Shensi, modern San-men-hsia), some seventy-five miles west of Lo-yang, K'ang I-ch'eng surrendered with the few troops that remained with him and was later executed with his family. A general sent Chu Hung-chao's head to Li Ts'ung-k'o, and Meng Han-ch'iung fled, later to be summarily executed by the roadside. Li Ts'ung-hou abandoned the capital, and Shih Ching-t'ang, en route from Ho-tung to the court, took him into custody as a bargaining counter for dealings with Shih's long-standing rival Li Ts'ung-k'o. At Lo-yang, Feng Tao led the officials to welcome Li Ts'ung-k'o and offer him the throne, and the dowager empress cleared the way by demoting Li Ts'ung-hou, who was soon killed. Shih Ching-t'ang was the first governor to attend on the new emperor, who ascended the throne in Lo-yang using the ceremony of a son before his father's coffin (T'ang Fei-ti, 934–6).[116]

Like Li Ssu-yüan, Li Ts'ung-k'o gained his throne from a weak military base as the representative of a general feeling of resentment that enabled him to enter the capital in the required fashion, at the head of an army. But whereas Li Ssu-yüan had discovered an unexpected following largely among governors and prefects in the provinces, Li Ts'ung-k'o's support came mostly from the Imperial Guard and was based less on dissatisfaction with the old regime than on the payments he made and promised them. Li Ts'ung-k'o relied more on material inducements because he lacked the expeditionary experience and thus the personal standing with the imperial armies that Li Ssu-yüan had enjoyed.[117] Accordingly, his main problem on accession was a lack of money. Paying military salaries had already caused hardship under Li Ssu-yüan. Li Ts'ung-hou had paid generous rewards for little return, and

[116] *TCTC* 279, pp. 9104–16; *CWTS* 45–6, pp. 618–32.

[117] See Chang, "Wu-tai cheng-ch'üan ti-shan chih k'ao-ch'a," pp. 26–7, who argues that the allegiance of the imperial armies was central to Li Ssu-yüan's successful takeover.

Li Ts'ung-k'o had encouraged his following by distributing booty seized in captured cities, including Lo-yang. When even the robes and treasures in the palace were inadequate to satisfy the troops, the inhabitants of the capital yelled abuse at soldiers in the streets, and Li realized that merely purchasing the military's loyalty would alienate the civilian population. He therefore made the hard decision to pay lower rewards than he had promised, knowing that this would compromise the army's allegiance. A special investigative commissioner encouraged Li to write off 3.38 million strings of uncollected taxes to please the people, who were then suffering the effects of a drought.[118]

Since almost all the dominant figures from Li Ssu-yüan's last years and Li Ts'ung-hou's reign had died in the rebellion, Li Ts'ung-k'o had to start afresh. Feng Tao remained chief minister, and Li Ssu-yüan's retainer Chang Yen-lang was soon placed back in charge of finances, but most of the senior ministers were new. Han Chao-yin (briefly military affairs commissioner and chief minister), Liu Yen-lang (promoted to assistant military affairs commissioner via the finance office), and Hsüeh Wen-yü (participant in the drafting of proclamations) had all been provincial administrators with literati backgrounds before joining Li Ts'ung-k'o's court. His reliance on such people has been construed as a deliberate attempt to increase the influence of bureaucrats over retainers like Chang Yen-lang.[119] But if this was so it did not necessarily produce better governance. Liu Yen-lang reputedly made appointment decisions in proportion to the size of his bribe, but even when found out he was not punished, and the bribe taking continued. But despite corruption and personal rivalries, intrigue of the kind that had felled Kuo Ch'ung-t'ao and An Ch'ung-hui was absent, precisely because there was no single figure dominating the scene.[120]

Li Ts'ung-k'o's position outside the court was insecure as long as the Imperial Guard commanders and the governors had doubts about his qualifications for holding the Mandate of Heaven. During Li's rebellion, the governors of Yang-chou2 and Hsing-yüan, in the mountainous Han River valley dividing Szechwan and Shensi, had transferred their allegiance to Meng Chih-hsiang of Later Shu after their armies joined Li Ts'ung-k'o. This provided a reminder that credible sources of alternative authority existed in the border regions, and it may have encouraged Li to keep his adopted brothers and erstwhile enemies, Li Ts'ung-chang and Li Ts'ung-min, in Lo-yang as private citizens, where they could do little to build a following. To secure his military position, Li tried to bring the Imperial Guard under control by appointing one of his

---

[118] *TCTC* 279, pp. 9105–24; *CWTS* 44, pp. 632–6.
[119] *TCTC* 279, pp. 9118–19, 9120, 9127, 9130–1, 9133, 9137; *CWTS* 69, p. 922; Wang, *Structure of power*, p. 156. Neither Han Chao-yin nor Hsüeh Wen-yü have biographies in the dynastic histories.
[120] *TCTC* 279, pp. 9133, 9137, 9128–9.

sons to command it, and he rewarded five of his early supporters – army officers and prefects – by entrusting them with provinces scattered all across the realm, apparently hoping to keep the older governors separated from each other. Gradually he managed to transfer or recall all the governors save two: Shih Ching-t'ang of Ho-tung (Li Ssu-yüan's son-in-law) and Chao Te-chün of Yu-chou (whose adopted son was Li Ssu-yüan's son-in-law).[121]

Li most feared Shih Ching-t'ang, an old rival from the days when both had been members of Li Ssu-yüan's retinue. Li Ts'ung-hou had transferred Shih from Ho-tung to Chen-chou but, crucially, had left him in charge of frontier defenses. Li Ts'ung-k'o returned Shih to Ho-tung, whence he requested more troops and supplies to deal with routine nomad activity and raids. Shih heard every detail of court affairs because he had sons residing in the palace and bribed servants of the dowager empress (his wife's mother) to gather information, so he knew that such requests compounded court suspicions about his allegiance. The court was further alarmed when some of Shih's troops tried to declare him emperor in 935. Shih executed the ringleaders and reported these events himself, suggesting that he may have been trying to reassure the court of his good intentions, but the news doubtless contributed to the imperial appointment of a deputy city governor for Shih's seat of T'ai-yüan, intended to weaken his authority. Shih thus knew the risks when, early in 936, he collected all his property from Lo-yang and other places and sent it to T'ai-yüan to help pay military expenses. Financing armies with private wealth was common practice, but naturally it heightened fears about Shih's intentions. Li Ts'ung-k'o responded by ordering Shih Ching-t'ang's transfer from Ho-tung to the tiny province of Yün-chou, south of the Yellow River, a test of imperial authority that transformed suspicion into reality. Shih had to either accept a humiliating demotion that marked him as disloyal or rebel against the throne to defend his political position and maybe his honor. Shih argued that he had been promised his Ho-tung posting for life, and the Sung chronicler Ssu-ma Kuang describes an aggrieved letter to Li Ts'ung-k'o accusing him, as an adopted son, of usurping the throne, and demanding restoration of the direct bloodline. Several leaders promptly joined Shih with units of troops, and the Imperial Guard units stationed at Wei-chou mutinied. Shih suggested to one follower that he was "abandoning the strong and pledging allegiance to the weak" and was informed in turn that once one had lost the confidence of superiors one might as well go down fighting.[122] Shih Ching-t'ang had nothing to lose.

---

[121] TCTC 279, pp. 9115, 9121–2, 9133; Wang, *Structure of power*, p. 188.
[122] TCTC 279–80, pp. 9104, 9119–20, 9124–31, 9139–45; CWTS 45, pp. 618–19; 46, pp. 634–5; 47, pp. 649–50. On private funding for armies, see Ku, "Fan-lun T'ang-mo Wu-tai."

Map 7. China under the Later Chin, c. 938.

Shih's sons and other family members were hunted down and killed, and his first supporters were defeated and executed. A section of the Imperial Guard under Chang Ching-ta laid siege to T'ai-yüan, and Shih turned to the Liao for help. The alliance surprised no one. Indeed, Shih's inner circle had discussed this possibility two months earlier. Moreover, Li Ts'ung-k'o's court had accepted plans to neutralize the Liao by offering annual payments. Li's officials had been attracted by the prospect of saving ninety percent of frontier expenses, but they abandoned the plans in the belief that the Liao would demand a princess in marriage – and that Shih Ching-t'ang would rebel anyway.[123]

---

[123] *TCTC* 280, pp. 9141–2, 9145–7; *CWTS* 48, pp. 660–3; 75, pp. 983–4; T'o-t'o et al., *Liao shih* 3, p. 38. On the willingness of the Ho-tung regimes to work with the Liao, see Jen Ch'ung-yüeh,

The Liao–Later Chin alliance, 936–942

Shih Ching-t'ang's agreement with the Liao emperor Te-kuang is probably the most famous event of the Five Dynasties period, taken to mark the beginning of the "barbarian" encroachment into northern China that culminated in the Mongol conquest of the whole country. Shih was only the latest of many who had turned to the Liao for supplementary forces, but he needed more than just a few extra cavalry. Li Ssu-yüan had concentrated military power in the Imperial Guard, and Shih Ching-t'ang had held day-to-day control of this force until 932, after which the dangers of sharing command with the volatile prince Li Ts'ung-jung had led Shih to extract himself from court and seek the Ho-tung command he had held ever since. Shih thus knew better than most that his own border defense forces were no match for the Imperial Guard, and accordingly the terms of Shih's deal with Te-kuang went far beyond what anyone had offered before. Shih promised annual payments of gold and silk, but he also undertook to hand over the districts that became known as the Sixteen Prefectures and to subordinate himself as Te-kuang's adopted son and subject.[124] The Sixteen Prefectures were Yu-chou (raised by the Khitan to Nan- or Yen-ching in 938), Chi-chou, Ying-chou, Mo-chou, Cho-chou, T'an-chou2, Shun-chou, Hsin-chou, Kuei-chou2, Ju-chou, Wu-chou, Yün-chou2, Ying-chou2, Huan-chou, Shuo-chou, and Yü-chou.[125] Such large promises imply a determination to succeed in seizing and retaining power, but it is not clear at this point whether Shih Ching-t'ang sought the throne in the Central Plains or simply regional autonomy such as that enjoyed by Meng Chih-hsiang of the Later Shu. That Te-kuang sent fifty thousand troops suggests his intention to avoid repeating the ill-fated ventures of 928, whose generals were still in Later T'ang custody.

The mutiny at Wei-chou tied down a section of the Later T'ang Imperial Guard for two months and so helped T'ai-yüan withstand a summer siege,

---

"Ch'i-tan yü Wu-tai Shan-hsi ko-chü cheng-ch'üan," in *Ch'i-tan shih-lun chu hui-pien*, ed. Sun Chin-chi et al. (Shen-yang, 1988), vol. 1, pp. 384–8, 368; and on the use of the Liao threat by people who usurped the throne (from Li Ssu-yüan to Kuo Wei), see Hsing I-t'ien, "Ch'i-tan yü Wu-tai cheng-ch'üan keng-tieh chih kuan-hsi," *Shih-huo yüeh-k'an* 1 No. 6 (1971), pp. 296–307.

[124] The original offer was "the circuit of Lu-lung and all the prefectures north of Yen-men pass" (*TCTC* 280, p. 9146).

[125] See *TCTC* 280, p. 9154. On the geography of this region, see the pair of articles by Chao T'ieh-han, "Yen–Yün shih-liu chou ti ti-li fen-hsi (shang)," *Ta-lu tsa-chih* 17 No. 11 (1958), pp. 3–7, and "Yen–Yün shih-liu chou ti ti-li fen-hsi (hsia)," *Ta-lu tsa-chih* 17 No. 12 (1958), pp. 18–22; and Ho T'ien-ming, "Shih-lun Liao-ch'ao chieh-kuan Yen-Yün ti-ch'ü," *Liao Chin Ch'i-tan Nü-chen shih yen-chiu tung-t'ai* 2 (1986), pp. 14–18; and on its significance, see Ho T'ien-ming, "Lun Liao cheng-ch'üan chieh-kuan Yen–Yün ti pi-jan-hsing chi li-shih tso-yung," in *Liao Chin shih lun-chi*, ed. Ch'en Shu (Peking, 1989), vol. 4, pp. 100–15.

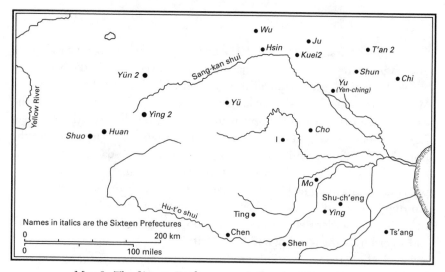

Map 8. The Sixteen Prefectures ceded to the Khitan in 937.

before the Liao armies arrived to relieve the city and in turn cut off the Later
T'ang camp at Chin-an-chai. Shih Ching-t'ang and Te-kuang met during the
long siege that followed, and in the eleventh month Te-kuang invested Shih as
emperor of Later Chin (Chin Kao-tsu, 936–42). The Later T'ang commanders
held in reserve two further sections of the Imperial Guard, which were placed
under Li Ts'ung-k'o's two most powerful governors: Fan Yen-kuang, who had
quelled the Wei-chou rebellion and been appointed to the governorship, and
Chao Te-chün of Yu-chou. Neither of them was keen to relieve T'ai-yüan. Chao
in particular tried to exploit the situation to get his adopted son appointed
to govern Chen-chou. Dissatisfied with Li Ts'ung-k'o's angry refusal, Chao
negotiated with Te-kuang to displace Shih Ching-t'ang as emperor in the
Central Plains in return for surrendering his armies and providing generous
payments thereafter. Although sorely tempted, Te-kuang did not abandon Shih
Ching-t'ang, and soon afterward received Chin-an-chai's surrender from the
Later T'ang general Yang Kuang-yüan, who had killed his stubbornly loyal
commander, Chang Ching-ta. This army was handed over to Shih Ching-
t'ang, who rewarded Yang Kuang-yüan by leaving him in command. Liao
cavalry pursued and killed many of the last effective fighting forces of the Later
T'ang, before their two commanders, Chao Te-chün and his adopted son Chao
Yen-shou, surrendered. The surviving forces seem to have been taken north
along with their commanders, and Chao Yen-shou was quickly promoted
at Te-kuang's court. Although benefiting from such changes of allegiance,

Te-kuang pointedly praised Chang Ching-ta's constancy and reprimanded the surrendering generals for their disobedience.[126]

Informed of the Liao victory, only one Later T'ang prefect and one minister declared continuing allegiance to Li Ts'ung-k'o. The powerful Fan Yen-kuang did nothing. Te-kuang despatched Shih Ching-t'ang to Lo-yang with an escort of five thousand troops, and Shih occupied the capital without resistance, while Te-kuang waited in Ho-tung to ensure a smooth takeover. When Li Ts'ung-k'o killed himself, few seemed sorry to see him go, and Te-kuang returned home.[127] Shih Ching-t'ang ordered the punishment of a few key ministers from Li Ts'ung-k'o's administration and a return to the ways of Li Ssu-yüan's court.

Shih Ching-t'ang's dissatisfaction with Li Ts'ung-k'o was shared by many of his peers, but Shih's own claim to the throne was problematical because of his relationship with the Liao emperor Te-kuang. The issue was not that Te-kuang was not Chinese – Shih and the Later T'ang rulers were themselves all of Sha-t'o origin – but that Shih Ching-t'ang fundamentally lacked legitimacy as emperor. Li Ssu-yüan had come to the throne by attracting a wide following, and Li Ts'ung-k'o by dispensing largesse. Both had taken over the capital at the head of an army, but with scarcely a blow struck. Shih Ching-t'ang marched on the capital as the result of much greater military achievement – a victory in battle, a siege, and a surrender – but this had been gained by reliance on another leader's troops and at the cost of Shih's formal subordination to that leader. As a result, Shih always struggled to be taken seriously as a ruler. The difficulty of Shih's position can be seen in the Later Shu's hostility toward the Later Chin envoys announcing Shih Ching-t'ang's accession, and again, six months later, when the state of Wu undertook a seaborne mission seeking an alliance with the Liao to conquer the Later Chin.[128] While neighboring rulers might have coveted each other's regimes, the usual procedure had been to acknowledge rival regimes first and fall out with them later. Such antagonism

---

[126] For this and the next paragraph: *TCTC* 280, pp. 9147–64; *CWTS* 48, pp. 663–8; 75–6, pp. 984–94; 70, pp. 933–4; 97, pp. 1296–7; 98, pp. 1309–10; 137, p. 1833; T'o-t'o et al., *Liao shih* 3, pp. 38–40; Wang, *Structure of power*, p. 189. Some of the sources suggest that Chao Te-chün had planned his claim to the throne months before, but on balance this seems unlikely. On Chao Yen-shou, see Naomi Standen, "Frontier crossings from north China to Liao, c. 900–1005" (diss., University of Durham, 1994), pp. 165–89.

[127] The response of the Wu-Yüeh regime is most striking; see *TCTC* 280, p. 9164.

[128] *TCTC* 281, p. 9173. Shih has been subjected to much criticism for giving away territory and for subordinating himself to another ruler. These points are reassessed by Wei Liang-t'ao, "I-erh, erh-huang-ti," *Li-shih yen-chiu* 1 (1991), pp. 164–7; Cheng Hsüeh-meng, "Kuan-yü Shih Ching-t'ang p'ing-chia ti chi-ko wen-t'i," *Hsia-men ta-hsüeh hsüeh-pao* 1 (1983), pp. 57–63; and (from Te-kuang's perspective) Standen, "What nomads want."

toward a new ruler at first greeting suggests that Shih Ching-t'ang lacked credibility.

Objections to the specific terms of Shih's agreement with the Liao also came from officials and leaders within the Sixteen Prefectures. Although Te-kuang did not receive the maps and registers for these districts until 938, he took possession straightaway, and he expected submission from the sitting officials. But even as the Liao withdrew north from Ho-tung in mid-937, an administrative assistant in Yün-chou2 (Ta-t'ung) closed his city to Te-kuang and asked Shih Ching-t'ang for help, while another regional general left for "the south," apparently ashamed to serve the Liao (whether from xenophobia or resentment of being given away we do not know). Shih Ching-t'ang could only ask Te-kuang to lift the siege of Yün-chou2, but resolving the situation required the offending assistant's recall to the south. Problems like these may have been behind Shih's offer of increased annual payments to buy back the Sixteen Prefectures, but Te-kuang refused.[129]

Doubts about Shih's authority made it harder for him to establish control over his governors, many of whom showed their uncertainty by being slow to offer their submission. However, the uncertain relationship of formal subordination that undermined Shih's position also gave him his major advantage over any challengers: their success was ultimately limited by the Liao's support for Shih. The significance of this quickly became apparent. North of the Yellow River, the Wei–Po governor Fan Yen-kuang still had with him at Wei-chou one of the two remaining sections of the Later T'ang Imperial Guard, and the danger he posed contributed to Shih Ching-t'ang's decision to move the Later Chin capital from Lo-yang to K'ai-feng, which was better placed strategically. Early in 937, Fan Yen-kuang rebelliously sought Liao support against Shih Ching-t'ang. Te-kuang, however, showed how seriously he took the alliance between the Liao and the Later Chin by not only refusing to help Fan but also discussing with Shih Ching-t'ang how he should respond. The conclusion seems to have been that Te-kuang would leave Shih to handle Fan Yen-kuang by himself. Shih first tried to appease Fan by giving him a noble title, but in the sixth month of that year Fan rebelled. Both sides had been maneuvering for position on opposite banks of the Yellow River, but Fan Yen-kuang now won over to his banner an imperial general who occupied the recently demoted capital, Lo-yang, rewarding his troops with the contents of the imperial store-houses. Panic gripped the court as Fan's army approached the new capital at K'ai-feng, and Shih Ching-t'ang contemplated fleeing to T'ai-yüan.

---

[129] *TCTC* 281, pp. 9169, 9175; T'o-t'o et al., *Liao shih* 3, pp. 40–1.

At this crucial juncture, rebellions broke out in major Yellow River cities downstream from Lo-yang, including an attempt by the troops of Imperial Guard general Yang Kuang-yüan to acclaim Yang emperor. Yang Kuang-yüan, crucially, maintained his allegiance to Shih Ching-t'ang, and Yang's Imperial Guard, together with a number of provincial forces, began to see some military success against the rebels. This enabled Shih Ching-t'ang to install demonstrably loyal Later Chin generals in the provinces around the old and new capitals and in the southern approaches to Ho-tung, while Fan Yen-kuang, unable to supplement his forces from outside the Later Chin realm, watched his following begin to dissipate. Nevertheless, Fan, besieged in Wei-chou by Yang Kuang-yüan, had still not surrendered after a year, at which point in 938 Shih Ching-t'ang offered Fan Yen-kuang a pardon and the governorship of a province. Shih pardoned all of Fan's adherents too and gave his generals prefectures, but Fan had to allow the regional troops (ya-chün) under his command – the core of any governor's following – to be incorporated into the Imperial Guard. While it was obviously not an overwhelming military triumph, Shih had nonetheless contained the rebellion and shown some military competence. Fan's submission confirmed Shih Ching-t'ang's superiority as emperor, and although Shih's governors never held him in enormous esteem, his surviving the rebellion – and without active Liao military help – signaled to them that he did, in fact, have the moral and military capabilities to be emperor. As a way of reinforcing this point, that winter he struck a military pose by bearing weapons at a court session.[130]

Shih Ching-t'ang, like Li Ssu-yüan, had taken over the empire with few troops of his own. Also like Li, Shih knew that he had to ensure that he controlled stronger military forces than any potential rival. The submission of Fan Yen-kuang allowed Shih to unite the Imperial Guard, but this placed all of Shih's forces under Yang Kuang-yüan, who, while siding with Shih against Fan Yen-kuang, had also used his military position to arrange for one of his sons to marry a daughter of Shih Ching-t'ang and to otherwise influence court affairs.[131] Immediately after giving Yang Kuang-yüan command of the surrendered Later T'ang expeditionary army in 936, Shih diluted Yang's military authority by appointing two of his own retainers, Liu Chih-yüan and Ching Yen-kuang, as, respectively, cavalry commander and infantry commander; moreover, during the campaign against Fan Yen-kuang another retainer, Liu Ch'u-jang, "join[ed] in discussions on military affairs" and effectively

acted as an army-supervising commissioner in all but name.[132] When Fan
Yen-kuang surrendered to Yang Kuang-yüan in 938, Shih appointed Yang to
replace Fan in the Wei–Po governorship at Wei-chou, neatly removing Yang
from day-to-day contact with the enlarged Imperial Guard. Two months later,
Shih achieved what none of his predecessors had managed by dividing Wei–
Po province into three, leaving Yang in control of just the city and prefecture
of Wei-chou itself and thus greatly reducing Yang's resources. Shih worked
throughout his reign to maintain and strengthen the allegiance of the Imperial
Guard, appointing palace commissioners – retainers – to command them and
bestowing honors and privileges upon the officers.[133] The army was a crucial
factor in keeping Shih on his throne.

Shih Ching-t'ang paid much less attention to other aspects of government,
content to continue the policies developed by Li Ssu-yüan. Shih was keen
to reemploy his predecessors' best servants. His reappointments included the
chief minister Feng Tao, who had also served Li Ssu-yüan, Li Ts'ung-hou,
and Li Ts'ung-k'o, and although Feng is singled out for criticism by the
writers of the eleventh-century sources, he was only one of many high-ranking
officials who served in several successive administrations in this period.[134]
Feng was known for his literary talent, in keeping with Shih Ching-t'ang's
expanded use of scholars in senior positions to the detriment of the palace
commissioners. Indeed, in 939 Shih abolished the Bureau of Military Affairs
and gave responsibility for administration to the chief ministers under Feng
Tao. This formally restored to the chief ministers their influence over political
and military matters that had been destroyed by Chu Wen two decades earlier.
But Feng Tao was never happy to have military responsibility, and the Bureau
of Military Affairs was revived in the 940s. Literati could now fill the highest
positions, and the court was becoming more subject to the back-and-forth of
group rivalries, but service in an emperor's retinue was still the key to obtaining
responsibilities in crucial areas. Accordingly, although Shih initially divided
the three financial offices among the chief ministers, in 938 he gave all three
posts to Liu Shen-chiao, a finance expert from Li Ts'un-hsü's retinue.[135]

The blended administration faced serious problems, not the least being the
impoverishment of the population by disrupted livelihoods and the depletion
of state granaries. A persistent difficulty was a shortage of coin, but a series

---

[132] Wang, *Structure of power*, pp. 162–3; *CWTS* 76, pp. 991–2; 94, p. 1250; *TCTC* 280, pp. 9158–9; 281,
    p. 9192.
[133] *TCTC* 281, pp. 9191, 9194; *CWTS* 77, pp. 1019, 1021–2; 97, p. 1291; Wang, *Structure of power*,
    pp. 186, 165–6; Mao, "T'ang-mo Wu-tai cheng-chih she-hui chih yen-chiu," p. 344.
[134] See Wang, "Feng Tao." Biography in *CWTS* 126, pp. 1655–66. He is criticized in Ou-yang, *Hsin
    Wu-tai shih* 54, pp. 611–12, and *TCTC* 291, pp. 9511–13.
[135] Wang, *Structure of power*, pp. 157–8, 162, 171–6; Worthy, "The founding of Sung China," pp. 228–30.

of edicts failed to prevent adulteration or the melting down of copper cash to make other things, or to impose standardized weights and patterns on private minting, which was banned in 939. Nevertheless, while Shih Ching-t'ang solicited ideas for relieving the plight of the deserving destitute, his chief administrator Sang Wei-han – presumably with the assistance of Liu Shen-chiao – attended to the revival of farming, sericulture, trade, and manufacturing, prompting claims that "within a few years" Sang's measures restored order to the realm. Benefits included the reduction and stabilization of the price of salt, and the apparent revival of the Silk Road trade. Noneconomic measures included better administration of the civil service examinations and periodic general pardons for those in prison.[136] Like Li Ssu-yüan, Shih Ching-t'ang understood the importance of acting in an exemplary fashion, which in the circumstances meant running a sound administration and giving the governors a relatively loose rein. If Shih Ching-t'ang's control of the army was crucial to sustaining his rule, producing order in the realm while not imposing too much on the privileges of the powerful made a less obvious, but just as essential, contribution.

Although Shih Ching-t'ang behaved like any other emperor of the Central Plains, he remained in the difficult position of also being formally subordinate to the Liao emperor. And because he was the autonomous emperor of an independent regime by virtue of an alliance that was responsible for placing and keeping him on the throne, he was obliged to stifle any misgivings about the formalities of rank and familial status. Thus in 938 Shih fired an official who regarded being an envoy to the Liao as a comedown from his former status, suggesting an impatience with overplayed sensitivities. Shih Ching-t'ang was no fool: he knew that his staying on his throne depended – even more than on his army or on his good governance – on the skill and determination with which he maintained the Liao alliance, however troublesome its implications.

Accordingly, Shih never forgot his debt to Te-kuang, nor did anything to risk the relationship, even though this exposed him to criticism for so fully accepting his subordination. Shih's envoys reluctantly tolerated arrogant treatment from their Liao hosts, and the subsidies to Liao were paid regularly. Compliance over such politically sensitive issues paid off, because when a Southern T'ang minister arranged for Liao envoys to be treated generously, but then had them murdered once they were on Later Chin soil, the Liao did not blame the Later Chin as the minister had intended.[137]

---

[136] On copper, see *TCTC* 281, p. 9195; 282, p. 9204; on Sang's measures, *TCTC* 280, p. 9168. See also Cheng, "Kuan-yü Shih Ching-t'ang," pp. 62–3, and his references. For Sang's biography, see *CWTS* 89, pp. 1161–9; for Liu Shen-chiao, see *CWTS* 95, pp. 1392–4.

[137] *TCTC* 281, pp. 9168, 9188–9, 9190. Wu had become Southern T'ang in 939.

But Shih's "good service" did not make him a doormat; he just had to be
subtle in seeking to protect and improve his status. Shih had accepted the
designation "subject," calling Te-kuang his "imperial father." According to
Ssu-ma Kuang, "although [the amount of the subsidy] was no more than the
taxes of a few counties, [the Later Chin] often cited the hardships of the people
as an excuse for not being able to fulfill the quota," which apparently prompted
Te-kuang to insist that Shih drop "subject" and use the less demeaning "imperial son" instead. The contemporary significance of such designations was great,
and so was Shih's achievement here, but Te-kuang could play the name game
too. After Fan Yen-kuang's surrender, Te-kuang invested Shih Ching-t'ang
with another imperial title, an ostensible honor that nevertheless highlighted
Shih's formal subordination.[138] Te-kuang sometimes exploited his superior
status (and the military power that backed it), as when he requested that a
refugee at the Liao court should succeed his late father Wang Ch'u-chih to
the vacant governorship of I–Ting, "in accord with the rules in our regime."
When Shih Ching-t'ang politely objected that "the Middle Kingdom's rules"
decreed that officials had to work their way up through the ranks, Te-kuang
angrily reminded Shih of his own promotion from governor to emperor. This
worried Shih, but he negotiated a compromise: appointing another of Wang
Ch'u-chih's descendants, already governor of another Later Chin province, to
the vacancy.[139]

The sources note that, like any virtuous ruler, Shih Ching-t'ang accepted
good advice. Hence he acknowledged that fostering the Liao relationship
should not mean neglecting frontier defenses. Too much activity might have
provoked aggrieved questioning from Te-kuang, but Shih did, for instance,
strengthen the Yellow River crossing at Te-sheng because of the potential danger from the Liao.[140] With the mountain passes now mostly in Liao hands,
the Yellow River had become the first major barrier against northern attack.
Since the capital, K'ai-feng, lay just to the south, such defenses would also be
useful against internal threats; the armies that Shih Ching-t'ang maintained
against challengers at home were available to fight external enemies if need be.
The alliance with the Liao meant that Shih did not have to delegate dangerous
amounts of authority to frontier generals and could concentrate his military
strength closer to his center.

This centralization was important, because Shih Ching-t'ang needed to
keep a watchful eye on the provinces. Upon Shih's accession Sang Wei-han had
advised him to "act with sincerity and abandon grudges in order to placate
the governors." Accordingly Shih had left the governors in place, and he

---

[138] *TCTC* 281, pp. 9188, 9191; *CWTS* 108, p. 1658.
[139] *TCTC* 282, p. 9204; Cheng, "Kuan-yü Shih Ching-t'ang," pp. 61–2.
[140] *TCTC* 281, p. 9194.

only gradually adjusted the policies of Li Ssu-yüan that limited governors' powers over finances and appointments.[141] By 940, however, Shih felt ready to undertake a major gubernatorial reshuffle. This went smoothly in the north, but in the south, where governors were still able to seek external support, two governors resisted. An Ts'ung-chin at Hsiang-chou in the middle section of the Han River valley occupied such a vital strategic position that Shih Ching-t'ang was obliged to let An's defiance pass. By contrast, when An Ts'ung-chin's neighbor, Li Chin-ch'üan at An-chou, pledged allegiance to the Southern T'ang, Shih Ching-t'ang did not hesitate to dispatch an army, retaining the province and incorporating Li Chin-ch'üan's Southern T'ang reinforcements into his own forces. Li fled to the Southern T'ang court but received a cool reception, and subsequently the ruler there rejected arguments for expanding north. This success doubtless helped to persuade the Emperor of Later Shu and the Ching-nan governor to refuse support to An Ts'ung-chin, and henceforth Shih's independent neighbors in the south ceased to be a potential source of assistance for discontented governors in the southern part of Later Chin territory.[142]

Most governors serving the Later Chin now had little inclination or ability to threaten their overlord, but individuals could still cause great trouble, even if they had received their positions from the emperor. By far the hardest governor to control was An Ch'ung-jung at Chen-chou. In 939, An apparently declared that "to become an emperor in these days, you just [need] strong troops and vigorous horses," and thereafter he became openly hostile to the regime. Shih Ching-t'ang did not act against him directly, but transferred away An's neighboring governor and relative by marriage, Huang-fu Yü of I–Ting. In 940, An Ch'ung-jung "enticed" a thousand "tents" of T'u-yü-hun tribesmen to submit to him and settle in his province, but Shih Ching-t'ang, chastised by Liao envoys, drove them back to their original lands. An Ch'ung-jung hated the Liao. He was rude to envoys and even had them murdered. Shih Ching-t'ang could not prevent this, and he found himself "humbly excus[ing]" An whenever Te-kuang complained about him.[143] Although often taken to indicate Later Chin subservience to the Khitan "barbarians," these events also show that Shih Ching-t'ang and Te-kuang were both determined to maintain peaceful relations between their states. Circumstances quite sufficient in themselves to provoke hostilities were negotiated away by these two allies, who deployed enormous patience and considerable creativity.

[141] TCTC 281, p. 9168. See discussion of one example of this tactic and further references in Sudō, "Godai setsudoshi no shihai taisei," pp. 398–9.

[142] CWTS 79, pp. 1038–41; TCTC 282, pp. 9211–22.

[143] TCTC 282, pp. 9203, 9219, 9222–3; CWTS 79, p. 1045; T'o-t'o et al., Liao shih 4, p. 48. For An Ch'ung-jung's biography, see CWTS 98, pp. 1301–4.

Nevertheless, in 941 An Ch'ung-jung precipitated a crisis in the relations between the Liao and the Later Chin. Seizing Liao envoys, as well as raiding over the border into Yu-chou, he demanded a war against the Liao, deploring Shih Ching-t'ang's patient submission and claiming that the Liao's nomadic subjects and the governors of the Sixteen Prefectures were all calling for an invasion to strike north. Under Sang Wei-han's prodding, Shih Ching-t'ang belatedly apologized to the Liao, but Te-kuang, understandably unsure of Shih's intentions, detained the Later Chin envoy. Meanwhile, the Ho-tung governor (and, until recently, Imperial Guard commander) Liu Chih-yüan gutted the support An Ch'ung-jung received from nomads by persuading several chieftains to switch their allegiance to the Later Chin, thus acquiring a force of elite T'u-yü-hun cavalry for his own service. An Ch'ung-jung had established communications with the troublesome An Ts'ung-chin at An-chou in the south, and at the end of 941 An Ts'ung-chin struck north, but Shih Ching-t'ang had anticipated this. An Ts'ung-chin was driven back, and the Later Chin received naval help against him both from the Ching-nan governor and from the King of Ch'u in Hunan. Those who previously might have supported the rebels were now lining up behind the recognized holder of superior authority. Hearing of this, An Ch'ung-jung desperately launched his rebellion from Chen-chou in the following month, which in Liao eyes demonstrated Shih Ching-t'ang's good faith toward them, prompting Te-kuang to release Shih's envoy. An Ch'ung-jung was executed by one of his own former generals, and his preserved head was sent in a box to Te-kuang. In the south, An Ts'ung-chin committed suicide a year later, after his city fell to an assault.[144]

Outright victories over provincial rebels increased Shih Ching-t'ang's political capital, even as his policy of external appeasement and internal forgiveness had brought a certain stability, lacking since the days of Li Ssu-yüan. Although it could not be said that Shih Ching-t'ang had fully united his domain, he had quelled repeated and sometimes serious resistance, fostered important developments in court and military institutions, and begun to rebuild the economy. Although taking control of the main armies of the realm had played an important part in this – giving him the military muscle to crush his several opponents – he had also greatly decreased the likelihood of widespread support for rebels by ruling in a manner deemed both proper and acceptable to most of the provincial leaders who were best placed to oppose him. Most important, the possibility of successful rebellion had been curtailed by Shih's alliance with the Liao emperor, which deprived rebels of the external support they needed

---

[144] See *TCTC* 282–3, pp. 9222–39; *CWTS* 79, p. 1048; 80, pp. 1054–6; 98, p. 1305; Ou-yang, *Hsin Wu-tai shih* 51, pp. 586–7; T'o-t'o et al., *Liao shih* 4, pp. 49–50. See *CWTS* 89, pp. 1163–6, for Sang Wei-han's memorial on the value of the alliance.

to challenge the sitting emperor. This situation in the north created ripple effects in the south, where Shih was able to use his strength without having to worry about his northern border at the same time. The alliance thus gave Shih a monopoly on authority, for there was now no external power, north or south, willing to act as an alternative source of legitimation for a rebel. Thus although the relationship with Te-kuang raised the serious problem of Shih Ching-t'ang's subordination to an external power, it also enabled him to safeguard his position so that when he fell ill in 942 his hope of securing an orderly succession was not unrealistic.

The Liao–Later Chin war, c. 943–947

Shih Ching-t'ang died in K'ai-feng in the sixth month of 942. The chief minister Feng Tao was entrusted with establishing Shih's young son Shih Ch'ung-jui on the throne, but instead installed an adult son, Shih Ch'ung-kuei (Chin Shao-ti, 942–7), then serving as city governor at Wei-chou, who was enthroned immediately. Thus the Imperial Guard was revealed as a new base for power, because Feng Tao had done the bidding of its chief commander, Ching Yen-kuang. Ching had been a palace commissioner working for Shih Ching-t'ang when he had commanded the Six Imperial Armies in the capital under Li Ssu-yüan, and subsequently Shih appointed him infantry commander of the Imperial Guard; Ching was to dominate the court for the next four years, together with other generals of the Imperial Guard.[145] Ching seems to have been particularly exercised about the theoretical inconsistency in Shih Ching-t'ang's relationship with the Liao ruler, and unlike his late emperor showed no concern at all to maintain peaceful relations with the Later Chin's northern neighbors.

Although Shih Ch'ung-kuei quickly informed the Liao of his accession, as was normal practice between states that maintained envoy relations, Ching Yen-kuang encouraged the impressionable new emperor to refer to himself only as the grandson of Te-kuang (since Shih Ching-t'ang had been Te-kuang's fictive son), not as his subject. Sang Wei-han lobbied for maintaining peaceful relations, but Feng Tao sat on the fence, and Ching Yen-kuang got his way, plus a seat among the chief ministers. When Te-kuang complained of Shih Ch'ung-kuei's breach of protocol and reminded him that his family owed the Liao for their kingdom, Ching Yen-kuang reiterated the refusal to accept subject status for Shih Ch'ung-kuei, on the grounds that, unlike his father, he had not been enthroned by Te-kuang. In the Liao regime such provocative behavior was

---

[145] TCTC 283, p. 9237. See Ching's biography in CWTS 88, pp. 1143–6.

seized upon by the governor of the Liao Southern Capital (previously called
Yu-chou), Chao Yen-shou. Chao coveted the throne that his father, Chao Te-
chün, had failed to win in 936 and now argued for an invasion in the hope
that he would be made emperor in Shih Ch'ung-kuei's place. Despite Ching
Yen-kuang's provocation, Te-kuang did not rush into war, suggesting again
the extent of the agreement that had been achieved between him and Shih
Ching-t'ang. With greater will from the south, that agreement could have
been institutionalized and peace maintained. As it was, the attitude of Shih
Ch'ung-kuei's court ensured that the 936 arrangement was interpreted as an
entirely personal deal between two individuals. Any benefits gained from the
alliance now became insignificant compared to the humiliation of accepting
subordination to an external ruler while claiming the supreme and indivisible
position of Son of Heaven.

Normal envoy relations continued for nearly a year, albeit amid rumors
of war, and Sang Wei-han was recalled to court.[146] But Ching Yen-kuang
continued to provoke, apparently ordering the killing of all Liao merchants
in Later Chin territory and the delivery of an aggressive message informing
Te-kuang that the Later Chin were ready for any military action the Liao
might take.[147] Having destroyed the external alliance so carefully nurtured
by Shih Ching-t'ang, Ching Yen-kuang then turned inward to provoke Yang
Kuang-yüan of Ch'ing-chou in western Shantung. Despite Yang Kuang-yüan's
efforts to expand his own influence and his complaints to the Liao emperor
about Shih Ching-t'ang, Yang had never actually raised a hand against Shih.
Now, however, Ching Yen-kuang alienated Yang by confiscating three thousand horses given him by the late emperor. The court mollified Yang with
gifts and with permission for his son to hold a prefecture within Ch'ing-chou
province, but it also strengthened the garrison 130 miles away at Yün-chou,
implying that Yang was not trusted. Yang responded as he had once before,
by complaining over Shih Ch'ung-kuei's head to his Liao overlord Te-kuang
that Shih had "turned his back on morality and broken the treaty." Yang also
reported on the weaknesses of the Later Chin. In simultaneously provoking
both a loyal governor and a staunch ally, Ching Yen-kuang had ensured a
return to the old pattern of cooperation between a disgruntled governor and
the Liao. Meanwhile, Chao Yen-shou mobilized fifty thousand troops from the

---

[146] See *TCTC* 283, pp. 9242–7; T'o-t'o et al., *Liao shih* 4, pp. 51–3; and *CWTS* 81, pp. 1068–76, which
reports entirely unexceptional envoy exchanges. Yang Lien-sheng raises some fascinating possibilities
regarding the crucial letter to Te-kuang in "A 'posthumous letter' from the Chin emperor to the Khitan
emperor in 942," *Harvard Journal of Asiatic Studies* 10 Nos. 3–4 (1947), pp. 418–28.

[147] See *TCTC* 283, pp. 9253–4; especially T'o-t'o et al., *Liao shih* 4, p. 52, where this incident is recorded
under the seventh month of 942; *CWTS* 88, p. 1144, and 137, p. 1834, allow for both earlier and later
dates.

Sixteen Prefectures, having apparently been promised the emperorship of the south if he conquered the region.[148]

Provoked by Ching Yen-kuang, the Liao turned to war to punish Shih Ch'ung-kuei for repudiating his father's relationship with Te-kuang, insisting on nothing less than Shih Ch'ung-kuei's dethronement. The war took three campaigns spread over four campaign seasons; each campaign was fought against a background of insect plagues, floods, and famines across much of the Later Chin domain. In each of the first two seasons (943–4 and 944–5) the Liao marched almost unhindered toward the Yellow River but withdrew once any substantial obstacle – an army or a defended fortification – was placed in their path. At this point in the second season the Later Chin, hoping to force a conclusion, attacked the Liao Southern Capital. This attack moved Te-kuang to also seek a decisive encounter to "pacify all-under-Heaven (*t'ien-hsia*)," but he was defeated in a dust storm near Ting-chou.[149]

Gleeful reports that Te-kuang had fled on a camel must have enhanced Shih Ch'ung-kuei's prestige, as did the general conduct of the fighting so far. Other events helped too. In the first season, Yang Kuang-yüan had rebelled to coincide with the Liao advance, but nobody joined him even though he resisted a siege of Ch'ing-chou for nearly a year. Eventually, his own son placed him under house arrest and surrendered the city to the Later Chin. Shih Ch'ung-kuei is also credited with sponsoring a rebellion in the Sixteen Prefectures that captured ten forts.

But the quality of governance had more impact than the war on Shih Ch'ung-kuei's standing with his followers, and Sang Wei-han's return to power at court after the war's first season was crucial. The plague and famine that accompanied the first season of fighting were compounded with reports of heartless rapacity by governors such as Tu Ch'ung-wei; any of these events could be taken as portents of impending dynastic collapse. The Later Chin court under Ching Yen-kuang's dominance not only failed to control such excesses but despite complaints also refused to reduce either taxes or court expenditures. Shih Ch'ung-kuei already regarded Ching Yen-kuang's behavior as intolerable, and in 944 Shih seized upon Ching's cowardly generalship during the first season to make him regent of Lo-yang and so remove him from court. This showed decisiveness and produced practical benefits. Ever since the Bureau of Military Affairs had been abolished in 939 and the chief ministers saddled with its responsibilities, Feng Tao had been arguing that the chief ministers lacked both time and qualifications for such tasks. He wanted the bureau reestablished,

---

[148] *TCTC* 283, pp. 9255–7; T'o-t'o et al., *Liao shih* 4, p. 53; *CWTS* 97, p. 1292; 98, p. 1311.

[149] The first two seasons of the war are discussed in *TCTC* 283–4, pp. 9257–90; *CWTS* 82–3, pp. 1082–1104; T'o-t'o et al., *Liao shih* 4, pp. 53–6.

and court opinion increasingly supported this policy. After the bureau was
revived, Sang Wei-han became, initially, its sole commissioner. He worked to
reform excesses at court and apparently won the cooperation of generals and
governors alike. A symbolic new reign era and an amnesty were announced.
These measures signaled some relief to the hard-pressed population. Yet even
as Sang Wei-han took over, disaster struck, as the Yellow River flooded five
prefectures, including the capital district. Other problems had human causes.
The war continued to require levies of soldiers, equipment, and taxes. Militia
numbers reportedly reached seventy thousand. Misappropriation, increasingly
widespread, diverted much tax revenue into governors' coffers. Sometimes the
only way for the court to collect revenue was to raid the governors' private
stores in their absence, although this could be hazardous. When an imperial
commissioner seized the illegally acquired grain stocks of Tu Ch'ung-wei,
then governor of Chen-chou, Tu's fury had to be assuaged with gifts, and the
commissioner was dismissed.[150]

Although Sang Wei-han's policies inspired hope that the court could restore
order, his authority was limited: Tu Ch'ung-wei could not be punished because
Shih Ch'ung-kuei dared not risk provoking defections to the Liao by others
who might fear similar treatment because they were just as guilty.[151] Worse
still, at court imperial favorites and generals of the Imperial Guard, such
as Li Yen-t'ao, continued to wield excessive influence even in Ching Yen-
kuang's absence, with Li apparently making official appointments on his own
authority. Sang Wei-han tried to curb these activities, but early in 945 Shih
Ch'ung-kuei's brother-in-law, Feng Yü, was appointed as a second military
affairs commissioner to dilute Sang's authority. The favorites joined forces
with Feng, and early in the third campaign season in 945, after just twenty
months in power, Sang Wei-han was ousted amid rumors of bribe taking. His
replacement, Li Sung, was in Sang Wei-han's mold but lacked unfettered access
to Shih Ch'ung-kuei. As a result, Li Yen-t'ao and Feng Yü were easily able to
ignore the new commissioner. Large-scale bribery returned and spending was
again uncontrolled.[152]

Sang Wei-han's departure made the following season (945–6) the crucial
year of the war, even though there was no official fighting because both states
were gripped by famine. Te-kuang directed no raids himself, so Liao incursions
reported throughout 946 were probably a response to drought. Within the
Later Chin state, famine led to widespread banditry, and bands sometimes
took over county seats and even defeated punitive forces, whose commanders

---

[150] *TCTC* 284, pp. 9271–4; 285, p. 9297; *CWTS* 89, pp. 1166–7.
[151] One such example was Mu-jung Yen-ch'ao. See *TCTC* 285, p. 9308.
[152] *TCTC* 284, p. 9285; 285, pp. 9295–6, 9300–1; *CWTS* 89, p. 1167.

were hampered by Li Yen-t'ao's mistrustful micro-management. During these difficult times, many villages and pastoralists switched their allegiance from the Later Chin to the Liao, including some of the T'u-yü-hun in the Ho-tung region who, hoping to escape the famine, returned to their old lands in Liao territory. Te-kuang treated them well to encourage others to come over too, but the Ho-tung governor, Liu Chih-yüan, who had deployed T'u-yü-hun forces against the Liao in 943, now engineered the confiscation of the T'u-yü-hun chieftain's riches to supply his own armies. A valuable ally had been selfishly sidelined, and others potentially alienated.[153]

Shih Ch'ung-kuei's poor handling of war and famine threw the people onto their own resources. In the strategic prefecture of Ting-chou, a Buddhist cult developed at a fortress built by the locals to protect themselves against bandit gangs. The cult was protected by Sun Fang-chien, who at first fought Khitan raiders but then became disaffected with the Later Chin court. The court had been suspicious of his motives and had refused him assistance. Sun then offered his allegiance to the Liao and apparently incited them to invade south.[154]

At court, meanwhile, Sang Wei-han's eclipse allowed Ching Yen-kuang to return to the field as deputy commander of the expeditionary armies, but preparations for the 946–7 season were limited. The defences of Chen-chou in the north and Shan-chou on the Yellow River were strengthened, and an alliance negotiated with the Koryŏ kingdom, but the Koryŏ army ultimately proved too weak even for a diversionary attack. The Later Chin were pinning their hopes on their secret invitation to the Liao commander in chief, Chao Yen-shou (originally from the Yellow River valley), to change sides. After an exchange of letters, Chao said that he "would like to come home to the Middle Kingdom" if an army was sent to meet him. Accordingly, as the season opened, commanders Tu Ch'ung-wei and Li Shou-chen led north the entire Imperial Guard, including Shih Ch'ung-kuei's personal guards, to join up with Chao's Liao force and capture the Sixteen Prefectures for Later Chin.[155]

But the Later Chin had been tricked. Chao Yen-shou had no intention of surrendering. He had drawn the Later Chin forces out of their defensive strongholds and dangerously exposed their field army. Later Chin morale flagged as ceaseless rain bogged them down. Tu Ch'ung-wei, retreating before the Liao advance, was persuaded to try to hold the Hu-t'o River crossing near Chen-chou, but in the end he was outflanked. Te-kuang reportedly promised

[153] *TCTC* 285, pp. 9306–8.
[154] *TCTC* 285, pp. 9303–4; *CWTS* 84, p. 1115; 125, pp. 1649–50; T'o-t'o et al., *Liao shih* 4, p. 57.
[155] *TCTC* 285, pp. 9297–9, 9306, 9311–14. The sources are not clear as to the exact sequence or dating of the exchange of letters with Chao Yen-shou. See especially *CWTS* 84, p. 1118; T'o-t'o et al., *Liao shih* 76, p. 1248.

Tu the Later Chin throne in place of Chao Yen-shou, and Tu handed over his entire army. Allegiance quickly cascaded away from Shih Ch'ung-kuei. Chen-chou submitted to the Liao as did several northern governors and prefects. The intemperate Ching-chou governor Chang Yen-tse joined the Liao and led an advance force to K'ai-feng, where a letter from Te-kuang convinced the dowager empress to stop Shih Ch'ung-kuei from killing himself and persuade him to submit instead. The first casualty of the conquest was Sang Wei-han, murdered by Chang Yen-tse as he settled scores with his critics. Ching Yen-kuang committed suicide. But Te-kuang allowed Shih Ch'ung-kuei to live out his natural life in Liao territory.[156]

The Liao occupation of the Central Plains, 947

The Liao emperor did not conquer and govern the Central Plains directly. His goal had been to punish Shih Ch'ung-kuei for repudiating his family's subordination, not to acquire territorial control. However, by dint of military success, he had become the legitimate emperor of the Central Plains. Familiar with T'ang protocols, and advised by formally educated ministers from both Liao and the Later Chin, Te-kuang observed such practices as declaring a new dynasty, wearing Chinese dress, and reemploying former officials. Crucially, from the ministers' viewpoint, Te-kuang consulted with them, and according to Ssu-ma Kuang it was they who advised against appointing a second emperor in the south. Like previous conquerors, he promised benefits for the common people: he would disband the armies, lighten the demands on the people, and inaugurate a new era of peace. Aware that the Liao had a fearsome image, Te-kuang sought to reassure the capital's population, ascending one of the city wall towers to explain through an interpreter that he too was a human being. Better still, Te-kuang did what no Later Chin ruler had dared, executing his recent accomplice, the reviled Chang Yen-tse, in the marketplace, and allowing the people to eat Chang's flesh as a mark of their disgust.[157]

Te-kuang consolidated his military and political position by disarming the Imperial Guard and receiving the submission of all but a couple of provincial governors. Indeed, Te-kuang faced less resistance than had Shih Ching-t'ang. Te-kuang promptly banned governors and prefects from keeping their own troops or from buying warhorses. He appointed new governors, demoted K'ai-feng from its capital status, and established Chen-chou as a capital instead.[158]

[156] *TCTC* 285–6, pp. 9313–29; *CWTS* 85, pp. 1121–6; T'o-t'o et al., *Liao shih* 4, pp. 57–8.

[157] *TCTC* 286, pp. 9327–30; T'o-t'o et al., *Liao shih* 4, p. 59; *CWTS* 85, p. 1126; 137, p. 1835. For discussion of Te-kuang's motives and the nature of the occupation, see Standen, "What nomads want."

[158] *TCTC* 286, pp. 9330–9; *CWTS* 99, p. 1324.

But Te-kuang did not intend to stay. Accordingly, despite his initial gestures of reconciliation, he treated the conquest as a very large raid, in which public relations were irrelevant and only loot mattered. Perhaps most damaging to Te-kuang's image was the policy of "smashing the pasture and grain" (*ta ts'ao-yü*), which he later regretted as a miscalculation. The Liao armies devastated the region around the capital, foraging to supply themselves and practicing the all-too-common cruelties of soldiers in wartime. To reward his troops, claimed to number three hundred thousand, Te-kuang demanded from an already overtaxed population cash and cloth to be stockpiled for transport north. Most ambitious of all was Te-kuang's attempt to take north every material element of the Later Chin imperial institution, including palace women and eunuchs, the complete contents of the imperial storehouses, and every last bureaucrat.[159]

In the third month of 947, Te-kuang ordered the capital stripped, and he departed for home in the fourth, leaving his brother-in-law Hsiao Han in charge. Formally, Te-kuang was going to pay his respects to his mother, but his departure conformed to the usual Liao practice of moving north in the summer to escape the heat. En route, Te-kuang was distressed by the scenes of devastation, which he blamed on Chao Yen-shou. He apparently wrote to his younger brother listing his own three faults in this venture: demanding cash from the people, ordering indiscriminate foraging and plundering, and failing to return the governors to their provinces in good time. The letter, preserved in the *Liao shih* (*Official history of the Liao*), describes the "foreignness" of the Khitan: they are raiders (rather than tax collectors) and pastoralists (rather than farmers), and they keep their governors at court (rather than giving them active responsibility in their provinces). In the hands of later writers, Te-kuang's mistakes become a warning to Chinese rulers of what to avoid if they wish to escape comparison with a "barbarian."[160]

Renewed independence: Liu Chih-yüan and the Later Han, 947–950

Te-kuang had received the submission of all but a few of the Later Chin governors, one of whom was Shih K'uang-wei at Ching-chou. His refusal to be transferred by Te-kuang has been credited with sowing the seeds for a backlash against Liao rule, but he was not approached to lead a resistance, nor did he organize one. Leaders in the provinces and in the independent states of the

---

[159] *TCTC* 286, pp. 9334–5, 9348–50; T'o-t'o et al., *Liao shih* 4, pp. 59–60. On the foraging policy, see Chao Kuang-yüan, "Lüeh-lun Ch'i-tan chün-tui tsai Chung-yüan 'Ta ts'ao-ku'," *Chung-kuo she-hui k'o-hsüeh-yüan yen-chiu-sheng-yüan hsüeh-pao* 6 (1986), pp. 67–71.

[160] *TCTC* 286, pp. 9348–54; T'o-t'o et al., *Liao shih* 4, p. 60; see also "The Later Han annals" in *CWTS* 99, pp. 1325–7, which gives a different cast to the events. See also Standen, "What nomads want."

south were all conscious that the most dangerous enemy was not the Liao, but each other. The expectation of more conflict was everywhere. Liu Chih-yüan of Ho-tung noted that "when [the Liao] have enough goods they will be certain to go north," and the Southern T'ang court heard calls to invade the Central Plains to provide them with a leader once the Liao had withdrawn.[161]

Because the Imperial Guard was scattered and its leaders subordinated to Te-kuang, preparations to cope with the impending power vacuum took place in the provinces. Liu Chih-yüan – a former retainer of Shih Ching-t'ang – was by far the strongest remaining governor. Ho-tung was almost impregnable and – unlike the rest of the provinces – still relatively well resourced. Mutual distrust between himself and Shih Ch'ung-kuei had apparently kept Liu out of the war, but Liu had recruited throughout, giving him control, now, of fifty thousand troops – a large force at any time but compellingly so after the four years of war in the region. Liu Chih-yüan sent letters congratulating Te-kuang, but he avoided attending court and claimed that his tribute had been delayed en route. Te-kuang, nervous about Liu's ambitions, sent him honorifics, along with a direct enquiry about how long Liu was going to equivocate, serving neither north nor south. Less powerful figures also hedged their bets or switched allegiance. Hence Kao Ts'ung-hui at Ching-nan notified Liu Chih-yüan of his support while at the same time sending tribute to Te-kuang. The governor of Ch'in-chou in the far west had already killed Te-kuang's envoys and taken three prefectures over to Later Shu, while several southern prefects and "bandits" offered their allegiance to the Southern T'ang.[162]

Six weeks after Te-kuang entered the Later Chin capital, K'ai-feng, Liu Chih-yüan declared himself emperor – apparently shamed into it by a Later Shu assault in the far southwest. But Liu did not change the dynastic name. He immediately sought to meet with Shih Ch'ung-kuei, then on his way to his new home in Liao territory, but Shih managed to escape an encounter he probably would not have survived. Liu Chih-yüan asserted his claim to authority by banning collections for the Liao coffers, by promising immunity to those forced to collaborate, and by commanding all circuits to punish the Liao, while his wife set a noble tone by promising the goods of the inner palace to reward the army rather than take yet more from the people.[163]

Liu expanded his following first to bandits, supporting one leader who attacked Hsiang-chou2, near Wei-chou, and making him provisional governor.

---

[161] *TCTC* 286, pp. 9330, 9333, 9336, 9338. The importance of the power vacuum is noted by Hsing, "Ch'i-tan yü Wu-tai cheng-ch'üan," p. 301; and Chang, "Wu-tai cheng-ch'üan ti-shan chih k'ao-ch'a," pp. 24–5.

[162] *TCTC* 286, pp. 9330, 9335–8.

[163] *TCTC* 286, pp. 9339–43.

A series of revolts then broke out across the Central Plains, with bandits playing a prominent role. Cities were occupied, Liao envoys were killed, and allegiance was transferred to Liu Chih-yüan rather than to Later Shu or the Southern T'ang.[164] Te-kuang, preoccupied with removing himself and his plunder north to the Liao homeland, was largely unresponsive to these events, although he did make an example of Hsiang-chou2, slaughtering some hundred thousand men and children, and taking away the women. Liu Chih-yüan now declared his intention to take control by appointing governors (with concurrent military commands) to provinces he did not hold, and selecting an entirely new set of ministers to replace those Later Chin bureaucrats currently on their way to service in the Liao regime.[165]

The Liao, for their part, did not vigorously defend the territory they had conquered. On the few occasions when they did fight, they did not try very hard. Hence the Liao occupiers in Lo-yang abandoned it for an apparent build-up against Lu-chou, but after clashing briefly with one of Liu Chih-yüan's generals they left Lu-chou behind and headed north. Soon afterward, Te-kuang suddenly took ill and died.[166] But this seems to have made little difference to Liao actions in the Central Plains, other than forcing Te-kuang's son Wu-yü (Yüan) to return more quickly to the Liao Supreme Capital, where he managed to secure his throne (Liao Shih-tsung, 947–51). This event had important repercussions for Liu Chih-yüan's future, because at Chen-chou Wu-yü abandoned all but two of the Later Chin officials in the entourage, although he did take with him the palace women, eunuchs, and musicians. Thus a generation of court-based officials was retained in the Central Plains, preserving an important element of continuity in the bureaucracy.[167]

With the new Liao emperor departed, Liu Chih-yüan's forces quickly occupied Lo-yang, Tse-chou, and the northwestern portion of the Later Chin empire. Hsiao Han, left to mind the southern realm by Te-kuang, needed to get home to participate in deciding the succession. At K'ai-feng Hsiao had installed Li Ssu-yüan's son, Li Ts'ung-i, to rule the south, but Hsiao and his mother – reluctant deputies – submitted to Liu Chih-yüan, only to be killed. Liu's advance met little resistance. At Lo-yang officials presented him with a letter of welcome from Li Ts'ung-i's officials, and as Liu approached K'ai-feng itself to declare his own dynasty, the Later Han, he received the submissions of the Later Chin governors. Dispensing pardons to collaborators, the new emperor, Han Kao-tsu (r. 947–8), confirmed all Te-kuang's provincial appointees in

[164] *TCTC* 286, pp. 9340–48; *CWTS* 99, pp. 1324–6.
[165] *TCTC* 286, pp. 9351–2; *CWTS* 99, pp. 1326–9.
[166] *TCTC* 286, p. 9356.
[167] *TCTC* 286–7, pp. 9352–64.

their posts. In 948 a Liao attempt to transfer Sun Fang-chien from Ting-chou provoked Sun to return his allegiance to the south, and with this move the last of the districts once held by the Later Chin came under Later Han authority. As usual, ambitious regional officials exploited the situation so that, for instance, two Liao-appointed generals killed their governor when he submitted to Liu Chih-yüan, and then themselves submitted, claiming the governor had rebelled. One got the province, the other a prefecture. South of the Yangtze the Ch'u ruler accepted titles from Liu Chih-yüan, but Kao Ts'ung-hui in Ching-nan rejected the Later Han envoys after he was refused a prefecture for himself. The Southern T'ang, though unprepared for a major expedition, made plans to attack north but did nothing once they heard that Liu Chih-yüan had taken the capital.[168]

None of this disturbed what was essentially a smooth takeover. Liu came to the throne at the head of the only credible military force remaining in the region and as the only governor who still controlled significant resources of his own. This strength, and the fact that the Liao forces had withdrawn from the Central Plains, had compelled the governors – however reluctantly – to join him; for they knew that no challenger could stand against Liu without outside assistance, but that anyone who sought such help would effectively rule themselves out as a potential emperor since they ran a strong risk of having to subordinate themselves to an external master. Liu may not have been first choice for emperor, but there were few credible alternatives. This, however, did not prevent challengers from arising subsequently, and several of them did seek Liao help.

Tu Ch'ung-wei, left behind by the Liao withdrawal and still commanding what was left of the Later Chin expeditionary army of 947, now submitted to Liu Chih-yüan, but promptly refused a transfer from Wei-chou and occupied the city, seeking help from a Liao general, Ma-ta. The one region the Liao seemed concerned to hold was the key strategic city of Chen-chou, which controlled the main access between the Central Plains and the Liao homeland. Chen-chou was now a Liao capital, and Ma-ta was garrisoning (and plundering) it. Ma-ta's Chinese troops, mistrusted and starved, mutinied with the support of the residents and the Later Chin ministers abandoned there by Wu-yü. Ma-ta eventually retreated northward to Ting-chou, which at the time was in Liao allegiance. Ma-ta's departure halted Liao military activity in the region and completed the Liao withdrawal. Thus denied Liao help, and with his fellow governors offering no support either, Tu Ch'ung-wei was besieged in Wei-chou, finally surrendering four months later after losing three-quarters of his population to starvation. The remnants of Tu's army were incorporated into the

---

[168] *TCTC* 287, pp. 9359–68; 288, p. 9389; *CWTS* 100, pp. 1331–5, 1338–9, 1347–8.

Later Han Imperial Guard, while Tu himself received senior court positions so that he could be carefully watched.[169]

The siege exhausted the Wei-chou region, which could no longer pose a major threat to Liu Chih-yüan. This made Chao K'uang-tsan, Chao Yen-shou's son and the governor at Ch'ang-an, potentially the most serious threat to Liu. Chao K'uang-tsan feared that Liu Chih-yüan would never trust him because he was the son of the Liao commander. Accordingly, he submitted to the Later Shu in the southwest and asked for military support. A Later Shu army of fifty thousand marched east to Feng-hsiang, where it received the submission of Chao's neighbor. Chao now asked the Later Shu to march on to the Wei River valley provinces of Kuan-chung – which included Ch'ang-an. But Chao had simultaneously submitted to Liu Chih-yüan, who sent a detachment from his Imperial Guard to reinforce Chao K'uang-tsan's provincial troops. When the Later Shu army heard of Chao's change of allegiance it began to withdraw, but it was intercepted by Chao's joint force with the loss of four hundred captured.[170]

Between dealing with Tu Ch'ung-wei and Chao K'uang-tsan, Liu Chih-yüan reshuffled most of his senior governors without incident. He had already reconstituted an Imperial Guard by recalling the scattered units of Shih Ch'ung-kuei's Guard force from their provincial postings, and when Tu Ch'ung-wei surrendered, the remnants of the Later Chin Imperial Guard and Imperial Bodyguard that he had led were incorporated into the Later Han force. Liu also chose a successor, who unfortunately died just a few weeks before Liu's own death early in 948.[171]

Before dying, Liu Chih-yüan had chosen a new successor, his eighteen-year-old son Liu Ch'eng-yu, but the young man was under the control of his mother and his regents, including the corrupt chief minister, Su Feng-chi. Keeping Liu's death secret, Su Feng-chi publicly executed Tu Ch'ung-wei and his sons, though carefully sparing his wife, Shih Ching-t'ang's sister. Only then did Ch'eng-yu's succession take place (Han Yin-ti, 948–50).[172]

However, a regime headed by a minor was open to challenge. But in 948 the only military forces in the region not under imperial control were two provincial armies in Kuan-chung. Shortly after Liu Ch'eng-yu's accession these two governors were recalled. Their troops were to be escorted to K'ai-feng for incorporation in the Imperial Guard. Instead, one of the provincial forces occupied Ch'ang-an, while two other major cites were also taken

[169] *TCTC* 287, pp. 9368–73, 9376–8; *CWTS* 100, pp. 1336–9; Mao, "T'ang-mo Wu-tai cheng-chih she-hui chih yen-chiu," pp. 349–50.

[170] *TCTC* 287, pp. 9377, 9380, 9382–4. Chao has a one-line biography at *CWTS* 98, p. 1313.

[171] *TCTC* 287, pp. 9370–80. On military reorganization, see Wang, *Structure of power*, p. 195; on the administration, Worthy, "The founding of Sung China," p. 231.

[172] *TCTC* 287, pp. 9384–5; *CWTS* 100, p. 1340.

over – Ho-chung by the governor and former commander of the Later Chin Imperial Guard, Li Shou-chen, and Feng-hsiang by a mutinous garrison. From the time of the last century of T'ang dynasty, Kuan-chung governors had formed sometimes powerful alliances, and in an echo of those times the rebel leaders plotted with and encouraged each other. However, the Kuan-chung provinces were now so much smaller than they had been that the three allies could not rely solely on their own resources. Accordingly, Li Shou-chen sought contact with the Liao whom he had so recently fought, despite the risk that he would end up subordinated to a Liao emperor. Bolstered by predictions that he would be emperor and a letter from the Ch'ang-an commander offering him imperial robes, Li Shou-chen assumed the title Prince of Ch'in. The rebels controlled most of the Wei River valley, depriving the Later Han of two of its best armies and providing a corridor to the Later Han capital should the hostile Later Shu regime become involved.[173]

The response from the Later Han court was hampered by internal wrangling. Resentment of Su Feng-chi, of his brother, and of the commander of the Imperial Guard, Shih Hung-chao, led to the concurrent appointment as chief minister of their rival, the military affairs commissioner Yang Pin. Thereafter all matters of state were referred to him. Yang dominated the court in the manner of a Kuo Ch'ung-t'ao or An Ch'ung-hui, but his methods were as irregular as Su Feng-chi's. The Sus, displaced, tried to bolster their position by attacking some former Chin ministers whose property the brothers had received after Liu Chih-yüan's victory. Li Sung and fifty family members were executed on charges of communicating with Li Shou-chen and the Liao, and of conspiring to "pillage the capital." The tax exactions of provincial officials and the arbitrary executions by Shih Hung-chao placed an extreme burden on commoners. Such poor behavior by Later Han officials only encouraged the opposition, so that while Yang Pin was appointing generals to fight Li Shou-chen at Ho-chung in 948, the Feng-hsiang commander was quietly establishing trade relations with the Later Shu, offering them his submission, and accepting titles from Li Shou-chen. Many others communicated their support to Li, but offered no material help. Li did not march on K'ai-feng and did not have to face an army. The Later Han generals hated each other too much to fight. Shih Hung-chao, although the obvious choice as Imperial Guard commander, was not given field command, probably from fear that he might rebel once he left the capital.[174]

[173] TCTC 287–8, pp. 9386–91; CWTS 101, pp. 1343–6; Wang, Structure of power, p. 196. For biographies of Li and his allies, see CWTS 109, pp. 1437–41 (Li Shou-chen); 1441–4 (Chao Ssu-wan at Ch'ang-an); Ou-yang, Hsin Wu-tai shih 53, pp. 603–5 (Wang Ching-ch'ung at Feng-hsiang).
[174] TCTC 288, pp. 9390–6; CWTS 101, pp. 1345–9; Worthy, "The founding of Sung China," pp. 232, 139.

Not until the autumn of 948 was the court finally compelled to appoint the military affairs commissioner Kuo Wei as commander in chief of an expeditionary army. Taking Feng Tao's advice, Kuo Wei focused all his efforts on Li Shou-chen in his Shan-hsi stronghold of Ho-chung. Since Li had previously commanded many of the troops that Kuo now led, Kuo offered them rewards to undercut their loyalty to their old commander, as well as sharing their hardships and mitigating some of the harsher elements of Later Han military discipline. Kuo, although not a regular general, won the allegiance of his expeditionary armies so well that he was able to suppress Li and his fellow mutineers by the end of 949.[175] In triumph, Kuo exercised his enhanced power – he was now a military affairs commissioner in firm control of a veteran Imperial Guard army – by removing without proper authority the city governor of Lo-yang, whom Kuo Wei felt had insulted him. The court refused Kuo Wei's calls to punish the governor but did not reinstate him. Kuo now made a point of refusing to take sole credit for the success of the western campaigns, emphasizing the importance of his logistical and administrative support. His praise seems warranted, but it was also calculated to assuage court fears that Kuo was becoming dangerously powerful, yet simultaneously display his virtue. Careful not to provoke Kuo Wei to rebellion, the court tried to woo top court ministers, the most important provincial governors, and the leaders of neighboring regimes, including Wu-Yüeh, Ch'u, and Ching-nan, offering them honors and titles.[176]

But this strategy was misplaced. There was little to fear from the ministers, who were preoccupied with infighting, and in the summer of 950 the court rotated most of the governors to different provinces without a murmur, demonstrating the remarkable extent to which – the recent rebellions notwithstanding – gubernatorial power had been curtailed. In addition to the measures continued from Li Ssu-yüan's time, the court was now able to appoint both administrators and military officers (in the guise of finance officials) directly to the provincial governments, effectively imposing court supervision. With military power entirely under court control and sections of the Imperial Guard patrolling the provinces under court-appointed officers, governors could only fume.[177]

Kuo Wei had scarcely reported at court before he was appointed, in the spring of 950, to be regent and provincial governor at Wei-chou and to lead a major expedition in retaliation for ongoing Khitan raids. Shih Hung-chao – formerly aligned with Su Feng-chi – suggested that Kuo should also retain

[175] *TCTC* 288, pp. 9396–9417; *CWTS* 101–2, pp. 1346–59; Worthy, "The founding of Sung China," pp. 139–40.
[176] *TCTC* 288, pp. 9412–15; *CWTS* 110, p. 1452; Worthy, "The founding of Sung China," pp. 232–3.
[177] *TCTC* 289, pp. 9419–23; Wang, *Structure of power*, pp. 196–7.

his post as military affairs commissioner alongside Yang Pin. Military affairs commissioners had led expeditions before and had held governorships while residing in the capital, but the combination of ministerial authority with both expeditionary command and a provincial base set a dangerous precedent. Su Feng-chi protested the "use of the outside to govern the inside," but he was overruled, creating a split between him and Shih Hung-chao and, it is said, between civil and military officials. Su Feng-chi and Shih Hung-chao were both regents, and the rift between them grew so deep that Yang Pin had to prevent Shih from killing Su. As more troops were sent against the Khitan raiders, the emperor's personal favorites increasingly obstructed the chief ministers, while the young emperor, Liu Ch'eng-yu, himself began to chafe at the restrictions placed on his decision making. Su Feng-chi encouraged one favorite to act against Yang Pin, Shih Hung-chao, and a third minister, Wang Chang, but became alarmed when Liu Ch'eng-yu took command and began a bloodbath, executing not only the three ministers but also their families and followers – events amounting to a coup d'état. Su Feng-chi was placed in charge of the Bureau of Military Affairs just as the purge was targeting Kuo Wei and other important allies of the three ministers. When a warning reached Kuo Wei, he blamed the young emperor's companions and decided to march south with his armies to "explain himself." His forces included his own governor's guard (*ya-chün*), created during his few months at Wei-chou, as well as the imperial forces mobilized to deal with the Khitan incursions. Reacting to this impending confrontation, the court promised rewards to the rest of the imperial armies, hoping to retain their allegiance, and issued a general summons to nearby governors, but received little response.[178]

Liu Ch'eng-yu's uncle, the governor at Shan-chou on the Yellow River, had refused to take part in the purge, and he allowed Kuo Wei to cross the river on his march toward the capital. As more governors and generals joined Kuo, he continued to declare himself subject to the emperor's will yet rewarded his troops in preparation for a fight and promised them ten days of plunder in the capital at K'ai-feng. In the end, the imperial troops all either defected, fled, or submitted to Kuo Wei, who had to use harsh methods to limit his army's looting.

The Later Han emperor Liu Ch'eng-yu was murdered by mutineers, and Su Feng-chi and his co-conspirators committed suicide. Kuo Wei had been careful to show that he did not seek the throne for himself, but he was now without any rival at court, and as the only surviving regent, he was the sole remaining power holder. Those who had conspired against Kuo and the three ministers

---

[178] *TCTC* 289, pp. 9422–34; *CWTS* 103, pp. 1369–70; 110, p. 1452. Worthy, "The founding of Sung China," pp. 139–43, gives a detailed account of Kuo Wei's rise to power.

were executed, and officials uninvolved in the plot reinstated. The general who had warned Kuo of the plot against him, Wang Yin, was rewarded with the position of commander of the Imperial Guard, replacing the murdered Shih Hung-chao.[179] Although Kuo Wei led a powerful military force, there were enough troops still outside his control to form concerted resistance. Nevertheless as in the cases of Li Ssu-yüan and Li T'sung-k'o, Kuo's following mushroomed rapidly, reflecting a general perception that he had more to offer than did the incumbent. The capacity to attract allegiance was at least as important as absolute military strength.

Kuo Wei did not immediately take the throne, but instead consolidated his hold on power behind the scenes while appearing to observe all the proper protocols of a loyal regent and army commander. He asked the dowager empress to choose a successor for Liu Ch'eng-yu, and she asked the officials to discuss the options. Kuo Wei proposed Liu Yün, Liu Chih-yüan's nephew and adopted son, and persuaded the dowager empress to hold court herself until Yün arrived from his distant province. In the first session of court, those who had shown early support for Kuo Wei were rewarded with commands in the Imperial Guard and posts giving them control of the military, palace, and financial administrations.[180]

Kuo Wei did not remain long at court. When a large Liao raid attacked Nei-ch'iu (south of Chen-chou) late in the year, Kuo went to deal with it in person. Shortly after crossing the Yellow River at Shan-chou, he was proclaimed emperor by his army, who, having pillaged the capital, now feared the revenge of the Liu family if they were restored to the throne. This time Kuo Wei made no protestations of unwillingness, but simply wrote to the dowager empress asking for permission to pay his respects at the Liu ancestral temple and to treat her as a mother; in effect, he was asking to be regarded as Liu Chih-yüan's adopted son and thus as legitimate an heir to the throne as the adopted sons Chu Yu-kuei or Li Ssu-yüan in their time. Kuo's willingness to ignore his mission and return forthwith to the capital suggests that the Liao raid was not so very dangerous, and indeed it was easily beaten off by local forces, leading to a peace request. Kuo Wei's followers quickly persuaded Liu Yün's bodyguard to join Kuo's side, and thus they effectively took Liu Yün into their custody. The dowager empress demoted Liu and made Kuo Wei regent, or *chien-kuo*, apparently with wide support both at court and in the provinces. Having done everything with absolute propriety, and without a blow being struck,

---

[179] *TCTC* 289, pp. 9434–40; *CWTS* 103, pp. 1370–3; 110, pp. 1452–5; Worthy, "The founding of Sung China," p. 142.

[180] *TCTC* 289, pp. 9440–3; *CWTS* 103, pp. 1373–6; 110, pp. 1455–7. Liu Yün's biography is in *CWTS* 105, pp. 1387–8.

Kuo Wei, in the first month of 951, proclaimed himself emperor (Chou T'ai-tsu, 951–4) and established the Later Chou dynasty. Liu Yün was murdered, and his provincial followers in Hsü-chou were eliminated after a two-month siege.[181]

MOVING TO CONSOLIDATION

Later Chou and Northern Han, 951–954

With the Later Chou regime came a return of the expansionism seen in the era of Chu Wen and Li Ts'un-hsü, twenty-five years earlier. This expansionism was built upon a much stronger base created by the struggles and consolidations of the three Sha-t'o-led dynasties. Most Five Dynasties governors had been content to accept the principle of formal subordination to superior authority provided they retained effective local autonomy. Later T'ang and Later Chin rulers from Li Ssu-yüan in the middle 920s onward had made incremental efforts to undermine provincial powers, but because the dynastic rulers needed to prevent the governors from offering their allegiance elsewhere, regional leaders were granted much of the autonomy they desired. By 950, however, after years of destructive warfare, governors had so few resources left that subordination was now not merely formal, but actual, for they could no longer resist court authority and still remain within the realm. Now governors could attain autonomy only by placing themselves outside Later Chou jurisdiction altogether. Allegiance with autonomy was no longer possible within northern China; governors could only be subordinate or independent.

Accordingly, Liu Ch'ung, an old enemy of Kuo Wei and a full brother of the Han founder (Liu Chih-yüan), was unwilling to accept his family's displacement. From his base at T'ai-yüan, he immediately declared himself the independent successor to the throne of the Later Han dynasty (Han Shih-tsu, 951–5). This continuation of the Later Han regime is known as Northern Han (951–79). Liu controlled twelve Ho-tung prefectures and appointed new ministers from his governor's retinue to replace those now working for Kuo Wei. Despite his declaration, Liu was himself dubious about his regime's imperial credentials, declaring to his ministers, "What kind of emperor am I, and what kind of governors are you!" He did not establish an imperial ancestral temple or make any sacrifices that distinguished him from a commoner, and he was only too aware of his financial limitations; his chief ministers were paid

---

[181] *TCTC* 289–90, pp. 9443–59; *CWTS* 103, pp. 1376–7; 110, pp. 1457–62; T'o-t'o et al., *Liao shih* 5, p. 65.

only half the going rate, leading Ssu-ma Kuang to comment that the regime "lacked incorrupt officials."[182]

Unsurprisingly, Liu Ch'ung sought an alliance with Liao, for Ho-tung could not have survived alone against the Later Chou. Liu offered Liao annual payments and subordination according to the "old ways of the [Later] Chin house" and received formal investiture from the Liao emperor as his fictive nephew. An immediate raid by the new allies on Chin-chou (in central Shansi) inside Later Chou territory prompted Kuo Wei to reinforce his northern defenses, even as he sought to protect his southern borders by publicly disavowing any aggressive intentions toward the domains in the Huai-nan region. Although the Liao sent their congratulations for Kuo Wei's accession, they subsequently detained the Later Chou envoys. The governor of Ting-nan, a western neighbor of the Northern Han, transferred his allegiance to Liu Ch'ung, thus protecting the new regime from a Later Chou flanking attack through his territory. Liao assistance was delayed by political unrest culminating in the assassination of the Liao emperor Wu-yü, but his cousin, Ching (Liao Mu-tsung, 951–69), who succeeded to the throne, continued the relationship with Northern Han. That winter an enormous force of Northern Han and Liao troops laid siege to Chin-chou until they were driven back by the lack of food and the arrival of Later Chou reinforcements. The Later Chou armies pursued the fleeing invaders and claimed to have destroyed a third of the allies' strength.[183]

The ripple effects of war worked against Liu Ch'ung and for Kuo Wei. The Ho-tung region had weathered the 940s better than anywhere in the Central Plains, but it was economically unproductive and its population small. To fund his armies and pay the Liao subsidies, Liu Ch'ung imposed such heavy taxes and corvée demands that many fled to Later Chou territory, thereby denuding Northern Han of its most important resource – people. The refuge Kuo Wei provided those fleeing from Northern Han so enhanced Kuo's power and attractiveness as a ruler that he managed to transfer Sun Fang-chien, governor of Ting-chou, without provoking him to defect northward, as Sun had done under the Later Chin and then Liao when they tried to transfer him in 946 and 948, respectively.[184]

Kuo Wei did face challengers. For example, Mu-jung Yen-ch'ao, governor of Yen-chou in western Shantung, first sent tribute to Kuo Wei, and then requested help from both Southern T'ang and Northern Han for a planned

[182] *TCTC* 290, pp. 9452–4; *CWTS* 110, p. 1464; 135, p. 1811. Ssu-ma Kuang states that Liu Ch'ung died in 954, *TCTC* 292, p. 9520; and see also *CWTS* 115, p. 1535; T'o-t'o et al., *Liao shih* 6, p. 73.
[183] *TCTC* 290, pp. 9455–71; *CWTS* 110–11, pp. 1464–79; see also T'o-t'o et al., *Liao shih* 5, pp. 66–7.
[184] *TCTC* 290, pp. 9462, 9470–1; *CWTS* 125, p. 1650.

rebellion. In 952 the Southern T'ang came to help Mu-jung but Kuo Wei defeated them and, by veiled threats, frightened them into staying out of the fray. Without allies and besieged in Yen-chou, Mu-jung resorted to savage extortion to pay his troops, but after four months, the city fell to an assault led by Kuo Wei in person. Mu-jung Yen-ch'ao committed suicide, and Kuo Wei made an example of the city, allowing his army to pillage savagely and to kill nearly ten thousand people, although he was persuaded not to execute Mu-jung's officials en masse.[185] Subsequent provincial challengers to Kuo Wei's authority, notably the governor at Yen-chou2 in the northwest in 953, and Wang Yin, the governor at Wei-chou, later the same year, were dealt with quickly and easily.[186] While governors outside Ho-tung could still cause trouble, their lack of military and financial resources made them almost totally reliant on support from outside the Central Plains, and these allies were rarely able to withstand the Later Chou imperial armies, over which Kuo Wei was particularly concerned to secure his control.

Having exploited his own expeditionary leadership of the Imperial Guard to build a following, Kuo was very conscious of the danger posed to him by the Guard commander. Wang Yin, the current incumbent, was Kuo's early supporter and appointee; nevertheless, Kuo still took the precaution of sending Wang Yin to govern Wei-chou to sever Wang's personal connection with his Imperial Guard troops. Following the lead of Yang Kuang-yüan and many previous Wei-chou governors, Wang Yin established his own governor's guard and brought several hundred troops with him when he attended court. But in 953, when Kuo ordered Wang's execution on charges of plotting rebellion, there was no supportive uprising in Wei-chou or rebellion from the Guard.[187] Control of armies depended as much as ever on day-to-day contact, but governorships were no longer automatically power bases.

To counterbalance the power of the Imperial Guard in the capital, Kuo Wei began to strengthen his personal bodyguard by appointing his sister's son, Li Ch'ung-chin, as commander in chief to bring the various uncoordinated units under a single general. When Wang Yin was sent to Wei-chou, someone still had to handle Guard affairs as his deputy in the capital, and in 952 Kuo gave this responsibility to Li Ch'ung-chin, who retained command of the personal bodyguard. As under Li Ssu-yüan, command of the main imperial forces was divided between an important follower and an imperial relative, but unlike

---

[185] *TCTC* 290, pp. 9453–78; *CWTS* 112, pp. 1479–82; (Mu-jung's biography is in *CWTS* 130, pp. 1716–18); Ou-yang, *Hsin Wu-tai shih* 53, pp. 608–10; T'o-t'o et al., *Liao shih* 6, p. 69.

[186] *TCTC* 291, pp. 9489–90, 9493, 9497–8. On the Wei-chou governor, Wang Yin, see Worthy, "The founding of Sung China," pp. 143–5, who suggests that the threat from Wang was much greater because of his formal position as commander of the Imperial Guard.

[187] Mao, "T'ang-mo Wu-tai cheng-chih she-hui chih yen-chiu," pp. 350–4.

those earlier cases, it was now the relative not the follower who held the practical authority, and the relative was not a potentially ambitious natural or adopted son, but a member of the emperor's natal family.[188] Tighter control of the central armies was accompanied by continued efforts to weaken the military strength of the governors by restricting their access to armaments: an order of 952 commanded that governors were to send to court the best of the weapons they produced rather than the second-rate, and that artisans were to be moved to the capital.[189]

Unlike most of his immediate predecessors, Kuo Wei had served mostly at court rather than as a governor, and so had not developed an extensive personal retinue. He did, however, have a group of associates at court. Even before his accession, Kuo had arranged for Wang Chün, his army-supervising commissioner and deputy at Wei-chou, to be military affairs commissioner. On becoming emperor, Kuo also appointed Wang to be chief minister, and made increasing use of several others from his Wei-chou staff. However, while previously serving at court Kuo Wei had been impressed by the court literati Li Ku and Fan Chih, both holders of the *chin-shih* degree, and while Kuo was at Wei-chou he had them appointed supervisor of the Finance Commission (*san-ssu shih*) and vice-commissioner for military affairs respectively. After Kuo ascended to the throne they took on the additional appointments of chief ministers.[190] Kuo Wei also reemployed long-standing figures like Feng Tao, but administrative continuity was no longer as critical since almost everyone that Kuo appointed was drawn from the same pool of career bureaucrats. Accordingly, the careers of many of the Later Chou senior ministers show a return to what had once been the normal pattern of regular transfers between both court and provincial positions. Among other things, this meant that bureaucrats were more frequently appointed to be generals or provincial governors.

In addition to his efforts to concentrate military and administrative control into his own hands, Kuo Wei made a dramatic change in his approach to governance, bringing a distinctive austerity and vigor to court. Within the first eight months of his reign Kuo abolished provincial tribute payments, capped his own income, signaled that he would listen to advice from any

[188] Worthy, "The founding of Sung China," p. 144. For Li Ch'ung-chin's biography, see T'o-t'o et al., eds., *Sung shih* [hereafter *SS*] (1345; Peking, 1977) 484, pp. 13975–9. On the advantages of emperors allying with their sisters, see Jennifer Holmgren, "Imperial marriage in the native Chinese and non-Han state, Han to Ming," in *Marriage and inequality in Chinese society*, ed. Rubie S. Watson and Patricia B. Ebrey (Berkeley, Calif., 1991) pp. 58–70.

[189] Worthy, "The founding of Sung China," pp. 145–6; *CWTS* 112, p. 1485 (weapons); 113, p. 1503; see also *SS* 484, p. 13975.

[190] For biographies, see Wang Chün, *CWTS* 130, pp. 1711–16; Li Ku and Fan Chih, *SS* 262, pp. 9051–6, and 249, pp. 8793–6, respectively.

bureaucrat, smashed precious objects from the treasuries in court to symbolize his attention to matters of state, and publicly consulted with his ministers. He rewarded households containing multiple generations, buried Liu Ch'eng-yu as an emperor, and sent home some Northern Han prisoners, perhaps trying to win over Liu Ch'ung. Although he was restricting his governors' activities, he also showed some respect for them by reversing the hated Later Han and Northern Han policy of directly appointing civil and military officials to provincial administrations.[191]

Kuo Wei highlighted the contrast between himself and the wartime Later Chin and the courts of Later and Northern Han by extending his accession amnesty back to 936, implying the illegitimacy of those regimes. Proportionate to the length of his reign, Kuo Wei seems to have made far more use than his Five Dynasties predecessors of symbolic acts of legitimation. In 952 he made obeisance at the Confucian temple, rejecting advice that an emperor should not prostrate himself before a mere official. Li Ssu-yüan had at least shown an interest in Confucian learning by ordering new editions of the Nine Classics, but it was Kuo Wei who benefited from their completion in 953, sponsoring their printing, sale, and wide dissemination. Kuo also attempted to ease the pressure at the top of the legal system by refusing to hear matters at court until local procedures had been exhausted. Kuo's measure doubtless reduced the caseload at court, but without reforms to increase accountability and enforce correct procedure at the lower levels, local events were often still governed by individual corruption. One example is the case of the Ch'ing-chou2 prefect in the northwest whose illegal seizure of livestock provoked an uprising in 952 that took two prefects and a governor two months to suppress.[192] Despite attempts to clamp down on such abuses of authority, imperial orders still had only limited impact outside the capital.

A more effective local measure was Kuo's abolition of the *ying-t'ien* system of military-agricultural outposts in southeastern Honan, a region that had suffered the worst of the fighting at the end of the T'ang dynasty. These outposts were government lands the taxes on which were payable in cattle. Herds had become depleted, yet the quotas had not changed, driving many to banditry. However, because these communities were administered directly by the Ministry of Revenue, the local authorities were not empowered to control the disorder. Resisting calls for the fertile *ying-t'ien* fields to be sold off for

[191] *TCTC* 290, pp. 9450–62; *CWTS* 110, p. 1460. See also Han Kuo-p'an, *Ch'ai Jung* (Shanghai, 1956), p. 18.

[192] *TCTC* 290, pp. 9478–9 (temple); 291, pp. 9485–90 (courts and Ch'ing-chou2 rising), 9495 (Classics). On symbolic legitimation in China, see Chan Hok-lam, *Legitimation in imperial China: Discussions under the Jürchen-Chin dynasty (1115–1234)* (Seattle, 1984).

profit, in 953 Kuo Wei ended the cattle levy; bestowed ownership of fields, homes, and implements on the *ying-t'ien* households themselves; and placed the *ying-t'ien* families under their local administrations, bringing thirty thousand households onto the registers and increasing agricultural productivity and thus state revenues. A similar concern for livelihoods had already been seen in a 952 edict reducing the number of cowhides owed to the court each year, permitting private possession of hides, and allowing trade in hides provided they were not sold to enemy states. Leather was a major constituent of armor, and possessing even a single hide had been made punishable by death under Later Han law, leaving the people without everyday items that they needed. Even as Kuo Wei was trying to control weapons production by governors, he was willing to give the general population a freer hand. These direct appeals to the people increased Kuo Wei's stature and further undercut the authority of local leaders. Thus when, in 953, Kuo restricted governors from sending their own appointees to collect taxes at county level, he was both limiting the governors' authority and displaying his concern over the burdens of his people.[193] Combined with Kuo's other economic measures, these policies seem to have contributed to a general economic recovery.

The effects of sound governance extended beyond Kuo Wei's borders. A Southern T'ang minister returning from travels on the Huai River reported that Kuo was perceived to be governing with increasing virtue, and accordingly might soon present a threat to the T'ang. Moreover, disenchanted examination candidates from Southern T'ang soon began heading north to seek work from the Later Chou state. Kuo Wei's prestige was high enough in the north that in 952 a Later Chin scholar who had gone north with the Liao ruler Te-kuang in 947 persuaded the governor of the Liao Southern Capital at Yu-chou, a member of the Liao consort clan, to offer his allegiance to the Later Chou.[194]

Kuo Wei also tried to display himself as a sage-ruler to win over the population of his northern borders, where the Northern Han and their Liao sponsors were Kuo's chief concerns. Confucius had claimed that sage-rulers would attract followers by their sheer virtue, and Kuo Wei recognized the utility behind the tradition: meeting current concerns enhanced a ruler's prestige. Many in the Liao frontier districts had formerly been ruled by the Later T'ang and before them by the T'ang dynasty; they clearly had much in common with their southern neighbors. In 952, Kuo Wei banned those on the Later Chou

[193] *TCTC* 291, pp. 9488–9 (*ying-t'ien*, the edict is in *CWTS* 112, p. 1488), 9486 (hides); *CWTS* 113, p. 1498 (tax collectors). On Kuo Wei's economic measures, see Han, *Ch'ai Jung*, pp. 16–17, and on landholding in particular, see Eberhard, "Remarks on the bureaucracy," p. 292.

[194] *TCTC* 291, p. 9490. For the story of this sympathizer, see *TCTC* 290, pp. 9479–80; T'o-t'o et al., *Liao shih* 6, p. 70; and see chapter 6 of Standen, *Unbounded loyalty*.

side of the border from raiding the Liao marches for captives and plunder, partly showing a desire to relieve a burden on the northerners but also demonstrating his confidence that his will would be obeyed.[195] Since the order was apparently not repeated, it may have been successful, enhancing Kuo's reputation as a virtuous ruler. When three Liao border prefectures suffered severe flooding, Kuo Wei provided relief for the refugees entering the Later Chou–held region of Ho-pei, and thus peacefully increased his own population. When Khitan raids – probably resulting from the same natural disaster – were not prevented by the Liao emperor, Kuo Wei's reputation was only enhanced by the contrast. In the south, too, in the following year, Southern T'ang refugees from a drought in Huai-nan were allowed to buy grain from the Later Chou, again showing Kuo Wei's humane qualities, although his image as a sage-ruler may have been undermined by subsequent reports of flooding across the eastern two-thirds of Chou.[196]

This virtuous behavior accompanied the development of what turned out to be Kuo Wei's terminal illness. Advised to exorcise his arthritis by disbursing charity, Kuo's immediate concern was to hold sacrifices in the southern suburbs and bring the state altars and imperial ancestral shrine from Lo-yang to K'ai-feng. On the evening after the sacrifices he became seriously ill. He spent two weeks giving instructions for a simple funeral and tomb arrangements, working to ensure an orderly succession, and arranging for flood defenses to be built.[197] Before Kuo Wei, only Li Ssu-yüan and Shih Ching-t'ang had attained sufficient stature and their regimes achieved enough stability for them to die natural deaths and procure a regular succession. Kuo Wei now successfully designated his adopted son Kuo Jung (formerly Ch'ai Jung) as his heir, and in the first month of 954 he tried to secure Jung's position by conducting the kind of reshuffle that was normally performed after an accession rather than before. Kuo Wei transferred several of his governors and gave many of them princely titles, and also replaced both the infantry and the cavalry commanders of the Imperial Guard. He left in place the senior commander of the Imperial Guard, his nephew Li Ch'ung-chin, but Kuo Jung – who already commanded Kuo Wei's palace army – received overall control of all military affairs, and Li Ch'ung-chin was made to bow to Kuo Jung as minister to emperor. On that same day, Kuo Wei died, and Kuo Jung acceded without incident (Chou Shih-tsung, 954–9).[198]

[195] *CWTS* 112, p. 1484. This order also makes it clear that frontier raiding for profit was not a nomadic prerogative. See Standen, "Raiding and frontier society."

[196] *TCTC* 291, pp. 9484, 9489, 9496.

[197] *TCTC* 291, pp. 9496–9500; see also *CWTS* 113, pp. 1498–1503.

[198] *TCTC* 291, pp. 9500–1; *CWTS* 113, pp. 1501–3; Worthy, "The founding of Sung China," pp. 148–9. Worthy notes that Li Ch'ung-chin was not given the commander in chief post, which had been vacant since Wang Yin's removal in 953.

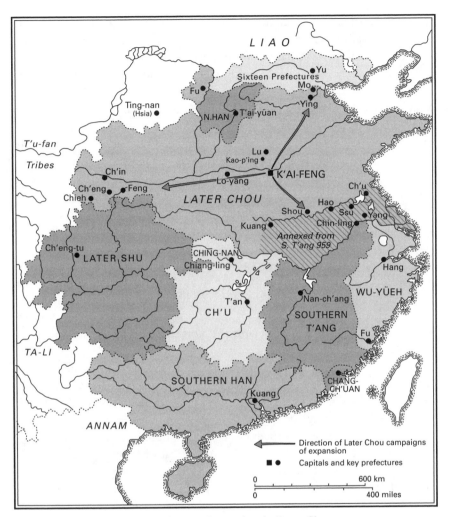

Map 9. Territorial expansion under the Later Chou, c. 959.

We must, of course, be skeptical about the saintly picture of Kuo Wei in the sources. The historians clearly approved of him, and the sense of a new order beginning is visible in the earliest sources. At the very least, Kuo Wei does seem to have avoided the personal failings, such as cruelty and corruption, that provoked contemporary unpopularity.

The revival of expansionism, 954–958

Kuo Wei had been able to focus on projecting a virtuous image because he enjoyed overwhelming military superiority within Later Chou territory. His heir, Kuo Jung, also had military experience, which was just as well, because

when the Northern Han ruler Liu Ch'ung heard of Kuo Wei's death he joined
with his Liao allies to march on Lu-chou with a large army. Inheriting personal
control of the Imperial Guard from his father, Kuo Jung led the Later Chou
armies to a dramatic and closely fought victory at Kao-p'ing, near Lu-chou, in
the third month of 954. This victory was crucial in limiting the Northern Han
forces to sporadic raids after it and in giving Kuo Jung claim to the Mandate of
Heaven not merely by inheritance but by the most powerful of means, his own
military merit. Throughout his reign he reinforced this merit by leading his
armies in person. The elderly Northern Han ruler, Liu Ch'ung, pursued after
the battle by Kuo Jung, nearly died from the exertions of the retreat home, and
was just able to prepare T'ai-yüan's defenses. The siege prompted numerous
Northern Han districts and one senior commander to submit to Kuo Jung,
but the Later Chou forces swiftly became overextended and halted their siege
after less than two months.[199]

In this uncertain military environment, the prefect of the northwestern
outpost of Fu-chou2 (at the northern tip of Shensi) – strategically positioned
as a Later Chou enclave outflanking the Northern Han and recently demoted
from provincial status – was able to achieve the reestablishment of the province
with himself as governor. In the captured Northern Han districts, rather than
following the previous practice of retaining the submitted prefects and county
magistrates, Kuo Jung installed his own people, seeking immediate integration of this territory. When he withdrew, he took his appointees with him.[200]
Mere allegiance was no longer an adequate basis for Kuo Jung's authority; it
was now all or nothing. If he could not exert complete control in captured
districts, he would abandon them rather than compromise his supremacy.

Kuo Jung had led the Kao-p'ing campaign against ministerial advice. His
success proved him right and revealed the ineffectiveness of the Imperial Guard,
now full of ill and elderly place keepers. Several units of the Imperial Guard
had fled during the battle, and dozens of officers of all ranks were subsequently
executed (including the recently appointed infantry and cavalry commanders),
allowing Kuo Jung to replace them with officers from the palace army, which
Kuo had been leading personally for over twelve months and which had fought
well at Kao-p'ing. With his own people in charge, later in 954 Kuo conducted
a long-needed fitness review that significantly reduced the size of the Imperial
Guard and increased its effectiveness. As a counterweight to the Imperial

---

[199] *TCTC* 291, pp. 9501–10, 9513; 292, pp. 9514–16; *CWTS* 114, pp. 1511–17; see also T'o-t'o et al.,
    Liao shih 6, p. 72. Discussion of the battle of Kao-p'ing and references to the literature can be found in
    Peter Lorge, "The entrance and exit of the Song founders," *Journal of Sung-Yuan Studies* 29 (1999), pp.
    43–62; and Lorge's "War and the creation of the Northern Song."
[200] *TCTC* 292, pp. 9515–16.

Guard, Kuo enlarged the palace army – which until now had functioned chiefly as the Later Chou emperor's personal bodyguard – by actively recruiting to it the finest fighters from all over the region, creating an elite fighting force. Many of these soldiers were poached from the armies of the governors, thus weakening them while enhancing Kuo's own forces. Kuo now monopolized control over the entire battlefield might of the empire – a dramatic contrast to the situation fewer than fifty years before. This control meant that Kuo no longer needed the allegiance of the governors to maintain his position as emperor. Combined with the Liao defeat at Kao-p'ing, it was now clearly impossible for any governor, or even an alliance of governors, to stand against Kuo, and it is striking that throughout his entire reign no Later Chou province rebelled against his authority. But the concentration of armed strength in the palace armies also meant that Kuo had altered a useful balance of power in which governors and palace armies offset each other. This new situation left Kuo precariously reliant on the loyalty of his commanders.[201]

Although the military was understandably Kuo Jung's first concern, he also followed Kuo Wei's lead in addressing issues of good governance. He punished prominent corrupt officials; ruled that degrees should be given only to those who had actually passed the examinations (and not on the basis of family connections); restored responsibility for local defense and policing to governors, prefects, and county magistrates (instead of sending central appointees); and built massive defenses along the Yellow River (deploying sixty thousand corvée laborers). In 955 he tried to encourage vagrants back onto the manorial estates (*chuang-t'ien*) they had fled, allowing the returning refugees to recover a portion of the land and wealth appropriated by others in their absence. He also ordered a carefully phased expansion of K'ai-feng's city walls, followed by the widening and straightening of the city's streets.[202] Kuo Jung also attempted to regulate the religious orders, whose membership in 954 was recorded as 61,200. In the fifth month of 955, he restricted entry to the monastic life to those whose grandparents, parents, and uncles had all died; banned ascetic mutilation; demanded more accurate counts of clergy; and abolished over thirty thousand temples. Such prohibitions were not intentionally anti-Buddhist: the main concern was financial. The practices of Buddhism had contributed

---

[201] *TCTC* 292, pp. 9518–19. Worthy, "The founding of Sung China," pp. 148–64, gives a detailed description of the new structure of the palace army and the Imperial Guard. On the relationship between the battle of Kao-p'ing and this reorganization, see Lorge, "The entrance and exit of the Song founders."

[202] See (provincial defenses) *TCTC* 292, p. 9519; (examinations) *CWTS* 115, pp. 1527–8, and Eberhard, "Remarks on the bureaucracy," p. 293; (vagrants) *CWTS* 115, p. 1525; Wang P'u, *Wu-tai hui-yao* (961; Shanghai, 1978) 25, pp. 406–7; and Kurihara Masuo, *Ransei no kōtei – "Kō-Shū" no Seisō to sono jidai* (Tokyo, 1968), pp. 203–11; (K'ai-feng) *TCTC* (1956) 292, pp. 9525, 9532.

significantly to a shortage of cash, as coins were melted down to make religious images. Later in the year, in order to free up the copper supply, Kuo Jung ordered that apart from statues in the remaining temples, military equipment, and official insignia, all copper implements and statues "among the people" must be surrendered, and compensation paid, with the death penalty for concealing more than five *chin* (6.5 pounds).[203] Unlike Shih Ching-t'ang's efforts in the same vein, Kuo Jung's appear to have been effective. Like Kuo Wei, Kuo Jung was successfully reasserting central authority.

All this organizational and administrative activity was conducted with the full cooperation of leading ministers who – in contrast even to the preceding reign – showed no sign of seeking overweening authority for themselves. Like his father, Kuo Jung drew his ministers from the ranks of the regular bureaucracy, yet personal relationships still remained important in guiding the emperor's choices; hence Kuo Jung's military affairs commissioners were already valued advisors before appointment. Cheng Jen-hui, a Wei-chou administrator favored by Kuo Wei, was made military affairs commissioner and chief minister immediately after the accession in 954. Cheng was soon joined at the commission by Wei Jen-p'u, who had helped Kuo Wei to secure the throne. Cheng Jen-hui died in 955; the following year Wang P'u was appointed vice-commissioner, and a year after that promoted to commissioner. He had served under Kuo Jung since 951 and was the architect of Later Chou territorial expansion. Shortly before Kuo Jung died in 959, he insisted that Wei also accept the appointment of chief minister, even though Wei lacked the necessary *chin-shih* degree. Unlike Kuo Ch'ung-t'ao or Yang Pin before him, but similar to his former colleague Cheng Jen-hui, Wei Jen-p'u did not exploit his powerful situation, even when Kuo Jung's young son came to the throne soon afterward.[204]

From 955 onward, Kuo Jung paid increasing attention to his northern borders. He refused to abandon strategic Fu-chou2 when the Ting-nan governor denied access to Later Chou envoys, instead forcing Ting-nan back into line by reminding its governor of his economic reliance on Later Chou. He also dredged the river on a north-south line between Shen-chou and Chi-chou2 in Ho-pei, improving navigability and making it harder for cavalry to cross; he established a new walled town and province at Chi-chou2; and further south

---

[203] *TCTC* 292, pp. 9527, 9530. The edicts are in *CWTS* 115, pp. 1529–31; Wang, *Wu-tai hui-yao* 12, pp. 196, 200–2; 27, p. 437. For discussion see Han, *Ch'ai Jung*, pp. 37–41; Kurihara, *Ransei no kōtei*, pp. 214–30. On the general fiscal impact of Buddhism, see Jacques Gernet, *Buddhism in Chinese society: An economic history from the fifth to the tenth centuries*, trans. Franciscus Verellen (New York, 1995).

[204] *TCTC* 291, p. 9499; 292, p. 9517; 293, pp. 9559, 9571; 294, p. 9601; Worthy, "The founding of Sung China," pp. 235–6. For biographies of Cheng Jen-hui, see *CWTS* 123, pp. 1620–1; Wei Jen-p'u, *SS* 249, pp. 8802–5; Wang P'u, *CWTS* 128, pp. 1679–82.

he allowed the energetic prefect of Te-chou a free rein to handle raids. While strengthening his defenses, Kuo Jung also began to look beyond them. Supposedly prompted by a request from "some people in Ch'in-chou [in Kansu]" to "restore the old borders," he ordered senior ministers to propose plans for territorial expansion.[205]

Whereas the expansions of Chu Wen and Li Ts'un-hsü had been based almost entirely on winning allegiance through military prowess, Kuo Jung's attractiveness as a ruler rested on military and moral bases. Wang P'u's famous memorial to Kuo Jung on how to expand Later Chou control exemplifies this emphasis on moral and military strategies by declaring that the first task was to recover the *Tao* (the Way) by appointing worthy officials and applying law and taxation fairly. Wang further suggested that military resources should be concentrated on one front at a time, listing the targets in order of difficulty: Chiang-pei in Southern T'ang, the far south, the west, and finally the Northern Han.[206] Wang's proposals to reform the internal before conquering the external were entirely conventional and practical – an internally strong state is more likely to expand successfully. But Kuo Jung, unlike his predecessors, was in a position to act on these expansion plans. He now had close control over large and powerful military forces, and no longer had to be concerned chiefly with the survival of his regime. Kuo Jung had built upon Kuo Wei's consolidation efforts, and on the progressive centralization of control over provincial resources begun by Chu Wen fifty years earlier and continued by each successive dynasty. Kuo's ambitions were further helped by the incompetence of the current Liao emperor, Mu-tsung, which greatly reduced the threat posed by the alliance between the Liao and the Northern Han. Wang P'u's listing of all the states surrounding Later Chou territory as targets for conquest indicates how much the balance of power had changed in only a few years, for the expansionary vision Wang presented to Kuo Jung denied the legitimacy of Kuo's fellow emperors and thus transformed them from tolerated neighbors into mortal enemies. It was now no longer acceptable for Later Chou subjects to place their allegiance elsewhere, which left governors and prefects with no recognized method of seeking outside help.

In what was to prove a warm-up for the later campaign of expansion, at the same time that Wang P'u was presenting his memorial in the summer of 955, Kuo Jung sent a surprise expedition to seize four prefectures (including Ch'in-chou) recently taken over by the Later Shu, even though Shu was not the

---

[205] *TCTC* 292, pp. 9520–5; *CWTS* 115, pp. 1528–9 (Ch'in-chou request).

[206] *TCTC* 292, pp. 9525–7; *CWTS* 115, pp. 1529–31; and see translation in Worthy, "The founding of Sung China," pp. 15–17. This sequence was not adhered to in practice, for success required a flexible approach. See Lorge, "The entrance and exit of the Song founders."

weakest adversary on Wang P'u's list. The Later Shu lost eight fortresses before expeditionary commanders could be appointed, and although they quickly formed an alliance with the Northern Han and Southern T'ang, no material help from them arrived, and Ch'in-chou fell in the autumn. Suing for peace, the Later Shu ruler clung to his prerogative, calling himself "emperor," but his letter went unanswered. Feng-chou fell before the end of the year, and Kuo Jung paid salaries to the surrendered troops and relieved burdens on the people to win them over. These Later Shu troops marched with Kuo to conquer Huai-nan.[207]

Preparing to conquer the wealthy region of Southern T'ang between the Huai and the Yangtze, Kuo Jung drained the marshland along the Pien River as far as the Huai and the Southern T'ang border. The Southern T'ang, however, proved to be no pushover. Late in 955 the Later Chou army under the chief minister and general Li Ku crossed the Huai River and laid siege to Shou-chou just to the south. Kuo Jung sought an alliance with the kingdom of Wu-Yüeh before setting off to take personal command of the siege early in 956. When the city did not fall quickly, Li Ku, concerned that Southern T'ang reinforcements would cut off his route of retreat, lifted his siege before Kuo Jung's countermand arrived. The Later Chou emperor sent his palace army commander, Li Ch'ung-chin, to reimpose the siege and to replace Li Ku as campaign commander. Kuo tried to turn the situation to some advantage by "comforting" the farmers who had returned briefly to their fields, encouraging them to resume their livelihoods and hoping to win them over. As the renewed siege of Shou-chou continued, military successes against the Southern T'ang navy and towns along the Yangtze and Huai rivers produced two peace offers from the Southern T'ang ruler, Li Ching. He first offered to make annual payments to Kuo, yet treat Kuo Jung as an older brother (and thus a near equal), but subsequently Li surrendered his claims to his imperial title and submitted as a "subject."[208]

Like the Liao emperor Te-kuang, Kuo Jung held out for complete conquest, and by the third month of 956 Later Chou troops had fought their way to control of most of the prefectures between the Huai and the Yangtze rivers, but not of the fortified border towns along the Huai River itself. Helped by Wu-Yüeh forces, Kuo Jung cut off the Southern T'ang capital of Chin-ling in a pincer movement; at the same time, Later Chou forces launched a major attack against Kuang-chou2, near the Huai River west of Shou-chou. Li Ching

[207] *TCTC* 292, pp. 9527–33; 293, p. 9569; *CWTS* 115, pp. 1528–33. For detailed discussion, see Lorge, "The entrance and exit of the Song founders."

[208] *TCTC* 292, pp. 9532–40; *CWTS* 115–16, pp. 1534–42. On the significance and difficulties of the Shou-chou campaign, see Worthy, "The founding of Sung China," pp. 34–7.

sent a mission to Kuo apologizing for his tardy acceptance of the Later Chou mandate, and he offered Kuo six prefectures and annual payments in return for an imperial title and an end to Chou aggression. But Kuo Jung wanted nothing less than the entire region north of the Yangtze River. An attempt to persuade the Southern T'ang ruler to accept these terms was foiled by Southern T'ang court rivalries, and a courageous Southern T'ang prince led a counterattack that made Kuo Jung and his generals briefly consider abandoning the campaign; but a new assault by Later Chou troops in the fourth month destroyed the Southern T'ang elite forces in battle at Liu-ho, just north of the Yangtze River near the Southern T'ang capital. The people in these captured territories at first welcomed Later Chou rule, resenting Li Ching's levies and especially the *ying-t'ien* system in Huai-nan, probably aware that Kuo Wei had abolished the *ying-t'ien* system in his own lands. Li Ching wisely followed suit during 956. Accordingly, when pillaging by Later Chou troops disillusioned many of the conquered, there was nothing to prevent a backlash. During the summer a spontaneously organized "White Armored Army" (*pai-chia chün*) brought many of the Later Chou gains back into Southern T'ang hands.[209]

For 957 the Southern T'ang threw everything into relieving the siege at Shou-chou on the Huai River. While Shou-chou remained uncaptured, Kuo Jung was unable to secure his conquests farther to the south. Consequently, some hope remained that the Southern T'ang might be able to recover control of the Huai-nan region. Early in the year, Southern T'ang troops linked a dozen fortresses to create a walled supply route intended to maintain communications between the defenders of Shou-chou and the rest of the Southern T'ang forces. Kuo Jung, however, had begun to create a navy, building several hundred warships near K'ai-feng and using surrendered Southern T'ang sailors to train units of the Later Chou. Kuo now sent these forces down a tributary of the Huai River that ran directly from K'ai-feng to Shou-chou. In the third month of 957 they cut the Southern T'ang supply link and forced the surrender of its commanding general and his ten thousand troops. Shou-chou continued to hold out, but Kuo Jung swept downstream along the Huai River basin by land and water, destroying the Southern T'ang relief army, and allowing the Later Chou forces to build their own walled supply and reinforcement route. Even with all hope of assistance gone, the commander at Shou-chou had to be incapacitated by illness before his subordinates could surrender, and Kuo Jung recognized his steadfastness with rewards and kind treatment.[210]

[209] *TCTC* 292–3, pp. 9540–58; *CWTS* 116, pp. 1542–9 (which quotes Li Ching's letters to Kuo Jung, pp. 1543–6).

[210] *TCTC* 293, pp. 9562–7; *CWTS* 116–17, pp. 1549–57.

Between campaigns Kuo Jung carefully consolidated his position. In 956 he had appointed officials to govern his territorial gains, and that year and the next he attended to affairs of state such as adopting a new calendar, commissioning new sacrificial vessels, displaying great respect to a senior minister, and refusing to choose an heir from among his own young children while there were adults better suited, thereby trying to avoid a destabilizing regency. Other measures included a decree that taxes would be collected only in the sixth and tenth months, and not earlier, allowing taxpayers time to gather the harvest and spin silk. After Shou-chou fell, Kuo issued an amnesty to its inhabitants and opened the prefectural granaries to feed the starving. He reorganized the surrendered Southern T'ang forces as the Huai-te army and rewarded the brilliant commander of the Huai-nan campaigns, Chao K'uang-yin, with a governorship. Kuo undertook more work on the waterways around his own capital, and ordered the compilation of the *Ta Chou hsing-t'ung* (*Law codes of the Great Chou*), containing explanations of the law. Crafting his image as a virtuous ruler, he received a series of memorials on topics ranging from rites and music to expeditionary logistics. He commissioned scholars from all over Later Chou territory to examine memorials and the Classics for ideas on military methods and on the improvement of officialdom.[211]

Displays of virtue were always reinforced by military success. Late in 957, Kuo Jung led a major land and water assault on Hao-chou, on the Huai River east of Shou-chou. The Hao-chou commander, valuing the perception of his loyalty, would not surrender formally to Kuo until he had consulted with the Southern T'ang court. Whereas the Shou-chou commander had refused to accept any commission from the Later Chou, his Hao-chou counterpart was not reluctant to join the Later Chou ranks.[212] Remembering the consequences of the pillaging of Huai-nan by Later Chou troops, Kuo Jung enforced strict discipline when Ssu-chou (east of Hao-chou) was captured. However, his most dramatic successes were on the waterways. At Ch'u-chou, the last city before the coast, a major advance by Kuo down the Huai River and along both its banks to Ch'u-chou destroyed or captured the entire Southern T'ang navy. Further south, Yang-chou on the Yangtze River was simply abandoned by the Southern T'ang. Kuo Jung wanted to move his navy from the Huai River onto the Yangtze, but the Southern T'ang still controlled access to the canal that connected the two waterways near Ch'u-chou. Kuo's response was to build a new channel and bypass the blockade. This feat astonished the Southern

---

[211] *TCTC* 293, pp. 9555, 9559, 9562–4, 9567–9, 9571–3.

[212] *TCTC* 293, pp. 9573, 9575. The province of which Shou-chou was the seat had been renamed Chung-cheng, "loyal and upright," further reflecting the important political use of the virtue of loyalty (*TCTC* 293, p. 9568).

T'ang forces on the Yangtze, and Kuo won several victories on and along the river. At Ch'u-chou, the Southern T'ang garrison fought in vain to the last breath. With both rivers effectively controlled by the ships of the Later Chou, the Southern T'ang imperial house descended into accusations and scheming among the princes, and in a final effort to stem the Later Chou advance Li Ching offered Kuo Jung the last four of the fourteen Huai-nan prefectures if Kuo would accept the Yangtze River as the border and cease hostilities. Li also offered to abdicate in favor of his heir apparent. This time Kuo Jung accepted. In the final agreement Li Ching did not abdicate, but accepted the subordinate title of *kuo-wang* (prince of the state), adopting the Later Chou calendar and surrendering the trappings of imperial status.[213]

Responding to the imminent Southern T'ang defeat, the ruler of the Southern Han regime had already offered tribute to Kuo Jung (never having accepted the legitimacy of the Central Plains regimes before), while mournfully preparing against an attack. Wu-Yüeh, employing a strategy of careful diplomacy, was rewarded for assisting the Later Chou, as was the independent governor of Ching-nan.[214] Southern T'ang itself, though firmly subordinated, was treated with considerable respect, and a special bureau established in K'ai-feng to provide diplomatic representation for the Southern T'ang. This institution resembles later handling of relations with particularly important foreign powers. It also may suggest the nature and significance of the relationship with Southern T'ang. A flurry of envoys discussing which Southern T'ang ministers should take the blame for their defeat seems to have established some parameters for relations between the Later Chou and Southern T'ang. Subsequently, Kuo Jung refused further subordination from Li Ching and permitted him to repair his defenses.[215]

The Huai-nan campaign proved to be the longest and most important campaign of the unification, making Kuo Jung fight at least as hard for his expansion as Chu Wen and Li Ts'un-hsü had fought for theirs.[216] The biggest gain for the Later Chou was economic, starting with the huge amounts of goods captured during the campaign and continuing with the large annual tribute from the remainder of the Southern T'ang regime, amounting to some million measures a year of silver, silk, coin, tea, and grain. The salt pans of Huai-nan

[213] *TCTC* 293, pp. 9574–81; see also *CWTS* 117, pp. 1562–70.

[214] *TCTC* 293, pp. 9576, 9581. On Wu-Yüeh's strategy, see Edmund H. Worthy, Jr., "Diplomacy for survival: Domestic and foreign relations of Wu Yüeh, 907–978," in *China among equals: The Middle Kingdom and its neighbors, 10th–14th centuries,* ed. Morris Rossabi (Berkeley, Calif., 1983), pp. 17–44; and the next chapter of this volume.

[215] *TCTC* 294, pp. 9584–90, 9599.

[216] See Lü, *Sui T'ang Wu-tai shih,* p. 694, who attributes Kuo Jung's victory to T'ang weakness rather than Chou strength.

had contributed significantly to making the regional regimes the wealthiest in the south, and they now greatly strengthened the economic basis for further Later Chou conquests. More important still, the productive land and dense population – 226,574 registered households in fourteen prefectures – provided a rice basket together with an infrastructure of waterways. The population increase for the Later Chou may have been as much as thirty percent. Kuo Jung extended dredging and repairs to reopen the major canal system to K'ai-feng and allow grain to be shipped from the south. Meanwhile, Later Chou naval patrols on the Yangtze River, and a reliance on the Later Chou for salt produced by the pans in Huai-nan, were a constant reminder of Southern T'ang inferiority and vulnerability.[217]

Returning to K'ai-feng in triumph, Kuo Jung continued his program of symbolic legitimation by promulgating his completed law code and promoting the study of rites and music.[218] In practical matters, Kuo was particularly concerned about agriculture, and he was at pains to display himself as its sponsor. His most important agrarian policy was an attempt to equalize the land tax. He sent a treatise to all circuits together with thirty-four commissioners to enforce the proposals. The intention was to distribute land equally to landless refugees, thereby settling the population, fostering prosperity, and increasing tax revenue. This measure necessitated a land survey, completed in a few months, and brought a huge area of land onto the registers. Some of this land was exempted to reduce resistance from those whose tax assessments were suddenly raised, but the increase in state revenues must still have been enormous. We have figures only for K'ai-feng prefecture, but there the registered land increased from 12,000 to 42,000 *ch'ing* (approximately 168,000 to 588,000 acres), of which 4,000 *ch'ing* were exempted.[219] Other economic measures included regularizing salary payments and further improving waterways around the capital. The latter facilitated grain transportation, producing a threefold increase in land-tax receipts from the capital district and making it easier to send relief when famine hit Huai-nan. Providing relief also gave Kuo Jung another opportunity to demonstrate his awareness of his responsibilities toward the common people, whom he now declared to be his children.[220]

---

[217] *TCTC* 294, pp. 9582–3, 9595; *CWTS* 118, p. 1570; Worthy, "The founding of Sung China," pp. 38–9.

[218] *TCTC* 294, pp. 9585, 9591–4. This code provided the basis for the Sung law code of 962. See Brian E. McKnight, *Law and order in Sung China* (Cambridge, 1992), p. 334.

[219] *TCTC* 294, pp. 9587–8, 9595; *CWTS* 118, p. 1574; Wang, *Wu-tai hui-yao* 25, p. 402. See also Worthy, "The founding of Sung China," pp. 39–40; Han, *Ch'ai Jung*, pp. 55–7.

[220] *TCTC* 294, pp. 9589, 9594–5.

The Later Chou assault on the north, 958–959

Kuo Jung now considered his next target for expansion. He sent an expeditionary force to the southwest, but the armies of the Later Shu, having geography and logistics on their side, annihilated them. Kuo then looked north to the Sixteen Prefectures,[221] a region desirable in itself and a means of distracting the Liao from supporting Northern Han. Liu Ch'ung of Northern Han had died in 955, and the forces of his successor, Liu Ch'eng-chün (Han Hsiao-ho-ti, 955–68), had reached Lu-chou's city walls while Kuo Jung was finishing off Huai-nan. Later Chou retaliation began with the capture of Shu-ch'eng by a local governor in the summer of 958, and was swiftly followed by the capture of six fortresses and a city in Northern Han. The Ts'ang-chou governor in southern Ho-pei had improved the waterways heading north toward Ying-chou and Mo-chou, well inside Liao territory. Using these newly connected watercourses, Kuo Jung led a land and water force straight to the border without disturbing the Ho-pei population. The Liao pass of I-chin-kuan surrendered, and Kuo Jung, abandoning his boats as the river narrowed, captured Wa-ch'iao Pass and then Yü-k'ou Pass, as well as the Liao prefectures of Ying-chou, Mo-chou, and I-chou. The southern part of the administrative territory controlled from the Liao Southern Capital (formerly Yu-chou) had fallen without bloodshed in less than three weeks, but Kuo Jung withdrew because of illness. As usual, the gains were incorporated administratively, defenses improved, and garrisons installed. Later Chou generals continued to nibble at the holdings of Liao's ally, the Northern Han, taking cities and fortresses with little resistance, and that autumn the Southern T'ang governor of Fu-chien at Ch'üan-chou offered his submission to Kuo.[222]

Much of Kuo's appeal derived from the program of expansion itself. Success in war was an important part of this, but the corollaries of the expansion policy also helped to persuade more people that their interests lay with supporting Kuo and the Later Chou state. War had been an almost constant feature of the Five Dynasties period, but until now much of the fighting had occurred within the Central Plains regimes rather than beyond them: Chu Wen's conquest of Honan, his wars with Li K'o-yung and Li Ts'un-hsü, the Liao conquest, and of course, innumerable rebellions, successful or otherwise. By contrast, although Kuo's armies brought widespread havoc to neighboring

---

[221] *TCTC* 294, pp. 9587–8.
[222] *TCTC* 294, pp. 9583–9600; *CWTS* 118, p. 1572; 119, pp. 1580–2; T'o-t'o et al., *Liao shih* 6, pp. 74–5. Lü Ssu-mien, in *Sui T'ang Wu-tai shih*, p. 697, presents a negative view of this campaign in particular and of Kuo Jung in general.

regions that had enjoyed significant periods of peace and prosperity, Kuo's campaigns did not wreak devastation on his own people, and even brought benefits to many levels of Later Chou society, in addition to the advantages to Kuo Jung and his central administration. The absence of war within Later Chou territory allowed the population to benefit from a sustained economic recovery. This recovery was further stimulated by policies such as the dredging of waterways, and other infrastructure improvements. Although Kuo's aim may have been to improve military communications, commerce benefited as well. Kuo's military success depended on the strength of his armies, and continual victorious campaigning kept those armies and their commanders occupied and well rewarded. This kept them happy as well and greatly reduced the potential danger they posed to Kuo himself. Kuo's military might also convinced the governors and prefects that there was nothing to be gained from resisting his authority, and the transformation of the Later Chou's neighboring states into implacable opponents meant that there was nowhere for the potential rebels to turn for outside assistance. This development of distinct external foes positioned Kuo Jung's subjects – including the governors – on the same side, and because the imperial armies could now offer a credible defense against those outside threats, most governors were willing to accept subordination in return for security. Kuo reinforced the advantages of this trade-off by leaving most of their privileges intact and consciously placing his trust in these governors.[223] He made no attempt to impose his authority on those few governors who remained effectively autonomous, notably the Ting-nan governors in the northwest. Kuo's program of expansion helped significantly in the effort to win over potential domestic challengers, whose support he then incorporated into his expansionist efforts, creating a cycle that only increased his appeal as a virtuous ruler.

Kuo Jung had enlarged the Later Chou empire from 96 to 118 prefectures, but at the age of thirty-nine he was dying. Despite his earlier rejection of a child successor, he spent his last few weeks selecting regents for his seven-year-old son, Kuo Tsung-hsün (Chou Kung-ti, 959), who came to the throne in the sixth month of 959. Although Kuo Jung's authority had been far stronger than that of any previous Five Dynasties ruler, its resonance was insufficient to sustain a child on the throne. That autumn the Southern T'ang began minting their own coins in response to a shortage of cash and decided to build a new capital at Hung-chou (modern Nan-ch'ang in Kiangsi province), strategically stronger than Chin-ling. These moves may have served to test the resolve of

---

[223] *TCTC* 293, p. 9560.

the Later Chou regency, but more dangerous to Chou was a potential alliance between the Southern T'ang and Liao. Later Chou subterfuge scuttled this alliance, however. When a Liao mission arrived in Southern T'ang territory, a Later Chou prefect in Huai-nan bribed some Southern T'ang officials to kill the lead envoy, a member of the Liao imperial house, causing the Liao emperor to sever relations and robbing the Southern T'ang of a much-needed ally.[224]

The ultimate test of the regime came six months later, in the new year of 960, with a report from Chen-chou and Ting-chou that the Northern Han and Liao had launched an attack. It is said that Chao K'uang-yin's palace army, which had long served under him, refused to fight against Liao as long as there was a minor on the throne. The soldiers ostensibly demanded that Chao seize power and become emperor. As in the case of Kuo Wei and the founding of the Later Chou, a Liao attack provided the justification for overthrowing the ruling house, and once again the claimant ignored the danger from the north in order to march to the capital (twenty miles to the southwest) and declare himself emperor (Sung T'ai-tsu, 960–76). Only two Later Chou governors resisted: Li Yün who had helped Kuo Wei take the throne and was now governor at Lu-chou, and Kuo Wei's nephew Li Ch'ung-chin, governor at Yang-chou in Huai-nan. Both were quelled easily, having failed to coordinate their efforts and rally allies in the face of the loyal and powerful Sung palace army. Li Ch'ung-chin was denied the Southern T'ang help he sought; Li Yün was slow to involve the Northern Han, and when he did seek their assistance he specified that the Liao were not to be involved.[225] Li Yün had imperial ambitions of his own and had no wish to become a second Shih Ching-t'ang, subordinate to another power. But without the assistance that could only be provided by another state, a regional rebel stood little chance of success.

Chao K'uang-yin and his brother, Chao K'uang-i (Sung T'ai-tsung, r. 976–97), continued the expansion begun by the Later Chou and did not cease until the Northern Han were finally beaten into submission in 979. Both brothers possessed considerable appeal as rulers, combining political skill with military leadership, bestowing generosity and trust, requiring propriety of themselves and their followers, and making direct requests to the common people. The Sung dynasty founders could rely on their followers to remain loyal partly because those followers lacked the independent resources to mount a challenge, and, significantly, because serving the Sung was the best option available for

[224] *TCTC* 294, pp. 9601–6; *CWTS* 119, pp. 1582–4.

[225] For detailed discussion and extensive references, see Worthy, "The founding of Sung China," pp. 42–4, and chapter 3 of this volume.

those at court, in the provinces, and at all levels of society. Potential challengers were now co-opted rather than coerced. This narrowing of alternatives had taken place in the preceding half century, partly from conscious effort, and partly from the unforeseen consequences of having to make immediate choices within highly constrained circumstances. These constrained circumstances and limited alternatives were themselves the legacy of a much longer period of uncertainty created by the An Lu-shan rebellion.

CHAPTER 2

THE SOUTHERN KINGDOMS BETWEEN THE T'ANG AND THE SUNG, 907–979

Hugh R. Clark

INTRODUCTION

The years between the collapse of T'ang dynastic authority that began in the mid-ninth century and the establishment of Sung authority in the later part of the tenth century were a period of great turmoil and change. The preceding chapter discussed the political history in north China through these decades. The present chapter focuses on the regions straddling and south of the Yangtze River. Historians have referred to the states that controlled this southern territory as the Ten Kingdoms, but this terminology is misleading. In fact, one of the so-called Ten Kingdoms is the Northern Han, located in northern Shansi. The Northern Han was a successor state to the Later Han dynasty of the north and belongs in a discussion of the northern dynasties. Of the nine kingdoms of the south that are covered in the following discussion, never more than seven existed at any one time (see figure 4 and table 3).

Four of these southern kingdoms governed their territories for almost the entire interregnum period: Wu-Yüeh (902–78), located in the Liang-che region of the Yangtze River delta, was the richest and most stable. Ch'u (907–64), centered in the region of modern Hunan, controlled the central Yangtze River valley. Ching-nan (907–63) was a tiny principality at the confluence of the Han and Yangtze rivers that survived among much larger kingdoms through diplomatic skill. Southern Han (909–71) occupied territory covered by the modern provinces of Kwangtung and Kwangsi. The Min kingdom (909–45) controlled the Fu-chien region (modern Fukien province) before it was assimilated by neighboring states after an internal fratricidal orgy of murder and mayhem. Only an autonomous warlord enclave (Chang-Ch'üan, 945–78) made up from the southern Fu-chien prefectures of Ch'üan-chou and Chang-chou endured until the close of the era. Chang-Ch'üan is not generally included among the southern kingdoms because it was nominally subordinate to the neighboring Southern T'ang. There were also two pairs of successor states: in the Chiang-Huai region straddling the middle section of the Yangtze

River, the Wu kingdom (902–37) was succeeded immediately by the Southern T'ang (937–75), and in Szechwan, the Former Shu kingdom (907–25) was
succeeded by the Later Shu (934–65).

Much as the Five Dynasties of the north inherited the legacy of the T'ang
dynastic heartland, the southern kingdoms were the product of developments
across the south in the eighth and ninth centuries. As preceding volumes
in this series have explained, these were the centuries when the south was
finally and irrevocably incorporated into the larger Chinese empire. This process began in the latter half of the Warring States period that preceded the
Ch'in dynasty (221–206 B.C.E.) and continued to unfold through the centuries and dynasties that followed. Even as late as the An Lu-shan rebellion
of the mid-eighth century, the long-time dynastic capital, Ch'ang-an, and
the North China Plain and its western extension along the Wei River valley
remained the political and cultural center for the Chinese-speaking world. If
population was gradually expanding in the south, especially in the fertile and
easily tilled river valleys, the vast reaches south of the Yangtze River remained
peripheral and exotic, lands to which losers in political struggles could be
banished in full expectation that they would succumb to the mysterious and
deadly miasmas that northerners so feared. These northern elites continued to
disparage the south as rustic and uncivilized well into the succeeding Sung
dynasty.

However, freed by the destruction of the An Lu-shan rebellion from the
limitations upon movement and relocation imposed by the *tsu-yung-tiao* (or
grain-labor-materials) tax system of the early T'ang dynasty, large numbers of
dislocated people had moved to the comparatively unaffected south. Through
the later eighth and ninth centuries new networks of settlement and trade
transformed the region. Old cores such as the lower reaches of the Yangtze
valley, the Ch'eng-tu Plain of Szechwan, and the maritime port of Kuang-
chou (Canton) in the far south were infused with new vitality, while new cores
emerged on the Tung-t'ing and P'o-yang lakes of the central Yangtze River
and along the coast of Fu-chien. The southern kingdoms formed around these
widely separated core regions.

As is so often the case in human history, the upheavals that gave birth
and context to these kingdoms featured an intriguing cast of disreputable
actors. Yang Hsing-mi, founder of the Wu kingdom, first emerged as a local
bandit in Huai-nan and capitalized on the chaos of Huang Ch'ao's rebellion
to build his own network of followers, who operated as freelancers without
giving loyalty to any cause. In the aftermath of the rebellion, however, as
loyalist forces regained control of the empire, Yang sought protection in the
restorationist armies before finally abandoning the T'ang cause and laying
the foundations of the first Huai-nan kingdom. Wang Chien, who founded

the Former Shu kingdom in Szechwan, likewise capitalized on the chaos of Huang Ch'ao's rebellion to transcend his early career as a bandit. In contrast to the freelance operations of Yang Hsing-mi, Wang, whose initial sphere of operations was in the plains south of K'ai-feng, actually joined Huang's uprising before the latter abandoned the north in 878. He nevertheless declined to follow Huang's subsequent march to the south, instead joining the army of Ch'in Tsung-ch'üan, one of the great warlords who emerged from the ashes of the rebellion. After Huang's rebellion had been suppressed, Wang Chien was among the loyalist forces who traveled to Szechwan to join the imperial court in its wartime refuge; when the court returned to the east, Wang remained in Szechwan where he laid the foundations of his state. The Ch'u founder, Ma Yin, had more obscure beginnings, but he too wound up joining Ch'in Tsung-ch'üan, albeit under the autonomous command of Sun Ju, himself one of the most nefariously intriguing characters of the time. When Sun broke with Ch'in late in the 880s, Ma Yin stayed loyal to his commander. But when Sun Ju's army broke up in factional strife in 892, Ma Yin struck off on his own on a path that took him to Hunan, where he stepped into a power vacuum and established his kingdom.

These men are only some of the figures who populate the narrative that follows. For all the morbid fascination they engender they are not what makes the history of the south through the long century of the interregnum important. As the following chapter will demonstrate, the tenth century was when the south emerged as the heart of the larger Chinese polity. Although the southern kingdoms were not above their own political intrigues and fratricidal strife, they were spared the regular chaos that so disrupted life in the north. This made them attractive to the countless men and women of the northern plain whose lives were uprooted and homes destroyed, and all the southern kingdoms benefited from the resulting migration of northerners to the south. Population in the region of the warlord enclave of southern Fu-chien, for example, rose fivefold, from approximately 30,000 households in the eighth century to over 150,000 in 978, when the enclave submitted to Sung authority; that of Fu-chou, the metropolitan center of northern Fu-chien, similarly though less dramatically rose from between 35,000 and 40,000 households in the eighth century to over 90,000 according to data submitted by the Wu-Yüeh authorities to the Sung government in 978.[1]

---

[1] Population data is taken from Yüeh Shih, *T'ai-p'ing huan-yü chi* [Ch'en Lan-sen 1793 ed.] (c. 980; Taipei, 1963), pp. 101–2. The *T'ai-p'ing huan-yü chi* is supplemented by the *Ying Sung-pen T'ai-p'ing huan-yü chi pu-ch'üeh* (1882–4; Taipei, 1963), which reconstitutes chapters missing from Ch'en Lan-sen's edition of *T'ai-p'ing huan-yü chi* from other sources. The *T'ai-p'ing huan-yü chi* is one of the earliest extant Chinese gazetteers and an immensely important source of T'ang, Five Dynasties, and Ten Kingdoms geographical and economic data.

The massive infusion of newcomers from the north energized the south. In many areas, indigenous elite structures were overwhelmed and heretofore déclassé men and their extended kin thrust into positions of political authority and the social prominence that goes with it. Throughout the south, moreover, the restoration of stability that had been accomplished by the first decade of the tenth century unleashed a surge of economic activity. Land was reclaimed and paddies extended. New crops such as the drought-resistant, quick-ripening strains of rice known as Champa rice were introduced, leading to unprecedented crop yields.[2] At the same time, production of textiles and other artisanal crafts expanded, and trade developed among the southern kingdoms themselves, between the southern kingdoms and the northern dynasties, and (of greatest long-term importance) between the coastal kingdoms and the further lands of southeast Asia and beyond.

These are the issues that will frame our discussion of this period through the following pages. In order to understand the southern kingdoms, however, we must begin with the late T'ang, with events that have been covered in detail by Robert Somers in volume 3 of this series.[3] As Somers demonstrated, the retreat of T'ang power and legitimate authority in the south was underway at least by the mid-ninth century.[4] Perhaps the first major overt sign of the unfolding process was the revolt of Ch'iu Fu, which devastated the critical lands of Che-tung (modern Chekiang) in 859–60. This revolt is of interest both for its causes and for the composition of its leadership.[5] Somers pointed to popular distress caused by heavy governmental taxation as an important though not the exclusive cause of the revolt. At least as critical to the subsequent history of the southern kingdoms, however, was the composition of Ch'iu Fu's following.

---

[2] For discussion, see Christian Lamouroux, "Crise politique et developpement rizicole en Chine: la region du Jiang-Huai (VIIIe-Xe siècle)," *Bulletin de l'École Française d'Extrême-Orient* 82 (1995), pp. 145–83.

[3] Robert Somers, "The end of the T'ang," in *The Cambridge history of China*, volume 3: *Sui and T'ang China, 589–906, part 1*, ed. Denis C. Twitchett (Cambridge, 1979), pp. 682–789. See also the extensive Chinese and Japanese secondary literature cited therein. For a recent study of early sources for the period, see Johannes L. Kurz, "Survey of the historical sources for the Five Dynasties and Ten States in Song times," *Journal of Sung-Yuan Studies* 33 (2003), pp. 187–224. For overviews of the Five Dynasties period in general, see the previous chapter and its sources.

[4] Somers, "The end of the T'ang." See also Somers's unpublished paper "Banditry, militarization, and state formation in late T'ang: The origins of Sung China," China Colloquium of the School of International Studies, University of Washington, Seattle, 31 May 1979.

[5] In addition to Somers's brief account of Ch'iu Fu's revolt, studies include Wang Shou-nan, "Lun wan T'ang Ch'iu Fu chih luan," *Kuo-li Cheng-chih ta-hsüeh hsüeh-pao* 19 (1969), pp. 283–308, and Matsui Shūichi, "Tōdai kōhanki no Kō-Wai ni tsuite – kōzoku oyobi Kō Zentai, Kyū Ho no hanran o chūshin to shite," *Shigaku zasshi* 66 No. 2 (1957), pp. 1–29. See also the synopses "Kyū no ran" in Tanigawa Michio and Mori Masao, eds., *Chūgoku minshu hanran shi* (Tokyo, 1978–83), vol. 1, pp. 301–18; and Chang Tse-hsien, *T'ang Wu-tai nung-min chan-cheng shih-liao hui-p'ien*, (Peking, 1979), vol. 1, pp. 241–54.

Ch'iu himself is described as a "bandit leader" (*tsei-shuai*) in contemporary sources.[6] Although a strongly pejorative term, it actually tells us very little about him. The surviving official sources are of the kind that tended to describe rebels in such terms, regardless of their precise background. As Ch'iu Fu's revolt gained momentum, other "bandit leaders" rallied around him, bringing their men to his cause. Ssu-ma Kuang tells us: "Bandits from the mountains and the sea, ne'er-do-wells and refugees from other provinces, came from all four directions and gathered like clouds around Ch'iu Fu."[7]

This was the first large-scale rebellion of the T'ang period south of the Yangtze River. This region had generally remained peaceful throughout the dynasty, although there was an ominous growth of banditry and lawlessness in the 830s and 840s. Somers maintained that Ch'iu Fu's rebellion "was the first revolt in late T'ang times to weld, however briefly, a large number of rural bandit gangs into a unified military and political force."[8] Of equal significance, and perhaps more revealing of who Ch'iu Fu may really have been, was Ch'iu Fu's apparent ability to find support among the local educated elites, the very class one would expect to have been most likely to support the T'ang dynasty and least likely to rally round the apparently quixotic cause of a local bandit. Among Ch'iu Fu's principal followers was one Wang Lu, whom Ssu-ma Kuang identified as a *chin-shih* degree holder and so a notable member of the regional elite.[9] Although Wang Lu is the only member of the elite whom we know joined Ch'iu Fu's rebellion, his participation suggests a growing alienation not just on the part of the common people but even of the more secure and protected strata of society.

Although Ch'iu Fu's revolt was crushed within a year, there is no indication that the T'ang court sought or was able to undertake steps to resolve the stresses that lay behind it. Indeed, at the close of the 860s a second major revolt, this one led by P'ang Hsün, enveloped eastern Huai-nan and Shantung.[10] Although this revolt began as an army mutiny, its rapid spread was the result of complex social factors, in part traceable to the same economic distress that lay behind the uprising of Ch'iu Fu. P'ang Hsün's uprising, like Ch'iu Fu's, appealed to a wide range of people, including "bandit gangs from modern Shantung, Huai-hsi, Huai-nan and even from as far south as Chekiang, and was supported by local

---

[6] See Ssu-ma Kuang, *Tzu-chih t'ung-chien* [hereafter *TCTC*], (1086; reprint of the 1956 edition, Hong Kong, 1972) 249, p. 8077; Liu Hsü et al. eds., *Chiu T'ang-shu* (945; Peking, 1975) 19, p. 650, refers to Ch'iu as a "rural bandit" (*ts'ao-tsei*).

[7] *TCTC* 250, p. 8080.

[8] Somers, "The end of the T'ang," pp. 688–9.

[9] *TCTC* 250, p. 8083.

[10] Somers, "The end of the T'ang," pp. 695–700. See also Robert des Rotours, "La révolte de P'ang Hiun, 868–869," *T'oung Pao* 56 (1970), pp. 229–40.

peasants, and by some members of the educated gentry."[11] Not insignificantly, except for Shantung, these were all areas that a few decades later would come under the authority of one or another of the southern kingdoms, revealing a groundswell of discontent across much of the south that affected all classes and types of men.

The greatest revolt, and the one that finally destroyed the remaining vestiges of imperial legitimacy for the T'ang court, was the rebellion of Wang Hsien-chih and Huang Ch'ao, which wrought havoc throughout central and south regions of the empire from 875 until 880, and then devastated the north and destroyed the T'ang capital, Ch'ang-an, before it was suppressed in 884. This revolt was truly one of the greatest uprisings in history, and its story has consequently been told many times.[12] The rebellion began in 874–5 in the same area of southwestern Shantung that had been devastated five years earlier by P'ang Hsün's rebellion. In the face of Wang Hsien-chih and Huang Ch'ao offensives, T'ang forces were incompetently led and acquitted themselves disastrously. But by 877, government forces stabilized control of the areas east of the imperial secondary capital, Lo-yang, and forced the rebels south toward the Yangtze River. Wang Hsien-chih was killed during this retreat, and leadership fell to Huang Ch'ao alone. Thereupon, Huang Ch'ao unexpectedly led the rebel army across the Yangtze River and into the heartlands of the south. Huang Ch'ao and his forces first marauded through the P'o-yang Lake region northeast to Hsüan-chou (in Anhwei), and then south through the wealthy port city of Fu-chou (Fu-chien) and on to Kuang-chou, which he sacked with great bloodshed.[13]

In the months that followed, Huang Ch'ao, pressured by his men who had grown unhappy and sickly in the sultry climate of the south, abandoned Kuang-chou and resumed his marauding. This time he headed back to the north. After spending the winter months of 879–80 just south of the Yangtze River, he recrossed the Yangtze in the seventh month of 880 and was never to bother the south again. But he had done extensive damage. His campaign through the south left local T'ang administrative structures a shambles. In their stead, local and regional structures of power began to develop. If the emerging leadership in the south did not immediately renounce their "loyalty" to the T'ang, it was mostly because no one else had come forth to fill the political vacuum and compete for their allegiance. This nominal allegiance to the T'ang dynasty should not, however, obscure the fact that the structures that arose

---

[11] Somers, "The end of the T'ang," p. 699.

[12] My account is based on Somers, "The end of the T'ang," pp. 727–45, and TCTC 253, as excerpted in Chang, T'ang Wu-tai nung-min chan-cheng, pp. 462–73.

[13] See map 21 in Somers, "The end of the T'ang," p. 738.

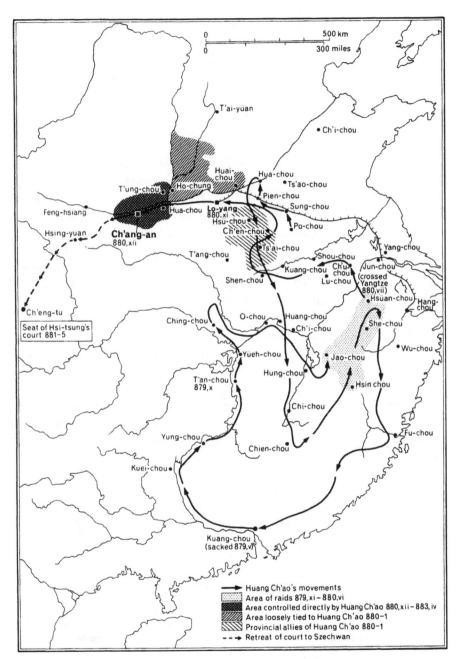

Map 10. Huang Ch'ao's movements, 878–880.

in the wake of Huang Ch'ao's rampage through the south were independent. From these independent structures came the new state structures of the tenth century.

FROM BANDITRY TO STATE FORMATION, 875–C. 910

Wu-Yüeh

In 875, one Wang Ying, a minor military official in a coastal garrison on the Yangtze River delta, rebelled, capturing Su-chou and Ch'ang-chou before taking to the sea to raid as far south as Wen-chou in coastal regions of Chekiang and Fu-chien. The court, after some delay, sent a large force from various garrisons in Honan to put down the rebellion and ordered the provinces around the lower Yangtze to mobilize their naval forces against Wang. They also directed local officials to recruit troops to suppress him.[14] It is in this context that two of the pivotal figures of the following years in the Liang-che region emerge: Tung Ch'ang, and his subordinate – and the future Wu-Yüeh founder – Ch'ien Liu. When faced with Wang Ying's assault on his home prefecture of Hang-chou, Tung Ch'ang organized a popular militia (t'u-t'uan) to provide resistance.[15] For his successes in the suppression of Wang Ying, who was finally cornered and killed in the spring of 877, Tung Ch'ang was named commander of the Shih-ching Garrison in Hang-chou. The years 878 and 879 were critical in the emergence of local power structures in the Che-tung (or greater Yangtze delta) area. In 878, as mentioned earlier, Huang Ch'ao passed through the area, avoiding any of the major population centers but causing alarm all the same. But more significantly, in that same year other rebels "swarmed like bees" in the areas recently affected by Wang Ying.[16] In response, each county in the Hang-chou area organized a militia force of one thousand men under local leadership. With Tung Ch'ang in charge of the whole structure, these forces came to be known as the Eight Battalions of Hang-chou (Hang-chou pa-tu). Ch'ien Liu served under Tung Ch'ang as a cavalry officer.[17]

[14] Regarding Wang Ying's uprising, see *TCTC* 252–3, especially pp. 8178–9.

[15] *TCTC* 253, p. 8210; Fan Chiung and Lin Yü, *Wu-Yüeh pei-shih* (11th c.; Taipei, 1966) 1, p. 21a. Sakurai Haruko (following Watanabe Michio) notes that Tung was most likely a prominent local landowner: "Without a doubt, the leaders of the Eight Battalions of Hang-chou, including Tung Ch'ang, Ch'eng Chi, Tu Ling, Wu Kung-yüeh and others, provided rural leadership and were from the major land-owning class." See Sakurai Haruko, "Godai Jikkoku no Go-Etsu ni tsuite," *Nara shien* 15 (1967), p. 13.

[16] On the rebels, see *TCTC* 253, p. 8210, and Fan and Lin, *Wu-Yüeh pei-shih* 1, p. 3a.

[17] See *TCTC* 253, p. 8210. On the Eight Battalions, see Tanigawa Michio, "Tōdai no hanchin ni tsuite – Setsusei no baai," *Shirin* 35 No. 3 (1952), pp. 297–8. Fan and Lin, *Wu-Yüeh pei-shih* 1, p. 3b date the formal organization of the Eight Battalions to the aftermath of defeating Huang Ch'ao.

Ch'ien Liu, the founder of the Wu-Yüeh state, was born in 852 in a village of Lin-an county in Hang-chou prefecture to a family of farmers and fishermen.[18] The family was poor, and the life it offered apparently had little appeal to young Ch'ien Liu. Instead, he spent his time with a band of similarly alienated youth who gathered together under a village tree. As the leader of this band, Ch'ien Liu would sit on a great rock and direct his friends in war games: "His orders had the force of law, and his comrades were generally fearful of him."[19] Although one source tells us that Ch'ien Liu was "a rascal who rejected all work,"[20] it would be more accurate to suggest only that he disdained all legitimate work. We are told by one source that he engaged in "resolving disputes and exacting revenge," and by another that he traded illegally in salt.[21] When he and his friends were not playing war games among the trees, they were available for hire for an assortment of disreputable tasks that could perhaps best be summarily described as thuggery, terrorism, and smuggling.

Although Ch'ien Liu may have run his gang through fear, there was apparently a measure of loyalty within it. He is described as "fond of chivalry" (*jen-hsia*), a code of martial behavior with ancient roots in Chinese culture that was applied to the warrior and so contrasted with the civil morality of the scholar.[22] In a story that may be apocryphal but is very revealing of the values on which Ch'ien Liu's gang was built, we hear of the Chung brothers, "drinking buddies" of Ch'ien Liu and the sons of Chung Ch'i, a clerk in the county office of Lin-an county.[23] Chung Ch'i, as we can well imagine of someone anxious to protect a marginal claim to membership in the civil elite, disapproved of the disreputable Ch'ien Liu and vainly sought to forbid his sons from seeing him. Their continued loyalty to Ch'ien Liu in the face of their father's objections is evidence of the strong ties that bound Ch'ien Liu's gang and of the degree to which Ch'ien's companions elevated *jen-hsia* over the civil morality by which the T'ang elite defined itself. Thus when Wang Ying's uprising erupted throughout the Yangtze delta in 875, Ch'ien Liu was

---

[18] There are many biographies of Ch'ien Liu. I have used the following: Hsüeh Chü-cheng et al., eds., *Chiu Wu-tai shih* [hereafter *CWTS*] (974; Peking, 1976) 133, pp. 1766–72; Ou-yang Hsiu, *Hsin Wu-tai shih* (1073; Peking, 1974) 67, pp. 835–41; Fan and Lin, *Wu-Yüeh pei-shih* 1; Wu Jen-ch'en, *Shih-kuo ch'un-ch'iu* (1669; Peking, 1983) 77–8, pp. 1045–1116. On the Ch'ien family occupation, see *CWTS* 133, p. 1768. See also Sakurai, "Godai Jikkoku no Go-Etsu ni tsuite," p. 13.

[19] Ou-yang, *Hsin Wu-tai shih* 67, p. 835. This passage is echoed in *TCTC* 267, p. 8727. See also Chan Chieh, *I-shih chi-wen* (Shanghai, 1927), p. 1a.

[20] Ou-yang, *Hsin Wu-tai shih* 67, p. 835. The term *wu-lai* was often used to describe the alienated men who led the many forces contributing to the collapse of the T'ang. See Somers, "Banditry, militarization, and state formation," p. 11.

[21] *CWTS* 133, p. 1766, and Ou-yang, *Hsin Wu-tai shih* 67, p. 835, respectively.

[22] *CWTS* 133, p. 1766.

[23] Ou-yang, *Hsin Wu-tai shih* 67, pp. 835–6.

the leader of a band of loyal followers tied by bonds of *jen-hsia*. It was this band, not just Ch'ien Liu, that Tung Ch'ang enrolled in his emerging regional defense alliance, though it was Ch'ien whom Tung Ch'ang made his second in command.

When Tung Ch'ang and Ch'ien Liu confronted Huang Ch'ao as he approached Hang-chou in 878, Huang swerved away rather than battle the Eight Battalions, confirming the potency of Tung Ch'ang and his troops. In the years that followed, the Eight Battalions ensured local stability. Between 882 and 887, for example, Liu Han-hung, the civil governor of Che-tung, attempted to consolidate his own power in the Liang-che region at the expense of the Eight Battalions.[24] Tung Ch'ang dispatched Ch'ien Liu to deal with this threat, allegedly telling Ch'ien that "If you can seize (Liu Han-hung's base at) Yüeh-chou, I will then grant you Hang-chou."[25] When Ch'ien eliminated Liu Han-hung in 887, Tung Ch'ang did indeed name him prefect of Hang-chou. Tung Ch'ang relocated to Yüeh-chou with the title director of military and civil affairs (*chih chün-fu shih*) in Che-tung.[26]

Ch'ien Liu, over the next few years, consolidated his power in Hang-chou, where he assumed Tung Ch'ang's former position as leader of the Eight Battalions, and expanded to the north as well. These advances brought Ch'ien Liu into conflict with the future Wu founder Yang Hsing-mi in the prefectures surrounding Lake T'ai just as Yang was consolidating his own power in Huai-nan and adjacent areas south of the Yangtze River. This proximity was to lead to near constant conflict between Yang Hsing-mi and Ch'ien Liu in the years to follow. Advancing to the north, however, enabled Ch'ien Liu to avoid conflict with his erstwhile patron Tung Ch'ang, located to Ch'ien's southeast. But in the middle 890s, this inherently unworkable situation broke down.

Tung Ch'ang had maintained a low and relatively benign profile while he consolidated his control over the southeastern reaches of Che-tung.[27] He soon

---

[24] Liu Han-hung first occurs in our sources in the context of Huang Ch'ao's rebellion; Ou-yang Hsiu, *Hsin T'ang shu* (1060; Peking, 1975) 225 *hsia*, p. 6451, lists Liu among Huang's "staff commanders," although Somers points out that Liu at times fought *against* Huang. For Liu's career, see Somers, "The end of the T'ang," p. 726, and the entries concerning him in *TCTC* 253–6.

[25] *TCTC* 256, p. 8339. Fan and Lin, *Wu-Yüeh pei-shih* 1, pp. 6b–7a, says that it was Ch'ien Liu who initiated the final assault after complaining to Tung that he could not bear the situation. Having defeated Liu Han-hung, Ch'ien was preparing to straighten out affairs in Yüeh-chou, but the people of Hang-chou appealed to Tung Ch'ang to name Ch'ien prefect of their city instead.

[26] *TCTC* 256, p. 8341.

[27] This and the following narrative is drawn from Ou-yang, *Hsin T'ang shu* 225 *hsia*, pp. 6466–9; *TCTC* 259, pp. 8460–1; 260, pp. 8463–5. See also Hsü Hsüan, *Chi-shen lu* [*Hsüeh-chin t'ao-yüan* 1805 ed.; 1922] (late 10th c.; Taipei, 1965) 1, pp. 2a–b. Given surviving information, the geographic extent of Tung's power can only be surmised.

began to abuse his power, though, courting favor with the desperate T'ang court by increasing his annual tribute offerings and thereby adding to the burden on the people. At some point he dedicated a shrine to himself and ordered the people to worship there, while the court showered him with ever more grandiose titles. Finally, in the mid-890s, Tung Ch'ang requested that the T'ang court name him King of Yüeh (*Yüeh wang*), but the court now balked. The infuriated Tung Ch'ang ranted that "the Court wishes to belittle me. I have sent uncounted tribute every year, but now the court will not grant me the title King of Yüeh!" Sycophants urged Tung Ch'ang on, saying, "Our Lord is King of Yüeh, but why not Emperor of Yüeh?" In early 895, Tung Ch'ang proclaimed himself emperor (*huang-ti*), calling his new state Ta-Yüeh Lo-p'ing.[28]

Tung Ch'ang's presumptuousness spurred Ch'ien Liu to action. After several months of posturing and negotiating, Ch'ien Liu launched an assault on Tung Ch'ang in the name of the T'ang court. When Tung Ch'ang appealed to Yang Hsing-mi, by now the emerging power in the Huai-nan region, for aid, Yang Hsing-mi attacked Ch'ien Liu's forces in Su-chou, Hang-chou, and elsewhere, but it was not enough to stave off Tung's defeat. In the summer of 896 Tung Ch'ang was captured and beheaded.

Ch'ien Liu had now established a measure of control across most of Che-tung and Che-hsi, a control that the ever-weaker T'ang court was able to confirm only after the fact.[29] Ch'ien Liu's control of the region set the stage for the founding, a decade later in 907, of the state of Wu-Yüeh, the longest-lived of all the southern kingdoms.

Wu

A collapse of central authority similar to that in the Che-tung and Che-hsi region had occurred over the same period and for much the same reasons in the broad area north and south of the lower Yangtze River known collectively as Chiang-Huai (now encompassed by modern Kiangsi province). This region contained two subregions: Huai-nan (an area south of the Huai River, north

---

[28] *TCTC* 259, p. 8460; 260, p. 8464. Somers refers to Lo-p'ing as the first of the southern kingdoms. See Somers, "The end of the T'ang," p. 788.

[29] Che-tung and Che-hsi denote the T'ang military commands on either side of the Che River that emptied into Hang-chou Bay. In 997 the commands were consolidated into the Sung administrative circuit of Liang-che, but then redivided at the beginning of the Southern Sung into Liang-che East and Liang-che West circuits. Liang-che West (or T'ang Che-hsi) encompassed the Yangtze River delta, including Lake T'ai and the wealthy cities of Su-chou and Hang-chou, in Southern Sung, to become the imperial capital; Liang-che East (or T'ang Che-tung) encompassed what is now part of Chekiang province, with its capital at Yüeh-chou (later Shao-hsing fu). For the locations of prefectures referred to in this chapter, refer to map 1 at the front of this volume.

of the Yangtze) and Chiang-nan (an area south of the Yangtze River).[30] Kao
P'ien, a member of a prominent T'ang military lineage and perhaps the foremost T'ang commander at the time of Huang Ch'ao's rebellion, was the first
to establish an independent governorship in Huai-nan. In late 879 he was
appointed military governor (*chieh-tu shih*) of Huai-nan and also salt and iron
commissioner, the most powerful financial authority in the southern and central parts of the empire. He was directed to block Huang Ch'ao's return to
the north.[31] When Huang managed to slip through Kao P'ien's defenses, Kao
lost credibility with the T'ang court. He was, nevertheless, well entrenched in
Huai-nan, and because the court was unable to dislodge him he remained as
an independent governor, with his base at Yang-chou.

Despite Huang Ch'ao's autonomy during the mid-880s there was an under-
current of instability throughout Huai-nan that finally culminated in Kao
P'ien's ouster in 887, engendering a period of incessant conflict.[32] In this context, Yang Hsing-mi, the founder of the state of Wu, emerged and consolidated
his own power.

Yang Hsing-mi was born in 851 to a peasant family of Ho-fei county
in Lu-chou2, a prefecture in the heart of the Huai-nan region.[33] Yang was
apparently no more attracted to a life of tilling the soil than was Ch'ien Liu,
and he too joined a band of local youth with whom he played war games and
from among whom he found his most trusted initial associates. At least two of
these associates – T'ien Chün and T'ao Ya – were natives of Yang's natal village.
T'ien Chün, we are told, "was like a brother to Yang as a youth,"[34] clearly an
echo of the values of *jen-hsia* that we have seen in Ch'ien Liu's gang. Although
T'ien Chün and T'ao Ya are the only two of Yang's trusted associates that the
sources definitely connect to Yang's gang, they were surely not the only gang
members to play prominent roles serving Yang Hsing-mi in the years to come.
Among his earliest associates for whom we have surviving biographies, five

---

[30] On the rise of the Wu founder Yang Hsing-mi as well as on the subsequent history of both Wu
and Southern T'ang, see Robert Krompart, "The southern restoration of T'ang: Counsel, policy and
parahistory in the stabilization of the Chiang-Huai region, 887–943" (diss., University of California at
Berkeley, 1973).

[31] For this and the following events, see the biographies of Kao P'ien in Liu, *Chiu T'ang-shu* 182, pp. 4703–
12, and Ou-yang, *Hsin T'ang shu* 225 *hsia*, pp. 6391–6405. See also Somers, "The end of the T'ang,"
pp. 742–4. Events are also recounted in *TCTC* 253–4.

[32] On these events, see *TCTC* 257, pp. 8351–5.

[33] Biographies of Yang Hsing-mi can be found in Ou-yang, *Hsin T'ang shu* 188, pp. 5451–61; *CWTS* 134,
pp. 1779–82; Ou-yang, *Hsin Wu-tai shih* 61, pp. 747–52; Wu, *Shih-kuo ch'un-ch'iu* 1, pp. 1–30. A useful
account in English is the second chapter of Krompart, "The southern restoration of T'ang."

[34] Ou-yang, *Hsin T'ang shu* 188, p. 5451. On T'ien Chün, see Ou-yang, *Hsin T'ang shu* 189, p. 5476; Lu
Chen, *Chiu-kuo chih* [*Shou-shan-ko ts'ung-shu* 1844 ed.; 1922] (c. 1000; Taipei, 1968) 3, pp. 3, 35; Wu,
Shih-kuo ch'un-ch'iu 13, p. 165. On T'ao Ya, see Lu, *Chiu-kuo chih* 1, p. 3; Wu, *Shih-kuo ch'un-ch'iu* 5,
p. 91.

others were natives of Ho-fei.[35] Additionally, among later associates – men who became prominent in the last years of the ninth century or under the Yang rulers early in the tenth – many were natives of Ho-fei, suggesting that they or their fathers had been among Yang Hsing-mi's early associates, surely including some who had been gang members.

In the years before Huang Ch'ao's rebellion, Yang Hsing-mi turned his gang from local thuggery to classic banditry. They broadened their sphere of activity beyond acts of petty delinquency at the village level to embrace a wider territory and more brazen behavior. The expanded range of activities must have included illegal trading in salt and raiding of poorly defended village storehouses, activities much like those of Ch'ien Liu. At some point in the early to mid-880s, after operating for a decade with general autonomy, but now faced with the growing power of Ch'in Tsung-ch'üan to his north, Yang Hsing-mi enrolled his gang in an emerging regional extraofficial defense force similar to that formed by Tung Ch'ang.[36] The *Chiu Wu-tai shih* tells us that the militia officials (*chün-chiang*) of Lu-chou2 and Shou-chou, who were apparently trying to maintain some loyalty to the T'ang court rather than succumb to the growing influence of Ch'in Tsung-ch'üan, recruited "men with military ability from among the bandits." Yang Hsing-mi took advantage of this program to bring one hundred of his bandit followers – very likely his whole gang – into the extraofficial frontier defense forces of Lu-chou2.[37] There, as Ssu-ma Kuang relates, Yang used his mastery of violence to become prefect of Lu-chou2:

> The commanders (of Lu-chou2) all feared Yang, and they persuaded the prefect Lang Yu-fu to dispatch him to defend the border. As Yang departed, the commanders sought to appease him with sweet talk, asking if there was anything he needed. Yang replied, "I need your heads," whereupon he cut them off. He then seized the several encampments and proclaimed himself commander of the eight encampments of infantry and cavalry. Lang Yu-fu was unable to control him, and appealed to Kao P'ien to appoint Yang Hsing-mi prefect in his stead.[38]

In the years that followed, Yang Hsing-mi consolidated his position in and around Lu-chou2, remaining nominally loyal to Kao P'ien although no doubt retaining a large measure of freedom of action. Thus when the assault on Kao P'ien began in Yang-chou in 887, Yang Hsing-mi was able to pick and choose among his friends and enemies depending on where he had the advantage. By the end of the conflict, early in 888, Yang had emerged in control of

---

[35] See Li Yu in Wu, *Shih-kuo ch'un-ch'iu* 6, p. 100. For Li Yü, see Lu, *Chiu-kuo chih* 1, pp. 7–8; for Luo Chih-hsiang, Wu, *Shih-kuo ch'un-ch'iu* 10, p. 139; for T'ai Meng, Lu, *Chiu-kuo chih* 1, pp. 6–7; for Wang Ching-jen (also known as Wang Muo-chang), *CWTS* 23, p. 317.

[36] It is most likely that this coincided with Ch'in's proclamation of his own dynasty in 883.

[37] *CWTS* 137, p. 1779.

[38] *TCTC* 255, p. 8290. See also Ou-yang, *Hsin Wu-tai shih* 61, p. 747.

Yang-chou, where he established his headquarters, and proclaimed himself commandant (*liu-hou*) of Huai-nan. He was now one of the two dominant forces in Huai-nan.

The other dominant force was Sun Ju.[39] Sun is yet another example of the men who had capitalized on Huang Ch'ao's rebellion to enhance their own standing. He was a village tough in the Lo-yang area who had enrolled in the local militia along with his gang. In the rebellion he had adhered to the cause of Ch'in Tsung-ch'üan, a T'ang officer who joined Huang Ch'ao during the latter's final assault on the T'ang capital, Ch'ang-an. Sun Ju stayed loyal to Ch'in Tsung-ch'üan as he battled with Chu Wen to inherit T'ang power in the north, even when Ch'in proclaimed himself emperor in 885.[40] As Ch'in Tsung-ch'üan grew increasingly ambitious, however, Sun Ju grew more and more alienated and finally broke their ties. From his base in Hao-chou, located on the south bank of the Huai River, Sun Ju led his army against Yang Hsing-mi for control of Huai-nan. Thus, with the fall of Kao P'ien, Sun Ju and Yang Hsing-mi entered a period of struggle for supremacy. Initially, Sun Ju held the upper hand, seizing Yang-chou in 888 and even campaigning as far south as Su-chou, where Yang and his proxies had been struggling against Ch'ien Liu. However, Yang Hsing-mi was finally able to capture and behead Sun Ju after a skirmish near Hu-chou in 892.[41]

If the struggle with Sun Ju was over, however, unrest was not. The years of constant warfare between the two rivals had devastated a huge area. Yang-chou, once a great and rich city, lay in ruins. There were still many men who had been loyal to Sun Ju, and they were reluctant to submit to Yang Hsing-mi's uncertain benevolence. Their resistance was encouraged by Chu Wen, who was now the dominant force in the north.[42] In 895, Yang Hsing-mi sought to forge an alliance with a variety of forces, including those of Li K'o-yung, the Sha-t'o Turk whose armies had occupied large areas of Ho-tung, against Chu Wen.[43] Late in 897, attempting to extend his authority into the Huai-nan region, Chu Wen ordered a major invasion of Yang Hsing-mi's territory.[44] But Chu Wen's commander greatly underestimated his adversary and was consequently dealt a smashing defeat. Of an initial invasion force of seventy thousand, fewer than a thousand managed to limp home: "Thereafter Yang Hsing-mi controlled the

---

[39] See Sun Ju's biography in Ou-yang, *Hsin T'ang shu* 188, pp. 5466–8.
[40] See the brief discussion in Somers, "The end of the T'ang," pp. 783–4.
[41] On Sun Ju's defeat and beheading, see *TCTC* 259, pp. 8429–31.
[42] On assistance received from Chu, see *TCTC* 260, p. 8468, with respect to Shou-chou; and *TCTC* 261, p. 8502, with respect to O-chou.
[43] See *TCTC* 260, p. 8463.
[44] On this invasion, see *TCTC* 261, pp. 8509, 8510–11.

land between the Yangtze and Huai rivers, and Chu Wen could not contest this."[45]

Although Yang Hsing-mi defeated Chu Wen's efforts to oust him, his own campaign to expand into western Huai-nan and Chiang-nan required another two decades of protracted war against Tu Hung in O-chou, which lay at the critical juncture of the Yangtze and Han rivers (completed 905); against Chung Chuan and his son in Hung-chou (modern Nan-ch'ang), on the Kan River south of P'o-yang Lake (completed 906); and finally against Lu Kuang-ch'ou in Ch'ien-chou (modern Kan-chou), further up the Kan River, which was not completed until 918.[46]

Ching-nan

Upstream from O-chou a similar pattern of turmoil raged in the aftermath of Huang Ch'ao's passage in 879. In the region known as Ching-nan, encompassing the three strategic Yangtze River prefectures just within and east of the Yangtze River gorges, there was near-constant turmoil as one adventurer supplanted another. The contest began to sort itself out in 885, when a man of violence named Ch'eng Ju took control of Kuei-chou, some forty miles inside the gorge itself.[47] In 888, Ch'eng Ju took advantage of further turmoil in the regional metropolis of Chiang-ling to seize control of the prefecture and assume the title commandant (liu-hou) of Ching-nan. Soon after, Ch'eng extended his authority west into K'uei-chou, one hundred miles into the gorge on the eastern fringe of Szechwan, at which point the T'ang court appointed him military governor of Ching-nan.[48] This arrangement brought some temporary stability to the region.

Ch'eng Ju remained governor with T'ang recognition until 903, when he heedlessly agreed to Chu Wen's request to send troops against Yang

---

[45] Although Yang's control over Huai-nan was henceforth firm, fighting resumed in 899; see TCTC 263, pp. 8522–3. For 902, see TCTC 263, p. 8577. The rivalry between Yang and Chu was a factor in numerous subsequent conflicts even when it did not pit them against each other directly.

[46] On Tu Hung, see Ou-yang, Hsin T'ang shu 190, pp. 5485–6; TCTC 256, p. 8343; 259, pp. 8455, 8459; and 261, pp. 8503–4. On Chung Chuan, see Ou-yang, Hsin T'ang shu 190, p. 5486–7; CWTS 17, p. 231; and Wu, Shih-kuo ch'un-ch'iu 8, p. 124. On Lu kuang-ch'ou, see Ou-yang, Hsin T'ang shu 190, pp. 5493–4, and Ou-yang, Hsin Wu-tai shih 41, pp. 443–4. On the capture of Ch'ien-chou, see TCTC 256, p. 8320.

[47] On the historical and strategic importance of Ching-nan, see Wang Gungwu, "The Middle Yangtse in T'ang politics," in Perspectives on the T'ang, ed. Arthur F. Wright and Denis C. Twitchett (New Haven, Conn., 1973) pp. 193–235. See, for example, TCTC 256, pp. 8319–20. On Ch'eng Ju, see Ou-yang, Hsin T'ang shu 190, pp. 5483–4; and CWTS 17, pp. 229–30.

[48] TCTC 257, p. 8378.

Hsing-mi.[49] Although Ch'eng Ju had no obligation to Chu Wen, he feared Chu's power and also saw a chance to expand his own authority. Ch'eng Ju, ignoring his advisors, dispatched one hundred thousand marines downriver, but his forces were routed by Yang Hsing-mi's besieging army, and Ch'eng Ju was drowned in the Yangtze River.

With Ch'eng Ju's death, Chu Wen sought a reliable replacement in Ching-nan, finally settling on Kao Chi-ch'ang. Kao was originally the household slave of one Li Jang, "a wealthy merchant of Pien-chou (K'ai-feng)," the headquarters of Chu Wen.[50] After Li Jang was adopted by Chu Wen, Kao Chi-ch'ang came to the attention of Chu Wen, who appointed him to a succession of military posts culminating in defense commissioner of Ying-chou4, a highly strategic prefecture on the north side of the Huai River confronting the territory of Yang Hsing-mi.[51] This was the post Kao Chi-ch'ang held when Chu Wen summoned him to assume control of Ching-nan in 907.[52] From this appointment the Kao family was to rule the Ching-nan region until they submitted to the Sung in 963.

Ch'u

South of Ching-nan, encompassing the basin of the Tung-t'ing Lake and the adjacent river valleys, was Hunan, the site of the future Ch'u kingdom of Ma Yin. When Huang Ch'ao left Kuang-chou and began his march back to the north, he went via the Hsiang River through the heart of Hunan. As always, he left behind turmoil and the collapse of established authority. The first to try and restore order was Min Hsü.[53] Min was from the Kiangsi region, but he had been commanding forces sent to defend the T'ang position in Vietnam. In 881, as he was heading north through rebellion-torn T'an-chou (modern Ch'ang-sha), he decided to stay in the city and proclaim himself commandant. In the years that followed he, like so many of the self-proclaimed administrators

---

[49] For the events of 903, see *TCTC* 264, pp. 8606–9.

[50] Ou-yang, *Hsin Wu-tai shih* 69, p. 855; Wu, *Shih-kuo ch'un-ch'iu* 100, p. 1427. Li's personal name is also given as Ch'i-lang; see *CWTS* 62, p. 831; and 133, p. 1751. All sources agree that Li was adopted by Chu Wen, who changed Li's name to Chu Yu-jang; see also Lu, *Chiu-kuo chih* 12, p. 123, and Kurihara Masuo, "Tō-Godai no kafushiteki ketsugō no seikaku," *Shigaku zasshi* 62 No. 6 (1953), p. 6, and especially chart 6 on p. 14. On Kao Chi-ch'ang (also known as Kao Chi-hsing), see *CWTS* 133, pp. 1751–2; Ou-yang, *Hsin Wu-tai shih* 69, pp. 855–7; Wu, *Shih-kuo ch'un-ch'iu* 100, p. 1427–36; T'ao Yüeh, *Wu-tai shih-pu* (1012; Nan-ch'ang, 1915) 2, pp. 4a–b; and Chou Yü-ch'ung, *San Ch'u hsin-lu* [*Hsüeh-hai lei-pien* 1831 ed.; 1920] (Taipei, 1967) 3, pp. 1a–3b.

[51] See *TCTC* 265, p. 8663; Lu, *Chiu-kuo chih* 12, p. 123; *CWTS* 133, p. 1751; and Ou-yang, *Hsin Wu-tai shih* 69, p. 856.

[52] See *TCTC* 265, pp. 8646, 8662; and 266, p. 8680.

[53] On Min Hsü, see Ou-yang, *Hsin T'ang shu* 186, pp. 5420–3; *TCTC* 254, p. 8260; 255, pp. 8269, 8299.

around the empire, was granted official titles by the powerless T'ang court in recognition of his de facto autonomous authority.

Although Min Hsü may have briefly brought some order to the situation, order in the region did not persist. In 886, Min was attacked by the prefect of Heng-chou. Min Hsü appealed to a local warlord to come to his aid, but the warlord instead killed him. The Heng-chou prefect then resumed his assault, seized T'an-chou, and killed the warlord. In the aftermath of these exchanges things again settled down, but the quiet was deceptive for Teng Ch'u-na, an ally of Min Hsü, was plotting to avenge him. Min Hsü had appointed Teng Ch'u-na prefect of Shao-chou, located on the Tzu River in southern Hunan, as a reward for many years of loyal service. For eight years following Min Hsü's death Teng Ch'u-na trained his troops in preparation. In 893 he launched his assault, took T'an-chou, and killed the former Heng-chou prefect.[54]

The instability in Hunan provided a much-needed opportunity for Ma Yin, then looking for a place to settle with his troops. Ma Yin was a native of Hsü-chou2 (in Honan), who wound up in the army of Ch'in Tsung-ch'üan under the command of Ch'in's general Sun Ju.[55] When Sun broke with Ch'in late in the 880s, Ma Yin remained loyal to Sun Ju, under whom he had risen to high command.

In the years that followed, Sun Ju's army marauded through Huai-nan and even into the Kiangsi region, seizing and pillaging as it went, behaving as a bandit army with no fixed territorial base.[56] When Sun Ju was captured and executed by forces loyal to Yang Hsing-mi in 892, this rootless army quickly broke up and most units switched their allegiance to Yang.[57] At this time, Ma Yin was second in command to Liu Chien-feng of a force dispatched by Sun to forage for supplies. Faced with the disaster that had befallen their associates, Liu Chien-feng and Ma Yin opted to strike out on their own with the army of seven thousand under their command.[58] As they traveled west to Hung-chou and then south along the Kan River through Kiangsi, they continued to act as one of the many bandit gangs that plagued the Yangtze River and adjacent valleys. Although they were able to expand their force from the original core of seven thousand, they were apparently unable to oust more powerful warlords

---

[54] See *TCTC* 259, p. 8451. On Teng Ch'u-na, see Ou-yang, *Hsin T'ang shu* 186, pp. 5420–1; Lu, *Chiu-kuo chih* 11, p. 115.

[55] On the origins and early history of Ma Yin, see Okada Kōji, "Godai So ōkoku no kenkoku seido," *Daitō Bunka Daigaku kiyō (Jinbun kagaku)* 19 (1981), pp. 73–89.

[56] One might note, for example, the comments of two generals in Yang Hsing-mi's army: "Sun sweeps the land clean from afar . . . He sends forth light cavalry in order to seize provisions and capture prisoners"; see *TCTC* 259, pp. 8424–5.

[57] *TCTC* 259, p. 8430.

[58] Wu, *Shih-kuo ch'un-ch'iu* 67, p. 931.

in the Kan River valley. Although we have no way of knowing whether they were aware that political structures in the regions of Hunan were less stable than in Kiangsi, they nevertheless opportunely turned west, across the rugged and hostile mountains between Kiangsi and Hunan, appearing on the fringe of T'an-chou in 894.

Teng Ch'u-na dispatched a small force to confront the intruders, but Ma Yin warned the local leaders that "My forces number 100,000, and they are highly trained soldiers. You have only a few thousand village militia. Your situation is difficult."[59] Ma Yin urged the T'an-chou forces not to fight, but rather to accept Liu Chien-feng's overlordship, an offer that the village militiamen accepted with alacrity. With T'an-chou thus exposed, Liu and Ma marched in and seized and executed Teng Ch'u-na. Liu Chien-feng then proclaimed himself commandant, but he proved less able as a governor than as a campaigner, and he was assassinated by a disgruntled associate in 896.[60] After some initial confusion over who should succeed Liu Chien-feng, Ma Yin inherited the position, a fact that the virtually irrelevant T'ang court officially confirmed later the same year.[61] Although these events established Ma's position in T'an-chou and Shao-chou, it took another two years to quell the independent rulers of the five remaining prefectures in the Hunan region (Heng-chou, Yung-chou, Tao-chou, Ch'en-chou2, and Lien-chou). By the close of 899, "all Hunan was at peace" and under the unified control of Ma Yin.[62]

Min

During the upheavals at the center of the T'ang empire that took place after Huang Ch'ao's passage through to the beginning of the tenth century, a similar process of displacement unfolded along the southeast and south coasts that eventually brought the Wang family to power in Fu-chien. When Huang Ch'ao's armies entered Fu-chien's northwest corner in 878, the region was still lightly settled. As happened elsewhere, Huang's depredations led to a collapse in the established structures of authority. In the face of the rebel threat, Ch'en Yen, a local landowner from Chien-chou, the mountainous prefecture where Huang first entered Fu-chien, capitalized on his formation of a private security army to earn appointment from the T'ang court as surveillance commissioner (*kuan-ch'a shih*). This appointment was another symbolic recognition of a situation that by the mid-880s had evolved beyond the court's

[59] *TCTC* 259, p. 8454.
[60] *TCTC* 260, p. 8485.
[61] *TCTC* 260, p. 8493.
[62] *TCTC* 261, pp. 8515, 8526, 8528.

control.[63] At that very same time, a band of migrants from the Huai River town of Kuang-chou2, led by Wang Hsü, entered Fu-chien via the remote and undeveloped southwest corner.[64] Wang Hsü had been a minor warlord in northern Huai-nan where he held power at the sufferance of Ch'in Tsung-ch'üan, Chu Wen's major rival in the north. In 884, Ch'in Tsung-ch'üan demanded subsidies from Wang Hsü that the latter was unable to pay. In the face of pending reprisals, Wang Hsü abandoned his fief with an army of about five thousand including three brothers who, although apparently unrelated to Wang Hsü, were also surnamed Wang: Wang Ch'ao, Wang Shen-kuei, and Wang Shen-chih.[65] After a journey of about eight hundred miles that probably followed Huang Ch'ao's earlier line of march, the band entered Fu-chien from the southwest. They first seized the remote and undeveloped prefecture of T'ing-chou, followed by the coastal prefecture of Chang-chou. Shortly afterward, Wang Hsü was ousted by the three brothers, who assumed control of the band under the leadership of Wang Ch'ao, the eldest. Although Wang Ch'ao set about returning the group to Huai-nan, their journey was interrupted when the elders of Ch'üan-chou caught up to them and begged them get rid of their prefect, Liao Yen-jou. The brothers agreed and directed a siege against that city that lasted a full year. In the fall of 886, Ch'üan-chou fell.[66] Once the Wangs gained control, they established Ch'üan-chou as their own fief. Wang Ch'ao formally submitted to the authority of Ch'en Yen, who granted him the title of prefect (*tz'u-shih*) from his base in Fu-chou, but this was a proforma action that did not alter the Wangs' functional autonomy.

The situation in Fu-chien remained static for the next six years. Wang Ch'ao and his brothers governed Ch'üan-chou, while Ch'en Yen continued as warlord in the north. Ch'en Yen's death in 891, however, brought this temporary stability to an end and set off a struggle between northern and southern Fu-chien that ended only after a year-long siege against Fu-chou that united Fu-chien under the Wang family.[67] Unfortunately, the Wang family itself was not united. Following his victory in the struggle between north and south, Wang Ch'ao moved his administrative headquarters north, settling in

[63] See *TCTC* 256, p. 8316; 256, pp. 8316–17; and Ch'en Yen's biography in Liang K'o-chia, *Ch'un-hsi San-shan chih* (1182; Peking, 1990) 21, p. 22b.

[64] The following discussion of the background to the founding of the Min kingdom of Fu-chien is based on the third chapter of Hugh R. Clark, *Community, trade, and networks: Southern Fujian province from the third to the thirteenth century* (Cambridge, 1991). Readers should also refer to Aoyama Sadao, "The newly-risen bureaucrats in Fukien at the Five Dynasty–Sung period, with special reference to their genealogies," *Memoirs of the Research Department of the Tōyō Bunko* 21 (1962), pp. 1–48.

[65] On Wang Ch'ao and his brothers, see Ou-yang, *Hsin T'ang shu* 190, pp. 5491–3; Ou-yang, *Hsin Wu-tai shih* 68, pp. 845–7; Wu, *Shih-kuo ch'un-ch'iu* 90, pp. 1297–1319; and T'ao, *Wu-tai shih-pu* 2, pp. 4b–6a.

[66] See *TCTC* 256, pp. 8320, 8325–6, 8339.

[67] *TCTC* 258, p. 8423.

Fu-chou. This was a sound strategic move. Fu-chou had been the center of opposition to the Wangs as well as the established center of unified regional government. Wang Ch'ao left the eldest of his brothers, the otherwise unknown Wang Yen-fu, to administer the south as prefect of Ch'üan-chou. Wang Yen-fu died in 894 and was succeeded by Wang Shen-kuei, now the eldest of Wang Ch'ao's surviving brothers. By 892 the Wang brothers ruled a central administration in Fu-chou and a nominally subordinate center in the south, based in Ch'üan-chou.

Although historians often treat Fu-chien of the ninth century as a single geopolitical entity, it is among the most topographically fractured regions of the T'ang empire. Fu-chou, located near the mouth of the Min River and linked to the interior by the river, was the political and economic center of the northern part of Fu-chien. Fu-chou and the territory tied to it had been the region most directly controlled by Ch'en Yen. By contrast, Ch'üan-chou was isolated from the north by mountains and formed a natural center for the southern coastal regions because of its excellent natural harbor. This had been the sphere Wang Ch'ao first controlled. These two geographic subdivisions of the Fu-chien region had been administratively unified since 742 when the southern prefectures were transferred from the jurisdiction of Ling-nan circuit to Chiang-nan circuit and a new network of circuit officials was formed.[68]

There is no reason to believe that relations between Wang Ch'ao and his brother Shen-kuei were strained. Wang Ch'ao's death in 898, however, set off a crisis. Wang Shen-kuei, as the oldest surviving brother, was in line to succeed as leader, and would likely have to move to Fu-chou, the established seat of regional administration. But Wang Shen-chih, the next oldest brother, was already established there, holding the all-embracing title director of military and civil affairs (chih chün-fu shih). Thus, while Wang Shen-kuei held uncontested authority in the south, his brother Wang Shen-chih controlled the entire military and civil apparatus in the north. Not surprisingly under such circumstances, Wang Shen-kuei declined to abandon his secure southern base and place himself at his younger brother's mercy, opting instead to yield his rights to the northern title to Wang Shen-chih.[69] As the tenth century began, there was a fundamental split in the emerging polity of the Wang family, a split that was to endure throughout the interregnum until the Sung unification.

---

[68] This division between north and south in Fu-chien is explored in chapter 3 of Clark, *Community, trade, and networks*; see also Hugh R. Clark, "Quanzhou (Fujian) during the Tang-Song interregnum 879–978," *T'oung Pao* 68 Nos. 1–3 (1982), pp. 132–49.

[69] *TCTC* 261, p. 8511.

Southern Han

South of Fu-chien lay Ling-nan, the territory of the Southern Han state. When Huang Ch'ao returned north after sacking Kuang-chou in 879, he must have left a shattered city and an absence of authority, as he did everywhere else. Unfortunately, there are no records of these events. However, the *Hsin T'ang-shu* tells us that one Liu Ch'ien occupied Feng-chou2, a small prefecture on the Hsi River west of Kuang-chou, and that he extended his power as far away as Kuei-chou3 (modern Kuei-lin). Liu Ch'ien's administration brought peace to the region, and refugees flocked to him, providing him with the base to build a sizable army as well as a navy.[70] Liu Ch'ien died in 894 and was succeeded by his son Liu Yin.[71]

Liu Yin is certainly unique among the founders of the interregnum states. He was not Han Chinese, although he was also not from the Middle East as was once claimed.[72] Most sources state that the family was native to Shang-ts'ai county (Honan). This claim probably derives from an attempt by Liu Yin's family to mask their ancestry and enhance their credibility in the Chinese world of the tenth century. In fact, the Lius were hereditary chieftains of one of the many non-Chinese tribes that lived in the far south, the people whom the Chinese lumped together as Man.

The first concrete evidence we have of the family concerns the marriage of Liu Ch'ien to the niece of Wei Chou, military governor of Ling-nan, during the Hsien-t'ung era (860–73).[73] Wei Chou had been dispatched to Ling-nan at a critical period in the T'ang struggle to control its southern frontier. In addition to the problems arising from the rebellions of Ch'iu Fu and P'ang Hsün in the lands below the Yangtze River, a pattern of local unrest and rebellion against Chinese rule that had persisted through much of the ninth century in the Annamese prefectures of the Red River valley was now being aggravated by threats on the T'ang dynasty's southwest frontier from the aggressive Nan-chao kingdom.[74] Wei Chou had earned a reputation for successfully cultivating cordial relationships with minority peoples,[75] and this was no doubt a factor

---

[70] See Ou-yang, *Hsin T'ang shu* 190, p. 5493. The *Hsin T'ang shu* gives Liu's personal name as Chih-ch'ien; however, all other sources call him Liu Ch'ien, including *TCTC* .

[71] On Liu Yin, see *CWTS* 135, pp. 1807–9; Ou-yang, *Hsin Wu-tai shih* 65, pp. 809–10; Wu, *Shih-kuo ch'un-ch'iu* 58, pp. 835–8.

[72] Fujita Toyohachi, "Nan-Kan Ryū-shi no sosen ni tsuite," *Tōyō gakuhō* 6 No. 2 (1916), pp. 247–57. Fujita's argument has been thoroughly debunked in Kawahara Masahiro, "Nan-Kan Ryū-shi no kōki," in his *Kan minzoku Kanan hattenshi kenkyū* (Tokyo, 1984), pp. 229–53. The following treatment is based entirely on Kawahara's excellent discussion.

[73] Sun Kuang-hsien, *Pei-meng so-yen* [Ya-yü t'ang ts'ang-shu 1756 ed.] (10th c.; Taipei, 1966) 6, p. 2b.

[74] See Somers, "The end of the T'ang," pp. 692–5.

[75] See Kawahara, *Kan minzoku Kanan hattenshi kenkyū*, pp. 134–5.

in his selection to serve in Ling-nan at this difficult time. Seen in this light, the marriage alliance Wei Chou forged with Liu Ch'ien was part of his policy for maintaining the loyalty and quiescence of those peoples, and was proof of the prominent role Liu Ch'ien played among them. Liu Ch'ien was no doubt the only figure to exercise any viable authority in the regions west of Kuang-chou in the aftermath of Huang Ch'ao's devastating campaign through the far south. T'ang authority in the region had been shattered. Thus when the T'ang court formally recognized Liu Ch'ien's control of Feng-chou2 early in the 880s it was a symbolic acceptance of a military reality and an effort to ensure Liu's ongoing loyalty to the declining T'ang cause. And although Liu Ch'ien and his heir, Liu Yin, could surely have rejected the overtures, they no doubt viewed the imprimatur of the T'ang court as a useful adjunct to their efforts to extend their control to additional prefectures and the Man who lived in them.

Liu Yin, in turn, demonstrated his loyalty to the T'ang dynasty in 896. The T'ang court appointed a prince of the royal family as the new military governor of Kuang-chou to maintain control over the lucrative revenues derived from the South Seas trade. In response to the T'ang court's efforts to reestablish a strong political presence in the region, two local militia leaders (*ya-chiang*) attempted to assert their independence and resist the new governor. The two militia leaders approached Liu Yin to seek an alliance, even promising a daughter in marriage. Liu Yin, however, launched a sneak attack against the militiamen, overwhelming them, and welcomed the prince to his post. In return, Liu was named adjutant (*hsing-chün ssu-ma*) in Kuang-chou.[76] In the years that followed, Liu Yin loyally served a succession of governors dispatched by the T'ang court.[77] Early in 902 he was rewarded again by being appointed commandant of Kuang-chou. This promotion was the first recognition of his own growing power.[78] Liu Yin's position was formalized when he was named military governor of Kuang-chou sometime around the fall of the T'ang and rise of the first of the northern dynasties, the Liang, in 907.[79] But his authority was probably not far-reaching, including just Kuang-chou and his original base of Feng-chou2, as well as the prefectures in between. To his north he was threatened by Lu Kuang-ch'ou, who controlled Shao-chou, located on the south side of the mountains from his base in the southern Kiangsi region, and by Ma Yin in Hunan, who had seized the northern prefectures of western

---

[76] *TCTC* 260, p. 8496.

[77] *TCTC* 262, p. 8533.

[78] *TCTC* 262, p. 8565.

[79] The first evidence that Liu Yin held the title military governor is in an entry dated 907 in *TCTC* 266, p. 8680; it does not tell us when the title was granted.

Ling-nan in 900.[80] Nor was Liu Yin's authority very effective to his west, which was brought under control only in 911, by Liu Yin's successor, Liu Yen, who formally established the Southern Han state in 917.[81]

Former Shu

The last region to consider in this preliminary survey is Szechwan, home of the successor states of Former and Later Shu. Even though Huang Ch'ao never entered the region, Szechwan was uniquely affected by his rebellion. For when Huang returned to north China and attacked the imperial capital of Ch'ang-an late in 880, he prompted Emperor T'ang Hsi-tsung (r. 873–88) to flee to the west and ultimately to Szechwan, where he remained until 885. Thus for five years Szechwan had to bear the burden of the imperial presence by itself, a burden that was magnified by the financial claims of the T'ang court and the rapacious corruption of the officials surrounding the emperor, especially the eunuch T'ien Ling-tzu and his brother Ch'en Ching-hsüan, the military governor of western Szechwan.[82]

Even as the T'ang court cowered in Ch'eng-tu, a pattern of breakdown and rebellion similar to that occurring elsewhere became manifest in Szechwan. The largest and most threatening uprising was that led by Ch'ien Neng, but Ch'ien was only one of several rebel leaders as unrest spread across Szechwan in the early 880s.[83] When imperial forces proved incapable of maintaining security, local structures led by indigenous leaders such as Wei Chün-ching evolved in their place.[84]

The emperor and his court returned to the capital in early 885. Order began to be restored in Szechwan late in the 880s as new, independent figures emerged and replaced the corrupt and discredited appointees of the T'ang court. Of these, Wang Chien was the most important.[85] Wang Chien probably was born

---

[80] On the incursion of Ma Yin into western Ling-nan, see *TCTC* 262, pp. 8535–6. On Lu Kuang-ch'ou seizing Shao-chou, see *TCTC* 263, p. 8589.

[81] See *TCTC* 267, p. 8733, and 268, pp. 8749–50.

[82] On the difficulties and burdens that Szechwan suffered while hosting the court, see Matsui Shōichi, "Tōdai kōhanki no Shisen – kanryō shihai to dogōsō no shutsugen o chūshin to shite," *Shigaku zasshi* 73 No. 10 (1964), pp. 73–9. For a more general discussion in the context of the history of the Former and Later Shu kingdoms, see chapter 1 of Yang Wei-li, *Ch'ien Shu Hou Shu shih* (Ch'eng-tu, 1986), and chapters 5 and 6 of Klaus-Peter Tietze, *Ssuch'uan vom 7. bis 10. Jahrhundert: Untersuchungen zur frühen Geschichte einer chinesischen Provinz* (Wiesbaden, 1980).

[83] On Ch'ien Neng, see Somers, "The end of the T'ang," pp. 748–50. See also Kuo Yün-tao, *Shu chien* [*Shou-shan-ko ts'ung-shu* 1844 ed.; 1922] (13th c.; Taipei, 1968) 7, pp. 5b–7b.

[84] On Wei Chün-ching, see the discussion in Somers, "The end of the T'ang," pp. 750–1, and the secondary literature Somers cites.

[85] Sources on the rise of Wang Chien are legion. For a sampling, see Chang T'ang-ying, *Shu t'ao-wu* [*I-hai chu-ch'en* c. 1800 ed.; 1850] (11th c.; Taipei, 1968) *shang*, pp. 2b–5a; Kuo, *Shu chien* 7, pp. 8b–14b; Wu,

in 848, making him very nearly the same age as his fellow brigands Ch'ien
Liu and Yang Hsing-mi.[86] Like Ma Yin, Wang was from Hsü-chou2, where
his father was a baker. Wang apparently tried a career as a butcher, but he was
no more attracted to the legitimate life than Ch'ien Liu or Yang Hsing-mi.

When we first hear of Wang Chien's illegal activities he was already rustling
livestock and trading illegally in salt, and had earned the sobriquet Bandit
Wang Eight (*Tsei Wang Pa*) from his villagers. By the 870s, however, Wang and
his gang had outgrown the limited sphere of village thuggery and had begun
to operate over a much wider area, a pattern that exactly echoes the evolution
of the careers of Ch'ien Liu and Yang Hsing-mi. Chang T'ang-ying (1029–71),
author of the *Shu t'ao-wu*, tells us that "Wang Chien and [his close comrade]
Chin Hui were united in banditry. They pillaged around Hsü-chou2 and Ts'ai-
chou, and they hid out in the wastelands."[87] As the group expanded its sphere
of operations, it began to exert a deep influence over the people, as is revealed
in a curious episode that must have occurred in the mid-870s.[88] Wang and
Chin had been captured following a raid in Hsü-chou2 and were about to be
executed. In the face of imminent death, however, they were inexplicably freed
by their jailor. Although this escape is attributed to the jailor's recognizing
that Wang Chien was a remarkable person, more plausibly it was because he
was afraid of offending so powerful a gang.

It is unclear whether Wang Chien formed an alliance with Huang Ch'ao,
but when Huang moved south early in 878, Wang Chien stayed behind in
Honan where he was again free to pursue his own agenda, one that apparently focused on the illegal trade in salt between the Honan and northwestern Hunan regions.[89] Yet in 880 when Huang Ch'ao headed north along a
route that aimed directly at western Honan, Wang Chien opted to enroll
his band under Ch'in Tsung-ch'üan, who while remaining loyal to the T'ang
court had emerged as a major force in Ts'ai-chou. Ch'in Tsung-ch'üan placed
Wang and his band under the command of Lu Yen-hung, himself a native of

Shih-kuo ch'un-ch'iu 35, pp. 481–503; and *TCTC* 257–66. For biographies of Wang, see additionally
CWTS 135, pp. 1815–19; Ou-yang, *Hsin Wu-tai shih* 63, pp. 783–96; Lu, *Chiu-kuo chih* 6, p. 51; and
Wu-kuo ku-shih (c. 11th c.; Shanghai, 1921) *shang*, pp. 9b–10b.

[86] The following discussion of the background of Wang Chien is drawn from the marvelous detective work
of Satake Yasuhiko, "Ō-Shoku seiken seiritsu no zentei ni tsuite," *Tōyō Bunka Kenkyūjo kiyō* 99 (1986),
pp. 21–69. On Wang's early life, see also Yang, *Ch'ien Shu Hou Shu shih*, pp. 15–49.

[87] Chang, *Shu t'ao-wu shang*, pp. 12a–b.

[88] This episode is closely examined by Satake, "Ō-Shoku seiken seiritsu," pp. 27–8. The several references
to this episode (Chang, *Shu t'ao-wu shang*, pp. 3a, 12b, and T'ao, *Wu-tai shih-pu* 1, p. 6a), show clearly
that there was a foundation to the story, although, as Satake argues, Wang was anxious to hide it from
later historians.

[89] Satake, "Ō-Shoku seiken seiritsu," pp. 25–33, may argue too strongly that Wang actually joined Huang's
rebellion. See also pp. 30–2 and especially the interesting discussion on pp. 42–52.

Hsü-chou2, and when Huang Ch'ao overwhelmed the T'ang capital of Ch'ang-an, Lu Yen-hung was dispatched with eight thousand troops, including those led by Wang Chien, to join the Chung-wu army commanded by the eunuch Yang Fu-kuang in a counterattack. After Huang Ch'ao had been expelled, Yang Fu-kuang organized these forces into eight regiments of one thousand troops each, giving Wang Chien one of the eight regimental commands.[90] When Yang died in 882, Lu Yen-hung assumed leadership of the eight regiments and set out to the west, ostensibly to join the T'ang court in Szechwan. Although Lu Yen-hung's unexpected seizure of Hsing-yüan, the strategic center of the upper Han River valley, estranged him from Wang Chien, Wang found an even more powerful sponsor in T'ien Ling-tzu, who assigned him to the Shen-ts'e army – the emperor's personal guard.

Just as Wang Chien prospered while T'ien Ling-tzu held power, Wang also suffered when T'ien withdrew from the T'ang court in 886. As part of T'ien Ling-tzu's retinue Wang Chien was demoted to serve as prefect of Li-chou2, which controlled the mountain roads between Hsing-yüan and the Szechwan Basin. At this point Wang Chien broke with the crumbling order of the T'ang court and began to operate on his own, a step that earned him the scornful label of "rural bandit" (ts'ao-tsei).[91] Wang Chien proceeded to consolidate his power over the rest of Szechwan through the remainder of the ninth century. By 891, Wang had wrested control of Ch'eng-tu and western Szechwan from Ch'en Ching-hsüan and his former patron T'ien Ling-t'zu.[92] Over the next decade Wang moved against Li Mao-chen in northern Szechwan and Ku Yen-hui in the east, eventually securing complete mastery over Szechwan and the upper Han River basin by 902. Szechwan was to remain under Wang family control until the 920s.[93]

In its final years, the T'ang court began to ennoble several men who were carving out autonomous spheres of power. In 902, Ch'ien Liu was enfeoffed as King of Yüeh (Yüeh wang) and Yang Hsing-mi as King of Wu (Wu wang).[94] In 903, Wang Chien was named King of Shu (Shu wang).[95] Others did not receive royal titles from the T'ang, but each was granted honorific titles, such as joint manager of affairs (t'ung p'ing-chang shih), that were normally granted to T'ang chief ministers, in addition to their designations as military governor. When they succeeded to power, the Later Liang court recognized such men with new titles: Ch'ien Liu was named King of Wu-Yüeh (Wu-Yüeh wang) in

[90] TCTC 254, p. 8252.

[91] Sun, Pei-meng so-yen 5, p. 8b. See also the description in Ou-yang, Hsin T'ang shu 224 hsia, p. 6407.

[92] On Wang's campaign against Ch'en and T'ien, see TCTC 258, especially pp. 8413–19.

[93] TCTC 259, p. 8438; 260, pp. 8501–9; 263, pp. 8580–1.

[94] See TCTC 263, p. 8575, and 263, p. 8573, respectively.

[95] TCTC 264, p. 8613.

907; Ma Yin became King of Ch'u (*Ch'u wang*); Wang Shen-chih was named King of Min (*Min wang*) in 909; and Liu Yin was appointed first King of Ta-p'eng (*Ta-p'eng wang*) in 907, and then King of Nan-p'ing (*Nan-p'ing wang*) in 909.[96] Although both the T'ang and the Later Liang title "king" (*wang*) might seem to convey the same significance, a note in the *Tzu-chih t'ung-chien* explains their import. The earlier T'ang enfeoffments as *wang* had been as *chün-wang* (commandery king).[97] The Later Liang titles were the more prestigious *kuo-wang* (nation king). Of the seven southern states, only tiny Ching-nan (i.e., Nan-p'ing), still in commandery status did not yet have a recognized *kuo-wang*.

EARLY POLITICAL RECRUITMENT

The founders of the southern kingdoms were mainly from ordinary back-grounds without strong claims to hereditary privilege. Only Wang Ch'ao, who established the foundations of the Min kingdom of Fu-chien, had any claim to standing among the elite, and even that claim appears to have been quite marginal. Not surprisingly, the early followers of the founders were of equally common stock. As these founders achieved political and military success they increasingly drew educated men into their service. Earlier, however, their political recruitment was largely locally based. The founders sought out and promoted followers who were trustworthy and above all good fighters.

This trend is most readily apparent in the rise of Wang Chien and his associates.[98] For example, the father of Chin Hui, one of Wang Chien's earliest and closest comrades, was probably a tradesman in Hsü-chou2 who opted to join Wang Chien in banditry.[99] Many of those who followed Wang Chien into Szechwan were first tied to him through the Chung-wu army, the force commanded by the eunuch Yang Fu-kuang into which Wang had enrolled his gang early in the 880s. No doubt many of these, like Chin Hui, had been Wang Chien's comrades even before he enrolled under Ch'in Tsung-ch'üan, and there are several who specifically traced their ancestry to the Hsü-chou2 prefectural city. But the most revealing group is the astonishingly large

---

[96] See *TCTC* 266, pp. 8674, 8680, 8708.

[97] *TCTC* 266, p. 8674.

[98] For a similar discussion, see Yang, *Ch'ien Shu Hou Shu shih*, pp. 55–6.

[99] Wu, *Shih-kuo ch'un-ch'iu* 40, p. 595. Lu, *Chiu-kuo chih* 6, p. 61, tells us that Chin Hui's father was an officer (*lieh-hsiao*) in the Chung-wu army – the force within which Wang Chien, Chin Hui, and others were enrolled under Yang Fu-kuang. Although possible, this conflicts with the evidence from the more immediately contemporary *Chien-chieh lu* (Ho Kuang-yüan, *Chien-chieh lu* [*Hsüeh-chin t'ao-yüan* 1805 ed.; 1922] [Taipei, 1965]) as well as with that in the much later *Shih-kuo ch'un-ch'iu*. I am inclined to view the *Chiu-kuo chih* as reflecting an effort to cover up Chin Hui's true origins and to accept the evidence of the *Chien-chieh lu*. See also Chang, *Shu t'ao-wu shang*, p. 11a.

number of men whom Wang Chien adopted and honored with his surname "Wang" and the same generational name "Tsung" as his natural sons. Ssu-ma Kuang claimed that there were over one hundred and twenty such adoptees.[100] Biographical information survives on forty-three of them, although in most cases it is very scant.[101] This group included several of Wang Chien's kinsmen, all of whom no doubt shared his social background and had presumably been members of his band from the early days. Others, such as Wang Tsung-pi and Wang Tsung-k'an – both of whom were important in the campaigns to gain control of Szechwan and subsequently held high office in Wang's kingdom – were natives of Hsü-chou2, raising the possibility that they too had served Wang before he joined the Chung-wu army. The majority of this group have left no trace of their origins, yet it is surely reasonable to conclude that almost without exception they came from undistinguished backgrounds. Nevertheless these men functioned at the core of Wang Chien's administration. They earned his favor not because of proper family background or because of scholarship, qualifications of the traditional elite, but because of merit earned on the battlefield. They represented, in short, an entirely new elite that had taken advantage of the unique context of the late ninth century and the emerging order of the interregnum to claim their position.

Similar patterns can be discerned among the early followers of all the founders. As the new order emerged across the south in the closing decades of the ninth century it propelled an entirely new elite to the fore. The leadership of the southern kingdoms was largely composed of men whose families had never been involved in positions of leadership before. One final specific case will help complete this point. As has been described in earlier passages, the Min kingdom was founded by Wang Ch'ao and his brothers after their long migration from Kuang-chou2 prefecture in Huai-nan. The brothers arrived in Fu-chien with an army of five thousand men; although we might imagine that they had picked up new followers and had lost some of their original ones as they made their way through the hills of the Kiangsi region, the band that finally settled in Ch'üan-chou in the mid-880s was identified as being "from Kuang-chou2." The group was clearly made up of men who were not native to Fu-chien, men who had abandoned their homes and set off on a venture, going they knew not where. They were men who could pick up and go because they had very little to leave behind. But once in Fu-chien, this

---

[100] *TCTC* 267, p. 8728; we know of approximately one-third of the adoptees. For discussions of this practice in general and as it was carried out by Wang Chien, see Kurihara, "Tō-Godai no kafushiteki ketsugō no seikaku," pp. 1–30; and his "Tōmatsu Godai no kafushiteki ketsugō ni okeru seimei to nenrei," *Tōyō gakuhō* 38 No. 4 (1956), pp. 61–88.

[101] This and the following discussion is based on Wu, *Shih-kuo ch'un-ch'iu* 40. Where possible, the discussion is supplemented with additional information from Lu, *Chiu-kuo chih*.

band became a reservoir from which a new elite was drawn. In later centuries, as the tradition of compiling family genealogies became deeply ingrained in the acutely lineage-conscious society of Fu-chien, many claimed descent from these migrants. Although modern scholarship has cast doubt on the validity of some of these lineage claims,[102] they would not have been made if there was not some benefit in doing so. In the society of the Min kingdom and of later Fu-chien it was socially advantageous to be connected with the migrants; that can only be because they had established themselves as the core of the local elite. This is a case where a truly déclassé group – wandering bandits who had left their homes on an uncertain journey because they had so little at stake to begin with – took advantage of the social and political upheaval of the period to completely change their social position and thereby to recast the social order of a whole region. And significantly, the enduring value of claiming descent from these migrants despite the passage of decades and centuries argues that many managed to firmly ensconce themselves in the local elite stratum for generations to come.

As the southern order took shape and stability returned, and in some cases even before then, the new rulers, despite their questionable backgrounds, began to attract men whose own origins placed them among the traditional elite. This was especially, but not uniquely, true of the three richest and most prominent states: the Chiang-Huai successor kingdoms of Wu and Southern T'ang, the lower Yangtze state of Wu-Yüeh, and the Szechwanese states of Former and Later Shu. Some of those who opted to join the new regimes were local natives, members of a nationally oriented elite that had gradually emerged throughout the south during the centuries of the T'ang dynasty that provided a reservoir of classically trained and traditionally oriented men on whom the new leadership could draw. Others were migrants from the north, men whose families had been part of the entrenched and powerful elite lineages that had dominated China's empires for centuries but who had now abandoned their ancestral homes in favor of the greater stability of the south.

As these new recruits joined the hard-edged regimes of the founders, they began to change the character of their states. Under Yang Hsing-mi, for example, there had been very few men with a civil – as opposed to military – background who held prominent positions in the Wu kingdom.[103] However, in the early years of the tenth century, as the Wu kingdom stabilized and matured

---

[102] See Aoyama, "Newly-risen bureaucrats."

[103] Nishikawa Masao claims there were only two: Yen K'o-ch'iu and Lo Chih-hsiang, both of whom were more closely associated with Yang Hsing-mi's advisor Hsü Wen than with Yang himself. All the rest, Nishikawa argues, had risen through the ranks of the military in Yang's early campaigns of conquest. See Nishikawa Masao, "Go, Nan-Tō ryō ōchō no kokka kenryoku no seikaku: Sōdai kokuseishi kenkyū josetsu no tame ni, sono ichi," *Hōseishi kenkyū* 9 (1958), pp. 95–171.

in a process closely tied to the emerging power of Yang Hsing-mi's advisor Hsü Wen and his adopted son Hsü Chih-kao, scholastic talent came to be more appreciated than military genius. As one modern scholar put it: "There occurred a shift from military prowess to political acumen as the measure for prestige and from the battlefield to the princely court as the main arena for action."[104] Or as Ma Ling wrote in his biography of Hsü Chih-kao: "When the Wu kingdom was first stabilized, local officials were all of military background, and the taxes were levied to aid the military. Only Hsü Chih-kao (who was appointed a prefectural magistrate in 912) was fond of scholarship. He welcomed those who practiced Confucian ritual, and was personally able to promote frugality. His administration was humane, and (people) were attracted to it from far and near."[105] Later, commenting upon Hsü Wen's appointment of Hsü Chih-kao to be his heir apparent, head of the Hsü family, and regent of the Wu kingdom, Ma wrote: "[Hsü Chih-kao] established a guest hall to accommodate scholars from every direction, and he promoted Sung Ch'i-ch'iu, Lo Chih-hsiang and Wang Ling-mou to be 'scholars in residence' (*kuan-k'o shih*)."[106] The changing character of the Wu kingdom is perhaps most clearly manifested by the reintroduction of civil service examinations in 909, shortly after Hsü Wen had usurped the power, though not the title, of the Wu throne. This development reflects Hsü's emphasis on the demilitarization of administration. Under Hsü Wen, Wu was the first post-T'ang state to revive the examinations.[107]

A similar process was underway in the other southern kingdoms. As Wang Chien in 907 pondered whether to assume the imperial title, for example, the debate was led by Feng Chüan, who opposed such a move, and Wei Chuang, who was its leading advocate. Feng Chüan was a native of the Liang-che region, a recipient of a *chin-shih* degree in 850, and the grandson of Feng Su, who had been president of the Board of Personnel early in the ninth century. Feng Chüan held prefectural office in Szechwan when Wang Chien was consolidating his state late in the ninth century, and Feng offered his service to the new order.[108] Wei Chuang, a native of Ling-nan, similarly held a *chin-shih* degree which he earned in the 890s. His father had been an official in the T'ang bureaucracy, and his grandfather had been a grand secretary under Emperor T'ang Hsiuan-tsung (846–59).[109] Neither man had been part of Wang Chien's military campaigns, and they are representative of a very

---

[104] Krompart, "The southern restoration of T'ang," p. 116.
[105] Ma Ling, *Ma-shih Nan T'ang shu* (1105; Shanghai, 1934) 1, p. 1b.
[106] Ma, *Ma-shih Nan T'ang shu* 1, p. 3a.
[107] *TCTC* 267, p. 8709.
[108] Wu, *Shih-kuo ch'un-ch'iu* 40, pp. 589–91. See also *TCTC* (1972) 266, p. 8685.
[109] Wu, *Shih-kuo ch'un-ch'iu* 40, p. 592.

important group within Wang's government. As Ssu-ma Kuang wrote of the debate, "At this time, many of the families of the great officials (*i-kuan chih tsu*) had fled to Shu [Szechwan] to avoid the chaos, and the Lord of Shu [Wang Chien] treated them with courtesy and utilized them."[110]

Similarly, as Ch'ien Liu consolidated his control over the Liang-che region he began to recruit men of more prestigious background. Wu Ch'eng, who rose to the pinnacle of the Wu-Yüeh bureaucracy during the tenth century, was the son of a T'ang *chin-shih*.[111] The father of Yüan Te-chao, who also rose to the highest ranks of the kingdom's bureaucracy, served the T'ang dynasty as prefect in a series of posts across Chiang-nan.[112] P'i Jih-hsiu came from an old family of Hsiang-chou. Like so many others, he fled the turmoil connected with the late-ninth-century rebellions and wound up in Su-chou, where he enlisted with Ch'ien Liu.[113] T'u Kuei-chih's family were long-time residents of Ho-tung. His grandfather had moved to the south for unspecified reasons. T'u Kuei-chih had tried his luck at the exams several times without success when Ch'ien Liu came to power. T'u Kuei-chih then abandoned scholarship, "grabbed a sword, and followed Ch'ien."[114] Shen Sung, a native of Fu-chou (Fu-chien), was the son of a T'ang magistrate in Fu-chou's Chang-hsi county. In 895, Shen Sung passed the palace examination in the imperial capital, thereby earning his *chin-shih*, and was returning home to Fu-chien in triumph when Ch'ien Liu detained and imposed offices upon him. Despite this inauspicious beginning, Shen Sung went on to have a brilliant career in the Wu-Yüeh bureaucracy.[115]

Many more examples of this trend in recruitment for the early southern states could be given. Biographical information survives from every one of the southern kingdoms on scholars who had fled the chaos of the north for the greater tranquility of the south and wound up serving a southern lord: Han Wo[116] and Yang I-feng[117] in Min, Li Yin-heng[118] and Liu Chün[119] in Southern Han, Liu Ch'ang-lu[120] and P'ang Chü-chao[121] in Ch'u. And as the south stabilized early in the tenth century, local scholars – men who shared the values

[110] *TCTC* 266, p. 8685. See also the discussion in Yang, *Ch'ien Shu Hou Shu shih*, pp. 59–63.

[111] Fan and Lin, *Wu-Yüeh pei-shih* 4, pp. 18a–b.

[112] Fan and Lin, *Wu-Yüeh pei-shih* 5, pp. 19b–20a.

[113] See *TCTC* 254, p. 8241; Fan and Lin, *Wu-Yüeh pei-shih* 3, pp. 3b–4a.

[114] Wu, *Shih-kuo ch'un-ch'iu* 84, p. 1231.

[115] Fan and Lin, *Wu-Yüeh pei-shih* 2, pp. 9a–b.

[116] Ou-yang, *Hsin T'ang shu* 183, p. 5387; Wu, *Shih-kuo ch'un-ch'iu* 95, p. 1371.

[117] Wu, *Shih-kuo ch'un-ch'iu* 95, p. 1372.

[118] Wu, *Shih-kuo ch'un-ch'iu* 62, p. 889; Ou-yang, *Hsin T'ang shu* 72 *shang*, p. 2591.

[119] Wu, *Shih-kuo ch'un-ch'iu* 62, p. 890.

[120] Wu, *Shih-kuo ch'un-ch'iu* 73, p. 1007; Lu, *Chiu-kuo chih* 11, p. 11b.

[121] Wu, *Shih-kuo ch'un-ch'iu* 73, pp. 1007–8.

of the elite scholarly class rather than the rough-hewn values of the rulers –
emerged to play active roles everywhere. The politics and recruitment practices
of the early interregnum markedly reshaped social structures across the south,
a process that continued through the turnovers of the middle interregnum and
into the Sung dynasty.

POLITICAL CHANGE, 920S–940S

Significant changes occurred in the political landscape as the interregnum
leadership moved into its second and third generations. In 925, Wang Yen,
son and successor to Wang Chien, the founder of the Former Shu kingdom
in Szechwan, was ousted from power by Later T'ang forces, whose campaign
commander Meng Chih-hsiang ten years later officially proclaimed a second, or
Later, Shu kingdom in 935. A smoother transition occurred in Chiang-Huai in
937 when Yang P'u, fourth son of Yang Hsing-mi and fourth to rule the region,
abdicated the throne in favor of Hsü Chih-kao, who took the surname Li and
proclaimed a restoration of the T'ang dynasty, the kingdom that historians call
the "Southern T'ang." The most fundamental change took place in Fu-chien.
After a succession of increasingly inept rulers, that kingdom collapsed in the
mid-940s in the rubble of ceaseless civil war. In contrast to Szechwan and
Chiang-Huai, where the new regimes generally continued along established
paths, in Fu-chien the old order totally disappeared when the Min kingdom
was divided up among three groups: the predatory forces of the Southern T'ang,
which took the mountainous prefectures of the interior; the defensive forces of
the Wu-Yüeh kingdom, which absorbed Fu-chou; and an independent warlord
who seized control of Chang-chou and Ch'üan-chou prefectures along the coast
south of Fu-chou.[122]

Historians have traditionally blamed the fall of the Former Shu kingdom
on Wang Yen, whom they portray as a dissolute and cowardly ruler who took
no interest in government, frittered away the kingdom's wealth, and refused to
acknowledge the threat presented by the Later T'ang: "Yen was young [he was
seventeen on assuming the throne] and given to carnal pleasures. He entrusted
his court to his officials . . . and surrounded himself with boors . . . Every night
he and his cronies drank and cavorted with women."[123] While there may well
be substantial truth to these characterizations, they oversimplify the matter in
the manner of the archetypal "bad last ruler" that is a stock figure in Chinese

---

[122] The political changes discussed in this section are depicted in Map 2 in this volume.
[123] Ou-yang, *Hsin Wu-tai shih* 63, p. 971. For other contemporary biographies of Wang Yen, see *CWTS*
136, pp. 1819–22; and Chang, *Shu t'ao-wu shang*, pp. 13a–23a. See also *TCTC* 270–3; Wu, *Shih-kuo
ch'un-ch'iu* 37, pp. 531–56, and Yang, *Ch'ien Shu Hou Shu shih*, pp. 81–94.

historiography. The fact is that much blame must be laid upon Wang Chien himself.

Although Wang Chien was an extremely able military leader, he seems to have been less able to judge the civil character of those who allied with him. This failing was overcome in part by the quality of the civil officials who flocked to the court in Ch'eng-tu. Many of these men had learned their craft under the civil traditions of the T'ang dynasty, and they carried those traditions with them. However, the security of the kingdom was disturbed several times by rebellions instigated by some of Wang's own early followers. These insurrections culminated in a major uprising launched in 912 by Wang Chien's designated heir apparent Wang Yüan-yung, whom Ssu-ma Kuang characterized as violent and uninterested in scholarship.[124] Once Wang Yüan-yung was killed and his uprising quelled, Wang Chien considered selecting either his son Wang Tsung-lu, "whose face resembled his own," or his son Wang Tsung-chieh, "the most able of his sons," as the new heir apparent. But since Wang Chien was "old and infirm," he could not make the decision. His favorite courtesan then stepped in and persuaded him instead to name her son, Wang Yen, the youngest and least prepared of his sons, to be the heir.[125] Unwisely, Wang Chien, who had managed to consolidate virtually all power in his own hands, on his death in the summer of 968 bequeathed that power to a woefully inadequate successor.

Wang Chien's administration had continued to pursue an aggressive policy against his neighbor to the north, Li Mao-chen, the autonomous ruler of the region that included Feng-hsiang and the upper Wei River valley. While a series of campaigns that the two fought between 911 and 918 proved inconclusive,[126] the conflict did weaken the forces of both Shu and Li Mao-chen. When the Sha-t'o Turks overthrew the Later Liang and founded the Later T'ang dynasty in 923, Li Mao-chen quickly submitted to the new order, thereby removing his realm as a useful buffer between Szechwan and the northern regime.

Li Ts'un-hsü, the Sha-t'o founder of the Later T'ang, quickly availed himself of this new opening to launch an invasion of Szechwan in late 925. Popular and elite alienation from Wang Yen led to massive defections and paved the way for the Later T'ang armies to enter Ch'eng-tu before the end of the year. After the conquest, the Later T'ang court restored the traditional division of Szechwan into two halves, appointing Meng Chih-hsiang to be military governor of the west and Tung Chang military governor of the

[124] See *TCTC* 266, pp. 8689, 8692–3; 268, pp. 8756, 8773–6.
[125] Ou-yang, *Hsin Wu-tai shih* 63, p. 791.
[126] See Yang, *Ch'ien Shu Hou Shu shih,* pp. 68–72.

east.[127] Meng Chih-hsiang and his father, though of Chinese descent, had both served in the Sha-t'o court of Li K'o-yung and Li Ts'un-hsü, where they had been close associates of the rulers and had held high office. Li K'o-yung had even given his niece to Meng Chih-hsiang to be his wife. But the good relations between Meng and the Later T'ang court collapsed following the assassination of Li Ts'un-hsü in 926 and the coup of Li Ssu-yüan, with whom Meng had no prior relationship. Both Meng Chih-hsiang and Tung Chang feared that the new emperor resented their control over the fabulous wealth of Szechwan, and they began laying plans to break away from the new court.[128]

For awhile, Meng Chih-hsiang and Tung Chang successfully overcame their rivalry over control of Szechwan salt revenues to form an alliance against the Later T'ang even as the court laid plans to invade Shu again.[129] Late in 930 the Later T'ang launched its forces against Tung Chang in the east, providing Meng Chih-hsiang an opportunity to assert control over the combined forces of eastern and western Szechwan. Two years later, Meng's troops killed Tung Chang, giving Meng Chih-hsiang control of all Szechwan.[130]

In the aftermath of Tung Chang's death and Meng Chih-hsiang's consolidation of authority, an effort at rapprochement between Meng and Li Ssu-yüan ensued, but the effort became irrelevant with Li Ssu-yüan's death late in 933. On hearing of the emperor's demise, Meng Chih-hsiang said to those around him: "The new emperor is young and weak, while those now in charge of the government are petty clerks and incompetents. We can just wait until everything breaks down."[131] Within a month Meng Chih-hsiang had proclaimed himself emperor of a revived Shu kingdom, which was to endure under his family until its eradication by Sung forces in 965.[132]

In the Chiang-Huai region the new order actually began to take shape long before the transition from Wu to Southern T'ang in 937. Through the first two decades of the tenth century, Hsü Wen had emerged as the preeminent power in the region. Although the children of Yang Hsing-mi continued to hold the throne of the kingdom in their capital at Kuang-ling (modern Yang-chou) following their father's death in 905, Hsü Wen had used his control over

[127] TCTC 274, pp. 8947, 8949. Biographies of Meng Chih-hsiang, on which most of the following discussion is based, can be found in CWTS 136, pp. 1822–3; Ou-yang, Hsin Wu-tai shih 64, pp. 797–803; Chang, Shu t'ao-wu hsia, pp. 1a–3b; Wu, Shih-kuo ch'un-ch'iu 48, pp. 679–704. See also the discussion in Yang, Ch'ien Shu Hou Shu shih, pp. 107–8.

[128] Ou-yang, Hsin Wu-tai shih 64, p. 798. See also TCTC 275, pp. 8991–2, for Meng Chih-hsiang's organization of defenses.

[129] On the control of salt, see TCTC 276, p. 9015. On the alliance between Meng Chih-hsiang and Tung Chang, see TCTC 277, pp. 9038–9.

[130] On the conflict and Tung Chang's death, see TCTC 277, pp. 9068–71.

[131] TCTC 278, p. 9097.

[132] TCTC 278, p. 9102.

personnel appointments to monopolize power by placing followers – notably his sons – in strategic positions in Yang-chou and throughout the kingdom. At his own base in Chin-ling (modern Nanking) he even created a second court that paralleled in many ways the official court in Kuang-ling.[133]

In the second decade of the tenth century Hsü Wen confronted perhaps his greatest challenge: how best to perpetuate the power of his family that he had so assiduously built up. His problem was that his oldest son, Hsü Chih-hsün, the designated heir, whom he had assigned to watch over the Wu ruler, Yang Lung-yen (r. 908–20), at the court in Kuang-ling, was an intemperate and mean-spirited person who alienated many of those around him. In 918 an angered courtier assassinated Hsü Chih-hsün.[134] Hsü Wen then designated his adopted son, Hsü Chih-kao, to be his eyes and ears in Kuang-ling. Hsü Wen returned "to [his own base in] Chin-ling, from where he managed the general policy of the Wu Kingdom. But the day to day issues of government were now all decided by Chih-kao."[135] In the decade that followed, the power of the Hsü family continued to grow. In 920, as Yang Lung-yen's health failed, Hsü Wen engineered the rejection of Yang Hsing-mi's third son, the mature and vigorous Yang Meng, as the heir apparent in favor of Yang Meng's younger and weaker brother, Yang P'u. When Yang P'u succeeded to the throne shortly afterward, the Hsüs had the most pliable Yang ruler thus far.

Hsü Chih-kao's rise to power encountered its most serious challenge in the fall of 927 when his adopted father and patron died. Many who had been close to Hsü Wen worried that Hsü Chih-kao might usurp the Hsü family patrimony and deny Hsü Wen's children and allies the fruits of their successes. In the end, that is exactly what happened, although it is impossible to be certain whether Hsü Chih-kao was driven by his desire to exclude his stepfather's sons and allies, or by their combined opposition to him.[136] By 931, however, following four years of maneuvering during which he maintained his base in Yang-chou,

---

[133] These and all the following events are discussed in chapters 3–5 of Krompart, "The southern restoration of T'ang." I have relied heavily on this work for narrative detail.

[134] *TCTC* 269, p. 8797; 270, pp. 8827–30.

[135] *TCTC* 270, p. 8831.

[136] Both Krompart's "The southern restoration of T'ang" and Nishikawa's "Go, Nan-Tō ryō ōchō" have examined the differences between the men who allied themselves with Hsü Wen and those who followed Hsü Chih-kao. Hsü Wen's adherents, they conclude, were primarily men of military background who had risen out of the turmoil of the collapsing T'ang; many had long been allies of Hsü Wen, and others simply shared his experience. Hsü Chih-kao's adherents, in contrast, were characteristically of civil background. Hsü Chih-kao was particularly a magnet to civil officials who had fled the turmoil of the north and sought shelter in the Chiang-Huai region. It may well be that the break that occurred between Hsü Chih-kao and his father's old allies was, in fact, forced by those old allies who had never looked favorably upon Hsü Chih-kao and had consequently not been included in his inner circle of advisors.

Hsü Chih-kao had overcome all opposition to his hegemony. He then invoked the model of his father by retiring to Chin-ling (Nanking) and assuming Hsü Wen's old titles. His own son, Hsü Ching-t'ung, remained in Yang-chou to serve as his eyes and ears, just as he himself had served Hsü Wen.[137]

While Hsü Chih-kao now held all effective power in the region, the Yang family remained on the throne. According to Ssu-ma Kuang, as early as 934 "Chih-kao had long planned to accept the abdication [of the Yang family], but because they had not yet lost their virtue he feared that the masses would not be supportive."[138] Between 934 and his formal assumption of the throne as the first ruler of a restored (Southern) T'ang, Hsü Chih-kao and those around him gradually built up his claim to rule while undermining the authority and legitimacy of Yang P'u. So successful were they that in 937 Yang P'u commanded Hsü Chih-kao to accept his abdication and assume an imperial mandate. Late in that year Hsü Chih-kao proclaimed himself ruler of a kingdom that he initially called Ch'i. This name was inspired by an honorary title Hsü Chih-kao had held since Hsü Wen's death and that Hsü Wen had held for many years. Henceforth the Wu kingdom ceased to exist.[139]

Hsü Chih-kao's final step in his consolidation of power was to claim the mantle of the defunct T'ang dynasty. It is uncertain when he first conceived of such a step. No doubt he was influenced by the collapse of the Later T'ang dynasty in the north in 935 and the absence of any current claimant to the T'ang mandate. But to take such a step was momentous. The T'ang mandate was not just to rule a kingdom, a piece of the whole, the T'ang mandate was to rule the entire empire. By invoking the T'ang mandate Hsü Chih-kao distinguished his kingdom from all others that ruled in the south throughout the interregnum. A carefully choreographed campaign to bolster Hsü's claim to the mandate got under way almost immediately after Hsü became King of Ch'i. Portents were cited, pleas that he accept the mandate were orchestrated, and a line of descent from the dynastic house of the T'ang (surnamed Li) concocted.[140] In 939, Hsü Chih-kao dropped the adopted surname "Hsü" in favor of "Li," changed his given name to "Pien," and changed the name of his kingdom to "T'ang." Like the Later Shu, the Southern T'ang empire founded by Li Pien (Hsü Chih-kao) was to persist until the close of the interregnum.

[137] *TCTC* 277, pp. 9062–3; Ma, *Ma-shih Nan T'ang shu* 1, p. 3b.

[138] *TCTC* 279, p. 9103. Krompart, "The southern restoration of T'ang," appears to assume that Hsü Chih-kao had resolved to usurp the throne much earlier; see especially pp. 228–37.

[139] Ma, *Ma-shih Nan T'ang shu* 1, p. 4a. *TCTC* 281, p. 9182, narrates the event but says that Hsü Chih-kao named his new kingdom "T'ang" from the beginning.

[140] The legitimacy of the presumed descent has been witheringly scrutinized in Krompart, "The southern restoration of T'ang," pp. 272–80, and found wanting.

Fu-chien was the last area to experience political upheaval. Following the possibly suspicious death in 925 of the able and popular Wang Shen-chih, the Min kingdom had been plunged into an era of civil war as Wang Shen-chih's natal and adoptive sons competed for advantage.[141] More than any other kingdom, Min was composed of sharply different geographical regions. These geographical differences were reflected in its fractured politics. In our earlier discussion, we have already observed the break between Ch'üan-chou, the major access point to the region's south coast, and Fu-chou in the north of Min, where the central court was located. T'ing-chou, located in the remote and mountainous southwest corner of Min and still today the most isolated part of Fu-chien, was probably never effectively under the sway of the interregnum courts. Even Chien-chou, up the Min River from the capital, Fu-chou, and presumably subject to the court's constant oversight, was regularly at odds with the rulers in Fu-chou. The inability of the Min court to extend effective sway over the kingdom's nominal territory was compounded by its own instability; from the mid-930s palace intrigue was chronic, assassination and regicide common.

Early in the 940s events in the region built toward a crescendo. Civil war between Wang Yen-hsi, based in Fu-chou and the recognized ruler of Min, and his brother Wang Yen-cheng, based in Chien-chou and the self-styled emperor of a breakaway state called Great Yin, was devastating. Min's finances were desperate. Early in 944 the courtiers Chu Wen-chin and Lien Chung-yü, most notable for their previous participation in the assassination of Wang Ch'ang, fourth ruler of the kingdom, again joined in assassination, this time against Wang Yen-hsi. Together they then announced to the shocked courtiers that the heirs to Wang Shen-chih's legacy were "licentious and cruel" and should be replaced by a man of virtue. Chu Wen-chin humbly presented himself as just such a person and took the title "Ruler of Min" (*Min chu*).[142] In the stunned aftermath of Chu Wen-chin's coup there was a general rally from beyond Fu-chou supporting Wang Yen-cheng, who was able to briefly restore his family's rule. However, the assassination of Wang Yen-hsi opened the doors to opportunists throughout the land, effectively ending the Wang family's control of the region.

In the northwest of Min, the neighboring Southern T'ang empire saw an opportunity to expand and sent its armies into the mountains of Chien-chou,

---

[141] The best account of events in Fu-chien remains Edward H. Schafer's *The empire of Min* (Rutland, Vt., 1954); see especially chapter 3. See also the narrative in T'ao, *Wu-tai shih-lüeh*, pp. 263–70. The prefectures named in this discussion can be located on map 1, where Chien-chou is designated by its alternate name of Chien-ning.

[142] *TCTC* 284, pp. 9268–9. To consolidate his victory Chu Wen-chin seized all the members of the Wang family and had them put to death; over fifty were executed in the ensuing carnage.

where they distracted Wang Yen-cheng even as he restored a short-lived unity to the kingdom. Because Wang Yen-cheng hesitated to return to Fu-chou in the face of the Southern T'ang threat, the way was open for an unhappy army leader named Li Jen-ta to seize control of the capital in the spring of 945. In the southern prefecture of Ch'üan-chou a militia leader named Liu Ts'ung-hsiao seized and executed Chu Wen-chin's prefect, and sent his severed head to Wang Yen-cheng in Chien-chou as a sign of submission. Although Yen-cheng then named a kinsman to serve as prefect, real power in Ch'üan-chou was now held by Li Jen-ta and his militia associates.

In the spring of 945, Southern T'ang forces attacked Chien-chou. By the fall they had gained control of the prefecture and also secured the submission of Wang Yen-cheng and the prefectural leaders in T'ing-chou, Ch'üan-chou, and Chang-chou, all of whom had been loyal to the Wang family. Wang family rule was now over. Only Li Jen-ta in Fu-chou held out against the Southern T'ang forces. Although the Southern T'ang court refused to authorize an assault against Li Jen-ta, preferring instead to negotiate his submission, the generals on the spot were hard to control and through the spring of 946 made their own plans. The Southern T'ang court learned of their assault, which began in the late summer of 946, only after the fact. Faced with a fait accompli, the Southern T'ang court then pursued the campaign vigorously. Li Jen-ta, in turn, appealed to neighboring Wu-Yüeh for assistance. Despite the opposition of most of his advisors the Wu-Yüeh ruler, Ch'ien Hung-tsou, opted to assist Fu-chou against the Southern T'ang forces. Subsequently, Li Jen-ta chafed under Wu-Yüeh control. He secretly planned to appeal to the Southern T'ang for help, but was discovered, and he was killed. Fu-chou was then completely integrated into the Wu-Yüeh kingdom.[143]

Liu Ts'ung-hsiao, the militia leader who had seized Ch'üan-chou, was nominally subordinate to the Southern T'ang. In early 946, as a reward for his loyal service on behalf of the Southern T'ang against Li Jen-ta, Liu was named prefect of Ch'üan-chou.[144] But the southeast coast of Fu-chien was beyond the effective control of Southern T'ang forces. This weakness became clear to the Southern T'ang court later in 946 when their appointed prefect of Chang-chou, south of Ch'üan-chou, rebelled. Although Liu Ts'ung-hsiao suppressed the uprising in the name of the Southern T'ang, he replaced the rebellious prefect with a long-time ally of his own. Three years later Liu's brother poisoned that prefect and took his place. As Ssu-ma Kuang put it: "The lord of T'ang was unable to control events, so he established the Ch'ing-yüan army in Ch'üan-chou and

[143] Fan and Lin, *Wu-Yüeh pei-shih* 3, p. 10a; Wu, *Shih-kuo ch'un-ch'iu* 86, p. 1252.
[144] *TCTC* 285, p. 9303.

named Liu its commander."[145] As the 940s closed, the Fu-chien region was divided into three parts: Southern T'ang had gained control of the mountain prefectures of the interior; Wu-Yüeh had seized Fu-chou, the largest and richest prefecture of the old Min kingdom, which also served as a buffer between the Wu-Yüeh heartland and the aggressive forces of T'ang; and along the southern coast a new political entity had arisen, based in Ch'üan-chou, under the control of Liu Ts'ung-hsiao. This region, all that remained of the defunct Min kingdom, was able to maintain its independence until it submitted to Sung rule in 978.

One last change, although not fully part of our narrative, also deserves a brief discussion: the rise of an independent state in Annam (An-nan), the northern portion of Vietnam centered around the Red River.[146] Annam had been under varying degrees of Chinese administrative control since the Han dynasty eight centuries earlier, and the regional elite had been highly sinified, but control of the Chinese court and of the sinified elite had been seriously threatened by the invasion of Nan-chao in the mid-ninth century.[147] Although the T'ang forces of Kao P'ien had been able to repel the invasion, T'ang authority was never again as strong as it had been previously, now having to rely on the local sinified elite to provide local officials rather than being able to appoint Han Chinese. When Liu Yin gained control over Ling-nan and established the Southern Han he claimed Annam as part of his kingdom, but it was an empty claim. Indigenous, albeit sinified, leadership was able to hold Southern Han at bay and manipulate the Liang court of the north to maintain their own autonomy. The politics of the moment, however, prevented those leaders from formally breaking their nominal dependence upon the Chinese court, thereby inadvertently giving some legitimacy to Southern Han's continuing claim.

But in 930, Liu Yen, who had succeeded his brother Liu Yin on the Southern Han throne, launched a successful invasion of Annam, sweeping away the sinified leaders. While the Southern Han armies encountered little opposition from those leaders, they were quickly confronted with a very different challenge. In late 931, Duong Dinh Nghe, a native of Ai province, the southernmost region of Annam and the area where Chinese political and cultural influence had traditionally been weakest and a sense of a separate Annamese identity consequently strongest, led an army against the Southern

[145] *TCTC* 288, p. 9417.
[146] The following narrative is drawn largely from chapters 6 and 7 in Keith W. Taylor, *The birth of Vietnam* (Berkeley, Calif., 1983). Also useful is "Godai Sōsho no Reinan to Betonamu dokuritsu ōchō no seiritsu," in Kawahara, *Kan minzoku Kanan hattenshi kenkyū*, pp. 229–70.
[147] See the discussion in Somers, "The end of the T'ang," pp. 692–5.

Han authorities and routed them. The Southern Han court, unable to offer any effective resistance to Duong's force, chose the path of least resistance and recognized him as a military governor. We can guess that this courtesy meant very little to Duong, for he was assassinated six years later by a leader of a pro-Chinese faction bent on restoring the sinified leadership he had displaced.

The brief return of that leadership, however, only prompted the rise of another native of the same southern reaches of Annam that had produced Duong Dinh Nghe and the strong sense of local identity that had legitimized his rule. Ngo Quyen had been a general under Duong and had served him as governor of Ai province. He was closely connected with the party that had just been overthrown. Ngo Quyen quickly disposed of the revanchist leaders and easily repulsed the efforts of Southern Han to defeat him. Two years later, in 939, he proclaimed himself king, a step that even Duong had been reluctant to take, and abandoned the capital of Dai-la (modern Hanoi), which he felt to be too closely identified with Chinese interests, in favor of Co-loa, farther to the south and long identified with Annamese culture. Subsequent Vietnamese historians have debated whether to acknowledge Ngo Quyen as the founder of an independent state, because he declined to take an imperial title and so nominally remained subordinate not only to the Chinese courts of the north but even to the Liu rulers of Southern Han who had taken that step in 917.[148] But the fact is that neither the Southern Han nor the Sung dynasty was able to project even nominal control over the Red River valley.

ECONOMIC STRUCTURES

The new kingdoms that had taken shape by the beginning of the tenth century all bore the burden of the several decades of turmoil that had wracked their lands, turmoil that had often been intended as a form of economic terrorism to destroy the people's livelihood.[149] Peasants had fled, cropland had fallen into disuse, cities had been besieged, and social and administrative infrastructures had collapsed. As the new ruling elites surveyed their realms and plotted courses of action, economic recovery was near the top of their priorities.

Agriculture was the basic source of wealth, and the new elites turned their attention to the restoration of agricultural productivity and the infrastructures of distribution. These were critical for the restoration of stability.

---

[148] See the discussion in Taylor, *The birth of Vietnam*, p. 275.

[149] See, for example, *TCTC* 265, p. 8638, which accuses Chu Wen of deliberately seeking the impoverishment of the peasantry of Huai-nan. For a general survey of immiseration in the Chiang-Huai region, see Matsui, "Tōdai kōhanki no Kō-Wai ni tsuite," pp. 1–29.

The most important step toward restoration of agricultural productivity and the distribution of goods was simply to restore order, and all areas showed signs of improvement by the early tenth century as order returned. As the new kingdoms consolidated, their rulers issued formulaic calls to their populations to promote agriculture.[150] But more concrete steps were possible as well, and in some combination were pursued almost everywhere. One such step was to ease tax burdens. In the years after Huang Ch'ao's campaigns, as the struggle for collapsing T'ang power unfolded across the south, the numerous contestants exacted ever-larger revenues from those under their control in order to finance their war efforts. Continuation of these heavy tax burdens marked the initial policies of the new states, but after a measure of peace was restored, large military expenditures were no longer necessary and tended to undermine the goal of restoring agricultural prosperity. Thus, at least some of the new rulers took steps to ease these burdens. Ssu-ma Kuang tells us that in 904: "Taxation under Wang [Chien] was onerous, but none dared to object. Then Feng Chüan took advantage of Wang's birthday celebration to mention the sufferings of the people. Wang was distraught, and thanked him. . . . From that time, the taxes of [the Former] Shu were eased."[151] Ssu-ma Kuang also tells us that under Wang Shen-chih "punishments were lenient and taxes were light" in the Min kingdom of Fu-chien.[152]

The establishment of peace and the easing of taxes helped to restore conditions that had underlain the prosperity of preceding centuries. Even more important to the increase of agricultural productivity were the active steps taken to promote new growth, such as the expansion of water conservancy networks and the reclamation of arable land. All the southern kingdoms lay within China's wet rice regions where irrigation is crucial to the success of the crop. Throughout the south such networks were already in place well before the late ninth century, the result of the many decades and even centuries of dramatic demographic and economic expansion that had transformed the Yangtze basin into the empire's premier rice basket long before the interregnum. But the fiscal needs of the new kingdoms demanded increases in agricultural productivity, which could be achieved only by expanding irrigation networks to support the creation of new paddy land. Irrigation projects were carried out throughout the southern kingdoms in the early tenth century. In Szechwan, for example, Chang Lin, prefect of the Ch'eng-tu Plain prefecture of Mei-chou around the turn of the century, restored the T'ung-chi Dike (*yen*), providing

[150] For a general survey of these policies, see Cheng Hsüeh-meng, "Wu-tai shih-ch'i Ch'ang-chiang liu-yü chi Chiang-nan ti-ch'ü ti nung-yeh ching-chi," *Li-shih yen-chiu* 4 (1985), pp. 32–44.

[151] *TCTC* 265, p. 8635.

[152] *TCTC* 267, pp. 8716–17.

water to 15,000 ch'ing (approximately 210,000 acres) of reclaimed paddy and earning a popular encomium that went: "Before we had Chang Ch'iu, and after came Duke Chang [i.e., Chang Lin]. Both expanded our irrigation, so our rice crops are rich."[153] In Ching-nan, Kao Chi-ch'ang took the lead in promoting reclamation projects, directing the construction of a dike that extended over thirty-three miles between the Han and Yangtze rivers and provided security from flooding to an extensive and highly productive floodplain.[154] In Ch'u, "because there were many springs in the mountains east of T'an-chou, the Ma family constructed dikes to collect the water and thereby provided irrigation to 10,000 ch'ing."[155] Even as small an entity as the warlord enclave on the southern coast of Fu-chien undertook projects such as the Ch'en Embankment, named for Ch'en Hung-chin who succeeded Liu Ts'ung-hsiao as leader of that domain in the last years before Sung unification; the embankment secured a coastal strip at the mouth of the Chiu-lung River from tidal encroachment and thereby opened up extensive new land to settlement and production.

Similar projects were undertaken in all the southern kingdoms,[156] but the state that pursued the expansion of water conservation networks most intensely was Wu-Yüeh. Although Wu-Yüeh encompassed different terrain – from the plains surrounding Hang-chou Bay to the highlands of the rugged interior – the low-lying coastal districts were among the most productive and heavily settled lands in all of China. The yield from the extensive paddylands was critical to the prosperity of the new kingdom of Wu-Yüeh. Without coastal dikes and catchment basins, these lands were subject to regular flooding, especially at times of storm surges in the spring and fall. The Wu-Yüeh leaders engaged in ambitious efforts to enhance those defenses. In 910, for example, the Warding off the Sea Catchment Basin (Han-hai t'ang) was constructed just outside the Hang-chou city wall to contain waters that were regularly flooding even the city gates. As Ssu-ma Kuang commented: "Today there are stone-lined catchment basins all along the city wall, and all were built by the Ch'ien rulers [of Wu-Yüeh]. . . . From this point, the wealth of Hang-chou was greatest in all the southeast."[157] The Warding off the Sea Catchment Basin may have been the most noted construction project of the interregnum, but

[153] Wu, Shih-kuo ch'un-ch'iu 40, p. 597. For a brief survey of trends in Szechwanese agriculture during the imperial era, see Paul J. Smith, "Commerce, agriculture, and core formation in the upper Yangzi, 2 A.D. to 1948," Late Imperial China 9 No. 1 (1988), pp. 22–41.

[154] Wu, Shih-kuo ch'un-ch'iu 100, p. 1430.

[155] T'o-t'o et al., eds., Sung shih [hereafter SS] (1345; Peking, 1977) 173, p. 4183.

[156] As general surveys of this process, see Pien Hsiao-hsüan and Cheng Hsüeh-meng, Wu-tai shih-hua (Peking, 1985), pp. 76–80, and T'ao Mao-ping, Wu-tai shih-lüeh (Peking, 1985), pp. 180–8.

[157] TCTC 267, p. 8726; Fan and Lin, Wu-Yüeh pei-shih 1, pp. 47b–48a. See the discussion in Cheng, "Wu-tai shih-ch'i Ch'ang-chiang liu-yu," p. 37.

many others, each equally important to those who benefited, are mentioned in surviving accounts.[158]

Perhaps the most significant innovation of the Wu-Yüeh rulers, however, was to establish the commissioner of waterways and agriculture (*tu-shui ying-t'ien shih*): "The commissioner of waterways and agriculture was established in order to manage irrigation. . . . He was directed to establish four corps around Lake T'ai with a total complement of 7,000–8,000 men to oversee the fields, to control the rivers, and to maintain the dikes. . . . If there was drought, then they brought water to the fields; at times of flooding, they drained water away from the fields."[159] Over a century later, Fan Chung-yen wrote of these men:

The corps specialized in matters pertaining to the fields, such as channeling rivers and building dikes in order to avoid flooding. At that time, the people could buy a picul (*shih2*) of rice for 50 cash. Ever since our dynasty [the Sung] unified the area, whenever the rice crop has failed in Chiang-nan relief supplies have been sought in Che-yu [the coastal regions north of the Yangtze River]. When the crop has failed in Che-yu, then relief has been sought in Huai-nan. [Our dynasty] has been careless about managing agriculture. The infrastructure has not been maintained, more than half the polders of Chiang-nan and the dikes of Che-hsi are in disrepair, and we thereby have forfeited the greatest advantage of the southeast. Today in Chiang-nan and Liang-che the price of a picul of rice is not less than 600–700 cash, or even 1,000 cash. If we compare it to the days of Wu-Yüeh, the cost has increased tenfold.[160]

Fan Chung-yen's praise for the commission's work was echoed by a twelfth-century gazetteer, which stated that "In the one hundred years of Ch'ien family rule the harvests were always good. Only during the Chang-hsing era [930–4] was there any flooding."[161]

Hand in hand with the restoration of agricultural productivity went the promotion of commercial agriculture, the expansion of handicraft and industrial production, and the building or restoration of trade networks. Tea, for example, was an important commodity in private trade. As early as 908, Kao Yü, a prominent advisor to Ma Yin of Ch'u, commented that "the people are cultivating vegetables and tea which they sell to northern merchants."[162]

---

[158] For a brief but specific overview of all the major water conservancy projects of Wu-Yüeh, see Pien and Cheng, *Wu-tai shih-hua*, pp. 77–8.

[159] Wu, *Shih-kuo ch'un-ch'iu* 78, p. 1090. See also Chu Ch'ang-wen, *Wu-chün t'u-ching hsü-chi* (1084; Peking, 1990) *hsia*, p. 1b, and Fan Ch'eng-ta, *Wu-chün chih* (1192; Peking, 1990) 19, p. 20b. It is not clear exactly when the Commission on Waterways and Agriculture was first established; there is no mention of it in *TCTC*.

[160] T'ao, *Wu-tai shih-lüeh*, p. 183, quoting the first *chüan*, "Ta yü chao t'iao-ch'en shih-shih," in *Fan Wen-cheng kung tsou-i-chi*.

[161] Fan, *Wu-chün chih*, 19, p. 20b.

[162] *TCTC* 266, p. 8702. See also Ma, *Ma-shih Nan T'ang shu* 29, p. 2b. See the discussion in Okada Kōji, "Godai Sō ōkoku no seikaku," in *Nakajima Satoshi Sensei koki kinen ronshū*, ed. Nakajima Satoshi Sensei Koki Kinen Jigyōkai (Tokyo, 1980–1), vol. 2, pp. 78–9.

Ch'u, of course, was not the only center of tea production. In 965 the Sung dynasty opened monopoly purchase centers for tea in five prefectures along the Yangtze and Huai rivers in territory that had just been reclaimed from the Southern T'ang.[163] These monopoly markets clearly reflected an earlier pattern of tea production in the hill country between the two rivers, land that in many ways is an extension of the tea country of Ch'u.[164] The northwestern corner of Fu-chien was a third center of tea growing as early as the late T'ang. Although we lack any concrete discussion of the relationship between the Min government and its tea producers, the references to tea in the notes on local products of the *T'ai-p'ing huan-yü chi* confirm that tea production was widespread at least by the close of the interregnum period.[165]

Without a doubt the most famous and best-documented center of tea production outside Ch'u was Szechwan, which had long been known for its teas.[166] Tea production remained important throughout the interregnum, a conclusion amply demonstrated by the long discussions on local teas in the *Ch'a-p'u* (*Monograph on tea*) of Mao Wen-hsi, an official of both the Former and Later Shu who was closely identified with Wang Chien.[167] Although there is evidence that the Former Shu kingdom did permit some private trade in the commodity,[168] Su Ch'e, younger brother of the famous statesman Su Shih, recalled that the Wang rulers had implemented a tea monopoly as well: "I have heard that in the Five Dynasties era when the Wang family ruled the land of Shu, government revenues were constricted and so they implemented a tea monopoly law."[169]

The cultivation of mulberry leaves and rearing of silkworms, sericulture, was becoming another important activity in many regions. Szechwan had a long tradition of producing fine silks, and the description of the silkworm

---

[163] Li T'ao, *Hsü Tzu-chih t'ung-chien ch'ang-pien* [hereafter *HCP* (1964)] [*Che-chiang shu-chü* 1881 ed.] (1183; Taipei, 1961–4) 6, p. 13a. See also the discussion in Kawahara Yoshirō, *Hoku-Sō ki tochi shoyū no mondai to shōgyō shihon* (Fukuoka, 1964), p. 322.

[164] On the prior history of tea production in these lands, see Matsui, "Tōdai kōhanki no Kō-Wai," pp. 20–1, and Hino Kaisaburō, "So no Ma In to tsūka seisaku no Godai jidai no kinyū gyōsha (jō)," *Tōyō gakuhō* 54 No. 2 (1971), pp. 28–9.

[165] See Yüeh, *T'ai-p'ing huan-yü chi* 101, p. 3b, regarding local products of Chien-chou; 100, p. 3b for Fu-chou; and 100, p. 9b for Nan-chien-chou. Hino, "So no Ma In (jō)," p. 37, also refers to evidence of tea from Ching-nan.

[166] For a survey of the history of tea in Szechwan, see chapter 2 of Paul J. Smith, *Taxing heaven's storehouse: Horses, bureaucrats and the destruction of the Sichuan tea industry, 1074–1224* (Cambridge, Mass., 1991). In addition to his own discussion, Smith makes reference to an extensive bibliography.

[167] See the discussion in Yang, *Ch'ien Shu Hou Shu shih*, pp. 178–9. On Mao Wen-hsi, see Wu, *Shih-kuo ch'un-ch'iu* 41, p. 609.

[168] See Kawahara, *Hoku-Sō ki tochi shoyū no mondai*, p. 50, which quotes this passage from Ho, *Chien-chieh lu* 4.

[169] See Yang, *Ch'ien Shu Hou Shu shih*, p. 180, which quotes *Luan-ch'eng chi* 36.

markets in the *Mao-t'ing k'o-hua*, an anecdotal collection compiled around the turn of the eleventh century, gives a feeling for the growing importance of sericulture under the Former and Later Shu kingdoms: "Shu has silkworm markets. They meet every year from the first to the third month [early spring] in the capital city [Ch'eng-tu], and they rotate among fifteen sites.... Trade is conducted in tools for silkworm rearing and agriculture as well as in goods from orchards and gardens and in medicines of all kinds."[170]

The origins of these markets stretch back at least as far as the late ninth century.[171] The *Wu-kuo ku-shih* adds that Wang Chien visited one such market and observed that "many are cultivating mulberry."[172] Ch'u was not the only source of tea among the southern kingdoms, nor was Szechwan the only flourishing producer of silk. In an entry for 925, Ssu-ma Kuang says of Ch'u: "The people of Hunan had not previously practiced sericulture. Kao Yü ordered the people to pay their taxes in cloth instead of cash. Soon looms were flourishing among them."[173] In 918, Sung Ch'i-ch'iu, a minister for the state of Wu, successfully advocated the policy of allowing people to pay their taxes in cloth or grain instead of in cash, after which "the lands of Huai were fully planted, sericulture was widespread, and the state grew rich and strong."[174] A Southern Sung edict of 1167 recalled that the Ch'ien rulers of Wu-Yüeh levied roughly one yard of cheap pongee silk (*chüan2*) on every *mou* of paddy land, and roughly four feet of silk on every *mou* of mulberry orchard. This retrospective evidence shows that silk cloth was integral to the local tax systems of these regions.[175]

Although it is generally unstated, it is implicit in all the foregoing passages that the several kingdoms often sought to promote the production of tea and silk as a way of enhancing their revenues. Another area of economic activity that they promoted at least in part for its fiscal advantages was handicraft and industrial production. Sericulture is, of course, inextricably tied to one such activity: the production of textiles. Virtually all the southern kingdoms were widely known for one textile or another, and several had government-run centers of production.[176] As is clear from the many entries that mention them among the tribute goods the southern kingdoms sent to the northern courts, textiles were very important commodities in the southern economies. Ceramic

---

[170] Huang Hsiu-fu, *Mao-t'ing k'o-hua* [*Lin-lang pi-shih ts'ung-shu* 1853 ed., 1887, 1888] (early 11th c.; Taipei, 1967) 9, pp. 2b–3b.

[171] See Chü Ch'ing-yüan, "T'ang-Sung shih-tai Ssu-ch'uan ti ts'an-shih," *Shih-huo pan yüeh k'an* 3 No. 6 (1936), pp. 28–34.

[172] *Wu-kuo ku-shih shang*, p. 10b.

[173] *TCTC* 274, p. 8953. See also Okada, "Godai So ōkoku no seikaku," p. 78.

[174] *TCTC* 270, p. 8832.

[175] Hsü Sung et al., *Sung hui-yao chi-pen* [hereafter *SHY* (1964)] (Sung, 1809, 1936; Taipei, 1964) *shih-huo* 70, p. 58a.

[176] See the discussions in Pien and Cheng, *Wu-tai shih-hua*, pp. 85–6, and T'ao, *Wu-tai shih-lüeh*, pp. 188–90.

production was another important craft in the south. Although production occurred widely and ceramic goods were another frequent tribute item, they were especially important to Wu-Yüeh, where state-run kilns existed beside private enterprises. A modern commentator has observed: "The Yüeh kilns at Yü-yao and Shang-lin Lake [in Chekiang] undoubtedly reached their peak in the tenth century when, under the Five Dynasties and early Sung, they enjoyed the direct patronage of the Wu-Yüeh rulers."[177] A third area of wide economic importance was mining. Not only did the southern kingdoms include large quantities of metal goods in their tribute to the northern dynasties, but many also issued their own coinage.

Important as the expansion and diversification of agricultural and craft production were to all the economies of the south, for several of the states they were not the key to prosperity or even to economic – and thus political – survival. These economies developed instead an unparalleled dependence upon trade. Of course interregional trade has a long history in China. It is well known, in particular, that the volume of trade, both interregional and local, expanded greatly through the eighth and ninth centuries. This growth was in no small part due to the movement of population into the lightly settled lands south of the Yangtze River, where administrative oversight was thin and bureaucratic regulation was consequently limited. These were also the centuries when the volume of overseas commerce increased greatly, stimulating the growth of coastal port cities such as Kuang-chou, Ch'üan-chou, Fu-chou, and Yang-chou. Thus trade was not a new variable in the economies of the lands of the south, nor were the trade patterns of the interregnum new. But the trade patterns are of particular interest for two reasons: because of what they say about interstate relationships during the era, and because of the critical role that trade revenues played in the survival of many of the interregnum kingdoms.

Trade generally was of three kinds: internal trade within a southern kingdom itself; direct trade in domestic goods among the southern kingdoms or between those kingdoms and the northern dynasties; and transshipment trade in imported goods from the South Seas. Internal trade within any of the kingdoms is paradoxically both the most self-evident and the most difficult of all trade patterns to demonstrate. Other than the relatively ample evidence for Szechwan, as exemplified by the passage on silkworm markets cited earlier, the references to internal trade in the remaining southern kingdoms are rare and almost exclusively anecdotal.[178]

---

[177] Basil Gray, *Sung porcelain and stoneware* (London, 1984), p. 30. See also T'ao, *Wu-tai shih-lüeh*, pp. 195–7, and Pien and Cheng, *Wu-tai shih-hua*, pp. 88–91. On Szechwan, see especially Yang, *Ch'ien Shu Hou Shu shih*, pp. 198–201.

[178] For a general discussion of trade in the two Shu kingdoms, see Yang, *Ch'ien Shu Hou Shu shih*, pp. 202–10. For two notices of trade (one about rice, the other about firewood) in the Fu-chien region, see Hsü, *Chi-shen lu* 3, pp. 7a–b; 5, pp. 11a–b.

Far more material survives on trade among the southern kingdoms and between them and the northern dynasties. In his extensive research Hino Kaisaburō identified three major inland routes of communication for both trade and official correspondence: the Kan River valley through Kiangsi, the Hsiang River valley through Hunan; and the Grand Canal.[179] Despite its enduring fame and mystery, the Grand Canal was the least important of the three routes. The chronic conflict between the kingdom that controlled the heart of the route and its great port Yang-chou, first Wu and then the Southern T'ang, and the states linked to the canal, Wu-Yüeh and the successive northern dynasties, made transit of the entire Grand Canal difficult if not impossible.

There was, of course, one other well-traveled route connecting north and south: the seaborne route along the coast as far as the ports of the Shantung peninsula and beyond to the northern lands of the Khitan, Korea, and even Japan. Because there were too many unpredictable dangers on the open sea, ranging from pirates to sudden storms, this was not a popular option and so was resorted to only when other inland routes became less safe. Ssu-ma Kuang alluded to this kind of difficulty in a comment appended to his account of the fall of Ch'ien-chou, the prefecture on the upper Kan River in southern Hunan that had been the center of an independent fief controlled by Lu Kuang-ch'ou. Under Lu this prefecture had been an important crossroads for both north-south and east-west communications, a role it held until it was overrun by Wu in 918: "Prior to this Ch'ien Liu had commonly sent his tribute [to the Later Liang dynasty] via Ch'ien-chou [i.e., through southern Kiangsi and into Hunan and points north]. Now [because of the enmity between Wu and Wu-Yüeh] that route was cut, and so Ch'ien's envoys began to use the sea route via Teng-chou and Lai-chou [ports on the Shantung peninsula] to enter Liang."[180] The Min rulers of Fu-chien had the same problem: "Yang Hsing-mi had occupied Chiang-tung and Huai-nan, and thus Min was cut off from [inland communications with] the Central Plains. Thereafter, when Wang Shen-chih sent tribute to the northern dynasties, the mission went by sea to Teng-chou and Lai-chou where they disembarked. But in going and coming

---

[179] Hino Kaisaburō, "Godai nanboku Shina rikujō kōtsūro ni tsuite," *Rekishigaku kenkyū* 11 No. 6 (1941), pp. 2–32. See, in addition, Hino's set of three articles: "Godai jidai ni okeru Kittan to Shina to no kaijōbōeki (jō)," *Shigaku zasshi* 52 No. 7 (1941), pp. 1–47; "Godai jidai ni okeru Kittan to Shina to no kaijōbōeki (chū)," *Shigaku zasshi* 52 No. 8 (1941), pp. 60–85; and "Godai jidai ni okeru Kittan to Shina to no kaijōbōeki (ge)," *Shigaku zasshi* 52 No. 9 (1941), pp. 55–82. See also, the pair of his articles: "Godai Binkoku no taichūgen chōkō to bōeki (jō)," *Shien* 26 (1941), pp. 1–50; and "Godai Binkoku no taichūgen chōkō to bōeki (ge)," *Shien* 27 (1942), pp. 1–41, and the pair "So no Ma In to tsūka seisaku" (jō) and "So no Ma In to tsūka seisaku to Godai jidai no kinyūgyōsha (ge)," *Tōyō gakuhō*, 54 No. 3 (1971), pp. 57–89. See, finally, the comments in his addendum to chapter 8 of *Zoku Tōdai no teiten no kenkyū* (Fukuoka, 1970), pp. 416–502.

[180] *TCTC* 270, pp. 8836–7.

they had to confront the dangers of wind and water, and four or five out of every ten ships were lost."[181]

All of the southern kingdoms except for the Former and Later Shu of Szechwan were tied to each other and to the northern dynasties by one or more of these routes, while the successive Shu kingdoms were linked to the north by roadways first cut through the mountains by Ch'in Shih-huang's engineers a millennium earlier.[182] Consequently, there was a great deal of movement among all the southern kingdoms and between those kingdoms and the northern dynasties. The latter trade is the best documented because of the court-oriented nature of the historical sources and because much of this trade was in the form of tribute. It would appear that most trade between south and north was directly controlled by the southern courts, either as tribute or as state-managed trade. Wu-Yüeh, Min, Ch'u, and Ching-nan all maintained regular tribute relations with the north, despite some occasional interruptions, and the goods offered as tribute were all commercially important. Ch'u annually sent two hundred and fifty thousand catties of tea. Wu-Yüeh sent large quantities of silks and metal goods. Min and Southern Han offered imported goods from the South Seas trade.[183] Ssu-ma Kuang spoke directly of the commercial importance of tribute: "Discussions at [the Later Liang] court all noted the great profits which Ch'ien Liu's tribute earned in the market. Many felt that it was inappropriate to further reward him with titles [as the emperor, Liang Mo-ti, was proposing to do]."[184] The relationship between tribute and trade is echoed in the events surrounding the tributary mission of Cheng Yüan-pi, representing the emperor of Min, Min K'ang-tsung, to the Later Chin emperor Chin Kao-tsu (r. 936–42). Cheng Yüan-pi and his company of three hundred and fifty found themselves imprisoned by the Later Chin emperor in response to the unacceptably arrogant tone of the Min emperor's letter that Cheng Yüan-pi presented to the Later Chin throne. After allowing its members to languish for several months, the Later Chin court relented and prepared to send the mission home, at which point the "tributary goods and private merchandise" (kung-wu ssu-shang) were returned to their rightful owners "according to the official list."[185] Obviously, most of the large number who accompanied Cheng

[181] In Hino, "Godai Binkoku (jō)" (1941), p. 20, quoting Ts'e-fu yüan-kuei 232.

[182] On the predominantly northern orientation of Szechwan's trade until the twelfth century, see Smith, "Commerce, agriculture, and core formation," pp. 42–5.

[183] On Ch'u, see TCTC 266, p. 8702. On Wu-Yüeh, see Hino, "Godai nanboku Shina," p. 8. On Min, see Clark, Community, trade, and networks, p. 65.

[184] TCTC 269, p. 8803. For the connection between tribute and trade between Min and the northern courts, see Hino's "Godai Binkoku" articles, especially "Godai Binkoku (ge)," pp. 12–28.

[185] On Cheng Yüan-pi's mission, see TCTC 282, pp. 9207–10. See also the discussion in Hino, Zoku Tōdai teiten no kenkyū, pp. 593–4.

Yüan-pi did so in pursuit of private trade, not in order to offer tribute, and this was an acknowledged, even official, part of the tributary process. The southern courts that pursued tributary ties with the northern dynasties were at least as interested in the profits they could earn through the relationship as they were in the ritual submission that it entailed.

Many if not all the southern courts also exercised control over nontributary trade relationships through court-managed trade outlets. In the early tenth century, for example, Ch'u initiated a system of state control over the production of tea and then opened a network of trading agencies to regulate its sale to the northern dynasties. Ssu-ma Kuang wrote that the policy was motivated by the suggestion of the court official Kao Yü that "the people are selling their vegetables and tea to northern merchants," and "if we collect taxes on this, we can support our army." Ssu-ma Kuang then says, "In 908 the Ch'u king, Ma Yin, petitioned [the Later Liang court for permission] to establish trading agencies (*hui-t'u wu*) in Pien-chou, Ching-chou2, Hsiang-chou, T'ang-chou, Ying-chou3, and Fu-chou3. . . . This request was granted, and from that time on Hunan prospered."[186] The profits that Ch'u agents realized through the sale of tea in these northern districts, where they had an effective monopoly, were used to purchase fine textiles and warhorses for the Ch'u court and army, essentially as Kao Yü had suggested. As Ssu-ma Kuang observed: "The territory of Ch'u produces large quantities of gold and silver, but the profits from tea are especially great."[187]

Wu-Yüeh also sought to control the profits of its trade with the north through state-sponsored agencies, although in contrast to Ch'u it did not seek the permission of the northern court to do so and was apparently much more aggressive in pursuit of profit:

At the time of the Later Han dynasty [947–50], because the route across Chiang-Huai had been cut, emissaries from Ch'ien Liu commonly came across the sea to the [Later Han territory]. In the coastal prefectures they established trading agencies (*po-i wu*, equivalent to *hui-t'u wu*) to carry out trade with the people. When the people failed to meet their debts on time, the agency officials themselves would seek to enforce them. They even established their own jails without regard to [the jurisdiction of] the local districts or counties. Because the [Later Han] officials had been heavily bribed, they tolerated this without question.[188]

It is clear that traders operating under the official imprimatur of the Wu-Yüeh court were engaged in direct and apparently unregulated trade with

---

[186] *TCTC* 266, p. 8702. Hino, "So no Ma In (jō)," pp. 26–7, argues that the textiles were also for military purposes. See the same essay on the tie between geography and the tea trade. See also the discussion in Okada, "Godai So ōkoku no seikaku," p. 77.

[187] *TCTC* 283, p. 9258.

[188] Ou-yang, *Hsin Wu-tai shih* 30, p. 335; see also *CWTS* 107, p. 1415.

private citizens of the north, the "Central Kingdom." Through a policy of bribery, they had bought off the local officials of the northern dynasties in order to pursue their profits without interference, even to the point of jailing local citizens to enforce the collection of debts.

Trade between the southern kingdoms and the northern dynasties was valuable not only to the participants but also to the states through which it passed. Ch'u, for example, adopted an ingenious method of indirect taxation on passing merchants:

Following the plan of Kao Yü, the Ch'u king, Ma Yin, minted lead and iron coins. Yü had argued that these coins would be useless to merchants outside Ch'u. Before leaving the kingdom, the merchants would exchange the coins for other goods. Thus Ch'u could barter what was surplus in Hunan for the myriad goods of the whole empire, and the kingdom would be rich.[189]

This obviously relates to the passage of merchants through Ch'u territory as they traversed the Hsiang River route mentioned earlier; without directly taxing the merchants, Ch'u had devised a way to make a significant profit nevertheless. Ching-nan was less subtle: "Ching-nan lay between Hunan [Ch'u], Ling-nan [Southern Han], and Fu-chien [Min]. . . . Since the time of Kao Chi-ch'ang, when envoys carrying tribute from these lands crossed Ching-nan territory [en route to the northern dynasties], Ching-nan seized a portion of their goods."[190] The degree to which Ching-nan had become dependent on these "revenues" is revealed in an incident that occurred in 948: "Ever since Kao Ts'ung-mei had broken with the Later Han dynasty [in 947], northern merchants had not come and the land was impoverished. So he sent an envoy [to the Later Han court] admitting his error and begging restoration of his tributary status."[191] Ching-nan lay along the one inland route between the southern kingdoms and northern dynasties that remained open, and it also commanded Yangtze River traffic between Wu and Nan T'ang, and Szechwan. This made it possible for Ching-nan to impose heavy transit charges, and the kingdom became heavily dependent on a system of transit taxes. When traffic on the route was interrupted, as it was in the year 947–8, the state was quickly reduced to begging.

In addition to trade between north and south, there was also extensive trade among the southern kingdoms themselves. An eleventh-century gazetteer of Su-chou, for example, comments: "Merchants from Fu-chien and Kuang-nan ride the wind to cross the sea, for there is no risk. Through them precious items

[189] *TCTC* 274, p. 8953.
[190] *TCTC* 287, p. 9375.
[191] *TCTC* 288, p. 9394.

and things from afar gather in the markets of Su-chou."[192] This is echoed in a passage from the *Wu-tai shih-pu*:

One morning [the monk Ch'i-ying] accompanied the King of Wu-Yüeh (Ch'ien Shu, r. 948–78) to the Pi-po Pavilion. At that moment the tide was full and ships were jammed together so tightly one could not see a beginning or an end to them. The king marveled: "This place is over 3,000 *li* from the capital [i.e., the northern court]. Who there could imagine that there could be so much profit [collected together] in one river?"[193]

The vibrant trade at the ports of the midcoast, such as Ming-chou and Hang-chou, and in inland cities on canal routes like Su-chou, was based upon ties with ports farther south in Min and Southern Han that gave access to the South Seas trade. Although such trade connections benefited all parties, the economies of the southernmost kingdoms were internally less developed than those of the more central kingdoms and were probably very dependent on the profits derived from these ties. Hu San-hsing, the Yüan dynasty commentator of the *Tzu-chih t'ung-chien*, suggested the many places along the midcoast where traders from the south might stop: "[Following the blockage of the overland route through Huai-nan, emissaries] had to travel from Fu-chien along the coast of Wen-chou. On reaching T'ai-chou they passed T'ien-men Mountain before approaching the coast of Ming-chou at Hsiang-shan. They then passed Ts'en-chiang and Lieh Harbor before heading out to sea en route to the coast of Teng-chou and Lai-chou."[194] Clearly the route from Fu-chien hugged the coast before heading out to the open sea somewhere north of Ming-chou (Ning-po) en route to Shantung.

In addition to trade ties along the coast, the southern kingdoms traded with one another along the inland routes. We see the evidence of trade ties between Southern T'ang and Min when the Southern T'ang court, planning an invasion of northwestern Fu-chien, turned for advice to the Han-lin academician Tsang Hsün, who had once been a merchant well versed in the topography of Fu-chien, to help draw up a strategy for capturing Chien-chou.[195] The *Ch'ing-i lu*, compiled as the interregnum closed, mentions the longan (*lung-yen*) fruit trade between Ling-nan and Ching-nan,[196] while the *Shih-kuo ch'un-ch'iu* tells of the merchant Shen Chia "who frequently passed between [Ch'u] and

---

[192] Chu, *Wu-chün t'u-ching hsü-chi shang*, p. 15a. The author's casual dismissal of risk stands in contrast to other claims of high danger on the ocean route. The risk, however, was greatest in the open water between the ports of Wu-Yüeh and the tip of the Shantung peninsula, a reach that was radically different from the coast-hugging stretches used farther south. The voyage between Fu-chou or Kuang-nan and Wu-Yüeh entailed much less danger than the voyage to the north.

[193] T'ao, *Wu-tai shih-pu* 5, pp. 13b–14a.

[194] *TCTC* 267, p. 8717.

[195] *TCTC* 284, p. 9278.

[196] T'ao Ku, *Ch'ing-i lu* [*Pao-yen t'ang pi-chi* 1606 ed.] (c. 960–70; Taipei, 1965) 2, p. 12b.

Kuang-chou."[197] All three anecdotes are references to trade along a north-south axis, reflecting the Kan and Hsiang river routes mentioned earlier. There was also an important east-west trade, with Ching-nan along the Yangtze River route that linked Chiang-Huai and Szechwan. In 913, for example, Kao Chi-ch'ang strengthened his local defenses and then announced "to all exiles and to those in transit between Wu and Shu" that he was no longer beholden to the northern dynasty.[198] The *Chiu Wu-tai shih* records: "Kao Ts'ung-mei [r. 929–48] abutted Wu to his east and Shu to his west. Both profited from the goods he sent in return for military supplies."[199] Similarly, Huang Hsiu-fu (?– c. 1006), in his biographical study of famous artists from Szechwan, recorded that merchants from the lower Yangtze River often sought to buy notable works in the local markets of Szechwan:

[In the Wu-ch'eng era (908–11)] the rulers of Ching-nan, Hu-nan, Huai-nan, and Liang-che sent men to Shu to scour the markets [for the works of the artist Chang Hsüan] which they then took back to their own lands. . . . While Shu was under the hegemonic rule [of the Wang family], merchants from Chiang-nan and Wu[-Yüeh] came to Shu. Many of them sought the paintings [of Tu Ching-an] which they took back to their own lands. . . . Early in the Kuang-cheng era (938–65) merchants came to Shu from Ching-nan and Hu-nan to seek the paintings of Yüan Wei-te. They took them back to their own lands, where they were deemed remarkable.[200]

Just as the southern kingdoms sought to maintain control over their trade with the northern dynasties, there is also evidence that they sought to control the interkingdom trade. For example, the second ruler of the Southern Han (Liu Yen, r. 917–42) established an official trading post in Ching-nan's capital of Chiang-ling in order to recover some of the profits generated by the transshipment of Southern Han tribute to the northern dynasties through that city.[201] Similarly, Min maintained a trade agency in the Southern Han capital of Kuang-chou (Canton). After Wang Yen-chün, the third Min ruler (r. 927–35), married the daughter of Liu Yen, ruler of Southern Han, he "then sent Lin Yen-yü to open a trade outlet (*ti*)[202] in Fan-yü (the port of Kuang-chou) in order to manage diplomacy (*chuan-chang kuo-hsin*)."[203] Once again, we see that trade was intimately connected to the formalities of interstate relationships.

---

[197] Wu, *Shih-kuo ch'un-ch'iu* 116, p. 1771.
[198] *TCTC* 268, pp. 8776–7.
[199] *CWTS* 133, p. 1753.
[200] Cited in Yang, *Ch'ien Shu Hou Shu shih*, p. 209, from Huang Hsiu-fu, *I-chou ming-hua-lu chung*.
[201] *HCP* (1964), vol. 1, reprinting *Yung-lo ta-tien* 12306, p. 3a.
[202] On the equivalence of *ti* with *hui-t'u wu* and other terms, see Hino, *Zoku Tōdai teiten no kenkyū*, pp. 591–7.
[203] *TCTC* 279, pp. 9134–5.

The last of the major trading patterns was the transshipment trade, the forwarding of imported goods from the South Seas, as the Chinese called the lands of the Southeast Asian archipelagoes and the coasts of the Indian Ocean, to the great cities of central and north China by the merchants of the port cities of China's south and southeast coasts. This trade cannot be entirely separated from the patterns of domestic trade just discussed, as its goods were often an important part of the cargoes of the domestic trade. The transshipment of South Seas trade nevertheless deserves to be separately recognized for three reasons: (1) because of the distinct goods that were part of it; (2) because it represents the continued development of ties between the ports of the south and southeast coasts and the lands beyond; and, most important, (3) because it was central to the economic survival of at least two of the southern kingdoms — Southern Han and Min.

The South Seas trade already had a long history by the ninth century, but without a doubt the latter half of the T'ang dynasty had seen an expansion in the volume of trade in the luxury goods that were its staple: aromatics such as frankincense, camphor, sapanwood, and sandalwood; spices and medicines such as ground rhinoceros horn (used as an aphrodisiac), pepper, and asafoetida; and unfinished wares such as ivory and tortoise shell. In return the major exports were Chinese silks, ceramics, and metalware. By the late ninth century at least three cities were particularly well established as regular ports of call to the foreign merchants who dominated the overseas links: Kuang-chou, which was the oldest and most active; Ch'üan-chou, which had supplanted Fu-chou as the principle port of Fu-chien; and Ming-chou (Ning-po), where much of the trade aimed at Hang-chou was off-loaded because Hang-chou Bay was too shallow to readily permit deep-draft ocean vessels to approach the great city itself.[204] All three ports continued to play important roles through the interregnum. The *Chiu Wu-tai shih*, for example, notes that "Kuang-chou amassed the precious goods of the South Seas . . . that were regularly traded with merchants from the north."[205] The *Wu-kuo ku-shih* says of Ch'üan-chou: "Wang Yen-pin [the nephew of Wang Shen-chih and autonomous governor of

---

[204] On the early history of the trade, see Fujita Toyohachi, "Sōdai shihakushi oyobi shihaku jōrei," *Tōyō gakuhō* 7 No. 2 (1917), pp. 159–246; Li Tung-hua, *Ch'üan-chou yü wo-kuo chung-ku ti hai-shang chiao-t'ung: Chiu shih-chi mo – shih-wu shih-chi ch'u* (Taipei, 1986); Wada Hisanori, "Tōdai ni okeru shihakushi no shōchi," in *Wada Hakushi koki kinen Tōyōshi ronsō: Shōwa 35-nen 11-gatsu*, ed. Wada Hakushi Koki Kinen Tōyōshi Ronsō Hensan Iinkai (Tokyo, 1961), pp. 1051–60; and Kuwabara Jitsuzō, "On P'u Shou-keng, part 1," *Memoirs of the Research Department of the Tōyō Bunko* 2 (1928), pp. 1–82. The three ports mentioned in the text were not the only major ports of the late T'ang. Fu-chou and Yang-chou were also important, but neither maintained prominent roles into the later tenth century. Sung maritime trade is the subject of a separate chapter by Angela Schottenhammer in the companion to this volume.

[205] CWTS 135, p. 1808.

Ch'üan-chou] governed for thirty years (904–34). Year after year the harvests were good and the trading ships of the southern barbarians never failed to stop."[206] This observation is reinforced by the *T'ai-p'ing huan-yü chi*, which was compiled within years of the consolidation of Sung rule in the Fu-chien region and lists the "spices and medicinals of the overseas trade ships" (*hai-po hsiang-yao*) among the "local products" of Ch'üan-chou and neighboring Chang-chou.[207] The enduring importance of these specific ports was quickly recognized by the Sung bureaucracy in the immediate aftermath of imperial consolidation later in the tenth century when a Trade Monopoly Office (*Chüeh-i yüan*) was established to control the trade, and monopoly clearinghouses were opened in all three prefectures.[208]

Control over the transshipment of imported goods was an important source of revenue for all of the coastal kingdoms. The T'ang dynasty had accomplished this control via the Office of the Trade Superintendent (*Shih-po ssu*), a monopoly purchasing agency established in Kuang-chou: importers sold their wares directly to the superintendency, which in turn sold them at a profit to domestic merchants for distribution within the empire. The coastal kingdoms apparently followed the T'ang model. The biography of Chang Mu, director of the Monopoly Tax Bureau (*Chüeh-huo wu*) in Fu-chou under Wang Shen-chih, relates that "[Mu] was gentle and not extortionate to the foreign merchants who responded [to Wang Shen-chih's invitation to trade through Fu-chou]. Thus the state's revenues daily grew richer."[209] While the passage does not refer specifically to a trade superintendency, the link between Chang and foreign traders is clear evidence that one existed in Fu-chou.

Although no such direct evidence of monopoly offices under the Southern Han or Wu-Yüeh survives, we can be quite sure they too existed. As just noted, Kuang-chou had been the site of the T'ang office that served as the model for the southern kingdoms, thus the infrastructure was in place prior to the Southern Han rulers. It is also apparent that these rulers had extensive access to the goods of the trade, as is suggested by Ou-yang Hsiu's later condemnation of Liu Yen, the second Han ruler, for immoral conduct: "He adored living in luxury, so he amassed the precious goods of the South Seas to make the Pearl Pavilion of the Jade Hall."[210] While there had not been a T'ang monopoly office in any of the ports of Liang-che, it is equally apparent that the Wu-Yüeh rulers had access to the same goods. As early as 920, Ch'ien Liu sent an envoy to the Khitan court to present that ruler with gifts of rhinoceros horn and

[206] *Wu-kuo ku-shih hsia*, pp. 9b–10a.
[207] Yüeh, *T'ai-p'ing huan-yü chi* 102, pp. 3a, 6a.
[208] SHY (1964) *chih-kuan* 44, p. 1b.
[209] Wu, *Shih-kuo ch'un-ch'iu* 95, p. 1377.
[210] Ou-yang, *Hsin Wu-tai shih* 65, p. 811.

coral, both goods of the South Seas trade.[211] Ch'ien Liu and his successors maintained a regular exchange of envoys with the Khitan; although this is the only occasion where specific gifts are recorded, it is very likely that such gifts were normal.[212] Years later, when the last Wu-Yüeh ruler, Ch'ien Shu, negotiated submission to the Sung dynasty, he sent huge quantities of tribute, prominent among which were the rhinoceros horn, ivory, frankincense, and a range of spices, medicinals, and aromatics commonly associated with the South Seas trade.[213]

Clearly, all three kingdoms exercised some form of control over the trade through their ports. For Min and Southern Han, neither of which had as sophisticated an economy as Wu-Yüeh, the revenues they realized from this control must have been critical to their survival, but even Wu-Yüeh must have benefited greatly. Benefit from the trade did not stop at state revenues. With the exception of Wu-Yüeh, none of the coastal kingdoms was an important consumer of the luxury goods that made up the trade. The market for these goods was concentrated, as it traditionally had been, in the great cities of the Yangtze and Yellow river valleys. The goods that entered through Kuang-chou, Ch'üan-chou, and the ports of Wu-Yüeh were in turn sent on via the domestic trade routes and became a critical source of earnings to the merchants involved, especially those of Min and Southern Han who had comparatively fewer local goods worthy of being sent to the markets of the north. The trans-shipment trade had a double advantage: for the administrators of the southern kingdoms, especially for those of Min and Southern Han, it made indepen-dence feasible, and for the merchants of the southern kingdoms, it made up for the general lack of local goods to trade in the great markets of the north and so gave them entrée to the north's domestic trade networks. In addition, it gave Chinese merchants access to overseas markets where there was tremen-dous demand for Chinese textiles, especially silks; for metals and metalwork; and, above all, for ceramics produced in the north as well as in the southern kingdoms.

Finally, we must consider currency policies, an issue of importance to all the southern kingdoms for political as well as economic reasons.[214] Hand in hand

---

[211] T'o-t'o et al., eds., *Liao shih* (1344; Peking, 1974) 2, p. 16.

[212] On relations between the Khitan and all the southern kingdoms, see Hino's "Godai jidai ni okeru Kittan to Shina to no kaijō bōeki" articles. On the relationship with Wu-Yüeh, see specifically "Godai jidai ni okeru Kittan to Shina to no kaijō bōeki (jō)," pp. 28–32.

[213] *SHY* (1964) *fan-i* 7, pp. 6b–8a.

[214] The most important study of medieval Chinese currency is Miyazaki Ichisada, *Godai Sōsho no tsūka mondai* (Kyoto, 1943); a highly abbreviated summary of this is his "Godai Sōsho no tsūka mondai kōgai," in *Ajia-shi kenkyū dai ni*, Miyazaki Ichisada (Kyoto, 1959), pp. 130–9. See also Hino's "So no Ma In" articles.

with the expanding commercial economy of southern China in the century preceding the interregnum went a growing demand for cash. As Denis Twitchett has discussed, throughout the ninth century a constant tension existed between the T'ang government, which sought to control the circulation of currency, and producers, merchants, and consumers who required ever-greater supplies of cash. The gap between supply and demand was increasingly filled by the illicit production of debased coins of lead, tin, or iron to supplement the available supplies of the standard copper cash. Twitchett cites evidence that already by the late eighth century debased coins of lead or tin were in circulation in the Yangtze valley without government authorization, a clear violation of existing law.[215] By the latter half of the ninth century, however, as many as thirteen of twenty-four official provincial mints were forced to issue iron coins, an acknowledgment that copper supplies were no longer adequate to meet society's need for cash.

Thus as the interregnum unfolded, two related phenomena – a chronic shortage of cash, and the precedent for minting cash from metals other than copper – combined to propel the southern kingdoms to issue their own coinages, in copper, lead, tin, and iron, in order to meet the expanding demand for cash within their own commercializing economies as well as to assert their political independence. Hino Kaisaburō has argued that economically backward kingdoms such as Ch'u, Southern Han, and Min, faced with shortages of the metal itself, were unable to amass the copper coinage that the monetary demands of their commercializing economies required. Economic need mandated that they find a substitute for the copper lest they abort their economic development.[216] These kingdoms took the initiative in minting coins of lead, tin, and iron, to the consternation of the northern dynasties whose markets were soon awash in the debased specie. In 924 the newly established Later T'ang issued a prohibition against using the lead or tin coins of the south, but the ban had to be reissued in 929 because "at this time Hunan [Ch'u] was using only tin coins which traded with copper coins at one hundred to one. These tin coins flowed into the north, and laws could not put a stop to this."[217]

This by no means exhausts references to debased currency circulating among the southern kingdoms. What is important and very clear is that not only were the southern economies commercializing, but they were beginning to monetize as well. While many parts of the south were dependent by necessity on debased coinage, the transformation that this monetization represented was essential

[215] See Denis C. Twitchett, *Financial administration under the T'ang dynasty*, 2nd ed. (Cambridge, 1970), pp. 66–84.
[216] Hino, "So no Ma In (ge)," pp. 57–9.
[217] *TCTC* 276, p. 9028; *CWTS* 146, p. 1948.

to the commercial development that occurred over much of the south in the centuries that followed.

STATE STRUCTURES AND INTERSTATE RELATIONSHIPS

Political identity

In the closing decades of the ninth century and early years of the tenth, as T'ang dynastic authority dissolved and a new order took shape across the south, most of the southern rulers accepted with reservations the claims to imperial authority of Chu Wen, founder of the first of the northern dynasties, the Later Liang. Significantly, the most powerful of the southern kingdoms, the Wu, Wu-Yüeh, and Former Shu, indicated their displeasure by refusing to adopt the Later Liang reign period for their calendars. Traditionally, a refusal such as this was considered a sign of rebellion and a reason for war. Both Yang Wo, who had just succeeded his father Yang Hsing-mi (d. 905) as ruler of Wu, and Ch'ien Liu of Wu-Yüeh continued to use the final T'ang reign period as a sign of loyalty to the fallen order. Wang Chien of the Former Shu went even further, retaining the reign period of the penultimate T'ang emperor, T'ang Chao-tsung, who had been killed by Chu Wen in 904. Wang Chien was thereby refusing to acknowledge the legitimacy of the very young successor, handpicked by Chu Wen, who reigned entirely at Chu's pleasure.

Over the next few years each of the southern kingdoms took steps to make its autonomy from the new imperial order more overt. As early as 908 in Wu-Yüeh, Ch'ien Liu proclaimed his own reign period for use within his kingdom, although he used the Later Liang system in all dealings with the north, a policy that was generally adhered to by his successors.[218] In Wu, Yang Wo and his successor, Yang Lung-yen, continued to use the last T'ang reign period even as the Later Liang went through a succession of changes, thus emphasizing Wu's break with the north. But the most direct actions were again those of Wang Chien. In 907, within months of Chu Wen's usurpation of the T'ang throne, Wang claimed the imperial title for himself, as a symbolic challenge to Chu Wen's legitimacy.[219] In 917, after denouncing the Later Liang as an "outlaw court" (wei-t'ing), the Southern Han ruler Liu Yen followed suit, urging the Wu leader Yang Lung-yen to do the same.[220] Liu Yen, like Wang Chien, was not motivated by a desire to claim the universal authority previously symbolized by the title of emperor. On the contrary, he was probably more interested in

---

[218] Wu, Shih-kuo ch'un-ch'iu 78, p. 1082.
[219] TCTC 266, p. 8685.
[220] TCTC 269, p. 8799; 270, pp. 8817, 8821.

using the title to further his claims to sovereignty over Ling-nan, including the Red River delta of modern Vietnam.

The defeat of the Later Liang's forces by the Sha-t'o forces of the Later T'ang stimulated a new round of imperial aspirations in the south. In 927, prompted by the force behind the throne, Hsü Chih-kao, the nominal Wu ruler Yang P'u joined the roster of competing emperors. There is no reason to think at this point that Hsü Chih-kao or the Yang rulers were seriously seeking to challenge the Later T'ang. They seem to have been questioning the legitimate transmission of the imperial mandate through a non-Chinese ruling order. When Hsü Chih-kao, himself having taken the throne in 937, changed his surname in 939 to "Li" and the name of his dynasty to T'ang (i.e., Southern T'ang), he was making a different statement. From then until 958, when Southern T'ang rulers abandoned the imperial title and reverted to styling themselves "king" (kuo-wang) in the face of pressure by the Later Chou,[221] the Southern T'ang court claimed to be the sole legitimate heir to the T'ang mandate and so ruler of its empire. Although Southern T'ang forces never campaigned against the northern dynasties until the Later Chou invasions of the mid-950s, its envoys frequently explored alliances with various forces, especially with the Khitan and Turkic kingdoms farther north, with the goal of expelling their rivals and controlling the northern plain.[222]

Bureaucratic governance

However the individual kingdoms of the south chose to acknowledge the successive dynasties of the north, they each had to confront the challenge of organizing their own bureaucracies, deploying their own armies, and raising their own revenues. Establishing the framework of bureaucracy was relatively easy. Each kingdom inherited a system of local and regional government from the T'ang dynasty. Although there were shifts in nomenclature over the following years as rulers gave new names to old offices or elevated subcounty units such as tax stations (ch'ang) to county (hsien) status in response to, for example, the administrative demands generated by population growth, the basic structures were continued without fundamental change.[223] Although none of the southern kingdoms inherited a central court or the attendant organs of bureaucracy, all shared in the T'ang dynastic legacy and each proceeded to replicate the imperial bureaucracy, often creating large and unwieldy

---

[221] TCTC 294, pp. 9583–4.

[222] See, for example, TCTC 292, pp. 9531–2. See also Hino's "Godai jidai ni okeru Kittan to Shina to no kaijō bōeki" articles.

[223] See, for example, Okada, "Godai So ōkoku no seikaku," pp. 73–6.

structures far too grandiose for the kingdoms they were designed to administer. The organization of armed forces was a parallel issue. All of the founders
not only headed the armies that brought them to power but also inherited
the T'ang regional militias and warlord forces that had been absorbed in the
course of state consolidation.

Two pressing challenges arose from the establishment of civil and military
structures: how to staff them, and how to fund them. The regions contained by
Ch'u, Ching-nan, the Southern Han, and Min had few families with extensive
high-level experience in government, whereas the advanced regions contained
by Wu-Yüeh, Wu, the Southern T'ang, and the two Shu kingdoms had much
stronger traditions of participation in bureaucratic government. But even they
were challenged by the burdens of staffing their new courts.

One short-term solution was to use bureaucratic appointments to reward
those who had helped the new rulers gain power. Many of the new administrations initially had a strongly militaristic flavor not unlike that found in the
northern dynasties.[224] Over time, the new states had to find more enduring
ways to recruit bureaucrats, and this meant either developing a tradition of
service where it did not exist or furthering that tradition where it did. In
some areas, especially Fu-chien, the initial preferences given to the associates
of the founders were transformed into long-term commitments to public service. In the Sung dynasty, when the Fu-chien region became a major source
of bureaucratic and scholastic talent, the descendents of those associated with
the founding Wang family occupied a disproportionately large share of the
province's *chin-shih* degree holders. Other kingdoms, notably Southern Han
and the two Shu kingdoms, relied heavily on elite migrants from the north.
This practice may have hurt the development of local elites oriented toward
high-level government service for in the following centuries neither Kuang-
nan nor Szechwan were prominent sources of *chin-shih* graduates.[225] The kingdoms that most successfully developed their own bureaucratic traditions were
Wu, the Southern T'ang, and Wu-Yüeh. Not incidentally, they also inherited
the most fully developed traditions of training and service and were best able
to perpetuate those traditions. Wu was the first state to revive examinations
for the selection of bureaucrats after the collapse of the T'ang. As early as 909
Wu initiated its own system of examinations.[226] Because the Wu-Yüeh rulers
continued to recognize the northern dynasties' imperial claim, its scholars were

[224] For example, on Wu, see Krompart, "The southern restoration of T'ang," and Nishikawa, "Go, Nan-Tō
      ryō ōchō." On Shu, see Kurihara, "Tō-Godai no kafushiteki ketsugō no seikaku" and his "Tōmatsu
      Godai no kafushiteki ketsugō ni okeru seimei to nenrei."

[225] See figures 5 and 6 in John W. Chaffee, *The thorny gates of learning in Sung China: A social history of
      examinations* (Cambridge, 1985), pp. 130–1.

[226] *TCTC* 267, p. 8709.

able to sit for the northern examinations. Wu-Yüeh never took the independent step of organizing its own examination system. Wu and Wu-Yüeh combined the judicious use of refugees from the north with the appointment of local talent to create able bureaucracies that made them two of the best-governed kingdoms of the era.

Taxation

To meet the fiscal burden of self-administration and defense, all the southern kingdoms initially relied on tax systems inherited from the T'ang dynasty, especially the double tax (*liang-shui*) levied on agriculture, to produce revenues.[227] As the era wore on, however, the yields from agricultural taxation proved inadequate to meet the needs of the courts. This was due at least in part to the flood of northern migrants to the south. Often these migrants were unable to find land of their own. As a result they resorted to tenancy or to life in the fast-growing cities of the south. In theory, of course, tenant production should have been included as part of the landowner's double-tax obligations. In many areas, however, land was increasingly held in the large estates called *chuang-yüan*.[228] The close ties between estate owners and the ruling elites — indeed, they must generally have been one and the same — made it very easy to hide the true yield of these properties, especially since estate owners used tenant labor to open new lands that had never been assessed, making the revenue from the double tax significantly less than it ought to have been.

In several areas the problem of a shrinking tax base was compounded by the growing economic power of Buddhist and Taoist institutions and the difficulty in taxing them. The most extreme example was in the region of Fuchien, where monasteries amassed vast land holdings of what were reported to be the very best lands.[229] But Min was hardly the only kingdom where monastic holdings grew dramatically. A gazetteer of the city of Shao-hsing, published at the beginning of the thirteenth century, recalled: "Ever since the Five Dynasties, Buddhist monasteries have been especially numerous in Chiang-nan. Wu-Yüeh, Min, and Ch'u all built them in untold numbers, and

---

[227] The double-tax system, also called the two-tax system, was a basic tax that could be paid in two annual installments. On the double tax and its implications in the latter half of the T'ang, see Charles A. Peterson, "Court and province in mid- and late T'ang," in *The Cambridge history of China*, volume 3: *Sui and T'ang China, 589–906, part 1*, ed. Denis C. Twitchett (Cambridge, 1979), pp. 498–501. See also Twitchett, *Financial administration under the T'ang dynasty*.

[228] On *chuang-yüan* in the interregnum, see Sudō Yoshiyuki, "Tōmatsu Godai no shōensei," in *Chūgoku tochi seidoshi kenkyū*, Sudō Yoshiyuki (Tokyo, 1954), pp. 7–64, and Matsui Shōichi, "Tōmatsu no minshū hanran to Godai no keisei," in *Iwanami Kōza Sekai rekishi 6 – Kodai 6* (Tokyo, 1971), pp. 274–7.

[229] See SS 173, p. 4191. See also the discussion in Clark, *Community, trade, and networks*, pp. 60–4.

one cannot count the number of monks."[230] It is not clear to what degree the southern kingdoms even attempted to tax the yields of monastic lands, but it is certain that in practice they were able to tax them very little. The monasteries also sheltered large numbers of lightly taxed tenants, just as occurred on the large private estates, a point echoed by the *Wu-tai shih-pu*: "The Ta-wei t'ung-ch'ing temple is in Ch'ang-sha. It has many monks and its fields are very extensive. There are over one thousand tenant households (*tien-hu*)."[231]

Not surprisingly, the southern rulers commonly attempted to solve their fiscal problems simply by raising the revenue generated from the land tax. This could be done either by improving land registration or by raising tax rates. In 943, for example, "Ch'u revenues were insufficient, so taxes were increased and officials were dispatched to survey the fields; they only earned merit if they could increase the number of *ch'ing* and *mou* [on the land registers]."[232] Such methods, however, would not allow the state to entirely realize the fullest revenues from the great estates. These methods could, in fact, exacerbate the problem, as happened in Ch'u following its just noted efforts to improve registration and increase yields: "The people could not meet their taxes and fled. . . . They had only just been able to meet their own needs, and from west to east many lost their livelihood."

Although many of the kingdoms resorted to a variety of supplementary taxes aimed at specific crops, in the long run the only real solution to their problem was to change the focus of taxes away from land and to more elastic sources of revenue, especially trade. Most if not all the kingdoms exercised some kind of control over interstate trade, including the taxation of trade goods or tribute goods in transit through their territory. Other methods of raising revenue included the establishment of monopolies over such products as salt and liquor, the imposition of levies on the wealthy, and the sale of office for revenue: "[In Ch'u] offices were rewarded according to a person's contribution, with rank depending on whether the contribution was great or small. Wealthy merchants and great traders appear on the lists of those holding office, and when officials finish tours in the countryside, they must offer a contribution [to get a new appointment]."[233]

It was the head tax, however, that in the end was the most significant innovation of the period.[234] The advantage of a head tax over other taxes,

---

[230] Shih Su et al., *Chia-t'ai Kuei-chi chih* (1201; Peking, 1990) 7, p. 1b.

[231] T'ao, *Wu-tai shih-pu* 3, p. 13a.

[232] *TCTC* 283, p. 9259. See also the discussion in Okada, "Godai So ōkoku no seikaku," pp. 78–9.

[233] *TCTC* 283, p. 9259. For a similar passage regarding Min, see *TCTC* 281, p. 9176.

[234] The two most thorough discussions of the head taxes of the southern kingdoms are Yanagida Setsuko, "Sōdai no teizei," in *Sō-Gen gōsonsei no kenkyū*, Yanagida Setsuko (Tokyo, 1986), pp. 324–50; and Shimasue Kazuyasu, "Sōdai shinteizei no shokeitō," *Tōyōshi kenkyū* 45 No. 3 (1986), pp. 119–44. Both provide further citations for this topic.

especially agrarian taxes, was twofold. First, a head tax could be levied on the urban population; and second, because head taxes are levied on individuals rather than on property, they could also be imposed directly on the landless tenants of the great estates, including those of the monasteries. Furthermore, because these taxes were assessed on the person, not on the land, the individual rather than the landowner was responsible for paying. This meant that the great landowners could not minimize their own taxes by shielding their tenants, a problem that undermined all taxes based on land. The head tax, at least in theory, overcame all the shortcomings of the various agrarian taxes.

All the southern kingdoms levied head taxes, with the possible exception of the Former and Later Shu about whose taxation policies little is known.[235] Although head taxes could be levied in a variety of goods, and at varying rates, one constant was to levy them on adult males between the ages of twenty and sixty. Women, children, and older men were not subject to the head tax. Ch'u may have been the first of the southern kingdoms to experiment with this tax: "Ever since the Ma family occupied Hunan they began to collect a tax in cash, silk, rice, or grain on each adult male in Yung-chou, Tao-chou, Ch'en-chou2, Kuei-yang chien, and Ch'a-ling county [in Heng-chou]."[236] In the absence of further information, we can only speculate as to why these prefectures and counties, all of which were clumped together in southeastern Ch'u, were singled out for the head tax, but a Sung dynasty source states that the tax was still in effect there in 1059, a century after Chu's absorption by the Sung.[237] The tax was levied equally on every adult male without distinction as to wealth or standing: "Under the Ma family, in Ch'en-chou2, Yung-chou, Kuei-yang, etc., a tax was levied on the people's produce. The amount was the same regardless of their wealth."[238]

If the tax in Ch'u was collected in a variety of goods – cash, rice, grains, textiles – this was not the case everywhere. In the Wu kingdom, for example, the head tax had to be paid in cash:

[Before 918] Wu had had a monetary head tax (*ting-k'ou ch'ien*) as well as a monetary tax on land. Thus cash was valued at the expense of goods, and the people were greatly oppressed. Sung Ch'i-ch'iu advised, "One doesn't get cash by tilling the land or sericulture. By forcing the people to get cash [to pay their taxes] we are teaching them to abandon what is basic [i.e., agriculture] for what is not [i.e., trade]. We should remit the head tax and collect the rest in grain and cloth."[239]

[235] See the brief comments in Smith, *Taxing heaven's storehouse*, pp. 77–9.
[236] Li Hsin-ch'uan, *Chien-yen i-lai ch'ao-yeh tsa-chi* [*Shih-yüan ts'ung-shu*, 1914 ed.] (c. 1202 *chia* volume, 1216 *i* volume; Taipei, 1967) 15, p. 1b.
[237] *SHY* (1964) *shih-huo* 70, p. 167b.
[238] See *SHY* (1964) *shih-huo* 70, p. 8b.
[239] *TCTC* 270, p. 8832.

Yang Lung-yen, the Wu king at the time, apparently followed Sung's advice and abandoned the head tax, but it was partially revived by the Southern T'ang in connection with levies on salt, as was explained by Fan Chung-yen in a memorial he submitted in 1033: "In the five counties of Chiang-ning the resident and migrant households all pay an annual tax called the 'adult male salt cash' (ting-k'ou yen-ch'ien). . . . This began when these counties were part of the Southern T'ang under which there was a salt production quota distributed among the population and collected in cash by the officials in T'ung-chou2 and T'ai-chou2 [both coastal districts between the Huai and Yangtze rivers]."[240]

In Ch'u and Southern T'ang it appears that the head tax was levied only in selected areas. But in Wu-Yüeh it was collected almost everywhere: "when men became adults they paid an annual tax of 360 cash. This was called 'adult male cash' (shen-ting ch'ien)."[241] When Wu-Yüeh had seized Fu-chou after the Min kingdom collapsed in the mid-940s, the tax was extended to all men there as well, although at a slightly lower rate: "In Fu-chou every adult male paid a tax of 325 cash."[242] In the warlord enclave of Chang-Ch'üan (southern Fu-chien) a head tax levied in rice was also extended to every adult male.[243] And in Kuang-nan, "the head tax began during the Five Dynasties when every adult male owed ten cash."[244]

Although the head tax was widely imposed in several variations it failed to solve the financial problems of the southern kingdoms, which one after another fell prey to fiscal crises that wore down the energy and spirit of their populations and made them vulnerable to the aggressions first of the Later Chou dynasty, the last and most vibrant of the northern dynasties, and finally to the Sung. Yet along with the unprecedented reliance on taxes on commerce, the head tax represents one of the most important and enduring developments of the southern kingdoms. Both forms of tax continued to be collected during the Sung dynasty, and while neither ever displaced the land tax as the largest source of revenue, they proved indispensable to the fiscal survival of the Sung.

Interstate relations

Ambitions for imperial supremacy put the successor kingdoms of Wu and Southern T'ang at the center of a contentious system of interstate relations.

[240] Shimasue, "Sōdai shinteizei," p. 140 n. 24, quoting (Ching-ting) Chien-t'ai chih. See also in Yanagida, "Sōdai no teizei," p. 335.
[241] Shimasue, "Sōdai shinteizei," p. 139 n. 6, quoting Ch'en Shih-tao, Hou-shan hsien-sheng chi. See also Yanagida, "Sōdai no teizei," p. 328.
[242] Shimasue, "Sōdai shinteizei," p. 139 n. 9, quoting Ch'en Fu-lang, Chih-chi wen-chi.
[243] SHY (1964) shih-huo 70, p. 166a.
[244] Shimasue, "Sōdai shinteizei," p. 141 n. 41, quoting Liu K'o-chuang, Hou-ts'un hsien-sheng ta-ch'üan-chi.

Only the Former and Later Shu kingdoms were isolated enough that they could remain aloof from other states, and there is no record that the Shu rulers initiated any exchanges with the other southern kingdoms. They did accept southern emissaries. On at least one occasion Liu Yen of Southern Han dispatched an envoy to Ch'eng-tu "to convey friendship," and in 937 Wu-Yüeh sent an envoy, probably to congratulate the Meng family on assuming the throne, which prompted Meng Ch'ang to send an emissary back as an expression of gratitude.[245] But if Shu was willing to receive friendly initiatives from the other kingdoms, it is nevertheless clear that the major focus of Shu policy was to cultivate ties with the non-Chinese peoples to the west and south from whom the Shu kingdoms could get horses and so ensure the strength of their defenses. Ssu-ma Kuang commented: "Wang Chien had originally been a cavalry general. Thus, after he gained control of Shu he traded for horses with the barbarians at Wen-chou2, Li-chou3, Wei-chou3, and Mao-chou [all strung along the kingdom's western frontier]."[246] We do not learn what Shu offered in these markets in exchange for the horses, although silk had been the favored commodity during the T'ang dynasty as tea was to become in later centuries. The cavalry that both Shu kingdoms could put in the field because of this trade was an integral part of their defense.[247]

The remaining southern kingdoms interacted regularly if not always amicably with one another. The Liu rulers of Southern Han, for example, sought to maintain good relations with their neighboring states of Ch'u and Min, which they cemented through marriage alliances among the ruling houses.[248] Relations among the Yangtze River states were generally less cordial, stirred as they often were by the imperial aspirations of Wu and the Southern T'ang or the expansionist designs of Ch'u. Through the first two decades of the tenth century, while the new order of the interregnum slowly unfolded, both Ch'u and Wu-Yüeh regularly found themselves pitched against Wu, despite the growing emphasis all the southern kingdoms placed on trade along the shared Yangtze River corridor. Wu-Yüeh reached a settlement with Wu in 919, but Ch'u's relations with Wu were constantly disrupted by Ch'u's designs on Ching-nan, which regularly appealed to Wu for help.[249] This particular

[245] *TCTC* 271, p. 8861; Chang, *Shu t'ao-wu hsia*, p. 4a.

[246] *TCTC* 264, p. 8607.

[247] On the horse trade in general and its connection to the Chinese military, see the discussion in Smith, *Taxing heaven's storehouse*, pp. 204–29. On the cavalry in the two Shu kingdoms, see Wu Chih-hao et al., *(Wan-li) Ch'ung-hsiu Ssu-ch'uan tsung-chih* [National Diet Library collection] (n.p., 1619) 22, pp. 52b–53a.

[248] On Southern Han relations with Ch'u, see Tanaka Seiji, "So to Nan-Kan to no kankei," in *Tamura hakushi shōju Tōyōshi ronsō*, ed. Tamura Hakushi Taikan Kinen Jigyōkai (Kyoto, 1968), pp. 359–74. On Southern Han marriage alliances with Min, see Schafer, *The empire of Min*, p. 20.

[249] On the foreign policy of Ch'u, see Tanaka, "So to Nan-Kan to no kankei," and Okada, "Godai So ōkoku no seikaku," pp. 79–82.

irritant was generally put to rest in 928, after a decisive military victory by Ch'u in which it was prepared to wipe Ching-nan off the map: "Ma Yin urged his general Wang Huan not to seize Ching-nan. Huan responded: 'Chiang-ling [i.e., Ching-nan] lies between the northern dynasty, Wu, and Shu. On all sides are enemies. It would be best if we permit it to endure as a buffer against our enemies.'"[250] This quieted Ch'u's desire to conquer Ching-nan, which in turn lowered the level of tension between Ch'u and Wu until the tumultuous late-interregnum decade of the 950s.

Neither of the remaining kingdoms, Ching-nan and Min, could readily afford to offend its neighbors. Ching-nan was especially vulnerable. As Wang Huan noted, it occupied a critical crossroad, yet it was surrounded by potential enemies on all sides. Its survival depended in large part on the continued acceptance of Wang's argument that Ching-nan served as a buffer. The Ching-nan rulers, in turn, attempted to cultivate their neighbors as a form of protection. In 947, Kao Ts'ung-mei, the Ching-nan ruler who had been on the throne for almost twenty years, sent an envoy to the Khitan who had just overthrown the Later Chin and were about to establish their own short-lived dynasty on the northern plain. This prompted Hu San-hsing to comment: "For the Kao family of Ching-nan, there was no more important task than protecting their kingdom."[251]

The interstate relations of Min resembled that of the two Shu kingdoms in one respect, since both the Fu-chien and Szechwan regions enjoyed the relative protection conferred by physical isolation. But whereas the two Shu states could afford to downplay relations with their neighbors Min could not. Min was much too dependent on revenues derived from trade with and through its neighboring kingdoms. From the beginning of the interregnum, the Wang family cultivated good relations with the Ch'ien family of Wu-Yüeh, relations that were cemented through marital exchanges in the 910s.[252] Similar ties were cultivated with the Southern Han, although these broke down briefly in 920 during a border skirmish that neither side apparently wanted.[253] Surprisingly, in a step that at first glance seems contradictory, in 909 Wang Shen-chih permanently broke ties with Wu. The reason was Wang Shen-chih's treatment of an envoy whom Yang Lung-yen, having just recently become King of Wu, had dispatched to establish friendly ties with the Min court. Wang

---

[250] *TCTC* 276, pp. 9015–16.

[251] *TCTC* 286, p. 9337.

[252] *TCTC* 269, p. 8808. On relations between Min and Wu-Yüeh, see Tanaka Seiji, "Go-Etsu to Bin to no kankei," *Tōyōshi kenkyū* 28 No. 1 (1969), pp. 28–51.

[253] *TCTC* 270, p. 8823. On the border skirmish, see *TCTC* 271, p. 8876; 273, p. 8919; see also Liu Chün's biography in Kuo Fei et al., *(Wan-li) Kuang-tung t'ung-chih* [Naikaku Bunko collection] (1602; n.p., n.d.) 22, p. 20a.

Shen-chih had the envoy beheaded, supposedly for arrogant behavior, but this was a step that was surely calculated to lead to a break. Wang Shen-chih's goal, no doubt, was to enhance his ties with Wu-Yüeh, which was at the time engaged in conflict with Wu. Wang Shen-chih was far more dependent on Wu-Yüeh than on Wu because of the critical position Wu-Yüeh held in Min's maritime trade ties to the north. Ties with Wu could presumably be broken with impunity, for Min did not rely on the overland route through Wu, and its successor the Southern T'ang, to ship its trade goods north, and the mountains of the Fu-chien interior that formed the mutual border could be relied on to provide some protection. Min's with Wu-Yüeh, however, appeared to be more critical, and any steps that might enhance them, such as establishing a mutual enemy, could seem advantageous. In fact, once Wang Shen-chih's control succumbed to family squabbles, Min proved vulnerable to both Wu-Yüeh and the Southern T'ang, each of which absorbed a major portion of Min's domain.

THE CLOSE OF THE INTERREGNUM

There are two components to the collapse of the southern kingdoms that marked the closing of the interregnum. One was the growing instability of many of the surviving kingdoms through the 950s and 960s, an instability caused by poor leadership and growing fiscal distress. The second, and equally important factor, was the emergence of stable leadership in the north. This stability began most conclusively with Kuo Wei and the Later Chou dynasty that he established in 951 and accelerated under Kuo's successor, Ch'ai Jung (Chou Shih-tsung, r. 954–9), culminating with the coup that brought Chao K'uang-yin to power as the founder of the Sung dynasty. Although only fully achieved under the Sung, Ch'ai Jung initiated the systematic unification of the lands south of the Yangtze.

Between the 920s and 940s, a pattern of political upheaval reordered the southern kingdoms. Two new and initially stable kingdoms, the Later Shu and the Southern T'ang, emerged outside of the Central Plains, while the least stable of the original kingdoms, the Min kingdom in Fu-chien, disappeared. At the same time, the short-lived authority exercised by the Later T'ang in the north evaporated in the turmoil enveloping the northern regimes during the 930s and 940s. In these middle decades it was the kingdoms of the Southern T'ang in Chiang-Huai, the Later Shu in Szechwan, and Wu-Yüeh in the lower Yangtze that seemed to hold the greatest promise for the future.

The death of the King of Ch'u, Ma Hsi-fan, in 947 initiated a second era of instability that precipitated the collapse of order in the southern kingdoms. The sequence of events in Ch'u brought about by Ma's death parallels the collapse of Min in the 940s.[254] Ma Hsi-fan's failure to name an heir caused a split between his brothers, Ma Hsi-o and Ma Hsi-kuang, that was temporarily resolved when the Later Han court of the north named Ma Hsi-kuang the new king. Ma Hsi-o resentfully retired to the western shore of Tung-t'ing Lake. Also living there was a large population of non-Chinese Man tribesmen who had never been fully included in the Ch'u polity nor felt particular loyalty to it.[255] From his retreat at the lake, Ma Hsi-o plotted rebellion. As part of his preparations, Ma Hsi-o appealed to the Later Han to partition the Ch'u kingdom between himself and Ma Hsi-kuang, but the court refused. In a strategy that echoed Kao Chi-ch'ang's attempt to play the northern court against the Wu empire twenty years earlier, Ma Hsi-o, in return for Southern T'ang's backing for his rebellion, pledged his subordination to Southern T'ang, which at the time was nearing the crest of its power and imperial pretensions. Li Ching, the second Southern T'ang ruler, accepted the bargain.

Late in 950, after almost a year of war, Ma Hsi-o's forces, heavily bolstered with Man troops, entered the Ch'u capital of T'an-chou (Ch'ang-sha), where they indulged in three days of looting and killing so violent that Ssu-ma Kuang later wrote: "Everything that had been built since the time of Ma Yin was burned to the ground, and all the wealth he had gathered was seized."[256] Ma Hsi-kuang was forced to commit suicide. Ma Hsi-o was now in control of Hunan and took for himself the titles that had been held first by Ma Yin and later by his brother, including King of Ch'u. He then sent an envoy to the Southern T'ang court, which in turn exercised its privilege as suzerain to formally acknowledge the titles he had taken. Ma Hsi-o's envoy, however, also advised Li Ching that the people of Ch'u were very unhappy with the violent and capricious administration of their new king: "The people of Hunan have been exhausted by his arrogance. You could seize it." And so Li Ching began preparations to do just that.[257]

Renewed civil war in the summer and fall of 951, when Ma Hsi-o's younger brother and former ally, Ma Hsi-ch'ung, rose against him, spelled the end of the Ch'u kingdom and of nearly six decades of Ma family rule. Both Mas appealed to Southern T'ang for help, but Li Ching ordered his forces to seize T'an-chou. All members of the Ma family were arrested and deported to the Southern

---

[254] These events are narrated in T'ao, *Wu-tai shih-lüeh*, pp. 270–8, and Okada, "Godai So ōkoku no seikaku," pp. 82–90. Both sources rely primarily on *TCTC*.

[255] On relations between the Man and Ch'u, see the following articles by Okada Kōji: "Godai So ōkoku no 'Keishū dōchū' ni tsuite," *Daitō Bunka Daigaku kiyō (Jinbun kagaku)* 22 (1984), pp. 123–43; and his "Tōmatsu Godai Sōsho Konan chiiki no minzoku mondai – toku ni Hō-shi no keifu to Tōcha-zoku to no kankei o chūshin to shite," *Tōyō kenkyū* 71 (1984), pp. 87–132.

[256] *TCTC* 289, p. 9445.

[257] *TCTC* 290, p. 9458.

T'ang capital in Chin-ling (Nanking), leaving the lands of Ch'u, minus six prefectures in the far south that Southern Han had seized for itself, under T'ang control. This peace was to be only an interlude in the history of Hunan. If the people were glad to be rid of Ma Hsi-o, the new Southern T'ang administration did not prove to be much better: "[Southern] T'ang forces seized all the gold and silk, the precious curios, the stored grain, and even the best of the ships and boats, the pavilions and courts, and the flowers and fruits; all were shipped to Chin-ling. Taxes were levied in Hunan to support the occupying troops; the exactions were harsh, and the people of Hunan lost hope."[258] Quickly the population turned against the Southern T'ang administration.

Had the attention of those in Chin-ling not been diverted by other matters, the unrest in Hunan may not have led to anything, but such was not the case. In 952 the Later Chou was consolidating control over the northern plain and there were rising tensions along the frontier between the Later Chou and Southern T'ang. This tension was exacerbated by Li Ching's support of anti-Chou forces. In one engagement Southern T'ang forces suffered losses of over a thousand dead and wounded.[259] This distraction between the Later Chou and Southern T'ang opened the way for new leaders in Hunan, many of whom were non-Chinese,[260] to expel the occupying army. By late 952 the Southern T'ang occupiers were gone and the land was once again in the hands of Hunanese, although peace was not fully restored until 956 when Chou Hsing-feng's forces invaded the region.

At the moment that Southern T'ang armies had taken control of Ch'u in 951, the power of the Southern T'ang appeared to be rising and the possibilities for conquest limitless. Despite their previous failure to consolidate control over Fu-chien, the Southern T'ang empire now embraced over thirty prefectures stretching from the Huai River in the north, to the mountainous frontier with Ling-nan in the south, and from the interior prefectures of Fu-chien in the east, to Tung-t'ing Lake and the river valleys of Hunan in the west. In the words of one author, writing in the eleventh century, Southern T'ang was "the most powerful" of all the southern kingdoms. Another wrote: "Compared to all the other states of that moment, T'ang territory was vaster, its strength greater, and its population more numerous." Ssu-ma Kuang added that Li Ching began to envision uniting the whole empire, daring to dream of the destiny implicit in the mandate his father had claimed.[261]

[258] TCTC 290, p. 9472. See also Ma, Ma-shih Nan T'ang shu 3, p. 5a.

[259] TCTC 290, pp. 9472–3; CWTS 112, pp. 1479–80.

[260] See Okada, "Godai So ōkoku no seikaku," pp. 88–9.

[261] CWTS 134, p. 1787; Lu Yu, Lu-shih Nan T'ang shu [Ch'ien Shu-pao handwritten Ming dynasty ed.] (12th c.; Shanghai, 1934) 2, p. 13a; TCTC 290, p. 9455.

Yet Southern T'ang power had reached its apogee, and began to wane. Much of the responsibility for this failure falls on Li Ching, for despite his musings about achieving a grand imperial ambition, he was plagued by indecision and hesitation. The best opportunities to realize his ambitions had come in the 940s, when turmoil and instability had enveloped the northern plain and his advisors had urged him to strike. Instead, he waited, afraid to make such a large commitment. When he did send out forces – this time to Fu-chien – it proved an unwise diversion of his resources. As a result of the defeat he suffered at the hands of the Wu-Yüeh army and the loss of twenty thousand men, the Fu-chien adventure weakened him at the very moment when, many argued, his forces should be moving north. Shortly after, as the Later Han collapsed, creating the power vacuum into which Kuo Wei ultimately stepped as the founder of the Later Chou, Li Ching sent his forces into Hunan. Hunan was a valuable prize, to be sure, but less valuable than the northern plain and, like the campaign in Fu-chien, Li Ching's campaign into Hunan was a military disaster.[262] By the end of 952, Li Ching was reeling from a succession of defeats. He announced that he would put an end to all military adventures, a decision the new dynasts of the north were not going to respect.[263]

But the inadequacies of Li Ching were not the only problem faced by the Southern T'ang. Paradoxically, the success of the five decades of Hsü and Li family control of the Chiang-Huai region had created its own weaknesses. The military had grown soft and indolent as a result of many years of inaction, its leadership inexperienced in the arts of war. This weakness contributed directly to the defeats suffered in the late 940s and 950s. More fundamentally, as Nishikawa Masao has argued, the upper ranks of the bureaucracy continued to be dominated by the refugee elite from north China who had surrounded Hsü Chih-kao in the 920s and 930s. This tight grip on power excluded the increasingly prosperous and sophisticated native population.[264] In 952, Li Ching made a half-hearted effort to address this situation by reinstituting an examination system for elite bureaucratic recruitment. The first exam yielded only three graduates. The system was then suspended.[265] Although it was reinstated the following year, over the next two decades many talented candidates did not sit for Southern T'ang examinations. They chose instead to go north and pursue careers in the bureaucracies of the Later Chou and the Sung. This movement of talented candidates suggests that alienation between the

---

[262] This is a common argument, see T'ao, *Wu-tai shih-lüeh*, pp. 283–7.
[263] *TCTC* 291, p. 9486.
[264] Nishikawa, "Go, Nan-Tō ryō ōchō," pp. 153–66.
[265] *TCTC* 290, pp. 9475, 9498. There is no record of when the examination system of the Wu kingdom had been suspended.

native elite and the entrenched circles around the emperor continued to be a problem. At the very time the Southern T'ang needed to reach out for support within its own territory, there was an indifference on the part of those whose support would have been instrumental in strengthening the kingdom.

The first serious confrontation between Southern T'ang and the northern dynasties began when the Later Chou emperor, Chou Shih-tsung, launched an invasion of Huai-nan, which had always been part of the Wu and Southern T'ang kingdoms. The Later Chou assault was a success. By 958, Li Ching was forced to surrender all the prefectures north of the Yangtze River and to acknowledge the Later Chou emperor as his suzerain. Li Ching also relinquished the imperial title that Southern T'ang rulers had claimed since Hsü Chih-kao in 937.[266] These concessions were more than a blow to Southern T'ang prestige. The surrendered Huai-nan prefectures were the heart of the state-run salt monopoly that was key to Southern T'ang finances. At the same time that the Later Chou victory deprived the Southern T'ang court of a major source of revenue, it claimed that revenue for itself and so enhanced its own coffers. The balance of power had now taken a major swing to the north.

By all accounts Chou Shih-tsung was intending to carry his campaign farther into Southern T'ang territory after a brief pause to consolidate his initial gains. In 959, however, the thirty-nine-year-old sovereign died from a sudden illness, before his plans could be put into action. Briefly, the stability of the north was disturbed. Within a year the Later Chou general Chao K'uang-yin (Sung T'ai-tsu r. 960–76) had usurped the Later Chou throne to establish the Sung dynasty. By 963, Sung T'ai-tsu was prepared to resume Chou Shih-tsung's campaigns of imperial expansion. Perhaps he would even have launched an invasion directly into the Southern T'ang heartland, as Chou Shih-tsung was probably going to do, but events in Hunan made that region a target too inviting to ignore. (See maps 9 and 11.)

Although Hunan had gone through a half decade of turmoil, by 956 Chou Hsing-feng had established order. Under Chou Hsing-feng taxes, which had risen dramatically in the preceding years, were eased and a measure of prosperity returned. His rule, which was stern, uncompromising, and often violent,[267] was nevertheless highly charismatic and, as is so characteristic of such rule, intensely personalized. When he died in 962, his ten-year-old son and heir, Chou Pao-ch'üan, who inherited neither his father's charisma nor the loyalties of those around him, was unable to perpetuate his authority, and rebellion again broke out. Following his father's deathbed instruction, Chou Pao-ch'üan appealed to Sung T'ai-tsu for help.

---

[266] *TCTC* 294, p. 9583.
[267] See, for example, *TCTC* 293, pp. 9555–8.

To the Sung court, anxious to resume the process of expansion, the turmoil in Hunan was an opportunity to incorporate the rich lands of the Tung-t'ing Lake drainage basin, whose wealth could be used to finance further campaigns against the stronger states in Szechwan and Chiang-nan. The new emperor Sung T'ai-tsu seized the opportunity without hesitation, gaining not only Hunan but Ching-nan as well. For when T'ai-tsu requested permission to send his forces through Ching-nan, Kao Chi-chung, fifth and last in his family to rule independently, was persuaded that while resistance would lead to death and destruction, compliance would spare his people and provide him continued wealth and existence. Kao Chi-chung yielded without a fight. He was the first of the southern rulers to give up his independence, opening a path for the Sung armies into Hunan.[268] By the summer of 963 all resistance in Hunan was overwhelmed and the territory absorbed into the new empire.[269] For the first time since the fall of the T'ang dynasty, a state from the northern plain had a secure foothold in the rich lands south of the Yangtze River.

The collapse of the kingdoms at the center of southern China touched off further reactions among the remaining kingdoms, especially in Szechwan. Meng Chih-hsiang, who had established the Later Shu kingdom in 934, died within months of taking the imperial title and was succeeded by his son, Meng Ch'ang (r. 934–65). Meng Ch'ang's long reign was initially prosperous and stable, and he was able to recover the four most northerly prefectures of Ch'in-chou, Ch'eng-chou, Chieh-chou, and Feng-chou (all in the southern part of modern Kansu) that had been lost with the fall of the Former Shu.[270] But as happened in the central Yangtze valley when Southern T'ang extended its territorial authority, Meng Ch'ang's successful reach into new territories undermined his ability to strengthen his kingdom. Also Meng Ch'ang was growing less interested in government, and in 951 he turned all responsibility over to a childhood friend, Yin Fan-cheng. According to Ssu-ma Kuang, "From this point the government of Shu began to decline."[271] In 955, Chou Shih-tsung began his program of unification by easily reclaiming Shu's four northern prefectures.[272] The cost of the unsuccessful defense of these prefectures was more than the Later Shu treasury could bear. The resulting fiscal crisis in Szechwan led to the confiscation of all privately owned iron implements, to be melted down and recast as debased iron coins.[273] The need to increase revenues,

---

[268] HCP (1964) 4, pp. 3b–4b.
[269] HCP (1964) 4, pp. 4b–6a.
[270] Ou-yang, Hsin Wu-tai shih 64, p. 804.
[271] TCTC 290, p. 9460.
[272] TCTC 292, pp. 9524–5, 9528–33.
[273] TCTC 292, p. 9531.

however, persisted, provoking Meng Ch'ang to intensify the collection of tax arrears as well as impose new levies.[274]

The Later Shu was spared from renewed Later Chou attacks when Chou Shih-tsung diverted his attention to the Southern T'ang. But then he died, and when the forces of Sung T'ai-tsu captured the territory of the central Yangtze basin, Meng Ch'ang grew justifiably afraid, and dispatched a secret message to the court of the Northern Han kingdom proposing an alliance. His message was discovered when his envoys passed through the new Sung capital, K'ai-feng, providing Sung T'ai-tsu with the excuse he sought to renew the campaign of expansion into Szechwan. Begun in late 964, the Sung assault proceeded with surprising speed. Within months Later Shu resistance had collapsed and Meng Ch'ang sued for peace, surrendering his land to the invaders.[275] Although sporadic unrest continued to disturb Szechwan for another quarter of a century, Meng Ch'ang's surrender meant that the Sung dynasty now controlled all southern territory west of Chiang-nan and north of Ling-nan.

It was five years before Sung T'ai-tsu resumed his campaigns in the south, having turned first to an unsuccessful attempt to subdue the Northern Han. The next kingdom to fall was the Southern Han. The Southern Han had experienced many years of stability under its first two rulers, Liu Yin and his brother Liu Yen, although Liu Yen had already begun the pattern of arbitrary rule and self-enrichment that was to characterize and discredit his successors.[276] Following Liu Yen's death in 942 the kingdom entered a steady spiral of decline and misrule. The Southern Han survived only because of the wealth it generated from its pivotal role in the overseas trade. Liu Ch'ang, the last member of the Liu family to rule, ascended the throne in 958 following the unmourned death of his tyrannical father. Liu Ch'ang is described as cruel and corrupt, with no interest in governing, choosing instead to drink and cavort with Persian girls.[277] Liu Ch'ang allowed the kingdom's military to deteriorate. Under the command of cruel and incompetent eunuchs, weapons went untended and troops unpaid.

Sung T'ai-tsu first turned his attention to the Southern Han in late 968, even as his unsuccessful campaign against Northern Han was unfolding. It was said that when Sung forces had retaken Ch'en-chou, a prefecture on the frontier between the Southern Han and Hunan, one of the eunuch prisoners was

[274] HCP (1964) 3, p. 15a; 6, p. 3b.
[275] The Sung campaign is narrated in Yang, *Ch'ien Shu Hou Shu shih*, pp. 159–63.
[276] The following is based on the account in Ou-yang, *Hsin Wu-tai shih* 65. See also Edward H. Schafer "The history of the empire of Southern Han, according to chapter 65 of the *Wu-tai shih* of Ou-yang Hsiu," in *Sōritsu nijūgo shūnen kinen ronbunshū {The silver jubilee volume of the Zinbun Kagaku Kenkyusyo, Kyoto University}*, ed. Kyōtō Daigaku Jinbun Kagaku Kenkyūjo (Kyoto, 1954), vol. 16, pp. 339–69.
[277] SS 481, p. 13920.

brought before the emperor. T'ai-tsu asked his captive about the government of his kingdom, to which the eunuch replied: "It has indulged itself in luxurious extravagance and merciless cruelty for many generations." Sung T'ai-tsu then sighed and said: "I must rescue the people of this place." The prefect of Tao-chou, in southern Hunan, then reported to the court that refugees were fleeing the evil oppressions of Liu Ch'ang's reign and called on the emperor to launch an invasion. Although an invasion was not feasible at that moment because of the ongoing campaign in the north, T'ai-tsu did direct Li Yü (r. 961–75), ruler of Southern T'ang, to appeal to Liu Ch'ang to desist from his abuses and to submit to northern suzerainty. Liu Ch'ang ignored the advice.[278] Finally in late 970, the northern campaign over, Sung T'ai-tsu directed his generals to launch their assault on the Southern Han. The campaign lasted several months, but Sung forces held the advantage from the beginning and gradually pushed the defenders back. By the late spring of 971, Liu Ch'ang was dead – the only one of the southern rulers to actually die in the unification campaigns.

There were now two kingdoms, T'ang and Wu-Yüeh, and the warlord enclave of Chang-Ch'üan (in southern Fu-chien) that had not yet fallen to Sung forces. Although they acknowledged the overlordship of the Sung, these remaining states continued to act independently, a situation T'ai-tsu was not willing to tolerate. Tributary suzerainty was not the same as imperial author-ity. Sung T'ai-tsu identified Southern T'ang as the cornerstone of continued resistance to Sung imperial claims, so it was to that kingdom that he turned his attention. Li Yü, as ruler of the Southern T'ang, had been a loyal and sub-servient tributary, regularly sending envoys to K'ai-feng to affirm his subordi-nate status. But following the successful conclusion of the campaign against the Southern Han, the Sung began deliberately to reduce Li Yü's status. Late in 971 he was directed to change his title from "Ruler of T'ang" to "Ruler of Chiang-nan," a demotion that attempted to end the connection between Li Yü and the imperial heritage of the T'ang dynasty.[279] The following year, Sung T'ai-tsu decided to increase the pressure by detaining Li Yü's brother, who had come to K'ai-feng on a tributary mission. Li Yü was greatly alarmed by this and restructured his bureaucracy to make it appear less imperial.[280] All this was in vain, however, for T'ai-tsu had determined that Li Yü would either yield his kingdom voluntarily or have it taken by force. Through 973 and 974 the two played a delicate minuet. Li Yü was fully aware that resistance to T'ai-tsu's appeal would lead to only one outcome, yet he continued to avoid a showdown. In late 975, T'ai-tsu's patience ran out and the invasion began.

---

[278] *HCP* (1964) 9, pp. 9b–10a.
[279] *HCP* (1964), 1, reprinting *Yung-lo ta-tien* 12306, pp. 6b–7a.
[280] *HCP* (1964), 1, reprinting *Yung-lo ta-tien* 12306, p. 9a.

Even Wu-Yüeh forces participated, launching an assault from the east at the same time that Sung forces crossed the Yangtze River and entered Chiang-nan from the north. Although Southern T'ang resources and power had been reduced by the loss of the Huai-nan prefectures nearly two decades before, the kingdom was still wealthy and its armies strong. The campaign was accordingly slow and difficult. But in late 975, Li Yü accepted the inevitable and surrendered.[281]

Neither of the remaining southern rulers, Ch'ien Shu (r. 948–78) of Wu-Yüeh and Ch'en Hung-chin (r. 962–78) (in southern Fu-chien), was under any illusion about the future. Both were preparing to yield their kingdoms voluntarily when Sung T'ai-tsu died in 976. The need to observe the formalities of mourning thus delayed their submission, which was not finalized until 978. Sung T'ai-tsu's evaluation of Southern T'ang as the last hurdle to surmount to accomplish unification was borne out. Neither surviving kingdom could prolong its conquest by the Sung empire, and the era of the southern kingdoms was over.

CONCLUSION

The southern kingdoms were critical to the character of the Sung dynasty that followed. As later chapters in this volume show, the new dynasty was increasingly oriented toward the lands they had conquered. The south was home to many of the pivotal figures of the first half of the Sung dynasty, including the great reformers of the eleventh century, Fan Chung-yen and Wang An-shih. As that century unfolded, southerners, many of whom were descendants of men who had taken advantage of the unsettled social conditions of the tenth century to rise from obscurity, increasingly dominated the civil service examinations and the governing bureaucracy. The south was the economic heart of the Sung in an era that was increasingly commercialized and dependent upon trade. It was the southern kingdoms that had consolidated the commercial character of the region and laid the groundwork for the great economic surge that followed. And as the new dynasty wrestled with what seemed to many to be unresolvable fiscal problems, the reformers turned to models of state finance that emphasized revenue sources other than land taxes, specifically models that had been adopted and refined by the southern kingdoms.

---

[281] The final year of the campaign is narrated in *HCP* (1964), 1, reprinting *Yung-lo ta-tien* 12307, pp. 1a–15a.

CHAPTER 3

FOUNDING AND CONSOLIDATION OF THE SUNG DYNASTY UNDER T'AI-TSU (960–976), T'AI-TSUNG (976–997), AND CHEN-TSUNG (997–1022)

Lau Nap-yin and Huang K'uan-chung

T'AI-TSU AND THE FOUNDING OF THE SUNG, 960–976

The last years of the Five Dynasties era

The end of T'ang imperial rule in 907 resulted in seventy-two years of political division, the emergence of nine kingdoms in the south, the Sha-t'o-ruled kingdom of Northern Han (951–79) (in Shansi), and a succession of five short-lived dynasties located in the traditional center of the Chinese imperium in the Yellow River valley. While the southern kingdoms (891–979) lasted for decades in relative peace and prosperity, the north was in a constant state of war, and each of the so-called Five Dynasties (907–60) rapidly supplanted one another through regicides, army mutinies, and war. This political fragmentation and instability invited military incursions and sometimes drew into the region armies of the Sha-t'o Turks and Khitan (Ch'i-tan). Further west, in the region of Kansu, former T'ang territories were controlled by Tibetan, Uighur, and Tangut warlord states. The most successful of these frontier groups were the Khitan, who incorporated the Sixteen Prefectures (a region encompassing modern Peking) into their own Liao empire (907–1125).

The decline of administrative order in the late T'ang dynasty gave rise to widespread banditry and separatist regional military governors (*chieh-tu shih*). The notorious Chu Wen (r. 907–12), for example, deserted the Huang Ch'ao rebellion (875–84) to become a T'ang military governor, then murdered and deposed the last two T'ang emperors to found his own Later Liang dynasty, which lasted sixteen years (907–23), the longest of the northern dynasties. Chu Wen's life, however, was taken in the fifth year of his reign by one of his sons, who was killed in turn by a half brother after only one year on the throne.[1]

---

[1] For Chu Wen and his Later Liang dynasty, see chapters 4 and 5 of Wang Gungwu, *The structure of power in north China during the Five Dynasties* (Kuala Lumpur, 1963); Robert Somers, "The end of T'ang," in *The Cambridge history of China*, volume 3: *Sui and T'ang China, 589–906, part 1*, ed. Denis C. Twitchett (Cambridge, 1979), pp. 781–7.

In the words of the historian Ma Tuan-lin (c. 1254–1323), the provincial military governors of the late T'ang empire were either insurgent soldiers or bandit leaders who had murdered or expelled former military governors and had their usurpations ratified by the helpless T'ang court.[2] The military governors expanded their territories at one another's expense in destructive battles, pillaging and ravaging whether they won or lost. Ch'ang-an (modern Hsi-an in Shensi) was ruined, Lo-yang (in Honan) was depopulated, and much of the north was devastated.[3] Under such leaders, the lawlessness of the late T'ang period spread and intensified.

Fragmentation also undermined the foundations of medieval tradition. The value of loyalty declined as ranking officials, high and low alike, prostrated themselves before whatever new ruler had just overthrown their old master. Ritually sworn brotherhood often ended in fratricide. Younger generals adopted as sons by their superiors frequently assassinated their "fathers." Personal loyalty was rare, loyalty to the state rarer still, since there was no lasting state. All was in flux, and betrayal motivated by self-interest was frequent. In determining the succession to the throne, naked force decided the outcome – emperors were raised to the throne by fellow generals and generals by their soldiers. Unsatisfied with the rewards accruing to them from such action or spurred on by their own ambitions, yesterday's supporters could easily turn into tomorrow's usurpers. In this age of constant and unpredictable conflict, when "emperors were enthroned like clerks and states were replaced like inns,"[4] most of the militarist rulers in the north before the Later Chou, even though they harbored dynastic pretensions, were generally preoccupied with war and seldom had either the leisure, the means, or the ambition to consider making changes in institutions, promoting cultural pursuits, or undertaking economic reconstruction.

However, a limited foundation of wealth and strength was gradually laid down during the Later Chou dynasty (951–60), the forerunner of the Sung and the first post T'ang regime able to claim to have been a stable dynasty. To briefly reprise events narrated in chapter 1, the Later Chou founder, Kuo Wei (r. 951–4), though himself a usurper, was determined to reform the economy

---

[2] Ma Tuan-lin, *Wen-hsien t'ung-k'ao* [*Shang-wu yin-shu-kuan*, 1935–7 ed.] (c. 1308; Taipei, 1965) 276, p. 2195. The Ch'ing historian Chao I (1727–1814) showed that almost thirty to forty percent of military governors during the late ninth and early tenth centuries were first appointed by their armies and then retrospectively confirmed in their posts by the central government. See Chao I, *Nien-erh shih cha-chi* (1799; Taipei, 1977) 21, pp. 460–3. His figure may be an underestimate; see Edmund H. Worthy, Jr., "The founding of Sung China, 950–1000: Integrative changes in military and political institutions" (diss., Princeton University, 1976), pp. 104, 132, n. 9. Worthy's pioneering work remains the best study of the founding of the Northern Sung.

[3] Liu Hsü et al., *Chiu T'ang-shu* (945; Peking, 1975) 123, p. 3513.

[4] See the introduction in Ou-yang Hsiu, *Hsin Wu-tai shih* (1073; Peking, 1974), p. 2.

and the military but died before he could accomplish much. His adopted son and successor, Ch'ai Jung (r. 954–9), achieved more. During the nine years of their reigns, heavy taxes were reduced and taxes imposed more equitably; vast areas of government land (in particular, the military garrison fields) were released to the common people, abandoned land was brought under cultivation; concealed landholdings were registered for taxation; irrigation canals and dikes were constructed; vagrants and refugees were settled; the selection of officials was carefully administered; and corruption was reduced. In 955, over thirty thousand Buddhist monasteries were abolished to free new land and obtain new taxpayers. The bells and statues from the monasteries were melted down and cast into coins to feed the rapidly expanding money economy. As a result, tax returns, economic output, and population all increased.[5] While implementing these improvements, Ch'ai Jung also set about expanding the territory under his control.

First, however, he had to strengthen the twin pillars of the imperial armies (chin-chün): the Metropolitan Command (Shih-wei ssu), and the Palace Command (Tien-ch'ien ssu). The ultimate goal was to transform these armies from "imperial power brokers" into "agents of centralized imperial power."[6] This process was begun as early as 954, soon after Ch'ai Jung ascended the throne and found himself fighting a massive invasion by Northern Han and Khitan troops. In a decisive battle at Kao-p'ing (in southern Shansi), when key units of the Metropolitan Command fled and defeat loomed, Ch'ai Jung heroically charged ahead with the Palace Command and saved the day.[7] Ch'ai Jung seized this opportunity to gain firm control over the Metropolitan Command. He executed commanders in chief and officers in the infantry and the cavalry for their cowardice and disobedience, and restaffed the Metropolitan Command with his own men. He then conducted a full-scale fitness review of the imperial armies, discharging the decrepit and unfit and promoting the ablest of their troops. This housecleaning reduced wasteful expenditures and revitalized the strength of the Metropolitan Command. At the same time, a recruitment campaign throughout Ch'ai Jung's realm began to draw the fittest stalwarts – including those serving the provincial military governors – into the Palace Command, making the Palace Command's strength and structure parallel

---

[5] For Kuo Wei's and Ch'ai Jung's reforms, see the accounts of their reigns written in 974 by Hsüeh Chü-cheng et al., eds., *Chiu Wu-tai shih* [hereafter *CWTS*] (974; Peking, 1976) 110–19, pp. 1447–1589; Han Kuo-p'an, *Ch'ai Jung* (Shanghai, 1956); Ch'üan Han-sheng, *T'ang Sung ti-kuo yün-ho* (Chung-ching, 1944), pp. 93–4; Kurihara Masuo, *Ransei no kōtei – "Kō-Shū" no Seisō to sono jidai* (Tokyo, 1968); and chapter 2 of Worthy, "The founding of Sung China," especially pp. 28, 32, 39.

[6] Quoted from the titles of chapters 3 and 4 of Worthy, "The founding of Sung China."

[7] *CWTS* 114, p. 1513.

to that of the Metropolitan Command.[8] Having effectively enacted these reforms during the first year of his reign, Ch'ai Jung became a strong military ruler.

The following year, Ch'ai Jung called for his ministers to propose unification strategies. Wang P'u (?–957), a bureau director in the Ministry of Justice, is usually credited by the historians with submitting the famous "South before North" strategy. Wang suggested that the first objective should be the Southern T'ang (937–75), since weak points along its border with the Later Chou could easily be penetrated and the riches of its main territories in the lower Yangtze valley would provide future campaigns with funds for manpower and resources. Wang further proposed that the Later Chou army should avoid conflict with the strong states in favor of attacking the weak. Only comparatively small forces would be needed to finish off the Southern T'ang, the Southern Han (917–71) in Kwangtung, and the Later Shu (934–65) in Szechwan, thus saving the major forces for a final expedition against the Northern Han and their allies the Khitan.[9]

Because of new and changing opportunities, Ch'ai Jung deviated slightly from Wang's proposal. Ch'ai Jung first captured four prefectures from the Later Shu. Then, in two and a half years, he annexed from the Southern T'ang fourteen fertile prefectures between the Yangtze and the Huai rivers. This annexation added 226,500 households and large tax revenues to the Later Chou coffers. It also provided a transportation route linking the Yangtze River and the productive Huai River areas to the Later Chou capital at K'ai-feng.[10] In 959, however, the southward campaign was diverted to counter an incursion on the northern frontiers by the Khitan, who were abetted by the Southern T'ang. The Later Chou counterattack more than halted the Khitan incursion: it captured three strategic passes and two of the so-called Sixteen Prefectures of Yen-Yün (Mo-chou and Ying-chou) from the Khitan (see map 9). The campaign faltered, however, at Yu-chou (the Liao Southern Capital), where Ch'ai Jung fell mortally ill. Ch'ai Jung returned to K'ai-feng, and one month later he died at the age of thirty-nine, leaving his five-year-old son on the throne. The Later Chou empire, enlarged from 96 to 118 prefectures, now needed strong leadership, and the position of emperor was coveted by powerful men.

---

[8] Wang P'u, *Wu-tai hui-yao* (961; Shanghai, 1978) 12, pp. 205–6; *CWTS* 114, p. 1522. For the political importance of the Metropolitan Command, see chapter 7 of Wang, *Structure of power*, especially pp. 205–6, and chapters 3 and 4 of Worthy, "The founding of Sung China."

[9] For Wang P'u's "South before North" strategy, see Chang Chia-chü, *Chao K'uang-yin chuan* (Nanking, 1959), pp. 27–8, and Worthy, "The founding of Sung China," pp. 14–17.

[10] *CWTS* 118, p. 1570.

The Coup at Ch'en-ch'iao

Legend has it that during his expedition against the Khitan, Ch'ai Jung was presented with a wooden plaque, mysteriously discovered on the ground, that bore a hexagram and the disturbing message: "The inspector-general is to be. . . ." According to the legend, the missing object sounded like the word "emperor" to Ch'ai Jung, and as a consequence he summarily dismissed the inspector-general of the Palace Command, Chang Yung-te (927–1000), an amateur astrologer and the son-in-law of Kuo Wei, and replaced him with the commander in chief – a military strongman named Chao K'uang-yin (926–76) who would in fact become the next emperor and founder of the Sung dynasty.[11]

Born into an official family in Lo-yang, Chao K'uang-yin had joined the regional army of Ch'ai Jung's predecessor, Kuo Wei, at the age of twenty-one. Chao followed in the footsteps of his father, Chao Hung-yin (?–956), who had served successively in the imperial armies of four dynasties beginning with the Later T'ang (923–36).[12] It did not take long for the receptive young Chao to learn firsthand how a new dynasty could, once established, turn around and victimize its subjects by neglecting to restrain its military. For example, toward the end of 950, the last emperor of the Later Han, Liu Ch'eng-yu (r. 948–50), had launched a bloody purge against his potential rivals. Three of the four officials Liu's predecessor had designated to advise him were executed with their families and followers, and an assassination plot was set in motion against another one. The fourth official was Kuo Wei – Ch'ai Jung's adoptive father and predecessor. Kuo Wei had just been posted as a military governor in Ho-pei. In response to the plot, Kuo marched with his troops to the capital, promising his army ten days of plunder if they took the city. When the city fell it was pillaged by the rebels, and the Later Han emperor executed. An adopted imperial relative was summoned from his prefecture of residence to succeed to the throne, but he never sat on it. In the last month of 950, a Khitan invasion was reported and Kuo Wei was dispatched to repel it. A few days after leaving the capital, Kuo was proclaimed emperor by the expeditionary troops. Among them was Chao K'uang-yin, who was soon promoted an officer.[13]

Chao K'uang-yin continued to win distinction and promotion under the new Chou emperor, Kuo Wei. Chao's talents furthermore endeared him to the then Prince Ch'ai Jung, who transferred Chao to his own command. The prince

---

[11] CWTS 119, p. 1583; T'o-t'o et al., eds., Sung shih [hereafter SS], (1345; Peking, 1977) 1, p. 3; 255, p. 8917. See also Liu Tzu-chien (James T. C. Liu), "Sung T'ai-tsung yü Sung-ch'u liang-tz'u ts'uan-wei," Shih-huo yüeh-k'an 17 Nos. 3–4 (1988), p. 1.

[12] For the Chao family, see Chang, Chao K'uang-yin chuan, pp. 1–6.

[13] Chang, Chao K'uang-yin chuan, p. 6; Worthy, "The founding of Sung China," pp. 140–4.

trusted Chao as though he were his own right arm during various expeditions. In the battle at Kao-p'ing, Chao distinguished himself by selflessly defending Ch'ai Jung, who, having succeeded Kuo Wei, was now emperor.[14] In the following year (955), when the Later Chou campaign against the Later Shu became bogged down in Ch'in-chou, Chao went to inspect the situation. Using Chao's recommendations, Ch'ai Jung was able to carry the campaign to victory. Later, during the invasion of the Southern T'ang in 956, Chao single-handedly captured an enemy general, earning himself appointment as inspector-general of the Palace Command.

In contrast to his counterpart in the Metropolitan Command, the high-handed Han T'ung (?–960), Chao K'uang-yin was politically adept and known to be a commander who was not only brave but also judicious and magnanimous. In the military he was popular with the rank and file. When Ch'ai Jung reformed the imperial armies in 954, Chao K'uang-yin was assigned the significant task of selecting the best new recruits for induction into the Palace Command, training them as a crack force. Through care and effective discipline, Chao earned the personal loyalty of his troops. In addition, he cultivated the acquaintance of many of his father's old friends and swore ritual brotherhood with promising new military commanders, many of them his subordinates.[15] He showed good administrative abilities, but these were less important than his skills in managing personal relationships and his political prowess.

As noted earlier, Ch'ai Jung died of illness in 959, leaving the throne to his young son, Kuo Tsung-hsün (Chou Kung-ti, 959) a small child of about five years of age. On the first day of the lunar year corresponding to 960, a joint invasion by Liao and Northern Han forces was reported by two frontier prefectures, Chen-chou and Ting-chou, in Ho-pei. Whether this invasion actually occurred is doubtful. The Liao had suffered defeats in 959, just before Ch'ai Jung's death, losing two strategic prefectures in northern Ho-pei to the Later Chou, and may have wished to recover them while the Later Chou court was preoccupied with succession. Acting on these invasion reports, the Later Chou court quickly mounted a defensive expedition. Despite early warnings from Han T'ung's son and other officials that Chao K'uang-yin was already too influential to be trusted with the overall command of the armies, Chao was dispatched to head the counterattack. When the army departed, rumors

---

[14] Chang, *Chao K'uang-yin chuan*, p. 7.

[15] See Chiang Fu-ts'ung, "Sung-tai i-ko kuo-ts'e ti chien-t'ao," *Ta-lu tsa-chih* 9 No. 7 (1954), pp. 21–36. Chao was one of a fraternity of "ten brothers," among whom Chao himself, Shih Shou-hsin (928–84), Han Ch'ung-yün (?–974), Wang Shen-ch'i (925–74), Liu T'ing-jang (929–87), and Li Chi-hsün (915–76) were prominent generals. At the time of Chao's coup, all of them except Li were in the Palace Command. See Worthy, "The founding of Sung China," pp. 165–8.

circulated through the capital that the troops were prepared to set up Chao K'uang-yin as emperor, because the troops feared that with a child on the throne and power in the hands of a woman (the dowager empress), their services to the state would not be recognized, and they would receive no promotions. These rumors brought terror to the capital. In anticipation of relentless plundering by uncontrollable troops set on king making, the citizens left K'ai-feng in droves, yet the court seemed indifferent.[16]

At dawn on the fourth day, in the camp of the expeditionary army at Ch'en-ch'iao, twenty miles northeast of K'ai-feng, the troops acclaimed the thirty-four-year-old Chao K'uang-yin as emperor, as rumor had predicted. According to the version of this event given in the official history, the throne was forced upon Chao K'uang-yin by a group of mutinous officers who, with drawn swords, burst into Chao's tent and robed their half-drunken commander in a gown of imperial yellow. Supposedly, they had already sent a secret messenger to inform two of Chao's sworn brother generals guarding the capital and the palace about the imminent coup.

The next day, Chao K'uang-yin returned to the defenseless capital K'ai-feng to seize the throne. General Han T'ung, the only major figure who attempted to muster resistance to the coup, was killed, and his peers prepared to greet their new master. The previously chosen child emperor of the Chou was given an honorary title and died in exile fourteen years later. By the afternoon, Chao had become the emperor (known posthumously as Sung T'ai-tsu, the Great Progenitor, r. 960–76) of a new dynasty, the Sung, named after the prefecture just southeast of K'ai-feng where he had served the Later Chou as military governor.

Chao's seizure of the throne appears at first sight to have been a repetition of Kuo Wei's earlier coup in 951,[17] in which Chao himself had participated. Most modern historians tend to agree that the coup was jointly engineered by Chao himself, his brother Chao K'uang-i (939–97, the future emperor Sung T'ai-tsung [r. 976–97], whose name was later changed to Chao Kuang-i to avoid the taboo on the new emperor's personal name), and some key advisors in his army.[18] Even if Chao K'uang-yin was not the prime instigator of the

---

[16] Ssu-ma Kuang, *Su-shui chi-wen* (c. 1180; Taipei, 1962) 1, pp. 1–2; 2, pp. 2–3; Li T'ao, *Hsü Tzu-chih t'ung-chien ch'ang-pien* [hereafter HCP (1964)] [*Che-chiang shu-chü* 1881 ed.] (1183; Taipei, 1961–4) 1, p. 1a.

[17] Chao, *Nien-erh shih cha-chi* 21, pp. 460–3; Chiang, "Sung-tai i-ko kuo-ts'e ti chien-t'ao," pp. 21–36.

[18] For example, see Teng Kuang-ming, "Ch'en-ch'iao ping-pien huang-p'ao chia-shen ku-shih k'ao-shih," *Chen-li tsa-chih* 1 No. 1 (1944), pp. 61–8; Chang, *Chao K'uang-yin chuan*, pp. 13–18; Ch'en Teng-yüan, *Kuo-shih chiu-wen* (Peking, 1958–62) 31, pp. 925–8; Wang Po-ch'in, "Sung ch'u erh-ti ch'üan-wei wen-t'i ti p'ou-hsi," *Ta-lu tsa-chih* 32 No. 10 (1966), pp. 16–17; Liu, "Sung T'ai-tsung yü Sung-ch'u liang-tz'u ts'uan-wei," pp. 1–2.

coup he was definitely a willing beneficiary, and adroitly took charge of the situation.

In a comparable mutiny in 935, Shih Ching-t'ang, the founder of the Later Chin dynasty (Chin Kao-tsu, r. 936–42), had deemed premature an attempt by his troops to carry out a unilateral coup and had crushed it immediately by executing some thirty of the instigators.[19] Given his undisputed control over the army, Chao K'uang-yin also could have refused the imperial yellow robe and pacified the mutineers had he so wished. Instead, he made a deal with the mutineers and threatened to refuse the crown unless they promised their obedience in all matters. Then he demanded that no harm be done to any member of the imperial house or to any court official; and, in unmistakable language, he vowed to execute the whole clan of "any officer or soldier who dared to loot the capital or to molest its inhabitants." On the other hand, he promised generous rewards to his obedient followers.

Under strict discipline, the army occupied the capital "without the slightest disturbance," so that even the street markets went on trading as usual.[20] Both troops and bureaucrats remained under tight control. This marked a notable break with the lawless successions during the Five Dynasties, most of whose rulers entered the capital at the head of plundering armies. Thanks to this peaceful and orderly takeover, the wealth and strength of the Later Chou was preserved and the goodwill of the population toward the new regime ensured. Consequently, T'ai-tsu was able to achieve internal security for his dynasty in a short time and proceed swiftly to the task of unification.

Legitimacy and internal stability

The founder of a new dynasty was usually concerned to establish a clean break with an inglorious past and to create a favorable image of himself for posterity. T'ai-tsu's orders prohibiting looting and bloodshed had already separated the Sung from the lawless Five Dynasties period, but his usurpation of the throne, whether voluntary or compelled, remained to be exonerated, and he needed quickly to transform himself from a usurper into the legitimate founder of a new dynasty. This could best be done by claiming he had received the Mandate of Heaven, which conferred legitimate power and authority on its bearer. Evidence of the conferral of the mandate was usually established by retrospective propaganda, in the form of legendary auspicious signs of heavenly approval.

---

[19] *CWTS* 75, p. 983.
[20] Ssu-ma, *Su-shui chi-wen* 1, p. 1; *HCP* (1964) 1, pp. 1a–3b.

One such legend about the founding of the Sung dynasty was related by a lieutenant and astrologer accompanying the 960 expedition, who claimed that when the army was leaving the capital, he saw the sun being eclipsed by another sun, perhaps symbolizing the advent of a new dynasty.[21] As the person to whom this legend supposedly referred, T'ai-tsu was said to have been confident of his having been chosen as the bearer of the mandate. When warned that it was dangerous to go out incognito to survey the state of society for himself, the newly enthroned emperor laughed at the prospect of danger, for he accepted the idea that when a person had been chosen by Heaven to be the true master of the world, no one could harm him; while without Heaven's mandate even the guarded doors of a secluded palace could not protect him.[22]

But T'ai-tsu needed real power to retain the Mandate of Heaven. There were other potential contenders for the throne as well as disgruntled holdovers from the ousted Later Chou dynasty to be dealt with. Among the generals and regional military governors, T'ai-tsu's enthronement aroused mixed emotions. Han Ling-k'un (923–68) and Mu-jung Yen-chao (913–63), T'ai-tsu's long-standing battlefield comrades, welcomed it. On the other hand, Kuo Ch'ung (908–65) and Yüan Yen (907–72), who had helped establish the Later Chou, were inclined to resist it, and Li Yün (?–960) in the north and Li Ch'ung-chin (?–960) in the south were firmly opposed.

Li Yün, who had been instrumental in founding the Later Chou, had since then been military governor of Lu-chou (modern Ch'ang-chih in Shansi). After the death of his old master Kuo Wei, Li's own imperial ambitions grew. He had begun to act independently and arbitrarily, and to swell his financial reserves with expropriated taxes and his army with refugees. When T'ai-tsu offered him a lofty honorary title and munificent gifts, Li refused them. He reluctantly sought an alliance with the Northern Han, whom he had attacked during the Later Chou. But his half-hearted overtures were matched by Northern Han misgivings about his dubious proposed strategy of marching straight on K'ai-feng. Li's hope of success was further dampened by opposition to his insurrection by his son and by some of his generals. As it turned out, the Sung army took the whole of Lu-chou in less than two months. With his thirty thousand troops routed, Li committed suicide.[23]

Li Ch'ung-chin, Kuo Wei's nephew, was isolated at his headquarters in Yang-chou, the greatest city in the southern territory and recently annexed

[21] *HCP* (1964) 1, p. 1b.

[22] Ssu-ma, *Su-shui chi-wen* 1, p. 3; *HCP* (1964) 1, pp. 25a–26a. See also Yao Ying-t'ing, "Lun T'ang Sung chih-chi ti t'ien-ming yü fan-t'ien-ming ssu-hsiang," in *Sung-shih yen-chiu lun-wen-chi: 1982 nien nien-hui pien-k'an*, ed. Teng Kuang-ming and Li Chia-chü (Cheng-chou, 1984), pp. 370–84.

[23] Wang Ch'eng, *Tung-tu shih-lüeh* (1186; Taipei, 1967) 22, pp. 1a–2b; *HCP* (1964) 1, pp. 10b–15a.

from the Southern T'ang by Ch'ai Jung. When T'ai-tsu was commander in chief of the Palace Command, Li Ch'ung-chin had held the parallel post of chief of the Metropolitan Command, a position he lost when the new dynasty demoted him to regional military governor of Yang-chou. Having decided to revolt, Li Ch'ung-chin sent an envoy to Li Yün to plan a synchronized pincer attack from the north and south, hoping to force the Sung forces to fight on two fronts a thousand miles apart. However, his envoy defected to the Sung and was induced to return to Yang-chou to delay Li Ch'ung-chin's offensive. This sealed Li Ch'ung-chin's fate. Soon besieged, Li Ch'ung-chin found that his hopes that the Southern T'ang would come to his relief had been nipped in the bud by a Sung threat of retaliation. In the eleventh month of 960, less than two months after his insurgency began, Yang-chou fell and Li Ch'ung-chin immolated himself and his entire family.[24]

The subjugation of these two potentially dangerous opponents by an overpowering central army sent a clear warning to other military governors. Even the unwilling Kuo Ch'ung and Yüan Yen could not but submit to the new dynasty. In return, T'ai-tsu allowed about four-fifths of the Later Chou provincial military governors (some forty-odd officials) to retain their posts.[25] As Wang Gungwu has pointed out, during the twenty-five years between 926 and 951 the power of individual provinces had gradually fallen "below the point where [they] could be a threat to imperial authority."[26] T'ai-tsu could now safely turn his attention to incorporating the territories of the various independent kingdoms that occupied parts of the former T'ang realm.

Military control and partial unification

The later historical view that T'ai-tsu, once in power, tilted the balance between military and civil elements in his regime toward civilian control should not obscure the strong military coloration of the early Sung period. Although T'ai-tsu certainly acknowledged the importance of the civil bureaucracy, he never slighted the military. Himself a military man, he needed to maintain a strong army to obviate any countercoups. Also, in the world beyond Sung borders, force and the threat of force was needed to achieve reconquest of large regions now controlled by independent regimes, and to defend against the persistent Liao threat to the Sung's northern borders. The survival of T'ai-tsu's

---

[24] Wang, *Tung-tu shih-lüeh* 22, pp. 2b–3b; *HCP* (1964) 1, pp. 20a–21b, 23b–24a.
[25] Wang, *Structure of power*, p. 203.
[26] Wang, *Structure of power*, pp. 191–4. This decrease in power was partly due to the Khitan invasion and occupation of northern China from 943 to 947, which had sapped the wealth and manpower of most military governors there to the point that none of them was strong enough to challenge the imperial government.

reign and the future of the Sung dynasty necessitated the establishment of tighter control over the army and improvement of its effectiveness through strict selection and vigorous training of its personnel.[27]

T'ai-tsu began to assert his control over the military by depriving all commanders, particularly his own accomplices in the 960 coup, of the ability to threaten the throne. He first removed from office all but one of these top generals. He then established permanent institutional control over the military by restructuring its command hierarchy to ensure that no single general could wield an unacceptable level of power. He also separated the military administration from the military command structure to ensure that no one except the emperor could exercise overall control of the military.

Immediately upon ascending the throne, T'ai-tsu began to tighten his grip over the Metropolitan Command, which had never been as responsive to his influence as had his loyal Palace Command. Within a few months the highest level of the Metropolitan Command was restaffed either by officers transferred from the Palace Command or by T'ai-tsu's sworn brothers or his most trusted generals. After the suppression of Li Ch'ung-chin, its former commander in chief, T'ai-tsu's control over the Metropolitan Command was practically unchallengeable. Within another few months, T'ai-tsu reappointed the chiefs of the Metropolitan Command and the Palace Command, Han Ling-k'un and Mu-jung Yen-chao, as regional military governors away from the capital. Soon other, top commanders were also reappointed to different posts.

During the interim between the founding of the Sung dynasty and the first unification campaign, amid the easy atmosphere of a wine-drinking party held in the seventh month of 961, T'ai-tsu complained to his top generals about the discomfort of occupying the throne. He constantly worried that the pampered subordinates of these top generals would some day force a yellow robe on one of them, as had been done to him. Startled and disoriented, the generals begged for the emperor's advice. T'ai-tsu first pointed out that the essence of happiness in the short life of man is to have wealth and prestige and to be able to bequeath them to one's descendants. Then he persuaded the generals to relinquish their current military authority in exchange for the wealth and prestige of appointment as regional military governors and the arrangement of marriages between their families and the imperial family.

The next day, all these generals offered to resign on the grounds of ill health.[28] True to his word, T'ai-tsu provided each of them with a comfortable

---

[27] For a general understanding of the Northern Sung military system, see Lo Ch'iu-ch'ing, "Pei Sung ping-chih yen-chiu," *Hsin-ya hsüeh-pao* 3 No. 1 (1957), pp. 169–270; and Wang Tseng-yü, *Sung-ch'ao ping-chih ch'u-t'an* (Peking, 1983).

[28] Ssu-ma, *Su-shui chi-wen* 1, pp. 6–7; Nieh Ch'ung-ch'i, "Lun Sung T'ai-tsu shou ping-ch'üan," *Yen-ching hsüeh-pao* 34 (1948), pp. 85–106; Ch'en, *Kuo-shih chiu-wen* 32, pp. 938–42.

official post and arranged a marriage linking them to the imperial family. Except for Han Ch'ung-yün (?–974), who was transferred to the Palace Command for the first time, all the top commanders of the imperial armies were thus pensioned off from their "dangerous" positions, and no longer posed a threat to the throne.[29] These commanders all lived well, until their deaths. For example, Shih Shou-hsin, the only top commander who retained his original position in the imperial armies concurrently (even though now in absentia), until he voluntarily relinquished it in the ninth month of the following year (962), became notorious for the vast fortune he subsequently amassed during his almost seventeen-year tenure (7/961–12/977) as a regional military governor.[30]

As for the promised marriages, except for Lo Yen-kuei, who seems to have been childless,[31] all of these top commanders became T'ai-tsu's in-laws: Shih Shou-hsin's second son, Shih Pao-chi (954–1010), married T'ai-tsu's second daughter in 972.[32] Chang Ling-to's third daughter was married to T'ai-tsu's second brother in 961.[33] Han Ch'ung-yün's second son, Han Ch'ung-yeh (960–1001), was married to T'ai-tsu's niece.[34] Kao Huai-te had already married T'ai-tsu's widowed younger sister in 960.[35] Wang Shen-ch'i's eldest son, Wang Ch'eng-yen (951–1003), married T'ai-tsu's eldest daughter in 970.[36] These marriages evidenced an intimate cordiality between T'ai-tsu and the families of these retired generals that had not existed between an emperor and his generals since the Later Han. (T'ai-tsu later adopted similarly conciliatory policies toward the regional rulers he defeated and their followers.[37]) At the same time, a new principle was also established that no regional military governor could concurrently hold a regular command in the imperial army.[38]

The purpose behind these institutional maneuvers was to downgrade the command hierarchy, to divide responsibilities, to break the close and lasting

---

[29] Chao Kuang-i was reappointed governor of K'ai-feng; Shih Shou-hsin (928–84), Chang Ling-to (911–70), Lo Yen-kuei (923–69), Kao Huai-te (926–82), and Wang Shen-ch'i (925–74) were all sent out to serve long terms as regional commissioners (*chieh-tu shih*). HCP (1964) 2, p. 11b; SS 250, pp. 8823–4, 8809–11, 8826–8, 8821–3, 8815–17.

[30] HCP (1964) 2, p. 11a; 3, p. 10a; 18, p. 20b.

[31] SS 250, pp. 8827–8.

[32] SS 248, p. 8772; 250, p. 8812.

[33] SS 250, p. 8826.

[34] SS 250, p. 8825.

[35] SS 248, p. 8771; 250, p. 8822.

[36] SS 248, p. 8772; 250, p. 8817.

[37] SS 244, p. 8676; 248, p. 8772; 251, pp. 8831–6.

[38] But Wang, *Structure of power*, pp. 204–5, has argued that most of the post-947 commanders of the Metropolitan Command continued as commanders even though they were designated as regional military governors. When they were serving in the capital, their provinces were administered by a staff chosen, or at least approved, by the court. Consequently, both imperial authority and central control over the provinces were enhanced.

links between commanders and their troops, and to elaborate the structure of surveillance and control. To solidify his own powers, T'ai-tsu left important posts vacant, including the two highest positions of the Metropolitan Command (commander in chief and vice–commander in chief) and the two highest positions of the Palace Command (inspector-general and vice–inspector-general). Other positions that were rarely or irregularly filled included the third highest post of the Metropolitan Command (inspector in chief) and the remaining three highest posts of the Palace Command (commander in chief, vice–commander in chief, and inspector in chief).[39] When T'ai-tsu did fill these positions, he chose low-ranked or docile men over people of distinction and initiative. Not only were the prestige and authority of the army leadership weakened, the previously unitary command of the Metropolitan Command was split between its two divisions: the cavalry and the infantry were each now placed under an independent commander. Therefore, the original dual command of the imperial army became tripartite, coming under the jurisdiction of the Three Military Bureaus (san-ya), that is, the Palace Command, and the Infantry and the Cavalry divisions of the Metropolitan Command. Each group was expected to check the others. The Metropolitan Command took care of regional defense, while the Palace Command guarded the capital and the palace. This arrangement was intended to maintain a functional separation of powers. Moreover, although they controlled the military command, the Three Military Bureaus had no authority to dispatch or transfer their troops. Military administration became the responsibility of the Bureau of Military Affairs (Shu-mi yüan), which commanded no troops of its own.[40] In addition, important personnel and administrative decisions, especially those regarding the appointment, promotion, or demotion of senior officers in the Three Military Bureaus, were handled by the emperor in person, and the appointees were directly answerable to him.

After the old personal links between officers and their troops had been severed by the resignation of senior generals, the development of new personal affiliations was averted by the "rotation system" (keng-hsü fa). Under this system, officers were transferred and soldiers rotated between the capital and the regions every three years, so that neither bonds between officers and troops nor relationships between persons and places could become too close or permanent.[41] Furthermore, the precise number of troops serving under

[39] See Worthy, "The founding of Sung China," pp. 174–7.

[40] SS 162, p. 3799.

[41] Ch'en, Kuo-shih chiu-wen 32, pp. 955–7. After 1074, this rotation system was overlapped by the localized "training command system" (chih-chiang fa) and the "community arms (or mutual security) system of local defense" (pao chia) initiated by the reformer Wang An-shih (1021–86). See Michael C. McGrath, "Military and regional administration in Northern Sung China (960–1126)" (diss., Princeton University, 1982), pp. 149, 166–8.

each high-ranking commander was frequently checked to prevent unauthorized expansion of the forces, and commanders were not allowed to maintain personal guards.

To ensure that such measures were observed, T'ai-tsu established an independent network of imperial informants (later called the Capital Security Office, *Huang-ch'eng ssu*) made up mostly of eunuchs, who were attached to every army on a campaign, in the capital, and in every region. In early 967, the chief commander of the Palace Command, though a sworn brother of T'ai-tsu, was summarily dismissed for allegedly maintaining private troops.[42] Another means of imperial control was for the court to withhold all military maps until the eve of a campaign. In addition, the moves to be made during a campaign were prescribed by the emperor in advance and operations continued to be directed by dispatches sent from the capital. After the campaign, the generals returned to the bureaus and the soldiers to their garrisons, so that "neither generals nor armies were consistently attached to each other," and "neither officers nor troops become familiar with each other."[43]

Despite these restrictions, T'ai-tsu knew his soldiers well, and he took personal care of them to ensure their fighting efficiency. After skimming off the best troops from the regions to replace the unfit soldiers of the imperial army, T'ai-tsu expanded the one hundred and twenty thousand men serving in the Later Chou armies to about two hundred thousand men. This weakened the regional armies controlled by the military governors and made the central government armies by far the strongest force in the empire.[44] Since the navy was indispensable to the conquest of the south, especially the Southern T'ang, T'ai-tsu was also concerned with naval buildup. He periodically inspected his new shipyards and conducted naval exercises in a new practice basin in K'ai-feng. In order to maintain capability and preparedness, to develop loyalty, and to instill discipline, exercises and imperial inspections of the army were also held frequently in the capital.[45] The distinction between ranks had to be strictly observed, and no more sworn brotherhoods were permitted. The least insubordination was punishable by death, to say nothing of failing to obey a

---

[42] *HCP* (1964) 8, pp. 4a–b. Another example of the use of informants was Ts'ao Pin (931–99), who was dismissed in 983 after being accused by an informer of falsely informing his border troops that their special allowance from the emperor actually originated from himself; see *HCP* (1964) 24, pp. 1a–b; John R. Labadie, "Rulers and soldiers: Perception and management of the military in Northern Sung China (960–1060)" (diss., University of Washington, 1981), p. 58. See also Ch'ai Te-keng, "Sung huan-kuan ts'an-yü chün shih k'ao," *Fu-jen hsüeh-chih* 10 Nos. 1–2 (1941), pp. 187–225; Yen Ch'in-heng, "Sung-tai tsou-ma ch'eng-shou kung-chih k'ao," *Kuo-li Cheng-chih ta-hsüeh hsüeh-pao* 9 (1964), pp. 319–37.

[43] Ma, *Wen-hsien t'ung-k'ao* (1965) 152, p. 1327.

[44] Worthy, "The founding of Sung China," pp. 162, 180–2; McGrath, "Military and regional administration," pp. 143–4, 167–8.

[45] Ma, *Wen-hsien t'ung-k'ao* (1965) 157, p. 1371.

superior's orders.[46] Looting and gratuitous killing, though not yet outlawed, were kept to a minimum.[47] At the start of the Southern T'ang campaign, for example, T'ai-tsu openly authorized the chief commander to execute any soldier guilty of excessive looting and killing.[48] Both in size and in quality, the Sung army during T'ai-tsu's reign was stronger than any possible competitors for the imperial throne.

THE WEAK FIRST, STRONG LATER STRATEGY

In early 963, T'ai-tsu was ready to expand his domain. Before him lay two equally tempting roads. Immediately to the southeast was the weakened Southern T'ang, which had lost some forty thousand troops, the bulk of its navy, and fourteen rich and productive prefectures north of the Yangtze River during the Later Chou invasion of 956 to 958. This exhausted dynasty now felt so vulnerable that it moved its capital from Chin-ling (modern Nanking) in prosperous Kiangsu to Nan-ch'ang (the modern city of the same name) in northern Kiangsi. Of the remaining lesser kingdoms, the Southern Han and Wu-Yüeh (895–978) continued to send royal hostages and tribute to K'ai-feng. The Later Shu in Szechwan had never posed a threat, while Ching-nan (907–63), Hunan (956–63), and Chang-Ch'üan (946–78), comprising two remnant prefectures of the Min kingdom in Fu-chien, were even weaker.

To the north, T'ai-tsu took advantage of the Later Chou victories over the Northern Han and the Liao. The Northern Han ruler, who escaped from the Kao-p'ing battle with only one hundred horsemen out of an army of thirty thousand, could no longer threaten the Sung but retained close links with the Liao. The Liao emperor, Liao Mu-tsung (r. 951–69), depraved and ineffectual, was nicknamed the "sleeping prince" for his habit of sleeping off his debaucheries rather than attending to government business. Even the loss of two prefectures and three passes in Ho-pei to Ch'ai Jung in 959 could not rouse him to take retaliatory action, because he considered the seized land to have been originally Han Chinese territories. His rule was so ineffective and unpredictable that he was unlikely ever to seriously threaten the Sung.

---

[46] Ma, *Wen-hsien t'ung-k'ao* (1965) 152, p. 1327; Chang, *Chao K'uang-yin chuan*, pp. 74–5; Wang, *Sung-ch'ao ping-chih ch'u-t'an*, pp. 300–3.

[47] *HCP* (1964) 5, p. 16a. Late in 964, T'ai-tsu granted the expeditionary troops fighting against the Later Shu the privilege of dividing during conquest all spoils except military equipment and provisions. This caused such ill feeling and resentment that in his later conquests looting and killing were strictly forbidden. See *HCP* (1964) 5, p. 16b; Ch'en Pang-chan et al., *Sung-shih chi-shih pen-mo* (1605; Peking, 1977) 4, p. 18.

[48] Chang, *Chao K'uang-yin chuan*, p. 49.

T'ai-tsu seems to have been originally inclined to attack the north first: to subjugate the Northern Han, which posed a threat to the western flank of any Sung operations in Ho-pei, and then move to recover the entire "Sixteen Prefectures of Yen-Yün" ceded to the Khitan in 937, thereby depriving the Liao of their strategic control of the Sung's northeastern border. Soon after establishing his dynasty, T'ai-tsu had asked Ts'ao Han (924–92), a general with long experience in border warfare, to draw up a battle plan for an attack northward. Other officials had also forwarded enthusiastic suggestions.[49]

Yet despite the initial interest in attacking the north, T'ai-tsu decided to conquer the south first. In a meeting held sometime in 962 or early 963 to decide the plan of conquest, Chao P'u (922–92), T'ai-tsu's confidant and commissioner of military affairs, strongly opposed the emperor's wish to begin with an attack on the Northern Han.[50] His objection was based on the military consideration that the Sung forces, after conquering the Northern Han, could be pinned down there and risk a retaliatory pincer attack launched by the Khitan from the northeast and nomadic tribes from the west. Such a stalemate would exhaust the new dynasty and force the postponement of its conquest of the south.[51] Chao P'u urged T'ai-tsu to first conquer the southern kingdoms and acquire their rich economic and human resources before facing the more formidable northern powers.

The northern threat was a real one. T'ai-tsu was aware that if he attacked the Northern Han, the Liao might attack the Sung in order to relieve their allies. The rulers of Northern Han had regularly received Liao investiture and military aid and, in return, had been serving as the Liao's forward line of defense. During the 950s the Liao had repeatedly come to Northern Han aid in the face of attacks by the Later Chou. Inside the Liao territory, which was considerably larger than the Sung, pastoralism was the main economic base, supplemented by flourishing agriculture in the south. The Khitan's surplus, along with large quantities of handiwork and other commercial goods, sustained a growing money economy. This territory also produced endless supplies of the best horses for the 500,000-strong Liao imperial cavalry, which alone outnumbered the Sung total of 193,000 cavalry and infantry by almost three to one.[52] These figures do not take account of the human and other resources the

[49] Sung Min-ch'iu, Ch'un-ming t'ui-ch'ao lu (c. 1070; Peking, 1980) shang, p. 15; Wang, Tung-tu shih-lüeh 22, p. 3b; HCP (1964) 4, p. 27a.

[50] T'ai-tsu enlisted Chao P'u under his command during the Later Chou invasion of the Southern T'ang in 956, when Chao advised T'ai-tsu of a little known route he could use to get behind and launch a surprise attack upon a military stronghold that T'ai-tsu had been ordered to take. Wang, Wu-tai hui-yao 116, pp. 1541–2.

[51] HCP (1964) 9, pp. 6a–b.

[52] T'o-t'o et al., eds., Liao shih (1344; Peking, 1974) 25, p. 401; SS 187, p. 4576.

Liao could mobilize from their vassal states and tribes in Inner Asia.[53] With superior horsemanship, archery, and mobility, Liao mounted warriors attacked and retreated with lightning speed, putting the Sung infantry, Sung's major military force, at a great disadvantage, especially on the flat plains of Ho-pei, where there were no natural defenses. T'ai-tsu must have calculated the risks of confronting such a formidable enemy, and it is not surprising that he decided instead to first subjugate the wealthy but militarily weaker southern kingdoms.

T'ai-tsu followed the Later Chin, Later Han, and Later Chou in designating K'ai-feng as his capital. This was a potentially dangerous move, for K'ai-feng lay without natural defenses in the midst of the North China Plain. The city was vulnerable to the Liao cavalry, which had briefly occupied K'ai-feng in 946 to crush the Later Chin's claim of independence from Khitan suzerainty. The Sung capital was chosen on economic grounds. It was almost three hundred miles closer to the affluent south than was the old T'ang capital Ch'ang-an to the west, and shipment of grain to K'ai-feng avoided the difficult stretches of the Yellow River between the old capital and the rice-producing Yangtze areas. More important was K'ai-feng's access to the Grand Canal system. K'ai-feng was seated at the northern terminus of the Pien Canal, which linked the Yellow and Huai river systems into one super transport network extending into the richest areas of the North China Plain. After the Later Chou partially reopened the south-to-north supply line by annexing the fourteen Southern T'ang prefectures between the Yangtze and Huai rivers, K'ai-feng could rely on the canal system, which now extended to the Yangtze River, to tap the resources of the lower Yangtze and southeast regions. Along the rivers and canals, transit granaries and relay stations had been built in the mid-T'ang dynasty to store the tax grain during the times when the waterways were unnavigable and to facilitate transshipment of cargo to boats suitable for the different sections of the canal system.[54]

Until the reform of the Later Chou, these waterways had fallen into disrepair because the previous dynasties were either too short-lived or too busy fighting to engage in maintenance projects. Even worse, in order to flood enemy locations or to destroy their transportation, these dynasties had frequently

[53] Karl A. Wittfogel and Feng Chia-sheng, *History of Chinese society, Liao (907–1125)* (Philadelphia, 1949). For Northern Han–Khitan relations, see Wang Min-hsin, "Liao Sung Shan-yüeh meng-yüeh ti-chieh ti pei-ching (shang)," *Chung-kuo shu-mu chi-k'an* 9 No. 2 (1975), pp. 38–40.

[54] Chi Ch'ao-ting, *Key economic areas in Chinese history – As revealed in the development of public works for water-control* (London, 1936), pp. 116, 127; Denis C. Twitchett, *Financial administration under the T'ang dynasty*, 2nd ed. (Cambridge, 1970), pp. 84–96, 182–9; Robert M. Hartwell, "A cycle of economic change in imperial China: Coal and iron in northeast China, 750–1350," *Journal of the Economic and Social History of the Orient* 10 No. 1 (1967), pp. 124–45.

breached the dikes of the Yellow River, deliberately causing inundations in eighteen of the fifty-three years of the Five Dynasties. The drainage and flood control system in the Ho-pei and Honan regions was subject to hazards at the best of times. Never before had this destructive tactic been used so frequently in the catastrophic history of the Yellow River.[55] Moreover, able-bodied male survivors of these wars and man-made disasters were repeatedly conscripted into the rival armies regardless of their age, and their faces were tattooed to prevent desertion.[56] Just as material resources were spoiled by intentional destruction of water-control works, human lives were squandered in warfare. As a consequence, the population of the North China Plain did not recover to T'ang dynasty levels for many centuries.

Meanwhile in the south, political fragmentation had not impeded economic growth. For example, in Szechwan, evocatively known as the "Land of Heavenly Abundance," the Later Shu had become a refuge for poets, artists, scholars, and officials fleeing from the fallen T'ang capital, who helped to preserve T'ang culture there. The kingdom's administrative structure and ritual followed T'ang models, and even its capital I-chou2 (modern Ch'eng-tu) was an imitation of Ch'ang-an. While its people increased and prospered in a self-sufficient economy, its famous textiles were sold far and wide beyond its easily defensible frontiers of mountains and torrents.[57]

The wealth of Later Shu, this western shield of the south, was rivaled by that of its eastern counterpart, the Southern T'ang in the Huai and lower Yangtze river valleys (Kiangsu, Anhwei, and Kiangsi). The Southern T'ang predecessor had been the Wu, whose policy of peace and rest had successfully restored its wartorn and desolated lands to cultivation and abundance. A glimpse of the wealth of the Southern T'ang can be seen from the huge indemnity and annual tribute it paid to the Later Chou: a total of one million units of tea, grain, cash, silk, and silver.[58] The smaller kingdoms also grew rich in their own particular ways. Ch'u depended on its silk and cloth industries and its mineral wealth in silver and copper, in addition to its profitable export of tea to the north. Min and Chang-Ch'üan, Min's diminutive successor in Fu-chien, isolated by topography, increased their maritime trade in silk and ceramics by exporting to the countries of the South China Sea and the Indian Ocean, as did the

---

[55] Shui-li-pu Huang-ho shui-li wei-yüan-hui "Huang-ho shui-li-shih shu-yao" pien-hsieh-tsu, *Huang-ho shui-li-shih shu-yao* (Peking, 1982), pp. 134–7.

[56] The practice of tattooing the faces of soldiers to discourage desertion was begun as early as the Later Liang dynasty. See Ma, *Wen-hsien t'ung-k'ao* (1965) 152, p. 1325. At least on one occasion even educated men were tattooed on their arms with the phrase *i-hsin shih-chu* (wholeheartedly serving the master). See CWTS 135, p. 1801.

[57] See Yang Wei-li, *Ch'ien Shu Hou Shu shih* (Ch'eng-tu, 1986), pp. 174–265.

[58] Worthy, "The founding of Sung China," p. 38.

Southern Han in the Kwangtung region.[59] The southern kingdoms suffered far less from warfare than did their contemporaries in the north, and as a result stability and prosperity were restored, population and production increased, commerce thrived, classical and Buddhist texts were printed and learning flourished; the role of south as China's new economic and cultural heartland was thus secured.[60]

Though centered in the north, the Sung dynasty derived much of its character – and ultimately the preponderance of its scholar-officials – from the vibrant south.[61] Through its strategy of unification, the Sung knitted the fragmented south into one integrated economic bloc, concentrating its scattered wealth, uniting its most productive areas, and releasing its boundless potential. With this economic power, the new dynasty first held off and then bought off its foreign enemies,[62] and sustained a cultural efflorescence centered on the south,[63] which finally enabled its successor, the Southern Sung (1127–1279), to survive and prosper after the dynasty's loss of the north.

T'ai-tsu began his efforts at unification in early 963 by annexing the smallest kingdoms, the middle Yangtze river state of Ching-nan and the Hunanese kingdom of Ch'u. Ching-nan and Hunan pierced the south like a dagger: along its edges were the Later Shu on the west and the Southern T'ang on the east. The dagger's point was the Southern Han in Kwangtung, and its hilt was the fledgling Sung. In late 962 the founder of the Hunan kingdom passed away, leaving his throne to an eleven-year-old son, who faced a revolt by his general Chang Wen-piao and called for the Sung's intervention. Seizing the opportunity, the Sung "relief" army traversed the tiny middle Yangtze state of Ching-nan and frightened its ruler into submission. Although Chang Wen-piao's revolt had already been suppressed by the government of Ch'u, the Sung army pressed on. Soon the Ch'u capital of T'an-chou (Ch'ang-sha) fell, amid riots and defections provoked by rumors that Sung soldiers had been seen practicing cannibalism. With this victory accomplished in less than three months, the Sung became the first northern dynasty in more than fifty years to

[59] Edward H. Schafer, *The empire of Min* (Rutland, Vt., 1954), pp. 75–7.

[60] See Chang Chia-chü, *Liang Sung ching-chi chung-hsin ti nan-i* (Wu-han, 1957), and Huang Ch'i-chiang, "Wu-tai shih-ch'i nan-fang chu-kuo ti ching-ying" (M.A. thesis, Kuo-li T'ai-wan ta-hsüeh, 1976).

[61] Yang Yüan, "Pei Sung tsai-fu jen-wu ti ti-li fen-pu," *Hsiang-kang Chung-wen ta-hsüeh Chung-kuo wen-hua yen-chiu-so hsüeh-pao* 13 (1982), pp. 147–211.

[62] In 963, T'ai-tsu had explained to his brother Kuang-i (the future T'ai-tsung) that the new dynasty needed to replenish its impoverished treasury from the resources of the south before it could deal with its northern enemies. Two years later T'ai-tsu established new palace treasuries to store the surplus wealth from the south in the hope of eventually redeeming the Sixteen Prefectures of Yen-Yün from the Liao. See Wang, *Tung-tu shih-lüeh* 23, pp. 10a–b; *HCP* (1964) 19, pp. 14a–b; Li Wei-kuo, "Lun Sung-tai nei-k'u ti ti-wei ho tso-yung," *Sung Liao Chin shih lun-ts'ung* 1 (1985), pp. 192–215.

[63] Ho Yu-sen, "Liang Sung hsüeh-feng ti ti-li fan-pu," *Hsin-ya hsüeh-pao* 1 No. 1 (1955), pp. 331–79.

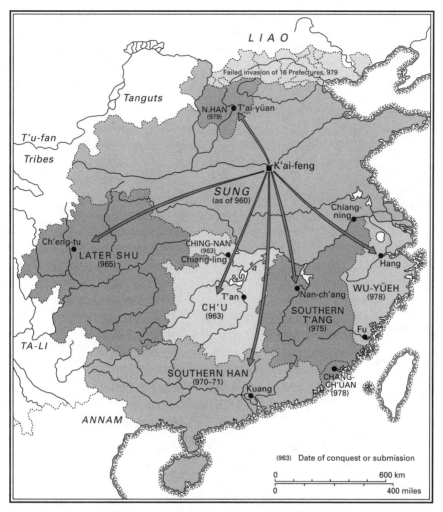

Map 11. Consolidation of the Sung, 960–979.

have a stronghold of seventeen prefectures and two hundred and forty thousand
households in the middle Yangtze, providing rich resources of fish, rice, tea,
and other agricultural products, and rich silver deposits and copper, tin, and
iron with which to make coins.[64] More important, the conquest completed
the Sung's encirclement of the Later Shu, whose northern border had already
been blockaded after it lost four key prefectures to the Later Chou, and whose
access to the middle Yangtze valley and communications with the Southern
T'ang were now severed.

[64] HCP (1964) 4, p. 1a–6a.

Meng Ch'ang (r. 934–65), the Later Shu ruler, had anticipated a Sung invasion, and in late 964 he secretly sent emissaries to seek military cooperation from the Northern Han. Information about the secret mission was sold by one of these emissaries in K'ai-feng, and the mission was used by the Sung as a pretext to launch a two-pronged invasion of Later Shu. One column moving southward through the mountains easily defeated a major counterattack led by the Later Shu's privy commissioner, Wang Chao-yüan. It then sealed the Later Shu's fate at Chien-men Pass, the difficult last obstacle before the Shu capital, launching a surprise attack that overwhelmed the Later Shu reinforcements commanded by Meng Ch'ang's incompetent son. In just over two months, the Later Shu had been forced to surrender, even before the second Sung column advancing westward along the Yangtze River had reached the Later Shu capital. However, the two Sung armies had behaved brutally, slaughtering surrendered troops, raping, and looting. Distressed and fearful over what might happen to them under Sung occupation, over one hundred thousand discontented peasants and surrendered soldiers rose in rebellion against the occupying forces. Pacifying this rebellion took the Sung armies almost two years, until the end of 966, to complete. All the commanding Sung generals except one, Ts'ao Pin (931–99), who did not permit looting, were discharged from their commands.[65] Despite the addition of forty-six prefectures and 534,029 households to the Sung empire, the ravages caused by the subjugation of the Later Shu cost the new dynasty a great part of these new resources, and delayed for two years its next campaign of conquest.[66] It also left a legacy of resentment in an important region. T'ai-tsu, after this costly mistake, always took pains to keep his armies under tight discipline.

In late 968 the Sung struck out again, but this time to the north. In the second half of the year, the Northern Han suffered a political crisis in which a chief minister of its recently deceased ruler assassinated the first successor to the throne and urged the second one to surrender to the Sung. In early 969, T'ai-tsu was able to surround the enemy capital, T'ai-yüan, and defeat the reinforcements sent by the Khitan. But an attempt to flood the city failed, and the ensuing stalemate reduced the Sung army's morale and depleted its supplies. Heavy rains brought disease, and as more Khitan relief forces neared in mid-969, T'ai-tsu reluctantly abandoned the siege that had lasted over three months. He was to compensate for this setback by renewed conquests in the south.[67]

Decades of expansion had enabled the Southern Han to occupy the regions of Kwangtung, the major half of Kwangsi and Kweichow, and the southern

[65] HCP (1964) 5, pp. 15a–20a; 6, pp. 1a–5b; 8, pp. 1b–2b.
[66] Worthy, "The founding of Sung China," p. 54.
[67] HCP (1964) 9, pp. 8a–9b, 11a–b, 12b; 10, pp. 1b–10a, 11a–b.

tip of Hunan. However, around the mid-tenth century, the Southern Han was led by a series of corrupt rulers, the last of whom was Liu Ch'ang (r. 958–71). He delighted in torture, and even more in extravagance. His thirst for pearls caused the drowning of numerous divers, and his irrational suspicion cost the lives of many of his capable generals. The army and the civil government were left in the hands of eunuchs. Liu also encroached on Hunanese territory after it was conquered by the Sung, and he flatly rejected a demand for submission forwarded by the Southern T'ang on behalf of the Sung. In the ninth month of 970, the Sung started a blanket invasion and within four months reached the outskirts of the capital Kuang-chou (modern Canton).

After his army with its war elephants had been routed, Liu Ch'ang resorted to constructing a palisade to halt the invading army, while his eunuchs fancied that destroying the treasures in his palace would dispirit the Sung troops. When the invaders set fire to the palisade, the defenders reduced Liu's immense wealth to ashes. Incensed at this, T'ai-tsu executed the eunuch arsonists. Despite the loss of the royal treasures, the conquest of Southern Han added sixty prefectures and 170,263 households to the Sung empire.[68]

The Southern T'ang had long been the wealthiest of the southern kingdoms, with thirty-three prefectures and 881,000 households at its peak. To avoid the waste of war T'ai-tsu had hoped for a peaceful annexation, especially since through his previous conquests he had encircled the Later T'ang in the north, west, and south, and had brought the Wu-Yüeh kingdom under his dominance in the east. Faced with this menace the Southern T'ang ruler Li Yü (r. 960–75) accepted a more subservient yet nontributary status for the Southern T'ang, observing the Sung calendar and receiving its state messages as edicts. Beginning in mid-974, however, the Sung increased its pressure on the Southern T'ang, detaining Li's younger brother after his diplomatic mission and displaying its naval forces along the Yangtze. After Li declined three times to go to K'ai-feng and pay respects in person, T'ai-tsu took his refusal as disobedience and declared war. Based on a careful study of the Yangtze, the Sung army crossed the river on a precisely constructed pontoon bridge of boats, arriving at the Southern T'ang capital in the first month of 975. Simultaneously, on T'ai-tsu's orders, Wu-Yüeh also invaded Southern T'ang, capturing two of its eastern prefectures. Although limiting the destructiveness of its attack in order to achieve the least costly conquest, the Sung army set fire to the entire enemy navy, on which rested the last hopes of Southern T'ang. In the eleventh month of 975 the Southern T'ang surrendered after fifteen months

---

[68] Wang, *Tung-tu shih-lüeh* 23, pp. 2b–5a; *HCP* (1964) 10, p. 10b; 11, pp. 7b–12b; 12, pp. 1a–3a; Edward H. Schafer, "The history of the empire of Southern Han, according to chapter 65 of the *Wu-tai shih* of Ou-yang Hsiu," in *Sōritsu nijūgo shūnen kinen ronbunshū {The silver jubilee volume of the Zinbun Kagaku Kenkyusyo, Kyoto University}*, ed. Kyōtō Daigaku Jinbun Kagaku Kenkyūjo (Kyoto, 1954), pp. 364–9.

of resistance, the longest among the southern kingdoms.[69] Its fallen ruler Li Yü, a lyricist of note, lamented the loss in a poem repenting the gullibility that led him to kill his own most capable general, who had been framed by the Sung to appear a defector.[70]

Prior to the Southern T'ang campaign, T'ai-tsu had also invited Ch'ien Ch'u (r. 948–78), the ruler of the Wu-Yüeh, to visit K'ai-feng, but he had declined. Two months after the fall of the Southern T'ang, Ch'ien anxiously appeared in the capital. He was given a sumptuous welcome and shown the wonderful mansions housing the former rulers of conquered kingdoms. T'ai-tsu's brother Chao Kuang-i (later T'ai-tsung) and many court officials urged T'ai-tsu to detain Ch'ien Ch'u, but T'ai-tsu honored a previous promise, and sent Ch'ien home with the demand that he pay tribute in person every three years. Shortly afterward, Ch'en Hung-chin (914–85, r. 964–78), ruler of the tiny Chang-Ch'üan state in southern Fu-chien, also set sail for K'ai-feng as a gesture of submission.

On the fourteenth of November 976 T'ai-tsu suddenly died. Two months before his death, T'ai-tsu had launched five armies to invade Northern Han from different directions, but the armies were recalled from their siege of the capital, T'ai-yüan, upon receipt of the sad news of T'ai-tsu's death. T'ai-tsu's original wish of integrating the north into the empire he had founded was not accomplished until two years after his death by his brother and successor, Chao Kuang-i.

The unification T'ai-tsu achieved was remarkable less for the military ease with which it was accomplished than for the conqueror's leniency toward the fallen states. Their people were granted amnesties and relieved of the most onerous taxes and corvée duties. Their soldiers were mostly returned to agriculture and the fittest enrolled in the Sung armies. Great numbers of their officials with proven abilities or special talents were reappointed to other parts of the empire, and the ruling families of the conquered kingdoms were given honorary titles, generous allowances, and splendid residences in K'ai-feng. Some members of former ruling families were even given court appointments.[71]

During the campaigns of unification T'ai-tsu, unlike his predecessors, seldom took the field himself, except in the 969 campaign against the Northern Han, but his presence was ubiquitous in every conquest. As a dynastic founder, he had great confidence in his prescribed battle plans, his control of generals,

---

[69] *Hsü Tzu-chih t'ung-chien ch'ang-pien*, cited in *Yung-lo ta-tien* (1408; Peking, 1960) 12307, pp. 2a–15a.

[70] The lyric is "The Beautiful Lady Yü," translated in Cyril Birch, ed., *Anthology of Chinese literature* (1965; Harmondsworth, U.K., 1967), p. 357.

[71] Chao, *Nien-erh shih cha-chi* 24, pp. 513–15; 25, pp. 524–5.

and his towering authority over his soldiers. Through this undisputed military authority, his government was characterized by centralized and absolute authority. This distinguished him from his predecessors and former military colleagues as a real emperor, not an all-powerful warlord, and his state as a newborn empire.

Centralization and imperial absolutism

At the very start of his reign, T'ai-tsu is reported to have asked his former tutor and close confidant Chao P'u how to secure his objectives of everlasting stability and peace. "The source of previous troubles was none other than the regional military governors becoming too powerful, rendering the dynasty weak and [themselves as] vassals strong," Chao replied. "The solution is to whittle down their power, check their revenues, and appropriate their crack troops."[72] Following these guidelines, T'ai-tsu gradually and peacefully imposed centralized bureaucratic supervision over local government in order to displace its former overlords, the military governors who were the last obstacle to the vigorous assertion of imperial power. Perhaps more importantly, at the local and central levels T'ai-tsu succeeded in embedding absolutist power into the administrative structure, thereby transforming it from something personal and transitory into a force that was institutionalized and enduring. The resulting Sung mode of centralization and absolutism became the model for the Chinese state system for centuries to come.

Although T'ai-tsu owed some of his success in suppressing autonomous regional authority to his Five Dynasties predecessors,[73] the groundwork was really laid when he used his overwhelming military strength to overpower his two Later Chou adversaries, Li Yün and Li Ch'ung-chin, in 960. But rather than depend solely on military muscle, T'ai-tsu was also a master of political manipulation. His success in attracting the loyalty of subordinates was facilitated by his display of military strength in smashing the two Lis. Furthermore, he artfully alternated between conciliatory and ruthless policies.

On the one hand, T'ai-tsu was willing to be generous and conciliatory. He tolerated the transgressions of dependable military governors, some of whom were his former colleagues who had helped him found the new dynasty. T'ai-tsu granted substantial income to those governors he forced into

---

[72] Ssu-ma, *Su-shui chi-wen* 1, pp. 6–7; *HCP* (1964) 2, p. 10b.

[73] For the control of the provinces during the T'ang and Five Dynasties, see chapters 5 and 7 of Wang, *Structure of power*, especially pp. 186–7, and 196; Charles A. Peterson, "The restoration completed: Emperor Hsian-tsung and the provinces," in *Perspectives on the T'ang*, ed. Arthur F. Wright and Denis C. Twitchett (New Haven, Conn., 1973), pp. 172–86.

retirement or confined to the capital. To those he deemed especially trustworthy and useful he granted long tenure in their positions, sometimes as long as five to ten years, while others were even kept in their posts for life.[74] New regional commissioners (*chieh-tu shih*) were occasionally appointed, including both military men assigned to defend the northern borders and retired generals given honorific appointments without much real power. Intermarriages were also arranged between the children of the imperial clan and those of the military governors. All T'ai-tsu's empresses and Kuang-i's second wife were daughters of military governors.[75] Such conciliatory measures helped to induce military men to give up forlorn hopes of resisting the centralization of power in his hands.

But, on the other hand, he could also be stern and pragmatic. T'ai-tsu removed potentially troublesome military governors at the first opportunity. It was said that during a wine party in 969, he rejected the complaints of four former Later Chou military governors about their treatment and retired them the next day.[76] While continuing Ch'ai Jung's policy of pressing the best regional troops into the imperial army, T'ai-tsu also wrested local control over civil, fiscal, judicial, and personnel matters away from the military governors by injecting court-appointed officials into local government.

At the county (*hsien*) level, civilians were appointed as law enforcement officials as early as 962, and high-ranking former court officials began to be appointed as magistrates in early 963.[77] By 977, when military governors could no longer appoint local officials within their jurisdiction, these new magistrates had already supplanted the personal retainers of the military governors, who had formerly filled most lesser posts in the general field administration. However, as there were still not enough capable men to fill the roughly fourteen hundred and fifty magistrate posts throughout the empire, "neither T'ai-tsu nor T'ai-tsung acquired an iron grip" on the county level of local government.[78]

---

[74] Charles O. Hucker's assumption that T'ai-tsu had summoned all the military governors (or commissioners, in his rendering) to the capital and retired them with princely pensions, as stated in his *A dictionary of official titles in imperial China* (Stanford, Calif., 1985), p. 45, represents the general view about the early Sung centralization, but this oversimplification has been shown to be incorrect by Worthy in "The founding of Sung China," pp. 272–9. Lo Ch'iu-ch'ing has also pointed out that T'ai-tsu continued to appoint military men as prefects along the northern and northwestern borders, "Pei Sung ping-chih yen-chiu," pp. 185–6, 198; see also Worthy, "The founding of Sung China," pp. 190–5.

[75] Ch'en, *Kuo-shih chiu-wen* 32, pp. 942–6; Worthy, "The founding of Sung China," pp. 273–8. See also John W. Chaffee, *Branches of heaven: A history of the imperial clan of Sung China* (Cambridge, Mass., 1999), pp. 55–6.

[76] *HCP* (1964) 10, pp. 15b–16a.

[77] *HCP* (1964) 4, pp. 13b–14a.

[78] Worthy, "The founding of Sung China," p. 281. See also Chang, *Chao K'uang-yin chuan*, pp. 84–5.

At the prefectural level, the post of administrator for public order (*ssu-k'ou ts'an-chün*), responsible for supervising police activities, was established.[79] In 961, civil officials from the capital were dispatched for the first time to regulate the tax collection and expenditures of the military governors. Two years later, the new post of controller-general (*t'ung-p'an*) was created and given extensive powers. Initially, the purpose of this official was to oversee the former prefects in newly conquered territories and to interpret Sung regulations and procedures for them. In 964, forty-three controllers-general were appointed to supervise all aspects of prefectural administration. They were charged with overseeing taxation and making sure that the full quota of taxes was forwarded to the capital. A controller-general held the same court rank as a prefect, and had the right to send confidential memorials directly to the throne. Without the controller-general's countersignature, no prefectural directive was considered valid. In 965, the controllers-general were ordered to send all surplus tax revenues from the prefectures to the capital. At the same time, military governors were prohibited from signing financial documents, and were confined to the use of revenues from their base prefecture alone.[80] Because they were court officials, some controllers-general tended to be imperious in overseeing the prefectures. In 966, in order to maintain a system of checks and balances, the controllers-general were ordered to obtain the prefects' countersignatures when issuing orders, and vice versa.[81] By that time, at intervals of three years, court officials were increasingly commissioned as prefects under the title of manager of the affairs of such-and-such prefecture (*chih mou chou-chün shih*).[82] Most of them were civilians, for T'ai-tsu optimistically thought that their excesses would be far less harmful than the abuses of military men.[83]

At the regional circuit (*lu*) level, similar progress toward centralization was accomplished by appointing fiscal intendants (*chuan-yün shih*). As the first such office established, the fiscal intendants served as the model for later regional intendants in charge of military and judicial matters.[84] The office of

---

[79] Chang, *Chao K'uang-yin chuan*, pp. 90–1. For some judicial cruelties of the Five Dynasties period, see Chao, *Nien-erh shih cha-chi* 22, pp. 472–3; *CWTS* 107, pp. 1414–15.

[80] Ch'en, *Kuo-shih chiu-wen* 32, pp. 951–3.

[81] *HCP* (1964) 7, pp. 14b–15a; Ou-yang Hsiu, *Kuei-t'ien lu* (1067; Peking, 1981) 2, p. 31.

[82] Ch'en et al., *Sung-shih chi-shih pen-mo* 2, pp. 7–12.

[83] *HCP* (1964) 13, pp. 12b–13a. For military men's abuses, see *CWTS* 98, pp. 1301–2. For T'ai-tsu's determination to suppress corruption, see Chang, *Chao K'uang-yin chuan*, pp. 108–10.

[84] The Sung territorial administration was organized on three levels: county, prefecture, and circuit. Later in the Sung period there were four kinds of circuit intendants: military, fiscal, judicial, and supply, collectively called the Four Circuit Supervisorates, serving as coordinators between prefectures and the central government while also checking and balancing each other. As James T. C. Liu has suggested, although some aspects of government were already highly centralized at the very beginning of the Sung, a distinction must be made "between centralization for the security of the state and the centralization of financial administration [which] . . . became established only with the coming of the New Policies

fiscal intendant answered T'ai-tsu's need for a unified program to provision his armies and to take logistical matters out of the hands of campaign commanders. In consolidating Sung control over new territories, some of these fiscal intendants were empowered to act as the representatives of the emperor.[85] Once their utility in implementing central control was proven, the fiscal intendants were assigned to take over the circuits administered by military governors. As early as 966, as the only regional-level administrators, the fiscal intendants saw their role expanded from financial management into the general administration of all civil matters falling between the central and the local governments. They collected taxes, estimated household populations, requisitioned corvée labor, reviewed judicial cases, supervised prefectural and district officials, and performed social and educational duties.[86] Two of the most important responsibilities were to oversee the transfer to the capital of certain local tax revenues[87] and to settle judicial cases involving death sentences.[88] By 973, central control over local finances had become so successful that a quota of surplus tax revenues was allowed to remain in the prefectures.[89] In 977, the hitherto provisional jurisdictions of the fiscal intendants were identified with the fifteen circuits newly institutionalized as the intermediate administrative

[during Shen-tsung's reign]." See Liu Tzu-chien (James T. C. Liu), *Reform in Sung China: Wang An-shih (1021–1086) and his New Policies* (Cambridge, Mass., 1959), pp. 85–6. Only the fiscal and judicial supervisorates were established by T'ai-tsu and T'ai-tsung. The military and supply supervisorates were established respectively by Chen-tsung and Shen-tsung. Michael McGrath has pointed out the differences in power and authority between the military and the fiscal intendants in the two distinct systems of regional administration: military intendants dominated military as well as civil affairs in border-zone circuits where they were needed to defend the borders, to recover lost territories, and to neutralize rival neighbors, whereas the fiscal intendants were more dominant in core-zone circuits. McGrath, "Military and regional administration," pp. 6, 22–4, 29, 32, 38.

85 For example, T'ai-tsu provided Li Fu (c. 924–c. 983), fiscal intendant of the circuit southwest of the capital, with a banner reading "Wherever Li Fu goes, it is as if His Majesty goes in person." See Lo Wen (Winston W. Lo), "Circuits and circuit intendants in the territorial administration of Sung China," *Monumenta Serica* 31 (1974–5), p. 70.

86 *HCP* (1964) 7, pp. 1a–2a. There was a significant degree of coincidence between the early Sung circuits and the formerly independent states of the Ten Kingdoms; see Lo, "Circuits and circuit intendants," p. 56. For a general description of the fiscal intendants' power and responsibilities, see Lo Wen (Winston W. Lo), "Provincial government in Sung China," *Chinese Culture* 19 No. 4 (1978), pp. 28–37; Hsü Huai-lin, "Pei Sung chuan-yün-shih chih-tu lüeh-lun," in *Sung-shih yen-chiu lun-wen-chi: 1982 nien nien-hui pien-k'an*, ed. Teng Kuang-ming and Li Chia-chü (Cheng-chou, 1984), pp. 287–318; Cheng Shih-kang, "Pei Sung ti chuan-yün-shih," in *Sung-shih yen-chiu lun-wen-chi: 1982 nien nien-hui pien-k'an*, ed. Teng Kuang-ming and Li Chia-chü (Cheng-chou, 1984), pp. 319–45.

87 *HCP* (1964) 5, p. 20a; 6, pp. 8a–b; Ch'en, *Kuo-shih chiu-wen* 32, pp. 957–8.

88 In 1013 capital cases were made the specific responsibility of judicial intendants. See McGrath, "Military and regional administration," pp. 54–5. For interintendancy rivalry, see Lo, "Provincial government in Sung China," pp. 26–8. See also *HCP* (1964) 5, p. 20a; 6, pp. 8a–b; Ch'en, *Kuo-shih chiu-wen* 32, pp. 957–8.

89 Chang, *Chao K'uang-yin chuan*, pp. 184–5; Ma, *Wen-hsien t'ung-k'ao* (1965) 23, pp. 228–9.

echelon between the central government and the prefectures.[90] In 981, fiscal intendants were further authorized to evaluate the performance of local officials throughout a circuit. As a check on the intendants, prefects and vice-prefects could communicate directly with the court. Since intendants, prefects, and controllers-general were court officials on what was called *ch'ai-ch'ien* (duty assignment), that is, on assignment away from the court, it was not unusual for a prefect or a controller-general to have a higher rank than the intendant. This difference in rank may have deterred intendants from encroaching upon the powers of the prefectures.[91] Furthermore, like prefects and controllers-general, circuit intendants generally served only three-year terms, a time short enough to prevent them from establishing their power in the region.

The year 977 marked a decisive point in undercutting the power of military governors. Within eighteen months after ascending the throne in 960, T'ai-tsu had transferred almost three-quarters of the remaining forty or so military governors away from their power base, which usually comprised two to five prefectures.[92] In one stroke in 977, T'ai-tsung ordered the remaining eighteen regional commissioners (*chieh-tu shih*) to surrender their forty or so subordinate prefectures to the central government. With few exceptions, they were reappointed as prefects of their headquarter prefectures under the supervision of the fiscal intendants.[93] At the same time, they were forbidden to conduct trade either within or outside their jurisdiction.[94] In time, military governors were replaced by court-appointed civil officials, and any new appointment as a *chieh-tu shih* was little more than an honorific title.[95]

The deployment and administration of military forces

The imperial army (*chin-chün*) was the mainstay of national defense. It guarded the emperor, secured the capital, garrisoned every circuit of the empire, and

---

[90] See Worthy, "The founding of Sung China," pp. 285–7, and McGrath, "Military and regional administration," pp. 43–50. The number of civil circuits – that is, circuits headed by a fiscal intendant – was steadily expanded through a process of subdivision to eighteen in the 1020s, twenty-three in the 1080s, and twenty-four by the end of the Northern Sung. That number fell to seventeen during the Southern Sung, when the fiscal intendant was replaced by the military commissioner (*an-fu shih*) as the chief administrative official. See the "Compiling Principles" section of the sixth volume (*Sung Liao Chin shih ch'i*) of T'an Ch'i-hsiang, ed., *Chung-kuo li-shih ti-t'u chi* (Shanghai, 1982).

[91] See Lo, "Circuits and circuit attendants" p. 63.

[92] Worthy, "The founding of Sung China," pp. 274–5.

[93] HCP (1964) 18, pp. 16b–17a; Ma, *Wen-hsien t'ung-k'ao* (1965) 61, p. 557. According to Worthy, "The founding of Sung China," p. 278, this was not completed until around 982.

[94] HCP (1964) 18, p. 1b.

[95] For a general understanding of the early Sung military governors, see Furugaki Kōichi, "Sōchō kenkokuki no kenkyū sono ichi: Sōho no setsudoshi o chūshin to shite," *Chūō Daigaku Daigakuin ronkyū* 4 No. 1 (1972), pp. 27–44.

prepared for foreign expeditions. It was so warily distributed and closely administered that, throughout the Northern Sung period, the dynasty was never jeopardized by army insurrections nor was the court ever commandeered by military men.[96]

The policy of concentrating the best armies in the capital region at the expense of all other regions had been used by the Later T'ang dynasty (923–36), but it was T'ai-tsu who brought this policy to perfection.[97] The capital, K'ai-feng, encircled by concentric walls, comprised an older, inner city and a newer, outer city. The palace was located within the inner city. Protecting the palace was the Imperial Elite (*Pan-chih*), chosen from the best soldiers of the Palace Command. They were the emperor's personal guard and were never stationed away from him or the palace. The Imperial Elite was counterbalanced by the Capital Security Office (*Huang-ch'eng ssu*) outside the palace, run by military officers and eunuchs.[98] Overall defense of the capital was assigned to the Upper Four Armies (*shang ssu-chün*), selected by the emperor himself: two armies from the Palace Command were stationed in the inner city, balanced by two armies from the Metropolitan Command stationed in the outer city. Each group had approximately thirty thousand troops.[99] At the same time, the two inner Upper Armies were counterbalanced by the palace security forces, and the two outer Upper Armies were offset by the imperial armies stationed in Ching-chi lu, the circuit encompassing the capital. When combined, the Upper Four Armies formed the largest and most powerful of all the imperial armies. The defense of the capital was primarily the responsibility of the more powerful Palace Command rather than of the Metropolitan Command. The selection system that continually siphoned the finest soldiers from the prefectures into the imperial armies, then into the Upper Four Armies, and finally into the Imperial Elite guaranteed that the best troops in the empire would be concentrated in the capital.[100]

In addition to the imperial army, the Sung military system included (1) the prefectural armies (*hsiang-chün*), (2) the local militias (*hsiang-ping*) provided

[96] For army rebellions during the Northern Sung, see Chang Ming-fu, "Shih-lun Pei Sung Ch'ing-li nien-chien ti ping-pien," *Shan-tung Shih-fan hsüeh-yüan hsüeh pao* 2 (1980), pp. 49–54, and Chia Ta-ch'üan, "Lun Pei Sung ti ping-pien," in *Sung-shih yen-chiu lun-wen-chi: Chung-hua wen-shih lun-ts'ung tseng-k'an*, ed. Teng Kuang-ming and Ch'eng Ying-liu (Shanghai, 1982), pp. 453–65. For overviews of Sung military administration, see Wang, *Sung-ch'ao ping-chih ch'u-t'an*, and Koiwai Hiromitsu, *Sōdai heiseishi no kenkyū* (Tokyo, 1998).

[97] Wang, *Structure of power*, p. 187; Chi Tzu-ya (Ch'i Hsia), "Chao K'uang-yin ho Chao Sung chuan-chih chu-i chung-yang chi-chüan chih-tu ti fa-chan," *Li-shih chiao-hsüeh* 12 (1954), pp. 13–18.

[98] Saeki Tomi, "Sōdai no kōjōshi ni tsuite – kunshu dokusaiken kenkyū no hitokoma," *Tōhō gakuhō (Kyoto)* 9 (1938), pp. 158–96; Ch'eng Min-sheng, "Pei Sung t'an-shih chi-kou – huang-ch'eng-ssu," *Ho-nan ta-hsüeh hsüeh-pao: Che-she pan* 4 (1984), pp. 37–41.

[99] McGrath, "Military and regional administration," pp. 145–7.

[100] *SS* 187, pp. 4570–1; Ma, *Wen-hsien t'ung-k'ao* (1965) 155, pp. 1325–6, 1351–2.

by villages and other local organizations for local defense, and (3) the frontier tribal troops (*fan-ping*). The combat capabilities of the latter two forces were generally negligible by the very nature of their composition. But the strength of the prefectural armies was deliberately kept inferior to that of the imperial army. The prefectural armies were recruited from four sources: mercenaries, conscripts from hereditary army families, refugees from natural calamities, and criminals consigned to serve their sentences in the armies. Because the prefectural army's best soldiers were routinely exchanged for unfit soldiers from the imperial army, the prefectural army's quality was such that it was commonly assigned to menial labor, reducing the corvée duties of the agricultural population.[101] The prefectural army also was used as a refuge for the destitute to prevent their becoming bandits or rebels.[102] Throughout most of the Northern Sung, the prefectural armies were smaller than the imperial army.[103] In size and quality, therefore, the imperial army was unchallenged.

A civil office, the Bureau of Military Affairs (*Shu-mi yüan*), wielded administrative control over the imperial army. During the early Sung the bureau was usually headed by one commissioner (rank 1B) and one assistant commissioner (2A). After consulting with the emperor, the bureau issued marching orders to the armies indirectly, through the agency of the Three Military Bureaus (*san-ya*). Although this system prevented any one bureau from monopolizing both administrative and command functions, this separation ultimately proved self-defeating. To begin with, it increasingly impeded communication between the army commanders and civil administrators, as veteran generals serving in the Bureau of Military Affairs were gradually replaced by scholar-officials at the very time that the two military founders of the dynasty were succeeded by emperors with no military experience. Consequently, these developments contributed to the declining status of the military. In addition, since the army commanders were subject to the personnel management of the Bureau of Military Affairs, they became vulnerable to the factional infighting among the bureau's ranking incumbents. As one modern historian has pointed out, "In some cases, a general's competence was less important than his support or opposition among civil officials."[104] In other words, while the separation of military administration from command secured civil control over the military, it also had the undesirable effect of sacrificing much-needed military autonomy.

---

[101] Teng Kuang-ming, "Pei Sung ti mu-ping chih-tu chi ch'i yü tang-shih chi-jo chi-p'an ho nung-yeh sheng-ch'an ti kuan-hsi," *Chung-kuo shih yen-chiu* 4 (1980), pp. 61–77; Wang Yü-chi, "Lun mu-ping chih-tu tui Pei Sung she-hui ti ying-hsiang," *Chung-kuo che-hsüeh-shih yen-chiu* 1 (1987), pp. 81–91.

[102] Shao Po, *Shao-shih wen-chien hou-lu*, ed. Liu Te-ch'üan and Li Chien-hsiung (1157; Peking, 1983) 1, p. 1.

[103] For a tabulated comparison of the deployment of imperial versus prefectural troops through Shen-tsung's reign, see McGrath, "Military and regional administration," p. 148.

[104] Labadie, "Rulers and soldiers," p. 199.

Military authority held by the Bureau of Military Affairs was also isolated from the paramount source of civil authority, held by the chief councilors (*tsai-hsiang*) in the Secretariat-Chancellery (*Chung-shu men-hsia*). This separation was first intended to protect the integrity of the civil administration. During the late T'ang and the Five Dynasties, the Bureau of Military Affairs (*Shu-mi yüan* or its precursors) was always occupied by illiterate military men who were relentless in usurping civil authority. Some commissioners from the Bureau of Military Affairs even held the concurrent title of chief councilor. Civil officials in the Secretariat-Chancellery, often unversed in military problems, were commonly reduced to powerless functionaries. This situation was changed during the Later Chou. The authority of the Bureau of Military Affairs, though still not clearly defined, was mostly exercised in military planning and administration, and the commissioners no longer enjoyed formal association with imperial army generals. At the same time, despite occasional appointments of commissioners as concurrent chief councilors, only those passing the civil service examinations were considered appropriate candidates for the top posts in the Secretariat-Chancellery.[105] Finally, the segregation of civil and military authority was institutionalized during the Sung by T'ai-tsu.

In common with other dynastic founders, T'ai-tsu dominated the military administration. There were no assertive commissioners in the Bureau of Military Affairs during his reign.[106] Neither did he allow anyone to be both chief councilor and military commissioner. For example, in 964 he transferred Chao P'u from the position of commissioner to chief councilor but would not appoint him to both offices concurrently, even though he continued to consult Chao P'u on both civil and military affairs. The restriction went further. In 972, after discovering that children of Chief Councilor Chao P'u and the Bureau of Military Affairs commissioner Li Ch'ung-chü had married, T'ai-tsu summarily dismissed Li to prevent the development of patronage ties between these two highest civil and military officials.[107] Referred to as the "Two Administrations" (*erh-fu*), the Bureau of Military Affairs and the Secretariat-Chancellery were "completely segregated from each other in the conduct of their affairs" during the first twenty-five years of the Sung dynasty.[108]

The separation of civil from military power served three purposes. First, it prevented military influence from undermining civil administration, replacing

---

[105] Wang, *Structure of power*, pp. 163–9; Worthy, "The founding of Sung China," pp. 214–37; Su Chi-lang, "Wu-tai ti shu-mi-yüan," *Shih-huo yüeh-k'an* 10 Nos. 1–2 (1980), pp. 3–19.

[106] McGrath, "Military and regional administration," p. 117.

[107] Liang T'ien-hsi, *Sung shu-mi-yüan chih-tu* (Taipei, 1981), p. 5; McGrath, "Military and regional administration," p. 118.

[108] Worthy, "The founding of Sung China," pp. 239, 242. For the responsibilities of the Bureau of Military Affairs, see McGrath, "Military and regional administration," pp. 55–6, 119–21, 141–2.

violence as the main tool of government with regular administrative procedures of the civil service. Second, it prevented the Bureau of Military Affairs commissioners from accumulating undue power beyond the military sphere. Third, and most important, this separation gave the emperor absolute control over the military and its highest officials, while excluding interference in military affairs by the chief councilors. This enhanced imperial power nourished imperial absolutism, since only the emperor could control the balance as well as the coordination between the civil administration and the military administration, and only he could simultaneously take charge of military command and military administration.

The civil service

T'ai-tsu seemed less concerned with reorganizing the civil administration than with reorganizing the military establishment.[109] In some areas that have been regarded as Sung contributions to the growth of imperial absolutism, such as reliance on civil service examination, the commission or duty assignment system, and the division of the chief councilor's power, T'ai-tsu merely adapted T'ang or Five Dynasties precedents.[110] T'ai-tsu was more a shrewd renovator than innovator.

T'ai-tsu seems to have had a practical nature, reflected in his insistence that his sons devote themselves to studying statecraft and not belles lettres.[111] However, seeking to increase the number of civil officials with a view to raising the intellectual standards of the administration, T'ai-tsu, in the second month of his reign, revived the civil service examinations; he passed a total of about four hundred and fifty men in fifteen examinations spread over seventeen years.[112] At this time, to increase the availability of examination texts, nine Confucian Classics and their commentaries were officially printed and widely promulgated.[113] In 962, to prevent nepotism, examiners and examinees were

---

[109] This neglect was due partly to the lack of advisors familiar with the organization of civil government; see *HCP* 5, p. 8a (commentary); 18, p. 10b; Wang Yung, *Yen-i i-mou lu* (c. 1227; Peking, 1981) 1, p. 6.

[110] See Sun Kuo-tung, "Sung-tai kuan-chih wen-luan tsai T'ang-chih ti ken-yüan – Sung-shih chih-kuan-chih shu Sung-tai luan chih ken-yüan pien," *Chung-kuo hsüeh-jen* 1 (1970), pp. 41–54; Lo Wen (Winston W. Lo), *An introduction to the civil service of Sung China: With emphasis on its personnel administration* (Honolulu, 1987), pp. 51–8.

[111] Ssu-ma, *Su-shui chi-wen* 1, p. 11.

[112] Different sources give different numbers of successful candidates; see Araki Toshikazu, *Sōdai kakyo seido kenkyū* (Kyoto, 1969), pp. 450–2, and John W. Chaffee, *The thorny gates of learning in Sung China: A social history of examinations* (Cambridge, 1985), p. 192. See also Chang, *Chao K'uang-yin chuan*, pp. 112, 114–15.

[113] Ch'en Le-su, "Pei Sung kuo-chia ti ku-chi cheng-li yin-hsing shih-yeh chi ch'i li-shih i-i," in *Sung Yüan wen-shih yen-chiu*, ed. Ch'en Le-su (Kuang-chou, 1988), pp. 66, 83.

forbidden to claim a patron-protégé relationship. And after the chief examiner was demoted in 973 for favoritism in passing inferior candidates from his native place, T'ai-tsu personally conducted a reexamination in the palace, with an eye to promoting fair competition between the upper and lower classes.[114] Thereafter, this palace examination was institutionalized as the third and final stage of the civil service examination.

The palace examination was inaugurated to validate the metropolitan examination that was supervised by court officials on ad hoc imperial assignment. The metropolitan examinations were in turn meant to screen those who had passed the preliminary examination conducted by prefectural officials. From 977, driven by the need to staff thousands of local administrative posts, T'ai-tsung began to pass candidates in great numbers, producing more than five thousand new officials during his reign.[115] Step by step, the examination system was improved to provide equal opportunity for most male commoners to enter officialdom,[116] and thereby in the long run change officialdom's character. As the product of an open examination system, the new ruling elite became far more heterogeneous than before, representing a variety of interests with little likelihood of uniting against the emperor.[117] Few members of this new governing class possessed the great wealth and hereditary status with which their aristocratic predecessors had survived imperial suppression. Since the power of the political elite was derived from the emperor, they were less willing to challenge his absolutist tendencies.

The commission or duty assignment (ch'ai-ch'ien) system that had originated in the T'ang dynasty was expanded by both T'ai-tsu and T'ai-tsung to apply to all important organs of the government. Many offices lost their authority, and their original functions were taken over by officials on ad hoc assignment approved or personally designated by the emperor. As such, an official's titular office (his formal title) bore little relation to his duties, and indicated only his rank in the civil service and his emoluments. His titular office was referred to as his salary or stipendiary office (chi-lu kuan). His responsibilities and corresponding authority were dependent on the duty assignment he obtained. This dual system of stipendiary office and duty assignment served two immediate

[114] HCP (1964) 14, pp. 2a–b.

[115] Chaffee, The thorny gates of learning in Sung China, pp. 49–50.

[116] Araki, Sōdai kakyo seido kenkyū, pp. 207–19; Chaffee, The thorny gates of learning in Sung China, pp. 51–3.

[117] Chang, Chao K'uang-yin chuan, pp. 112–13. Although more than half of the officialdom was occupied by the beneficiaries of the protection privileges (yin2) that allowed high officials to nominate sons or relatives for official appointments, most chief councilors, vice–chief councilors, and commissioners of military affairs possessed the elite (chin-shih) degrees acquired from their participation in the highest level civil service examinations. See Li Chün, Chung-kuo tsai-hsiang chih-tu (Taipei, 1966), pp. 136–40; Lo, Introduction to the civil service of Sung China, pp. 85, 93–4.

and two long-term purposes. It pensioned off Later Chou holdovers by granting them salaried offices but withholding the authority of a duty assignment, thereby ameliorating the "relaxation of bureaucratic standards" that had beset governments in Five Dynasties.[118] Governmental irregularities and arbitrary practices had become rife during the Five Dynasties and the Ten Kingdoms, and not a few civil administrative posts had been occupied by substandard bureaucrats or by agents who furthered the interests of the military. By preserving these men's former ranks and emoluments but assigning them only nominal duties, the dual system facilitated the standardization and demilitarization of the administration. In the long run, it accommodated retired high officials and imperial relatives in the same way as it had accommodated the Later Chou holdovers. Most important, it allowed the emperor the utmost flexibility in personnel administration. Since duty assignments were not formally ranked, the emperor could commission a low-ranking but capable official to perform the work of a high-ranking office or assign a high court official to a county office.[119] Moreover, the tenure of a stipendiary office was in general three years, but a duty assignment could be made open-ended as circumstances warranted.

A vexing problem in early Sung administration was determining how much power the chief councilor should hold. To understand this problem we must distinguish between the chief councilor's personal influence and his institutional power; a chief councilor with force of character and great personal influence could surmount the limitations of his institutional authority.[120] Following Five Dynasties precedents, the powers of the chief councilors were split into three parts during the early Sung. Civil power was vested in the Secretariat-Chancellery, which indirectly controlled the six ministries: Personnel, Revenue, Rites, War, Justice, and Works. Military power was vested in the Bureau of Military Affairs (*Shu-mi yüan*), and the locus of fiscal power was in the Finance Commission (*San-ssu*). Each of the three parts was autonomous in making and implementing policies in its own field, and each was answerable only to the emperor. This division of power placed the military and fiscal administrations under the direct control of the emperor at the expense of the chief councilors. Moreover, the civil authority of the chief councilors was further reduced in that personnel management ceased to be the responsibility of

---

[118] Wang, *Structure of power*, p. 174.

[119] Chang, *Chao K'uang-yin chuan*, pp. 111–2.

[120] Wang Jui-lai failed to make this distinction in his argument that the early Sung chief councilors were more powerful than has generally been believed; see Wang Jui-lai, "Lun Sung-tai hsiang-ch'üan," *Li-shih yen-chiu* 2 (1985), pp. 106–20. For the evolution of the chief councilor's institutional power, see Chin Chung-shu, "Sung-tai san-sheng chang-kuan fei-chih ti yen-chiu," *Hsin-ya hsüeh-pao* 11 No. 1 (1974), pp. 89–147.

the Secretariat-Chancellery. Recruitment by means of the civil service examinations, formerly under the jurisdiction of the Ministry of Rites, was now administered by court officials commissioned directly by the emperor. Appointments and evaluations of general officials, formerly the responsibilities of the Ministry of Personnel, were now handled by independent organs such as the Bureau of Personnel Evaluation (*Shen-kuan yüan*).[121] Also, the final say of the Ministry of Justice in critical legal matters was delegated to the Judicial Control Office (*Shen-hsing yüan*) established by T'ai-tsung.

Like the palace examination and the duty assignment system, the division of power into isolated administrative organs without a "prime" minister resulted in the emperor's substantial participation in making decisions, coordinating policies, and even supervising their execution. The emperor's workload was increased by the need for separate audiences, especially between the Secretariat-Chancellery and the Bureau of Military Affairs. Leading officials of these two offices were not permitted to appear together at imperial audiences in the State Meeting Hall (*Tu-t'ang*). This practice allowed the emperor to cross-examine their reports, and to maintain the division of power at top-level meetings where national policies were formed. Accordingly, the two offices each kept exclusive records of their separate audiences. Such insistence on confidentiality was carried further after the mid-Sung. High-ranking officials were prohibited from receiving guests at home except on national holidays. All officials involved in formulating policies, particularly the councilors, the drafters, the censors, and the remonstrators, were prohibited from private association or communication with one another.[122] At the highest level of governance, the throne was the only point of contact. The emperor was the linchpin of the empire, arbitrating and making the final decisions on all state policy.

Did the seventeen years of T'ai-tsu's reign witness the development of the civilian-dominated bureaucratic government for which the Sung is famous? Or to put the question another way, were the approximately four hundred and fifty most qualified candidates for civil offices sufficient to form such a government? It seems safer to believe that T'ai-tsu's government was still dominated by survivors of the old political elite from the late Five Dynasties, of whom only a minority had civil or bureaucratic origins, and most of whom

---

[121] Edward A. Kracke, Jr., *Civil service in early Sung China, 960–1067; with particular emphasis on the development of controlled sponsorship to foster administrative responsibility* (Cambridge, Mass., 1953), pp. 43–5.

[122] Liu Tzu-chien (James T. C. Liu), "An administrative cycle in Chinese history: The case of Northern Sung emperors," *Journal of Asian Studies* 21 No. 2 (1962), p. 139.

were of military or clerical (*li2*) origin.[123] Also, the question might be asked, had T'ai-tsu himself adopted a civilian frame of mind? One answer might be provided by the fact that T'ai-tsu once asked two finalists of the civil service examination to resort to boxing to decide who deserved the highest honors.[124]

Even late in his reign, T'ai-tsu continued to search for civil officials with military abilities.[125] According to some anecdotes, T'ai-tsu demanded that men of learning should be exempted from capital punishment and that only they could be appointed chief councilors.[126] However, he did not allow civil officials to replace military governors or to dominate the Bureau of Military Affairs or the Finance Commission.[127] Neither was he eager to revive the practice of policy criticism or the opinion organs.[128] Even if T'ai-tsu had foreseen a civilian government to which scholar-officials were indispensable, his unification plans needed substantial participation by military and financial specialists in the administration. In sum, T'ai-tsu opened up the path that led from the militarily dominated government he inherited from the Five Dynasties to the civilian-dominated government his successors consolidated.

T'ai-tsu, for the most part, cleared the civil administration of military influence and entrusted it to the Secretariat-Chancellery, though he persisted in giving independence to the Bureau of Military Affairs. He reduced the role of the military in government and increased that of the civilians, but this action was intended to balance out the former dominance by the military and not to create a new imbalance under civilian dominance.[129]

---

[123] See Sun Kuo-tung, "T'ang Sung chih chi she-hui men-ti chih hsiao-jung," *Hsin-ya hsüeh-pao* 4 No. 1 (1959), pp. 246–50, and the chart between pp. 280 and 281. Wang Gungwu, "The rhetoric of a lesser empire: Early Sung relations with its neighbors," in *China among equals: The Middle Kingdom and its neighbors, 10th–14th centuries,* ed. Morris Rossabi (Berkeley, Calif.,1983), p. 171. Ch'en I-yen, *Pei Sung t'ung-chih chieh-ts'eng she-hui liu-tung chih yen-chiu* (Taipei, 1977), pp. 24, 29–30, 34–5, 59, 61, 136. Robert M. Hartwell, "Demographic, political, and social transformations of China, 750–1550," *Harvard Journal of Asiatic Studies* 42 No. 2 (1982), pp. 405–11.

[124] *SS* 287, p. 9650; Ssu-ma, *Su-shui chi-wen* 3, p. 26.

[125] Worthy, "The founding of Sung China," p. 302; Chaffee, *The thorny gates of learning in Sung China,* p. 48.

[126] *HCP* (1964) 7, p. 6a; Chang Yin-lin, "Sung T'ai-tsu shih-pei chi cheng-shih-t'ang k'o-shih k'ao," *Wen-shih tsa-chih* 1 No. 7 (1940), pp. 15–16; Hsü Kuei, "Sung T'ai-tsu shih-yüeh pien-hsi," *Li-shih yen-chiu* 4 (1986), pp. 190–2.

[127] Worthy, "The founding of Sung China," p. 275, 304. Hartwell, "Demographic, political, and social transformations of China," pp. 408, 410. All four finance commissioners (*san-ssu shih*) during T'ai-tsu's reign were military men. See Ko Shao-ou, "Pei Sung chih san-ssu-shih," *Shih-huo yüeh-k'an* 8 No. 2 (1978), pp. 113–15. The ratio of commissioners and assistant commissioners of military affairs with civil ranks to those with military ranks steadily increased from 40 percent under T'ai-tsu, to 60 percent or more under T'ai-tsung and Chen-tsung, to over 90 percent from the 1060s through the end of the Northern Sung. See Liang, *Sung shu-mi-yüan chih-tu,* pp. 12–14.

[128] Liu, "An administrative cycle in Chinese history," p. 142.

[129] For a theoretical discussion of these questions, see Worthy, "The founding of Sung China," pp. 299–305.

War and peace under T'ai-tsung, 976–997

T'ai-tsu died unexpectedly in the fall of 976.[130] He was survived by two sons, the twenty-six-year-old Chao Te-chao (950–79) and the eighteen-year-old Chao Te-fang (959–81), and by their young stepmother, the twenty-five-year-old Empress Sung (951–95), but he left no officially designated successor. Contrary to the tradition of primogeniture, T'ai-tsu's thirty-seven-year-old brother Kuang-i (posthumously T'ai-tsung) installed himself as emperor, as is recorded in the *Liao dynastic history*.[131] Because of the scarcity of evidence, the bias of the official *veritable records* (*shih-lu*) of T'ai-tsu and T'ai-tsung,[132] and the hyperbole of the anecdotes relating to it, modern historians are unsure which version, if any, of these events is credible.

One story hints that T'ai-tsu was murdered by Kuang-i. On one snowy night, T'ai-tsu invited Kuang-i for a drink and dismissed all the attendants. From far away Kuang-i was seen by dim candlelight frequently leaving his seat as if dodging something. Subsequently, T'ai-tsu struck an "axe" against a pillar and told Kuang-i, "Do it well, do it well." Then T'ai-tsu went to sleep, snoring like thunder. Kuang-i stayed in the palace that night. Early next morning, T'ai-tsu was found dead.[133] From this evidence, a Ming dynasty commentator adduced two further points to speculate that T'ai-tsu was murdered. First, the new emperor impatiently replaced T'ai-tsu's reign title only twelve days before it was due to terminate. Second, the new title, T'ai-p'ing hsing-kuo (Ascendent State in Grand Tranquility, 976–84),[134] implied his transcendency over T'ai-tsu. Such disrespect for the deceased emperor might suggest that Kuang-i acquired the throne by wrongdoing.[135] But one modern historian assumes that

---

[130] The cause of T'ai-tsu's death is unclear. T'eng Kuang-ming suspected illness; see T'eng Kuang-ming, "Sung T'ai-tsu T'ai-tsung shou-shou pien," *Chen-li tsa-chih* 1 No. 2 (1944), p. 192; see also Pi Yüan, *Hsü Tzu-chih t'ung-chien* [Te-yü-t'ang tsang-pan ed. 1801] (1792; Peking, 1957) 8, p. 205. However, there is no evidence of any illness nor any record of T'ai-tsu's sons being asked to attend in the palace. Araki Toshikazu suggested alcoholism; see Araki Toshikazu, "Sō Taiso sakekuse kō," *Shirin* 38 No. 5 (1955), pp. 41–55, but Chang Ch'i-fan argues that T'ai-tsu had abstained from heavy drinking as early as 961. Chang's own inference of poisoning by Kuang-i is based on flimsy evidence; see Chang Ch'i-fan, "Sung T'ai-tsung lun," *Li-shih yen-chiu* 2 (1987), pp. 101–2.

[131] T'o-t'o et al., *Liao shih* 8, p. 96.

[132] See Chiang Fu-ts'ung, "Sung T'ai-tsung shih-lu tsuan-hsiu k'ao," in *Sung-shih hsin-t'an, Chiang Fu-ts'ung pien-chu*, ed. Chiang Fu-ts'ung (Taipei, 1966), pp. 61–72.

[133] Wen-ying, *Hsiang-shan yeh-lu* (c. 1073; Peking, 1984), p. 74. Teng, "Sung T'ai-tsu T'ai-tsung shou-shou pien," p. 191, has deciphered Wen-ying's account for hidden suggestions of T'ai-tsu's unnatural death.

[134] For translations of reign titles, see James M. Hargett, "A chronology of the reigns and reign-periods of the Song dynasty (960–1279)," *Bulletin of Sung-Yüan Studies* 19 (1987), pp. 32–4.

[135] Liu Ting-chih, *Tai-chai ts'un-kao* [1506–21 ed; Kuo-li Pei-ching t'u-shu-kuan microfilm ed.; Fu Ssu-nien tu-shu-kuan] (15th c.; Taipei, 20th c.) 5, pp. 2b–3a. Though disagreeing with Liu, Chiang Fu-ts'ung points out that such a change of reign title was unusual even in the chaotic years of the

T'ai-tsu confirmed the fraternal succession in that private meeting and that the "axe" was only an axe-shaped piece of stationery.[136] In addition, few historians believe that Kuang-i would have resorted to violence in the palace.[137]

Another version attributes the legitimacy of Kuang-i's succession to his mother's assessment of the political situation. Intelligent and shrewd, the dowager empress Tu (901–61) helped T'ai-tsu make decisions on state affairs early in his reign. Sixteen years before, on her deathbed, the dowager empress is said to have asked T'ai-tsu why he became emperor. T'ai-tsu was supposed to have ascribed his accession to the virtue and blessings she and his ancestors had bestowed upon him. "No," his mother is said to have replied, "It is precisely because the Ch'ai house [of the Later Chou] let a child become master of all under Heaven." With this in mind, she instructed T'ai-tsu to leave the throne to his second and third brothers in succession so that the future of his own sons could also be secured. T'ai-tsu allegedly promised to do so, and she was supposed to have asked Chao P'u to sign a special document, which he was to keep in a golden box in the palace.[138] It was said that Chao P'u revealed this secret document some twenty years later, in 981, to T'ai-tsung to curry favor with him.[139] However, the timing of this supposed revelation is not credible. First, if these events had really happened, why did Chao P'u not reveal them in 976, when T'ai-tsung needed to legitimate his own succession?[140] Second, why would T'ai-tsung want the issue of succession reopened after he had already been on the throne for five years? Finally, would T'ai-tsung have let the court know that the third brother was mentioned in the secret document when he himself was about to remove this brother from the line of

Five Dynasties. See Chiang Fu-ts'ung, "Sung T'ai-tsu chih peng pu yü-nien erh kai-yüan k'ao," in *Ch'ing-chu Chu Chia-hua hsien-sheng ch'i-shih-sui lun-wen-chi*, ed. Ch'ing-chu Chu Chia-hua hsien-sheng ch'i-shih-sui lun-wen-chi bien-chi wei-yüan-hui (Taipei, 1962), pp. 457–60.

[136] Ku Chi-kuang, "Sung-tai chi-ch'eng wen-t'i shang-ch'üeh," *Ch'ing-hua hsüeh-pao* 13 No. 1 (1941), pp. 90–1, and p. 92 n. 9.

[137] See Teng, "Sung T'ai-tsu T'ai-tsung shou-shou pien," pp. 191–2; Miyazaki Ichisada, "Sō no Taiso hishū setsu ni tsuite," *Tōyōshi kenkyū* 9 No. 4 (1945), pp. 5–8; and Liu, "Sung T'ai-tsung yü Sung-ch'u liang-tz'u ts'uan-wei," p. 2.

[138] Ssu-ma, *Su-shui chi-wen* 1, p. 6. Whether the dowager empress had included the third brother in the succession line is an important question, but even Li T'ao was puzzled by authoritative but contradictory sources, such as the original *Veritable records* (comp. 978–80) of T'ai-tsu, which did not record the secret will at all; its revised edition (994–9, revised again in 1016), which excluded the third brother; and the *Veritable records* (997–8, revised in 1016) of T'ai-tsung and Ssu-ma Kuang's *Su-shui chi-wen* (c. 1180), both of which included the third brother. Therefore, Li omitted the third brother in *HCP* (1964) 2, pp. 8a–b, but included him in *HCP* (1964) 22, pp. 11b–12b, with a note that by Ssu-ma Kuang's time he was widely believed to be in the succession line. See also Teng, "Sung T'ai-tsu T'ai-tsung shou-shou pien," p. 178.

[139] *HCP* (1964) 22, p. 11b.

[140] Chang Yin-lin, "Sung T'ai-tsung chi-t'ung k'ao-shih," *Wen-shih tsa-chih* 1 No. 8 (1941), p. 29; Wang, "Sung ch'u erh-ti ch'üan-wei wen-t'i ti p'ou-hsi," p. 22.

succession?[141] Although historians are not unanimous about the authenticity of this document,[142] it seems plausible to believe either that it was fabricated by Chao P'u with T'ai-tsung's acquiescence,[143] or that the story was fabricated by the compilers of the *Veritable records* of T'ai-tsung to justify his succession.[144]

Whatever the truth of the matter, Kuang-i was the most dominant of all the potential successors to the throne. Furthermore, the current situation, complicated as it was by the menacing Northern Han–Khitan alliance, the problem of recovering the Sixteen Yen-Yün Prefectures, and T'ai-tsu's highly centralized government, all required a strong and decisive emperor. No imperial clansman was more experienced than Kuang-i in dealing with the military and civil measures these protocols demanded.

Kuang-i and Ch'ai Jung (the second emperor of the Later Chou) had shared the same father-in-law.[145] From 954 or so until 961, Kuang-i fought on the battlefield alongside his father Chao Hung-yin (until his death in 956) and his brother T'ai-tsu.[146] Kuang-i thrived under their aegis, filling a series of relatively minor but sensitive military positions within the Palace Guard and the attendant staff. He was believed to have been a chief instigator of the 960 coup at Ch'en-ch'iao.[147] As a reward, Kuang-i was made the third-ranking inspector in chief in the Palace Command, until he was appointed the governor of K'ai-feng in 961.[148] This important post controlled the entire capital area and had been given only to the most likely imperial successor during the

---

[141] Chang, "Sung T'ai-tsung chi-t'ung k'ao-shih," p. 30 n. 9.

[142] For believers, see Ku, "Sung-tai chi-ch'eng wen-t'i shang-ch'üeh," pp. 88–90; Curtis Chung Chang, "Inheritance problems in the first two reigns of the Sung dynasty," *Chinese Culture* 9 No. 4 (1968), p. 35; Chiang Fu-ts'ung, "Sung T'ai-tsu shih T'ai-tsung yü Chao P'u ti cheng-cheng," *Shih-hsüeh hui-k'an* 5 (1973), p. 7; for dissenters, see Chang, "Sung T'ai-tsung chi-t'ung k'ao-shih," pp. 28–30; Teng, "Sung T'ai-tsu T'ai-tsung shou-shou pien," pp. 178–80; Wang, "Sung ch'u erh-ti ch'üan-wei wen-t'i ti p'ou-hsi," pp. 21–2.

[143] Miyazaki, "Sō no Taiso hishū setsu ni tsuite," p. 14, suggests that T'ai-tsung and Chao P'u cooperated in the fabrication. Chang, "Sung T'ai-tsung lun," p. 105, argues that it was done by either T'ai-tsung or Chao P'u; but we believe that Chao P'u took the initiative, because of the second and third points mentioned earlier. Wang, "Sung ch'u erh-ti ch'üan-wei wen-t'i ti p'ou-hsi," pp. 18 and 22, guesses that the dowager empress Tu might have spoken of "passing the throne to a mature person," or "passing the throne to your brothers," which Chao P'u transformed into a written will.

[144] Teng, "Sung T'ai-tsu T'ai-tsung shou-shou pien," pp. 179, 185. However, it seems doubtful that the compilers would dare to fabricate such an important event without some sort of reference from someone high up.

[145] For its significance, see Liu, "Sung T'ai-tsung yü Sung-ch'u liang-tz'u ts'uan-wei," p. 1.

[146] This, T'ai-tsung's own account, contains some temporal errors; see *HCP* (1964) 29, p. 2b; Chang, "Sung T'ai-tsung lun," p. 97.

[147] Wang, "Sung ch'u erh-ti ch'üan-wei wen-t'i ti p'ou-hsi," pp. 17 and 22, even suspects that T'ai-tsu was pushed by Kuang-i to stage the coup and then might have reached some sort of agreement about their succession.

[148] See Worthy, "The founding of Sung China," p. 167, table I.

Five Dynasties era.[149] When T'ai-tsu took to the field himself, against Li Yün and Li Ch'ung-chin in 960, Kuang-i was appointed chief administrator of the imperial residence, and when Tai-tsu again left to attack the Northern Han in 969, Kuang-i was made resident defender (*liu-shou*) in the capital.[150] These appointments may indicate T'ai-tsu's intention to elevate Kuang-i's status, as well as suggesting his trust in him.[151]

Kuang-i always held rank superior to T'ai-tsu's son Chao Te-chao. Though already in his twenties, Te-chao had never been appointed to any important post. Moreover, contrary to convention, he was not ennobled as a prince (*wang*) when he reached maturity and moved out of the palace. In 973, he was made an honorary military governor and a grand mentor, a high-sounding sinecure with a rank equal to chief councilor. At the same time, however, Kuang-i was ennobled one rank higher than Te-chao and made a prince, the first and only living prince during T'ai-tsu's reign, and placed above the chief councilors in regular audiences.[152] It seems clear that by that time Kuang-i was already T'ai-tsu's intended successor.[153]

Kuang-i's personal entourage was also formidable. During his fifteen years (961–76) as governor of K'ai-feng, he recruited talented people from all walks of life, mostly fighters, some fugitives, and a few literati. Also he exchanged favors with many nobles, court officials, and eunuchs.[154] Indeed, following the dismissed of his archrival, Chao P'u, as the lone chief councilor after nine years' service (964–73) because of his corruption and dictatorial tendencies, Kuang-i became the second most powerful man in the empire.[155] Furthermore, Kuang-i alone had been able to dissuade T'ai-tsu from moving the capital from K'ai-feng to Lo-yang.

The new emperor worked very hard. He tried to hold daily audiences and worked late each night, reading every memorial, carefully checking the accounts of the Finance Commission, handpicking central and local government officials, judging criminal cases in K'ai-feng, and even rectifying the

[149] Chiang Fu-ts'ung, "Sung T'ai-tsung Chin-ti mu-fu k'ao," *Ta-lu tsa-chih* 30 No. 3 (1965), p. 16.

[150] *SS* 1, pp. 6–7; 2, p. 28.

[151] Chang, "Inheritance problems in the first two reigns of the Sung dynasty," p. 15.

[152] *SS* 3, p. 40; 244, p. 8676; Chang, "Inheritance problems in the first two reigns of the Sung dynasty," p. 15.

[153] Chang, "Sung T'ai-tsung chi-t'ung k'ao-shih," p. 26; Ku, "Sung-tai chi-ch'eng wen-t'i shang-ch'üeh," pp. 87–9; Wang, "Sung ch'u erh-ti ch'üan-wei wen-t'i ti p'ou-hsi," pp. 15–17. Teng, "Sung T'ai-tsu T'ai-tsung shou-shou pien," pp. 181–4, disagrees, but his arguments are made only against some anecdotes rather than against the facts mentioned earlier.

[154] Teng, "Sung T'ai-tsu T'ai-tsung shou-shou pien," pp. 187–8; Chiang, "Sung T'ai-tsung Chin-ti mu-fu k'ao," pp. 15–23; Wang Huai-ling, "Lun Sung T'ai-tsung," *Hsüeh-shu yüeh-k'an* 3 (1986), p. 63.

[155] See Chiang, "Sung T'ai-tsu shih T'ai-tsung yü Chao P'u ti cheng-cheng," pp. 1–14; Chang, "Sung T'ai-tsung lun," pp. 98–100; Wang, "Sung ch'u erh-ti ch'üan-wei wen-t'i ti p'ou-hsi."

misbehavior of clerical staff.[156] To further the development of governmental centralization and imperial absolutism, T'ai-tsung deprived most military governors of their power bases, replacing the governors and their protégés with officials selected through civil service examinations, and he also whittled down the power of the chief councilors and border generals.

Despite an early Sung precedent that required state councilors to submit memoranda (*cha-tzu*) on every state affair for the emperor's approval before they were drafted into edicts, influential councilors still used council directives (*t'ang-t'ieh*) to give administrative orders independent of imperial power. In 996, however, T'ai-tsung ordered that the method of handling major affairs should follow the memorandum precedent, and that even the council directives for minor affairs must first pass his scrutiny.[157] Moreover, after a suspension of six years (976–82), T'ai-tsung again appointed assistant councilors of state (*ts'an-chih cheng-shih*) with powers roughly equivalent to those of the chief councilors.[158] Also in 996, new measures regarding governmental checks and balances were imposed: only chief councilors could command the seal of the Secretariat-Chancellery, and assisting councilors were now required to stand behind chief councilors at court, though all councilors could deliberate state affairs in the Council of State.[159] As a result, civil authority was no longer concentrated in the hands of the highest-ranking chief councilors, since they were always outnumbered by the assisting councilors, who, though very powerful, ranked below them. Then too, most of the chief councilors T'ai-tsung preferred were quiet, careful, and even timid, carrying no weight in policy decisions.[160]

Early in his reign T'ai-tsung reviewed the troops often, as a way of cultivating and securing their loyalty to him. Although the Bureau of Military Affairs had been entrusted to members of his former entourage, he rated all officers, himself, first according to their ability to control their subordinates and then according to their bravery.[161] This approach reflected his preference for firm control, particularly over the border generals whose power and autonomy posed a potential threat to him. The contentious state of Sung-

---

[156] Liu, "An administrative cycle in Chinese history," p. 142; Karl F. Olsson, "The structure of power under the third emperor of Sung China: The shifting balance after the peace of Shan-yüan" (diss., University of Chicago, 1974), pp. 46–8; Liu Ching-chen, "Pei Sung ch'ien-ch'i huang-ch'üan fa-chan chih yen-chiu – huang-ti cheng-chih chiao-se ti fen-hsi" (diss., Kuo-li T'ai-wan ta-hsüeh, 1987), pp. 60–78.

[157] *HCP* (1964) 40, pp. 5a–6a; Olsson, "The structure of power under the third emperor of Sung China," pp. 106–8; Worthy, "The founding of Sung China," pp. 246–8.

[158] *HCP* (1964) 37, p. 6a.

[159] *HCP* (1964) 40, p. 7a.

[160] Liu, "An administrative cycle in Chinese history," p. 142; Liu, "Pei Sung ch'ien-ch'i huang-ch'üan fa-chan chih yen-chiu," pp. 102–4.

[161] Chiang, "Sung T'ai-tsung Chin-ti mu-fu k'ao," pp. 22–3; Worthy, "The founding of Sung China," p. 183.

Liao relations necessitated the elevation of major border posts to the status of Chief Deployment Commands (*tu-pu shu*), and their incumbents carried much higher military rank and commanded many more troops than had been prescribed under T'ai-tsu. To offset their high rank, T'ai-tsung did not grant the border generals the same level of privileges and autonomy that T'ai-tsu had allowed them.[162] They were now forbidden to retain personal guards, a restriction that resulted in the killing of at least one expeditionary commander by the Khitan.[163] Their transgressions were also no longer tolerated. For example, a veteran general was castigated for beating to death a lieutenant found guilty of malfeasance.[164] At the tactical level, the generals' previous freedom in military actions was largely circumscribed by T'ai-tsung's obsession with control.[165] Moreover, frontier commanders were prohibited from trading and from appropriating local taxes. These prohibition's prevented self-enrichment but deprived frontier commanders of revenues to pay spies, grant bounties, or meet urgent needs.[166] In short, T'ai-tsung was unwilling to give the generals the free rein they needed to cope flexibly with fluid border circumstances.

SINO-LIAO RELATIONS AND THE TWO SONS OF HEAVEN

The Sung empire was much smaller than the cosmopolitan T'ang. The Sung never controlled any part of Central Asia, from which area Indian Buddhism and the best warhorses had come. It never reincorporated Annam (Northern Vietnam), its southwestern neighbor, whose independence in 968 ended centuries of Chinese hegemony over the Red River flood plain. Instead, the Sung was continually humiliated by its neighbors. Attempts to recover the Sixteen Prefectures of Yen-Yün from the Liao ended in disastrous defeats, and the policy of *i-i chih-i* (playing the barbarians off against each other) used against the Tangut (or Hsi Hsia from 1038) only hastened the Tangut achievement of autonomy. Given its place in a geopolitical triangle formed by the Sung, Liao, and Hsi Hsia states, the Sung empire has been described by modern historians as just one state "among equals."[167]

---

[162] Tseng Kung (1019–83) summarized the essence of T'ai-tsu's approach to managing border generals as follows: "Exalt them [the generals] with rewards. Treat them with sincerity. Enrich them with wealth. Denigrate their titles but elevate their powers. Overlook their minor [faults] and demand their major [accomplishments]. Prolong their [tenure as] officials and expect their success." Tseng Kung, *Tseng Kung chi* (1078–83; Peking, 1984) 49, pp. 663–4, translated by Worthy in "The founding of Sung China," p. 190.

[163] Worthy, "The founding of Sung China," p. 192.

[164] Chang, "Sung T'ai-tsung lun," pp. 107–8.

[165] Worthy, "The founding of Sung China," p. 188.

[166] Worthy, "The founding of Sung China," pp. 192–5; Chang, "Sung T'ai-tsung lun," p. 107.

[167] For the term and its many ramifications, see Morris Rossabi, ed., *China among equals: The Middle Kingdom and its neighbors, 10th–14th centuries* (Berkeley, Calif., 1983).

Sung-Liao relations began well. Although T'ai-tsu had not followed the Five Dynasties' practice of announcing his enthronement to the Khitan court, he took great care throughout his reign to avoid direct provocation. In late 974, after officials suggested that they become "eternal allies," the Sung and the Liao entered a relationship of equality, exchanging envoys with state letters on New Year's Day.[168] For the next four years, their relationship was harmonious. In 975 alone, the Liao dispatched several missions to the Sung; one was even sent especially to congratulate T'ai-tsu on his conquest of the Southern T'ang. The next year, Liao envoys presented condolences for T'ai-tsu's death and brought T'ai-tsung congratulations upon his succession. T'ai-tsung was also conciliatory, sending courtesy missions to the Liao emperor, allowing trade with the Liao, and arresting troublemakers along the border.[169]

This cordial relationship with the Liao was shattered by T'ai-tsung's campaign to conquer the Northern Han. In 979, one year after the submission to the Sung of the last two southern kingdoms (Chang-Ch'üan and Wu-Yüeh), T'ai-tsung launched an imperial campaign against the Northern Han. Frustrated in its diplomatic attempts to halt the Sung campaign, the Liao declared war. Learning from the failure of T'ai-tsu's invasion of the Northern Han from the south, T'ai-tsung attacked them instead from the northwest, crushing a major Liao reinforcement head-on. Isolated, the Northern Han resisted for only fifteen days before surrendering its ten prefectures and 35,220 households.[170] Acting without T'ai-tsu's leniency, T'ai-tsung downgraded the Northern Han capital T'ai-yüan from prefectural to county status, and set the city on fire, killing many of the trapped inhabitants.[171]

With the reluctant consent of most of his generals, T'ai-tsung, ambitious to fulfill his plans for a grand unification, immediately advanced toward the Sixteen Prefectures of Yen-Yün with no regard for the fatigue of his soldiers or for the shortage of his army's provisions. The campaign proceeded with deceptive smoothness until the army was caught between the city of Yu-chou (modern Peking, the southern capital of Liao) and approaching Khitan reinforcements. The disastrous defeat suffered by the Sung at the Kao-liang River (southeast of Ch'ang-p'ing, Peking), where over ten thousand Sung

---

[168] For basic studies of Sino-Liao relations see: Tao Jing-shen (T'ao Chin-sheng), *Two sons of heaven: Studies in Sung-Liao relations* (Tucson, Ariz.,1988); Wang, "Liao Sung Shan-yüan meng-yüeh ti-chieh ti pei-ching (shang)," pp. 35–49; Melvin Thlick-Len Ang, "Sung-Liao diplomacy in eleventh- and twelfth-century China: A study of the social and political determinants of foreign policy" (diss., University of Pennsylvania, 1983), pp. 97–9; Wang, "The rhetoric of a lesser empire," p. 51.

[169] Wang, "The rhetoric of a lesser empire," p. 51; Tao, *Two sons of heaven*, p. 13.

[170] Worthy, "The founding of Sung China," pp. 78–9; Tao, *Two sons of heaven*, p. 13.

[171] *HCP* (1964) 20, pp. 10a–b.

troops were killed and T'ai-tsung himself was wounded by arrows,[172] ushered in twenty-five years of warfare between the Sung and the Liao, who now faced each other directly, without the Northern Han between them as a buffer state.

In the following six years, the Liao initiated all the attacks, using hit-and-run tactics to exhaust the Sung armies. For example, after plundering the strategic Wa-ch'iao Pass (south of modern Hsiung county in Hopei) in 980, they retreated in the face of a counterattack led by T'ai-tsung in person. This tactic was aimed at dislocating the economy and sapping the military strength of the Sung border areas.[173] During these years, T'ai-tsung's continual requests for military cooperation from Koryŏ and the Parhae (Po-hai) people, inhabitants of eastern Liaoning who had been incorporated into the Liao state by the Khitan in the 920s, bore no results. In contrast, the Liao continued to build up its hegemony in the region south of the Gobi Desert, thereby securing their western borders before concentrating on attacking the Sung. According to *Liao dynastic history* (*Liao shih*), in early 983 T'ai-tsung had sent congratulations accompanied by peace overtures to the new emperor of Liao, the thirteen-year-old Liao Sheng-tsung (r. 982–1031), but to no avail.[174] In early 986 even the Tanguts turned their back on the Sung and submitted to the Liao.[175]

Hoping to take advantage of Sheng-tsung's inexperience and Liao preoccupation with northern expansion, T'ai-tsung launched a new attack in 986. Nearly two hundred thousand Sung troops invaded the Sixteen Yen-Yün Prefectures from three directions, achieving some victories in the mountain areas. In the plain of Ho-pei, however, the Sung infantry, commanded by generals whose tactics were poorly coordinated, were no match for the Liao cavalry led by seasoned generals like Yeh-lü Hsiu-ko (953–998) and Yeh-lü Hsieh-chen (?–999), under the capable leadership of the dowager empress Hsiao (?–1009).

---

[172] Tao, *Two sons of heaven*, pp. 13–14. For a brief description of this defeat, as recorded in the *Liao shih*, see Wittfogel and Feng, *History of Chinese society*, p. 582. Wang Gungwu argues that T'ai-tsung's confidence in attacking the Liao was not unjustified, for Sung power had reached its climax in 979, with the envoys from important non-Chinese states such as Koryŏ, Champa, and the Tanguts arriving with tribute; see Wang, "The rhetoric of a lesser empire," pp. 51–2. Sung Ch'ang-lien suggests that a mutiny was possible and that a large majority of the Sung forces did not participate in the battle; see Sung Ch'ang-lien, "K'ao-liang-ho chan-i k'ao-shih," *Ta-lu tsa-chih* 39 No. 10 (1969), pp. 33–6. Ch'eng Kuang-yü has documented most of the important primary sources on T'ai-tsung's battles with the Liao in his *Sung T'ai-tsung tui Liao chan-cheng k'ao* (Taipei, 1972).

[173] T'o-t'o et al., *Liao shih* 34, pp. 398–9.

[174] T'o-t'o et al., *Liao shih* 10, p. 108.

[175] Wang, "The rhetoric of a lesser empire," pp. 52–3. Wittfogel and Feng, *History of Chinese society*, pp. 317–25, 405–8. Tao, *Two sons of heaven*, p. 80, states that a Korean army of twenty-five thousand had advanced toward the Liao in cooperation with the Sung expedition of 986, but nothing more about this army is recorded.

The debacle at Ch'i-kou Pass (southwest of modern Cho county in Hopei), where some thirty thousand Sung soldiers were reportedly lost, was followed by further defeats and finally by the total retreat of the expedition. Soon the Liao took revenge for the invasion at the strategic Chün-tzu Pass (northwest of modern Ho-chien in Hopei), where they killed several generals and tens of thousands of Sung soldiers. Having lost most of his crack troops, including a most capable general, Yang Yeh (?–986), T'ai-tsung now had to take a defensive rather than an offensive stance against the Liao.[176]

During the 986 expedition, T'ai-tsung conferred only with the Bureau of Military Affairs, issuing six edicts in a single day without informing the Secretariat-Chancellery. After the defeat, T'ai-tsung forswore such exclusive reliance on the Bureau of Military Affairs, but he soon broke his resolution. In 988, troops were recruited for a campaign without the chief councilors' knowledge. The next year, however, to ease the councilors' irritation at not being informed on military affairs, T'ai-tsung ordered the Bureau of Military Affairs to send a copy of its log to the Secretariat-Chancellery. One councilor even dared to stop an assistant commissioner returning from an imperial audience and, on learning that foreign affairs had been discussed, insist on voicing his own opinions before the emperor.[177] This suggests that external crises may have provided opportunities for the councilors to gain ground in their tug-of-war with the emperor over the division of civil and military powers. In fact, councilors would serve as concurrent commissioners in the Bureau of Military Affairs in 1042–5, during the Sung-Hsi Hsia wars, and again, during the Southern Sung, as a consequence of ongoing crises with the Jurchen and later the Mongols.[178]

T'ai-tsung's wars against the Liao were very costly. Liao counterraids inside Sung borders devastated the region's human and economic resources, forcing T'ai-tsung to grant years of land tax remissions to landowners in Ho-pei, and to abandon the recruitment of soldiers in the region of Honan. During this period T'ai-tsung also lost potential allies. In 991 and 994, after their requests for military aid were turned down by T'ai-tsung, the Jurchen in the region of northern Manchuria and the Koryŏ kingdom accepted Liao suzerainty. As

[176] HCP (1964) 27, pp. 1a–b, 18a–19b, 21b–23a; 28, p. 1a; Ang, "Sung-Liao diplomacy in eleventh- and twelfth-century China," pp. 68–71, 99–100. For a succinct analysis of the failure of this expedition; see Chin Yü-fu, Sung Liao Chin shih (1936; Shanghai, 1946), p. 32. T'ai-tsung blamed the defeat on some commanders' violation of his prescribed strategy; see HCP (1964) 27, p. 14a.

[177] Olsson, "The structure of power under the third emperor of Sung China," pp. 110–12; Worthy, "The founding of Sung China," pp. 239–41.

[178] Chou Tao-chi, "Sung-tai tsai-hsiang ming-ch'eng yü ch'i shih-ch'üan chih yen-chiu," Ta-lu tsa-chih 17 No. 12 (1958), pp. 14–15; Lin T'ien-wei, "Sung-tai ch'üan-hsiang hsing-ch'eng chih fen-hsi," Ssu yü yen 10 No. 5 (1973), pp. 37–9.

the hope of victory over the Liao dimmed, advocates of a diplomatic rather than a military solution began gaining ground at the Sung court. T'ai-tsung himself became increasingly tired of fighting. Two Sung appeals for peace were recorded in the *Liao dynastic history*, but they came to nothing.[179]

Relations with the Tanguts, or the "western barbarians"

In contrast to the their attitudes toward the Liao, the Sung usually looked down on the Tanguts, whether the tribes were subservient or hostile, calling them "western barbarians," "recalcitrant caitiffs in the west," or "western bandits."[180] In the late ninth century, in return for his help in putting down the Huang Ch'ao rebellion (875–84), the Tangut leader had been rewarded by the T'ang court with the imperial surname Li, granted the title Duke of the Hsi Hsia state, and given a hereditary title of military governor of the Ting-nan army controlling Hsia-chou, Sui-chou, Yin-chou, and Yu-chou2 prefectures on the southern border of the Ordos Desert (see map 13 in chapter 4). During the Five Dynasties, the Tanguts strengthened their hold on Ting-nan, while remaining allies of the Later Liang and Later T'ang. Under the Later Han, Tangut territory increased, and in 954 their leader was enfeoffed as Prince of Hsi-p'ing. The Hsia-chou regime remained on good terms with both the Later Chou and the Sung dynasties, for whom they were an important source of horses. In general, their dependence on trade for salt, food, and consumer goods kept the Tanguts subordinate. At one point they even assisted T'ai-tsung in his conquest of the Northern Han.[181]

From 982 on, with the establishment of an independent Hsia state and ensuing Tangut encroachment on Sung territory, a hostile relationship emerged that would last for the duration of the Northern Sung. Li I-yin, who had governed Hsi Hsia since 935, died in 967, and was granted the posthumous title King of Hsia. The Sung duly appointed his son Li K'o-jui as king in his place. But in 978, Li K'o-jui died, and his brother Li Chi-p'eng usurped the throne. In 979, when the Northern Han state that had formed a buffer state to the east was annexed by Sung, the Tanguts now had a long frontier with Sung

---

[179] T'o-t'o et al., *Liao shih* 13, p. 145.

[180] Tao Jing-shen (T'ao Chin-sheng), "Barbarians or northerners: Northern Sung images of the Khitans," in *China among equals: The Middle Kingdom and its neighbors, 10th–14th centuries*, ed. Morris Rossabi (Berkeley, Calif., 1983), p. 78; Herbert Franke, "Sung embassies: Some general observations," in *China among equals: The Middle Kingdom and its neighbors, 10th–14th centuries*, ed. Morris Rossabi (Berkeley Calif., 1983), pp. 116–48.

[181] Wang, *Wu-tai hui-yao* 29, pp. 462–4; Shiba Yoshinobu, "Sung foreign trade: Its scope and organization," in *China among equals: The Middle Kingdom and its neighbors, 10th–14th centuries*, ed. Morris Rossabi (Berkeley, Calif., 1983), p. 101.

both to their south and east. After two years as Tangut ruler, the unpopular Li Chi-p'eng surrendered his land to the Sung in 982. T'ai-tsung, who wanted to remove the Tanguts as a potential enemy, planned to take control of the strategic Ordos region in order to establish a northwestern defense against the Liao and to maintain commercial access to Tangut warhorses.[182] However, while Li Chi-p'eng's entire clan was in the process of moving to K'ai-feng, his cousin Li Chi-ch'ien (?–1004) and various Tangut tribes rebelled against the high-handedness of the Sung occupation forces. They gradually took back some territory and even outmaneuvered the Sung diplomatically by submitting themselves to the Liao on the eve of T'ai-tsung's 986 expedition. In addition, during the next year, Li Chi-ch'ien married a Liao princess with a dowry of three thousand horses.

To avoid a two-front war, T'ai-tsung adopted Chao P'u's policy of divide and rule, and reinstated Li Chi-p'eng as Tangut ruler.[183] Li Chi-ch'ien feigned submission to the Sung to buy time and eventually induced Chi-p'eng to fight for autonomy. But Li Chi-ch'ien's plan backfired. Enraged, the Liao raided and looted the Tangut territory in 992 to punish them for their apparent submission to the Sung. In 994 the Sung in their turn deposed Li Chi-ch'ien, destroying the Tangut citadel of Hsia-chou, and rigidly prohibited the exchange of Tangut salt for Sung food in the Shensi and Kansu regions.[184] Reinforced by a great number of starving Tanguts, Li Chi-ch'ien defeated a Sung expedition in 996 after intercepting its supply train with its hugh quantities of grain. These wars encouraged the various Tangut tribes to consolidate, and they began to expand westward into what is now Ningsia province. In 998, under a new appeasement policy, the Sung appointed Li Chi-ch'ien military governor in command of all the Tangut territories. This unwisely legitimized a power base that the Tanguts steadily expanded. By 1036 they controlled all of the Ordos region, Ningsia, and almost all of Kansu. Shortly afterward they invaded the Tibetan domains east of the inland sea known as the Ch'ing-hai (Lake Kokonor). With this action the Tanguts won a favorable treaty from the Sung in 1044, as described in the following chapter.[185] Thereafter, the Sung were cut off from the land route across Turkestan to Western Asia and Europe.

---

[182] Ang, "Sung-Liao diplomacy in eleventh- and twelfth-century China," pp. 25–6.

[183] See Tsutomu Iwasaki "A study of Ho-hsi Tibetans during the Northern Sung dynasty," *Memoirs of the Research Department of the Tōyō Bunko* 44 (1986), pp. 57–132, especially pp. 57–8.

[184] For a discussion of the significance of salt in the Sung–Hsi Hsia relations, see Liao Lung-sheng, "Sung Hsia kuan-hsi chung ti ch'ing-pai yen wen-t'i," *Shih-huo yüeh-k'an* 5 No. 10 (1976), pp. 14–21.

[185] Chin, *Sung Liao Chin shih*, p. 90, also pp. 93–5 for a succinct analysis of Liao–Hsi Hsia relations. For a general survey of the Sung–Hsi Hsia relations, see Ch'üeh Hao-tseng, "Sung Hsia kuan-hsi chih yen-chiu," *Kuo-li Cheng-chih ta-hsüeh hsüeh-pao* 9 (1964), pp. 267–317. For a more detailed overview see Li Hua-jui, *Sung Hsia kuan-hsi shih* (Shih-chia-chuang, 1998).

The closure of the northern frontiers accelerated the shift of political and economic centers to the south and southeast, at the same time that the wars in the northwest thrust scholar-officials into positions of military command.[186] The closure of these frontiers also impeded Sung trade with Central Asia and confined Sung expansion mostly to the south, turning its attention from the interior of Asia toward the oceans. Consequently, the Sung developed a prosperous maritime trade and expanded their overseas relations with Koryŏ, Japan, Southeast Asia, and the Indian Ocean.[187] Whereas in the north the shortage of warhorses put the Sung at a disadvantage before Tangut and Khitan cavalry, in the south the sophisticated marine technology and naval strategies invented during the Sung eventually elevated the empire to the status of a sea power.[188] Maritime trade helped the Sung spread the influence of Confucianism in Koryŏ and Japan, leaving imprints that exist today.[189] However, the decline of Indian Buddhism and the obstruction of its eastward transmission deprived the Sung empire of a significant source of stimulation by foreign ideas, although some contact did continue. Both T'ai-tsu and T'ai-tsung seriously attempted to revive contacts and continue the translation of Indian Buddhist texts.[190] But the program died in the mid-eleventh century; the Indian masters were few, and Chinese skills in Sanskrit had declined. Besides, Buddhism in India and China had begun to follow separate paths.

Military defeats reduced the Sung's supremacy within this multistate environment. Koryŏ transferred the tribute formerly offered the Sung to the Liao, the Tanguts played the Liao off against the Sung, and the Vietnamese finally established their independent state of Ta Yüeh.[191] Yet residents of the Sung capitalized on the hard-earned peace to attain economic prosperity and cultural efflorescence.[192] Modern historians have pointed out that the Sung leaders, though sometimes given to rhetorical excess in their external and internal communications about foreigners, were actually flexible, realistic, and pragmatic

---

[186] Yang Te-ch'uan and Liu Tzu-chien (James T. C. Liu), "The image of scholar-generals and a case in the Southern Sung," *Saeculum* 37 No. 2 (1986), p. 184. For examples of quasi- "scholar-generals" during the early reigns of the Northern Sung, see Labadie, "Rulers and soldiers," pp. 194–7.

[187] Lo Jung-pang, "Maritime commerce and its relation to the Sung navy," *Journal of Economic and Social History of the Orient* 22 No. 1 (1969), pp. 57–101.

[188] Lo Jung-pang, "The emergence of China as a sea power during the late Sung and early Yüan periods," *Far Eastern Quarterly* 14 (1954–5), pp. 489–503. On the problem of Sung horse supply, see Paul J. Smith, *Taxing heaven's storehouse: Horses, bureaucrats and the destruction of the Sichuan tea industry, 1074–1224* (Cambridge, Mass., 1991).

[189] Kenneth K. S. Chen, *Buddhism in China: A historical survey* (Princeton, N.J., 1964), pp. 389–90, 394–400.

[190] See the recent study of Sen Tansen, *Buddhism, diplomacy, and trade: The realignment of Sino-Indian relations, 600–1400* (Honolulu, 2003), especially pp. 102–39.

[191] Wang, "The rhetoric of a lesser empire," pp. 61–2.

[192] This is especially so after the peace of 1005; see Tao, *Two sons of heaven*, pp. 23–4.

in dealing with foreign states. Recognizing their own military weakness, they acknowledged the Liao as a diplomatic equal.[193]

The rewards of peace: Literary pursuits and internal security

Supplied with nearly five thousand men who had passed at least one level of the civil service examinations,[194] T'ai-tsung began producing a bureaucratic regime dominated by civil officials. Of the top posts in the central government, all the chief councilors except Chao P'u possessed high academic credentials and examination degrees. In T'ai-tsung's reign only six of the twenty-two finance commissioners came from the military, and twenty-one (or 60 percent) of the thirty-five commissioners or assistant commissioners of the Bureau of Military Affairs had civil ranks, of whom eleven held the highest *chin-shih* degree.[195]

Himself a poet and a famous calligrapher,[196] T'ai-tsung founded three new imperial libraries and the Historiography Institute. He also initiated the compilation of what are know as the *Four great compendia of the Sung dynasty* (*Sung ssu ta shu*).[197]

The first of these four great works, the *T'ai-p'ing yü-lan* (*Imperial encyclopedia of the T'ai-p'ing hsing-kuo era*), in one thousand *chüan* (chapters), was compiled over almost six years (977–82) by seventeen officials, of whom at least four were former officials of the Later Chou and seven of the Southern T'ang.[198] In order to provide a broad foundation of general knowledge, the encyclopedia was organized in fifty-five categories according to the traditional conception of

---

[193] Labadie, "Rulers and soldiers," pp. 90–8; Ang, "Sung-Liao diplomacy in eleventh- and twelfth-century China," pp. 72–4; Wang, "The rhetoric of a lesser empire," pp. 47–65, especially pp. 52–4; Tao, "Barbarians or northerners," pp. 66–86, especially pp. 75–9.

[194] Araki, "Sō Taiso sakekuse kō," pp. 451–2; Chaffee, *The thorny gates of learning in Sung China*, p. 192.

[195] Worthy, "The founding of Sung China," p. 306; Ko, "Pei Sung chih san-ssu-shih," pp. 7–10; Liang, *Sung shu-mi-yüan chih-tu*. Worthy's figures differ from Ko's, but both indicate a large number of civil officials.

[196] Liu, "Pei Sung ch'ien-ch'i huang-ch'üan fa-chan chih yen-chiu," pp. 98–9.

[197] The following survey of these four compendia, unsurpassed in scope until the production of the *Yung-lo ta tien* (*Encyclopedia of the Yung-lo era*, compiled in 1408) of the Ming dynasty (1368–1644), is based on Kuo Po-kung, *Sung ssu-ta-shu k'ao* (Taipei, 1967); John W. Haeger, "The significance of confusion: The origin of the T'ai-p'ing yü-lan," *Journal of the American Oriental Society* 88 No. 3 (1968), pp. 401–10; Teng Ssu-yu and Knight Biggerstaff, *An annotated bibliography of selected Chinese reference works*, 3rd ed. (Cambridge, Mass., 1971); and Yves Hervouet, ed., *A Sung bibliography (Bibliographie des Sung)* (Hong Kong, 1978).

[198] The completion date is still not clear, but the work was presented to T'ai-tsung in 982; see Kuo, *Sung ssu-ta-shu k'ao*, pp. 8–11; Haeger, "The significance of confusion," pp. 401–3, 407; and Johannes L. Kurz, "The politics of collecting knowledge: Song Taizong's compilations project," *T'oung Pao* 87 No. 4–5 (2001), pp. 289–316.

the world order, beginning with Heaven, and covering such categories as time, Earth, legitimate sovereigns, medicines, and flowers. The *T'ai-p'ing yü-lan* is now the only source for a great number of pre-Sung texts, as nearly eighty percent of the 2,579 works that it quotes and two of the three collectanea from which it was compiled are lost today. This compilation was a forerunner of such later compilations as the Ming dynasty *Yung-lo ta-tien* (*Encyclopedia of the Yung-lo era*, 1408) and the Ch'ing dynasty *Ch'in-ting ku-chin tu-shu chi-cheng* (*Imperially approved synthesis of books and illustrations past and present*, 1726–8). T'ai-tsung himself read three *chüan* a day to complete the entire work in one year, suggesting corrections throughout and proudly comparing himself to a scholar working hard on ten thousand *chüan* of books.

The *T'ai-p'ing kuang-chi* (*Extensive records of the T'ai-p'ing hsing-kuo era*), in five hundred *chüan*, was compiled in one and a half years (977–9) by the same officials who had worked on the *T'ai-p'ing yü-lan*. Most of the 475 works anthologized in the *T'ai-p'ing kuang-chi* – overwhelmingly historical novels, short stories, and other "unorthodox" writings from the Han dynasty (206 B.C.E.–220 C.E.), the Six Dynasties (220–589), and particularly the T'ang dynasty – are lost today. Its ninety-two subject categories included Taoist arts, Buddhist tales of reward and retribution, tales of immoral acts, dreams, oddities and grotesques, and the like. Aside from its literary value, it is an excellent source of material on the mythology, religion, ethnology, and natural history of early China.

The *Wen-yüan ying-hua* (*Finest blossoms from the garden of elegant writing*), in one thousand *chüan*, was finished in fifty-one months, spanning 982 to 987. Of its twenty-two compilers, the three from the Later Chou and four of the five from the Southern T'ang were replaced during their work on the compendium by new personnel who had passed the civil service examination under the Sung. As a continuation of the *Wen-hsüan* (*Anthology of literature*) compiled in the sixth century by Hsiao T'ung (better known as Prince Chao-ming, 501–53), this anthology subsumed, under thirty-seven genres, nearly twenty thousand pieces of poetry and prose written by 2,200 authors. Ninety percent of these works were T'ang products.

Conceived by T'ai-tsung and completed under his successor Chen-tsung, the *Ts'e-fu yüan-kuei* (*Outstanding models from the storehouse of literature*), in one thousand *chüan*, supplemented these other three great compilations with a major work of historical synthesis. It was compiled in eight years (1005–13) by eighteen officials, half of whom were southerners. In order to give an authoritative account of the histories of pre-Sung emperors and ranking officials, the compilers took great pains to exhaustively comb the standard histories and classics, producing an indispensable source for the study of the government and political history of the T'ang and the Five Dynasties.[199] Chen-tsung actively participated in the editing, especially in including in the work overt moral judgments concerning past events, which later influenced Ssu-ma Kuang (1019–86) in his compilation of the *Tzu-chih t'ung-chien* (*Comprehensive mirror to aid in government*, comp. 1067–84), and which reflected the rise of imperial absolutism that characterized the Sung period. The book's thirty-one sections were arranged in the topical framework similar to that used in the compilation of the official *hui-yao* (*Compendium of the institutions of the dynasty*) since the T'ang period.

T'ai-tsung's encyclopedic projects not only satisfied his literary interests (or what some have termed his "bibliomania") but also justified his first reign title, T'ai-p'ing hsing-kuo (Ascendent State in Grand Tranquility), which implied his superiority to his brother. From the dynasty's perspective, the compilation projects also served to provide work and titles for the officials of the various newly conquered southern states, while also affording a career path for the rising scholar-officials of the new dynasty. Just as the civil service examination helped replace holdovers from former dynasties with new Sung officials, the editing of the encyclopedias allowed Sung scholars and their emperor to appropriate the achievements of the past, thus paving the way for the emergence of a new culture that favored literary pursuits over martial endeavors and values.[200]

Literary pursuits were interrupted in 993, when the first extensive peasant rebellion of the Sung dynasty broke out in Szechwan. Ever since its submission in 965, this remote region had experienced years of popular unrest, first triggered by the brutality of the Sung expeditionary troops during the original conquest. Their rapacity had provoked an uprising that took almost two years to suppress, and local resentment was kept alive by taxation of the region's salt, brocade, and tea industries and heavy-handed state intervention that seriously disrupted Szechwan's regional economy.[201] The rebels, driven by the severe drought of 993 and excited by a slogan proclaiming the equalization

---

[199] Teng and Biggerstaff, *An annotated bibliography of selected Chinese reference works*, p. 89.

[200] The *T'ai-p'ing yü-lan* was popular from the eleventh century on; see Haeger, "The significance of confusion," pp. 406–7. The *T'ai-p'ing kuang-chi*, because it contained a huge collection of prose narratives, many of them fictional, was scarcely circulated until 1566; see Kuo, *Sung ssu-ta-shu k'ao*, pp. 66–73. The *Ts'e-fu yüan-kuei* was first printed in 1015, almost two centuries before the printing of the *Wen-yüan ying-hua* in 1204; see Kuo, *Sung ssu-ta-shu k'ao*, p. 95, 129.

[201] This rebellion in Szechwan is generally but wrongly attributed to the governmental monopoly of the tea business, which in fact did not exist until 1076. See Ssu-ch'uan ta-hsüeh li-shih-hsi "Wang Hsiao-p'o Li Shun ch'i-i" tiao-ch'a tsu-pien, *Wang Hsiao-p'o Li Shun ch'i-i tzu-liao hui-pien* (Ch'eng-tu, 1978), pp. 126–39; Richard von Glahn, *The country of streams and grottoes: Expansion, settlement, and the civilizing of the Sichuan frontier in Song times* (Cambridge, Mass., 1987), pp. 76–7; and Smith, *Taxing heaven's storehouse*, pp. 93–101.

of wealth, captured city after city, under the leadership of Wang Hsiao-po (?–993), a small-scale tea planter. Wang died during the fighting. In 994, however, his brother-in-law Li Shun (?–c. 994) rebelled and proclaimed an independent Ta Shu state in the regional capital of I-chou2 (modern Ch'eng-tu), establishing government institutions, a monetary system, and even ties with its neighbor state, the Nan-chao in Yunnan.

Shaken by the ferocity of the rebellion, T'ai-tsung gave free rein in the pacification campaign to the loyal and battle-experienced eunuch general Wang Chi-en (?–999), whose eunuch status and proven loyalty reduced the risk of his creating a personal power base in Szechwan and using the turmoil against T'ai-tsung. Yet despite Wang Chi-en's long experience in previous wars, he nearly reproduced the tragedy of the initial Sung conquest of Szechwan thirty years before. After crushing the main force of the Wang Hsiao-po rebellion, Wang Chi-en came close to losing the region again when some prefectures and counties fell back into rebel hands while Wang indulged himself in feasting and his troops engaged in an orgy of looting. It was only after T'ai-tsung assigned some able officials to assist him that Wang finally mopped up the remnants of the rebellion and restored order in 995.[202]

Following the Szechwan rebellion some of the most flagrant forms of misgovernment by local officials were corrected and extortionate taxes were reduced. At the same time, the number of circuits into which Szechwan was divided doubled from two to four to strengthen centralized control of the region. Since tensions were still running high, some of the counterrebellion measures that had been suspended elsewhere in the empire were reinstituted in Szechwan. To prevent self-entrenchment, court officials serving there were not allowed to bring along their families, and until the mid-eleventh century Szechwan natives were so strictly subjected to the rule prohibiting officials from serving in their home provinces that the officials were not even permitted to retire to their ancestral homes.[203]

Tragedy and the problems of succession

When T'ai-tsung died in 997 there was no longer any competition for the throne from his younger brother Chao T'ing-mei (947–84) or from T'ai-tsu's sons Chao Te-chao (d. 979) and Chao Te-fang (d. 981), all of whom were long dead. Although Te-fang's death from illness was sad, the death of T'ing-mei

[202] SS 466, pp. 13602–4.
[203] Lo Wen (Winston W. Lo), Szechwan in Sung China: A case study in the political integration of the Chinese empire (Taipei, 1982), pp. 25–6; Lo, Introduction to the civil service of Sung China, pp. 204–5; von Glahn, Country of streams and grottoes, p. 63. For the reversal of the rule prohibiting Szechwanese from serving in their home region, see Smith, Taxing heaven's storehouse, pp. 99–108.

and especially that of Te-chao can be regarded as tragic.[204] On the night of
T'ai-tsung's defeat at the Kao-liang River in 979, some troops, presuming that
the missing T'ai-tsung was lost or dead, speculated that T'ai-tsu's son Te-chao
should be proclaimed emperor on the spot. T'ai-tsung was infuriated by this,
and when on their return to the capital Te-chao requested the expeditionary
troops be granted their suspended rewards, T'ai-tsung exploded, "It won't be
too late to grant the rewards when you yourself become [emperor]" (*tai ju tzu
wei chih shang wei wan yeh*).[205] Terrified, Chao Te-chao committed suicide with
a kitchen knife.

Chao T'ing-mei's elimination was more indirect. Only seven days after T'ai-
tsung's accession to the throne, T'ing-mei was made a prince and appointed to
T'ai-tsung's former position as governor of K'ai-feng. In addition, T'ing-mei
was given court standing above the chief councilors, and his children were
officially called "imperial sons" (*huang-tzu*) and "imperial daughters" (*huang-
nü*).[206] At least in appearance, T'ing-mei had become T'ai-tsung's intended
successor.[207] In a few years, however, T'ing-mei would lose everything as a
result of accusations against him.

In 981, T'ai-tsung heard rumors that T'ing-mei was hatching a conspiracy,
and the emperor reappointed Chao P'u as chief councilor with the specific
task of exposing the plot.[208] Early the next year T'ing-mei was accused of
conspiring to overthrow T'ai-tsung. Instead of being executed, however, he
was transferred from the governorship of K'ai-feng to the regency of Lo-yang.
His "plot" was allegedly kept secret by T'ai-tsung, who even granted him a
generous travel allowance and an official farewell feast.[209] But rather than let
the scandal die down, Chao P'u tried to capitalize on it to secure the downfall
both of T'ing-mei and of his own life-long rival, Chief Councilor Lu To-hsün
(934–85), by accusing them of forming a clique. Upon the "self-confessions" of
Lu and some clerks who allegedly had transmitted secrets from the Secretariat-
Chancellery to T'ing-mei, seventy-four court officials found Lu and T'ing-mei

---

[204] These events are recounted in Chaffee, *Branches of heaven*, pp. 25–30.

[205] *HCP* (1964) 20, pp. 15b–16a; *SS* 244, p. 8676. The ambiguous Chinese original can also be interpreted
as "when you make yourself [emperor]." Perhaps punctuating after "shang," Curtis Chung Chang
translates the passage as "It would not be too late if some day you could reward them yourself." See
Chang, "Inheritance problems in the first two reigns of the Sung dynasty," p. 20.

[206] *HCP* (1964) 17, pp. 18a, 19a.

[207] Wang, "Sung ch'u erh-ti ch'üan-wei wen-t'i ti p'ou-hsi," p. 18. Teng, "Sung T'ai-tsu T'ai-tsung shou-
shou pien," p. 181, suspects that it was a deal made between T'ai-tsung and T'ing-mei to isolate
Te-chao. Curtis Chung Chang maintains that it was a political gesture showing to the public that T'ai-
tsung's precedent of fraternal succession was legitimate and thus to be followed; see Chang, "Inheritance
problems in the first two reigns of the Sung dynasty," p. 23.

[208] *HCP* (1964) 22, p. 11b.

[209] *HCP* (1964) 23, pp. 3a–b.

deserving of execution for their covetousness and for wishing an early death upon T'ai-tsung. All the clerks were executed, and Lu was exiled to Yai-chou, on Hainan Island. T'ing-mei was first put under house arrest and, after several days, having been charged with being unrepentant and resentful, was exiled to Fang-chou; his sons were demoted to the position of "imperial nephews" (*huang-chih*).[210]

Under the watchful eyes of T'ai-tsung's special custodians, the thirty-seven-year-old T'ing-mei died of fear and grief on an unknown date in 984.[211] Later, T'ai-tsung denigrated T'ing-mei to his councilors, claiming that T'ing-mei had been only his half brother, born to his wet nurse; but this contradicts Dowager Empress Tu's biography in the *Sung dynastic history* (*Sung shih*).[212]

The tragedy in the Chao clan continued. T'ai-tsung's eldest son, Yüan-tso (965–1027), who alone had remonstrated against T'ing-mei's exile, was driven insane by his uncle's unjust death. While he was recuperating in 985, he was not invited to the family gathering for the Autumn Festival. Feeling deserted, he got drunk and set fire to the palace. As punishment he was reduced in rank to that of a commoner.[213] In the same year T'ai-tsung's second son, Yüan-hsi (966–92), was made prince and governor of K'ai-feng. Majestic and self-possessed, his conduct as governor was considered impeccable, and he was greatly loved by T'ai-tsung. In 992, however, he died of a sudden illness in T'ai-tsung's presence, and his father then spent many sleepless nights lamenting his death and composing elegies.[214] For the next two years none of the remaining six sons of T'ai-tsung was given the K'ai-feng governorship that designated status as heir apparent. In the meantime, no officials dared memorialize T'ai-tsung about the succession question. In any event, it is noteworthy that none of Tai-tsu's descendants came under consideration. T'ai-tsung had made his own branch of the family the imperial line. In 994, as the old arrow wounds of the aging emperor troubled him more and because the thirty-four-year-old Empress Li (960–1004) remained barren, T'ai-tsung's third son, Chao Heng (968–1022), was appointed governor of K'ai-feng at the age of twenty-six

---

[210] *HCP* (1964) 23, pp. 4b–5a, 5b–6a, 8a. There is no extant evidence supporting the accusations, which were likely to have been invented by Chao P'u and T'ai-tsung's confidants; see *SS* 244, p. 8669; Ku, "Sung-tai chi-ch'eng wen-t'i shang-ch'üeh," pp. 94–5; Wang, "Sung ch'u erh-ti ch'üan-wei wen-t'i ti p'ou-hsi," p. 21; Chang, "Inheritance problems in the first two reigns of the Sung dynasty," pp. 24–6.

[211] *HCP* (1964) 23, p. 8a; 25, p. 1b; Wang, "Sung ch'u erh-ti ch'üan-wei wen-t'i ti p'ou-hsi," p. 20.

[212] *HCP* (1964) 25, pp. 1b–2a; *SS* 242, p. 8606. Although Li T'ao loyally believed T'ai-tsung's account (*HCP* [1964] 2, pp. 8b–9a), most historians discount it as a flat-out lie; see Ku, "Sung-tai chi-ch'eng wen-t'i shang-ch'üeh," pp. 97–8; Wang, "Sung ch'u erh-ti ch'üan-wei wen-t'i ti p'ou-hsi," p. 19.

[213] *SS* 245, p. 8694; *HCP* (1964) 26, pp. 4a–5a.

[214] This title was later withheld, mainly for the past misbehavior of a concubine of this son; see *SS* 245, pp. 8697–8; *HCP* (1964) 33, pp. 8a–b. The son had once been impeached by a censor and punished accordingly, but the impeachment is not extant; see *HCP* (1964) 29, p. 9a.

and elevated to heir apparent the next year. It is recorded that T'ai-tsung was initially displeased by the popularity of the new heir apparent, although he was finally coaxed into accepting it as evidence that he had made the right decision.[215] Two years later, T'ai-tsung died, and Chao Heng (posthumous name Chen-tsung) succeeded to the throne.

A NEW TYPE OF EMPEROR: THE DIFFIDENT CHEN-TSUNG, 997–1022

Compared with the founders as well as the senior officials of the Sung, the thirty-year-old new emperor, Chen-tsung (r. 997–1022), was indeed a beginner, with merely two years of administrative experience as the governor of K'ai-feng. His father had once said, "My children are brought up in the seclusion of the palace. Without knowing the affairs of the world, they will need the advice and guidance of good scholars."[216] While scholars lectured them on the merits of entrusting the administration to the councilors and of respecting the opinion of the officials, T'ai-tsung himself taught his sons to be modest, even ordering the heir apparent to stand below the chief councilors at court; to treat his tutors with deference; and to respect the counsel of subordinates during his governorship of K'ai-feng, which indeed was closely watched by T'ai-tsung himself.[217] However, long before he finished providing the guidance he thought his sons needed, T'ai-tsung died of illness in the seclusion of the inner palace, leaving the heir apparent at the mercy of a conspiracy.

Influenced by Wang Chi-en, Assistant Councilor Li Ch'ang-ling (937–1008), and drafter Hu Tan (*chin shih* 978), Empress Li sent Wang Chi-en to seek agreement from Chief Councilor Lü Tuan (935–1000) to replace the heir apparent with his eldest brother. Instead, Lü Tuan locked Wang Chi-en up and protested to the empress that T'ai-tsung's will could not be reversed by her claim of primogeniture. In the succession ceremony, to ensure that the new emperor really was Chen-tsung, Lü Tuan ordered the removal of the throne screen, approached the throne, looked carefully at the occupant, and only then led the court to cheer the emperor. In the following two months, the three conspirators were sent into exile: Hu Tan for improperly drafting a commemorative edict, Li Ch'ing-ling for lobbying in the court, and Wang

---

[215] *HCP* (1964) 36, p. 12b; 38, pp. 1b–2b, which also recorded that T'ai-tsung made the choice in a private meeting with Assisting Councilor K'ou Chun (961–1023). See also Chang, "Inheritance problems in the first two reigns of the Sung dynasty," pp. 31–2.

[216] Quoted from Liu, "An administrative cycle in Chinese history," p. 142. Liu, "Pei Sung ch'ien-ch'i huang-ch'üan fa-chan chih yen-chiu," pp. 137–8.

[217] Liu, "An administrative cycle in Chinese history," p. 142; Olsson, "The structure of power under the third emperor of Sung China," pp. 40–1; Liu, "Pei Sung ch'ien-ch'i huang-ch'üan fa-chan chih yen-chiu," pp. 139–41.

Chi-en for deceit and forming a clique.[218] The mystery and details surrounding this conspiracy, which was recorded by Lü Tuan's family and by Ssu-ma Kuang, may never be solved,[219] but the banishment of one assistant councilor and one powerful eunuch was enough to boost Chen-tsung's authority.

In fact, the new emperor worked hard to appear strong. Twelve days after his enthronement, when the vice-minister of works, also a respected member of his royal staff, declined a new appointment, Chen-tsung disallowed the refusal, telling the state councilors who recommended following precedents for accepting the refusal that a new emperor should be firm in his orders.[220] Early in his reign, Chen-tsung tried hard to emulate almost everything that his father had done during his prime. Chen-tsung even attempted to interest himself in military affairs, inspecting the borders as a ceremonial matter and drawing up diagrams of battle formations with senior generals.[221] However, though giving him energy, his youth, coupled with his inexperience and the limited training he had received, made Chen-tsung somewhat diffident and deferential.

The new emperor respected the chief councilors, especially Lü Tuan, whose style was to pay little attention to small matters, but to focus on big issues and to emphasize stability in the court and the bureaucracy. Although the emperor still insisted on separating civil and military authorities, he sanctioned venues for the Bureau of Military Affairs and the Secretariat-Chancellery to exchange important information. Chen-tsung was exceptionally tolerant of private contacts between high officials, allowing them to entertain visitors in their homes.[222] With such a trusting nature, Chen-tsung tended to delegate more and more authority to his officials.

In a meeting with the state councilors in 1001, Chen-tsung claimed that he always discussed state affairs, however big or small, with them, and never made decisions alone.[223] In 1003, the three sections of the Finance Commission (the Salt and Iron Monopoly Bureau, the Tax Bureau, and the Census Bureau), which T'ai-tsung had separated to increase imperial control over financial policies, were recombined under the single leadership of the commissioner, so that Chen-tsung could shed the burden of coordinating the suggestions from each

---

[218] *HCP* (1964) 41, pp. 3a–b, 5a, 5b–6b; *SS* 281, pp. 9516, 9535 n. 2.

[219] *HCP* (1964) 41, pp. 3a–b; Ssu-ma, *Su-shui chi-wen* 6, pp. 62–3. Although Ku Chi-kuang in his "Sung-tai chi-ch'eng wen-t'i shang-ch'üeh," pp. 99–104, has attempted to solve the mystery of this alleged conspiracy, it is almost impossible to do so because of the scarcity of evidence.

[220] Liu, "Pei Sung ch'ien-ch'i huang-ch'üan fa-chan chih yen-chiu," pp. 142–3.

[221] Olsson, "The structure of power under the third emperor of Sung China," pp. 48–51; Liu, "Pei Sung ch'ien-ch'i huang-ch'üan fa-chan chih yen-chiu," pp. 145–7, 164–6.

[222] Olsson, "The structure of power under the third emperor of Sung China," pp. 40, 114–15; Liu, "Pei Sung ch'ien-ch'i huang-ch'üan fa-chan chih yen-chiu," p. 136.

[223] *HCP* (1964) 49, p. 2b.

branch of the commission.[224] This tendency to delegate and to consolidate authority accelerated after the ever-present threat from the Liao was eased by a peace agreement in 1005.

Appeasement and the peace of Shan-yüan

In 1004 the Liao launched their largest invasion of Sung territory since 946. The Liao army, under the command of Dowager Empress Hsiao and Emperor Sheng-tsung, was reportedly made up of two hundred thousand crack troops, and penetrated Ho-pei in sixty days, reaching the outskirts of Shan-yüan (or Shan-chou, modern P'u-yang), less than two hundred miles from K'ai-feng. The Liao's objectives, which undoubtedly affected the nature of the peace agreement of 1005, should be understood from the Liao's perspective. After they had taken revenge for T'ai-tsung's two large-scale invasions, the Liao had three options in dealing with the Sung: they could continue their short-range raids across Sung borders; they could immediately try to obtain an advantageous peace settlement; or, they could try to obtain peace by continuing and intensifying the war.

The first alternative was increasingly difficult to carry out, since the Sung had strengthened their defenses by creating swamps and waterways that bogged down the Liao cavalry.[225] In 989, for example, the famous Liao general Yeh-lü Hsiu-ko was so seriously wounded during one foray that he had to desert his troops.[226] In 999, one year after the death of Yeh-lü Hsiu-ko, another hero in the victories over the last two Sung expeditions, Yeh-lü Hsieh-chen, also passed away.[227] In the three years from 999 to 1001, almost all major Liao attacks either incurred heavy losses or were turned back without significant gain.[228] Moreover, Chen-tsung's inspection trips to the border and his exiling of a cowardly commander in chief helped boost Sung troop morale.[229] With fewer victories and more defeats, the Liao faced a choice between either

---

[224] Olsson, "The structure of power under the third emperor of Sung China," p. 57; Liu, "Pei Sung ch'ien-ch'i huang-ch'üan fa-chan chih yen-chiu," p. 148.

[225] Yen Ch'in-heng, "Pei Sung tui Liao t'ang-ti she-shih chih yen-chiu," *Kuo-li Cheng-chih ta-hsüeh hsüeh-pao* 8 (1963), pp. 247–58.

[226] *HCP* (1964) 30, pp. 15b–16a; Ch'en et al., *Sung-shih chi-shih pen-mo* 13, pp. 90–1. Akisada Jitsuzō [Tamura Jitsuzō], "Sen-en no meiyaku to sono shiteki igi (jō)," *Shirin* 20 No. 1 (1935), pp. 7–8.

[227] For comments on their contributions, see T'o-t'o et al., *Liao shih* 83, p. 1305.

[228] For details of these battles, see Ch'eng Kuang-yü, "Shan-yüan chih-meng yü t'ien-shu (shang)," *Ta-lu tsa-chih* 22 No. 6 (1961), pp. 11–13; Wang Min-hsin, "Liao Sung Shan-yüan meng-yüeh ti-chieh ti pei-ching (chung)," *Chung-kuo shu-mu chi-k'an* 9 No. 3 (1975), pp. 46–50. Ch'eng Kuang-yu compares the *Sung shih*, the *Hsü Tzu-chih t'ung-chien ch'ang-pien*, and the *Liao shih* to give careful accounts of the Sung-Liao encounters.

[229] Wang, "Liao Sung Shan-yüan meng-yüeh ti-chieh ti pei-ching (chung)," pp. 47–8, 52.

abandoning their strategy of having a buffer zone between the two states or paying an unpredictably high price to maintain that buffer. Since either choice jeopardized Liao security, a different alternative had to be found.[230]

After T'ai-tsung died, the Liao seemed to be willing to maintain the buffer zone despite the cost. However, given the danger from the last two Sung invasions, the Liao considered that any permanent peace should be predicated upon Sung renunciation of irredentism and should require Sung to recognize Liao sovereignty over the strategic Yen-Yün region and to return the area south of the mountain passes – that is, the so-called Kuan-nan (south of the passes) area in Ho-pei that the Later Chou had reconquered.[231] Permanent peace to the Liao, however, meant permanent menace to the Sung. Even without these incompatible diplomatic objectives, the door to negotiation was temporarily closed. Upon ascending the throne, Chen-tsung had ordered Ho Ch'eng-chü (946–1006), a veteran border official, to inform the Liao of T'ai-tsung's death and of Chen-tsung's desire for peace, but the Sung had received no response.[232] The Sung court did not make any further initiative for peace. Fearing Liao infiltration, the Sung court turned down the suggestion from some officials to reopen border markets to trade tea with the Khitan. In 1002, perhaps as a probe, the Liao requested the opening of border markets that had all been closed in 991.[233] Annoyed by intermittent Liao attacks, the Sung court refused. It was only upon the later insistence of Ho Ch'eng-chü that one market was opened.[234] The next year, to prevent Khitan espionage, the market was again closed,[235] as was the channel to reconciliation.

In the following year (1004), the Liao attempted to resolve their dilemma by implementing a third alternative – to achieve an advantageous peace by means of war – but their timing was bad. In the fourth month of the previous year they had captured Wang Chi-chung (?–1023), a high-ranking border general and, more important, a long-time confidant of Chen-tsung. Wang's capture greatly alarmed the Sung. Assuming that Wang Chi-chung had been killed in action, Chen-tsung severely punished two chief commanders for their desertion of Wang. Chen-tsung also solicited frontier policies from the court and from border officials, which enhanced "the visibility and influence enjoyed by

---

[230] *HCP* 57, p. 15b, states that Dowager Empress Hsiao "is tired of wars."

[231] The Liao apprehension of another Sung expedition to recover the Yen-Yün region was an important component of the 1004 invasion: *HCP* (1964) 57, p. 16a. For comments on the threat of T'ai-tsung's two expeditions to the Liao, see T'o-t'o et al., *Liao-shih* 83, p. 1305. For a comparison of the strength of Sung and Liao, see *Liao-shih* 36, p. 433; 48, p. 828.

[232] *SS* 273, p. 9329; *HCP* (1964) 44, pp. 14b–15a.

[233] *SS* 277, pp. 9420–1. For the closing of the border markets in 991, see *SS* 186, p. 4562.

[234] *HCP* (1964) 51, p. 19b.

[235] *HCP* (1964) 54, p. 16b.

high-ranking generals in policy discussions."[236] The Bureau of Military Affairs
and the Secretariat-Chancellery were allowed joint discussion on these matters.[237] Old strategies were adjusted, new commanders were appointed, and
Chen-tsung was prepared to lead a counterattack in person. From the autumn
of 1003 to late summer of 1004, in anticipation of Khitan invasions, the Sung
went on the highest alert.[238]

Sung preparedness paid off. At least one month before its start, the Khitan expedition was detected by Sung intelligence units. After conferring with
the Secretariat-Chancellery and the Bureau of Military Affairs, Chen-tsung
accepted the suggestion of Chief Councilor Pi Shih-an (938–1005) to lead
a counterattack in winter, looking forward to a victory that could end the
Liao incursions once and for all. Chen-tsung also ordered close coordination among these officials and sent additional rewards and provisions to the
front.[239]

No longer a mere episode of border warfare, the Liao invasion force, at the
risk of exposing its rear, penetrated rapidly and deeply into Ho-pei; easily
breaking through the first defensive line on the Sung frontier, the Liao overran
ten prefectures, but captured only two of the ten prefectural cites it attacked.[240]
Ahead lay no more than a thin deployment of Sung infantry covering a plain
stretching some hundred miles to K'ai-feng.[241] Shocked by the Liao approach,
uncertain of its aims, and frightened by the inflow of distress messages (as many
as five on some days), most court officials urged the wavering Chen-tsung to
escape. However, he was eventually persuaded by Chief Councilor K'ou Chun
(961–1023) to personally lead the army at Shan-yüan.

On the battlefield, Liao troops began to meet strong resistance from the
Sung defense forces, headed by Chen-tsung himself, who had been convinced
by some court officials to take the lead. The invasion's close approach to K'ai-
feng and the memory that during the Five Dynasties period a Liao army
had occupied K'ai-feng alarmed the Sung court. But in northern Ho-pei an
all-out Liao offensive had failed to capture the strategic strongholds of Ting-
chou (modern Ting county in Hopei). Then the Liao dowager empress Hsiao
beat the war drum herself to launch day-long attacks on another vital Sung

---

[236] Labadie, "Rulers and soldiers," pp. 66–7; see also pp. 62, 204.

[237] *HCP* (1964) 54, pp. 17b–20a.

[238] Wang Min-hsin, "Liao Sung Shan-yüan meng-yüeh ti-chieh ti pei-ching (hsia)," *Chung-kuo shu-mu chi-k'an* 9 No. 4 (1975), pp. 54–7.

[239] *HCP* (1964) 57, pp. 5b–6a; Wang, "Liao Sung Shan-yüan meng-yüeh ti-chieh ti pei-ching (hsia)," pp. 57–9.

[240] Wang, "Liao Sung Shan-yüan meng-yüeh ti-chieh ti pei-ching (hsia)," pp. 59–60.

[241] *HCP* (1964) 57, pp. 13b–14b; 8, p. 7b; Wang Min-hsin, "Shan-yüan ti-meng chih chien-t'ao," *Shih-huo yüeh-k'an* 5 No. 3 (1975), pp. 6–7.

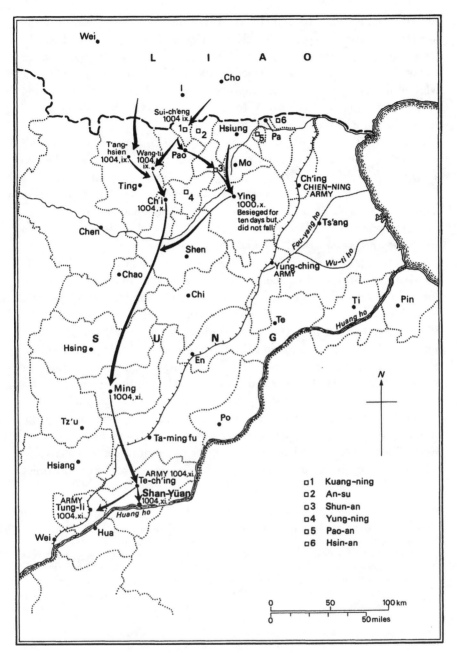

Map 12. Liao invasion of the Sung, 1004.

military stronghold, Ying-chou (modern Ho-chien in Hopei). She reportedly lost thirty thousand troops within three weeks, again in vain.[242] At about the same time, Sung border garrisons took the offensive, some closing in on the rear of the advancing Liao expedition. They succeeded in occasional ambushes, while other garrisons took the offensive, crossing the frontier and scoring minor victories against the Liao.[243] Meanwhile, Wang Chi-chung's "personal" appeal for peace had reached Chen-tsung.

The role in the peace negotiations of Wang Chi-chung is controversial.[244] It is certain that Wang revealed to the Liao dowager empress that he had a close relationship with the Sung emperor. She then appointed him Tax Commissioner and married him to a woman of her own clan.[245] It is very likely that Dowager Empress Hsiao recognized Wang's potential usefulness in initiating peace negotiations with the Sung court, and made use of him. In any event, the Liao initiated the peace negotiations.[246]

Chen-tsung, for his part, was willing to buy off the Liao, but not to cede the Kuan-nan area south of the mountain passes.[247] In his second appeal to the Sung court, Wang Chi-chung emphasized the importance of this area to the Liao and requested that Chen-tsung send a negotiator first.[248] But the Sung envoy, Ts'ao Li-yung (?–1029), was already on his way when the Liao again attacked Ying-chou, in an attempt to increase their bargaining power. Shortly afterward, just as Chen-tsung was leading his army out to confront the invaders, Dowager Empress Hsiao announced her willingness to negotiate peace.[249]

The Liao's growing anxiousness for a settlement was accelerated by the accidental death of their leading general, a cousin of Dowager Empress Hsiao, Hsiao T'a-lan (?–1004), who was struck by an arrow during a reconnaissance mission.[250] In contrast, Sung troop morale was greatly boosted by Chen-tsung's

---

[242] HCP (1964) 57, pp. 17a–b; 58, pp. 1b–3a, 5a.

[243] HCP (1964) 57, pp. 17a–b; 58, pp. 1b–3a, 5a.

[244] Chiang Fu-ts'ung asserts that Wang Chi-chung's capture was planned by Chen-tsung and his advisors as an important step toward peace negotiations; see Chiang Fu-ts'ung, "Sung Chen-tsung yü Shan-yüan chih-meng (shang)," Ta-lu tsa-chih 22 No. 8 (1961), pp. 26–30; Chiang Fu-ts'ung, "Sung Chen-tsung yü Shan-yüan chih-meng (hsü)," Ta-lu tsa-chih 22 No. 9 (1961), pp. 27–34; Chiang Fu-ts'ung, "Sung Chen-tsung yü Shan-yüan chih-meng (mo)," Ta-lu tsa-chih 22 No. 10 (1961), pp. 32–6. But Wang Min-hsin persuasively discounts this in his "Shan-yüan ti-meng chih chien-t'ao," pp. 3–5, 8–9; see also his "Liao Sung Shan-yüan meng-yüeh ti-chieh ti pei-ching (shang)," pp. 43–4.

[245] HCP (1964) 57, p. 16a; T'o-t'o et al., Liao shih 81, p. 284.

[246] For arguments about which dynasty took the initiative for peace, see Akisada, "Sen-en no meiyaku to sono shiteki igi (jō)," p. 19; Wang, "Shan-yüan ti-meng chih chien-t'ao," pp. 2–5.

[247] HCP (1964) 57, pp. 16a–b.

[248] HCP (1964) 58, p. 5b.

[249] T'o-t'o et al., Liao shih 14, p. 160.

[250] HCP (1964) 58, pp. 9b, 11b–12a.

appearance at the front.[251] After two sessions of negotiations failed to reach an accord on the issue of sovereignty over Kuan-nan, the Liao plundered a nearby prefecture, but then showed signs of retreating. Chen-tsung, also tired of fighting, prepared to return to K'ai-feng.[252] In the third round of negotiations, the Liao assertion that their main objective was the recovery of the Kuan-nan area was again rejected. However, the Liao accepted the Sung offer of annual payments. They stated their conditions through a confidential petition from Wang Chi-chung directly to Chen-tsung. The conditions outlined in this petition became the foundation of the so-called Treaty of Shan-yüan:

1. The establishment of friendly relations between the two states
2. Annual payments to the Liao of one hundred thousand taels of silver and two hundred thousand bolts of silk
3. The demarcation of borders that would be mutually respected
4. The agreement that both sides would repatriate fugitives from justice
5. The agreement that neither side would disturb the farmland and crops of the other
6. The agreement that neither side would construct new fortifications and canals along the border
7. The pledge of a solemn oath whose contravention would bring about religious sanctions[253]

The treaty was costly to the Sung, in territory and in long-term security. Article 3 annulled Sung claims to the land and to jurisdiction over the Han Chinese in the major part of the Yen-Yün region. It dampened all Sung hopes of recovering this critically strategic region and precluded the basic military activity required to do so. It also left a legacy of revanchism at the Sung court, which became politically divisive. As the reformer Fan Chung-yen (989–1052) later exclaimed, "Yen and Yün are lost. This is the greatest insult inflicted on China by the barbarians in a thousand years, but it has not been avenged."[254] Article 4 of the treaty prohibited the Sung from accepting into their service Liao officials, who had been deserting in increasing numbers, bringing valuable skills and information with them.[255] Article 6 undermined

---

[251] The *Liao shih* ascribes the Liao acceptance of the 1005 peace treaty to the death of Hsiao T'a-lan; see T'o-t'o et al., *Liao shih* 85, p. 1319. See also *HCP* (1964) 58, pp. 12b, 15a.

[252] *HCP* (1964) 58, pp. 13a–14b, 15b. Tao, *Two sons of heaven*, p. 15, blames the conclusion of the "humiliating" treaty of 1005 on Chen-tsung's weak leadership, which negated the military advantages of the Sung.

[253] *HCP* (1964) 58, pp. 15a–17b, 22a–23b; the translation is taken from Tao, "Barbarians or northerners," p. 68; Wang, "The rhetoric of a lesser empire," p. 51.

[254] Quoted from Tao, "Barbarians or northerners," p. 79.

[255] See Chiang, "Sung Chen-tsung yü Shan-yüan chih-meng (hsü)," pp. 30–1.

one of the Sung's most effective means of defense against the Liao (and later against the Jurchen cavalry) – the flooding of artificial swamps and waterways that acted as moats. Except for the exchange of the Kuan-nan area in return for the annual payments,[256] the Liao received everything they wanted, thanks to the mediation of Wang Chi-chung.

To the lives and economic activities of the people along the Sung northern borders, Articles 1 and 5 restored peace and normality. It was estimated that the annual payments amounted to only 1 or 2 percent of the Sung military expenditures required during war times,[257] and to merely 0.3 to 0.5 percent of the total state expenditures.[258] Moreover, these payments were easily offset by the surpluses acquired from the seven new border markets that were established. On average, Sung official trade annually netted 400,000 to 500,000 strings of cash (one string nominally contained 1,000 cash) out of a total trade profit of 800,000 strings, more than enough to recoup the costs of the silver paid to the Liao.[259] Enriched by the bargain struck in the treaty, the Liao used the annual payments to subsidize the construction of their central capital, and exported the silk in large quantities to Central Asia and to frontier peoples such as the Tanguts, at a price three to four times higher than the Sung charged in peacetime and forty times higher than the price during wartime, stimulating a cycle of multistate trade.[260] Furthermore, to avoid future conflicts, a buffer zone was established inside the border prefecture of Hsiung-chou (modern Hsiung county, northern Hopei). The conditions of the buffer zone's neutrality were that its inhabitants would pay no taxes but would provide labor service to both the Sung and the Liao, and that, being demilitarized, its inhabitants would maintain neither troops nor local self-defense forces.[261] To both parties, the most important result of the treaty was a century of peace bought at an acceptable price.

Though this was not stipulated in the treaty, the two parties also treated each other nearly as diplomatic equals. This exceptional practice was expressed in diplomacy by the use of a protocol of brotherly kinship between the two rulers. Immediately after the conclusion of the treaty, Chen-tsung abolished all place-names that included pejorative terms such as "caitiffs" or "barbarians." The Liao, in turn, refrained from calling the annual payments "tribute" in

---

[256] See Tao, *Two sons of heaven*, p. 128 n. 12.

[257] *HCP* (1964) 70, p. 16b; 150, p. 16a.

[258] Wong Hon-chiu, "Government expenditures in Northern Sung China (960–1127)" (diss., University of Pennsylvania, 1975), p. 158.

[259] Akisada Jitsuzō [Tamura Jitsuzō], "Sen-en no meiyaku to sono shiteki igi (ge)," *Shirin* 20 No. 4 (1935), pp. 175–205; Shiba, "Sung foreign trade," p. 98. See also Wang, "Shan-yüan ti-meng chih chien-t'ao," pp. 9, 12 n. 12; Tao, *Two sons of heaven*, p. 16.

[260] Shiba, "Sung foreign trade," pp. 93, 99, 100; Tao, *Two sons of heaven*, p. 24.

[261] Saeki Tomi, "Sōdai Yūshū ni okeru kanshōchi ryōyuchi ni tsuite," *Tōa jinbun gakuhō* 1 No. 2 (1941), pp. 127–56.

communications with the Sung, though using the term internally to please its own people and vassals.[262] The two dynasties officially addressed each other as "the northern dynasty," "the southern dynasty," "the Great Liao," and "the Great Sung." According to seniority of age rather than of status, Chen-tsung called Liao Sheng-tsung his "younger brother" and Dowager Empress Hsiao his "junior aunt."[263] Both states observed a mourning period for a deceased emperor and made his name a national taboo.[264] A special agency, the Office of Diplomatic Correspondence (*Wang-lai kuo-hsin so*) in the Court of State Ceremonial (*Hung-lu ssu*), was specially established to handle only diplomatic exchanges with the Liao. Great attention was paid to the proper selection of capable envoys, may of whom were famous men, several later becoming chief councilors.[265]

The restoration of peace enabled Chen-tsung to reestablish the civilian-oriented policy of "strong trunk and weak branches." In 1000, the acting governor of K'ai-feng had already warned against the concentration of troops on the border at the expense of the rear.[266] Twice in 1002, Chen-tsung reminded the court officials of the danger of delegating undue military power to prefectural officials.[267] During the peace negotiations, even the chief councilor, K'ou Chun, was suspected of using the war for self-aggrandizement, an allegation that apparently made him so uneasy that he dropped his objections to the peace treaty.[268] As soon as the treaty was concluded, almost all militia in Ho-pei were demobilized, and a great number of the imperial troops gathered there were sent back to their home bases. Nearly four hundred military officers were relieved of their posts, and fifty percent of the Ho-pei garrisons and thirty percent of the border garrisons were stood down.[269] Moreover, just as civilians made up two-thirds of the top officials in the Bureau of Military Affairs,[270] Chen-tsung also began the process of installing civil officials in regional military posts once reserved for soldiers, thereby increasing the predominance of civilians in the lower levels of military administration and command.[271]

---

[262] Tao, *Two sons of heaven*, p. 16.

[263] Tao, *Two sons of heaven*, pp. 17–18, 107 (Appendix 3).

[264] Tao, "Barbarians or northerners," pp. 69–70; Tao, *Two sons of heaven*, pp. 18–20.

[265] See Herbert Franke, *Diplomatic missions of the Sung state, 960–1276* (Canberra, 1981), pp. 2–5; Franke, "Sung embassies," pp. 120, 122–4. See also chapters 4 and 5 of Ang, "Sung-Liao diplomacy in eleventh- and twelfth-century China."

[266] *HCP* (1964) 46, pp. 15a–b.

[267] *HCP* (1964) 52, p. 2b; 53, p. 2b; Liu, "Pei Sung ch'ien-ch'i huang-ch'üan fa-chan chih yen-chiu," p. 166.

[268] *SS* 281, p. 9531.

[269] *HCP* (1964) 59, pp. 1a, 2b, 3b, 5b, 6a.

[270] Liang, *Sung shu-mi-yüan chih-tu*, p. 13. See also Labadie, "Rulers and soldiers," p. 196; McGrath, "Military and regional administration," pp. 55–6.

[271] Labadie, "Rulers and soldiers," p. 204; McGrath, "Military and regional administration," pp. 24, 32, 55–6, 301.

Overall, although the Liao were able to use the treaty to gain additional advantages from the Sung (especially in 1042 and 1075), the pragmatic approach to foreign relations shown by the Sung recognition of the Liao as a legitimate empire and diplomatic counterpart makes the Treaty of Shan-yüan an "epoch-making event" in Chinese history.[272]

Burnishing the imperial image with "documents from Heaven"

Only a year after the peace treaty with the Liao, K'ou Chun was dismissed as chief councilor after Wang Ch'in-jo (962–1025), the head of the Bureau of Military Affairs, maligned him to the emperor for negotiating a humiliating treaty. Wang Ch'in-jo's vilification of the Shan-yüan Treaty and its architect so demoralized Chen-tsung that he had K'ou Chun cashiered.[273] Having undermined the emperor's confidence, Wang Ch'in-jo (like Chen-tsung, a follower of Taoism) now sought to build it up again by encouraging the emperor to perform the *feng-shan* sacrifices to Heaven and Earth, which would offset the humiliation of Shan-yüan by "pacifying the Four Quarters and intimidating the barbarians."[274] Before these sacrifices could be performed however, tradition decreed that Heaven had to provide auspicious omens as a sign of divine approval of the sacrifices that signified the high point of dynastic success. Because the appearance of such omens could not be counted on, Wang proposed to fabricate them, as the sage-rulers of antiquity had done when they created the *Yellow River chart* (*Ho-t'u*) and the *Lo River text* (*Lo-shu*).[275] Chen-tsung remained uncertain about the legitimacy of fabricated omens, but when an eminent but unsuspecting classical scholar corroborated Wang's interpretation, the emperor finally relented.[276]

---

[272] Tao, *Two sons of heaven*, pp. 23–4. See also Franke, *Diplomatic missions of the Sung state*, p. 1; Ch'en et al., *Sung-shih chi-shih pen-mo* 22, pp. 150–4, 156–9; Ang, "Sung-Liao diplomacy in eleventh- and twelfth-century China," pp. 83–91; Chin, *Sung Liao Chin shih*, pp. 35–7; Tao, "Barbarians or northerners," pp. 69, 71, 76.

[273] *HCP* (1964) 57, pp. 14b–15a; 62, pp. 6a–7a. See also Wolfgang Franke, "Historical precedent or accidental repetition of events? K'ou Chun in 1004 and Yu Ch'ien in 1449," in *Études Song: In memoriam Étienne Balazs*, ed. Françoise Aubin (Paris, 1976), pp. 200–1.

[274] *HCP* (1964) 67, p. 10b. This goal is explained in Ssu-ma, *Su-shui chi-wen* 6, p. 62, and in the comments appended to Chen-tsung's annals in *SS* 8, p. 172. A full translation of the latter appears in Suzanne E. Cahill, "Taoism at the Sung court: The Heavenly Text affair of 1008," *Bulletin of Sung-Yüan Studies* 16 (1981), p. 36.

[275] For an explanation of *Ho-t'u* and *Lo-shu*, see Richard Wilhelm, *The I Ching or Book of Changes*, 3rd ed., trans. Cary F. Baynes (1950; Princeton, N.J., 1977), pp. 309–10, 320.

[276] *HCP* (1964) 67, pp. 10b–11a; Ch'eng Kuang-yü, "Shan-yüan chih-meng yü t'ien-shu (hsia)," *Ta-lu tsa-chih* 22 No. 7 (1961), p. 21. For Chen-tsung's devotion to Taoism, see Cahill, "Taoism at the Sung court," pp. 39–41. As Cahill explains, "To a person of Sung, a document purporting to be of divine origin but made by human hands was not necessarily a forgery; . . . what matters is that the omen be appropriate, accurate, and legitimate in religious terms. Far from tricking the emperor or advising him to practice a cynical deception, Wang may in fact have been urging him to follow ancient usages."

During the winter and spring of 1008, three Heavenly Texts "appeared" at auspicious locations in the palace complex. The first one read, "The Chao have received the mandate and brought it to glory with the Sung. It will be handed down in perpetuity (*heng*) [or it could be understood as, 'It has been handed down to (Chao) Heng (the present emperor)']."[277] With this reassurance of the legitimacy of the Sung state and the potency of his own rule, Chen-tsung changed his reign title to Ta-chung hsiang-fu (Great Centrality and Auspicious Talisman, 1008–16) and ordered a five-day bacchanal. This was just a prelude to Chen-tsung's performance of the most expensive, lavish, ancient, and prestigious of all the imperial ceremonies, the twin sacrifices to Heaven and Earth at Mount T'ai in Shantung (performed in 1008) and followed by those to the Earth deity at the Fen River in Shansi (carried out in 1011).

Every effort was made to portray the rituals as signs of Chen-tsung's imperial power and efficacy. Chief Councilor Wang Tan (957–1017), for example, assured the emperor that "Heaven has given Your Majesty the divine talismans of the Grand Ultimate. One cycle is completed and another is about to begin. There will be eternal peace for the multitude of men." As one modern historian points out, these words were intended "to glorify the emperor and suggest that the dynasty is rejuvenated, a new cycle of history is beginning, and the Mandate of Heaven is reaffirmed."[278]

Chen-tsung's devotion to Taoism, plainly visible in the Heavenly Texts affair, was also clearly reflected in Chen-tsung's paying a special visit to the temple of Lao Tzu (the traditional founder of Taoism) in Po-chou in 1014, and in the storage of the Heavenly Texts in the newest and greatest Taoist temple in the capital. Most conspicuously, when the "earliest ancestor" of the imperial clan appeared to Chen-tsung in a dream, claiming to be the bearer of the Heavenly Texts, Chen-tsung rendered the name of his imagined ancestor taboo and ordered that Taoist temples throughout the empire add a belvedere (*kuan*) dedicated to this progenitor.[279]

Not everyone in the region was impressed by Chen-tsung's attempt to manufacture religious charisma. Shortly before the sacrifices on Mount T'ai in 1008, the Liao, in an attempt to test Chen-tsung's resolve, requested allowances beyond the annual payments. As a concession, thirty thousand taels of silver and thirty thousand bolts of silk, amounting to one-fifth of the annual payments, were "lent" to the Liao for the year, with no expectation of repayment.[280]

[277] *HCP* (1964) 68, pp. 1a–2a. See also Ch'eng, "Shan-yüan chih-meng yü t'ien-shu (hsia)," p. 22. Translation adapted from Cahill, "Taoism at the Sung court," pp. 26–7.
[278] Cahill, "Taoism at the Sung court," p. 38; Ch'en et al., *Sung-shih chi-shih pen-mo* 22, p. 165.
[279] Cahill, "Taoism at the Sung court," p. 31.
[280] *SS* 282, p. 9547.

Cognizant of this precedent, in 1010 the Tanguts – whom the Sung had bought off four years earlier with military commissions and copious amounts of silver, silk, cash, and tea – requested ten million additional bushels of grain for famine relief. Although most officials suggested that the request be dismissed as an attempt at blackmail, Wang Tan prudently purchased continued peace by accepting the Tangut petition.[281] Ritual claims notwithstanding, it was obviously the combination of generous concessions and compliant diplomacy that kept the foreign states at bay, not the religious charisma represented by the Heavenly Texts.

Nor was Chen-tsung's domestic audience uniformly impressed. The five most prominent advocates of the Heavenly Texts affair – Wang Ch'in-jo, Ting Wei (966–1037), Ch'en P'eng-nien (961–1017), Liu Ch'eng-kuei, and Lin T'e – were ridiculed as the "Five Devils" by disbelieving contemporaries, and some officials came out openly against the affair.[282] "How could Heaven use words? How could there possibly be a document?" taunted the edict attendant Sun Shih (962–1033) in the first of six passionate remonstrations he submitted between 1008 and 1019.[283] In 1015, the minister of rites, Chang Yung (946–1015), requested in a posthumously presented memorial that one of the Five Devils be beheaded for deceiving the emperor.[284] In 1017, Wang Tan, now ill and close to death, confessed to his sons that he regretted his involvement in the affair, which he considered the one mistake that had stained his life. In contrition, he asked to be buried with his head shaved and clothed in the robes of a Buddhist monk.[285] For a brief time the emperor lost faith in the gush of heavenly auspices, and in 1016 he forbade the presentation of auspicious objects as tribute. The next year, however, he changed his mind and ordered that further concealment of any reports of calamities and visitations would be considered a crime.[286]

In 1016, a natural omen shook Chen-tsung's dream of heavenly favor. A plague of locusts struck the capital area. At first, Chen-tsung still believed that his faith could minimize the calamity or even quicken the death of the locusts. As proof that it could, some councilors presented heaps of dead locusts and suggested a court celebration. Before the celebration could be held, swarms of live locusts flew over the audience hall darkening the sky, making it obvious

---

[281] SS 282, p. 9547; 485, pp. 13989–90. For another incident, see HCP (1964) 73, p. 20a.

[282] See Ch'en et al., Sung-shih chi-shih pen-mo 22, especially p. 170.

[283] Hung Mai, Jung-chai sui-pi (1180–1202; Shanghai, 1978) san-pi, 7, pp. 493–5; Ch'en et al., Sung-shih chi-shih pen-mo 22, pp. 163, 166–9, 171–2, 174–5; Cahill, "Taoism at the Sung court," pp. 27, 29–30, 34–5.

[284] HCP (1964) 85, p. 9a.

[285] HCP (1964) 90, p. 12b; Cahill, "Taoism at the Sung court," pp. 33–4.

[286] Cahill, "Taoism at the Sung court," pp. 33–4.

that both the emperor and his councilors were mistaken. From then on, Chen-tsung reportedly began to feel sick.[287] In 1022 the Heavenly Texts were buried with Chen-tsung, putting an end to the hoax. "Ah! How wise!" exclaimed the compilers of the *Sung dynastic history*.[288] In 1029, all but two small halls of the greatest Taoist temple in which they had been housed were completely destroyed in a mysterious fire.

Court politics and intrigue

Chen-tsung had good reasons for delegating more authority than T'ai-tsu or T'ai-tsung. After the conclusion of the Shan-yüan Treaty, the Sung experienced a period of peace and prosperity that required a less firm hand on the reins of government. Despite the immense cost of the *feng-shan* sacrifices and of maintaining Taoist establishments, as well as the payments to the Liao and the Hsi Hsia, Chen-tsung's reign enjoyed the greatest surplus of income over expenditure of any period during the Northern Sung. Income was 150,850,100 strings of cash in 1021 – more than double that of 997 – and expenditures were only 126,775,200 strings.[289] But there was an ever-increasing array of governmental affairs to be overseen, most of which would have seemed routine in times of peace, but which were still burdensome to an emperor preoccupied with such other matters as the Heavenly Texts affair.[290] And after half a century of unification, the bureaucracy had grown to an unwieldy size.

As early as 999, Chen-tsung was receiving no fewer than one hundred memorials per day. The varied counsel confused him, and the mutual accusations eventually annoyed him. In 1007, inundated with both regular and sealed memorials, Chen-tsung ordered that an outline be attached to each memorial to facilitate his selective reading. This did not guarantee the quality of the memorials, and Chen-tsung continued to complain about the misrepresentation and trifling content found in some of them.[291] Also, the frequency of rotating audiences and deliberative meetings declined, depriving most lower-ranking officials of the chance to express their opinions. Between 1004 and his death in 1022, Chen-tsung issued only one general request for frank remonstrance, a sharp contrast to the three such requests he made in his first two years

---

[287] Liu, "Pei Sung ch'ien-ch'i huang-ch'üan fa-chan chih yen-chiu," pp. 202–3.

[288] Worthy, "The founding of Sung China," p. 54.

[289] Wong, "Government expenditures in Northern Sung China," pp. 161–2, table 25.

[290] *HCP* (1964) 62, p. 6a: "After peace had been concluded with the Khitan, there was a dearth of important matters at court." For some administrative difficulties facing ordinary emperors, see Liu, "An administrative cycle in Chinese history," pp. 146–50.

[291] Olsson, "The structure of power under the third emperor of Sung China," pp. 67–8, 75, 149–50.

as emperor.[292] In 1017, the Censorate was enlarged with six new posts and the Remonstrance Bureau (*Chien-yüan*) was established. One of the duties of its six remonstrators was to criticize proposals and policy decisions. Although this was intended to give criticism greater weight at court, it actually circumscribed the formerly wide participation by officials in the remonstrance process. For the right to speak on state affairs that all officials had enjoyed before 1017 was now limited to a mere handful of "opinion officials."[293]

Though the numbers of officials and the amount of state affairs requiring decision increased, imperial audiences were held less and less frequently. After 1018, they were not held on days when banquets were given for departing or returning officials. They were not held on state holidays after 1019, nor, after 1020, on alternate days. Prior to this, Chen-tsung had already displayed signs of lethargy. In a series of proclamations beginning in 1006, the emperor reduced the number of officials who could attend imperial audiences and circumscribed the types of subjects to be memorialized. In 1010, he ordered the Finance Commission to make secondary decisions independently or according to precedents. In 1011, he ordered that officials should, in general, request audiences only when they had important matters to discuss, and otherwise make decisions themselves and report these to him.[294] This willingness to delegate imperial power was not necessarily bad, since a power structure too strongly centered on the emperor might not have benefited the state after the ratification of the Shan-yüan Treaty. To achieve peacetime goals, the bureaucratic leadership required more independent authority, more autonomy, and a more hierarchical structure.[295] However, this decentralization of executive power increasingly brought with it conflicts of interests among bureaucratic leaders.

Chen-tsung retained a very static political leadership at the highest levels; in the fourteen years from 1005 to 1019, there were only nineteen holders of the top offices in the Secretariat-Chancellery and the Bureau of Military Affairs. Power was largely concentrated in the hands of the southerners Wang Ch'in-jo, Ting Wei, and Ch'en P'eng-nien – all of them members of the so-called Five Devils.[296] As a modern historian persuasively concludes, "Wang Ch'in-jo and his friends, especially Ting Wei and Ch'en P'eng-nien, were concerned

---

[292] See chapter 3 of Olsson, "The structure of power under the third emperor," especially pp. 63–5, 75–8, 89.

[293] *HCP* (1964) 89, pp. 4b–5a; Olsson, "The structure of power under the third emperor of Sung China," pp. 92–3.

[294] See chapter 3 of Olsson, "The structure of power under the third emperor," especially pp. 51–2, 56–60.

[295] Olsson, "The structure of power under the third emperor of Sung China," pp. 94–5.

[296] This conclusion is based on the information in Hsü Tzu-ming, *Sung tsai-fu pien-nien lu* (early 13th c.; Peking, 1986), pp. 100–57.

primarily with their own personal positions, and any views different from their own, whether those of northerners or fellow southerners, were considered a threat to their personal power and influence."[297] The stage was set for a power struggle. The emperor was increasingly lethargic, some top officials were unscrupulously self-aggrandizing, and bureaucratic power was concentrated in the hands of a few officials long entrenched in the rival Secretariat-Chancellery and Bureau of Military Affairs, each of whom was ready to encroach upon their counterparts' jurisdiction in order to enhance his own bureaucratic domain.

Of all his officials, Wang Tan was most trusted by Chen-tsung. "Wang Tan is expert at handling important matters; he is a true chief councilor," said the emperor when Wang Tan alone found a solution to an impending army revolt triggered by a commander's tough policy of demobilization.[298] Quite often, even for decisions concerning the Bureau of Military Affairs and the Finance Commission, Chen-tsung first consulted Wang Tan, whom he valued for his political wisdom. Occupying the paramount post of chief councilor for twelve years, Wang Tan was the most senior minister in the Secretariat-Chancellery. The power and importance of the Secretariat-Chancellery was relatively greater than that of the Bureau of Military Affairs during the long time of peace when civil matters outweighed military concerns. This eminence notwithstanding, Wang Tan was cautious at court, keeping a polite distance from subordinates, refraining from open association with persons he sponsored for promotions, assuming a low posture before his colleagues, and always deferring to the imperial will, as in the Heavenly Texts affair.[299]

In 1016, upon discovering that Wang Tan had decided certain matters without informing the emperor, the chief councilor's disgruntled colleagues, including Ch'en P'eng-nien, complained. They obtained no more than apologies from Wang. Surprised by their complaints, the emperor asked them whether Wang Tan's decisions had been fair. Receiving a unanimous yes, the emperor revealed that, having found no selfishness in Wang after many years of observation, he had given him plenipotentiary authority over minor matters from the time of the sacrifices. Accepting his colleagues' apologies, Wang Tan explained that he felt it inappropriate to disclose this authorization on his own, but promised further reliance on their advice in the future.[300]

Even with this imperial trust, Wang Tan could not save Chen-tsung from the machinations of Wang Ch'in-jo, who blamed Wang Tan for obstructing

[297] Olssen, "The structure of power under the third emperor of Sung China," p. 182, see also pp. 151, 181–3, 196–8, 217–18.
[298] HCP (1964) 86, p. 1b.
[299] SS 282, pp. 9542–52; Olsson, "The structure of power under the third emperor of Sung China," pp. 68, 142–4, 188–9, 198–207; Liu, "Pei Sung ch'ien-ch'i huang-ch'üan fa-chan chih yen-chiu," p. 200.
[300] HCP (1964) 88, pp. 1b–2a.

his own advancement to the post of chief councilor.[301] Wang Ch'in-jo tried to erode Wang Tan's influence by removing Wang Tan's close associates. The first to go was Chao An-jen (958–1018), a discreet and able assisting councilor. In 1012, Wang Ch'in-jo answered the emperor that the most virtuous person at court was Chao, because he had always tried to repay a former chief councilor for his patronage. Alert to the hint of favoritism and unhappy with Chao An-jen's reticence during court audiences, the emperor dismissed him.[302] To replace Chao, Wang Tan consulted with Wang Ch'in-jo about recommending a poor friend of his, Li Tsung-o (964–1012). After telling Wang Tan that he agreed with his choice, Wang Ch'in-jo secretly told Chen-tsung that Li was heavily indebted to Wang Tan, who looked forward to getting the official presents that would be conferred upon Li on his appointment as a new councilor. This, Wang Ch'in-jo insisted, was not the way to select worthy men for government office. The following day, when Wang Tan mentioned Li, the emperor got angry and instead accepted Wang Ch'in-jo's recommendation of Ting Wei.[303] In the same year, the emperor also accepted the request of the Bureau of Military Affairs that its monthly record, which previously had been sent to the Secretariat-Chancellery for compilation, should now be compiled independently and sent directly to the Historiography Institute.[304] Even though the institute was under the jurisdiction of the chief councilors, by cutting out the Secretariat-Chancellery this at least structurally enhanced the autonomy of the Bureau of Military Affairs.

In 1014, Wang Ch'in-jo was suspended for almost a year, largely as a result of his domineering manner at the Bureau of Military Affairs. As an example of his high-handedness, Wang Ch'in-jo often discussed only a select handful of the memorials he had brought to the audience. When the audience ended, despite his colleague Ma Chih-chieh's strong objections, Wang alone would make decisions on the undisclosed memorials, pretending that these decisions had been made during the audience with the emperor's assent. Enraged by Wang's conduct, Ma Chih-chieh often disagreed heatedly with Wang in the audiences. This tactic finally backfired.

Chen-tsung, irked by an altercation between Wang Ch'in-jo and Ma Chih-chieh, summoned Wang Tan to mediate, but Wang Ch'in-jo kept on protesting. After the audience adjourned, the emperor wanted to send Wang Ch'in-jo and Ma Chih-chieh to the Censorate for trial, but he was dissuaded by Wang Tan. The following day, Chen-tsung told Wang Tan that Wang Ch'in-jo and

[301] SS 282, p. 9548.
[302] HCP (1964) 78, pp. 15b–16b.
[303] HCP (1964) 78, pp. 16b–17a.
[304] HCP (1964) 78, p. 3b.

Ma Chih-chieh were to be dismissed on the charge of "discourteous wrangling." Wang Tan suggested instead that they first be admonished and dismissed only if the admonition had no effect, lest a scandal harm the imperial image among foreign states. The emperor agreed.[305] Slightly over a month later, Wang Ch'in-jo and Ma Chih-chieh again deadlocked over meting out appropriate rewards for a military commander. Extremely angry at their endless squabbling, and discovering that the Bureau of Military Affairs had made a decision behind his back, the emperor dismissed the two men and, upon Wang Tan's recommendation, recalled Wang Ch'in-jo's archrival, K'ou Chun.[306] But K'ou Chun proved equally domineering and was dismissed the next year; Wang Ch'in-jo was reinstalled.[307] There was no ultimate winner in this see-saw battle.

The death of Wang Tan in 1017 and the deteriorating health of Chentsung ushered in a period of intensified political struggle. Under the influence of the new chief councilor, Wang Ch'in-jo, the emperor dismissed Assisting Councilor Wang Tseng (978–1038) and permitted the resignation of another assisting councilor, Chang Chih-pai (?–1028), who could no longer tolerate Wang Ch'in-jo's hostility.[308] In 1019, however, Wang Ch'in-jo himself was dismissed on charges of accepting bribes and of befriending a Taoist who possessed forbidden books and claimed to have the power to summon heavenly troops (traditionally signs of treasonable intentions).[309] Wang Ch'in-jo's replacement was K'ou Chun, who had earlier been persuaded by his son-in-law to report to the court another Heavenly Text found in his jurisdiction, which actually had been fabricated by a favorite military officer of K'ou's.[310]

Chen-tsung's mental state steadily deteriorated during the 1010s. His sixth son and heir, Chao Chen (1010–63), was born to a palace attendant surnamed Li. Chen-tsung's wife, the empress Liu (969–1033), took over the rearing of the son and kept his real mother, Lady Li, in obscurity, paving the way for her own ascent to power as dowager empress and regent. Chou Huai-cheng (?–1020) was much concerned with the growing influence of the empress, now stepmother of the heir apparent. Strong-willed, able, and astute, Empress Liu displayed a great interest in court politics, helping Chen-tsung manage state affairs in the inner palace, and also having two of her close relatives appointed commanders of the imperial army. From a humble family with no political background at court, she had allied herself with Ting Wei and Hanlin academician Ch'ien Wei-yen (962–1034) by forming marriage relations.

[305] SS 282, pp. 9548–9.
[306] HCP (1964) 82, pp. 18b–19b.
[307] HCP (1964) 84, pp. 11a–12b.
[308] HCP (1964) 90, p. 10a; 92, p. 14b.
[309] HCP (1964) 93, pp. 13a–b.
[310] HCP (1964) 93, pp. 6b–7a; SS 466, p. 13615; HCP (1964) 93, p. 6b; 96, p. 6a.

Ch'ien Wei-yen's younger sister was the wife of Empress Liu's adopted older brother, and Ch'ien's daughter was the wife of Ting Wei's son. When she was made empress in 1012 at the age of forty-two, her humble background and barrenness prompted opposition from some senior officials, including K'ou Chun. Furthermore, some of the elite, mostly the southern scholar-officials, objected to a female regency reminiscent of the ill-fated T'ang dynasty empress Wu Tse-t'ien.[311] Nonetheless, when Chen-tsung died in the second month of 1022 their objections were disregarded, and Empress Liu assumed power as dowager empress and the dynasty's first regent.

---

[311] Chiba Hiroshi, "Sōdai no kōhi – Taiso, Taisō, Shinsō, Jinsō shichō," in *Aoyama Hakushi koki kinen Sōdai shi ronsō*, ed. Aoyama Hakushi Koki Kinen Sōdai-shi Ronsō Kankōkai (Tokyo, 1974), pp. 209–38.

CHAPTER 4

THE REIGNS OF JEN-TSUNG (1022–1063) AND YING-TSUNG (1063–1067)

Michael McGrath

JEN-TSUNG'S EARLY REIGN: THE REGENCY OF EMPRESS LIU
(1022–1033)

Chao Chen, whose temple name was Sung Jen-tsung, was born 30 May 1010. He reigned for just over forty-one years, longer than any other Sung emperor.[1] His mother was named Lady Li, but Empress Liu (969–1033) claimed him as her own in 1014 when he was three years old. Pure Consort Yang (Yang Shu-fei, 984–1036) was another lesser consort of Chen-tsung, and a close friend of Empress Liu. Pure Consort Yang played an important role in raising and watching over Jen-tsung. Jen-tsung did not learn his birth mother's identity until 1033, when the death of Dowager Empress Liu ended her eleven-year regency.[2]

Empress Liu, a capable and ambitious woman of lowly origins from Szech-wan who had been appointed Chen-tsung's empress in 1012, developed the skills she would need in her regency during the last years of her husband's reign. She capitalized on Chen-tsung's increasing despondency and ill health following the 1016 locust infestation that terminated the Heavenly Texts affair, offering advice, reading memorials, and even deciding policy for the emperor. The future Jen-tsung was designated heir apparent (*t'ai-tzu*) in 1018, and two years later Chen-tsung instructed his senior ministers that so long as his son remained a minor Empress Liu should be relied upon to make decisions with their advice.[3] The primary beneficiaries of that injunction were Empress Liu

---

[1] Jen-tsung's original name was Chao Shou-i but was changed to Chao Chen when he was appointed heir apparent in 1018. He was Chen-tsung's sixth and last son. Pi Yüan, *Hsü Tzu-chih t'ung-chien* [hereafter *HTC* (1957)] [*Te-yü-t'ang tsang-pan* 1801 ed.] (1792; Peking, 1958) 34, p. 759.

[2] *HTC* (1957) 31, p. 698.

[3] *HTC* (1957) 35, pp. 786–7. Liu Ching-chen, "Ts'ung huang-hou kan-cheng tao t'ai-hou she-cheng – Pei Sung Chen-Jen chih chi nü-chu cheng-chih ch'üan-li shih-t'an," in *Kuo-chi Sung-shih yen-t'ao-hui lun-wen-chi*, ed. Kuo-chi Sung-shih yen-t'ao-hui (Taipei, 1988), p. 585. For a recent study of Empress Liu as "the fourth ruler of the Song," see John W. Chaffee, "The rise and regency of Empress Liu (969–1033)," *Journal of Sung-Yuan Studies* 31 (2001), pp. 1–26.

and the chief councilor, Ting Wei, who was relentlessly securing control over
the State Council, and who in the final month of 1020 secured the establishment of the future Jen-tsung as temporary regent on account of his father's
incapacity, albeit under the strict control of Empress Liu.[4] With Chen-tsung's
death in the second month of 1022, and because Jen-tsung was still a child,
Empress Liu formally assumed the regent's powers for herself, on the authority
of Chen-tsung's testament, which the chief councilors drafted into a decree:
"The Heir Apparent assumes the throne, the Empress will be called Dowager
Empress (*huang t'ai-hou*), the Pure Consort Yang will be called Dowager Consort (*huang t'ai-fei*). All important matters of state will temporarily be decided
by the dowager empress."[5]

Chen-tsung's testamentary decree gave executive authority to the now dowager empress Liu, who attended the court hidden behind a screen. For the most
part, she ruled unobtrusively and exercised her power through her councilors.
Initially, her dominance did nothing to stop the competition for ministerial
authority swirling around her. Chief Councilor Ting Wei moved first to consolidate his hold on power, by demoting political rivals like Li Ti and K'ou
Chun and K'ou's associates, and by collaborating with the eunuch Lei Yün-
kung (?–1022) to commandeer the reins of government.[6] But Ting Wei's
assignment as commissioner of the imperial tomb, responsible for the location
and construction of Chen-tsung's tomb, gave Ting's antagonist, Wang Tseng
(978–1038) – a senior minister who showed himself unusually concerned with
the young emperor's welfare – an opportunity to undo both Ting Wei and Lei
Yün-kung.[7] As codirector of construction for the tomb project, Lei Yün-kung
ordered a change in the tomb's location. But this move threatened to inundate
the burial vault with water. Although Ting Wei tried to cover up for Lei,
other officials reported the fiasco to the dowager empress, who asked Wang
Tseng, along with the K'ai-feng prefect Lü I-chien (978–1044) and Han-lin
academician Lu Tsung-tao (966–1029), to investigate. As a result, Lei Yün-
kung was charged with unlawfully moving the site of Chen-tsung's burial vault
and with stealing large quantities of silver, gold, pearls, and imperial burial
accoutrements. As punishment he was beaten to death, his family's property
was expropriated, and his brother was banished to the region of Hunan.

---

[4] Li T'ao, *Hsü tzu-chih t'ung-chien ch'ang-pien* [hereafter *HCP* (1979)] (1183; Peking, 1979–95) 96, pp. 2232–
   3; *HTC* (1957) 35, p. 790; Yang Chung-liang, *Tzu-chih t'ung-chien ch'ang-pien chi-shih pen-mo* [hereafter
   CPPM] (1253; Taipei, 1967) 27, pp. 805–6.

[5] *HCP* (1979) 98, p. 2271. Liu, "Ts'ung huang-hou kan-cheng tao t'ai-hou she-cheng," p. 587, emphasizes
   that despite the existence of variant texts, this is the first instance where her governing role is legalized.

[6] *HTC* (1957) 35, pp. 796–8; Liu, "Ts'ung huang-hou kan-cheng tao t'ai-hou she-cheng," p. 589.

[7] On Wang Tseng, see Tonami Mamoru, "Wang Tseng," in *Sung biographies*, ed. Herbert Franke (Wiesbaden,
   1976), vol. 3, pp. 1159–61.

Lei Yün-kung's downfall provided Wang Tseng with the wedge he needed to dislodge Ting Wei. In a private audience with Dowager Empress Liu, Wang charged Ting Wei with conspiring with Lei Yün-kung in shifting the burial vault to a geomantically forbidden location. Anger and outrage were added to the dowager empress's previous annoyance with Ting Wei for objecting to her holding court without the young emperor in attendance. She demanded Ting Wei's execution. Although other senior ministers, including Feng Cheng and Wang Tseng, were happy enough to see Ting fall, they persuaded Dowager Empress Liu that dismissal, demotion, and public disgrace would be punishment enough. The dowager empress thereupon promoted Wang Tseng to senior councilor, brought Lü I-chien and Lu Tsung-tao in as assistant councilors (ts'an-chih cheng-shih), and had Chief Councilor Feng Cheng replace Ting Wei as commissioner of the Imperial Tomb.[8] Although Ting Wei lived for fifteen more years, his official career was over.

As of mid-1022, the dowager empress was no longer ensnared by Lei Yün-kung and Ting Wei, but she also no longer had a Ting Wei to support her ambitions. As the ranking minister, Feng Cheng longed to emulate Ting Wei, but could not match his intelligence, learning, or cunning.[9] Nor was Feng Cheng as willing to allow the dowager empress as much latitude. Moreover, Wang Tseng was strongly opposed to her participation in governance, and in the seventh month of 1022 he attempted to restore the previous arrangement for holding court: every five days and always in the presence of the young Jen-tsung. Three times the dowager empress rejected Wang Tseng's request for the change, but when Wang submitted the request to the young emperor, she gave in and approved it, realizing that if she resisted too much she might provoke Wang Tseng and the others to push the young emperor to depose her.[10] Not until 1029, when Lu Tsung-tao had died and Wang Tseng was dismissed, did she again show signs of any grander ambitions.

The dowager empress's rule soon settled into a routine. She devoted great care to the governance of the palace but left control of public policy to her ministers, making few interventions and acting as a figurehead. The composition of the Council of State was stable for the next six years. Lü I-chien and Lu Tsung-tao were the only assisting civil councilors, Ts'ao Li-yung (?–1029) was commissioner of military affairs from 1018 until 1029, and Chang Shih-hsün (964–1049) served as assistant commissioner of military affairs until he was promoted to chief councilor in the spring of 1028.[11] Chang Chih-po

---

[8] *HCP* (1979) 98, pp. 2283–7; 35, pp. 800–2.
[9] *HTC* (1957) 35, p. 803.
[10] *HTC* (1957) 35, pp. 803–4; *HCP* (1979) 99, p. 2293; *CPPM* 27, p. 810.
[11] Ch'ang Pi-te et al., eds., *Sung-jen chuan-chi tzu-liao so-yin* (Taipei, 1974–6), pp. 2345–6.

(?–1028) served as assistant commissioner of military affairs and joint chief councilor with Wang Tseng until Chang's death in 1028.[12] Feng Cheng was dismissed in fall of 1023, and Wang Ch'in-jo (962–1025) was recalled as a chief councilor.[13] Chang Chi,[14] one of Chen-tsung's longest serving officials and a favorite of Dowager Empress Liu, served as assistant commissioner and commissioner of military affairs between 1025 and 1033. Yen Shu and Hsia Sung (985–1051) also served as assistant commissioners of military affairs.[15] This was a configuration that generally left the dowager empress hemmed in by men of talent, probity, and traditional views about dynastic succession and sovereignty. Nevertheless, her strength of character, the weight of the imperial testament, and Jen-tsung's youth counterbalanced the efforts of these men and others to convince her to withdraw from governing and to limit herself to ceremonial matters. Even so, she exercised her power discreetly, and her activities were largely confined to the dynastic, ceremonial, and familial: she had her birthday declared a holiday (*ch'ang-ning chieh*), three generations of her ancestors ennobled, and her father's name declared taboo. She added more eunuch officials, instituted an exchange of envoys between dowager empresses of the Sung and of the Liao, and assumed some of the ceremonial trappings usually reserved for emperors.[16]

The start of the new lunar year of 1023 was marked by the inauguration of a new reign title – T'ien-sheng (Celestial Sageness, 1023–32).[17] The nine years of this reign period coincided with all but two years of Dowager Empress Liu's regency. During that time, as the dowager empress sought to maintain her own power, the chief ministers tried to offset her influence by imbuing the young emperor with Confucian learning and norms. The centerpoint of Jen-tsung's education, in which the dowager empress took a close interest, was the Imperial Seminar (*ching-yen*), where Sun Shih (962–1033),[18] the head of the Directorate of Education, and Academician Feng Yüan (975–1037)[19] would lecture to the emperor on the Confucian canonical texts and the *Analects* and

---

[12] Tonami Mamoru, "Chang Chih-po," in *Sung biographies*, ed. Herbert Franke (Wiesbaden, 1976), vol. 1, pp. 10–11; Ch'ang et al., *Sung-jen chuan-chi tzu-liao so-yin*, pp. 2390–1.

[13] Yamauchi Masahiro, "Wang Ch'in-jo," in *Sung biographies*, ed. Herbert Franke (Wiesbaden, 1976), vol. 3, pp. 1105–9; Ch'ang et al., *Sung-jen chuan-chi tzu-liao so-yin*, pp. 350–1.

[14] Ch'ang et al., *Sung-jen chuan-chi tzu-liao so-yin*, p. 2267. Originally his personal name was Min. *HTC* (1957) 36, p. 830.

[15] Ch'ang et al., *Sung-jen chuan-chi tzu-liao so-yin*, pp. 1807–8.

[16] *HCP* (1979) 100, p. 2322; Ch'en Pang-chan et al., *Sung-shih chi-shih pen-mo* (1605; Peking, 1977) 24, p. 188; *HCP* (1979) 104, p. 2401.

[17] James M. Hargett, "A chronology of the reigns and reign-periods of the Song dynasty (960–1279)," *Bulletin of Sung-Yüan Studies* 19 (1987), p. 32.

[18] Ch'ang et al., *Sung-jen chuan-chi tzu-liao so-yin*, pp. 1904–5.

[19] Ch'ang et al., *Sung-jen chuan-chi tzu-liao so-yin*, pp. 2737–8.

on the histories.[20] Initially the seminar was to have been held only on even-numbered days, but Wang Tseng insisted on rigorous daily lecturing and reading of selected texts, some of them specifically written for Jen-tsung's instruction. Wang believed that it was essential for the young emperor to have a close association with worthy scholars as his teachers. Sun Shih was so strict that he would not start lecturing or reading until the emperor stopped squirming in his throne, and when expounding history Sun always repeated accounts of disorders and dynastic collapse. Jen-tsung was a studious and avid learner, and was becoming an accomplished calligrapher. He was praised for listening respectfully and attentively to his teachers.[21]

There were also more than enough current problems for Jen-tsung's tutors to lecture on, had they chosen to do so. Many of these problems concerned finance, particularly how to pay for a rash of new expenses. Of these, one of the most pressing was repair of the breach in the long-neglected Yellow River dikes at Hua-chou2, just north of K'ai-feng, that was caused in 1026 by torrential rains. These dikes had collapsed previously in 1018. The new breach had caused widespread flooding throughout the capital and in the floodplain to the east. In K'ai-feng, soldiers were set to work reinforcing the dike walls. Officials were also sent out to coordinate relief efforts in the southern portion of the flood area. By late spring, corvée laborers were drafted from the eastern and western circuits of Ching-tung, Ho-pei, Shan-hsi, and Huai-nan to transport fascines of straw and sticks to fill in the break at Hua-chou2. During the summer Jen-tsung forgave all outstanding arrears of taxes as part of the grand act of grace (*ta-she*) promulgated on his accession to the throne. The timing suggests his action was occasioned by the flooding. Nevertheless, forgiving all back taxes on the occasion of a grand act of grace became a precedent.[22] The breach was not fully repaired until the tenth month of 1027, through the efforts of 38,000 corvée laborers and 21,000 soldiers, and expenditures of 500,000 strings of cash.[23]

[20] See Robert M. Hartwell, "Historical analogism, public policy, and social science in eleventh- and twelfth-century China," *American Historical Review* 76 No. 3 (1971), pp. 690–727, for an account of its significance. For example, see Wang Tseng's emphasis on historical guidance, *HTC* (1957) 37, p. 834 (May 1026), or Jen-tsung's historical consciousness, *HCP* (1979) 107, p. 2504 (May 1029).

[21] *CPPM* 28, p. 849.

[22] *HTC* (1957) 36, p. 815. Jen-tsung subsequently promulgated grand acts of grace in 1024, 1029, 1032 (twice), 1033 (twice), 1034, 1045, and 1056. Certainly the practice of forgiving back taxes on these occasions diminished imperial income by some amount, yet its overall effect was probably negligible.

[23] T'o-t'o et al., eds., *Sung shih* [hereafter *SS*] (1345; Peking, 1977) 9, pp. 183, 184; and *SS* 91 and 92, which detail the flooding of the Yellow River and the various attempts to solve this perennial problem. See also Klaus Flessel, *Der Huang-ho und die historische Hydrotechnik in China: Unter besonderer Berücksichtigung der Nödlichen-Sung-Zeit und mit einem Ausblick auf den vergleichbaren Wasserbau in Europa* (Tübingen, 1974).

The recent funeral expenses for Chen-tsung, although not borne by the people directly, merely emphasized the sense of a straitened fisc, attributed to a combination of Chen-tsung's profligacy, the growth of the army and officialdom, the burgeoning numbers of Buddhist and Taoist clergy, and the peace payments to the Liao. Yü Hsien-ch'ing, a Finance Commission official, observed that the tax burden was becoming noticeably heavier, especially in the central circuits along the Huai and Yangtze rivers.[24] Following the request of Finance Commissioner Li Tzu (d. 1036),[25] an ad hoc agency, the *Chi-chih ssu*, was established under the direction of Chang Shih-hsün, Lü I-chien, and Lu Tsung-tao to curb excessive expenditures, to examine income and expenditure, and in particular to increase revenues from the government's tea monopoly.

Tea, like salt, was used by the government in place of cash to pay merchants for shipments of grain to the northern frontier. Beginning in the 980s the government employed the so-called provisioning (*ju-chung*) method of exchange, whereby merchants who delivered grain to staging areas in the northern circuits encompassed by modern Shensi, Shansi, and Hopei provinces were paid with exchange vouchers (*chiao-yin*) that could be redeemed in the capital for money, or in the official monopoly markets of the southeast for government tea. But the linkage of tea to frontier provisioning tended to devalue the worth of government tea stocks, while the costs of maintaining centralized monopoly markets grew faster than did overall revenues. To enhance the value of government tea, the 1023 committee recommended severing tea's connection to the frontier, while also requiring tea merchants to collect their tea not at high-cost government warehouses, but in the local tea markets. There they would be given a certificate of verification – the so-called *t'ieh-she* certificate – that gave the reform its name. Advocates of the measure predicted that this decentralization of tea sales would increase government revenues and that the *t'ieh-she* certificate would prevent illegal tea sales.[26]

Although the *t'ieh-she* reform reduced cash expenditures for the government, it was resisted by merchants whose profits were cut, and it was soon rescinded as unworkable. In late 1025, Sun Shih and others pointed out that the thirteen tea plantations had an unsold accumulation of 6,130,000 catties of tea, and recommended a return to the old system of government purchase of tea combined with merchant purchase of tea certificates. This remained the usual procedure until the tea monopoly was abolished in 1059. In early

[24] *HCP* (1979) 100, p. 2311.

[25] Ch'ang et al., *Sung-jen chuan-chi tzu-liao so-yin*, p. 913.

[26] There is a substantial literature in Chinese and Japanese on the Northern Sung tea reforms. A good place to start is Hua Shan, "Ts'ung ch'a-yeh ching-chi k'an Sung-tai she-hui," in his *Sung-shih lun-chi* (Chi-nan, 1982), pp. 55–111.

1026 the principal officers of the tea and salt monopolies were fined various amounts. Two Finance Commission accountants were impeached for falsifying the income generated so as to garner performance bonuses for themselves and were sent to Sha-men Island. Chang Shih-hsün, Lü I-chien, and Lu Tsung-tao were required to justify their behavior, and even though Lü strenuously argued that despite accounting irregularities the reform itself had been a success, all three men were fined for failures in their oversight of the monopoly reforms.[27]

Tea policy was not the only sphere that saw reforms begun and aborted during Dowager Empress Liu's regency. In personnel management, a short-lived change was attempted in the way officials' salaries were augmented to encourage honesty. In 1028 the old system, in which the income from government lands was used to provide supplementary allowances that varied with the wealth of the individual prefectures, was replaced by a system of uniform allowances distributed by the central government. Despite the equity of this new approach, in 1031 it was discontinued as administratively unworkable in favor of simply assigning officials to rich and poor prefectures in alternation.[28] Policy officials had somewhat better success persuading Jen-tsung to authorize a new edition of the imperial orders, which the Han-lin academicians Hsia Sung and Ts'ai Ch'i and the drafter Ch'eng Lin were assigned to produce in 1026.[29] In twelve years, the number of imperial decrees had grown to 6,783. Jen-tsung had expressed his reluctance to change anything, but Wang Tseng assured him that flatterers had deceived him, mentioning the revision of T'ai-tsung's decrees carried out under Chen-tsung in which only ten or twenty percent of the original number were retained. Wang emphasized that the recension was done for the good of the people and that each decree would be examined carefully before discarding or retaining it. A month later comments were solicited concerning the value of any imperial decree. Six months later, the less learned but more politically and bureaucratically adept Lü I-chien was put in charge. The project was not completed until late in 1029. Every prefectural administrator was instructed to read the new compilation and offer comments. If after a year no more changes were found necessary, the new edition was to be printed and distributed. Even so, the T'ien-sheng era recension was not implemented as law of the land until the spring of 1032.

Overall, it was politics rather than policy that dominated the court during Dowager Empress Liu's regency, particularly the political wrangling between

[27] HCP (1979) 104, pp. 2403–4.

[28] HCP (1979) 108, p. 2520; 110, pp. 2554, 2557; Hsü Sung et al., Sung hui-yao chi-kao (1809, 1936; Taipei, 1964) chih-kuan 5, pp. 5–7.

[29] HCP (1979) 104, p. 2423; CPPM 32, pp. 989–91; SS 9, p. 183; see also Robert M. Hartwell, "Financial expertise, examinations, and the formation of economic policy in Northern Sung China," Journal of Asian Studies 30 No. 2 (1971), p. 295.

senior ministers and the dowager empress herself. In the second month of 1029, Lu Tsung-tao, one of the regent's staunchest opponents, died after seven years' service in the State Council.[30] On several occasions Lu had asked Dowager Empress Liu to relinquish her rule to Jen-tsung. Once, when the dowager empress asked the court about Empress Wu Tse-t'ien of the T'ang dynasty, no one was willing to comment except Lu Tsung-tao. By characterizing Wu Tse-t'ien as a criminal who almost brought the T'ang dynasty down, Lu undermined the dowager empress's attempt to use Wu Tse-t'ien as a precedent for her own ambitions. On another occasion, following the submission of a memorial by a low-ranking sycophant requesting that the dowager empress establish seven ancestral temples for the Liu clan, Lu Tsung-tao commented that if the Liu clan had seven temples (a practice reserved for the imperial clan), what would be left for the ruling Chao clan? Lu thereby deftly blocked the dowager empress's attempt to secure an imperial prerogative. Once, when she and Jen-tsung were to visit the Tz'u-hsiao Temple, Dowager Empress Liu wanted her carriage to precede Jen-tsung's. When Lu Tsung-tao instructed her that women are subject to the "three obediences" (*san-ts'ung*) – obedience to father, to husband, and to son – she was obliged to order her carriage to follow Jen-tsung's. Following this particularly annoying and embarrassing incident, Lu was given the nickname "Fish-head Minister," as a pun on the Chinese character for his surname, Lu, and a reference to one who gives advice that sticks in one's throat like a fish bone. However, it seems that Jen-tsung appreciated Lu's efforts, for at the end of Lu's life, as his illness intensified, Jen-tsung visited Lu and gave him three thousand ounces of silver. Court was suspended for a day after Lu's death; and even Dowager Empress Liu attended the funeral.

After Lu Tsung-tao's death, other officials rallied to check the dowager empress's quest for power. During a heavy thunderstorm in the summer of 1029, the Yü-ch'ing chao-ying Palace was struck by lightning and all but a few buildings burned to the ground. The next day one of the newly appointed assistant commissioners of military affairs, Fan Yung, suspecting that Dowager Empress Liu intended to have the palace complex rebuilt, said that the construction of the palace complex had sapped the empire's strength and that because the destruction of the Yü-ch'ing chao-ying Palace was not a human act, to rebuild it would contravene Heaven's warning.[31] Lü I-chien and Wang Tseng also opposed rebuilding. They crafted arguments based upon the Confucian textual tradition, quoting from the *Hung-fan* chapter of the *Book of documents* (*Shu-ching*) to support their opposition. Wang Shu, the highest-ranking censor, also opposed rebuilding. Dowager Empress Liu was silent in the face of

[30] *HCP* (1979) 107, p. 2494.
[31] *HCP* (1979) 108, p. 2515.

this strong opposition to rebuilding the palace complex. Wang Tseng, as the custodian of the Yü-ch'ing chao-ying Palace, had to take responsibility for the destruction of the palace, and this provided Dowager Empress Liu with the opportunity to remove the last of Chen-tsung's senior ministers from office.

Wang Tseng was widely esteemed for his honesty and fairness. While he was still living, people even set up shrines containing his portrait. Jen-tsung clearly held him in high regard, and in 1035, three years before he died, Wang Tseng was returned to service as a chief councilor. In the early 1050s, Jen-tsung wrote the calligraphy for the stone tablet for Wang Tseng's tomb, and years later, during Ying-tsung's reign (1063–7), Wang Tseng was enshrined in Jen-tsung's temple.

In the fall of 1029, Lü I-chien was confirmed as the new senior councilor, replacing Wang Tseng. As had now become customary on the winter solstice, Jen-tsung led his officials to wish Dowager Empress Liu a long life. This time, the fast-rising Fan Chung-yen (989–1052),[32] now a subeditor in the Imperial Archives, had the temerity to point out that there was no precedent for any ritual in which the emperor faced north, that such behavior diminished the imperial office, and that it should certainly not become a precedent for the future. The memorial was delivered but not answered. Fan's sponsor, Yen Shu, was disturbed by Fan's apparent glory hunting, but Fan Chung-yen replied that he was unaware that loyal criticism would make Yen Shu culpable. In the spring of 1030, Fan submitted a memorial asking Dowager Empress Liu to hand the government over to Jen-tsung. This memorial also went unanswered. Soon afterward Fan Chung-yen requested assignment out of the capital, and he was sent as vice-prefect (t'ung-p'an) to Ho-chung fu (Shan-hsi, Yung-hsing-chün circuit).

That the emperor would face north – an act symbolizing subordination – was an invitation for other irregularities, including the deliberate withholding of memorials from imperial scrutiny. Such violations had not yet occurred in the Sung.[33] Over the next three years, Sung Shou, Liu Sui, Teng Tsung-liang, Liu Yüeh, Lin Hsien-k'o, and Sun Tsu-te, concerned about the disorder that her regency was causing, memorialized the throne asking Dowager Empress Liu to step down.

[32] See Liu Tzu-chien (James T. C. Liu), "Fan Chung-yen," in *Sung biographies*, ed. Herbert Franke (Wiesbaden, 1976), vol. 1, pp. 321–30; Liu Tzu-chien (James T. C. Liu), "An early Sung reformer: Fan Chung-yen," in *Chinese thought and institutions*, ed. John K. Fairbank (Chicago, 1957), pp. 105–31; Denis C. Twitchett, "The Fan clan's charitable estate, 1050–1760," in *Confucianism in action*, ed. David S. Nivison and Arthur F. Wright (Stanford, Calif., 1959), pp. 97–133; Ting Ch'uan-ching, *A compilation of anecdotes of Sung personalities*, ed. and trans. Chu Djang and Jane C. Djang (Taipei, 1989), pp. 310–21.
[33] Karl F. Olsson, "The structure of power under the third emperor of Sung China: The shifting balance after the peace of Shan-yüan" (diss., University of Chicago, 1974), p. 69.

Sung-Liao relations remained stable and peaceful during the early part of Jen-tsung's reign, until 1041 when the war between Sung and Hsi Hsia threatened to involve the Liao.[34] In mid-1031, Emperor Liao Sheng-tsung died after fifty years of rule and was succeeded by his son, Tsung-chen, later known as Liao Hsing-tsung (r. 1031–55). As a display of respect, the Sung court was suspended for seven days and the playing of music was also forbidden for seven days in the Ho-pei and Ho-tung circuits that neighbored Liao.[35] By a curious coincidence, the new Liao emperor was controlled by the powerful dowager empress Ch'in-ai (r. 1032–9), who was formally recognized by Dowager Empress Liu. Even as Dowager Empress Liu reached out to a sister female regent she was extending her perogatives into interstate relations, a realm usually reserved for sovereigns. She was also encroaching on the emperor's perogatives in other ways. In the summer of 1031, Han-lin Academician Sung Shou and two commissioners of the Palace Audience Gate of the West submitted a newly edited *Compendium of rituals and paraphernalia of the Dowager Empress (Huang-t'ai-hou i-chih)* that regularized practices Wang Tseng had opposed during his term as chief councilor.[36] In the absence of a Wang Tseng or a Lu Tsung-tao the dowager empress supported her favorites more openly, and late in the year had Sung Shou dismissed for reminding her of the original limits of Chen-tsung's testamentary orders. Those orders allowed the regent to decide on major policy and promotions, but these meetings were to be held in one of the smaller pavilions with very few officials present. Sung Shou proposed that Jen-tsung hold a separate court where he might rule on less important matters. Sung Shou's advocacy forced the dowager empress to approve of several much-needed reforms, including giving policy critics (*chien-kuan*) their own separate headquarters and an enhanced status.[37] The dowager empress retaliated by forcing the dismissal of three censors and a censorial staff officer for giving preferment to more than eighty persons on the death of a court favorite, Liu Ts'ung-te.[38] Most conspicuously, shortly before her death in the spring of 1033, the dowager empress held the imperial clan

---

[34] The leading authority on Sung-Liao relations is Tao Jing-shen. Consult Tao Jing-shen (T'ao Chin-sheng), *Two sons of heaven: Studies in Sung-Liao relations* (Tucson, Ariz.,1988), pp. 53–67; Tao Jing-shen (T'ao Chin-sheng), "Yü Ching and Sung policies towards Liao and Hsia, 1042–1044," *Journal of Asian History* 6 No. 2 (1972), pp. 114–22; and Tao Jing-shen (T'ao Chin-sheng) and Wang Min-hsin, eds., *Li T'ao Hsü Tzu-chih t'ung-chien ch'ang-p'ien Sung Liao kuan-hsi shih-liao chi-lu* (Taipei, 1974). See also Melvin Thlick-Len Ang, "Sung-Liao diplomacy in eleventh- and twelfth-century China: A study of the social and political determinants of foreign policy" (diss., University of Pennsylvania, 1983).

[35] *HCP* (1979) 110, pp. 2559–63; Karl A. Wittfogel and Feng Chia-sheng, *History of Chinese society, Liao (907–1125)* (Philadelphia, 1949), p. 588.

[36] *HCP* (1979) 110, p. 2562.

[37] *HCP* (1979) 110, pp. 2564, 2570.

[38] *HCP* (1979) 110, pp. 2571, 2576; 111, pp. 2591–2; 112, p. 2604.

sacrifice in the Chao clan temple wearing an emperor's ritual robes. Her two assistant officiants were Dowager Empress Yang and Empress Kuo. Only the T'ang empress Wu Tse-t'ien had ever worn the ritual clothing of an emperor.[39] Although Dowager Empress Liu was fascinated with the life of Wu Tse-t'ien, she had no ambitions to overthrow her own son and seize the throne. When Ch'eng Lin (988–1056) presented her with a painting entitled *Empress Wu Serves as Regent*,[40] she threw it to the ground, saying that she could never do what Empress Wu Tse-t'ien had done.[41]

Despite Dowager Empress Liu's ascendancy, her position was not secure. Only a year earlier, in 1032, Jen-tsung's biological mother, the silent Lady Li, had died.[42] Dowager Empress Liu wished to keep her passing as quiet as possible, since Jen-tsung still did not realize that the dowager empress was not his biological mother. And although Lü I-chien's intercession gained Lady Li a proper burial, Jen-tsung remained ignorant of his real mother's identity until the third month of 1033, when the dowager empress Liu died, garbed in imperial robes.[43] Aged twenty-three, Jen-tsung was at last in a position to rule on his own behalf.

JEN-TSUNG AND LÜ I-CHIEN'S MINISTRY (1033–1043)

With Dowager Empress Liu's death, the story of Jen-tsung's birth mother finally surfaced. Jen-tsung probably learned of his biological mother from his paternal uncle, Chao Yüan-yen, Prince of Ching.[44] For days Jen-tsung wept for the mother who had been hidden from him. Recovering somewhat, he had Lady Li posthumously promoted to dowager empress and ordered that she be buried with Chen-tsung. To put his mind at rest, Jen-tsung sent his maternal uncle, Li Yung-ho, to examine the corpse to see if she had died naturally and to verify that she had been given proper honors. When Li Yung-ho confirmed that all was as it should be, the surviving relatives of Dowager Empress Liu were treated generously, confirming the wisdom of Lü I-chien's advice to Dowager Empress Liu to bury Lady Li as if she were an empress.

Dowager Empress Liu had left instructions that her old friend, Dowager Consort Yang, should be appointed dowager empress and regent. Jen-tsung did not object to the dowager empress's wishes, and Lü I-chien seemed content to prolong a weak imperial office managed by a strong chief councilor. But the

[39] *HCP* (1979) 112, p. 2605.
[40] Ch'ang et al., *Sung-jen chuan-chi tzu-liao so-yin*, pp. 3011–102.
[41] Ch'en et al., *Sung-shih chi-shih pen-mo* 24, p. 190.
[42] *HCP* (1979) 111, pp. 2577, 2579.
[43] *HCP* (1979) 112, pp. 2609–13.
[44] *HTC* (1957) 39, p. 890; *HCP* (1979) 112, p. 2610.

senior censor, Ts'ai Ch'i, confronted the councilors of state and objected to the new regency, persuading them that the emperor was now of age and should begin to rule in his own right. The decree based on the Dowager Empress Liu's dying testament was quietly suppressed.

Jen-tsung began his personal rule in the spring of 1033. His first act was to award a prestige title to Lin Hsien-k'o for having asked Dowager Empress Liu to return the government to Jen-tsung. Over the next two years he honored eighteen officials for having challenged Dowager Empress Liu to relinquish her regency in favor of the young emperor.[45] In the first month of 1035, he publicly rewarded more than one hundred and forty men who had served him while he was heir apparent and during the regency.[46] Jen-tsung's appreciation of the loyalty shown him extended to his generous posthumous award of high titular office – generally reserved for imperial princes – to K'ou Chun, one of his earliest supporters. Some of the men who supported Jen-tsung included Fan Chung-yen and Sung Shou, whom he recalled within a week. He dismissed all senior officials closely associated with Dowager Empress Liu – the same ones who had been willing to allow another regency – including Lü I-chien, Chang Chi, Hsia Sung, Ch'en Yao-tso, Fan Yung, Chao Chen2, and Yen Shu. The new Council of State consisted of Chang Shih-hsün, Li Ti, Wang Sui, Sung Shou, Li Tzu, and Wang Te-yung. This was Jen-tsung's first opportunity to act relatively unobstructed. He had moved decisively to rid the court of Dowager Empress Liu's followers and the most annoying sycophants. He also dismissed the powerful eunuchs Chang Te-ming and Lo Ch'ung-hsün, as well as others, and he eliminated the extra eunuch positions Dowager Empress Liu had created.[47]

But any hope of realizing a new vision of government soon foundered. Jen-tsung's lack of forcefulness and the inertia of an entrenched bureaucracy made significant change extremely difficult.[48] Although Jen-tsung admired the renewed Confucian orientation of the senior bureaucrats, he was not resolute enough to force this agenda on the careerists, the conventional, and the powerful. He seemed to prefer strong chief councilors, and he greatly expanded the number of scholarly offices and policy critics. He encouraged both centralization and criticism of the conventional ways of running the empire. In many instances these tendencies stymied rather than promoted change.

---

[45] *HTC* (1957) 39, pp. 891, 893, 897, 899, 901, 906.

[46] *HCP* (1979) 116, p. 2717.

[47] Liu, "Ts'ung huang-hou kan-cheng tao t'ai-hou she-cheng," pp. 593–5, citing Jen-tsung's comment that he had kept note of who was upright and who was not. See Wang Ch'eng, *Tung-tu shih-lüeh* (1186; Taipei, 1967) 56, p. 829.

[48] *HTC* (1957) 39, p. 891.

By the summer of 1033, his stepmother's regency was behind him. Fu Pi convinced Jen-tsung to burn all the paraphernalia of her regency. Jen-tsung also removed the official taboo against using the characters in the name of Dowager Empress Liu's father. Nonetheless, Fan Chung-yen reminded Jen-tsung that the dowager empress had acted with the authorization of his father, Chen-tsung. Dowager Empress Liu had been keenly aware of Jen-tsung's ambivalence toward power, and her attempt to pass the regency on to Pure Consort Yang, who had helped raise Jen-tsung, reflected a possibly genuine belief that Jen-tsung was too ambivalent to rule effectively.[49]

Jen-tsung was also a sentimental man and was especially assiduous in expressing his filial duties. In the fall of 1033 the Feng-tz'u Temple was completed. He visited the coffin of his mother three times that season. In the late fall of that year, Dowager Empresses Liu and Li were interred at Chen-tsung's imperial tomb site. Shortly afterward, Jen-tsung made offerings to their spirit tablets in the Feng-tz'u Temple. Some three hundred thousand strings of cash were spent in the construction of their tombs, paid for by a grant from the Palace Treasury (Nei-tsang k'u). Indeed, that fall the Palace Treasury disbursed one million strings to the Finance Commission to help cover the expenses of gifts given during the last Ritual Plowing – the agricultural rite in which the emperor reaffirmed his link with the earth and the seasons by plowing and thereby beginning the new growing season. Jen-tsung said to chief councilor Chang Shih-hsün that since there was no fundamental difference between state and imperial funds he ought to help with expenses. Chang Shih-hsün responded that this was not so, since officials had not stopped "overfishing" the people.[50]

Despite his desire for fiscal discipline and his avowed reluctance to assist Jen-tsung in overspending, Chang Shih-hsün's still had to contend with the political and financial costs of Jen-tsung's spending. In the summer of 1033 drought and locusts in the capital region and throughout the north, and in the Huai and Yangtze river valleys, had become so serious that pacification officials had been sent out to deal with the refugees and starving commoners.[51] Various remedies were attempted, including tax remissions and widespread soup kitchens, but to little avail.[52] Fan Chung-yen blamed the crisis on unrestrained imperial spending and urged the emperor to make specific tax and corvée reductions in the appropriate districts, to reduce the excessive number of troops and officials, to curtail construction, and to limit spending in

[49] HTC (1957) 41, p. 972.
[50] HCP (1979) 113, p. 2634.
[51] HCP (1979) 113, p. 2647.
[52] HCP (1979) 114, p. 2661.

the capital district – actions that would increase the availability of grain in the famine-stricken regions of the Huai and Yangtze.[53] Jen-tsung complied, but he also settled a score with Chang Shih-hsün – who had previously abandoned an imperial ceremony for Dowager Empress Liu to go drinking at the home of his Bureau of Military Affairs counterpart Yang Ch'ung-hsün – by blaming Chang for failing to alleviate the effects of drought and famine. As a result, Jen-tsung cashiered both Chang Shih-hsün and Yang Ch'ung-hsün in the tenth month of 1033, replacing Chang as chief councilor with Lü I-chien, whose cooperation and effectiveness Jen-tsung had begun to miss, while Yang Ch'ung-hsün was replaced as military affairs director by Wang Shu.[54]

Once Lü I-chien was back in high office, Jen-tsung came to rely on him almost completely to run the government. But Jen-tsung's long-standing problems with his consorts drew Lü into the affairs of the inner quarters. Late in 1033, Jen-tsung symbolically severed his subordination to the late Dowager Empress Liu by posthumously appointing his beloved Lady Chang as empress.[55] Nine years earlier, when Jen-tsung was fourteen, Lady Chang had been his favorite, but Empress Liu had instead chosen Lady Kuo to be Jen-tsung's empress. Empress Kuo was a protégé of Dowager Empress Liu and had assisted her earlier in 1033 at the ceremony where the Dowager Empress Liu had worn the robes of an emperor. Almost as soon as Dowager Empress Liu died, Jen-tsung entered into intense sexual liaisons with Lady Shang and Lady Yang that lasted for about a year and a half. By year's end, he had dismissed Empress Kuo, committing her to live out her life as a Taoist nun.[56] The pretext for this dismissal was that during an argument with Lady Shang, Empress Kuo, consumed with jealousy, had accidentally scratched Jen-tsung's neck when she was trying to slap Lady Shang for her impertinence. After some effort, the eunuch Yen Wen-ying connived with Lü I-chien and Fan Feng to convince Jen-tsung to divorce Empress Kuo on the grounds that she had not produced an heir, that she had struck him, and that she wanted to withdraw from the world and live as a Taoist nun. The divorce edict outraged Fan Chung-yen and the senior censor, K'ung Tao-fu, both of whom led the policy critics and censors to the palace gate to demand an interview with the emperor.[57] Jen-tsung had Lü I-chien tell them the trumped-up reasons for divorcing the woman who had been forced on him by his stepmother. The next day, both K'ung Tao-fu and Fan Chung-yen were transferred to regional posts, and the censors and policy critics were forbidden to ask for an audience as a group.

[53] Chao Ju-yü, *Chu-ch'en tsou-i* (1186; Taipei, 1970) 11, pp. 574–5.
[54] *HTC* (1957) 39, p. 900.
[55] *HTC* (1957) 36, p. 901; 36, p. 825.
[56] *HTC* (1957) 39, p. 902.
[57] Chao, *Chu-ch'en tsou-i* 28, pp. 1083–94.

Jen-tsung also extended his purge to two hundred palace women, whom he saw as partisans of Dowager Empress Liu and Empress Kuo.

Jen-tsung's marital affairs were not effectively settled until the fall of 1034, after an onslaught of natural disasters, a humbling military defeat, unusual astronomical portents, mourning for two mothers, debauchery, divorce, and political in-fighting drove the emperor to his sickbed. Lü I-chien, Sung Shou, and his other councilors asked him to take care of his health, to ensure that there would be an heir, and to appoint an empress. In response, Jen-tsung announced that Pure Consort Kuo (the title given the deposed empress) was to be housed outside the palace, Lady Shang was to enter Taoist orders, and Lady Yang was also to be sent to a monastery. Lady Yang was later reinstated as a lesser consort after Lady Shang's death in 1050. Lady Yang died in 1072. In addition, the numerous women who had been sent to the palace by officials and in-laws in the hopes of winning the emperor's favor were returned to their families. Lastly, a proper candidate for empress was to be sought to restore order to the inner palace. Lady Shang and the young Lady Yang were blamed for Jen-tsung's physical collapse, but at first not even Dowager Empress Yang could convince him to send them away; the indefatigable eunuch Yen Wen-ying, however, finally succeeded.[58] Earlier, Lü I-chien had voiced doubts that Jen-tsung could manage the women in the palace, and he appears to have been correct. Lady Shang was the most troublesome. She issued illegal palace orders, took bribes, arranged official and palace staff appointments, and allowed unauthorized visitors.[59] During Jen-tsung's illness, the usual remedies from the palace medical staff were ineffectual. Jen-tsung's oldest daughter, the Princess of Wei, finally recommended a Han-lin physician who was able to help the emperor. Jen-tsung resumed holding court late in the year.

The first candidate for empress, recommended by Dowager Empress Yang, was a Lady Ch'en, daughter of a Shou-chou tea merchant who held a minor official title. Sung Shou, Lü I-chien, Ts'ai Ch'i, and others disapproved. The emperor sent her back, not so much because her father was a merchant, but because she had been a servant. Late in the fall of 1034, Lady Ts'ao, granddaughter of Ts'ao Pin, one of T'ai-tsu's founding generals, was selected empress. The official investiture of Empress Ts'ao took place a month after the announcement, the necessity of assuring an heir taking precedence over mourning rules. Empress Ts'ao was a painter, calligrapher, and gardener, and proved a good choice as empress: unlike Empress Liu, who had lavishly favored her own family, Empress Ts'ao did not request or permit favors for her relatives.[60]

[58] *HCP* (1979) 115, p. 2696.
[59] Chao, *Chu-ch'en tsou-i* 29, pp. 1101–2.
[60] *HTC* (1957) 39, p. 921.

The emperor still felt regret about demoting Empress Kuo in a fit of rage about the dowager empress. Late in 1035 he renewed contact with her, sending her gifts and asking after her health. By chance she fell ill. The ever-watchful Yen Wen-ying, who was acting for the emperor, conveyed medicine to her. Within days she suddenly died, and it was widely believed Yen had poisoned her. She was buried with the rites proper to an empress, and the episode was closed.

Jen-tsung's flawed character made both him and his chief councilor vulnerable to unwelcome criticism. In the last month of 1034, the censor Sun Mien was dismissed for criticizing Lü I-chien, for criticizing Jen-tsung's behavior since his liaisons with Ladies Yang and Shang, for cataloguing the problems for which the emperor was responsible, and for pointing out that Jen-tsung held court on barely one hundred days a year.[61] Jen-tsung's apathy toward active rule and holding court continued throughout his reign. But the emperor did enjoy the company of learned men and regularly met with close advisors, Han-lin academicians, and other scholar-officials to appreciate texts, calligraphy, and readings, and to discuss Confucian thought. In the spring of 1035, Jen-tsung invited Sheng Tu, Chia Ch'ang-ch'ao, and other lecturers, readers, and close advisors to attend the opening of two new halls, in which Jen-tsung had calligraphed screens with the "Wu-yi" chapter from the *Book of documents*.[62]

One cultural project initiated by Jen-tsung was a catalogue of the four imperial libraries. It was begun in 1034 under the direction of Chang Kuan and with the help of two drafting officials and the directors of the four libraries. By late 1035, the 8,435 *chüan* of classics and histories had been catalogued and edited. The project was completed in 1041 by Wang Yao-ch'en, Wang Chu, Ou-yang Hsiu, and the others who compiled the annotated catalogue, modeled on the T'ang dynasty *K'ai-yüan ssu-pu lu*, and a model, itself, for later imperial catalogues. The four libraries held 3,445 titles in 30,669 *chüan*. Books missing from the collections of the scholarly institutes were to be acquired by purchase on the open book market.[63]

Jen-tsung also sponsored significant reforms in the education system. Just months after Jen-tsung ascended the throne, Sun Shih, Jen-tsung's tutor and the director of the Imperial University (*T'ai-hsüeh*), established the precedent

---

[61] *HCP* (1979) 115, pp. 2709–12; *SS* 289, p. 9687.

[62] *HTC* (1957) 40, p. 924.

[63] *HCP* (1979) 114, p. 2681; 117, p. 2760; 118, p. 2783; 134, p. 3206; Yves Hervouet, ed., *A Sung bibliography (Bibliographie des Sung)* (Hong Kong, 1978), p. 195; Liu Tzu-chien (James T. C. Liu), *Ou-yang Hsiu: An eleventh century Neo-Confucianist* (Stanford, Calif.,1967), p. 102. See also John H. Winkelman, *The imperial library in Southern Sung China, 1127–1279: A study of the organization and operation of the scholarly agencies of the central government* (Philadelphia, 1974).

of endowing prefectural schools with income land.[64] In the first month of 1034, the Shan-hsi circuit capital of Ching-ch'ao fu (modern Hsi-an) was authorized to establish a prefectural school, which was provided with an edition of the Nine Classics and an endowment of five ch'ing (approximately 70 acres) of rental land to support the school. By mid-1034, Ch'en-chou (Ching-hsi North) and Yang-chou were also authorized to set up prefectural schools, and were each given rental land and a set of the Nine Classics. This was the usual practice for endowing all subsequent prefectural schools during Jen-tsung's reign.[65] By the end of 1037, it was decided to limit the establishment of schools to only the most populous prefectures, which in practice meant about one-sixth of the approximately two hundred and fifty prefectures in the empire.[66] Thirty-seven prefectural schools were established before the Ch'ing-li reforms in 1044. In all, eighty prefectural schools and eighty-nine county schools were established during Jen-tsung's reign.

The civil service examinations were another important element of Sung education. Early in 1034, Jen-tsung had the selection ratio for the chin-shih degree increased to twenty percent instead of the usual six to seven percent of the examinees. This became the standard selection ratio for his reign. That year yielded 783 new graduates, a result of the extremely generous standards set. As the number of students involved increased, the number of qualified graduates far exceeded the posts available, and the problems of unfairness and favoritism in selection for appointment increased. At the beginning of 1037 it was ordered that the quota for the various prefectures be equalized to restore the principle of fairness that had been distorted by occasional ad hoc changes. Also in 1037 the practice of recopying examination papers to ensure that examiners would not recognize the handwriting of protégés was instituted.[67]

The rapid, state-sponsored expansion of the education system yielded some unexpected side effects. The fast-growing group of literati graduates began

---

[64] HCP (1979) 99, p. 2303.

[65] HTC (1957) 39, p. 911. See HCP (1979) 114, pp. 2659, 2677, 2681; 115, p. 2705; 116, pp. 2725, 2728, 2757, 2761, 2767; 118, pp. 2775, 2778, 2783, 2785–7, 2789–91; 119, pp. 2795, 2802, 2810; 120, pp. 2819, 2822, 2825, 2836, 2840, 2843; 121, pp. 2861, 2867; 122, p. 2875; 123, pp. 2896, 2900; 125, p. 2941; 145, p. 3516. For a full account of prefectural schools, especially following Jen-tsung's reign, see Thomas H. C. Lee, Government education and examinations in Sung China (New York, 1985), pp. 105–37. See also John W. Chaffee, The thorny gates of learning in Sung China: A social history of examinations (Cambridge, 1985), p. 75, table 10, which shows that Jen-tsung established more prefectural and county schools per decade than any other emperor.

[66] Michael C. McGrath, "Military and regional administration in Northern Sung China (960–1126)" (diss., Princeton University, 1982), p. 71.

[67] Chaffee, The thorny gates of learning in Sung China, pp. 51, and 53, quoting HCP (1979) 120, p. 2819; HTC (1957) 40, p. 956; HCP (1979) 114, p. 2661; Lee, Government education and examinations in Sung China, p.148.

to challenge the lingering ideals of what had been a more rigidly stratified social order. In 1036, the unprecedented spread of literati culture throughout society compelled the emperor and scholar-officials to promulgate sumptuary regulations for the people of the capital district specifying status-appropriate headgear and clothing, housing, carts and horses, and articles of daily living for them. Knowledge of decrees and laws was restricted by forbidding private individuals from copying out collections of legal documents. The number of scholar-officials, drawn from the ranks of the literati, grew by virtue of the doubling of the size of the civil service in Jen-tsung's reign. The ability of the government to absorb new candidates was quickly saturated. As more men were recruited, more officials were supported, increasing the number of individuals eligible for pensions. Privileges of official status were also extended more widely when, at the end of 1036, all officials, their sons, and their grandsons were relieved from obligations to serve as village officers, a privilege that had previously been restricted to officials of rank 7b and up in the nine-tier system of stipendiary grades. Officials were even allowed to use the official postal system to send letters to their family.[68]

To further curtail the political powers of the bureaucratic elite, restrictions on the socializing of officials were reiterated: officials of the Finance Commission, Censorate, and K'ai-feng prefecture were not permitted to meet officially with each other's "guests" or retinue. Between 1039 and 1059 restrictions were enforced and gradually enlarged to include judicial review officials and senior Justice Board officials, Han-lin academicians, drafting officials, remonstrators, and councilors of state; after 1059 the rules were gradually relaxed.[69]

Another group in Sung society whose wealth and fecundity caused unwelcome side effects was the imperial clan. Because imperial clansmen were scattered all over the capital and because they were forbidden to meet except at court or at imperial sacrifices, Jen-tsung ordered a Hostel for Imperial Clansmen (Mu-ch'in chai) to be built on the grounds of the burned down Yü-ch'ing chao-ying Palace. There, members of the ten princely houses could live in proximity to each other. Finance Commissioner Ch'eng Lin oversaw the project, and the eunuch Yen Wen-ying directed the work, which was completed in

[68] Edward A. Kracke, Jr., Civil service in early Sung China, 960–1067; with particular emphasis on the development of controlled sponsorship to foster administrative responsibility (Cambridge, Mass., 1953), p. 164; Kracke also explains the official ranking system. See also HCP (1979) 118, pp. 2776–7, 2786; Lo Wen (Winston W. Lo), An introduction to the civil service of Sung China: With emphasis on its personnel administration (Honolulu, 1987), pp. 134–7. See also Brian E. McKnight, "Fiscal privileges and social order in Sung China," in Crisis and prosperity in Sung China, ed. John W. Haeger (Tucson, Ariz.,1975), pp. 79–100.

[69] HCP (1979) 118, p. 2776; 125, p. 2945; 143, p. 3449; 160, p. 3873; 189, pp. 4564–5; 193, pp. 4661–2. See also Gung Wei Ai, "The participation of censorial officials in politics during the Northern Sung dynasty (960–1126 A.D.)," Chinese Culture 5 No. 2 (1974), pp. 30–4, 41.

the fall of 1035.[70] In the same way that the *Mu-ch'in chai* was built to accommodate imperial clansmen, a guesthouse complex was built for court officials while they were in the capital. Twelve years later, in 1047, Jen-tsung had the *Kuang-ch'in chai* constructed to house the children and grandchildren of T'ai-tsu's youngest son, the Prince of Ch'in, who had outgrown their originally allocated space. By this time there were approximately 1,080 recognized members of the imperial clan. Jen-tsung apparently achieved a high level of clan participation in imperial rites, for only sixty of the imperial clansmen did not practice the austerities necessary to take part in the triennial worship of Heaven. Yet clan socializing threatened to swell out of control, and within a few years so many imperial clan members were visiting the imperial palace that Jen-tsung forbade further unannounced visits.[71] In 1036, to help manage the affairs of the increasingly large imperial clan, Jen-tsung set up a new Chief Office of Imperial Clan Affairs (*Ta tsung-cheng ssu*), without eliminating the older Court of the Imperial Clan (*Tsung-cheng ssu*). The concern of the new office was the education and good behavior of imperial clansmen. Jen-tsung selected his cousin Chao Yün-jang (995–1059) as the first director of the Chief Office of Imperial Clan Affairs. He was the third son of Chao Yüan-fen and a grandson of T'ai-tsung, and he had been Chen-tsung's choice to become heir after Chen-tsung's oldest son had died and before Jen-tsung was born.[72]

Although without Lü I-chien's energy little would have been accomplished during these early years of Jen-tsung's majority, to those on the outside it appeared as though the chief councilor was usurping imperial authority. In 1036, Fan Chung-yen denounced Lü for blatant favoritism in the selection and promotion of officials, and also challenged Jen-tsung to take personal responsibility for managing personnel affairs. Fan went so far as to suggest that Lü I-chien could be another Wang Mang or Chang Yü, infamous usurpers of the past. Lü I-chien responded by charging Fan with forming a faction (*p'eng-tang*) and with trying to drive a wedge between the ruler and his loyal minister. Fan Chung-yen's suggestion that Jen-tsung's cousin, Chao Yün-jang, be designated as heir apparent also had disconcerted the emperor. As the

---

[70] *HCP* (1979) 117, pp. 2757–8.

[71] *HCP* (1979) 117, p. 2762; 161, pp. 3887, 3889. On these issues see John W. Chaffee, "From capital to countryside: Changing residency patterns of the Sung imperial clan," *Chinese Culture* 30 No. 1 (1989), pp. 21–34.; John W. Chaffee, "The marriage of Sung imperial clanswomen," in *Marriage and inequality in Chinese society*, ed. Rubie S. Watson and Patricia B. Ebrey (Berkeley, Calif., 1991), pp. 133–69. See also John C. Chaffee, "Two Sung imperial clan genealogies: Preliminary findings and questions," *Journal of Sung-Yuan Studies* 23 (1993), pp. 99–109; Robert M. Hartwell, "The imperial treasuries: Finance and power in Song China," *Bulletin of Sung-Yüan Studies* 20 (1988), pp. 44–5; and Han Ch'i's memorial in Chao, *Chu-ch'en tsou-i* 23, pp. 949–50.

[72] *HCP* (1979) 119, pp. 2796, 2799; *SS* 245, p. 8708; Ch'ang et al., *Sung-jen chuan-chi tzu-liao so-yin*, p. 3413.

prefect of K'ai-feng, Fan Chung-yen was not a court official, so his memorial went beyond his direct administrative purview, and on these grounds he was removed from K'ai-feng. Even though Fan had shown that it was possible to criticize Lü I-chien, continued fear of the chief councilor prevented censors or remonstrance officials from objecting to Fan Chung-yen's demotion.[73] It was left to Li Hung, Wang Chih, Yü Ching, Yin Shu, and Ou-yang Hsiu, all junior scholarly officials, to protest against Fan's punishment.[74] All were themselves demoted and sent out of the capital. Ts'ai Hsiang (1012–67) wrote a poem praising the stalwarts, and Han Ch'i managed to divert a retaliatory impeachment launched against Ts'ai Hsiang. But following Lü I-chien's lead, a junior censor suggested that officials be forbidden to exceed the authority of their office by discussing matters outside their specific responsibilities. Su Yao-ch'in argued unsuccessfully that the restraining order was a bad policy.[75]

Nonetheless, by 1037 Lü I-chien was no longer as unassailable as he had been. In the spring of that year he was removed from office in a widespread reshuffling of the Council of State that also led to fellow councilor Wang Tseng's transfer.[76] Lü I-chien and Wang Tseng had been unable to get along, for Wang – who had once been Lü's superior – could not tolerate Lü's authoritarian control of the government. When Wang Tseng requested a transfer and reappointment, Jen-tsung asked him why. Wang replied that Lü abused his powers and sold favors. Wang Tseng's criticism of Lü in some sense was possible only because Fan Chung-yen had already denounced Lü. Nonetheless, the new chief councilors, Wang Sui and Ch'en Yao-tso, were proxies who had been secretly recommended to the emperor by Lü himself. Clearly, Lü I-chien intended Jen-tsung to suffer under ineffectual chief councilors until Jen-tsung could be persuaded to recall him as chief councilor.

But Lü's I-chien reputation was further buffeted by an earthquake that rocked the capital district for five days at the end of 1037.[77] Ting-chou and Hsiang-chou (in Ho-pei West) were also affected. Two weeks later, Ping-chou, Tai-chou, and Hsin-chou3 (all in Ho-tung) suffered earthquakes. It was said that earthquakes continued for several years with as many as four or five shocks a day. The earth cracked, geysers spouted, and more than twelve thousand people were killed with some fifty-six hundred people injured and

[73] HCP (1979) 118, pp. 2783–6, 2788; Liu, "An early Sung reformer: Fan Chung-yen," pp. 105–31; Liu, "Fan Chung-yen," pp. 321–30; and Liu Tzu-chien (James T. C. Liu), "Lü I-chien," in Sung biographies, ed. Herbert Franke (Wiesbaden, 1976), vol. 2, pp. 713–19.

[74] Peter K. Bol, "This culture of ours": Intellectual transition in T'ang and Sung China (Stanford, Calif.,1992), p. 169.

[75] Chao, Chu-ch'en tsou-i 18, pp. 786–93.

[76] HTC (1957) 40, pp. 952–3.

[77] HCP (1979) 120, pp. 2844–5.

fifty thousand cattle injured or killed. The day after the report from Ho-tung, Ch'eng K'an, a censor, was sent to investigate and to manage disaster relief. Han Ch'i and P'ang Chi memorialized the emperor about the portents in the past five months, admonishing him to maintain closer control of the military, to keep palace women and their friends out of official matters, and – in an indirect reference to Lü I-chien – to prevent despotic government. Han Ch'i, in particular, expressed concern over the construction of Taoist ritual spaces in the Ta-ch'ing Pavilion and other places.[78] Yeh Ch'ing-ch'en, a scholar attached to the Historiography Institute, reminded the emperor that for the two years since Fan Chung-yen, Yü Ching, and the others had been demoted and dismissed because of speaking out, no one had dared discuss matters of court or governance. He asked Jen-tsung to hold himself responsible and to relent in his treatment of loyal but outspoken officials. As a result, Jen-tsung had Fan Chung-yen, Yü Ching, and Ou-yang Hsiu transferred to posts closer to the capital. Even this small transfer of Fan Chung-yen made his detractors fear his return, and they quickly raised false accusations, incurring the emperor's wrath. But the polarizing of political discourse that was to poison late Northern Sung political culture had begun its vogue, and before long any association of officials could be discredited by calling it a "faction" of Fan Chung-yen's.

The 1030s were a period of prolonged bad weather and famines. Severe thunderstorms and heavy rains followed the earthquakes of 1037, and two days afterward a meteor shower prompted Jen-tsung to lift the prohibition on discussing public matters. In response, Sung Ch'i, Su Hsün-ch'in, Chang Fang-p'ing, Han Ch'i, Su Shen, Chang Kuan, and Yeh Ch'ing-ch'en all warned Jen-tsung against allowing Lü I-chien to dominate the government, suppress open discussion, or appoint favorites.[79] One result of Su Hsün-ch'in's memorial was the resumption of the daily court assemblies in the main hall. Because of the earthquakes and the continuous thunderstorms, fiscal intendants and judicial intendants were ordered to evaluate their subordinate officials for competence and to take measures to reduce or discontinue the harsh treatment of the people. More to the point, collection of the 1037 autumn tax was canceled for earthquake victims in Ping-chou (T'ai-yüan), Tai-chou, and Hsin-chou3 prefectures in Ho-tung.

The most dramatic outcome from the advice Jen-tsung had received was a clean sweep of incompetents and of Lü I-chien's favorites, especially Wang Sui, Ch'en Yao-tso, Han I, and Shih Chung-li. Jen-tsung was ready for a steadier, more active Council of State that could repair the damage done by the ominous portents and withstand the rising tide of political criticism made

[78] HCP (1979) 120, p. 2842; Chao, Chu-ch'en tsou-i 38, pp. 1368–75.
[79] Chao, Chu-ch'en tsou-i 38, pp. 1379–1424; HTC (1957) 41, p. 964; HCP (1979) 121, pp. 2849–64.

possible by the proliferation of advisory positions. Furthermore, Wang Sui and
Ch'en Yao-tso were so sick that the Secretariat-Chancellery was referred to as
the "Convalescent Room" (indeed, Wang Sui died early in 1039). Jen-tsung
then appointed Chang Shih-hsün and Chang Te-hsiang as his chief councilors,
Wang Tsung and Li Jo-ku as the two assistant executives, and Wang Po-wen
and Ch'en Chih-chung as the two deputies at the Bureau of Military Affairs.
Wang Po-wen, however, died within a month and was replaced by Chang
Kuan, a *chin-shih* honors graduate, who had earlier recommended Wang Po-
wen as a censor.[80] To this team of state councilors fell the initial responsibility
of managing a new crisis: the Sung's first major war with the Tangut Hsia,
known in Chinese sources as the Hsi Hsia (Western Hsia).

THE WAR WITH HSI HSIA (1038–1044)

From the time of the signing of the Shan-yüan Treaty in 1005 until war with
the Sung in 1038, the Hsi Hsia domain had grown from a handful of towns
inside the loop of the Yellow River to an extensive cavalry empire that spanned
the Ordos region and the Kansu Corridor.[81] Li Yüan-hao's father, the Tangut
leader, Li Te-ming, had acknowledged both the Sung and the Liao as overlords,
but he had systematically expanded into the west. In 1028, Li Te-ming sent his
son to capture Kan-chou2 (near Chang-yeh, Kansu) from the Hui-ku; Li Yüan-
hao's success confirmed him as Li Te-ming's rightful heir. Under Li Yüan-hao
the Tanguts also gained control of Liang-chou, at the eastern side of the fertile
plains area bounded on the west by Kan-chou2, thereby displacing the Tibetan
federation headed by Ku-ssu-lo (997–1065) south to the Huang-shui valley
town of Ch'ing-t'ang, east of Kokonor Lake (Ch'ing-hai).[82]

As soon as Li Yüan-hao, far less attached to Chinese culture than his father
had been, inherited the rulership of the Hsi Hsia at the end of 1032, he began
to carve out a distinct Tangut political and cultural realm. In his first year and
a half as ruler he consolidated his regime and transformed the Tangut polity
into a militarized state. In 1034, Li Yüan-hao attacked Fu-chou2 (in Ho-tung
circuit) and Ch'ing-chou2 (in what was to become Yung-hsing-chün circuit).

---

[80] Ch'ang et al., *Sung-jen chuan-chi tzu-liao so-yin*, p. 2339. Liang T'ien-hsi, "Ts'ung Tsun-yao-lu k'an Sung-
ch'u ssu-ch'ao chih chün-shih yü cheng-chih," *Ta-lu tsa-chih* 31 No. 6 (1965), p. 28, sees this purge as
one of the decisive steps in the factional struggles which contributed to the fall of the Sung. See also
HCP (1979) 121, pp. 2864–6.

[81] See Ruth W. Dunnell, "The Hsi Hsia," in *The Cambridge history of China*, volume 6: *Alien regimes and
border states, 907–1368*, ed. Herbert Franke and Denis C. Twitchett (New York, 1994), p. 171, map 10.
See the front endpaper map in Wu T'ien-ch'ih, *Hsi Hsia shih-kao* (Ch'eng-tu, 1981), and maps 11–402
and 11–403 in Li Chen and Ch'en T'ing-yüan, *Chung-kuo li-tai chan-cheng shih* (Taipei, 1976), vol. 11.

[82] See Ruth W. Dunnell, "Tanguts and the Tangut state of Ta Hsia" (diss., Princeton University, 1983),
pp. 100, 105–6.

Earlier, a non-Chinese patrol leader (*hsün-chien*) had raided Hsi Hsia territory, destroying fortified settlements there. In reaction Li Yüan-hao defeated the local district commander (*tu-chien*), who had ignored an interpreter's warning of an ambush. In a demonstration of moral superiority, Li Yüan-hao returned the captured Sung officers and soldiers. In the fall of 1034, Jen-tsung sent Chou Wei-te, one of his eunuch troubleshooters, to the Huan-ch'ing military subcircuit to assess the situation.[83] He also sent General Liu P'ing, a prefectural administrator, as deputy general commandant for Huan-ch'ing. Earlier, Liu P'ing had warned Jen-tsung that Li Yüan-hao was preparing for cultural and political independence, but had been ignored. Now Jen-tsung charged Liu P'ing to take care of the matter, giving him a million strings of cash. At the time, Jen-tsung was incapacitated by illness and afterward preoccupied with preparations for the investiture of the new empress in 1034. For a few years Li Yüan-hao was not regarded as a serious threat. Initially, the only action taken by the Sung was to cashier various eunuchs and generals in the circuit. Indeed, Sung Shou, one of the councilors of state, was more concerned about Jen-tsung's banqueting, music, and women. Otherwise the empire appeared to be at peace.[84] Normal relations seemed to have resumed by early 1035, when Li Yüan-hao sent fifty horses to the court and requested a copy of the *Buddhist canon*, which was sent to him. Until Li Yüan-hao asked for official recognition in 1038, the Sung court did not pay close attention to Hsi Hsia military and political developments; all the while, however, the Tanguts were solidifying their hold over crucial Kansu Corridor trade routes and developing their military resources.

Besides establishing a Chinese-style central government for the militarized kingdom, Li Yüan-hao also designated eighteen military control commissions spread among five military zones, defended by as many as three hundred and seventy thousand men under arms.[85] These were mounted forces, who had been stretched thin by hard warfare and whose ranks had probably been swelled by nonwarrior horsemen impressed to fill the army. Li Yüan-hao also maintained a six-unit bodyguard of five thousand and an elite cavalry force of three thousand. It was a fearful concentration of military might overlaying a shallow economic base. Preparing for campaigns in Sung territory, Li Yüan-hao requested permission in early 1038 to send a group to visit the five sacred Buddhist mountains by way of the transport routes of the official postal system.

[83] For an explanation of the civil and military subdivisions of greater Shan-hsi, see the Introduction, note 31.

[84] *HCP* (1979) 115, p. 2694.

[85] For the location of the military control commissions see Dunnell, "The Hsi Hsia," pp. 184–5 map 12; *HCP* (1979) 119, pp. 2813–14, 2845.

Even though everyone knew that his real intention was to reconnoiter Ho-tung, permission was granted.

Between Li Yüan-hao's preliminary raids on Lin-chou, Fu-chou2, Ch'ing-chou2, and Huan-chou2 in 1034 and his proclamation of the Hsi Hsia empire in 1038, the Sung had responded by repairing the San-pai irrigation system in the Wei River valley in Shan-hsi, reestablishing the *ju-chung* delivery system to move grain and supplies into the border garrisons,[86] and distributing a compendium on military science. Orders were issued in mid-1037 to conduct the secret repair and construction of defensive works in Ho-pei and Ho-tung circuits which were main areas of concern because of the Liao threat. This last measure was backed up by the expenditure of one and half million *liang* of silver and more than three hundred thousand bolts of silk. Throughout the war with Hsi Hsia, Ho-pei and Ho-tung continued to receive Palace Treasury support because of their proximity to Liao and to the imperial capital. Not until mid-fall of 1038 did the Palace Treasury begin disbursing resources for Shan-hsi, which faced the brunt of the Hsia threat,[87] when one million bolts of silk were allocated for buying supplies.

In late fall the zone commander (*ch'ien-hsia*) of Fu-yen circuit reported that Li Yüan-hao's stepfather, Shan-yü Wei-liang, and others had sent messengers ahead to request permission to surrender to the Sung. The court ordered the commander not to accept the surrender, which was induced by Li Yüan-hao's execution of chiefs who opposed his plan to attack the Sung. Because Shan-yü Wei-liang had tried to stop Li Yüan-hao from taking this course several times with no success, he feared he would be killed also. As a result, he kidnapped Li Yüan-hao's wife and son as hostages in order to escape to the Sung. But the Sung frontier commander sent him back under military escort to Li Yüan-hao to face execution by massed archers. At the same time, Yüan-hao sent an envoy to request recognition of his rule as Emperor of Hsia (*Ta Hsia huang-ti*), on the grounds that he was descended from the Northern Wei dynasty (386–534); that he had patterned the Tangut script, clothing, rituals, music, and implements after the Chinese model; that the peoples of the region all submitted to him; and that his people desired to have their own state (*chien pang-chia*). A month before Jen-tsung conducted the worship of Heaven in late 1038, Li Yüan-hao had already constructed an altar to announce his self-appointment as Emperor of Hsia. Li had also declared a new reign title and ennobled his deceased grandfather and father as emperors. Although

---

[86] On the *ju-chung* provisioning system, see Peter J. Golas, "The Sung financial administration," in *The Cambridge history of China*, volume 5: *The Sung dynasty and its precursors, 907–1279, part 2*, ed. John W. Chaffee and Denis C. Twitchett (New York, forthcoming).

[87] *HCP* (1979) 122, p. 2879.

Li Yüan-hao still accepted subservience to Sung, he requested a patent of title from his majesty Jen-tsung, the south-facing sovereign, and expressed hope for good relations. However, the timing of Li Yüan-hao's ceremonies on his own altar was a clear affront that was exacerbated by Li's refusal to send annual tribute to the Sung as a further means of publicly proclaiming his new independent status.[88]

In the four years from Li Yüan-hao's elevation to emperor to his preliminary acceptance of peace with the Sung at the end of 1042, the war between Hsi Hsia and Sung was primarily driven by Li Yüan-hao's actions and Sung reactions to them. The war can be divided into five phases: (1) a preparatory phase from late 1038 to late 1039, culminating in the Hsi Hsia attack on Pao-an chün; (2) 1040 and the consequences of the Hsi Hsia siege of Yen-an fu; (3) 1041 and the aftermath of the Sung defeat at Hao-shui-ch'uan; (4) an interlude from late 1041 to autumn of 1042, as Sung attention is diverted by the threat of a Liao invasion; and (5) from the battle of Ting-ch'uan-chai in the autumn of 1042 through the summer of 1044, when Li Yüan-hao agrees to refer to himself as "subject" (ch'en) when addressing the Sung emperor.[89]

Phase 1 (late 1038–late 1039)

Consideration of how to respond to Yüan-hao was postponed while Jen-tsung and his officials organized the triennial cycle of worship of Heaven and Earth in late 1038. Among the military preparations that were undertaken, the Ch'ing-t'ang Tibetan ruler Ku-ssu-lo was promoted to chieh-tu shih (military governor) – by this time an honorary post used largely to reward compliant native chieftains[90] – for his support against Li Yüan-hao. In addition, a reward of one hundred thousand strings of cash was offered for Li's capture. Hsia Sung and Fan Yung were appointed pacification intendants of the circuits along the Sung–Hsi Hsia frontier. But decisions were made so slowly that the court did not strip Li Yüan-hao of his ranks, titles, offices, and the Chao surname until the middle of 1039. To bolster their loyalty, money in varying amounts was given to troops in Shan-hsi and Szechwan, and pearls and jewels worth three hundred thousand strings were issued to the Finance Commission to pay for border zone military provisions, thereby both buttressing military preparations and easing the burden on local taxpayers. The pattern of spending suggests that Jen-tsung

---

[88] HCP (1979) 122, p. 2888.

[89] HCP (1979) 149, pp. 3616–17.

[90] See Charles O. Hucker, A dictionary of official titles in imperial China (Stanford, Calif., 1985), p. 144. Though honorary from the Sung perspective, these titles served as potent sources of political capital for their native incumbents.

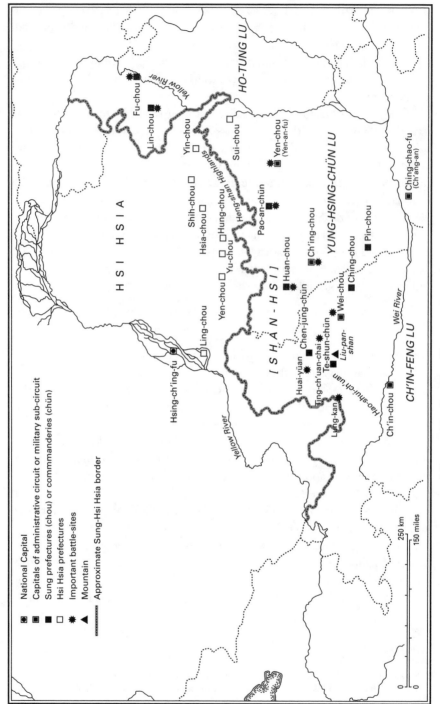

Map 13. The first Sino-Tangut war, 1038–1044.

National Capital
Capitals of administrative circuit or military sub-circuit
Sung prefectures (chou) or commmanderies (chün)
Hsi Hsia prefectures
Important battle-sites
Mountain
Approximate Sung-Hsi Hsia border

HSI HSIA

HO-TUNG LU

YUNG-HSING-CHÜN LU

I SHÂN - H SI I

CH'IN-FENG LU

Fu-chou
Lin-chou
Yellow River
Yin-chou
Sui-chou
Yen-chou
(Yen-an-fu)
Shih-chou
Hsia-chou
Hung-chou
Hengshan Highlands
Pao-an-chün
Ch'ing-chou
Pin-chou
Ching-chao-fu
(Ch'ang-an)
Yen-chou
Yu-chou
Huan-chou
Ching-chou
Ling-chou
Huai-yüan
Chen-jung-chün
Wei-chou
Hsing-ch'ing-fu
Ting-ch'uan-chai
Te-shun-chün
Liu-pan-
shan
Hao-shui-ch'uan
Yellow River
Lung-kan
Ch'in-chou
Wei River

250 km
150 miles

sought to assert control over the crucial disbursements for a war that was costing more than the government had in hand. The dual problem of liquidity and budget balancing once again produced a rash of money-saving measures. Jen-tsung ordered the release of two hundred and seventy palace women, and had his close advisors work with the finance commission to discuss how to reduce excessive and fluctuating expenses. Han Ch'i recommended spending less money on the imperial women and imperial paraphernalia, and a few other officials proposed reducing salaries and allowances (which Jen-tsung opposed) and tightening eligibility for appointing children to official rank by hereditary privilege.[91] In Ho-pei, military and economic oversight were strengthened simultaneously by giving the Ho-pei fiscal intendant overall direction of agricultural and military colonies.

Late in 1039 Hsi Hsia attacks on Pao-an chün were repulsed by Lu Shou-ch'in, zone commander for Fu-yen circuit.[92] The Hsia also surrounded Ch'eng-p'ing-chai with some thirty thousand mounted troops while Hsü Huai-te, the deputy circuit military commander (*fu-pu-shu*) for Fu-yen circuit, was in the city. Hsü led a thousand or so troops to break through the encirclement and attack the Hsia, after which the Tangut forces disengaged. Sung troops then destroyed several Hsi Hsia outposts. Lu Shou-ch'in was promoted for his victory. Ti Ch'ing distinguished himself so greatly that he was promoted four ranks, from ordinary soldier to military official.

In the following month, the last of the lunar year, Su Shen offered Jen-tsung advice, speaking from his junior position at the Historiography Institute.[93] Although he warned Jen-tsung to guard his health and to avoid squandering his energy and treasury on the distractions of luxury and sex, he also urged the emperor to order his border generals and commanders to submit plans for an offensive war, because ten years of defense had not paid off. Many others also submitted recommendations, but no one else advocated taking the offensive.[94] The two basic military issues were force concentration and training. The main frontier districts were in the Kansu region along the Ordos Desert and west of the Liu-p'an Mountains. Apart from the few river valleys, this area was mostly sparse grasslands with very low rainfall. Its population, made up of mostly non-Han pastoralists, was few and scattered. Distances between settlements were so great that more horses, mounted archers, local militias, tribal allies, and fortified bases were needed to counter Li Yüan-hao's ability to bring large concentrations of mounted forces together for massive raids. The distances,

[91] Chao, *Chu-ch'en tsou-i* 101, pp. 3365–7; *HCP* (1979) 123, pp. 2902, 2904–6, 2908.
[92] Ch'ang et al., *Sung-jen chuan-chi tzu-liao so-yin*, pp. 4028–9.
[93] Ch'ang et al., *Sung-jen chuan-chi tzu-liao so-yin*, pp. 4310–11; *HCP* (1979) 125, pp. 2950–3.
[94] *HCP* (1979) 125, pp. 2953–60; Chao, *Chu-ch'en tsou-i* 132, pp. 4477–80.

terrain, and enemy tactics required mounted warfare, preparation for which would need two or three years to train troops and to augment and replace detrained imperial garrison forces. There were also economic concerns, for Jen-tsung was informed that support for the military and the court was absorbing the entire tribute grain delivery from Huai-nan, Liang-che, and Chiang-nan.

Phase 2 (early to late 1040)

The second phase of the war dates from early 1040, when Li Yüan-hao attacked Chin-ming Fort near Yen-an fu, capturing the local commanding officer and his son. Li Yüan-hao then moved to encircle Yen-an fu, whose prefect, Fan Yung, had been duped by the Tanguts into leaving the city unprepared.[95]

That spring of 1040, Han Ch'i convinced Jen-tsung to restore Fan Chung-yen as a junior drafting official, and both Han and Fan were concurrently appointed deputy military intendants of Shan-hsi. Fan Chung-yen was also appointed to be prefect of Yen-an fu in the fall. Prior to his appointment, troops and commanders had been disposed as follows: each regional comman-dant (or circuit military commander) commanded 10,000 troops, each zone commander commanded 5,000 troops, and each district commander com-manded 3,000. Whenever there was an incursion the lowest-ranking com-mander was sent to respond. Fan Chung-yen argued that this was a self-defeating response to military threats, and he redeployed the troops within Yen-an fu into six commands. Each commander led 3,000 troops, trained them within their own units, and responded swiftly to Hsi Hsia incursions on the basis of the number of attackers. Fan's method, which the entire region later adopted, was so successful that even the Tanguts were impressed, warning each other to avoid attacking Yen-an fu "because nowadays Young Master Fan has several myriads of soldiers and isn't as easy to dupe as Old Master Fan [Yung]."[96]

Fan's success notwithstanding, the military situation in early 1040 was so serious that the emperor ordered the Bureau of Military Affairs to deliberate with the chief councilors concerning the war with Li Yüan-hao, overturning a long-standing dynastic policy to keep civil and military authority separate. A few months later, Jen-tsung expanded the deliberative group to include assis-tant councilors, and had a special meeting room set up by the Secretariat just south of the Bureau of Military Affairs compound. So desperate was the emperor for strategic advice that he permitted officials at court and on assignment in the outlying regions to comment on affairs of state. This was the first time since Fan Chung-yen had been demoted a little less than four years earlier that officials were allowed to comment on matters outside the immediate jurisdiction of their office.[97] Several weeks later, Jen-tsung ordered his senior officials to submit policy recommendations on whether to take a defensive or an offensive approach in Shan-hsi. By mid-spring, Li Yüan-hao had already overrun Chin-ming and attacked the An-yan, Sai-men, and Yung-p'ing forts. Because of these defeats, Jen-tsung reinstalled the old reliable Lü I-chien as chief councilor, and dismissed his military councilors, Wang Tsung, Ch'en Chih-chung, and Chang Kuan, replacing them with Yen Shu, Sung Shou, and Wang I-yung.[98] Yen Shu, while serving as finance commissioner, had asked Jen-tsung to discontinue using eunuchs as military supervisors (referring in particular to Lu Shou-ch'in), to require his field commanders to follow set-piece battle plans, to draft and train archers, and to relinquish some of the treasures in the palace to pay for the war. Further advice came from Han-lin Academician Ting Tu (later, the editor of the *Wu-ching tsung-yao* [*Essentials of the military classics*]), who submitted his *Pei-pien yao-lan* (*Conspectus of border region defense preparedness*), which emphasized paying careful attention to fortifications and protective walls (battlements), long-range patrolling, and the strict control of critical strategic locations.[99] Concerned about the possibility of an alliance between the Hsia and the Liao, Jen-tsung sent an emissary to the Liao to announce an impending campaign against Li Yüan-hao. Yet through the fall the situation continued to deteriorate, culminating in the disastrous loss of some five thousand men at San-ch'uan near Wei-chou4, the third defeat of 1040.[100] The court, desperate for skilled commanders and troops, recruited sixty-one new tactical experts for office at various grades. But it was strategy that was so lacking among Jen-tsung's military planners. At the end of the year Han Ch'i's widely approved policy of aggression was adopted, and Fu-yen (capital Yen-an fu) and Ching-yüan (capital Wei-chou4) circuits were ordered to have their troops attack Li Yüan-hao within two weeks. No preparations were made in advance of the attack, however, and only after the order was sent down was any thought given to assembling the necessary pack animals: K'ai-feng, Ching-tung, Ching-hsi, and Ho-tung were ordered to assemble fifty thousand mules for the campaign in two weeks.[101]

Phase 3 (early 1041–summer 1041)

Even as war raged the empire was beset by natural disasters and financial crises. In 1039 famine in the North China Plain left 1.9 million people needing relief

[97] *HCP* (1979) 126, p. 2986.
[98] *HCP* (1979) 128, pp. 2987–8.
[99] *HTC* (1957) 42, p. 1011.
[100] *HCP* (1979) 128, p. 3042.
[101] *HTC* (1957) 42, p. 1021.

payments. In 1043 2.5 million people in Shansi would require relief. With the
start of the new year 1041, Han-lin Academician Wang Yao-ch'en and fifteen
others were appointed as investigating pacification intendants throughout the
empire to deal with the widespread problems associated with famine, heavy
taxation and corvée service obligations, economic destitution, the war with
Hsi Hsia, border conflicts in the north and south, and uprisings. Jen-tsung
accepted their recommendation to remit taxes for two years, made possible
because a surplus of four million strings had been discovered in the Finance
Commission.[102]

Despite his battlefield victories, in the first month of the new year Li Yüan-
hao sent emissaries to Fan Chung-yen in Yen-an fu asking for peace. Fan
dismissed the overture as insincere, but at the same time he convinced Jen-
tsung to postpone counterattacking until the spring thaw, when Yüan-hao's
cavalry would be at its weakest for lack of fodder.[103] Pursuing his long-term
approach of deep defense based on a chain of walled and fortified settlements,
Fan Chung-yen actively walled Ch'eng-p'ing and eleven other outposts where
Chinese and Tibetan tribesmen resumed their interrelated livelihoods.

This third phase of the war was marked by the Sung's catastrophic loss
in the second month middle of the year of six thousand men at Hao-shui-
ch'uan, in Shan-hsi's Te-shun commandery (Ch'in-feng circuit). The disaster
began when Han Ch'i, intendant for Huan-ch'ing circuit, tried to preempt
a Tangut attack on Wei-chou4. Han Ch'i sped to Chen-jung chün (about 30
miles north of Wei-chou4) where he enlisted some eighteen thousand local
stalwarts (kan-yung) and placed them under field commander Jen Fu to attack
Li Yüan-hao. Sang I commanded the vanguard. From just outside Hsin-hao,
Jen Fu rushed with several thousand light cavalry to Huai-yüan (about 35–40
miles due west of Chen-jung chün) where they killed several hundred Hsi
Hsia soldiers. Feigning escape, the Hsi Hsia troops abandoned horses, sheep,
and loaded camels. Sang I and Jen Fu divided their troops and gave chase,
recombining their forces at Hao-shui-ch'uan near dusk. Heedless of the Hsi
Hsia ruse, they had dissipated their forces in the chase. When the Hsi Hsia were
north of Lung-kan-ch'eng their advance brigade joined up with a large attack
force following the river; once beneath Liu-p'an Mountain, they attacked the
Sung army. The Sung generals, realizing they had been tricked, were unable
to regroup. Tangut shock troops hit them in front while others ambushed

---

[102] *HCP* (1979) 128, pp. 3037–8; 130, p. 3083; 132, p. 3148.

[103] *HCP* (1979) 130, pp. 3085–9. See Janet McCracken Novey, "Yü Ching, a Northern Sung statesman, and his treatise on the Ch'i-tan bureaucracy" (diss., Indiana University, 1983), pp. 53–8. Near
the end of the year Chang Fang-p'ing suggested a policy that any offer or communication should
be sent to K'ai-feng for evaluation rather than be rejected outright on the spot. *HCP* (1979) 134,
p. 3187.

the Sung flank. When the fighting ended Jen Fu, the field commander for Huan-ch'ing circuit, a number of his subordinate generals including Sang I, and more than six thousand troops, died in battle at Hao-shui-ch'uan. This was the worst Sung defeat since the founding of the dynasty. For ten days the chief councilors deliberately delayed telling the emperor of the flash reports sent to the capital from the front. Jen-tsung first learned of the defeat from an old soldier sweeping a courtyard who had read about it in a letter. The emperor upbraided his councilors for "trying my patience."[104]

Military response to the Hao-shui-ch'uan disaster was indecisive. In keeping with traditional border practice, Fan Chung-yen, now prefect of Ch'ing-chou2, asked the court for permission to give gifts and rewards to the various Tibetan tribal chiefs who had aided the Sung and to make treaties with them.[105] But the policy of attack was now in abeyance, and the Sung went on the defensive. The Shan-hsi regional commands were alerted to be prepared to resist any incursion, but not to penetrate Hsi Hsia territory. In addition, Jen-tsung consolidated twenty battalions from among the best of three infantry regiments into a new Ever Victorious Army (*Wan-sheng chün*), which not only transferred some of the costs out of K'ai-feng but also contributed to the defense against the Liao. Toward the end of 1041, these twelve thousand troops, originally intended for the Ho-pei circuits, were assigned to Lin-chou and Fu-chou2 of Ho-tung.[106] In Shan-hsi some efforts were made to train border zone garrison troops by transferring them to interior prefectures.[107]

Phase 4 (late 1041–autumn 1042)

The year spanning late 1041 to late 1042 was complicated by fears of a Liao attack and thus a war on two fronts.[108] Responding to reports of a possible Khitan invasion, twenty-one prefectures in Ho-pei were ordered to repair

[104] Ting Ch'uan-ching, *Sung-jen i-shih hui-pien* (1935; Peking, 1981) 1, p. 26. This was not the only time information was withheld from Jen-tsung: reports of Wang Lun2's uprising in 1043 and of the Nung Chih-kao insurrection of 1052 were also delayed. See Klaus Flessel, "Early Chinese newspapers (tenth to thirteenth centuries)," in *Collected papers of the XXIXth Congress of Chinese Studies, 10th–15th September 1984, University of Tübingen*, ed. Tilemann Grimm et al. (Tübingen, 1988), p. 65.

[105] See Lo Ch'iu-ch'ing, "Pei Sung ping-chih yen-chiu," *Hsin-ya hsüeh-pao* 3 No. 1 (1957), pp. 169–270, and his "Sung Hsia chan-cheng-chung-te fan-pu yü pao-chai," *Ch'ung-chi hsüeh-pao* 6 No. 2 (1967), pp. 223–43.

[106] *HCP* (1979) 132, p. 3151; 134, pp. 3195–6.

[107] *HCP* (1979) 132, p. 3149.

[108] See Denis C. Twitchett and Klaus-Peter Tietze, "The Liao," in *The Cambridge history of China*, volume 6: *Alien regimes and border states, 907–1368*, ed. Herbert Franke and Denis C. Twitchett (New York, 1994), pp. 114–23, and the map on pp. 118–19. See also Ang, "Sung-Liao diplomacy in eleventh- and twelfth-century China," pp. 83–8; Tao, *Two sons of heaven*, pp. 53–67; Tao, "Yü Ching and Sung policies towards Liao and Hsia," pp. 114–22.

their walls and moats in the late winter of 1041.[109] During the past thirty years, relations between the Liao and the Sung had been routine and peaceful. But conflict between Hsi Hsia and Sung provided an opportunity, after the stunning Hsi Hsia victory over the Sung at Hao-shui-ch'uan, for the Liao to press for territorial gains. Despite divided opinion among his senior advisors, the Liao emperor Hsing-tsung ordered his troops to start assembling along the Sung-Liao border.[110] Even though the Sung were ineffective in dealing with the Hsi Hsia threat in Shan-hsi, they were in a much better geographic and strategic situation on the Ho-pei frontier. Chen-ting fu, Ting-chou, and Shan-chou each had reserves of one hundred thousand troops, two years of grain and fodder, and fifty thousand sets of armor and weapons. Sixty-four battalions of imperial troops (approximately fourteen thousand men) were assigned to Shan-chou. Ho-pei's defense also included five hundred boats that had been secretly built in Ching-tung and Ching-hsi. One million strings of cash and two million bolts of silk were allocated for military expenses in Ho-pei.[111]

In the spring of 1042 two Liao emissaries, Hsiao T'e-mo and Liu Liu-fu, arrived in K'ai-feng to demand the ten counties south of Wa-ch'iao Pass (southwest of modern Hsiung county, Hopei). In addition, they pressed for an explanation as to why the Sung was attacking Hsi Hsia, why they were violating the Shan-yüan Treaty by building defensive works, and why they were building up troop strength in Ho-pei. Earlier, Lü I-chien had recommended that Fu Pi escort the Liao delegation from the northern border to K'ai-feng. During the escort, Fu Pi challenged Hsiao T'e-mo to make proper obeisances toward Jen-tsung's official greeting. Hsiao T'e-mo feigned illness as an excuse to refuse, but the challenge was so forceful that Hsiao T'e-mo had to abandon his pretense and he and the others, full of fear, rose and made proper obeisances. After this, Fu Pi became very forthright and Hsiao T'e-mo responded in kind, revealing his ruler's intentions. Fu Pi reported in full to Jen-tsung, who was willing only to increase the annual tribute or to offer an imperial princess in marriage to the Liao emperor's son. While Lü I-chien did not particularly like Fu Pi, he nevertheless recommended him for the mission to the Liao court to negotiate for the Sung. Between the time Fu Pi left K'ai-feng and the time he arrived at the Liao capital, the Liao had assembled troops south of their Southern Capital (Yu-chou) along the Ho-pei border. By midsummer, Fu Pi had convinced the Liao to agree to drop their territorial demands and accept instead an increase in the annual gift, now referred to as tribute (*na*).[112] Fu Pi

---

[109] *HCP* (1979) 134, p. 3187.
[110] *HCP* (1979) 134, p. 3208.
[111] *HCP* (1979) 135, p. 3226.
[112] *HCP* (1979) 135, pp. 3229–31, 3234–6; 137, pp. 3283–7. See Tao, *Two sons of heaven*, pp. 60–2.

and Liang Shih offered the Liao emperor Hsing-tsung an extra one hundred thousand strings a year if he would convince the Hsi Hsia to negotiate.[113] At the same time, at the Sung court, Lü I-chien recommended making Ta-ming (the capital of the Ho-pei East circuit) the Northern Capital of the Sung to indicate to the Liao that Jen-tsung might personally lead a campaign against them. Jen-tsung approved, and in the fifth month Ta-ming fu, the very place where Chen-tsung had encamped during the last conflict between the Liao and the Sung, was designated the Northern Capital.[114] The next month Wang Te-yung was appointed supervising prefect of Ting-chou and concomitant general commandant of Ho-pei, with the task of openly training combat troops in the hope that reports from Liao spies would help dissuade the Liao from attacking.[115]

These demonstrations of resolve helped avert a Liao invasion but could not preserve Sung dignity. In the autumn of 1042 the Liao ambassadors Yeh-lü Jen-hsien and Liu Liu-fu arrived in K'ai-feng to deliver a treaty of friendship that obliged the Sung to add 100,000 bolts of silk and 100,000 ounces of silver per annum to their tribute, bringing the annual total to 200,000 ounces of silver and 300,000 bolts of silk. The treaty also made Jen-tsung elder brother to Liao Hsing-tsung.[116] These costs, however, paled in comparison with the level of emergency spending in the Ho-pei circuits at the height of the Liao threat, when Jen-tsung had allocated the equivalent of twelve million strings in silks in a single month to assist in border expenses and reward Ho-pei's "righteous braves" (*i-shih*).[117]

The threat of Liao intervention was averted, but Hsi Hsia remained to be dealt with. Throughout late 1041 to late 1042 strategies for managing Hsi Hsia were debated. Han Ch'i, Fan Chung-yen, and P'ang Chi all offered advice on how to deal with the intermittent war in Shan-hsi. All three were serving as prefects and military intendants in Shan-hsi, and all three had concluded that it would require two or three more years of war to wear down Li Yüan-hao. P'ang Chi noted that Li usually had only ten days of supplies, did not do well with sieges, and took many casualties. From this he concluded that all fortified settlements should be prepared to withstand up to ten days of siege, which would give time for supporting Sung forces to arrive.[118] Han Ch'i insisted that

[113] Tao, "Yü Ching and Sung policies towards Liao and Hsia," p. 116; *HCP* (1979) 139, p. 3342. Tao Jing-shen writes that "From the 1040s onward, the Khitans often intervened in Sung-Hsi Hsia relations." See Tao, *Two sons of heaven*, p. 30.

[114] *HCP* (1979) 136, pp. 3260–5.

[115] *HCP* (1979) 136, pp. 3267–8.

[116] Tao, *Two sons of heaven*, pp. 17, 107.

[117] Hartwell, "The imperial treasuries," p. 57; *HCP* (1979) 137, p. 3276.

[118] *HCP* (1979) 135, p. 3222.

a long-term defense would eventually defeat Li Yüan-hao and in any case would
be necessary to allow time for generals and troops to gain sufficient combat
experience. He suggested adding thirty thousand more troops for Fu-chou2,
Ch'ing-chou2, and Wei-chou4. Expenses for these troop increases would not
be a problem if the emperor's own expenditures were kept within bounds.[119]
Fan Chung-yen deftly redefined attack as what was necessary to consolidate the
empty spaces in Shan-hsi through which Li Yüan-hao had been able to move his
forces. Interlocking fortifications chosen for their control of the strategic space
was the key to defeating the Hsi Hsia. Fan Chung-yen also pleaded with the
emperor to stop issuing secret orders because such interference made the war
impossible to manage. Perhaps as important was Fan's argument that the Sung
should rely on the strength of its economy to defeat Li Yüan-hao, whose own
economic resources were incomparably smaller. The relatively small size of the
annual tribute he had already extorted from the Sung revealed the narrowness
of his expectations and the limited threat that he represented in the overall
calculus of international power. Lü I-chien sent the advice back for discussion
among the Shan-hsi military intendants.[120]

Conceding the failure of coordinating its four constituent circuits into one
unified command, in late 1041 Shan-hsi was divided into four military circuits: Ch'in-feng, Ching-yüan, Huan-ch'ing, and Fu-yen, whose seats were
Ch'in-chou, Wei-chou4, Ch'ing-chou2, and Yen-an fu, respectively.[121] Shan-
hsi Agricultural Colony Offices for Ch'in-feng, Ching-yüan, Huan-ch'ing, and
Fu-yen also were established to help reduce military expenses by making the
armies at least partly self-supporting. Each was to be under the joint direction
of the circuit military commander and the fiscal intendant.[122] Besides transferring imperial troops from K'ai-feng, locals were drafted into additional militia
battalions of archers.[123] According to one reckoning, three million strings of
cash were needed to pay for the additional seventy thousand troops transferred
into Shan-hsi over the preceding year. Southeastern foundries in Chiang-chou,
Jao-chou, and Ch'ih-chou in the Yangtze valley were ordered to mint three
million strings of iron coins to help pay for the military campaign in Shan-hsi,
where there was a cash shortage.[124]

At the time of the triennial worship of Heaven in winter of 1041, Jen-
tsung retroactively implemented a new reign title, Ch'ing-li (Felicitous

[119] *HCP* (1979) 133, pp. 3176–8.
[120] *HCP* (1979) 135, pp. 3216–18.
[121] See *HCP* (1979) 132, pp. 3146–9; 133, p. 3170.
[122] *HCP* (1979) 134, pp. 3192, 3197, 3205–6.
[123] *HCP* (1979) 132, p. 3150; 134, p. 3196; 137, p. 3291.
[124] *HCP* (1979) 134, p. 3196.

Chronometry, 1041–8).[125] The emperor greatly desired to change the unfavorable circumstances, and he assigned Ting Tu and Liang Shih to work with the finance commissioner to forgive all outstanding taxes. A few months later, Jen-tsung ordered censors and policy critics to work with the Finance Commission to eliminate all nonessential expenses. A preliminary cost-cutting measure was to halve the gifts distributed to imperial clan members and in-laws at the annual sacrifices to Heaven.[126]

Jen-tsung also asked for recommendations of suitable field commanders from the Palace Command and from the eunuch service agencies. These were the obvious sources for trustworthy military talent. However, the risk of patronage, rather than merit, appointments was high. Chang Fang-p'ing, director of the Remonstrance Bureau (*Chien-yüan*), observed that in a period of fifty days some twenty eunuchs, in-laws, and physicians had been given various appointments and promotions.[127] The impulses that created an environment of favoritism and nepotism within the palace also encouraged regular military and civil officials to exploit it. The development of familial influence networks became increasingly institutionalized. At Chang Fang-p'ing's suggestion, Jen-tsung had officials study the question of permitting private family temples as a reward for service to the Sung.[128] It would be another decade before this crucial element of modern Chinese clan organization became an officially sanctioned practice.

The most distinctive measure taken to deal with the Shan-hsi war was a short-lived attempt to abolish the Bureau of Military Affairs. Fu Pi had initially suggested having the chief councilor act concurrently as the commissioner of military affairs. Jen-tsung said that overall control over military affairs ought to be brought under the civil bureaucracy because the Bureau of Military Affairs was not a canonical office. However, he did not wish to abolish the office, but merely have the councilors of state deliberate with senior officials at the bureau. When Chang Fang-p'ing suggested abolishing the bureau, Jen-tsung countered by suggesting that the chief councilors should manage it. In mid-1042, Lü I-chien was appointed supervisor of the Bureau of Military Affairs, Chang Te-hsiang was appointed concurrent commissioner, and Yen Shu was appointed commissioner.[129]

[125] *HCP* (1979) 134, p. 3198.
[126] Hartwell, "Financial expertise, examinations, and the formation of economic policy in Northern Sung China," p. 294; *HCP* (1979) 134, p. 3205.
[127] *HCP* (1979) 133, p. 3165.
[128] *HCP* (1979) 134, pp. 3198–9.
[129] *HCP* (1979) 137, p. 3283.

Phase 5 (autumn 1042–summer 1044)

The lull in fighting was shattered in late fall of 1042 when 100,000 Hsi Hsia troops attacked the Ting-ch'uan-chai area (in southern Ningsia) using a mix of running battles and focused attacks. The deputy circuit military commander, Ko Huai-min, was killed along with thirteen generals and about 9,400 soldiers. From Ting-ch'uan-chai, Li Yüan-hao headed southeast toward Wei-chou4, plundering the countryside along the way. When Fan Chung-yen, now prefect of Ch'ing-chou2, arrived at Wei-chou4 with 6,000 troops from Pin-chou and Ching-chou, Li Yüan-hao's troops were forced to withdraw to their own territory.[130] Superior knowledge of the terrain and superior generalship were on Li's side, but he no longer enjoyed superiority in numbers. Since his first victory at Yen-an fu, Li Yüan-hao had lost half his forces.[131] On the Sung side, Fu-Yen circuit now had 68,000 troops, Huan-Ch'ing circuit had 50,000, Ching-yüan circuit had 70,000, and Ch'in-feng circuit had 27,000; in addition, there were almost 400,000 militia in Shan-hsi to back them up. Yet despite massive Sung troop strength the strategic initiative remained with Hsi Hsia, and the Sung military was unable to choose its own battle locations and still had no well-integrated defensive strategy.[132]

By early 1043, however, the protracted war had exacted an enormous toll on Hsi Hsia resources, and a weakened Li Yüan-hao sent an emissary to negotiate a rapprochement.[133] Li Yüan-hao was even willing to refer to Jen-tsung in correspondence as his father. The Sung had also helped force the peace overture by sowing dissension among some of Li Yüan-hao's border officials, who had ambitions of independence from their ruler. By the time the Liao emissary informed the Sung court that Yüan-hao was willing to negotiate, the court had become increasingly weary of the war. Rumors had begun to spread that Li Yüan-hao had been defeated by the Hsi-fan Tibetans, that the Yeh-li clan had rebelled, that rats had eaten their grain stores, that there was a great famine, that Sung gifts and border markets had been suspended for a long time, that there was no more tea, that cloth was scarce, and that the people were weary.[134] In the spring of 1043, Shao Lang-tso, a staff officer at Pao-an chün knowledgeable in Hsi Hsia affairs, was authorized to offer enfeoffment to Li Yüan-hao as ruler of Hsi Hsia, with an annual gift of one hundred thousand bolts of silk and thirty thousand catties of tea, but only if Li would accept

---

[130] *HCP* (1979) 137, pp. 3300–3; 138, p. 3310.

[131] See Li, *Chung-kuo li-tai chan-cheng shih* (1976), vol. 11, p. 297.

[132] *HCP* (1979) 138, p. 3311; 139, p. 3345.

[133] *HCP* (1979) 138, pp. 3330–3; 139, p. 3343; 140, pp. 3358, 3361–2; 142, pp. 3403–5, 3408; 145, pp. 3500–1, 3507–8, 3513–15; 146, pp. 3536–7; 149, pp. 3613, 3616.

[134] *HCP* (1979) 138, p. 3330; Dunnell, "The Hsi Hsia."

the subordinate status of subject (*ch'en*) in diplomatic correspondence with the Sung court. By this time, Li Yüan-hao had become engaged in a conflict with the Liao, and could not sustain a two-front war.[135] Yet by late summer of 1043, Li Yüan-hao had still not agreed to terms. The Sung officials Ou-yang Hsiu and Han Ch'i, suspicious of Li's intentions, continued to oppose détente with Hsi Hsia. Both sides remained ambivalent during the next year, but in the fifth month of 1144, drawn by the prospect of selling Tangut salt across the borders to the Sung, Li Yüan-hao formally agreed to call himself "subject."[136]

In general, this first war between the Sung and Hsi Hsia revealed military strengths and weaknesses that were characteristic of the Sung. Compared to wars fought under T'ai-tsung, Chen-tsung, and Shen-tsung, Jen-tsung's loss of twenty thousand troops to Hsi Hsia was relatively small.[137] Spending was much greater for the Shan-hsi theater than the Ho-pei theater (33.6 million units compared to 25.4 million units in 1042), but the war with Hsi Hsia was emotionally more significant because such a small state had held the great Sung hostage.[138] Tangut tactics had demonstrated the effectiveness of horse warfare in challenging the greater economic power of agriculturally based empires. The Sung defense was directed by civil officials at the policy level, as well as at the level of the theater of military operations. Civilian dominance, indifference to military preparedness, and overreliance on non-Chinese tribal allies had all reduced Sung military effectiveness. But military deficiencies were offset by economic resources and large-scale static defenses. An enemy like Li Yüan-hao lacked the resources to penetrate major geographical obstacles and overwhelm settled populations in order to conquer and hold central territory. In the four years of fighting, Li Yüan-hao launched only five major attacks: in late 1039, mid-1040, early 1041, mid-1041, and late 1042. Jen-tsung, who was easily impressed by military prowess, was nonetheless intimidated by Yüan-hao's limited success.[139] Moreover, despite its fear of the Tanguts, the Sung court, in most cases, quite reasonably continued to be far more concerned about the threat to it on the more vulnerable Liao border with the Ho-tung and Ho-pei circuits than about the threat on the Hsi Hsia border in Shan-hsi. This is not

---

[135] Dunnell, "Tanguts and the Tangut state of Ta Hsia," pp. 126–8; Tao, *Two sons of heaven*, pp. 62–3.

[136] *HCP* (1979) 149, pp. 3616–17.

[137] Ch'en et al., *Sung-shih chi-shih pen-mo* 13, p. 80, notes losses of ten thousand. See Twitchett and Tietze, "The Liao," p. 86.

[138] For Wang Yao-ch'en's budget report of 1043 comparing income and expenditure in Shan-hsi, Ho-tung, Ho-pei, and the capital before and during the war, see Chao, *Chu-ch'en tsou-i* 13, pp. 621–4; *HCP* (1979) 140, p. 3366.

[139] Dunnell, "Tanguts and the Tangut state of Ta Hsia," p. 136, observes that "Wei-ming Yüan-hao's legacy of prowess haunted the Chinese for generations."

surprising considering that during the preceding century the Liao had twice overrun the border and invaded and occupied much of the Yellow River plain. As a precaution against such an attack, a Northern Capital was designated in Ho-pei to be a forward command center, but a Western Capital was not established at Lo-yang. The difference in annual gifts delivered to the Liao and to the Hsi Hsia also clearly reveals the priority of interests. Jen-tsung and his civilian court had dithered away the war, never fully accepting the opportunity to go on the offensive because of their fear of delegating adequate autonomous power to regional governments or to the military.[140]

THE CH'ING-LI REFORMS (1043–1045)

The war was just one of several factors that impelled Jen-tsung from 1043 to 1045 to back a reform movement spearheaded by Fan Chung-yen and his ideological associates. The Ch'ing-li reforms (named after the 1041–8 reign period), while only a brief episode in Jen-tsung's reign, were significant far beyond the two years when the reformers enjoyed the emperor's backing. For this was the first Confucian political movement of the dynasty, a manifestation not only of the revival of Confucian political discourse but also of the political coming-of-age of a cohort of local and regional elites who owed their success to the examination system, and to the economic and institutional developments that made learning, examinations, and government service the premier channel of social mobility.[141] The principal reform advocates, including Fan Chung-yen and his younger associates, all in their thirties, Fu Pi, Han Ch'i, and Ou-yang Hsiu, were prominent representatives of this new political cohort, but it took Lü I-chien's illness to give them the chance to put their reform program into practice.

Jen-tsung's decision to support reform

War with Hsi Hsia, exacerbated by opportunistic saber rattling by the Khitan Liao, was the central preoccupation of the Sung court from 1038 until the beginning of 1043. Adding to this prolonged military crisis were famines and epidemics in the Szechwan, Liang-che, and Chiang-nan regions, accompanied between 1040 and 1044 by widespread peasant uprisings, mutinies, and bandit depredations that spared only the regions of Szechwan and Kwangsi. In 1043

[140] Li and Ch'en, *Chung-kuo li-tai chan-cheng shih* (1976), vol. 11, p. 290.

[141] On these developments, see Robert M. Hartwell, "Demographic, political, and social transformations of China, 750–1550," *Harvard Journal of Asiatic Studies* 42 No. 2 (1982), pp. 365–442; Bol, "*This culture of ours*"; and Chaffee, *The thorny gates of learning in Sung China*.

more than 2.5 million people in the eastern plain had to be granted relief because of famine. In order to address these dangers, Jen-tsung recalled the sixty-one-year-old Lü I-chien in the spring of 1040. But in the winter of 1042, Lü suffered a stroke from which he never fully recovered.[142] From then on, critics declared him responsible for failing to prosecute the war more effectively, for weak government, and for ignoring capable officials.[143] When Sun Mien, fiscal intendant of Shan-hsi, chastised Lü for blocking remonstrance, sowing dissent, and impeding the careers of men of worth, not only did Jen-tsung not punish Sun, but the wounded Lü even expressed regret at not having received such good advice ten years earlier.[144] Finally, in the spring of 1043, Lü was dismissed as chief councilor at his own request and his critics' insistence.[145] This is not to say that Jen-tsung shook off Lü's influence voluntarily, for the emperor's attachment to Lü I-chien and others whom he loved, respected, or trusted always expressed itself in personal loyalty and sentimental attachment to that person. Thus when Lü I-chien fell ill, Jen-tsung cut a lock of his own hair for use in a curative decoction, and when Lü died in the fall of 1044, Jen-tsung openly wept, grieving for his loyal councilor and mentor of twenty years.[146] Jen-tsung now had no choice but to turn elsewhere for advice, and the next most viable group of advisors were the reform coalition centered around Fan Chung-yen, Han Ch'i, P'ang Chi, Ou-yang Hsiu, and Fu Pi. By the fall of 1043, Fan, Han, and P'ang had been appointed to the State Council, Ou-yang Hsiu was made a policy critic, and Fu Pi (having declined an appointment as deputy commissioner of military affairs) was assigned to the Han-lin Academy.[147] The way was now clear to proceed with their reforms.[148]

The reform program

Han Ch'i launched the reform process with a pair of memorials exhorting Jen-tsung to strengthen overall military preparedness, improve personnel procedures at every level of government, and improve economic performance while easing the fiscal burdens on the people.[149] But it was a joint memorial, submitted by Fan Chung-yen and Fu Pi in the ninth month of 1043, that defined the

---

[142] HCP (1979) 138, pp. 3329–30.
[143] HCP (1979) 138, pp. 3329, 3345–7; 140, pp. 3367–70.
[144] HCP (1979) 139, pp. 3345–7.
[145] Ch'ang et al., Sung-jen chuan-chi tzu-liao so-yin, p. 413; SS 432, pp. 12833–6.
[146] HCP (1979) 138, pp. 3329–30; 152, pp. 3698–9.
[147] HCP (1979) 140, pp. 3359, 3361; 142, pp. 3398–9.
[148] HCP (1979) 143, pp. 3431–44; Liu, "An early Sung reformer: Fan Chung-yen," pp. 112–22; Liu, Ou-yang Hsiu, pp. 40–51; Bol, "This culture of ours," pp. 171–2; Lee, Government education and examinations in Sung China, pp. 233–4.
[149] HCP (1979) 142, pp. 3412–15.

reform agenda.[150] In this memorial the two men offered ten major recommendations: (1) improve the merit-rating system for assessing the performance of those in office; (2) reduce the favoritism created through the widespread use of the protection privilege (*yin2*) that allowed sons and other relatives of senior officials to be appointed to office without having to write the examinations; (3) purify the examination system by stressing the conduct of candidates and testing their knowledge of the Classics rather than their skill in literary composition; (4) select officials for local office through sponsorship to ensure competence and honesty; (5) equalize the income from prefectural office lands to minimize corruption; (6) increase agricultural productivity through land reclamation and water-control works; (7) improve military preparedness by reinstituting the T'ang dynasty militia system of self-supporting farmer-soldiers (*fu-ping*); (8) reduce the need for corvée service by consolidating administrative units; (9) enact imperial decrees of amnesty and grace systematically and properly; and (10) draft regulations and orders using appropriate language, based on verified precedents, and enact them fully, uniformly, and universally. In a separate and more provocative memorial, Fu Pi also recommended removing unqualified circuit intendants and reducing the size of their staffs.

With the exception of the suggested revival of the T'ang system of farmer-soldiers, the nonactivist members of the State Council (Chang Te-hsiang, Yen Shu, Tu Yen, and Chia Ch'ang-ch'ao) were prepared to agree to all other components of the reform agenda. Three of the proposals – increased land reclamation and water control, proper implementation of amnesties and acts of grace, and reevaluation of laws and regulations – resulted in no specific legislation. Policies meant to address performance review rather than automatic promotion of officials, examination reform, selection and appointment of local officials based on recommendations and sponsorship, raising and equalizing the salaries local officials received from office land, and reducing corvée service were implemented over the next eight months, only to be aborted in early 1045 when the reformers were ousted by their opposition's efforts.

Changes in the examination system and in the school system were the most enduring aspects of the reforms, and these changes were important to the literati class as a whole. Official local schools were not disestablished with the rest of the reforms, but continued as undeniably desirable Confucian institutions. In the spring of 1044, Fan Chung-yen, Sung Ch'i, Wang Kung-ch'en, Chang Fang-p'ing, Ou-yang Hsiu, Mei Chih, Tseng Kung-liang, Wang Shu, Sun Fu, and Liu Shih recommended establishing schools in every prefecture and in counties that had an adequate number of students. In contrast with the earlier practice of endowing schools on an ad hoc basis, now every prefecture was allocated five *ch'ing* (about 70 acres) of school land, a set of the Nine Classics, and a supervisory educational official. In deference to the reformers' preference, *ku-wen* (ancient style of) writing, statecraft discussions, and plain prose were given temporary precedence over literary style and the writing of poetry in the civil service examinations.[151] Although the debate over competing educational approaches – in particular, proponents of belles lettres, with its focus on literary embellishment, and cultural entertainment versus advocates (like the reformers) of a more Confucian approach based on a knowledge of ritual, music, and the Classics – was not yet permanently resolved by the reforms, the priority given to local schools, examinations, and an Imperial University (*T'ai-hsüeh*) continued well beyond the end of the reform movement.

Social and economic problems

One of the concerns of Jen-tsung and the reformers was how to relieve the populace of the heavy burdens of taxation and service. Sung Ch'i had strongly urged cutting the size of the civil service and the military in 1039, but nothing was done. That this proposal was more than inflammatory rhetoric can be judged from Wang Yao-ch'en's 1043 fiscal report on revenue and expenditure in the capital, and the Shan-hsi, Ho-pei, and Ho-tung circuits.[152] Revenue raised from the capital district had risen from 19.5 million strings in 1038 to a bit more than 29 million strings in 1042; in Shan-hsi revenue had increased from 19.8 million to 33.9 million between 1038 and 1042; in Ho-pei from 20 million to 27.5 million; and in Ho-tung from 10 million to 11.8 million. In short, the revenue collected from the taxable populace in these four northern regions had increased by 33 percent, 70 percent, 38 percent, and 18 percent, respectively. In 1038 and in 1042 there were revenue surpluses, but at the same time military spending in 1034 and during the decade from 1038 to 1048 were the highest for the Northern Sung as a whole by margins of 10 million to 20 million strings compared to all other years of the dynasty.[153]

In their quest for the causes of excessive taxation, the reformers focused on such perennial problems as the high number of supernumerary officials and soldiers, expensive gifts lavished on court favorites, tax-exempt Buddhist and Taoist temples, and the inadequate number (despite the overall surplus)

---

[151] *HCP* (1979) 147, pp. 3563–4. See also Bol, "*This culture of ours,*" pp. 169–75; Chaffee, *The thorny gates of learning in Sung China*, pp. 51, 66–77; Liu, *Ou-yang Hsiu*, pp. 17, 69–70, 87–8, 148–52; Lee, *Government education and examinations in Sung China*, pp. 62–4, 70–2, 129–30.

[152] Chao, *Chu-ch'en tsou-i* 13, pp. 621–4; *HCP* (1979) 140, p. 3366.

[153] Wong Hon-chiu, "Government expenditures in Northern Sung China (960–1127)" (diss., University of Pennsylvania, 1975), pp. 182–93.

of truly effective local and regional officials.[154] It was thought that war and defense on two fronts, banditry, trouble with resistant indigenous tribes along the expanding southern frontiers, and natural disasters would only be more effectively and justly dealt with by men of good character and education and that it was basically the lack of such men that had produced all the problems facing the empire.

Reformers like Ts'ai Hsiang thought that local government was more effective than its central counterpart, especially when it came to prosecuting the war between Sung and Hsi Hsia.[155] The contrast between the inertia of the central government and the activism of the locally based reformers can be seen in an incident that occurred in late spring of 1043.[156] A crisis was looming because tribute grain deliveries to the capital were not sufficient to feed the armies in K'ai-feng through to the next harvest. Fan Chung-yen, newly installed as deputy commissioner for military affairs, recommended an experienced fiscal and regional official who immediately coordinated the shipments of grain from seventy-two prefectures spread over six circuits, quickly restoring the K'ai-feng grain stock. Such individual administrative and reformist activities, however, were inadequate to provide a long-term solution to extensive and prolonged lapses in the local and regional management of civil, military, and fiscal affairs. Moreover, the grain delivery system itself was breaking down.[157]

In the reformers' view, the lack of effective local and regional administration left the empire unable to defend itself, to collect taxes effectively, or to maintain law and order.[158] But for all his moral outrage, Fan Chung-yen was not prepared to struggle against an entrenched bureaucracy. For one thing, he was able neither to gain Jen-tsung's complete trust nor to shake the emperor out of his complacency. More crucially, the reformers committed the tactical mistake of openly threatening the livelihoods and status of thousands of sons, nephews, cousins, protégés, and followers of officials, military officers, imperial kinsmen, and eunuchs, by eliminating or reducing their easy access to office and promotion. The initial threat to established career interests stemmed from Ou-yang Hsiu's requests to evaluate the performance of all local officials by

---

[154] On excessive spending, see *HCP* (1979) 123, p. 2908; 125, pp. 2941–4; 135, p. 3233; 141, pp. 3387–8; 142, pp. 3412–15; 143, p. 3482; 154, p. 3742; 161, pp. 3895–6; on the bloated army, *HCP* (1979) 154, p. 3742; 159, p. 3839; 161, pp. 3895–8; 163, p. 3923; 163, p. 3930; on supernumerary officials, *HCP* (1979) 123, p. 2893; 125, pp. 2941–4; 143, p. 3464; 158, p. 3823; 163, p. 3924; on the shortage of good local officials, *HCP* (1979) 116, p. 2732; 141, p. 3386; 163, p. 3932; 166, p. 3985.

[155] *HCP* (1979) 141, p. 3368.

[156] *HCP* (1979) 141, p. 3373; *HTC* (1957) 45, pp. 1086–7.

[157] *HCP* (1979) 147, p. 3556; Robert M. Hartwell, "Markets, technology, and structure of enterprise in development of 11th-century Chinese iron and steel industry," *Journal of Economic History* 26 No. 1 (1966), p. 30.

[158] *HCP* (1979) 141, p. 3386; 148, p. 3593; 150, pp. 3622–4.

appointing fiscal intendants as surveillance commissioners (*an-ch'a shih*), with the objective of eliminating incumbent officeholders who were too old, sickly, corrupt, or incompetent.[159] The resistance to this program was so great that it was allowed to lapse in 1045.[160] The zeal of Fan Chung-yen, Fu Pi, Yin Shu, Shih Chieh, Ou-yang Hsiu, and their followers was not enough to overcome the resentment of large numbers of officials, including powerful, experienced politicians who would have lost their powers of patronage. Although officials such as Han Ch'i and P'ang Chi avoided much of this animus through their restraint and impersonal approach to reform, the reform agenda was too provocative to escape a backlash from well-entrenched bureaucratic interests.

Ousting the Ch'ing-li reformers

The ideals of the reformers, sustained and expressed intermittently over the preceding twenty years, reflected the shared vision of an ideological faction. It was this vision that had moved Jen-tsung to choose these like-minded men to solve the problems of the empire. But complaints against the reformers were immediately lodged by senior ministers, local officials, eunuchs, and favorites – all who feared that customary practices for promotion, grace, and favors would be limited or eliminated. Personal animosity drove Hsia Sung to oppose the reforms, for he had been ousted as commissioner of military affairs in favor of Tu Yen after a strenuous campaign by policy critics and censors in early 1043. Hsia plotted revenge, particularly against Shih Chieh, a reputation-seeking lecturer at the Directorate of Education, who had written a poem gloating over the dismissals of Lü I-chien and Hsia himself, and crowing over the appointments of Chang Te-hsiang, Yen Shu, Chia Ch'ang-ch'ao, Han Ch'i, Fan Chung-yen, Fu Pi, Ou-yang Hsiu, Ts'ai Hsiang, Wang Su, Yü Ching, and Tu Yen.[161] The fastidious and brilliant Hsia Sung trained a servant girl to write in Shih Chieh's hand, using a note Shih Chieh had written to Fu Pi as a model for the forging of a more incriminating version that raised the specter of factional plotting. This forgery exacerbated the doubts already implanted in Jen-tsung's mind by Fan Chung-yen's almost flippant response to the emperor's question about whether

---

[159] *HCP* (1979) 136, pp. 3251–9; 143, p. 3463; 144, p. 3480; 146, p. 3539; 148, pp. 3582–3.

[160] *HCP* (1979) 155, p. 3772; 157, p. 3803. In 976, Chao P'u, at that point serving T'ai-tsung as chief councilor, briefly instituted surveillance responsibilities for fiscal intendants to evaluate local officials. *HCP* (1979) 17, pp. 385–6.

[161] *HCP* (1979) 140, pp. 3364, 3370; 148, pp. 3580–2. See Jonathan Chaves, *Mei Yao-ch'en and the development of early Sung poetry* (New York, 1976), pp. 71–4; Bol, *"This culture of ours,"* pp. 181–3, 162, who make clear that Shih Chieh's attack is literary as well as political; Liu, *Ou-yang Hsiu*, pp. 48–9. Even after Shih Chieh died, Hsia Sung viciously implied that Shih Chieh was still alive and was involved in a complex plot with the Tanguts and Fu Pi.

the reformers constituted a faction: "It is for you to decide," Fan had replied. "If a faction is good, what harm is done to the state?" Ou-yang Hsiu further inflamed the matter when he submitted an essay, "On Factions," that argued that men of principle working together could not be regarded as criminal, even if they could be regarded as a faction.

Factionalism was not new to the Sung, but Fan Chung-yen's reform movement transformed ordinary factional maneuverings into a debilitating crisis in Sung government.[162] If during Jen-tsung's reign factionalism was a troubling but passing issue, by the end of the eleventh century it would become the most incendiary and destructive political trend at court.[163] Fan Chung-yen's role in this process cannot be ignored, for Fan's own denunciation of Lü I-chien, using a chart to show Lü's favoritism in appointments, brought factionalism into the open by exposing the practice. It also provoked counterfactional dismissals, while eliciting support for Fan Chung-yen in Confucian ethical terms.[164]

The remainder of Jen-tsung's reign factions, once they had been named, had to overcome both the weight of opposition and the weight of being identified with the improper pursuit of self-interest. The reformers themselves practiced a principled favoritism that set up a putative opposition to the dynasty in the form of an impersonal loyalty to a set of values that transcended the state. As Ou-yang Hsiu and others understood, there was no rhetorical escape, and ideological groupings went underground in the face of careerists' pragmatic opposition. Factional conflict did not end, of course, and Jen-tsung and others periodically decried the harm caused by anonymous factional denunciations and the damage done to innocent bystanders.[165] But factionalism was not only a sensitive issue for Jen-tsung, it was also a convenient and effective weapon for the opponents of reform, as Fan Chung-yen and Fu Pi came to realize. Both were made especially nervous by the forged letter, and they soon began to ask for appointments outside the capital.[166] By the end of 1044,

[162] For background on factionalism, see Gung, "The participation of censorial officials in politics during the Northern Sung dynasty," pp. 30–41. Emperor T'ai-tsung was twice advised to make an effort to distinguish between factions composed of virtuous like-minded men and factions of those seeking personal advantage. *HCP* (1979) 24, p. 547; 42, pp. 896–901.

[163] See Chapter 6 in this volume. Robert P. Hymes, *Statesmen and gentlemen: The elite of Fu-chou, Chiang-hsi, in Northern and Southern Sung* (Cambridge, 1986), pp. 1–6, 115–23, expands on the work of Robert M. Hartwell to explain the shifts in elite patterns of self-advancement and status maintenance whose roots are to be seen in the intensified factional politics of the reigns from Jen-tsung through Shen-tsung.

[164] *HCP* (1979) 118, p. 2783; 122, pp. 2881–2.

[165] *HCP* (1979) 151, p. 3691; 153, p. 3718; 160, p. 3861; 166, pp. 3983, 4001; 174, p. 4212; 176, p. 4268; 177, pp. 4285–9, 4293–4; 191, p. 4627; 192, pp. 4635, 4637–8; 193, pp. 4661–2, 4680–3; 194, pp. 4691–2; 205, p. 4968; *SS* 285, pp. 9606–7, 9619; Chao, *Chu-ch'en tsou-i* 13, pp. 642–3; 18, pp. 793–6; 61, pp. 2247–9; 76, pp. 2668–9.

[166] *HCP* (1979) 150, p. 3636.

Wang Kung-ch'en, an opponent of the reforms, was able to implicate Fan Chung-yen and Tu Yen because of Su Shun-ch'in's misuse of office money to hire a dancing girl.[167] Chia Ch'ang-ch'ao, one of the chief councilors, secretly directed Wang Kung-ch'en, Sung Ch'i, and Chang Fang-p'ing against Han Ch'i. Chang Te-hsiang, the other chief councilor, could not refute the charges, which further undermined Jen-tsung's confidence in Fan Chung-yen.[168] At the beginning of 1045, following the recent triennial worship of Heaven, Jen-tsung let Fan Chung-yen and Fu Pi take up prefectural seats and senior circuit military intendancies. Tu Yen, who had been their supporter, was dismissed shortly thereafter. The reformers had all been ousted by the time Han Ch'i was dismissed in the early spring of 1045. Over the next year almost all the reforms were either rescinded or allowed to lapse.

The retreat from reform (1042–1045) to inertial administration (1045–1063)

Court government was relatively quiet between 1046 and the deaths of Jen-tsung (in 1063) and his cousin and successor, Ying-tsung, in 1067.[169] Jen-tsung continued to increase the size of the consultative group at court and of the entire civil service. The experimentation and rapid turnover of chief officials that had characterized the period after the end of Empress Liu's regency in 1032 until 1045 was replaced by institutional stability combined with steady turnover of smaller numbers of chief officials.[170] Between 1045 and 1067, thirty-nine officials served Jen-tsung and Ying-tsung as councilors of state. Of these, only fourteen served fewer than three years, while the remaining twenty-five served from three to thirteen years. Wang I-yung was commissioner of military affairs from 1045 to 1054; P'ang Chi served between 1045 and 1053, eventually becoming chief councilor; Sung Hsiang, who had previously been a councilor of state, served again between 1045 and 1051, obtaining the rank of chief councilor; and Kao Jo-na, who served from 1047 to 1053, reached the rank of commissioner of military affairs. For almost a decade, these four men provided stability, but no particular program. Over the next several years Jen-tsung appointed four more councilors of state – Chang Sheng, Chao Kai, Ch'en Chiu (aka Ch'en Sheng-chih), and Ou-yang Hsiu – who continued to serve for several years into Ying-tsung's reign. A new, stable configuration of senior officials was created in 1056 with the appointment of Han Ch'i and

[167] HCP (1979) 153, pp. 3715–16.

[168] HCP (1979) 154, p. 3740.

[169] Liu Tzu-chien (James T. C. Liu), "An administrative cycle in Chinese history: The case of Northern Sung emperors," Journal of Asian Studies 21 No. 2 (1962), pp. 143–4, characterizes Jen-tsung as a maintenance or normalcy-type emperor.

[170] McGrath, "Military and regional administration in Northern Sung China," pp. 124, 257.

Tseng Kung-liang, who each served as chief councilors through to the end of Ying-tsung's reign.

Despite episodes of factional conflict, favoritism, and crisis, these high officials preserved an appearance of administrative order. Officials regularly pointed out areas of excessive expenditure, but spending was not curtailed. During the fifteen years from the end of the Ch'ing-li reforms until the end of Ying-tsung's reign in 1067, the number of civil and military officials steadily grew from between 17,000 and 20,000 in the period 1049–53, to 24,000 in the period 1064–67. Four to seven thousand more officials were added to the imperial payroll in seven years, a growth necessary to accommodate the men who had passed the civil service exams, the continuation of the hereditary protection privilege (yin2), and imperial clan official appointments.[171]

After Fan Chung-yen and his associates had been ousted from office, Jen-tsung backed away from an activist, programmatic administration with its attendant factional conflict, and turned instead to a leisurely form of "cultural glamour."[172] Jen-tsung was instinctively opposed to conflict within his court, even to the point of dismissing chief and assistant councilors of state for arguing and wrangling.[173] Officials became reluctant to discuss issues forcefully. Factional politics remained at the heart of much of the wrangling, making any issue at hand an opportunity for politicization. Reforms and programs only intensified and clarified the lines of factional demarcation. Such was the traditional fear of disorder (luan) in politics, and such was Jen-tsung's dislike of discord, that the idealistic programs of the reformers were easily undermined by claiming that they were the result of the conniving of a political faction.[174]

But Jen-tsung's desire for civility and quiet must have rested uneasily with his sense of obligation to heed frank speech and sincere criticism. Jen-tsung solicited public advice from the civil service as a whole twelve times in his reign – once in 1032, once in 1038, twice in 1040, twice in 1042, and once each in 1043, 1047, 1048, 1049, 1053, and 1056. In contrast, Ying-tsung "opened up the channels of remonstrance" (k'ai yen-lu) just once, in 1065. The first time Jen-tsung asked for advice, the dowager empress Liu's pretensions were beginning to cause concern, the empire was beset by famine and locusts, and part of the inner palace had just burned down.[175] In 1038, the emperor

---

[171] Wong, "Government expenditures in Northern Sung China," pp. 62–73; Lo Wen (Winston W. Lo), *Szechwan in Sung China: A case study in the political integration of the Chinese empire* (Taipei, 1982), pp. 79–80.

[172] S. A. M. Adshead, *China in world history* (New York, 1988), p. 102; *HCP* (1979) 120, p. 2841.

[173] In 1046 and 1047 Jen-tsung shifted and dismissed councilors of state for these reasons. *HCP* (1979) 160, p. 3865.

[174] *HCP* (1979) 122, pp. 2881–2; 176, pp. 4264–7; 193, pp. 4680–3.

[175] *HCP* (1979) 111, p. 3587.

asked for advice following earthquakes in the capital district and in the Ho-pei region.[176] In 1040, 1042, and 1043, Jen-tsung solicited advice about the war with Hsi Hsia, the threats from the Liao, mutinies, uprisings, banditry, famine, massive expenses, currency problems, insufficient grain to supply the military in the capital, and the need to mobilize hundreds of thousands of men, militias, and regional and imperial military units.[177] In 1047, Jen-tsung asked for advice concerning the drought in the capital district.[178] In 1048, the circumstances were much more dramatic; Wang Tse's sixty-five-day rebellion in the heart of Ho-pei had caused major disruptions close to the capital, and unrest still simmered. Moreover, the palace was hit with a mutiny, and military spending remained extremely high.[179] In 1049, Jen-tsung must have felt overwhelmed from both the flooding in the Ching-tung and Ching-hsi circuits and the resulting masses of refugees, and an outbreak of banditry that had followed an inauspicious solar eclipse in the first month.[180] In 1056, Jen-tsung became very ill, and heavy rains had overloaded the Yellow River, producing widespread flooding and a major shift in the river's course.[181] After his illness in 1056, Jen-tsung continued his gradual withdrawal from public affairs that had begun after the death of his Precious Consort Chang in 1054. By and large, the advice he received on these occasions was sensible but predictable, and produced little in positive results.

There were many reasons for the passivity of Jen-tsung's court following the failed Ch'ing-li reforms. At the broadest level, growth of the official class through hereditary protection (*yin2*), special grace following major ceremonies and rites, enlargement of the examination quotas, and the establishment and support of prefectural schools met with complacency among the majority of officials. Only a few spoke out against the "too many" and the "too much."[182] Moreover, once the war with Hsi Hsia had been resolved and military spending decreased, most of the social and economic issues sank below the horizon of official awareness. Administration became increasingly routine, relying on precedent.[183] In particular, few changes were made to the byzantine welter of regulations and procedures used to govern ritual and sumptuary practices;

---

[176] *HCP* (1979) 121, p. 2851.

[177] *HCP* (1979) 126, pp. 2978, 2982, 2986; 136, p. 3250; 143, pp. 3430–1.

[178] *HCP* (1979) 160, p. 3865.

[179] *SS* 11, p. 225; *HCP* (1979) 163, p. 3922.

[180] *HCP* (1979) 166, p. 3988.

[181] *HCP* (1979) 182, p. 4416.

[182] See Lo, *Introduction to the civil service of Sung China*, pp. 29–30. He refers to *yin2* as "the institutionalization of the self-perpetuating propensity of the ruling elite." *HCP* (1979) 158, p. 3824; 167, pp. 4018, 4023–8; 169, p. 4059; 181, pp. 4374–6; 187, p. 4505; 208, pp. 5052, 5058–62; Chao, *Chu-ch'en tsou-i* 49, pp. 1864–5; 70, pp. 2499–2502.

[183] *HCP* (1979) 176, p. 4270.

management of the imperial clan, harem, and eunuchs; and military, regional, and local administration.[184] Pragmatic institutional memories were compiled into books of precedents that improved conventional and ad hoc responses to routine events but did not address issues of goals or purposes – only reformers raised these issues and usually only when disasters or crises brought them to the fore.

Although there were few outright crises, the list of problems facing the Sung at midcentury remained daunting. During Jen-tsung's reign the clearest problem in regional and local administration was the persistent shortage of officials in prefectural and county-level positions despite an abundance of officials of the correct rank waiting for posts. This shortage was matched by problems in the north with support services for local officials,[185] as well as by unequal taxation and tax collection, banditry, disaster relief, and the rapacity of officials and clerks.[186] Granaries for price stabilization, disaster relief, and poor relief were established with regular deposits of grain by late in Jen-tsung's reign.[187] Disaster relief, however, sometimes meant enrolling disaster victims into military units.[188] Attempts were made right to the end of the Sung dynasty to resolve unequal taxation, although this was structurally incompatible with the growth of the estates that reemerged at this time. By contrast, few attempts were made to control the constant flooding of the Yellow River, even though, as Klaus Flessel has shown, the technical knowledge and experience available at the time might have made this possible. What was lacking was imperial and central government commitment.[189] In the absence of large-scale water-control measures, flooding routinely beset the Ho-pei and Ching-tung circuits, and the Yellow River shifted its course with hugh damage and loss of life in 1036, 1048, 1056, 1060, and 1081.[190]

[184] *HCP* (1979) 157, p. 3805; 160, p. 3861; 161, p. 3887; 181, p. 4380; 184, p. 4447; 185, pp. 4478–9; 186, pp. 4486, 4492; 187, pp. 4509, 4512; 188, p. 4536; 194, p. 4713; 195, pp. 4726, 4730–1; 196, p. 4744; 205, pp. 4966, 4968; 208, p. 5053.

[185] *HCP* (1979) 168, pp. 4045–6; 188, p. 4539; 189, p. 4570; 190, p. 4597; 206, p. 5007; Kracke, *Civil service in early Sung China*, p. 89.

[186] *HCP* (1979) 151, pp. 3670–3; 161, p. 3887; 164, p. 3956; 165, p. 3975; 170, p. 4077; 170, p. 4097; 174, p. 4214; 175, pp. 4219, 4227, 4235; 176, p. 4256; 180, p. 4355; 183, p. 4424; 187, pp. 4508–9; 190, pp. 4590–1; 192, pp. 4654–7; 194, p. 4691.

[187] *HCP* (1979) 175, p. 4219; 179, pp. 4331–3; 186, p. 4488; 189, p. 4570; 199, p. 4841; 202, p. 4901; 204, pp. 4954–5; 206, p. 5014; *SS* 176, pp. 4275–9.

[188] *HCP* (1979) 107, p. 2499; 109, p. 2536; 111, p. 2578; 112, p. 2627; 127, p. 3009; 135, p. 3213; 139, p. 3342; 164, p. 3957; 166, pp. 2985–6; 204, p. 4941; *SS* 192, pp. 4767, 4773, 4777, 4780–1; 193, pp. 4799, 4801–6; 199, pp. 4976–7, 4979, 4989, 5015, 5020; 313, p. 10259. See also Lo, "Pei Sung ping-chih yen-chiu," pp. 232–5; Chien Po-tsan, *Chung-kuo shih kang-yao* (1962; Peking, 1979), vol. 3, p. 13; Ts'ai Mei-piao et al., *Chung-kuo t'ung-shih: ti wu ts'e*, 5th ed. (Peking, 1978), p. 130; McGrath, "Military and regional administration in Northern Sung China," p. 305.

[189] Flessel, *Der Huang-ho und die historische Hydrotechnik in China*, pp. 128, 140.

[190] *HCP* (1979) 118, p. 2787; 183, p. 4448; 191, p. 4610; *SS* 91, pp. 2266–74; 299, p. 9932.

Tax collection was the essential administrative function necessary to sustain the state. Prefectures and counties collected the basic land-tax revenue partly in the form of cash, and partly in grain and other commodities; they arranged the levying of labor services, and they relied on local sub-bureaucratic service organizations for commodity delivery, tax collection, and the maintenance of local defenses. Fiscal and transport intendants insured the delivery of taxes to K'ai-feng. During Jen-tsung's reign and especially in the latter half, tax revenue was increasingly paid in cash and increasingly derived from taxes on commerce and from the state's monopolies on tea, salt, and wine. This high level of reliance on taxing commerce was not seen again until the middle of the nineteenth century, but it was necessitated by a decline in land-tax revenue due to the unequal application of the tax.[191]

Iron currency and paper money were used in Ho-tung, Shan-hsi, and Szech-wan to compensate for an unmet demand for currency and to protect the Sung from the outflow of copper coin from the frontier circuits to Hsi Hsia or Liao, both of which were deficient in metals. Within the iron currency areas, coun-terfeiting was a problem. This was usually solved by adjusting the exchange rate between copper and iron coin. In 1048 the currency systems in the north were in shambles but were quickly restored to normal.[192] Deficits arising dur-ing the 1038–45 war with Hsi Hsia were covered directly by the throne from the Palace Treasuries and repaid later. Fresh deficits built up in 1056 and 1057, primarily as a result of the remission of taxes, the reinstitution of the Ho-pei grain delivery, and the breakdown of the grain delivery system.[193] Fortunately, in contrast to the deficits of the 1040s, the deficits of 1056 and 1057 occurred during a decade of surplus revenue.[194] Even so, the problems were significant enough for Wang An-shih (1021–86), future architect of Shen-tsung's New Policies (hsin-fa), to submit a memorial on the subject.[195] But given the insti-tutional inertia of the last years of Jen-tsung's reign, it would take ten more

[191] Golas, "The Sung financial administration"; Chou Chin-sheng, An economic history of China, ed. and trans. Edward H. Kaplan (Bellingham, Wash., 1974), p. 91; Edmund H. Worthy, Jr., "Regional control in the Southern Sung salt administration," in Crisis and prosperity in Sung China, ed. John W. Haeger (Tucson, Ariz., 1975), pp. 101–41; HCP (1979) 190, pp. 4590–1; 192, pp. 4654–7; 194, p. 4691; SS 326, pp. 10530–3.

[192] HCP (1979) 164, pp. 3954–6; 183, p. 4441; 189, p. 4552; SS 180, pp. 4375, 4381; 185, p. 4525; Golas, "The Sung financial administration"; Robert M. Hartwell, "The evolution of the early Northern Sung monetary system, A.D. 960–1025," Journal of the American Oriental Society 87 No. 3 (1967), pp. 280–9, for insight into the workings of the Sung monetary system; Peter J. Golas, "A copper production breakthrough in the Song: The copper precipitation process," Journal of Sung-Yuan Studies 25 (1995), pp. 153–68; Yang Lien-sheng, Money and credit in China: A short history (Cambridge, Mass., 1952), pp. 153–68.

[193] SS 175, pp. 4252–3; HCP (1979) 176, p. 4271; 181, p. 4382; 182, pp. 4409, 4414; 183, p. 4423; 185, pp. 4472–3; 186, p. 4488; 188, pp. 4531–2; Chao, Chu-ch'en tsou-i 40, pp. 1471–2.

[194] Hartwell, "The imperial treasuries," p. 62; SS 179, p. 4353.

[195] HCP (1979) 188, pp. 4531–2.

years before Wang's suggested reform would be implemented. In 1065 the
government once again was unable to cover all its expenditures, revealing the
depth and pervasiveness of the problems the empire faced.[196]

THE SOUTHERN FRONTIER REGION

Jen-tsung's policy makers also had to confront problems in the regions of the
south. Although the south may have been politically underrepresented until
the latter part of the Northern Sung, it was geographically and economically
an essential part of the empire. By the Ch'ing-li period (1041–8), the circuits along the southwest borders – Tzu-chou, K'uei-chou, Ching-hu South,
Kuang-nan East, and Kuang-nan West – having absorbed immigrants, min-
ers, soldiers, and officials in search of wealth and territory, erupted in a series of
small and large frontier wars, uprisings among the indigenous population, and
banditry.[197] The southern frontier districts of Fu-chien and most of Szechwan
were by now more fully incorporated in the empire and went largely untouched
by the upheavals of the late 1030s and early 1040s.[198]

   The Ching-hu and Kuang-nan circuits and Szechwan's southernmost frontier prefectures of Jung-chou and Lu-chou3 were three regions where conflict
broke out between the Sung and indigenous non-Han populations. In part,
these conflicts resulted from the Sung court's inclination, despite its tolerance of Buddhism and Taoism, to suppress the heterodox rituals they associated with southern peoples.[199] The Sung court dealt with these conflicts by
posting rewards for the capture of bandits, organizing local braves to maintain order, establishing military patrol units (hsün-chien), building walls and
strongholds, bringing in or assembling imperial expeditionary forces, and

---

[196] Wong, "Government expenditures in Northern Sung China," pp. xxxix, 60–1.

[197] Richard von Glahn, The country of streams and grottoes: Expansion, settlement, and the civilizing of the Sichuan
   frontier in Song times (Cambridge, Mass., 1987), pp. 75, 208–9; Peter J. Golas, "Rural China in the
   Song," Journal of Asian Studies 39 No. 2 (1980), p. 295; Hartwell, "Demographic, political, and social
   transformations of China," pp. 369–71, 375–7; Brian E. McKnight, Law and order in Sung China
   (Cambridge, 1992), pp. 79–81, 115.

[198] See Hugh R. Clark, "Consolidation of the south China frontier: The development of Ch'uan-chou, 699–
   1126" (diss., University of Pennsylvania, 1981), pp. 259–60, 359–77. Fu-chien had three recorded
   problems with salt smugglers and bandits in the 1040s, and in 1054 and 1059. Szechwan had one local
   uprising in 1028 and two famine-generated local uprisings in 1040 and 1057.

[199] For examples of suppression, see HCP (1979) 24, p. 554; 159, p. 3847; 192, p. 4653; 203, p. 4928; von
   Glahn, Country of streams and grottoes, p. 212; McKnight, Law and order in Sung China, pp. 75–9. Chang
   Fang-p'ing noted that twenty out of seventy cases he reviewed when he directed the Judicial Control
   Office (Shen-hsing yüan) involved questions of heterodoxy. HCP (1979) 163, p. 3928. See Guillaume
   Dunstheimer, "Some religious aspects of secret societies," in Popular movements and secret societies in China,
   1840–1950, ed. Jean Chesneaux (Stanford, Calif., 1972), pp. 23–8, for clarification of the concept of
   heterodoxy.

enticing leaders to call off their rebellion or banditry in exchange for local office.[200] But the administration of these regions was difficult and very thinly spread: local officials often had to confront rugged terrain and tropical diseases, and had inadequate military force at their disposal. Even the frontiers were ill-defined, with many local communities subject to conflicting influence not only by Sung but also from the Viet state and the local Ta-li kingdom in Yunnan.[201]

The Nung Chih-kao uprising (1049–1053)

During Jen-tsung's reign there were seven multiyear conflicts with groups in the south: (1) the native tribes of An-hua county in I-chou3 prefecture of Kuang-nan West in 1038–9;[202] (2) the Yao2 people of Kuei-yang chien, Ching-hu South, 1043–51;[203] (3) locals led by Ch'ü-pu-fan in I-chou3, Kuang-nan West, 1044–5;[204] (4) aboriginal groups in Yü-ching chien, in Lu-chou3 prefecture of Tzu-chou circuit, 1044–9;[205] (5) Nung Chih-kao's uprising centered on Yung-chou2, Kuang-nan West, 1049–53;[206] (6) P'eng Shih-hsi's conflict with the Sung in Hsia-hsi-chou in Ching-hu North, 1055–8;[207] and (7) the indigenous peoples of Yung-chou2 in 1058–61.[208] Of these, the second disrupted a very important silver-mining center for some years, but most were of minor importance. Only Nung Chih-kao's uprising posed a significant threat to the dynasty on a wider scale. Nung Chih-kao captured dozens of forts, markets, towns, and cities in Kuang-nan West and East. Based in the border region between the Sung and the Vietnamese Ly dynasty (*Chiao-chih* in Chinese), which was only lightly patrolled by the Sung, Nung brought his two

[200] *HCP* (1979) 145, p. 3514; 146, p. 3541; 148, p. 3591; 149, p. 3616; 151, p. 3665; 158, pp. 3819, 3822; 160, p. 3873; 177, pp. 4292, 4295; 178, p. 4304; 182, p. 4398; 187, pp. 4504, 4514; 188, pp. 4527–8; 192, pp. 4634, 4652; 194, p. 4687.

[201] Von Glahn, *Country of streams and grottoes*, p. 105; *HCP* (1979) 127, p. 2884.

[202] *HCP* (1979) 122, p. 2886; 123, p. 2892.

[203] *HCP* (1979) 141, p. 3390; 143, pp. 3430, 3462; 144, pp. 3476–8; 145, p. 3513; 146, pp. 3558–63; 152, pp. 3701–3; 157, p. 3812; 158, p. 3819; 159, pp. 3847–8; 160, pp. 3859, 3873; 161, p. 3869; 170, p. 4098; 190, p. 4595.

[204] *HCP* (1979) 121, p. 2874; 146, p. 3541; 148, pp. 3578–9; 151, p. 3665; 152, pp. 3701–3; 155, p. 3760; 156, p. 3777; 157, p. 3812.

[205] *HCP* (1979) 148, p. 3591; 166, p. 3998; von Glahn, *Country of streams and grottoes*, pp. 73–5, 80, 86–7, 90, 92–5.

[206] *HCP* (1979) 167, pp. 4014–5; 168, pp. 4041–2; 170, p. 4078; 172, pp. 4140, 4142, 4147–55; 173, pp. 4162, 4165, 4170, 4175, 4178, 4182–5; 174, pp. 4190, 4197; 175, pp. 4221, 4239; 180, p. 4355; 186, p. 4493; 192, p. 4647.

[207] *HCP* (1979) 181, p. 4382; 183, p. 4440; 185, pp. 4468, 4475; 186, pp. 4490–1, 4494; 187, p. 4514; 188, pp. 4525–6; von Glahn, *Country of streams and grottoes*, p. 99.

[208] *HCP* (1979) 119, p. 2795; 178, p. 4304; 182, p. 4398; 187, p. 4517; 190, p. 4593; 191, p. 4628; 192, pp. 4634, 4636, 4647, 4654; 193, p. 4664.

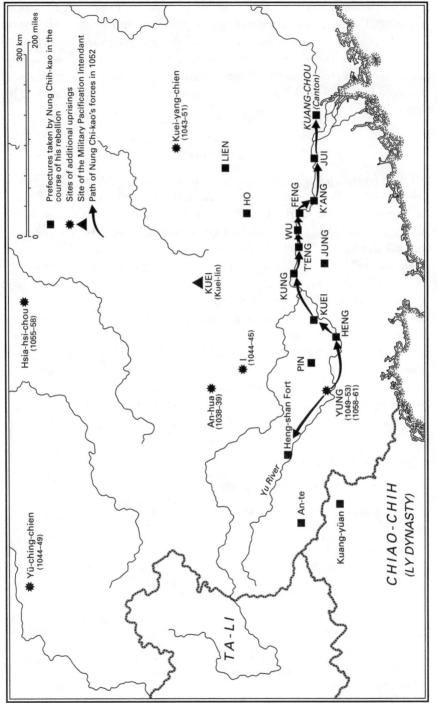

Map 14. Nung Chih-kao's uprising, 1049–1053.

greater neighbors into a confrontation in a contested border zone populated with multiple non-Han and non-Vietnamese groups.[209]

In the fall of 1049, Nung Chih-kao declared himself ruler of a kingdom with its own reign title, a direct challenge to Jen-tsung's authority as the Son of Heaven. Nung Chih-kao was a distaff descendant of an elite non-Chinese lineage in Kuang-yüan-chou, southwest of Yung-chou2. Kuang-yüan-chou lay within Sung jurisdiction but was also claimed, but not controlled, by the Ly dynasty. Yung-chou2 was a large frontier territory of nearly fifty-eight hundred square miles, with two counties, one outpost, one gold market, and sixty settlements of local non-Chinese with a registered population of approximately five thousand households. Initially the conflict was local and did not involve many Chinese residents. Not until some fifty Chinese towns and cities in Kuang-nan West were attacked or captured by the rebels in the spring of 1052, did the Sung government react. By year's end, the high-ranking eunuch, Kao Huai-cheng, was sent to oversee the capture of the Yung-chou2 bandits.

Caught between the hostile Ly kingdom and a Sung empire unwilling to accept him as a vassal ruler, Nung Chih-kao started to carve out his own state in the spring of 1052. This was not the first time a member of his clan had made such an attempt. In 1038 his father, Nung Tsun-fu, had rebelled against the Viet kingdom and set up an independent state (Ch'ang-shen kuo). In 1041, Nung Chih-kao and his mother had tried to set up a Ta-li kingdom (Ta-li kuo) in Tang-yu prefecture, his father's base, only to be suppressed again by Vietnamese forces. In 1048, Nang Chih-kao initiated another unsuccessful revolt, escaping to An-te prefecture where he set up the Nan-t'ien kingdom (Nan-t'ien kuo), about 155 miles west of the prefectural seat, Yung-chou2. With the assistance of Huang Wei and Huang Shih-mi, two *chin-shih* degree holders from Kuang-chou, he planned to establish an independent kingdom. His first step was to move his five thousand followers some 70 miles east and capture Heng-shan Fort, an important outpost on the Yu River 90 miles upstream from Yung-chou2.[210]

On the first day of the fifth month of 1052, Nung captured Yung-chou2, declared himself the Jen-hui emperor, and took the reign title of Ch'i-li (Annunciatory Calendar). In three weeks his forces had advanced almost 185 miles downriver, capturing Heng-chou2, Kung-chou, T'eng-chou,

[209] For a monographic study of Nung Chih-kao's rebellion in the larger context of Sino-Vietnamese relations, see James A. Anderson, *The rebel den of Nùng Trí Cao: Eleventh-century rebellion and response along the Sino-Vietnamese frontier* (Seattle, Wash., 2006).

[210] See Araki Toshikazu, "Nung Chih-kao and the k'o-ch'ü examinations," *Acta Asiatica* 50 (1986), pp. 73–5, 82–3; and Ch'en et al., *Sung-shih chi-shih pen-mo* 31, p. 273.

Wu-chou2, Feng-chou2, K'ang-chou, Tuan-chou, and finally Kuang-chou (Canton), overrunning a huge territory that had been only lightly garrisoned by the Sung. Not until the twenty-eighth day of the month did the Sung emperor respond, by ordering Ch'en Shu, the prefect of the untouched river town Kuei-chou3 (Kuei-lin, about 150 miles north of Wu-chou2), to lead an expedition against Nung Chih-kao. Around the same time, the trusted courtier Yü Ching was appointed both pacification intendant for Kuang-nan West and prefect of Kuei-chou3 (Kuei-lin), on account of his earlier experience in Shao-chou2 in Kuang-nan East. Yang T'ien, formerly attached to the Historiography Institute, was appointed investigating pacification intendant and supervisor of bandit suppression, based on his experience in dealing with the Man tribes. These field assignments were matched at court by the appointment of Ti Ch'ing as the deputy commissioner of military affairs. Critics observed that Ti Ch'ing's rise through the ranks to become a councilor of state had been unprecedented and, further, that allowing a military man to become a councilor of state might make the Sung the object of ridicule. Jen-tsung was unmoved. The emperor did ask Ti Ch'ing to remove his tattoos, but when Ti said that they reminded him of his origins and would also encourage other military men to be proud of their service Jen-tsung's respect for his general only increased.[211] Nonetheless, there was widespread opposition to Ti Ch'ing's appointment when he left for Kuang-nan to supervise the war against Nung Chih-kao.

Although Nung Chih-kao had captured and looted Kuang-chou, he could not hold the great city. Yet attempts to stop Nung Chih-kao as he withdrew from Kuang-chou, including the deployment of a river fleet carrying two thousand locally recruited braves, were unsuccessful. However, Nung's forces were prevented from advancing northward into the regions of Kiangsi and Hunan. In the fall of 1052, Sun Mien, an auxiliary academician of the Bureau of Military Affairs, was sent to keep the region of Ching-hu South and Chiang-nan West peaceful and isolated from the Kuang-nan campaign. During his interview with the emperor, Sun Mien so impressed Jen-tsung with a correct prediction about the defeat of one of the imperial forces in Kuang-nan that Jen-tsung granted him plenipotentiary authority and widened his jurisdiction to include Kuang-nan. Fearing that Nung Chih-kao might set his sights northward, Sun Mien transferred some troops and openly repaired and built fortifications so that Nung would not dare to attack northward. Meanwhile Nung's western path of retreat along the Hsi River was blocked by barricades and troops so that he was forced to skirt north and then head west

---

[211] *HTC* (1957) 52, pp. 1272–3.

through the hills to Lien-chou and Ho-chou, and, ultimately, back to Yung-chou2.

Now five months into the campaign and with Sung military units still making little headway, Jen-tsung and his councilors decided they needed a different pacification leadership group: Yü Ching was appointed supervisor of soldiery and bandit suppression, Ti Ch'ing was appointed pacification intendant for Kuang-nan and chief supervisor of bandit suppression (*tu-ta t'i-chü kuang-nan-tung-hsi lu ching-chih tao-tsei shih*), and Sun Mien was appointed deputy pacification intendant. Two weeks later, Jen-tsung decreed that Ti Ch'ing would be reappointed deputy commissioner of military affairs upon his return from the Yung-chou2 campaign. On his return Sun Mien was also appointed a deputy commissioner of military affairs. The first response to the Sung military problem was to reduce the span of control by dividing Kuang-nan West into three military circuits, with headquarters in I-chou3, Jung-chou, and Yung-chou2, coordinated from Kuei-lin by a military pacification intendant. Fifteen thousand northern infantry and cavalry from Shan-hsi were eventually brought into the campaign. Initially, Ti Ch'ing was criticized for trying to use cavalry in Kuang-nan, but Kao Jo-na, now commissioner of military affairs, concurred with Ti Ch'ing's plan. Sun Mien conscripted more local troops to transport supplies to the armies, enticing the conscripts with a thirty percent reduction in their fall tax payment. The Vietnamese ruler, Li T'ai-tsung (r. 1028–54), offered to send twenty thousand of his own troops to help exterminate Nung Chih-kao, but his offer was declined.

On the sixth day of the new year 1053, and prior to Ti Ch'ing's arrival, the hot-headed Ch'en Shu, hungry for glory, led eight thousand infantry to K'un-lun Pass, the fastest route from Pin-chou2 to Yung-chou2, where he was defeated once again. Two days later, Ti Ch'ing arrived at Pin-chou2 with the combined forces of Sun Mien and Yü Ching. Lack of discipline on the part of both troops and commanding officers continued to be a problem. No coherent strategic or even tactical plan could be implemented without reliable troops and responsive leaders. Ti Ch'ing executed Ch'en Shu and thirty-two reckless commanders and imperial military officers for acting irresponsibly, effectively bringing the expeditionary forces under his own control. Even Sun Mien and Yü Ching were cowed by the violence. Ti Ch'ing absolved Yü Ching for having urged Ch'en Shu to attack, informing him, "The Drafting Official is a civil official, so commanding the army is not within his jurisdiction."[212] Ti Ch'ing then announced, as a ruse, that the army would remain in place for ten days, but instead he attacked the unsuspecting Nung Chih-kao on the ninth day.

---

[212] *HTC* (1957) 53, p. 1286.

Ti Ch'ing's forces captured Yung-chou2 and beheaded more than five thousand of Nung Chih-kao's followers, but Nung himself escaped to the Ta-li kingdom in Yunnan. Immediately, rewards were distributed to all Sung military units.

As soon as Jen-tsung received word of Ti Ch'ing's victory, he asked P'ang Chi to arrange to honor Ti with a promotion to commissioner of military affairs and chief councilor. P'ang Chi pointed out that T'ai-tsu had never rewarded a general with so high a civil post, but Jen-tsung insisted. In the wake of the Nung Chih-kao rebellion the Kuang-nan fiscal intendancy was ordered to relieve the impoverished population in Yung-chou2 by making a loan of grain to each household. Following the recommendation of Chou Hang, who had gone to Kuang-nan after the rebellion as an investigating pacification intendant, displaced people were given one year to return to their land and were to be relieved of up to three years of labor service. At the end of the year, officials in Kuang-nan West reported that Nung Chih-kao's mother and his sons and younger brother had been captured. They were kept imprisoned until the middle of 1055, when they were executed following the news of Nung Chih-kao's death in Ta-li. But even now the Nungs were not quelled: between 1057 and 1062 a bandit named Nung Tsung-tan harassed Yung-chou2 until he was finally allowed to submit and was given a Sung official rank.

THE IMPERIAL WOMEN

Women played an openly influential role in Jen-tsung's life and also in the politics of his court, especially during Dowager Empress Liu's regency.[213] Over his forty-year reign, Jen-tsung had four empresses and twelve consorts. Empress Kuo, his first empress, and Empress Ts'ao, his second, were his only two actual empresses. The other two were favorites whom he posthumously elevated to the status of empress. Jen-tsung had thirteen daughters, nine of whom died in childhood.[214] His eldest daughter, the Chou-ch'en Princess (1038–70), was born to Lady Miao and married to a maternal cousin, Li Wei. The emperor treated them indulgently. In 1060 and 1061, she and her husband not only had marital problems, but they also broke the sumptuary laws by maintaining a household with more than their permitted quota of eunuchs and low-ranking military officials, many of whom had been given sinecure monopoly-tax offices. Jen-tsung did little about the complaints, about the

[213] For a general study, see Priscilla C. Chung, "Political power and social prestige of palace women in the Northern Sung (960–1126)" (diss., University of Pennsylvania, 1977).
[214] SS 248, pp. 8776–8; Li Chih, Huang Sung shih-ch'ao kang-yao (c. 1213; Taipei, 1980) 4, pp. 126–7.

couple, and in general allowed his daughters to come and go freely.[215] Jen-tsung had no surviving sons. He fathered only three boys, none of whom lived for more than three years.[216] Jen-tsung's eventual heir was his cousin, Chao Tsung-shih, the thirteenth son of Chao Yün-jang, himself the third son of T'ai-tsung's third son.[217]

Jen-tsung was often criticized for his excessive generosity to his relatives and favorites and their families. For example, when Lady Chang, his favorite during the Ch'ing-li years, died in 1054, Jen-tsung promoted her to the posthumous title of Wen-ch'eng Empress (Wen-ch'eng huang-hou). He also bestowed various posthumous ranks on an unprecedented three generations of her male ancestors; assigned her brother to office and her paternal uncle, Chang Yao-tso, to a number of prestigious posts; and granted her mother honorary titles. This display of favoritism provoked much criticism, which he ignored.[218] Favors also went to palace wet nurses, to princesses, to Lady Miao, to another one of Jen-tsung's deceased sons, and to the Chou-chen Princess.[219]

In contrast, troublesome groups of palace women could always be expelled on the basis of omens; for example, the day after a partial solar eclipse in 1059, 214 women were released from palace service, and the following month another 236 women were released, including two particular troublemakers.[220]

THE DEATH OF JEN-TSUNG AND THE ACCESSION OF YING-TSUNG

Jen-tsung died at the beginning of 1063, passing the throne on to a cousin, Chao Tsung-shih, leaving no princely houses of his own. Chao Tsung-shih, known to us as Ying-tsung (r. 1063–7), was the fifth emperor of the Sung dynasty and the third palace emperor. Although not born in the imperial palace, Ying-tsung was raised there and was a palace emperor unacquainted with the world outside – like his two immediate predecessors, Jen-tsung and Chen-tsung, and unlike his great-grandfather, T'ai-tsung, and great-granduncle, T'ai-tsu. Even Jen-tsung traveled further afield than Ying-tsung, traveling

---

[215] HCP (1979) 124, p. 2924; 192, pp. 4646–7; Chao, Chu-ch'en tsou-i 126, pp. 4281–2; 31, pp. 1170–6; 33, pp. 1221–2; SS 242, p. 8617.

[216] The Prince of Yang, Fang, was born in 1037 to Lady Yü. The Prince of Yung, Chin, was born in 1039 to Lady Chu. The Prince of Ching, Hsi, was born in 1041 to Lady Miao. HCP (1979) 120, p. 2831; 124, p. 2922; 129, p. 3050; 131, pp. 3103, 3109, 3127; 133, p. 3161; SS 245, p. 8708.

[217] SS 245, p. 8708; Po-yang, Chung-kuo ti-wang huang-hou ch'in-wang kung-chu shih-hsi lu (Taipei, 1977).

[218] HCP (1979) 136, p. 3246; 137, p. 3300; 147, pp. 3555–6; 158, p. 3826; 169, p. 4061; Chao, Chu-ch'en tsou-i 23, pp. 950–1; 34, pp. 1250–6.

[219] HCP (1979) 124, p. 2924; 134, pp. 3189, 3208; 135, p. 3228; 137, p. 3300; 155, p. 3766; 185, p. 4478; 186, p. 4484.

[220] HCP (1979) 189, p. 4571; 190, p. 4579; Chung, "Political power and social prestige of palace women in the Northern Sung," pp. 97–107.

once to Kung county where the imperial tombs were located, only seventy-five miles from the capital, K'ai-feng. Dowager Empress Ts'ao served as regent for the first full year of his reign. Ying-tsung died on the 25th of January 1067. His forty-four-month reign was significant only as a transitional period between Jen-tsung's reign and Shen-tsung's reign.

Chao Tsung-shih (the future Ying-tsung), thirteenth of the twenty-eight sons of Chao Yün-jang (995–1059), was born on 17 February 1032.[221] He was brought into the palace under the care of Empress Ts'ao in 1035, where he was appointed *t'ai-tzu* (heir apparent) and given the name Tsung-shih. It is clear from the advice of Dowager Empress Yang that Chao Tsung-shih had not been formally designated or chosen as Jen-tsung's heir.[222] In 1039, when Jen-tsung's second son was born, Tsung-shih was returned to his father's household at the Hostel for Imperial Clansmen. Chao Tsung-shih's natural father, Chao Yün-jang, was the third son of Chao Yüan-fen who was a son of T'ai-tsung. Chao Yün-jang had many years before been brought into the palace by Chen-tsung as a potential heir before Jen-tsung was born, and became the inseparable companion of Jen-tsung before Jen-tsung was himself designated heir. When Chao Yün-jang became ill in late 1059 Jen-tsung visited the prince and thereafter asked after him daily. When the prince died in mid-December, the emperor personally visited the family to offer his condolences and suspended court for five days. Chao Yün-jang was posthumously enfeoffed as Prince of P'u with the posthumous name An-i. He had served as director of the Chief Office of Imperial Clan Affairs for twenty years. Chao Yün-jang's largesse and generosity were matched by a rigorous sternness. His son, the future Ying-tsung, learned an emotional and punctilious form of filial piety from him and from his elder cousin, Jen-tsung. At the end of 1060, Jen-tsung appointed Chao Yün-pi and Chao Ts'ung-ku as director and acting codirector of the Chief Office of Imperial Clan Affairs.[223] One year later, when Chao Tsung-shih had mourned his father for twenty-four months, Jen-tsung asked him to take office as head of the imperial clan agency, but he refused to do so until he had completed the full obligatory twenty-seven months of mourning. Six months later, in the fall of 1062, Jen-tsung held a solemn ceremony designating Chao Tsung-shih as heir apparent (*t'ai-tzu*) and giving him a new personal name, Shu (dawn light).[224] Jen-tsung reported to Heaven

[221] *CPPM* 51, pp. 1627–8; *SS* 245, pp. 8708–11; Miyazaki Ichisada, "Ying-Tsung," in *Sung biographies*, ed. Herbert Franke (Wiesbaden, 1976), vol. 3, pp. 1257–8; Li, *Huang Sung shih-ch'ao kang-yao* 7, p. 197; *HCP* (1979) 120, p. 2833.

[222] *HCP* (1979) 119, p. 2811.

[223] For a complete study of the imperial clan, see John W. Chaffee, *Branches of heaven: A history of the imperial clan of Sung China* (Cambridge, Mass., 1999).

[224] *HCP* (1979) 120, p. 2833; 197, pp. 4473, 4776–7.

and Earth as well as to the ancestors that he had designated Chao Tsung-shih as his heir, but Chao Tsung-shih accepted this honor with great reluctance, in part because he was still in mourning for the death of his father. This tension between his feelings for his father and his duties to the emperor would later fuel the factionalism that was increasingly complicating all aspects of Northern Sung political life.

The new heir apparent would be summoned to the throne sooner than he expected, for by early 1063 the emperor was mortally ill. For six weeks before his death, Jen-tsung fitfully attended to business of state from his sickroom in the Fu-ning Pavilion. The week before he died he appeared to have recovered, but then on the night of 30 April 1063 he rose suddenly from his bed to seek medicine and called for the Empress Ts'ao. When she arrived he could only point to his chest. Neither medicine nor moxibustion helped. Around midnight, Jen-tsung died. Everyone but Empress Ts'ao wanted to open the gates at once and call the councilors of state. Instead she had them ordered to come to the palace at dawn. During the night, in Jen-tsung's bed chamber, the now dowager empress Ts'ao worked out the details of the succession with Han Ch'i and Tseng Kung-liang (998–1078). The leadership group that would work together for the next four years included Han Ch'i, Tseng Kung-liang, Chao Kai, Ou-yang Hsiu, Chang Sheng, Fu Pi, Hu Su, and Wu K'uei, many of whom had been active in the Ch'ing-li reforms. The heir apparent, Chao Tsung-shih, was summoned and informed that he was emperor. In shock he replied, "I can't! I can't!" He then turned to leave. Han Ch'i and Tseng Kung-liang took hold of him and loosened his hair while someone else placed the imperial robe on him. All upper-ranked imperial clansmen and military officers were called in to receive the imperial order establishing Ying-tsung as the new emperor. Han Ch'i cried as he read the testamentary decree before the kinsmen and officials assembled in front of the Fu-ning Pavilion. Then Ying-tsung accepted the obeisance of his assembled officials. Ying-tsung immediately asked Han Ch'i to take charge of the government while he himself undertook a three-year period of mourning, but he relented at the insistence of his councilors.[225] In order to assure a smooth transition, four million strings of cash were paid out as largesse to eunuchs and soldiers in K'ai-feng, and some seven million strings were distributed to troops throughout the empire.[226] Funeral arrangements, under Han Ch'i's supervision, were made for a modest tomb and for modest expenditures. Some forty-eight thousand soldiers from various circuits worked on the tomb. Immediately, the Finance Commission asked to borrow 1.5 million strings, 2.5 million bolts of silk, and

[225] HCP (1979) 198, pp. 4791–4.
[226] HCP (1979) 198, pp. 4791, 4794.

50,000 ounces of silver to meet the costs of the tomb and various associated gifts.[227]

On his fourth evening as emperor Ying-tsung suddenly became ill, losing the power of speech and the ability to recognize people. The demoted physicians were recalled to examine him. A few days later he was found shouting, walking about wildly, and unable to control his behavior. Han Ch'i asked Dowager Empress Ts'ao to serve as regent for the duration of Ying-tsung's incapacity, which she did until the spring of 1064, when Ying-tsung's recovery prompted Han Ch'i to demand that the reins of government be returned to Ying-tsung.[228] Ying-tsung's three living sons and three daughters were promoted in rank and honors. His eldest son, Chao Chung-chen (later renamed Chao Hsü) (1048–85), was officially designated heir apparent (*t'ai-tzu*) in 1064. The future Shen-tsung was set up in his own household outside the palace. The separation was tearful and he returned every day to visit.[229] Lady Kao, Ying-tsung's wife since 1047 and the mother of his three sons, was appointed empress. She was the maternal niece of Dowager Empress Ts'ao. Eventually, Empress Kao would become dowager empress and regent during Che-tsung's reign, during which time she repealed Wang An-shih's reform measures, dismissed his followers, and appointed Ssu-ma Kuang and his associates to high office.

Jen-tsung was entombed in the fall of 1063, and the commemorative service was held in the spring of 1064.[230] Ying-tsung's absence because of illness and Dowager Empress Ts'ao's regency contributed to a relatively subdued nine months of ceremony and construction work.[231] The year of Dowager Empress Ts'ao's governance was not disturbed by any major conflicts, invasions, crises, or issues, and she conducted a very restrained regency. Ying-tsung barely spoke before the end of the year, and the two chief councilors, Han Ch'i and Tseng Kung-liang, kept the caretaker administration on an even keel. By the end of 1063, Ying-tsung was well enough to order the writing of the veritable record of his predecessor's reign and to announce his own reign title, Chih-p'ing

---

[227] *HCP* (1979) 198, pp. 4794, 4802.

[228] *HCP* (1979) 198, pp. 4755, 4795, 4802, 4804, 4809, 4812, 4816; 201, p. 4865; Chao, *Chu-ch'en tsou-i* 26, p. 1039; Yang Lien-sheng, "Female rulers in Imperial China," *Harvard Journal of Asiatic Studies* 23 (1960–1), pp. 51, 56–7; *CPPM* 54, pp. 1721–48, provides a succinct account of the dowager empress's regency. Ying-tsung was well enough in December to attend his first session of the Imperial Seminar. *HCP* (1979) 199, pp. 4839–40.

[229] *HCP* (1979) 199, p. 4840.

[230] *HCP* (1979) 199, p. 4829; 200, p. 4851; 204, p. 4953.

[231] Construction for the tomb, the enlargement of the Chao clan ancestral temple, and the funeral cost about a million and a half strings, two and a half million bolts of silk, and half a million *liang* of silver. His burial complex was known as Yung-chao ling. *HCP* (1979) 198, pp. 4794, 4806, 4809–11; 199, p. 4829.

(Ordered Tranquility, 1064–7), which began on the first day of 1064.[232] Han Ch'i was the nominal editorial director of the *Jen-tsung veritable record* (*Jen-tsung shih-lu*), but Wang Kuei (1019–85) did most of the work. The project was prolonged because Jen-tsung's reign was so long, and because Wang Kuei had to reconstruct the information that would normally have been included in the *Court calendar* (*chü-ch'i lu*) and the *Record of current government* (*shih-ch'eng chi*), neither of which had been kept up between roughly 1049 and 1061. Han Ch'i finally presented the *Jen-tsung veritable record* in the summer of 1069, after Ying-tsung's death and at the same time as the *Ying-tsung veritable record* (*Ying-tsung shih-lu*) was presented to the emperor Shen-tsung.[233]

Han Ch'i's steady governance during the Ts'ao regency did not translate into harmonious relations with his fellow councilors, especially with the now sixty-year-old Fu Pi. After the collapse of the Ch'ing-li reforms, Han Ch'i and Fu Pi, among others, had been demoted to regional posts. Both were reappointed to positions on the Council of State in the mid-1050s, but in 1061 Fu Pi had taken mourning leave and refused to return until he had completed the full period. Fu Pi was appointed commissioner for military affairs as well as chief councilor in the spring of 1063. Although Fu accepted the position, he soon asked to be released from ministerial duties because of tensions with the temperamentally quite different Han Ch'i. Han Ch'i never consulted Fu Pi. Han Ch'i decided matters quickly, Fu Pi ruminated. Han Ch'i thought Fu Pi talked too much. Fu Pi thought Han Ch'i was a bit shallow. Under Han Ch'i, all questions to the Bureau of Military Affairs were handled informally by his subordinates. When Fu Pi complained about this, Han Ch'i replied superciliously that if the Bureau of Military Affairs was not consulted, Fu Pi ought to complain to the dowager empress, not to him. Fu Pi took a strong dislike to Han Ch'i. Beginning in the fall of 1064, Fu Pi stayed home in bed on the pretext of a foot ailment. Over the next six months he asked Ying-tsung some twenty times to send him to a prefectural or circuit appointment. In the meantime, Han Ch'i and Tseng Kung-liang had been appointed to manage the affairs of the Bureau of Military Affairs while Fu Pi was on sick leave. Finally, in the summer of 1065, Fu Pi got his wish and was assigned to a regional post; a few weeks later Ying-tsung appointed Wen Yen-po (1006–97)

---

[232] Another cultural activity that confirmed imperial authority was issuing a calendar. The calendar finally issued in the spring of 1065 was unworkable as a replacement. *SS* 74, pp. 1685–1708; 75, pp. 1709–41; *HCP* (1979) 204, p. 4951.

[233] *HCP* (1979) 194, p. 4690; 199, p. 4840; 200, p. 4852; 206, p. 4995; 207, p. 5023; *HTC* (1957) 65, p. 1589; 66, p. 1617; 67, p. 1650; Ts'ai Ch'ung-pang, *Sung-tai hsiu-shih chih-tu yen-chiu* (Taipei, 1991), pp. 78–82; Yang Lien-sheng, "The organization of Chinese official historiography: Principles and methods of the standard histories from the T'ang through the Ming dynasty," in *Historians of China and Japan*, ed. William G. Beasley and Edwin G. Pulleyblank (London, 1961), pp. 44–59.

as commissioner of military affairs, in part because he was grateful to Wen for supporting him as heir to the throne.[234]

The controversy over the ritual status of the Prince of P'u

By the spring of 1064 Ying-tsung was healthy enough to resume his duties as emperor: he read memorials, asked questions, understood implications, and made decisions. Earlier Ssu-ma Kuang had raised the issue of how to differentiate ritually between Chao Yün-jang, the Prince of P'u and the emperor's deceased biological father, and Jen-tsung, Ying-tsung's deceased adoptive father.[235] The question was raised again when Ying-tsung had resumed direct rule. But Ying-tsung explicitly postponed all discussion until his mourning for Jen-tsung was completed in the early summer of 1065. Then the issue came to dominate the political stage.

Ying-tsung's reign was largely taken up by the complexities of accession, regency, and mourning, which, under a morose, passive, and withdrawn emperor, became political fodder for factional conflict.[236] Once the regency was over and the mourning for Jen-tsung completed, Ying-tsung was determined to honor and promote his biological father. These events unfolded in two phases. The first phase comprised discussions on how Ying-tsung was to ritually address and behave toward his adopted father and predecessor, the deceased Jen-tsung, on the one hand, and his deceased natural father, the Prince of P'u, on the other. These discussions began in spring of 1065 and were terminated by Ying-tsung's imperial order in the winter of 1066. The second phase was marked by conflict over the limits of censorial responsibility waged between the emperor and chief councilors on one side, and the policy critics, censors, drafting officials, ritual experts, and Han-lin academicians on the other. This phase lasted two months in early 1066.[237]

Ying-tsung's reign, from the very beginning, was caught up in debates over ritual. During the regency of Dowager Empress Ts'ao and the completion of Ying-tsung's mourning for Jen-tsung, debates swirled around Jen-tsung's status as ancestral deity (*p'ei*), Ying-tsung's filial duties toward Dowager Empress Ts'ao, and the obligations and requirements of an adopted son.[238] During the

---

[234] *HCP* (1979) 201, p. 4866; 205, pp. 4967, 4976–8.

[235] *HCP* (1979) 199, p. 4837.

[236] See Ch'en et al., *Sung-shih chi-shih pen-mo* 36, pp. 311–22; *CPPM* 55, pp. 1749–80, and Carney T. Fisher, "The ritual dispute of Sung Ying-tsung," *Papers on Far Eastern History* 36 (1987), pp. 109–38, for accounts of this episode in Ying-tsung's reign.

[237] Fisher, "The ritual dispute of Sung Ying-tsung," pp. 110, 128.

[238] *HCP* (1979) 199, pp. 4832–5; 200, pp. 4846–51, 4853–6; 201, pp. 4868–9; Chao, *Chu-ch'en tsou-i* 86, pp. 2983–90.

course of Ying-tsung's illness, Ssu-ma Kuang and Lü Hui offered advice to both Ying-tsung and the dowager empress Ts'ao on filial responsibility within the adoptive relationship. But the relationship between Ying-tsung and the dowager empress had become strained by Ying-tsung's deranged behavior.[239] At the same time, Han Ch'i and the other councilors of state pressed Ying-tsung to discuss what to do about the Prince of P'u and his three wives, a discussion that Ying-tsung, as already noted, wished to postpone until he had completed his mourning for Jen-tsung.[240] Two months before that milestone was reached, Ying-tsung instructed his ritual experts to reengage the question that Han Ch'i and the other ministers of state had posed about Ying-tsung's ritual relationship to his natural father, the Prince of P'u.[241] No one responded during the last two months of mourning, using the time for discussion and to search for precedents. Ying-tsung then enlarged the circle of discussants to include censors, policy critics, and Han-lin academicians.[242]

Discussion swiftly grew into a political controversy that continued for almost a year. Confucian idealists led by Lü Hui and pragmatic ministers of state led by Han Ch'i engaged in a struggle that evolved into a constitutional dispute over the role of censors as a counterbalance to the factional rivalries embodied in imperial and ministerial absolutism.[243] Ssu-ma Kuang proposed that Ying-tsung's filial obligations ought to be decided according to Confucian values, irrespective of emotional attachments. Representing the opposite pole, Ou-yang Hsiu insisted that it was precisely these contingent, embodied, human values that ought to decide the issue.[244] Throughout the summer of 1065, Policy Critic Ssu-ma Kuang, Policy Critic Lü Hui, Han-lin Academician Recipient of Edicts Wang Kuei, and Censors Lü Ta-fang, Fan Chen, Fan Ch'un-jen, Chao Chan, Fu Yao-yü, and Chao Ting2 submitted dozens of memorials individually and as a group. The specific problem of establishing which titles would be applied to the Prince of P'u and which to Jen-tsung was paralleled by the debate over which set of criteria should define familial behavior: natural feelings or universal (if dispassionate) values. Ou-yang Hsiu, who had just completed the then-definitive text on court ritual, joined Han Ch'i in siding with Ying-tsung's wish to recognize his obligations to his natural father as well as those to his adoptive father. But Lü Hui, Fan

---

[239] HCP (1979) 199, pp. 4832–5.

[240] HCP (1979) 201, pp. 4872–7; Chao, *Chu-ch'en tsou-i* 34, pp. 1265–6; 89, pp. 3031–2.

[241] HCP (1979) 204, p. 4957.

[242] HCP (1979) 205, p. 4968.

[243] Liu, *Ou-yang Hsiu*, pp. 77–8; Fisher, "The ritual dispute of Sung Ying-tsung," pp. 113–14; Chao, *Chu-ch'en tsou-i* 89, pp. 3034–53; Gung, "The participation of censorial officials in politics during the Northern Sung dynasty," pp. 30–41.

[244] Bol, "*This culture of ours*," pp. 177, 238, 268.

Ch'un-jen, Ssu-ma Kuang, Wang Kuei, Lü Ta-fang, Fan Chen, Fu Yao-yü, Chan Ting, and Chao Chan believed that ritual paternity trumped biological fatherhood: because Jen-tsung had adopted Ying-tsung, bringing him into the main branch of the dynastic family, Ying-tsung was obliged to honor Jen-tsung above his natural father, the Prince of P'u. As they saw it, Jen-tsung had to be referred to as "deceased father" (*k'ao*), while the Prince of P'u had to be referred to as "deceased imperial paternal uncle" (*huang-po*). For the proponents of universal values, the designations "imperial deceased father" (*huang-k'ao*) or parent (*ch'in*) could not be properly applied to the Prince of P'u.[245] Even Dowager Empress Ts'ao rejected the use of *k'ao* for the prince.

The debate was interrupted by massive floods in K'ai-feng in the fall, as well as by the efforts of Han Ch'i, Ou-yang Hsiu, and Tseng Kung-liang to cut off further discussion of the matter.[246] With the dowager empress's consent, Han Ch'i and his associates convinced Ying-tsung to summarily announce that henceforth the Prince of P'u would be called emperor (*huang*), P'u's wives would be called empress (*hou*), and Jen-tsung would be addressed as parent (*ch'in*).[247] Although this was intended to be definitive, the order simply unleashed a new storm of protest – against using the title *ch'in* (parent) for both the Prince of P'u and Jen-tsung, against establishing a taboo for the Prince of P'u, against setting up a separate memorial garden, and against Dowager Empress Ts'ao's meddling.[248]

At this point, Ying-tsung was unsure what to do. His diffidence, his affection for his natural father, the reluctance with which he had entered into adoption, the ambiguity of the adoption, and his respect for the opposition officials left him confused.[249] But Han Ch'i successfully pressed Ying-tsung to choose sides, since the other officials had impeached Han Ch'i, Ou-yang Hsiu, and Tseng Kung-liang. The opposing faction, including Lü Hui, Fan Ch'un-jen, Lü Ta-fang, Fu Yao-yü, Chao Ting2, Chao Chan, and Lü Kung-chu, were transferred to other appointments during the first two months of 1066. Ying-tsung emphasized that they were not to be treated harshly for their opposition. Even so, the imperial orders were delivered to their homes directly rather than through Han Wei, who might have blocked the orders in his role as drafter or as concurrent controller of the Memorial Forwarding Office

[245] *HCP* (1979) 205, pp. 4971–6.
[246] *HCP* (1979) 206, pp. 4984, 5004, 5010–12; 207, pp. 5020–9; Chao, *Chu-ch'en tsou-i* 49, pp. 1865–6; 56, pp. 2098–2102; 89, pp. 3054–67; 90, pp. 3069–76.
[247] *HCP* (1979) 207, pp. 5029–37, 5043.
[248] *HCP* (1979) 207, pp. 5032–7; Fisher, "The ritual dispute of Sung Ying-tsung," p. 127.
[249] *HCP* (1979) 200, p. 4583; 201, pp. 4867–8, 4878; and 204, p. 4946 reveal elements of ambiguity in Jen-tsung's adoption of Ying-tsung. In general, the consensus was that Ying-tsung was the adopted son of Jen-tsung. See *HCP* (1979) 197, p. 4773; *HTC* (1957) 60, p. 1470.

(*T'ung-chin yin-t'ai ssu*). Nevertheless, Ssu-ma Kuang, Han Wei, Fu Yao-yü, Chao Chan, and P'eng Ssu-yung continued to criticize the decision.[250] Finally, in the third month of 1066, Ying-tsung issued a personal decree in his own hand declaring his decision and chiding Lü Hui and others for their intransigence.[251] Arrangements were made to promote the lineal descendants of the Prince of P'u, and to enlarge the memorial garden of his mother, Lady Jen, to the dimensions of a proper mausoleum.[252]

POLITICS FROM SPRING 1065 UNTIL THE DEATH OF YING-TSUNG IN JANUARY 1067

As the ritual controversy was winding down, the Liao announced in early 1066 that they had upgraded their self-designation to Great Liao (Ta Liao), and that henceforth they would refer to themselves as the Northern Country in relation to the Sung Southern Country.[253] While this elicited some discussion, Ying-tsung was not well enough to handle both the Prince of P'u controversy and this new issue. Ironically, this unilateral change in relative Sung and Liao status in the regional tributary and diplomatic arena did not attract as much attention from censors, policy critics, and Han-lin academicians as did the personal relationship of Ying-tsung to his "fathers." In general, Sung and Liao relations had been quite uneventful since the 1042 treaty revision. The Liao–Hsi Hsia conflict of 1049–54 had been announced at court, as was the death and succession of the Liao emperor in 1055, but to no great fanfare; and several minor border problems involving trade and river fishing were resolved through negotiations and discussions between the relevant military intendants and their Liao counterparts.[254]

Few outside events spurred the court to great efforts. Raids led by Liang-tso (1046–67), the Hsi Hsia ruler, did provoke a massive recruitment of peasants into the Shan-hsi militia in 1064. In the fall of 1066, Liang-tso mounted two further raids against the Sung.[255] In late September, Liang-tso led attacks on Ta-shun ch'eng (in Ch'ing-chou2, Yung-hsing-chün circuit), burning and

---

[250] *HCP* (1979) 207, pp. 5040–2; Fisher, "The ritual dispute of Sung Ying-tsung," p. 132.

[251] *HCP* (1979) 207, p. 5043.

[252] It is worth noting that in the retrospective opinion of Chu Hsi (1130–1200), it was Ou-yang Hsiu rather than Ssu-ma Kuang who had been wrong, because, as Chu put it, it is "improper to extend paternity to both a natural and adoptive parent." See Fisher, "The ritual dispute of Sung Ying-tsung," p. 133.

[253] *HCP* (1979) 207, p. 5021.

[254] *HCP* (1979) 151, p. 2668; 167, p. 4020; 168, p. 4034; 176, pp. 4281–2; 179, p. 4329; 180, pp. 4363–4; 182, p. 4399; 186, p. 4492; 187, pp. 4502, 4509; 193, p. 4671; 204, p. 4958; 207, p. 5021; 208, p. 5057.

[255] *HCP* (1979) 208, pp. 5062–3, 5067–8.

destroying several fortified settlements. The military pacification intendant for Huan-ch'ing circuit, having learned that Liang-tso intended to attack, made preparations to repel him by positioning troops at critical points, especially at Ta-shun ch'eng. However, Liang-tso's force of around twenty thousand considerably outnumbered the Sung troops, who were surrounded for three days before an allied cavalry commander came to their aid. Liang-tso was wounded by crossbow fire and forced to withdraw. A subsequent Hsi Hsia raid against a fort defended by a deputy military intendant and military commander failed. The Sung commander raised three thousand braves to harass the Hsi Hsia camp at night, scattering the Tangut forces. Liang-tso regrouped at Chint'ang, where, instead of mounting another offensive, he merely traded insults with the Sung officials. Initially, Han Ch'i suggested withholding the annual tribute, but Wen Yen-po, the new commissioner of military affairs, said this would only serve as a pretext for further conflict. Ch'en Chiu (aka Ch'en Shengchih) and Lü Kung-pi cited the example of 1038–9 to convince Ying-tsung not to provoke Liang-tso. Han Ch'i retorted sarcastically that "the war specialists" ought to understand the difference between then and now, for Sung preparedness and capability were far greater now, and Hsi Hsia was led by Liang-tso, a young fool with nothing like the military prowess of Li Yüan-hao.

With the time for the annual tribute payment close at hand, Ying-tsung chose Han Ch'i's aggressive strategy. Meanwhile, Liang-tso attacked and surrounded Ta-shun ch'eng again in December. The Fu-yen military intendant, frustrated by the passive military response to Hsi Hsia, sent a memorial urging the emperor to do something about the raids, but the result was only a letter of disapproval upbraiding Liang-tso for improper behavior. However, when a letter was delivered to Liang-tso threatening to withhold the muchdesired annual tribute of tea and silver, Liang-tso backed off, concocting a story that a Sung border official had started the confrontation. By this time, Ying-tsung was bedridden. During one morning audience, Han Ch'i tapped on the screen in front of the emperor's bed to ask the news from the western zone. Ying-tsung exerted himself to look at Han Ch'i and told him, "It was as you predicted." Even so, Liang-tso's reply was ambiguous enough that another emissary was sent to insist on a solemn oath reaffirming his recognition of Sung sovereignty.

Throughout Ying-tsung's reign the central government's growing fiscal problems showed themselves in various and increasingly insidious ways. One of the immediate consequences of the already costly recruitment of one hundred and fifty thousand militia men in Shan-hsi as part of the defensive military response to Hsi Hsia aggression was an intensified need to transport supplies into the region. Yet despite the mounting problems with fiscal liquidity and effective tax collection, the only economic issues chosen for discussion at court were the excessive numbers of officials and excessive imperial spending on ritual.[256] More far-reaching than establishing limits on the number of officials that could be appointed to certain ranks was the decision in the fall of 1066 to hold the *chin-shih* civil service examination only once every three years, a practice that endured until 1905.[257]

Ying-tsung's reign saw no change in the political leadership. The four leading civil officials – Han Ch'i, Tseng Kung-liang, Chao Kai, and Ou-yang Hsiu – had all served for at least one year before Ying-tsung came to the throne and served at least one year after his death. The military leadership was less settled, and included one unusual appointment, that of General Kuo K'uei as cosignatory deputy commissioner of military affairs in 1066. Kuo K'uei, a senior general and a former protégé of Fan Chung-yen, was recommended by Han Ch'i in place of Chang Fang-p'ing (1007–91), whom Han resented for refusing to join his coterie.[258] Han Ch'i craftily suggested to Ying-tsung that it had been a long time since a military man had been appointed to the Bureau of Military Affairs, asserting that Kuo K'uei was a less objectionable alternative than the other eligible general. Remonstrance officials and censors pointed out that while other emperors had appointed military men to the Bureau of Military Affairs, they had been men of substance, like Ts'ao Pin, Ma Chih-chieh, or Wang Te-yung, and not crafty sycophants like Kuo K'uei. Whether or not their characterization of Kuo was accurate, Ying-tsung agreed to Han Ch'i's proposal to appoint Kuo K'uei. However, just six months later Kuo was reassigned out of the capital to Shan-hsi.

Significant changes did occur below the top level of bureaucrats. Chang Fang-p'ing had been appointed Han-lin academician recipient of edicts at the beginning of 1066, to compensate for the transfer of Wang Kuei to write Jen-tsung's veritable record. Chang Fang-p'ing and Ou-yang Hsiu, although dissimilar in many ways, each appreciated the outstanding talents of Su Hsün (1009–66) and his sons, Su Shih (1037–1101) and Su Ch'e (1039–1112), and through their efforts Su Hsün and Su Shih gained recognition and office. In 1060, Ou-yang Hsiu had sponsored Su Shih for a special decree examination, while Ssu-ma Kuang had sponsored Su Ch'e. Although Ying-tsung was so impressed that he wanted to appoint Su Shih as a Han-lin academician, Han Ch'i proposed a less prestigious appointment as an auxiliary in the Historiography Institute (*Kuo-shih kuan*). Su Hsün died in 1066, just after he and his sons returned to K'ai-feng from the Ch'eng-tu area, having been in mourning for his wife and their mother.[259] Such links between sponsors and patrons,

[256] *HCP* (1979) 204, pp. 4955, 4957; 205, pp. 4965, 4968; 206, pp. 4992–5; 208, pp. 5052, 5058–61.
[257] *HCP* (1979) 208, pp. 5063–4.
[258] *SS* 290, pp. 9722–6; *HCP* (1979) 208, pp. 5051–2, 5064; *HTC* (1957) 64, pp. 1572, 1579.
[259] *HCP* (1979) 192, pp. 4639–40; 207, p. 5039; 208, pp. 5054–6; Ting, *Compilation of anecdotes of Sung personalities*, pp. 391, 475–94; George C. Hatch, "Su Hsün," in *Sung biographies*, ed. Herbert Franke (Wiesbaden, 1976), vols. 2–3, pp. 885–968; Ch'ang et al., *Sung-jen chuan-chi tzu-liao so-yin*, pp. 4304–5.

and their protégés and followers, were important social and political ties, and they were reinforced by formal measures to nurture talented men from among whom the upper echelons of advisors and councilors of state would be drawn. In late 1066, Han Ch'i, Tseng Kung-liang, Chao Kai, and Ou-yang Hsiu recommended twenty men for assignment to the imperial academies and institutes.[260] But at the same time that potential future ministers of state were being identified and appointed to such low-ranking but prestigious posts, attempts were made to slow down the overall growth in the number of men on the roll of officials. One such measure was the extension of the civil service examination cycle to once every three years.[261]

In order to perpetuate the Chao clan's dynastic line, a suitable marriage partner for Ying-tsung's eldest son, Chao Hsü (formerly named Chao Chung-chen), was sought among proper official families. In April 1066, the granddaughter of Hsiang Min-chung was married to Chao Hsü. It was not long before the status of the new couple would change dramatically. Throughout his reign Ying-tsung had been sick, recovering, or feeling unwell, and between November 1066 and his death on 25 January 1067 he was terminally ill.[262] As was the usual practice, prayers were offered at the Ta-ch'ing Pavilion – the location for the Ming-t'ang rituals and the other formal great state ceremonies. One day, as Han Ch'i and others were withdrawing from a visit to ask after the emperor's health, Chao Hsü asked Han Ch'i if there was anything he could do. Han Ch'i replied that he hoped His Highness would stay with the emperor day and night. The young man replied that this was his duty, and Han Ch'i told the prince that that was not what he had meant. The succession was still technically unsettled, and since Ying-tsung could no longer talk, he could only write his instructions or gesture in reply to questions. Between Han Ch'i and Chang Fang-p'ing, the Han-lin academician who drafted major decrees of state, Ying-tsung was coaxed to specify in his weak handwriting that Chao Hsü was his heir apparent. Before the formal ceremony of investiture could be held, Ying-tsung died at age thirty-six.

---

[260] *HCP* (1979) 208, pp. 5064–5.
[261] *HCP* (1979) 204, p. 4957; 208, pp. 5052, 5058–64.
[262] *HCP* (1979) 208, pp. 5063, 5066, 5068.

CHAPTER 5

SHEN-TSUNG'S REIGN AND THE NEW POLICIES OF WANG AN-SHIH, 1067–1085

Paul Jakov Smith

SHEN-TSUNG'S ASCENSION AND THE CRISIS OF THE MID-ELEVENTH CENTURY

The nature of the midcentury crisis

In 1067 the nineteen-year-old Chao Hsü (1048–85) ascended the throne with an acute sense of shame for his country's foreign humiliations and a fierce ambition to redress the crises that beset his empire.[1] The young Shen-tsung emperor and his ministers had many reasons to feel uncertain, for the death of his father, Ying-tsung (r. 1063–7), after only three and a half years on the throne could be taken only as a bad omen. But the sense of crisis that pervaded Shen-tsung's empire had been brewing throughout Jen-tsung's reign (1022–63),

---

[1] Shen-tsung's reign and the New Policies spearheaded by his chief minister, Wang An-shih, have inspired a vast and growing literature. For background information and a guide to the sources, the first places to go are the two encyclopedic works by Higashi Ichio, Ō Anseki shinpō no kenkyū (Tokyo, 1970), and Ō Anseki jiten (Tokyo, 1980). Three of the most useful interpretations are Ch'i Hsia, Wang An-shih pien-fa, 2nd ed. (Shanghai, 1979); Liu Tzu-chien (James T. C. Liu), Reform in Sung China: Wang An-shih (1021–86) and his New Policies (Cambridge, Mass., 1959); and Wang Tseng-yü, "Wang An-shih pien-fa chien-lun," Chung-kuo she-hui k'o-hsüeh 3 (1980), pp. 131–54, which set off a wave of revisionist critiques in China of the New Policies. For a recent biography of Shen-tsung, see Chung Wei-min, Sung Shen-tsung (Ch'ang-ch'un, 1997). The most important primary source for Shen-tsung's reign is Li T'ao's Hsü tzu-chih t'ung-chien ch'ang-pien, which supplements the official record with a rich array of diaries, memoirs, and unofficial histories, many of them no longer extant. The punctuated edition, Hsü tzu-chih t'ung-chien ch'ang-pien [hereafter HCP (1979)] (1183; Peking, 1979–95), is supplemented by the Shang-hai ku-chi ch'u-pan-she reprint, Hsü Tzu-chih t'ung-chien ch'ang-pien [hereafter HCP (1986)] [Che-chiang shu-chü 1881 ed.] (1183; Shanghai, 1986), of the once standard 1881 edition. Because the HCP chapters for the period from the second month of 1067 through to the third month of 1070 have been lost, the first three years of Shen-tsung's reign must be reconstructed from the Southern Sung historian Yang Chung-liang's Tzu-chih t'ung-chien ch'ang-pien chi-shih pen-mo [hereafter CPPM] (1253; Taipei, 1967), which has been rearranged, along with many other sources, into chronological order by Ch'in Hsiang-yeh et al., Hsü tzu-chih t'ung-chien ch'ang-pien shih-pu [hereafter HCP (1986) shih-pu], published as volume 5 of the Shang-hai ku-chi ch'u-pan-she edition. In addition to the HCP, this chapter relies primarily on Hsü Sung et al., Sung hui-yao chi-pen [hereafter SHY (1964)] (1809, 1936; Taipei, 1964), and T'o-t'o et al., eds., Sung shih [hereafter SS] (1345; Peking, 1977).

ever since the Sino-Tangut war of 1038–44 had exposed troubling weaknesses in the fundamental pillars of the dynastic system itself – the military, the financial system, and the bureaucracy.

The four-year war with the Tangut Hsi Hsia had demonstrated that the Sung's mercenary armies were unfit for active combat. Although the Sung mustered some 1.25 million men against 826,000 Tangut troops, the aged and inexperienced Sung soldiers, hired from among the flotsam of the marketplace, were likely to scatter at their first sight of a Tangut soldier. The war confirmed the status of the Tangut state as a major Asian power, even as the cessation of hostilities exacerbated defensive pressures on the Sung as just one of several players in a multistate geopolitical setting. With the Tanguts solidly entrenched in the Ordos, and the Khitan Liao sitting implacably along the northern borders of Ho-tung and Ho-pei, Sung ministers saw little short-term alternative to maintaining their huge if unreliable standing armies in the north. Efforts were made to pare the size of the regular, imperial troops, but by the mid-1060s the court still had 1,162,000 men on the rolls, over half of whom (663,000) were costly imperial troops.[2]

Of course, the war had exacted an enormous toll on the Sung state, which was in turn forced to raise taxes by fifty percent in the three northern circuits of Shan-hsi, Ho-pei, and Ho-tung to meet emergency needs.[3] But what dismayed contemporary observers even more was that the end of the war brought no financial relief. The need to pay, outfit, and provision troops stationed along the resource-poor northern frontier forced the Sung state to dig ever deeper into the commercial and agrarian economies, transforming the Sung fisc into what the historian Sogabe Shizuo has referred to as a perpetual "wartime economy."[4] As routine defense costs absorbed an increasing portion of the state's income, official efforts to generate more revenues undermined trade in the state's two most important monopolized commodities, tea and salt. Yet even so it was impossible to keep up with the costs of a cumbersome but

---

[2] On the origins and characteristics of the Sung's troops during the war, see SS 187, p. 4574; on the war itself, see Wu T'ien-ch'ih, Hsi Hsia shih-kao (Ch'eng-tu, 1981), pp. 59–68; Li Hua-jui, Sung Hsia kuan-hsi shih (Shih-chia-chuang, 1998), pp. 40–57; Feng Tung-li and Mao Yüan-yu, Pei Sung Liao Hsia chün-shih shih (Peking, 1998), pp. 248–61; Ruth W. Dunnell, "The Hsi Hsia," in The Cambridge history of China, volume 6: Alien regimes and border states, 907–1368, ed. Herbert Franke and Denis C. Twitchett (New York, 1994), pp. 154–205. Wang Tseng-yü discusses the weaknesses of the Sung armies in the mid-eleventh century in his Sung-ch'ao ping-chih ch'u-t'an (Peking, 1983), pp. 90–5; for a contemporary assessment, see "Shang huang-ti shu" in Su Ch'e, Luan-ch'eng chi (1541; Taipei, 1965–6) 21, pp. 7b–10a.

[3] Expenditures in the three northern circuits rose from 42.3 million to 72.1 million mixed units between 1038 and 1043, forcing an increase in taxes from 50.3 to 73.1 million units. See HCP (1979) 140, p. 3366.

[4] See Sogabe Shizuo, Sōdai zaiseishi (Tokyo, 1941), p. 3. The most frequently cited contemporary analysis of the impact of war on the midcentury Sung economy is by the two-term finance commissioner Chang Fang-P'ing (1007–91) in his memorial "Lun kuo-chi ch'u-na shih," in Chang Fang-P'ing, Le-ch'üan chi [Ssu-k'u ch'üan-shu, Wen-yüan ko 1779 ed.] (c. 1100; Taipei, 1969) 23, pp. 2b–5a.

ineffective system of defense: by 1065 defense expenditures consumed fifty of the state's sixty million strings of cash income – eighty-three percent – while the government registered its first overall financial deficit.[5]

Defense was not the only budgetary item that had swelled out of control by midcentury. The state's financial capacity was also stretched thin by what contemporaries called the problem of *jung-kuan*, supernumerary officials. The numbers of men with ranked civil service status (including civil and military officials) almost tripled during the reigns of Chen-tsung (997–1022), Jen-tsung, and Ying-tsung, from 9,785 to roughly 24,000 individuals. All of these men drew salaries commensurate with their civil service rank, or stipendiary grade (*chi-lu kuan*), even if they held no active post (*ch'ai-ch'ien*). And starting sometime during Chen-tsung's reign the number of ranked civil servants increased well beyond the number of available posts, a trend that only continued to worsen. This glut of officials had several unfavorable consequences: in order to maintain a large enough candidate pool to ensure elite loyalty to the dynasty and at least a minimum flow of new blood into government, the state had to pay men for whom it had no jobs. This resulted in a large, though unspecified, financial burden. But poor career prospects and the long waiting period between posts undermined the morale of the civil service, especially the majority of civil servants in the junior, or executory (*hsüan-jen*), division. The professional spirit of these men could erode if they were kept too long in lowly provincial posts or were forced to go without posts altogether. Yet the court had to be wary of promoting too many junior men to the much smaller senior, or administrative, division (*ching-ch'ao kuan*) – the critical *kai-kuan* promotion – where appropriate posts were even rarer. By the 1040s the problem of job competition and underemployment had expanded beyond the executory division into the upper reaches of the administrative class as well, inducing powerful members of the bureaucracy to unduly manipulate the personnel system to favor their relatives and protégés.[6]

---

[5] For a recent survey of the secular increase in taxes that began in Jen-tsung's reign, see Ch'i Hsia, *Sung-tai ching-chi shih* (Shanghai, 1987–8), vol. 1, pp. 393–410. Shiba Yoshinobu discusses military spending in his "Sōdai shiteki seido no enkaku," in *Aoyama Hakushi koki kinen Sōdai shi ronsō*, ed. Aoyama Hakushi Koki Kinen Sōdai-shi Ronsō Kankokai (Tokyo, 1974). Ch'eng Min-sheng disputes the standard interpretation that the figures preserved in *SS* 179, p. 4353, for 1065 demonstrate a chronic fiscal deficit. See Ch'eng Min-sheng, "Lun Pei Sung ts'ai-cheng ti t'e-tien yü chi-pin ti chia-hsiang," *Chung-kuo shih yen-chiu* 3 (1984), pp. 33–4. These doubts are amplified by Ji Xiaobin, "Pei Sung chi-p'in hsin-chieh – shih-lun 'kuo-yung pu-tsu' yü Wang An-shih hsin-fa chih cheng," in *Kuo-shih fu-hai k'ai-hsin-lu: Yü Ying-shih chiao-shou jung-t'ui lun-wen-chi*, ed. Chou Chih-p'ing and Willard J. Peterson (Taipei, 2002), pp. 283–300.

[6] On the reasons for and problems spawned by the growth of the Sung civil service, see Furugaki Kōichi, "Sōdai no kanryō sū ni tsuite," in *Sōdai no shakai to shūkyō*, ed. Sōdai-shi Kenkyūkai (Tokyo, 1985), pp. 121–58; Lo Wen (Winston W. Lo), *An introduction to the civil service of Sung China: With emphasis on its personnel administration* (Honolulu, 1987), pp. 60–2, 158–65; and Umehara Kaoru, *Sōdai kanryō seido kenkyū* (Kyoto, 1985), chapter 1 and pp. 249–66.

Responses to the midcentury crisis

The Sino-Tangut debacle forced leading thinkers to reevaluate the state of Sung rule eighty years after the founding, and prompted the first major reform movement of the dynasty, the Ch'ing-li reforms of 1043 to 1045. Under the leadership of Fan Chung-yen (989–1052) the reform partisans insisted that the only way to reverse the military deterioration that the war had exposed was to undertake a comprehensive campaign to dismantle privilege and promote efficiency in the bureaucracy, rejuvenate the agrarian economy, and revive peasant participation in national defense.[7] But, as documented in the previous chapter, in little more than a year the Ch'ing-li reform movement was abruptly suppressed, after highly placed opponents convinced Jen-tsung that the reform faction under Fan Chung-yen, Fu Pi (1004–83), and Han Ch'i (1008–75) constituted a threat to both imperial power and well-entrenched bureaucratic interests. Indeed, it was the failure of the Ch'ing-li reforms that paved the way for the more radical reforms of Shen-tsung's reign, for despite Jen-tsung's volte-face, public-spirited men grew increasingly uneasy. Or so at least the Yüan-yu partisan Liu An-shih (1048–1125) thought, as he tried to account for Shen-tsung's reforms to his student Ma Yung-ch'ing (chin-shih 1109). Relating what he must have learned from his own teacher Ssu-ma Kuang (1019–86), Liu explained that "Between the time of the founders, who ruled the world with loyalty and benevolence, and the end of the Chia-yu era [1056–63], the affairs of the world appeared to unravel, and all were dispirited and lackluster. The scholarly elite (shih-ta-fu) of the time deplored this state of affairs, and many of them wrote about it."[8] It was in this very period, in 1058, that Shen-tsung's future chief councilor, Wang An-shih (1021–86), submitted his manifesto for achieving dynastic greatness through comprehensive reform, the so-called Myriad word memorial; three years later, Ssu-ma Kuang followed with a set of memorials that offered an alternative approach to the problems of the day, rooted in prudence and a conservative eschewal of adventurism.[9] Nevertheless,

---

[7] See Liu Tzu-chien (James T. C. Liu), "An early Sung reformer: Fan Chung-yen," in *Chinese thought and institutions*, ed. John K. Fairbank (Chicago, 1957), pp. 105–31. For Fan's ten-point call for reform, issued in the ninth month of 1043, see Fan Chung-yen, *Fan Wen-cheng kung cheng-fu tsou-i* (1053; Taipei, 1967) *shang*, pp. 176–82. The text is reproduced in substantially complete form in *HCP* (1979) 143, pp. 3431–44.

[8] Ma Yung-ch'ing, *Yüan-ch'eng yü-lu*, quoted in Ch'i, *Wang An-shih pien-fa*, p. 63. Ch'i Hsia discusses the political responses to the midcentury crisis on pp. 57–97. For a sense of the intellectual ferment of these times, see chapter 6 of Peter K. Bol, *"This culture of ours": Intellectual transition in T'ang and Sung China* (Stanford, Calif., 1992).

[9] Wang's memorial, "Shang Jen-tsung huang-ti yen-shih shu" in Wang An-shih, *Wang Lin-ch'uan ch'üan-chi*, 2nd ed. (c. 1100; Taipei, 1966) 39, pp. 217–27, is discussed more fully later. For Ssu-ma's "Five Guidelines," see Ssu-ma Kuang, *Ssu-ma Wen-cheng kung ch'uan-chia chi* (mid-12th c.; Shanghai, 1937) 21, pp. 307–14, analyzed in Bol, *"This culture of ours,"* pp. 220–1.

despite heated debate about the problems of the day, it was impossible to undertake major initiatives without an emperor dedicated to change, and Jentsung no longer was. Some efforts were made at the top to tinker with those fiscal and military institutions that were dangerously close to collapsing, such as the tea and salt monopolies and the cavalry horse procurement system.[10] But the really significant reforms in the post-Ch'ing-li era were initiated by local and provincial officials to address problems faced by the people of their own jurisdictions. These localized measures included at least two preharvest loan measures, one of them by the magistrate of Yin county (Liang-che, modern Ning-po), Wang An-shih; a service exemption fee for supply masters (*yach'ien*); and two prototypical mutual security systems (*pao-chia*) established by local administrators to quell banditry in Ts'ai-chou and K'ai-feng.[11] Although without imperial support none of these experiments spread very far, they all served as precedents and prototypes for the New Policies (*hsin-fa*) promulgated under Shen-tsung's reign.

What Shen-tsung faced

When Jen-tsung died with no male heir in 1063, his nephew Chao Shu was elevated to the throne at age thirty-one. Although contemporaries such as Tseng Kung (1019–83) thought the new emperor Ying-tsung was eager for change and reform, Ying-tsung's short reign was so paralyzed by factionalism and an acrimonious ritual controversy that little was accomplished.[12] Thus when Ying-tsung abruptly died in the first month of the new lunar year (1067) his nineteen-year-old son Chao Hsü inherited all the problems that had bedeviled the Ch'ing-li reformers, but in even more intensified form.

On the financial front, the imperial coffers were still empty from the huge costs of Jen-tsung's interment, and now another imperial funeral impended. Although the young emperor ordered that expenditures on his father be kept to one-third the cost of Jen-tsung's funeral, Chief Councilor Han Ch'i was still forced to borrow three hundred thousand strings of cash from the Inner

---

[10] See, for example, Saeki Tomi, "Sōsho ni okeru cha no senbai seido," in *Chūgoku-shi kenkyū*, Saeki Tomi (Kyoto, 1969), vol. 1, pp. 377–408; Tai I-hsüan, *Sung-tai ch'ao-yen chih-tu yen-chiu* (Shanghai, 1957); and chapter 1 of Paul J. Smith, *Taxing heaven's storehouse: Horses, bureaucrats and the destruction of the Sichuan tea industry, 1074–1224* (Cambridge, Mass., 1991).

[11] For these and additional examples of reforms initiated locally between the late 1040s and early 1060s see Ch'i, *Wang An-shih pien-fa*, pp. 67–70.

[12] On the ritual dispute over whom Ying-tsung should call his father, see Bol, "*This culture of ours,*" p. 213, citing Carney T. Fisher, "The ritual dispute of Sung Ying-tsung," *Papers on Far Eastern History* 36 (1987), pp. 109–38; and Liu Tzu-chien (James T. C. Liu), *Ou-yang Hsiu: An eleventh century Neo-Confucianist* (Stanford, Calif., 1967), pp. 76–9. For Ying-tsung's abortive "activism" (*chih tsai yu-wei*) see Tseng Kung, *Yüan-feng lei-kao* (c. 1038; Taipei, 1968) 30, p. 330, cited, among other examples, by Ch'i, *Wang An-shih pien-fa*, p. 96.

Treasury and to conscript into service thirty-five thousand laborers and four thousand stonemasons.[13] More fundamentally, official morale seemed to be at a nadir as the surplus of officials began to affect the entire civil service. Many commentators lamented that the glut of executory grade officials had worsened over the years, with far more men than the system could absorb clamoring for posts, sponsors, and promotion to senior administrative status.[14] And now the need to accommodate the demands of junior men had also produced a surfeit of administrative-grade officials: in 1068 a censor complained that there were ten times more administrative-grade officials than there had been under the first two emperors, forcing the Bureau of Personnel Evaluation (*Shen-kuan yüan*) to furlough senior- as well as junior-grade officials.[15] Moreover, according to the great scholar Ou-yang Hsiu (1007–72), the choicest senior-level positions – those in the Three Institutes (*San-kuan*, of History, Literature, and Worthies), the training ground for future chief councilors – were no longer assigned to the most talented *chin-shih* graduates, but rather to those men with technical experience in finance, law, and defense. As Ou-yang saw it, learning and good reputation no longer mattered, leaving the most steadfast members of the civil service dispirited.[16]

But perhaps the most immediately troubling problem inherited by the new emperor was the growing aggressiveness of the Tanguts under Liang-tso (r. 1048–67), son and successor of the Tangut state builder Li Yüan-hao (r. 1032–48). Liang-tso's ambitions were aided and inspired by the political deterioration of the Tibetan federation in the Kansu and Ch'ing-hai border-lands that had long been the Sung's only northern ally. Disaffected tribal leaders occupying the vulnerable northwestern perimeter of the Lung-hsi basin that divided the Tanguts, the Sung, and the Ch'ing-hai federation had begun defecting to the Hsi Hsia side from the late 1050s on, encouraging the Tanguts to launch an expansionist campaign throughout the unstable border region. Starting in 1063 the Tanguts repeatedly sent large expeditionary forces against Tibetan tribal capitals, against the sinified border tribes, and in 1066 against Chinese commanderies themselves. These Tangut probes presented an immediate threat to the always fragile Sung horse-supply system, but in the long term they threatened the Sung state itself. Ying-tsung's chief ministers had been confused about how to deal with Liang-tso and the Tanguts, and could still not agree on a plan to present to Shen-tsung.[17]

---

[13] *HCP* (1979) 209, pp. 5074–6.

[14] *HCP* (1979) 208, pp. 5052, 5058–60.

[15] *HCP* (1986) *shih-pu* 3 *shang*, pp. 11b–12a.

[16] *HCP* (1979) 208, pp. 5064–5.

[17] See *SS* 485, p. 14002; 492, p. 14162; and *HCP* (1979) 208, pp. 5067–8. For a discussion and sources, see Smith, *Taxing heaven's storehouse*, p. 43.

Shen-tsung and the old guard

Shen-tsung, however, had his own ideas about what needed to be done, for he saw himself as the heir to the founders' dreams of recovering the sixteen prefectures of Yen-Yün occupied by the Khitan Liao in the north, and the Ordos prefecture of Ling-chou lost to the Tanguts in 1001. He came to the throne "determined to wipe away generations of shame," not by relying on conciliation and passive defense, as had every predecessor since T'ai-tsung (r. 976–97), but by redefining the political map through conquest and expansion.[18] This irredentist dream also shaped Shen-tsung's attitude toward his empire's fiscal crisis: very simply, the state needed riches to finance its wars, for as Shen-tsung told his war minister Wen Yen-po (1006–97), "if we are to raise troops for our frontier campaigns, then our treasuries must be full."[19] And finally, Shen-tsung's ambitions were animated by a vision of himself as an activist, hands-on ruler. Although it was not until Wang An-shih's ouster in 1076 that Shen-tsung took direct control of the affairs of state, he ascended the throne with an expansive sense of imperial power and an abiding dissatisfaction with the absolutist powers built up over the years by the great ministers – particularly Han Ch'i, still in the chief councilor's office he had held under the last two emperors.[20]

Shen-tsung had reason to expect an enthusiastic response to his goals from his leading officials, since many of them had spearheaded the reform movement of 1043. But time and prominence had dulled their edge, and many of the emperor's "venerables" (yüan-lao) had turned conservative. Chu Hsi (1130–1200) stressed this point to his students a century later, commenting that when such men as Han Ch'i and Fu Pi came to power again following the failure of the Ch'ing-li reforms, "they had forgotten [the excitement of] those early days. Master Fu was afraid of acting, and wanted only to read the classics and recite Buddhist sutras."[21] Fu Pi, who "knew the emperor was devoted to activism (yu-wei)," made a special point of counseling restraint at every opportunity, especially on matters of war. When in 1068 the emperor asked him about border affairs, Fu replied that "Your Majesty has not been [on the throne] for very long; it would be best if you spread virtue and act benevolently, and not speak of war for twenty years."[22]

---

[18] SS 16, p. 314.

[19] Ma Tuan-lin, Wen-hsien t'ung-k'ao [Shang-wu yin-shu-kuan 1935–7 ed.] (c. 1308; Taipei, 1965) 24, p. 232c.

[20] HCP (1986) shih-pu 1, p. 2a.

[21] Chu Hsi, Chu-tzu yü-lei, cited in Ch'i, Wang An-shih pien-fa, p. 97.

[22] SS 313, p. 10255.

Fu Pi's homily was not especially useful at a time when the country was drifting into a war with the Tanguts, and Shen-tsung received it in "stony silence." But Fu was hardly alone in resisting the emperor's desire to confront the Tanguts. In 1066, after three years of Tangut attacks on Chinese surrogates and military installations, the Shan-hsi fiscal intendant Hsüeh Hsiang had sent up a comprehensive plan for border defense that emphasized setting Tangut surrogates against their masters. In mid-1067 Hsüeh's plan assumed greater urgency when the border official Ch'ung O kidnapped Tangut general Wei-ming Shan and his followers, unleashing an escalating spiral of violence punctuated by the Tangut execution of a Sung emissary and Ch'ung O's walling of the Tangut town of Sui-chou (Shan-hsi, renamed Sui-te chün).[23] All agreed that Ch'ung O had acted without authorization, but Shen-tsung dismissed calls that he and Hsüeh Hsiang be punished to placate the Tanguts and bring the matter to an end.[24] For Shen-tsung was desperate to launch an offensive campaign, and the Ch'ung O fiasco was all he had. Perhaps for this reason he was especially incensed by a memorial that his new chief censor, Ssu-ma Kuang, sent up in the ninth month of 1067. Although Ssu-ma allowed that the emperor's desire to recover the territories of the Kansu Corridor (held by the Uighurs and Tibetans), the Ordos (held by the Tanguts), and the sixteen prefectures (held by the Khitan) were laudable goals, they could not be achieved by Ch'ung O's policy of turning Liang-tso's allies against the Tanguts. First of all, insisted Ssu-ma, since the Chinese people were by nature and livelihood ill-equipped to do battle with the war-loving barbarians, the only sage policy was to seek a stable border through diplomacy and compliance – literally by embracing them and being soft (huai-jou). Every Sung emperor who pursued an offensive policy against the Tanguts, such as T'ai-tsung in 1001 and Jen-tsung in the 1040s, saw his troops cut down in battle, his people killed off by the exhaustion of transport duty, and his coffers emptied by war and the annual bounties paid to the barbarian victors. Second, although Liang-tso may have transgressed from time to time, he never openly cut off relations with the Sung; he still called himself "vassal" (ch'en). Thus from a diplomatic standpoint it would be humiliating to break faith with a vassal by suborning his ministers. And finally, if the destabilizing plan failed and the country found itself in an outright war with the Tanguts, its resources would be stretched beyond capacity, for the Sung was not at all ready for war. On the contrary, stressed Ssu-ma,

---

[23] Ch'ung O had bribed Wei-ming Shan's younger brother into turning in Wei-ming, and then preemptively kidnapped Wei-ming when it looked like the plan was unraveling. See *CPPM* 83, pp. 2627–39, and the useful synopsis in Pi Yüan's late-eighteenth-century reconstruction of the Sung and Yüan chronicles, the *Hsü tzu-chih t'ung-chien* [hereafter *HTC* (1957)] (Peking, 1957) 65, p. 1609.

[24] *HCP* (1986) *shih-pu* 2, pp. 18b–21a.

to the extent that the emperor's revanchist goals were at all laudable, they could be realized only after a thorough revamping of the imperial bureaucracy, the fiscal system, the army command structure, the system of military recruitment and training, and the arsenal. Since none of these had been attended to, to go on the offensive prematurely could lead only to disaster.[25]

Because of their antipathy toward offensive war, Shen-tsung's early advisors were also lukewarm about creating a national war chest. Although all agreed that the nation was in the midst of a financial crisis, they continued the tradition of indicting irresponsible spending for impoverishing the people and the state, and proposed cost-cutting measures that were more appropriate for a minimalist approach to government than to the activist ambitions harbored by the new emperor. Early in 1067, for example, Chang Fang-p'ing urged that the emperor first reduce the size of his armies, and then seek to cut costs in the imperial household and the bureaucracy by eradicating everything that conflicted with "plainness and simplicity."[26] A year later Ssu-ma Kuang declined a post in the new Office of Economizing (Ts'ai-chien chü), which he thought was itself a wasteful bureaucratic accretion, by admonishing the emperor that "the current deficits in the national treasury have been caused by wasteful administrative expenditures, unrestrained bestowal of emoluments and rewards [attendant on the deaths of two emperors in four years], an overly lavish imperial household, a bloated bureaucracy, and an inefficient army." Ssu-ma cautioned that reducing expenditures had to be a long-term project, and he wondered why it could not be assigned to the Finance Commission, rather than to yet another wasteful office. Although Shen-tsung did dutifully institute a campaign to trim expenses in the imperial household, he declined, despite Ssu-ma's advice, to dismantle the new cost-cutting agency.[27]

The issue that most provoked Shen-tsung's dissatisfaction with his elder statesmen was not war or finance, but the scope of monarchical power. Within months of Shen-tsung's accession prominent officials sought to curtail the new emperor's ambition to initiate and direct reforms from the throne, and to press on him the importance of leaving the management of affairs of state to his bureaucracy. In a memorial of the second month of 1067 the academician Han Wei (1017–98) begged Shen-tsung not to intervene directly in the governing process: "The hundred affairs of government each have their appropriate officials, who exercise their utmost skills to fulfill their duties. There can be no

---

[25] "Lun Heng-shan shu," in Ssu-ma, Ssu-ma Wen-cheng kung ch'uan-chia chi 41, pp. 525–9. Shen-tsung fumed about Ssu-ma Kuang's memorial to his war minister, Wen Yen-po, and demanded to know how Ssu-ma knew about the deliberations in the first place. See HCP (1986) shih-pu 2, p. 7b.

[26] HCP (1979) 209, p. 5091.

[27] "Ts'u-mien ts'ai-chien kuo-yung cha-tzu," in Ssu-ma, Ssu-ma Wen-cheng kung ch'uan-chia chi 42, pp. 533–5, and Ma, Wen-hsien t'ung-k'ao (1965) 24, p. 232c.

greater sacrifice of the essence of government than for the monarch to take over
from his officials in the management of affairs." Han Wei urged Shen-tsung
to confine his decision making to only the most important issues, and only
when his officials were stalemated; and above all he stressed that the ruler
could not hasten to do great things, but must proceed systematically and with
great caution.[28] As Anthony Sariti has argued, it was Ssu-ma Kuang who
most forcefully contended that the emperor should act as a final arbiter who
stood aloof – and sequestered – from the actual process of bureaucratic decision
making.[29] Two months after Han Wei's memorial, Ssu-ma Kuang inaugurated
his appointment as chief censor by urging Shen-tsung to eschew "the many
bothersome details of government" in favor of first rectifying his own heart
(*hsiu-hsin*), and then selecting and motivating the best men to govern the
nation (*chih-kuo*).[30] It was just this division between imperial and bureaucratic
spheres of influence that Shen-tsung was disinclined to honor, however, and
four months later Ssu-ma Kuang was forced to complain that the emperor was
interfering in the normal process of government by sending out his own agents
(*nei-ch'en*) to investigate affairs and line officials in the field.[31]

It must be stressed that although Shen-tsung did not get the encouragement
he wanted from such men as Fu Pi and Ssu-ma Kuang, he did not on that
account want them out of his way. On the contrary, he continued to value the
opinions of the most fervent critics of his revanchist, reforming ambitions, and
sought to keep the critics by his side. Shen-tsung kept Fu Pi in the capital
until 1072 despite the old man's opposition to change, for example, because
he felt that Fu Pi's "prominence helped to hold together all under Heaven."[32]
And Ssu-ma Kuang remained Shen-tsung's closest confidant – perhaps even
closer intellectually than Wang An-shih – despite his intransigent opposition

---

[28] *HCP* (1979) 209, p. 5077.

[29] See Anthony W. Sariti, "Monarchy, bureaucracy, and absolutism in the political thought of Ssu-ma
Kuang," *Journal of Asian Studies* 32 No. 1 (1972), pp. 53–76.

[30] "Ch'u ch'u chung-ch'eng shang-tien cha-tsu," in Ssu-ma, *Ssu-ma Wen-cheng kung ch'uan-chia chi* 38,
pp. 493–4, and *HCP* (1986) *shih-pu* 1, pp. 9b–10a. The first part of Ssu-ma's injunction is translated in
Sariti, "Monarchy, bureaucracy, and absolutism in the political thought of Ssu-ma Kuang," p. 62.

[31] "Yen Wang Chung-cheng ti erh cha-tzu," in Ssu-ma, *Ssu-ma Wen-cheng kung ch'uan-chia chi* 39, p. 511, and
HCP (1986) *shih-pu* 2, pp. 1a–2b. Anthony Sariti is right to conclude (contra James T. C. Liu) that this
question of the delegation of authority to the bureaucracy does not distinguish between conservatives and
reformers. Once he was in power Wang An-shih made many of the same arguments as Han Wei and Ssu-
ma Kuang had made. The dividing line comes over what kind of power (extractive and entrepreneurial
versus ameliorative and advocatory) and to what kinds of officials (special-function fiscal agents versus
regular line officials).

[32] *HCP* (1979) 231, pp. 5614–16, citing the *Yeh-shih* of Lin Hsi (c. 1035–c. 1101), compiler in the
mid-1090s of the *Veritable records* of Shen-tsung's reign. For capsule biographies of Lin and many of the
individuals mentioned in this chapter, see Sung-shih chüan pien-tsuan wei-yüan-hui, *Chung-kuo li-shih
ta tz'u-tien: Sung-shih chüan* (Shanghai, 1984).

to every facet of the emperor's reform agenda. For as Shen-tsung told Lü Kung-chu (1018–81) in the tenth month of 1067, "I want Ssu-ma Kuang by my side not for his opinions on affairs of state [for as they both agreed Ssu-ma, like Wang An-shih, was rather impractical] but because of his moral power (*tao-te*) and learning."[33]

Thus it was not simply over ideas about how to rule that Shen-tsung turned away from the leading midcentury intellectuals to Wang An-shih, but also because of politics. More importantly, Shen-tsung resented what he perceived as the autocratic powers built up over three reigns by his chief councilor Han Ch'i. Shen-tsung's resentment was fanned by his former tutor, Wang T'ao (1020–80), who repeatedly charged that "since the end of the Chia-yu era [1056–63] Han Ch'i has monopolized the handles of government, with the result that the monarch's position is weak and the minister's position is strong." Starting in the third month of 1067 Wang T'ao used his post as head of the Censorate to launch an impeachment campaign against Han Ch'i and his co-councilor Tseng Kung-liang (998–1078) for taking advantage of a new emperor to violate the rules of office protocol. Shen-tsung himself quashed the impeachment process, but a political free-for-all between Wang T'ao and the assistant civil councilor, Wu K'uei (1010–67) ensued that revived the factional animosities of the 1060s and undermined the power of the old leadership. On the one hand Han Ch'i, seriously compromised by Wang T'ao's attacks and the public perception of Shen-tsung's displeasure with him, repeatedly begged permission to resign his post. On the other hand, Tseng Kung-liang, corespondent in the impeachment memorials, sought to distance himself from Han Ch'i by forcefully sponsoring a new and as yet unaffiliated rising star – Wang An-shih. Shen-tsung finally accepted Han Ch'i's resignation in the ninth month of 1067, by which time he had become obsessed with the idea of meeting and using Wang An-shih.[34]

Shen-tsung and Wang An-shih

In many ways Wang An-shih was typical of the men who moved into the bureaucratic elite during the second half of the eleventh century. The Wangs were part of the wave of sojourners who migrated from the old northern heart-land (in their case from T'ai-yüan) to the new political and economic centers of

---

[33] *HCP* (1986) *shih-pu*, 2, pp. 13a–15b.

[34] The basic sources on Han Ch'i's resignation and Tseng Kung-liang's promotion of Wang An-shih are anthologized in *HCP* (1986) *shih-pu* 2, pp. 8a–11a. See also Henry R. Williamson, *Wang An-Shih, a Chinese statesman and educationalist of the Sung dynasty* (London, 1935–7), vol. 1, pp. 101–2. Williamson's chief narrative source is Pi Yüan's *Hsü tzu-chih t'ung-chien.*

the south during the upheavals of the Five Dynasties era.[35] The family settled in Fu-chou5 (Chiang-nan West), a region that was just beginning to rise in economic and political significance during the early eleventh century.[36] With Wang's father, Wang I (993–1039), a *chin-shih* graduate of 1015, the family entered the bureaucratic stream: Wang I held a series of local offices culminating as vice-prefect (*t'ung-p'an*) of Chiang-ning fu (modern Nanking), where he died in 1039 and which Wang An-shih came to regard as home. Between the beginning of the century and 1068 the Wang lineage produced eight *chin-shih* graduates, including An-shih (*chin-shih* 1042). In conjunction with their migration out of their native place to Chiang-ning, this achievement reflects the kind of academic focus and geographic mobility characteristic of families specializing in government service during the eleventh century. Known from his youth as a dazzling scholar (he placed fourth in his *chin-shih* class), Wang earned early recommendations from such luminaries as Ou-yang Hsiu and Wen Yen-po. Nonetheless, Wang spurned opportunities to break into official circles in the capital, preferring to serve in local posts in Chiang-nan where he could better discharge his family and financial responsibilities. In 1147 he took a post as magistrate of the coastal Yin county (modern Ning-po), where he promoted the kinds of agricultural policies he would apply empirewide during the New Policies, including irrigation and land reclamation projects and an early version of an agricultural loan measure that provided grain in the off-season to be paid back with interest at harvest time.[37]

In 1058, after a decade of staff positions in prefectural and central government earned him the judicial intendancy of Chiang-nan East circuit, Wang sent to Jen-tsung the "Myriad word memorial" that was to become Wang's

---

[35] Wang reviews his family's history in a short biographical notice for his father called "Hsien ta-fu shu," in Wang, *Wang Lin-ch'uan ch'üan-chi* 71, pp. 448–9. The basic source for Wang's life remains Ts'ai Shang-hsiang, *Wang Ching kung nien-p'u k'ao-lüeh* (1804; Shanghai, 1974). Ts'ai reconstructs Wang's life and career from a wide variety of sources, including literary collections and local gazeteers. H. R. Williamson's biography of Wang An-shih, in Williamson, *Wang An Shih*, vol. 1, pp. 1–388, is based largely on Ts'ai Shang-hsiang and on Wang's biography in *SS* 327, pp. 10541–51. For modern studies of Wang's early life and career, see Saeki Tomi, "Ō Anseki," in *Chūgoku-shi kenkyū*, Saeki Tomi (Kyoto, 1969), vol. 3, pp. 365–81; Higashi, *Ō Anseki shinpō no kenkyū*, pp. 924–33, and Higashi, *Ō Anseki jiten*, pp. 129–35; and Liu, *Reform in Sung China*, pp. 1–4. For a parallel study of the evolution of the careers and thought of Wang An-shih and Ssu-ma Kuang, see Bol, *"This culture of ours,"* pp. 212–53.

[36] The political and demographic trends exemplified by Wang and his family are outlined in Robert M. Hartwell, "Demographic, political, and social transformations of China, 750–1550," *Harvard Journal of Asiatic Studies* 42 No. 2 (1982), pp. 365–442. For an examination of those trends in Wang An-shih's home region, see Robert P. Hymes, *Statesmen and gentlemen: The elite of Fu-chou, Chiang-hsi, in Northern and Southern Sung* (Cambridge, 1986).

[37] Higashi devotes a special section to Wang's tenure in Yin county. See Higashi, *Ō Anseki shinpō no kenkyū*, pp. 930–3, and *SS* 327, p. 10541. The parallel chronologies of the lives and careers of Wang and Ssu-ma Kuang are conveniently tabulated in Higashi, *Ō Anseki jiten*, pp. 221–35. See also Saeki, "Ō Anseki," pp. 439–50.

reform manifesto.[38] Wang's memorial exemplifies the alarm intellectuals felt as they saw their country head toward crisis in the decades following the Sino-Tangut war:

Within the empire the security of the state is a cause for some anxiety, and on our borders there is the constant threat of the barbarians. Day by day the resources of the nation become more depleted and exhausted, while the moral tone and habits of life among the people steadily deteriorate. On all sides officials who have the interests of the nation at heart are fearful that the peace of the empire may not last.[39]

The underlying cause of the crisis, for Wang, was that men of the present had moved too far from the laws and institutions of the ancient kings. At its heart, Wang's memorial is an indictment of the prevailing political culture, a culture dominated by self-serving and convention-mired men selected by the examination system for their strong memories and literary skills rather than for the practical experience essential for good government. It was these men, Wang may well have thought, who had suppressed the Ch'ing-li reforms; and it was certainly these men who would ensure that even when emperor and court did promulgate the right kinds of measures, either they would not be acted on or they would be turned against the people. Consequently, Wang insisted, "the most urgent need of the time is to secure men of talent," for only then will it be possible to transform the decadent institutions that cause human suffering and approach the ideals of the ancient kings. And the only way to secure such men is to follow the example of the ancients – that is, to create a nationwide school system "to mold and train them" through a four-stage process: Instruction, nurturance, selection, and employment. This process would produce activist, practical-minded men, trained and experienced in the specialties for which they were best suited, who could be given great latitude to carry out their projects "without being hampered by this or that regulation."[40] Wang did not expect his new bureaucrats to forgo their own interests; on the contrary, he proposed to cement their interests to the well-being of the state by paying them well enough to keep them honest. But he did expect them to all share the same values – "to be uniformly instructed in the way of the ancient kings," as were the scholars of old, when "the heterodox learning of the hundred schools was all rejected, and no one dared study them." And he insisted on a return to that

[38] "Shang Jen-tsung huang-ti yen-shih shu" in Wang, *Wang Lin-ch'uan ch'üan-chi* 39, pp. 217–27. For English translations, see Williamson, *Wang An Shih,* vol. 1, pp. 48–84; and Wm. Theodore de Bary et al., eds., *Sources of Chinese tradition* (New York, 1960), pp. 413–19. Wang's memorial is analyzed in Higashi, *Ō Anseki shinpō no kenkyū,* pp. 921–77; see also Bol, *"This culture of ours,"* pp. 216–18.

[39] Wang, *Wang Lin-ch'uan ch'üan-chi* 39, p. 218, translation from de Bary et al., *Sources of Chinese tradition,* p. 414.

[40] Wang, *Wang Lin-ch'uan ch'üan-chi* 39, p. 220. For an interpretation of Wang An-shih's memorial as a call for the mobilization of bureaucratic entrepreneurs, see Smith, *Taxing heaven's storehouse,* pp. 117–18.

ancient *shih* ideal that held the civil and military arts to be inseparable, so that the defense of the borders and the palace would be in the hands of the scholarly elite (*shih-ta-fu*), rather than sloughed off on the most corrupt, ruthless, and irresponsible elements of society, men who could not even maintain themselves in their native villages but had to leave their families to muster in the army.[41]

In Wang An-shih's view, then, the only way to meet the challenges of the day was to revitalize the bureaucracy by creating the widest possible pool of like-minded, action-oriented specialists who were devoted to the civil and military interests of the state. But even a revitalized bureaucracy did not mean that reform would proceed automatically or that the emperor could remain aloof from the political process. On the contrary, Wang warned that activist rule (*yu-wei*) could proceed only if the emperor himself was firm and resolute and enforced political discipline. In the past – and again Wang must have had the Ch'ing-li reforms in mind – whenever some "vulgar opportunist" (*liu-su chiao-hsing chih jen*) disliked and opposed reform, "the court just called a halt and would not dare to proceed." The sage-kings of antiquity, by contrast, never failed to push relentlessly forward:

Whenever the ancients aspired to great deeds they never failed to exterminate (*cheng-chu*) [their opportunist opponents] as a prelude to attaining their goals. Thus the *Book of poetry* says "By punishment and extermination we eliminate opposition." In this way did King Wen [the Chou progenitor] first exterminate his opposition and only then achieve his goals for the world.[42]

Because they inhabited an especially corrupt world the ancient kings had to overcome their reluctance to exterminate their adversaries, "for they knew that otherwise they could not accomplish great deeds." Wang assured Jen-tsung that his own task would be easier, since opportunistic nay-sayers were far outnumbered by the many who would welcome reforms. But this made it all the more ignoble for the emperor to allow himself to be swayed from the imperative to reform officialdom and the world. "If Your Majesty sincerely hopes to bring the world's talents to the fore then this minister urges that you decide once and for all."[43]

Although his imagery would become less sanguinary, this was the same message that in his six years as chief councilor Wang would repeat over and over again to Shen-tsung: be resolute, crush dissent, and disregard the murmuring opposition of vulgar opportunists. And although Jen-tsung had had his one chance at reform and was not about to try again, under Shen-tsung "when

---

[41] Wang, *Wang Lin-ch'uan ch'üan-chi* 39, pp. 221, 223. See Bol, *"This culture of ours,"* p. 218 and his sources for further examples of Wang An-shih's stress on the need for unity of values and customs.

[42] Wang, *Wang Lin-ch'uan ch'üan-chi* 39, p. 226.

[43] Ibid.

An-shih came to the head of the country, all his proposals found their origins [in the "Myriad word memorial"]."[44]

Following the submission of his memorial, Wang was appointed to a series of capital posts, including staff supervisor in the Office of Funds (*san-ssu tu-chih p'an-kuan*) of the Finance Commission, auxiliary in the Academy of Worthies (*Chi-hsien yüan*), and in 1061 drafting official (*chih-chih-kao*) for the Secretariat. During this period Wang's mother had resided in the capital, but when she died in the eighth month of 1063, five months after the death of Jen-tsung, Wang An-shih returned to bury her in Chiang-ning. Yet even though Wang spent all of Ying-tsung's reign in Chiang-ning, his name was constantly brought to the future emperor Shen-tsung's attention by Shen-tsung's tutor, Han Wei. For whenever Han's discourses met with the young prince's approval Han would say, "This is not my idea, it is the idea of my friend Wang An-shih."[45] When Shen-tsung ascended the throne his interest in Wang was fanned by Tseng Kung-liang as well, who insisted that Wang was "ministerial material"; and although Wang refused an imperial summons for an audience in the third month of Shen-tsung's reign (1067), he surprised even his friend Han Wei by accepting at the same time an appointment as prefect of Chiang-ning. But Wang was still out of the capital and out of sight of the emperor who wanted to meet him. Shen-tsung kept pressing his ministers for their opinions on Wang – Wu K'uei and Han Ch'i both thought Wang appropriate for an academic post but not for a position on the Council of State – and when Han Ch'i resigned as chief councilor in the ninth month of 1067, Shen-tsung appointed Wang to the Han-lin Academy, along with Ssu-ma Kuang. Seven months later, burning with impatience, Shen-tsung ordered the "newly appointed Han-lin Academician Wang An-shih to appear for an audience immediately."[46]

That first meeting between the twenty-year-old emperor and the forty-seven-year-old political maverick must have convinced Shen-tsung that here was an advisor whose activist ambitions matched his own. Wang An-shih even counseled the emperor to abandon T'ang T'ai-tsung as his model, and to reach back to the sages Yao and Shun, heretofore thought by "the scholars of this decadent age" (*mo-shih hsüeh-shih tai-fu*), content to accept the ordinary as their goal, to be beyond the reach of men of today.[47] Shen-tsung replied that perhaps with Wang's help he could attain such heights; but he did probe for the cause of Wang's sense of urgency, by asking how his predecessors had

---

[44] *SS* 327, p. 10542. For the self-protective rerouting of dissent into art and poetry during Shen-tsung's reign, see chapter 2 of Alfreda Murck, *Poetry and painting in Song China: The subtle art of dissent* (Cambridge, Mass., 2000), pp. 28–50.

[45] Ts'ai, *Wang Ching kung nien-p'u k'ao-lüeh* 9, pp. 143–5; *SS* 327, p. 10543.

[46] *CPPM* 59, p. 1888.

[47] *CPPM* 59, p. 1888; Williamson, *Wang An Shih*, vol. 2, p. 34.

managed to hold all under Heaven for one hundred years "without a major disaster." Wang's response, presented following the audience in a formal memorial entitled "[Why] this dynasty has enjoyed a hundred years without disaster," supplied just the rationale for action that Shen-tsung had been seeking.[48]

In essence, Wang argued that the survival of the dynasty had heretofore depended on the imperial virtues of care for the welfare of the people, open-mindedness toward the opinions of officials, fairness in the application of the laws, prudence and compliance toward the barbarians, and above all good fortune. But fortune and imperial virtue just barely offset the "the problems of slavish conventionality typical of a period of decline (yin-hsün mo-su chih-pi)." In the court, Wang charged, the ruler spends his time surrounded by eunuchs, women, and nit-picking bureaucrats, and "has not yet emulated those activist rulers of old who discoursed with learned scholars on the methods used by the former kings to order the world." At the institutional level, no changes had been made in the methods of training, selecting, and employing officials, and consequently the few capable men who did rise through the bureaucracy were so outnumbered by selfish, obstructionist mediocrities that nothing could be accomplished by government. Meanwhile, the peasantry was being destroyed by the burdens of labor service, yet no effort had been made to offer them relief, or to create offices devoted to improving irrigation and agricultural productivity. Similarly, the army was still mustered from among the sick and aged dregs of society, with no provisions made for training and drilling them or for putting them under the long-term command of dedicated generals. In sum,

There is no method to the management of resources, so that even if the government economizes the people will not prosper; even if we worry and strive the nation will not become strong. The reason the empire has suffered no great calamity is because the time has not yet arrived for the barbarians to explode on the scene, and we have not yet been visited by great floods or droughts. Although it is attributed to the doings of men, it is in fact because of the aid of Heaven. . . . I beg Your Majesty to aim for the highest sageliness and to lay claim to the unending strand [that links you to the ancient kings]. You must know that the aid of Heaven cannot be counted on, nor can the affairs of men be idly left to their own. The time for doing great deeds (ta yu-wei chih shih) is right now.

However much Shen-tsung might disagree with certain elements of Wang An-shih's advice in the coming months, no other advisor so excited the emperor with a vision of great achievements – achievements he announced that only Wang An-shih could help him realize.[49] From this time on, Shen-tsung

---

[48] Wang, Wang Lin-ch'uan ch'üan-chi 42, pp. 242–3; "Pen-ch'ao pai-nien wu-shih cha-tzu," anthologized in CPPM 59, pp. 1888–92.
[49] CPPM 59, p. 1894.

determined to bring Wang An-shih into the Council of State as an assisting civil councilor (*ts'an-chih cheng-shih*), but he met strong opposition from the incumbent assisting councilor T'ang Chieh (1010–69), a man with a formidable reputation as a "straight speaker." T'ang Chieh rejected Wang as stubborn and impractical, and he predicted publicly to the emperor and privately to Wang's sponsor Tseng Kung-liang that "if Wang is made a councilor he will change many things and disrupt the empire . . . and everyone already knows this."[50] But Shen-tsung could not be dissuaded, and in the second month of 1069 he offered the assistant councilor's post to Wang with the command that he could not turn it down.

For his part, Wang responded that it was indeed his hope to "assist the emperor to accomplish great deeds." But he cautioned that it would be difficult, for the court was filled with mediocrities (*yung-jen*) and outright villains (*chien-jen*), who through jealousy or sheer ignorance would conspire to block the few clear-thinking and independent men in office from accomplishing anything of merit, by overwhelming them with dissenting opinions (*i-lun*).[51] Therefore in his answer to Shen-tsung's question about the first task before them, Wang An-shih replied that it was to "transform customs and mores and establish laws and institutions," by "strengthening the superior men and eliminating the petty ones (*ch'ang chün-tzu, hsiao hsiao-jen*)," with their pernicious power to corrupt the people and preclude all possibility of moral rule. The first step in Wang's reform vision, in short, was to eliminate all those – like T'ang Chieh – who opposed him. And with this "the emperor agreed." Wang's appointment to the council was announced in the second month of 1069, and the very next month he began to systematically neutralize his opponents.

GAINING POWER

While discussing possible appointments in the fall of 1070, Tseng Kung-liang urged the emperor to heed Chen-tsung's belief that "it is important to have people of different opinions stirring each other up, so that no one will dare to do wrong." But Wang An-shih forcefully disagreed: "If everyone at court agitates one another with different opinions then how will it be possible to govern? This minister humbly believes that if the court ministers in charge of affairs of state do not share one mind and one morality (*t'ung-hsin t'ung-te*) nor cooperatively strive for unanimity, then none of the tasks facing the empire can be accomplished."[52] For Wang, nothing so impeded progress as the constant

---

[50] Shen-tsung's discussions with and about Wang An-shih are reported in *CPPM* 59, pp. 1894–5.
[51] See *CPPM* 59, pp. 1895–6, for the exchange between Wang and Shen-tsung.
[52] *HCP* (1979) 213, p. 5169.

babble of contending opinion, and therefore change could be founded only on unanimity of opinion and the elimination of dissent. In the long run the most effective way to eliminate disagreement was to imbue the next generation of officials with "moral unity" (*i tao-te*), or a common ideology.

This quest for ideological uniformity underlay almost all of Wang's educational measures, including his proposals for the creation of a national school system, his reform of the examination system, the promulgation of his own commentaries to the Classics as the key to passing the exams, and his attempt to pack such leading educational institutions as the Directorate of Education (*Kuo-tzu chien*) and the new Bureau for the Interpretation of the Classics (*Ching-i chü*) with his own relatives and followers.[53]

But ultimately, Wang insisted, it was the emperor's responsibility to silence the critics of change, by exercising the imperial prerogative (*jen-chu chih ch'üan*) to decide issues of substance. In 1070 the emperor, torn as ever between Wang's insistence on uniformity and the remonstrances of such senior statesmen as Ssu-ma Kuang and Ou-yang Hsiu, wondered at the continuing controversy surrounding the reforms. Wang, as he would throughout his tenure as head of government, blamed the persistence of dissent on the emperor himself: "Although Your Majesty is far more sagacious than his predecessors, because you are insufficiently resolute (*kang-chien*) you have not yet succeeded in transforming civic culture by unifying morality (*i tao-te i pien feng-su*). As a result the cacophony of opinions continues."[54] In Wang's view, it was up to the emperor to

awe and intimidate the multitudes into compliance, so that the court can attend to affairs.... It is just like Heaven itself, which uses the *yang-ch'i* to activate the myriad things. Heaven does not let the different things saturate one another, but rather conceives

---

[53] After Wang An-shih's *San-ching hsin-i* (*New Meaning of the Three Canons* [the *Chou-li*, *Shih-ching*, and *Shu-ching*]) was made the basis of the civil service examinations in 1075, Pi Chung-yu (1045–1119) observed that "if a candidate's interpretation of the classics did not accord with Wang An-shih's, then no official would dare choose him." See Pi's "Li-hui k'o-chang tsou-chuang" in his *Hsi-t'ai chi* 1, quoted in Wang, "Wang An-shih pien-fa chien-lun," p. 145. On packing educational institutions, see *HCP* (1979) 228, pp. 5545–6; 243, p. 5917; on efforts to canonize Wang An-shih's commentaries, see *HCP* (1979) 215, pp. 5245–7; 265, pp. 6514–16. Wang An-shih first proclaimed the need to promote a uniform morality or ideology in his *Ch'i kai k'o t'iao-chih cha-tzu* [*Request to reform the examination system*] in Wang, *Wang Lin-ch'uan ch'üan-chi* 42, p. 245. For this and for Wang An-shih's educational reforms in general, see Thomas H. C. Lee, *Government education and examinations in Sung China* (New York, 1985), pp. 239–43. John W. Chaffee, *The thorny gates of learning in Sung China: A social history of examinations* (Cambridge, 1985), pp. 76–84, examines the consequences of Wang An-shih's school reforms, which took root in the postreform era under Ts'ai Ching and Hui-tsung. For sources and more specific treatment, see Kondo Kazunari, "Ō Anseki no kakyo kaikaku o megutte," *Tōyōshi kenkyū* 46 No. 3 (1987), pp. 21–46. The intellectual foundation of Wang An-shih's educational reforms and the debate they spawned are discussed in Peter K. Bol, "Examinations and orthodoxies: 1070 and 1313 compared," in *Culture and state in Chinese history: Conventions, accommodations, and critiques*, ed. Theodore B. Huters et al. (Stanford, Calif., 1997), pp. 29–57.

[54] *HCP* (1979) 215, p. 5232.

them all with the one essence. Just so, if the imperial resolve is strong, then all under Heaven will comply without being commanded; if not, the factions of the vast party of conventionalists (*liu-su ch'un-tang*) will strengthen by the day, while the imperial authority will daily wither.[55]

The exercise of imperial prerogative meant two things for Wang: the steadfast enactment of imperial decisions, and unwavering support for reform activists. Wang continuously pressed Shen-tsung to stick to decisions he had made or approved, lest the power of imperial authority fall to the "factionalists" – the reform opponents – within the government. One key arena for the exercise of imperial power was the promotion and demotion of officials, which became increasingly politicized during the 1070s as the fulfillment of reform goals came to dominate personnel decisions. New Policies opponents who invoked procedural and ethical precedents to protect their own members from demotion and block the unilateral ascent of reform partisans inevitably encountered Wang's imperial prerogative argument. In mid-1070, for example, Wang denounced critics of an imperial order appointing his protégé Li Ting (1028–87) to the Censorate by warning the emperor that "if Your Majesty . . . revokes the order appointing Li Ting . . . then your majesty's authority to appoint and dismiss (*yü-tuo chih ch'üan*) will have been compromised, and straight-speaking officials will no longer dare rely on your majesty as their leader."[56] In a separate incident a short time later, an imperial rescript demoting K'ung Wen-chung (1038–88) for an allegedly impertinent examination essay was repeatedly returned by officials in the Memorial Forwarding Office (*T'ung-chin yin-t'ai ssu*), with the support of the prominent reform opponent Han Wei. Wang An-shih charged K'ung with slandering the emperor, and successfully convinced Shen-tsung that if he did not enforce his decision "then the authority of the emperor will be usurped by the multitude of evil [factionalists], and the conventionalists will so incite one another that in the future there will be nothing that we can do."[57] But Wang urged the emperor

---

[55] *HCP* (1979) 214, pp. 5206–7.

[56] *HCP* (1979) 213, p. 5174. Critics attacked Li Ting not directly for his policy views, but for his failure to mourn as mother the concubine who had nursed and possibly even bore him. For an analysis of the case as one example of the anxieties provoked by the intrusion into scholarly elite life of the market in women, see Patricia B. Ebrey, "Women, money, and class: Ssu-ma Kuang and Sung Neo-Confucian views on women," in *Chung-kuo chin-shih she-hui wen-hua-shih lun-wen-chi*, ed. Chung-yang yen-chiu-yüan li-shih yü-yen yen-chiu-so ch'u-pan-p'in pien-chi wei-yüan-hui (Taipei, 1992), pp. 629–30.

[57] *HCP* (1979) 215, pp. 5245–7. Wang An-shih was apparently gaining revenge for the demotion of one Hou P'u for a sycophantic exam essay on natural disasters that quoted Wang's own commentary to the *Hung-fan*. According to an excerpt from Lin Hsi's *Yeh-shih*, the demotion of K'ung Wen-chung had ramifications that chilled officialdom. K'ung's younger brother Wu-chung declined a lecturer's post, further fueling the court's anger; then K'ung's father, Yen-chih, turned down the post of prefectural judge of K'ai-feng out of fear of residing in the capital, requesting a provincial post instead. He was granted the same position in Yüeh-chou (Liang-che), but when salt returns there fell below quota he was impeached for "defying the New Policies" (*wei-pei hsin-fa*). K'ung Yen-chih was subsequently transferred

to be unyielding on broader policy issues as well. For example, when Shen-tsung worried that the Bureau of Military Affairs (under Wen Yen-po) would reject Wang's proposal to replace mercenaries with a popular militia, Wang responded that "if the emperor genuinely wishes to enact a militia policy then who will be able to oppose it? This is for the emperor to decide."[58] In the end, ideological uniformity came down to a question of obedience to the emperor's (and Wang's) decisions, for as Wang insisted to Shen-tsung in 1072, "one may see an issue as right or wrong, but if one sees it as wrong when the court disagrees and deems it right, then one must obey the court's commands."[59]

As long as Wang had the emperor's ear and support, the exercise of impe-rial prerogative provided the best possible protection for Wang's own reform policies. But it was equally important to extend that protection to Wang's lieutenants in the field, by immunizing them from outside criticism and inter-ference. In his "Myriad word memorial" Wang had insisted on granting broad discretionary authority to field officials, arguing that "there has never been a single case in history that has shown it possible to obtain good govern-ment even with the right man in power if he is bound by one regulation or another so that he cannot carry out his ideas."[60] But where those ideas were as controversial and disruptive as the reform measures there was inevitable resistance against carrying them out, and it was precisely the most successful agents of reform who were most bitterly attacked as cruel and mean-spirited seekers of profit for the state and rewards for themselves (*hsing-li chih ch'en, chü-lien chih ch'en*). As a young man with a keen sense of mission and imperial responsibility, Shen-tsung took these charges very much to heart, but Wang An-shih saw every such expression of imperial concern as an abandonment of the reform cause. In the fourth month of 1072, for example, Wang complained about the continued attacks on his chief water-control engineer Ch'eng Fang, chiding the emperor for investigating every charge made by "villainous, self-interested" partisans against the loyal and diligent officials working hard for the reforms.[61] Two months later, in one of his many tirades against the detrac-tors of the border official Wang Shao, Wang An-shih warned the emperor that the multitude of evil-doers were in danger of blocking the reforms and overwhelming the few real activists (*chien-kung chin-li-che*) in government with their baseless rumors and slander. Wang charged that by punishing reformers

to Hsüan-chou (Chiang-nan East), where he was cashiered in the middle of his term. See *HCP* (1979) 215, p. 5247.

[58] *HCP* (1979) 213, pp. 5171–2.

[59] *HCP* (1979) 230, p. 5605.

[60] Wang, *Wang Lin-ch'uan ch'üan-chi* 39, p. 224.

[61] *HCP* (1979) 232, pp. 5634–5.

for the slightest misstep while letting slander and rumormongering go unquestioned the emperor was not only chilling the ardor of his most effective reformers, he was also encouraging factionalism. Wang appreciated that the emperor tolerated critics and dissenters out of a desire to "broaden what he hears and sees," but he insisted that by opening himself to lies and falsehoods the emperor was only blocking the path to knowledge. The solution, Wang concluded, was to honor the emperor's desire for accurate information by punishing the purveyors of slander and lies.[62]

In the end, Wang was enormously successful in garnering Shen-tsung's support for his policies and his men, and the entire New Policies era was characterized by an unusual devolution of authority and autonomy to agents in the field.[63] But Shen-tsung never lost his respect for the many prominent critics of reform tactics and policy, and these men battled endlessly with Wang for the mind and heart of the emperor. At moments of natural disaster or political turmoil Shen-tsung often heeded the urgings of his senior statesmen "to open up the channels of remonstrance" (k'ai yen-lu); but inevitably those channels would be reclosed. For Wang was relentless in his campaign to stamp out dissent, which he made a fundamental feature of his political vision. Even Lü Hui-ch'ing (1032–1110), Wang's closest associate until their falling out in 1075, was appalled by Wang's obsession with quelling dissent:

Wang An-shih is fond of saying that in the management of troops it is essential to enforce ranks, so that even those with the will to differ will not dare give voice to their opinions, and unanimity will be maintained. But in fact An-shih acts this way not only towards the army but towards the entire nation. Wang regards all under Heaven as an enemy – but even if he can manage to silence those close to him, can he really silence all under Heaven?[64]

However intolerant Wang may have been he did still adhere to long-established rules of political competition, which meant that he could not silence all dissent. But he could hound all dissenters out of office, and that is precisely what he did. The successful enactment of the New Policies was predicated on a threefold political coup: capturing the Council of State, ousting all opponents of reform from office, and appointing his followers to all key policy and remonstrance agencies.

---

[62] *HCP* (1979) 234, pp. 5678–9.

[63] The question of decentralization of authority is discussed in Paul J. Smith, "State power and economic activism during the New Policies, 1068–1085: The tea and horse trade and the 'Green Sprouts' loan policy," in *Ordering the world: Approaches to state and society in Sung dynasty China*, ed. Robert P. Hymes and Conrad Schirokauer (Berkeley, Calif.,1993), pp. 76–127.

[64] *HCP* (1979) 268, p. 6574.

Capturing the Council of State

The Ch'ing-li reforms demonstrated that no reform program could be mounted unless its advocates gained firm control of the government. After his appointment as assistant councilor in the second month of 1069, Wang An-shih moved swiftly to monopolize power for the reform coalition. Within weeks of receiving the emperor's mandate Wang launched a systematic campaign to wrest control of the Council of State, neutralize the Censorate, create a reform-specific bureaucratic apparatus, and place his followers in key posts throughout the government.

The key to creating a political apparatus dedicated to reform was to monopolize the Council of State, the paramount policy organ of government, with control over administration and policy making for both civil and military affairs. The council was headed by one to three chief councilors (*tsai-hsiang*, or more formally *t'ung chung-shu men-hsia p'ing-chang shih*), who were concurrently the heads of the Secretariat-Chancellery (*Chung-shu men-hsia*). The chief councilors were joined on the civil side by one to three assistant civil councilors (*chih-cheng*, or *ts'an-chih cheng-shih*). On the military side the council included the commissioner of the Bureau of Military Affairs (*shu-mi shih*), which was paired with the Secretariat-Chancellery as the "two authorities" (*liang fu*). Joining the commissioner on the council were the administrator or coadministrator (*chih shu-mi yüan shih, t'ung-chih shu-mi yüan shih*) and one or two assistant commissioners (*shu-mi fu-shih*).[65] As an advisory committee to assist the emperor, who needed to approve all its measures, the council was designed more to facilitate sharp differences of opinion than to foster unanimous political action. But if one of the contending groups within government could pack the Council of State with its own adherents, it was then possible to ostracize political opponents from the capital, capture the Censorate and the Remonstrance Bureau, and push government in a single direction;[66] and it was just this strategy that Wang An-shih pursued.

When he was appointed assisting civil councilor in the second month of 1069, Wang joined a body that had no unified plan of action, headed by two men (Fu Pi and Tseng Kung-liang) who "want only not to offend the

[65] Edward A. Kracke, Jr., *Civil service in early Sung China, 960–1067; with particular emphasis on the development of controlled sponsorship to foster administrative responsibility* (Cambridge, Mass., 1953), pp. 30–9. Despite the functional division into civil and military spheres, all councilors were drawn from the civil bureaucracy and many incumbents passed through all or some of the four levels. For a convenient table of incumbents in the Council of State from 1041 to 1125, see Higashi, *Ō Anseki jiten*, pp. 211–20. For more detail, see Hsü Tzu-ming, *Sung tsai-fu pien-nien lu chiao-pu*, ed. Wang Jui-lai, (c. 1220; Peking, 1986).

[66] This paraphrases Kracke's discussion of monopolizing the ear of the emperor; see Kracke, *Civil service in early Sung*, p. 30.

'conventionalists' and have no interest in reforming our corrupted institutions. I am afraid that [with men like this in power] we cannot long rely on peace nor look forward to improving governance."[67] Armed with an imperial mandate for change, Wang immediately began to arrogate to himself powers of command that conventionally belonged to the chief councilors and even to the emperor, and to intimidate his fellow councilors. After just two months in office Wang pressed his point on a legal issue with such vehemence that when Shen-tsung sided with Wang against (as Wang put it) T'ang Chieh and his clique, the infuriated T'ang Chieh abruply died at age fifty-nine. Contemporaries regarded T'ang as the only councilor with the courage to oppose Wang, and with his death "Tseng Kung-liang (age 71) begged to retire because of age, Fu Pi (age 65) begged to be excused from attending to affairs because of illness, and Chao Pien (age 61), lacking the strength [to withstand Wang], just spent his days sighing.... As a result people said of the Secretariat that it included 'the quick (Wang), the old (Tseng), the sick (Fu), the dead (T'ang), and the embittered (Chao)."[68]

Although T'ang's death opened a potential opportunity for Wang it also unleashed the hostility of officials who resented his hold on the emperor, and especially his creation (in the second month of 1069) of a separate base of power in the Finance Planning Commission (*Chih-chih san-ssu t'iao-li ssu*). That hostility exploded in the fifth month of 1069, when Executive Censor Lü Hui (1014–71) sent up a ten-point memorial of impeachment. Among a wide-ranging list of abuses past and present, Lü accused Wang of nepotism; of suborning the emperor during illicit private conferences (*liu-shen chin-shuo*); of usurping chief ministerial powers of appointment in order to oust his adversaries; and of using the Finance Planning Commission to circumvent established agencies (such as the Finance Commission and the Council of State itself) and monopolize control over military and financial affairs. Wang reacted to Lü's charge as he would many times in the future, by threatening to resign. But Shen-tsung dissuaded Wang by issuing a personal edict reiterating his support and allowing Lü to be cashiered from the Censorate.[69] In the tenth month of 1069, Fu Pi was allowed to resign as chief councilor, and was replaced by Wang's

---

[67] *CPPM* 58, p. 1871.

[68] See Hsü, *Sung tsai-fu pien-nien lu chiao-pu* 7, p. 377, citing the *Ting-wei lu*. Wang An-shih's specific battle with T'ang Chieh was over the issue of whether a Teng-chou2 woman who tried but failed to kill her abusive husband should suffer the death penalty, as T'ang and most members of the court agreed, or be more leniently penalized under the statutes for "injury committed in an attempt to kill" (*mou-sha shang*), as Wang insisted. See also *CPPM* 59, pp. 1896–7, and *SS* 327, p. 10544.

[69] For the affair, see *CPPM* 58, pp. 1867–77; for the text of Lü's memorial, see *HCP* (1986) *shih-pu* 4, pp. 22a–23a, and Ts'ai, *Wang Ching kung nien-p'u k'ao-lüeh* 14, pp. 204–6. The memorial is summarized in Williamson, *Wang An Shih*, vol. 1, pp. 127–30.

own candidate, the administrator of the Bureau of Military Affairs and Wang's cochief of the Finance Planning Commission, Ch'en Sheng-chih. As bureau administrator, Ch'en had sat on the council since 1065, but as soon as he was promoted to chief councilor, he tried to break free of Wang, inciting a feud that culminated in his ouster one year later (see shortly). At the time, however, Ch'en's promotion testified to Wang's growing ability to shape council membership to his needs.[70]

In order to fully control the council, Wang not only had to persuade Shen-tsung to appoint Wang's associates, he also had to dissuade the emperor from promoting Wang's rivals. It was especially important to Wang to keep potential dissenters out of policy-making positions during his first year in office, when such critical measures as the "green sprouts" rural credit act (*ch'ing-miao fa*) and the agricultural lands and irrigation policy (*nung-t'ien shui-li fa*) were taking shape (see Table 4). Thus in the first month of 1070, Wang persuaded the emperor to post Chang Fang-p'ing to the provinces despite Shen-tsung's desire to have him at hand in the capital.[71] But Wang scored an even greater coup by dissuading Shen-tsung from appointing Wang's chief ideological rival, Ssu-ma Kuang, to the Council of State. Whereas Shen-tsung valued Wang as an instrument of dynastic revival he reserved his warmest personal admiration for Ssu-ma Kuang, whom he would have liked always to keep by his side.[72] Though Wang too had enormous respect for Ssu-ma, whom he regarded as a man of great distinction, Ssu-ma's views were the antithesis of his own, and for the moment Wang convinced Shen-tsung that putting Ssu-ma on the council would hinder the emperor's own program: "Although Ssu-ma Kuang is disputatious (*hao wei i-lun*) his own talents would prevent him from harming government policy. But if he is employed in high office then he will become a 'red banner' (*ch'ih chih*) for other disputatious men," including the Szechwanese luminaries Su Shih (1037–1101) and Su Ch'e (1039–1112), and their followers.[73]

But even though Wang An-shih exerted enormous influence over the emperor, Shen-tsung was by no means his pawn, and imperial support could be shaken by adverse public and political opinion. A crisis of confidence was incited in the second month of 1070 by Han Ch'i's denunciation of

---

[70] Hsü, *Sung tsai-fu pien-nien lu chiao-pu* 7, pp. 409–10.

[71] *CPPM* 63, pp. 2026–7.

[72] See, for example, *HCP* (1979) 220, pp. 5338–41.

[73] *CPPM* 63, pp. 2028–9; on Wang An-shih's praise of Ssu-ma Kuang the man, *HCP* (1979) 213, pp. 5167–9. For an analysis of the many points of intersection and divergence in the careers and ideas of Wang and Ssu-ma, see Peter K. Bol, "Government, society, and state: On the political visions of Ssu-ma Kuang and Wang An-shih," in *Ordering the world: Approaches to state and society in Sung dynasty China*, ed. Robert P. Hymes and Conrad Schirokauer (Berkeley, Calif.,1993), pp. 128–92.

the "green sprouts" policy that almost toppled Wang An-shih from power. Han Ch'i's charge that the government set out to raise revenues by forcing or enticing poor peasants into taking loans that they couldn't repay shook Shen-tsung's faith in the measure, which was then the cornerstone of Wang's reforms. When Wang retired to his sickbed in fury at the emperor's vacillation, the door was opened to a political revolt. Ssu-ma Kuang, in his capacity as Han-lin academician, composed an imperial rescript stating that owing to the reforms "the world is in ferment and the people are distressed"; and though Shen-tsung apologized to Wang for the unfortunate wording, he nonetheless took advantage of Wang's self-imposed removal to appoint Ssu-ma Kuang to the council, as assistant commissioner of military affairs. Shen-tsung simultaneously ordered his councilors to abolish the green sprouts measure, prompting the chief councilors Tseng Kung-liang and Ch'en Sheng-chih to mount the growing anti-Wang, anti-*ch'ing-miao* bandwagon by altering the original green sprouts edict to exclude Wang's own prohibition against forced loans. At this point the reform movement was very close to collapsing. But faced with Wang's melodramatic but effective threat to resign, the emperor capitulated: Shen-tsung admitted to Wang that he had been deluded by the mass uproar over the green sprouts measure, and agreed to put the weight of his authority against the "conventionalists" who sought to block the reforms.[74]

Once again Wang emerged from a crisis with renewed influence. Thwarted in his efforts to reverse the green sprouts policy, Han Ch'i requested assignment to a relatively minor post in the north; at the same time Ssu-ma Kuang realized that with Wang back in power his own position was untenable, and he insisted that his appointment to the Bureau of Military Affairs and the council be annulled.[75] Shen-tsung continued to urge Ssu-ma to play a role at court, but Ssu-ma protested that there was no point in his remaining at court when the emperor would neither heed his advice nor give him real power; he even argued that with Wang An-shih setting his brother-in-law, Hsieh Ching-wen, on his adversaries like a dog, remaining in the capital was unsafe. In the fourth month of 1071, Ssu-ma Kuang retired to Lo-yang, the opposition capital for the next fourteen years.[76]

---

[74] For Han Ch'i's memorial, see *CPPM* 68, pp. 2165–9. On the efforts to undermine Wang, see *CPPM* 68, pp. 2172–3, 2176–7. For a synopsis, see *SS* 327, p. 10545.

[75] *CPPM* 63, p. 2029. Han Ch'i was reassigned from pacification commissioner of Ho-pei to the single subcircuit of Ta-ming fu.

[76] *HCP* (1986) *shih-pu* 7, pp. 35a–36a; *HCP* (1979) 214, pp. 5201–2; and Ssu-ma Kuang's *nien-p'u*, appended in Ssu-ma, *Ssu-ma Wen-cheng kung ch'uan-chia chi*, p. 1068. On Lo-yang as the opposition capital, see Michael D. Freeman, "Lo-yang and the opposition to Wang An-shih: The rise of Confucian conservatism, 1068–1086" (diss., Yale University, 1973).

With his chief ideological competitors neutralized Wang turned on those one-time supporters who had sided against him in the green sprouts imbroglio: Tseng Kung-liang, Ch'en Sheng-chih, and Chao Pien. Chao, Wang's fellow assistant councilor, was the only one of the three men to urge that no action on green sprouts be taken while Wang was out of office; but his disagreements with the policy, and his abomination of Wang's custom of dismissing all criticism as "prattle of the conventionalists," forced him to resign his post in the fourth month of 1070.[77] Chao was replaced by the fifty-eight-year-old Han Chiang (1012–88), a *chin-shih* classmate and ardent supporter of Wang, who was (as the censor Ch'en Hsiang complained) the second man in a row to move from co-leadership of Wang's Finance Planning Commission, with its focus on revenue gathering rather than on good governance, to a post as civil councilor.[78]

Though Chao Pien resigned his post in the council voluntarily, Tseng Kung-liang and Ch'en Sheng-chih were driven out by the venom of Wang's animosity. Immediately after resuming his duties Wang had vehemently denounced the two men for scheming against the green sprouts measure, so shaking them that they in turn "withdrew because of illness."[79] Ch'en had particular reason to fear Wang, whose enmity he had earned by contemptuously abandoning his co-leadership of the Finance Planning Commission as soon as Wang had him named chief councilor. One month after the green sprouts affair (the third month of 1070) Ch'en took advantage of his mother's illness to beg permission to resign, but to forestall gossip Shen-tsung forced the now ineffective man to stay on until his mother's death in the tenth month of 1070.[80] Tseng Kung-liang – the man most responsible for getting Wang appointed to the Secretariat – was completely unnerved by Wang's vituperative attack, and by the defamation campaign waged against him by Wang and his followers. As Wang assumed an increasingly despotic hold on government, Su Shih berated Tseng for not "saving the court." But Tseng replied that "the emperor and Wang An-shih are like one man; that is Heaven's doing." Tseng withstood Wang's abuse as long as he could – gossip maintained that he held out long enough to secure a career for his son – but after he fell prostrate before

---

[77] *HCP* (1979) 210, pp. 5101–2. Chao Pien accepted the post of prefect of Hang-chou.

[78] *HCP* (1979) 210, pp. 2102–3. Han, like his Finance Planning Commission predecessor Ch'en Sheng-chih, was also already in the council as an executive of the Bureau of Military Affairs. Han's younger brother Wei (1017–98), though a trusted advisor to the emperor, was a staunch opponent of the reforms. For capsule biographies of Wang An-shih's relatives and associates, see Higashi, *Ō Anseki jiten*, pp. 94–119; for biographies of those adversaries later termed the "Yüan-yu clique," see Higashi, *Ō Anseki jiten*, pp. 149–211. For greater detail, consult the sources listed in Ch'ang Pi-te et al., eds., *Sung-jen chuan-chi tzu-liao so-yin* (Taipei, 1974–6).

[79] *CPPM* 68, p. 2181.

[80] *CPPM* 66, pp. 2102–3; 68, p. 2183; *HCP* (1979) 215, p. 5234; 216, p. 5261.

Shen-tsung in the ninth month of 1070 the emperor allowed him to retire.[81] With Ch'en out of office the following month, the way was cleared for Wang's elevation to chief councilor. In the final month of 1070, Wang and his older protégé, Han Chiang, were both promoted to the chief position, but three months later Han was cashiered for errors made on an assignment along the northwestern frontier.[82]

Thus, from 1071 to his first resignation in the fourth month of 1074, Wang was the unrivaled chief of government. Most of the empire's elder statesmen – including Ou-yang Hsiu (age 65), Ssu-ma Kuang (age 50), Wang T'ao (age 50), Fan Chen (age 63), Lü Hui (age 58), and Fu Pi (age 68) – had been forced into retirement at the height of their powers.[83] Meanwhile, in the council itself only Feng Ching (1021–94) and the Bureau of Military Affairs chief Wen Yen-po could stand up against Wang, but their influence was limited. Feng Ching's protests carried no weight, and Wang systematically emasculated the Bureau of Military Affairs by putting reform advocates such as Han Chiang and Wang's relative Wu Ch'ung into the assistant bureau positions; by overwhelming Wen and his associates in council deliberations; and most important by aggrandizing the authority over military financing, personnel, and war making for the Wang An-shih coalitions in the Finance Planning Commission, in the Secretariat, and in the field.[84]

Controlling remonstrance offices

Yet even capturing the Council of State did not guarantee Wang a free hand in promoting his policies, since under a division of responsibilities that by Sung times was accepted as conventional, the arbitrary exercise of power by the chief councilor – or even by the emperor – was intended to be checked by independent remonstrance agencies. The two most important remonstrance organs, the Censorate (*Yü-shih t'ai*) and the Remonstrance Bureau (*Chien-yüan*), were responsible for informing the emperor and the central authorities of local conditions and government effectiveness throughout the empire, for providing

---

[81] *HCP* (1979) 215, pp. 5238–9. Tseng's son Hsiao-k'uan was named assistant commissioner of the Bureau of Military Affairs in 1075, but Li T'ao dismisses the claim that this was Tseng Kung-liang's motive.

[82] *HCP* (1979) 218, p. 5301; *HCP* (1979) 221, pp. 5389–91. Han Chiang was brought back as chief councilor from the fourth month of 1074 to the eighth month of 1075.

[83] Or so charged the censor Yang Hui, himself a victim of Wang's climb to power. See *HCP* (1979) 224, pp. 5449–50.

[84] For examples, see *HCP* (1979) 211, pp. 5138–9; 213, pp. 5166–7; 244, pp. 5944–5. As one indication of how the reformers circumvented Wen Yen-po, until 1075 the *pao-chia* militia system was controlled by the reform-dominated Court of Agricultural Supervision rather than by the Bureau of Military Affairs. See *SS* 192, p. 4770.

a channel for complaints and suggestions from all sources, and for criticizing policy recommendations and, where deemed necessary, returning them to the council for reconsideration. According to Edward Kracke, "The institutional expression of the information and rectification functions, and the protection afforded those performing the functions, formed the closest Chinese parallel to the constitutional separation of powers."[85]

But however autonomous the Censorate and the Remonstrance Bureau were intended to be in theory, in practice their privileged status emanated from an emperor whose respect for their independence was buttressed only by convention and public opinion, and not by law. In a regime as determined to flout convention as that of Shen-tsung and Wang An-shih, officials who actually exercised their remonstrance prerogative could expect very little protection. With Lü Hui's ouster as executive censor in mid-1069 the precedent was set for removing any remonstrance official who dared attack Wang's policies or his tactics. In the eighth month of 1069 three censors (Liu Shu, Liu Ch'i, and Ch'ien I) were cashiered for denouncing Wang's reckless, ruthless tampering with time-honored institutions, signaling an all-out war by Wang's forces against the remonstrance bureaus.[86]

Wang An-shih and the emperor sought to exempt reform policies and personnel as appropriate targets of remonstrance. In the early months of 1070, Probationary Censor Chang Chien, youngest brother of the philosopher Chang Tsai, joined the chorus of green sprouts opponents with a series of memorials denouncing the Finance Planning Commission and all its enterprises; Wang An-shih and his fiscalist confederates Lü Hui-ch'ing and Han Chiang; and the timorous accomplices to Wang's crimes, Tseng Kung-liang, Ch'en Sheng-chih, and Chao Pien. In the fourth month of the year, with Wang firmly returned to power, an imperial edict charged Chang Chien with "insulting state ministers and laying false charges," and demoted him to a post as county magistrate.[87] Although Shen-tsung was deeply distressed by the uproar over the green sprouts measure, Wang An-shih convinced him that the Censorate was at the center of a conspiracy against the emperor's reform program: "It is the role of remonstrance officials to uphold the policies of the court. Where then is the justice in [their] banding together with the 'conventionalists' like this?" Shen-tsung agreed with Wang, later adding that the reason for all the

---

[85] Kracke, *Civil service in early Sung*, p. 33.

[86] *CPPM* 63, pp. 2025–6; *HCP* (1986) *shih-pu* 5, pp. 3b–4a.

[87] *HCP* (1979) 210, pp. 5107–8. Chang's colleague Wang Tzu-shao was also demoted for "giving the appearance of rectitude while secretly embracing an evil clique" by condemning the green sprouts policy even though he had recommended his own brother to be one of its administrators.

agitation over the rural credit measure was because "I have put the wrong men in the Censorate and the Remonstrance Bureau." Thus just a few days before dismissing Chang Chien the emperor cashiered the executive censor Lü Kung-chu, Chang's superior and the spearhead of censorial remonstrance against the policy.[88]

In essence, then, Wang and the emperor viewed the Censorate as an administrative arm of the court rather than as an independent political entity. Consequently, censorial opposition to any regime decisions constituted grounds for dismissal. Indeed, in the fifth month of 1070, Shen-tsung even authorized the use of preemptive dismissals, cashiering the acting director of the Censorate, Ch'en Chien, simply on the expectation that he would "veto" the controversial promotion of Wang's protégé Li Ting from a junior position as civil aide to a position as investigating censor.[89] This restrictive view of censorial power applied equally to regime members who crossed Wang. In the sixth month of 1070, Shen-tsung took the initiative in dismissing Hu Tsung-yu (1029–94) from his concurrent posts as chief of the Remonstrance Bureau and codirector (with Lü Hui-ch'ing) of the Court of Agricultural Supervision, the successor to the Finance Planning Commission as the nerve center of reform economic policy (see later discussion). In an angry denunciation before his state councilors, the emperor lashed out at Hu for obstructing court policy, citing in particular Hu's opposition to the transfer of personnel powers from the Bureau of Military Affairs to the West Bureau of Personnel Evaluation of the Secretariat. Han Chiang chimed in that it was the responsibility of remonstrance officials to adhere to imperial directives, and Wang An-shih capped the denunciation by adding that though it was not wrong for censors to disagree with a given measure, it was totally unacceptable for them to harbor evil designs to obstruct policy.[90] For it was the enactment of policy that was paramount for Wang and the emperor, and there were few constitutional principles that they would not bend to ensure that reform policies were vigorously prosecuted. It was this imperative that Wang invoked in mid-1071 when he urged that Executive

---

[88] *CPPM* 68, pp. 2188–9; *HCP* (1986) *shih-pu* 7, pp. 33b–34b; *HCP* (1979) 210, pp. 5095–9.

[89] *HCP* (1979) 211, p. 5121. This was just the opening salvo in a war between Wang and the established civil service over the emperor's prerogative to make appointments based on skills (and ideological conformity) rather than formal civil service status. The entries from the *HCP* are anthologized in *CPPM* 61, pp. 1997–2004.

[90] *HCP* (1979) 212, pp. 5159–60. According to Hu's biography in the *Sung shih*, Hu earned Wang's enmity by opposing the appointment of Li Ting; see *SS* 318, p. 10370. Another regime member to be ousted from the Censorate for crossing Wang was Wang's brother-in-law Hsieh Ching-wen. Hsieh was put in the Censorate specifically to attack Su Shih, but when, in 1071, he began to attack Hsüeh Hsiang and Wang Shao as well, Wang An-shih had him dismissed; *HCP* (1979) 219, pp. 5321–2; 230, pp. 5085–6.

Censor Yang Hui be dismissed for his opposition to the hired service (or service exemption) measure (*mu-i fa*):

> If I commit transgressions in the service of Your Majesty none of the great ministers will want to conceal them, so there is no need for a Yang Hui to keep watch on my actions. But with a man such as Hui occupying the path of remonstrance then those officials in the provinces who should exert themselves to administer the laws will [hold back on the assumption] that the policies are going to be blocked, and then how will anything get completed? . . . The court has been prosecuting the reform program for years now without accomplishing very much, because each time our initiatives have been stalled; therefore I fear that we are unlikely to see any results.[91]

The very next month (the seventh month of 1071) Yang Hui and his staff member Liu Chih were demoted out of the Censorate, completing the purge of Wang's opponents from key remonstrance positions.[92] As surveyed by the fourteenth-century authors of the *Sung dynastic history*, Wang's coup seemed quite stunning: seventeen censors, four policy critics, and three drafting officials (*chih-chih-kao*) ousted from office in Wang's first two years in office.[93] With most other spokesmen for the opposition driven into retirement or assigned to the many temple posts that were created as sinecures for dissenters, Wang's purge of the government was virtually complete.[94]

Of course, with every opponent expelled from a critical post room was made for a Wang An-shih supporter. Wang's open campaign to pack the government with his followers gave rise to his reputation for "exclusively employing mean and petty men" (*chuan yung hsiao-jen*), and it naturally precipitated charges of factionalism.[95] But the force of such accusations diminished as Wang strengthened his grip on government. In mid-1070, for example, Wang's opponents complained that he was appointing fresh *chin-shih* holders to editorial positions in the Institute for the Veneration of Literature (*Ch'ung-wen yüan*), including a disciple (Lu Tien), a "guest" member of his entourage (Chang An-kuo), and a finance expert who was notoriously incompetent in the classics (Lü Hui-ch'ing's younger brother Lü Sheng-ch'ing). But by this time Wang controlled

---

[91] *HCP* (1979) 224, p. 5439.

[92] *HCP* (1979) 225, pp. 5487–8.

[93] *SS* 327, p. 10546. The number of censors includes Lü Hui and Lü Kung-chu.

[94] On the temple posts created for dissidents, see *HCP* (1979) 211, p. 5128.

[95] *CPPM* 64, pp. 2053–71, devotes a chapter to Wang's "mean and petty men," among whom are included Li Ting, Tseng Pu, Teng Wan, Chang Tun, Lü Chia-wen, and many more. Fan Tsu-yü (1041–98) delivered a postreform diatribe against Wang's "promotion of petty men to mislead the nation" that indicted all the chief financial specialists and border officials of Shen-tsung's reign, including one of the most brilliant scientific minds of his day, Shen K'uo. See *SS* 337, pp. 10798–9. On Shen K'uo as an example of the quintessential New Policies reformer, see chapter 3 of Paul C. Forage, "Science, technology, and war in Song China: Reflections in the Brush talks from the Dream Creek by Shen Kuo, 1031–1095" (diss., University of Toronto, 1991).

the Remonstrance Bureau through his brother-in-law Hsieh Ching-wen, who transformed the complaint into an attack on a fourth newcomer to the post (Hsing Shu), a protégé of Wang's opponent Lü Kung-chu who was demoted out of the institute while Wang's followers all remained.[96] One month later Wang's longtime associate Hsüeh Hsiang (1016–81) was named edict attendant in the Han-lin Academy, and when Feng Ching complained about the appointment of an amoral fiscalist – for Hsüeh was known above all as a financial expert – to so delicate a post, Emperor Shen-tsung personally intervened with a rescript of praise for Hsüeh proclaiming that "among those things that are foremost in the governance of affairs, finance is the most urgent."[97] Occasionally, a follower of Wang's would refuse an assignment that appeared too blatantly political. In the ninth month of 1070, for example, the rising star Tseng Pu (1036–1107) cited his low rank as a reason for declining a lectureship in the Hall for the Veneration of Governance (Ch'ung-cheng tien), where Wang wanted to put him to control Classics Mat debates before the emperor and scrutinize the flow of memorials from the opposition.[98] But in a career environment that had become increasingly competitive most men were eager to accept all the spoils of the conservatives' political defeat, and in a few short years Wang had thoroughly consolidated his hold on power. As the memoirist Wei T'ai (c. 1050–1110), a friend of Wang's and a brother-in-law of Tseng Pu, observed:

Wang [An-shih] grasped the reins of state and dedicated himself to transforming the world. Since through their memorials and opinions the old men of accumulated virtue refused to cooperate with Wang, he instead reached down to employ men newly advanced [into the civil service], appointing them to posts without regard for formal rank. Thus in no time at all the policies that were to characterize the entire period were all launched, and in the forbidden recesses of the Han-lin Academy, [in] the halls of the Censorate, and in the strategic positions at court and in the provinces, there were no vacancies that were not filled by these newly advanced scholars.[99]

Ssu-ma Kuang viewed the situation even more ominously just before retiring to Lo-yang in the fourth month of 1071. By this time, as Ssu-ma saw it, Wang's hold on government was complete: his own party of friends and

---

[96] HCP (1979) 211, p. 5129. On Lü Sheng-ch'ing's shortcomings as a classical scholar, see HCP (1979) 253, pp. 6196–7.

[97] HCP (1979) 212, pp. 5155–7.

[98] HCP (1979) 215, p. 5236. Until the seventh month of 1071, when he accepted a post as provisional proclamation drafting official (shih chih-chih-kao) in place of a man who refused to do Wang's bidding, Tseng Pu preferred to occupy low-ranked but extremely powerful positions at the top of such New Policies nerve centers as the Office for the Compilation of Secretariat Regulations (pien-hsiu chung-shu t'iao-li-ssu) and the Court of Agricultural Supervision (Ssu-nung ssu). For Yang Hui's review of Tseng Pu's meteoric rise, see HCP (1979) 225, pp. 5480–1.

[99] Cited in HCP (1979) 260, p. 6336.

relatives were in power, all those who disagreed with him were purged, and the emperor had become such a slave to Wang's views that imperial authority really emanated from Wang himself.[100]

Creating a reform apparatus

By commandeering existing posts for reform partisans Wang could suppress dissent, control the flow of documents and information, and dominate routine administrative affairs. But the routine administrative apparatus, with its checks and balances, multiple and often mutually conflicting responsibilities, and elaborate chain of command, was never intended to foster rapid decision making or flexible implementation of policy. Therefore, in order to meet the extraordinary demands of the New Policies, Wang and his colleagues preferred to circumvent the existing administrative structure altogether by creating new institutions to carry out specific reform tasks.[101]

At the top of this reform-dedicated administrative apparatus sat the Finance Planning Commission (*Chih-chih san-ssu t'iao-li ssu*), established in the second month of 1069 to "dominate and restrain the engrossers, equalize wealth and assist the poor, and liberate the flow of wealth through the world."[102] On a more mundane political level, the Finance Planning Commission was created as a vehicle for excluding potentially obstreperous state councilors, particularly Fu Pi, Tseng Kung-liang, and Wen Yen-po, from reform deliberations. Headed directly by Wang and his closest associates – Han Chiang, the "Propagating Abbot" (*ch'uan-fa sha-men*) of the New Policies, and Lü Hui-ch'ing, their "Divine Protector" (*hu-fa shan-shen*) – the Finance Planning Commission assumed the status of "a mini-secretariat within the Secretariat," and "anything Wang needed to accomplish he enacted directly out of the commission."[103]

It was through the Finance Planning Commission that Wang assembled his reform cadre and launched his first reform measures, including the "tribute transport and distribution act" (*chün-shu fa*, the seventh month of 1069),

---

[100] *HCP* (1979) 220, pp. 5338–41.

[101] Lo Wen (Winston W. Lo), "Circuits and circuit intendants in the territorial administration of Sung China," *Monumenta Serica* 31 (1974–5), pp. 39–107, especially p. 89. For a good example of the cumbersome and inflexible administrative process, see Ssu-ma Kuang's description of the prereform price-control system managed by the Ever-normal Granaries, *HCP* (1979) 384, pp. 9350–2.

[102] *HCP* (1986) *shih-pu* 4, p. 5b. The chief study of the Finance Planning Commission is Higashi, *Ō Anseki shinpō no kenkyū*, pp. 264–327.

[103] *CPPM* 66, p. 2105; Higashi, *Ō Anseki shinpō no kenkyū*, p. 335. Han Chiang and Lü Hui-ch'ing earned their sobriquets when they kept the reforms in motion during Wang's first retirement, in 1074. See *SS* 327, p. 10548.

the "green sprouts act" (*ch'ing-miao fa*, the ninth month of 1069), and the "agricultural lands and irrigation policy" (*nung-t'ien shui-li fa*).[104] The executive affairs of the commission were entrusted to an Executive Secretariat (*chih-chih-ssu chien-hsiang wen-tzu kuan*), charged with collating reports from the provinces and planning policy initiatives. The first incumbents were Lü Hui-ch'ing, a *Chou-li* (*Rites of Chou*) scholar whom Wang regarded as one of the finest thinkers in memory, and Su Ch'e, the Szechwanese finance expert and brother of Su Shih. Su's philosophy of fiscal restraint proved wholly incompatible with the expansionist thrust represented by the Finance Planning Commission, and he left his post and his dalliance with the reformers in the eighth month of 1069.[105] Lü Hui-ch'ing was assigned to a court post one month later, but as Wang's most trusted lieutenant he continued to dominate the commission and its appointees, whom Lü Kung-chu (no relation) charged were all his sycophants.[106]

The basic information necessary for policy planning was supplied to the Executive Secretariat by a contingent of special "commissioners for the consideration of benefit and harm" (*hsiang-tu li-hai kuan*), who were dispatched throughout the empire to conduct on-the-spot investigations of agriculture, irrigation, taxes, and labor service. Despite Lü Kung-chu's charge of sycophancy, the eight men appointed to the investigative post (including Ch'eng Hao, who was to break with Wang over the issue of interest on the "green sprouts" loans) were chosen largely for their interest and experience in agriculture and water control, and to a lesser degree finance.[107] The policies that came out of the Finance Planning Commission planning process, particularly the green sprouts rural credit program, the agriculture and water-control measure, and later (under the direction of the Court of Agricultural Supervision) the service exemption (*mien-i*) act, were executed by a new addition to the Sung circuit administrative structure previously dominated by the fiscal

---

[104] Unless otherwise specified, the following discussion is drawn from Higashi, *Ō Anseki shinpō no kenkyū*, pp. 264–363. For a clear synthesis of Higashi and other Japanese scholars on the structure, personnel, and responsibilities of the Finance Planning Commission, see Mira A. Mihelich, "Polders and the politics of land reclamation in southeast China during the Northern Sung dynasty (960–1126)" (diss., Cornell University, 1979), pp. 48–60.

[105] *HCP* (1986) *shih-pu* 5, pp. 13b–19a, anthologizes Su Ch'e's memorials on the Finance Planning Commission, including his "Chih-chih san-ssu t'iao-li ssu lun-shih chuang," in Su, *Luan-ch'eng chi* 35, pp. 1a–5a.

[106] *CPPM* 66, p. 2106. For capsule biographies of all incumbents in the Executive Secretariat, see Higashi, *Ō Anseki shinpō no kenkyū*, pp. 284–302.

[107] Higashi, *Ō Anseki shinpō no kenkyū*, pp. 336–7; for capsule biographies see pp. 304–15. As Mihelich points out, the eight investigators were characterized by men who had demonstrated a strong disposition toward activism in water control and agricultural affairs in low-level offices, with more experience in their home regions than in the capital. See Mihelich, "Polders and the politics of land reclamation," p. 55.

intendant (*chuan-yün shih*) and the judicial intendant (*t'i-tien hsing-yü*): the intendants for Ever-normal Granaries, agriculture, and water conservancy (*t'i-chü ch'ang-p'ing nung-t'ien shui-li kuan*).[108] By late 1069 forty-one intendants or assistant intendants (*kuan-kou kuan*) had been dispatched to virtually every circuit of the empire, filled by men at the lower levels of the civil service (including at least three from executory-class posts as civil aides) who fit the typical Finance Planning Commission profile of proven skills in finance and agricultural improvement.[109] The intendants supervised a network of officials designated from among the existing administrative staff of every prefecture and county to manage the Ever-normal Granaries (a traditional mechanism for stabilizing grain prices and supplies), and to collect the enormous sums of money generated by the green sprouts loans and the service exemption fees. This new command structure, extending from the Finance Planning Commission chiefs through the intendants to their designated functionaries in local government, circumvented the traditional financial nerve system dominated by the Finance Commission and the circuit fiscal intendants, and channeled surpluses from the new revenue-generating enterprises directly to Wang and his reform coalition in the State Council.[110]

The creation of a parallel administrative apparatus devoted purely (as opponents saw it) to generating revenues inspired a barrage of outraged criticism. A memorial submitted by Su Shih in late 1069 captures the flavor of the complaints voiced by Ssu-ma Kuang and Lü Kung-chu, and by his own brother, Su Ch'e:

From the founding of the dynasty to the present, the fiscal administration of the empire has been entrusted solely to the commissioner, assistant commissioners, and the supervisors of the Finance Commission, who for more than one hundred years have left no matter untended. Now, for no cause, another commission has been set up in the name of "Coordinating the regulations of the Finance Commission." Six or seven young men are empowered to discuss fiscal policies day and night within the bureau, while more than forty emissaries have been sent out to enact their policies in the provinces. The vast scale of their initial

---

[108] For the evolution of the Sung system of circuit administration, see Lo, "Circuits and circuit intendants."

[109] For an analysis of the professional traits of seventy-one of the men appointed intendant or assistant intendant between 1069 and 1086, see Smith, "State power and economic activism during the New Policies." For capsule biographies of the first wave of intendants, see Higashi, *Ō Anseki shinpō no kenkyū*, pp. 317–34.

[110] Smith, "State power and economic activism during the New Policies"; Wang Tseng-yü, "Pei Sung ti Ssu-nung-ssu," in *Sung-shih yen-chiu lun-wen-chi: 1987 nien nien-hui pien-k'an*, ed. Teng Kuang-ming et al. (Shih-chia-chuang, 1989), pp. 8–35, especially p. 9; Robert M. Hartwell, "The imperial treasuries: Finance and power in Song China," *Bulletin of Sung-Yüan Studies* 20 (1988), p. 65. For Winston Lo's model of the Sung system of dual control over county magistrates see his "Circuits and circuit intendants," pp. 92–5.

operations has made people frightened and suspicious; the strangeness of the new laws adopted has made officials fearful and puzzled. Worthy men seek for an explanation, and failing to get any, cannot relieve their anxiety; small men simply conjecture as to what is going on at court and give voice to slander, saying that Your Majesty, as the master of 100,000 chariots, is interested in personal profit, while the state councilor [Wang An-shih], acting as chancellor of the Son of Heaven, is concerned only with managing wealth (*chih-ts'ai*).[111]

The uproar raised against the Finance Planning Commission convinced Shen-tsung to abolish the office in the fifth month of 1070, sooner than Wang An-shih had wanted.[112] But the entire planning and administrative apparatus was simply transferred to a moribund but long-established – and therefore more legitimate – agency, the Court of Agricultural Supervision (*Ssu-nung ssu*). The Court of Agricultural Supervision inherited the Finance Planning Commission's position as financial command center of the reforms, amassing huge surpluses through the course of Shen-tsung's reign while the routine fiscal apparatus under the finance commissioner slid ever deeper into debt.[113] The top posts in the Court of Agricultural Supervision were filled by the chief reform policy makers, including Lü Hui-ch'ing and Tseng Pu; these men occupied the Court of Agricultural Supervision directorship in conjunction with their concurrent assignments in key policy, remonstrance, and drafting positions, creating an interlocking directorate that merged advisory and operational functions in the reform leadership and subordinated the government's most important operations to the fiscal imperatives of Shen-tsung and Wang An-shih.[114]

The financial apparatus created by Wang and his associates by no means exhausted the new reform-dedicated organizations. Reformers consolidated their power with the creation of other new agencies at the central and provincial levels. The most important new policy-making agency was the Subcouncil for

---

[111] See "Shang Shen-tsung huang-ti," in Su Shih, *Ching-chin Tung-po wen-chi shih-lüeh* (c. 1173; Taipei, 1967) 24, pp. 141–2, translation revised from de Bary, *Sources of Chinese tradition*, p. 481. HCP (1986) *shih-pu* 6, p. 19b, argues persuasively that the correct date of this memorial is the twelfth month of 1069, and not the second month of 1071 as indicated in the original text. Other influential denunciations of the Finance Planning Commission include Su Ch'e's, cited earlier; Lü Kung-chu, HCP, 210, pp. 5095–9; and Ssu-ma Kuang; see "Ch'i pa t'iao-li-ssu ch'ang-p'ing-shih shu," in Ssu-ma, *Ssu-ma Wen-cheng kung ch'uan-chia chi* 44, pp. 559–63.

[112] HCP (1979) 211, p. 5122.

[113] Wang, "Pei Sung ti Ssu-nung-ssu," pp. 26–7.

[114] On the concurrent posts, see Wang, "Pei Sung ti Ssu-nung-ssu" pp. 10–11. It was this subordination of government to finance that most outraged the opponents of the reforms, as reflected in outgoing censor Ch'en Hsiang's charge (in the fourth month of 1070) that "ever since Your Majesty has put Wang An-shih in charge of the government he has done nothing but plot to raise revenues." HCP (1979) 210, pp. 5102–3.

the Compilation of Secretariat Regulations (*pien-hsiu chung-shu t'iao-li-ssu*), established in mid-1069 as a reform "think tank" within the Secretariat to consider issues of policy and administrative restructuring. The subcouncil was answerable directly to Wang An-shih and helped him consolidate his power vis-à-vis the other state councilors and the emperor himself.[115] The executive level of Wang's special agency was staffed by five secretariat examiners (*chien-cheng chung-shu wu-fang kung-shih*) – one for each division (*fang*) of the Secretariat. These five examiners and their staff were under the overall supervision of a chief examiner (*tu chien-cheng*). The chief and divisional positions were filled by the most promising members of the reform clique, including Lü Hui-ch'ing, Tseng Pu, Shen K'uo, Teng Wan, and P'u Tsung-meng, and always included the director of the Court of Agricultural Supervision on concurrent assignment.[116] In addition, the administrative range and authority of the secretariat examiners were enhanced by sending many of them into the field on ad hoc assignments as investigative commissioners (*ch'a-fang shih*), a New Policies trouble-shooting post that enabled reform policy makers to directly monitor the progress of policy initiatives and the compliance of officials in the field.[117] As Yang Hui complained in the second month of 1071 in reference to Tseng Pu, the new bureau facilitated Wang's domination of the government by allowing him to settle all matters pertaining to the Secretariat with his chief examiner, without reference to the other civil councilors.[118] When Shen-tsung assumed direct control of the government after Wang's final retirement in 1076, however, he began recouping executive power from the Secretariat, reducing the secretariat examiners to little more than clerks.[119]

At the regional level, the administrative reach and extractive capacity of the reformers were extended by the creation of new multicircuit superintendancies, in particular, the Superintendancy for Tea and Horses (*tu-ta t'i-chü ch'a-ma-ssu*) that dominated the economies of Szechwan and Shan-hsi, and the Superintendancy for State Trade (*tu t'i-chü shih-i-ssu*) that presided over state whole-sale and credit operations in the capital and the provinces. Unlike the Ever-normal intendancies, which were linked through a direct chain of command to the central government, these two superintendancies were autonomous state

---

[115] Higashi, *Ō Anseki jiten*, p. 79; *SHY* (1964) *chih-kuan* 5, pp. 8b–9a.

[116] On the secretariat examiners, see Kumamoto Takashi, "Chūshoken seikan – Ō Anseki seiken no ninaite-tachi," *Tōyōshi kenkyū* 47 No. 1 (1988), pp. 54–80, especially the table of incumbents, pp. 62–3.

[117] Secretariat examiners who served concurrently as investigative commissioners included Li Ch'eng-chih, Chang Tun, Hsiung Pen, Lü Hui-ch'ing, P'u Tsung-meng, and Shen K'uo. See table in Kumamoto, "Chūshoken seikan," pp. 62–3; *HCP* (1979) 251, p. 6116. On the post itself, see *SHY* (1964) *chih-kuan* 42, pp. 62a–63a.

[118] *HCP* (1979) 220, pp. 5346–7.

[119] Kumamoto, "Chūshoken seikan" pp. 75–7.

enterprises that traded revenues for independence, operating under the protection, but not the direct supervision, of the reform leadership.[120] And other circuit intendancies, such as the *pao-chia* (mutual security) militia intendants, were also created in the course of the New Policies. In conjunction with the expansion of traditional circuit positions, the new network of regional intendancies tightened the reformers' control over the people and the resources of the empire, as Ssu-ma Kuang lamented just prior to his death in 1086:

When Wang An-shih got hold of the reins of government he wanted to press forward vigorously with his New Policies. In every circuit he set up an intendant of Ever-normal and Universal Charitable granaries and Farming Lands and Irrigation. Afterward he added intendants' positions for every type of affair; moreover, investigators (*an-ch'a kuan*) were also appointed [for each of these new functions], all of whom wielded the same authority as a [regular] circuit official. At the same time, he also increased the number of fiscal vice-intendants and fiscal supervisors. And for each post he selected young, low-ranked, frivolous officials, with seniority status no higher than vice-prefect, county magistrate, or market inspector. . . . Officials such as these showed no concern for the affairs of state nor sympathy for the plight of the common people, but just devoted themselves to collaborating in schemes aimed at gaining promotions [for themselves] and revenues [for the state].[121]

It is to this search for revenues under Wang An-shih that we now turn.

THE FIRST PHASE OF THE NEW POLICIES: ECONOMIC REFORM UNDER WANG AN-SHIH

Their effective control of all the major organs of policy making, implementation, and remonstrance allowed Wang's coalition to mount a sweeping program of political, economic, and military reform. Under the banner of "activist statecraft" (*ta yu-wei chih cheng*), the reformers enacted a wide array of educational, administrative, and legal measures designed to reshape the outlook of the civil service, improve administrative efficiency, and extend government control over the populace.[122] But for reformers and opponents both, it was the measures

---

[120] On the Superintendancy for Tea and Horses, see Smith, *Taxing heaven's storehouse*; on the Superintendancy for State Trade, see Liang Keng-yao, "Shih-i fa shu," *Kuo-li T'ai-wan ta-hsüeh li-shih hsüeh-hsi hsüeh-pao* Nos. 10–11 (1984), pp. 187–8.

[121] *HCP* (1979) 368, pp. 8875–7.

[122] The chief administrative measure enacted before Shen-tsung's Yüan-feng administrative reforms was the Granary System (*ts'ang-fa*) or "increased clerical salaries" (*tseng li-lu*), promulgated in 1070 as an effort to professionalize the clerical service. Salaries were followed by the introduction of examinations and merit promotions to move effective clerks into minor offices, and the opening up of clerical positions to irregular executory-class officials and military servitors with the appropriate experience. See Liu, *Reform in Sung China*; Miyazaki Ichisada, "Ō Anseki no rishi gōitsu saku – sōhō o chūshin to shite," in his *Ajiashi kenkyū* (Kyoto, 1957), vol. 1, pp. 311–64; and Liu K'un-t'ai, "Wang An-shih kai-ke li-chih te she-hsiang yü shih-chien," in *Sung-shih yen-chiu lun-wen-chi*, ed. Teng Kuang-ming and Hsü Kuei (Hangchou, 1987), pp. 282–96. From 1071 on, to contain the persistent unrest that accompanied

devoted to "enriching the nation and strengthening its military power" (*fu-kuo ch'iang-ping*) that came to define the substance – and the tragedy – of the New Policies.[123]

Wang An-shih's own focus was on the economy. In his "Myriad word memorial" of 1058, Wang had identified bureaucratic rejuvenation as the key to social, military, and economic renascence: create a bureaucracy of ideologically uniform but highly motivated specialists drawn from all segments of the society, and all the other problems facing the empire will fall into place. By the time he assumed power under Shen-tsung, however, a decade of fiscal crisis had altered the balance to make the "management of resources" (*li-ts'ai*) the defining feature of the art of government, and economic rejuvenation the paramount concern of the day. This was the bridle Wang repeatedly used to restrain Shen-tsung from precipitately pursuing *his* own ambition – an irredentist war: "The reason we have not yet begun our [great] enterprise (*chü-shih*)," Wang advised the emperor in 1071, "is because our financial resources are inadequate. That is why I say that the management of resources (*li-ts'ai*) is our most urgent priority."[124]

Wang An-shih's economic thought

Wang's emphasis on finance was not surprising. By the late 1060s even men who were to part company over the New Policies could agree that both the

---

the enactment of the New Policies, the government began expanding the regions in which it applied the "heavy laws" (*chung-fa*), which made punishments more severe, extended liability on the part of accomplices and kin further, and offered rewards that were greater than under ordinary penalties. In addition to the frontier war zones where they were routinely invoked, the government ultimately extended the "heavy penalties" to selected counties of K'ai-feng, parts of Ching-hsi, and all of Huai-nan, Ho-pei, and Ching-tung. See Wang, "Wang An-shih pien-fa chien-lun," p. 143, and Saeki Tomi, "Sōdai ni okeru jūhō chibun ni tsuite," in *Chūgoku-shi kenkyū*, Saeki Tomi (Kyoto, 1969), vol. 1, pp. 464–8.

[123] For Ssu-ma Kuang the definitive components of the New Policies were the green sprouts (*ch'ing-miao*), hired service or service exemption (*ku-i, mu-i, mien-i*), state trade (*shih-i*), and mutual security (*pao-chia*) measures; the large-scale irrigation projects; and the disruptive frontier campaigns. See, for example, his "Ying chao yen ch'ao-cheng ch'üeh-shih chuang" (Memorial in response to the Court's order for criticism of its failures) of 1074, in Ssu-ma, *Ssu-ma Wen-cheng kung ch'uan-chia chi* 45, pp. 574–5. The authors of the *Sung shih* identify the "new policies" as *nung-t'ien shui-li* (agricultural lands and irrigation), *ch'ing-miao* (green sprouts), *chün-shu* (equalized tribute and transportation), *pao-chia* (mutual security), *mien-i* or *mu-i* (service exemption or hired service), *shih-i* (state trade), *pao-ma* (mutual security horse pasturage), and *fang-t'ien* (square-fields land survey). See *SS* 327, p. 10544.

[124] *HCP* (1979) 220, p. 5351. For other statements on the primacy of finance, see also "Ta Tseng Kung-li shu" in Wang, *Wang Lin-ch'uan ch'üan-chi* 73, p. 464, cited in Liu, *Reform in Sung China*, p. 50. As Ch'i Hsia points out, Wang An-shih ascribed his emphasis on finance to the *Rites of Chou* (*Chou-li*), "half of which," wrote Wang, "is concerned with the management of resources." See Ch'i, *Sung-tai ching-chi shih*, vol. 2, p. 1149. Ch'i Hsia analyses Wang An-shih's economic thought in general at *Sung-tai ching-chi shih*, pp. 1142–52.

Table 4. *Chronology of the New Policies during Shen-tsung's reign*

1067 (Chih-p'ing 4)	
1st month	Ying-tsung dies; Shen-tsung enthroned.
1069 (Hsi-ning 2)	
2nd month	Wang An-shih appointed assistant civil councilor.
	FINANCE PLANNING COMMISSION established.
6th month	Subcouncil for Compilation of Secretariat Regulation (*Pien-hsiu chung-shu t'iao-li-ssu*) established.
7th month	TRIBUTE TRANSPORT AND DISTRIBUTION MEASURE (*chün-shu fa*) announced for six circuits of Huai basin and Chiang-nan, under Transport Intendant Hsüeh Hsiang.
9th month	"GREEN SPROUTS" RURAL CREDIT POLICY (*ch'ing-miao fa*) promulgated.
11th month	POLICY TO PROMOTE LAND DEVELOPMENT AND IRRIGATION (*nung-t'ien shui-li fa*) promulgated.
12th month	HIRED SERVICE (*mu-i;* or service exemption, *mien-i*) proposal submitted.
1070 (Hsi-ning 3)	
3rd month	REFORMS OF THE EXAMINATIONS to emphasize policy issues, the classics, and later law begin.
5th month	COURT OF AGRICULTURAL SUPERVISION (*ssu-nung ssu*) replaces Finance Planning Commission as policy nerve center.
8th month	GRANARY SYSTEM (*ts'ang-fa*) of salaries for government clerks in the capital and the provinces established. (*HCP* 214/5223; other sources say the 12th month).
12th month	Wang An-shih and Han Chiang named chief councilors.
	MUTUAL SECURITY (*pao-chia*) experiment begins in Kaifeng.
1071 (Hsi-ning 4)	
2nd month	REVISED EXAMINATION CURRICULUM based on classics and policy issues promulgated.
3rd month	Han Chiang cashiered as chief councilor.
10th month	HIRED SERVICE POLICY promulgated (*HCP* 227/5521-24).
1072 (Hsi-ning 5)	
3rd month	STATE TRADE POLICY (*shih-i fa*) promulgated.
5th month	LOCAL HORSE-PASTURAGE SYSTEM (*pao-ma fa*) promulgated in the north to graft horse pasturage onto the mutual security system.
8th month	LAND SURVEY AND EQUITABLE TAX MEASURE (*fang-t'ien chün-shui fa*) promulgated.
10th month	Hsi-ho circuit established in the Tibetan tribal lands of the T'ao River valley, Kansu.
1073 (Hsi-ning 6)	
3rd month	BUREAU FOR THE INTERPRETATION OF THE CLASSICS (*ching-i chü*) established under Lü Hui-ch'ing and Wang Pang.
6th month	Directorate of Armaments (*chün-ch'i chien*) established.
8th month	*Pao-chia* made universal.

(*continued*)

Table 4 *(continued)*

9th month	GUILD EXEMPTION TAX (*mien-hang ch'ien*) introduced to commute guild assessments in kind to cash.
10th month	Plan to straighten the Yellow River begun.
1074 (Hsi-ning 7)	
4th month	Wang An-shih resigns, forced out by Cheng Hsia's memorial on drought and the destructiveness of the New Policies. Replaced by Lü Hui-ch'ing (assisting civil councilor) and Han Chiang (chief councilor).
7th month	SELF-REGISTRATION MEASURE (*Shou-shih fa*) enacted.
1075 (Hsi-ning 8)	
2nd month	Wang An-shih reappointed chief councilor.
6th month	New Interpretations (*hsin-i*) of the *Shih-ching*, *Shu-ching*, and *Chou-li* presented to the throne for use by education officials.
8th month	Han Chiang resigns.
10th month	Lü Hui-ch'ing cashiered.
11th month	Chiao-chih (Vietnam) invades, resolved in the tenth month of 1076.
1076 (Hsi-ning 9)	
7th month	Wang Pang dies.
10th month	Wang An-shih resigns, replaced by Wu Ch'ung and Wang K'uei.
1079 (Yüan-feng 2)	
5th month	Ts'ai Ch'üeh appointed assistant councilor of state.
1080 (Yüan-feng 3)	
3rd month	Wu Ch'ung resigns.
8th month	Shen-tsung begins his administrative reforms (*kai-kuan*).
1081 (Yüan-feng 4)	
8th month	Shen-tsung launches campaign against Tangut Hsi Hsia.
1082 (Yüan-feng 5)	
9th month	Campaign against Tanguts ends in disaster at Yung-le, though hostilities simmer.
1085 (Yüan-feng 8)	
3rd month	Shen-tsung dies, Che-tsung enthroned under Dowager Empress Hsüan-jen as regent. New Policies gradually rolled back.
1086 (Yüan-yu 1)	
int. 2nd month	Ts'ai Ch'üeh forced out, replaced as chief minister by Ssu-ma Kuang.
4th month	Wang An-shih dies.
9th month	Ssu-ma Kuang dies.

finances of the state and the prosperity of the economy were imperiled. Just after Ying-tsung's death in 1067, Han Chiang and Chang Fang-p'ing, soon to be in opposite political camps, sent up a joint memorial declaring that to ensure the livelihoods of the people and the very foundation of the state nothing was more essential than getting the nation's financial affairs in order.[125] But the relatively large arena of shared economic opinion that characterized the 1050s and 1060s was to shrink with the onset of the New Policies, when disagreements became much more sharply pronounced.[126]

As the reform agenda began to take shape, a conservative fiscal position emerged that clustered around three main points. First, conservatives such as Ssu-ma Kuang held that "the production of Heaven and Earth is constant"; that is, despite increases in the size of the population (as Ssu-ma Kuang acknowledged) the size of the economic pie remained relatively fixed.[127] Second, although fate, natural endowment, and the inelasticity of economic output induced great inequalities in wealth, conservatives such as Ssu-ma Kuang, Su Hsün, Su Ch'e, Cheng Hsia, Fan Chen, and others insisted that the relationship between rich and poor was both benign and mutually beneficial: the wealthy served as the pillars of local society and the state and as the providers of capital (land and credit) and security to the poor, who in turn assisted the wealthy with their labor.[128] And third, the fixed size of the economic pie defined the proper relationship between the economy and the state: the economy functioned best when it was least burdened by the government.

Although conservatives acknowledged that economy and finance were both in crisis, then, in their view that crisis was caused solely by the irresponsible spending of the state. Because of the inelasticity of economic output, there was no way to increase government revenues beyond traditional limits (which Chang Fang-p'ing defined as the land tax, taxes on the products of the mountains and the marshes, and commercial taxes assessed on goods in transit and at the point of sale[129]) without in turn decreasing the incomes of the people. In fact, the way to increase the prosperity of the nation, wrote Su Ch'e in the memorial that earned him a temporary position on the Finance Planning Commission, is not to demand more wealth (in the form of taxes), but rather to root out those things that harm the formation of wealth in the first place: excess officials, excess troops, and excess expenditures.[130] Ssu-ma Kuang made the same point even more forcefully in a debate with Wang An-shih before the emperor, where he reiterated his view that "the output of the world in money and goods is of a fixed and definite amount. If it is in the hands of the state

---

[125] *HCP* (1979) 209, pp. 5074–5.

[126] During the 1060s, Ssu-ma Kuang promoted many of the same ideas on finance as Wang An-shih, and even anticipated key aspects of the reforms. See, for example, his memorial on finance from 1062 entitled "Lun ts'ai-li shu" (On wealth and profit), in Ssu-ma, *Ssu-ma Wen-cheng kung ch'uan-chia chi* 25, pp. 353–62, analyzed in Bol, "Government, society, and state."

[127] Ssu-ma, *Ssu-ma Wen-cheng kung ch'uan-chia chi* 25, p. 361.

[128] For a survey of conservative views on the harmonious relationship between rich and poor, see Ch'i, *Sung-tai ching-chi shih*, vol. 2, pp. 1163–8.

[129] See Chang Fang-p'ing's memorial "Lun lu-ch'ien mu-i shih," quoted in *HCP* (1979) 277, p. 6787.

[130] *CPPM* 66, p. 2096.

then it is not in the hands of the people." And he reminded Shen-tsung of the lesson learned by the emperor Han Wu-ti (r. 141–87 B.C.E.) when he let himself be deluded by his economic minister Sang-hung Yang: when the state extracts wealth from the people, "bandits swarm like wasps."[131]

The reformers harbored an entirely more robust view of the economy. By the mid-eleventh century China could no longer be characterized by the relatively closed natural economy envisioned by the conservatives. Particularly in south China, commerce had increasingly transformed economic relations, breaking down self-sufficiency and fostering regional specialization and household production for and reliance on the market. And with commerce came a concomitant expansion in the role of money as a medium of exchange for goods and services. Although Northern Sung finance officials may have been relatively slow to recognize the distinctive properties of money, which they lumped with such commodities as grain and textiles in their statistical summaries of national income and expenditure, by Shen-tsung's reign the reformers seemed more attuned to the unique role of money as an exchange medium and a unit of value.[132] If anything, the reformers exaggerated the role of money in the Chinese economy, mesmerized as they were by the ways that money multiplied itself through commercial transactions and interest on loans. And it was this very multiplication that caught their attention and distinguished the reformers from the conservatives: for whereas conservatives viewed the economy as static, the reformers saw the economy as dynamic and expanding. In yet another strict contrast with the conservatives, who saw the state as the greatest single threat to economic well-being, the reformers held that economic dynamism could be sustained only by the involvement of the state. As early as 1058, Wang insisted that it was the responsibility of public finance (chih-ts'ai) "to utilize the energy of all under Heaven to produce wealth for all under Heaven, and to use the wealth of all under Heaven to meet the needs of all under Heaven."[133] Just one year later Wang memorialized that "If the state improves its institutions so as to make the [productive] base grow strong and the [consumer] end diminish, then the wealth of the country will be so great that no matter how much the state uses it cannot possibly exhaust all

---

[131] "Er-ying tsou-tui," in Ssu-ma, Ssu-ma Wen-cheng kung ch'uan-chia chi 42, pp. 543–5; CPPM 57, pp. 1840–5.

[132] The locus classicus on commerce in Sung China remains Shiba Yoshinobu, Sōdai shōgyōshi kenkyū (Tokyo, 1968), which should now be supplemented by his Sōdai kōnan keizaishi no kenkyū (Tokyo, 1988), and Ch'i, Sung-tai ching-chi shih. The importance of commerce and monetization to understanding the New Policies is discussed in Higashi, Ō Anseki shinpō no kenkyū, pp. 113–71. On the propensity to lump money with other commodities, see Miyazawa Tomoyuki, "Hoku-Sō no zaisei to kahei keizai," in Chūgoku sensei kokka to shakai tōgō, ed. Chūgokushi Kenkyūkai (Kyoto, 1990), pp. 281–332.

[133] Wang, Wang Lin-ch'uan ch'üan-chi 39, pp. 222–3.

of it."[134] And in his debate with Ssu-ma Kuang before the emperor, Wang argued that in a fiscal system run by "men who are skilled at finance (*shan li-ts'ai che*)" it was possible to "secure a surplus for the state without increasing the tax burden on the people."[135]

Skilled financial officials were needed to counter the aggrandizing instincts of the rich and powerful. This too was a key distinction between conservative and reform visions of the economy, for instead of the benign, mutually bene-ficial relationships between rich and poor identified by the conservatives, the reformers saw the economic landscape as dominated by coercive and preda-tory "engrossers" (*chien-ping*), magnates who preyed on the poor and usurped the fiscal prerogatives of the state. Wang had associated himself with this antiengrosser sentiment, which reached all the way back to Hsün-tzu (fl. 298–238 B.C.E.), as early as 1053, in a poem denouncing the "wicked engrossers" who had ensnared the wealth of the empire and encroached on the authority of the monarch, thus shattering the ancient unity between public (*kung*) and pri-vate (*ssu*) wealth.[136] In the idealized Chou dynasty that served as Wang's model, the former kings delegated the protection of the public interest from private encroachment to their treasury officers (*ch'üan-fu*), who "controlled and reg-ulated would-be engrossers, measured and equalized the differences between rich and poor, transformed and circulated the wealth of all under Heaven, and caused the benefits to all flow from a single source."[137] For Wang, the con-temporary analog of the treasury officer was the well-trained, virtually heroic financial specialist, upholding the power of the state to protect the common good. Nowhere did he make this clearer than in an encomium of about 1060 to the officers of funds (*tu-chih fu-shih*) of the past:

Now it is wealth that holds all the people of the world together, laws that bring order to the empire's wealth, and officials who uphold the empire's laws. If the officials are inadequate then though there are laws they will not be upheld; if the laws are not good then though there is wealth it won't be put in order. And if there is wealth but it is not regulated, then churlish people in the villages and towns will all be able to capture the power to collect and disburse for themselves and to usurp the benefits of the myriad things, in competition with the monarch. . . . Not even Yao and Shun of high antiquity could avoid making it their most urgent priority to improve the laws and appoint officials to uphold them in order to regulate the wealth of all under Heaven.[138]

---

[134] Wang, *Wang Lin-ch'uan ch'üan-chi* 70, p. 444; "I ch'a-fa," quoted in Liu, *Reform in Sung China*, p. 50.

[135] *CPPM* 57, p. 1843. Ssu-ma Kuang predicted that it was these very finance experts who would drive the people into poverty and banditry.

[136] See Wang's poem "The engrossers" in Wang, *Wang Lin-ch'uan ch'üan-chi* 5, p. 22.

[137] *HCP* (1986) *shih-pu* 4, pp. 5a–b.

[138] Wang, *Wang Lin-ch'uan ch'üan-chi* 82, pp. 521–2, "Tu-chih fu-shih t'ing-pi t'i-ming chi," cited by Liang, "Shih-i fa shu," p. 178.

But the task of regulating wealth and restraining the engrossers was made more difficult by the engrossers' ubiquity. In 1072, for example, Wang complained that: "In each and every district and prefecture there are 'engrosser' families who do nothing but collect interest of tens of thousands of strings of cash each year. Aside from violating and devouring the masses and tax-paying households to enhance their spendthrift extravagance, what do they do for the country to deserve such rich rewards?"[139]

Because there were too few officials trained in the techniques of economic management, the state had forfeited its regulatory authority to the ubiquitous predatory rich. Wang highlighted this point in the second month of 1069, in his plea for establishing the Finance Planning Commission that inaugurated the New Policies. There Wang emphasized that because incompetent officials relied on an outmoded and inflexible command structure to siphon off goods and services from a complex market-oriented economy, "most of the commodities used by the court are levied from places where they are not produced, or demanded before their season. Wealthy merchants and great traders have taken advantage of the crises this causes both public and private interests to usurp control over the ratios of exchange (ch'ing-chung) and the collection and disbursement of money and goods."[140] Because Sung financial institutions lagged behind changes in the economy, well-capitalized merchants were handed rich opportunities to profit from the gap between outmoded quotas and economic reality.

To close this gap and reestablish "public authority over the ratios of exchange and the collection and disbursement of money and goods," Wang proposed to use the new Finance Planning Commission to spearhead intensified state participation in the market economy. This commitment to expanding the scope of state power was doubly controversial. First, in direct contrast with Shen-tsung's conservative advisors, Wang openly counseled expanding rather than pruning the bureaucracy as a means of stimulating economic activity and generating greater revenues. In his very first month on the Council of State, Wang wrote that "only with many officials can essential tasks be accomplished. So long as these tasks are accomplished there is nothing wrong with official activity. And large expenditures will stimulate the production of wealth. So long as they stimulate prosperity, what is the harm in great expenditures?"[141]

---

[139] *HCP* (1979) 240, p. 5829, for the eleventh month of 1072.

[140] "Ch'i chih-chih san-ssu t'iao-li," in Wang, *Wang Lin-ch'uan ch'üan-chi* 70, p. 445.

[141] Wang, *Wang Lin-ch'uan ch'üan-chi* 62, p. 391; "K'an-hsiang tsa-i" (A series of responses to imperial queries), quoted in Liu, *Reform in Sung China*, p. 48. Wang repeated his argument in 1074, when he instructed Shen-tsung on the economic benefits of appointing additional officials to administer the labor exemption funds: "The number of [county-level] officials in charge of distribution and collection of the labor exemption and Ever-normal funds does not exceed 500 men, with combined salaries of no

As proof of Wang's intent, under his direction the number of qualified officials registered the greatest increase of the entire dynasty, jumping forty-one percent, from twenty-four thousand men in 1067 to over thirty-four thousand men in 1080.[142]

Second, if the state were to compete successfully with powerful private interests in the expanding marketplace, then it was not enough simply to make government larger: the agents of the state had to think and act not like rule-bound bureaucrats, but like innovative entrepreneurs. As Wang had argued in 1058, this meant selecting men for office based on their skills rather than for their formal credentials, and then granting them the authority and autonomy they needed to perform their intended tasks free of bureaucratic interference. Shen-tsung must have found Wang's argument persuasive, for as the author of the *Tzu-chih t'ung-chien ch'ang-pien chi-shih pen-mo* wryly observed: "the emperor tested talented men from all over the empire in governmental affairs, even reaching down to the most distant commoners. If a prefectural or county clerk made a few useful remarks, without even knowing him [the emperor] would pluck him up and in less than a day he would be appointed an imperial attendant."[143] Even more galling to the New Policies critics was Wang's employment of "anyone with an opinion on finance, from traveling merchant to market trader to butcher."[144] These potential bureaucratic entrepreneurs – or "mean-minded practitioners of profit," as their opponents called them – were assigned to the panoply of new intendancies created to extend the economic power of the state and were granted unusual autonomy over their own operations. In the case of such price-equalizing institutions as the Ever-normal Granaries, officials were encouraged "to imitate the activities of the [very merchants whose price-gouging they were seeking to break] and call it 'the art of enriching the nation.'"[145] And in the new state-run commercial enterprises that were spawned by the New Policies, especially the state trade agency, merchants were routinely given official positions.[146]

---

more than 100,000 strings annually. This year profits [from the two accounts] reached three million strings, at a [total administrative] cost of but 300,000 strings. Establishing new offices does not lead to unnecessary expenses." *HCP* (1979) 250, p. 6095.

[142] See Chaffee, *The thorny gates of learning in Sung China* (1985), p. 27, table 4.

[143] The editorial comment is appended to an order promoting an imperial affine, Hsiang Ching. See *CPPM* 81, p. 2596.

[144] *HCP* (1979) 225, p. 5484. The complaint was by Liu Chih, as he was driven from the Censorate because of his opposition to the hired service policy. In 1075 even Han Chiang complained when Wang An-shih appointed the "mean-minded practitioner of profit" Liu Tso to head the state trade agency. But Wang responded, "If a state trade official is not expert in matters of profit, how then can he manage [the affairs of the agency]?" *HCP* (1979) 264, p. 6468.

[145] Author's introduction in Ma, *Wen-hsien t'ung-k'ao* (1965), p. 5a.

[146] The state trade agency is discussed below.

Wang charged his expanded corps of financial specialists with two specific tasks: rationalizing the state's financial operations, and displacing the engrossers from their monopolistic positions. The key element of financial rationalization was to put money at the center of the relationship between the state and the economy. The first policy to come out of the Finance Planning Commission, the tribute transport and distribution measure (*chün-shu fa*), proposed to replace the clumsy command extraction of goods with a market-oriented procurement system that authorized the transport intendant (*fa-yün shih*) to buy necessities and sell surpluses on the market.[147] Although the policy was in the end aborted, other key measures, including state trade, hired service, and green sprouts, inherited its monetizing thrust.

This fiscal accommodation to the role of money in the economy was also meant to promote the state's second objective, displacing the engrossers. Under Wang's prodding, "smashing the engrossers" (*ts'ui chien-ping*) became the ideological foundation of the New Policies, and the magic key to enriching the state. In one exhortation after another Wang urged Shen-tsung to see smashing the engrossers as the very foundation of his reforms: "Heaven devolved the Nine Continents and Four Seas on the emperor just so he could suppress the great and the powerful, raise the poor and the weak, and enable poor and rich alike to enjoy the benefits [of his rule]."[148] In particular, he insisted that suppressing the engrossers was the key to financing Shen-tsung's longed-for frontier campaigns. For just as financial reforms were the prerequisite to subduing the Tanguts and the Liao, revitalizing the peasant economy lay at the heart of financial reform, "and in order to eradicate the burdens on the peasantry we must suppress the engrossers."[149] Yet while the rewards of smashing the engrossers were great, Wang warned that completely destroying their power would be difficult:

The Ch'in was able to unify the Six Kingdoms but even they could not control the engrossers, and in fact they even erected a memorial to the rich Widow Ch'ing. From the Ch'in to the present no one has known how to smash and control the engrossers. But [I] believe that if the engrossers could be smashed and controlled then the state's revenues would meet its needs and there would be no need to worry about inadequate resources.[150]

Enacting the economic reforms

At its broadest, then, Wang's economic policy was animated by the conviction that by charging financial specialists to rationalize and expand the presence of

---

[147] Ch'i, *Wang An-shih pien-fa*, pp. 153–7; Liang, "Shih-i fa shu," pp. 180–1.
[148] *HCP* (1979) 232, p. 5641.
[149] *HCP* (1979) 220, p. 5351.
[150] *HCP* (1979) 262, p. 6407, for the fourth month of 1075; Liang, "Shih-i fa shu," p. 223.

the state in the monetized, commercialized economy, government agents could appropriate the illicit profits of the engrossers and thereby assist the poor, stimulate production, and enhance government revenues without increasing the tax burdens on the people. Under the direction of the Finance Planning Commission and its successor, the Court of Agricultural Supervision, Wang's economic corps did realize several significant successes. The many water-control projects pursued as part of the policy to promote land development and irrigation (*nung-t'ien shui-li fa*) certainly provided a direct stimulus to agricultural productivity. Between 1070 and 1076 the reform administration initiated 10,793 water-control and land reclamation projects around the empire, reclaiming a total of 361,178 *ch'ing* 88 *mu* (approximately 38,829,779 acres) of agricultural land. In addition, such directors of waterways (*tu-shui chien*) as Ch'eng Fang and Hou Shu-hsien contributed to both productivity and fiscal solvency by remedying conservancy and flood control problems along the Yellow River and the Pien Canal.[151]

The redistributive goal of the reformers was most closely approximated in the "land survey and equitable tax policy" (*fang-t'ien chün-shui fa*) enacted in the "five [northern] circuits" (*wu-lu*) (Ho-tung, the two Ho-pei circuits, Yung-hsing-chün, and Ch'in-feng). Initiated in the eighth month of 1072, the new measure sought to redistribute some of the tax burden that had been sloughed off onto small, politically powerless landowners by the powerful "official families and families of substance" (*kuan-hu hsing-shih-hu*) whose large landholdings were protected by tax exemptions. In a concession to powerful landowners that would later be followed by early Ch'ing dynasty (1644–1911) rulers, the reformers traded the promise of readjustment but no total tax increase for the right to institute a new series of cadastral surveys. Although this concession preempted any increase in the total land tax from the five northern circuits, by the time the policy was rescinded in 1085 a reported 2,484,349 *ch'ing* (c. 34.7 million acres) of land – fifty-four percent of the national total of 4.6 million *ch'ing* as of 1082 – had been revealed. And while the overall impact of the measure is difficult to assess, it is quite possible that the exposure of these previously untaxed lands allowed some shifting of the tax burden away from poor northern households already encumbered by the severe labor service (*fu-i*) burdens occasioned by militarization of the borders with the Liao and Hsi Hsia.[152]

---

[151] For sources and discussion of New Policies water-control measures, see Higashi, *Ō Anseki shinpō no kenkyū*, pp. 394–509, and Mihelich, "Polders and the politics of land reclamation," pp. 48–118. For a tabulation by region of the figures on reform water-control projects (from *SHY* [1964] *shih-huo* 61, pp. 68a–70b), see Higashi, *Ō Anseki shinpō no kenkyū*, p. 509.

[152] Ch'i, *Wang An-shih pien-fa*, pp. 144–7; Higashi, *Ō Anseki shinpō no kenkyū*, pp. 815–88; Sudō Yoshiyuki, "Ō Anseki no shinpō to sono shiteki igi – nōmin seisaku o chushin to shite," in *Sōdai-shi kenkyū*, Sudō Yoshiyuki (Tokyo, 1969), pp. 11–14. Wang, "Wang An-shih pien-fa chien-lun," p. 146, doubts the

Ultimately, however, the redistributive and productivity goals that gave the New Policies their moral persuasiveness were overwhelmed by the state's fiscal imperatives. One after another, policies that began as efforts to rationalize the mobilization of goods and services, assist poor peasants, equalize tax burdens, or break commercial monopolies were metamorphosed into the claws of a predatory bureaucracy whose sole purpose was to gouge new revenues out of the economy. These policies did indeed enrich the state, but only at great political and economic cost. For not only did the fiscalization of the reforms undermine broader economic objectives, it also produced a sharp backlash that turned reformers as well as conservatives against the New Policies, first bringing down Wang An-shih and then the reform movement as a whole. Because this transformation of redistributive policies into unbridled revenue extraction shaped the final outcome of the reforms, it is worth examining in detail the four measures most thoroughly tarred with the fiscalist brush: green sprouts, hired service, state trade, and mutual security – a local militia system that was ultimately turned by exigency and opportunity into the tax collection arm of the state.

Rural credit (ch'ing-miao) and hired service (mu-i or mien-i)

New Policies economic reforms as a whole drew heavily on experiments under-taken locally during Jen-tsung's reign, and Wang An-shih had himself devised a prototype of the green sprouts rural credit measure. The green sprouts policy took aim at the inequalities created by the progressive monetization of the economy. As land and the entire agrarian regime were drawn deeper into the commercial vortex, the peasant's ability to hold onto his land came to depend increasingly on his access to money and credit. The enveloping cash nexus fostered a cycle of rural debt and propertylessness that seemed to be intensify-ing throughout the eleventh century. By midcentury roughly eighty percent of the ten million rural landowning households (that is, resident – chu-hu – versus "guest" or tenant – k'o-hu – households) were ranked in the lowest two grades (4 and 5) of a hierarchy consisting of five grades of commoners and a single grade of officials, and possessed only about twenty-two percent of the empire's cultivated lands. With average holdings of just fifteen mu (c. two acres), roughly three mu less than was needed to feed a family of five, these

---

validity of the figure of over 2.4 million ch'ing. Higashi, Ō Anseki shinpō no kenkyū, pp. 869–70, takes another tack, by noting that Wen-hsien t'ung-k'ao's author, Ma Tuan-lin, doubted the validity of the figure for total acreage of 4.6 million ch'ing, suspecting that the real arable amount was more like 30 million ch'ing. See Ma, Wen-hsien t'ung-k'ao (1965) 4, p. 59b. If Ma Tuan-lin is correct, the amount of land uncovered in the north suggests what kind of inroads the state might have made had it been able to extend its policy to the south as well.

households lived at the margins of economic dependence: not only were they often forced to supplement their incomes as hired laborers or tenants on other people's lands, but "[m]any of them were chronically in debt, and mounting debts led all too often to forced sale or foreclosure of their land."[153]

Forced sales and debt foreclosures presented problems for the state as well as for the peasantry, since propertylessness and the concentration of land ownership increased the possibilities of rural unrest and diminished the state's access to the taxes and labor of the peasantry. Up through the eighth century the principal lever utilized by the state to protect peasant solvency and independence involved periodic land redistribution, but even Wang An-shih admitted that the state no longer possessed the power to reestablish the old land-equalizing measures.[154] Instead, Wang and like-minded reformers came to view rural credit as the fulcrum through which state power could best protect the peasantry.

The most vulnerable time for peasants fell in the lean months between consumption of the previous year's crop and the planting and harvest of the new crop, when peasants were forced to borrow food and seed grain or the cash to buy them. Sometime in the 1040s the Shan-hsi finance official Li Ts'an devised a policy that incidentally filled this credit gap by making advance payments of "green sprouts cash" (ch'ing-miao ch'ien) to peasants in the off-season for the purchase of grain at harvest time. Although Li Ts'an's measure lent its name to the later measure, his was intended more to assure a reliable supply of grain for the army than to remedy rural distress.[155] But Wang An-shih did target the credit squeeze during his term as magistrate of Yin county (Liang-che) around 1049, though instead of paying cash for future crops he lent grain for immediate needs, allowing lenders to redeem their loans with interest at harvest time.[156] Wang An-shih's measure was well received locally, and he revived the plan very soon after joining the Council of State in early 1069, this time replacing grain with interest-bearing loans of "green sprouts cash." With Wang and his coalition not yet in firm control, Su Ch'e was able to block this first green sprouts proposal. But shortly thereafter Wang Kuang-lien, a managing supervisor in the Ho-pei Fiscal Intendancy, requested

[153] Peter J. Golas, "Rural China in the Song," *Journal of Asian Studies* 39 No. 2 (1980), pp. 302–4. As of 1075, the population consisted of 10.6 million *chu-hu* and 5 million *k'e-hu*. See Ch'i, *Sung-tai ching-chi shih*, vol. 1, p. 47. The household categories raise a number of descriptive and analytical problems and have spawned a considerable literature, which Golas surveys in "Rural China in the Song," pp. 305–9. Much of this discussion of the green sprouts policy is drawn from Smith, "State power and economic activism during the New Policies."

[154] *HCP* (1979) 223, p. 5419.

[155] *SS* 330, p. 10619; Higashi, *Ō Anseki shinpō no kenkyū*, pp. 546–8.

[156] *SS* 327, p. 10541; Higashi, *Ō Anseki shinpō no kenkyū*, pp. 548–50.

permission to sell several thousand ordination certificates in order to capitalize a green sprouts loan policy in Shan-hsi, and this time Wang and his lieutenant Lü Hui-ch'ing were strong enough to force adoption of the "Shan-hsi green sprouts loan act" on a regional, experimental basis.[157]

By the ninth month of 1069 the reformers were ready to push for empirewide enactment of the measure, which they advertised as an attack on the monopoly over agricultural credit enjoyed by the rural "engrossers": "The reason people are burdened by deficits is because in that seasonal gap separating the old harvest from the new, engrossing households take advantage of the crisis to demand interest rates of 100 percent. Consequently, would-be borrowers are often denied the funds they need."[158]

In order to break this private credit monopoly the reformers proposed to create a state-run rural credit system, to be capitalized by liquidating the fifteen million piculs of grain and strings of cash that sat idly in the moribund system of Ever-normal (Ch'ang-p'ing ts'ang) and Universal Charity (Kuang-hui ts'ang) granaries. Traditionally, the Ever-normal Granaries were authorized to buy up grains when prices were cheap for resale when prices were dear, or in times of natural disaster. By the onset of Shen-tsung's reign however the system had become so cumbersome that the mechanism had ceased to work effectively, and stocks were rarely circulated.[159] Nonetheless these idle grain reserves represented an enormous capitalizing potential, and in its directive the Finance Planning Commission proposed a simultaneous solution to the problems of price equalization, disaster relief, and seasonal credit crises that transformed the nation's granary stocks into a green sprouts fund for rural investment. Control of the granaries was transferred from the circuit judicial intendants to the new satellites of the Finance Planning Commission – the circuit intendants for Ever-normal Granaries – who were empowered to convert the reserves into a liquid loan fund that would be administered by county magistrates and local village officers.[160] The loans were to be made in the spring and repaid in two installments after taxes in the summer and fall, and a series of rules were established to protect borrowers against unfair manipulation by officials. For example, loans could be repaid in either currency or grain, with exchange rates set to ensure only that the government lost none of its basic capitalization (pen-ch'ien); forced loans (i-p'ei) were expressly prohibited.

---

[157] SHY (1964) shih-huo 4, p. 17a–b; Higashi, Ō Anseki shinpō no kenkyū, pp. 550–2.

[158] SHY (1964) shih-huo 4, p. 16a. This key text, which comprises the basic legislation for the green sprouts policy, is analyzed in Sudō Yoshiyuki, "Ō Anseki no seibyoho no shiko katei," Tōyō Daigaku Daigakuin kiyō 8 (1972), pp. 172–4.

[159] On the granary systems, see SS 176, pp. 4275–91.

[160] For details of the administration, see SHY (1964) shih-huo 4 and 5, and Smith, "State power and economic activism during the New Policies."

Nothing less than a complete rejuvenation of the agrarian economy was expected from the new measure, which was perceived as a means of rationalizing the distribution and collection of grain and money to equalize commodity prices, minimize the unequal geographic distribution of resources, and ensure adequate supplies of relief grain. The policy's authors likened it to the measures by which the ancient kings "aided agriculture, equalized wealth, and prevented the powerful from plundering the people," for by supplanting private landlords and moneylenders as the principal source of rural credit, the state could "enable the peasants to hasten to the management of their affairs so that monopolist households will be unable to take advantage of their crises." Above all, the Finance Planning Commission disavowed any fiscal interest in the measure, insisting that "the loan policy is for the sake of the people; the government (*kung-chia*) will claim no benefit from its receipts."[161]

The stated objectives of the green sprouts policy, then, were explicitly redistributionist: the establishment of a state-run rural credit system that would keep the two poorest grades of landowning peasants solvent, by breaking their dependence on usurious rural moneylenders. But poor property owners were not the only endangered segment of the landed population. By the mid-eleventh century the three highest grades, comprising the same middle to wealthy peasants who in other contexts could be labeled "engrossers," were also showing signs of vulnerability. For while the roughly twenty percent of all landed peasants in these three upper grades might enjoy adequate lands and financial resources, their very prosperity made them eligible for a variety of burdensome and often ruinous government obligations. Because the traditional Chinese state never had the financial or organizational resources to expand its bureaucratic tendrils below the county level it was forced to conscript local villagers into fulfilling those functions on which its survival depended, especially tax collection and local security. On the eve of the New Policies, the principal village positions included the household chiefs (*hu-chang*) and canton scribes (*hsiang shu-shou*), responsible for tax assessment and collections, and the village elders (*ch'i-chang*) and stalwart men or guardsmen (*chuang-ting*), responsible for local security. Incumbents for these posts were mustered through the "drafted service system" (*ch'ai-i fa*), which conscripted villagers for fixed terms into posts requiring resources appropriate to their household grade.[162]

---

[161] *SHY* (1964) *shih-huo* 4, p. 16b.

[162] Though the periodical literature on local government service during the Sung is growing steadily, among the standard works that still demand attention are Sogabe Shizuo, "Ō Anseki no boyakuhō," in *Sōdai zaiseishi*, Sogabe Shizuo (Tokyo, 1966), pp. 143–98; and Sudō Yoshiyuki, "Ō Anseki no boyakusen chōshū no sho mondai," in *Sōdai-shi kenkyū*, Sudō Yoshiyuki (Tokyo, 1969), pp. 189–259, the main points of which are summarized in Sudō, "Ō Anseki no shinpō to sono shiteki igi," pp. 1–26; Nieh

Although the tax officials, particularly after 1055 the household chiefs, were obliged to make up shortfalls below quota out of their own incomes, on the whole village service did not become especially onerous until the financial and military collapse of the Northern Sung. Much more burdensome was the stipulation that after completing their local duties village servicemen could be drafted into "government service" (*chih-i*) attached to the county and prefectural yamen. These official posts, which numbered over a million at any one time, included office messengers (*ch'eng-fu*) and miscellaneous servants (*san-ts'ung kuan*), bookkeepers (*tien-li*) and scribes (*shu-piao shih*), a wide variety of granary and supply functionaries and laborers (*k'u-tzu, t'ou-tzu, jen-li*), and yamen police for the arrest of thieves (*kung-shou*) and people charged in law suits (*yü-hou*). But the most onerous post was that of supply master (*ya-ch'ien*).[163] Drafted from the wealthiest households, the supply masters were responsible for managing government granaries, hosting prefectural guests, and two functions that required extensive travel: accompanying civil officials to and from office and overseeing the transmission of taxes and tribute goods from their local yamen to designated destinations throughout the empire, including the capital.[164] During the course of the eleventh century the supply master's post became semiprofessionalized in the most commercially advanced regions of the empire, such as Chiang-nan and parts of Szechwan; there volunteers (called *t'ou-ming ya-ch'ien* or *ch'ang-ming ya-ch'ien*) were reimbursed with the rights to manage government ferry crossings (*ho-tu*) and wine-mash franchises (*fang-ch'ang*), and might profit handsomely from their enterprises. But in most parts of the country the post was filled by unremunerated conscripts who were ill-prepared to finance their long trips to the capital, bribe clerks to accept their shipments, or cover the costs of goods lost or damaged in transit.[165]

Shen-tsung's accession was accompanied by a flurry of memorials calling for reform of the government service draft, especially the supply master system.

Ch'ung-ch'i, "Sung i-fa shu," rpt. in his *Sung-shih ts'ung-k'ao*, (Peking, 1980), pp. 1–70; Liu, *Reform in Sung China*, pp. 98–113; and Brian E. McKnight, *Village and bureaucracy in Southern Sung China* (Chicago, 1971), pp. 20–37. For a more recent example, see Yü Tsung-hsien, "Lun Wang An-shih mien-i fa," in *Sung-shih lun-chi*, ed. Chung-chou shu-hua-she (Cheng-chou, 1983), pp. 107–23.

[163] Liu, *Reform in Sung China*, pp. 100–1; McKnight, *Village and bureaucracy*, pp. 23–5; Sudō, "Ō Anseki no shinpō to sono shiteki igi," pp. 4–5.

[164] Sudō, "Ō Anseki no shinpō to sono shiteki igi," p. 4. See also his "Sōdai shuken no shokuyaku to shuri no hatten," in *Sōdai keizaishi kenkyū*, Sudō Yoshiyuki (Tokyo, 1962), pp. 661–704. For a more recent discussion, see Wang Tseng-yü's "Sung ya-ch'ien tsa-lun (1)," *Pei-ching shih-yüan hsüeh-pao* No. 3 (1986), pp. 76–82; and "Sung ya-ch'ien tsa-lun (2)," *Pei-ching shih-yüan hsüeh-pao* No. 1 (1987), pp. 49–57.

[165] McKnight, *Village and bureaucracy*, p. 26. On volunteers, see Sudō, *Sōdai keizaishi kenkyū*, pp. 662 ff. For a useful summary of how the government controlled the manufacture and distribution of wine during the Sung, see Ch'i, *Sung-tai ching-chi shih*, vol. 2, pp. 875–904.

Early in 1067, Han Chiang, as finance commissioner, memorialized that the supply master conscription was the single greatest threat to peasant productivity. A single term, lasting two to three years, could prove so costly to the incumbent (up to one thousand strings of cash in one report) that eligible household heads would commit suicide, break up their families, or sell or abandon their lands in order to lower their household grade. More important, the threat of conscription was a disincentive to agricultural investment: "people rely on the productivity of the land for their livelihoods. But now if they exhaust themselves to succeed, once they have attained a certain level of prosperity they are hit with drafted service. If we want to encourage more people to farm and more lands to be opened, then how can this situation be tolerated?"[166] A year later Wu Ch'ung described how once an upper-grade family was assigned supply master duties an official arrived at their door to register all their belongings, from cups and pestles to baskets and chopsticks, to be counted against losses incurred in service. Wu Ch'ung complained that

it even gets to the point that when household property is exhausted, but the debts not yet requited, then the children and grandchildren are in turn impoverished and neighboring guarantors sought out. Therefore in order to avoid ruinous draft service the people do not dare to cultivate much land so as to avoid high household rank, and men of the same bones and flesh do not dare live together out of fear of raising their eligibility for corvée.

Wu emphasized that since supply master service was destroying the upper-grade families the duties had to be pushed down onto poorer households even less able to bear the costs, a process that inevitably squeezed peasants out of farming and even into vagrancy.[167]

Reports such as these from his father's senior officials moved Shen-tsung to call for urgent action on the government service draft. Drafted service had received far more attention than rural credit over the years, and Shen-tsung's policy makers could draw upon a long if ultimately unsuccessful history of reform precedents. In 1022, for example, a group of officials recommended that limits be placed on the amount of land officials could keep exempt from financial obligations, in order to expand the tax base for local services and restrict official families' (*kuan-hu*) engrossment of land.[168] The 1030s saw the first local attempts to levy special taxes to subsidize the hiring of volunteer supply masters, including the imposition in 1041 of a service exemption fee (*mien-i ch'ien*) in the Ching-hu South circuit.[169] And in the decade prior to the

[166] *SHY* (1964) 65, pp. 1a–b. The figure of one thousand strings per term is supplied by Teng Wan; see *HCP* (1979) 227, pp. 5522–3.

[167] *SHY* (1964) *shih-huo* 65, pp. 2a–b.

[168] McKnight, *Village and bureaucracy*, pp. 27–8; Ma, *Wen-hsien t'ung-k'ao* (1965) 12, pp. 128c–129a.

[169] McKnight, *Village and bureaucracy*, p. 30; Ma, *Wen-hsien t'ung-k'ao* (1965) 12, p. 129a.

New Policies both Tseng Kung and Ssu-ma Kuang – who was to vehemently oppose the service exemption (*mien-i*) policy – proposed utilizing income from the wine monopoly, supplemented by imposts on the rural or urban rich, to create a fund for compensating hired government servicemen.[170]

But government service reforms encountered far more opposition than did reform of the rural credit system. For whereas the green sprouts credit mechanism competed with private moneylenders, it did not impose any new costs on the wealthy – indeed, wealthy families soon became eligible for loans themselves. All of the proposed solutions to the drafted service problem, however, shifted part of the burden to families who had previously been exempt by law, such as officials and town dwellers, or by practice, such as the powerful local families whose influence over government clerks gave them de facto immunity from conscription.[171] Consequently, reform of the drafted service system was touted as an antiengrosser issue, even though the beneficiaries of reform were in the highest household categories.[172]

Precisely because drafted service reform did challenge powerful entrenched interests in a way that the green sprouts measure did not, it took a much longer time to enact a workable policy. In the last month of 1069 – a year and a half after Shen-tsung's first calls for action – the Finance Planning Commission produced a proposal to replace government service conscripts with paid volunteers.[173] The funds to pay this new semiprofessionalized corps were to come from three sources: a tax on the households eligible for drafted service, called either a service exemption (*mien-i*) or hired service (*mu-i*) fee, graduated according to their assessed wealth; the auctioning off of franchises to manage the state's twenty-six thousand wine and ferry installations for a fixed period;[174] and the imposition of a tax, called a "service assistance fee"

---

[170] McKnight, *Village and bureaucracy*, p. 31, citing *SS* 319, p. 10390; *HCP* (1979) 196, pp. 4755–6.

[171] See Teng Wan's description in *HCP* (1979) 227, p. 5522.

[172] For Wang An-shih's comments, see *HCP* (1979) 220, p. 5351; 223, p. 5427.

[173] The directive is excerpted in *SS* 177, p. 4299, and Ma, *Wen-hsien t'ung-k'ao* (1965) 12, pp. 129a–130c, but the fullest version, from the original *shih-huo chih*, is anthologized in Li T'ao's commentary in *HCP* (1979) 227, p. 5521. Li T'ao's notes, *HCP* (1979) 227, pp. 5521–4, are the best source for recreating the history of the *mien-i* policy up to its universal enactment in the tenth month of 1071.

[174] The old method of granting these franchises to supply masters as compensation for their services had cost the state the market value of an important financial operation at a time of commercial expansion. By selling the franchise rights to the highest bidders, the state acquired a buoyant revenue source, worth three million strings of cash by 1076. Total returns by region to the 26,341 stations as of 1076, as part of the total revenue stream produced by the green sprouts and service exemption measures as tabulated in the *Chung-shu tui-pei*, are preserved in *Yung-lo ta-tien* (repr. Peking, 1960), 7507, pp. 3360–2, and tabulated in Sudō "Ō Anseki no boyakusen chōshū no sho mondai," pp. 200–2; the entire revenue package is tabulated by Miyazawa, "Hoku-Sō no zaisei to kahei keizai," pp. 327–32. For a description of the sealed-bid procedure used to auction off franchises in Shan-hsi in the eleventh month of 1070, see *HCP* (1979) 217, pp. 3274–5.

(*chu-i ch'ien*), on all households with property and wealth but not themselves liable for service. This last innovation was the most politically daring, although it too had been raised before. Some of those now taxed in this new category, such as households with no taxable males (*ting2*), or only a single taxable male, or headed by a woman, did not necessarily wield much power on their own. But the inclusion of all urban households, households of Buddhist and Taoist temples, and particularly the households of ranked officials directly challenged a very influential constituency. In addition to putting government service on a paid, volunteer basis, the commissioners called for an overall reduction in the number of service positions needed in long-distance transport, and a prohibition on the many abuses and expenses to which supply masters in transit were liable.

The commission's proposal contained all but two elements of the final policy – the *k'uan-sheng ch'ien* (surplus emergency fee) surtax and an explicit levy on the lowest-grade households – but it was only an "instruction," sent to Ever-normal Granary intendants, fiscal intendants, and prefects and county magistrates for discussion. The proposal had still not been enacted half a year later when the Finance Planning Commission was abolished and all its functions, including the rural credit program, irrigation, and the persistent drafted service dilemma, were transferred to the Court of Agricultural Supervision under the leadership of Lü Hui-ch'ing.[175] Although Lü fervently agreed that conscription for prefectural and county service was the most urgent problem facing rural society, he feared that the Finance Planning Commission proposal made too many enemies among the powerful who could evade service and the local functionaries who benefited from its abuses.

> Those who receive the most liberal benefits from the proposal are the poorest peasants, who as the simplest members of their villages are unable to represent their own interests; while those who are selected [to pay for service] include the baronial families of officials and engrossers who can easily get others to speak for them. Moreover, if the policy is enacted uniformly then prefectural legal aides and county clerks will not be able to exploit the people and will therefore oppose the measure, making it very difficult to enact.

Lü argued that it was because of this alliance between elites and local officials that the policy was so slow to take shape, writing that because of the powerful opposition to the measure "officials are not able to view the intent of the policy clearly, and are confused by the many different opinions of those who plot [against it] behind their walls. Therefore it will be difficult to bring the measure to fruition." As a result, Lü counseled that the government should

---

[175] *HCP* (1979) 211, p. 5130; *SHY* (1964) *shih-huo* 65, pp. 3b–4a.

slowly experiment with the policy in one or two prefectures, and then if
successful there expand to the rest of the country.[176]

Under Lü and (after Lü's leave for mourning) his successor, Tseng Pu, experimental programs were mounted in Shan-hsi, Szechwan, and Ho-pei.[177] But
the most influential experiment was in K'ai-feng itself, where sometime in late
1070 the commissioner-general for K'ai-feng (*t'i-tien fu-chieh kung-shih*), Chao
Tzu-chi, submitted what was to become the prototypical service exemption
policy.[178] As approved and enacted by the Court of Agricultural Supervision
in the first month of 1071, Chao's proposal followed the original Finance
Planning Commission outline. First, in order to calibrate each household's
fee fairly, all rural households were subdivided into fifteen subgrades and all
urban households into ten grades, with the poorest rural grades (4 and 5) and
poorest urban grades (6 through 10) exempt from payment. Second, in order
to neutralize the opposition of those propertied classes previously exempt from
service, the households of ranked officials, households headed by women, families without taxable males, and temple households were required to pay only
half the rate for their assessed grade.[179] Finally, the fees collected from these

---

[176] Taken from *Lü Hui-ch'ing chia-chuan* and quoted with notes on dating in *HCP* (1979) 215, p. 5237;
227, p. 5522.

[177] All three were reported in the eleventh month of 1070; *HCP* (1979), 217, pp. 5274–5, 5283–4. For
Ssu-ma Kuang's opposition to the Shan-hsi experiment, see "Ch'i mien Yung-hsing-chün Lu mien-i-
ch'ien cha-tzu," in Ssu-ma, *Ssu-ma Wen-cheng kung ch'uan-chia chi* 44, pp. 565–6. As all sources repeat,
without explanation, after taking over in the ninth month of 1070 Tseng Pu earned Lü Hui-ch'ing's
enmity by changing *chü-i* (service assistance) to *mien-i* (service exemption). What this may mean is that
Tseng wanted to charge exemptees in full, which Lü – and Wang – thought would destroy political
support for the measure. See, as an example, *HCP* (1979) 215, p. 5237.

[178] The sources preserve only the response to Chao's proposal by Tseng Pu and his new co-leader of the
Ssu-nung ssu, Teng Wan. See Li T'ao's appended notes in *HCP* (1979) 227, pp. 5522–3, and *SS* 177,
p. 4300.

[179] Although Wang An-shih admitted the need to compromise with the privileged rich, it galled him. If
the service exemption fees for official families and urban dwellers were not reduced, he admitted to the
emperor, "official households would block and undermine the measure, while urban households would
congregate into mobs and beat the drums to intimidate the state councilors. Not even the emperor
would be able to move their hearts." But Wang did hold the emperor partly to blame: "If Your Majesty
were truly able to plan for benefit and harm, to distinguish true from false, and to clearly distinguish
good and evil with rewards and punishments so that everyone would be awed, then [no one] would dare
speak evil talk or rumor nor put forth wild and malicious plans, and powerful and cunning officials
and commoners would naturally be stilled. If this were the case, then without doing any harm even
more could be extracted from the engrossing magnates (*chien-ping hao-ch'iang*) in order to assist the
poor." See *HCP* (1979) 223, p. 5427. Information on overall rates is spotty. In K'ai-feng county, 22,600
households were charged 12,900 strings of cash annually as of 1071, or about 570 cash each per year;
HCP (1979) 227, p. 5522. Teng Wan estimated that the richest families would be charged 250 strings
every decade – the typical cycle for reconscription under the old system – or 25 strings annually, while
middle households would pay 80 to 90 strings each decade. Teng claimed that the fees were half of what
families would have to pay as draftees; *HCP* (1979) 227, pp. 5522–3. But, in 1082, the Ever-normal
Granary intendant of Chiang-nan, Liu I, estimated that the richest families in Liang-che paid up to

two sources – draft-liable and draft-exempt households – would be used exclusively to hire volunteers from households of grade 3 and higher – the middle and rich peasantry – for the three most important government-service posts: supply masters, who had to put up property as collateral; county militiamen (literally, "bowmen," *kung-shou*), who had to be tested in martial arts; and scribes (*tien-li*), who had to be tested in accounting. Terms of service were set at two to three years, and actual salaries were to vary with the labor market in each locale, and the difficulty and number of workdays required by each position.

Even the K'ai-feng prototype was experimental, and in the fifth month of 1071 local citizens and censors rallied against the plan. By this time, however, Wang An-shih had solidified his hold on government, and despite the temporary embarrassment of the "Tung-ming affair" (discussed later), in the tenth month of 1071 the service exemption policy was made the law of the land.[180]

State trade (shih-i)

Taken as a whole, the green sprouts and hired service measures were intended to revive an agrarian economy that was endangered by rural credit markets controlled by the rich and a regressive service burden that favored the powerful. But the rural rich were not the only targets of the reformers' redistributionist zeal: Wang An-shih's "Request for a Finance Planning Commission" had launched the New Policies with an attack on "the wealthy merchants and great traders" who manipulated the market for commodities to their own advantage. Wang's memorial had spawned the "equalized tribute measure" (*chün-shu fa*), which charged Transport Intendant Hsüeh Hsiang to close the gap between local quotas and a supply manipulated by engrossers, by replacing tribute quotas with government purchases of necessities and sales of surpluses on the market. Although the measure was never enacted, reformers continued to worry that by using their powers to manipulate prices, dominate access to markets, and control the supply of goods, the great urban merchants had created commercial monopolies that locked out small traders and harmed the consumers, and they sought a policy that would open up bottlenecked markets and free the circulation of goods.[181]

800,000 cash (nominally, 800 strings) annually in service exemption fees; eight times more than the draft had cost them. See *HCP* (1979) 324, p. 7798.

[180] *HCP* (1979) 227, p. 5521.

[181] On the *chün-shu fa* as progenitor of the state trade measure, see Hartwell, "The imperial treasuries," p. 69. For studies of the state trade measure see Liang, "Shih-i fa shu," and Miyazawa Tomoyuki, "Sōdai no toshi shōgyō to kokka – shiekihō shinkō," in *Chūgoku kinsei no toshi to bunka*, ed. Umehara Kaoru (Kyoto, 1984), pp. 321–58.

The reformers' prototype was supplied by Wang Shao's state trade policy (*shih-i fa*), an openly revenue-oriented measure that eyed merchant monopolies not as an evil to be eradicated but as an opportunity to be admired and appropriated. In early 1070, in the midst of his campaign to colonize the Tibetan tribal lands between the Ch'ing-hai Lake and Ch'in-feng circuit, Wang Shao recommended that the thriving private Sino-Tibetan trade be appropriated and monopolized by the state in order to subsidize the frontier campaign. Wang Shao complained that although hundreds of thousands of strings of cash worth of Tibetan goods were imported into China each year, "the profits created by these merchant travelers all revert back to the people [rather than go to the state]. I wish to establish a state trade agency in [Ch'in-feng circuit] that will use government funds as capital [to buy domestic goods for trade to foreign merchants], in order to capture for the state the profits that now flow to merchants and traders." Wang anticipated returns of two hundred thousand strings of cash on the monopolized trade, which he promised would be enough to finance the frontier campaign without further government funds.[182]

As Wang Shao's chief patron in the capital, Wang An-shih strongly promoted the plan as an effective way of bolstering Tibetan loyalties, while at the same time providing crucial revenues for the troop buildup and campaigns in the northwest.[183] Shen-tsung was also much taken with the idea, which he envisioned as a lucrative source of cash, generating endless revenues through the magic of interest. As the emperor saw it,

The government uses its funds to buy up goods brought to market by Tibetan merchants, saving them the trouble of waiting around for a buyer. The officials then resell these goods to resident merchants on credit, [saving them the trouble of having to have cash on hand. In addition to its markup on the sale] the government also collects interest on the credit transaction. And that is why the plan is advantageous.[184]

Although Wang Shao proposed to commandeer the wholesalers' profits from private merchants, his plan was neither antiengrosser in tone nor redistributionist in intent. But the basic outline of his policy meshed with the antiengrosser zeal of the more radical reformers, and within two years of its enactment in 1070 in the northwest frontier a more redistributionist version of Wang Shao's measure was introduced in K'ai-feng. The new version was

---

[182] *SHY* (1964) *shih-huo* 37, p. 14a; *HCP* (1979) 226, p. 5502.

[183] *HCP* (1979) 214, p. 5205; 224, p. 5460; "Yu Wang Tzu-ch'un (Shao) shu," in Wang, *Wang Lin-ch'uan ch'üan-chi* 73, pp. 464–5.

[184] *SHY* (1964) *shih-huo* 37, p. 14b. This imperial endorsement is an early indication of the fascination with the power of usury as a fiscal tool that suffused New Policies economic planners.

proposed in early 1072 by the self-described commoner Wei Chi-tsung in response to a growing trade crisis in the capital caused by price fixing and monopolistic hoarding.[185] In the memorial that launched the state trade venture in K'ai-feng, Wei Chi-tsung lambasted the "rich men and great families" (*fu-jen ta-hsing*) who took advantage of temporary imbalances in supply and demand to buy up and hoard the commodities brought into the city by traveling merchants at deflated prices, then waited until demand peaked before releasing them onto the market at inflated prices. Faced with these monopolistic tactics, provincial merchants had stopped transporting essential goods to the capital, depriving the city's consumers of these goods and the state of necessary revenues. In keeping with reform rhetoric, Wei Chi-tsung invoked the ancient adage that the true way to rule all under Heaven required the ability "to confiscate from the rich in order to be able to give to the poor," an ability he lamented that officials had lost. As evidence, Wei noted that although the capital's Bureau of Monopoly Goods (*Ch'üeh-huo wu*) was overflowing with surplus cash and commodities, because of official incompetence none of this surplus was used to equalize prices.[186] In a recommendation that merged the credit and wholesalers' functions of Wang Shao's frontier trade bureau with the price-equalizing function of the Ever-normal Granaries, Wei Chi-tsung called on the government to use surplus Bureau of Monopoly Goods funds to capitalize an Ever-normal State Trade Agency (*Ch'ang-p'ing shih-i ssu*) in the capital, managed by financial officials assisted by "worthy merchants" (*liang-ku*). Like its Ever-normal Granary prototype, the state trade agency would pay relatively generous prices to buy unmoved goods in a stagnant market, to the advantage of the traveling merchants, and would charge relatively cheap prices to sell high-demand goods in a robust market, to the advantage of the consumer. In this way the state could equalize commodity prices, break the private monopolies held by the rich, stimulate commerce, and protect the consumption needs of the people – yet still obtain a modest profit to meet the financial needs of the state.

Wang An-shih and his men in the Secretariat heartily endorsed the antiengrosser thrust of Wei Chi-tsung's memorial, agreeing that "when merchants from around the empire bring goods to the capital, they are often exploited by the engrosser houses of the city. Everywhere livelihoods are lost, and guild shops and petty traders are being drained and exhausted by the need to eke

---

[185] *HCP* (1979) 231, p. 5622; *SHY* (1964) *shih-huo* 37, pp. 14b–15a.

[186] The Bureau of Monopoly Goods was subordinate to the Court of the Imperial Treasury (*T'ai-fu ssu*). It managed the resale or exchange of commodities collected through the commercial operations that financed the privy purse; see *SS* 165, pp. 3907–8.

out even a small profit." Arguing that in order to equalize prices and stimulate trade it was necessary to emulate the ancients by suppressing the engrossers, the reformers called for the establishment of a state trade bureau (*shih-i wu*) that would make the state an active partner in commerce in the capital.[187]

The Metropolitan State Trade Bureau was established in the third month of 1072 under the direction of Lü Chia-wen, a talented young financial expert who had earned Wang An-shih's patronage – and the hand of his daughter – by informing on the antireform views of his granduncle, Lü Kung-pi (1007–73).[188] Lü was assisted by three senior managers, although actual commercial transactions were entrusted to a consortium of brokers and guild members drawn from the K'ai-feng commercial community. These brokers were authorized to use the government's funds to purchase slow-moving commodities either for themselves or for the state. In the first instance, the government used the power of credit to induce guild merchants to purchase stagnating commodities: loans were made to guild merchants (who put up collateral and formed a five-man guarantee group or *pao*) who agreed to purchase depressed commodities from traveling merchants, at a price negotiated among the merchant, guild member, and broker. The size of the loans was limited by the amount of collateral, offered at an interest rate of twenty percent per annum. Even at these terms not all goods could find a guild buyer, and in such cases the proposal authorized the state trade functionaries to purchase those commodities that might realistically be warehoused for later government sale at appropriate market prices.[189]

Because it aimed at the intersection of K'ai-feng's commercial and political elite, including (said Wang) the empress's family, the state trade measure ignited controversy from the very start.[190] Within months of its enactment, complaints that state trade functionaries harassed merchants, encroached on the sale of essential commodities, and drove up the price of such staples as sesame, hair combs, and cooking oil swamped the worried emperor. With his typical bravado, Wang blamed all the charges on engrossers, middlemen, and hangers-on who because they were disadvantaged by the new policy sought to

---

[187] *SHY* (1964) *shih-huo* 37, p. 14a.

[188] See Lü Chia-wen's biography in *SS* 355, pp. 11187–90. For his act of "family treason" (*chia-tsei*), as the Lü family called it, the *Sung shih* authors separated Chia-wen's biography from the rest of the Lüs, p. 11190.

[189] The operating principles are described in *SHY* (1964) *shih-huo* 37, pp. 15a–b, and *HCP* (1979) 231, pp. 5622–3. Wang firmly believed in authorizing merchants to manage state trade affairs, telling the emperor in the eleventh month of 1072 that "it is just because state trade matters are detailed and picayune that the bureau employs merchants to serve as its managers (*kuo-tang-kuan*)." See *HCP* (1979) 240, p. 5827.

[190] *HCP* (1979) 251, p. 6125.

reverse it through slander. To illustrate his point, Wang related the price-fixing practices of the tea merchants guild:

In the tea merchants guild (*hang*), there are more than ten engrosser firms (*chien-ping chih chia*). When traveling merchants bring tea to the capital, the engrossers first invite them to a feast where they arrange to buy their tea at a set price so low that it includes no markup; the engrossers then sell the tea to poorer members of the tea guild at double the price, out of which they take enough profit to reward [the traveling merchants as well]. Now that the state trade act is in effect, these engrosser firms have to buy tea at the same price as the poorer members of the guild, and so they slander the new law as inappropriate. I learned this from the deposition of a tea guild member, but the other guilds are all like this as well.

Wang then asked rhetorically if the purpose of the new law was to equalize wealth, or to allow treacherous engrossers to profit from and encroach on the working poor as before. "If it is to equalize profits," Wang concluded, "then those engrossers who because of the new law might lose their livelihoods are not worth pitying."[191]

Shen-tsung could not easily ignore the complaints of either his relatives or of such reform leaders as Tseng Pu, who eventually repudiated the state trade measure, and periodic doubts about the policy helped force Wang into his first retirement in the fourth month of 1074. But Shen-tsung's worries were always overcome by that fascination with the power of interest to generate revenues that he had expressed in 1070, and the emperor himself became one of the policy's biggest investors, providing massive subventions from the Inner Treasury to seed the state trade agency and help it grow.[192]

Mutual security system (pao-chia)

The mutual security system (*pao-chia*), the fourth major reform, originated in response to heightened violence and banditry in the capital and was not originally conceived of as an economic measure at all. The formal security apparatus of the Sung was clustered at the level of the prefecture, under the control of the military inspector (*hsün-chien*) with the assistance of local troops (*ping-shih*); the county, under the jurisdiction of the sheriff (*wei*) assisted by bowmen (*kung-shou*) conscripts; and the canton (*hsiang*), the largest sub-bureaucratic administrative unit, under the control of the conscripted elder (*ch'i-chang*) and his stalwart (*chuang-ting*) underlings. Below the canton level, villages formed

---

[191] *HCP* (1979) 236, p. 5738.

[192] Shen-tsung provided a subvention of 1 million strings to establish the Metropolitan State Trade Bureau in K'ai-feng, and another 2 million strings in late 1074 to help it expand its operations. See *SHY* (1964) *shih-huo* 37, p. 15b; *shih-huo* 55, p. 32b; *HCP* (1979) 257, p. 6280; and Hartwell, "The imperial treasuries," p. 69.

into a variety of voluntary defense organizations to foster local security, including the "neighborhood mutual guarantee group" (*lin-chü-hsiang-pao*) and the "local elder–stalwart township plan" (*ti-fen ch'i-chuang lin-li*).[193] Over time, these voluntary associations tended to deteriorate, opening the way for local banditry and unrest. In 1070, the K'ai-feng commissioner-general Chao Tzu-chi reported that when he had served as a civil aide in K'ai-feng residents had blamed local unrest on the collapse of the old, voluntary "*pao-chia* organization, in which rural families organized to keep watch on evil and treacherous activities, and to put a stop to banditry." At just the same time that he was formulating his service exemption plan, Chao also called for a state-sponsored resuscitation of the mutual security system, "so that the wealthy can live in peace, without fear of thieves, by grouping together with the poor for survival, while the poor can live securely on the land by relying on cooperation with the wealthy for their livelihoods."[194]

Building on Chao Tzu-chi's proposal, Wang An-shih and Tseng Pu announced in the last month of 1070 a complete set of *pao-chia* regulations for K'ai-feng and its subordinate counties. The regulations imposed a formal leadership and organizational structure over the local population: every ten (later reduced to five) households were organized into a small guard, headed by a capable landowner as the small guard chief (*pao-chang*). At the next level of organization, every five small guard units formed a large guard (*ta-pao*), headed by the most capable and wealthiest landowner as large guard chief (*ta-pao-chang*). Finally, every five large guard units formed one superior guard (*tu-pao*), headed by two influential landowners as superior guard leader (*pao-cheng*) and assistant leader (*fu pao-cheng*). The rank and file were drawn from the remaining families, irrespective of wealth: all master or guest (landlord or tenant) families with two mature males or more could be called upon to supply a guardsman (*pao-ting*), and all other families were regarded as "auxiliaries to the local guards" (*chiu-chin fu-pao*). Both guardsmen and auxiliaries were allowed to train with bows and arrows and any nonproscribed weapons. In contrast to the older system recalled by Chao Tzu-chi, participation in the new mutual security apparatus was compulsory. County officials in the capital supervised the formation of guard units, and in order to ensure compliance and population control each unit had to erect a tablet listing all its members, by household, individual, and designated guardsmen, and to report all families moving into or out of its territory. The responsibilities of the guard

---

[193] The clearest discussion of the *pao-chia* system during the Sung is still Sogabe Shizuo, "Ō Anseki no hokōhō," in *Sōdai seikeishi no kenkyū*, Sogabe Shizuo (Tokyo, 1974), pp. 1–63, which can be usefully supplemented by McKnight, *Village and bureaucracy*.
[194] *HCP* (1979) 218, pp. 5298–9.

units were all connected with security and social control, and included nightly patrols; pursuit of thieves; and informing on bandits, murderers, arsonists, rapists, practitioners of unorthodox religious cults, and anyone who might harbor such evildoers.[195]

As the authors of the *Sung shih* emphasize, the initial *pao-chia* proposal was concerned entirely with banditry and social control; it had no links to larger military objectives, and was under the control of the *Ssu-nung ssu* rather than the Bureau of Military Affairs.[196] Moreover, geographic expansion of the mutual security system was quite slow: it was over a year before the *pao-chia* regulations were extended to six prefectures surrounding the capital, in the seventh month of 1072; and they were only made universal in the eighth month of 1073.[197] By that time, however, Wang An-shih had begun to push the mutual security measure toward his ultimate goal – replacing the regular mercenary army. From the very beginning Wang had envisioned *pao-chia* as the cornerstone of his plan to rejuvenate the Sung military, by replacing the mercenaries (*mu-ping*) on whom the dynasty had come to rely with a people's army (*min-ping*) drawn from the peasantry. Wang had only contempt for the hirelings who made up the backbone of the Sung army, whom he derided as shiftless and unruly riffraff "who cannot even see to their own safety." Peasants, in contrast, Wang glorified as "simple, strong and single-minded men who know how to obey commands. From this perspective it is clear that in a crisis, there is nothing so useful as a people's army."[198]

Beyond the strategic effectiveness of militarizing the peasantry, Wang was also convinced that it was the irreducible foundation of fiscal solvency. In contrast to his typical belief in expanding government spending as a way to stimulate the economy, Wang felt that military costs had to be cut sharply by replacing hired mercenaries with the kind of people's army that the militarists of the Five Dynasties had used so effectively: "If we are unable to reform our

---

[195] *HCP* (1979) 218, pp. 5297–8. By 1075 five households, including tenants (*k'e-hu*), had become standard for the small guard, yielding household ratios of 5 (small guard):25 (large guard):250 (superior guard). See *HCP* (1979) 267, p. 6553.

[196] *SS* 192, p. 4768.

[197] *HCP* (1979) 235, pp. 5710–11; 246, pp. 5999–6000. The spread of *pao-chia* often induced panic among the citizenry. In the seventh month of 1072 the *Ssu-nung ssu* reported that people outside K'ai-feng's Feng-ch'iu county were shaking down potential *pao-ting* conscripts who had not yet registered, and Shen-tsung worried that the panic might spread to the newly targeted prefectures. Wang as usual dismissed the emperor's fears, blaming the problem on criminals who had already been driven to outlying counties by the *pao-chia* system; now that these counties too were being organized – thus threatening their criminal livelihoods – the hoodlums had taken to shaking down potential *pao-ting* conscripts. On the whole, Wang assured the emperor, *pao-chia* registration had gone quite smoothly, and out of hundreds of thousands of families registered in K'ai-feng's seventeen counties only twenty or so individuals had come to the capital to complain.

[198] *HCP* (1979) 236, p. 5743.

army so that it is more like their system [of peasant soldiers] then there will be no hope of enriching and strengthening the Middle Kingdom."[199] In Wang's view, *pao-chia* was the key to creating a peasant-based army that would cost only ten or twenty percent of the current mercenary system.[200]

As it happened, the principal economic benefit of the *pao-chia* system was an unintended consequence of militarization, for by tightening up the *pao-chia* organization to enhance its military readiness, the reformers created a command structure that could take over the very functions the state now paid for through the hired service policy. The consummation of this latent opportunity had to await the transformation of the service exemption fees into an outright source of unencumbered funds, which is discussed in greater detail later. Here we will survey the two paths Wang took to militarize the mutual security apparatus: the system of detached service (*shang-fan*), which rotated *pao-chia* guardsmen into paramilitary service under the prefectural military inspector or county sheriff, and the system of military drill and review (*chiao-yüeh*), which trained *pao-chia* members for service as a form of national guard, or for absorption into the regular military.

In early 1071, even as he sought to calm Shen-tsung's worries about reports that some K'ai-feng residents had mutilated themselves to avoid *pao-chia* duty, Wang expressed his ultimate hope of rotating *pao-chia* troops into active service under the prefectural military inspectors (*hsün-chien*) and eventually mixing them into the national army.[201] A year later the first part of Wang's hope had crystallized in the detached service system, which was enacted in K'ai-feng in the seventh month of 1072. The detached service system appended the local *pao-chia* structure to the prefectural military inspector: property-owning (*chu-hu*) guardsmen who volunteered to serve under the military inspectors were organized into squads of fifty guardsmen and placed under a rotating command of two large guard chiefs (*ta-pao-chang*) and one superior or deputy superior guard leader (*tu-fu pao-cheng*).[202] Guardsman volunteers received monthly compensation in grain and "sustenance cash" (*hsin-ts'ai ch'ien*), in return for

---

[199] Ma, *Wen-hsien t'ung-k'ao* (1965) 153, p. 1334a.

[200] Ma, *Wen-hsien t'ung-k'ao* (1965) 153, p. 1335c; *HCP* (1986) *shih-pu* 5, pp. 22b–23a.

[201] *HCP* (1979) 221, pp. 5380–1; 5391–2. Likening laws to medicine – "without some dizziness there cannot be a cure" – Wang reluctantly agreed that there might be a few cases of self-mutilation, but he blamed them on rumors that *pao-chia* participants would be tattooed and impressed into militia service along the northern border. His solution was to offer rewards to those who informed on rumormongerers.

[202] For the regulations, see *HCP* (1979) 235, pp. 5697–9. After Wang An-shih first outlined the measure in the fifth month of 1072, the court apparently experimented with a more stringent set of controls that included tattooing of participants and month-long terms of active duty; see *HCP* (1979) 233, pp. 5650–1. By the seventh month of 1072 Wang An-shih argued for abolition of the tattoos and a reduction in the term of service in order to make the policy more attractive. Wang Tseng-yü discusses both the *shang-fan* and *chiao-yüeh* policies in his *Sung-ch'ao ping-chih ch'u-t'an*, pp. 122–6.

which they served detached service rotations of ten days duration. Off-duty guardsmen who participated in bandit sweeps were also eligible for fees, and received time off their next detached service terms. While on detached service guardsmen received three *sheng* of rice and between 10 and 80 cash per diem. Payments for supervisors were far more generous: 3,000 cash per term for the large guard chiefs, and 7,000 cash for the superior guard leaders and assistant leaders.[203] All volunteers for detached service were obliged to undergo military training, and those guardsmen who achieved the top three (of eight) levels of skill were eligible for grants of between three and fifteen piculs (*tan*) of relief grain in times of dearth. In addition to their training in the martial arts, while on duty the civilian guardsmen and their large guard and superior guard supervisors were all subject to a strict schedule of military discipline that put them directly under the command of the military inspectors and mandated corporal punishments for any acts of insubordination.[204]

Financial considerations certainly entered into Wang's promotion of the detached service plan. In preliminary discussions of the measure, Wang estimated that by replacing six thousand local troops permanently attached to the military inspectors in the K'ai-feng region with one hundred thousand guardsmen (*pao-ting*) on ten-day terms of detached service, the court could save one hundred thousand strings of cash annually.[205] Wang even hoped to use *pao-chia* to cut the costs of the labor service system, by assigning *pao-chia* units to the county sheriff to replace the bowmen, only recently put on salary by the service exemption reforms.[206] But Wang also hoped that the combination of cash incentives, grain, tax exemptions, and relief-grain credits built into the system would heighten the military readiness of the entire population, by driving the populace to "compete toward greater levels of military skill, so that they will not even have to go on detached service to learn satisfactorily. . . . In a few years time not only will the *pao-chia* guardsmen exceed the skills of righteous brave militia, they will even surpass the regular troops . . . who are not driven in their

---

[203] Compensation for supervisors is stated explicitly in *HCP* (1979) 235, p. 5699. Wang An-shih estimated that guardsmen would be paid 80 cash a day for a ten-day rotation, but in 1084, Fan Ch'ün-ts'ui reported that under the "old regulations" – presumably those of 1072 – guardsmen received only 10 cash per day. See *HCP* (1979) 233, p. 5651, and *HCP* (1979) 343, pp. 8235–6.

[204] *HCP* (1979) 237, pp. 5769–70. As the system spread, terms of detached service came to vary by place and season, with ten days to half a month being standard; see Wang, *Sung-ch'ao ping-chih ch'u-t'an*, p. 123.

[205] *HCP* (1979) 233, p. 5651. The annual compensation bill for the six thousand military inspectorate troops (*hsün-chien ping-chi*) came to 180,000 strings. If an apparent textual corruption is disregarded, Wang An-shih's figures work out to a cost of 30 strings per soldier per year (or 82.19 cash per diem), as opposed to 800 cash per rotation (or 80 cash per diem) for each guardsman. It should be noted that as of 1076, K'ai-feng had only 73,718 men on active *pao-chia* duty. See *SHY* (1964) *ping* 2, pp. 12b–15a.

[206] *HCP* (1979) 235, p. 5697.

hearts like the guardsmen." Tseng Pu added that the tax and cash incentives would induce commoners to use their leisure time to practice martial arts: "without exhortation everyone will compete to improve their skills, and soon no one, including the bandit gangs in the capital, will be able to withstand [the guardsmen on detached service]."[207]

Wang and Tseng Pu had enormous confidence in the new system, for they immediately ordered military inspectors to replace all but a handful of the *hsiang-chün* prefectural troops necessary for corvée duty with *pao-chia* men. Four months later, the eleventh month of 1072, the system was extended to county sheriffs as well.[208] By the eighth month of 1073 *pao-chia* guardsmen had replaced one-third of the assorted troops under the control of the military inspectors in K'ai-feng and were deployed as supplements to the bowmen assigned to the county sheriffs. Though somewhat slower to take root in the north, where the emphasis was on military drill rather than bandit control, by mid-1075 the detached service system was enacted throughout the empire.[209]

The detached service system represented the court's attempt to pare administrative costs by shaping *pao-chia* into the primary mechanism for social control at the county and prefectural levels. In K'ai-feng and the five circuits of the north, the reformers also pushed for outright militarization of the *pao-chia* system, through the institution of a military "drill and review" (*chiao-yüeh*) program. Like detached service, the new program, when it was first tried out in K'ai-feng in the ninth month of 1071, was described as purely voluntary, driven by an incentive system. During the slack season guardsmen (*pao-ting*) could undergo testing in archery, horsemanship, and foot-soldiery, with rewards that included imperial review and an official post for the most accomplished, and two thousand cash and one month's corvée exemption for the second rank. The government made a special effort to bring superior guard leaders and assistant leaders – by law the wealthiest and most able members of their communities – into the procedure: even leaders with no particular military skills could be "benevolenced" (*en-shih*) into the highest grade if their guardsmen showed particular zeal in training, or if the level of bandit activity in their guard unit was low.[210] By the eighth month of 1073 drill and review had become standard in the five northern circuits of Ho-pei East, Ho-pei West, Ho-tung, and the two subcircuits of Shan-hsi as well, making it a fixture of rural life at the capital and throughout the entire region of north China that bordered the Liao and the Tanguts.[211]

[207] *HCP* (1979) 235, p. 5698.
[208] *HCP* (1979) 237, p. 5669.
[209] *HCP* (1979) 246, pp. 5999–6000; *SHY* (1964) *ping* 2, p. 10a.
[210] *HCP* (1979) 226, p. 5516. See also *SS* 192, p. 4768.
[211] *HCP* (1979) 246, pp. 5999–6000.

Two years later, in 1075, the pace of militarization was heightened when control over *pao-chia* was transferred from the Court of Agricultural Supervision to the Bureau of Military Affairs.[212] That same year the size of *pao-chia* units in K'ai-feng and north China was halved to tighten the density of control, guest households with two adult males were made full rather than auxiliary members of a regular unit, and *pao-chia* drill and review procedures were standardized and merged with those of the *i-yung* (righteous brave) militia.[213] Then in mid-1076 the court sought to transform the *pao-chia* organization into tight tactical fighting units in the event of war, by superimposing over the large guard units a new "squad structure" (*tui-fa*), developed only two years earlier for troops on the Sino-Tangut border.[214] But no complex tactical reorganization could be undertaken without intensifying the drill and review procedures for guardsmen and their leaders, and in the eleventh month of 1079 the drill program was put under higher-order supervision with the designation of intendants for military drill and review (*t'i-chü chiao-yüeh-shih*) for K'ai-feng and for each of the five circuits of north China.[215] The new drill regimen brought the *pao-chia* organization into direct contact with the regular military: drill chiefs (*chiao-t'ou*) drawn from the imperial troops and military servitors (*shih-ch'en*) were assigned to train the large guard chiefs (*ta-pao-chang*) in archery, crossbows, and horsemanship, who in turn divided their local *pao-chia* guardsman into drill "teams" (*t'uan*). This "team drill measure" (*t'uan chiao-fa*) not only buttressed the power of the already wealthy and influential men who stood at the top of the *pao-chia* hierarchy but also made participation in military drill and review virtually compulsory for *pao-chia* men in K'ai-feng and north China.[216]

---

[212] *SS* 192, p. 4770.

[213] *HCP* (1979) 267, p. 6553; *SHY* (1964) *ping* 2, p. 10a. *I-yung* militiamen, conscripted from among the peasantry of Ho-pei, Ho-tung, and Shan-hsi, were tattooed on the hand and obliged to undergo military drill in the off-season. In 1081 the *i-yung* militia were absorbed into the *pao-chia* system. See Ma, *Wen-hsien t'ung-k'ao* (1965) 153, p. 1335; SHY, *ping* 2, pp. 17a–23b. For the impact of drill and review reforms on the provincial armies, see Koiwai Hiromitsu, *Sōdai heiseishi no kenkyū* (Tokyo, 1998), pp. 171–201.

[214] *SHY* (1964) *ping* 2, pp. 11a–b; *HCP* (1979) 275, p. 6723. See Sogabe, "Ō Anseki no hokōhō," p. 14; on the new "squad structure," see Wang, *Sung-ch'ao ping-chih ch'u-t'an*, p. 108.

[215] *HCP* (1979) 301, pp. 7324–5; *SS* 192, p. 5770.

[216] *SS* 192, pp. 4770–1; Sogabe, "Ō Anseki no hokōhō," p. 23. In 1084, Fan Ch'un-jen reported that in Ho-chung fu, in eastern Shan-hsi (Yung-hsing-chün circuit), not only were drills and inspections conducted during the summer agricultural season but "no one not old or weak was allowed to remain at home." Fan added that "these days most relatively healthy peasants must serve as guardsmen and drill for five days. When the travel time [to the drill site] is included, it can be seen how this seriously interferes with the harvest." See *HCP* (1979) 345, pp. 8289–90. Fan exaggerates somewhat: as of 1083, Yung-hsing-chün circuit had 155,536 men in the *pao-chia* system, of whom 103,865 were guardsmen. This equals roughly one *pao-chia* member for every 5.4 households (at a total population of 836,759 households) – close to the statutory number – and one guardsman for every eight households. See *HCP* (1979) 337, pp. 8121–4.

How deeply did the *pao-chia* system reach into local Chinese society? According to the statistical portrait of the *pao-chia* system preserved in the *Essential regulations of the Sung* (*Sung hui-yao*), as of 1076 there were 6.9 million men on the active *pao-chia* rosters. If we assume that no family supplied more than one *pao-chia* member, then almost half (46 percent) of the empire's fifteen million households supplied an active *pao-chia* member overall. Of course, there was great regional variation in *pao-chia* participation, as is shown in table 5. Excluding Kuang-nan West, it may appear as though the capital of K'ai-feng and the five circuits of north China were the least affected by the *pao-chia* system, which drew only 25.7 to 31.3 percent of the northern population. But more significant than total membership is the percentage of members involved in formal drill and review: virtually all *pao-chia* conscripts in north China and the capital were subject to military drill. Elsewhere the total numbers of households in *pao-chia* were much higher: 70 percent of the populations of Ching-hsi and Huai-nan were organized in *pao-chia*, probably reflecting the high incidence of banditry south and west of the capital; and in the rest of China some 45 percent of the population was enfolded into the *pao-chia* system. But outside of K'ai-feng and north China none of the population was put under drill and review, suggesting that whereas the goal in the north was tilted toward military preparedness, in the south it was social control. Moreover, as the reformers became ever more obsessed with generating new revenues, the huge organizational capacity of the *pao-chia* system could be used to help squeeze out financial surpluses as well, as we will see.

FROM ECONOMIC REDISTRIBUTION TO REVENUE EXTRACTION

Rural credit

In a policy-making environment dominated by the quest for funds to finance new state initiatives and the emperor's northern campaigns, the redistributionist rationale that justified the new economic policies was soon sacrificed to the need for revenues. The green sprouts policy was the first measure to succumb to the hunger for revenues, despite the government's explicit disavowal of a fiscal interest in the loan fund. In the eyes of critics of the policy, fiscalization was signaled by the imposition of interest charges on the green sprouts loans. No provisions were made for interest charges in the original directive of the ninth month of 1069, but within a few months rates of twenty to thirty percent annually were imposed in order to finance the plan.[217] Critics such as Han Ch'i, Ou-yang Hsiu, and Ssu-ma Kuang denounced the unseemliness

---

[217] *SHY* (1964) *shih-huo* 4, p. 19a; *CPPM* 68, pp. 2164–9.

Table 5. *Percentage of the population in active* pao-chia *service, 1076*

Circuit	Pop. in 1080, hu[a]	Total pao-chia in 1076, individuals[b]	Total drill/review (chiao-yüeh)	Percentage in pao-chia	Percentage in drill/ review
Ho-pei E. & W.	984,195	252,647	200,568	25.7	20.4
Shan-hsi (Yung-hsing & Ch'in-feng)	962,318	272,253	184,419	28.3	19.2
Kuang-nan W.	242,109	69,994		28.9	
Ho-tung E. & W.	450,869	135,638	115,196	30.1	25.5
Capital Region (K'ai-feng)	235,599	73,718	70,642	31.3	30.0
K'uei-chou	246,521	91,172		37.0	
Kuang-nan E.	565,534	213,780		37.8	
Li-chou	301,991	115,382		38.2	
Cheng-tu Fu	771,533	310,512		40.2	
Liang-che	1,830,096	810,770		44.3	
Tzu-chou	478,171	219,355		45.9	
Ching-tung	1,370,800	629,993		46.0	
Fu-chien	992,087	487,507		49.1	
Chiang-nan W.	1,365,533	674,806		49.4	
Chiang-nan E.	1,073,760	568,813		53.0	
Ching-hu Nan	811,057	443,161		54.6	
Ching-hu Pei	589,302	344,052		58.4	
Huai-nan	1,079,054	751,356		69.6	
Ching-hsi	651,742	467,535		71.7	
Total	15,002,271	6,932,444	570,825		

[a] Pi Chung-yen, *Chung-shu tui-pei* in Ma, *Wen-hsien t'ung-k'ao* (1965) 11, pp. 114–16, supplemented by Wang Ts'un, *Yüan-feng chiu-yü-chih* (1089; Peking, 1984), pp. 2, 320–34, 363–74 for figures in italics.

[b] Pao-chia figures for 1076, from *SHY* (1964) *ping* 2, pp. 12b–15a, tabulated by Sogabe, "Ō Anseki no hokōhō," pp. 17–20.

of government usury, and predicted that the collection of interest fees would soon supersede rural credit relief as the primary operations goal of the farming loan policy. Wang countered that although charging interest on the government loans was by no means ideal, the practice, which was sanctioned by the canonical *Chou-li*, was the only way to keep the loan fund solvent.[218]

But Wang's critics were right in that the imposition of interest charges opened the door to government profit seeking, for maximizing the revenue potential of the loan fund soon became the first priority of the green sprouts

[218] *HCP* (1986) *shih-pu* 7, pp. 24a–29b, for the debate on interest rates, drawn primarily from Han Ch'i's *Chia-chuan*. For Wang An-shih's argument, see "Ta Tseng Kung-li shu," in Wang, *Wang Lin-ch'uan ch'üan-chi* 73, p. 464.

measure. In evaluating the performance of officials connected with the green
sprouts measure, from the Ever-normal Granary intendants down to the local
officials who actually transacted the loans, much greater emphasis was placed
on meeting the quotas for loan distribution and collection than on effective
administration of the disaster-relief operation. As Ou-yang Hsiu pointed out
in mid-1070, despite government pronouncements against forced loans (*i-
p'ei*), officials up and down the chain of command knew that they would be
penalized if funds went undistributed or loans uncollected.[219]

This pressure to maximize financial returns to the loan fund inevitably
prompted officials to make as many loans as possible, which led to a predictable
array of abuses, including (in the eyes of opponents) the seduction of poor
peasants into an escalating cycle of debt and extravagance.[220] But it was just
these poor peasants who were least able to repay their loans, making both them
and their guarantors subject to confiscation first of their collateral, and then
of their immovable property. These properties could be sold by the state, and
as of 1071 the returns from these debt sales were funneled back into the rural
loan fund, where it could generate more revenue.[221] Indeed, it was this seizure
and sale of property from the very segment of the population that the loan
policy was intended to aid that underscored the conflict between the social and
fiscal objectives of the green sprouts measure. To balance these competing aims
the government attempted to create a consistent policy on payment deferrals
(*i-ko*), but through the very end of the New Policies, Ever-normal Granary
officials were caught between the court's reluctance to press poor peasants too
hard and its insistence that repayments not fall below quota.[222]

Ultimately, the most effective way to maximize green sprouts revenues
without undermining the poor peasantry was to disregard the targeted beneficiaries of the measure and make loans to anyone who could be counted on to
repay them. Consequently, in early 1070 the Finance Planning Commission
pegged loan limits to the household grading system, and extended eligibility
to virtually all residential (as opposed to itinerant, *fou-lang*) families. The new
order entitled grade 5 and guest households to 1,500 cash; grade 4 to 3,000
cash; grade 3 to 6,000 cash; grade 2 to 10,000 cash; and the highest grade,

---

[219] See, for example, *HCP* (1979) 211, p. 5133.

[220] Su Shih's retrospective denunciation of the green sprouts loans is typical of the conservative efforts to
extol the natural, demonetized economy: "Peasant households balance expenditures against income,
and economize in clothing and food, so that even if they are poor they still meet their basic needs.
But when the peasants get more money than they need their expenses naturally increase, and there is
nothing they will not do to get more money still." See *HCP* (1979) 384, p. 9360.

[221] *HCP* (1979) 228, p. 5547. See also *HCP* (1979) 279, p. 6845; *HCP* (1979) 294, p. 7170.

[222] *SHY* (1964) *shih-huo* 4, p. 16b. For further discussion, see Smith, "State power and economic activism
during the New Policies."

grade 1, to 15,000 cash. The order then added that "if there are remaining funds, county officials are authorized to assess the situation and offer additional loans to households of grade three and above; if there are still surpluses, then interested households from the urban wards and suburbs with property and businesses to offer as collateral will be allowed to form into five-family guarantee groups and obtain loans under the green sprouts statutes."[223]

This extension of loans to anyone who could pay immediately inflamed opponents of the green sprouts measure. In his plea of the second month of 1070 to abolish the policy, Ssu-ma Kuang predicted that the new ruling would encourage administrators to force loans on the rich:

Now county officials are issued interest funds to lend to the people in spring and fall. None of the wealthy people want the loans, but the poor people do. Because administrators want to distribute loans on a wide scale in order to accumulate official merit, they just force loans on the people according to their household grade, without inquiring into their actual circumstances. The wealthy are assigned relatively large loans, the poor somewhat smaller. Large loans go up to fifteen strings, small ones not less than 1,000 cash. Prefectural and county officials and clerks fear getting stuck with the responsibility of absconders and defaulters, so they order the poor and rich to array themselves together in *pao-chia* guarantee groups. The wealthy are made the chiefs (*k'uei-shou*), the poor obtain money, and in no time at all the money is gone. In the future if the millet or wheat harvests are inadequate, the people will not even be able to pay their twice yearly tax, let alone the interest payments. Since they cannot repay, the fears of the clerks will be spread to all four quarters and, inescapably, the wealthy will have to repay the accumulated debts of the many households.[224]

At the same time, Han Ch'i embarrassed the reformers by insisting that by making loans available to everyone, the court was providing public monies to the same group – the engrossers – that the green sprouts measure was intended to suppress:

It is the rural households of grade three and above and the propertied urban and suburban households that have heretofore been the "engrossing families." Now they are all given loans and charged 1,300 cash for every 1,000. The government is simply chasing after interest payments. This measure absolutely contradicts the stated intent of the policy to suppress engrossers and aid those in need.[225]

[223] *SHY* (1964) *shih-huo* 4, p. 19a.

[224] "Ch'i pa t'iao-li-ssu ch'ang-p'ing-shih shu," in Ssu-ma, *Ssu-ma Wen-cheng kung ch'uan-chia chi* 44, p. 560. Ssu-ma Kuang then goes on to outline a scenario for disaster in which the poor will be exhausted, the rich made poor, and the state forced to forgo its revenues through widespread payment deferrals. "And once the wealthy are completely exhausted, if the nation (*kuo-chia*) should have the misfortune of a border emergency, and have to raise many troops, then from whom will the monies for grain, cloth, and military provisions be raised?"

[225] *SHY* (1964) *shih-huo* 4, p. 19b.

Wang An-shih tried to downplay the ideological contradiction, countering that even wealthy families could encounter hard times and be forced into ruin by private lenders. "How can they all be 'engrosser families'?" Wang asked, insisting that lending them surplus funds was exactly what was meant by repressing engrossers.[226] But Han Ch'i utterly rejected Wang's response, contending that "everyone under Heaven" knows that these wealthy rural, urban, and suburban families are engrossers. "The only reason the Finance Planning Commission denies that they are engrossing households is because they want to push even more green sprouts funds on them in order to generate still more interest."[227]

The government's effort to wring as much money as possible out of the rural credit measure also threatened to undermine a basic function of the Ever-normal Granary system, disaster relief. Critics drew the emperor's attention to granary officials who withheld relief grain from the hungry poor in order to build up the size of the loan fund. In 1074, Shen-tsung complained that although loan revenues were substantial, over seventy percent of the total Ever-normal Granary reserves in cash and grain had been distributed as loans, at a time when widespread drought and famine made adequate relief grain essential. From this point on, the granaries were ordered to hold half their resources in reserve.[228]

In the end, however, all Shen-tsung's doubts about the rural credit program were overwhelmed by its revenue potential. For example, when in 1074 Shen-tsung worried that local loan officials might be violating the laws, Wang An-shih recommended creating five hundred new county-level recorder's posts to keep the loan accounts. Any anxiety Shen-tsung had about the additional expense evaporated when Wang An-shih assured him that by spending 100,000 strings of cash to hire five hundred new recorders, the court could protect its annual profits of 3 million strings of cash from the loans.[229] From 1071 to 1085 the green sprouts loan fund was paired with the service exemption fees as the chief source of money for reform projects, including flood and famine relief, irrigation works, and border provisioning and defense; and in 1082, two years after Shen-tsung built the Yüan-feng Treasury (*Yüan-feng k'u*) to hold the growing New Policies bounty, 8 million strings in surplus farming loan funds from around the country were deposited in its vaults.[230] Overall, the farming loan system operated under a minimum quota of 13.9 million

[226] *SHY* (1964) *shih-huo* 4, p. 23a.

[227] *SHY* (1964) *shih-huo* 4, p. 27b; *HCP* (1986) *shih-pu* 7, pp. 26a–27b.

[228] *HCP* (1979) 256, p. 6263; 272, pp. 6663–4.

[229] *HCP* (1979) 250, p. 6095.

[230] *HCP* (1979) 330, pp. 7958–9. The *HCP* contains extensive material on farming loan subventions to other agencies.

strings collected on loans of 11 million strings, for a net-profit quota of 26.5 percent. Individual officials were in turn judged for promotion or demotion primarily (though not exclusively) on the basis of their success in meeting local loan targets, which were not abolished until 1086.[231] Although social welfare ideals could not be ignored in an agency ostensibly dedicated to agrarian relief, it is clear that for the duration of the New Policies making money became the chief objective of the farming loans measure, and economic welfare was delegated to a secondary role.

Hired service and pao-chia

Because of philosophical antipathy to state usury, the green sprouts measure encountered immediate and strident opposition from officials at court and in the field, but was welcomed by a populace hungry for new sources of cash. The hired service measure met less strident opposition from acting officials, many of whom supported its basic goals; instead, it provoked an immediate reaction from politically aware and well-connected sectors of the public, who saw the service exemption fees as nothing more than a new and obnoxious tax. The first outpouring of discontent took place in Liang-che circuit in the fourth month of 1071, when local residents learned that two circuit administrators had been recommended for promotion for proposing an exemption-fee quota that was twice what the services would actually cost. Their outrage was seized on by Vice–censor in chief Yang Hui as evidence that revenue gathering (chü-lien, or "fiscalism") had already begun to supplant tax equitability as the main goal of the measure. Shen-tsung initially added the imperial voice to Yang Hui's concerns, but his anxiety gave way to anger when Wang An-shih gave the incident a more insidious spin: for Wang, the episode just proved that even though they had not yet been greatly harmed by the measure, the "engrossers" were powerful enough to manipulate the opinions of the scholarly elite (shih-ta-fu), and even to confuse the emperor with their babble.[232]

A second incident of public protest against the hired service measure was harder for Wang An-shih to gloss over. In the fifth month of 1071, eleven hundred residents of K'ai-feng's Tung-ming county marched on the prefectural yamen to complain that their household grades had been arbitrarily

---

[231] *HCP* (1979) 226, p. 5506; for the memorial by Ssu-ma Kuang that heralded the suspension of the green sprouts measure, see *HCP* (1979) 368, pp. 8875–8.

[232] *HCP* (1979) 223, pp. 5421, 5433–4. Liang-che residents reacted against a reform initiative more publicly in early 1073, when two hundred residents of Su-chou confronted the waterworks intendant Chia Tan, leading to his dismissal. See Lin Hsi's report in *HCP* (1979) 240, pp. 5824–5, excerpted and analyzed in Mihelich, "Polders and the politics of land reclamation," pp. 96–101.

raised in order to increase their service assistance fees. Whipped into a fury
by the yamen's refusal to hear their case, the crowd converged on Wang
An-shih's residence to vent their anger. Though Wang succeeded in driving them away he was emotionally shaken by the incident, which he tried to
portray as a provocation incited by the Tung-ming county magistrate, Ku Fan.
Ku Fan was ultimately impeached, but not before the censors Yang Hui and
Liu Chih denounced the transformation of the service exemption fees into a
new layer of taxes on the entire population, including the lowest classes explicitly excluded by the original order. For Liu Chih in particular, the Tung-ming
affair illustrated the inevitable consequence of "activist statecraft" (ta yu-wei
chih pi): that "the petty men who actually administer the policies will devote
themselves to raising revenues in order to earn rewards, thereby transforming
the best-intentioned of measures into outright fiscalism."[233]

Although the attack by Yang Hui and Liu Chih embarrassed the reformers
into reiterating the prohibition against manipulation of the household registration process, Wang and Tseng Pu launched a counterattack that drove Yang and
Liu to lesser posts outside the capital.[234] Their ouster marked the end of pointed
censorial opposition to the reforms and enabled Wang to extend the hired service measure to the entire nation in the tenth month of 1071.[235] Between 1071
and Wang's resignation in 1076, the hired service policy was transformed from
a progressive attempt to professionalize county- and prefectural-level service
and equalize the financial burden it imposed on middle- and upper-grade
households, to a regressive cluster of fees and surcharges imposed on the entire
population in order to swell revenues.

The first great departure from the original progressive, egalitarian rhetoric
of the hired service policy came with the extension of service exemption fees to
the poorest property-owning peasants, those ranked grades 4 and 5. Initially,
fees were collected only from those households that were directly liable for
government service – the service exemption fee (mien-i ch'ien) – or those households that possessed adequate resources but were exempt from service because
of privilege – the service assistance fee (chu-i ch'ien) charged to officials, widows,
and urban dwellers. Although rural households of grades 4 and 5 were still
liable for conscription as local patrolmen, or "stalwarts" (chuang-ting), by the

---

[233] HCP (1979) 224, pp. 5442–3. See also HCP (1979) 223, pp. 5425–30; 224, pp. 5439–40, 5444–8;
225, pp. 5479–88.

[234] As a parting shot, Liu Chih denounced Wang An-shih and his followers for "summoning to government
every proponent of 'finance,' including merchants, tradesmen, and butchers, and employing every
possible way of making money, including selling calendars on the streets." See HCP (1979) 225, p.
5484. For Tseng Pu's detailed rebuttal of the two censors' charges, see HCP (1979) 225, pp. 5469–74;
also in SHY (1964) shih-huo 65, pp. 8b–11a.

[235] HCP (1979) 227, p. 5521.

terms of the original statutes of the hired service policy they were exempt from paying any fees.[236] By the time the measure was universally enacted, however, the imposition of service exemption fees of between 200 and 1,000 cash on grade 4 and grade 5 households had become routine.[237]

In 1072, Shen-tsung asked that grade 5 families be exempted, but demurred when Wang An-shih pointed out the fiscal utility of those fees:

Although families in grade five do not pay very much, in Liang-che circuit we have collected 40,000 strings of cash despite exempting the lower half of the grade five category. If there are poor harvests in Liang-che, this money might be enough to assist the hard-working peasants by hiring them for water-control projects or to replace ponds and drainage ditches. As long as your majesty does not use this money frivolously, then it is not cruel to collect it.[238]

Although collecting fees from poor households to fund local relief programs may not have been cruel, it certainly did not meet the original goals of the service exemption measure. And observers inside and outside the reform administration agreed that however insignificant, the new fees placed an unwarranted burden on the poorest households. The size of the cash fee varied from place to place, but even the smallest sum could be a burden. In Liang-che circuit as of 1073, the roughly one million grade 5 households (out of a total population of 1.8 million households) paid an average of fifty to sixty cash in service fees per family, for services they themselves were not liable to perform.[239] Although fifty cash might seem insignificant, Chang Fang-p'ing asserted that in Honan's Ying-t'ien-fu (Ching-tung West) fifty cash might be all the money a peasant family saw in a year.[240] And in Kuang-nan West, the Ever-normal Granary Intendant Liu I reported in 1082 that even a service exemption fee of five or eight cash could be ruinous, since it forced timid and isolated peasants to come up with cash and then, at the height of the growing season, travel to the yamen to pay.[241] Finally, though in less rustic places the yamen officials came to the peasants, for the poor peasants of Hang-chou, as Su Shih points out, this was not necessarily any cheaper:

[Prior to the service exemption measure] families of grade 4 and below were not liable for government service at the county and prefectural level, but merely served as stalwart men.... Once the measure was established, however, they all had to pay service fees. Although the fees were not great, even the poorest people had to come up with 300 to

---

[236] SHY (1964) shih-huo 65, pp. 4b–5a; on extension of fees to lower households, see Sudō, "Ō Anseki no boyakusen chōshū no sho mondai," pp. 241–56.
[237] HCP (1979) 227, pp. 5526–7.
[238] HCP (1979) 237, p. 5779.
[239] HCP (1979) 248, p. 6055.
[240] HCP (1979) 277, p. 6789.
[241] HCP (1979) 324, pp. 7797–8.

500 cash for no reason. Before they were even ready the clerks and soldiers would be at their doors, and it would take 100 cash just to avert disaster; even before they had paid the government, the cost was heavy.[242]

Even as service exemption fees were being extended to all property owners, a second assault on the progessivity of the hired service measure was in the offing: the introduction of new surcharges. When service exemption quotas were first being estimated for the entire country, in late 1071, officials were ordered to add a percentage to the anticipated annual wage bill for each locale, to serve as an emergency fund to offset arrearages caused by famine or drought. This additional charge, called the "surplus emergency fee" (k'uan-sheng ch'ien), was calculated as an increase in the total fee quota assessed each locale, which was then distributed among all the households based on their grade and status as rural or urban.[243] Officials were initially instructed to allow 10 percent for the emergency fund, but the first set of quotas (in turn the basis for individual assessments) was considerably higher: out of a total quota of 12,343,670 strings of cash, 9,258,585 strings were earmarked for distribution, and 3,085,022 designated as surplus. By this reckoning, the "surplus" emergency fund constituted 33.3 percent of the wage bill, or 24.9 percent of the total collection quota. Moreover, in many circuits the percentage of total collections set aside as "surplus" – to take the second approach – was considerably higher: Ching-tung East and Ching-tung West stood at 39.1 and 38.3 percent respectively, and Ho-tung and Ching-hu South circuits were at 42.1 percent and 44.8 percent.[244]

In 1074 service exemption fees were raised further with the addition of a new surtax, the t'ou-tzu head surtax of 5 cash per 1,000 levied on all mien-i payments. This new fee was meant to pay for those local services, such as maintenance of official buildings, porterage, and the provision of implements,

---

[242] HCP (1979) 435, p. 10480, cited in Sudō, "Ō Anseki no boyakusen chōshū no sho mondai," p. 244.

[243] SHY (1964) shih-huo 65, p. 12b; SS 177, p. 4300; for discussion, see Sudō, "Ō Anseki no boyakusen chōshū no sho mondai," pp. 203–22.

[244] The figures come from the Chung-shu tui-pei enumeration of returns to the green sprouts, service exemption, and winery and ferry installation funds for 1076, as preserved in the Yung-lo ta-tien entry for ts'ang (granaries), 7507, pp. 3357–66. For the service exemption funds, the Chung-shu tui-pei first gives each circuit's quota for receipts, expenditures, and surplus emergency fees (k'uan-sheng ch'ien). Sudō Yoshiyuki tabulates the surplus emergency fee figures by circuit in Sudō, "Ō Anseki no boyakusen chōshū no sho mondai," pp. 216–17. Following the quotas, the actual returns for 1076 are given, broken down into four categories of income flow: receipts (shou), expenditures (chih), current balance (hsien-tsai), and "earmarked funds" (ying-tsai), which Sudō interprets as funds earmarked but not yet spent, a measure of the progressive transfer of control over tax revenues from the local and regional to the central government; see Sudō, "Ō Anseki no boyakusen chōshū no sho mondai," pp. 221–2. The figures are aggregated by circuit, and each category is further broken down by exchange medium. Sudō tabulates the circuit figures on pp. 218–19; Miyazawa Tomoyuki tabulates the entire set of accounts by circuit and exchange media in his "Hoku-Sō no zaisei to kahei keizai," pp. 327–32.

that had formerly been the responsibility of draftees.[245] In practice, however, it simply joined the "surplus emergency fee" to help swell the total *mien-i* fund well beyond what might be needed for the service wage bill under any circumstances. For example, according to the perceptive Szechwanese reform opponent Lü T'ao, in 1076 the most prosperous region of his province, Ch'eng-tu-fu circuit, spent only 66 percent of its service exemption fund on salaries.[246] At the same time, the country as a whole spent only 60.7 percent of its hired service funds on wages, or 6,487,688 out of 10,414,553 strings.[247]

What became of the remaining forty percent? The fiscal success of the green sprouts measure suggested one use to cash-hungry administrators. In the third month of 1072, just a few months after universal promulgation of the service exemption policy, K'ai-feng administrators were ordered to use their surplus-fee fund to make interest-bearing loans to the public. Five months later, beguiled by the service exemption surplus already building up in northern Szechwan, Wang An-shih declared that the interest collected on all unused service exemption funds could be diverted to finance clerical salaries, and thereby promote his program to professionalize the clerical service and merge clerical and official streams.[248] By 1075 the interest generated by hired service funds had joined the income from wineries, ferry crossings, and other fees as a source for the roughly 1.1 million strings needed annually for the salaries of clerks in the capital (413,400 strings) and in circuit and prefectural offices (689,800 strings).[249]

Not surprisingly, the revenue potential of the service exemption accounts induced officials to maximize financial surpluses by drawing funds away from the funds' designated purpose – the hiring of service personnel. Between 1070 and 1076 *mien-i* administrators experimented with a variety of ways to spend as little of their service funds as possible. One such experiment, the "land in return for service" policy (*kei-t'ien mu-jen*), was enacted by Lü Hui-ch'ing in mid-1074, while he was standing in for Wang An-shih. The new plan (devised by Lü's brother Lü Wei-ch'ing) was designed to preserve the liquidity of the service exemption fund by continuing to collect the fees without actually using them to pay service agents; in their place, the government would pay agents with

---

[245] *HCP* (1979) 251, p. 6113. These services were collectively termed *yüan-jung*.

[246] That is, 406,024 strings out of 615,673 strings. See "Tsou wei mien-i-ch'ien ch'i-chuang er-fen chün-pei chih-yung chuang," in Lü T'ao, *Ching-te chi* (c. 1100; n.p., 1899) 1, pp. 2a–3b. Lü's memorial is analyzed in Sudō, "Ō Anseki no boyakusen chōshū no sho mondai," pp. 214–15.

[247] *Chung-shu tui-pei*, in *Yung-lo ta-tien* 7507, p. 3357. For tabulations of the circuit figures see Sudō, "Ō Anseki no boyakusen chōshū no sho mondai," pp. 218–19, and Miyazawa, "Hoku-Sō no zaisei to kahei keizai," p. 329.

[248] *HCP* (1979) 231, p. 5614; 237, pp. 5764–5.

[249] *HCP* (1979) 248, p. 6052, cited in Sudō, "Ō Anseki no boyakusen chōshū no sho mondai," p. 208; *SS* 177, p. 4306.

tenancies on official lands. Although the government actually tried the policy in a few places it turned out to be too costly, and Wang An-shih peremptorily abolished it when he returned to office in the second month of 1075, thereby exacerbating the tension between him and his closest lieutenant.[250]

Other stratagems were more successful in accumulating service exemption surpluses. Most important, by either reducing the number of government service positions needed or transferring the responsibilities to civil service and military personnel, financial officials reduced the number of functionaries paid out of hired service funds even as the officials increased the total amount of money collected. Reform of the drafted service system was always intended to reinforce market mobilization with a reduction in the number of functionaries, especially supply masters, that would be needed. The original reductions were aimed more at administrative efficiency than revenue production, and they were quite successful. In the eleventh month of 1070, the fiscal intendant of Tzu-chou circuit, in central Szechwan, was commended by Wang An-shih and the emperor for consolidating tribute shipments out of his circuit by 136 convoys, for a savings of 283 supply master posts and 501 service personnel (kung-jen).[251] A month later Han Wei, the prefect of K'ai-feng and no supporter of the reforms despite being Han Chiang's brother, was also praised for abolishing 835 rural supply master posts (hsiang-hu ya-ch'ien) in the capital prefecture.[252] Even after unnecessary supply master positions were squeezed out of the system, further savings were made by replacing the protoprofessional supply masters – the generic t'ou-ming ya-ch'ien – with civil and military officials. In early 1072, the concurrent judicial and Ever-normal Granary intendant of Chiang-nan, Chin Chün-ch'ing, realized substantial savings on the shipment of spice and silks from Chiang-nan to the capital by hiring fifty "officials whose replacements had arrived" (who would have had to return to the capital anyway) and military servitors to muster porters and lead the convoys, all at prices below what former local supply masters were willing to accept. Wang An-shih immediately seized upon Chin's plan as a prototype for transferring supply master responsibilities to replaced or cashiered officials, whom he insisted "would compete for transport duty

---

[250] Because the fiscal rights to government land, including pastureland and abandoned plots, belonged to the fiscal intendant of each circuit, the fiscal intendants had to be reimbursed the amounts of money they would have earned through sale or rental of the property. In areas where the value of land was high, such as Liang-che circuit, mien-i administrators spent more money on the land transfers than it would cost to pay their wage bill. See HCP (1979) 253, p. 6198; 260, p. 6345; SHY (1964) shih-huo 65, p. 14b; SS 177, pp. 4306–7. For a discussion, see Higashi, Ō Anseki shinpō no kenkyū, pp. 727–35.

[251] HCP (1979) 217, pp. 5283–4.

[252] HCP (1979) 218, p. 5301.

without cease" if they were given cash incentives to escort convoys back to the capital.[253]

It was also common to replace supply masters with military personnel, a recommendation made early in the hired service policy debates.[254] Even military men had to be paid something for their services: in Ching-hsi North's Hsü-chou2 prefecture in 1071, military functionaries (rank not specified) were paid a "sustenance fee" of three thousand cash per month to manage the prefecture's public storehouse (*kung-shih-k'u*) in place of civilian supply masters, who one after the other were being sucked dry by the position's vulnerability to clerical corruption.[255] On the whole, however, replacing civilian supply masters with soldiers allowed the government to shelter its wage fund and "deposit" (*chuang*) or "stockpile" (*feng-chuang*) the surplus for other purposes.[256]

In general, then, professionalization of the supply master position and the concomitant shift from command to market mobilization was at least partly supplanted by a parallel effort to save money by absorbing the supply master functions into the civil service and military bureaucracies. The expansion of *pao-chia* organizations throughout the country had a similar effect on reform of the bowman (*kung-shou*) or county militiaman's position, the second post targeted by the hired service measure. Wang An-shih had always hoped that the system of detached service under the county sheriff would enable the court to replace hired bowmen with conscripted *pao-chia* guardsmen.[257] By 1076 Wang's hope had been partially realized. According to a report by the censor Teng Jun-fu, in the five circuits of north China bowman strength had been cut by seventy or eighty percent, from a range of 70 to 140 bowmen per county down to a mere 15 or 30. The remaining troop strength was made up by the *pao-chia* guardsmen and *i-yung* militia men, rotated in from the outside for half-month tours of detached service (*shang-fan*). Though Teng deplored the extent to which reducing the number of bowmen undermined local security, from the fiscal perspective the replacement of hired bowmen by conscripted *pao-chia* guardsmen allowed the government to save even more of its hired service funds.

Inevitably, the reduction of government service personnel and replacement of civilians by civil and military officials prompted calls for a parallel reduction

---

[253] *HCP* (1979) 229, pp. 5576–7. Chin offered 100 full strings of cash for every 10,000 bolts of silk transported, and 70 full strings for each 10,000 strings of cash. An earlier official had proposed 500 full strings for every 10,000 count of either silk or cash.

[254] *HCP* (1979) 227, p. 5523.

[255] *HCP* (1979) 222, p. 5399.

[256] *HCP* (1979) 268, p. 6569.

[257] *HCP* (1979) 235, p. 5697.

in the various service exemption fees.[258] But the whole point of reducing the number of hired civilians, from the perspective of the New Policies planners, was to free up the service funds for other, potentially more remunerative, uses. In the ninth month of 1075, after it boasted about the success of the hired service policy in cutting supply master positions, paring costs, and regaining control over ferry and winery profits, the *Ssu-nung ssu* was ordered to "deposit" (*chuang*) one part of its surplus, lend out a second part to the public as interest-bearing loans, and distribute a third part – one million strings of cash *a year* in winery and ferry installation fees – to state trade bureaus around the country to finance their purchase of commercial goods for resale in the capital.[259] One year later the revenue stream from both the wineries and ferries and the entire surplus-fee fund were formally severed from the hired service policy; transformed now into unencumbered revenue, they were to be pumped back into the Ever-normal Granary system, where they could beget still more money.[260]

By the end of Wang An-shih's tenure the service exemption funds, like the green sprouts loans, had become a robust source of revenues. In 1076 the government spent only 6.4 million strings of the 10.4 million strings it collected in service exemption fees, for a surplus of 4 million strings. At the same time, the fund contained 8.5 million strings of unused "current funds" (*hsien-tsai*) – in some circuits equal to an entire year's income – built up through underspending and the accumulation of surplus emergency fees (*k'uan-sheng chien*) up to 1076. The winery and ferry account was equally well capitalized, with an income of 2.1 million units (primarily cash) over expenditures (1.7 million units).[261] Nor did the fiscalization of the hired service funds end with Wang An-shih's retirement. Despite the efforts of officials such as Chou Yin and Shen K'uo in late 1076, Lü T'ao in 1077, and Liu I in 1082 to reduce hired service collections to the actual wage bill or relink the wine and ferry fund to hired service, both accounts continued to grow as the number of civilian government service agents hired shrunk or stayed stable. In 1084 the government collected or held 18,729,300 million strings in service exemption fees, and 5,050,090 strings in wine and ferry fees. The transformation of the hired service policy into a mechanism of revenue extraction was complete.[262]

---

[258] For examples by Chou Yin and Shen K'uo, see *HCP* (1979) 279, pp. 6825–6. The Court of Agricultural Supervision (*Ssu-nung ssu*) insisted that such calls were misguided, since they ignored the expense incurred in hiring soldiers to replace service men; *HCP* (1979) 268, p. 6569.

[259] *HCP* (1979) 268, p. 6569.

[260] *SHY* (1964) *shih-huo* 65, p. 16a.

[261] Miyazawa, "Hoku-Sō no zaisei to kahei keizai," pp. 329–32; Sudō, "Ō Anseki no boyakusen chōshū no sho mondai," pp. 218–19.

[262] *HCP* (1979) 350, p. 8397; *SS* 177, p. 4310; Sudō, "Ō Anseki no boyakusen chōshū no sho mondai," p. 222. For Lü T'ao's complaint, see Lü, *Ching-te chi* 1, p. 2b; for Chou Yin, Shen K'uo, and Liu I, see *HCP* (1979) 279, pp. 6825–6, and *HCP* (1979) 324, pp. 7795–801.

It is doubtful whether this transformation could have proceeded so far had not the entire population been organized into *pao-chia* mutual security units, thereby providing administrators with a relatively cheap system of conscription.[263] For not only did expansion of the *pao-chia* system enable the government to replace county-level bowmen with cheaper *pao-chia* guardsmen on detached service; it also reversed the trend toward putting the village-level posts of elder (*ch'i-chang*), household chief (*hu-chang*), and stalwart (*chuang-ting*) on a hired basis.

Because the trend toward monetizing village service never went beyond an ad hoc, localized movement, its full extent is impossible to trace. But from two Southern Sung sources it is clear that as early as 1069 some parts of the country began to hire rather than conscript men for the village posts of household chief (*hu-chang*), with responsibility for tax collection, and the elder (*ch'i-chuang*) and his subordinates, the stalwarts (*chuang-ting*), with responsibility for bandit and fire control.[264] The experiment was short-lived, however, for between 1071 and 1074 hireage was abandoned in favor of a return to the conscription of men for all three posts.[265]

Why the monetization of village posts lapsed just as hireage was being pushed at the county and prefectural level is unclear, but the spread of *pao-chia* certainly provided both incentive and opportunity. The *pao-chia* system was made universal in 1073, and one year later the court abolished the positions of household chief and its urban counterpart, the neighborhood headman (*fang-cheng*), and transferred their tax-pressing duties to the *pao-chia* organization.[266] Then in 1075 the regulations were tightened up and the mutual security apparatus made the unified representative of the state at the village level responsible for all local public functions: in all counties where *pao-chia* was in effect, all elder and any remaining household chief and stalwart positions were abolished, and their collective duties subsumed into the *pao-chia* system. The *pao-ting* guardsmen were designated as the primary collection agents of

[263] The critical links between *pao-chia* and the hired service measure are stressed in Sudō Yoshiyuki, "Sōdai gōsonsei no hensen katei," in *Tō-Sō shakai keizaishi kenkyū*, Sudō Yoshiyuki (Tokyo, 1965), pp. 561–644, especially pp. 577–96, and in Sudō, "Ō Anseki no shinpō to sono shiteki igi," pp. 2–10; and by Higashi, *Ō Anseki shinpō no kenkyū*, pp. 691–812.

[264] The two sources are the 1182 Fu-chou gazeteer by Liang K'o-chia, *Ch'un-hsi San-shan chih* (1182; Taipei, 1980) 14, p. 7744, and a memorial by Ch'en Fu-liang (1137–1203), "Chuan-tui lun i-fa cha-tzu," in Ch'en Fu-liang, *Chih-chai hsien-sheng wen-chi* (Taipei, 1979) 21, pp. 119–20. For analysis, see Sudō, "Sōdai gōsonsei no hensen katei," p. 578.

[265] In place of salaries, the elder, stalwarts, and household chief received tax and *mien-i* fee exemptions during their term of service. See Ch'en, *Chih-chai hsien-sheng wen-chi* 21, p. 120.

[266] *HCP* (1979) 257, pp. 6277–8. Tax pressers (*ts'ui-shui chia-t'ou*) were mustered from among master households and were obliged to keep up the tax lists and to supervise one tax collection, in addition to their security service. See Sudō, "Sōdai gōsonsei no hensen katei," pp. 579–80.

the state, responsible for collecting all taxes, service exemption fees, and green sprouts repayments. At the same time the tasks of the elder, including fire control and bridge and road repair as well as security, were transferred to the top echelons of the *pao-chia* system – the superior or deputy superior guard leaders (*tu-fu pao-cheng*) and the large guard chiefs (*ta-pao-chang*). One new position, termed the "messenger" (*ch'eng-t'ieh jen*), was created to assist the local *pao-chia* leaders in their new tasks. Each superior guard leader – who was responsible for 250 households – was allowed to hire two messengers, who were charged with managing the unit's documentation and communication. The fact that messengers were hired made them the sole exception to the return of command mobilization at the village level, but because the position required literacy it was not easily subject to conscription.[267]

Shen-tsung did worry that because service exemption fees were now universal, the people would view the transfer of tax-collection responsibilities to the *pao-chia* guardsmen as a breach of trust; moreover, he felt that it was improper to require superior guard leaders to take on new tasks in addition to overseeing military training. But Wang An-shih minimized the impact of the tax-collection burden on the guardsmen and, at the same time, revealed his basic ambivalence toward relying on the market to mobilize labor for government functions. In the times of the former kings, Wang insisted, everyone in the population performed multiple tasks; "if [now] the people are ordered to do nothing more than military drill, I do not know who could be counted on to perform the remaining tasks [of local government]."[268]

In the end, the reformers were unable to backtrack completely on enlisted local service. In 1081, an official of the Bureau of Military Affairs reiterated Shen-tsung's complaint about foisting tax-pressing duties on men who had paid service exemption fees, and reported that in the K'ai-feng region, poorer guardsmen proved powerless to compel rich households to pay their taxes and fees. As a result, in K'ai-feng, drafted guardsmen were replaced as tax pressers by paid "messengers." But in a compromise that embedded market mobilization within the *pao-chia* command structure, overall supervision of tax collection still rested with the superior guard leader.[269]

Because of lacunae in the records there is no way of knowing whether the spread of the *pao-chia* system subverted plans by the reform leadership to

---

[267] The messengers were paid with funds that would otherwise have gone to the elder and stalwart, either as maintenance fees or as vestiges of their hired service wages. For the entire reform, see *HCP* (1979) 263, pp. 6436–7. Every ten to thirty master households had to put up their own guardsmen to collect taxes, but any single guardsman had to undertake the responsibility for only a single tax period and, according to Wang An-shih, do so only once every decade or so; *HCP* (1979) 263, p. 6451.

[268] *HCP* (1979) 263, pp. 6450–1.

[269] *HCP* (1979) 311, p. 7536.

extend the voluntary, marketized provisions of the hired service measure to village- as well as county-level service. But contemporaries and near-contemporaries assumed, with Shen-tsung, that the payment of service exemption fees ought to confer immunity from village-level service, and hence that *pao-chia* undermined the progressive aspects of the service exemption policy and exacerbated its fiscalist potential. In 1076, for example, the censor Chou Yin urged the court to sever the ties between *pao-chia* and village-level administration, and to return to the hiring of elders and household chiefs, as specified in the original service exemption regulations.[270] Nine years later, as Shen-tsung's death put the reforms under attack, the county magistrate Shang-kuan Kung-ying protested that the replacement of village-level posts by the *pao-chia* system contravened the goal of the service exemption policy "to collect money from the people exclusively to provide wages for service, and not to meet the ordinary financial needs of the nation," and he insisted that if the posts of elder, stalwart, and household chief were no longer necessary, then the service exemption fees should be commensurately reduced.[271] But perhaps with hindsight the Southern Sung observer Ch'en Fu-liang saw the situation most clearly: from the perspective of the reformers, the *pao-chia* system provided an opportunity "to make profits on and stockpile (*feng-chuang*) the hired service wage fund."[272]

State trade

The state trade act was less hampered by competing and contradictory goals than were the green sprouts, hired service, or *pao-chia* policies, and despite its resounding redistributionist rhetoric it was the most thoroughly transformed into a mechanism for generating revenues. Early on, Wang An-shih had assured the emperor that the interest payments generated by commercial loans would provide ample funds for the state's financial needs.[273] Despite sharp resistance that jeopardized even the emperor's support of the reforms, Wang and Lü Chia-wen resolutely expanded the organizational domain, geographic range, and operational scope of the State Trade Bureau, transforming it from a capital-centered regulatory agency intended to promote commerce,

---

[270] *HCP* (1979) 279, p. 6825.

[271] *HCP* (1979) 360, pp. 8620–1. Shang-kuan was serving in An-fu county, Chiang-hsi, at the time.

[272] Ch'en, *Chih-chai hsien-sheng wen-chi* 21, p. 120. During the Southern Sung, the *pao-chia* system developed into the basic unit of rural administration, while the service exemption fee joined the list of local taxes that were funneled out of their region to finance the military budget. See Sudō, "Sōdai gōsonsei no hensen katei," pp. 600–23; Sogabe, "Ō Anseki no hokōhō," pp. 33–63.

[273] "Shang wu-shih cha-tzu," in Wang, *Wang Lin-ch'uan ch'üan-chi* 41, p. 239, cited in Liang, "Shih-i fa shu," p. 185. This section draws heavily on Liang Keng-yao's sources and analysis.

to an empirewide credit and wholesaling operation dedicated to amassing revenues.

Demonstrating a keen understanding of organizational power, Lü Chia-wen quickly asserted control over all the government's commercial operations in the capital. In the single month of June (the fifth month of 1072) the state trade bureau gained dominion over the Bureau of Monopoly Goods (*Ch'üeh-huo wu*), the Central Commercial Tax Bureau (*Tu shang-shui yüan*), and the General Sales and General Purchase Markets (*Tsa-mai ch'ang, Tsa-mai wu*). With these acquisitions the state trade bureau ruled over the sale of commercial permits for the trade in government-controlled tea, salt, and imported incense and medicinals; the collection of commercial taxes in the capital; and the procurement and resale of commercial goods acquired for the court.[274] The state trade bureau's control over commerce in the capital also increased the funds available to it for investment in interest-bearing loans, for as chief collector of commercial taxes in the capital, the bureau inherited the market usage surtax (*shih-li ch'ien*) of six cash that was added to every hundred cash of commercial taxes.[275] This revenue stream was further augmented by the imposition in mid-1073 (the fifth month of 1073) of the "guild exemption fee" (*mien-hang ch'ien*), a cash fee paid by all of K'ai-feng's commercial guilds in lieu of providing actual goods or services to the government. Although intended like its model, the service exemption fee, to be progressive, the guild exemption fee ended up as a flat levy imposed on all vendors, including such petty traders as the water sellers (*t'i p'ing-che*), who despite having had no previous responsibilities to the state now had to form into guilds before they could ply their wares in K'ai-feng.[276] To provide an outlet for its expanded supply of cash, the state trade bureau took over the Central Collateralized Loan Bureau (*Ti-tang so*), a unit of the K'ai-feng prefectural financial administration that accepted valuables from the public as security for interest-bearing cash loans. The bureau soon opened five installations around the city to lend out surplus market usage and guild exemption funds. By the fourth month of 1074 the credit operation had been pushed out to the suburban county of Hsiang-fu, where, according to Assisting Councilor of State Feng Ching, officials encouraged ignorant poor folk to pawn their grain in addition to valuables to get emergency cash loans. "They just see that the government is handing out money," Feng complained,

---

[274] *SHY* (1964) *chih-kuan* 27, pp. 8b, 38a; Liang, "Shih-i fa shu," p. 187.

[275] See Cheng Hsia, *Hsi-t'ang chi* [*Ssu-k'u ch'üan-shu, Wen-yüan ko* 1779 ed.] (Taipei, 1973) 1, pp. 9a–10b; Liang, "Shih-i fa shu," p. 190. The surtax was initially designated for the pool of funds used to pay clerical salaries under the new *ts'ang-fa* measure; but by 1073, Lü Chia-wen had raised the surtax to ten cash per transaction, regardless of the size of the basic commercial tax, in order to swell overall revenues.

[276] Cheng, *Hsi-t'ang chi* 1, pp. 8a–9a; *HCP* (1979) 245, p. 5962; Liang, "Shih-i fa shu," p. 191.

"and there are none who can turn it away. So they pile up debts, and when the time comes they cannot repay."[277]

The financial success of the state trade bureau in K'ai-feng, as well as of its progenitor in western Shan-hsi, encouraged Wang An-shih and Lü Chia-wen to open branch bureaus throughout the country. In the tenth month of 1073 the K'ai-feng state trade bureau was upgraded to the status of Superintendancy of State Trade (*tu t'i-chü shih-i-ssu*) and all provincial branches placed under its authority. By the end of the first phase of expansion in 1074, seven provincial bureaus were in operation around the empire; by the end of Shen-tsung's reign at least twenty provincial bureaus had been opened, providing access to every commercial center except western Szechwan, which was dominated by the Superintendancy for Tea and Horses.[278]

Geographic expansion provided an irresistible temptation to Lü Chia-wen to enlarge the agency's role from passive recipient of commercial goods in the capital to active buyer, and finally seller, of goods in the provinces. Any move away from the agency's original designation as a mediating agent between resident and traveling merchants drew censure, and in late 1072 Wang An-shih had to defend the direct sale of fruit in K'ai-feng by explaining that fruit was the medium in which some peddlers wanted to repay their commercial loans, and so state trade officials had to resell the fruit to consumers.[279] But this was still an ad hoc method of disposing of a surplus; at the end of the year Lü Chia-wen made the agency's involvement more active by financing private contractors to go out into the provinces to buy up marketable commodities for the State Trade Bureau.[280]

This use of commoners and merchants to act as agents of the state was of course controversial, and on several occasions Wang An-shih had to intercede with the emperor.[281] But the state trade agency incurred even greater censure

---

[277] *SHY* (1964) *chih-kuan* 27, p. 65b; Liang, "Shih-i fa shu," p. 192. For Feng Ching's comments, see *HCP* (1979) 252, pp. 6155–6. Smith, "State power and economic activism during the New Policies," misidentifies the green sprouts loans as the target of Feng's criticism.

[278] *SHY* (1964) *shih-huo* 37, p. 17b. For sources on and the distribution of provincial state trade bureaus, see Liang, "Shih-i fa shu," pp. 188–90, 206, and Higashi, *Ō Anseki jiten*, pp. 54–7, tables 15 and 16. On the battle between the state trade agency and the tea and horse agency for dominion over the lucrative Ch'eng-tu market, see Smith, *Taxing heaven's storehouse*, pp 154–5.

[279] The original complaint was made by Wen Yen-po, who blamed the collapse of a mountain in Hua-chou (eastern Shensi) on cosmic anger at the government's intrusion in the fruit market. See *HCP* (1979) 239, pp. 5810–11; 240, pp. 5826–8.

[280] *HCP* (1979) 241, p. 5874; Liang, "Shih-i fa shu," p. 192.

[281] In the eleventh month of 1072, Wang An-shih told Shen-tsung that "it is precisely because state trade matters are detailed and picayune that the bureau employs merchants to serve as its managers." In the eighth month of 1073, he insisted that a commoner-broker sent out on behalf of the state trade agency to trade with the Liao was no less trustworthy or decorous than any of the emperor's intimates. See *HCP* (1979) 240, p. 5827; 246, pp. 5995–6.

by sending out officials to trade directly in the provinces. In 1074, after Tseng Pu himself complained about officials buying tea in Hunan, salt in Shan-hsi, and silk in Liang-che, Shen-tsung demanded to know where in the state trade legislation it authorized sending officials into the provinces to trade.[282] But the imperial pique was somewhat disingenuous, for it was Shen-tsung's own hunger for revenues, as manifested in the rewards and promotions granted Lü Chia-wen and his associates for exceeding revenue quotas, that encouraged the bureau's growing expansion into provincial commerce.[283] The lure of funds finally moved Shen-tsung to openly embrace the revenue goals of the state trade agency, and in late 1074 he lent the agency two million strings of cash from the Inner Treasury to send out "men of special talent" to buy up salt permits and grain in the provinces.[284] Four months later, in the second month of 1075, the agency extended its reach by opening purchase stations (chü) in all commercially strategic places throughout the country.[285] Now, in the eyes of reform opponent Su Ch'e, "there were no goods [the state trade agency] would not stoop to buy, no profits it would not seek to commandeer, as it ordered officials and dispatched commoners to buy and sell goods in north and south, and to hand out loans in search of interest."[286]

Up through the end of Wang An-shih's tenure the agency focused on purchasing goods that could be resold to small merchants, but the scope of its operations continued to expand even when Shen-tsung took over the reins of state. By 1078 the state trade agency had acquired such a stockpile of commodities that the court authorized it to begin retailing its stocks in the provinces for cash (pien-chuan), with an incentive schedule for officials pegged to specific sales targets.[287] This explicit intervention into local consumer markets was followed by the expansion of Collateralized Loan Stations (Ti-tang so) throughout the country, to generate funds for Shen-tsung's war on the Tanguts. New loan stations were opened in K'ai-feng and in the capital region in 1081 and

---

[282] HCP (1979) 252, p. 6159; 253, p. 6188. Tseng Pu's complaint was part of a wider uproar, dealt with in the next section, that forced Wang An-shih into temporary retirement.

[283] HCP (1979) 245, p. 5962; 256, p. 6256; Liang, "Shih-i fa shu," p. 194.

[284] HCP (1979) 257, p. 6280; Liang, "Shih-i fa shu," p. 208. By repurchasing salt permits at extremely low prices from merchants who had already paid cash for the licenses, the state increased the amount of money it squeezed out of the merchants by devaluing the permits.

[285] HCP (1979) 260, p. 6331.

[286] "Tzu Ch'i-chou hui lun shih-shih shu," in Su, Luan-ch'eng chi 35, p. 14a. Su Ch'e dates the memorial at seven years after his resignation from the Finance Planning Commission, in the eighth month of 1069. In the last month of 1075 the agency was authorized to buy three million catties worth of tea a year for resale on credit to itinerant peddlers who hawked it throughout Ho-pei and Shantung, earning a rebuke from Lü T'ao; see "Tsou ch'i pa Ching-tung Ho-pei lu she-fang ta-fang ch'a chuang," in Lü, Ching-te chi 3, pp. 9b–10b; SHY (1964) shih-huo 37, pp. 23b–24a.

[287] HCP (1979) 294, pp. 7174–5.

1082, and then in every circuit in 1083, when they were capitalized by green sprouts and service exemption funds. Even as late as the fifth month of 1085, two months after Shen-tsung's death, the Ministry of Finance recommended that loan stations be set up in all but the most commercially backward areas of the empire.[288] By the end of Shen-tsung's reign an agency that was meant to curb the power of the engrossing monopolists had itself turned into the largest engrosser in the empire, "stockpiling any goods the people might use, monopolizing any transaction that might bring them profit . . . and forcing merchants to a halt."[289]

Like all monopolies, however, the state trade agency was extremely profitable. For the single year of the tenth month of 1076 to the tenth month of 1077, the state trade agency reported net returns (*hsi-ch'ien*) of 1.41 million strings of cash, a return of 28 percent on its basic capitalization of 5 million strings at that time.[290] By 1085 the basic capitalization had more than doubled, to 12.26 million strings, which at the same rate of return should have yielded 3.45 million strings in interest. But by then the state trade agency and its debtors were overextended, forcing the court to issue reductions or cancellations on the interest owed on loans and credit purchases, while seeking to protect its principal.[291]

We can be more precise about the profitability of the New Policies as a whole, which very significantly enriched government coffers. One historian estimates that in 1077 the major revenue measures – state trade, green sprouts, and hired service – added an extra 18 million strings, or 33 percent, to the 54 million strings of cash obtained through traditional currency sources.[292] Other than state trade, this new currency stream was collected almost entirely from the agricultural sector of the economy.

In the absence of comparable data on net returns for the rest of the reign period, the surviving figures on cash surpluses can serve as a surrogate measure

---

[288] Liang, "Shih-i fa shu," p. 225; *HCP* 322, p. 7770; 332, pp. 8000–1; 356, p. 8515.

[289] The quote is from Censor Chao Ju-li (1041–94), in Yang Shih-ch'i, *Li-tai ming-ch'en tsou-i* (1416; Taipei, 1964) 269, pp. 15a–b. Chao's memorial, written around 1077, focuses on the Chiang-nan region, where he claims that state trade agents had undermined the tea, silk, and manufacturing trades that local people relied on for their livelihoods.

[290] *SHY* (1964) *chih-kuan* 27, pp. 39a–b; *HCP* (1979) 282, p. 6907. *SS* 186, p. 4551, reports a lower figure of 1.3 million strings, made up of interest payments and *shih-li* fees. The profits earned a bonus of 300,000 cash for director Lü Chia-wen. See also Liang, "Shih-i fa shu," p. 205.

[291] See *SHY* (1964) *shih-huo* 37, pp. 31b–32b.

[292] Miyazawa, "Hoku-Sō no zaisei to kahei keizai," p. 300, table 4. The traditional cash sources were the cash portion of *liang-shui* (5.59 million strings), commercial taxes (8.07 million strings), the wine monopoly (12.28 million strings), the salt monopoly (22.3 million strings), and new currency (5.95 million strings). Of the new measures, state trade provided 1.41 million strings, service exemption 10.17 million strings, wine and ferry stations 3.87 million strings, and Ever-normal Granaries – that is, the interest on green sprouts loans – 2.3 million strings.

of the revenue-generating powers of the New Policies. By the end of 1076, the Court of Agricultural Supervision (*Ssu-nung ssu*) had built up a surplus of unspent reserves (*hsien-tsai ch'ien*) from the rural credit, service exemption, and winery and ferry franchise funds totaling 49.9 million mixed units, including 27.7 million strings of cash.[293] These and later surpluses were used to fill Shen-tsung's treasuries: in 1079 the *Ssu-nung ssu* was instructed to deposit one million strings of winery franchise funds annually in Shen-tsung's Inner Treasury; three years later 13 million strings of accumulated funds from the green sprouts, service exemption, and winery and ferry franchise accounts were transferred to the Yüan-feng Treasury, established in 1080 specifically to house profits from enterprises controlled by the *Ssu-nung ssu*.[294] For Shen-tsung these hoards were to be the life's blood of his campaign against the Tanguts. And though the Tangut war of 1081–3 exacted an enormous toll in money and men, New Policies revenues were so robust that imperial treasuries remained full into the next reign period. In 1087 the head of the Ministry of Finance, Li Ch'ang, reported:

Our former emperor labored year after year to build up a surplus for border defense. As of now, the green sprouts, service exemption, and winery franchise accounts have yielded surpluses of 56 million strings, while another ten million strings worth of money, goods, and precious metals have accumulated from the sales of rice and salt in the capital and funds stockpiled in the Yüan-feng Treasury. Moreover, another half [of] this amount was spent on the frontier [war].[295]

In sum, the surviving figures on surplus revenues suggest that the key reform financial policies generated in the range of one hundred million strings of cash for Shen-tsung and the reformers, though little of this money was seen by mainstream budgetary agencies.[296] But did reform financial measures "multiply the state's revenues without adding to the people's taxes," as Wang An-shih had promised? Contemporaries thought not. Yang Shih (1053–1135), a disciple of the Ch'eng brothers who received his *chin-shih* degree when Wang

[293] See the *Chung-shu tui-pei* figures tabulated in Miyazawa, "Hoku-Sō no zaisei to kahei keizai," pp. 327–32.

[294] *SHY* (1964) *chih-kuan* 26, p. 13a; *SHY* (1964) *shih-huo* 52, p. 14a; Wang, "Pei Sung ti Ssu-nung-ssu," p. 26.

[295] *HCP* 407, p. 9904.

[296] Shen-tsung and his chief ministers controlled revenues generated by the New Policies, through the *Ssu-nung ssu*, and, after 1082, the Agency of the Right of the Board of Revenue (*hu-pu yu-ts'ao*). The fiscal agencies in charge of routine budgetary matters, such as the Finance Commission and its successor, the Agency of the Left of the Board of Revenue (*hu-pu tso-ts'ao*), were short of cash throughout the reform era. In the specific case of state trade revenues, Chao Ju-li complained that everything the agency gained through its monopolistic practices came at the expense of commercial taxes lost to the Finance Commission; Yang, *Li-tai ming-ch'en tsou-i* 269, p. 15b. For general discussions, see Wang, "Pei Sung ti Ssu-nung-ssu," p. 26, and Hartwell, "The imperial treasuries," pp. 70–2.

An-shih was at the height of his power, lamented what he saw as the unintended slide into confiscatory revenue gathering: "Although the idea behind the New Policies was laudable, in less than a decade even though imperial treasuries overflowed with revenues, the people were put in terrible distress."[297] Another observer, Pi Chung-yu, was less willing to give the reformers, including Shen-tsung, the benefit of the doubt. Just after Shen-tsung's death had revived hopes for a conservative restoration, Pi wrote to his mentor, Ssu-ma Kuang, that "Wang An-shih stirred the late emperor's heart with his talk of great deeds. But although the late emperor believed in Wang he feared that funds would be inadequate, so he distributed green sprouts loans, set up state trade bureaus, collected service exemption fees, and changed the salt laws. There was no method that might get money out of the people that the government would not employ."[298] Throughout the fifteen years of the reforms, opponents argued that although in the short term the New Policies did enrich the state, they did so only by sacrificing the long-term stability and productivity of the economy. Critics catalogued a wide range of abuses perpetrated by the reforms but focused on three issues that especially highlight the unintended consequences of state activism: opponents collectively asserted that reform financial measures sundered the bonds of the natural community, confronted the natural economy with the demands of a hypermonetized state, and wound up harming most the relatively poor and unprotected classes they were intended to assist.

The impact of the New Policies: The opposition critique

In contrast to Wang An-shih, who depicted rural life as an arena of unbridled domination and mutual antagonism, many other contemporary observers believed that rural society was held together by bonds of communal solidarity and mutual interdependence that were stronger than the centrifugal forces of inequality. Ssu-ma Kuang was perhaps the most persistent advocate of the belief that "although bitterness and happiness are not equally distributed, at least rich and poor mutually aid one another in order to guarantee their livelihoods."[299] But he was by no means alone. Cheng Hsia, a one-time protégé of Wang An-shih's who became disenchanted with the reforms, reported that

[297] Yang Shih, *K'uei-shan chi* 15, cited in Liang, "Shih-i fa shu," p. 171.

[298] "Shang men-hsia shih-lang Ssu-ma wen-kung shu," in Pi Chung-yu, *Hsi-t'ai chi* (c. 1117; Taipei, 1986) 7, p. 92.

[299] See "Ch'i pa t'iao-li-ssu ch'ang-p'ing-shih shu," in Ssu-ma, *Ssu-ma Wen-cheng kung ch'uan-chia chi* 44, p. 562.

he was told the same thing in 1074 when he interviewed refugees from the prolonged drought that had plagued north China for years:

Families rich and poor, great and small, all rely on one another for survival. The poor and small depend on the rich and great for nurturance in the face of their poverty and powerlessness, while the rich and powerful depend on the poor to complete their well-being. The rich and powerful possess property and grain, whereas the weak own no land or dwellings. They must serve as the tenants of others, and there is nothing that they need for peddling or cultivating that they do not obtain through interest-bearing loans from the rich and powerful. The rich in turn prosper daily, and exert themselves on behalf of the tenants who rent their houses and their land.[300]

According to men who observed the impact of the reforms on the local level, by projecting state power more deeply into local society, the New Policies fractured time-honored relationships of mutual dependency, at great cost to the people and ultimately to the state itself. They were especially adamant about the disruptive effect of the green sprouts loan policy, arguing that instead of protecting poor peasants from the avarice of the rich, the collection of government loans subjected poor peasants to the coercive powers of the state. In one of the flood of critiques that emerged as the reforms were being rolled back in mid-1086, the censor Shang-kuan Chün (1038–1115) asserted that although before the green sprouts reform private lenders had charged nominally high interest rates, when it came time to collect they were at least relatively flexible and benign. By the time a peasant finished off paying the ruthlessly efficient agents of the state, however, the price of a loan had risen from the statutory twenty percent to fifty or even one hundred percent of the principal.[301] At the same time the left policy critic Wang Yen-sou (1043–93) graphically depicted the many minions of the state that a green sprouts borrower had to confront: first, in order to register for a loan, he had to pay off the local *pao-chia* leaders, including the large guard chief, tax-pressing *chia-tou*, and notary for household registrations. Then at the other end of the process, if he fell behind on his payments a government clerk would appear at the door, who had to be bought off with food and drink. But even the clerks could not be bought off forever, and eventually the collection agents would arrive to seize the debtor's property and drag him off to be beaten. Moreover, Wang did not assume that the maliciousness perpetrated by the green sprouts measure was intentional; it was simply the unavoidable consequence of government interference in the rural economy: "To strive intentionally for the benefit of the peasantry is not as good as bringing them benefit by leaving them alone."[302]

[300] "Liu min" in Cheng, *Hsi-t'ang chi* 1, p. 13a.
[301] *HCP* (1979) 378, pp. 9192–4.
[302] *HCP* (1979) 376, pp. 9131–2.

The disruption of communal solidarity was even more insidious in the case of the hired service policy, in the eyes of critics, since here the attempt to replace community-based service agents with semiprofessional mercenaries also undermined the interests of the state. According to Wang Yen-sou, the old system of drafted service was built on a solid communal foundation, in which "households on duty" (*ying-tang men-hu*) with propertied roots in the community were kept afloat during their period of service by neighbors who came to their aid with labor and material assistance. Under the hired service system, however, well-established local families were replaced by "vagrant riff-raff from the marketplace" who used their positions as guardians and scribes at the government's granaries, tax stations, treasuries, and financial bureaus to intimidate local citizens and embezzle state property. Wang Yen-sou was just one of many conservatives who doubted that the marketplace could provide reliable and responsible professionals. For Wang, as for Ssu-ma Kuang, Chang Fang-p'ing, Liu Chih, and Yang Hui, only local men with property in the region could be trusted to manage the government's property; no bond or collateral could prevent sojourning mercenaries from engaging in graft or absconding with the government's property, then changing their names and volunteering for work elsewhere.[303]

The hired service measure was also held responsible for subverting the communal focus of the *pao-chia* system, which if anything was intended to reinforce communal organizations by transforming them into compulsory, bureaucratized units. In 1076 the censor Teng Jun-fu (1027–94) charged that the use of local *pao-chia* guardsmen on detached service to replace county-level bowmen, one of the *mien-i* hiring categories, had shattered a natural defense and surveillance network built on personal relationships, leaving local communities powerless to control rising banditry in the Shantung and Fu-chien regions. Teng memorialized that

under the old system [prior to hired service and *pao-chia*] a large county claimed about 140 bowmen, a medium county one hundred, and a small county not less than seventy to eighty bowmen. Although in name only one person was drafted into service, in fact when it came time to quell bandits all the remaining men rose up as well. The rural compatriots and relatives all acted as the eyes and ears [of the bowmen]. . . . People were at peace in their old villages and did not lightly dare to leave them, and it was this that allowed them to control banditry.[304]

Although critics no doubt exaggerated the harmoniousness and solidarity of rural communities prior to the reforms, their anecdotal portraits do

[303] *HCP* (1979) 364, pp. 8703–6. The last charge is by Ssu-ma Kuang; see "Ch'i pa mien-i i chiu ch'ai-i cha-tzu," in Ssu-ma, *Ssu-ma Wen-cheng kung ch'uan-chia chi* 49, pp. 626–8. For Yang Hui and Chang Fang-p'ing, see *HCP* (1979) 224, pp. 5444–6; 277, pp. 6787–91.

[304] *HCP* (1979) 279, pp. 6834–5.

highlight the disruptive intrusiveness of the state under the New Policies. Moreover, there was a broad consensus that the disruption of local communities was exacerbated by what may be termed the hypermonetized demands of the state under Wang An-shih and Shen-tsung. Despite the considerable spread of commerce and market relationships that characterized the eleventh-century economy, money was distributed very unevenly through Sung society. During the momentary flowering of criticism that the emperor allowed in 1074, Ssu-ma Kuang offered a widely shared view of the limited place of money in the economy:

There are some rich merchants and great traders who possess great stores of cash, but among the peasantry wealth is measured by the possession of more land and larger stocks of grain, [and is acquired by] maintaining better buildings and dwellings and working their oxen without cease. Nowhere do peasants amass tens of thousands of cash in their homes As for the poor peasants, their tattered rags do not even cover their bodies, nor does their coarse fodder fill their bellies. In the fall they hope their crops will ripen in the summer; come summer they look towards the harvest in the fall. Some of them must even work as share-cropping tenants for others. Surely there are none among them with any knowledge of money.[305]

Ssu-ma's contention was shared by Chang Fang-p'ing, who in 1076 wrote that in the poor hamlets of Ying-t'ien-fu (Ching-tung West), "at the time of the winter sacrifices the poor peasants carry their firewood and straw into the town market, a round trip of ten *li*, where they sell it for 50 or 70 cash. With this money they buy some onions, eggplant, salt, and vinegar, and young and old regard it as sweet and beautiful. Throughout their days, what do they know of a single [extra] cash?" Even the reform lieutenant Teng Wan (1028–86) described an autarkic rural economy in which stubborn and fearful peasants raised silkworms for their clothes, worked the land for their food, and from youth to old age never passed through a market gate or saw a government yamen.[306]

By contrast, Shen-tsung, Wang An-shih, and their followers were obsessed with the idea of money, whose role in the economy they seem to have seriously exaggerated. The reformers valued money because it was liquid, and could be exchanged for goods and services when and where they were needed; because it was indestructible, and could be stored in treasuries with no fear of spoilage; and because it was expandable, and could be made to grow through minting, of course, but also through government control over commutation

---

[305] "Ying chao yen ch'ao-cheng ch'üeh-shih chuang," in Ssu-ma, *Ssu-ma Wen-cheng kung ch'uan-chia chi* 45, p. 575. In 1086, Ssu-ma Kuang insisted that "even the richest landowner never has more than several hundred strings of cash at most." See "Ch'i pa mien-i," in Ssu-ma, *Ssu-ma Wen-cheng kung ch'uan-chia chi* 49, pp. 626–8.

[306] *HCP* (1979) 277, p. 6789; 269, p. 6605.

rates between money and goods, and by the seemingly inexhaustible power of interest on money constantly recirculated into the economy. The government's obsession with the idea of turning goods into cash and pumping cash into the economy was no more clearly manifested than in the Szechwan tea monopoly, where official placards enjoined tea market functionaries to "expedite the rapid purchase and sale of tea, prevent the stagnation of capital."[307]

If Wang An-shih was obsessed with increasing the flow of revenues to the state, the fundamental rationale of his reform program was that he could do so without diminishing the resources of the people. To recapitulate Wang's argument, under the stimulation of the state, goods and money would circulate freely, unimpeded by either private monopolies or bottlenecks from outmoded quotas for command-mandated goods and services; this free circulation of goods and money would in turn produce new wealth for the state without increasing fiscal claims on the people. According to his opponents, however, Wang's policies led to a very different set of outcomes: in their view, the confrontation between a cash-hungry state and an imperfectly monetized economy resulted in increased monetary taxes, a currency crisis, and economic dislocation and stagnation.

The chief contributor to the rise in taxes came from the service exemption fees and the surplus emergency fee (*k'uan-sheng ch'ien*) surtax. Although by monetizing government service the reformers hoped to minimize the burden borne by upper-grade households, critics adduced statistics to prove that the annual fees on rich households were far higher than the cost of periodic service had ever been before. In 1082, Liu I, the Ever-normal Granary intendant for Chiang-nan, estimated that the richest households in neighboring Liang-che circuit paid up to eight hundred thousand cash annually in service exemption fees, eight times more than the periodic draft had cost them prior to the reforms.[308]

Critics were divided on how harmful the hired service policy was to the rich in general, since in counties with low overall *mien-i* quotas spreading out the costs of government service could work to the advantage of the wealthy.[309] But they all joined Chang Fang-p'ing in condemning the extension of service

---

[307] "Tsou wei ch'a yüan-hu an-che san-fen chia-ch'ien . . . ," in Lü, *Ching-te chi* 1, p. 11a. For a recent article on the manipulation of commutation rates, see Chang Hsi-wei, "Sung-tai che-pien-chih t'an-hsi," *Chung-kuo shih yen-chiu* No. 1 (1992), pp. 26–33.

[308] *HCP* (1979) 324, p. 7798.

[309] When Chang Tun tried to halt the rising tide against the hired service policy in early 1086, he seized on the fact that Ssu-ma Kuang himself was not sure whether the measure was good or bad for the wealthy. See *HCP* (1979) 367, p. 8822, which also cites Ssu-ma's arguments. Some critics, such as Wang Yen-sou, thought that the hired service policy might work well if the exemption fees were limited to those families that were liable for the service. See *HCP* (1979) 364, pp. 8703-6.

exemption fees to lower-grade households as a way of "taxing those too poor
to meet their needs in order to subsidize the powerful who possess more than
they need."[310] The intrinsic regressivity of the measure was exacerbated by
the practice of arbitrarily upgrading lower-grade households in order to meet
or surpass revenue quotas. As the hired service policy spread from K'ai-feng to
the rest of the country after its universal promulgation in the tenth month of
1071, officials in each county were required to set collection quotas based on
the distribution of households in the five-grade hierarchy. This initial grading
was the specific job of clerical staff, whom Chang Fang-p'ing charged were
spurred by a court-issued incentive schedule to set collection quotas as high
as possible. As a result, "the grasping clerks counted everything as property –
land, huts, ox-tackle, produce, mulberry and jujube trees, even down to the
tools, spades, kettles, dogs, and pigs of the most downtrodden families. Since
the clerks were aiming for rewards and bonuses, everything was given a cash
value [in order to maximize the amount of money each family would have to
pay]."[311] Nor did a peasant's problems end with the first grading. As Liu Chih
pointed out on his return to the Censorate in 1086, once the richest families
were ruined by annual service exemption burdens of hundreds of strings of
cash, officials passed their fees onto the remaining population by arbitrarily
upgrading the poorer households. Liu's colleague Wang Yen-sou provided a
specific example: in Ting-chou's An-hsi county (Ho-pei West), some sixteen
hundred out of a total of thirteen thousand households were ranked in grade 4
prior to the hired service measure. But because upper-grade households could
not continue to meet their disproportionate share of the total county quota,
officials simply moved everyone up the ladder: thirty-four hundred households
were upgraded from rank 5 to 4, and over seven hundred rank 4 families were
upgraded to rank 3. And unlike past times, when regrading was predictable
and realistic, now "the poorest households can get upgraded at any time even
if there is no increase in the value of their meager property, in order to make
them pay more in service exemption fees." In every county in the land, Wang
Yen-sou declared, the poor were being reassessed to provide *mien-i* and even
more spurious fees that government functionaries ground out of them through
the power of the lash.[312]

By increasing the amount of money taken out of an economy that was
only partially monetized to begin with, Wang An-shih's reformers decreased

---

[310] *HCP* (1979) 277, p. 6788.

[311] *HCP* (1979) 277, pp. 6789–90.

[312] *HCP* (1979) 364, pp. 8700, 8704. At least in some places, arbitrary upgrading provided the same
disincentive to agricultural expansion that drafted service did; in 1073, Shen-tsung complained that
because of fear of the *mien-i* assessor, peasants were refusing to plant mulberry trees. See *HCP* (1979)
245, p. 5969.

rather than increased the volume of money in circulation, thereby depressing agricultural production. Clearly this was not their intention: during Shen-tsung's reign, Sung mints pumped more copper currency into the economy than at any time before the eighteenth century – an annual quota of 5.06 million strings, or about 60 cash per capita annually as of 1080.[313] This was supplemented by currency introduced into the economy by the green sprouts rural credit measure, which distributed a quota of 11 million mixed units annually, about half of which was in cash.[314] But despite these annual injections of currency into the economy, more still was taken out by the service exemption fees, the twenty percent surplus emergency fee (*k'uan-sheng ch'ien*) surtax, the nominal twenty percent interest charged on the green sprouts loans, and the welter of nuisance fees and surtaxes, such as the *t'ou-tzu* and *shih-li* fees, that proliferated during Shen-tsung's reign.[315] This outflow of currency from the local economy hit peasant producers especially hard, for by assessing these new fees in cash the government forced peasants to sell their produce at disadvantageous rates to obtain currency to pay their taxes. Yet as local currency became increasingly scarce, the value of a peasant's produce declined. In the parlance of the time, money became dear and goods cheap (*ch'ien-chung huo-ch'ing*). As Chang Fang-p'ing, a close observer of the deflationary phenomenon, described it: "Because of the green sprouts and service assistance measures, peasants all sell their grain and textiles so they can pay their fees in cash. But cash has become increasingly hard to get, driving down the price of grain and cloth and putting the people in even greater distress. They all call it the 'cash famine' (*ch'ien-huang*)."[316]

In principle, a significant portion of these funds was supposed to be recirculated back into the local economy: service exemption fees in the form of

---

[313] Yüan I-t'ang, "Pei Sung ch'ien-huang: ts'ung pi-chih tao liu-t'ung t'i-chih ti k'ao-ch'a," *Li-shih yen-chiu* No. 4 (1991), pp. 129–40, especially p. 131. By contrast, Ming dynasty mints produced 3 copper cash per capita in 1393, and Ch'ing dynasty mints produced 4.3 cash per capita in 1721. I have adjusted Yüan's figures to reflect a household:individual ratio of 1 to 5.

[314] For distribution and collection quotas and the actual figures for 1080 and 1081, see *HCP* (1979) 332, p. 8006. The percentage represented by specie is not given, and no obvious surrogates are available. In 1077 currency constituted around half of the discretionary funds (*hsien-tsai ch'ien*) account for the rural credit operation, or 15.5 million strings out of a total of 37.3 million mixed units. See Miyazawa, "Hoku-Sō no zaisei to kahei keizai," p. 328, table 2, citing *Yung-lo ta-tien*.

[315] On the proliferation of fees, see "Tsou ch'i fang-mien k'uan-sheng i-ch'ien chuang," in Lü, *Ching-te chi* 1, pp. 1a–2a. In 1076, Chang Fang-p'ing reported that although the green sprouts measure added 83,600 strings of cash to the Ying-t'ien-fu economy every year, after interest charges there was a net loss of 16,600 strings. See *HCP* (1979) 277, p. 6789.

[316] Quoted in Yeh T'an, "Lun Pei Sung 'ch'ien-huang,'" *Chung-kuo shih yen-chiu* No. 2 (1991), pp. 20–30. As Yeh Tan points out, Chang Fang-p'ing also indicted Wang An-shih's relaxation of the prohibitions against the private sale of copper and the export of copper coins as causes of the cash shortage.

wages, surplus emergency fee (*k'uan-sheng ch'ien*) surtaxes in the form of collateral for shortfalls, and even the green sprouts interest payments as payment
for the administration of the Ever-normal Granary operation. But as we have
seen, the government made every effort to divert these new revenue streams
from their intended purposes, drawing local funds out of the place of collection to government repositories in the capital and the provinces. Some of this
money was pumped back into the economy in the form of clerical salaries
and still more interest-bearing loans. But the interest frenzy that overtook
Shen-tsung and the reformers was matched by an irrepressible instinct for
government hoarding, and much of the cash collected from the peasantry sat
uselessly in imperial treasuries. In 1077, Lü T'ao warned that because half of
the currency collected in service exemption and surplus-tax fees in the Szechwanese prefecture of P'eng-chou (Ch'eng-tu-fu circuit) was siphoned out of
the economy by the government, there was little currency left to circulate
in local markets.[317] A decade later Lü's fellow Szechwanese Su Ch'e reported
that the cash famine threatened to stall the once-robust southeastern economy: "Ever since the Hsi-ning period the people have had to pay out cash for
service exemption fees and the interest on green sprouts loans. Now strings
of cash just pile up uselessly in government storehouses, while officials scour
for more cash among the people until there is nothing left. In the markets
people have taken to using privately minted small cash, but even so goods
do not move and peasants and their wives cannot sell what they grow or
spin."[318]

Even without a cash shortage the monetization of agricultural taxes was
destabilizing, since it forced poor peasants to produce for the market in order
to obtain cash for their taxes. When coupled with the deflation brought on
by the currency shortage, monetization could be ruinous, forcing peasants to
sell their meager working capital – land, oxen, the firewood created by disman-
tling their houses or cutting down their mulberry trees – to get cash for their
taxes. And here, for conservatives, was the most ironic consequence of Wang
An-shih's economic reforms. For the direct beneficiaries of these forced sales
was the very class of "engrossers" that the reforms were intended to suppress:
families wealthy enough to pay their own new taxes and yet still have enough
cash left to buy up the property of poorer peasants at vastly reduced rates, or to
provide usurious loans so they could pay their green sprouts interest. Thus as
Ssu-ma Kuang, Liu Chih, Wang Yen-sou, and their associates all agreed, rather

[317] Lü, *Ching-te chi* 1, pp. 1a–b.
[318] "Ch'i chieh ch'ang-p'ing-ch'ien mai shang-kung chi chu-chou chün-liang chuang," in Su, *Luan-ch'eng chi* 37, p. 13a, quoted in Yeh, "Lun Pei Sung 'ch'ien-huang,'" p. 22.

than suppressing the rural engrossers, Wang An-shih's two agrarian reforms wound up working to the engrossers' advantage.[319]

Although opponents singled out green sprouts and hired service as the most pernicious of the New Policies, they were no less quick to condemn the state trade and *pao-chia* measures for subjecting the very categories of people they were meant to protect to the disruptive powers of a state apparatus driven beyond legitimate bounds by the frenzy for revenues. The state trade policy, justified as a way to protect small merchants and itinerant traders from the grip of the great guild monopolists, soon mirrored the regressivity of the hired service act by charging nonguild vendors a guild exemption fee (*mien-hang ch'ien*) and exacting the market usage surtax (*shih-li ch'ien*) on transactions too small even to warrant a commercial tax.[320] Perhaps even more damaging to small traders and their customers was the concerted effort by state trade officials to insert themselves into the place once held by private commercial monopolists. State trade functionaries violated the original intent of the policy so egregiously that in 1074 both its originator – Wei Chi-tsung – and its chief sponsor – Tseng Pu – turned against the agency:

> Lü Chia-wen and his minions devote themselves solely to taking in profits in order to garner rewards. All traveling merchants must sell their wares to the state trade agency, all vendors in the markets must buy what they need from the agency. Moreover the agency buys cheap and sells dear in order to swell its income and pare down its expenditures, so as to bring in profits from every quarter. As Wei Chi-tsung has said, this is nothing less than using the power of the government to act just like the engrossers.[321]

As already shown, the charges by Tseng Pu and Wei Chi-tsung were just a part of the widespread denunciation of state trade agents who monopolized (*lung*) commerce in the provinces and the capital. By mimicking the monopolistic practices of the private engrossers, state trade agents could have the same depressing effect on trade that the engrossers were accused of. This was illustrated by the trade in glutinous rice (*no-mi*). Around 1074 the agency monopolized all the glutinous rice shipped by merchants to the capital, a monopoly that it protected by offering rewards of up to three hundred thousand cash to residents who informed on violators. The agency in turn sold the glutinous rice on credit to the city's wineries, who were its principal consumers. By 1075, however, rice importers reacted against the state trade agency's unrealistically low prices by cutting off K'ai-feng's supply, so undercutting the wine

---

[319] See Ssu-ma, *Ssu-ma Wen-cheng kung ch'uan-chia chi* 47, pp. 608–9, 626–8; *HCP* (1979) 364, p. 8700; 376, pp. 9131–2.

[320] See Cheng, *Hsi-t'ang chi* 1, pp. 8a–10b.

[321] *HCP* (1979) 251, p. 6134.

industry that local winemakers were unable to meet the interest payments for their earlier purchases.[322]

Like its counterpart measures in the countryside, the state trade agency also enforced its financial claims in a far more draconian way than could private monopolists. The K'ai-feng winemakers were relatively fortunate, for faced with the disruption of an essential industry the court was obliged to forego half the interest accrued by the wineries. Left to its own, the state trade agency could be relentless in collecting its fees. In 1073, Cheng Hsia saw state trade debtors wearing cangues around their necks, their hands laden with house beams and tiles, being led off to the public market to sell the remains of their dismantled homes in order to requite their debts to the state.[323] And finally, the state trade act shared one further trait with its rural counterparts – its utility to the same rich and influential "engrossers" it was meant to suppress. In 1075, Wang An-shih boasted that because of the success of the state trade act in "smashing engrossers," the only occupation left for the "great names" of the capital was to open pawnshops.[324] But as the historian Liang Keng-yao argues, these pawnshops were probably financed by state trade agency loans. For having shut the rich merchants and residents of K'ai-feng out of commerce, agency officials then clamored to swell revenues by lending these same people money at interest. Despite periodic efforts to exclude the most influential people, including officials and members of the imperial clan, from taking state trade loans, prudence often succumbed to greed, as state trade officials, in their eagerness for revenues and rewards, became the principal financiers of the rich and powerful. Among the chief beneficiaries of this largesse were state trade officials themselves and their kin, who were among the most prodigal borrowers of agency funds. By 1078, for example, the maternal relatives of Chi Feng, the state trade intendant for the lucrative frontier bureaus in Ch'in-chou and the recently created Hsi-chou2 (Ch'in-feng circuit), had amassed a debt of 120,000 strings of cash; one year later the one-time state trade official and Szechwan tea and horse intendant Liu Tso owed 180,000 strings of cash.[325] And the rich and powerful continued to amass debts to the state trade agency throughout the 1080s. By mid-1085, when the restoration government began discounting the loans, a total of 27,155 K'ai-feng families owed combined

[322] HCP (1979) 260, pp. 6329–30.

[323] See "T'u-hui ch'eng-wai min chi K'ai-feng jen-hu che-wo mai-wa mu teng shih," in Cheng, Hsi-t'ang chi 1, pp. 14a–b. A year later Shen-tsung also complained about the borrowers of state trade agency loans having their property confiscated and their necks placed in the cangue. See HCP (1979) 251, p. 6117.

[324] HCP (1979) 262, p. 6407. See Liang, "Shih-i fa shu," pp. 222–5.

[325] HCP (1979) 294, p. 7168; 298, p. 7251.

debts of 2.37 million strings of cash to the State Trade Superintendancy. Sixty-five percent of this debt was owed by only sixty-two families – thirty-five "great names" (*ta-hsing*) and twenty-seven winemakers – who averaged 24,838 strings of cash per borrower. The remaining 830,000 strings of cash were distributed among 27,093 "small names" (*hsiao-hsing*), at an average of 30 strings per borrower.[326]

Finally, the *pao-chia* system, the last piece in Wang An-shih's program to expand state control over society and the economy, also wound up impeding economic productivity and enhancing the power of rural magnates. The chief cause of both problems was the extension of the program of military drill and review (*chiao-yüeh*). Originally, the drill program for K'ai-feng and the circuits of north China was voluntary and was timed for the slack months of late fall and winter. During the 1080s, however, under the pressure of war with the Tanguts, military drill became compulsory in practice if not in law, and it increased in frequency to one training session every five days throughout the agricultural season.[327] In 1084, Fan Ch'un-jen described the impact of compulsory drill on agriculture in eastern Shan-hsi:

In Shan-hsi this summer's wheat and barley are about to ripen, and all hands are needed to harvest and store it. Otherwise if bandits swarm or winds and rain hit before the harvest is in, then most of it will be lost. . . . But now, because all the strongest men must serve in the *pao-chia* units and drill once every five days, agriculture is hampered. . . . Every commoner family with two adult males must send one into *pao-chia*, thereby losing the labor they need to see to their livelihoods. This is especially trying for poor families with little land.[328]

Observers such as Wang Kung-ch'en, Ssu-ma Kuang, and Wang Yen-sou confirm Fan's claim that compulsory drill drew scarce labor out of the fields at critical agricultural times.[329] They confirm also that the training procedures subjected the *pao-ting* guardsmen, who were mustered from the poorest households, to the whims of the *pao-chia* leaders, who were selected by law from

[326] "Ch'i fang shih-i ch'ien-ch'ien chuang," in Su, *Luan-ch'eng chi* 38, pp. 11a–13a; Liang, "Shih-i fa shu," p. 222. In the fourth month of 1085, the Secretariat ordered the state trade agency to forgive seventy percent of the interest owed by the great names and all of the interest owed by the small families. See *HCP* (1979) 354, p. 8472.

[327] Though no statute can be found supporting either change, descriptions by Fan Ch'un-jen and Ssu-ma Kuang indicate that by the end of Shen-tsung's reign military drill was constant and compulsory. See *HCP* (1979) 345, pp. 8289–90; "Ch'i pa pao-chia chuang," in Ssu-ma, *Ssu-ma Wen-cheng kung ch'uan-chia chi* 46, p. 592.

[328] *HCP* (1979) 345, p. 8290. Compare this with the regulations of 1072 that put the guardsmen under the power of their *pao-chia* superiors and the military inspectors; *HCP* (1979) 237, pp. 5769–70.

[329] In addition to Ssu-ma, *Ssu-ma Wen-cheng kung ch'uan-chia chi* 46, p. 592 and 47, pp. 606–8, see *HCP* (1979) 343, p. 8242; 361, pp. 8641–2.

the richest and most powerful families of each neighborhood. In 1085, Wang Yen-sou described some of the most exploitative demands made on the *pao-ting* guardsmen by their *pao-chia* and official superiors:

> During training, the large guard chief and the superior guard leader will beat [the guardsman], then the military inspector and his sergeant (*chih-shih*) will take turns flogging him, followed by the lieutenant (*chih-hui shih*) and civilian administrator (*kan-tang kung-shih*) of the *pao-chia* intendant, who will whip him, and then perhaps another lashing by their superior. And if the guardsman tries to flee then he will be flogged by the county magistrate as well.... Beyond [this physical abuse] he must make his own garb, buy his own headgear and bow, and repair his own arrows.... Moreover, even when at their leisure in their homes, the superior guard leader and assistant leader and the large and small guard chiefs all demand gifts for weddings and funerals, as well as tributes of silk, hemp, rice, and wheat at the autumn and summer harvests; or they demand that the guardsman treat them to a drink and a meal in the walled markets. Yet even though the guardsman fears falling into the clutches of these men he dare not refuse to do their bidding, for if even one thing is not as they want it then he will be charged with violating the regulations, and be subjected to unlimited thrashing and humiliation.[330]

Wang Yen-sou and his fellow conservatives warned that training the guardsmen in military skills while filling them with hatred for their superiors could only foment rather than suppress banditry. This is precisely how Southern Sung critics viewed the consequences of the *pao-chia* system. Hu Shun-chih (1083–1143), just a child when Shen-tsung died, wrote in 1135 that "Bandits swarmed everywhere during the Yüan-feng period, and it was *pao-chia* men who were responsible. The policy intended to prevent banditry instead promoted it."[331] Nor did training peasants for military service save much money in military expenses. According to the historian Sogabe Shizuo, although in 1081 the *pao-chia* system allowed the government to save 1.3 million strings of cash in wages and maintenance for soldiers, the court paid almost the same amount, one million strings of cash, in incentives and rewards for the drill and review program.[332] Even more critically, under the successors to Shen-tsung and Wang An-shih, especially Hui-tsung and his chief minister, Ts'ai Ching, reliance on *pao-chia* at the expense of the regular mercenary troops eviscerated the nation's defenses. When the Jurchen threatened in 1126, a rattled court was forced to scour the markets for riff-raff to hire to supplement its ill-trained and panic-stricken *pao-chia* brigades.[333]

---

[330] *HCP* (1979) 361, p. 8642.

[331] Li Hsin-ch'uan, *Chien-yen i-lai hsi-nien yao-lu* (1253; Peking, 1956) 96, p. 1585.

[332] Sogabe, "Ō Anseki no hokōhō," pp. 17–22; Ma, *Wen-hsien t'ung-k'ao* (1965) 153, p. 1335.

[333] Ma, *Wen-hsien t'ung-k'ao* (1965) 153, p. 1440. For a review of *pao-chia* policy under Che-tsung and Hui-tsung, see Sogabe, "Ō Anseki no hokōhō," pp. 27–33.

THE NEW POLICIES UNDER SHEN-TSUNG

Although the conservative portrayal of a rapacious fiscal administration preying on Shen-tsung's hapless subjects may not represent the entirety of Wang
An-shih's economic measures, its credibility is reenforced by the number of
reformers who themselves renounced the policies. Such renunciations must be
seen in the context of a political environment heated to the boiling point by
the competition for the extraordinary career leaps made possible by the reforms
and by the smouldering resentments of those who were passed over. Yet even
so, it was often differences over economic policy that served as the lightning
rod for political defections, sparking such tensions within Wang's inner circle
that in 1076 the coalition finally collapsed, putting Shen-tsung himself at the
helm of the reforms.

The collapse of Wang An-shih's coalition

After Wang ousted Tseng Kung-liang and Ch'en Sheng-chih from the Council
of State in late 1070 internal dissent against the reforms was muted. But in
the fall of 1072, T'ang Chiung, a young man who had earned Wang's approval
by recommending that Han Ch'i be beheaded for opposing the green sprouts
measure, turned against his patron when he was passed over for a promotion to the Remonstrance Bureau (*Chien-yüan*). T'ang retaliated with a flurry
of memorials condemning the reforms, but when these were all ignored he
boldly seized upon a general audience before the emperor to publicly humiliate Wang An-shih. Ignoring Shen-tsung's efforts to make him desist, T'ang
read out a memorial denouncing Wang, Tseng Pu, and their circle as despots,
and lambasting the *pao-chia*, service exemption, and state trade measures for
embittering the people.[334]

T'ang Chiung's attack, for which he was demoted to a minor post in Kuang-
nan, was deeply embarrassing to Wang, but it was so obviously tied to personal
ambition that it had little further effect. Moreover, Wang was then at the height
of his influence over Shen-tsung, who had just reaffirmed his trust in Wang
by demoting and rusticating an imperial favorite outside the reform circle
whose relentless criticisms had triggered another Wang resignation threat.[335]
But two years later the situation had changed dramatically, prompting doubts
and defections from Wang's followers, his lieutenants, and even the emperor
himself. The chief cause of the change was a prolonged drought in north

---

[334] *HCP* (1979) 237, pp. 5778–82; Williamson, *Wang An Shih*, vol 1, pp. 271–3.

[335] The official was Li Ping, chief edict recorder in the Bureau of Military Affairs. The Li Ping affair is
summarized in *HCP* (1979) 235, pp. 5712–15.

China, a drought so severe that Wang's efforts to minimize it earned him an imperial rebuke. Thousands of refugees fled the parched, famine-ridden north for relief in the capital, where they congregated as a direct reproach to the emperor. Shen-tsung was persuaded by his Han-lin advisor Han Wei that the disaster was Heaven's punishment for the economic exploitation and military adventurism that characterized the reforms, and in the third month of 1074 the emperor "opened the route of remonstrance," calling on all officials to memorialize him personally on the failings of his government.[336]

In Lo-yang, seat of the opposition, Shen-tsung's call for remonstrance was greeted with tears by Ssu-ma Kuang, who sent up his first comprehensive critique of the New Policies since his vow of silence in 1070.[337] Far more damaging to Wang An-shih, however, was a shocking portrait of the victims of the drought, of tax-gouging, and of military mobilization that was secreted into the court through illicit channels by Wang's erstwhile protégé Cheng Hsia (1040–1119). Acknowledged as a disciple by Wang around 1065, Cheng was appointed to a staff position in the Kuang-chou2 (Huai-nan West) prefectural administration at the start of the reform era. On his return to the capital in late 1073, Cheng sought to convince his mentor that despite their good intentions the economic reforms, exacerbated by military adventurism, had turned into cruel and oppressive burdens on the people. Meeting nothing but silence from Wang, Cheng Hsia decided to take his case directly to the emperor. With the encouragement of Wang's younger brother Wang An-kuo, an associate of the Lo-yang opposition who resolutely opposed the New Policies, Cheng Hsia vividly portrayed the weak, sick, and naked refugees who thronged the roads out of the northeast with their families and possessions in tow, driven along by the wind and sand. Though the ostensible cause of this panicked migration was drought and famine, the real source of the misfortune was Heaven's anger at a government that filled its storehouses to overflowing through such rapacious policies as the green sprouts, state trade, guild exemption, and service exemption measures. The only solution was to placate Heaven, by opening the nation's granaries to the people, abolishing Wang An-shih's oppressive fiscal policies, and cashiering Wang himself: "The drought is Wang An-shih's doing; cashier him, and the heavens will give rain."[338]

---

[336] *HCP* (1979) 251, pp. 6137–8; 252, pp. 6147–8.

[337] See "Ying chao yen ch'ao-cheng ch'üeh-shih chuang," in Ssu-ma, *Ssu-ma Wen-cheng kung ch'uan-chia chi* 45, pp. 571–8.

[338] The basic source is Cheng Hsia's composite "Shang Huang-ti lun hsin-fa chin liu-min t'u," in Cheng, *Hsi-t'ang chi* 1, pp. 1a–16b, which includes the eight points of Cheng's exposé and a synopsis of the explosion at court; it was based on information that the reform clique charged Cheng came by illegally. For this charge, and for Wang An-kuo's involvement, see *HCP* (1979) 259, pp. 6310–15. In late 1071, in an audience with the emperor that slowed down his career, Wang An-kuo lamented the fiscalist orientation that his brother and the reforms had taken, and he warned Wang An-shih that the enmity engendered by the New Policies would endanger the family. But An-kuo placed most of the blame not

Despite Shen-tsung's vow to read every criticism personally, it was only after Cheng's memorial was routed past reform henchmen to the Office of Transmission (*Yin-t'ai ssu*) controlled by Han Wei that it even got to the emperor.[339] Its impact on the emperor was made more acute by the fact that it coincided with a dispute over the state trade policy that involved the reform leadership itself. At the heart of the dispute stood Lü Chia-wen, who with Wang An-shih's support had turned the state trade agency into a fiscal empire that made Lü even more powerful than his nominal superior, the finance commissioner Hsüeh Hsiang. In early 1074, Hsüeh launched an investigation into charges that state trade agents routinely beat and imprisoned brokers and merchants who bypassed the agency. Lü Chia-wen convinced Wang An-shih that the charges were false, but rumors of abuses in the state trade operation, and especially in the collection of guild exemption fees, continued to surface. When Tseng Pu replaced Hsüeh Hsiang as finance commissioner in the third month of 1074, Shen-tsung secretly urged him to press on with the inquiry, and that month Tseng and Wei Chi-tsung issued their denunciation of Lü Chia-wen and his minions as reward-seeking usurious monopolists (as noted earlier). Though Wang continued to defend Lü Chia-wen to the emperor the affair was getting out of control, and toward the end of the month Wang tried to neutralize the issue by appointing his closest trustee, Lü Hui-ch'ing, to co-opt the state trade inquiry from Tseng. Lü Hui-ch'ing had long resented Tseng because of changes Tseng made in the service exemption measure, and he now joined with Lü Chia-wen to undermine Tseng and kill the affair, not least by intimidating clerks and merchant witnesses, altering their depositions, and seeking to suborn Wei Chi-tsung.[340] But any hope of suppressing the state trade affair was dashed by Cheng Hsia's exposé, whose lurid portrayal of petty traders hauled off in cangues for defaulting on their state trade fees confirmed Shen-tsung's worst fears about the reforms in general. The day after reading Cheng's memorial, Shen-tsung ordered reductions in the guild exemption and market usage fees, temporary suspension of the green sprouts and service exemption measures, and a halt to new registration for *pao-chia* and the "square-fields" (*fang-t'ien*) cadastral survey then in progress. When the promised rain fell within a week,

---

on his brother, but on Tseng Pu and Lü Hui-ch'ing. See *HCP* (1979) 227, pp. 5531–42, citing Lin Hsi's *Yeh-shih*. For Cheng Hsia's letter denouncing the green sprouts, service exemption, state trade, and guild exemption policies see "Shang Wang Ching-kung shu," in Cheng, *Hsi-t'ang chi* 6, pp. 1a–10b, as well as *HCP* (1979) 252, pp. 6152–4; 254, p. 6206; and Williamson, *Wang An-Shih*, vol. 1, pp. 281–2.

339 See Cheng, *Hsi-t'ang chi* 1, p. 4b. Cheng was later charged with abusing the emergency horse-relay postal route. According to Cheng's biography, as cited in *HCP* (1979) 252, p. 6168, very few of the remonstrance memorials ever got through Wang's gatekeepers to the emperor.

340 The state trade affair, which runs through *HCP* 251 and 252, is examined by Li Han, "Ts'ung Tseng Pu ken-chiu shih-i wei-fa-t'iao ti fen-cheng k'an hsin-tang nei-pu ti mao-tun yü wen-t'i," in *Sung-shih yen-chiu lun-wen-chi: 1984 nien nien-hui pien-k'an*, ed. Teng Kuang-ming et al. (Hang-chou, 1987), pp. 267–81.

Shen-tsung divulged Cheng's memorial to his shaken state councilors. Wang An-shih had no choice but to proffer his resignation, while for his part Shen-tsung was so pressed by his brother and the two dowager empresses to drop Wang that he had no choice but to accept. Thus in the fourth month of 1074 Wang was relieved of his post as chief minister, and reassigned as prefect of Chiang-ning fu (Nanking).[341]

Wang An-shih's departure put the reform policies in peril, but in the end Shen-tsung reversed himself on overturning the reforms. Shen-tsung left the choice of a successor to Wang himself, who selected Han Chiang as chief minister, and Lü Hui-ch'ing as Han's replacement as assisting civil councilor. It was Lü Hui-ch'ing who had personally crafted much of the actual reform legislation, and he quickly mobilized reform supporters throughout the bureaucracy to close ranks against the many conservatives who hoped to see the New Policies dismantled in the wake of Wang's ouster. Shen-tsung came down firmly on the side of the reforms, and though he issued an edict promising to rectify shortcomings in the New Policies, at the same time he warned that any attempt by the scholarly elite (*shih-ta-fu*) to "capitulate to conventionality and try to undermine his laws" would be treated as an unpardonable offense.[342] This provided the signal Lü needed to reverse the emergency policy of open remonstrance. His first target was the audacious Cheng Hsia, who since Wang's removal had immediately begun an attack on Lü. As the bearer of bad tidings, Cheng Hsia earned Shen-tsung's wrath, and although the emperor balked at having Cheng executed he did allow Lü Hui-ch'ing to banish him to administrative arrest in Kuang-nan.[343] Shen-tsung also let Lü Hui-ch'ing bring the state trade affair to a conclusion, by silencing the principals: in the eighth month of 1074, Tseng Pu, who had been as instrumental in bringing the reforms to life as Lü, was demoted from finance commissioner to prefect of Jao-chou (Chiang-nan East), on a charge of falsifying financial statistics and merchant depositions; Wei Chi-tsung, the real founder of the state trade measure, was cashiered. Lü Chia-wen also received a demotion, to forestall public censure, but in eight months he was back at the helm of the state trade agency.[344]

It was because of his devotion to the New Policies that Lü Hui-ch'ing earned from his contemporaries the derisive sobriquet "Divine Protector"

---

[341] See especially *HCP* (1979) 252, pp. 6168–70, and *SS* 327, pp. 10547–8.

[342] *HCP* (1979) 252, pp. 6168–70, 6172.

[343] *HCP* (1979) 254, pp. 6207–8; 259, pp. 6310–15. As late as 1077, Shen-tsung punished four officials who recommended that Cheng Hsia's punishment be lightened; see *HCP* (1979) 284, p. 6953. Another victim of the change in political wind was Li Shih-chung, who was rusticated to Huai-nan West for demanding the return to high office of Ssu-ma Kuang and the Su brothers; see *HCP* (1979) 253, pp. 6187–8.

[344] *HCP* (1979) 255, pp. 6237–8; 262, pp. 6407–8.

(*hu-fa shan-shen*), while the senior but less powerful Han Chiang was termed the "Propagating Abbot" (*ch'uan-fa sha-men*). Lü Hui-ch'ing sought not only to save the reforms, however, but also to displace Wang An-shih as the reform leader. As the contemporary political observer Wei T'ai noted, once men of ambition saw that Lü had gained the ear of the emperor and a chance to topple Wang, they all began to attach themselves to Lü,[345] who actively promoted his own cause by destabilizing the Wang An-shih faction. On the one hand, Lü tried to co-opt Wang's dissatisfied affinal kinsmen, men whose marriages to Wang's relatives had not advanced their careers as far as they had hoped. One month after Wang's resignation, for instance, Lü Hui-ch'ing tried to promote Chu Ming-chih to a lectureship in the Imperial University; this was the same position that Chu, who married two Wang women (Wang's sister, and when she died, Wang's niece), had lost in 1071, when it was given instead to Wang's brilliant but imperious son, P'ang. Shen-tsung rejected the promotion out of a personal dislike for Chu, but he allowed Lü Hui-ch'ing to give the position to another dissatisfied Wang brother-in-law, the classicist Shen Chi-chang, who had also incurred Wang P'ang's hatred.[346] On the other hand, Lü also fomented attacks on Wang An-shih's reputation, first by attacking Wang An-kuo for his role in Cheng Hsia's memorial, and then by unleashing Teng Wan to play up Wang An-shih's relationship to the Szechwanese Taoist and fortune-teller Li Shih-ning, who was implicated in a seditious plot that reached into the imperial family.[347] And of course Lü used his new position to build up a private clique (*ssu-tang*) of his own by demoting enemies and promoting his favorites, especially his brothers Lü Wen-ch'ing, Lü Sheng-ch'ing, and Lü Ho-ch'ing and his in-laws, the P'u-t'ien Fangs.[348]

Lü Hui-ch'ing's bid to supplant Wang An-shih sundered the fragile coalition of patron-client relationships that had come together under a single unquestioned leader, and turned policy debate into the unfettered instrument of political ambition. The two adjustments to the service exemption policy that Lü Hui-ch'ing advocated were universally denounced, but whether on their merits or because Lü's fortunes had begun to decline is impossible to ascertain. In the fifth month of 1075, Lü introduced the "land in return for

---

[345] *HCP* (1979) 260, p. 6336. For a credible attempt to refurbish Lü Hui-ch'ing's reputation, see Chou Pao-chu, "Lüeh-lun Lü Hui-ch'ing," in *Sung-shih yen-chiu lun-wen-chi: Chung-hua wen-shih lun-ts'ung tseng-k'an*, ed. Teng Kuang-ming and Ch'eng Ying-liu (Shanghai, 1982), pp. 335–49.

[346] See *HCP* (1979) 226, pp. 5507–10, citing Lin Hsi's *Yeh-shih* on the Chu Ming-chih tale; and *HCP* (1979) 253, pp. 6196–7.

[347] For the case of Li Shih-ning and Chao Shih-chü, see especially *HCP* (1979) 260, pp. 6336–8; 262, p. 6403; 264, pp. 6459–62; 271, p. 1775.

[348] See especially the twenty-one-point indictment and retrospective assessment of Lü Hui-ch'ing by the resolutely independent censor Ts'ai Ch'eng-hsi, in *HCP* (1979) 269, pp. 6584–90; 280, pp. 6874–6.

service" (*kei-t'ien mu-jen*) measure, which aimed at building up surpluses in the *mien-i* fund by letting certain counties pay government service agents with land rights rather than with cash; two months later he tried to address the household registration system that made the service exemption policy so controversial, by experimenting with a system of self-registration (the *shou-shih fa*) that let households report their own wealth according to a set of universally promulgated formulas, enforced by rewards for local informants. These reforms can never have been enacted very extensively, but they quickly earned widespread condemnation and are said to have undermined support for Lü. Wang An-shih memorialized against the land for service measure from his home in Chiang-ning, even as popular outrage against the measures "made everyone under Heaven think once again of Wang Ching-kung." By early 1075, Han Chiang, the nominal head of state, could no longer tolerate Lü Hui-ch'ing's policy – and political – machinations, and he begged Shen-tsung to bring Wang An-shih back. This was just the opening Shen-tsung needed to recall his mentor, who was more than ready to return: after receiving his summons in the second month of 1075, Wang made the trip from Chiang-ning to K'ai-feng in a remarkable seven days.[349]

But some of the bloom was off the reform movement during Wang An-shih's second term as chief minister. For one thing, the long-term problems of drought and famine still plagued north China, forcing the government to cut back on some lucrative reform programs. So many officials advocated food handouts and debt amnesties that Wang An-shih complained that everyone was "competing to indulge the commoners with sympathy," without thinking about the long-term solvency of the economic policies.[350] There was also a change in Shen-tsung's attitude, for the twenty-five-year-old emperor was no longer as ready as he had been to accept the often facile arguments of his fifty-four-year-old mentor. In the tenth month of 1075, Shen-tsung was shaken by a series of astronomical portents, culminating in the appearance of a comet in the constellation *chen* that was traditionally interpreted to betoken a sweeping away of the old order. The fearful emperor responded with a fast and seclusion from the public, and he issued another call for frank criticism of his government that elicited memorials from Fu Pi, Chang Fang-p'ing, Lü Kung-chu, and Wang's younger brother, the reform opponent Wang An-li. Wang An-shih disparaged the significance of astronomical phenomena, and urged Shen-tsung to once

---

[349] *HCP* (1979) 260, pp. 6336–8.

[350] Ironically, one of the officials singled out by Wang was Li Chi, a man so reviled by the public for his cruelty that he was compared in a popular ditty to the black death. See *HCP* (1979) 297, p. 7234. Further instances of Li Chi's cruelty are noted later. Wang An-shih also opposed Shen-tsung's plan to give famine victims in Ting-chou cooked rice gruel (*chu*) instead of uncooked rice, out of a fear that cooked gruel would make victimization overly attractive. *HCP* (1979) 264, p. 6458.

again crush critics of the reforms. But this time Shen-tsung refused, retorting that "the people are seriously troubled by the New Policies." Again Wang tried to minimize the problem: "The people resent all manner of things, like intense cold, heat, and rain. Why does their resentment of the New Policies merit special sympathy?" And once again Shen-tsung demurred: "I wish they did not even have these to resent."[351]

Shen-tsung's temerity drove the melodramatic Wang to his sickbed for thirteen days. Ssu-ma Kuang thought that after Wang returned from seclusion at the urging of Wang's nervous followers, Shen-tsung was even more compliant toward his chief minister than before. But in fact Shen-tsung was growing weary of his mentor and of the disorder in Wang's faction. In the seventh month of 1075, Han Chiang, who despite his position as the head of state had endured five years of self-abnegation and humiliation on behalf of the New Policies, resigned in protest over Wang's selection of a man charged with an administrative offense to head the state trade agency.[352] More destructively still, Wang's return signaled that Lü had been eclipsed, and forced Lü's partisans to scramble to protect themselves. Under the prodding of Wang's son P'ang, whom Southern Sung historians blamed for all the most despotic traits of Wang An-shih's regime, the one-time Lü supporter Teng Wan and Teng's client Lien Heng-fu began a widespread attack on Lü Hui-ch'ing's family, especially Lü's brother Sheng-ch'ing, and on such "evil associates" of Lü as Chang Tun.[353] Late in the year they were joined by Ts'ai Ch'eng-hsi, who charged Lü with factionalism and with conspiring to use his influence in a land purchase. By the ninth month of 1075, Lü Hui-ch'ing had had enough: he beseeched the emperor for a complete investigation of all the charges, and he was allowed to resign to an outside post as prefect of Ch'en-chou while the case progressed. Although indictments continued to pour in, the evidence of real wrongdoing was scanty, and in the sixth month of 1076, Lü Hui-ch'ing counterattacked with a scathing denunciation of Wang An-shih, who had tried to remain above the fray. When Wang sought an explanation from his son, Wang P'ang admitted that in order to prosecute Lü he had pushed Teng Wan, Lien Heng-fu, and Lü Chia-wen into manipulating the evidence. Wang reproached

---

[351] HCP (1979) 270, p. 6628; Williamson, *Wang An Shih*, vol. 1, pp. 357–9. See also HCP (1979) 269, pp. 6596–6600.

[352] The official was Liu Tso, later to head the Szechwan Tea Market Agency. Shen-tsung was extremely puzzled by Han Chiang's intransigence over the Liu Tso affair. See HCP (1979) 264, pp. 6467–8; 266, pp. 6530–1.

[353] For examples, see HCP (1979) 264, pp. 6480–1; 266, pp. 6532–4; 268, pp. 6563–7; 269, pp. 6598–6600. Williamson, *Wang An Shih*, vol. 2, pp. 251–6, recapitulates Liang Ch'i-ch'ao's argument that Southern Sung observers sought in Wang P'ang a scapegoat for Wang An-shih, just as they used Wang as a scapegoat for the emperor.

his son, who worked himself into such a fury that a boil broke out on his back, from which he died the following month. Distraught over the death of his son and in fear for his position, Wang turned on his proxies Teng Wan and Lien Heng-fu, but the emperor's patience had come to an end: in a line that echoes in every source, "the emperor was increasingly weary of Wang An-shih's behavior." In the tenth month of 1076, Shen-tsung let Wang An-shih retire to Chiang-ning.[354]

Shen-tsung and Ts'ai Ch'üeh

More than in 1074, conservatives now had reason to hope that the emperor's exasperation with Wang An-shih and the entire reform coalition heralded a reversal of Wang's policies. For in the tenth month of 1076, unlike two years earlier when Wang was replaced by his closest lieutenants, Shen-tsung filled the chief minister's post with Wu Ch'ung, a man who despite affinal connections to Wang and long service in the reform-dominated State Council was a persistent critic of the New Policies. Wu Ch'ung made it his mission to reform if not abolish the New Policies, and he excited the conservative party by calling for the return to court of many of Wang's most prominent victims, including Ssu-ma Kuang, Lü Kung-chu, Han Wei, Ch'eng Hao, and Su Sung. For their part, conservatives outside and moderates inside the government welcomed Wu's appointment with public memorials denouncing the New Policies and with private communications to Wu Ch'ung lending him support.[355] Ssu-ma Kuang sent Wu Ch'ung a letter from Lo-yang portraying north China as a land where rich and poor alike had been uprooted by the reforms, spawning swarms of bandits who openly attacked walled cities and murdered officials; and he urged Wu Ch'ung to help awaken Shen-tsung to the evils of the New Policies, sweetening his exhortation with the flattering claim that travelers returned from the capital with Wu Ch'ung's name on their lips.[356]

---

[354] SS 327, pp. 10549–50, translated in Williamson, Wang An Shih, vol. 2, pp. 51–3. For greater detail, see HCP (1979) 266, pp. 6532–4; 268, pp. 6563–7, 6570–9; 269, pp. 6582–90; 276, pp. 6742–3; 278, pp. 6797–8, 6803–4.

[355] SS 312, pp. 10238–41. The HCP entries for 1077 are replete with denunciations of the reforms by censors such as Chou Jun-fu and Chou Yin and by prefects such as Lü T'ao, Chang Fang-p'ing, Wen Yen-po, and even Han Chiang and Wang Shao (now vice-director of the Bureau of Military Affairs), who declared that the exploiter Lü Chia-wen "should be boiled alive to show thanks to Heaven"; HCP (1979) 280, p. 6866. The jockeying for position caught Shen K'uo, then provisional finance commissioner, in the middle, when he was impeached by Censor Ts'ai Ch'üeh for covertly turning against the service exemption measure once it became clear that political currents were running against the New Policies. See HCP (1979) 283, pp. 6933–5. Wu Ch'ung's son An-ch'ih resigned his post as intendant of the state trade agency as soon as his father was appointed chief minister; see HCP (1979) 278, p. 6808.

[356] "Yü Wu ch'eng-hsiang Ch'ung shu," in Ssu-ma, Ssu-ma Wen-cheng kung ch'uan-chia chi 61, pp. 735–7; HCP (1979) 286, pp. 7002–5.

Hopes for a conservative restoration were short-lived, however, thwarted by Shen-tsung's own autocratic aspirations and the opportunities autocracy provided to political opportunists more interested in riding the emperor's agenda to power than in advancing reform. For despite Shen-tsung's willingness to give conservatives a place at court, he was not ready to abandon his reformist ambitions. On the contrary, he was more resolved than ever to be the activist ruler, running his own government from the throne. As Chu Hsi retrospectively explained to a disciple, having acquired all he needed in the way of political skills from Wang An-shih in the Hsi-ning period, Shen-tsung was eager during the new Yüan-feng era (1078–85) to manage affairs by himself, using officials only to do his bidding.[357] Indeed, in the fifth month of 1077, less than a year after Wang An-shih's resignation, departing censor Ts'ai Ch'eng-hsi charged officials with abetting the drift toward bureaucratic paralysis and autocracy:

Why is it that despite the emperor's abundant virtue, the world is still not well governed? The reason for this tragedy is that the hundred officers do not perform their duties. [In particular,] the Secretariat-Chancellery [headed by Wu Ch'ung] has abrogated to the emperor its duty to promote and select men of talent, while the Bureau of Military Affairs [under Feng Ching] has forfeited its responsibility for managing troops and selecting generals. Decisions on all matters now come from the emperor alone, and if those decisions do not accord with public opinion, then officials simply say that "It was all decided by his majesty."[358]

One reason that officials were so compliant was fear: by mid-1077 the "road of remonstrance" was again being closed, once more endangering the careers of New Policies critics. The assault on remonstrance came from many quarters – in 1077 the head of the Szechwan tea monopoly alone had four prominent critics of its revenue-gathering practices transferred or dismissed from office – but they all reflected Shen-tsung's own decision to take up the mantle of reform leader. The man most responsible for chilling the political debate was the forty-year-old Ts'ai Ch'üeh (1037–93), who used his facility for reading political winds and manipulating weaker men to quash Wu Ch'ung and the restorationists. The first of the *Sung dynastic history's* "evil ministers," Ts'ai had earned an appointment to the Censorate by criticizing his mentor Wang An-shih's punishment of a dutiful palace guard in the Hsüan-te Gate incident of 1073.[359] Following Wang's retirement, Ts'ai used his censorial powers to check

---

[357] Chu Hsi, *Chu-tzu yü-lei* 130, quoted in Ch'i, *Wang An-shih pien-fa*, p. 223.

[358] *HCP* (1979) 282, pp. 6908–9.

[359] In the first month of 1073, when Wang tried to escort the imperial chariot through the Hsüan-te Gate on horseback, a palace guard hailed Wang and beat back his horse. Though Shen-tsung let the guard and his some nine other men be cudgeled to placate Wang, he was also pleased by Ts'ai Ch'üeh's remonstrance. The event is given a line each in *SS* 327, p. 10546, and *SS* 471, p. 13698, but for the full story and its restorationist interpretation, see *HCP* (1979) 242, pp. 5898–5901.

the rise of potential rivals, such as Acting Finance Commissioner Shen K'uo, who had tilted in the direction of Wu Ch'ung; and to impeach men whose posts Ts'ai coveted, such as the drafting official and director of the *Ssu-nung ssu*, Hsiung Pen. Ts'ai's attacks had the implicit approval of the emperor, who in late 1077 rewarded Ts'ai with Hsiung Pen's two posts as well as with the concurrent post of director of the Remonstrance Bureau, making Ts'ai by far the most powerful of those officials who "did his bidding": as head of the *Ssu-nung ssu* Ts'ai Ch'üeh "presided over the New Policies," while as chief remonstrator and drafting official he could monitor people and communications to root out remaining opponents of Shen-tsung's management of affairs.[360]

Ts'ai Ch'üeh's effectiveness was enhanced by a cruel streak that helped him intimidate opponents: in early 1078, Ts'ai took charge of a case in which two officials of the Court of Judicial Review (*Ta-li ssu*) were accused of taking bribes to cover up a provincial murder case. Ts'ai had the two men cangued and exposed in the sun for fifty-seven days, to the horror of both Chief Censor Teng Jun-fu (who imagined he heard their screams at night) and Teng's assistant, Shang-kuan Chün. Teng and Shang-kuan took their concerns about the case to the emperor; but despite their convincing evidence of wrongdoing Shen-tsung eventually sided with Ts'ai Ch'üeh. The two censors were demoted and forced to write confessions admitting to malfeasance and factionalism, while Ts'ai was rewarded with Teng Jun-fu's post as chief censor to add to his quiver.[361] By mid-1078, Ts'ai Ch'üeh had managed to use the bribery case to taint Wu Ch'ung's son An-ch'ih and Wu's son-in-law Wen Chi-fu as well, and both men were cashiered with the original defendants. When Ts'ai Ch'üeh complained that Wu An-ch'ih had been treated too leniently Shen-tsung finally realized that the real target of Ts'ai's campaign was Wu Ch'ung himself; but although the emperor berated Ts'ai, he was captivated by the logic of Ts'ai's defense: "If one man (Ts'ai) cooperates to bring what His Majesty has founded to completion, and another man (Wu) bears grudges and tries to destroy that foundation, how will the people know where to put their hands and feet?"[362] Ts'ai's attack on Wu Ch'ung bore its first fruit in the fifth month of 1079, when Ts'ai was named to the State Council. Wu Ch'ung was still chief minister, but five months later Wu lost his closest ally with the death of the dowager empress, spearhead of the anti–New Policies faction at court. Broken and bereft, Wu Ch'ung was finally allowed to resign in the third month of the new year, and

---

[360] SS 471, pp. 13698–701. For the war of Ts'ai Ch'üeh on Shen K'uo, whom he denounced as a "devious character," see *HCP* (1979) 283, pp. 6933–5; 291, pp. 7114–15, and Forage, "Science, technology, and war in Song China," p. 56. On his acquisition of Hsiung Pen's posts and the remonstrance directorship, see *HCP* (1979) 286, pp. 6999–7000; 287, pp. 7015, 7019; 288, p. 7053.

[361] *HCP* (1979) 289, pp. 7059–63; 7066–8.

[362] *HCP* (1979) 290, pp. 7090–1; *HCP* (1979) 298, p. 7249.

one month later he was dead. In four years he had gone from being the hope of the conservatives to an object of pity, commended for his upright character but held in derision for his weakness and his refusal to stand up for his beliefs by resigning earlier.[363] Meanwhile, though Ts'ai Ch'üeh remained only an assisting councilor of state, the chief minister Wang Kuei (1019–85) was a man of weak character whom Shen-tsung held in contempt.[364] Ts'ai Ch'üeh completely dominated the fearful older man, whom he manipulated like a puppet in the service of both his own political ambitions and Shen-tsung's agenda.

The Yüan-feng administrative reforms

Shen-tsung's agenda was dominated by two paramount objectives. Of course, his most abiding goal – the one that had preoccupied him since before ascending the throne – was to recover the northern territories. But by the time of his new Yüan-feng reign period, the emperor was also convinced that the structure of his government itself was badly in need of reform.

The Sung bureaucracy was an amalgam of two very different administrative systems, both inherited from the T'ang and Five Dynasties periods. On the one hand, the Sung founder, Chao K'uang-yin (T'ai-tsu), inherited the elaborate bureaucratic apparatus of the high T'ang: the three departments (san-sheng), six ministries (liu-pu), nine courts (chiu-ssu), and five directorates (wu-chien) that in theory covered every aspect of civil administration. Because it located the dynasty's new officials – many of them holdovers from the T'ang and Five Dynasties regimes – in a familiar pyramid of job descriptions and authority relations, this formal T'ang model served the needs of political consolidation. But even by the eighth century many of these offices had lost their functional importance, supplanted by a welter of ad hoc organizations such as the Bureau of Military Affairs (Shu-mi yüan), the Finance Commission (San-ssu), the censorates, and the increasing number of circuit intendancies that assumed the primary responsibilities for defense, finance, law, and regional administration.[365] In contrast to the formal T'ang model, which strengthened ministerial authority at the expense of the ruler, the system of ad hoc organizations could be used to enhance monarchical power, by siphoning away responsibilities

---

[363] HCP (1979) 300, pp. 7313–15; 303, pp. 7374–5.

[364] See HCP (1979) 291, pp. 7115–16.

[365] This section draws heavily on Lo, Introduction to the civil service of Sung China, pp. 35–78, and Kung Yen-ming, "Pei Sung Yüan-feng kuan-chih kai-ko lun," Chung-kuo shih yen-chiu No. 1 (1990), pp. 132–43, and on the assistance of Professor Wang Tseng-yü. For a comprehensive study of the Yüan-feng reforms in the broader context of the late Northern Sung administrative change, see Chang Fu-hua, Pei Sung chung-ch'i i-hou chih kuan-chih kai-ko (Taipei, 1991).

of the formal bureaucratic structure and serving as a direct extension of the imperial will. Because each administrative model met a different need, the Sung founders retained both, creating the characteristic Sung system of dual appointments. In order to consolidate their control over newly conquered territories, "respectable holdovers" from the preceding regime were retained in their positions in the formal bureaucratic hierarchy, but the positions themselves were stripped of functional importance: they became purely titular or stipendiary offices (chi-lu kuan) that conferred rank and salary. Those officials who won the confidence of the new rulers were additionally granted functional commissions (ch'ai-ch'ien) or offices (chih) in the still vital prefectural and county bureaucracies or in the ad hoc organizations, where the real work of the empire was conducted.[366] Thus every active official held at least two (though possibly more) concurrent appointments: a purely titular appointment in the formal bureaucracy, such as grand master of remonstrance of the Secretariat (yu chien-i ta-fu), and an active assignment or commission, such as fiscal intendant-general of the Ho-pei circuits.[367]

The Sung system of dual appointments served the useful purpose of differentiating an official's civil service rank, which was ideally a function of his seniority and merit, from his actual job at a given time, which shifted with his own special skills and the needs of the court. But the use of actual if moribund office titles simply to designate rank and to provide sinecures to officials awaiting active assignments proved confusing and expensive. For to mollify the large surplus of conquered scholarly elite (shih-ta-fu) and their families the court continued to fill the quota of officials in the departments, ministries, courts, and directorates, even as parallel organizations absorbed more and more of their functions, fostering the proliferation of redundant offices (ch'ung-san tie-ssu). For example, in finance, although officials were appointed to the Ministry of Finance (Hu-pu) and its subordinate bureaus, such as the Accounting Bureau (Tu-chih ssu), they performed no function; meanwhile, in the Finance Commission, where the real fiscal administration took place, a different set of officials were assigned to the Accounting Bureau (Tu-chih ssu) and the Census Bureau (Hu-pu ssu). And a similar redundancy of offices characterized the parallel personnel, judicial, and military administrations.[368]

---

[366] Lo, *Introduction to the civil service of Sung China*, pp. 59–60.

[367] These were the positions held by the first fiscal intendant-general (tu chuan-yün-shih), Fan Chih-ku, in 988. See *HCP* (1979) 29, p. 657. Note that by this time membership in the senior or administrative class of officials – that is, officials designated as worthy of posts in the capital and the court (ching-ch'ao kuan) – no longer denoted actual service in the capital or the court.

[368] There were times when an official actually performed the function associated with his titular office. In those case his title was prefaced with such terms as "acting" (ch'uan), "managing" (kou-tang), "supervising" (p'an), and others. See Kung, "Pei Sung Yüan-feng kuan-chih kai-ko lun," pp. 132–3.

Over the course of the eleventh century, officials charged that the growth of these parallel bureaucracies – one mostly titular and one entirely functional – promoted turf wars, administrative inefficiency, and above all a glut of supernumerary officials and clerks. But up to the Yüan-feng era few solutions had been offered. Even Wang An-shih showed little interest in administrative reform for its own sake. To promote his own reforms Wang was perfectly willing to create such new agencies as the Finance Planning Commission, the Commission for Reform of the Secretariat, and Secretariat examiners, as well as a host of new intendancies, or to revitalize such old T'ang vestiges as the Court of Agricultural Supervision and, to administer *pao-chia* militia training, the Ministry of War. Yet however much these new agencies streamlined the pursuit of reform objectives, their addition to the existing structure just compounded the larger problem of bureaucratic redundancy. Thus Shen-tsung made it his own mission to overhaul Sung government and to untangle the bureaucratic chaos that in his eyes had become an embarrassment to the memory of the founders.[369] Moreover, until he was ready to announce his reforms in 1080 he kept his mission private: according to Wang An-shih, who witnessed the Yüan-feng reorganization of government with some alarm from his retirement post in Chiang-ning fu, whereas Shen-tsung had never before done anything without prior discussion, in this most important matter he proceeded with no consultation at all.[370]

At the core of his administrative reforms, Shen-tsung aimed to reorganize the Sung central government according to the *T'ang statutes of government* (*T'ang liu-tien*), whose departments, ministries, courts, and directorates provided the hollow shell of the Sung's titular, stipendiary offices. The first stage of the reform, announced in the eighth month of 1080, involved the "rectification of office titles" (*cheng kuan-ming*). This "rectification" involved two steps. First, the functional responsibilities of the entire T'ang roster of offices were revived, except for those with no current applicability, which were abolished outright.[371] With this change the six ministries, and to a lesser extent the courts and directorates, took over the administrative tasks of the central government, either displacing their counterpart ad hoc organizations completely or reducing them to their original functions. For instance, the financial affairs of the central government, which had been divided between the Finance Commission and since 1070 the Court of Agricultural Supervision, were now centralized in the Ministry of Finance (*Hu-pu*): the Finance Commission was

[369] HCP (1979) 307, p. 7462.
[370] Kung, "Pei Sung Yüan-feng kuan-chih kai-ko lun," p. 141, citing Chu Hsi, *Chu-tzu yü-lei* (Taipei, 1962) 128, p. 3070.
[371] HCP (1979) 307, p. 7462; HTC (1957) 75, p. 1880.

abolished completely, and its financial concerns shifted to the Left Section (*tso-ts'ao*) of the Ministry of Finance; at the same time the Court of Agricultural Supervision was reduced from its powerful role as financial center of the New Policies to its original task as manager of the government's granaries, while its revenue-generating operations were transferred to the Right Section (*yu-ts'ao*) of the Ministry of Finance.[372] Similarly, the personnel functions of the civil and military bureaucracies, which had been scattered among four separate agencies answering to as many oversight boards, were all centralized in the Ministry of Personnel.[373] In the same manner the entire roster of ministries, courts, and directorates were revived as the administrative apparatus of the central government.

The second step in the "rectification of office titles" aimed at creating a new set of titles to designate rank and salary level, now that the old set had been turned into functioning offices. For this purpose Shen-tsung's Administrative Reform Commission (*Hsiang-ting kuan-chih so*) employed the so-called prestige titles (*chieh-kuan*) in vogue during the T'ang and early Sung. In the ninth month of 1080 the commission submitted a roster of twenty-five new stipendiary titles, organized in a hierarchy of nine major steps (*kuan-p'in*) and arrayed for the sake of continuity in a one-to-one relationship with the old stipendiary offices. The new roster had two distinct benefits: it was elegant, with all lower titles ending in the suffix *lang* (gentleman) and all but the two highest titles ending in the suffix *ta-fu* (grandee); and it was unambiguous, since none of the titles had ever been associated with functional offices.[374] The virtues of the reform can be illustrated by the changes in the titles of Fan Ch'un-jen's stipendiary rank: just before the reform Fan held the stipendiary title of gentleman of the interior of the Ministry of Justice (*shang-shu hsing-pu lang-chung*) – a grade 6B office in the middle of the hierarchy – with the functional assignment as prefect of Hsin-yang Commandery. When the reform took effect Fan kept his assignment, but acquired the new stipendiary title of *ch'ao-san ta-fu*, also grade 6B; meanwhile his old stipendiary title had become a functioning post in the Ministry of Justice.[375]

---

[372] SS 163, pp. 3846–8; 165, pp. 3904–5; Wang, "Pei Sung ti Ssu-nung-ssu," pp. 30–1.

[373] Kung, "Pei Sung Yüan-feng kuan-chih kai-ko lun," pp. 136, 138; Lo, *Introduction to the civil service of Sung China*, p. 71. Executory class officials were administered by the Bureau of Executory Personnel (*Liu-nei ch'üan*) under the Board of Personnel; administrative class officials were administered by the Bureau of Personnel Evaluation (*Shen-kuan yüan*) under the Secretariat-Chancellery; military servitors were administered by the *Hsüan-hui yüan* under the Three Echelons (*San-pan yüan*); and senior military officers were administered directly by the Bureau of Military Affairs (*Shu-mi yüan*).

[374] Lo, *Introduction to the civil service of Sung China*, p. 71.

[375] See "Fan Ch'un-jen kai-kuan ming-chih," in Wang An-li, *Wang Wei kung chi* (Nan-ch'ang, 1915–20), p. 3. For tables of equivalencies, see Miyasaki Ichisada, "Sōdai kansei josetsu," which introduces Saeki Tomi's *Sō-shi shokkanshi sakuin* Dai 2-han (Kyoto, 1974); or see *Chung-kuo li-shih ta t'zu-tien: Sung-shih chüan*, pp. 158–60.

The Yüan-feng reforms were limited to the central government, and had little impact on the structure of circuit, prefectural, and county administration. Initially the "rectification of office titles" affected only the stipendiary titles of senior civil officials – that is, of officials in the administrative class (*ching-ch'ao kuan*) – since at the probationary executory (*hsüan-jen*) level there was much less discrepancy between titular office and the actual function performed as a staff member of local government. But there were some exceptions, and consequently during Hui-tsung's reign new stipendiary titles were adopted for the seven grades of executory officials as well.[376] Overall, the first phase of the reforms solved the most vexing problems of the Sung's dual system of classificatory rank and functional office, and helped reduce the number of redundant offices and supernumerary officials – though according to some contemporaries not as much as the abolition of the courts and directorates, which duplicated functions of the six ministries, would have done.[377] In this respect, the first phase of the Yüan-feng reorganization did foster Shen-tsung's explicit goal of administrative rationalization. But Shen-tsung also aimed at a second, less explicit, objective, which was to strengthen the authority of the emperor over his ministers.[378] One way he chose of maintaining imperial authority was to preserve the Bureau of Military Affairs, despite its overlap with the Ministry of War. The Sung founders had used the Bureau of Military Affairs to maintain imperial control over military matters by segregating military policy making from the civilian bureaucracy. Despite pressure from many officials to maintain the consistency of the reforms by transferring all military matters to the Ministry of War, Shen-tsung refused to abandon the "household regulations" (*chia-fa*) of his dynastic forebears. Consequently, only relatively routine matters were routed to the Ministry of War, while major policy-making authority – and seats on the Council of State – were reserved for the director and vice-director of the Bureau of Military Affairs.[379] But if preserving the bureau constituted a step back from the principle of administrative reform, Shen-tsung also pushed the reforms forward to consolidate his power over the bureaucracy: in the second phase of the Yüan-feng reorganization, in mid-1082, Shen-tsung turned his attention to the top echelon of the bureaucracy, the "three departments" (*san-sheng*).

---

[376] Lo, *Introduction to the civil service of Sung China*, pp. 72–3. Lo also describes the creation of new titles for military officials during the Yüan-feng period, which "imposed a uniform terminology on the rank systems of both the civil and military officials and brought them under the same personnel agency," thereby reducing the psychological distance between the two services. See p. 73.

[377] For the views of Ssu-ma Kuang, Liu An-shih, and Chu Hsi, see Kung, "Pei Sung Yüan-feng kuan-chih kai-ko lun," p. 139.

[378] See Kung, "Pei Sung Yüan-feng kuan-chih kai-ko lun," p. 139.

[379] Kung, "Pei Sung Yüan-feng kuan-chih kai-ko lun," p. 139.

The three departments – State (*shang-shu sheng*), the Chancellery (*Men-hsia sheng*), and the Secretariat (*Chung-shu sheng*) – had stood as the collective pinnacle of government since the post-Han period of division. By the eighth century, however, functional distinctions among them had become blurred. This led to the formation of a combined Secretariat-Chancellery (*Chung-shu men-hsia*) whose heads normally served as the chief councilors (*tsai-hsiang*), supported by a structure of staff offices (*fang*) that duplicated and supplanted the six ministries of the Department of State Affairs. By the early Sung the Secretariat-Chancellery controlled all civilian affairs except remonstrance, and with the Bureau of Military Affairs comprised the two administrations (*liang fu*) – civil and military – of government.[380]

Intent as he was on running his own government, Shen-tsung saw the three departments as a way of breaking up the concentrated power of the Secretariat-Chancellery and its chief ministers, by dividing the single unified civil authority into three separate components. In new administrative protocols announced in the fourth and fifth months of 1082, the three departments were revived in a way that diluted their overall authority as much as possible: rather than making each department responsible for a particular set of issues, all three departments were made to share different aspects of every issue: the Secretariat was to consider and deliberate, the Chancellery was to investigate policy alternatives, and the Department of State Affairs – pinnacle of the six ministries – was to put the final policy decisions into effect. Except in the most unusual circumstances each department was required to perform and memorialize about its own function alone.[381]

Only under the guidance of a superordinate coordinator could such an extreme division of responsibilities function effectively. Under the T'ang Statutes of Government that paramount position would have been filled by the Secretariat director (*chung-shu ling*), often the de facto chief councilor (*ch'eng-hsiang*) to the emperor and the man most directly responsible for civil and military governance.[382] But it was just this paramount chief official that Shen-tsung wanted to avoid, and in this he was assisted by the wily and ambitious Ts'ai Ch'üeh, still an assisting civil councilor of state under the ineffective Wang Kuei. In Ts'ai Ch'üeh's eyes, the absence of a superordinate minister provided the opportunity he needed to attain supreme power in the

---

[380] For useful background information, see the Introduction and relevant entries in Charles O. Hucker, *A dictionary of official titles in imperial China* (Stanford, Calif., 1985).

[381] *HCP* (1979) 325, pp. 7823–4; 326, pp. 7837–8; 327, pp. 7871–2. See also the "San-sheng tsung-lun," in *Yüan-feng kuan-chih* [Kyoto University photocopy of T'ai-pei kuo-li chung-yang t'u-shu-kuan holding] (1081; n.p., 1972).

[382] Hucker, *Dictionary of official titles*, p. 193, item 1616; Li Lin-fu et al., comps., *Ta T'ang liu-tien* [1515 ed.] (738; Taipei, 1974), 9, p. 7a.

bureaucracy. When the new departmental structure was enacted in the fourth month of 1082, Wang Kuei's post was changed from chief executive of the Secretariat-Chancellery (*t'ung chung-shu men-hsia p'ing-chang-shih*) – the de facto chief minister – to left codirector of the Department of State Affairs (*shang-shu tso p'u-yeh*); Ts'ai's post was changed from assisting civil councilor (*ts'an-chih cheng-shih*) to right codirector (*yu p'u-yeh*) of the Department of State Affairs. Just after the change, it is reported, Ts'ai instructed the credulous Wang Kuei that since under the old system he had been chief minister, then under the new one he should be named director of the Secretariat. But to Shen-tsung, Ts'ai insisted that no such position was needed: the same level of coordination could be achieved by naming the left codirector a concurrent vice-director (*shih-lang*) of the Chancellery, and the right codirector a concurrent vice-director of the Secretariat. Since this suited Shen-tsung's plan to keep political authority divided, the emperor agreed. As a result, Ts'ai Ch'üeh came to be known as the "second chief councilor" (*tz'u hsiang*), although "in reality it was Ts'ai who monopolized the handles of government, while Wang Kuei could only fold his hands in deference."[383]

Although Ts'ai Ch'üeh found additional ways to benefit from the new departmental structure – including having documents routed to his domain in the Secretariat marked *shang* or "submitted up" – Shen-tsung emphasized his own authority by playing up the subservience of his chief councilors. In sharp contrast to his relationship with Wang An-shih, which was marked by genuine friendship and the respect of a disciple for his mentor, Shen-tsung publicly humiliated Ts'ai and Wang Kuei, fining them sums of gold for the smallest infractions and then obliging them to thank the emperor for their punishment (*men-hsieh*). Although Ts'ai Ch'üeh was no favorite of officialdom, many were embarrassed by this unprecedented imperial discourtesy, which the new censor Huang Lü warned would erode official morale.[384]

Although the strict division of administrative tasks mandated for the three departments may have enhanced imperial authority, it also prompted an immediate decline in administrative efficiency. Within a month of promulgating the new rules, in the fifth month of 1082, Shen-tsung himself complained that government had become paralyzed by a dangerous administrative backlog. The emperor seemed on the verge of reviving the old system, in which functionally specialized agencies, such as the Finance Commission and the Court of Agricultural Supervision, reported to a paramount Secretariat. But

---

[383] *SS* 471, p. 13699. The remaining civilian councilors were Chang Tun and Chang Tsao as *men-hsia* and *chung-shu shih-langs*; P'u Tsung-meng as *shang-shu tso-ch'eng*; and Wang An-shih's brother An-li as *shang-shu yu-ch'eng*. See *HCP* (1979) 325, p. 7825.

[384] *SS* 471, pp. 13699–700; *HCP* 325, p. 7825; 335, p. 8079.

Ts'ai Ch'üeh, whose power if not his dignity had been significantly enhanced by the reform, convinced Shen-tsung that the new system saved over twenty thousand strings of cash monthly in official salaries.[385] Nonetheless the strict departmental division of labor proved the least successful aspect of the Yüan-feng administrative reforms: routing every policy initiative through each of the three department, then down to the ministries, and then back up to the departments, was just not conducive to administrative efficiency. Moreover, after Shen-tsung's death in 1085 the problems became insuperable. For as Lü Kung-chu pointed out in the seventh month of 1085, under Shen-tsung the flaws in the system could be overcome, since he essentially made policy himself and then his chief ministers did what he ordered; but with Shen-tsung's eight-year-old son on the throne there was a critical need for a strong unified council of ministers, working and memorializing on all aspects of policy in concert. As a result of Lü's memorial the three departments and the Censorate were given permission to cooperate and to memorialize jointly on policy issues.[386] Ssu-ma Kuang wanted to go even further, by recombining the Secretariat and the Chancellery as before and giving the chief minister more latitude to decide issues directly.[387] Certainly Hui-tsung's chief councilor, Ts'ai Ching, lacked no opportunity to decide matters on his own, but that was because power flows as much from personality as it does from institutions. Institutionally, the three departments were not formally recombined until right after the fall of the Northern Sung, in 1129, nor were their chief officers abolished until 1172. Until then, the three departments survived as another redundant layer, a residue of Shen-tsung's attempt to lead the reform movement on his own.

THE CAMPAIGN AGAINST THE TANGUT HSI HSIA

If Shen-tsung's administrative reforms enjoyed only limited success, his war policy was an unmitigated disaster: the debacle at Yung-lo ch'eng in the ninth month of 1082 not only sapped the emperor's faith in his reforms, it also cut short his life at age thirty-seven.

Foreign policy under Wang An-shih

As a young man Shen-tsung was fixated on recovering the northern territories occupied by the Tanguts and the Khitan, and he ascended the throne in 1067

---

[385] *HCP* (1979) 326, p. 7848.

[386] *HCP* (1979) 358, pp. 8561–2.

[387] "Ch'i he liang-sheng wei-i cha-tzu," in Ssu-ma, *Ssu-ma Wen-cheng kung ch'uan-chia chi* 57, pp. 685–7, quoted in Kung, "Pei Sung Yüan-feng kuan-chih kai-ko lun," p. 138.

eager to wage offensive wars. In Shen-tsung's mind, recovering the northlands was the raison d'être of the New Policies, and so it is ironic that only Wang An-shih, the architect of the New Policies, was able to restrain the emperor's irredentist ambitions. But unlike Fu Pi and Ssu-ma Kuang, who admonished the emperor for even thinking about conquest, Wang An-shih fed the emperor's hopes of "mastering the Hsia state and recovering the old borders of the Han and T'ang" – but only after essential reforms had been completed.[388] For as Wang demonstrated in a court debate of 1071, he was keenly aware of the power of Sung's northern neighbors, and of the folly of engaging them prematurely:

There are projects that we should pursue but for which our power is still inadequate. For example quelling the barbarians and opening up the frontier, however desirable they seem at the moment, are still beyond our capacity. His majesty must deeply consider that our financial resources are inadequate and reliable men of talent rare. For the moment, therefore, we should concentrate on quieting down border affairs. If we can quiet things down on the border so that the barbarians cannot harm us then we can put our internal affairs in order; once our internal affairs are in order, there is an adequate supply of talented men, and we are prosperous and strong (fu-ch'iang), then there will be nothing that we cannot do.[389]

Wang believed that of the two northern states the Sung had more to fear from the Liao, which he described as the most vast, most populous barbarian nation in many generations; and he warned Shen-tsung that if he did not first devote himself to "establishing order throughout society," then there could be no hope of encompassing and controlling the Khitan.[390] Wang put this prudent view to effect in a series of border issues that embroiled the two empires between 1072 and 1076, when he consistently sought to preserve peace, even where peace meant adopting a compliant attitude toward the Liao.[391]

It sometimes seemed that Wang took a much more defiant attitude toward the Tangut Hsi Hsia, who because of the accession of a child ruler (Ping Ch'ang, r. 1067–86) and their political disarray could appear relatively vulnerable.[392]

---

[388] *HCP* (1979) 230, p. 5605. On Wang An-shih's cautious approach to war, see Liu, *Reform in Sung China*, p. 57, and Tao Jing-shen (T'ao Chin-sheng), *Two sons of heaven: Studies in Sung-Liao relations* (Tucson, Ariz., 1988), p. 68.

[389] *HCP* (1979) 221, p. 5371.

[390] *HCP* (1979) 236, pp. 5725–6.

[391] See Tao, *Two sons of heaven*, pp. 72–8. The principal issues were the border incursion of 1072, the Khitan establishment of observation posts in Sung territory in 1073, and Sung fortification of the border and renegotiation of the Sung-Liao boundary between 1074 and 1075, an issue on which Wang was less inclined to be submissive. Although traditional historiography charges Wang with the abandonment of land to the Liao in the final settlement of 1076, Tao Jing-shen argues that Wang probably played little role in the final decision.

[392] *HCP* (1979) 236, p. 5752.

But in practice Wang preached a cautious approach to the Tanguts as well. Wang's real views were revealed in 1070, after Sung incursions into Tangut territory had provoked retaliatory attacks in Ching-yüan circuit:

What if we show a strong front to the [Tanguts] and they decline to obey; how will the court then deal with them? We are not now strong enough to match troops (*chiao-ping*) with them; and if we do not match troops, then what else can we do? It would be most inappropriate if we first put up a show of strength and are then forced to humble ourselves. Under the current circumstances, we should make a point of being accommodating (*jou*) toward [the Hsia]; by being accommodating we are least likely to miscalculate.[393]

What then did Wang offer an emperor whose motivating ambition was to recover the lost territories of the north? In brief, he offered Shen-tsung a policy of expansion, colonization, and economic exploitation in the frontier regions of Hunan and Szechwan, and in the Tibetan tribal lands of the Tsinghai and Kansu region.[394] This long border between the Sung and the tribes of the forest, mountains, and steppe contained abundant natural resources, including war horses, and hosted a wide range of lucrative foreign trades that could be exploited for the eventual campaign against the Tanguts. The prototype for Wang An-shih's policy of conquest along the weak frontier was created by the frontier adventurer Wang Shao. In 1068, Wang Shao sent up a proposal to colonize the Tibetan tribal lands between Hsi-ning2 (in modern Tsinghai province) and the T'ao River valley (in soutwestern Kansu), then highly unstable and vulnerable to Tangut annexation, and to finance the conquest with a state monopoly over the region's substantial foreign trade. Wang Shao offered his policy as the first step in creating a Sino-Tibetan alliance that would surround the Tanguts from front to rear, and put the Hsia state "in the palm of [Sung] hands."[395] As an expression of his commitment to employing any man who could get things done the emperor immediately charged Wang Shao with

---

[393] *HCP* (1979) 214, p. 5197.

[394] For overviews and sources on Wang An-shih's policies in the northwestern and southwestern frontiers, see Smith, *Taxing heaven's storehouse*, pp. 41–7; Richard von Glahn, *The country of streams and grottoes: Expansion, settlement, and the civilizing of the Sichuan frontier in Song times* (Cambridge, Mass., 1987), pp. 98–104; and (on Hunan) Richard von Glahn, "The country of streams and grottoes: Geography, settlement, and the civilizing of China's southwestern frontier, 1000–1250" (diss., Yale University, 1983).

[395] For Wang Shao's "Three part proposal for pacifying the Western Barbarians," see *SS* 328, p. 10579, translated in Williamson, *Wang An Shih*, vol. 1, pp. 305–6. The fullest study of Wang Shao's frontier policy is Enoki Kazuo, "Ō Sei no Kasei keiryaku ni tsuite," *Mōko gakuhō* 1 (1940), pp. 87–168. For its continuation under Che-tsung and Hui-tsung, see Paul Jakov Smith, "Irredentism as political capital: The New Policies and the annexation of Tibetan domains in Hehuang (the Qinghai-Gansu highlands) under Shenzong and his sons, 1068–1108," in *Emperor Huizong and late Northern Song China: The politics of culture and the culture of politics*, ed. Patricia B. Ebrey and Maggie Bickford (Cambridge, Mass., 2006), pp. 78–130.

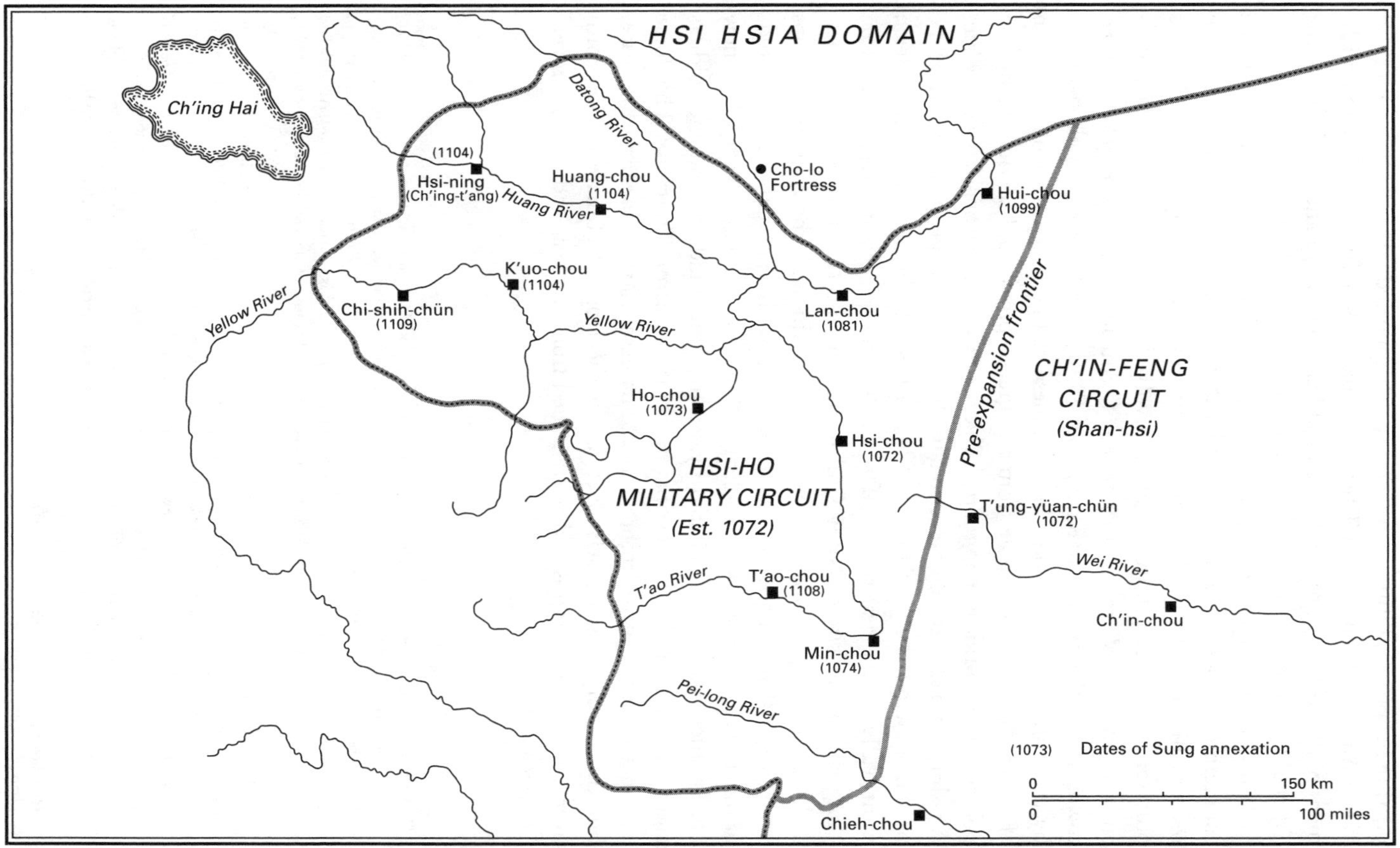
HSI HSIA DOMAIN
Ch'ing Hai
Datong River
Cho-lo Fortress
Hui-chou (1099)
(1104) Hsi-ning (Ch'ing-t'ang)
Huang-chou (1104)
Huang River
K'uo-chou (1104)
Yellow River
Chi-shih-chün (1109)
Yellow River
Lan-chou (1081)
Pre-expansion frontier
CH'IN-FENG CIRCUIT (Shan-hsi)
Ho-chou (1073)
Hsi-chou (1072)
HSI-HO MILITARY CIRCUIT (Est. 1072)
T'ung-yüan-chün (1072)
Wei River
Ch'in-chou
T'ao River
T'ao-chou (1108)
Min-chou (1074)
Pei-long River
(1073) Dates of Sung annexation
0 150 km
0 100 miles
Chieh-chou

Map 15. Annexation of Tibetan territories under Shen-tsung and his sons, 1072–1109.

putting his proposal into action. Fervently supported by both Shen-tsung and Wang An-shih, Wang Shao's Tibetan campaign bore fruit with the establishment of the new Sung military circuit of Hsi-ho in 1072 and the defeat of the Tibetan leader Mu-cheng in 1074.[396]

Whenever the policy of expansion in the weak frontiers provoked nervous countermeasures by the Tanguts and the Khitan, Wang An-shih acted to restrain his more bellicose emperor from responding impetuously. Wang's only serious strategic miscalculation involved the Annamese state of Chiao-chih, in modern Vietnam. In late 1075, Annamese troops attacked walled towns across the border in Kuang-nan West, searching for rebels harbored by the Chinese. In addition, the Annamese claimed they were on a mission of mercy, "to save the people from the green sprouts and service exemption policies of the Middle Kingdom." Taking this as a personal affront, Wang An-shih persuaded the emperor to launch a punitive expedition, for which he personally wrote the proclamation.[397] But from the beginning the expedition went badly: in the first month of 1076 the Annamese launched an attack on Yung-chou2, the site of Nung Chih-kao's uprising twenty-five years earlier; and despite Wang's insistence that the city would hold, the Annamese troops overcame stiff resistance to breach the city's walls and slaughter thousands of functionaries, troops, and residents.[398] Ten months later, with Wang now out of office, the court retaliated by sending one hundred thousand soldiers and twice as many labor consripts deep into Annamese territory. This force was massive enough to frighten the Annamese leader into suing for peace, but the victory was a costly one; for in the tropical climate of the south over half the Sung troops and porters died from the heat and "swamp fever" (she-chang).[399]

---

[396] Two constituent prefectures of Hsi-ho circuit, Ho-chou2 and Min-chou, were not taken until 1073, in battles that brought down on Wang Shao the charge of genocide against Tibetan tribals. Wang's chief Tibetan adversary, Mu-cheng, did not submit until 1074. See *HCP* (1979) 239, p. 5818; 243, pp. 5912–16, 5945–56; 252, p. 6160. When he retired in 1077, after his relations with Wang An-shih had soured over the war with Annam, Wang Shao claimed that because of the cost he had never wanted to create a separate circuit of Hsi-ho, but that Wang An-shih had insisted. See *HCP* (1979) 280, p. 6865.

[397] *HCP* (1979) 271, pp. 6650–1; 273, pp. 6674–5. On the Sino-Vietnamese war, see James A. Anderson, "Treacherous factions: Shifting frontier alliances in the breakdown of Sino-Vietnamese relations on the eve of the 1075 border war," in *Battlefronts real and imagined: War, border, and identity in the Chinese middle period*, ed. Donald J. Wyatt (New York, 2008); and chapter 4 of James A. Anderson, *The rebel den of Nùng Trí Cao: Eleventh-century rebellion and response along the Sino-Vietnamese frontier* (Seattle, Wash., 2006). Anderson argues that the Vietnamese Ly court was prompted to invade the Chinese side of the frontier out of fear that Sung authorities were overly successful in cultivating relations with the upland followers of Nung Chih-kao and his clan.

[398] *HCP* (1979) 272, pp. 6664–5.

[399] *HCP* (1979) 279, pp. 6843–4.

Shen-tsung's Tangut wars

The Annam campaign further exacerbated the political turmoil of Wang An-shih's second term as chief minister, driving a wedge between him and Wang Shao and further alienating the emperor.[400] But if conservatives thought that Wang's departure would bring an end to frontier expansion and war mobilization they were deeply disappointed. With no one left to speak to Shen-tsung as an equal, the emperor was finally free to pursue the linchpin of his plan to recover the northern territories, the conquest of the Tangut Hsi Hsia.

Shen-tsung had to know that the conquest would be difficult, for the Tanguts had already demonstrated how formidable they were at the beginning of his reign. In 1067 the Sung general Ch'ung O captured the Tangut town of Sui-chou, a strategic key to the river valleys leading southeast to the Yellow River and the Sung heartland.[401] When a deal to exchange Sui-chou for Sung stockades held by the Tanguts fell through in 1069 the Sung court tightened its hold by walling the old town and renaming it Sui-te Commandery (Sui-te chün). The Tanguts responded in the fifth month of 1070 by throwing "one hundred thousand" troops southwest of the contested zone into Shan-hsi's Huan-ch'ing military circuit, in a probe that exposed the incompetence of the Sung generals and the lack of discipline among their troops, who slaughtered hundreds of Tibetan residents of the area long after the Tangut troops had withdrawn.[402] Tangut forces took one Huan-ch'ing stockade after another, at the same time diverting twenty thousand men against Sui-te, but even at this point the hostilities could have been stepped down, as Wang An-shih recommended. Arguing that the Tanguts were just trying to provoke the Sung into wasting men and provisions, Wang urged Shen-tsung to let the Tanguts keep the small stockades and not to make a show of massive retaliation before Sung troops were ready. But Shen-tsung was not yet willing to abandon the prospect of an offensive campaign, and in the ninth month of 1070 he dispatched State Councilor Han Chiang to Shan-hsi to oversee war preparations.[403]

In a campaign that served as a dress rehearsal for the debacle at Yung-lo ch'eng in 1082, Han proposed mixing a defense based on "strengthening the walls and clearing out the countryside" (chien-pi ch'ing yeh) with an offensive tactic of political and military provocations that would incite the Tanguts into

---

[400] HCP (1979) 273, p. 6684; 280, p. 2865.

[401] For descriptions of the border terrain, see Forage, "Science, technology, and war in Song China," p. 71; and Li, Sung Hsia kuan-hsi shih, pp. 158–63.

[402] HCP (1979) 214, pp. 5203–5; SS 486, pp. 14007–8.

[403] HCP (1979) 214, pp. 5195–7, 5203–5; 215, pp. 5236–7. The emperor had wanted to send Wang, who had no military expertise at all, but Han Chiang requested the assignment for himself.

overcommitting themselves.[404] The cornerstone of Han's plan was to build a
line of stockades along the border from Heng-shan to the Yellow River, despite
the warnings of court officials and field commanders that the arid, grassless
wasteland would be difficult to provision and impossible to defend.[405] In
the last month of 1070, Han armed Ch'ung O with twenty thousand troops
and a license to behead uncooperative commanders, and ordered him to wall
Luo-wu-ch'eng just south of the Tangut outpost of Yü-lin. In the next month
Ch'ung O secured the area and threw up walls around Luo-wu, using wood
from buildings and watchtowers farther south that he had dismantled and carried in. Before he could move on to the next site, however, logistical problems
began to intrude: Luo-wu had no wells, the fifty-mile provisioning road was
indefensible, conscription of Chinese and Tibetan men left only women available to carry grain, and the enormous provisioning needs of the campaign had
begun to suck up the scarce resources of a twenty-prefecture regional economy
that was already exhausted by drought. On top of the logistical problems, the
command structure had been short-circuited by Han Chiang and Ch'ung O,
leaving field generals in complete confusion.[406] In the second month of 1071
Tangut troops moved in to take advantage of the misconceived campaign,
meeting no significant opposition. Once the first stockade fell the Sung court
ordered Luo-wu-ch'eng abandoned, while Ch'ung O "panicked so badly that
he could not even hold a brush" to write for help. Moreover, the confusion
spread into neighboring Ch'ing-chou2, where a former Tangut slave whom
Han Chiang had promoted to commander led a mutiny of some two thousand
men, humiliating Han and further exposing the disorder within the Sung
armies.[407]

The Luo-wu-ch'eng fiasco, for which Han Chiang was cashiered, ended
Shen-tsung's first attempt to conquer the Hsi Hsia. Although the Tanguts
did not recover Sui-te, the campaign and related military activities cost the
Sung over seven million strings of cash, and further destabilized a north Chinese population already buffeted by drought and famine.[408] The debacle also
underscored the need for fundamental reforms before Shen-tsung could realize
his irredentist ambition. In addition to militarization of the *pao-chia* system,
reform leaders enacted other significant military reforms. In mid-1072 the
court reestablished a national military institute to improve the training of

---

[404] *HCP* (1979) 215, pp. 5241–2. The Sung court cut off yearly payments to the Hsi Hsia and closed down
the mutual trade (*ho-shih*) markets.

[405] *HCP* (1979) 217, p. 5273; 219, p. 5324.

[406] *HCP* (1979) 218, pp. 5305–6; 218, pp. 5312–15; 220, pp. 5337–8, 5343–6.

[407] *SS* 486, p. 14009; *HCP* (1979) 220, pp. 5361–2.

[408] For Ssu-ma Kuang's "Chien Hsi-cheng shu" (Admonition against the western campaign), see Ssu-ma,
Ssu-ma Wen-cheng kung ch'uan-chia chi 45, pp. 569–71, quoted in *HCP* (1979) 218, pp. 5312–15.

Sung military leaders, for whom Wang An-shih had little respect.[409] Wang An-shih also tried to alleviate the odium of military service, which he saw as a cause of unrest and potential rebelliousness, by abolishing the practice of branding soldiers and by reducing the punishments for desertion.[410] And in an effort to improve troop training and cooperation, the court introduced the "combined battalion" and "cohesive squad" measures (*chiang-ping, chieh-tui fa*).[411] On other fronts, reformers crafted a reliable horse-supply system to help offset the Tangut and Liao advantage in cavalry mounts. Starting in 1074, administrators of the Szechwan-Shan-hsi Tea and Horse Agency took advantage of Wang Shao's extension of the northwest frontier to create a marketing system that regularly traded Szechwanese tea for over ten thousand Tibetan cavalry horses annually for the remainder of the Northern Sung.[412] At about the same time Wang An-shih and his followers dismantled the expensive attempt to maintain a national herd in government pastures radiating out from K'ai-feng, and instead stabled a small number of horses throughout the north Chinese population through the *pao-ma* (*pao-chia* horse), *hu-ma* (household horse), and *chi-ti mu-ma* (land in return for a horse) measures.[413] In addition, Wang P'ang and Lü Hui-ch'ing established the Directorate of Armaments in 1073 in order to extend China's overall advantage in military technology.[414] And of course throughout the 1070s the reformers built up Shen-tsung's war chest with surplus cash and grain generated by the green sprouts and service exemption funds, as well as through more local measures like the Szechwan tea monopoly.

---

[409] *HCP* (1979) 234, pp. 5689–91. For examples of Wang's contempt for the Sung general staff, see *HCP* (1979) 232, pp. 5631–2; 234, p. 5675.

[410] *HCP* (1979) 223, p. 5420; 235, pp. 5704–5. See also Teng Kuang-ming, "Wang An-shih tui Pei Sung ping-chih ti kai-ko ts'o-shih chi ch'i she-hsiang," in *Sung-shih yen-chiu lun-wen-chi: Chung-hua wen-shih lun-ts'ung tseng-k'an*, ed. Teng Kuang-ming and Ch'eng Ying-liu (Shanghai, 1982), pp. 318–20.

[411] These two measures sought to regularize military training and to institute greater troop solidarity by combining imperial troops, and in frontier regions the Tibetan soldiers and "archers" from different commands (*chih-hui*), into mixed battalions (*chiang*) of several thousand to ten thousand men, subdivided into companies (*pu*) and squads (*tui*) under a hierarchy of officers charged with upgrading overall training. See Wang, *Sung-ch'ao ping-chih ch'u-t'an*, pp. 107–14; Ch'i, *Wang An-shih pien-fa*, pp. 283–5; and, for an overall survey of Shen-tsung's military reforms, Feng and Mao, *Pei Sung Liao Hsia chün-shih shih*, pp. 277–312.

[412] Smith, *Taxing heaven's storehouse*, pp. 264–5.

[413] See Sogabe Shizuo, "Sōdai no basei," in his *Sōdai keizaishi no kenkyū*, pp. 77–91; *SS* 198, pp. 4946–50; Ma, *Wen-hsien t'ung-k'ao* (1965) 160, pp. 1391a–1392c; *CPPM* 75, pp. 2381–93; 109, pp. 3443–54. The numbers involved were relatively insignificant: *pao-ma* operated under a quota of 8,000 head; *hu-ma* distributed 11,662 head by 1080 but stopped replacing animals after 1084; and *chi-ti mu-ma* placed a total of 23,500 horses under the care of 87,000 households by 1124.

[414] *HCP* (1979) 245, pp. 5972–4. Paul Forage discusses the relationship between Shen-tsung's expansionism and military technology in his "Science, technology, and war in Song China."

As the military reforms took shape and the funds poured in, only Wang An-shih stood between Shen-tsung and a new expedition against the Hsi Hsia. When in 1074 the emperor demanded to know why now was not the time to attack the Tanguts, Wang urged him to let Wang Shao complete his pacification of the Tibetans, lest the Tanguts take advantage of the Sung's pre-occupation to combine forces with the Khitan.[415] Once Wang was out of office, however, Shen-tsung was surrounded by ineffective men like Wu Ch'ung, too weak to restrain the emperor, or by opportunists like Ts'ai Ch'üeh, willing to say anything the emperor wanted to hear. And all the emperor did want to hear, lamented Chang Fang-p'ing in 1077, was talk of war.[416] Ambitious men in and out of government knew that the best way to advance their careers was to promote Shen-tsung's war goals. Thus Ts'ai Ch'üeh goaded Wang Kuei into supporting the Tangut expedition, in order to put the out-of-favor chief minister in Ts'ai's debt by saving his position; while Shen K'uo circumvented Ts'ai Ch'üeh's efforts to keep him out of government by presenting the emperor with an actual expedition plan.[417]

Meanwhile, as officials fed the emperor's irredentist yearnings, Shen-tsung made his own preparations for war. In the eleventh month of 1077, the Directorate of Armaments announced that weapons had been stockpiled in the five circuits of north China.[418] A year later Shen-tsung renamed the thirty-three treasuries that had grown out of T'ai-tsu's original war chest, and commemorated them with a poem: "In succession the Five Dynasties lost their bearings, while the northern dogs flourished. T'ai-tsu founded our nation, and with the aim of disciplining the barbarians he established an inner storehouse to pay for raising troops. [This dream] his descendant must honor; could I dare forget his ambition?"[419]

Now all Shen-tsung needed was an appropriate opportunity to launch his new campaign.

The collapse of the Yüan-feng invasion

The Hsia dowager empress Liang, who in early 1081 imprisoned her son Ping-ch'ang, the emperor Hsia Hui-tsung, for drifting ritually and diplomatically

---

[415] HCP (1979) 250, pp. 6103–4.

[416] HCP (1979) 286, pp. 7005–9. Li T'ao attributes this memorial, which ranks bellicosity as destructive as an addiction to sex, to Su Shih.

[417] HCP (1979) 291, pp. 7115–16; HCP (1979) 313, pp. 7593–4. On the connections between Ts'ai Ch'üeh, Shen K'uo, and the Yüan-feng expedition, see Forage, "Science, technology, and war in Song China," pp. 56–8.

[418] HCP (1979) 285, p. 6989.

[419] HCP (1979) 295, p. 7192. This poem is also translated, following Liang Ch'i-ch'ao, in Williamson, Wang An Shih, vol. 2, p.160.

toward the Sung provided Shen-tsung with the opportunity he needed to justify his new compaign.[420] The coup was reported to Shen-tsung by none other than Ch'ung O, who had survived the Luo-wu-ch'eng embarrassment to become commandant of Fu-yen military circuit. To restore the rightful ruler Ch'ung O recommended launching a "punitive expedition" against the Tanguts in Ling-chou and their capital of Hsing-chou2. Ch'ung was ordered to draw up a battle plan with Shen K'uo, then serving as Fu-yen military commissioner (*ching-lüeh an-fu shih*), and after Ch'ung boasted that he would conquer the leaderless Hsia nation and bring the child Ping-ch'ang back to K'ai-feng, Shen-tsung could be restrained no longer: in the sixth month of 1081, all circuits of Shan-hsi were ordered to prepare for the arrival of expeditionary forces.[421]

The battle plan called for a five-pronged attack on the Tangut capital, led largely by men who had served in Wang Shao's Hsi-ho campaign: in addition to Ch'ung O, the commanders included the eunuch generals Li Hsien, Wang Chung-cheng, and Liu Ch'ang-tso, and Shen-tsung's maternal uncle, Kao Tsun-yü. These five men commanded combat troops of about three hundred and seventy thousand men, supported by about the same number of transport troops, arrayed to converge on the Tangut capital from the south, southeast, and southwest.[422]

The logistical demands of the expedition were enormous, requiring the tactical expertise of individual commanders, smooth communication among all the commanders, and the rapid coordination of forces and provisions across the vast, inhospitable terrain bounded by the southern half of the Yellow River loop. Coming on the tenth anniversary of Ch'ung O's Luo-wu-ch'eng disaster, which had failed on just these same criteria, the Yüan-feng expedition would test how much the offensive capacity of the Sung armies had improved over ten years of reform.

The campaign was launched in the eighth month of 1081, and at first it enjoyed quite stunning success. The next month Li Hsien's troops took Lan-chou, which had been in Tibetan or Tangut control for four centuries, giving him access to the Yellow River routes up to the Tangut capital.[423] Ch'ung O, heading in from the western side of the loop, took Mi-chih, Shih-chou, and Hsia-chou in the tenth month of 1081, thus gaining control of the

---

[420] *HCP* (1979) 312, p. 7578. Ping-ch'ang had replaced Tangut with Chinese ceremony and allegedly planned to turn over the southern Ordos to the Sung. See Dunnell, "The Hsi Hsia."

[421] *HCP* (1979) 313, pp. 7593–4; Forage, "Science, technology, and war in Song China," p. 59.

[422] For a discussion of troop strength and the ratio of combat to transport troops, see Forage, "Science, technology, and war in Song China," pp. 59–60, 65–6.

[423] *HCP* (1979) 316, pp. 7638, 7641. The battles are summarized in *SS* 486, pp. 14010–11; and analyzed in Forage, "Science, technology, and war in Song China," pp. 61–73; and Li, *Sung Hsia kuan-hsi shih*, pp. 180–93.

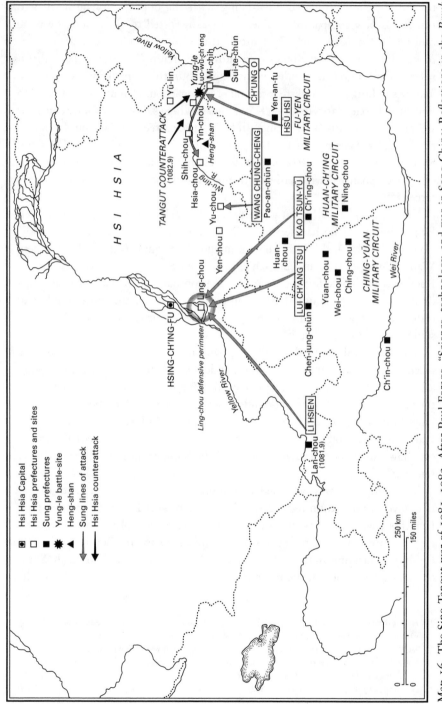

Map 16. The Sino-Tangut war of 1081–1082. After Paul Forage, "Science, technology, and war in Song China: Reflections in the *Brush talks from the Dream Creek* by Shen Kuo, 1031–1095," (diss., University of Toronto, 1991), Map 4, p. 61.

Heng-shan highlands where he had fared so poorly a decade earlier.[424] At the same time Kao Tsun-yü and Liu Ch'ang-tso, leading armies from Huan-ch'ing and Ching-yüan respectively, fought their way north toward Ling-chou.[425]

The Tangut court was caught off guard by the initial Sung victories, which cost thousands of Tangut lives. Desperate for a strategy to save the capital, the dowager empress Liang rejected the plea of her younger generals to confront the Sung forces directly in favor of a plan to "strengthen the walls and clear the fields" advocated by one of her older generals: to concentrate Tangut forces around Ling-chou in the west and Hsia-chou in the east and to let the Sung armies penetrate deeply into Tangut territory, then attack their supply lines with light cavalry to cut off their provisions.[426] Whether or not this account of the Tangut war council is apocryphal, it accurately summarizes the fate of the Sung invasion. Supply problems soon beset Kao Tsun-yü and Liu Ch'ang-tso at one end of the campaign in Ling-chou, and Ch'ung O and Wang Chung-cheng at the other end in the Heng-shan highlands, sowing discord among the generals and between them and their civilian supply masters. In the east, shortages kept Ch'ung O from advancing from Hsia-chou to Ling-chou, and precipitated the grizzly slaughter of hundreds of labor conscripts at the hands of the Fu-yen circuit fiscal intendant Li Chi, who personally joined his troops in slicing through the foot tendons of fleeing porters and left them to crawl helplessly to their deaths.[427] At the same time, two other Fu-yen fiscal officials had sold off provisions intended for Wang Chung-cheng and his troops in Yu-chou2, compounding Wang's sense of dread at the eerie emptiness of an area completely abandoned by the Tanguts. Because of his fear that lurking Tangut soldiers would spy on his encampment Wang forbade his soldiers from lighting fires, forcing the men to eat their dwindling supply of rice uncooked. Already weakened by exhaustion and exposure to the cold, many of the soldiers got sick from the dirty, raw rice, provoking angry calls to murder their commander and the two fiscal officials. Wang Chung-cheng barely escaped with his life before his troops were ordered to retreat back to Yen-chou2, losing twenty thousand soldiers to starvation and Tangut harassment.[428]

In Ling-chou, supply problems were exacerbated by poor communications and sheer incompetence: neither Kao Tsun-yü nor Liu Ch'ang-tso were able to coordinate their arrival at Ling-chou, and when Kao did begin to attack

---

[424] Ch'ung O was joined in Hsia-chou by Wang Chung-cheng. *HCP* (1979) 316, p. 7653; 317, p. 7669; 318, p. 7682.

[425] *HCP* (1979) 319, p.7699.

[426] *SS* 486, p. 14011. Forage suggests that the event is a "post facto historical reconstruction." See Forage, "Science, technology, and war in Song China," p. 65 n. 74.

[427] *HCP* (1979) 319, p. 7702. Li Chi was seconded from the Szechwan Tea and Horse Exchange, where he had been superintendant.

[428] *HCP* (1979) 319, pp. 7700–2, 7705. Half of the civilian transport conscripts fled.

in the eleventh month of 1081 he discovered that his troops had brought no
siege equipment. After eighteen days of their ineffective siege, punctuated by
squabbles between Kao and Liu and threats of mutiny from the troops, the
Tanguts cut the irrigation canals that watered the city and inundated the Sung
camps. The Sung forces were ordered by the court to withdraw, but Tangut
harassment turned their retreat into a rout.[429]

In four short months the Tangut invasion, for Shen-tsung the capstone of
the New Policies, had gone from stunning success to humiliating defeat. But
despite the rout, the northern armies were still geared up for war, and in the
spring of 1082 many officials called on the emperor to continue his campaign.
In the fourth month of 1082, Li Hsien, whose capture of Lan-chou was one
of the few successes of the expedition, advocated a new expedition against the
Tangut capital; when Lü Kung-chu resolutely opposed repeating the earlier
mistake an irritated Shen-tsung let him resign as codirector of the Bureau of
Military Affairs.[430] The next month Shen K'uo and Ch'ung O recommended
an alternative plan to wall Wu-yen-ch'eng, on the headwaters of the Wu-ting
River, in order to control the strategic resources of the Heng-shan highlands
(salt, iron, pastures, and war-loving locals) and gain access to the southern
Ordos. It was this more limited proposal that Shen-tsung endorsed. But rather
than delegating it to Shen K'uo and Ch'ung O, who at least knew the terrain,
he placed it in the hands of Hsü Hsi, a cunning political manipulator who
had won the emperor's favor by denouncing Sung generals as too cowardly
to conquer the Tanguts.[431] Hsü Hsi reached Yen-an fu and the campaign
staging ground in the eighth month of 1082, and immediately revised the
original proposal. Instead of focusing on Wu-yen and the arc of sites north
of Heng-shan, which he rejected as too close to the prefectures that Ch'ung
O had lost the previous fall, Hsü Hsi proposed to wall Yung-lo ch'eng to
the south of Heng-shan, which overlooked the Wu-ting River valley leading
southeast to Sui-te. But Yung-lo ch'eng was just across a stream from Luo-wu,
the site of Ch'ung O's first disaster, and Ch'ung O forcefully opposed Hsü
Hsi's choice with the same argument he himself had ignored in 1071: Yung-lo
ch'eng had no independent water supply, it was indefensible, and walling it
could only lead to carnage. Hsü Hsi remained obdurate, however, and after
ordering Ch'ung O to return to Yen-chou2 he himself undertook the walling
of Yung-lo ch'eng, which Shen-tsung elevated with the title of "Yin-ch'uan
Fortress."[432]

---

[429] HCP (1979) 320, p. 7720; Forage, "Science, technology, and war in Song China," p. 69.

[430] HCP (1979) 225, pp. 7828–9. For court discussion of the plan, see HCP (1979) 327, pp. 7868–71.

[431] HCP (1979) 330, pp. 7955–6.

[432] CPPM 89, pp. 2757–9; SS 486, p. 14011. The HCP entries on Hsü Hsi's campaign are anthologized
in CPPM 89, pp. 2757–67. General Kao Yung-heng also criticized the project, for which he was
dispatched to Yen-chou2 and placed under arrest. See HTC (1957) 77, p. 1929.

Official opinion held that because of Yung-lo ch'eng's strategic importance the Tanguts would have to contest it, but Hsü Hsi welcomed their arrival, proclaiming that it would be his moment of glory. When in the ninth month of 1082 the Tanguts actually converged, however, Hsü Hsi's braggadocio turned to horror: for as he looked out over his new walls to the west, there stood three hundred thousand Tangut troops stretched out as far as the eye could see. And now the fates of his thirty-five thousand troops were sealed, for Hsü Hsi's stubbornness was compounded by incompetence. Twice he refused to heed his generals when they begged him to attack before the Tanguts, with their awesome armored cavalry called the Iron Hawks (*t'ie-yao*), could get into formation; and twice he refused to let his troops retreat before the Tangut onslaught, one time even forcing them to stand outside the gates and take the Tangut attack head on. Half of the troops who made it back inside the walls died of thirst, as Tangut control of the water supply forced parched soldiers to drink what liquids they could wring out of horse manure. When heavy rains did fall it was too late for the exhausted troops, who were cut down or fled as the Tanguts swarmed the walls. Li Chi and Hsü Hsi's eunuch lieutenant Li Shun-chü were killed by the panicking soldiers, as was Hsü Hsi himself thought to have been, although some reported sighting him alive.[433]

The tragedy at Yung-lo ch'eng brought an end to Shen-tsung's irredentist ambitions. From a military perspective, the costs had already been too high: in return for Lan-chou and six Tangut border towns, the Sung lost 230 officers and 12,300 troops at Yung-lo ch'eng, and an estimated 600,000 officers, Chinese and Tibetan regulars, and militia for the Ling-chou and Yung-lo ch'eng campaigns combined.[434] Emotionally, the debacle broke Shen-tsung's spirit. After receiving the report of Yung-lo ch'eng's fall in the tenth month of 1082 he appeared in tears before his state councilors, berating them for not giving him better advice. "Not a single one of you said that the Yung-lo ch'eng campaign was wrong," the emperor charged, casting about for a scapegoat. It is true that ever since Wang An-shih's departure officials had tried to advance their own careers by urging the emperor on to war, even after the Ling-chou rout had "caused all under Heaven to yearn for the court to bring an end to war." Yet by the emperor's own admission there were men who had counseled against war, including the state councilors Lü Kung-chu and Wang An-li – who had also warned that Hsü Hsi would destroy the nation – and the field commander Chao Hsieh. Shen-tsung had simply chosen not to listen. It was the failure of the Yüan-feng invasions that finally forced Shen-tsung to confront

[433] *HCP* (1979) 329, pp. 7935–7; *SS* 486, p. 14012.
[434] *HCP* (1979) 330, p. 7945; *SS* 486, p. 14012. Although the figure of 600,000 is undoubtedly exaggerated, it suggests how stunning the actual losses must have been.

the limitations of his armies: after Kao Tsun-yü was routed at Ling-chou and Hsü Hsi was overwhelmed by a Tangut army whose strength he had completely underestimated, "the emperor began to realize that his frontier officials could not be trusted; moreover he had become weary of war, and had no more ambition to conquer the Western (Hsia)."[435]

After a decade of military reform the Sung army was no more able to project power out into the desert and the steppe than before. Of course, the Tanguts had also suffered devastating losses and could no longer be regarded as an offensive threat. But in the eyes of such Yüan-yu critics as Su Shih, Su Ch'e, and Ssu-ma Kuang they never had been an offensive threat; it was the Sung that constituted the threat, driven on by "ambitious and provocative ministers" who started the wars for territory and personal glory.[436] In the aftermath of the fall of Yung-lo ch'eng, hostilities continued to simmer, as the Tanguts sought to regain Lan-chou and their six border towns. Neither side had the strength for an extended offensive campaign, however, and a stalemate persisted between the two countries until Che-tsung's majority in 1094, when (as described in the next chapter) Chang Tun, Ts'ai Ching, and T'ung Kuan gradually returned to a more aggressive strategy.

SHEN-TSUNG'S DEATH AND THE OUSTER OF THE REFORMERS

The collapse of his Tangut expedition sapped Shen-tsung's reforming zeal and pushed him increasingly toward the "old-party" (chiu-tang) men. In fact, Shen-tsung had planned to use the second stage of his administrative reforms, the reestablishment of the T'ang table of offices in 1082, as a vehicle for mixing conservatives in with the "new" men. He had hoped to start by appointing Ssu-ma Kuang to the resuscitated position of censor in chief (yü-shih ta-fu), unfilled for at least three reigns, but bowed to the objections of Ts'ai Ch'üeh and Wang Kuei.[437] After Yung-lo ch'eng, however, Shen-tsung was much less tolerant of what he saw as the reformers' obsession with keeping Ssu-ma Kuang out of court, and in the eighth month of 1083 he gave vent to his frustration by cashiering State Councilor P'u Tsung-meng for railing against Ssu-ma Kuang's "perverted views."[438] Soon after, the emperor began to bring Ssu-ma Kuang's associates back into the government. In the first month of 1084, Shen-tsung ordered that Su Shih be allowed to move to the lively Yangtze delta

[435] HCP (1979) 330, pp. 7945, 7955.
[436] For representative memorials, see HCP (1979) 380, pp. 9221–2 (Ssu-ma Kuang); 381, pp. 9278–83 (Su Ch'e); and 405, pp. 9862–6, 9872–5 (Su Shih); cited by Wu, Hsi Hsia shih-kao, pp. 84–5.
[437] HCP (1979) 350, pp. 8390–2. On the censor in chief, see Kracke, Civil service in early Sung, p. 36.
[438] HCP (1979) 338, pp. 8148–9.

city of Ch'ang-chou from the backwater river town of Huang-chou (Huai-nan West) where Wang Kuei had banished him under "administrative restraint" (*an-chih*) for writing an allegedly seditious poem.[439] Four months later the emperor also revived the career of the prominent New Policies opponent Fan Ch'un-jen, blocked like Ssu-ma Kuang from a new office under the Yüan-feng administrative reforms; Shen-tsung appointed Fan prefect of Shan-hsi's Ho-chung fu, the critical transport center at the intersection of the Wei and Yellow rivers, where he immediately began detailing the disruptions caused by *pao-chia* mobilization.[440]

By the autumn of 1084, Shen-tsung turned with even greater urgency to the old-party men, for though only thirty-six-years old he was ill and sensed he was dying. It was time, the emperor announced to his ministers, to designate an heir, whose training and protection he would entrust to Ssu-ma and Lü Kung-chu. To Ts'ai Ch'üeh, always good at reading the emperor's mind, it was clear that Ssu-ma Kuang could no longer be kept from court; so rather than squandering his influence trying to oppose Ssu-ma Kuang, Ts'ai sought instead to ingratiate himself with him.[441] This he could not do directly, for Ssu-ma would be unlikely to deal directly with a man like Ts'ai Ch'üeh; an intermediary was needed. For this purpose Ts'ai chose Hsing Shu, in the 1060s a disciple of Ch'eng Hao, Lü Kung-chu, and Ssu-ma Kuang himself. Hsing Shu had also attracted the attention of Wang An-shih, who tried to mould him into a New Policies partisan. When factional lines began to form Hsing Shu chose the conservative side, deprecating the reforms to Wang An-shih and his son, but Hsing paid a heavy price for his principled stand, spending most of the Hsi-ning years wandering around Lo-yang with no employment. Wu Ch'ung brought him back to court in an academic position, which he valued all the more because of his years out of office. Ts'ai Ch'üeh's purge of Wu Ch'ung's men filled Hsing Shu with dread, but he was saved from expulsion by the emperor's favorable notice. But Ts'ai must have sensed that Hsing Shu had become accustomed to office and hence was easy to suborn. As soon as Ts'ai approached Hsing Shu in late 1084, Hsing offered to put his connections with the conservative luminaries at Ts'ai's service, and transmitted a message from Ts'ai Ch'üeh to Ssu-ma Kuang's son K'ang urging K'ang to encourage his father to accept an academic post at court – an act of fawning servility that Ssu-ma Kuang dismissed with a laugh. Hsing Shu even used his connections with

---

[439] *HCP* (1979) 342, pp. 8228–9. Wang Kuei had succeeded in enforcing the banishment despite Shen-tsung's protestations against overinterpreting poetry, suggesting that one key element of imperial power was simply how committed the emperor was to exercising his will.

[440] *HCP* (1979) 345, pp. 8289–90.

[441] *HCP* (1979) 350, pp. 8390–2.

the dowager empress's nephews to try to alter the imperial succession from Shen-tsung's eight-year-old son, Chao Hsü2, to an older collateral prince, who might be inclined to exercise his independence from the imperial family by favoring Ts'ai Ch'üeh. Although Hsing Shu and Ts'ai Ch'üeh were not punished for their interference until 1089, Hsing's scheme was immediately denounced by the two nephews.[442] In the second month of 1085, with the emperor nodding weakly from his sickbed, Chao Hsü2 was named heir apparent and his grandmother designated as temporary regent, "until the emperor should recover."[443]

Shen-tsung's strength was spent, however, and in the third month of 1085 he died. Chao Hsü2 was proclaimed the new emperor, and authority over all national and military affairs was transferred to Shen-tsung's mother, Ying-tsung's empress Kao and now the regent and dowager empress Hsüan-jen.[444] As the two chief ministers, Ts'ai Ch'üeh and Wang Kuei controlled official ceremonial in their capacity as the masters of imperial interment (*shan-ling shih*), but they were powerless to control the unofficial demonstrations set off by the emperor's demise. Ssu-ma Kuang was again in Lo-yang mulling over the offer of a court post when he learned of Shen-tsung's death, and despite his reluctance to be sucked into the politics of an imperial transition he let Ch'eng Hao persuade him to go to the capital to pay his respects. As it happened, Ssu-ma's welcome was even more tumultuous than he could have imagined: the palace guards alerted the populace to Ssu-ma's arrival by saluting him as "Prime Minister Ssu-ma." The thousands of people who thronged the palace gates at the passing of an emperor pressed in to embrace Ssu-ma's horse, shouting "Please do not return to Lo; stay here to assist the Son of Heaven bring the people back to life." Ssu-ma Kuang took fright at the demonstration and, making his excuses, rushed directly back to Lo-yang.[445]

At sixty-seven and in poor health, Ssu-ma Kuang was understandably reluctant to leave the quiet of Lo-yang; but from a distance he was ready to advise the dowager empress on how to repair the damage done by the reformers. And first priority, he insisted, must go to "opening up the route of remonstrance" to officials and commoners, and to keeping it open with placards in the provinces, drum calls in the capital, and punishments for anyone who stood in the way.[446]

---

[442] *HCP* (1979) 350, p. 8391; *SS* 471, pp. 13702–3. Hsing Shu's perfidy earned him a position among the biographies of the evil ministers.

[443] See *HCP* (1979) 351, pp. 8409–14. For detailed contemporary accounts, see *HCP* (1979) 352, pp. 8417–50.

[444] *HCP* (1979) 353, pp. 8456–9.

[445] *HCP* (1979) 353, p. 8465.

[446] "Ch'i k'ai yen-lu cha-tzu," in Ssu-ma, *Ssu-ma Wen-cheng kung ch'uan-chia chi* 46, pp. 585–6, quoted in *HCP* (1979) 353, pp. 8465–7.

Yet the response to Ssu-ma Kuang's memorial illustrates the resiliency of the reform faction, which still controlled the State Council and the key organs of government. Two months after Che-tsung's accession the government did issue a call for criticism, but to Ssu-ma Kuang's chagrin it was so limited in scope as to be useless. For Ts'ai Ch'üeh had intervened in the drafting process to prohibit on pain of punishment any real criticism of the government's leaders or policies, in order to stem the personal attacks against him that had proliferated since Shen-tsung's death.[447] If the conservatives were to reverse the policies they so abhorred more would be needed than the support of the dowager empress; they would have to oust the new-party men from power and take over the government themselves.

The battle for political power took a full year. In the first months of the new reign the dowager empress assembled her forces: Ssu-ma Kuang accepted a post as prefect of Ch'en-chou, just south of K'ai-feng, while Lü Kung-chu, Su Shih, and Ch'eng Hao all came to the capital directly.[448] Then in the fifth month of 1085 she could make her first big move, for after sixteen undistinguished years as a state councilor Chief Minister Wang Kuei finally died, letting Hsüan-jen put her own stamp on the State Council.[449] Since Ts'ai Ch'üeh's power was still intact he could not be kept from assuming Wang Kuei's post as left codirector of the Department of State Affairs, but in the ensuing cabinet shuffle Hsüan-jen did win two major victories: she prevented Ts'ai from elevating his own candidate, Chang Tun, to the cochief ministership, or right codirector of the Department of State Affairs, obliging Chang to become head of the Bureau of Military Affairs instead; and she convinced Ssu-ma Kuang that for the sake of the nation and the boy emperor he had to take the Chancellery position (*men-hsia shih-lang*) vacated by Chang, even though that meant serving in the State Council under Ts'ai Ch'üeh.[450] Two months later Dowager Empress Hsüan-jen's hand was strengthened even further when Lü Kung-chu was appointed to the council as an assistant director of the Department of State Affairs (*shang-shu tso-ch'eng*).[451]

---

[447] "Ch'i kai ch'iu-chien chao-shu cha-tzu," in Ssu-ma, *Ssu-ma Wen-cheng kung ch'uan-chia chi* 47, pp. 602–3; *HCP* (1979) 356, pp. 8508–11.

[448] *HCP* (1979) 356, pp. 8508, 8513–14.

[449] *HCP* (1979) 356, p. 8517.

[450] The cochief minister's position went to Han Chen, which Hsüan-jen found preferable to having Ts'ai's man in power even though she personally disliked Han. Chang Tun's move still constituted a promotion, from the equivalent of assisting civil councilor to chief military councilor. The reshuffling of the State Council also prompted changes in the academic institutes and the six boards: Wang An-li returned from Chiang-ning fu to serve in the Han-lin Academy, Lü Hui-ch'ing returned to court as an academician in the Hall of the Aid to Governance (*Tzu-cheng tien*); and Tseng Pu was named director of the Board of Revenue. See *HCP* (1986) 356, pp. 8520–5.

[451] *HCP* (1986) 358, pp. 8561–2.

Ssu-ma Kuang's presence in the council had a dramatic impact on conservative efforts to overturn the New Policies, for as leader of the opposition
throughout Shen-tsung's reign he was the only man with the prestige needed
to offset the entrenched power of the reformers. Much as Wang An-shih had
defined the horizons of the reforms fifteen years earlier, Ssu-ma Kuang defined
the scope of the conservative restoration. Indeed, it was Ssu-ma Kuang who
assured Hsüan-jen that a conservative restoration was ritually appropriate –
that it was legitimate, in short, to reverse a deceased emperor's policies and
expel his ministers even before the three years of mourning had passed, if that
was the only way to save the nation and its people.[452] Ssu-ma Kuang's passionate memorials lay the foundation for the conservative critique of activist
government and opened a floodgate of denunciations of the policies it had
spawned. But as Pi Chung-yu argued in a letter to Ssu-ma Kuang on his mentor's return to office, critiques and denunciations could accomplish little in
the absence of political power:

Now we would move to abolish green sprouts, suspend state trade, remit service exemption
taxes, and eradicate the salt monopoly laws – all those so-called profitable measures that
harm the people. But as soon as we try to weed them out or change them then those men
who managed the New Policies will become unhappy; and they will not only complain
that "we cannot abolish green sprouts, suspend state trade, remit service exemption taxes,
or eradicate the salt monopoly," but will also manipulate the emperor's fears that financial
resources are inadequate, and harp on the issue, in order to sway the emperor's mind. . . . And
because of this, [even if we eradicate the New Policies fiscal measures] the green sprouts
funds will be distributed again, state trade will be reestablished, remitted exemption funds
will be recollected, and the salt monopoly will be revived.

How then, asked Pi Chung-yu, could the fiscalist policies be irrevocably
eradicated? In the long term, it was necessary to remove the fear of fiscal shortages by slowly building up surpluses through prudent economic policies that
measured expenditures against income, and by returning funds and resources
to the regions from which they were collected. In the short term, however, it
was necessary to extirpate the agents of the New Policies who still controlled
the government:

When Wang An-shih was in office there was no one in office at court or in the provinces who
was not his follower, and that is why he could enact his policies. Now we wish to undo the
shortcomings of those days, yet out of every ten senior court officials, circuit intendants and
departmental directors, and military officers, seven or eight are Wang An-shih's followers.
Although we have raised two or three venerables to power, and have put six or seven men
of virtue in office, there are still tens of their men throughout the hundred offices. Where
then is the power to accomplish our objectives?[453]

---

[452] "Ch'i ch'ü hsin-fa chih ping-min shang-kuo che shu," in Ssu-ma, *Ssu-ma Wen-cheng kung ch'uan-chia chi*
    46, pp. 588–91.
[453] *SS* 281, pp. 9525–6.

Ssu-ma Kuang did not himself have the ruthlessness to wrest political power the way Wang An-shih had done, nor did he have the energy – for he like Wang was now tired and old. Yet by serving on the State Council Ssu-ma Kuang could advise Hsüan-jen on whom to use, and recruit men who did have the drive and energy to purge the reformers and build up a conservative power base. Neither Wang An-shih, who died in the fourth month of 1086, nor Ssu-ma Kuang, who died five months later, lived to fully comprehend the consequences of that purge, which is taken up in the following chapter.

CHAPTER 6

CHE-TSUNG'S REIGN (1085–1100) AND THE AGE OF FACTION

Ari Daniel Levine

RETROGRESSION: 1085–1086

Turning back the clock: The coming of the Hsüan-jen regency

As Emperor Shen-tsung (1048–85, r. 1067–85) lay dying at the age of thirty-seven, an era of relative political stability was fading along with him.[1] Long held dormant by the force of Shen-tsung's will, the personal and political animosities of his past and present ministers were stirring, now that their emperor's untimely death would effect a new political alignment. Since his heir apparent was an eight-year-old boy, after the emperor's passing executive powers would be wielded by a regent for the foreseeable future. Upon assuming the regency, Dowager Empress Hsüan-jen, a longtime opponent of Shen-tsung's New Policies, would become the dominant force at court, throwing her support behind the conservative opposition and dooming the current reformist ministerial coalition. In the early spring of 1085, the specter of factional infighting was casting its shadow upon the corridors of power, as two

---

[1] Compared to the burgeoning field of studies of Shen-tsung, Wang An-shih, and the New Policies, the political history of the Che-tsung reign remains largely uncharted territory. For a recent biography of Che-tsung, see Wang Han, *Sung Che-tsung* (Ch'ang-ch'un, 1997). For a condensed introduction to the political history of the Che-tsung reign, see Liu Po-chi, "Yüan-yu tang-cheng chih yen-pien yü liu-tu," in *Shih-hsüeh lun-chi*, ed. Chung-hua hsüeh-shu yüan (Taipei, 1977), pp. 240–66. For a more recent and in-depth study of factional politics in the late Northern Sung, see Lo Chia-hsiang, *Pei Sung tang-cheng yen-chiu* (Taipei, 1993). The most important primary source for the Che-tsung reign is Li T'ao's *Hsü tzu-chih t'ung-chien ch'ang-pien* [hereafter *HCP* (1979)] (1183; Peking, 1979–95), which provides a day-by-day account of events at court from 1086 to 1101, supplemented by a near-limitless variety of unofficial sources. This *Chung-hua shu-chü* punctuated edition of *HCP* is preferable to the reprint of the standard 1881 *Che-chiang shu-chü* edition (1183; Shanghai, 1986). Also indispensable to the historian is Yang Chung-liang's *Tzu-chih t'ung-chien ch'ang-pien chi-shih pen-mo* [hereafter *CPPM*] (1253; Taipei, 1967), a thematic compilation of and companion to *HCP*. A three-year lacuna exists in the *HCP*, between the seventh month of 1093 and the fourth month of 1097, and was reconstructed from various chapters of *CPPM*. Other essential sources are T'o-t'o et al., eds., *Sung shih* [hereafter *SS*], (1345; Peking, 1977), the official dynastic history of the Sung, and Hsü Sung et al., *Sung hui-yao chi-kao* [hereafter *SHY* (1997)] (1809, 1935; Peking, 1997), a compendium of official court documents.

hostile court coalitions readied themselves for a protracted and acrimonious struggle for dominance. When the conflict ended a year and a half later, after the most sweeping political purge thus far in the history of the dynasty, a new conservative ministerial regime would establish firm control over policy and polity and would reverse – they thought for good – the reform policies of the Shen-tsung reign.

In the second month of 1085, cracks were already beginning to show in the current coalition government, in which advocates and adversaries of the New Policies (*hsin-fa*) maintained an edgy truce. Wang Kuei (1019–85), the elderly éminence grise of the Yüan-feng era, clung to the senior ministerial post of chief councilor of the left (*tso-p'u-yeh*) for dear life.[2] Despite the semihostile yet ineffectual presence of Wang at the head of the Council of State, the reformists still controlled the central government machinery. Real decision-making power over the details of administration had been wielded for several years by Ts'ai Ch'üeh (1037–93), the reformist chief councilor of the right (*yu-p'u-yeh*) and a former disciple of Wang An-shih.[3] For the past six years, Wang Kuei and Ts'ai Ch'üeh had uneasily shared power at Shen-tsung's behest; the emperor had played Wang and Ts'ai off against each another, while maintaining his personal dominance over state policy.[4]

Shen-tsung had ensured the continued survival of the New Policies by deflecting criticism from the antireform coalition, to whom he had partially extended the olive branch in the last years of his reign. While holding the brunt of opposition to the New Policies at bay, Shen-tsung had attempted to co-opt the conservatives into the Yüan-feng regime, partially rehabilitating such prominent opponents of reform as Ssu-ma Kuang (1019–86), Lü Kung-chu (1018–89), and Su Shih (1037–1101).[5] While such moves had contained the antireform opposition, they could not conciliate it. Now that Shen-tsung was on his deathbed, some opponents of the Hsi-ning reforms were hesitantly preparing to return to the capital, after having spent more than a decade in exile. Although the New Policies remained in force and the reform faction (*hsin-tang*) still dominated the Council of State, with the monarch in critical condition the political situation at court was becoming ever more fluid and

---

[2] For Wang Kuei's exceptionally undistinguished biography, see *SS* 312, pp. 10241–7. Also see Shiba Yoshinobu, "Wang Kuei," in *Sung biographies*, ed. Herbert Franke (Wiesbaden, 1976), pp. 1115–17.

[3] *SS* 471, pp. 13699–700.

[4] Although Wang and Ts'ai had shared power for six years as the emperor's chief councilors, the partisan and personal rivalry between the two men was so intense that they "changed colors merely looking at each other." See *SS* 312, p. 10242.

[5] Unwilling to entrust the education of his heir apparent to Wang Kuei and Ts'ai Ch'üeh, Shen-tsung even considered appointing Ssu-ma Kuang and Lü Kung-chu as tutors to the crown prince. See *HCP* (1979) 350, p. 8930.

uncertain, as long-simmering policy disputes and personal rivalries came to a boiling point.

Ministers on both sides of the partisan divide understood that a tectonic shift in court politics was at hand, and that the impending imperial succession would not bode well for the reform faction. Late in the second month of 1085, Dowager Empress Hsüan-jen – the widow of Ying-tsung (r. 1063–7), the mother of Shen-tsung, and the grandmother of the future Che-tsung – was officially declared regent and vested with full monarchical authority in the ailing emperor's stead.[6] A representative of the dynastic old guard, the newly invested regent was a member of the Kao lineage, one of the leading military clans of the Northern Sung. Hsüan-jen's political sympathies and antipathies were no secret. As far back as 1074, she had implored her son to abolish the Hsi-ning reforms and to break free of the baleful influence of Wang An-shih, and her opposition to the New Policies and the reformists had never wavered.[7]

Hence, upon the sudden death of their imperial patron, the reformists faced uncertain prospects in a court dominated by Hsüan-jen and her trusted conservative ministers-to-be, Ssu-ma Kuang and Lü Kung-chu. Fighting for his political life, Ts'ai Ch'üeh mobilized his faction for a preemptive counteroffensive. Long-dormant personal animosities came to the forefront, as Ts'ai mounted a campaign of character assassination against Wang Kuei, portraying him as Hsüan-jen's shameless lackey. Failing to discredit Wang or engineer his dismissal as chief councilor, Ts'ai and his cohort turned to more desperate measures, attempting to alter the imperial succession itself in an abortive palace coup.

Hastily named heir apparent mere days before Shen-tsung's death on the fifth day of the third month of 1085, Chao Hsü2, the Prince of Yen-an, the future Emperor Che-tsung, was only eight years old, far too immature to be trusted with the reins of imperial power.[8] Ts'ai Ch'üeh and his co-conspirators Chang Tun, Hsing Shu, and Ts'ai Ching hatched a plot to depose Chao Hsü2, and replace him with his younger brother, Chao Hao, the Prince of Yung.[9] But the

---

[6] *HCP* (1979) 351, pp. 8409–10. When Wang Kuei urged Hsüan-jen to take up the regency, she declined a customary three times before accepting with calculated and ritualized reluctance.

[7] *HCP* (1979) 252, pp. 6169–70. For an anecdotal account of a debate between Dowager Empress Hsüan-jen and Shen-tsung over Wang An-shih and the New Policies, which transpired some time in the mid-1070s, see Shao Po-wen, *Shao-shih wen-chien lu* (1151; Peking, 1983) 3, p. 25. In Shao's account, the dowager empress actually succeeded in persuading Shen-tsung to dismiss Wang as chief councilor.

[8] *SS* 17, p. 317.

[9] *HCP* (1979) 351, pp. 8411–12. Ts'ai Ch'üeh and Hsing Shu attempted to enlist the assistance of Hsüan-jen's nephews, Kao Tseng-kung and Kao Chi, to place the Prince of Yung upon the throne. See *SS* 471, pp. 13702–3, for Hsing Shu's biography, which was classified under the ignominious rubric "Traitorous Ministers" (*chien-ch'en*). Also, the youthful Ts'ai Ching, the future chief councilor of the Hui-tsung reign, participated in the plot, an act of political treachery that would prefigure his later career, if we take the moralistic biases of the *HCP* at face value. Not surprisingly, Ts'ai Ching's biography can also be found in the "Traitorous Ministers" section of the *Sung shih*; see *SS* 471, pp. 13721–8.

reformists' plot to alter the imperial succession failed; their futile palace coup only aggravated Hsüan-jen's animus toward reformists and further incited the wrath of their political adversaries. Thus began a far-reaching transformation within the realm of court politics, one of the most extensive political changes in the history of the dynasty. The regency of Hsüan-jen was now a fait accompli, since the dowager empress could not be casually shoved aside by a reformist minister on the pretext of restoring a juvenile emperor's personal rule. Once the regent chose her prospective ministers, the current reformist-dominated Council of State, along with the New Policies, would not long survive the interregnum.

Caught beneath a landslide: The conservative takeover of 1085

Engaging Dowager Empress Hsüan-jen as their monarchical patron, the conservatives seized the opportunity of Che-tsung's accession to orchestrate a political comeback, bringing their lengthy political exile to an end. Ssu-ma Kuang, the most visible and audible opponent of the New Policies in the early years of Shen-tsung's reign, was certain to be at the core of Hsüan-jen's ministerial cabinet. After his resignation from court in 1070, the conservative statesman and eminent historian had spent fifteen years in exile in Lo-yang. There, Ssu-ma had supervised the compilation of his comprehensive history of China, the *Tzu-chih t'ung-chien*, and had forged a sort of government-in-exile with other like-minded opponents of the New Policies.[10]

When he heard the news of Shen-tsung's death, Ssu-ma was at home in Lo-yang, contemplating whether to return to court and accept an academic office. After fifteen years of painstaking historiographic labors, Ssu-ma Kuang was physically and mentally spent at the advanced age of sixty-six, and was understandably reluctant to dive back into the political fray in the capital.[11] But Ch'eng Hao, the Confucian fundamentalist theoretician and an intellectual progenitor of what would later become the *Tao-hsüeh* movement, persuaded Ssu-ma to return to K'ai-feng, if only to attend the imperial funeral rites.

[10] For a detailed portrait of Ssu-ma Kuang's years in exile, and an analysis of the transformation of Confucian conservatism to meet the threat of the New Policies of Wang An-shih, see Michael D. Freeman, "Lo-yang and the opposition to Wang An-shih: The rise of Confucian conservatism, 1068–1086" (diss., Yale University, 1973). Also see Ko Chao-kuang, "Lo-yang yü Pien-liang: Wen-hua chung-hsin yü cheng-chih chung-hsin ti fen-li – kuan-yü shih-i shih-chi pa-shih nien-tai li-hsüeh li-shih yü ssu-hsiang ti k'ao-ch'a," *Li-shih yen-chiu* 267 (2000), pp. 24–37.

[11] For an intellectual and political biography of Ssu-ma Kuang, see Ji Xiaobin, "Conservatism and court politics in Northern Song China: The thought and career of Ssu-ma Kuang (1019–1086)" (diss., Princeton University, 1998).

Arriving in the capital, Ssu-ma Kuang received a fervidly enthusiastic wel-come from a crowd of several thousand who vied to embrace his horse, and was even saluted by overeager palace guardsmen as "Prime Minister Ssu-ma."[12] Alarmed by this excessive show of popular adulation, he returned to Lo-yang, remaining noncommittal about returning to court and assuming the post of chief councilor. A few days later, Ssu-ma submitted a memorial in which he entreated Hsüan-jen and her ministers "to open wide the roads of remonstrance. Whether they are officials or private citizens, those who possess an understanding of the court's failures and of the people's suffering should present factual memorials, with utmost feeling and emphatic words."[13] By bringing grievances against the New Policies into the open, Ssu-ma Kuang hoped to bypass Ts'ai Ch'üeh, who still possessed sufficient residual power to block any antireform memorials. Indeed, remonstrance would later serve as the conservatives' main weapon in their campaign to win over the imperial bureaucracy and change the direction of state policy.

Within a week of Shen-tsung's death, it was clear that the winds were shift-ing, when the first edict of the regency expressed veiled criticism of the New Policies and Ts'ai Ch'üeh's role in executing them in recent years.[14] Not long after, Ssu-ma Kuang finally committed himself to leading the opposition to the New Policies, and to sacrificing his own health for that of the dynasty. Late in the fourth month of 1085, Ssu-ma fired off a series of scathing memo-rials, petitioning for the immediate "abolition of the New Policies which have ravaged the people and injured the state (*ping-min shang-kuo*)." Through the power of his rhetoric, Ssu-ma manufactured a villain with which to contrast his self-styled heroism, launching into a vitriolic ad hominem attack on the architect of the reforms, Wang An-shih:

[He] was self-satisfied and self-righteous, and considered himself to be unparalleled by figures past and present. . . . Often, he recklessly reformed the old statutes, substituting them with his own ideas, which he called the New Policies. Whatever this man wanted to do, the ruler could not prevent him from doing so. . . . He assisted those who agreed with him to ascend to the skies, while he banished those who disagreed with him, casting them into the ditch.[15]

---

[12] According to the *HCP*, the K'ai-feng crowds pleaded with Ssu-ma Kuang, crying: "Please do not return to Lo-yang. Remain here to serve as minister to the Son of Heaven, in order to bring the common people back to life." See *HCP* (1979) 353, p. 8465.

[13] *HCP* (1979) 353, pp. 8465–7.

[14] See *HCP* (1979) 354, pp. 8473–4.

[15] See *HCP* (1979) 355, pp. 8489–8501. Also see "Ch'i ch'ü hsin-fa chih ping-min shang-kuo che shu," in Ssu-ma Kuang, *Ssu-ma Kuang tsou-i*, ed. Wang Ken-lin (T'ai-yüan, 1986) 46, pp. 588–91. Ssu-ma followed this general memorial with more specific attacks on the mutual security (*pao-chia*) and hired service (*mien-i*) policies. See Ssu-ma, *Ssu-ma Kuang tsou-i* 46, pp. 591–4; 47, pp. 608–9.

In the harshly moralistic worldview of Ssu-ma Kuang, Wang An-shih was the very model of the deceitful and self-serving minister, and Shen-tsung was to blame for employing him and granting him carte blanche to enact his ill-considered schemes. It followed, then, that the New Policies were nothing but pernicious, as Wang had

relinquished what was right and embraced what was wrong, and promoted what was harmful and rejected what was beneficial. In name alone, he loved the people, but in fact he brought them harm. In name alone he benefited the state, but in fact he brought injury to it. He created the green sprouts (*ch'ing-miao*), hired service (*mien-i*), and state trade (*shih-i*) policies in order to illegally amass wealth and to mercilessly exploit the people.[16]

And not only had the activist domestic policy of the reformists been a complete debacle, but their belligerent border policy had carelessly incited an unwinnable war with the Hsi Hsia in 1081–3, a war in which hundreds of thousands of troops had perished for nothing. After the debacle at Yung-lo ch'eng, the Sung-Tangut border remained heavily militarized, and was the scene of the occasional deadly skirmish. As Ssu-ma viewed it, the carnage and insanity were spawned by

officials on the border who recklessly pressed their luck and spoke arrogantly with bald-faced lies. They negligently went into battle and needlessly disturbed the northern barbarians. Deploying troops is a weighty matter of state; its rise and fall hang in the balance. But these men carelessly sought glory and advancement for themselves, regardless of the deaths of the common people. They planned thoughtlessly and plotted recklessly, regardless of whether this would benefit or harm the state. . . . They caused the corpses of hundreds of thousands of soldiers to litter the wasteland, and they abandoned untold millions of weapons in a strange land.[17]

For Ssu-ma Kuang, the New Policies had brought the empire to the edge of certain collapse: "Everyone in the empire – the high and low, the wise and the ignorant – knows of the evils of the New Policies . . . [for they] ravage the people and injure the state." Three separate memorials followed, assailing what Ssu-ma Kuang considered to be the most noxious of the New Policies: the mutual security (*pao-chia*) and hired service measures.

Casting himself as the savior of the dynasty, Ssu-ma Kuang believed he possessed the key to delivering the Sung from the brink of destruction from within and without: the immediate abolition of the New Policies. Tragically quixotic, Ssu-ma persisted in his political crusade even as his health deteriorated and his rationality deserted him. During his brief tenure as Hsüan-jen's chief councilor, Ssu-ma pushed through a negative and reactionary policy agenda, advocating

[16] *HCP* (1979) 355, p. 8490.
[17] *HCP* (1979) 355, p. 8490.

the complete rollback of the reforms of the Shen-tsung reign and the rever-
sion to the policies of Jen-tsung and Ying-tsung. Instead of creating new
institutions, Ssu-ma advocated a moral renewal of preexisting institutions,
and the restoration of proper hierarchy within the imperial bureaucracy.[18]
By recruiting moral exemplars into the civil service and employing them in
a well-delineated chain of command, the Sung regime could be revived, to
triumph over internal insolvency and external hostility. Moreover, although
abolishing Shen-tsung's policies at the beginning of mourning would be a
gesture of unbridled unfiliality on Che-tsung's part, it was the lesser of two
evils, forgivable when compared to the alternative: allowing the New Policies
to remain in effect. In Ssu-ma's failing eyes, the new emperor's duty to the
dynasty as a whole outweighed his duties as a son. In a famous oration, Ssu-ma
placed himself in a near-messianic role, describing the immediate abolition
of the New Policies as a necessary and heroic undertaking: "If what Wang
An-shih. . . . established has injured the empire, and was not in accordance
with the intentions of the former emperor, then eliminating them is like
extinguishing a fire or rescuing the drowning."[19]

But overblown and extremist rhetoric alone could not abolish the New Policies while the reformists still controlled access to the roads of remonstrance
and still dominated the major policy-making positions at court.[20] The antire-
formers would need to emulate Wang An-shih's own approach fifteen years
earlier and mount a hostile takeover of the central government. This entailed
monopolizing the Censorate and other remonstrance offices, purging their
major antagonists from the capital, and then abolishing the reform statutes
one by one. This battle for power at court proceeded at a nearly glacial pace,
requiring more than a year, and incurring many prominent casualties, before
the antireform faction finally succeeded. Ssu-ma Kuang and Lü Kung-chu
were the first of their cohort to establish a beachhead at court in the fourth

---

[18] For an adept analysis of the political and ethical thought of Ssu-ma Kuang and Wang An-shih, see
Peter K. Bol, *"This culture of ours": Intellectual transition in T'ang and Sung China* (Stanford, Calif., 1992),
pp. 212–53. For an expanded version of this chapter, see Peter K. Bol, "Government, society, and state:
On the political visions of Ssu-ma Kuang and Wang An-shih," in *Ordering the world: Approaches to state
and society in Sung dynasty China*, ed. Robert P. Hymes and Conrad Schirokauer (Berkeley, Calif., 1993),
pp. 128–92. Also see Anthony W. Sariti, "Monarchy, bureaucracy, and absolutism in the political thought
of Ssu-ma Kuang," *Journal of Asian Studies* 32 No. 1 (1972), pp. 53–76.

[19] Wang Ch'eng, *Tōto jiryaku* [*Shinshūkan* 1849 ed.], ed. and ann. Nagasawa Kikuya (1186; Tokyo, 1973)
87 *hsia*, p. 2a. Also see Lü Chung, *Sung ta-shih-chi chiang-i* [*Ssu-k'u ch'üan-shu*, Wen-yüan ko 1779 ed.]
(Taipei, 1983) 18, pp. 3a–b.

[20] When a call for criticism of the New Policies and the current ministerial regime was finally issued,
Ts'ai Ch'üeh, facing a barrage of personal attacks, had rendered the new remonstrance policy toothless,
emending the edict so that all who dared criticize the chief councilor or his policies would be punished.
See *HCP* (1979) 356, pp. 8507–8.

month of 1085, and others soon followed them into the Censorate and other critical positions.[21] Serving as vice–censor in chief (yü-shih chung-ch'eng) in the first years of Shen-tsung's reign, Lü had been forcibly dismissed from his post in 1070 for his opposition to the green sprouts agricultural loan policy. Now that the balance of power had shifted in favor of Hsüan-jen and the antireform cause, the Censorate and Remonstrance Bureau could again be employed as weapons against the New Policies. And by monopolizing remonstrance and surveillance posts, newly appointed conservative censors hoped to impeach reformists from the Council of State, or at least to forestall their nomination as high ministers.[22]

Yet when Wang Kuei died in the fifth month of 1085, after serving as a councilor for more than a decade without any notable distinction, the antireformists were powerless to prevent Ts'ai Ch'üeh from ascending to the post of chief councilor of the left.[23] Ts'ai would prove difficult to dislodge as the new emperor's prime minister, retaining his lofty position despite a year-long torrent of censorial indictments that clamored for his dismissal. However, the antireform faction was successful in denying the junior councilorship to Chang Tun, Ts'ai's lieutenant, who had to settle for the post of administrator of the Bureau of Military Affairs (chih shu-mi yüan shih).[24] The same day, Ssu-ma Kuang entered the Council of State as the vice-director of the Chancellery (men-hsia shih-lang), a position that to his great dismay was subordinate to that of his archenemy Ts'ai Ch'üeh. Although the conservatives had lost the first battle, they would eventually win the war, chipping away at the foundations of Ts'ai's authority until his position became indefensible.

Once he was ensconced in the Council of State, Ssu-ma Kuang wasted little time in facilitating the high-level appointments of his allies, in preparation for an assault on the upper echelons of the imperial bureaucracy. In an audience with Hsüan-jen in the sixth month of 1085, he recommended the names of Liu Chih, Wang Yen-sou, Fan Ch'un-jen, Fan Tsu-yü, Su Ch'e, Su Shih, and the elder statesmen Lü Kung-chu and Wen Yen-po as possible candidates for an antireformist-dominated Council of State.[25] One month later, Ssu-ma's recommendations were already being heeded, when Lü Kung-chu was appointed assistant director of the left in the Department

---

[21] HCP (1979) 354, p. 8476. For a brief biography of Lü Kung-chu, see Michael D. Freeman, "Lü Kung-chu," in Sung biographies, ed. Herbert Franke (Wiesbaden, 1976), pp. 719–22.

[22] The prominent antireformists Sun Chüeh, Wang Yen-sou, and Liu Chih were all appointed to high censorial posts in 1085 and set about making life at court extremely uncomfortable for the reformists. See HCP (1979) 354, p. 8476; 357, p. 8537; 359, p. 8597.

[23] HCP (1979) 356, pp. 8517, 8520.

[24] HCP (1979) 356, p. 8521.

[25] HCP (1979) 357, pp. 8552–4.

of State Affairs (*shang-shu tso-ch'eng*), giving the conservatives another powerful voice in the Council of State.[26] Throughout the summer and autumn
of 1085, Ssu-ma and his factional allies built up their political capital at
court. Remonstrance and surveillance posts were packed with conservatives,
who issued an unceasing barrage of memorials that harshly criticized the
reforms of the Shen-tsung reign and recommended their immediate abolition.[27] Intended as a check on ministerial prerogatives, the powers of the Censorate (*Yü-shih t'ai*) and the Remonstrance Bureau (*Chien-yüan*) had been sharply
curtailed under the reformist administrations of Wang An-shih and Ts'ai
Ch'üeh.[28]

But after the death of Shen-tsung, censors and remonstrators assumed their
customary privileges with a vengeance, using their offices as a pulpit from
which to fulminate against the ministers of the reform coalition, whose members and policies had long been immune from criticism. Lü Kung-chu memorialized to abolish the jurisdictional limits that had governed the Censorate
and Remonstrance Bureau ever since the Yüan-feng administrative reforms
of 1082. By removing remonstrators from under the thumb of the Council of
State, and by expanding their purview to encompass broad-based criticism of
state policy and the Council of State, Lü hoped to utilize them as a weapon
against the New Policies and the ministerial regime of Ts'ai Ch'üeh: "Let
there be an edict that censors and remonstrance officials will jointly remonstrate without taboos, advise the ruler on his shortcomings, enumerate the
flaws of the court, point out the treacherous faction among officialdom, and
manifest the suffering of the common people."[29]

After Lü's wish had been granted, a flood of indictments followed, revealing
the fatal flaws of the New Policies and excoriating the reformists. For example,
in a single day in the eighth month of 1085, the censor Fan Tsu-yü argued
that it was ritually appropriate to abolish Shen-tsung's reforms even at the
start of the three-year imperial mourning period for him, and Wang Yen-
sou described the suffering of the common people under the New Policies
in heartbreaking detail.[30] But with their foes maintaining an obstructionist
stance, the antireformists would have to attack each of the New Policies one

---

[26] *HCP* (1979) 358, p. 8561.
[27] For an example of Ssu-ma's invective, see *HCP* (1979) 358, pp. 8563–6, for his attack on the *pao-chia* policy.
[28] For more information on the curtailment of censorial powers during the Shen-tsung reign, see the preceding chapter. Also see Shen Sung-ch'in, "Pei Sung t'ai-chien chih-tu yü tang-cheng," *Li-shih yen-chiu* 254 (1998), pp. 32–5. For details on the restructuring of the remonstrance system during the Che-tsung reign, see Tiao Chung-min, "Lun Sung Che-tsung chih Kao-tsung shih-ch'i chih t'ai-chien chih-tu," *Ssu-ch'uan ta-hsüeh hsüeh-pao* 105 (1999), pp. 61–9.
[29] *HCP* (1979) 357, pp. 8546–7.
[30] *HCP* (1979) 359, pp. 8592–4.

at a time, a war of attrition that would require the better part of a year. For if the reformists could not prevent the ascendancy of their foes, who were now packing the Censorate and the Council of State, they could at least obstruct them at every turn, in an effort to bring the political process to a standstill. When Ssu-ma Kuang and Lü Kung-chu nominated five of their allies to censorial posts in the tenth month of 1085, Chang Tun protested the move as a hostile conspiracy to monopolize the remonstrance organs of the central government. In a heated debate with Hsüan-jen and Ssu-ma Kuang, Chang charged that the recommenders were of insufficient rank to nominate officials to the Remonstrance Bureau. Chang succeeded in overturning the appointments of Fan Ch'un-jen and Fan Tsu-yü, but he was unable to block the appointments of Chu Kuang-t'ing and Su Ch'e to remonstrance posts.[31] More important, Chang's obstructionist schemes only fanned the flames of resentment and did little to endear him to the regent or to the ministers of her shadow cabinet.[32] By this point in the factional struggle, remonstrance and surveillance offices were under the sway of the antireformists, who would be certain to retaliate against the chief targets of their wrath – Ts'ai Ch'üeh and Chang Tun.

But even as the censorial offensive against them increased in force and frequency in the winter of 1085–6, the leaders of the reformist ministerial regime remained more or less untouchable. Month after month, memorials of impeachment were drawn up, indicting both Ts'ai and Chang for their ritual irreverence and administrative incompetence, but none succeeded in dislodging the chief councilor of the right and his lieutenant from the Council of State. Liu Chih denounced Ts'ai Ch'üeh for violating ritual protocol as the master of imperial interment (*shan-ling-shih*), and Wang Yen-sou chastised Chang Tun for his irreverence toward Hsüan-jen during the debate over censorial nominations.[33] And countless memorials simply clamored for the dismissal of the so-called three traitors (*san-chien*) Ts'ai Ch'üeh, Chang Tun, and Han Chen, and then urged the promotion of the "three worthies" (*san-hsien*) Ssu-ma Kuang, Lü Kung-chu, and Han Wei.[34] While Ts'ai and Chang survived the storm for more than a year, many of their junior comrades were

[31] *HCP* (1979) 360, pp. 8606–8. Chu Kuang-t'ing was successfully appointed exhorter of the left (*tso-cheng-yen*), and Su Ch'e exhorter of the right (*yu-cheng-yen*).

[32] Six days later, on the ninth day of the tenth month of 1085, Liu Chih would retaliate by overturning the nominations of two second-generation reformists, Ts'ai Pien and Lu Tien, to academic posts in the Dragon Diagram Pavilion (*Lung-t'u ko*) of the Han-lin Academy. They were replaced with Chao Yen-jo and Fu Yao-yü, both of whom Ssu-ma Kuang had recommended earlier. See *HCP* (1979) 360, pp. 8616–17.

[33] *HCP* (1979) 360, p. 8629; 361, pp. 8650–1.

[34] For a typical example of the genre by Chu Kuang-t'ing, see *HCP* (1979) 363, pp. 8674–6.

caught in the undertow.[35] By the beginning of 1086, the conservatives managed to monopolize the Ministry of Personnel, gaining complete control over the bureaucratic appointment process. Now that the rank-and-file members of the reform faction were being exiled to regional administrative posts, the antireform opposition could pack the central government with its own men. It was only a matter of time before the takeover would be accomplished and a new conservative ministerial regime would consolidate its hold on power.

Tabula rasa: Eradicating the New Policies, 1085

Meanwhile, the New Policies were being abolished one by one, with only token resistance, in the second half of 1085. Ssu-ma Kuang was managing to unite his antireform coalition behind a policy agenda that was simplistically negative: the immediate and total eradication of the New Policies and the revival of the old policies of the Jen-tsung and Ying-tsung reigns in their entirety. Realizing that Ssu-ma's conservative juggernaut was unstoppable, the dwindling number of reformist ministers at court allowed several elements of their policy agenda to fall by the wayside. Perhaps Ts'ai Ch'üeh and Chang Tun were occupied with fending off censorial indictments, or perhaps they were saving their strength for a final showdown on the core New Policies – the hired service and green sprouts (ch'ing-miao) measures – frameworks that they believed were worth salvaging. In either case, reformist recalcitrance was remarkably limited, and intriguingly nonideological. While Ts'ai Ch'üeh was fighting tooth and nail to retain his chief councilorship, Chang Tun was disputing the abolition agenda on practical grounds. The death knell of state activism, with its intrusive mechanisms of bureaucratic entrepreneurship and revenue extraction, had been sounded.[36]

The first of the New Policies to be abolished was the mutual security (pao-chia) system, which arguably penetrated deeper into Sung society than did any other reform measure. Across the empire, nearly seven million men – from close to half of the empire's fifteen million households – were enrolled in the system by 1076.[37] In the eyes of Ssu-ma Kuang, there was no question that the militarization of the peasantry should be immediately put to an end: "The mutual security (pao-chia) and horse-pasturage (pao-ma) policies are harmful

---

[35] HCP (1979) 360, pp. 8630–2; 362, pp. 8670–1; 363, pp. 8683–8. Ts'ai Ching was dismissed from his post as prefect of K'ai-feng for alleged dirty dealings with the Central Buddhist Registry. Hsing Shu was punished for assisting Ts'ai Ch'üeh in his plot to meddle with the imperial succession.

[36] For application of the concept of bureaucratic entrepreneurship to the late Northern Sung, see Paul J. Smith, *Taxing heaven's storehouse: Horses, bureaucrats and the destruction of the Sichuan tea industry, 1074–1224* (Cambridge, Mass., 1991).

[37] SHY (1997) ping 2, p. 12b.

without a single benefit, and the people of the empire all know this. Your servant does not understand why the court is so reluctant, and has taken so long to abolish them!"[38] Under the compulsory *pao-chia* system, farmers were prevented from performing necessary agricultural tasks and, moreover, had learned martial skills that could make them a potential threat to the peace they were intended to maintain.

In the seventh month of 1085, an imperial edict abolished the mutual security (*pao-chia*) system in the K'ai-feng area and the surrounding circuits in the north (Ho-pei, Ho-tung, and Shan-hsi) where the policy had had its greatest negative impact.[39] For the past ten years, participation in military drills and reviews had become compulsory for almost every man on the *pao-chia* rolls in the north and the capital region. If a memorial by Ssu-ma Kuang can be believed, for several years those enlisted as *pao-chia* militiamen were required to participate in training every fifth day, which would have represented an enormous drain of labor from agricultural pursuits.[40] Investigating Censor (*chien-ch'a yü-shih*) Wang Yen-sou had also violently objected not to the intrusiveness of the militia training regimen, but to its unnecessary brutality, which would only increase peasants' resentment of their superiors, and would make the men potentially dangerous as trained bandits and rebels.[41] With a single brushstroke, an onerous obligation for hundreds of thousands of men was ended. As of the first month of 1086, the "team drill" (*t'uan-chiao*) program that had been enacted throughout the north and capital region would be replaced by the old *i-yung* militia system, with a more lenient drill and review program (*chiao-yüeh*) of one month a year.[42] Late in 1086, the poorest (grade 5) households, and those with landholdings under twenty *mou*, were exempted from militia training altogether, on the request of the palace censor (*tien-chung shih yü-shih*) Lü T'ao.[43]

Although the *pao-chia* system was the military cornerstone of the New Policies, there is a dearth of evidence of reformist opposition to its abolition.[44] Now

[38] *HCP* (1979) 358, pp. 8563–5.

[39] *HCP* (1979) 358, p. 8562. For a more detailed discussion of the legal and institutional intricacies of the *pao-chia* system as they existed during the Shen-tsung reign, see the preceding chapter.

[40] *HCP* (1979) 355, p. 8494. These figures were possibly distorted for rhetorical effect.

[41] *HCP* (1979) 361, pp. 8641–5; *SS* 192, pp. 4783–5.

[42] *HCP* (1979) 358, p. 8562.

[43] *SS* 192, p. 4786.

[44] The historiographic record of the early Yüan-yu period tells only one side of the story: that of the antireformists. The primary sources for the study of late Northern Sung political culture are themselves deeply suffused with political culture. Blatant airbrushing has occurred at both stages of the compilation of the period's most crucial source, *HCP*. First, the source material for the *HCP*, the veritable records (*shih-lu*) of the Shen-tsung and Che-tsung reigns, was reedited long after the fact in the early years of the Southern Sung by those sympathetic to the antireform cause. Second, the *HCP* itself is suffused with the political biases of Li T'ao, its compiler. As a result, the prominent reformists of the period

that Ts'ai Ch'üeh and Chang Tun were treading water just to retain their posts for another day or two, their objections to the elimination of the New Policies were pragmatic rather than ideological. In a debate with Ssu-ma Kuang, Chang Tun objected not to the conservatives' determination to eliminate the mutual security system, but to the haste and heavy-handedness with which they planned to do so, to say nothing of their lack of any detailed framework for its replacement. Endeavoring to accommodate himself to Ssu-ma and remain on the Council of State, Chang pleaded for moderation, maintaining that no administrative structure as complex and pervasive as the *pao-chia* system could be dissolved within a five-day limit, at least not without precipitating massive bureaucratic chaos.[45] Chang's arguments were apt, for Ssu-ma Kuang's immediate abolition of the mutual security system would indeed cause massive headaches for regional administrators in the months and years to come.

The next of the New Policies to be eliminated, without as much as a whimper from the reformists, was the land survey and equitable tax policy (*fang-t'ien chün-shui fa*), in the eleventh month of 1085.[46] Unlike other planks in the reformist policy program, which had begun as redistributive measures but were quickly transformed into instruments of revenue extraction, the *fang-t'ien* policy successfully realized Wang An-shih's vision of redistributing capital from wealthy "engrossers" (*chien-ping*) to the poor and powerless. Implemented in 1072 in five northern circuits, the policy initiated a large-scale cadastral survey, which divided lands into standard units, graded them for quality, and determined their actual ownership.[47] The *fang-t'ien* surveys were intended to reveal tax abuses by large landowners, who had employed tax exemptions and various other subterfuges to make vast swaths of land "disappear" from the registers. By uncovering lands that had previously gone untaxed, Wang hoped to make the map correspond to the terrain – to make state tax registers correspond more closely to rural socioeconomic realities. This entailed shifting the burden of land taxes away from small farmers, perhaps offsetting the

---

have been silenced – very few of the memorials of Ts'ai Ch'üeh and Chang Tun have survived in this period's documentary record. For more information on the political forces that influenced the revision of the *shih-lu*, see Ts'ai Ch'ung-pang, *Sung-tai hsiu-shih chih-tu yen-chiu* (Taipei, 1991), pp. 82–102. For more information on the compilation of the *HCP*, see Sudō Yoshiyuki, "Nan-Sō no Ri Tō to *Zoku Shichi tsugan chōhen* no seiritsu," in *Sōdai-shi kenkyū*, Sudō Yoshiyuki (Tokyo, 1969), pp. 469–512.

[45] Chang Tun's urging moderation in the abolition of *pao-chia* represents one of the two prominent exceptions to the silencing of the reformists in the *HCP*. Perhaps Chang's statements were included for their relative political inoffensiveness, as some prominent antireformists like Fan Ch'un-jen and Su Shih were also opposed to the immediacy with which Ssu-ma Kuang planned to eradicate the New Policies. For Chang's arguments, see *HCP* (1979) 367, pp. 8821–30.

[46] *HCP* (1979) 360, p. 8618.

[47] See the previous chapter, as well as *SS* 174, pp. 4199–4200; Ch'i Hsia, *Wang An-shih pien-fa*, 2nd ed. (Shanghai, 1979), pp. 145–7; Higashi Ichio, *Ō Anseki jiten* (Tokyo, 1980), pp. 70–2.

onerous labor and military service obligations they would endure under the mutual security (*pao-chia*) and hired service (*mien-i*) policies. Once the *fang-t'ien* system was abolished, farm lands would again be accumulated by the powerful, and tax burdens would again be shifted from the wealthy to the poor. But for Ssu-ma Kuang and his allies, who believed that the state should not interfere in local society or expand the peasant economy, traditional – and necessary – socioeconomic divisions in the countryside would be restored at last. As for the actual repercussions of the abolition of the land survey and equitable tax policy in the Sung countryside, impressionistic conclusions are all that can be drawn.

The rollback of the New Policies gathered further momentum in the twelfth month of 1085, when the state trade (*shih-i*) policy was stricken from the statute books.[48] Designed to break the commercial cartels of wealthy merchants, who aggrandized themselves through hoarding and price gouging, the state trade system had created an extensive government monopoly that gave the engrossers a run for their money. By buying products cheap and selling them dear, the state trade agency (*shih-i ssu*) had cornered the market in staple goods. Under the financial expertise of Lü Chia-wen, a disciple and son-in-law of Wang An-shih, the agency spread its tentacles almost everywhere, reaping vast profits.[49] Branch trade bureaus spread into every corner of the empire and had been a major source of revenue to finance the protracted border war with the Hsi Hsia in 1081–3.[50]

Over the course of 1085, the authority of the state trade agency was slowly whittled away by a series of executive orders. First, in the fourth month of the year, the Secretariat ordered the state trade agency to forgive 70 percent of the interest owed by great families, and a full 100 percent of interest owed by commoners, in order to rescue K'ai-feng's commercial community from permanent indebtedness.[51] Next, in the eighth month of 1085, two imperial edicts abolished the agency's loan bureaus at the prefectural and county levels, as well as those in northern border outposts.[52] Still, a steady trickle of memorials warned the emperor and his regent that piecemeal measures were

[48] *SHY* (1997) *shih-huo* 37, pp. 32a–b.

[49] For an in-depth analysis of the state trade policy, see Liang Keng-yao, "Shih-i fa shu," in *Sung-tai she-hui ching-chi shih lun-chi*, ed. Liang Keng-yao (Taipei, 1997), pp. 104–260.

[50] In 1084, a state trade bureau was established even in the newly occupied territory of Lan-chou, which had recently been gained through a war of conquest with the Hsi Hsia to monopolize cross-border trade. See *SS* 186, p. 4553. For a quantitative assessment of the regional penetration of the state trade system, see Higashi, *Ō Anseki jiten*, pp. 54–7 (tables 15 and 16).

[51] *HCP* (1979) 354, p. 8472. The balance of the interest owed to the state trade agency by the "great names" (*ta-ming*) was forgiven on the eighteenth day of the eleventh month of 1085. See *HCP* (1979) 361, p. 8647; *SHY* (1997) *shih-huo* 37, p. 32a.

[52] *SS* 186, p. 4553.

insufficient, urging the complete termination of the state trade policy, which was finally decreed in the last month of 1085. As punishment for his corrupt administration of the state trade policy, not to mention his inept bungling of border relations with the Hsi Hsia, Lü Chia-wen was dismissed from court in the first month of 1086 and demoted to a humiliating prefectural-level post. The Censorate had indicted Lü for his corrupt direction of the state trade agency, which had out-engrossed the engrossers and had pushed millions to the edge of poverty.[53]

By the end of 1085, Ssu-ma Kuang and his factional allies had reached the turning point of their political war. Although more than half of the reform agenda was now eradicated, the hired service and green sprouts policies, the core of Wang An-shih's agrarian reform agenda, remained in force. Half the Council of State was occupied by Ts'ai Ch'üeh and his lieutenants, who were still in high places, even as the ground beneath their feet was giving way. The reformist resistance had been neutralized but not eliminated, and its remaining ministers would fight to the last man against overwhelming odds to ensure their political survival first, and the continuation of the New Policies second.

One last push: The fall of Ts'ai Ch'üeh and Chang Tun

The year 1086, the first of the newly proclaimed Yüan-yu era, began on an ambiguous note, indicative of the current situation at court, where the conservative ascendancy was not yet complete. Even the selection of the new reign title was a consequence of a political compromise between the reform and antireform coalitions.[54] The name Yüan-yu itself was representative of the schizophrenic character of the current ministerial regime of winter 1085–6, suggesting that the reforms of the Yüan-feng era (1078–85) would survive somehow, balanced by the stolid conservatism of the Chia-yu era (1056–63) of Jen-tsung's reign.[55] But such a state of political indeterminacy would not persist for long; by the early spring, the partisan stalemate would be conclusively resolved in favor of the antireformists.

Sung political culture was governed by ritual practices, and politics and policy were inextricably linked to cosmological phenomena. Despite recent

---

[53] According to the censor Sun Sheng's indictment: "When the [state trade] policy was initially enacted, Lü Chia-wen had jurisdiction over its affairs. . . . He selfishly and cunningly recommended the disciples of engrossers, and put an end to the profits of merchants. He deceived the emperor and destroyed the law, and practiced treachery and deceit." See HCP (1979) 364, p. 8707; SHY (1997) shih-huo 37, pp. 32b–33a.

[54] For Liu Chih's and Ssu-ma Kuang's suggestions on what to name the new reign period, see HCP (1979) 362, pp. 8663–5. As for the reformist side of the story, HCP has (predictably) preserved none of their proposals on this matter.

[55] For Lü Tao's explanation, see the commentary to HCP (1979) 364, p. 8697.

changes in monarchs, ministers, policy, and reign devices, which were intended to recenter an age of political, ritual, and cosmological imbalance, K'ai-feng remained in the grip of a lengthy drought in the winter of 1085–6. In the eyes of antireform ministers, the snowless winter was a direct consequence of the unsettled situation at court, and of the continued presence of Ts'ai Ch'üeh and his cronies in the Council of State. Two querulous censors went so far as to argue that Che-tsung's reluctance to dismiss his father's treacherous chief ministers had thrown the seasonal cycle out of kilter, and was directly responsible for the drought that had plagued K'ai-feng all winter long.[56]

When conservative remonstrators were not blaming the current drought on the reformists, they were engaging in that old standby of political discourse: character assassination. Su Ch'e, the exhorter of the left, repeatedly argued that moral defects or sheer incompetence or both made Ts'ai and Chang unfit to remain on the Council of State: "Ts'ai Ch'üeh's obsequious streak runs deep; he must be punished. . . . Chang Tun possesses the talent to perform his duties, but his character makes him unemployable."[57] Policy disputes also figured into the equation, as remonstrators such as Liu Chih continually indicted Ts'ai not just for being treacherous and disloyal but also for obstructing the abolition of the hired service system.[58] Su Ch'e continued to rail against Ts'ai and his reformist colleagues in the Council of State, arguing that their administrative talent was "so insufficient as to make them unemployable, and their wicked transgressions numerous."[59] Continually on the defensive against censorial indictments, Ts'ai Ch'üeh had been pushed to the end of his tether. In the intercalary second month of 1086, he resigned as chief councilor of the right, and was appointed administrator of Ch'en-chou, close to the capital.[60] Much to the chagrin of his critics, Ts'ai managed to retain his full rank and his academic position at court, despite having been demoted to this humiliating prefectural-level post. Ssu-ma Kuang was now awarded the prize his eyes had been set on for decades, and he assumed the post of chief councilor of the left, from whence he could finally dictate state policy, free from opposition or obstruction.

But even in a conservative-controlled Council of State, Ssu-ma's triumph was to be short-lived. Afflicted by an increasingly debilitating illness,

---

[56] These memorials, authored by Chu Kuang-t'ing and Wang Yen-sou, link the microcosm of court politics to the macrocosm, opening a window onto the ritualized mentality and political cosmology which prevailed in the Northern Sung. See *HCP* (1979) 365, pp. 8745–6; 364, pp. 8711–13.

[57] *HCP* (1979) 367, pp. 8818–20; "Ch'i hsüan-yung chih-cheng chuang," in Su Ch'e, *Su Ch'e chi*, ed. Ch'en Hung-t'ien and Kao Hsiu-fang (Peking, 1990) 36, pp. 634–5.

[58] *HCP* (1979) 364, pp. 8716–24, 8729–30.

[59] *HCP* (1979) 368, pp. 8849–51.

[60] *HCP* (1979) 368, p. 8854.

Ssu-ma was not equal to the physical or intellectual demands of his court duties. On account of his worsening condition, he made a show of refusing the chief councilorship, recommending his senior colleague Wen Yen-po (1006–97) for the post, and beseeching Hsüan-jen for a sinecure instead.[61] His request was refused, and Ssu-ma Kuang would spend the last eight months of his life as the regent's prime minister. To his horror, Ssu-ma had ascended the political stage too late to save the empire from its "four perils," as the green sprouts, hired service, and military reforms remained in force, and the Sung war with the Hsi Hsia continued. During the first month of 1086, he lamented: "the four perils have not yet been eliminated, and I will die discontented."[62] Even worse, the conservative coalition began to splinter apart during the months-long debate over the hired service policy, the next of the New Policies on the Ssu-ma's abolition agenda.

Eradicating the hired service system and reviving the old drafted service (*ch'ai-i*) regulations had formed the cornerstone of Ssu-ma Kuang's antireform platform. The hired service policy, enacted empirewide in 1071, had supplanted the state's conscripted service labor force with a professional corps of laborers, who were remunerated with state funds, drawn from service exemption fees (*mien-i ch'ien*) assessed upon eligible rural households.[63] For the purpose of assessing these fees in an equitable fashion, rural households were divided into five grades, with the poorest households in grades 4 and 5 exempt from payment. As with the state trade policy, the hired service system was originally designed to alleviate savage socioeconomic inequalities with massive state intervention. But in practice, *mien-i* had mutated into a mechanism of revenue extraction, after a series of executive orders expanded both the number of fees to be paid and the number of households that were required to pay them. Not surprisingly, these extra surcharges swelled the coffers of the central government, which in 1076 directly received almost forty percent of the service exemption fees.[64]

Needless to say, Ssu-ma Kuang and such fellow members of the antireform coalition as Wang Yen-sou could not tolerate the extent to which the hired service system and its associated service exemption levies had expanded state revenue extraction. In a memorial presented not long after his return to court in mid-1085, Ssu-ma argued that the arbitrary surcharges and fees of *mien-i* had impoverished millions of households by monetizing the rural

---

[61] *HCP* (1979) 368, pp. 8854–5.

[62] Lü, *Sung ta-shih-chi chiang-i* 18, p. 4b.

[63] See the previous chapter and *SS* 177, pp. 4299–4301; Ch'i, *Wang An-shih pien-fa*, pp. 133–8; Higashi, *Ō Anseki jiten*, pp. 61–2.

[64] *SHY* (1997) *shih-huo* 66, p. 40b; Ch'i, *Wang An-shih pien-fa*, p. 144.

economy.[65] Forcing all peasants to pay service exemption fees in cash had thrown them at the mercy of the market and the seasons, driving many into abject penury. The extractive state brought into being by Wang An-shih had utterly destroyed Ssu-ma Kuang's illusory ideal of a self-sufficient agrarian order. But Chang Tun laid his political career on the line to defend the hired service system against the censorial and ministerial onslaught. On the twenty-eighth day of the third month of 1086 he memorialized the throne with a point-by-point rebuttal of Ssu-ma Kuang's plan to abolish hired service and revive drafted service.[66] Notably, his defense of hired service was less ideological than it was pragmatic.

Even so, for Chang to stand alone against Ssu-ma and to reveal the glaring logical inconsistencies in the chief councilor's rhetoric was to invite certain disaster.[67] In one memorial, Ssu-ma Kuang had claimed that rich peasant households would benefit from the revival of drafted service, since they suffered from the yearly imposition of hired service fees; half a month later, he argued that these same households enjoyed preferential treatment in the hired service system.

In Chang's words:

Your servant examines the contents of Ssu-ma Kuang's memorial of the third day of the first month, which claims that: "upper-grade households (*shang-hu*) will consider drafted service to be advantageous, and will consider hired service payments to be harmful." But in his memorial of the seventeenth day of the first month, he claims: "Although hired service payments make lower-grade households (*hsia-hu*) suffer hardship, upper-grade households enjoy preferential treatment." Within a dozen days, in two memorials, what he has said about the benefits and harm to upper households is contradictory.[68]

In an earlier memorial, Ssu-ma had parried detailed policy critiques with crude generalizations, claiming that the hired service system was causing extreme suffering for all peasants everywhere: "Officials and commoners have offered up reports which state that the people are suffering. Of the several thousand statements which have been offered, not one has not said that hired service was harmful. From the above, we can conclude this is indubitably a peril to the empire."[69] But Chang took exception to the expedience with which Ssu-ma

---

[65] *HCP* (1979) 355, pp. 8497–9. See "Ch'i pa mien-i chuang," in Ssu-ma, *Ssu-ma Kuang tsou-i* 32, pp. 345–6.

[66] *HCP* (1979) 367, pp. 8821–30.

[67] This statement represents the second exception to the complete exclusion of the reformists from the documentary record of the period. For an expanded explanation of the hired service–drafted service debate between Chang Tun and Ssu-ma Kuang, see Teng Kuang-ming, *Wang An-shih: Chung-kuo shih-i shih-chi ti kai-ko-chia*, rev. ed. (Peking, 1975), pp. 174–6.

[68] *HCP* (1979) 367, p. 8822.

[69] *HCP* (1979) 365, p. 8759.

wished to abolish hired service and revive drafted service, arguing that such complex policy problems could not be solved within a mere five days:

> Your servant sees that today's policy proposals are concerned with their benefit and harm to living people. The hired service and drafted service policies are indeed important, but they must be carefully examined, and cannot be changed lightly.... In five days from now, how can the various county magistrates make an assessment of its benefit and harm? ... Although Kuang has a heart which commiserates with the state and loves the people, [his] methods of reforming [hired service] have not been discussed, no plan exists, and it will be implemented recklessly.[70]

Chang was dismissed twenty-one days after Ts'ai Ch'üeh, but went down with far more fighting spirit than his factional patron. In a feverish debate on hired service held in front of the dowager empress's screen, Chang offended Hsüan-jen with his irreverence, and was immediately dismissed from the Council of State and demoted to a prefectural-level post.[71] Now that Ts'ai Ch'üeh and Chang Tun were out of the way, the conservatives enjoyed unchallenged control of the Council of State. On the day of Chang's dismissal, Wang Yen-sou celebrated his coalition's conquest of the central government, arguing that "now that Ch'üeh and Tun have been dismissed, no more great malefactors remain."[72] In Wang's judgment, the remaining reformist nonentities at court were "obsequious and malleable, and can be easily managed." Two months later, the reform coalition would be bereft even of its founding figure, making its regeneration all the more unlikely. For in the spring of 1086 an embittered Wang An-shih died in retirement at the age of sixty-five, not long after hearing of the repeal of the New Policies.[73] After a year-long struggle, the Council of State was the sole province of the antireform coalition, but this coalition would itself become increasingly unstable in the months to come, fracturing over personal and policy disputes.

The seeds of disunion: Eradicating the New Policies, 1086

As the debate over hired service raged on, the antireform coalition began to fissure, foreshadowing the factional infighting that would paralyze the court for the remainder of the regency.[74] While Ssu-ma Kuang myopically and

---

[70] *HCP* (1979) 367, p. 8827.

[71] Chang was appointed prefect of Ju-chou2 (Ching-hsi North). He was replaced as director of the Bureau of Military Affairs by his former assistant director, the reformist An T'ao. The prominent conservative Fan Ch'un-jen took An's place as assistant director. See *HCP* (1979) 370, p. 8934.

[72] *HCP* (1979) 370, pp. 8935–7.

[73] *SS* 327, p. 10550; *HCP* (1979) 374, pp. 9069–70.

[74] For a detailed discussion of how the antireform coalition fractured over the hired service issue, see Lo, *Pei Sung tang-cheng yen-chiu*, pp. 112–21.

unyieldingly insisted upon the immediate eradication of the evils of the hired service measure, a considerable number of high-placed conservatives urged caution. The moderate wing of the conservative coalition shared many points of agreement with the recently dismissed reformist Chang Tun. Arguing that an entire system could not be abolished overnight without serious repercussions, these dissenters demanded that a detailed scheme for the reimplementation of drafted service be formulated first. As Su Ch'e put it: "Since the court enacted hired service close to twenty years have passed, and officials and private citizens have long been accustomed to it. Now, if we begin to implement drafted service, there will unavoidably be some disagreements and disparities."[75] For Su Ch'e, the countless details of the revived drafted service system would need to be worked out first.[76]

In the rancorous debates at court that ensued during the intercalendary second month of 1086, other prominent antireformists shared Su's skepticism. Even Lü Kung-chu, a longtime conservative stalwart since the 1060s, memorialized that Ssu-ma's plan was strong in theory, but weak on details, and many other remonstrators, including Wang Yen-sou and Liu Chih, also urged restraint.[77] Another notable dissenter was Fan Ch'un-jen, who agreed that while hired service was not without its negative aspects, "it also has aspects which should not be immediately abolished, for the way of governance consists of only eliminating the most extreme" failings of hired service. But Ssu-ma Kuang would brook no dissent from within the ranks, and responded with characteristic ideological fervor, accusing Fan and his associates of heel dragging and apostatizing.[78] After service exemption payments were ultimately abolished in the third month of 1086, a ministerial commission was at last appointed to flesh out the details of drafted service, including local and regional quotas, and worked through the summer and autumn.

With the antireform camp already divided into hard-liners and moderates on the issue of corvée policy, Su Shih broke ranks with what remained of the conservative coalition, proposing a compromise between hired service and drafted service.[79] While his younger brother Su Ch'e was a more mainstream figure at court, Su Shih's principled iconoclasm made him a constant source

---

[75] CPPM 108, pp. 3393–6; "Lun pa mien-i-ch'ien hsing ch'ai-i-fa chuang," in Su, Su Ch'e chi 36, pp. 626–7.

[76] For a more specific policy memorial by Su Ch'e, see HCP (1979) 369, pp. 8895–8, 8901–2.

[77] HCP (1979) 367, p. 8837.

[78] In Ssu-ma Kuang's rebarbative words, "Certainly, there are ministers who owe their advancement to the New Policies, who are taking advantage of this opportunity to argue that hired service fees should not be abolished." See HCP (1979) 367, pp. 8838–9.

[79] For a literary and political biography of Su Shih, see Ronald C. Egan, Word, image, and deed in the life of Su Shi (Cambridge, Mass., 1994). For an intellectual biography of Su Shih, see Bol, "This culture of ours," pp. 254–99.

of irritation to those in power. One of the most outspoken and persistent opponents of Wang An-shih in the 1070s, Su Shih had undergone something of a political change of heart, relenting in his antagonism to the New Policies and questioning the self-righteous extremism of Ssu-ma Kuang.[80] Su had belatedly come to understand the positive aspects of hired service, which he now hoped to combine with the strong points of drafted service. Memorializing the throne in the fourth month of 1086, Su Shih noted that the surplus emergency fee (*k'uan-sheng ch'ien*) that had been extorted through the hired service system had remained unspent since its inception. In the sixteen-odd years since the fee was arbitrarily imposed upon every commoner, he wrote, "it has accumulated to as much as 3 million plus strings of unused cash. . . . Your servant states that these monies came forth from the people's labor, and in principle they should return to the people's use."[81] Su proposed that this surplus be used to buy up public lands, which could be granted to volunteer laborers in lieu of paying them wages, thereby cutting state payroll expenditures and reducing service exemption fees. When his proposals went unheeded, Su became a source of irritation to the rest of the drafted service working group, from which he was dismissed in the seventh month of 1086.[82] Su Shih's defiance of the political consensus would make him a constant irritant at court and would result in his eventual dismissal in 1089. Until then, his dissent from the antireform bloc would only intensify, as he formed a splinter group with his brother Su Ch'e and his fellow Szechwanese Lü T'ao. Su Shih's nonconformity foreshadowed a broader political trend: the fissuring of the conservative coalition into factions that would square off over both personal disagreements and policy issues for the remainder of the regency.

The abolition of the green sprouts policy, the second of Ssu-ma Kuang's "four perils," became another source of dissension at court, but, compared with the paralyzing debates over hired service, the disputes over green sprouts were rather mild. As described in chapter 5, although the policy was redistributive in intent, it quickly became yet another instrument of revenue extraction once annual interest rates of twenty to thirty percent were assessed upon green sprouts loans and the loan fund was opened up to people from all classes of rural society. Given the previous hostility of Ssu-ma Kuang and his coalition toward hired service, the extractive nature of green sprouts policy naturally roused their ire.[83] The antireformist forays against green sprouts were roughly

[80] See Su Shih's letter to his friend Teng Fu, "Yü T'eng Ta-tao pa," in Su Shih, *Su Shih wen-chi*, ed. K'ung Fan-li (Peking, 1986) 51, p. 1478.

[81] *HCP* (1979) 374, pp. 9071–5; "Lun chi tien mu-i chuang," in Su, *Su Shih wen-chi* 26, pp. 768–71.

[82] *HCP* (1979) 382, pp. 9299–9300; "Tsai ch'i pa hsiang-ting mien-i chuang," in Su, *Su Shih wen-chi* 26, p. 781.

[83] For Ssu-ma Kuang's memorial on green sprouts, see *HCP* (1979) 368, pp. 8875–7; "Ch'i pa ti-chü-kuan cha-tzu," in Ssu-ma, *Ssu-ma Kuang tsou-i* 36, pp. 389–91.

coterminous with criticism of hired service, extending through the spring and summer of 1086. In a memorial of the fourth month of 1086, Wang Yen-sou voiced the mainstream view that government expansion into loan-sharking had succeeded in enriching the state and impoverishing the peasantry. And another conservative remonstrator maintained that even private moneylenders were more lenient than government agents, who raised interest on farm loans from an acceptable twenty percent to an extortionate sixty percent.[84]

Compared to the protracted hand-wringing over hired service, court opinion against green sprouts loans was far more unified. Even Su Shih fell into line with the political mainstream, memorializing against the evils and abuses of the green sprouts system: "For the past twenty years, these policies have grown more harmful by the day, the people have grown more impoverished, penalties have grown more bothersome, graft has grown more intense.... To detail and number its numerous harms would be impossible."[85] Apparently, the sole dissenting voice within the conservative camp was Fan Ch'un-jen, then serving as assistant director of the Bureau of Military Affairs. Perhaps the most significant voice of moderation within the antireform coalition and the son of the eminent 1040s statesman Fan Chung-yen, Fan Ch'un-jen would later be promoted to chief councilor of the right in 1088. By expressing his qualms over the abolition of green sprouts, arguing that interest from the loans would benefit the state's bottom line, Fan enraged Ssu-ma Kuang, who nearly dismissed Fan from court for disobedience.[86] At this point, Ssu-ma alone could not enforce factional discipline; when Wang Yen-sou and others vouched for Fan's integrity, Fan managed to retain his post. By the summer of 1086, an ailing Ssu-ma Kuang could no longer be assured of the loyalty of his allies, and his coalition began to fracture over each and every major policy issue that came to the table.

Peace in our time: Rapprochement with the Hsi Hsia

Border tensions with the Tangut Hsi Hsia represented the last great peril Ssu-ma Kuang needed to eliminate before he could die in peace. After the conservative takeover of 1085–6, conciliation and vacillation became the guiding principles in Sung foreign policy, supplanting the expansionism and militarism of the reform era. During Shen-tsung's reign, the conflict with the Hsi Hsia had been prosecuted but at a prohibitive cost. While the total war of 1081–3

---

[84] *HCP* (1979) 378, pp. 9192–4.
[85] *HCP* (1979) 384, pp. 9359–61; see "Ch'i pu chi-san ch'ing-miao-ch'ien chuang," in Su, *Su Shih wen-chi* 27, pp. 783–5.
[86] *HCP* (1979) 384, pp. 9366–7.

had neutralized the offensive threat of the Hsi Hsia, the Sung had squandered innumerable lives and vast quantities of resources to win a few small plots of land. The painful lesson of the Sung army's disastrous defeat at Yung-lo ch'eng in 1082, in which two hundred thousand troops had been massacred, remained fresh in the collective memory of everyone at court.[87] After the mass carnage of the early 1080s campaigns, the conflict continued on a smaller scale along the heavily militarized northwestern border, where the Hsi Hsia conducted pinprick raids on Sung positions but failed to regain them. For the ascendant antireform faction who now dictated military and border policy, all that the Sung required was an exit strategy, and this stalemated conflict could be ended once and for all.

An opportunity for a lasting peace came in the summer of 1086, when a Tangut embassy arrived in K'ai-feng to initiate peace negotiations, following the death of the Hsi Hsia ruler Wei-ming Ping-ch'ang (Emperor Hsia Hui-tsung, r. 1068–86). The terms of the truce were costly, for the Hsi Hsia envoys demanded the immediate return of territories that the Sung had occupied in the war of 1081–3: Lan-chou plus four stockades in the Heng-shan highlands on the Hsi Hsia–Shan-hsi border (see map 17).[88] Both of these areas formed the bulwark of Sung defenses along the northwestern marches, controlling access to the upper Yellow River valley. Under the reformists, who had pursued a policy of militant irredentism, surrendering even a square inch of hard-won borderland would have been inconceivable. But now that the antireform coalition held sway over the Sung court, the pacific overtures of the Tanguts met with an enthusiastic reception.

As with the eradication of the New Policies, Ssu-ma Kuang approached border relations with bold strokes and grand gestures, hoping to accomplish an abrupt and permanent reversal of what the reformists had wrought. In the sixth month of 1086, Ssu-ma Kuang spoke out in favor of rapprochement with the Hsi Hsia, forcefully arguing that the loss of a few small plots of distant land was a small price to pay for a lasting peace.[89] In Ssu-ma's eyes, reformist irredentism and adventurism represented a far greater threat to the multistate balance of power than did the Tanguts themselves. Even Su Shih concurred with the chief councilor, arguing that the reformists alone had destabilized the northwestern border by instigating a futile war with the Hsi Hsia in an act

---

[87] For the political and military history of the Hsi Hsia empire in this period, see Ruth W. Dunnell, "The Hsi Hsia," in *The Cambridge history of China*, volume 6: *Alien regimes and border states, 907–1368*, ed. Herbert Franke and Denis C. Twitchett (New York, 1994), pp. 154–214, and Wu T'ien-ch'ih, *Hsin Hsi Hsia shih* (Taipei, 1987). The most thorough monograph on Sung-Tangut relations is Li Hua-jui, *Sung Hsia kuan-hsi shih* (Shih-chia-chuang, 1998).

[88] *SS* 486, p. 14015.

[89] *HCP* (1979) 380, pp. 9221–2.

of vainglorious folly.[90] In the early Yüan-yu consensus, now that a dangerous internal enemy – the reformists – had been purged from the Sung court, the last barrier to peace with an external enemy had fallen.

While many at court concurred with Ssu-ma Kuang, the debates over ceding Lan-chou and the four border stockades were especially prolonged and intense. Several sources indicate that prominent conservatives, including Lü Ta-fang and Wang Ts'un, protested the cession of territory to the Tanguts.[91] But the most outspoken opponent of a negotiated peace was An T'ao, one of the remaining reformists on the Council of State, and currently the director of the Bureau of Military Affairs, who refused to relinquish hard-won territories to the Tanguts.[92]

However, many antireformists took exception to An T'ao's invocation of Shen-tsung's memory. The brothers Su Ch'e and Su Shih insisted that the occupation of Lan-chou and the five border stockades "was originally not the sagely intention of the former emperor," but rather the consequence of the incompetence and cowardice of the eunuch general Li Hsien, so that "abandoning them would not violate his [Shen-tsung's] testament."[93] By the end of the debate, the cession of the occupied territories had become a thinkable option at court. Lan-chou (established in 1081) had been decoupled from Shen-tsung's legacy and rendered into non-Sung territory through the smoke and mirrors of rhetoric. But the case for abandoning these areas was not just academic, for they had originally belonged to the Tibetans and had not been under Chinese rule since the T'ang. In the vivid words of Su Ch'e, the northwestern border was "a wilderness littered with bones, not worthy of begrudging."[94] With most figures at court favoring appeasement as the only way out of an untenable situation, a costly truce would ultimately be pushed through.

Ssu-ma Kuang did not live to see the conclusion of the Sung–Hsi Hsia peace treaty, which was finally signed in the sixth month of 1089. For the time being, negotiations remained deadlocked over the final status of Lan-chou, which the Sung adamantly refused to relinquish. Even when the Sung

---

[90] HCP (1979) 405, pp. 9872–5; "Yin ch'in kuei-chang lun hsi-ch'iang Hsia-jen shih-i cha-tzu," in Su, *Su Shih wen-chi* 28, pp. 798–800.

[91] No memorials opposing the truce agreement have survived in HCP (1979), but other sources reveal that many in the antireform coalition opposed the cession of territory. A 1094 memorial by Kuo Chih-chang, preserved in the CPPM, claims that Sun Chüeh and Wang Tsun opposed the deal; see CPPM 101, pp. 3124–6. According to Lü Chung, Lü Ta-fang opposed ceding Lan-chou to the Hsi Hsia; see Lü, *Sung ta-shih-chi chiang-i* 19, p. 4a. And other antireformists were far more wary than Ssu-ma Kuang in accepting the terms of the truce agreement. For a voice of caution, see Liu Chih's memorial in HCP (1979) 382, pp. 9307–9.

[92] HCP (1979) 382, pp. 9311–12.

[93] HCP (1979) 382, pp. 9304–5.

[94] HCP (1979) 381, p. 9280; "Lun Lan-chou teng ti chuang," in Su, *Su Ch'e chi* 39, pp. 684–8.

conceded four stockades in Shan-hsi's Yung-hsing-chün circuit — Mi-chih, Chia-lu, Fu-t'u, and An-chiang, all crucial positions without which the Heng-shan highlands were untenable — their boundaries were never clearly delineated.[95] In exchange for these four border forts, the Sung received the approximately one hundred and fifty prisoners of war who had survived the Yung-lo ch'eng massacre.[96] Clearly, this was not the lasting peace that Ssu-ma Kuang had expected, for the limited and sketchy terms of the truce would probably not have met with the chief councilor's approval. For the rest of the Yüan-yu era, Lan-chou and the Heng-shan region remained points of contention along an unstable boundary line dividing the Sung and the Tanguts. Throughout the regency, the Sung court would generally respond to Hsi Hsia raids with characteristic inaction, and no further efforts were made to peaceably resolve the border conflict. To a certain extent, Ssu-ma Kuang and his successors had succeeded in overturning the irredentist border policies of Wang An-shih and Ts'ai Ch'üeh, but a permanent peace remained beyond their grasp. The fragile truce between the two empires would hold until 1096, when the restored reformist regime of Chang Tun would launch a full-scale assault upon the Tanguts.

The end of an era: The death of Ssu-ma Kuang

Having vanquished the empire's great perils and succeeded in his quixotic mission to turn back the clock to the 1060s, Ssu-ma Kuang could at last die in some semblance of peace. Under the aegis of Dowager Empress Hsüan-jen and the domineering influence of Ssu-ma Kuang, a negative policy agenda had been pushed through court, substituting conservatism for activism, withdrawal for expansionism. But the antireformist victory was to be ephemeral, for on the first day of the ninth month of 1086 their leader, Ssu-ma Kuang, succumbed to lingering illness at the age of sixty-seven. In a eulogistic memorial, Wang Yen-sou acknowledged that the passing of such a singularly dedicated statesman as Ssu-ma Kuang had left behind a void at court that could never be filled by mere mortals:

When Your Majesty assumed the throne, the empire hoped that You would employ Ssu-ma Kuang to administer the government, and that You would trust his counsel in order to eliminate the harm which has been done to the empire. Only Kuang possessed a sincere

---

[95] For the terms of the truce, see *SS* 486, p. 14016; and *HCP* (1979) 429, p. 10370. Mi-chih corresponds to modern-day Mi-chih county in Shensi, and Chia-lu corresponds to modern-day Chia county in Shensi. Fu-t'u lies to the west of modern-day Sui-te county, Shensi, while An-ch'iang is located to the northwest of modern-day Ch'ing-yang county, Kansu.

[96] For more details on the prisoner exchange, see *SS* 17, p. 330; *HCP* (1979) 432, pp. 10425–6; 434, pp. 10467–9; 435, p. 10489; and 438, pp. 10533–4.

heart which sympathized with the state and cherished the people.... Who will again take the empire's heart as his own, the people's intentions as his own? Who will toil to exhaustion all night long and sacrifice himself as Kuang did?[97]

Even for Su Shih, who had acrimoniously broken ranks with his patron over the issue of hired service, the death of Ssu-ma Kuang was an epochal moment that "touched the hearts of men, and shook Heaven and Earth."[98] According to the *Hsü Tzu-chih t'ung-chien ch'ang-pien*, Ssu-ma's death incited a great popular outcry among the inhabitants of K'ai-feng, who snapped up huge quantities of his printed portrait and mourned him as if he were their own kinsman.[99] The death of Ssu-ma Kuang was acknowledged by contemporaries to be an irreparable loss, and by later historians to be a watershed moment in political life. In the following years of the regency, and for the remainder of the Northern Sung, the antireform coalition would never surpass the heroics of the early regency. Dominated by the stellar figure of Ssu-ma Kuang, 1085 and 1086 would be known as the golden years of the conservative coalition, a brief but spectacular event. The chief councilor had managed to temporarily short-circuit the deep divisions within the antireform coalition, which erupted to the surface soon after its moment of triumph.

POLITICAL GRIDLOCK: 1086–1093

The splintering of the antireform coalition: Shuo versus Lo versus Shu

Left without a paramount leader to guide them and without an organized resistance to fight, and already partially disunited by protracted policy debates, the members of the antireform coalition began to attack each other. As far as domestic policy was concerned, the remainder of the Hsüan-jen regency was relatively eventless. Policy debates were few and far between, and only incremental adjustments were made to the policies established in 1085–6. What did occupy the attentions of courtiers was the endless cycle of indictments and recriminations that gridlocked the imperial court for the next eight years. Even before the death of Ssu-ma Kuang, fissures had developed within the coalition, but they now threatened its very foundations. Annals of the years from 1087 to 1093 read like a litany of political infighting, in which ministers and remonstrators volleyed polemics at each other, seeking to purge the court of their political and personal adversaries. The traditional historiography of the Yüan-yu period identifies three discrete regional court

[97] *HCP* (1979) 387, pp. 9416–17.
[98] *HCP* (1979) 387, p. 9416.
[99] See n. 12 and *HCP* (1979) 387, p. 9415.

factions (*tang*): the Shuo faction, comprised largely of men from Ho-pei; the Lo faction, associated with Lo-yang; and the Shu faction, headed by men from Szechwan. When these three coalitions were not contending for power and jockeying for position, they were besieging a fourth faction: the defeated reformists, who were assumed to be waiting in the wings and poised for a comeback.

Dominant at court throughout the regency, the Shuo faction claimed to be the ideological heirs of Ssu-ma Kuang, and boasted such stalwart antireformist remonstrators as Liu Chih, Liang T'ao, Wang Yen-sou, and Liu An-shih within its ranks. Political pragmatists who sought truth from facts, the men of Shuo viewed statecraft through the prism of historical analogy. Over the course of the regency, its members managed to control the commanding heights of the bureaucracy, with Liu Chih and Liang T'ao ensconced in positions of administrative authority, and Wang Yen-sou and Liu An-shih placed in powerful censorial and remonstrance posts. Occupying the political mainstream, the men of Shuo would subdue their rivals by expelling the most voluble dissident elements – the iconoclasts of Shu and the zealots of Lo – from court. At the same time, the leaders of the Shuo faction would co-opt more pliant political figures into its patronage organization. By the early 1090s, the governing coalition of Liu Chih would ultimately absorb many members from both the Lo and Shu factions.

To the right of the Shuo faction stood the Lo faction of Ch'eng I, who would earn himself a place of honor in Southern Sung historiography as the progenitor of the *Tao-hsüeh* movement, and his supporters Chia I and Chu Kuang-t'ing. Serving in prominent academic and remonstrance posts, Ch'eng and his lieutenants were in the ascendant in the early years of the regency. Their fundamentalist approach to ethics and ritual – and their eventual persecution by the reformist ministry of the Hui-tsung reign – would earn them a place of honor in the twelfth- and thirteenth-century histories of the *Tao-hsüeh* movement. While the Shuo faction were pragmatic historicists, the men of Lo were classical ideologues, radicals in the original sense of the word, envisioning the revival of the Way of antiquity through ritual practice and textual exegesis. But in the context of the late eleventh century, the men of Lo were generally considered to be extremists.[100] Ch'eng I himself was out of his element in the world of politics; he would fail to establish himself as a lasting presence at court, serving only a year and a half as Che-tsung's principal tutor. But Chia I and Chu Kuang-t'ing would survive the infighting of early Yüan-yu, as the

---

[100] For an intellectual biography of Ch'eng I and an adept analysis of his central role in Sung intellectual history as a transitional figure between *ku-wen* and *Tao-hsüeh*, see Bol, *"This culture of ours,"* pp. 300–42.

remaining men of Lo would gradually merge into the Shuo coalition of Liu Chih by the end of the regency.[101]

Ch'eng I's principal antagonist was the political iconoclast and literary lion Su Shih, who had been accused of forming a Shu faction with his brother Su Ch'e and his fellow Szechwanese Lü T'ao and K'ung Wen-chung. Due to their preeminent positions in Sung intellectual history, Su Shih's bitter contention with Ch'eng I has become the stuff of legend. During the Hsüan-jen regency, Su Shih's position at court was extremely precarious. Caught up in a series of literary inquisitions for alleged slanders against the throne, Su was exiled from the capital nearly every other year, only to be rehabilitated after serving a single tour of duty outside the capital. Su Ch'e and Lü T'ao, in contrast, were adept political survivors, remaining in high positions at court for most of the regency, and continuing to launch reprisals against Chia I and Chu Kuang-t'ing, their counterparts in the Lo faction. And when the brothers Su or Lü T'ao were denounced by their antagonists from Shuo or Lo, they were frequently accused of being closet reformists. Traditional historiography has maligned the Shu faction, accusing them of instigating factional discord, but their political tenacity throughout the regency would suggest otherwise.

The internal dissension that plagued the antireform coalition during the Yüan-yu era, and diverted attention from the real business of governing, was far less destructive than the preceding (and succeeding) hostilities between the reformists and antireformists. The gates of the imperial court became revolving doors, as those who were purged from court for one reason or another – whether men of Shuo, Lo, or Shu – invariably found their way back to K'ai-feng after a year or two. Only members of the Yüan-feng reformist coalition, or those suspected of being reformist sympathizers, were the prominent exceptions to this rule. Once the antireform coalition had first purged and then pardoned its own for two or three years, they began to unite against a manufactured enemy. While they were scapegoating such exiled and powerless reformists as Ts'ai Ch'üeh and Chang Tun, prominent antireformists from all three cliques lived in constant fear of a reformist comeback. Hence, most of the casualties of Yüan-yu factionalism were actual reformists or those members of the antireform coalition who were suspected of concealing reformist sympathies.

Although useful as a heuristic device, the historiographic division of the antireform coalition into three discrete factions belies the chaos and complexity of political life in the late Northern Sung. First of all, the members of these so-called factions and cliques (*tang* and *p'eng-tang*) would never have applied those words to describe their own court coalitions. While councilors and censors

---

[101] Ch'eng I had been appointed tutor to Che-tsung in the third month of 1086, from near obscurity, on the recommendation of Ssu-ma Kuang and Lü Kung-chu. See *HCP* (1979) 373, p. 9029.

constantly accused their opponents of the egregious offense of factionalism, no one at court would ever have admitted to actually having formed a faction. In late Northern Sung political discourse, factions were seen as inherently inimical to the primary ministerial virtue of public mindedness (*kung*), and as the embodiment of nefariously self-serving behavior (*ssu*).[102] Only one's political enemies deserved the appellation *tang*. In countless indictments of the Yüan-yu period, the accused were invariably charged with the heinous crime of having formed factions.

Second, during the Yüan-yu era, factional battle lines were not as clearly drawn as traditional historiography would have its readers believe. For these political divisions were by no means hard and fast, and perhaps court factions should be conceptualized as constantly shifting coalitions rather than as monolithic party blocs. Nor were they either discrete regional groupings of northeasterners, northwesterners, and Szechwanese or representatives of distinct regional socioeconomic interests, such as northwestern magnates or southeastern merchants. Furthermore, not everyone joined coalitions, for several notable figures at court, such as Lü Ta-fang, Fan Ch'un-jen, and Fan Tsu-yü, remained neutral and nonaligned. Moreover, Yüan-yu factions were unstable, readily fissioning into smaller agglomerations of scholar-officials, as policy debates and personal animosities drove their members apart. In the absence of major debates over policy after 1086, factional infighting tended to revolve around personality clashes. Perhaps the infighting between Lo and Shu would be better thought of as an extension of the personal animosity between Ch'eng I and Su Shih. These were not tightly disciplined political machines, but rather loose affiliations that clustered around central figures.

Third, traditional and modern historians have associated the Shuo, Lo, and Shu factions, as well as the reform group, with discrete regional traditions of intellectual production and learning. The clash between Lo and Shu has been depicted as an ideological schism between northeastern *Tao-hsüeh* (Learning of the Way) and the "Szechwanese learning" (*Shu-hsüeh*) of the brothers Su.[103] A broad chasm indeed separated the philosophies of Ch'eng I and Su Shih, and their most fundamental point of disagreement revolved around the relationship of culture and values. The most prominent literatus of his time, Su Shih

---

[102] For an analysis of factional discourse during the Yüan-yu era, see chapter 5 of Ari D. Levine, "A house in darkness: The politics of history and the language of politics in the late Northern Song, 1066–1126" (diss., Columbia University, 2002).

[103] See Lei Fei-lung, "Pei Sung hsin-chiu tang-cheng yü ch'i hsüeh-shu cheng-ts'e chih kuan-hsi," *Kuo-li Cheng-chih ta-hsüeh hsüeh-pao* 11 (1965), pp. 201–44. Also see Ho Man-tzu, "Yüan-yu Shu-Lo tang-cheng ho Su Shih ti fan Tao-hsüeh tou-cheng (shang)," *Sung-liao hsüeh-pao: She-hui k'o-hsüeh pan* 2 (1984), pp. 1–7; Wang Tseng-yü, "Lo, Shu, Shuo tang-cheng pien," in *Chin-hsin-chi: Chang Cheng-lang hsien-sheng pa-shih ch'ing-shou lun-wen-chi*, ed. Wu Jung-tseng (Peking, 1996), pp. 351–69.

viewed the literary (*wen*) as the embodiment of moral values, and cultural forms as the articulation of the sagely Way. Denying the centrality of literary expression, and severing the link between culture and ethics, Ch'eng I preached that true values could be found within, through a rigorous process of self-cultivation.[104] However, while the ideologies of Ch'eng I and Su Shih were diametrically opposed, one would be mistaken to characterize Su Shih as a vociferous opponent of *Tao-hsüeh*, which did not exist as a clearly defined philosophical system until the Southern Sung.[105] Since the boundaries between Shuo, Lo, and Shu learning were drawn and rigidified long after the fact, it makes far more sense to describe the factional infighting of the Yüan-yu era as primarily a political rather than an intellectual phenomenon. Though the collision between Ch'eng I and Su Shih did indeed take on philosophical overtones, it was basically a personal struggle for power between two extreme personalities.

Fourth, to complicate matters even further, overall political discord was exacerbated by the separation of powers between the Council of State and the Censorate, which inevitably kindled hostilities between councilors and remonstrators.[106] During the late 1080s and early 1090s, chief councilors and censors engaged in a drawn-out game of tug-of-war, whose players were not divided by factional battle lines. Throughout the Hsüan-jen regency, remonstrance and surveillance organs remained firmly under the thumb of chief councilors. Councilors succeeded in manipulating the Censorate and the Remonstrance Bureau into vilifying their political enemies and shielding themselves from hostile remonstrance. When individual censors remonstrated against ministerial high-handedness or called attention to the failings of court policy, councilors would frequently have them dismissed and purged for what they perceived as slander. As the three factions battled each other, an institutional conflict simultaneously unfolded, as councilors consolidated their dominance over the workings of the central government by increasing their control over remonstrance and surveillance.

Hence, the constant state of political flux during the Hsüan-jen regency defies any historiographic attempt to extract signal from noise, to impose a rational analysis upon chaos. To be sure, the nine years of the Yüan-yu era (1086–94) witnessed protracted hostilities between three coalitions, and this factional infighting paralyzed the imperial court. But one must be careful not to overdraw the boundaries between these coalitions, and not to describe them

---

[104] See Bol, *"This culture of ours,"* pp. 254–345.

[105] See Lo, *Pei Sung tang-cheng yen-chiu*, pp. 181–4.

[106] For an analysis of the central role played by the Censorate and the Remonstrance Bureau in the factional conflict of the late Northern Sung, see Shen, "Pei Sung t'ai-chien chih-tu yü tang-cheng," pp. 27–44.

as stable entities with regionally exclusive memberships and distinct ideologies. When the men of Shuo attempted to purge the men of Shu from the metropolitan bureaucracy, and when the men of Shu launched invective at the men of Lo, their rivalry was primarily personal and political. The political history of these nine years is extremely convoluted and involuted, and limitations of space prevent anything but a summary of its highlights.

Missing the mark: Su Shih versus Ch'eng I

According to the received narratives of Yüan-yu era political history, the death of Ssu-ma Kuang marked the official starting point of factional infighting. As the thirteenth-century commentator Lü Chung described the unsettled situation at court in late 1086: "Ssu-ma Kuang died one day, and the factional disputes began the next. If Ssu-ma Kuang were still alive, then the true gentlemen (chün-tzu) would still have remained, and the calamity of factions certainly would not have occurred."[107] In traditional historiography, the point of origin of the Lo-Shu feud was Ssu-ma Kuang's funeral, where the animosity between Ch'eng I and Su Shih first reared its ugly head. According to most retellings, Ch'eng I was responsible for administering protocol at the funeral, where his punctilious adherence to ancient ritual forms provoked a burst of mockery from Su Shih. Before attending the funeral, Su had participated in an amnesty-conferral ceremony, at which music had been played and sung. Ch'eng adamantly refused to admit Su to the funeral hall, citing the Analects passage "On the day the Master mourned, he never sang." Su struck back with the witty epigram, "I have heard of not singing after you mourn, but I have never heard of not mourning after you sing," after which all assembled mocked Ch'eng I for being ridiculously inflexible.[108]

While Su Shih had clearly made a laughingstock of Ch'eng I, it is doubtful that nine years of vicious infighting could have begun with a single jest at Ssu-ma Kuang's funeral. The antireform coalition had already been cracking apart for a year, and it is unlikely that Su Shih cast the final stone that shattered its fragile unity. Such accusations were made long after the fact, after the intellectual lineage of Ch'eng I had triumphed over that of Su Shih in the twelfth century. Moreover, Su Shih was not alone in criticizing Ch'eng for

---

[107] Lü, Sung ta-shih-chi chiang-i 19, p. 11b.

[108] For an extended narrative of Su Shih's personal, political, and ideological disputes with Ch'eng I, see Egan, Word, image, and deed in the life of Su Shi, pp. 93–8. For a discussion of the discrepancies between each of the retellings, see Lo, Pei Sung tang-cheng yen-chiu, pp. 180–1. For one version of the story, plus extensive commentary, see HCP (1979) 393, pp. 9569–73. Also see Shao Po, Shao-shih wen-chien hou-lu, ed. Liu Te-ch'üan and Li Chien-hsiung (1157; Peking, 1983) 20, pp. 159–60; and Ch'eng Hao and Ch'eng I, Erh Ch'eng chi, ed. Wang Hsiao-yü (Peking, 1981) 11, pp. 415–16.

his rigidly dogmatic approach to classical texts and ancient ritual. Even so mainstream a political figure as Liu Chih, a leader of the Shuo faction, had expressed his doubts about Ch'eng I's approach to classical hermeneutics, and questioned his harsh approach to tutoring Che-tsung.[109] Many at court, from both the Shu and Shuo factions, resented the meteoric rise of Ch'eng I – who two years before had been a commoner with no history of bureaucratic service whatsoever – to the lofty (and to some, undeserved) position of the emperor's principal tutor. Almost immediately, Ch'eng had attracted several well-placed followers, including Chia I, Chu Kuang-t'ing, and Wang Yen-sou; his formation of a clique naturally aroused the suspicion of many at court. Moreover, his rivals were apprehensive about the way Ch'eng was discharging his tutorial duties, believing that he was abusing his privileged position at court to isolate and manipulate the young emperor and thus to further his own career. Clearly, then, Su Shih was not the only one who suspected Ch'eng I of treachery and factiousness.

Whatever the origins of the strife between Lo and Shu, Su Shih's alleged mockery of Ch'eng I did not go unpunished. The factional infighting began in earnest in the final month of 1086, when Chu Kuang-t'ing remonstrated to have Su Shih dismissed from his post as Han-lin academician (*Han-lin hsüeh-shih*). Chu accused Su Shih of having slandered the deceased Emperors Jen-tsung and Shen-tsung in this examination question:

The court wishes to model itself after the loyalty and magnanimity of Jen-tsung, but is concerned that bureaucrats would not perform the duties for which they are responsible, and that this would result in laxity. On the other hand, it wishes to make laws with the dedication and determination of Shen-tsung, but fears that the supervisory and prefectural officials would not understand the intent behind them, and that this would result in harshness.[110]

In Chu's forced interpretation, Su Shih was supposedly denigrating Jen-tsung for "laxness," and Shen-tsung for his "harshness." Censors and remonstrators of the Shuo faction, including Wang Yen-sou and Fu Yao-yü, also concurred that Su Shih had blasphemed the memory of the late emperors, urging Su Shih's dismissal from court.[111] Ironically, many members of the antireform coalition had employed far more polemical and offensive language to describe the reign of Shen-tsung as a time of misrule and corruption.

Events soon turned in Su Shih's favor, when Palace Censor Lü T'ao came to his defense, unable to remain silent while his comrade (and fellow Szechwanese) was being victimized by factional collusion. Quite convincingly, Lü

---

[109] *HCP* (1979) 373, pp. 9031–3.
[110] *HCP* (1979) 393, pp. 9564–6.
[111] *HCP* (1979) 394, pp. 9598–9601.

claimed that Chu's indictment of Su Shih was a factionally motivated frame-up, a misguided attempt to avenge Su's insult of Ch'eng I.[112] In his own defense, Su Shih denied any intention of slandering the former emperors, explaining that he had used the terms "laxity" and "harshness" to allude to ministerial incompetence in the present court. Eloquently rising to the occasion, Su proclaimed his innocence, accusing his accusers of deliberately misinterpreting and misrepresenting his words: "The pattern of the writing is extremely clear, as plain as black and white – how could there even be a single hair which merits suspicion?"[113] Convinced by Su Shih's arguments in his own defense, Hsüan-jen exonerated him in the first month of 1087 of the trumped-up charges.[114] A few weeks later, Chu Kuang-t'ing was dismissed from the capital and sent to supervise disaster relief in Ho-pei, a move that was not entirely unrelated to his assaults upon Su Shih.[115] Disappointed with Hsüan-jen's ruling, the enemies of Su Shih continued to call for his dismissal. In the third month of 1087, a censorial cabal comprised of Ch'eng I's allies branded Su a traitor for his stubborn opposition to drafted service, but again did not succeed in forcing his resignation.[116]

Meanwhile, there were increasing calls from several remonstrators, including Supervising Secretary (chi-shih-chung) Ku Lin, for the resignation of Ch'eng I as imperial tutor. Ch'eng attributed the hostility of his aggressors to the general depravity and ignorance of a fallen age, portraying himself as the savior of the Way of antiquity, and accusing them of precipitating a general crisis of culture and values.[117] The political writings of Ch'eng I, marked by moralistic severity and fundamentalist messianic fervor, inhabit an entirely different discursive universe than those of his contemporaries, who would never have accused their accusers in such terms. At any rate, Ch'eng still possessed sufficient influence at court to move against his accusers, engineering Ku's dismissal from his remonstrance post, a move that met with broad-based protest from such representatives of the Shuo and Shu factions as Liang T'ao and Su Shih.[118] But the time would soon come when Ch'eng I could no longer defend himself from his adversaries, who were more powerful and better protected than the hapless Ku Lin.

---

[112] *HCP* (1979) 393, pp. 9568–9.

[113] *HCP* (1979) 394, pp. 9594–8; "Pien shih-kuan chih ts'e-wen cha-tzu," in Su, *Su Shih wen-chi* 27, pp. 788–93.

[114] *HCP* (1979) 394, p. 9607.

[115] *HCP* (1979) 395, p. 9626.

[116] *HCP* (1979) 397, pp. 9681–2.

[117] *HCP* (1979) 397, pp. 9674–9; "You shang Taihuang Taihou shu," in Ch'eng and Ch'eng, *Erh Ch'eng chi* 6, pp. 549–52.

[118] *HCP* (1979) 398, pp. 9703–5. Ku Lin was dismissed from the capital and appointed fiscal commissioner in chief (*tu chuan-yün shih*) of Ho-pei.

Institutional tensions: Councilors versus remonstrators

As illustrated by the forcible dismissal of Ku Lin, the tripartite Lo-Shuo-Shu struggle was intertwined and concurrent with an institutional conflict between the Council of State and the Censorate. During the Hsüan-jen regency chief councilors restricted the ambit of remonstrance, continuing an organizational trend that originated during the ministerial regime of Wang An-shih.[119] Despite the antireformists' professed desire to open the roads of remonstrance during their takeover of the bureaucracy in 1085, their ministerial regime in fact seriously infringed upon the independence of remonstrators. But by 1087, free and autonomous remonstrance had become a political liability for the antireformist regime, which could no longer tolerate dissent from within its own ranks. Those unfortunate members of the Censorate and Remonstrance Bureau who dared speak out against ministerial abuses of power were summarily dismissed, thereby provoking the outrage of their fellow remonstrators, regardless of their factional affiliations.

A case in point was the dismissal of the investigating censor (*chien-ch'a yü-shih*) Chang Shun-min in the fourth month of 1087. Chang had issued an outspoken critique of the border policies and the patronage system of Wen Yen-po, the elderly conservative who had replaced Ssu-ma Kuang as chief councilor of the left.[120] When Wen and Lü Kung-chu ordered Chang purged from the Censorate, howls of protest immediately erupted from his fellow remonstrators, who objected to the arbitrary circumstances behind his dismissal. Fu Yao-yü and Wang Yen-sou, the acting administrators of the Censorate, spoke valiantly in defense of Chang Shun-min: "Censors are Your Majesty's eyes and ears. If chief councilors are harboring treachery, embracing wickedness, and forming cliques, then [censors] must speak out about their crimes and call for their dismissal."[121] According to Fu and Wang, the Council of State had abrogated the autonomy of remonstrance organs, a high-handed move to obstruct the censure of ministerial malfeasance.

In the days to follow, nearly the entire Censorate and Remonstrance Bureau memorialized the throne to demand Chang's return, chastening the Council of State for their high-handedness. Chang's supporters were a diverse group, comprising members of all three factions – Liang T'ao, Fu Yao-yü, and Wang Yen-sou of Shuo; Chu Kuang-t'ing of Lo; and Lü T'ao of Shu – all of whom would be dismissed and demoted before long. After his demotion to a prefectural post in the fifth month of 1087, Liang T'ao went down fighting,

---

[119] Shen, "Pei Sung t'ai-chien chih-tu yü tang-cheng," pp. 32–6.
[120] *HCP* (1979) 399, pp. 9722–3.
[121] *HCP* (1979) 399, pp. 9723–5.

offering a spirited defense of censorial prerogatives in "rectifying institutions
and revering the court," which were being undermined by state councilor
interference.[122] But despite his factional loyalties to his fellow men of Shuo,
Liu Chih, the influential assistant director of the right of the Department of
State Affairs (*shang-shu yu-ch'eng*), could not prevent the demotion of Liang
T'ao. Nor could he intervene when his comrades Wang Yen-sou and Fu Yao-
yü were both demoted to similarly humiliating posts outside the capital mere
days later.[123] In the process of purging Chang Shun-min and his supporters from the metropolitan bureaucracy, the Council of State had reestablished
its control over remonstrance organs. While the Censorate and the Remonstrance Bureau could be employed in a lateral fashion by political antagonists
to indict one another, vertical remonstrance against chief councilors was now
out of bounds.

The widening chasm: Lo versus Shu

The defenders of Chang Shun-min had spanned factional fault lines in a failed
effort to protect the autonomy of remonstrance organs from ministerial interference. But this spirit of cooperation was extremely short-lived, giving way to
renewed bickering between Lo and Shu. Both sides manipulated the Censorate
and the Remonstrance Bureau for partisan advantage, using allied remonstrators to fire off broadsides against their rivals. In its first phase, from 1087
to 1088, the Lo-Shu factional feud claimed all of the prominent members of
both sides (with the sole exception of the moderate Su Ch'e) as casualties.
These years would witness a progressive polemicization of political culture,
as mean-spirited debates and character assassinations permanently fractured
what remained of the antireform coalition.

Even though such members of the Lo faction as Chu Kuang-t'ing had rallied to the defense of Chang Shun-min, Ch'eng I and his lieutenant Chia I
apparently exploited the case for partisan gain. After their efforts to prosecute a literary inquisition against Su Shih proved fruitless, the Lo faction
utilized the last of their dwindling political capital to strike against Lü T'ao,
Su Shih's staunchest supporter. In the seventh month of 1087, Lü was belatedly
indicted for his opposition to Chang's dismissal, sacked from the Censorate, and
demoted to a circuit-level post in Ching-hsi. Firing off parting shots against
the Lo faction, Lü represented himself as the innocent victim of a factionally

---

[122] *HCP* (1979) 401, pp. 9761–2. Liang was demoted to the post of prefect of Lu-chou.

[123] For Liu Chih's condemnation of Liang Tao, see *HCP* (1979) 401, pp. 9763–5. Fu Yao-yü and Wang
Yen-sou were demoted to the posts of administrator of Ch'en-chou and Ch'i-chou, respectively. See
HCP (1979) 401, p. 9780.

motivated frame-up, naming Ch'eng I and Chia I as the hidden agents who initiated his expulsion from court, and issuing a blanket denial of any personal participation whatsoever in partisan hostilities. According to Lü, Ch'eng and Chia were the agents provocateur who had initiated his expulsion from court, and the true perpetrators of factional treachery, for they had exploited the Censorate to avenge a private vendetta.[124]

Such subterfuges would not go unpunished, and Ch'eng I and Chia I soon met with their retribution. Once the Shuo faction became involved, political momentum slipped away from the men of Lo and into the hands of its enemies. Early in the eighth month of 1087, Chia I was dismissed from his censorial position, banished from the capital, and appointed prefect of Huai-chou.[125] After failing in his bid to indict Su Shih for having written a slanderous exam-ination question, Chia had accused Wen Yen-po, the venerable chief councilor of the right, of protecting Su and of being the real leader of the Shu faction. Understandably, Wen was enraged at these allegations, as were Lü Kung-chu and Hsüan-jen, who arranged for Chia I's dismissal from the Censorate.[126] By accusing Wen Yen-po of factional collusion, Chia I had aroused the ire of the Shuo faction and sealed the fate of the men of Lo. Censorial attempts to impeach chief councilors could not be tolerated, especially not careless mudslinging.

The very same day, Ch'eng I was expelled from his post as chief tutor to Emperor Che-tsung, and demoted to an inconsequential post in the Lo-yang branch of the Directorate of Education (*Kuo-tzu chien*). Su Shih's ally K'ung Wen-chung, the grand master of remonstrance (*chien-i ta-fu*), had indicted Ch'eng I on several counts. K'ung first charged Ch'eng with exploiting his position as Classics Mat lecturer for personal gain, and with attempting to brainwash and isolate the young and impressionable emperor.[127] Moreover, he questioned Ch'eng I's scholarly pedantry and assailed his approach to classical hermeneutics as rife with misinterpretations. Even worse according to K'ung, Ch'eng had formed a faction with his cronies Chu Kuang-t'ing and Chia I to impugn righteous men like Lü T'ao and to mount a hostile takeover of the state apparatus. Another censor linked to Su Shih further elaborated upon the shortcomings of Ch'eng I, recommending Cheng's immediate expulsion from court. His political career was over. For the rest of his life, Ch'eng would not return to K'ai-feng, and would serve only intermittently in Lo-yang. He had failed to single-handedly halt the moral decline of the empire, to change the system from within. Ch'eng I's fall from grace at court would lead him to

[124] *HCP* (1979) 403, pp. 9814–16.
[125] *HCP* (1979) 404, p. 9828.
[126] *HCP* (1979) 404, p. 9828.
[127] *HCP* (1979) 404, pp. 9829–31.

permanently distrust political solutions to what he considered to be a fundamental cultural crisis and would influence the *Tao-hsüeh* movement to assume
an oppositionist stance toward the state.

Su Shih managed to survive the partisan friction for another year, but he was
ultimately forced to request his own dismissal from court after being constantly
hounded by remonstrators. While the Lo faction no longer represented a serious
threat to his political survival, he had made many enemies in the course of
his political career, with his iconoclastic views and combative personality.
Evidently, Su Shih's clashes with Ssu-ma Kuang over drafted service had earned
him the everlasting scorn of the Shuo faction. In a memorial to Che-tsung, Su
protested the lockstep political conformity of Ssu-ma's successors: "The various
censors and remonstrators all desired to conform to Kuang's intentions, in
order to seek advancement.... They formed a faction and blocked dissenting
opinions.... They never understood that Kuang had devoted himself to the
people with extreme sincerity, and did not intend for men to conform with
him."[128]

Furthermore, Su Shih and Lü Tao had recently been denounced as a Szechwanese faction by Han Wei, the current vice-director of the Chancellery.[129]
Su's words and actions in recent years had done little to endear him to the
political mainstream, and it was no great shock when various remonstrators
set upon him. In the twelfth month of 1087 and the first month of 1088,
two conservative remonstrators accused Su of exhibiting favoritism toward
certain degree candidates before they had even sat for examination.[130] Later
in 1088, Chao T'ing-chih, a long-standing enemy since the Yüan-feng era,
sought revenge against Su Shih, repeatedly demanding Su's dismissal from
the Han-lin Academy.[131] Chao fabricated slander charges against Su, bringing back his examination question of 1086, and also accusing him of having
slandered Emperor Che-tsung by citing a line from the *Book of poetry* (*Shih-
ching*) that alluded to the suffering of the common people. Su dismissed Chao's

---

[128] *HCP* (1979) 415, pp. 10077–80; "Ch'i chün cha-tzu," in Su, *Su Shih wen-chi* 29, pp. 827–30.

[129] In the seventh month of 1087, Lü T'ao and Su Ch'e were involved in a successful plot to dismiss Han
Wei from the Chancellery and demote him to the post of prefect of Teng-chou2. For more details, see
HCP (1979) 403, pp. 9807–19.

[130] *HCP* (1979) 407, p. 9914; 408, pp. 9922–3.

[131] Chao T'ing-chih's enmity toward Su Shih had many roots. First, during the late Yüan-feng era, when
Chao T'ing-chih had served as vice-prefect (*t'ung-p'an*) in Te-chou (Ho-pei East), Su Shih's protégé
Huang T'ing-chien criticized him for his excessive zeal in implementing the state trade policy in an
area where the peasantry was already impoverished. Second, in early Yüan-yu, when Chao T'ing-chih
was summoned to court as an examination official (*shih-kuan*), Su Shih memorialized to overturn the
appointment, arguing that Chao was ignorant and petty. Third, Su Shih's brother Su Ch'e had once
memorialized against Chao T'ing-chih's father-in-law, Kuo Kai. For Su Shih's explanation, see *HCP*
(1979) 415, p. 10078; "Ch'i chün cha-tzu," in Su, *Su Shih wen-chi* 29, pp. 827–8.

charges as utterly laughable: "If Chao T'ing-chih considers this to have slandered the emperor, this is like saying black is white and west is east. His accusations are without even the slightest semblance of truth."[132] Unable to endure an unending censorial assault, and without defenders in the Council of State, Su made frequent requests for a transfer away from the capital. In the third month of 1089, Su was appointed prefect of Hang-chou, where he enjoyed a well-deserved respite from his legion of detractors.[133]

By early 1089, the Lo-Shu factional conflict had run its course, and the principal combatants from both sides had been expelled from the capital. But their sentences would be commuted in the very near future, when all but Ch'eng I would be politically rehabilitated and returned to influential academic and censorial positions. Lü T'ao would be the first to return to court, after his reappointment to the Censorate in the summer of 1089. Chia I worked his way back into the Censorate by mid-1090, and Su Shih would be reappointed to the Han-lin Academy early in 1091. Of course, the backbiting between Lo and Shu would continue in more subdued form for the rest of the regency. But after several years of purging each other from court on various trumped-up charges, members of the ruling coalition would find their chief enemies elsewhere. The first half of the Yüan-yu era had been wasted with partisan infighting, but political life in the succeeding years would be marked by antagonism of a different kind.

The cultivation of hatred: The banishment of Ts'ai Ch'üeh

There was one cause that could unify nearly everyone at court during the Hsüan-jen regency: fear and loathing of the reformists. No longer distracted by infighting at court, remonstrators sought hard-to-miss targets outside the capital. Upon their dismissal in 1086, both Ts'ai Ch'üeh and Chang Tun had been permitted to retain their honorary titles, a fact that still rankled their foes. Thus, no one was taken aback when the censor Liu An-shih accused Chang Tun of having coerced Su-chou commoners into illegal land deals in the final month of 1088, and Chang was subsequently demoted one titular rank.[134] Compared to his factional patron, Chang Tun got off with a mere slap on the wrist in this darkly farcical purge of the purged.

For Ts'ai Ch'üeh, the exiled leader of the reformists, stood as the embodiment of the collective hatred of the governing coalition. Although Ts'ai was

[132] *HCP* (1979) 415, p. 10080; "Ch'i chün cha-tzu," in Su, *Su Shih wen-chi* 29, pp. 829–30. For an extended narrative of this episode see Egan, *Word, image, and deed in the life of Su Shi*, pp. 100–1.

[133] *HCP* (1979) 424, pp. 10251–3.

[134] *HCP* (1979) 420, pp. 10174–81; 464, p. 11085.

conveniently out of the way far from the capital, and hence no longer a threat
to the survival of the current regime, many lived in constant (and irrational)
apprehension of his possible return to the capital. In a memorial of early 1089,
Liu An-shih, ever the alarmist, issued a general warning to his comrades about
the ever-present danger of a reformist comeback: "The greater part of Ts'ai
Ch'üeh's faction remains at court," and await their chance to "seize power and
make chaos of governance."[135] The next month, Liu Chih warned Hsüan-jen
that the followers of Ts'ai Ch'üeh and Chang Tun had formed a fifth column,
waiting for their chance to strike at the heart of the empire.[136]

The collective hatred of Ts'ai Ch'üeh would take on concrete form once word
reached court of his scandalous and seditious activities in exile. In the fourth
month of 1089, Wu Ch'u-hou, the administrator of Han-yang chün (modern
Wu-han), memorialized the throne to accuse Ts'ai of having slandered and
satirized Hsüan-jen. Wu offered a critical reading of a cycle of ten quatrains
(*chüeh-chü*) entitled "Ascending the Carriage Canopy Pavilion in Summer,"
written while Ts'ai was serving as prefect of neighboring An-chou (Ching-hu
North). He alleged that two of these pieces of verse were "slanderous in the
extreme," possessing "nuanced meanings, of which Ch'üeh desired the reader
to be oblivious."[137] According to Wu, the most abominable poem in the cycle
bemoaned the plight of Hao Ch'u-chün, a loyal minister who had served T'ang
Kao-tsung during the 670s and had once resided in An-chou:

> Peerless was the famed minister Hao Ch'u-chün
> During the Shang-yüan era, his words were loyal and his conduct just.
> His fishing platform is overgrown with weeds, and none know its whereabouts;
> Sighing in contemplation of this, I look down upon the jade bay.

In Wu's interpretation of the quatrain, by associating himself with Hao,
Ts'ai was also drawing an analogy between Dowager Empress Hsüan-jen and
the T'ang dynasty empress Wu Tse-t'ien, the most infamous female usurper in
history. When the sick T'ang Kao-tsung wished to appoint the empress rather
than the heir apparent as temporary regent, Hao Ch'u-chün had protested
the move as an act of feminine encroachment upon the masculine sphere of
legitimate rulership. Thus, by honoring the memory of Empress Wu Tse-
t'ien's famed detractor, Ts'ai Ch'üeh was held to be casting aspersions at the
legitimacy of the Hsüan-jen regency.

An uproar ensued at court during the fifth month of 1089, with remonstrators falling over themselves to censure Ts'ai for his crime of blasphemy.

---

[135] *HCP* (1979) 422, pp. 10222–3.
[136] *HCP* (1979) 423, pp. 10239–45.
[137] *HCP* (1979) 425, pp. 10270–3.

Liang T'ao averred that Ts'ai deserved the ultimate punishment for his vicious slanders: "Ch'üeh admires Hao Ch'u-chün, and I observe that his intention was to claim that Hsüan-jen should not be ruling as regent.... Your servant has repeatedly memorialized on the crimes and wickedness of Ts'ai Ch'üeh, begging for his punishment according to the statutes. But this has not yet been accomplished, and public-minded opinion is seething."[138]

Many other hard-line members of the Censorate and the Remonstrance Bureau, including Liu An-shih, Wang Yen-sou, Wu An-shih, and Fan Tsu-yü, asserted that these poems were sufficient evidence of the overwhelming treachery of Ts'ai Ch'üeh, and an indication that the reformists were waiting for their chance to overthrow Hsüan-jen. The consensus at court urged the application of the strictest penalty in the book to Ts'ai Ch'üeh: permanent banishment to the malarial wastes of Kuang-nan, a rarely applied punishment that amounted to a virtual death sentence.[139]

Facing certain punishment, Ts'ai Ch'üeh valiantly defended himself with solicitous denials, but his words fell on deaf ears. First, he denied harboring any ill will toward the current regime or the regent, claiming that his self-appointed poetry critics were seeing only what they wanted to see:

Your servant wrote several short poems, but neither a single verse nor a single charac-ter touched upon current affairs.... Officials have offered several commentaries that are extraneous to these poems, and they arbitrarily consider them to be slanderous, ascribing hidden meanings to them. If this is so, when everyone opens his mouth or sets down his brush, even though these are unrelated to a certain matter, anyone can be incriminated for a certain matter by those who claim that it has hidden meanings.[140]

Adhering to a literalist interpretation of his own verse, Ts'ai denied that his allusion to Empress Wu Tse-t'ien was a veiled slander of Dowager Empress Hsüan-jen, and affirmed his support for the legitimacy of her regency. His poems, he professed to an incredulous audience, were purely evocative of natu-ral scenes and allusive of past events, with no political implications whatsoever.

While they too refused to believe Ts'ai's casuistic arguments in his own defense, several major court figures voiced their principled defiance of the bloodthirsty chorus who demanded his banishment to Kuang-nan. Su Shih, recently exiled to Hang-chou and no stranger to literary inquisitions, begged clemency for Ts'ai. While his crimes were indeed heinous, Su argued that throwing the book at Ts'ai Ch'üeh would only harshen the current political

---

[138] *HCP* (1979) 425, pp. 10273–6.
[139] *HCP* (1979) 426, pp. 10305–7; 427, pp. 10315–16, 10319–20.
[140] *HCP* (1979) 426, pp. 10301–5.

climate and intensify the proscription of dissent.[141] Fan Ch'un-jen, who replaced the recently deceased Lü Kung-chu as the chief councilor of the left, was appalled by the lack of evidence that Ts'ai Ch'üeh had even formed a faction at court.[142] Fan's protests were quickly overruled by Hsüan-jen, assisted by Lü Ta-fang, Wen Yen-po, and Liu Chih, who maintained that Ts'ai was indeed the leader of a hidden faction at court. In this show trial atmosphere, it is no wonder that the prosecution prevailed, and that Ts'ai received the maximum sentence allowed by law. When the matter was debated before Hsüan-jen, who was out for blood against her long-standing foe, the vengeful elements at court rode roughshod over the voices of moderation. Plagued by fears that a reformist conspiracy had penetrated the ranks of the metropolitan bureaucracy, and united by a common hatred of Ts'ai and his past machinations, the Council of State achieved near unanimity on the issue.

Fan Ch'un-jen and Wang Ts'un – the assistant director of the right in the Department of State Affairs – jeopardized their own careers to voice their loyal opposition, a move that ultimately cost them their positions. Fan expressed his deep anxiety that the regent's decree would set a disastrous precedent for the future of court politics.[143] If a former minister could be entrapped in a literary inquisition after a change of regimes had swept his adversaries into power, then the members of the current regime would be liable to face similar charges in the not-so-distant future. Whether good or evil, all who were accused of factional intrigue would suffer a similar fate as Ts'ai Ch'üeh. Moreover, pronouncing a virtual death sentence upon a former chief councilor could not cure the epidemic of factionalism but would help perpetuate it, and make rational political discussion impossible.[144]

Regardless of Fan's impassioned arguments, Dowager Empress Hsüan-jen decreed that Ts'ai Ch'üeh would be banished to Hsin-chou, Kuang-nan East circuit (present-day Hsin-hsing, Kwangtung). Wang Ts'un and Fan Ch'un-jen both begged for clemency for Ts'ai, pleading that "It is not permissible to send Ts'ai Ch'üeh to a place of death."[145] When the regent and Wen Yen-po refused to hear their appeals, Fan stood his ground, offering prescient words of protest: "This road has been overgrown by thorns for seventy years. Why should it be opened now? I fear that we will not avoid walking it ourselves."[146] To permanently exile Ts'ai to the miasmic tropics would break with many decades

---

[141] *HCP* (1979) 425, pp. 10277–8; "Ch'i hsing-ch'ien Ts'ai Ch'üeh cha-tzu," in Su, *Su Shih wen-chi* 29, p. 837.

[142] *HCP* (1979) 426, p. 10298.

[143] *HCP* (1979) 427, p. 10323.

[144] *HCP* (1979) 427, pp. 10323–5.

[145] *HCP* (1979) 427, p. 10326.

[146] *HCP* (1979) 427, p. 10326.

of dynastic tradition. When compared to past and future regimes, the Sung was lenient as far as capital punishment was concerned. Court executions were all but unknown in the Sung, and ministers had not been banished to the miasmic fringes of the empire since Jen-tsung's reign, when chief councilor Ting Wei had also been banished to the far south. Hence, in the history of Northern Sung politics, the banishment of Ts'ai Ch'üeh represented a crossing of the Rubicon, ushering in an age of unprecedented brutality. If the reformists ever returned to power, they would never forgive the current regime for ordering the death of their leader on trumped-up charges, and the ministers of the Yüan-yu regime would certainly be the first to be similarly punished.

Thus despite the eloquent pleas of Fan Ch'un-jen, the antireform era's most outspoken moderate, Ts'ai Ch'üeh was forcibly exiled to Kuang-nan. But he was not to be the only political casualty of the day, as the same censorial clique who had impeached Ts'ai Ch'üeh then turned on Fan Ch'un-jen and Wang Ts'un as well. Liang T'ao and Liu An-shih memorialized that Fan and Wang were closet reformists, somehow in league with Ts'ai.[147] On the first day of the sixth month of 1089, after Wen Yen-po and Lü Ta-fang insisted to Hsüan-jen that Fan and Wang were key members of the nefarious faction of Ts'ai Ch'üeh, Fan and Wang were dismissed from the Council of State and demoted to prefectural-level positions. Fan and Wang would both return to high positions in the capital after spending a few years away, but Ts'ai Ch'üeh was not so fortunate. Having lived nearly four years in Hsin-chou, Ts'ai Ch'üeh died in the first month of 1093, at the age of fifty-six. In a cruel irony, the reformists would indeed stage a political comeback the next year, and, as predicted by Fan Ch'un-Jen, they proved not to be kindly disposed toward the men who had orchestrated their former leader's show trial.

Conciliation and provocation: Politics in the late regency

The final years of the Hsüan-jen regency witnessed continued political gridlock and renewed factional infighting. In the second month of 1090, when Wen Yen-po retired as chief councilor at the age of ninety-one, having been forced from office by Liu Chih and Wang Yen-sou, the old guard of the antireformists was succeeded by a younger and more pragmatic generation. Even after the more extreme elements were purged from court in the late 1080s, and the conflict between Lo and Shu had petered out, long-term unity proved an elusive goal for the conservative coalition. During the early 1090s, a rivalry of sorts was slowly simmering between Lü Ta-fang and Liu Chih, the chief councilors of the left and right. A caretaker figure at court who considered

---

[147] *HCP* (1979) 428, pp. 10348–2.

himself above petty partisanship, Lü resented the increasing power of Liu Chih's clique, but tacitly condoned Liu's actions.[148] Building upon the core membership of the Shuo faction, Liu secured the allegiances of several of the principal men of Lo to create a broad political coalition, not to mention a serviceable patronage machine. Liu endeavored to further expand the reach of his faction, and to palliate the enmity of the followers of Ts'ai Ch'üeh, however belatedly, by recruiting reformists back into the metropolitan bureaucracy. Not surprisingly, Liu Chih's policy of reconciliation, an issue about which Hsüan-jen remained indecisive, became a lightning rod for reproof from the militant wing of the antireformists. Somewhere along the line, Lü Ta-fang broke ranks with Liu and sided with his detractors, precipitating Liu's dismissal from the Council of State. Embodying both the conciliatory and provocative aspects of court politics, Liu Chih affords a central figure around which to recount the history of the late regency, a time in which the political system was afflicted with paralysis and myopia.

When Liu Chih initiated his policy of factional détente in 1090, with the implicit approval of Lü Ta-fang, it offered too little and came too late to assuage the resentment of the reformists. Liu's policy also alienated the more militant elements at court, men who counted themselves outside of his governing coalition. Owing to the resistance of militantly antireformist remonstrators, the campaign of propitiation was brought to a near standstill. When Yüan-feng partisans were summoned back to court, their appointments were invariably overturned, only exacerbating the alienation of reformists. Regardless of how badly they had failed in conciliating opposition from both without and within court, the chief councilors of the late regency would draw the scorn of Li T'ao, the compiler of the *Hsü Tzu-chih t'ung-chien ch'ang-pien*: "Lü Ta-fang and Liu Chih desired to promote and employ the Yüan-feng faction in order to pacify old grievances, calling it 'conciliation' (*t'iao-t'ing*), and Hsüan-jen was somewhat deluded by this."[149] However, the comments of Li T'ao must be received with a certain skepticism, for Lü Ta-fang merely condoned this political triangulation maneuver, which was in all likelihood the brainchild of Liu Chih, who monopolized control over bureaucratic appointments.

When the conciliatory process began in early 1090, it met with resistance from the right flank of the Censorate. The first reformist sympathizer to be co-opted into the metropolitan bureaucracy was Teng Wen-po (also known

---

[148] For biographical accounts of the two chief councilors of the late Yüan-yu era, see Michael D. Freeman and Chikusa Masaaki, "Lü Ta-fang," in *Sung biographies*, ed. Herbert Franke (Wiesbaden, 1976), pp. 735–8, and Michael D. Freeman and Chikusa Masaaki, "Liu Chih," in *Sung biographies*, ed. Herbert Franke (Wiesbaden, 1976), pp. 634–6.

[149] *HCP* (1979) 443, p. 10669.

as Teng Jun-fu), a former associate of Ts'ai Ch'üeh. Almost immediately after Teng was appointed Han-lin academician in the third month of 1090, an outcry arose from such unreconstructed antireformists as Wang Yen-sou, Liu An-shih, and Liang T'ao. The three remonstrators not only considered Teng to be of dubious scholarly merit, but also linked him with the unholy reformist trinity of Wang An-shih, Lü Hui-ch'ing, and Ts'ai Ch'üeh.[150] Soon thereafter, Liu An-shih and Liang T'ao were removed from their remonstrance posts for their defiant stance against Teng's appointment.[151] Without a doubt, the most impassioned and articulate opponent of partisan conciliation was Su Ch'e, the current vice–censor in chief, who drew a line in the sand between the noble antireformists and such petty men as Teng Wen-po. For Su Ch'e, to incorporate reformists into the ruling coalition was to flirt with certain disaster:

If true gentlemen are brought close and if petty men are banished, then the ruler will be honored and glorious and the polity will be peaceful and joyous. If true gentlemen are alienated and distanced and petty men are promoted and entrusted, then the ruler will be anxious and disgraced, and the state will be imperiled and precarious.

If men like Teng were allowed to gain a beachhead in the capital, they would soon be back to their old dirty tricks:

Disputers have deluded with glib words, intending to invite and include [the reformists] to jointly administer affairs, desiring to conciliate (*t'iao-t'ing*) their faction. Your servant claims that if these men return. . . . they will certainly harm and bring ruin to righteous men.[152]

Intransigent antireformists like Su Ch'e were fighting a lost cause, however, as Teng Wen-po could not be dislodged from his new post without the assent of the chief councilors, which was not forthcoming.[153]

The campaign of propitiation continued through the remainder of the Hsüan-jen regency, as the chief councilors attempted to rehabilitate a considerable number of reformists. But such forced and calculated moves of factional détente were only marginally successful, and many appointments were overturned by the Censorate and the Remonstrance Bureau, and infrequently by the regent herself. Hence, the most prominent Yüan-feng partisans were forced to add a few more years onto their half-decade in ignominious exile, a fact that would have drastic repercussions in the near future. The first and foremost

---

[150] *HCP* (1979) 439, pp. 10577–8; 441, pp. 10612–17.

[151] Liang was appointed minister of revenue, and Liu was demoted to the post of secretariat drafter. See *HCP* (1979) 442, p. 10640.

[152] *HCP* (1979) 443, pp. 10669–72; "Tsai lun fen-pieh hsieh-cheng cha-tzu," in Su, *Su Ch'e chi* 43, pp. 760–2.

[153] Despite the opposition of Sun Sheng, Chu Kuang-t'ing, and Su Ch'e, Teng Wen-po was promoted and appointed minister of rites in the second month of 1091. See *HCP* (1979) 455, p. 10902.

potential beneficiary of factional appeasement was Ts'ai Ch'üeh, who had already served two years in Kuang-nan. But in the eighth month of 1091, Liu Chih and Lü Ta-fang failed in their bid to grant Ts'ai amnesty after a deafening chorus of disapproval arose from the obstinate Hsüan-jen and several unyielding censors such as Su Ch'e and Chu Kuang-t'ing.[154] Simultaneous efforts to restore Chang Tun to his previous honorary rank also met with hostility from Chu, who would not countenance the pardoning of "such a treacherous, wicked, base, corrupt and lawless man."[155] Subsequent attempts to transfer reformists back to the capital failed repeatedly, as Ts'ai Ching, Lü Hui-ch'ing, Tseng Pu, and a host of minor Yüan-feng partisans were denied positions in the metropolitan bureaucracy in 1091 and 1092. Aside from Teng Wen-po, the only other reformist of note to establish a brief foothold in the capital during the late regency were Yang Wei and Li Ch'ing-chen, who would both play a pivotal transitional role once Che-tsung began his personal rule.[156] All of Liu Chih's efforts to mitigate the destructiveness of a future reformist takeover came to naught.

Hence, Liu Chih's precipitous fall from power after censorial denunciations intensified in late 1091 could not be called unexpected. Exasperated by his efforts to co-opt reformists into the metropolitan bureaucracy, more ideologically minded antireformists accused Liu of a heinous crime against the state: factional treachery. In the tenth month of 1091, Cheng Yung, the current vice–censor in chief, accused Liu of constructing a factional patronage machine that monopolized control over the bureaucratic appointment process for private gain:

Liu Chih has long occupied the corridors of power. . . . He and those who agree with him control the promotion and demotion of men. . . . Since Chih has wielded authority, his subordinates have been promoted to crucial positions, either to the Secretariat and Chancellery or to the roads of remonstrance. Those with whom Chih is displeased are attacked by the Secretariat drafters and supervising secretaries, or indicted by remonstrators.[157]

Cheng, a man apparently without factional allegiances to Lo or to Shu, proceeded to name names, listing thirty men as members of Liu Chih's faction.[158]

---

[154] In Hsüan-jen's words: "Ts'ai Ch'üeh [was punished] not because of his slanderous poems, but only because he was detrimental to the state and dynastic altars. If the state and dynastic altars are to flourish, then Ch'üeh must die." See *HCP* (1979) 464, pp. 11088–9.

[155] *HCP* (1979) 464, p. 11085.

[156] Yang Wei was appointed palace censor in the fourth month of 1091, on the recommendation of Liu Chih, and remained in the Censorate for the duration of the regency. After being repeatedly denied a transfer from his regional post to the capital in 1091–2, Li Ch'ing-ch'en was appointed minister of personnel in the fourth month of 1094 and transferred back to a regional post the following month. See *HCP* (1979) 457, p. 10948; 484, p. 11493.

[157] *HCP* (1979) 467, pp. 11151–2.

[158] *HCP* (1979) 467, p. 11152.

This curious miscellany seemed to include nearly every major and minor figure at court, with the exceptions of Lü Ta-fang and Su Ch'e. Among the ranks of Liu Chih's so-called faction, Cheng Yung included not only stalwart members of the Shuo-dominated ruling coalition like Liang T'ao and Wang Yen-sou but also such men of Lo as Chia I and Chu Kuang-t'ing. More problematic was Cheng's inclusion of such opponents of factional reconciliation as Liu An-shih and Wang Ti, not to mention several men who were opposed to banishing Ts'ai Ch'üeh. While Cheng's list was clearly a politically motivated document in its linkage of strange bedfellows, perhaps one can discern therein a certain blurring of boundaries between the Shuo and Lo factions by the end of the regency.

For the rest of 1091, Liu Chih was the subject of several months of indictments and ad hominem attacks upon his character. As if the crime of factional treachery were insufficient reason to dismiss Liu as chief councilor, remonstrators further accused him of having deceitfully quashed the criminal investigation of a kinsman.[159] Speaking in his own defense, Liu Chih accused his accusers of being covert reformists, and of obeying the orders of their sinister handlers, Chang Tun and Hsing Shu.[160] Liu's political position became untenable, however, and he resigned from the Council of State in the eleventh month of 1091 to be appointed prefect of Yün-chou (Ching-tung West).[161]

The rise and fall of Liu Chih was indicative of the paralytic state of the state in the late regency. Liu's dismissal in late 1091 did little either to rouse the court from its paralysis or to promote the formation of a stable coalition government. Su Sung and Fan Ch'un-jen, Liu Chih's successors as chief councilor of the left, fared little better; the former was implicated in a guilt-by-association scandal, and the latter was deposed by the resurgent reformists. No matter who made up the Council of State, the court remained walking in circles, caught up in a recurrent cycle of personal recriminations that precluded political unity.

With a whimper: The end of the Hsüan-jen regency

The last years of the Yüan-yu era were a time of extreme and protracted inaction, in which the successes of 1086 were never truly consolidated or built upon. While the antireform coalition had succeeded in turning back the clock to the 1060s and repealing the New Policies, their policy agenda was basically reactionary; Hsüan-jen had restored peace to the empire and reestablished the status quo. And as the antireform coalition fractured into warring factions, its

---

[159] HCP (1979) 467, p. 11152.
[160] HCP (1979) 467, pp. 11158–60.
[161] HCP (1979) 468, p. 11167.

members became preoccupied with political infighting. Ch'eng I would later bemoan the degradation of political life and the ensuing partisan struggles that crippled the regency: "During the Hsi-ning era the struggle against the New Policies emerged from differing views of the public need but during Yüan-yu [these factional struggles] were based on pure selfishness."[162] Whether purging their own or calumniating their often imaginary foes, the men of Yüan-yu had practiced a brand of politics that lacked any long-term vision, remaining narrowly focused upon immediate and expedient objectives. And their attempts to conciliate their opposition after the show trial of Ts'ai Ch'üeh were ultimately abortive. Thus, when the inevitable reformist backlash came, no member of the antireform coalition would be spared, regardless of his factional alignment or political inclination.

Even worse, the antireformists had taken no account of the political threat to their dominance posed by the young emperor himself, and had never formulated a viable fallback plan for their political survival after Hsüan-jen's death. Che-tsung idolized his late father and had been forced to swallow his bitterness toward his grandmother and her ministers throughout his adolescence.[163] When they were not entirely ignoring the presence of the teenage emperor, as was their usual practice, members of the Council of State had only alienated him with their tactless meddling. Che-tsung clearly detested his tutors, whose ranks included such intellectual luminaries as Ch'eng I and Fan Tsu-yü, for their moralistic pedantry. Moreover, the regent and her ministers had intervened in the choice of his consort in 1091–2. Hsüan-jen, seconded by Wang Yen-sou, had vetoed Lady Ti, Che-tsung's choice as empress, substituting Lady Meng, a candidate whom they deemed more politically amenable. This further estranged the emperor, who was sixteen at the time of his betrothal to Empress Meng.[164] Unfortunately for the ruling coalition at court, Che-tsung's obvious antipathy toward the antireformists could be contained only for a brief span of time.

Once Hsüan-jen had passed away, no one could obstruct Che-tsung from beginning his personal rule upon attaining his majority. By the autumn of 1093, Emperor Hsüan-jen's health had deteriorated, but her callous grandson would not even visit her sickbed.[165] When the councilors paid their final

[162] Lü, *Sung ta-shih-chi chiang-i* 20, pp. 3a–b.

[163] For anecdotes about Che-tsung's resentment of the antireformists and Hsüan-jen, see Ts'ai T'ao, *T'ieh-wei shan ts'ung-t'an*, ed. Feng Hui-min and Shen Hsi-lin (c. 1130; Peking, 1983) 1, p. 5. Also see the biography of Su Sung in *SS* 340, p. 10867.

[164] See *HCP* (1979) 457, pp. 10945–8; *CPPM* 113, pp. 3565–8.

[165] *CPPM* 91, pp. 2821–2. Because of the three-year lacuna in *HCP*, for which the chapters for the seventh month of 1093 through the third month of 1097 (Yüan-feng 8, seventh month through Shao-sheng 4, third month) have not survived, the narrative of the early personal rule of Che-tsung had to

respects to the dying regent, she offered them some portentous last words, sensing that her death would have drastic repercussions for the antireformists: "After my old self has died, there will certainly be many who will toy with Che-tsung. You should not listen to them, and you should seek early retirement."[166] As with the death of Shen-tsung, the coming dynastic transition would precipitate a sweeping political realignment at court. After Hsüan-jen finally succumbed to the ravages of old age in the ninth month of 1093, the antireformists did not stand a chance, and their political dominance simply evaporated. Despite the bang with which it began, the Hsüan-jen regency would end with a whimper.

RESURRECTION: 1093–1100

The pendulum swings back: The personal rule of Che-tsung

In a major reversal of fortune, after the death of dowager empress Hsüan-jen, the tide swiftly turned against the forces of conservatism. As the unfolding history of the late Northern Sung would demonstrate, the nine years of the regency were an isolated instance of reaction and regression in the midst of six decades of reformist experimentation. The beginning of Che-tsung's personal rule (*ch'in-cheng*) witnessed the resurrection of the reform coalition, and the next three decades would represent its undisputed political heyday. By consolidating their political gains, constructing a relatively stable court coalition, and maintaining an enduring patronage machine, the reformist regimes of the Che-tsung and Hui-tsung reigns acquired nearly unstoppable momentum. In the 1090s, the surviving disciples of Wang An-shih and Ts'ai Ch'üeh would restart unfinished business, reviving the New Policies with greater reach than ever before and initiating a thorough transformation of society and the economy. Moreover, preliminary evidence indicates that the resuscitated reform measures of the Che-tsung reign were not as extractive and intrusive as those of the Hsi-ning and Yüan-feng eras had been.

However, the expanded reform agenda of the Shao-sheng era (1094–8) could not have been enacted without the wholesale elimination of the conservative opposition. Late Northern Sung politics entered its most virulent and divisive stage during the personal rule of Che-tsung. The purges of 1093–4 and their

---

be reconstructed from entries in relevant chapters in *CPPM*, which boasts far less detail than *HCP* and provides only attenuated descriptions of crucial events. Even more frustrating to the historian, the *CPPM*, is not without its own gaping lacunae. Chapters 113 to 119, which offer a topical reorganization of the annals of the late Che-tsung reign, have been missing for centuries.

[166] *CPPM* 91, pp. 2822–3.

aftermath made the bloodless palace coup of 1086 look like a dress rehearsal. Soon after their takeover at court, the reformists retaliated with a vengeance against their past victimizers, forcing them to walk the thorny path toward banishment in Kuang-nan. Blacklisting their political enemies, the reformists officially excluded hundreds of men and their immediate kin from officeholding altogether. Reigning unchallenged, Che-tsung and his reformist councilors redrew the political landscape ruthlessly and irrevocably.

When Che-tsung began his personal rule late in 1093, the leaders of the antireformist regime, fearful of losing their positions, apprehensively waited for the end, in the calm before the storm. For the time being, the roads of remonstrance remained occupied by conservatives, who would endeavor to belatedly convert the emperor to their cause. Days after the death of Hsüan-jen, Fan Tsu-yü desperately admonished Che-tsung to resist the blandishments of the reformists:

Now there certainly are petty men who will advance to say, "The dowager empress should not have altered the governance of the former emperor, and should not have expelled the former emperor's ministers." These rift-widening words cannot but be investigated. In the days when Your Majesty first ascended the throne and the dowager empress took control of governance, the officials and commoners who memorialized the throne numbered in the tens of thousands, and they all said that governmental directives had disadvantageous aspects. Because the hearts of the men of the empire intended to alter them [i.e., the New Policies], the dowager empress and Your Majesty together altered them, and did not do so with her own selfish intentions.[167]

The next month, Lü T'ao pleaded with Che-tsung to ignore the siren song of the reformists and to maintain the political settlement of the Yüan-yu era:

Ever since the dowager empress began her regency, the ferocious and the wicked have been banished.... Of the hearts of petty men, none does bear resentment. When they speak treacherously and wickedly, it is only to confound Your Majesty.... The matters that the dowager empress reformed were all beneficial to the common people. All of the ministers whom she expelled were the malefactors of the empire. How could anyone ever doubt this?[168]

In the conservatives' judgment what the reformists had wrought during Shen-tsung's reign had been a sheer abomination, and rehabilitating these known malefactors would push the empire back to the brink of ruin. Swimming against the current of history and sealing their own fates, Fan Tsu-yü and Lü T'ao were not only addressing their monarch but also leaving behind testaments for posterity. In the next century, their principled opposition to the

[167] *CPPM* 91, pp. 2824–5.
[168] *CPPM* 101, pp. 3113–15.

resurgent reformists would ultimately earn Fan and Lü pride of place in the pantheon of political martyrs.

The era of personal rule was inaugurated early in 1094, when the first batch of reformists were rehabilitated and a new reformist manifesto was promulgated. Perhaps to forestall an outcry from the Censorate and the Remonstrance Bureau, Li Ch'ing-ch'en and Teng Wen-po, two malleable and accommodating reformists, were appointed to the Council of State in the second month of 1094.[169] A moderate member of the Yüan-feng reform ministry, Li had recanted his political views and paid lip service to the antireform cause during the early regency, which now made him a politically acceptable candidate as vice-director of the Secretariat-Chancellery.[170] Another active participant in the Hsi-ning and Yüan-feng reforms, Teng Wen-po, had broken ranks with Ts'ai Ch'üeh over border military strategy, which made Teng a palatable choice as vice-director of the Bureau of State Affairs.[171] An apparent sleeper agent for the reformist cause, Palace Censor Yang Wei was responsible for recommending the two to the Council of State, and for facilitating the return of Chang Tun and An T'ao to court.[172] Serving as Che-tsung's transition team, Li and Teng acted as standard-bearers for the mass return of the reformists to court and paved the way for the sweeping political changes to come. Soon thereafter, Lü Ta-fang was permitted to resign as chief councilor of the left in the third month of 1094, leaving the top post in the bureaucracy open for Chang Tun, the ranking member of the reform coalition.[173]

Year zero: The reformist takeover of 1094

In political discourse and practice, the first year of the new era represented a complete rupture with the past eight years of antireformist domination. The first verbal indication that Che-tsung would revive his father's policies came in the third month of 1094, in a palace examination question purportedly authored by Li Ch'ing-ch'en. Illuminating the intellectual underpinnings of

---

[169] *CPPM* 100, p. 3085. There is no textual evidence that these appointments met with irate opposition from the antireformists. Given the sparseness of the documentary record in the *CPPM*, not to mention the fact that the veritable records of the reformist regimes were continually subject to historiographic revisionism, the absence of evidence should not be construed as the evidence of absence.

[170] *SS* 328, p. 10562.

[171] *SS* 343, p. 10912.

[172] Back in 1091, Fan Ch'un-jen had adamantly opposed the appointment of Yang Wei to the Censorate, and Wang Yen-sou had accused Yang of being a crony of Lü Hui-ching. See *CPPM* 100, pp. 3093–6; *HCP* (1979) 468, pp. 11161–3.

[173] *CPPM* 101, p. 3120. Lü was demoted to the post of prefect of Ying-ch'ang *fu* but was permitted to retain both his honorary rank and his former academic position.

the new order, Li's question lionized the emperor's dearly departed father as the exemplar of righteous rule:

The virtue of Emperor Shen-tsung was numinous and enlightened, and he possessed the learning of Shun and Yü.... For the nineteen years of his rule, rites and music, policies and institutions, were all benevolently bequeathed to the empire. We consider his methods and will to have been sincere and diligent. Day and night, We do not dare forget this.[174]

For the first time in almost a decade, after having been slanderously portrayed as an overly suggestible and tragically flawed monarch, the former emperor had become the subject of unqualified and glowing praise. In a series of linked rhetorical questions, the text proceeded to heap obloquy upon Hsüan-jen and her ministers, presenting a scathing indictment of the Yüan-yu regime as a time of reaction and inaction:

During the ten years of the regency, although official selection by poetic examination has been revived, gentlemen have not increased in ability. Although the Ever-normal Granary officials have been abolished, farmers have not increased in wealth. Although there have been a variety of arguments on whom to hire and whom to draft, corvée policy is still faulty.... Although territory has been ceded to mollify those from afar, the Tangut barbarians' incursions have not yet ceased. Although profit making has been rescinded in order to be advantageous to the common people, merchants' routes go untraveled. Why have matters come to this, when clerical personnel are rampant and numerous, when military preparations have been trimmed and deficient, when hunger and famine is so acute that grass is eaten, when rebels and felons still increase?[175]

A manifesto of reformism, the examination question clearly indicated that the pendulum had begun to swing back toward reform, and official ideology had shifted 180 degrees almost overnight. Outside the sphere of rhetoric, the text was not without far-reaching practical consequences for bureaucratic recruitment. The question just quoted was explicitly designed as a political and ideological litmus test to incorporate like-minded reformists into the civil service and to weed out the opponents of reform, for whom this question would have been all but unanswerable.

Such an unsubtle statement of vision naturally drew last-ditch resistance from conservatives in the Council of State. In another act of calculated defiance, seeking the judgment of future historians rather than that of his contemporaries, Su Ch'e voiced his opposition to this examination question in particular and to the reformist revival in general: "Your servant sees that the palace examination question slandered the policies enacted in recent years, and had the intention of reviving the policies of the Hsi-ning and Yüan-feng eras.... Your

---

[174] *CPPM* 100, pp. 3086–7.
[175] *CPPM* 100, pp. 3086–7.

servant cannot but remonstrate against this."[176] Su distinguished himself from the reformists, painting himself as a steadfast councilor: "It is said that for petty men, love of the ruler depends upon expediency, and that for loyal ministers, love of the ruler is for the sake of the security of the dynastic and state altars. This is the situation at hand."[177] He launched into a litany of the most flagrant abuses of the reformist regimes of Hsi-ning and Yüan-feng, describing the New Policies as an utter debacle. For sticking his neck out so conspicuously, Su Ch'e became the first notable victim of the purge of 1094. Enraged, Che-tsung sacked Su from his post as vice-director of the Chancellery (*menhsia shih-lang*), and demoted him to the post of prefect of Ju-chou2 (Ching-hsi North).

In the first year of Che-tsung's personal rule, political culture underwent a dramatic and abrupt revolution, a disjuncture that was reflected in the realm of symbol and ritual. As with other transformative moments in recent political history, a change in regimes was marked by a change in reign titles. In the fourth month of 1094, after the auspicious sighting of a white halo around the sun, the current reign title was retroactively changed; the ninth year of Yüan-yu was decreed to be the first year of the Shao-sheng era.[178] Meaning "Continuing Sagacity," the name of the new era clearly evoked the policies of Shen-tsung, the eponymous sage to whom Che-tsung and his newly appointed councilors were paying metaphorical homage. Hence, 1094 represented a year zero, in which the intervening years of the regency could be bridged as if they had never occurred at all. As the symbolic center of the new era, Che-tsung could bask in the reflected glow of his father's achievements, which were being polished to a sheen by the new historical revisionism.

The reformist takeover of 1094 was accomplished at unprecedented speed. Within the span of a single month, remonstrance posts were packed with loyal men, the upper echelons of the metropolitan bureaucracy were purged of antireformists, and the Council of State was commandeered by Chang Tun and his factional allies. Early in the fourth month, five reformists – Chai Ssu, Shang-kuan Chün, Chou Chih, Liu Cheng2, and Chang Shang-ying – were appointed to the Censorate and the Remonstrance Bureau.[179] The very same day, these newly appointed reformist remonstrators began to mount a vitriolic offensive against their political enemies. Chang Shang-ying memorialized the throne with a blanket critique of the past nine years, blaming the regent for her inaction and inattention to governance: "Dowager Empress Hsüan-jen. . . . was

---

[176] *CPPM* 100, pp. 3087–8.
[177] *CPPM* 100, pp. 3087–8.
[178] *CPPM* 100, p. 3096; *SS* 18, p. 340.
[179] *CPPM* 101, p. 3120.

convinced to entrust her ministers and to consign supervision of the Censorate and Remonstrance Bureau. Under their influence, she was beset by a swarm of flatterers, sycophants, and opportunists."[180]

In dismissal after dismissal, the reformist-dominated court expelled the leaders of the Yüan-yu faction to regional posts, regardless of where they stood on the political spectrum. Steadfast conservatives such as Fan Tsu-yü, Che-tsung's despised tutor, were purged from court alongside more accommodating figures such as Fan Ch'un-jen, one of the few defenders of Ts'ai Ch'üeh.[181] At this point, the antireformists had simply been demoted from the Council of State and sent down to prefectural-level posts. The real bloodletting would be postponed for a few months, until the reformists and their imperial patron had consolidated their control of the bureaucratic machinery.

In a mere thirty days, the antireform regime of the regency had simply evaporated, and the corridors of power had been cleansed of the opposition. The path had been cleared for the return of Chang Tun, who swept back into power as Che-tsung's chief councilor of the left in the fourth month of 1094.[182] As the most eminent survivor of the Yüan-yu purges, Chang earned himself a place by the emperor's side as the architect of the revived New Policies. Back in K'ai-feng after an eight-year enforced absence, Chang moved quickly to appoint his junior reformist comrades to high positions, incorporating Lin Hsi and the brothers Ts'ai Ching and Ts'ai Pien into his ruling coalition. By the sixth month of 1094, the basic cabinet of the Shao-sheng era had taken shape, with the appointment of Tseng Pu as assistant director of the Bureau of Military Affairs. With the central government under his directorship, and with the emperor hanging on his every word, Chang Tun and his reformist comrades could now settle some old scores, exacting their revenge upon all those who served in the antireform ministerial regime of Yüan-yu.

Measure for measure: Persecuting the Yüan-yu faction

Back in 1089, the forced exile of Ts'ai Ch'üeh to the malarial wastes of Kuang-nan had been a rare and isolated instance of political brutality, an act that the reformists could neither forgive nor forget. In such a sharply polarized polit-ical climate, factional reconciliation was simply unthinkable. Under the new regime, what Ts'ai had suffered would be visited tenfold upon his persecutors. The ministers and remonstrators of Shao-sheng would avenge the death of

---

[180] *CPPM* 101, pp. 3120–1.

[181] *CPPM* 101, pp. 3121–2. Fan Tsu-yü was made prefect of Hsia-chou, and Fan Ch'un-jen was made prefect of Ying-ch'ang *fu*.

[182] *CPPM* 101, p. 3122.

their departed leader by banishing not just a handful of scapegoats but rather the entire Yüan-yu ministry to the lethal borderlands of the far south. Thus the vicious circle of political practice, in which violence simply bred more violence, remained unbroken.

By the 1090s, political discourse had become so degraded that factions would condemn each other for the cardinal sin of factional treachery (*chien*), while maintaining their own sacrosanct innocence. The remonstrators of early Shao-sheng censured the Yüan-yu partisans for high treason, for selfishly and willfully abandoning the glorious reform legacy of Shen-tsung. In the fifth month of 1094, a censorial indictment blamed such sacred cows of the antireform ministry as Ssu-ma Kuang and Wen Yen-po for having pursued a weak-kneed policy of accommodation toward the Hsi Hsia and deceiving the young Che-tsung into abandoning the martial glory of his father.[183] The next month, a formidable onslaught upon the Yüan-yu ministry began in earnest, when the remonstrators Huang Lü and Chai Ssu condemned such prominent antireformists as Liu Chih, Liu An-shih, and Liang T'ao for arrogating their authority to pronounce a virtual death sentence upon Ts'ai Ch'üeh.[184] Lü Ta-fang, the long-serving conservative chief councilor of the late regency, was named as the foremost malefactor of Yüan-yu, for "monopolizing the governance of the state," "cherishing wickedness and shamelessly delighting in profit," and "abandoning himself to treachery and evil."[185] Similar opprobrium was heaped upon the other chief councilors of the regency, as Ssu-ma Kuang, Lü Kung-chu, and Liu Chih were also indicted (the first two posthumously) for "promoting their own faction, acting willfully, and arguing slanderously," and for going to such treacherous extremes as arbitrarily abolishing hired service and packing remonstrance posts with their malicious followers.[186] The torrent of censorial indictments pronounced against the antireformists in 1094 bore an odious resemblance to those that had been issued eight years earlier against the reformists in the purges of 1086. While both factions subscribed to radically divergent conceptions of statecraft, the discourse they employed to attack each other was remarkably similar, employing the same black-and-white distinctions.

As far as political practice was concerned, however, the reformists went several giant steps beyond their rivals. Beginning in mid-1094, the surviving members of the Yüan-yu ministry were forcibly exiled to distant prefectures, and their deceased colleagues were posthumously stripped of honors.

---

[183] *CPPM* 101, pp. 3124-5.
[184] *CPPM* 101, pp. 3125-7.
[185] *CPPM* 101, pp. 3126-7.
[186] *CPPM* 101, pp. 3127-8.

Lü Ta-fang was the first to go; deprived of his prestige titles, he was banished to the post of prefect of Sui-chou2 (Ching-hsi South). Liu Chih and Su Ch'e were also dismissed from their honorary academic posts, demoted several ranks in the hierarchy of prestige titles, and given administrative posts in similar hinterland prefectures. Su Shih, a perpetual irritant to any ministerial regime, received an even harsher punishment, commensurate with that of Ts'ai Ch'üeh: banishment to Hui-chou2, in the far south of Kuang-nan East.[187] This second round of personnel transfers effectively neutralized the antireform opposition, from whom little more was heard for the rest of the Che-tsung reign. In the seventh month of 1094, the remonstrators Chou Chih and Chang Shang-ying, seconded by Chang Tun, urged that Lü Ta-fang and his cronies be dismissed as regional administrators and banished to even more distant territories.[188] Moreover, the Shao-sheng purges extended to the deceased as well as to the living members of the Yüan-yu regime. Denouncing Ssu-ma Kuang and Lü Kung-chu for their sinister and factious words and deeds as chief councilors, an imperial edict rescinded the posthumous honors they had been granted by the regency upon their deaths in 1086 and 1089, respectively.[189] Once regarded as the first among equals of the antireform coalition and as the foremost statesman of his age, Ssu-ma Kuang was now blamed for all the failings of the Yüan-yu regime, accused of treacherously monopolizing power, arbitrarily overturning the New Policies, intolerantly purging the loyal opposition, and deceiving the dowager empress.

Purging and punishing the conservative opposition was only one tactic employed during the reformist offensive, which also entailed a sweeping revision of recent history. To the victors of the factional conflict went the spoils of writing its chronicles. Portrayed as nefarious villains in Yüan-yu era political discourse, the reformists now were described as the noble victims of the treacherous antireformists; the long-maligned New Policies were now described in the most glowing of terms. But the official history of the reform era was still stained by the broad brush of regency politics. Compiled in the early years of the Hsüan-jen regency, the *Veritable records* (*shih-lu*) of Shen-tsung's reign represented the Hsi-ning reforms as extractive and destructive, and depicted the reformists as traitorous ministers.[190] Under the personal rule of Che-tsung, official history would have to be revised to conform to the new political realities. In the sixth month of 1094, control over the Historiography Institute

[187] *CPPM* 101, p. 3129.

[188] *CPPM* 101, pp. 3134–6.

[189] *CPPM* 101, pp. 3138–40.

[190] For a textual history of the *Shen-tsung shih-lu*, see chapter 2 of Levine, "A house in darkness." Also see Ts'ai, *Sung-tai hsiu-shih chih-tu yen-chiu*, and P'eng Chiu-sung, "Pei Sung 'Shen-tsung shih-lu' ssu hsiu k'ao," *Wen-shih* 24 (1985), pp. 179–88.

was wrested away from the antireformists upon the dismissal of the institute's directors Fan Tsu-yü, Chao Yen-jo, and Huang T'ing-chien.[191] Soon thereafter, Ts'ai Pien, a junior member of the Yüan-feng ministry and the son-in-law of Wang An-shih, was entrusted with the recompilation of the official history of the reform era.[192] The antireform biases of the original compilers of the *Shen-tsung shih-lu* would be erased, and the record supplemented by entries from Wang An-shih's personal diaries.[193] Harsher punishments awaited the three antireformist historiographers at the end of 1094, when Fan, Chao, and Huang were summarily dismissed from the civil service, and exiled to distant south-central prefectures.[194] After the first year of Che-tsung's personal rule, factional reconciliation became a thing of the past, following the first of a series of purges that escalated the brutality of court politics beyond the previous high-water mark set during the regency.

And far worse was yet to come. After a debate before the throne in the eighth month of 1095, in which Chang Tun urged the emperor to deny amnesty to Lü Ta-fang and his cronies, Che-tsung promulgated an edict that permanently banned the leaders of the crushed antireform coalition from bureaucratic service. Ever the voice of caution and moderation, an exiled Fan Ch'un-jen protested the edict, pleading clemency for his partisan comrades, but he only succeeded in infuriating Chang, who had Fan stripped of his academic honors and transferred to Sui-chou2.[195] The reformist governing coalition similarly squelched dissent from within the ranks of the metropolitan bureaucracy, cleansing the Censorate and the Remonstrance Bureau of the defiant and the disloyal. Under the personal rule of Che-tsung, prevailing institutional trends continued, as councilors brooked no opposition from remonstrators. When Investigating Censor Ch'ang An-min spoke out against the nepotism and factionalism of Chang Tun, he was dismissed from his post in the ninth month of

---

[191] *CPPM* 101, pp. 3131–2.

[192] *CPPM* 120, p. 3601.

[193] For the historian, frustratingly little information on the revision of the *Shen-tsung shih-lu* can be found in the standard primary sources for Northern Sung political history. The first three years of the Shao-sheng era have been swallowed up by a gaping lacuna in *HCP*. Even worse, chapter 114 of *CPPM*, "Hsiu shih-lu," which purports to chronicle the revision of the Shen-tsung veritable records, also falls within a seven-chapter lacuna. But according to the memorialist Shao Po-wen, whose *Shao-shih wen-chien lu* reads like a hagiography-cum-martyrology of the Yüan-yu faction, when Ts'ai Pien seized the Wang An-shih diaries to revise the official history of the Shen-tsung reign, "he falsified entries from the diaries, and the text was rife with treacherous falsehoods. Above, Shen-tsung was insulted. Below, the old ministers of Yüan-yu were slandered. The official history of the Shen-tsung reign, compiled during the Yüan-yu era, was completely amended"; see Shao, *Shao-shih wen-chien lu* 12, p. 128. Shao Po-wen's account is corroborated by Ts'ai Pien's *Sung shih* biography; see *SS* 472, p. 13729.

[194] Fan Tsu-yü was exiled to Yung-chou, Chao Yen-jo to Feng-chou2, and Huang T'ing-chien to Ch'ien-chou. See *CPPM* 101, p. 3141.

[195] *CPPM* 101, p. 3144.

1095 on Chang's orders.[196] But Ch'ang An-min would not go quietly. Mustering one final broadside against the chief councilor and his coterie, Ch'ang insisted that the revival of Shen-tsung's way of governance was a mere smokescreen for ministerial absolutism: "Those who have pressured Your Majesty for a restoration only desire to employ the former emperor as a pretext to implement their treacherous schemes. . . . They desire to advance their selfish enmity and entrap the virtuous, in order to distract Your Majesty's intentions. This must be investigated."[197]

Unlike its Yüan-yu predecessor, the reformist ministry of Chang Tun evinced remarkable party discipline, quashing dissent from within its own ranks. By the second year of the Yüan-yu era the antireform faction had been crippled by infighting, but all available sources indicate that the restored reform coalition remained a united and potent political force until the late 1090s.

Simply neutralizing and displacing the opposition was not enough for the leaders of the revived reform coalition. By the third year of his personal rule, Che-tsung was becoming more dependent upon his chief councilors, who were granted free reign to eliminate the Yüan-yu faction once and for all. Earlier in the Shao-sheng era, the purge of the antireformists had been conducted on a case-by-case basis. Now that Chang Tun and his comrades had achieved near-dictatorial powers, political persecution was becoming formalized and systematized, with the creation of institutional mechanisms to prosecute crimes against the state. In the winter of 1095–6, Chang Tun and Tseng Pu persuaded the emperor to approve a comprehensive investigation and classification of Yüan-yu memorials for sedition and slander, targeting those antireformists who had heretofore escaped punishment.[198] The process of justice became recursive in the sixth month of 1098, when the attendant censor (*shih yü-shih*) An Tun memorialized the throne to investigate the Investigation and Prosecution Bureau (*Su-li so*), which had been created back in 1086 to vet the political content of memorials that had been submitted during Shen-tsung's reign. During the early Yüan-yu era, the bureau had investigated the words and deeds of officials who served in the reformist administrations of Hsi-ning and Yüan-feng, resulting in the forced dismissal of many followers of Wang An-shih and Ts'ai Ch'üeh.[199] In An Tun's judgment, the treacherous factionalists of the Yüan-yu era had exploited the bureau's investigations to purge

---

[196] *CPPM* 106, pp. 3311–12.

[197] *CPPM* 106, pp. 3313–14.

[198] *CPPM* 101, pp. 3145, 3148–9.

[199] *SHY* (1997) *chih-kuan* 3, pp. 75–6. For the most thorough institutional history of the *Su-li so*, see Lo Chia-hsiang, *P'eng-tang chih cheng yü Pei Sung cheng-chih* (Wu-han, 2002), pp. 186–7.

reformists from the imperial bureaucracy as a false faction.[200] Only weeks after the bureau's establishment, Tseng Pu extravagantly claimed, the Yüan-yu-era bureau had investigated the remonstrance of 897 individual reformist officials, but the actual total was probably closer to one hundred.[201] Later, in the third month of 1099, An Tun memorialized the throne to implore Che-tsung to punish the entire Yüan-yu-era staff of the Investigation and Prosecution Bureau, all the way down to the minor paper pushers who had survived Liu Chih, the project's mastermind.[202] Regardless of the total casualty count, the activities of the Investigation and Prosecution Bureau illustrate the extent to which political persecution during the regency had become almost an end in itself, a bureaucratized final solution to a protracted factional conflict.

In the ultimate act of revenge, the conservative coalition of the Hsüan-jen regency would not only be decimated but decapitated, incapable of ever again posing a threat to reformist hegemony. An official ministerial report of the second month of 1097 perfectly encapsulated the vengefulness of the factional proscription campaign:

Ssu-ma Kuang and Lü Kung-chu initiated treacherous schemes. They deluded and flattered the former emperor, modified policies and institutions, and their crimes and evil were extremely profound.... [This] malignant faction united in evil for mutual benefit. Some of its leaders and followers have been fated to die by now, so they are unable to receive the appropriate punishment. But even after death.... their surviving sons, grandsons, kinsmen, and associates who survive will be punished, regardless of the severity of their crimes ... and future generations will know these men as rebellious ministers and felons.[203]

An appended imperial edict stripped Ssu-ma and Lü – along with Wang Yen-sou, who had passed away in 1094 – of all remaining prestige titles, and banned their descendants from officeholding in perpetuity.[204] The surviving leaders of the antireform coalition were far less fortunate than those who predeceased them. Also promulgated in the second month of 1097, an official blacklist cited the names of thirty-seven members of the Yüan-yu ministry, all of whom were deprived of their honorary titles and their descendants similarly barred from bureaucratic service.[205]

Perhaps the most salient example of the politics of revenge was the Korean Relations Institute (*T'ung-wen kuan*) case of 1097, which was nearly the mirror image of the Ts'ai Ch'üeh poetry inquisition. With the emperor under their thumb and the wheels of justice turning according to their whim, the

---

[200] *SHY* (1997) *chih-kuan* 3, p. 76.
[201] *HCP* (1979) 499, pp. 11886–7.
[202] *HCP* (1979) 507, p. 12079.
[203] *CPPM* 102, pp. 3156–8.
[204] *CPPM* 102, p. 3158.
[205] *CPPM* 102, pp. 3158–63.

reformists had finally arrived at payback time to avenge Ts'ai's wrongful death. As had happened in 1089, charges of high treason were trumped up against the banished leaders of the opposition on the basis of the flimsiest of circumstantial evidence and hearsay, and the charges were prosecuted with extreme prejudice. In a finger-pointing memorial of the eighth month of 1097, Ts'ai Wei, the eldest son of Ts'ai Ch'üeh, alleged that his colleague Hsing Shu had received a letter from Wen Chi-fu, the son of Wen Yen-po, that alluded to the existence of a nefarious plot to depose Che-tsung in the first months of the Hsüan-jen regency.[206] As if the bare outlines of the case were not complicated enough, the affair grew ever more entangled. Enraged by the allegations, Che-tsung ordered Ts'ai Ching and An Tun to interrogate Wen Chi-fu at the Korean Relations Institute, where it was somehow revealed that the putative leaders of the purported and abortive palace coup were none other than Ssu-ma Kuang, Liu Chih, Wang Yen-sou, and Liang T'ao.[207] As far as the historian can discern, the current accusations were sheer fictions; while a plot was indeed afoot to depose Che-tsung back in 1085, it is possible that Ts'ai Ch'üeh, Hsing Shu, and Ts'ai Ching had been its masterminds. However, by appealing to Che-tsung's deeply ingrained sense of victimization, the reformists of Shao-sheng managed to launch a baseless inquisition against their old adversaries. When the emperor ordered Ts'ai Ching and a eunuch to carry out a joint investigation of the charges, they did not uncover any more corroborating evidence. Even so, the Korean Relations Institute inquisition became a pretext for a renewed offensive against the Yüan-yu faction.

In a mordantly ironic instance of retributive justice, Liu Chih, Liang T'ao, and Liu An-shih, the chief instigators of the Ts'ai Ch'üeh poetry inquisition, were banished to lethal places themselves. Exiled to Kuang-nan, Liu Chih and Liang T'ao died in Hua-chou3 and Hsin-chou, respectively, in the eleventh and twelfth months of 1097, while Liu An-shih survived his banishment to Mei-chou2.[208] Moreover, Lü Ta-fang, the leading figure of late regency politics, and one of the chief objects of reformist resentment, died of illness en route to his place of mandated exile in Hsün-chou. The ignominy of exile awaited the defeated leaders of the shattered antireform coalition. Su Ch'e, Su Shih,

---

[206] *HCP* (1979) 490, p. 11628.

[207] One nagging question remains: why did Wen Chi-fu accuse Liu Chih and others of being the chief instigators of the alleged cabal to dethrone the young Che-tsung, if no evidence exists linking Liu to the reform faction? According to *HCP* (1979) 490, p. 11628, Wen bore a longtime resentment against Liu Chih for slighting his father by urging his retirement from the Council of State in 1090.

[208] *CPPM* 102, p. 3175. Hua-chou3 was located in Kuang-nan West circuit (present-day Hua-chou3, Kwangtung). Hsin-chou (present-day Hsin-hsing, Kwangtung) had also been Ts'ai Ch'üeh's place of death. An imperial edict in the fourth month of 1098 forbade the return of Liang Tao's corpse to his home county for burial. See *CPPM* 102, p. 3177.

Chu Kuang-t'ing, Fan Tsu-yü, and Ch'eng I were all sentenced to extended stays in the miasmic far south, a fate that befell even Fan Ch'un-jen, one of Ts'ai's sole defenders back in 1089, when virtual death sentences were still an outrageous rarity. And a staggering number of their lieutenants, including K'ung Wen-chung, Wang Ti, Ch'in Kuan, and Chia I, were also shipped off to the fringes of the empire. Fan's grim prophecy had been realized at last; the men of Yüan-yu were all forced to walk the thorny path that they had cleared not long ago.

The Korean Relations Institute case concluded with yet another proscription against the sons and grandsons of the Yüan-yu councilors.[209] Their descendants and kinsmen were also banned from officeholding for life, effectively alienating a large number of elite lineages from court politics for the remainder of the Northern Sung. In an ever-widening vicious circle, political brutality produced ever more political brutality. Twelfth-century historiographers, influenced by the ascendant *Tao-hsüeh* movement, would portray the Shao-sheng partisan proscriptions as the height of treacherous infamy. Moreover, North American historians of the late twentieth century have hypothesized that the sheer destructiveness of factional politics made bureaucratic service such a risky prospect for the *shih-ta-fu* class that it caused a sea change in elite orientation and mobility strategies from national politics to local activism.[210] The forced exile of Ts'ai Ch'üeh to Kuang-nan had come back to haunt the surviving members of the Yüan-yu ministry, who were systematically persecuted with great vindictiveness. Memories of brutality would tarnish the history and historiography of the restored reform regime and the personal rule of Che-tsung, with far-reaching consequences for the future of the Sung dynasty.

Continuing Sagacity: Resuscitating the New Policies

While persecuting its political adversaries with unprecedented ruthlessness, the reformist ministerial regime of Shao-sheng pursued a comparatively moderate policy agenda. When they spearheaded the revival of the New Policies of the Shen-tsung reign, Chang Tun and his fellow councilors endeavored to alleviate the measures' most extractive aspects and eliminate their most flagrant

---

[209] *CPPM* 107, pp. 3378–9.

[210] See Robert M. Hartwell, "Demographic, political, and social transformations of China, 750–1550," *Harvard Journal of Asiatic Studies* 42 No. 2 (1982), pp. 420–5, and Robert P. Hymes, *Statesmen and gentlemen: The elite of Fu-chou, Chiang-hsi, in Northern and Southern Sung* (Cambridge, 1986), pp. 121–3. The Hartwell-Hymes hypothesis has recently been critiqued by Beverly Bossler, who argues that the elite transformation from Northern Sung to Southern Sung was more a historiographic than a historical phenomenon. See Beverly J. Bossler, *Powerful relations: Kinship, status, and the state in Sung China (960–1279)* (Cambridge, Mass., 1998), pp. 203–10.

abuses. During the early years of the Hsi-ning era, Wang An-shih originally proposed the trinity of hired service, green sprouts, and state trade as a means of alleviating socioeconomic inequalities, but these core New Policies had been expediently and expeditiously transformed into tools of wealth extraction. By their return to court in 1094, the remaining reformists had mellowed in their ideological fervor and had come to a realization that the opposition critique of the New Policies was not entirely off base. Chang Tun, the chief councilor of the left throughout the period of Che-tsung's personal rule, was by no means an ideological extremist. Back in 1085–6, Chang had attempted to prevent the abolition of the Hsi-ning and Yüan-feng reform measures with remarkably pragmatic arguments, acknowledging their failings while resisting their arbitrary elimination. Once in power, Chang Tun and his factional allies ushered in a new era of fiscal reform, preserving the pump-priming aspects of the New Policies while curbing the policies' widespread excesses.

In the fourth month of 1094, when Chang Tun assumed the chief councilorship, his newly installed reform ministry quickly seized the initiative on the policy-making front. The first order of business for the new regime was the revival of the hired service policy, which Ts'ai Ching, the newly appointed minister of revenue, convinced Chang to move to the top of the reformist agenda. Notorious in official historiography for his cynical opportunism, Ts'ai had performed a complete about-face on the issue of corvée policy within the span of eight years. While serving as prefect of K'ai-feng in 1085–6, Ts'ai had curried favor with Ssu-ma Kuang by implementing drafted service (ch'ai-i fa) in the capital region within a five-day deadline; now that the reformists had recaptured the Council of State, he hoped to impress Chang Tun with his zealous advocacy of hired service.[211] At any rate, when summoned before the throne on the fourth day of the fourth month of 1086, Chang and his fellow ministers announced their intention to radically restructure the empirewide corvée system according to the abolished Yüan-feng guidelines. Che-tsung assented to his ministers' entreaties, agreeing that the people of the empire would benefit from the revival of hired service, but on one condition: that the notoriously exorbitant surplus emergency fees (k'uan-sheng ch'ien) be reduced.[212] Moreover, the reformists attempted to exempt grade 5 households from the obligation of paying service exemption fees entirely, a glaring injustice that Ssu-ma Kuang himself had singled out for elimination in 1085. Token words of disapproval

---

[211] According to Ts'ai Ching's biography in the *Sung shih*, "[Chang] Tun and [Ssu-ma] Kuang disagreed about the two corvée policies [i.e., drafted service and hired service]. Within the span of ten years, Ts'ai had twice faced this issue, but he had backed down, when both councilors relied upon him for assistance. Those who knew him saw his treachery." For the whole story, see *SS* 472, pp. 13721–2.

[212] *SHY* (1997) *shih-huo* 65, pp. 63a–b.

came from Fan Ch'un-jen, soon to be purged, who argued that reviving hired service on an empirewide scale would neglect the irregularities of local conditions and the welfare of the masses.[213]

In the charged political atmosphere of the early days of Che-tsung's personal rule, all such dissent was effectively stifled, and the change in corvée policy was accomplished in a matter of weeks, a feat that had taken Ssu-ma Kuang and his bickering comrades six months to achieve. The official revival of hired service was hastily enacted by an imperial edict of the twenty-sixth day of the fourth month of 1094, without any more recorded opposition from within the reform coalition.[214] Despite the high-handed manner with which they were implemented, the Shao-sheng hired service regulations did indeed mitigate the most glaring failures of the Yüan-feng system, at least on paper. Surplus emergency fees, the most exorbitantly extractive aspect of the old system, were capped at a maximum of ten percent, and exemptions were granted to the poorest grade of rural households.

But no matter how expeditiously Chang Tun orchestrated its revival, hired service still met with bureaucratic resistance from below. Seven months later, in the eleventh month of 1094, Ts'ai Ching, the current minister of revenue (*hu-pu shang-shu*), reported that local administrators in the capital region were still enforcing Yüan-yu-era drafted service regulations.[215] Ignoring the specific difficulties in adapting hired service to varying conditions in localities across the empire, the reformist ministry of Shao-sheng apparently utilized the Censorate and the Remonstrance Bureau to coerce regional officials into obeying mandated deadlines and quotas.[216] Whereas the antireform coalition had foundered over drafted service in 1086, the Shao-sheng reform faction possessed far greater discipline and unity, and internal dissent on policy issues was simply quashed. When a lone remonstrator attempted to break ranks with the factional consensus, he was summarily dismissed. After critiquing the bureaucratic overreach of hired service in a memorial of the fifth month of 1096, the exhorter of the right Sun O was immediately purged from the ranks of remonstrators. Ts'ai Ching, the hired service advocate, indicted Sun for treachery and engineered his dismissal to a prefectural-level post.[217]

---

[213] *SHY* (1997) *shih-huo* 65, p. 63b.

[214] *SHY* (1997) *shih-huo* 65, p. 63b.

[215] *SHY* (1997) *shih-huo* 65, p. 69a.

[216] In the first month of 1095, the palace censor Kuo Chih-chang memorialized the throne urging stricter discipline for circuit-level officials who failed to implement the new hired service guidelines. See *SHY* (1997) *shih-huo* 65, pp. 68a–b.

[217] *SHY* (1997) *shih-huo* 65, pp. 69a–70b; *CPPM* 100, p. 3105. Sun O was appointed prefect of Kuang-te commandery.

All the available evidence indicates that the empirewide imposition of hired service reaped some tangible successes, but that even factional discipline and top-down coercion could not counter the widespread inertia of regional administrators. And one must wonder whether the ten percent cap on surplus emergency fees and the fee-exempt status of grade 5 households were actually maintained in practice, even though both restraints remained on the statute books throughout the Che-tsung reign. No matter how the Council of State attempted to enforce compliance by running roughshod over local officials, bureaucratic abuses and extractive excesses must have occurred. Still, without any solid quantitative data on the collection of hired service fees and their impact upon the balance sheet of the imperial treasury, conclusions on the policy's short- and long-term effects must remain largely presumptive and impressionistic.

Once hired service was pushed through, the Shao-sheng ministry turned its attention to reviving the green sprouts policy, the next item on its reform agenda. As he had with hired service, the ubiquitous Ts'ai Ching directed every stage of the fast-track implementation of the green sprouts policy, which took all of two months. In a memorial of the seventh month of 1095, Ts'ai sang the praises of Shen-tsung's agrarian loan measure, which, he argued, had been enacted with the most noble of intentions: to benefit small farmers at the expense of exploitative engrossers (*chien-ping*). Ever since the abolition of green sprouts by the misguided ministers of Yüan-yu, Ts'ai maintained that rural magnates had flourished, to the detriment of poor agricultural households. Claiming that "the way of making money (*sheng-ts'ai chih tao*) will benefit the common people of the state," he made a case for extending government credit to farmers, "the foundation of the empire."[218] A series of concurrent memorials followed from loyal members of the reformist rank and file, one of whom urged the imposition of a ten percent limit on yearly compounded interest, so that the state would not out-engross the engrossers.[219] When Che-tsung assented to the measure on the fourteenth day of the ninth month of 1095, no contrary voices were recorded in the *Sung hui-yao*, but given the attenuated state of the documentary record of Shao-sheng fiscal policy, the absence of evidence should not be assumed to be the evidence of absence. Even more frustrating for the historian, no tangible information whatsoever remains on the implementation of green sprouts on the local level for the entire Che-tsung reign, so not a single conclusion about its administration or maladministration can be surmised.

State trade (*shih-i*) represented the final piece of the puzzle, the last of the New Policies to be revived by the Shao-sheng reform ministry. Starting in the

---

[218] *SHY* (1997) *shih-huo* 5, pp. 15b–16a; *CPPM* 110, p. 3103.
[219] *SHY* (1997) *shih-huo* 5, p. 17a.

first year of Che-tsung's personal rule, the various components of the Yüan-feng commercial regulation and monopoly system gradually fell into place.[220] First, in the seventh month of 1094, Chang Tun prompted the emperor to initiate the process of state intervention into the private sector by reimposing "guild exemption fees" (*mien-hang ch'ien*) within the capital area. All mercantile guilds in K'ai-feng were now required to remit these monies to the central government, commensurate with the value of provisions that the state would now purchase for itself. While the guild exemption fee had been employed as a coercive tool of revenue extraction during the Shen-tsung reign, efforts were made to limit the collection of interest to a far from usurious ten percent, in similar fashion to the surplus emergency fee assessed upon hired service payments.

Full implementation of the remainder of the Yüan-feng commercial monopoly system did not occur until the twelfth month of 1097. A ministerial report recommended the revival of state trade bureaus (*shih-i wu*) to enhance commerce, to "restrain engrossers," and to rescue the common people from the "suffering" that had ensued after the bureaus' abolition.[221] Promulgated at the very end of 1097 by an amenable Che-tsung, an imperial edict approved the empirewide reestablishment of branch trade bureaus, which would purchase bulk staple goods cheap and sell them dear, and plow the profits back into the issue of loans to merchants.[222] As with hired service fees and green sprouts interest, strict limits were enforced upon interest payments for state trade loans, and capped at twenty percent. However, given the paucity of the historical record with reference to fiscal policy during Che-tsung's personal rule, the question of whether these controls over officially sanctioned usury were ever enforced must go unanswered.

Pitiably scant as it is, all available evidence suggests that the revival of the New Policies was a qualified success. First, the expeditious implementation of hired service, green sprouts, and state trade suggests that the Shao-sheng ministry was a tightly disciplined political machine, attaining its policy goals while silencing dissent and crushing resistance. Whereas the Yüan-yu coalition had agonized and bickered for the better part of a year over the abolition of the Shen-tsung reform agenda, the restored reform regime reimplemented the Yüan-feng systems of labor management, agricultural loans, and commercial monopolies from scratch in a matter of months. Moreover, the policy achievements of the resurgent reformists would have been unthinkable without

---

[220] For an analysis of the state trade policy during Che-tsung's personal rule, see Liang, "Shih-i fa shu," pp. 212–15.

[221] *HCP* (1979) 493, p. 11720.

[222] *SHY* (1997) *shih-huo* 37, p. 33b; *HCP* (1979) 493, p. 11720.

the patronage of Che-tsung, a pliant and dependent emperor who shared the
reformists' vision of statecraft. Second, on paper at least, the revived New Policies were intended to stimulate the economy and enhance state revenue, while
reining in the extractive excesses of the Yüan-feng era. Although no quantitative data can corroborate this impression, the Shao-sheng reform agenda
attempted to strike some sort of pragmatic compromise, alleviating the most
glaring of the abuses by the bureaucratic entrepreneurs of the 1080s. Regardless
of (or perhaps despite) the maximum legal limits placed upon the extraction of
hired service fees, and the reduction of green sprouts and state trade interest,
the Sung court was able to finance a renewed offensive against the Tanguts
in 1095–9. Any further conclusions on the consequences of state policy during Che-tsung's personal rule would be unwarranted speculation based on a
disappointingly inadequate documentary record.

Turning the tide: Renewed war against the Hsi Hsia

During the personal rule of Che-tsung, the resurgence of reformist statecraft
extended beyond fiscal policy into the long-disputed realm of border relations.
From the very beginning of the Shao-sheng era, remonstrators had excori-
ated the regency ministry of Ssu-ma Kuang and his successors for pursuing a
fragile détente with the Hsi Hsia, a weak-kneed policy of appeasement that
had erased the military legacy of Shen-tsung. Even after the four outposts of
Mi-chih, Chia-lu, Fu-t'u, and An-chiang had been ceded in 1089, the Tanguts
had taken advantage of the Sung court's passivity and docility to advance across
the frontier. Since its final status had not been conclusively settled by the end
of the Hsüan-jen regency, the Hsi Hsia had made every effort to redraw the
northwestern border in its favor. Abandoning the conciliatory stance of their
factional adversaries, the reformists contended that a renewed military offensive would stabilize the deteriorating border situation. In 1095, Chang Tun
convinced the increasingly dependent emperor to continue the expansionist
policies of his father, devising a new "advance and fortify" (*chin-chu*) plan to
tilt the balance of power back toward Sung dominance.[223] By seizing strategic
positions along the frontier – along the Hu-lu River valley and in the T'ien-tu
and Heng-shan plateaus – and rendering them impregnable to assault, the
Sung exploited its military superiority to effectively destroy the power position of the Hsi Hsia. When the Tanguts sued for peace in 1099, Che-tsung's
reform ministry had accomplished what Shen-tsung's best and brightest never
could: the projection of Sung hegemony into the northwest.

---

[223] For a well-documented analysis of the Sung-Tangut wars of the 1090s, see Wu, *Hsin Hsi Hsia shih*,
pp. 110–15; and Li, *Sung Hsia kuan-hsi shih*, pp. 91–6, 193–7, 221–31.

The revival of irredentism was accompanied by a more bellicose turn in political discourse. Reformist remonstrators portrayed the leaders of the Yüan-yu ministry not only as nefarious traitors but as cowardly weaklings who had bought an inconclusive peace by surrendering Sung territory to the Tanguts. In the fifth month of 1095, the palace censor Kuo Chih-chang issued a strident and scathing condemnation of the regency's border policies, which had needlessly forsaken the patrimony of Shen-tsung:

> The former emperor opened lands by pushing forward and choking the throats of the western barbarians. An-chiang, Chia-lu, Fu-t'u, and Mi-chih were occupied under his lofty governance, and their redoubts were assaulted. At the onset of the Yüan-yu era, the ministers who were then employed abandoned the four outposts, thereby manifesting weakness to the exterior, and emboldening the hearts of the barbarians.[224]

Kuo demanded both the punishment of all those who had supported the cession of the four border outposts in the Heng-shan highlands and the assumption of a more aggressive stance toward the Hsi Hsia. But it was only after the New Policies had been resurrected, providing sufficient revenue for rearmament, that the reform ministry could turn from bellicose rhetoric to action. Over the course of 1095 and 1096, Chang Tun persuaded Che-tsung to abandon the Yüan-yu policy of appeasement and to adopt an offensive posture toward the Tanguts. Annual tribute offerings to the Hsi Hsia were abruptly cut off, and orders were given to mobilize armed forces for deployment along the northwestern frontier. In 1097 a two-pronged "advance and fortify" strategy was devised, based on an assessment of the weak points in the Hsi Hsia defenses. Learning from the debacle of Yung-lo ch'eng, in which entire legions of Sung troops had perished in the defense of the indefensible, the general Chang Chieh (1027–1102) proposed a campaign of lightning attacks against the most strategic positions in the Heng-shan range and the Hu-lu River valley, which could be heavily fortified against any desperate Tangut offensive.[225] The supreme commander of Sung forces in Hsi-ho, Ch'in-feng, and Huan-ch'ing circuits, Chang Chieh argued that the Sung offensive into the disputed frontier territories would force the Hsi Hsia to retreat north: "Recently, the court has developed and constructed walled cities and fortifications, thereby expanding its territory. The first objective has been to seize territorial gains, and to topple the rebel lairs."[226]

As they systematically expanded into Tangut-occupied areas, the Sung forces proceeded from strength to strength. By the fourth month of 1097, Chang Chieh's troops occupied Hung-chou2 and Yen-chou3, and had wrested

[224] CPPM 101, pp. 3124–5.
[225] HCP (1979) 485, pp. 11518–19; SS 328, pp. 10589–90.
[226] HCP (1979) 505, pp. 12034–5.

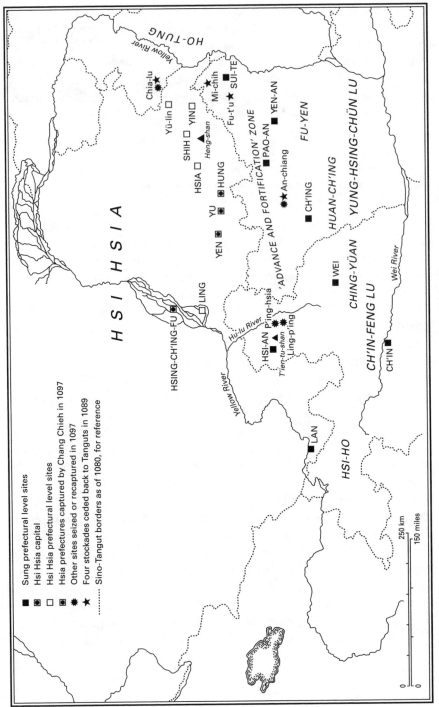

Map 17. Revived campaign against the Tanguts, 1097–1099.

Legend:

- ■ Sung prefectural level sites
- ◉ Hsi Hsia capital
- □ Hsi Hsia prefectural level sites
- ▣ Hsia prefectures captured by Chang Chieh in 1097
- ✹ Other sites seized or recaptured in 1097
- ★ Four stockades ceded back to Tanguts in 1089
- ‒‒‒‒‒ Sino-Tangut borders as of 1080, for reference

HO-TUNG

Yellow River

H S I   H S I A

Chia-lu ★
Yü-lin □
Mi-chih ★   SUI-TE ★
SHIH □   YIN □
HSIA □   Heng-shan ▲   Fu-t'u ★   YEN-AN ■
YU ▣   HUNG ▣   PAO-AN ■
YEN ▣   An-chiang ★   FU-YEN
'ADVANCE AND FORTIFICATION' ZONE
CH'ING ■   HUAN-CH'ING
YUNG-HSING-CHÜN LU

HSING-CH'ING-FU ◉
LING □

Yellow River
Hu-lu River   P'ing-hsia
HSI-AN ▲   Tien-tu-shan ▲   Ling-p'ing ✹
WEI ■   CHING-YÜAN

LAN ■

HSI-HO

CH'IN-FENG LU
CH'IN ■
Wei River

250 km
150 miles

Yu-chou from the hands of the Hsi Hsia. Moreover, the Chin-cheng pass in Hsi-ho circuit had been seized and fortified, and the Chia-lu and An-chiang stockades in Yung-hsing-chün and Ho-tung circuits, ceded in 1089, had been recovered.[227] Soon thereafter, Chang Chieh led his troops to seize and refortify P'ing-hsia and Ling-p'ing, crucial positions on either bank of the Hu-lu River that would enable the Sung troops to strike the very heart of the Tangut empire: its capital city of Hsing-ch'ing.[228] Between the autumn of 1097 and the winter of 1099, at least forty separate fortifications were constructed in the four circuits of Fu-yen, Huan-ch'ing, Ching-yüan, and Ho-tung, thereby cementing Sung hegemony over the northwestern frontier. With the occupation of the T'ien-tu range and the establishment of Hsi-an prefecture, several vital supply lines and key horse-producing areas now belonged to Sung, furthering the progress of its war machine.

The "advance and fortify" strategy was put to a final test in late 1098, when Dowager Empress Liang of the Hsi Hsia dispatched more than a hundred thousand troops in what became a suicide mission to recapture P'ing-hsia. Having learned from the fatal lessons of 1082, the Sung armed forces held the high ground to soundly defeat the Hsi Hsia besiegers, capturing the famed Tangut generals Wei-ming A-mai and Mei-lo-tu-pu in the process.[229] The broken siege of P'ing-hsia was the massacre of Yung-lo ch'eng in reverse, a ruinous loss that at least temporarily eliminated the Hsi Hsia as a threat to Sung hegemony. Backed into an increasingly untenable position, Emperor Hui-tsung of the Hsi Hsia had no choice but to sue for peace through a Liao intermediary in the ninth month of 1099, a move that was welcomed with much celebration by the Sung court.[230] The bellicose irredentist policies of Che-tsung had been brought to fruition, achieving what all of Shen-tsung's horses and men could not: blotting out the stain of the defeat at Yung-lo ch'eng.

Broken stalemate: Politics in the Yüan-fu era and the interregnum

As the most disciplined political organization of its time, the Shao-sheng coalition had achieved great triumphs in the spheres of fiscal and border policy, not just consummating but surpassing the attainments of Shen-tsung and his ministers. When they swept back into power in 1094, the reformists

---

[227] *SS* 18, p. 347.
[228] *SS* 18, pp. 347–8.
[229] Wang, *Tōto jiryaku* 128, p. 3b; *SS* 328, p. 10590.
[230] *HCP* (1979) 515, pp. 12234, 12240.

enjoyed both an exceptional degree of unanimity and unqualified imperial support. Throughout the mid-1090s, the ministry of Chang Tun functioned as a well-lubricated political machine, uniting behind clear-cut policy objectives and silencing dissent from the bureaucratic rank and file. With Che-tsung increasingly shut out of the loop, the reform ministry possessed virtual carte blanche, unchecked by imperial oversight. But after the members of the "Yüan-yu faction" had been persecuted, the New Policies had been renovated, and the northwestern borderlands had been all but pacified, the reform coalition was riven asunder by personal rivalries within the Council of State. By 1098, the first year of the new Yüan-fu era, the tacit agreement that had once prevailed among the reform cabinet of Chang Tun, Tseng Pu, Ts'ai Ching, and Ts'ai Pien gave way to incessant backbiting. Unlike the tripartite conflict of Lo, Shuo, and Shu a decade earlier, this bout of political infighting pitted man against man rather than faction against faction.

These internal rivalries were mostly personal rather than political in nature, grounded in spitefulness, jealousy, and resentment. When Ts'ai Pien was appointed assistant director of the right in the Department of State Affairs (*shang-shu yu-ch'eng*) in the tenth month of 1096, his older brother, Ts'ai Ching, succumbed to sibling rivalry, resenting that he himself had been passed over for a promotion. After being refused a seat on the Council of State yet again in early 1097, Ts'ai Ching became permanently estranged from Chang Tun as well, but Ts'ai's bureaucratic expertise rendered him immune from dismissal.[231] Apparently, Chang could not control the bureaucratic machinery without Ts'ai's assistance, and could not risk dismissing him from office. Once a loyal lieutenant to Chang Tun, Ts'ai Pien also fell out with his factional patron.[232] As Chang Tun increasingly delegated de facto authority to Ts'ai Pien, the two were bound together by mutual dependency and enmity, and neither could succeed in dislodging the other from court. Hence, the chief councilor and two of his leading protégés were caught up in an unwinnable struggle that remained stalemated to the end of Che-tsung's personal rule.

Whereas personality conflicts had alienated both Ts'ai Ching and Ts'ai Pien from Chang Tun, Tseng Pu took a principled stance of opposition to the chief councilor. Long loyal to Chang Tun, Tseng Pu broke away from his former patron to oppose Chang's absolutist rule as chief councilor. On many occasions in the Shao-sheng era, Tseng Pu had adamantly refused any hope of amnesty for the purged Yüan-yu partisans, and had coordinated and

---

[231] *HCP* (1979) 490, p. 11621; 492, pp. 11688–9.
[232] *HCP* (1979) 506, p. 12062; *SS* 472, p. 13729.

systematized the bureaucratic aspects of the factional proscriptions. But as the factional persecution campaign continued, Tseng could no longer stomach its brutal consequences, and experienced what appears to have been a serious change of heart. Making a calculated effort to triangulate his way through political life, Tseng Pu broke with the mainstream of the reform coalition and its leaders, striking out upon a solitary middle path between the extremes of Yüan-yu and Shao-sheng. In mid-1097, he begged for a measure of clemency for the banished Lü Ta-fang and Liu Chih; five months later, he advocated the rehabilitation of Ch'en Kuan, a banned member of the antireform coalition.[233] The same year, in a series of private audiences with Che-tsung, Tseng Pu further distanced himself from the reformist ministerial regime by casting aspersions on Chang Tun and Ts'ai Pien, accusing them of monopolizing power and stifling all dissent.[234] In a later dialogue in 1099, the final year of the emperor's reign, Tseng insisted that the factional persecutions had gone too far: "When Chang Tun and Ts'ai Pien enacted [the persecution] of the Yüan-yu faction, their assembled arguments were entirely excessive, and when they slandered the former court, it was mostly to avenge their selfish grudges."[235] By regretfully rejecting the darkest aspects of the reformist past, Tseng Pu had offered himself as a politically viable alternative to Chang Tun, employing a strategy of compromise that would, in the short term, prove to be both shrewd and prescient.

But Che-tsung suddenly died of an unspecified illness in the first month of 1100, at the age of twenty-four. The latent hostilities within the reformist leadership now burst to the surface. When Dowager Empress Ch'in-sheng (1045–1101), the widow of Shen-tsung and a steadfast opponent of the New Policies, assumed the role of regent, the political climate was abruptly transformed. In the ensuing debate over the imperial succession, Chang Tun invoked the dynastic ritual code to advocate the enthronement of the Prince of Chien, Che-tsung's younger brother of the same mother. But the dowager empress and Tseng Pu begged to differ, arguing that Chao Chi, the Prince of Tuan, was truly next in line for the throne, maintaining that his robust health and filial benevolence would make him an ideal emperor. When the remainder of the Council of State, including Ts'ai Pien, sided with the dowager empress, and the Prince of Tuan was enthroned as Emperor Hui-tsung at the age of seventeen, Chang Tun was stunned into silence.[236]

[233] *HCP* (1979) 487, p. 11563; 492, p. 11686.
[234] *HCP* (1979) 491, p. 11654.
[235] *HCP* (1979) 506, p. 12062.
[236] *HCP* (1979) 530, pp. 12356–8.

Having chosen the losing candidate in the succession controversy, Chang Tun incurred the permanent enmity of the newly enthroned emperor. And despite having supported Hui-tsung's succession, Ts'ai Pien was guilty by association with Chang, a definite political liability in the new regency. The only viable contender to the councilorship was now Tseng Pu, who had effectively distanced himself from the reformist mainstream. Tseng swiftly seized the advantage of the mounting tensions between Chang Tun and Hui-tsung to begin rehabilitating such banished antireformists as Fan Ch'un-jen, Han Chung-yen, and Ch'en Kuan. Packing the Censorate with Yüan-yu sympathizers in the summer of 1100, Tseng Pu opened the roads of remonstrance to begin the process of dislodging Chang Tun and the brothers Ts'ai from the Council of State. Drawing upon the support of his new allies in remonstrance posts, Tseng Pu engineered the dismissals of Ts'ai Ching and Ts'ai Pien in the third and fifth months of 1100.[237] After repeatedly bearing the brunt of censorial indictments for "monopolizing power . . . betraying the state, and misleading the court," Chang Tun was cashiered and demoted to a regional post in the ninth month of 1100, effectively eliminating the Shao-sheng faction from the corridors of power for the time being.[238]

With his rivals for power finally dispensed with, Tseng Pu ascended to the councilorship in the tenth month of 1100, serving alongside the rehabilitated antireformist Han Chung-yen in a bipartisan ministry. Symbolic of Tseng Pu's attempts to transcend factionalism, the reign title was changed to Chien-chung ching-kuo (Establishing the Mean and Stabilizing the State) early in 1101. But this conciliatory experiment in establishing a middle path between the excesses of Yüan-yu and Shao-sheng was to prove ephemeral. And Tseng Pu's attempts to be everything to everyone were ultimately abortive, for he was too deeply implicated in the Shao-sheng persecutions to ever appeal to the Yüan-yu survivors, and too much of a betrayer and apostate to ever endear himself to the reformists.

Upon the sudden death of the dowager empress in the first month of 1101, Hui-tsung began his personal rule, bringing the experiment in factional conciliation to an end. Having lost faith in Tseng Pu and his coalition government, Hui-tsung expressed his desire to continue the policies of Shen-tsung and Che-tsung. The reign title was changed again to Ch'ung-ning (Revering the Hsi-ning Era) in 1102. The implications were clear: the reform coalition would regain its dominance over politics and polity, and Tseng Pu's bipartisan coalition would be doomed to failure. When Ts'ai Ching was appointed chief councilor of the right in the seventh month of 1102, he immediately

---

[237] *CPPM* 120, pp. 3616, 3620.
[238] *CPPM* 120, pp. 3618–19, 3624.

unleashed another series of severe proscriptions against the Yüan-yu faction and its recent sympathizers. The short-lived reconciliation campaign of 1101–2 came to a crashing halt, as it became abundantly clear that factional conflict could not be conciliated by imperial fiat. Under the ministry of Ts'ai Ching, a new political alignment would take shape, and reformist dominance would remain unchallenged until the end of the Northern Sung.

CHAPTER 7

THE REIGNS OF HUI-TSUNG (1100–1126) AND CH'IN-TSUNG (1126–1127) AND THE FALL OF THE NORTHERN SUNG

Ari Daniel Levine

APPROACHES AND DEPARTURES: HISTORIOGRAPHIC ISSUES

Ensconced within his palace pleasure gardens, a dissolute aesthete-emperor paints exquisite birds and flowers, even as the empire rots from corruption within and succumbs to invasion from without. Such is the classical historio-graphic image of Emperor Hui-tsung (1082–1135, r. 1100–26), the penulti-mate monarch of the Northern Sung.[1] Occupying a tantalizingly ambiguous position in history, he has been simultaneously celebrated as a magnificent patron and practitioner of the arts and reviled as a negligent ruler who nearly doomed the dynasty. For centuries of Chinese historians, Hui-tsung has func-tioned as a metonymic figure, embodying the contradictions of the Sung dynasty as a whole, symbolizing the ascendancy of *wen*, the refinements of culture, over *wu*, the arts of war. Rich in tragedy and irony, the contradictions and contrasts of Hui-tsung's reign have been suppressed by historians, who have reconstructed a fragmentary corpus of primary sources into a didactic and moralistic narrative.

Judgments of the Hui-tsung era have tended toward high levels of general-ization, for the documentary record of his reign poses a minefield of historio-graphic problems. Foremost of these issues is the moralistic praise-and-blame bias of traditional Chinese historiography. In the standard dynastic histories of the Sung, and in privately compiled works of historiography, Hui-tsung and his long-serving chief councilor Ts'ai Ching (1046–1127) have been held responsible for a litany of crimes against the moral and territorial integrity of

[1] The most critical primary source for the Hui-tsung reign is Yang Chung-liang's *Tzu-chih t'ung-chien ch'ang-pien chi-shih pen-mo* [hereafter *CPPM*] (1253; Taipei, 1967). *CPPM* is a thematic compilation of and companion to Li T'ao's *Hsü tzu-chih t'ung-chien ch'ang-p'ien* [hereafter *HCP* (1979)] (1183; Peking, 1979–95), the surviving edition of which contains only the first month of Hui-tsung's reign. Other essential sources are T'o-t'o et al., eds., *Sung shih* [hereafter *SS*] (1345; Peking, 1977), the official dynastic history of the Sung. The motherlode of administrative documents for the Hui-tsung reign is Hsü Sung et al., *Sung hui-yao chi-kao* [hereafter *SHY* (1997)] (1809, 1935; Peking, 1997). Another crucial collection of documents for political history is Hsü Tzu-ming, ed., *Sung tsai-fu pien-nien lu chiao-fu* (Peking, 1986).

the state. Ts'ai and his fellow state councilors, pejoratively referred to as the "Six Felons" (*liu tsei*), were blamed for prosecuting the most sweeping factional purge in Sung history, allowing governmental corruption to run rampant, and pushing the subjects of the empire toward impoverishment and rebellion. In the judgment of posterity, the greatest crime of these so-called felonious ministers was their bungling of border diplomacy and military strategy, which precipitated the Jurchen Chin invasion, the sack of K'ai-feng, and the fall of the north.

Moral outrage has pervaded the primary and secondary sources of the Hui-tsung reign so deeply that it has become a challenge for present-day historians to strip away these layers of revisionism and to separate events from interpretation. For example, the *Sung shih* biographies of the leading statesmen of the Hui-tsung reign have been placed under the rubric "treacherous ministers" (*chien-ch'en*), portraying Ts'ai Ching and his colleagues in an unfailingly negative light.[2] The surviving unofficial chronicles of the period have been deliberately arranged to indict the failures and crimes of Hui-tsung's state councilors. Historians can attempt to correct for the biases of our late-imperial predecessors, but moralistic judgments pervade the very fabric of the historiography, turning primary sources into secondary sources.

The traditional ideals of moralistic historiography not only have determined the composition of the primary sources for the history of the Hui-tsung reign, they have also determined the sources' distribution and survival. In other words, few sources that deviate from the trend of condemnatory historiography have survived. The moralistic biases of traditional historians have influenced which primary sources they deemed worthy of recopying and reprinting. Hence, nine centuries later, almost no counterhistories of the Hui-tsung reign have been preserved. Only a very limited number of texts veer in the opposite interpretational direction from the standard histories to try to glorify the emperor and his most prominent courtiers.[3] Perhaps the most authoritative chronicle of this period could be mined and reassembled from the *Sung hui-yao*, a topical compendium of administrative documents. At any rate, the so-called

---

[2] *SS* 472, pp. 13271–8, for the "treacherous minister" biography of Ts'ai Ching. For a textual archeology of this historical narrative, see Charles Hartman, "A textual history of Cai Jing's biography in the *Song shi*," in *Emperor Huizong and Late Northern Song China: The politics of culture and the culture of politics*, ed. Patricia B. Ebrey and Maggie Bickford (Cambridge, Mass., 2006), pp. 517–64. For an analysis of the moralistic strain of official Sung historiography, see also Charles Hartman, "The making of a villain: Ch'in Kuei and Tao-hsüeh," *Harvard Journal of Asiatic Studies* 58 No. 1 (1998), pp. 59–146.

[3] For example, one of the most valuable primary sources for the history of the Hui-tsung reign is Ts'ai T'ao's *T'ieh-wei shan ts'ung-t'an*, ed. Feng Hui-min and Shen Hsi-lin (c. 1130; Peking, 1983), a slender volume of *pi-chi* anecdotes which provides access to the imperial court. Since Ts'ai T'ao was the son of the chief councilor, Ts'ai Ching, his narratives tend to eulogize Hui-tsung and his ministers with self-serving glorification.

primary sources of the Hui-tsung reign must be read with a skeptical eye, for what they can and cannot recount.

In both quantity and quality, the documentary record of the Hui-tsung era pales in comparison to the reign chronicles of the emperor's immediate predecessors, Shen-tsung and Che-tsung. The exact reason for the disappearance of major source texts pertaining to the Hui-tsung reign remains unknown. Doubtless, some portions of the pertinent dynastic chronicles were destroyed during the Chin conquest and the subsequent southbound flight of the imperial court. Because of the paucity of the documentary record, the compilation of the *Veritable records* (*shih-lu*) of the Hui-tsung reign occupied Southern Sung court historiographers for several decades, starting in the late 1130s. This text was not completed until 1177, and its compilation was undertaken during the Kao-tsung and Hsiao-tsung reigns, at a time when political circumstances had dramatically changed.[4] By the middle of the twelfth century, the official interpretation of recent history blamed the ministry of Ts'ai Ching for the collapse of the Northern Sung. Documents that might have portrayed the achievements of the Hui-tsung reign in a positive light were systematically excluded from both the pertinent *Veritable records* and the *State history* (*kuo-shih*). These works of official history were collated into the *Sung shih*, the standard dynastic history, and the unofficial chronicles that survive. Hence, the present-day disposition of the documentary record has been skewed by the condemnatory attitudes of historians in the Southern Sung and later.

The most basic source for Northern Sung political history, the *Hsü tzu-chih t'ung-chien ch'ang-pien* (1183) of Li T'ao (1115–84), is now missing all but a month of the Hui-tsung reign. Compiled from the basic annals of the *Veritable records* and *State histories* of the Northern Sung, this text is an indispensable chronicle of prior reigns, but extends only as far as the month after Hui-tsung's enthronement. A fraction of entries from the *Hsü Tzu-chih t'ung-chien ch'ang-pien* has been collected and classified in a shorter topical compilation, Yang Chung-liang's *Tzu-chih t'ung-chien ch'ang-pien chi-shih pen-mo* (1253), but this text is problematic as well, for its entries present an uncertain quantity of selections from the *Hsü Tzu-chih t'ung-chien ch'ang-pien*, and it fails to devote much space to the history of state policies and institutions. The *Chi-shih pen-mo* devotes a preponderant amount of space to the early and final years of Hui-tsung's twenty-six year reign, leaving a gap that must be filled by other sources. These include the aforementioned *Sung hui-yao* and Hsü Meng-hsin's

---

[4] For an extended textual history of the official historiography of the Hui-tsung reign, see chapter 2, Ari D. Levine, "A house in darkness: The politics of history and the language of politics in the Late Northern Song, 1066–1126" (diss., Columbia University, 2002). Also see Ts'ai Ch'ung-pang, *Sung-tai hsiu-shih chih-tu yen-chiu* (Taipei, 1991), pp. 100–4.

(1126–1207) *San-chao pei-meng hui-pien* (1196), a collection of documents chronicling the Sung court's wars and treaties with the Liao and Chin.

Presenting another set of problems, in both primary and secondary sources, the history of the late Northern Sung has inevitably been narrated in teleological fashion. With the benefit of hindsight, later historians have portrayed the Hui-tsung era as a period of inevitable decline and fall, conceptualizing nearly three decades – the second longest reign of the Northern Sung – as a slippery downward slope toward humiliation and disintegration. To replicate such a teleological narrative is to elide the random and fortuitous factors that precipitated the collapse of the Northern Sung and to ignore the moments of stasis and equilibrium that punctuate its history. The primary sources and secondary literature for the period offer little guidance to the historian who seeks to write a narrative that does not assume that the "Calamity of Ching-k'ang" – that is, the Jurchen conquest of north China in 1126–7 – was a foregone conclusion.

To bring the problem of sources back into the picture, in traditional historiography the decadence and dissolution of a ruler and his court are portrayed as harbingers of dynastic collapse. Since the primary sources for the penultimate reign of the Northern Sung have been subject to historiographic revisions, present-day historians cannot entirely avoid reiterating the interpretations of their predecessors. Standard historiography has determined the conventional interpretation of the Hui-tsung reign, as well as the composition and distribution of the documentary record. Even if such a thing were desirable, this chapter is not a rehabilitation project, an attempt to peel away historiographic accretions to discover what lies beneath. The story narrated here does not deviate from the documentary record, but it will interrogate it at every opportunity, revealing the extent to which it has been compromised by the moralistic agenda of traditional historiography.

COURT POLITICS DURING THE CH'IN-SHENG REGENCY

If it had not been for his older brother's premature death, Chao Chi, Shen-tsung's eleventh son, would never have been enthroned as emperor.[5] Unburdened by the demands of rulership and excluded from involvement in court politics, this imperial prince surely would have devoted his life to artistic patronage and production. A connoisseur and practitioner par excellence, the future Emperor Hui-tsung was infatuated with painting, calligraphy, and other refined aesthetic pursuits. His skill with the brush has been described as

[5] For a recent biography of Hui-tsung, which offers a detailed history of his reign, see Jen Ch'ung-yüeh, *Sung Hui-tsung Sung Ch'in-tsung* (Ch'ang-ch'un, 1996).

prodigious, and he has joined the art-historical canon as a creator, organizer, and patron.[6] With the passing of the heirless Emperor Che-tsung (1077–1100, r. 1085–1100), his younger brother Chao Chi was thrust into a role he had not been prepared to play. Compared to his activist predecessors Shen-tsung and Che-tsung, both of whom immersed themselves in the quotidian affairs of governance, Hui-tsung was largely a hands-off monarch, setting the general direction of state policies and delegating broad powers to his ministers to formulate and implement them.[7]

According to the traditional interpretation of his reign, the emperor Hui-tsung allowed himself to be manipulated by his chief councilor, Ts'ai Ching, surrendering his oversight of governance in return for a constant supply of luxuries. Accused of buying Hui-tsung's compliance with art objects and garden supplies, Ts'ai Ching enjoyed the perquisites of the councilorship for twenty-five years, with minimal interruptions. Long maligned in classical historiography as a "treacherous minister" (chien-ch'en), Ts'ai succeeded in maintaining political stability at a court that had been a factional battleground for more than thirty years. Perhaps his ministerial regime endured because Ts'ai Ching was politically astute enough (or, as his biographers alleged, ruthless and cynical enough) to succeed where his predecessors had failed. Granted, he marginalized political dissenters from the imperial bureaucracy and formed an enduring factional patronage network at court. As long as Hui-tsung remained upon the throne, Ts'ai Ching and his affiliates could dictate state policy as they saw fit. Caught up in a web of mutual dependence, the emperor's ministers clung to power until they were ultimately brought down by a military crisis of their own making. By instigating the Chin invasion of 1126–7, Hui-tsung's ministers earned themselves the scorn of traditional historians, who reinterpreted the emperor's entire reign as a downward spiral, heading inexorably toward dynastic collapse.

But few who attended his enthronement could have foreseen that Hui-tsung and his ministers would have pushed the Sung dynasty to the brink of extinction. In fact, in the first month of 1100, when Emperor Che-tsung died at the age of twenty-four under suspicious circumstances, Hui-tsung assumed the throne to nearly unanimous acclaim from his Council of State.

---

[6] For three recent art-historical studies of Hui-tsung, see Maggie Bickford, "Emperor Huizong and the aesthetic of agency," Archives of Asian art 53 (2002–3), pp. 71–104; Peter C. Sturman, "Cranes above Kaifeng: The auspicious image in the court of Huizong," Ars Orientalis 20 (1990), pp. 33–68; and Maggie Bickford, "Huizong's paintings: Art and the art of emperorship," in Emperor Huizong and late Northern Song China: The politics of culture and the culture of politics, ed. Patricia B. Ebrey and Maggie Bickford (Cambridge, Mass., 2006), pp. 453–513.

[7] For a brief analysis of court politics and state policy during the Hui-tsung reign, see Wang Tseng-yü, "Pei Sung wan-ch'i cheng-chih chien-lun" Chung-kuo-shih yen-chiu 4 (1994), pp. 82–7.

In the crowded field of Shen-tsung's surviving heirs, Chao Chi had emerged as the leading candidate for enthronement. And in the first year of his reign, during which he shared power with Dowager Empress Ch'in-sheng, the new monarch took an activist approach to governance. Hui-tsung assented to a balanced policy of factional reconciliation, steering a middle course between the reformist extremism of the Shao-sheng era and the antireform fervor of the Yüan-yu regency. From the standpoint of the early Hui-tsung reign, a time of contingency and uncertainty at court, the fall of the Northern Sung was by no means inevitable.

Long live the king: The enthronement controversy of 1100

The controversy over the imperial enthronement brought an end to politics as usual as it had been practiced during the previous two decades of factional conflict. With the young monarch's death came the abrupt fall of the reformist Chang Tun (1035–1105) and the rise of his moderate rival Tseng Pu (1036–1107). Breaking ranks with his old patron and the political mainstream in the final years of Che-tsung's reign, Tseng had opposed the partisan proscriptions that Chang's ministry had orchestrated in the mid-1090s. Nevertheless, Tseng Pu failed to convince the monarch that the brutal excesses of factionalism had jeopardized any hope of political stability at court.[8] In audiences with the previous emperor, Tseng had repeatedly attacked Chang and his lieutenant Ts'ai Pien (1058–1117), accusing them of monopolizing power and silencing dissent at court.[9] By breaking with the darkest aspects of the reformist past, Tseng Pu offered himself as a politically viable alternative to Chang Tun, if only the monarch would listen.

In a political culture where the survival of a ministry was dependent upon monarchical patronage, Che-tsung's death loosened Chang's grip on ministerial power and granted Tseng Pu an opportunity to stage a challenge for the councilorship. As had happened with the death of Shen-tsung in 1085, the monarchical transition of 1100 tipped the balance of power in favor of the opponents of the reformists' New Policies. Shen-tsung's consort, Dowager Empress Ch'in-sheng (1045–1101), assumed the regency, influencing the imperial succession and the direction of state policy. Like Dowager Empress Hsüan-jen before her, Ch'in-sheng was a critic of the New Policies and rehabilitated antireformist councilors and remonstrators almost as soon as she was named

---

[8] As Tseng argued in an audience with Che-tsung held in 1099: "When Chang Tun and Ts'ai Pien persecuted the Yüan-yu faction, their arguments were entirely excessive, and when they slandered the former court, it was mostly to avenge their selfish grievances." See *HCP* (1979) 506, p. 12062.

[9] *HCP* (1979) 491, p. 11654; 492, p. 11686.

regent.[10] As had occured at the beginning of the Hsüan-jen regency, when the reformist councilor Ts'ai Ch'üeh was deposed, the early months of the Ch'in-sheng regency initiated a dramatic shift in court politics that ended the long-lived reform ministry of Chang Tun.

Adjudicated by the dowager empress, the ensuing debate over the imperial succession provided a pretext for Chang's dismissal from the Council of State. Since Che-tsung had died without issue and had not nominated an heir apparent, one of his brothers would be nominated to succeed him as emperor. But which brother? For nearly every prominent figure at court but Chang Tun, the choice of whom to enthrone was unequivocal. When the regent summoned her councilors to debate the succession in the ninth month of 1100, Chang spoke first, presumably without having canvassed the opinions of his colleagues. Such presumption might have gone unquestioned when Che-tsung occupied the throne, but it now threatened Chang's political survival.[11] Rigidly interpreting the ritual code of the dynasty, which postulated consanguinity as the principle for a fraternal succession, Chang supported the enthronement of Chao Ssu, the Prince of Chien, Che-tsung's younger brother by the same mother.[12] The dowager empress sternly objected to Chang's efforts at king making, asserting that at age nineteen, Chao Chi, the Prince of Tuan, enjoyed the advantages of seniority and maturity over Chao Ssu.[13] In the ensuing debate, she overrode the increasingly desperate protestations of Chang Tun, who insinuated that the Prince of Tuan was too frivolous to be an acceptable choice as ruler. The chief councilor's judgment might have been borne out by future events, but his casting of aspersions at Chao Chi was a reckless maneuver at the time. Ultimately, the regent prevailed in arguing for the enthronement of Chao Chi, whose "longevity, benevolence, and filiality" she claimed distinguished him from his brothers. All of Chang's colleagues in the Council of State, Tseng Pu and Ts'ai Pien among them, seconded the dowager empress's choice. Speaking for the other assembled ministers, Tseng affirmed the Prince of Tuan's candidacy, denouncing Chang for attempting to dictate the imperial succession.[14] Later that day, Chao Chi assumed the throne as Emperor Hui-tsung, an event that was witnessed by a speechless Chang Tun, who could no longer take monarchical patronage for granted.

---

[10] According to Dowager Empress Ch'in-sheng's *Sung shih* biography, she supported the antireform policies of the Hsüan-jen regency. See *SS* 243, p. 8630.

[11] Such was the moralistic interpretation of the compilers of the *Sung shih*. See *SS* 471, p. 13713.

[12] *HCP* (1979) 530, pp. 12356–8.

[13] Chao Pi, the Prince of Shen, was Shen-tsung's eldest surviving son, but he was rejected as a serious candidate for enthronement because of his poor vision. For his biography, see *SS* 246, p. 8722.

[14] *HCP* (1979) 530, pp. 12356–8.

Shifting winds: The return of the antireformists and the fall of Chang Tun

During the first months of Hui-tsung's reign, Chang Tun's political position became increasingly untenable. The new monarchical regime, guided by Dowager Empress Ch'in-sheng, made preliminary moves to rehabilitate prominent antireformists who had endured the factional proscriptions that had been advanced during Che-tsung's personal rule. Fearing his impending dismissal and the elimination of the New Policies, Chang sought to convince the dowager empress and Emperor Hui-tsung to retain his ministerial regime by appealing to the reforming legacy of Shen-tsung.[15] His entreaties fell on deaf ears, since the regent firmly grasped the reins of power. In the early months of 1100, the surviving members of the antireform coalition and their second-generation supporters returned to the capital, after almost a decade of being marginalized by Chang Tun's reform ministry.

As Tseng Pu continued to maneuver toward the political center, reformist dominance of the Council of State was further undermined. With the regent's approval, surviving opponents of the New Policies began to return to court. Two potential leaders of the antireform opposition emerged, when Fan Ch'un-jen (1027–1101) and Han Chung-yen (1038–1109), prominent members of the antireform coalition of 1085–93, were rehabilitated and summoned back to the capital in the first month of 1100.[16] Both men had exceptional pedigrees, both political and familial, that could make them the standard-bearers of a restored antireform ministry. Frequently the lone voice of moderation during the Hsüan-jen regency, Fan Ch'un-jen had notably opposed the forced banishment of Ts'ai Ch'üeh, the former chief councilor and leader of the reformist opposition, in 1089. Even so, Fan had suffered political persecution during Chang Tun's regime, enduring years of exile in the far south. The son of Jen-tsung's famed chief councilor Fan Chung-yen, Fan would have been the natural standard-bearer of the resurgent antireform coalition of 1100, but his ill health and advancing blindness forced him to decline the councilorship.[17]

---

[15] See memorials by Chang Tun and Ts'ai Pien, both presented days after Hui-tsung's enthronement, in *HCP* (1979) 520, pp. 12368, 12371.

[16] In the first month of 1100 a messenger was sent to Yung-chou2 (in Kuang-nan West), to summon Fan Ch'un-jen back to the capital. See the topical history by the Southern Sung compiler P'eng Pai-chuan, *T'ai-p'ing chih-chi t'ung-lei* (c. 13th c.; Taipei, 1966) 24, p. 30a. Han Chung-yen was officially recommended to the Council of State in the first month of 1100, along with several other nonmainstream political figures: Kuo Chih-chang and Huang Lü, both moderate reformists loyal to Tseng Pu; and Lu Tien, Kung Yuan, and Tseng Chao, all of whom were individualists who had served under both factions. See *HCP* (1979) 520, p. 12378.

[17] According to his *Sung shih* biography, Fan Ch'un-jen's forced exile to Yung-chou (Ching-hu South circuit) was ended after Dowager Empress Ch'in-sheng intervened to restore his honorary official rank and to arrange for his transfer to Cheng-chou, much closer to the capital. Imperial boons of medical herbs

Han Chung-yen, another scion of the antireform movement, took Fan's place as the formal leader of the antireform opposition. The son of Han Ch'i (1008–75), a renowned councilor of the 1050s and 1060s, Han Chung-yen also opposed the New Policies but was more amenable to serving under a bipartisan ministerial regime. In the third month of 1100, Han was appointed chief councilor of the right (*yu-p'u-yeh*), a move that foreshadowed the impending dismissal of Chang Tun.[18]

In the meantime, other survivors of the antireform coalition were making their way back to K'ai-feng to form the nucleus of an opposition movement at court. By the second month of Hui-tsung's reign, such stalwart antireformists as Liu An-shih, Ch'eng I, Su Shih, and Lü T'ao were released from their exiles and restored to the ranks of officialdom.[19] But because most prominent members of the antireform coalition of the 1080s were deceased, infirm, or simply unwilling to serve at court, younger associates took their places. By the spring of 1100, both the Censorate and the Remonstrance Bureau were packed with a second generation of Yüan-yu sympathizers. The most voluble conservatives at court during the first year of the Hui-tsung reign were the remonstrators Ch'en Kuan (1057–1122), Tsou Hao (1060–1111), and Kung Kuai (n.d.).[20] Long barricaded under Chang Tun's ministry, the roads of remonstrance were reopened by an edict affirming that in the new monarchical regime, "upright words will be heeded, with no restrictions."[21] With the promulgation of this edict, antireformist remonstrators were granted permission to clamor for Chang's dismissal, which the dowager empress had sought ever since the enthronement debates.

Chang Tun was soon buried beneath a heap of hostile indictments from the Censorate and the Remonstrance Bureau. Ch'en Kuan, the exhorter of the left (*tso-cheng-yen*), led the resistance, inspiring his colleagues in remonstrance posts to demand the chief councilor's summary dismissal. In a memorial of the fourth month of 1100, the likes of which had not been read for more than a decade, Ch'en attacked Chang with extreme viciousness and moralistic fervor: "Chang Tun has monopolized power as chief councilor for eight years

---

and tea could not save Fan's health, which had sharply deteriorated during his exile. In 1101, a year after declining the councilorship, Fan died at the age of seventy-five. See *SS* 314, p. 10292. For a brief English-language biography, see Michael D. Freeman and Chikusa Masaaki, "Fan Shun-jen," in *Sung biographies*, ed. Herbert Franke (Wiesbaden, 1976), pp. 334–7.

[18] P'eng, *T'ai-p'ing chih-chi t'ung-lei* 24, p. 30b.

[19] P'eng, *T'ai-p'ing chih-chi t'ung-lei* 24, pp. 30a–b. Another ten antireformists, mostly rank-and-file members of the Yüan-yu coalition, were rehabilitated in the second month of 1100.

[20] P'eng, *T'ai-p'ing chih-chi t'ung-lei* 24, p. 30b. Ch'en Kuan was appointed exhorter of the left (*tso cheng-yen*), Tsou Hao was appointed exhorter of the right (*yu cheng-yen*), and Kung Kuai was made palace censor (*tien-chung shih yü-shih*).

[21] *CPPM* 123, pp. 3708–9.

running. He has confused the state and misled the court, and his crimes cannot be concealed. All of the resentment and anger in the empire is focused upon him."[22]

But Ch'en's words failed to sway the mind of Hui-tsung, who refused to allow Chang to retire from the Council of State on several occasions. The emperor's ambivalence on this issue cannot be easily explained away, since he did not lack a reason to dismiss the sole opponent of his enthronement from the councilorship. Nonetheless, when it came to dismissing Chang's lieutenants from the Council of State, Ch'in-sheng and Hui-tsung were much less hesitant. Largely responsible for the revival of the New Policies and the brutal purge of the antireformists during Che-tsung's personal rule, Ts'ai Pien was the first to fall from grace. In mid-1100, the palace censor Kung Kuai railed against Ts'ai, employing polemical and language reminiscent of the days of the Yüan-yu regency: "[Your servant] observes that Ts'ai Pien's heart is profoundly venomous, and his nature is endowed with wickedness. . . . If he was not loyal to the Former Emperors [i.e., Shen-tsung and Che-tsung], then how can he possibly be loyal to Your Majesty?[23]

Soon thereafter, Ts'ai was cashiered as the assistant director of the left in the Department of State Affairs (*shang-shu tso-ch'eng*), and demoted to a prefectural-level administrative post in the Yangtze Delta.[24] With the subsequent dismissals of Hsing Shu and Ts'ai Pien's older brother Ts'ai Ching, the reformist majority on the Council of State collapsed. Yet although his maneuvering it managed to win him the councilorship, Tseng Pu's move to eliminate his former comrades in the reform faction would come back to haunt him. As an apostate to the reform cause, Tseng had cut off a bloc of potential supporters on the left, and he would be the first to be purged from court if an unreconstructed reformist ever returned to power.

Set free by Tseng Pu, conservative remonstrators stepped up their campaign to remove Chang Tun from the councilorship. Ch'en Kuan and his colleagues indicted Chang for a slew of crimes against the state: absolutism, favoritism, factionalism, blasphemy, heresy, and irredentism.[25] Hui-tsung finally heeded the calls of his censors and granted Chang's requests for retirement in the ninth month of 1100, dismissing him from the Council of State and demoting him to a post in prefectural administration.[26] Even after his dismissal to Yüeh-chou (Liang-che), where he was appointed prefect, Chang was still singled out for

---

[22] *CPPM* 120, pp. 3618–19.

[23] *CPPM* 120, pp. 3619–20.

[24] Ts'ai was appointed prefect of Chiang-ning *fu*. See *CPPM* 120, p. 3620.

[25] For a series of censorial indictments against Chang Tun, see *CPPM* 120, pp. 3622–4.

[26] Chang was initially appointed prefect of Yüeh-chou in the ninth month of 1100, but he was soon stripped of his honorary ranks and was banished to T'an-chou the next month. See *CPPM* 120, p. 3627.

further punishment, for his dismissal failed to satisfy his enemies in either the
Censorate or the Remonstrance Bureau. The subject of an unceasing stream
of indictments, Chang Tun was stripped of his honorary rank and ultimately
banished to the far south by imperial fiat in early 1101. As the victim of what
his future biographers would deem retributive justice, Chang received the
same sentence as he had arranged for his own political adversaries during the
factional purges of the 1090s.[27] After his former protégé Ts'ai Ching ascended
to the councilorship in 1102, Chang remained unwelcome at court.[28] Never
to return to the capital, Chang Tun died in 1105, during a period of exile to
the southern fringes of the empire generically known as Ling-nan, just like the
antireformists whom he had systematically purged during his councilorship.[29]

Broken stalemate: The failure of factional conciliation

Chang Tun's dismissal paved the way for Tseng Pu's ascendancy to the councilorship the next month, causing the court to drift closer to the political
center.[30] While formally subordinate to Han Chung-yen as chief councilor of
the right, Tseng (as the *Sung shih* compilers claimed) in fact wielded the reins
of governance, influencing Hui-tsung to implement a policy of bipartisan conciliation.[31] An imperial edict of the tenth month of 1100 officially initiated an
era of centrist politics in that political pragmatism and centrism, not factional
or ideological extremism, would serve as the guiding principles of governance:
"From now on, those managing the government who use distorted scholarship
to be biased and who make unreasonable changes will be publicly rejected."[32]
Aware of the excesses of factional politics during the Hsüan-jen regency and
the personal rule of Che-tsung, Tseng Pu convinced Hui-tsung that the good
of the dynasty required putting an end to the destructive partisanship that had
divided the court for the past thirty years. A bifactional unity government,
presided over by Tseng, was formed to palliate both reformists and their opponents. By co-opting more moderate elements from both sides of the factional

---

[27] For a textual archeology of Chang Tun's "treacherous minister" biography in the *Sung shih*, see the third
chapter of Levine, "A house in darkness."

[28] Chang Tun was even listed prominently in the factional blacklist of 1104. For his "disloyalty as a state
councilor," see *CPPM* 122, p. 3699.

[29] For the documents pertaining to Chang's dismissal, see *CPPM* 120, pp. 3632–3. For the somewhat
ironic circumstances of Chang's exile to Lei-chou and Mu-chou, see *SS* 471, p. 13713.

[30] *CPPM* 130, p. 3939. According to the compilers of the *Sung shih*: "When the reign title was changed to
Chien-chung ching-kuo, those who controlled the state desired to harmonize the men of Yüan-yu and
Shao-sheng; hence the use of the character *chung* (centrality) in the reign title." See *SS* 345, p. 10965.

[31] According to Tseng's biography in the *Sung shih*: "Although Chung-yen held the higher post, he was
weak and pliant, and the majority of decisions were Pu's." See *SS* 471, p. 13715.

[32] P'eng, *T'ai-p'ing chih-chi t'ung-lei* 24, p. 33b.

struggle into the center of court politics, Tseng sought to defuse tensions and alleviate grievances, and to prepare for an eventual return to governance as usual. But traditional historiography has maligned this policy of factional conciliation as a cynical political ploy.[33] Indeed, perhaps the idealistic language of Tseng Pu's public pronouncements had been a calculated political move to position himself to the right of Chang Tun and transform himself into a viable alternative candidate for the councilorship, although in the long run this repositioning maneuver undermined his long-term political survival.

Signaling a break with the preceding age of faction, Hui-tsung decreed that in the coming new year of 1101 the reign title would be changed to Chienchung ching-kuo (Establishing the Mean and Stabilizing the State, 1101).[34] However, Tseng Pu's attempt to palliate political grievances did not meet with any real success beyond the realm of signs and symbols. After thirty years of unending bitterness, factional hatreds were too profound to be conciliated by imperial fiat, and partisan rivalries had been passed on to a new political generation. Leaders of both factions had been forcibly deported to Ling-nan in ever-larger numbers, and such breaches of "civilized" political practice could never be healed. Escalating in fervor ever since the 1070s, political rhetoric and practices had been polemicized and degraded to the point where civility, let alone basic tolerance, could no longer be restored.[35]

While Tseng Pu had co-opted some junior members of the antireform coalition into his court coalition, he could not manipulate them to ensure his own political survival. Soon to be threatened on his right flank, Tseng lacked any effective means of damage control. Once unleashed upon Chang Tun, the pack of conservative remonstrators could not be tamed to spare Tseng Pu. Whatever his current political leanings, he was too deeply implicated in the policies and purges of the 1090s to remain acceptable as a chief councilor in a unity government. Conservative elements at court distrusted Tseng and believed that his conversion to the cause of factional conciliation had been duplicitous. In an indictment of late 1100, an attending censor (shih-yü shih), Chen Tz'usheng, tarred him with the same brush as Chang Tun: "Tseng Pu's character is treacherous and wicked; his heart harbors fiendishness and venom. . . . Since he was recently elevated to the councilorship, he has monopolized state power and slighted his bureaucratic colleagues."[36] The extremism of antireformist remonstrators, expressed in a flood of hostile memorials, would frustrate Tseng

---

[33] Such are the aspersions cast by Tseng's *Sung shih* biography. See *SS* 471, p. 13716.

[34] P'eng, *T'ai-p'ing chih-chi t'ung-lei* 24, pp. 33b–34a.

[35] For a discursive analysis of political rhetoric from 1070 to 1104, see chapter 5 of Levine, "A house in darkness."

[36] See *CPPM* 130, pp. 3939–40.

Pu's attempts at bifactional government, regardless of whether they were motivated by sincerity or by cynicism.[37]

Knowing that his councilorship was being jeopardized by hostile remonstrators, Tseng Pu appealed to Hui-tsung to maintain a conciliatory policy and
to continue to steer a centrist course. In the seventh month of 1101, during
an audience before the throne, he urged the emperor to continue with this
experiment in bipartisanship:

> Your Majesty desires to uphold impartiality and employ centering to break through the
> discourse of factionalism, which will conciliate and unify the empire. Who would dare
> consider this [policy] to be incorrect? Men with biased views and deviant opinions each
> privately favors his own faction. . . . I wish Your Majesty would deeply consider this, and
> not allow either of these factions to succeed. Thereafter, harmony and tranquillity will
> prevail, and the empire will be without incident.[38]

On the surface, Tseng's attempt at consensus building evinced a spirit of
magnanimity, but he was actually moving to silence his most vocal critics on
the right, who had intensified their ad hominem attacks against his councilorship. Throughout 1101, conservative remonstrators presented a united front
of resistance to Tseng Pu's councilorship, seeking his dismissal and replacement. For Ch'en Kuan, Tseng's involvement in the restored reformist regime
of the 1090s, notably his participation in the factionally motivated revision of
official historiography, proved that he was little different from the pernicious
reformist Chang Tun.[39] In the end, Hui-tsung sided with Tseng, ordering
Ch'en Kuan's dismissal from the Remonstrance Bureau, and his demotion to
a regional post in the eighth month of 1101.[40] Several months earlier, Tseng
had also arranged for the summary dismissal of Tsou Hao, another of his most
outspoken adversaries.[41] By purging his most recalcitrant critics from court,
Tseng managed to shore up his sagging position as councilor in the short term,
but he soon met with even more damaging opposition from a former colleague.

---

[37] Most private accounts of the early Hui-tsung reign, written by antireformist sympathizers, consider
that Tseng Pu's move to co-opt conservatives into a bipartisan government was motivated by self-
serving cynicism, and that he was an opportunistic reformist to the core. See Yeh Meng-te, *Pi-shu lu-hua*
[*Ts'ung-shu chi-ch'eng ch'u-pien* 1935–7 ed.] (1135; Peking, 1985) *hsia*, pp. 52–3.

[38] *CPPM* 130, pp. 3942–3.

[39] In 1094, Tseng had served for several months in the Historiography Institute, and had argued for the
inclusion of Wang An-shih's *Diaries* in a newly revised edition of the *Veritable records of Emperor Shen-tsung*
(*Shen-tsung shih-lu*). As chief councilor, Tseng had resisted Ch'en Kuan's calls to recompile these *Veritable
records* to exclude the writings of Wang An-shih. For the text of Chen's attacks, see *CPPM* 129, pp. 3892–
5. For more information on the influence of court factionalism on official historiography, see chapter 3
of Levine, "A house in darkness."

[40] For the text of the court debate over Ch'en Kuan's dismissal, see *CPPM* 129, pp. 3896–8.

[41] *CPPM* 129, p. 3910.

Expedient means: The rise of Ts'ai Ching

Now embattled on both sides, Tseng Pu alienated both conservatives and reformists by maneuvering himself into the councilorship as a conciliating centrist. The precariousness of Tseng's situation was exacerbated by the emperor's vacillation. Beginning his personal rule in the first month of 1101, after the death of Dowager Empress Ch'in-sheng, Hui-tsung increasingly asserted his own prerogatives. He ceased pursuing the politics of conciliation by midyear, when he officially expressed his desire to continue the reform legacy of Shentsung and Che-tsung. After supporting the rehabilitation of the antireformists, and then purging them when they grew obstreperous and unmanageable, Tseng had undermined his credibility with his imperial patron, who now ruled unchecked. By agreeing to another change in the reign title from Chienchung ching-kuo to Ch'ung-ning (Revering the Hsi-ning Era), Hui-tsung symbolically sanctioned a return to the reformist course of the Shen-tsung reign.[42]

Han Chung-yen, the figurehead chief councilor of the left, resented sharing the councilorship with Tseng. Doubting that Tseng Pu's co-optation of the antireformists had been a sincere move to heal political divisions, Han considered his rival to be an unreconstructed reformist to the core and frequently disagreed with Tseng in court debates.[43] Han repeatedly requested retirement from his official duties, but Hui-tsung would not grant him that wish, thereby intensifying divisions within the Council of State.[44] Powerless to move against Tseng from the right, perhaps Han sought to undermine his rival from the left by encouraging the emperor to rehabilitate the reformist Ts'ai Ching. An alternate interpretation of the documentary record is that Tseng Pu, not Han Chung-yen, was responsible for Ts'ai Ching's return to court, by abandoning his efforts at factional reconciliation and casting his lot with the reformists.

Recently cashiered from the metropolitan bureaucracy by Tseng Pu as a "treacherous" and "disloyal" reformist minister, the Fukienese arriviste Ts'ai Ching has become known to history as an exceptionally unscrupulous political operator.[45] Since the primary sources for the Hui-tsung reign have been distorted by moralistic revisionism, historians have found it difficult to describe

---

[42] *SS* 19, p. 363. The Hsi-ning era (1068–77) of Shen-tsung's reign had witnessed the implementation of Wang An-shih's New Policies.

[43] According to one source, "[Han] Chung-yen resented [Tseng] Pu. He said: 'Pu is selfishly plotting to restore Shen-tsung's reforms (*shao-shu*). I have been employed so that he can accomplish this.'" See Hsü, *Sung tsai-fu pien-nien lu chiao-pu* 11, p. 701.

[44] *CPPM* 130, p. 3949.

[45] See Hartman, "A textual history." For a detailed social history of Ts'ai and his extended lineage, see Hugh R. Clark, "An inquiry into the Xianyou Cai: Cai Xiang, Cai Que, Cai Jing, and the politics of kinship," *Journal of Sung-Yuan Studies* 31 (2001), pp. 67–101.

Ts'ai Ching as anything but the apotheosis of ethical and political depravity. His biographers asserted that Ts'ai had distinguished himself from his
reformist colleagues by his naked pursuit of political power throughout his
bureaucratic career, when he served under the ministries of Ts'ai Ch'üeh and
Chang Tun. The compilers of his standard biography asserted that he sacrificed
his reformist principles to accommodate himself to Ssu-ma Kuang during the
debates over the abolition of the New Policies in 1085–6.[46] In what later
historians deemed another expedient volte-face, when Chang Tun had been
rehabilitated as chief councilor in 1094 Ts'ai pressured him to revive the
New Policies, with no questions asked.[47] If the traditional histories are to
be believed, Ts'ai Ching was willing to discard his political principles and
personal integrity to advance his own career at every turn.

According to the conventional interpretation of his rise to the councilorship,
Ts'ai Ching cunningly manipulated Hui-tsung by appealing to the emperor's
insatiable craving for aesthetic pleasure. During his exile from court in 1101,
Ts'ai had been posted to the Yangtze delta as a regional administrator. In
Hang-chou, Ts'ai encountered the eunuch T'ung Kuan, who had been dispatched south to collect scrolls and paintings for the imperial collection.[48]
The compilers of the *Sung shih* allege that by appending persuasive memorials
to T'ung Kuan's daily shipments of art objects to the palace, Ts'ai managed to
win the emperor's unconditional trust. While Tseng Pu and Han Chung-yen
were working at cross-purposes, Ts'ai broke through the bipartisan gridlock
at court, swaying Hui-tsung to appoint him to the councilorship. Sources
indicate that the emperor decided to reappoint Ts'ai to the Council of State
by the end of 1101. Once he was rehabilitated at court, Ts'ai could not be
contained or controlled by those who opposed his rapid ascent to the councilorship. Returning to the capital in an academic capacity in the third month
of 1102, Ts'ai was appointed to his old post of assistant director of the left in
the Department of State Affairs (*shang-shu tso-ch'eng*) two months later.[49] Han
Chung-yen was the first to be pushed aside, earning dismissal from bureaucratic

---

[46] According to Ts'ai Ching's *Sung shih* biography: "When Ssu-ma Kuang controlled governance, he revived
the drafted service policy. [Ts'ai] and his colleagues were compelled [to implement it] within a span
of 5 days, but only Ching was able to entirely change the capital district and the surrounding county
over to drafted service, without a single violation." See *SS* 472, p. 13722. This was the first chapter in
traditional historiography's condemnation of Ts'ai Ching as a "treacherous minister." See Hartman, "A
textual history."

[47] According to the compilers of the *Sung shih*, "[Chang] Tun and [Ssu-ma] Kuang disagreed about the
two corvée policies. Within the span of ten years, Ts'ai Ching had twice faced this issue. But he turned
over his hand, and both councilors relied upon him for assistance. Those who knew him witnessed his
treachery." See *SS* 472, p. 13723.

[48] *SS* 472, p. 13722.

[49] *CPPM* 131, p. 3983.

service even before Ts'ai's return to the capital. But Tseng Pu went down fighting, attempting to salvage his policy of factional conciliation and hoping to forestall the reformist revival that Ts'ai would likely spearhead.

Yet Hui-tsung had already made up his mind about whom to trust. In mid-1102, Ch'ien Yü, a censor loyal to Ts'ai impeached Tseng Pu for having been a turncoat to the cause of reform and for having abetted the conservative opposition.[50] Ultimately, Tseng's efforts to resolve the factional deadlock palliated neither the reformists nor the antireformists, paving the way for his downfall. In the intercalary sixth month of 1102 Tseng was dismissed from court and demoted to a regional post. He was banished (*an-chih*) to Ling-nan three months later.[51] With Tseng Pu joining Chang Tun in banishment, Ts'ai Ching's appointment as chief councilor of the right in the seventh month of 1102 was assured. During the first three years of the Ts'ai Ching ministry, the factional conflict would be resolved through systematic proscription. For most of the remainder of the Hui-tsung reign, Ts'ai established an unchallenged power, inaugurating an era of political stability at court. Perhaps even his detractors would admit that the chief councilor was a masterful political operator, able to build lasting coalitions and to implement radical policy initiatives where his predecessors had failed.

COURT POLITICS AND STATE POLICY DURING HUI-TSUNG'S REIGN

Traditional historians have claimed that Ts'ai Ching manipulated Hui-tsung into dependency and submission, usurping monarchical prerogatives to dictate state policy unchallenged. There are elements of truth to this moralistic interpretation of political history, in which Ts'ai was portrayed as an absolute villain and scapegoated for the collapse of the Northern Sung. He was far from blameless, but he was not culpable to the extreme extent claimed by his biographers. It is undeniable that Ts'ai Ching was responsible for eliminating all of his potential rivals and proscribing an enemies list of hundreds. During his councilorship, the rank and file of officialdom was packed with loyal members of Ts'ai Ching's patronage machine, men who were recruited through an expanded state educational system that replaced the civil service examination system. Through institutional restructuring, the chief councilor granted himself enhanced powers over the workings of the imperial bureaucracy. Reviving the New Policies, Ts'ai transformed the fiscal administration of the state into a mechanism of revenue and resource extraction. Historians have further alleged that the empire was ransacked to construct and stock Hui-tsung's extravagant

---

[50] See Palace Censor Ch'ien Yü's indictment in *CPPM* 130, pp. 3958–9.
[51] *CPPM* 130, pp. 3959–62.

pleasure gardens, sparking several destructive and widespread popular rebellions. According to the traditional historiography, the emperor and his ministers strayed far from the ethical path of governance, thereby precipitating the collapse of the dynasty.

A more nuanced reading of the documentary record of Hui-tsung's reign tells a more complex and ambiguous story, painted in shades of gray. Opponents of reform (the so-called Yüan-yu faction) were not the only victims of the partisan purges, whose victims also included Ts'ai Ching's reformist rivals for the councilorship. Moreover, these factional bans were lifted after only two years, shielding the antireformists from further damage, and allowing their descendants to survive into the Southern Sung. Reformed and restructured educational institutions succeeded in channeling loyal men into the imperial bureaucracy to implement the chief councilor's reforms. But once opposition had been nearly eliminated from the ranks of officialdom, state schools became hotbeds of political protest and dissent, as students memorialized the throne to criticize the Ts'ai Ching ministry and its policies. And the chief councilor's monopoly on political power was neither guaranteed nor unchallenged, since his adversaries pressured the emperor into dismissing Ts'ai from court several times.

Where state policy was concerned, Hui-tsung walked in the footsteps of his imperial predecessors. Like those of the Shen-tsung and Che-tsung reigns, the reform measures of the Hui-tsung reign were initially meant to improve the livelihoods of the poor and dispossessed and to restrain the dominance of socioeconomic elites. Although the revived New Policies became prone to corruption and malfeasance by local officials, similar abuses of power had occurred under the reformist regimes of the 1070s, 1080s, and 1090s. The reform program of the Ts'ai Ching ministry represented a coherent and systematic set of institutional mechanisms, conceived of and administered by the central government, that were designed to uplift public morality and to accomplish the moral revival of the empire. To further complicate the traditional interpretation of state policy, the early twelfth century was notable for the creation and elaboration of a comprehensive network of institutions that promoted social welfare and public health. When viewed from a more balanced perspective, the history of the Hui-tsung reign appears less anomalous, and the Ts'ai Ching ministry appears less cynical, than traditional-minded historians have asserted.

The factional proscriptions of 1102–1104

During the first three years of Ts'ai Ching's tenure as chief councilor, a wave of political proscriptions pushed the political system of the late Northern Sung close to its breaking point. The factional proscriptions of 1102–4 extended the blacklists of the 1090s, banning the political opposition from officeholding and exiling them en masse to the fringes of the empire. In a radical departure from past political practice, Ts'ai ensured that all potential contenders for power were not just marginalized or indicted on an ad hoc basis but were systematically excluded from the imperial bureaucracy.

The political persecution of the so-called Yüan-yu faction (*Yüan-yu tang*) became the first order of business for the new ministerial regime.[52] Ts'ai Ching convinced Hui-tsung that his earlier policy of partisan conciliation had been an abortive failure, and the two openly discussed the imposition of a series of partisan proscriptions. After his first audience with Hui-tsung in the fifth month of 1102, Ts'ai presented an anonymous memorial to the throne denouncing the antireform ministry of the Hsüan-jen regency (1085–93). He urged the immediate investigation of the earlier generation of antireformists, accusing them of committing crimes against the state and of poisoning the glorious memory of Emperor Shen-tsung.[53] In the words of this blanket indictment, the ministers of the Yüan-yu era had "formed a treacherous clique which deluded the emperor" and "committed crimes against Shen-tsung."[54]

Shortly thereafter, Ts'ai presented the emperor with a follow-up memorial in which he denounced the perfidy of the antireformists who had served at court under the Ch'in-sheng regency, accusing them of "uniting into a faction and harboring disloyal discourse."[55] The chief councilor, searching for what he deemed seditious content, initiated a thorough investigation of all the memorials submitted during the interregnum of 1100–1. After Hui-tsung's enthronement, the roads of remonstrance had been unblocked for the purpose of purging Chang Tun and his fellow reformists from court. Just a year later, these solicited memorials had become a political liability for their authors, now that the antireformists had become targets of official persecution yet again. Hundreds of remonstrators were officially categorized into two blocs: the "correct" (*cheng*) and the "wicked" (*hsieh*), which had by now become thinly veiled code words for "reformist" and "antireformist."[56]

In moving to eliminate his rivals for power, Ts'ai Ching manipulated political language to serve his own purposes, widening the ironic gulf between

---

[52] The most thorough scholarly account of the factional proscriptions of 1102–4 is Lo Chia-hsiang, *Pei Sung tang-cheng yen-chiu* (Taipei, 1993), pp. 287–97. Also see Ari D. Levine, "Terms of estrangement: Factional discourse in the early Huizong reign," in *Emperor Huizong and late Northern Song China: The politics of culture and the culture of politics*, ed. Patricia B. Ebrey and Maggie Bickford (Cambridge, Mass., 2006), pp. 131–70.

[53] Immediately after the submission of Ts'ai Ching's first anonymous memorial, a number of antireform sympathizers were dismissed from court. See *CPPM* 121, p. 3641.

[54] *CPPM* 121, pp. 3639–41.

[55] *CPPM* 121, pp. 3641–2.

[56] *CPPM* 123, pp. 3712–22.

political discourse and practice. Only 41 men were deemed to have submitted proper memorials, while a total of 542 men were classified under the rubric of the "wicked," and were subsequently indicted and prosecuted. The investigation and categorization of recent memorials for seditious content paved the way for the mass banishment of antireformist ministers and remonstrators. In this phase of the factional conflict, the members of the conservative coalition were prosecuted for the crime of factionalism itself. The rhetoric justifying the Ch'ung-ning purges promised a solution to the recurrent problem of factionalism. In the utopian language of reformist remonstrators, an everlasting age of ideal governance awaited Hui-tsung in the near future if he committed himself to banishing the Yüan-yu faction from court.

Exiling members of the political opposition to the far south had become an increasingly common practice during the Shen-tsung and Che-tsung reigns. At the beginning of the dynasty, Emperor T'ai-tsu had issued an injunction against the legal execution and corporal punishment of high officials, but this tradition of restraint was honored in the breach by shipping ministerial offenders off to the far south of the empire, where it was hoped they would die.[57] During the 1080s and 1090s, this extreme sentence was pronounced only on a case-by-case basis, after extensive investigation and deliberation; the ranks of the condemned were usually limited to the leaders of a previous ministerial regime. In contrast, the factional purges of 1102–4 were broader in scale, involving the systematic prosecution of hundreds of antireformists, both living and dead.

The first members of the Yüan-yu faction to be persecuted were deceased, having already succumbed to either the advance of old age or the political purges of the mid-1090s. An imperial edict of the fifth month of 1102 stripped dozens of prominent antireformists – including the former chief councilors Ssu-ma Kuang, Lü Kung-chu, Lü Ta-fang, and Liu Chih – of all honors and prestige titles they had received posthumously during the Ch'in-sheng regency.[58] The text of the edict rhetorically exhumed these deceased ministers of the Hsüan-jen regency and defiled their reputations, censuring them for "monopolizing the state, commanding a wicked faction, and slandering the former emperor."[59]

But the deceased leaders of the conservative coalition of 1085–93 were the fortunate ones. Their descendants and kin were permanently banned from service in the metropolitan bureaucracy by a series of imperial edicts; later

---

[57] Liu Tzu-chien (James T. C. Liu), "An administrative cycle in Chinese history: The case of Northern Sung emperors," *Journal of Asian Studies* 21 No. 2 (1962), p. 139.

[58] *CPPM* 121, pp. 3642–6.

[59] *CPPM* 121, pp. 3648–9. According to the *CPPM*, the edict was authored by Tseng Pu, thereby implicating him in the factional proscriptions before his dismissal from court in the intercalary sixth month of 1102.

on, they were even prohibited from entering the gates of K'ai-feng.[60] In 1105 these bans were extended to five circles of kinship, excluding the kinsmen of the "treacherous faction of Yüan-yu" from bureaucratic officeholding, which denied the privileges of elite status to thousands of men.[61] The purges of 1102–4 were intended to systematically uproot the entire antireform faction so that they could never again stage a political comeback. Reformist dominance was achieved by excluding thousands of members of the political opposition from the imperial bureaucracy, perhaps contributing to a sea change in elite orientation from national service to local involvement in the Southern Sung.[62]

In the ninth month of 1102, the first partisan blacklist (*tang-chi*) was imposed, officially proscribing 117 men, naming nearly every official who had served in the highest echelons of the antireformist ministerial regime of the Hsüan-jen regency. Whether dead or alive, every state councilor of the Yüan-yu era (1086–94) was included, as was every prominent academic and remonstrance official.[63] Their blacklisted names were written personally by Hui-tsung in his renowned calligraphy and inscribed into a stele placed outside the Tuan-li Gate of the imperial palace.[64] The ranks of the blacklisted were summarily dismissed from bureaucratic service, and many were placed under strict surveillance and virtual house arrest in their native places.[65] A literary inquisition soon followed, with the banning and destruction of the collected works (*wen-chi*) of such noted antireform literati as Su Shih, Fan Tsu-yü, and Huang T'ing-chien, and the prosecution of Ch'eng I for scholarly heresy.[66] Furthermore, a subsequent imperial edict officially banned Yüan-yu

---

[60] *CPPM* 121, pp. 3652–3, 3661–2.

[61] *CPPM* 121, pp. 3661–4. This ban on officeholding was so thorough that it included the adopted descendants of blacklisted eunuchs.

[62] Both Robert M. Hartwell and Robert P. Hymes have hypothesized that the increasing casualty count of court factionalism was one primary cause of a shift in elite orientation from the Northern Sung to the Southern Sung, causing national officeholding to be perceived as a risky prospect by members of the elite. See Robert M. Hartwell, "Demographic, political, and social transformations of China, 750–1550," *Harvard Journal of Asiatic Studies* 42 No. 2 (1982), pp. 416–25, and Robert P. Hymes, *Statesmen and gentlemen: The elite of Fu-chou, Chiang-hsi, in Northern and Southern Sung* (Cambridge, 1986), pp. 210–18.

[63] Among the twenty-two state councilors named were Wen Yen-po, Ssu-ma Kuang, Lü Kung-chu, Lü Ta-fang, Liu Chih, Liang T'ao, Wang Yen-sou, Fan Ch'un-jen, and Wang Kuei. Among the thirty-five subordinate officials were Su Shih, Fan Tsu-yü, K'ung Wen-chung, Chu Kuang-t'ing, Liu An-shih, Tsou Hao, and Chang Shun-min.

[64] The actual extent of Hui-tsung's involvement in the factional proscriptions is unknown, given the extensive revision of the historical record to portray him as a benevolent monarch led dangerously astray by treacherous ministers. It remains debatable whether the emperor was actively involved in the blacklist or simply manipulated by Ts'ai Ching, but no evidence survives to corroborate either theory.

[65] *CPPM* 121, p. 3661.

[66] *CPPM* 121, pp. 3663–4; 122, p. 3675. This attempt at a burning of the books was unsuccessful, since complete editions of all of these collected works are still extant.

learning (*Yüan-yu hsüeh*) as "heterodox discourse" (*hsieh-shuo*).[67] In the eleventh month of 1102, eighty men whose recent memorials had been categorized as "extremely wicked" were exiled to remote border prefectures. The memorial justifying this decision equated and implicated the antireformists of both regency regimes.[68] By the middle of 1103, the majority of the blacklisted antireformists were on their way to Ling-nan.

As if the widespread fallout from the first blacklist had been insufficient to destroy the antireform coalition, a second edition was promulgated in the ninth month of 1103. Ninety-eight men (nearly half of them deceased) were named as members of the Yüan-yu faction, including every one of Ts'ai Ching's major adversaries and omitting only minor figures who had been included in the first blacklist. Immediately before the second blacklist edict was announced, an anonymous remonstrator (probably Ts'ai himself) implored Hui-tsung to disseminate it throughout the empire:

Even though the court has promulgated their names, going so far as to carve them with imperial calligraphy, this is still not widely known.... [Your servant] implores Your Majesty to promulgate an enlightened pronouncement, arraying all the names of the treacherous faction which have been inscribed with imperial calligraphy upon the Gate of Rectified Ritual, and to disseminate it to the offices of the highest officials in exterior circuits and prefectures, who should set up steles with an inscribed record to manifest [their names] for a myriad generations.[69]

The public humiliation of the antireform coalition, whose names were to be carved into steles prominently placed in every prefectural seat, was supposed to be abject, total, and eternal.[70] These political purges were also extended to the realm of court ritual and to the state cult, as another edict ordered the removal of the images of the Yüan-yu faction from imperially sponsored temples and shrines in the capital and across the empire.[71] The deportation of the conservative coalition continued, and by the beginning of 1104, several hundred former officials had been banished to the southern fringes of the empire.

Issued in the sixth month of 1104, the third round of blacklists was an exercise in overkill, marginalizing an already broken and discredited opposition.

---

[67] *SS* 19, p. 366.

[68] *CPPM* 123, pp. 3722–3.

[69] *CPPM* 121, p. 3668.

[70] A copy of one of these steles remained incised into the surface of a cliff outside Kuei-lin, Kwangsi province, for nine centuries, until its destruction during the Cultural Revolution of 1966–76. See Ch'en Le-su, "Kuei-lin shih-k'o 'Yüan-yu tang-chi,'" *Hsüeh-shu yen-chiu* 61 No. 6 (1983), pp. 63–71. Another stele reportedly remains standing in the Miao autonomous region of Kwangsi.

[71] *CPPM* 121, p. 3671.

Literally carved into stone in steles erected across the empire and upon the west wall of the palace precincts, the names of three hundred and nine former officials were permanently condemned as "wicked" (*hsieh*) and "treacherous" (*chien*).[72] These included the usual suspects from the first two blacklists – the prominent members of the ministerial regime of the Yüan-yu regency and the antireformist remonstrators of the Ch'in-sheng regency. To these names were added two hundred more supernumeraries, drawn from the lower reaches of the bureaucracy.[73] And whereas earlier blacklists had consisted solely of known antireformists, the "treacherous faction of Yüan-yu," the 1104 edition represented the personal enemies list of Ts'ai Ching.[74] It included prominent members of the reform coalition who had either challenged Ts'ai for the councilorship or had refused to join his ministry, among them Tseng Pu and Chang Tun, both of whom were singled out for their "ministerial disloyalty." By including the names of his major reformist rivals on the third and final blacklist, Ts'ai Ching was able to liquidate all potential rivals for power from within his own faction.

With the ranks of the antireformists sentenced to administrative detention in Ling-nan, alongside his former reformist allies, Ts'ai succeeded in consolidating his hold on the councilorship. The partisan proscriptions of 1102–4 represented not only the most extreme phase of the late Northern Sung factional conflict but also its endgame. Ts'ai conclusively ended the struggle for power at court between reformists and their opponents by proscribing the former. And while the antireformists were also being purged from the imperial bureaucracy, silencing the opposition to the New Policies, Ts'ai Ching's ministry had the breathing room to pursue its policy goals unchallenged. Between 1102 and 1104, the chief councilor and his subordinates pushed through a series of domestic and policy initiatives that surpassed those of the Shen-tsung and Che-tsung reigns in scale and ambition. For almost the entire Hui-tsung reign, Ts'ai monopolized the councilorship (with occasional interludes) and established an era of political stability.

---

[72] *CPPM* 122, pp. 3692–9.

[73] The names of many of these men are now difficult to discern, and biographical information on hundreds of them no longer exists. Two Southern Sung commentators have claimed that a majority of the blacklisted did not belong there. According to both Fei Kun and Wang Ming-ch'ing, only seventy-eight (or ninety-eight) "superior men" (*chün-tzu*) were truly members of the "Yuan-yu faction," while the remainder were "wicked men" (*hsieh-jen*). See Fei Kun, *Liang-hsi man-chih* [*Ts'ung-shu chi-ch'eng ch'u-pien*, 1935–7 ed.] (1192; Peking, 1991) 3, pp. 5b–6a; see "Hui-chu hou-lu," in Wang Ming-ch'ing, *Hui-chu lu* (1194; Peking, 1961), pp. 64–5.

[74] Lo Chia-hsiang, *Pei Sung tang-cheng yen-chiu*, pp. 301–5. For a Ming dynasty investigation of the partisan blacklist, see Hai Jui, *Yüan-yu tang-chi pei-kao* [*Ts'ung-shu chi-ch'eng ch'u-pien* 1935–7 ed.] (c. 1570; Peking, 1985). For a detailed analysis of the 1104 blacklist, also see Helmolt Vittinghoff, *Proskription und Intrigue gegen Yüan-yu-parteiganger* (Bern, 1975).

However, one can only surmise whether these proscriptions and prohibitions were ever rigorously or widely enforced. No matter how permanently they had been intended to stand as a warning against factionalism, the factional blacklist steles were demolished in 1106, less than two years after the third series of proscriptions. While many major figures of the antireform coalition (not to mention two reformist councilors) died in exile, many antireformists and their descendants survived into the Southern Sung. Even so, the purges of 1102–4 succeeded in excluding the antireformists from the imperial bureaucracy, and the relaxation did not bring about their rehabilitation. The partisan proscriptions of the Ch'ung-ning era should not be anachronistically conflated with twentieth-century forms of political warfare, but they did represent the most virulent outbreak of factionalism in the history of the Northern Sung.

Political stability: The long-lived ministry of Ts'ai Ching

In many ways, the history of the Hui-tsung reign is the history of the Ts'ai Ching ministry. From any perspective, Ts'ai Ching was indisputably a master politician, able to perpetuate his power against all odds and at all costs. Punctuated by occasional interruptions, he managed to cling to the chief councilorship from 1102 to 1124, longer than any ministerial predecessor from the Shen-tsung and Che-tsung reigns.[75] Sheer persistence and skill are insufficient to explain Ts'ai Ching's longevity at court, which was ultimately dependent upon continued imperial patronage and trust. Yet Hui-tsung's confidence in his long-serving chief councilor was not unconditional. Cosmological portents and political considerations compelled the emperor to dismiss Ts'ai from court on three occasions, but each time Ts'ai managed to claw his way back into power, despite his advancing infirmity and blindness. Even from his pampered exile, the chief councilor continued to exert an influence over court policy from afar, while his trusted subordinates remained in control of the imperial bureaucracy, which was virtually devoid of opposition. Although some of Ts'ai's reform measures were abolished after his repeated dismissals from court, these were invariably revived and expanded upon his return. During the extended councilorship of Ts'ai Ching, the rules of court politics changed irrevocably, as the alternating factional regimes of the late eleventh century were replaced by a stable bureaucratic machine that endured for more than two decades.

After the third factional blacklist was promulgated in 1104, Ts'ai Ching ruled the commanding heights of the imperial bureaucracy, and with no

---

[75] This section draws heavily on John W. Chaffee, "Huizong, Cai Jing, and the politics of reform," in *Emperor Huizong and late Northern Song China: The politics of culture and the culture of politics*, ed. Patricia B. Ebrey and Maggie Bickford (Cambridge, Mass., 2006), pp. 31–77.

discernible opposition he pushed through a comprehensive package of fiscal, educational, and welfare reform policies. Having served as sole councilor for three years, with most of his political and policy initiatives accomplished, Ts'ai recommended the political veteran Chao T'ing-chih (1040–1107) to assist him as chief councilor of the right in the third month of 1105.[76] Several years before, during the Tseng Pu ministry, Chao had been unstinting in his partisan attacks upon the antireformists, and perhaps his promotion was a well-deserved plum for past assistance rendered to Ts'ai Ching. But almost immediately after he was installed Chao apparently sought to dislodge Ts'ai, repeatedly accusing him of treachery and duplicity and refusing to serve alongside him.[77] When Hui-tsung sided with Ts'ai Ching, Chao T'ing-chih was left to dangle, and his desperate requests for dismissal were not granted until the sixth month of 1105. Even if Ts'ai had emerged unscathed from this minor squabble with an outmatched opponent, it demonstrated that his political survival was dependent upon the emperor's continued favor.

While the sweeping political purges of 1102–4 and the revival of the New Policies had been designed to harmonize and stabilize the realm, such idealistic visions of everlasting order were invalidated by a cosmological portent of imminent disaster. When a long-tailed comet was sighted in the first month of 1106, a terrified emperor read the ominous skies above as a sign of heavenly disapproval of Ts'ai Ching, his reform policies, and his ruthless proscription of the opposition. According to the *Sung shih* account, Hui-tsung immediately ordered the destruction of the factional blacklist steles. He issued an edict to restore the banished to the ranks of officialdom and to assure that remonstrance would no longer be censured or obstructed.[78] Soon thereafter, the emperor promulgated an empirewide amnesty, and lifted the prohibitions against the blacklisted members of the Yüan-yu faction. He invalidated two crucial components of the New Policies agenda by ordering the abolition of the land survey and equitable tax measure and the restoration of the Ever-normal Granary system.[79] And for the first time, Hui-tsung signaled his extreme displeasure with Ts'ai Ching by dismissing him from the councilorship. The emperor reappointed Chao T'ing-chih as chief councilor of the right, praising his powers of judgment and conceding to him that "everything that Ching did was just as you said it was."[80]

---

[76] *SS* 351, p. 11094; *CPPM* 131, p. 3985.

[77] For an excerpt from Chao's official obituary (*hsing-chuang*), see *CPPM* 131, pp. 3985–7.

[78] For a condensed account of these events, see *SS* 20, p. 375. The most detailed account of comet-sighting matters is Chao Ting-chih's (1040–1107) official obituary, portions of which were cited in *CPPM* 131, pp. 3985–7. Also see Chaffee, "Huizong, Cai Jing, and the politics of reform," pp. 44–5.

[79] *SS* 20, pp. 375–6.

[80] *CPPM* 131, p. 3986; *SS* 351, p. 11094.

During Ts'ai Ching's first absence from the councilorship, Chao shared ministerial power with Liu K'uei. Like Chao T'ing-chih, Liu had previously been one of Ts'ai's most loyal supporters, but he seized upon the comet sighting to remonstrate against his mentor's policies and to urge the demolition of the blacklist steles.[81] Rewarded with a promotion to vice-director of the Secretariat, Liu K'uei actively collaborated with Chao. But according to his *Sung shih* biography, Liu's arbitrary manner and lust for glory made enemies at court, who charged him with monopolizing state power.[82] These accusations of malfeasance were not lodged by disinterested parties, but by Cheng Chü-cheng and Liu Cheng-fu, two of Ts'ai Ching's loyal lieutenants. Evidence exists that prior to his abrupt departure from court, Ts'ai had ordered his subordinates to memorialize in praise of their factional patron and in support of the New Policies; they ostensibly succeeded in convincing Hui-tsung that Liu K'uei had rashly suspended the reform program and forsaken the legacy of Shen-tsung and Che-tsung.[83] The emperor bowed to pressure, dismissing Liu K'uei from the Council of State at the end of 1106.

After spending a single year in exile, Ts'ai Ching swept back into court at the start of 1107. Little in the way of evidence has survived to document his second term as chief councilor. For reasons unexplained, Ts'ai regained his rapport with Hui-tsung, almost as if he never had left. During the first half of 1107, the emperor entertained his chief councilor in his palace gardens, the two engaged in poetic composition, and Ts'ai was awarded an ornate jade belt as an imperial boon.[84] More important, the Ts'ai Ching ministry moved to expand its educational reform program with implementation of the Eight Conduct (*pa-hsing*) policy in government schools in the sixth month of 1107.[85] To be discussed in detail later, this policy ensured greater ideological conformity among students, and created a fast track for the promotion of loyal men from regional schools into the imperial bureaucracy. To further confirm reformist dominance of the central government, the imperial court relaxed the ban against the now harmless members of the Yüan-yu faction in 1108, granting an amnesty to the majority of them and formally erasing ninety-five names from the blacklists.[86] Presumably, Ts'ai Ching would not have assented to such a move if he believed the discredited antireformists still posed a threat to his

[81] *SS* 351, p. 11109.

[82] *SS* 351, p. 11109.

[83] *SS* 351, p. 11103; Ch'in Hsiang-yeh and Huang I-chou, *Hsü tzu-chih t'ung-chien ch'ang-pien shih-pu* (1881; Taipei, 1964) 26, p. 10b.

[84] *CPPM* 131, p. 3988.

[85] *CPPM* 126, pp. 3791–8.

[86] Pi Yüan, *Hsü tzu-chih t'ung-chien* [*Shih-chieh shu-chü* 1935 ed.] (c. 1880; Shanghai, 1987), pp. 472b, 473a.

unchallenged dominance. In any case, opposition to the chief councilor had been driven outside the bureaucracy or emerged from among activist students at the Imperial University.[87] The only ones who stood any chance of dislodging Ts'ai from court were opportunistic members of his court coalition who could exploit circumstances to depose their patron.

Ts'ai Ching's second fall from power in 1109 was a more overdetermined affair than his first, combining a rebellion in the Censorate with the sighting of another inauspicious portent in the heavens. Shih Kung-pi, who had been awarded the position of censor in chief for enabling Ts'ai to return to court in 1107, along with the censor Mao Chu, repeatedly memorialized the throne to urge the chief councilor's dismissal.[88] In mid-1109, the Imperial University student Ch'en Ch'ao-lao submitted a memorial indicting Ts'ai on fourteen counts of political crimes, including deluding the monarch, promoting a faction, and perverting state policy.[89] Confirming these caustic critiques was the Bureau of Astronomy, which announced the sighting of sunspots that an alarmed emperor interpreted as an omen of celestial disapproval. Now sixty-three years old, Ts'ai Ching petitioned Hui-tsung for retirement on grounds of ill health. Although the emperor granted this request, he also assented to what were extraordinary demands for a dismissed state councilor. Ts'ai was permitted to remain in the capital, to attend court audiences, and to supervise the compilation of the *Veritable records* of Emperor Che-tsung, the authoritative documentary record of the preceding reign.[90] In the meantime, only minor aspects of the reform program were scaled back. Even after he was officially dismissed, Hui-tsung's favorite minister was proving extremely resilient, and his patronage network was still entrenched at court.

What finally persuaded the emperor to remove Ts'ai Ching from court was the sighting of another comet in the fifth month of 1110, after which more hostile memorials reached the throne.[91] Among these was a searing indictment by the censor Chang K'o-kung, who accused Ts'ai of all manner of political corruption and influence peddling: "His power makes all inside and outside court tremble. He has frivolously bestowed honors to corrupt the state, and has seized upon salaries and emoluments to traffic in private favors.... He

---

[87] For a treatment of political activism at the Imperial University, see Thomas H. C. Lee, *Government education and examinations in Sung China* (New York, 1985), pp. 186–92.

[88] Hsü, *Sung tsai-fu pien-nien lu chiao-pu* 12, pp. 747–9; *CPPM* 131, pp. 3990–1.

[89] *SS* 472, p. 13725; *CPPM* 131, pp. 3989–90. It is likely that Ch'en was an obscure figure whose remonstrance was not apt to be heeded by the throne. His role in history was no doubt magnified by the compilers of the standard histories, who sought to incorporate as much condemnatory material as possible into their narrative of Ts'ai Ching's councilorship. See Hartman, "A textual history."

[90] *CPPM* 131, pp. 3989–91. For a textual history of the *Veritable records* of Shen-tsung, Che-tsung, and Hui-tsung, see chapter 2 of Levine, "A house in darkness."

[91] *SS* 20, p. 382.

has promoted petty men to form a faction."[92] Arguing that this dismissed councilor was continuing to meddle with court affairs to disastrous effect, Chang implored Hui-tsung to remove Ts'ai from the capital entirely. Issuing an edict whose condemnatory language echoed that of Chang K'o-kung, the emperor transferred Ts'ai Ching to Hang-chou, where he would serve as prefect, not exactly a hardship assignment.[93]

Filling an enormous void and signaling a major shift in court politics, Chang Shang-ying (1043–1122) ascended to the councilorship in the sixth month of 1110. A rough contemporary of Ts'ai Ching, Chang had served with distinction in two reformist ministerial regimes; he had been a prominent lieutenant of Chang Tun as well as a leading member of the Advisory Council. His name had been added to the Yüan-yu faction blacklist after running afoul of Ts'ai, but his opposition to the chief councilor and his support of the New Policies made him a clear candidate for rehabilitation, not to mention promotion to the Council of State.[94] In an audience with Hui-tsung, Chang Shang-ying voiced his desire to follow the reforming legacy of Shen-tsung even as he thoroughly assessed the success and failure of each reform policy on a case-by-case basis.[95] During his tenure as chief councilor Chang abolished the land survey and equitable tax policy and initiated a series of austerity measures that limited the expansion of social welfare institutions, the state educational system, and imperial clan residences.[96] Chang Shang-ying faced considerable opposition in downsizing the New Policies, and this was used as ammunition against him by those who sought Ts'ai Ching's return to court. The state councilors Ho Chih-chung and Cheng Chü-chung unstintingly attacked Chang for his policy initiatives, as well as for his unsavory personal connections with Buddhist monks and imperial astronomers.[97] Facing increasing bureaucratic opposition, Chang Shang-ying was demoted to a regional post in the autumn of 1111, a move that left the councilorship wide open for Ts'ai Ching's return in the spring of 1112.[98]

Back in Hui-tsung's good graces and with naysayers out of his way, Ts'ai had all the room he needed to dictate state policy yet again. During his third term as chief councilor, Ts'ai Ching not only overturned Chang Shang-ying's limited austerity program but also pursued the expansion of the New Policies, to which he committed large sums from the imperial treasury. Social service

---

[92] SS 472, p. 13725; CPPM 131, pp. 3991–2.
[93] SS 472, p. 13725; CPPM 131, pp. 3992–3.
[94] SS 351, pp. 11096–7.
[95] SS 351, p. 11097.
[96] SS 20, pp. 383–4.
[97] SS 351, p. 11097.
[98] CPPM 131, p. 3979.

and public health institutions were placed under tighter supervision by fiscal intendants and granted a mandate to provide care on the basis of need instead of quotas.[99] The emperor also expanded the number and scope of state-funded schools, and devoted increased largesse to the imperial clan. Perhaps these institutional expansions were linked to the growth of Ts'ai Ching's patronage machine, increasing opportunities for graft among the bureaucratic rank and file.

Moreover, the Cheng-ho era (1111–17) was a time of profligate imperial spending on pleasure gardens and religious patronage, so these institutional enhancements and funding increases were not out of place. The second decade of Hui-tsung's reign represented a definite break with what had gone before, as the emperor shifted his focus from reviving the New Policies to promoting Taoist religion and ritual. Analyzing a set of palace examination questions from the Hui-tsung reign, Peter Bol has asserted that these texts reflected the monarch shifting his attention from fiscal reform to Taoist rulership, "depicting the emperor as the agent producing change in society and nature, eliding the mediating role of government institutions."[100] In a sense, however, Hui-tsung's religious initiatives represented a parallel instance of state penetration into society through the establishment of a centralized hierarchy of regulatory systems, through which a sage-ruler could revive antiquity and morally revitalize the body politic.

Over the course of the 1110s, Ts'ai Ching gradually retreated from active involvement in court policy, allowing his lieutenants to formulate policy and his patronage machine to implement it. According to his *Sung shih* biography, the chief councilor aided and abetted the emperor's efforts to reform court rites and music, to promote Taoist institutions, and to expand the imperial palace.[101] This standard history also recounts that Ts'ai Ching's sons and grandsons were showered with imperial favor (his son Ts'ai T'iao even married an imperial princess), and received appointments as court academics and high officials.[102] At the age of seventy-three, Ts'ai was visibly failing and a spent political force. In the sixth month of 1120, Hui-tsung granted him the last of many requests to retire from official service, thus ending Ts'ai Ching's third term as chief councilor.[103]

[99] *SHY* (1997) *shih-huo* 60, pp. 6a–b. Cited in Chaffee, "Huizong, Cai Jing, and the politics of reform," p. 51.

[100] Peter K. Bol, "Emperors can claim antiquity too – emperorship and autocracy under the New Policies," in *Emperor Huizong and late Northern Song China: The politics of culture and the culture of politics*, ed. Patricia B. Ebrey and Maggie Bickford (Cambridge, Mass., 2006), p. 199.

[101] *SS* 472, p. 13726.

[102] *SS* 472, pp. 13726–7.

[103] *CPPM* 131, pp. 4002–3.

A new generation of loyal men, whose entire official careers were coexten-
sive with the Ts'ai Ching ministry, now controlled the Council of State and
the imperial bureaucracy. Wang Fu (1079–1126) had been an early beneficiary of the Three Halls policy in the early years of Hui-tsung's reign, and
was the leading figure at court in the early 1120s. Maligned in the *Sung
shih* as a "sycophant" (*ning-hsing*), Wang first rose to prominence in 1111 by
attacking Chang Shang-ying, thereby enabling Ts'ai Ching's rehabilitation
and return to the councilorship.[104] But Wang Fu's obsequiousness and loyalty must have been exaggerated; once Ts'ai retired from court and Wang
was sole councilor, he ordered the comprehensive rollback of the New Policies agenda. In 1120–1, Wang abolished the land survey and Three Halls
policies, curtailed the salt and tea certificate programs, and cut back social
welfare institutions.[105] The fortuitous timing of these moves indicates that
the reforms were clearly linked with Ts'ai Ching himself, and their continuation required his presence at court. And given the potent military threats
the Sung empire was facing in the year 1120, Hui-tsung and his ministers
were pressured to make difficult budgetary choices. The New Policies were
consuming revenues that were needed elsewhere, since the imperial court had
to simultaneously prosecute military campaigns on two fronts, quashing the
Fang La rebellion while attempting to reconquer the Sixteen Prefectures from
the Liao.

In the midst of a diplomatic and military crisis, Ts'ai Ching ascended to
the councilorship for a brief fourth term in 1124, replacing Wang Fu. Almost
blind and a virtual figurehead, he relied on his son Ts'ai T'ao to attend to his
governmental paperwork and to compose memorials in his name.[106] The *Sung
shih* alleges that Ts'ai the younger abused his position utterly, dominating
court affairs and siphoning state funds, which eventually led to demands for
his father's dismissal. Under pressure from the state councilor Pai Shih-chung
and the commander in chief T'ung Kuan, Ts'ai Ching retired in disgrace in
the fourth month of 1125, heading south with his family and retinue. But
military and diplomatic events had long since escalated beyond the control
or competence of anyone at court. With the Chin invasion force preparing to
overrun the Sung empire, the feeble former councilor and his reform policies
were blamed for the increasingly desperate predicament of the imperial court.
A thorough assessment of the expansion of the New Policies during the Ts'ai
Ching ministry demonstrates that the collapse of the Northern Sung was by
no means inevitable, even after Ts'ai's reform agenda had been abolished.

---

[104] *SS* 470, p. 13681.
[105] *SS* 470, p. 13682.
[106] *SS* 471, p. 13727.

In their own image: Educational policy and elite orientations

After marginalizing the political opposition with blacklists and banishments in 1102–4, the Ts'ai Ching ministry asserted intellectual control over the imperial bureaucracy through institutional reform. In John Chaffee's analysis, Ts'ai's educational reforms were designed for the purpose of "propagating the reformers' political vision while chastising [Ts'ai's] enemies."[107] By radically restructuring the recruitment of scholar-officials, and by dramatically expanding the state educational system, Ts'ai planned to create a new political elite almost from scratch.[108] His ministry abolished the examination system and replaced it with a unified system of county and prefectural schools, designed both to educate students and to recruit bureaucrats. By employing state-financed schools to force-feed state-approved teachings to prospective officials, his educational reforms sought to ensure political and intellectual uniformity within the bureaucracy. Peter Bol has suggested that the "New Policies educational program sought to inculcate in the literati a vision of an activist state that would transform society."[109] The Ts'ai Ching ministry's educational policies remade political culture in its own image, packing the bureaucratic rank-and-file with loyal reformists. Building a patronage network through institutional reforms, Ts'ai ensured political stability at court while perpetuating his ministry's hold on power.

The educational reforms of the Ts'ai Ching ministry were built upon foundations laid during the Shen-tsung reign by the first generation of reformists. In the early 1070s, the chief councilor Wang An-shih had implemented a reform package that dramatically expanded the state educational system. By establishing state-sponsored schools as bureaucratic recruitment mechanisms, Wang sought to impose intellectual orthodoxy upon the scholar-official elite.[110] Endeavoring to create, mold, and recruit like-minded bureaucrats, Wang restructured the form and content of civil service examinations to emphasize statecraft over poetic composition. Wang An-shih's ministry also enacted the Three Halls policy (*san-she fa*), which divided the Imperial University (*T'ai-hsüeh*) into three grades; graduates of the highest grade, the "Superior College"

---

[107] John W. Chaffee, *The thorny gates of learning in Sung China: A social history of examinations*, new ed. (1985; Albany, 1995), p. 79.

[108] For a balanced treatment of the educational reforms of the Ts'ai Ching ministry, see Chaffee, *The thorny gates of learning* (1995), pp. 77–84. Also see Kondo Kazunari, "Sai Kei no kakyō – gakkō seisoku." *Tōyōshi kenkyū* 53 No. 1 (1995), pp. 25–49.

[109] Peter K. Bol, "Whither the emperor? Emperor Huizong, the New Policies, and the Tang-Song transition," *Journal of Sung-Yuan Studies* 31 (2001), p. 121.

[110] For an analysis of the examination policies of Wang An-shih, see Peter K. Bol, "Examinations and orthodoxies: 1070 and 1313 compared," in *Culture and state in Chinese history: Conventions, accommodations, and critiques*, ed. Theodore B. Huters et al. (Stanford, Calif., 1997), pp. 29–43.

(*shang-she*), were promoted directly into the bureaucratic ranks. Hampered by funding constraints, efforts were made to promote prefectural schools (*chou-hsüeh*) across the empire and to appoint executory-class officials to supervise them. After Shen-tsung's death, Wang An-shih's educational reforms had been overturned during the Hsüan-jen regency. Poetic composition was restored as a requirement for civil service examinations, and the expansion of state-funded schools was brought to a standstill. During Che-tsung's personal rule, composition of poetry was again eliminated as an examination subject, and the restored reform regime of Chang Tun oversaw a slight expansion of the state educational system by extending the Three Halls hierarchy to prefectural schools.[111]

Directly benefiting from Wang An-shih's reforms of the examination system, Ts'ai Ching was a graduate of the *chin-shih* class of 1070, the first civil service examinations to emphasize statecraft skills over poetic composition.[112] Soon after his ascent to the councilorship in 1102, Ts'ai Ching spearheaded a comprehensive educational reform program that dramatically expanded the institutional innovations of the Shen-tsung reign. In the eighth month of 1102, he convinced Hui-tsung that "schools were today's foremost order of business," successfully petitioning the emperor to order the establishment of a unified network of state-funded schools in every county and prefecture of the empire.[113] This state educational system assumed not only the responsibility of educating students but also the political purpose of training and recruiting prospective bureaucrats. Extending Wang An-shih's Three Halls policy from the Imperial University to county schools (*hsien-hsüeh*), each level of the educational system was divided into three "halls" or grades: the "outer" (*wai*), "inner" (*nei*), and "upper" (*shang*).[114] Students advanced from grade to grade and were transferred upward from county school to prefectural school to the Imperial University by passing a regular cycle of examinations and receiving character recommendations from educational officials. Moreover, the Ts'ai Ching ministry entirely abolished the graduated system of civil service examinations. Only graduates of the upper level of the Imperial University were permitted to sit for the *chin-shih* degree examinations; if they passed, they were promoted directly into the lower ranks of the imperial bureaucracy. Once these institutional innovations took hold, establishing an empirewide hierarchy of schools, an entire generation of hopeful scholar-officials was required to work their way up into the bureaucracy through local schools.

Later in the Hui-tsung reign, the Three Halls policy was amended to ensure ideological conformity within state schools and the imperial bureaucracy. Since

---

[111] *SHY* (1997) *ch'ung-ju* 2, p. 7a.

[112] *SS* 472, p. 13721.

[113] See *CPPM* 126, pp. 3978–80; passage cited in Chaffee, *The thorny gates of learning* (1995), p. 77.

[114] *SHY* (1997) *ch'ung-ju* 2, pp. 7b–9a.

the institutional reforms of 1102 did not mint degree candidates quickly enough, Hui-tsung's ministers created a fast-track exception to the Three Halls policy. In 1107, the emperor promulgated an edict implementing the *pa-hsing* (Eight [kinds of virtuous] Conduct) system.[115] Students who were judged to embody the eight cardinal virtues were selected to receive an expedited prebureaucratic education and were rapidly promoted from their home villages into prefectural schools. After spending a year there, these exemplary scholars were permitted to bypass several levels of examinations and were sent up to the upper hall of the Imperial University. After being investigated to determine that they held correct views, they were granted *chin-shih* degrees and official ranks. In practice, moral virtue was equated with ideological conformity, and the *pa-hsing* system was exploited to pack the civil service with men loyal to Ts'ai Ching's ministry. At the same time, students with dissenting words and deeds were investigated and sometimes imprisoned in "self-criticism rooms" (*tzu-sung chai*) where they could reflect upon their ethical transgressions and ideological lapses. Students who received "eight punishments" (also pronounced *pa-hsing2*, but written with a different second character) for immoral (i.e., dissident) behavior were summarily expelled from the Imperial University.[116]

By educating prospective bureaucrats and inculcating them with reformist ideology, the Ts'ai Ching ministry created a new bureaucratic elite and inserted it into the power structure. But educating this new elite was extremely expensive, and supporting a vastly expanded educational system came at high price for the central government. Vast quantities of resources were allocated to finance county and prefectural schools, each of which required salaries and upkeep, as well as students' room and board fees. Regional administrators were ordered to seize uninherited land, as well as to siphon the proceeds from Ever-normal Granaries to endow schools with plots of agricultural land.[117] Across the empire, income from more than one hundred thousand *ch'ing* (nominally, 1.4 million acres) of farmland was reserved for the support of prefectural and county schools, which educated, housed, and fed approximately two hundred thousand students.[118] However, these massive outlays of resources were an invitation to corruption, as local officials were tempted to embezzle education

[115] *CPPM* 126, pp. 3791–5.

[116] Ma Tuan-lin, *Wen-hsien t'ung-k'ao* [*Shang-wu yin-shu-kuan* 1935–7 ed.] (c. 1308; Taipei, 1965) 42, p. 433. Cited in Chaffee, *The thorny gates of learning* (1995), p. 78. Also see Chaffee, "Huizong, Cai Jing, and the politics of reform," p. 47.

[117] See *SHY* (1997) *ch'ung-ju* 2, p. 7b; passage cited in Chaffee, *The thorny gates of learning* (1995), p. 78.

[118] According to John Chaffee's calculations, this figure represented approximately 0.4 percent of the male population of the Sung empire, which totaled around one hundred million in 1100. See Chaffee, *The thorny gates of learning* (1995), p. 78.

funds.[119] Official corruption became so rampant that few protested the abolition of the Three Halls policy in 1121.

To supplement the Imperial University, the Ts'ai Ching ministry established a number of technical and specialty schools in the capital to educate bureaucrats who would be expert in medicine and mathematics, as well as to train masters of painting and calligraphy to serve at the imperial court.[120] Placed under the aegis of the Directorate of Education (*Kuo-tzu chien*), some of these schools were built upon earlier precedents, but several were new creations of the Hui-tsung reign. Each was organized according to the Three Halls model, in which passing examination scores permitted students to progress through three grades and, finally, to graduate with a certificate entitling them to employment by the central government. The continued existence and funding of these institutions were dependent upon the patronage of Ts'ai Ching, and the schools were invariably abolished when he was forced out of the councilorship in 1109 and 1120. The School of Medicine (*I-hsüeh*), reorganized in 1103, was designed to raise the status of imperially licensed physicians to parallel that of Imperial University graduates.[121] Progressing through the Three Halls hierarchy by examination, physicians-in-training mastered the medical canon and received clinical experience, qualifying them to serve in the expanding state medical bureaucracy and government-funded clinics. Founded in 1104, the School of Mathematics (*Suan-hsüeh*) was structured according to the Three Halls system, and channeled experts directly into bureaucratic posts, generally those involving state finance.[122] The brainchild of Hui-tsung, himself a master with the brush, the School of Painting (*Hua-hsüeh*) and the School of Calligraphy (*Shu-hsüeh2*) trained and certified practitioners to serve at court, where they participated in the emperor's collective artistic enterprises.[123] All of these schools were centralized and hierarchical institutions designed to select and train human talent, experts who would serve the empire.

It is possible that the dramatic enlargement of the state educational system encouraged a degree of upward socioeconomic mobility in the short term. But since the Three Halls policy was in force only for twenty years, and was not revived in the Southern Sung, its overall influence was probably negligible.

[119] *SHY* (1997) *ch'ung-ju* 2, p. 18a.

[120] For an institutional history of these technical schools, see Lee, *Government education and examinations in Sung China,* pp. 91–101.

[121] See *SHY* (1997) *ch'ung-ju* 3, pp. 12a–b; passage cited in Asaf Goldschmidt, "Huizong's impact on medicine and on public health," in *Emperor Huizong and late Northern Song China: The politics of culture and the culture of politics,* ed. Patricia B. Ebrey and Maggie Bickford (Cambridge, Mass., 2006), pp. 285–6.

[122] See *SHY* (1997) *ch'ung-ju* 3, pp. 2a–b; passage cited in Lee, *Government education and examinations in Sung China,* p. 94.

[123] See *SHY* (1997) *ch'ung-ju* 3, pp. 1a–2a; passage cited in Lee, *Government education and examinations in Sung China,* p. 100.

In the long term, the expansion of local schools adversely affected the bureaucratic prospects of both preexisting and emerging elites. The sheer numbers of degree candidates increased exponentially in the early twelfth century, but the imperial bureaucracy did not grow commensurately. Hence, competition for bureaucratic posts became more intense as increased numbers of degree candidates vied with one another to fill a more or less fixed number of bureaucratic positions.[124] By expanding the state educational system to ensure the ideological control of officialdom, Hui-tsung's ministers exacerbated the already intense competition for bureaucratic posts. Robert Hartwell and Robert Hymes have hypothesized that the increase in competition for bureaucratic posts encouraged elites to turn away from national officeholding to embrace a localist strategy.[125] While intended to make the *shih-ta-fu* elite shift their orbit ever closer to the state, the Three Halls policy had the reverse effect, contributing to an epochal change in elite orientation from court politics to local involvement.

Institutionalized rapacity: Fiscal policy and revenue extraction

With all traces of opposition eliminated from court, Ts'ai Ching controlled state policy unchallenged.[126] Not long after his appointment as Hui-tsung's chief minister, Ts'ai moved to expand substantially the executive powers of the chief councilorship. Following the precedent of Wang An-shih's Finance Planning Commission (*Chih-chih san-ssu t'iao-li ssu*), which had concentrated ministerial powers over state policy in order to override the resistance to the New Policies, Ts'ai Ching established the Advisory Office (*Chiang-i ssu*) in the seventh month of 1102.[127] On paper, this administrative body was meant to provide a mechanism for the expeditious discussion of policy issues by the Council of State and the chief administrators of a wide range of government organs. Staffed by twenty-seven officials, the Advisory Office was granted oversight over such wide-ranging matters as the imperial clan, supernumerary officials, state expenditure, itinerant merchants, livestock management, and the salt monopoly.[128] Ts'ai himself was appointed director of the office, which he packed with "bright but junior officials loyal to him and without vested

---

[124] See Chaffee, *The thorny gates of learning* (1995), pp. 187–8; also see Peter K. Bol, "The Sung examination system and the *Shih*," review of *The thorny gates of learning in Sung China: A social history of examinations*, John W. Chaffee, *Asia Major*, 3rd series, 3 No. 2 (1990), pp. 151–5.

[125] See Hartwell, "Demographic, political, and social transformations," pp. 420–5, and Hymes, *Statesmen and gentlemen*, pp. 121–3.

[126] This section draws on Chaffee, "Huizong, Cai Jing, and the politics of reform," p. 36.

[127] *SHY* (1997) *chih-kuan* 5, p. 13a; *CPPM* 132, pp. 4009–10. For an extended analysis of the structure and function of the *Chiang-i ssu*, see Lin T'ien-wei, "Ts'ai Ching yü chiang-i ssu," *Shih-huo yüeh-k'an* 6 No. 4 (1971), pp. 137–43.

[128] *SHY* (1997) *chih-kuan* 5, pp. 12a–13b.

interests of their own."[129] Since all dissenting voices had already been forcibly eliminated from court, the Advisory Office served as a conduit through which Ts'ai Ching could practically dictate the formulation and implementation of state policy. Once the office was staffed, Ts'ai expeditiously enacted a coherent program of reforms, which took shape in the second half of 1102. Having served its purpose in expediting the formulation of state policy, the Advisory Office was abolished in the fourth month of 1104, at a time when Ts'ai Ching's control of the bureaucracy had been assured through partisan proscription and factional patronage.[130]

Endeavoring to restore and extend the New Policies (hsin-fa) of the Shen-tsung and Che-tsung reigns, Ts'ai Ching transformed state fiscal policy into a blunt instrument of extortion. Although originally designed to restrain the influence of "engrosser" (chien-ping) landlords and plutocratic merchants, and thereby assist poor farmers, the fiscal reform policies of Wang An-shih had been manipulated since their inception in the early 1070s to squeeze revenue from both the agricultural and mercantile sectors.[131] But during the councilorship of Ts'ai Ching, resource extraction reached astronomical heights. Corrupt regional administrators succeeded in swelling state coffers to the bursting point and along the way feathered their own nests. According to the standard historical accounts, the New Policies initiatives of Hui-tsung's reign drove legions of farmers into bankruptcy and pushed some rural areas to the brink of rebellion. Salt and tea monopolies were substantially expanded to enhance state revenue, strangling the commercial sector of the economy. Hui-tsung's government bled the private sector to enrich the state, and the monarch and his courtiers.

During the Hui-tsung reign, tax revenues from agricultural landholdings were increased through bureaucratic and extrabureaucratic means. The first of the New Policies to be restored was the land survey and equitable tax policy (fang-t'ien chün-shui fa). The measure had been enacted during the early Shen-tsung reign to ameliorate inequalities in the land-tax structure, but had been abolished early in the Hsüan-jen regency. An imperial edict of the seventh month of 1104 revived the fang-t'ien policy, and ordered an empirewide cadastral survey.[132] By uncovering previously untaxed farmlands that had been removed from the registers by engrossing magnates and redistributing them

---

[129] Chaffee, "Huizong, Cai Jing, and the politics of reform."

[130] SHY (1997) chih-kuan 5, pp. 13b–14b.

[131] For an interpretive survey of the New Policies, see Paul Jakov Smith's chapter on Shen-tsung's reign in this volume.

[132] For the text of the edict and the memorial that prompted the implementation of fang-t'ien policy, see CPPM 138, pp. 4155–7; SS 174, pp. 4200–1. Also see Chaffee, "Huizong, Cai Jing, and the politics of reform," pp. 40–1.

to impoverished households, it was hoped that rural socioeconomic disparities could be ameliorated.[133] In practice, however, corrupt local administrators were frequently bribed by large landholders to remove productive lands from the registers. Moreover, small and large landholders were burdened with supplementary fees and taxes assessed on uncovered lands.[134] Acknowledging that "many *fang-t'ien* officials throughout the empire had not realized the court's intentions, stopping at nothing to harass good people," the court issued an edict that effectively abolished the *fang-t'ien* policy in 1110.[135] After attempting to redress the grievances of remonstrators who complained that the tax structure in many rural areas remained inequitable, the court formally abandoned the policy as a dismal failure in 1120.[136]

Starting in the mid-1110s, Hui-tsung and his ministers employed extra-bureaucratic means to orchestrate a massive land grab. A series of eunuch-controlled agencies, such as the Western Wall Bureau (*Hsi-ch'eng so*), were created to confiscate vast swaths of cultivated and fallow lands in several northeastern circuits. In 1116, the eunuch Yang Chien2 established a Public Lands Bureau (*Kung-t'ien so*) in Ching-hsi to seize wastelands and tax-exempt lands, forcing commoners to become tenant farmers and to pay rent for farming these public fields.[137] According to the *Sung shih*, those who dared to resist being ensnared in such an oppressive arrangement were cangued and jailed. After Yang's death, the eunuch Li Yen redoubled Yang's efforts, confiscating more than thirty-four thousand *ch'ing* of land in circuits around the capital.[138] Rent proceeds from these public lands were remitted directly to the emperor for his own personal use. Available evidence indicates that during the Hui-tsung reign, state penetration into the agricultural sector increased revenue extraction and heightened inequalities in the rural socioeconomic order.

In reimplementing the hired service policy (*mu-i* or *ku-i fa*, also known as the service exemption policy, *mien-i fa*), Ts'ai Ching's ministry, as well as local administrators, went overboard in their effort to extract revenue from the rural economy. A cornerstone of Wang An-shih's New Policies, the hired service measure required rural households to make cash payments (*mien-i ch'ien*, or service exemption fees) in lieu of providing state labor service. During

---

[133] *CPPM* 138, pp. 4155–7; *SS* 19, p. 370.

[134] For example, in Hui-ch'ang county (in Ch'ien-chou, Chiang-nan West circuit) the *fang-t'ien* system was used to extract tax revenue at exorbitant rates. See *SS* 174, p. 4202.

[135] For the text of the edict, see *CPPM* 138, pp. 4160–1.

[136] For memorials critical of the unequal implementation of the *fang-t'ien chün-shui fa*, see *CPPM* 138, pp. 4157–9; *SHY* (1997) *shih-huo* 4, pp. 11a–12b. For the text of the edict which abolished the policy, see *CPPM* 138, p. 4165.

[137] *SS* 174, p. 4212; 468, p. 13664.

[138] The Public Lands Bureau and its successor organizations administered lands in Ching-hsi, Ching-tung, Ho-pei, and the capital region. For more information, see *SS* 174, p. 4212: 468, p. 13664–5.

Che-tsung's personal rule, the extractive excesses of the policy had been restrained, at least on paper, as strict limits were imposed on the assessment of the service exemption levy. In 1101, during the Ch'in-sheng regency, the pros and cons of the hired service policy were debated, and regional administrators were permitted a degree of flexibility in implementing labor service policy.[139] However, this period of pragmatic moderation was too ephemeral to result in the full-scale rollback of the hired service policy.

After Hui-tsung began his personal rule, local administrators were no longer granted flexibility in administering the labor service regime. When it was revealed that some district-level officials had adopted the drafted service policy that had prevailed during the Yüan-yu regency, strict central government control of labor service policy was reasserted. In 1102, the hired service guidelines of the Shao-sheng era were reimposed by imperial edict, and local administrators were required to adhere to them.[140] Following the precedent of the mid-1090s, efforts were made in the early years of the Hui-tsung reign to prevent extractive abuses by local administrators eager to enhance revenue collection. In 1103, a ten percent cap was imposed on the assessment of surplus emergency fees (*k'uan-sheng ch'ien*), and fee increases were limited to once in a decade.[141]

It cannot be ascertained from available evidence whether these mandated limitations actually succeeded in curbing excessive revenue extraction by local administrators during the first five years of Hui-tsung's personal rule. But later entries in the documentary record indicate that in the following years, the hired service system became rife with official corruption and abuses. In 1107, an imperial edict scrapped the Shao-sheng-era hired service regulations and revived the Yüan-feng-era rules of the early 1080s.[142] This measure most likely abolished the ten percent rate caps imposed in 1103, freeing local administrators to extract supplementary fees without limit. Incomplete evidence indicates that the hired service system was transformed into a mechanism of revenue extraction, as it had been during the first phase of the New Policies. And a reading of the fragmentary documentary record suggests that in the middle years of the Hui-tsung reign, hired service fees were assessed at astronomical rates, far surpassing the extortionate sums that had been collected during the 1080s. In the northwestern prefecture of Kung-chou2 (Ch'in-feng circuit), the only area for which numerical data survives, the annual collection of service exemption fees had been capped at four hundred strings of cash

---

[139] *SHY* (1997) *shih-huo* 65, p. 72b; *SS* 178, p. 4331.
[140] *SHY* (1997) *shih-huo* 65, p. 73a; *SS* 178, p. 4331.
[141] *SHY* (1997) *shih-huo* 65, pp. 73a–b; *SS* 178, p. 4332.
[142] *SS* 187, p. 4332.

around 1080, but almost thirty thousand strings of cash were collected in 1111.[143] After this report came to light, further moves were made to limit the collection of service exemption fees in the mid-1110s, but the efficacy of these regulations cannot be ascertained.[144] The hired service policy remained on the books until its abolition in 1127, and the admittedly scanty evidence suggests that throughout Ts'ai Ching's tenure it was employed to exact extraordinary sums from the rural economy.

Aside from the service exemption levy, agricultural tax revenues also increased significantly, placing further strain upon farmers. Before Hui-tsung's reign, the central government was responsible for shipping several million bushels of tax grain from the various circuits to the capital. Each circuit in the southeast, the rice bowl of the empire, shipped its quota of tax grain to K'ai-feng, storing the surplus in granaries to compensate for future shortfalls. During the first decade of Hui-tsung's reign, the court ordered the seizure of these surplus reserves from circuit granaries, and the circuits remitted several million strings of cash as tribute to the emperor.[145] Established in 1109, the direct networking (chih-ta wang) system required regional administrators to assume the responsibility for financing annual grain transport to the capital.[146] Indicative of a manifold increase in revenue extraction from the most productive agricultural areas of the empire, circuit granaries were overflowing, with surpluses estimated at millions of piculs a year. It can be argued, then, that the Hui-tsung reign witnessed the extensive taxation and exploitation of the agricultural economy for the benefit of the state treasury and the imperial purse.

Just as changes in state fiscal policy squeezed the agrarian sector dry, government monopolies on salt and tea were transformed into mechanisms for extorting vast sums of revenue from the mercantile sector. State mercantile monopolies fell under the purview of the Advisory Office, through which Ts'ai Ching wielded control over fiscal policy. In 1102, Ts'ai succeeded in expanding the state salt monopoly to include sea salt produced along the southeastern coast.[147] Henceforth, merchants who desired to trade in salt were required to

---

[143] SS 187, p. 4332. Given the fragmentary nature of fiscal data for the Hui-tsung reign, it cannot be known whether the numbers for Kung-chou2 were the most egregious example of extortionate revenue extraction in the empire or were representative of a general empirewide pattern.

[144] SHY (1997) shih-huo 65, pp. 74b–75b.

[145] SS 175, p. 4257.

[146] SS 175, pp. 4255, 4258–9.

[147] SHY (1997) shih-huo 24, p. 37b. The most thorough English-language study of the Sung salt monopoly is Edmund H. Worthy, Jr., "Regional control in the Southern Sung salt administration," in Crisis and prosperity in Sung China, ed. John W. Haeger (Tucson, Ariz., 1975), pp. 101–41. For an exhaustive treatment of the salt certificate policy during the Hui-tsung reign, see Tai I-hsüan, Sung-tai ch'ao-yen chih-tu yen-chiu (1957; Taipei, 1982), pp. 318–30. Also see Ch'i Hsia, Sung-tai ching-chi shih (Shanghai, 1987–8), pp. 841–9.

buy salt certificates (*yen-ch'ao*) from the government, which they could then
exchange for salt when they arrived in the salt-producing areas of the southeast.[148] To dramatically enhance the revenues it could collect from the salt
monopoly, the central government continually printed additional salt certificates. Since older certificates were devalued, more certificates were required to
buy the same quantity of salt.[149] To make matters worse, the price of salt was
subject to continual inflation, reducing the mercantile sector to near penury.
According to the purple prose of Ts'ai Ching's biography in the *Sung shih*: "Rich
merchants and great magnates, who had once wielded hundreds of thousands of
strings of cash, suddenly were transformed into drifters and beggars. . . . Some
went so far as to drown or hang themselves."[150] Although such impressionistic
evidence can be somewhat discounted, it can be conclusively proved that the
new salt certificate policy quickly became a phenomenally successful source of
state revenue. In the five months from the twelfth month of 1103 to the fourth
month of 1104, more than five million strings of cash entered state coffers as
a result of the expansion of the sale of salt certificates.[151] State revenues from
the salt monopoly have been estimated at ten to twenty million strings per
annum in the middle of the Hui-tsung reign.

Paralleling the expansion of the salt monopoly in the southeast, the tea
monopoly was similarly enlarged to increase state revenue and to enrich the
emperor and his ministers.[152] In 1102, soon after his ascent to the councilorship, Ts'ai Ching memorialized to revive the state monopoly over southeastern
tea and prohibit growers and merchants from participating in private trade.[153]
Ts'ai argued that the abolition of the tea monopoly in seven southeastern circuits had resulted in the loss of millions of strings, and that this long-dormant
source of wealth could be tapped.[154] Under the new southeastern tea monopoly,
prospective tea merchants were required to buy tea certificates (*ch'a-yin*) from

[148] *SS* 182, pp. 4444–5.

[149] *SS* 181, p. 4425; 182, p. 4445.

[150] *SS* 471, p. 13723.

[151] This figure represented the total revenues collected through the sale of salt certificates in Shan-hsi and Ho-pei circuits. *SHY* (1997) *chih-kuan* 27, pp. 18a–b.

[152] Since the 1070s, a parallel state tea monopoly had existed in Szechwan. For an analysis of state interven-
tion in the Szechwanese tea trade in the Northern and Southern Sung, see Paul J. Smith, *Taxing heaven's storehouse: Horses, bureaucrats and the destruction of the Sichuan tea industry, 1074–1224* (Cambridge, Mass., 1991).

[153] For an extended treatment of the expansion of the state tea monopoly during the Hui-tsung reign, see Ch'i, *Sung-tai ching-chi shih*, pp. 788–94.

[154] Ts'ai claimed that annual state proceeds from the southeastern tea monopoly (in Ching-hu, Chiang-
nan, Huai-nan, Liang-che, and Fu-chien circuits) had once exceeded 5 million strings of cash, but had
recently dwindled to only 500,000 strings. For a précis of his memorial to revive the monopoly, see *SS* 184, p. 4502.

the central government and then to use these certificates to buy tea from tea-growing households.[155] Like the salt monopoly, the tea monopoly quickly became a phenomenally profitable means of revenue extraction. Estimates of annual central government revenue from the sale of tea certificates in the mid-1110s range from two million to four million strings of cash.[156] A substantial portion of these profits – more than one million strings of cash per annum – were remitted directly to Hui-tsung's imperial purse. Moreover, the *Sung shih* alleges that a million strings a year were redirected to Ts'ai Ching and his coterie as an imperial boon.[157] The southeastern tea monopoly became a tool of mercantile exploitation, and a large share of the profits were siphoned off by the emperor and his courtiers.

Thus, the fiscal policies of the Hui-tsung reign and the Ts'ai Ching ministry entailed the active state penetration of the agricultural and commercial economy for the sole purpose of revenue confiscation. During the early twelfth century, the extraction of revenues from the private sector far surpassed the already sizable sums exacted by the reformist ministries of the Shen-tsung and Che-tsung reigns. Initially designed to ameliorate socioeconomic inequalities in the countryside, the land survey and hired service policies were abused by corrupt local administrators, who employed these fiscal reforms as instruments of revenue extraction. In the final stage of their implementation, these two elements of the New Policies enabled the central government to parasitically feast upon the rural economy. Moreover, the expansion of the salt and tea monopolies seems to have crippled the commercial sector of the economy and to have impoverished once wealthy merchant households. Bureaucratic expansion into the commercial sector diverted untold millions of strings of cash into the state treasury, and into the private purses of the emperor and his ministers. As Paul J. Smith has concluded, "By the twelfth century the Song state was draining far more out of the economy than it was contributing to society as a whole.... Economic activism degenerated into confiscatory taxation."[158] Primarily extractive rather than ameliorative, the fiscal policies of Hui-tsung and his ministers continued the growth of state activism that had begun during Shen-tsung's reign. Led by Ts'ai Ching, Hui-tsung's reformist

---

[155] SS 184, p. 4502.

[156] According to the *Sung shih*, between 1112 and 1116, revenues from the tea monopoly totaled more than ten million strings of cash. See SS 184, p. 4503. According to Li Hsin-ch'uan, annual revenues during the Cheng-ho era (1111–17) could be estimated at 4 million strings of cash. See Li Hsin-ch'uan, *Chien-yen i-lai ch'ao-yeh tsa-chi* [*Shih-yüan ts'ung-shu* 1914 ed.] (c. 1202 *chia* volume, 1216 *i* volume; Taipei, 1967) *chia* 14, pp. 197–8.

[157] SS 184, p. 4303.

[158] Smith, *Taxing heaven's storehouse*, p. 313.

councilors promoted intrusive policies that expanded revenue collection and resource extraction far beyond the wildest dreams of Wang An-shih and his immediate successors.

Imperial munificence: The expansion of social welfare institutions

The reform policies of Hui-tsung's reign and Ts'ai Ching's ministry were not motivated solely by exploitation, extraction, and embezzlement. Some elements of the reform program evinced an idealistic concern for the public welfare, and these aspects of state policy have been overlooked by many historians of the period. Portions of the vast sums that flowed into the imperial treasury as a result of extractive fiscal policies were not misappropriated by Hui-tsung and his courtiers, but were redistributed to fund institutions that benefited some of the neediest subjects of the empire. The Hui-tsung reign was a time of massive state intrusion into the agrarian and commercial economy, but it also witnessed state intervention in local society through the creation of a centralized and comprehensive system of regulatory institutions that actively promoted public health and welfare.

Rather predictably, the *Sung shih* compilers accused Ts'ai Ching and his subordinates of exploiting and corrupting this network of charitable institutions and of squandering large sums from the imperial treasury.[159] Even if this were the case, the creation and expansion of state welfare programs remained an integral aspect of the ministry's package of reforms. In funding and establishing poorhouses, charitable clinics, and paupers' cemeteries, the emperor's public pronouncements manifested a reforming zeal.[160] In the words of one imperial edict, social welfare institutions such as "clinics, poorhouses, and cemeteries were the chief aspect of humane governance," and were established for the relief of the destitute of the empire.[161] Each of these relief institutions had precedents in the latter half of the eleventh century but had never before been integrated into a single, wide-ranging, state-funded system. By improving the well-being of the emperor's subjects, these centralized networks of institutions were intended to revitalize popular morality, and ultimately to usher in an era of perfect governance. Building upon foundations laid during the Ying-tsung and Shen-tsung reigns, these institutions represented the high point of direct state involvement in social welfare in early modern Chinese history. While little

[159] *SS* 178, p. 4339.
[160] This section draws heavily upon Goldschmidt, "Huizong's impact on medicine and on public health," pp. 275–323. For a treatment of public welfare institutions, see Hugh Scogin, "Poor relief in Northern Sung China," *Oriens Extremus* 25 No. 1 (1978), pp. 30–46.
[161] *SHY* (1997) *shih-huo* 68, p. 134b.

hard quantitative evidence exists, it is probable that establishing and supporting these empirewide networks of social welfare and public health institutions
required substantial sums. More important, the empirewide implementation
of these programs indicates that during Hui-tsung's reign the state was making, in John Chaffee's assessment, "a radical assumption of responsibility for
at least minimum levels of welfare for the poor."[162]

One of the first actions of Ts'ai Ching's Advisory Office was to mandate
the establishment of Security and Relief Clinics (*An-chi fang*) in every prefecture and county of the empire in the eighth month of 1102.[163] Three
years later, similar institutions were established within the capital, completing an empirewide state-funded hospital network.[164] During the late T'ang
and the late eleventh century, a limited network of poorhouses had served as
all-purpose social welfare institutions for providing food, shelter, and health
care. The charitable clinics of the Hui-tsung reign were apparently modeled
after a similar institution that had been founded as a public-private partner-
ship by Su Shih in 1089, when he was serving as prefect of Hang-chou.[165]
The functional specialization of state-funded hospitals, maintained separately
from relief homes, represented an institutional innovation of the early twelfth
century. Providing free medical services to the poor and needy, these charitable clinics were established to save the lives of commoners and to combat the
spread of epidemics. Patients were divided into separate wards according to the
severity of their illness to minimize cross-contamination, and salaried physicians were awarded bonuses on the basis of positive treatment outcomes.[166]
Paralleling the Security and Relief Clinics, a network of Public Pharmacies
(*Ho-chi chü*) was extended beyond the capital into the circuits in 1103, and was
designed to provide physicians with medications, thereby serving as a second
line of defense against contagion.[167] During the Hui-tsung reign, the central
government actively involved itself in public health as no prior Sung monarch
had done, assuming a new mandate to control the outbreak of epidemics.[168]

Founded with a similar reforming mission as charitable clinics, poorhouses
(*chü-yang yüan*) were the second system of social welfare institutions to be
implemented by the Ts'ai Ching ministry. Hui-tsung and his councilors' efforts

---

[162] Chaffee, "Huizong, Cai Jing, and the politics of reform," p. 41.

[163] *SHY* (1997) *shih-huo* 68, pp. 129a–130a.

[164] See *SHY* (1997) *shih-huo* 68, pp. 130b–131a; passage cited and translated in Goldschmidt, "Huizong's
impact on medicine and on public health," p. 295.

[165] See *SHY* (1997) *shih-huo* 68, p. 130a; passage cited in Scogin, "Poor relief," p. 32. For an assessment
of Su Shih's promotion of social welfare as prefect of Hang-chou, see Ronald C. Egan, *Word, image, and
deed in the life of Su Shi* (Cambridge, Mass., 1994), pp. 108–27.

[166] *SHY* (1997) *shih-huo* 68, pp. 131b–132a.

[167] *SHY* (1997) *chih-kuan* 27, p. 17b.

[168] Goldschmidt, "Huizong's impact on medicine and on public health," p. 295.

to establish a system of relief homes across the empire followed earlier precedents in government aid to the destitute. During the late T'ang, an attenuated system of poorhouses had existed on paper, and small-scale homeless shelters had been established in K'ai-feng during Ying-tsung's reign. What differentiated the new social welfare institutions from their predecessors was the systematic and pervasive manner in which they were implemented. In 1103, the Poorhouse policy (*chü-yang fa*), first enacted by Che-tsung in 1098, was extended from the capital to the prefectures. Managed by prefects and county magistrates, the relief homes were to be financed with property confiscated from subjects who died without heirs and from interest and fees from the Ever-normal Granary system; they operated on a permanent rather than ad hoc basis.[169] The chief beneficiaries of government aid were the most vulnerable members of society: the elderly (over 50 years of age), widows, orphans, and abandoned children. Aid grants of food were calculated to match local conditions and the age of the recipient, and sometimes included such items as fuel, clothing, bedding, and cooking utensils.[170] Elderly aid recipients were conferred special grants of food and clothing according to a sliding scale, and wet nurses were employed to care for infants. To wrestle with bureaucratic paperwork and to handle increased caseloads in winter, the imperial court appointed petty officials to render extra clerical assistance.

But given the unwieldy nature of the poorhouse system and its sweeping mandate, not to mention the piles of money and the warehouses of goods it was intended to disburse, maladministration became endemic. Like the land survey and hired service measures, the Poorhouse policy had been established to improve the lives of the lower socioeconomic orders, but soon fell prey to the corruption of local officials. In 1105 the first reports of fraudulent record keeping and the padding of welfare rolls were submitted in memorials to the throne from several regional administrators.[171] Responding to these repeated allegations of malfeasance, an imperial edict dispatched additional officials to ensure that aid truly reached the needy rather than be pocketed by officials or the undeserving.[172] When investigators could not prevent embezzlement, austerity measures to decrease official opportunities for graft were imposed under the short-lived councilorship of Chang Shang-ying. An edict of 1110 imposed aid quotas to shrink the number of relief homes in the capital (these quotas were later relaxed) but left the poorhouse system outside the capital

---

[169] *SHY* (1997) *shih-huo* 68, pp. 128b, 130a–b.

[170] Such presumably nonessential items as mosquito nets were sometimes issued to poorhouse residents, a fact seized upon and amplified by this policy's critics. See Scogin, "Poor relief," pp. 33–4.

[171] *SHY* (1997) *shih-huo* 68, pp. 131a–b.

[172] *SHY* (1997) *shih-huo* 68, p. 132a.

virtually untouched.[173] In the succeeding years, more reports of official mismanagement reached the court, which inevitably responded by reiterating social welfare regulations and sending investigators to ferret out corruption on the local level. Nevertheless, the temptation to exploit the system for the benefit of administrators and undeserving aid recipients was too great ever to be countered by central government regulation and surveillance. In 1120 the imperial court announced cutbacks in aid that revived the Yüan-feng social welfare regulations, forbade relief administrators to dispense anything but food and money to their charges, and set a minimum age of sixty years for the receipt of assistance.[174] The expanding ranks of the urban homeless were hardest hit by the curtailment of state aid institutions, and the Poorhouse policy was revived in 1125 and remained on the statute books until the end of the Northern Sung.[175] From the attenuated documentary record that survives, it is difficult to ascertain whether this system of relief homes benefited the destitute or those who exploited it.

The third social welfare system to be expanded during the early Hui-tsung reign was the Pauper's Cemetery (*Lou-tse yüan*), established in the second month of 1104.[176] This policy followed a precedent of the Shen-tsung reign, when prefects were ordered to establish public cemeteries for the destitute and to subsidize their funeral rites.[177] Providing proper burials for the indigent and itinerant, these cemeteries were places of interment for the urban poor who had died without family or far from home. And like the charitable clinics established two years earlier, paupers' cemeteries were meant to control the spread of contagious diseases in areas of high population density. Prefects were instructed to set aside a plot of infertile public land to serve as a cemeter and to provide a grave site, a coffin, and a carved headstone for each person to be buried.[178] A central shrine was to be constructed in each cemetery to provide a place for ancestral sacrifices to be made. Hugh Scogin has suggested that paupers' cemeteries served as a means of ensuring the proper performance of death ritual in an increasingly mobile, commercialized, and urbanized society in which kinship connections were fraying.[179]

The New Policies enacted by the Ts'ai Ching ministry have traditionally been described as tools of economic exploitation, which enhanced the powers

---

[173] *SHY* (1997) *shih-huo* 68, pp. 133b–134a.
[174] *SS* 178, p. 4340; *SHY* (1997) *shih-huo* 68, pp. 137a–b.
[175] *SHY* (1997) *shih-huo* 68, p. 137b.
[176] *SHY* (1997) *shih-huo* 68, p. 130b.
[177] *SS* 178, p. 4339.
[178] *SHY* (1997) *shih-huo* 68, pp. 130a–b.
[179] Scogin, "Poor relief," pp. 35–7; Goldschmidt, "Huizong's impact on medicine and on public health," pp. 302–3.

of the state at the expense of society. Even worse, the reform measures gave rise to widespread corruption among local administrators as well as among state councilors. The ministry's fiscal reforms were indeed prone to official malfeasance, and similar abuses no doubt occurred in the empirewide network of social welfare institutions, at least within the poorhouse system. Yet despite its widespread corruption and abuses, the system did provide a safety net for the destitute and dispossessed, and aid must have reached some deserving recipients in county seats and prefectural capitals.[180] In the official pronouncements which justified these institutional innovations, Hui-tsung portrayed himself as an exemplar of humane governance and as rightful heir to the reforming legacy of Shen-tsung and Che-tsung. By expanding the central government's mandate to provide for the health and welfare of the poor, the emperor was demonstrating his benevolence and munificence toward his subjects, especially toward the urban poor, who benefited most from these policy initiatives. Furthermore, social welfare and public health policies were clearly conceived as part of a comprehensive system to improve the lives of the dispossessed, sparking a chain reaction that would result in nothing less than the moral resurgence of the empire. Through a series of institutional innovations, Hui-tsung took an active interest in improving the health, education, and welfare of his subjects, creating programs that surpassed those of his imperial predecessors in scope and ambition. Through its fiscal policies, the imperial bureaucracy extracted large sums from rural commoners, but only a fraction of these revenues were redistributed to the urban poor through poorhouses, charitable hospitals, cemeteries, and dispensaries. Examining the creation and expansion of social welfare and public health institutions provides a corrective to the interpretation that the emperor and his ministers presided over a dark and dissolute age. During the reign of Hui-tsung and the Ts'ai Ching ministry, idealism and munificence coexisted in ironic tension with corruption and cynicism.

Recovering the satellites: Expanding imperial clan institutions

Aside from the urban poor, Hui-tsung's court extended its munificence to a less numerous, albeit burgeoning, group of beneficiaries: members of the imperial Chao clan.[181] Through the establishment of the Advisory Office in

---

[180] Recent excavations in Shan-chou2 (Yung-hsing-chün circuit) show that local paupers' cemeteries provided interment for indigent commoners and soldiers well to the west of the capital. See San-men-hsia-shih wen-wu kung-tso tui, comp., *Pei Sung Shan-chou lou-tse-yüan* (Peking, 1999). Cited in Goldschmidt, "Huizong's impact on medicine and on public health," p. 303.

[181] This section draws heavily on John Caffee's comprehensive treatment of imperial clan institutions during the Hui-tsung reign. See John W. Chaffee, *Branches of heaven: A history of the imperial clan of Sung China* (Cambridge, Mass., 1999), pp. 95–111.

1102, Ts'ai Ching granted the Council of State broad powers to formulate and implement policies to reform imperial lineage institutions. As John Chaffee has explained the situation, in the second century of the house of Chao, "the clan was undergoing a fundamental reorientation resulting from a crisis in numbers, money, and attenuated genealogical relationships."[182] Entire branches of the lineage now fell outside the five circles of mourning (*wu-fu*), and an increasing number of clansmen were dispersed outside official residences in the capital, left to their own devices. Thousands of sixth- and seventh-generation imperial descendants required state support through living allowances, which were placing an ever-greater burden upon state finances, even as many clansmen were moving outside state control.

In a memorial of late 1102, Ts'ai Ching urged Hui-tsung to address clan problems, and to provide clan members with enhanced access to education, examinations, and bureaucratic posts that would allow some clansmen to better support themselves.[183] For Ts'ai, a true believer in large-scale institutional initiatives, the solution was to grant land to imperial kinsmen beyond the five circles of mourning. In the Western Capital of Lo-yang and the Southern Capital of Ying-t'ien-fu, local administrators were ordered to assemble unsold parcels of government land (*kuan-t'ien*), a portion of rent proceeds from which would be used to endow and support residences for imperial clan members.[184] Called Halls of Extended Clanship (*Tun-tsung yüan*), these residential centers in secondary capitals were intended to house those without official stipends, and their numbers grew to several hundreds. Seven years later, not long before Ts'ai Ching's second fall from the councilorship in 1109, an imperial edict abolished the halls and evicted clan members, claiming they were incorrigible and lawless.[185] Perhaps these institutions were regarded as revenue drains, like the state-funded educational and social welfare institutions that were scaled back around the same time by Chang Shang-ying's short-lived councilorship.

After Ts'ai's return to office in 1112, the Halls of Extended Clanship were revived and augmented, coinciding with a parallel expansion of the state's mandate to provide for the health, education, and welfare of commoners. Over the Cheng-ho era, a time of profligate spending by Hui-tsung's court, residential complexes grew at an astounding rate, fueled by funding from large swaths of public lands. In 1120, the two secondary clan centers in Lo-yang and Ying-t'ien-fu encompassed a total of more than twenty thousand rooms,

---

[182] Chaffee, *Branches of heaven*, p. 91.
[183] See Chaffee, *Branches of heaven*, p. 97; also see *SHY* (1997) *chih-kuan* 20, pp. 34a–b; *ti-hsi* 5, pp. 15b–18a.
[184] Chaffee, *Branches of heaven*, p. 98.
[185] See Chaffee, *Branches of heaven*, p. 100; also see *SHY* (1997) *chih-kuan* 20, pp. 35a–b.

and were endowed with 44,000 *ch'ing* (615,560 acres) of fields.[186] Chaffee
estimates that approximately ten thousand clan members resided in the halls,
meaning that each resident was supported by proceeds from more than 4
ch'ing (about 56 acres) of land.[187] When compared to the government school
system, which housed and educated more than one hundred and sixty thousand
students on a land endowment of 100,000 *ch'ing*, this represented a generous
subsidy indeed. With the growth of the Halls of Extended Clanship in the
second half of Hui-tsung's reign, the central government earmarked resources
and established institutions to support even distant branches of the imperial
clan in perpetuity. In creating these secondary clan centers, Hui-tsung and his
ministers inadvertently ensured the continuation of the imperial lineage, not
to mention a pool of potential imperial heirs, after the fall of K'ai-feng, when
the emperor and almost all of his kinsmen residing in the capital were taken
prisoner by the Jurchen.[188]

COURT CULTURE AND STATE RELIGION DURING HUI-TSUNG'S REIGN

In traditional historiography, the extravagance of Hui-tsung's court and his
promotion of religious Taoism are interpreted as harbingers of dynastic collapse. Hui-tsung is portrayed as a Neronic figure who frolicked in his sumptuous pleasure gardens while the empire was impoverished, eventually succumbing to rebellion from within and conquest from without. And by declaring the
Divine Empyrean sect of Taoism to be the state religion, the emperor invited
the moralistic scorn of later historians. Moreover, the standard accounts of the
reign accuse Ts'ai Ching and his ministerial colleagues of distracting Hui-
tsung from the responsibilities of rulership by feeding his appetite for luxury
and encouraging his ritual and religious initiatives. It has been alleged that the
political stability of Ts'ai's ministry was ensured by Hui-tsung's complicity and
collusion, which allowed the councilor and his cronies to remain entrenched
in near-absolute power for two decades. No assessment of Hui-tsung and his
times would be complete without detailing the exceptional extravagance in
which the emperor lived, and without documenting his imperial ritual and
religious initiatives. The source materials for these aspects of Hui-tsung's reign
are extremely fragmentary, as well as riddled with the moralistic biases of their
compilers, who sought to portray the emperor's court as depraved and dissolute.
And since the authors of these colorful anecdotes were prone to exaggeration,
it is difficult to corroborate any of these narratives. To summarize this limited

---

[186] See Chaffee, *Branches of heaven*, p. 101; also see *SHY* (1997) *chih-kuan* 20, pp. 37a–b.
[187] Chaffee, *Branches of heaven*, p. 101.
[188] Chaffee, *Branches of heaven*, pp. 110–1.

corpus of source texts without echoing their condemnatory tone poses an even greater challenge.

An embarrassment of riches: Imperial extravagance and corruption

Extracted through fiscal reforms and extraordinary levies, unknown millions in state revenues were directly channeled into the imperial purse to finance the emperor's aesthetic pursuits. Some regions of the empire were ransacked to build and stock a park for Hui-tsung's personal enjoyment. After a critical reading of the documentary record, it is undeniable that Hui-tsung's reign witnessed imperial extravagance on a grand scale. Whether this extravagance was a cause of dynastic decline, as traditional historiography asserts, is another story altogether.

As a young prince, Hui-tsung was "learned in painting, skilled in brush-work, and delighted in ancient vessels and mountain rocks."[189] During his period of exile in Hang-chou in 1101, Ts'ai Ching trafficked with palace eunuchs and commoners who were well positioned to satisfy the emperor's aesthetic cravings. At the beginning of his reign, Hui-tsung had dispatched the eunuch T'ung Kuan (d. 1126) to Hang-chou and Su-chou, the wealthiest cities of the Chiang-nan region, to confiscate exceptional examples of paint-ing and calligraphy for the imperial collection. It is alleged that by attaching memorials and missives to these shipments, Ts'ai won Hui-tsung's uncondi-tional trust, rising to the councilorship from exile. T'ung also quickly rose into the emperor's inner circle as a result of his successful procurement mis-sions, which forcibly acquired and manufactured art objects and curios to fill Hui-tsung's palaces. In early 1102, Fabrication Bureaus (*Tsao-tso chü*) were established in Hang-chou and Su-chou, under T'ung Kuan's direction, to fab-ricate luxury items for the palace.[190] Large-scale protoindustrial operations, these workshops employed several thousand workers, who crafted jewels and textiles from confiscated materials. Luxury items produced in these imperial ateliers filled a vast new complex of palace halls, the ironically named Palace of Extended Blessings (*Yen-fu kung*). Built in 1114, this parklike compound extended the palace precincts to the north.[191] The complex encompassed more than thirty buildings, surrounded by a pleasure park, including an artificial mountain and lake, that housed thousands of birds and beasts.[192] If the standard

---

[189] For an excerpt from Ts'ai T'ao's personal memoirs of Hui-tsung, see *CPPM* 128, p. 3881–4.

[190] Ch'en Pang-chan et al., *Sung-shih chi-shih pen-mo* (1605; Peking, 1977) 50, p. 505.

[191] Patricia Ebrey, "Taoism and art at the court of Song Huizong," in *Taoism and the arts of China*, ed. Stephen Little and Shawn Eichman (Chicago, 2000), p. 100.

[192] Ch'en et al., *Sung-shih chi-shih pen-mo* (1977) 50, p. 506. For an anecdotal account of Hui-tsung's palaces, see Hung Mai, *Jung-chai sui-pi* (1180–1202; Shanghai, 1996) *san-pi*, 13, pp. 568–9.

histories are to be believed, this great construction project only whetted the emperor's appetite for extravagance.

In the following years, a wide-ranging transshipment network was established for the sole purpose of conveying strangely shaped rocks, exotic trees, and flowering plants to stock Hui-tsung's pleasure gardens. In 1105, two Imperial Provisioning Bureaus (*Ying-feng chü*) were established in Hang-chou and Su-chou to stock the emperor's palaces with trees and flowers. These bureaus were supervised by the commoner Chu Mien (1075–1126), who had been lifted from regional obscurity to join Ts'ai Ching's ministerial retinue.[193] Late in Hui-tsung's reign, Chu's name would be included among the "Six Felons." Initially, Chu Mien's shipping operation was comparatively small in scale; before 1110, he seized exotic plant specimens from private gardens and presented them as tribute several times a year.[194] By the year 1111, the operation had grown too large and complex to keep secret, as fleets of riverboats were required to ship the volume of specimens to the capital. Employing thousands of laborers, the Provisioning Bureaus procured and transported huge quantities of rocks and flowers up the Grand Canal to K'ai-feng. The entire operation was unofficially referred to as the "flower and rock network" (*hua-shih wang*), and its jurisdiction expanded throughout the south and southeast of the empire.[195] The transportation network required an enormous outlay of capital; according to one anecdotal account, it cost several hundred thousand strings of cash to ship a single boulder from the Liang-che region to the capital.[196]

By the middle of the 1110s, the network extended throughout the empire. From Fu-chien to Szechwan to the Kuang-nan circuits, the extraction of resources by imperial fiat began to affect the regional economies of the southeast, southwest, and far south.[197] Merchant vessels and grain boats were pressed into service to join the tribute convoys, which proceeded to the capital inland, up the Grand Canal, or by sea. District and prefectural administrators were required to finance the shipment of these rocks and flowers from their own local treasuries, which were emptied by these extraordinary exactions. Battalions of

[193] *CPPM* 128, p. 3882; Ch'en et al., *Sung-shih chi-shih pen-mo* (1977) 50, p. 505. In 1100–1, when Ts'ai Ching had been banished to Chiang-nan, he built a Buddhist temple hall in Su-chou, enlisting the apothecary Chu Ch'ung to supervise the project. Ts'ai was so pleased with Chu Ch'ung's work that he enlisted his son Chu Mien to join his retinue. When Ts'ai was appointed chief councilor, he placed Chu in charge of the Provisioning Bureau. For Chu Mien's biography, see *SS* 470, p. 13684.

[194] *SS* 470, p. 13684.

[195] According to the memoirs of Ts'ai T'ao, "All the flowers and stones were moved in several tens of ships, forming a fleet (*wang*)." See *CPPM* 128, pp. 3883–4.

[196] Ch'en et al., *Sung-shih chi-shih pen-mo* (1977) 50, pp. 505–6.

[197] *CPPM* 128, p. 3884. For an extended treatment of the "flower and rock network" and the construction of Hui-tsung's pleasure park, see James M. Hargett, "Huizong's magic Marchmount: The Genyue Pleasure Park of Kaifeng," *Monumenta Serica* 38 (1988–9), pp. 11–15.

troops were enlisted to accelerate the progress of the treasure fleet to K'ai-feng. Furthermore, the expansion of the "flower and rock network" allegedly wreaked havoc on the economic infrastructure of the empire. According to one anecdotal source, "some of the articles of tribute were so excessively large that river dikes had to be breached, bridges destroyed, and city walls bored through" in order to transport them to the capital.[198] Perhaps resorting to hyperbole, Ts'ai Ching's second son, Ts'ai T'ao, claimed that exotic flowers were shipped to the palace so expeditiously – in a matter of three or four days – that their scent remained fresh.[199] The logistics of the system were simply staggering: available sources indicate that colossal boulders, some fifty feet high, were swiftly shipped to the capital by thousands of conscript workers. These organized depredations incurred popular resentment, and the network temporarily ceased operations in 1120, after the outbreak of a major popular rebellion.[200] Fang La and his comrades took up arms to protest the tax burdens that had impoverished the peasants of Liang-che circuit, the area most directly affected by the "flower and rock network." After T'ung Kuan led more than a hundred thousand troops to suppress the uprising in 1121, the Provisioning Bureaus were revived, and the transshipment network resumed operations.[201] Under the continued direction of Chu Mien, goods were transported to the capital, until K'ai-feng's supply chain was interrupted by the siege in 1126.

Laboriously transported to the imperial capital, these cargoes of flowers, trees, and stones were assembled within the palace precincts to form Hui-tsung's personal pleasure park. Supervised by the eunuch Liang Shih-ch'eng (d. 1126), another of the "Six Felons," work on the project began in 1118 and was completed four years later, possibly delayed by the Fang La rebellion.[202] The garden originally referred to as the Myriad Years Mountain (*Wan-sui shan*), was formally renamed Northeast Marchmount (*Ken-yüeh*) in 1122, after a Taoist verse that described an auspicious convergence of cosmic forces.[203] The park occupied an area several miles in circumference in the northeastern quadrant of K'ai-feng and ostensibly displaced entire residential neighborhoods.[204] Its centerpiece was an artificial minimountain that towered nearly one hundred feet high, assembled from boulders transported

---

[198] *CPPM* 128, p. 3883.

[199] *CPPM* 128, p. 3883.

[200] Ch'en et al., *Sung-shih chi-shih pen-mo* (1977) 50, p. 507.

[201] *CPPM* 128, pp. 3886–7. Fang La's rebellion is treated in greater detail later.

[202] Wang, *Hui-chu lu* 2, p. 72; Ch'en et al., *Sung-shih chi-shih pen-mo* (1977) 50, p. 508.

[203] *CPPM* 128, pp. 3877–9. The name *Ken-yüeh* (Northeast Marchmount) derived from the verse "The Northeast Marchmount is aligned in the vacuous empyrean." The mountain peak at the center of the park represented Emperor Hui-tsung, a "high center" whose divine influence ordered the world.

[204] Hargett, "Huizong's magic Marchmount," p. 16.

by the "flower and rock network." Representing the world in microcosm, the *Ken-yüeh* garden was stocked with exotic flora and auspicious fauna. Its visitors proceeded through scenic vistas of streams, cliffs, and groves that replicated the natural splendors of the empire. After an expenditure of enormous sums from the imperial treasury, the park survived for only four years. It was plundered and disassembled in the early months of 1127. During the Jurchen siege, the desperate citizens of the besieged capital tore down its wooden structures for firewood, and its stones were used as shot for catapults.[205]

According to the traditional interpretation, the wealth of the empire was plundered to support Hui-tsung in sumptuous splendor. Moreover, the construction of these palace halls, ritual complexes, and pleasure gardens was financed through fiscal reforms and outright confiscation, provoking some subjects of a restive empire into rebellion. Doubtless, these grand projects undermined the regime of the emperor and his "felonious" ministers. And arguably these initiatives drained the imperial treasury at a time when these financial resources were most needed for the defense of the empire against Jurchen aggression. However, it must not be forgotten that Hui-tsung's grand projects were not motivated by mere aestheticism; even the *Ken-yüeh* pleasure park formed part of a unified ritual and ideological program. By recreating the rites and music of antiquity, and by building a splendid pleasure garden, the emperor sought to harmonize his realm with the primal forces of the cosmos. Despite these noble hopes, ritual and ideology alone could not bring peace and prosperity to Hui-tsung's empire, even as it was threatened from without and collapsed from within.

Harmonizing the realm: Reinventing ritual and promoting Taoism

In their postmortem search for the causes of the fall of the Northern Sung, historians past and present have condemned Hui-tsung and his advisors for undertaking a radical transformation of court ritual and state religion, which began almost as soon as Hui-tsung became monarch.[206] Starting in 1104, the first of a series of "wonder-workers" or "occult masters" (*fang-shih*) persuaded Hui-tsung to initiate a series of sweeping changes to the sacrificial ceremonies of rulership. The rites and music of antiquity were reconstituted to ensure the longevity of the monarch and the perpetual glory of the dynasty. During the

---

[205] SS 85, p. 2102.

[206] This section draws heavily on Patricia Ebrey's study of Hui-tsung's promotion of and involvement in religious Taoism. See her "Taoism and art," pp. 94–111. For a well-documented overview of Hui-tsung's promotion of Taoism, also see Sun K'o-k'uan, *Sung-Yüan tao-chiao chih fa-chan* (Taichung, 1965), pp. 93–122.

Cheng-ho era (1111–17), alternative ideologies were adopted to legitimize the Sung court and delegitimize its alien adversaries, as Divine Empyrean (*Shen-hsiao*) Taoism was proclaimed the official state religion. Seeking enhanced sanction for his reign, Hui-tsung portrayed himself as the incarnation of a powerful deity in the loftiest reaches of the Taoist heavens. In an unprecedented and exceptional development, monasteries and temples across the empire were endowed with imperial funds to perform Taoist rites that were designed to glorify Hui-tsung as a god-emperor.[207]

Traditional historians of the Northern Sung claimed that Hui-tsung's involvement with Taoism and experimentation with ritual had hastened the end of the dynasty. They compared him to Emperor T'ang Hsüan-tsung (r. 712–56) of the T'ang dynasty, drawing parallels between the tragic historical circumstances of their respective reigns. A Taoist patron and believer, as well as a great supporter of the performing and occult arts, Hsüan-tsung was accused of negligence that provoked the An Lu-shan rebellion, which nearly destroyed the T'ang dynasty. Ever since the "Calamity of Ching-k'ang" and the fall of the Northern Sung, historians have condemned Hui-tsung's promotion of religious Taoism as an aberration and abomination and have blamed Taoist practitioners for leading the emperor down the road to ruin. To be fair, only some of the blame was laid upon the emperor's shoulders; Ts'ai Ching and his clique were accused of using Taoism as a smokescreen to distract Hui-tsung from active involvement in government. Historians who accepted the Neo-Confucian (*Tao-hsüeh*) movement's privileged claims to doctrinal supremacy situated Taoist religion beyond the pale of their exclusionary conception of ethical and political thought. Furthermore, they portrayed the emperor's efforts to reconstruct and revive the rites and music of antiquity as quixotic and overwrought attempts to bring peace and prosperity to a dynasty in collapse.

These deviations from Confucian forms of political culture antagonized those who constructed the historical narratives of Hui-tsung's reign. Reading past the moralistic and teleological biases of standard historiography, it is clear that Hui-tsung's imperial religious and ritual initiatives represented essential aspects of his reign. From our contemporary historiographic perspective, the fall of the Northern Sung resulted largely from strategic and diplomatic blunders, not from any ideological heterodoxy of the emperor and his court establishment. Despite the tragic consequences of his border and military policies, Hui-tsung was convinced that his policies were reviving his empire and

---

[207] See Chao Shin-yi, "Huizong and the divine Empyrean palace temple network," in *Emperor Huizong and late Northern Song China: The politics of culture and the culture of politics*, ed. Patricia B. Ebrey and Maggie Bickford (Cambridge, Mass., 2006), pp. 338–48.

permanently ensuring its integrity. Through his patronage of Taoist religion
and his ritual reform program, the emperor was seeking to harmonize his
realm with Heaven and Earth, thereby ensuring the eternal dominance of the
imperial house of Chao. In a time of conflict with hostile border regimes, he
and his political and religious advisors sought to assert Sung hegemony and
legitimacy and to proclaim its possession of heavenly favor.

Early in his reign, Hui-tsung encouraged the formulation of a new court
ritual program, which was developed to revive the rites and music of the ancient
sage-kings.[208] In the political culture of the imperium, the performance of rites
and music served as a means of morally and spiritually legitimizing a dynasty.
Moreover, proper performance of ritual was part of the proper performance
of emperorship, ensuring that a monarch embodied the ethical and cosmic
principles of rulership. Ritual officials and practitioners at Hui-tsung's court
claimed that court music had declined and decayed in recent centuries. Tones
and scales, they argued, required rectification in order for the emperor to rival
the achievements of the ancient sage-kings by bringing everlasting harmony
to the empire. All the while, the Sung was contending with the border regimes
of Liao and Hsi Hsia for hegemony, and ritual served as an affirmation of Sung
legitimacy.

In 1105, the occult master (*fang-shih*) Wei Han-chin, Hui-tsung's personal
chaplain for a time, designed a new system of musical intervals, based on
the lengths of the emperor's fingers, called *ta-sheng* ("great brightness").[209]
Reviving classical designs from the Eastern Chou, a new set of bells was cast
to play the scales Wei had invented and was employed in conjunction with a
newly improvised regimen of imperial rites. Under Wei's influence, Hui-tsung
ordered the casting of nine colossal ritual tripods (*ting*), which required the
astronomical amount of more than two hundred thousand catties of copper.[210]
These vessels symbolized sovereignty over the subcelestial realm, "providing
a direct line of communication with the utopian age of the sage-kings."[211]
The emperor employed the nine tripods in imperial sacrifices that revived
and recreated the royal rites of antiquity. Keyed to resonate with an elaborate
correlative cosmology, they involved offerings to such mythic and ancient
exemplars of rulership as the Yellow Emperor and the Duke of Chou, whom
Hui-tsung sought to emulate.

---

[208] For a brief treatment of Hui-tsung's ritual program, see Sturman, "Cranes above Kaifeng," pp. 40–1.

[209] *SS* 128, pp. 2998–9; *CPPM* 135, pp. 4098–4100. For more on Hui-tsung's reform of rites and music,
see Joseph S. M. Lam, "Huizong's dashengyue: A musical performance of emperorship and officialdom,"
in *Emperor Huizong and late Northern Song China: The politics of culture and the culture of politics*, ed. Patricia
B. Ebrey and Maggie Bickford (Cambridge, Mass., 2006), pp. 395–452.

[210] *CPPM* 128, pp. 4102–3.

[211] Sturman, "Cranes above Kaifeng," p. 43.

Sacrificial vessels were part of a larger effort to restore the rites and music to the standards of antiquity. A voracious collector of antiquities, Hui-tsung noted the disparity in design between the bronzes currently used at court and those unearthed from ancient Shang and Chou dynasty tombs. Proclaiming in an edict of 1113 that "We are distant from antiquity, and the transmission of rites has been lost," the emperor officially stated his intention to bring court rituals into line with classical norms.[212] He formally established the Ritual Regulations Office (*Li-chih chü*) within the Department of State Affairs to standardize ritual protocol. Until its abolition in 1120, bureaucrats attached to the service reformed nearly every aspect of imperial rites and music; correlative cosmology influenced the casting of new vessels, the redesign of altars, and the sequence of activities. Accordance with ancient models guaranteed the correct sacrificial ceremonies. By extension, Hui-tsung's ritual reforms would ensure the legitimacy and supremacy of the Sung dynasty's challenge to the competing claims of border empires.

Coinciding with the emperor's revival of ancient rites and music, massive palace building projects were also undertaken as ritual stages. First, a colossal palace pavilion, called the Palace of Nine Movements (*Chiu-ch'eng kung*), was constructed to house the newly cast bells and tripods. In 1106, each circuit intendant was required to purchase and ship large quantities of timber to the capital, and tens of thousands of laborers were conscripted to erect an imposing new sacrificial hall, based on classical precedents, called the Hall of Enlightenment (*Ming-t'ang*).[213] Constructed in the final years of his reign, Hui-tsung's *Ken-yüeh* pleasure park was designed to rectify a perceived imbalance of cosmic forces within the capital, and to ensure the integrity and survival of the polity.[214] Essential elements of Hui-tsung's transformation of imperial ideology and practice, each of these grand ritual projects was either informed by the ideas of religious Taoism or initiated by Taoist practitioners.

In the annals of imperial history, Hui-tsung's reign earned notoriety as an era in which religious Taoism was extolled to the exclusion of Confucianism and Buddhism. However, the penultimate emperor of the Northern Sung was not the first of his lineage to have granted imperial patronage to Taoist religion. Both T'ai-tsung (r. 976–97) and Chen-tsung (r. 997–1022) also employed the arcane and wondrous talents of *fang-shih*. Emperor Chen-tsung committed imperial funds to the construction of a grand Taoist temple in K'ai-feng, which was probably the most elaborate building project sponsored by any Sung monarch, even exceeding Hui-tsung's construction programs.

---

[212] *CPPM* 134, pp. 4061–2.
[213] *CPPM* 125, p. 3766; *SS* 101, pp. 2473–4.
[214] For a study of Hui-tsung's pleasure park, see Hargett, "Huizong's magic Marchmount," pp. 1–48.

According to one anecdotal account, the emperor's infatuation with things Taoist began before his enthronement, when he was visited in his dreams by one of several divinities, who nominated him as the bearer and reviver of teachings of the *Tao*.[215] Perhaps encouraged by these nocturnal visions, Hui-tsung began to grant imperial patronage and subsidies to Taoist religious institutions and practitioners. In 1103 the emperor received Liu Hun-k'ang (1035–1108), the twenty-fifth patriarch of the Highest Purity (*Shang-ch'ing*) sect, and granted him funds for the reconstruction of his sect's central monastery at Mao-shan.[216] A Taoist ritual hall and a splendid monastic residence were built within the palace precincts, where Liu engaged in a series of sacrificial ceremonies for the preservation of the empire. Soon thereafter, he and other Mao-shan practitioners were granted imperial titles. When the abbot returned to his own monastery in Liang-che circuit, he continued to correspond with Hui-tsung, encouraging him to reject Buddhism and embrace Taoist teachings for the sake of the imperial polity.[217]

In 1107, state promotion of Taoist religion began in earnest, when an imperial edict mandated that Taoist clergy would be superior in rank and honors to their Buddhist counterparts.[218] The following year, Hui-tsung promulgated an edict establishing an examination system for Taoist clergy to receive state accreditation, with an annual recruitment quota set at seventy priests. Also in 1108, the emperor ordered that copies of the liturgy for Rites of the Golden Register (*chin-lu chiao*), a ceremony of fifth-century origin, be distributed to temples in every prefecture and county to ensure the preservation of the imperial house of Chao. In the words of Michel Strickmann, the codification and performance of these rites would "ensure that a vast chorus of supplication in the interests of the Sung would rise from every corner of the empire."[219] Increasingly, preexisting Taoist liturgies and institutions were employed to advance and articulate the interests of the empire and its ruler.

By sponsoring the first printed edition of the *Taoist canon* (*Tao-tsang*), Hui-tsung established himself as a preeminent figure in the revival and dissemination of Taoist textual learning in the Sung.[220] He was following in the footsteps of Emperors T'ai-tsung and Chen-tsung, who had sponsored the collection and

---

[215] *CPPM* 127, pp. 3841–2.

[216] *CPPM* 127, pp. 3839–40. For a brief history of the Shang-ch'ing school of Taoism, see Isabelle Robinet, *Taoism: Growth of a religion*, trans. Phyllis Brooks (Stanford, Calif., 1997), pp. 115–20.

[217] Ebrey, "Taoism and art," p. 99.

[218] *CPPM* 127, p. 3817.

[219] Michel Strickmann, "The longest Taoist scripture," *History of Religions* 17 Nos. 3–4 (1978), pp. 343–4.

[220] The most authoritative English language study of the *Taoist canon*'s compilation is Strickmann, "The longest Taoist scripture." Also see Judith M. Boltz, *A survey of Taoist literature: Tenth to seventeenth centuries* (Berkeley, Calif., 1987), pp. 5–6; and Edward L. Davis, *Society and the supernatural in Song China* (Honolulu, 2001), pp. 34–44.

collation of Taoist texts into a small number of hand-copied exemplars of an earlier version of the *Taoist canon*.[221] In 1114, Hui-tsung ordered that Taoist scriptures should be searched out and forwarded to the capital, where invited religious scholars would begin collating them into an authoritative canonical edition.[222] Submitted texts included earlier Taoist scriptures from the *Ling-pao* and *Shang-ch'ing* schools, as well as scriptures of more recent provenance from the Celestial Heart (*T'ien-hsin*) and other religious movements that had originated and developed in the Northern Sung.[223] Also included were Divine Empyrean (*Shen-hsiao*) texts dating from Hui-tsung's own reign and several canonical commentaries and hymn collections attributed to the emperor himself. Completed in 1116, the manuscript of the *Taoist canon of the longevity of the Cheng-ho reign* (*Cheng-ho wan-shou Tao-tsang*) was engraved and printed in Fu-chou, Fu-chien circuit, between 1118 and 1120. For scholars who have focused on the textual foundations of Chinese religion, this publishing project represented Hui-tsung's greatest contribution as an imperial patron of Taoism.

Meanwhile, the expanded state educational system became a conduit for channeling Taoist scholars into court positions, and a medium for the promotion of Taoist learning. Instructorships in canonical Taoist texts were established at the Imperial University and at prefectural schools, and a separate examination track was created to award civil service degrees to Taoist adepts.[224] Regional administrators were ordered to employ the Eight Conduct (*pa-hsing*) system to recruit Taoist scholars and practitioners into official posts. A number of classical Taoist texts became part of the curriculum of government schools in 1118, and early Taoist sages were incorporated into the state cult. For a brief time, Taoist learning was placed on an equal footing with Confucian education, and supported with state resources, a fact that no doubt rankled the Neo-Confucian historians of the Hui-tsung reign.

While he was promoting Taoist textual scholarship, the emperor became entangled with wonder-workers and ritual experts. Both the spirit medium Wang Lao-chih and the faith healer Wang Tzu-hsi temporarily won his favor before their hasty departures from court. By far the most influential practitioner was the Thunder Rites (*lei-fa*) master Lin Ling-su, who arrived at court from coastal Wen-chou (Liang-che) in 1114.[225] When Lin gained access to

[221] Boltz, *Survey of Taoist literature*, p. 5.

[222] *CPPM* 127, p. 3819.

[223] For more information about Celestial Heart Taoism, see Davis, *Society and the supernatural*, pp. 21–4, and Robert Hymes, *Way and byway: Taoism, local religion, and models of divinity in Sung and modern China* (Berkeley, Calif., 2002), pp. 26–8.

[224] *CPPM* 127, pp. 3825–7.

[225] For a study of the relationship between Hui-tsung and Lin Ling-su, see Miyakawa Hisayuki, "Rin Reiso to Sō no Kisō," *Tōkai Daigaku kiyō: Bungaku bu* 24 (1975), pp. 1–8. See also Strickmann, "The Longest

the emperor, the Sung court's promotion of religious Taoism reached unprecedented heights. Originally invited to K'ai-feng to participate in the compilation of the *Taoist canon*, Lin brought with him a new set of revelations and
claimed supremacy over all previous forms of religious Taoism. He purported
to possess exclusive access to the uppermost layer of the heavens, the Divine
Empyrean, a realm that superseded all other levels in the celestial hierarchy.[226]
The new *Shen-hsiao* scriptures foretold that an age of purification was imminent, and that the world would soon be transformed through the perfection
of the true *Tao*, embodied by a sage-ruler. When summoned before the throne
in 1117, Lin Ling-su proclaimed that Hui-tsung himself was the incarnation of the Great Emperor of Everlasting Life (*Ch'ang-sheng ta-ti*), the eldest
son of the Jade Emperor and the brother of the current governor of Heaven,
the Sovereign of Ch'ing-hua (*Ch'ing-hua wang*).[227] Moreover, these imperially
sanctioned shrines, and the deities worshipped therein, were decreed to rank
above all local temples and shrines. As Robert Hymes explains the significance
of this association of Hui-tsung and a powerful Divine Empyrean deity, "Lin
and the emperor had managed, for the only time in Sung history, to establish
a living emperor as a god, and a very high god indeed."[228]

   The patronage of *Shen-hsiao* Taoism was not limited to court and capital, but
radiated out from the capital to affect local religious institutions and practices,
at least for a short time. An edict of 1117 mandated the establishment of
Divine Empyrean temples in every prefecture of the empire for the worship
of the Great Emperor of Everlasting Life, ordering the forcible conversion and
Taoicization of Buddhist temples in areas without Taoist temples.[229] Hui-
tsung's glorification of Taoism – and his self-glorification through Taoism –
coincided with prohibitions against Buddhist institutions and practitioners.
Ten years earlier, Buddhist monks had been formally declared to be inferior to
Taoist priests in the eyes of the state, and an edict of the seventh month of 1117
urged Buddhist monks empirewide to convert voluntarily to Taoism.[230] In the
first month of 1119, the emperor officially prohibited Buddhist monasteries

---

   Taoist scripture." Davis, *Society and the supernatural*, pp. 61–6, examines the role of spirit mediums
   during the Sung.
[226] For an analysis of the earliest Divine Empyrean liturgical and ritual texts dating from this period of
   the Hui-tsung reign, see Boltz, *Survey of Taoist literature*, pp. 26–30.
[227] *CPPM* 127, pp. 3819–20.
[228] Hymes, *Way and byway*, p. 120.
[229] *CPPM* 127, pp. 3823, 3836. Michel Strickmann and Patricia Ebrey have both found evidence in
   Southern Sung memorabilia literature (*pi-chi*) that Buddhist temples were indeed converted to Taoist
   temples around this time. See Strickmann, "The longest Taoist scripture," p. 246 n. 44; Ebrey, "Taoism
   and art," p. 104.
[230] See Pi, *Hsü tzu-chih t'ung-chien* (1987) 93, p. 485c; passage cited in Strickmann, "The longest Taoist
   scripture," p. 346.

and temples from enhancing or expanding their landholdings, buildings, or financial assets. Henceforth, Buddhist monks would be known as "clergy of virtue" (*te-shih*), and were ordered to dress and behave like Taoist clergy (*tao-shih*); in another official name change, Buddhist temples and monasteries (*ssu2*, *yüan*) were renamed as Taoist temples and monasteries (*kung3*, *kuan2*).[231]

Rather than banning Buddhism outright, these changes subsumed it within the structure and nomenclature of Taoism, in what Strickmann deemed a "rectification of names" rather than a "wholesale persecution of the Sangha."[232] Most likely, Hui-tsung's promotion of Taoism represented an attempt to delegitimize the Liao, whose state religion was Buddhism, just as the Sung was embroiled in efforts to wrest back the disputed Sixteen Prefectures from the Khitan.[233] In any case, the forced Taoicization of Buddhist institutions met with criticism from the heir apparent and from the chief councilors Ts'ai Ching and Chang Shang-ying. Most of these official prohibitions were overturned early in 1120, not long after Lin Ling-su was forced to return to Wen-chou in order to placate his critics at court.[234] But Lin's departure did not mean that Hui-tsung severed his connection with the Divine Empyrean sect, nor did it mean that the court ceased to patronize religious Taoism. Supplanting Lin Ling-su, his affiliate Wang Wen-ch'ing (1093–1153) led the imperial Taoist establishment in the early 1120s and completed several major textual and liturgical projects before his sudden departure from court.

By granting imperial patronage to Taoism, Hui-tsung was not radically breaking with dynastic tradition, since both T'ai-tsung and Chen-tsung had pursued some similar projects, albeit on a much smaller scale. When imposing restrictions upon Buddhist clergy and religious institutions, Hui-tsung's short-lived policies did not match the persecutions of the late T'ang. Still, they were extreme moves for a Sung monarch whose predecessors had supported institutional Buddhism. His attempted subordination of Buddhism into a state-approved hierarchy of Taoist deities and temples was an unprecedented development. As a patron and practitioner of Taoism, Hui-tsung transformed state religion and transformed court ritual in radical ways, even if his initiatives were ultimately abandoned.

Furthermore, Hui-tsung's promotion of Taoism represented a departure from the reforming legacy of his immediate imperial predecessors, Shen-tsung and Che-tsung. The majority of the emperor's religious and ritual initiatives were initiated during the second half of his reign, a decade after he

[231] *SS* 22, p. 403; *CPPM* 127, p. 3830.
[232] Strickmann, "The longest Taoist scripture," p. 347.
[233] Strickmann, "The longest Taoist scripture," p. 349.
[234] *CPPM* 127, pp. 3848–50. Also see Ebrey, "Taoism and art," p. 107.

had revived and extended the New Policies.[235] Perhaps similar structuring impulses informed the reform policies and religious transformations of Hui-tsung's court, since both programs represented parallel instances of state intrusion into society through the creation and elaboration of regulatory systems. Enshrining *Shen-hsiao* Taoism as the state religion, Hui-tsung and his advisors created an empirewide hierarchy of Divine Empyrean temples to glorify the monarch and the dynasty, and employed the state educational system as a means of disseminating Taoist learning. By the second decade of his reign, Hui-tsung had deviated from the political legacy of his father and brother, but he was guided by equally idealistic impulses to develop new institutions to accomplish similar reforming aims. The emperor's extension of the New Policies and his patronage of religious Taoism were both informed by similar impulses: to become a sagely ruler who brought order to his empire by radiating virtue into society through centralized state institutions, which gave him the power to revive the ethical and political orders of antiquity.

POPULAR UPRISINGS, BORDER CONFLICTS, AND THE FALL OF THE NORTHERN SUNG

Contrary to the teleological narrative of traditional history, neither the profligacy of Hui-tsung's court nor the policies of the Ts'ai Ching ministry were responsible for the fall of the Northern Sung. What doomed the dynasty was a concatenation of diplomatic and military crises, into which the emperor and his ministers blundered, and from which they proved incapable of extricating themselves. While the Sung armed forces were not outnumbered by their adversaries, they were ineptly commanded from the center, by an imperial court overconfident of certain victory. Unaware of their own strategic and tactical blind spots, Hui-tsung's unaccountable councilors and generals could not marshal and coordinate the necessary fiscal and human might to defend the empire. More than any inherent disadvantages, a lack of will and leadership caused the collapse of the Northern Sung.

From the beginning of his personal rule, Hui-tsung pursued an aggressive expansionist military and diplomatic policy against the empire's border adversaries, with ephemeral successes followed by total failures. In a series of ultimately fruitless campaigns against the Tangut Hsi Hsia, in 1103–6 and 1113–19, Hui-tsung pursued the conquest of territories that had already been gained and lost by Shen-tsung and Che-tsung. While they did succeed in destroying the Tanguts' preeminent position on the northwestern frontier,

---

[235] Chaffee, "Huizong, Cai Jing, and the politics of reform," p. 53.

Sung commanders overextended themselves, snatching defeat from the jaws of victory.

If the imperial armed forces could not hope to defeat the Hsi Hsia after years of campaigns, they were clearly outmatched by the declining Khitan Liao empire, which occupied the Sixteen Prefectures coveted by Sung emperors since the dynasty's inception. In 1119, tempted by the desire to reconquer this *terra irredenta*, Hui-tsung's court entered into a diplomatic pact with the Jurchen, whose emerging and expansionist Chin empire threatened the Liao from the north. Planning to mount concerted attacks upon the Liao, the Sung and Chin leadership agreed to split the conquered territories between them. But the need to suppress the massive popular rebellions of Fang La in 1120 prevented the Sung court from fully mobilizing its forces against the Liao, and when they finally proceeded with their invasion plans a year later the imperial troops suffered severe setbacks. After the Jurchen conquered the Liao dynasty with little assistance from the Sung, Hui-tsung's diplomats repeatedly enraged the Chin leadership with their excessive demands for more territory. Late in 1125, the Jurchen launched a punitive invasion of the Sung empire, breaking through border defenses and capturing strategic cities in the north. Although symbolic of renewed imperial resolve, Hui-tsung's abdication in favor of his son Ch'in-tsung in the twelfth month of 1125 could not stave off disaster, for the new emperor and his revolving-door councilors vacillated between appeasement and resistance. Concluding peace at any price in 1126, the Sung extricated itself from its first war with the Chin only to have its diplomatic incompetence provoke a second, fatal conflict. In the second month of 1127, Jurchen forces invaded the North China Plain, sacked K'ai-feng, and took both Hui-tsung and Ch'in-tsung prisoner, effectively decapitating the dynasty. The dynasty fell because Hui-tsung's councilors and commanders failed to acknowledge the military might of their adversaries or to accept accountability for their ill-conceived schemes, causing them to overconfidently stumble into war against an invincible foe.

All for nothing: The final phase of the Sung–Tangut conflict, 1101–1119

When he ascended the throne, Hui-tsung succeeded to a legacy of aggressive expansionism along the northwestern frontier.[236] In the 1070s, Shen-tsung

---

[236] For the political and military history of the Hsi Hsia empire in this period, see Ruth W. Dunnell, "The Hsi Hsia," in *The Cambridge history of China*, volume 6: *Alien regimes and border states, 907–1368*, ed. Herbert Franke and Denis C. Twitchett (New York, 1994); Wu T'ien-ch'ih, *Hsin Hsi Hsia shih* (Taipei, 1987); and Li Hua-jui, *Sung Hsia kuan-hsi shih* (Shih-chia-chuang, 1998). For an analysis of military policy during the reformist ministries of the Shen-tsung and Che-tsung reigns, see Chao

had initiated Sung military incursions into Tangut territory, only to be mired in an inconclusive war of attrition. The premature end of Shen-tsung's reign was perhaps hastened by the bloodbath of Yung-lo ch'eng in 1082, which broke the emperor's spirit and ruined his health. However, during his personal rule, Che-tsung and his ministers had overturned Dowager Empress Hsüan-jen's policy of appeasement, ultimately succeeding in undermining the power position of the Hsi Hsia. Pursuing an "advance and fortify" (*chin-chu*) strategy of occupying enemy territory and holding it with strategic fortifications, Sung forces had soundly defeated the Tanguts in the climactic battle of P'ing-hsia in 1099.

But even if Hui-tsung desired to follow in the footsteps of his father and older brother, his hands were tied. He was constrained not only by a peace treaty concluded in the last months of Che-tsung's reign but also by the pacifistic presence of Dowager Empress Ch'in-sheng and the ascendant antireformists. In the first years of the Hui-tsung reign, opinion at court turned against the adventurism of the Chang Tun ministry and favored a return to the accommodationist border policy of the Yüan-yu regency. When Chang was indicted for political crimes and dismissed from the councilorship in 1101, the conservative censor Ch'en Kuan accused him of "delighting in the deployment of troops and opening up great border rifts."[237] Perhaps the greatest military failure of Chang's ministry was the collapse of an invasion of the Tibetan stronghold of Ch'ing-t'ang (modern Hsi-ning2) in the Huang-shui valley east of Lake Kokonor (Ch'ing-hai), which left Sung troops stranded deep behind enemy lines.[238] In the third month of 1101 the Sung court admitted defeat in the Ch'ing-t'ang campaigns by completely withdrawing from the Huang-shui valley, which policy makers had hoped to annex as part of Hsi-ho military circuit, and returning it to the Tibetans. After Chang Tun fell from power, an increasing number of remonstrators were emboldened to memorialize against the misguided irredentism of his ministry. True to form, this peace lobby argued that the campaigns of the late 1090s had wasted the empire's limited military and fiscal resources to occupy an empty and unproductive swath of mountainous territory in the far northwest.[239]

Ti-hsien, "Shih-lun Pei Sung pien-fa-p'ai chün-shih kai-ko te ch'eng-kung," *Li-shih yen-chiu* 250 (1997), pp. 143–60.

[237] Hsü, *Sung tsai-fu pien-nien lu chiao-pu* 11, p. 668.

[238] The following discussion is based on Paul J. Smith, "Irredentism as political capital: The New Policies and the annexation of Tibetan domains in Hehuang (the Qinghai-Gansu highlands) under Shenzong and his sons, 1068–1108," in *Emperor Huizong and late Northern Song China: The politics of culture and the culture of politics*, ed. Patricia B. Ebrey and Maggie Bickford (Cambridge, Mass., 2006), pp. 99–105.

[239] For memorials by Fan Ch'un-ts'ui and Chang Shun-min which criticize the "advance and fortify" strategy, and for Che-tsung's border policies in general, see Chao Ju-yü, *Sung-ch'ao chu-ch'en tsou-i* (1186; Shanghai, 1999) 140, pp. 1583–5.

But once Hui-tsung began his personal rule, he adopted the expansionist border policy of his imperial predecessors. With the death of Dowager Empress Ch'in-sheng and the banishment of the antireformists from court, he and his ministers were unrestrained to make further incursions into Hsi Hsia territory. When Ts'ai Ching was appointed chief councilor in 1102, he convinced the emperor to commit to military campaigns without end on the northwestern frontier. The next year, troops were mobilized for a revival of the Ch'ing-t'ang campaign, to be commanded by Wang Hou, the son of Shen-tsung's onetime military advisor Wang Shao. Wang had devised a two-pronged invasion strategy, simultaneously pushing into the valleys of Ch'ing-t'ang and the highlands of Heng-shan. Rising meteorically from collecting artwork for Hui-tsung to commanding his majesty's armed forces, the eunuch T'ung Kuan was appointed Wang's second-in-command.[240]

In the valleys of Ch'ing-t'ang, Wang and T'ung pursued a blitzkrieg strategy, committing a massive force to besiege and reoccupy strategic outposts that had been surrendered several years before. In the sixth month of 1103, Sung forces recaptured Shan-chou3 (the old Ch'ing-t'ang) and Huang-chou2 and dozens of attached fortifications.[241] Wang claimed that this move had pacified an area of fifteen hundred square *li* (about 65 square miles), which supported a population of a hundred thousand, belonging to more than twenty different tribes.[242] By the end of 1104, native resistance was extinguished, and the independent rulers of K'uo-chou and Ch'ing-t'ang (soon renamed Hsi-ning-chou) surrendered.[243] Hui-tsung honored Wang Hou and T'ung Kuan for conquering the region, which afforded the Sung control over the southern border of the Hsi Hsia and brought an estimated seven hundred thousand subjects under direct imperial administration. In 1104 and 1105, Hsi Hsia forces reacted defensively to the Sung invasion, which threatened their southwestern border and cut off their empire from Tibetan territory. Launching pinprick attacks on Sung stockades, and later sending armies of a hundred thousand men to besiege fortifications in Huang-chou2 and Lan-chou, the Tanguts failed to wrest Ch'ing-t'ang away from Sung domination. Most of the credit for this military triumph went to T'ung Kuan, who replaced Wang Hou as supreme commander over the entire northwestern frontier in the first month of 1105.[244] In many ways, T'ung Kuan's rise to power at court resulted

---

[240] *CPPM* 140, pp. 4217–18.

[241] Huang-chou2 corresponds to modern Lo-tu, and Shan-chou3 to modern Hsi-ning2, both in Tsinghai province.

[242] *CPPM* 139, pp. 4182–6.

[243] *CPPM* 140, pp. 4227–8.

[244] Li Chih, *Huang Sung shih-ch'ao kang-yao* (c. 1213; Shanghai, 1995) 16, p. 23a. T'ung was appointed pacification commissioner (*ching-lüeh an-fu chih-chih-shih*) of Ch'in-feng and Hsi-ho-Lan-Huang circuits.

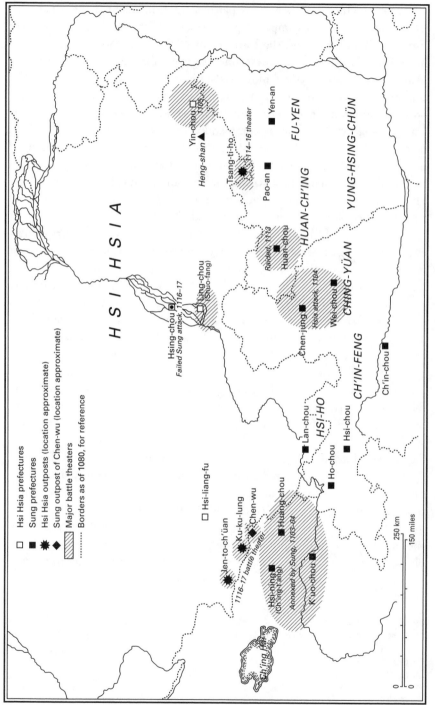

Map 18. Hui-tsung's wars in the northwest, 1103–1117.

from his victorious involvement in the Ch'ing-t'ang campaigns, which, in Paul Smith's assessment, "promoted Hui-tsung's continuing dream of pursuing his father's irredentist vision."[245]

Farther east, in the main theater of battle against the Tanguts, Sung troops mobilized for a second-wave offensive that would push into the Heng-shan highlands. In retribution for the Sung conquest of Ch'ing-t'ang, Hsi Hsia troops went on a rampage in northwestern Ch'in-feng circuit in the ninth month of 1104, killing tens of thousands of civilians in the two border prefectures of Wei-chou4 and Chen-jung chün. Alarmed at these atrocities, Ts'ai Ching appointed the general T'ao Chieh-fu as pacification commissioner (ching-lüeh an-fu shih) of Fu-yen circuit, entrusting him with defending the eastern stretch of the Sung–Hsi Hsia frontier.[246] Like his former commander Chang Chieh, T'ao formulated an "advance and fortify" strategy to defend the Heng-shan highlands from future Tangut incursions and reprisals by establishing a solid defense perimeter. In the spring of 1105, Sung forces captured and fortified the strategic walled city of Yin-chou, later staving off a large-scale Hsi Hsia offensive to recapture the surrounding area.[247] By projecting Sung military power ever closer to the heartland of the Hsi Hsia empire, T'ao Chieh-fu managed to bring the Tanguts back to the bargaining table. After his troops were defeated in the battle over Yin-chou, Emperor Ch'ung-tsung of the Hsi Hsia sued for peace through a Liao emissary.[248] A cease-fire was proclaimed in the seventh month of 1106, but diplomatic negotiations soon bogged down over the issue of ceding captured territory. In the end, a compromise treaty was reached, in which the Sung retained its hegemony over the Ch'ing-t'ang region, but returned Yin-chou as a concession to the Tanguts. Through the demotion of T'ao Chieh-fu to a prefectural post, the Sung court demonstrated its willingness to abandon its "advance and fortify" strategy for the foreseeable future.

The truce held for seven years, while Hui-tsung's court remained divided between proponents of aggression and appeasement. Frustrated by his demotion and the cession of hard-won territory to the Tanguts, T'ao Chieh-fu advocated extreme measures. Apparently, he managed to convince several members of the Council of State that the only way to stabilize the border and to prevent further incursions was to decapitate the Hsi Hsia regime with an all-out assault

---

[245] Smith, "Irredentism as political capital," p. 123.

[246] SS 348, p. 11039.

[247] CPPM 140, pp. 4239–40.

[248] In the standard sources of Sung history, which refuse to acknowledge the Hsi Hsia as a legitimate empire, Emperor Ch'ung-tsung is known as Wei-ming Ch'ien-shun. At the beginning of the twelfth century, the Hsi Hsia empire concluded a diplomatic alliance with the Liao, cemented by the marriage of Emperor Ch'ung-tsung of the Hsi Hsia to an imperial princess of the Liao in 1104.

upon its heartland of Hsing-chou2 and Ling-chou.[249] Chao T'ing-chih, who briefly served as chief councilor in 1107, after Ts'ai Ching's first departure from court, opposed T'ao's invasion plan as costly and imprudent. Unswayed by the hawks at court, Hui-tsung was either unwilling or unable to commit troops and resources on another prolonged border campaign. A few years later, external pressures finally tipped the balance, providing the emperor with a legitimate casus belli. Starting in 1109, a series of escalating disagreements over the demarcation of the unfixed Sung–Hsi Hsia frontier brought the rulers of both empires to the brink of war. In 1113, in an attempt to convince the Sung to agree on a redrawn borderline, the Hsi Hsia ruler Ch'ung-tsung resumed the construction of fortifications in the disputed frontier territory. To further destabilize an already precarious situation, the Ch'iang chieftain Li O-to switched allegiance to the Hsi Hsia and began raiding Sung positions in Huan-chou2.[250] The Tanguts continued to buttress their position in Heng-shan, in 1114 building a strategic fortification at Tsang-ti-ho, on the northern edge of the Sung commandery of Pao-an.[251] After this provocation, bellicose elements at court convinced Hui-tsung to commit tens of millions of strings of cash and hundreds of thousands of soldiers to a renewed offensive in the northwest.

At the onset of hostilities in the fourth and final Sung-Tangut conflict, Hui-tsung appointed T'ung Kuan supreme commander of the imperial forces in all six border circuits. For the next five years, T'ung overcommitted Sung forces to fight in a conflict with unattainable objectives. Just as they had a decade before, Sung troops made simultaneous incursions into Ch'ing-t'ang and Heng-shan. Never achieving the final breakthrough they had expected, the emperor's generals squandered massive resources and caused the deaths of (according to one estimate) several hundred thousand imperial troops. In 1115, a force of one hundred and fifty thousand soldiers under the command of Liu Fa moved north from Huang-chou2 to reoccupy the Ch'ing-t'ang region. Pushing deep inside enemy territory, Liu's army slaughtered a Tangut garrison to conquer the stockade at Ku-ku-lung, on the Tibeto-Tangut border.[252] The same year, the Chin-feng military commissioner Liu Chung-wu and a man identified as Wang Hou led imperial troops from four circuits to besiege the newly constructed Tangut fort at Tsang-ti-ho, where nearly half of them – more than a hundred thousand men, by one estimate – were massacred. According to the *Sung shih* account, Wang bribed T'ung to conceal these massive casualties

[249] SS 348, p. 11039.
[250] SS 356, p. 11221; 486, pp. 14019–20.
[251] SS 486, p. 14020.
[252] SS 486, p. 14020. Ku-ku-lung is located to the northeast of modern Hsi-ning2 in Tsinghai province.

in his reports to the emperor.[253] In 1116, Liu Fa and Liu Chung-wu united two circuit armies to penetrate farther into the Hao-tan valley, forcing the surrender of Jen-to-ch'üan, a Hsi Hsia walled town upstream from Ku-ku-lung.[254] Undaunted by the carnage of the previous year, a hundred thousand Sung troops conquered the strategic fortress at Tsang-ti-ho, the original bone of contention in this final phase of the Sung–Tangut conflict.

But after these promising initial victories, the tide of battle turned against the Sung, as mounting casualties forced the court to admit defeat. Seeking to even the score, the Tanguts staged a successful surprise attack on the Sung walled town of Ching-hsia during the relatively snowless midwinter of 1116–17.[255] In the final analysis, what forced the Sung court to abandon the campaign was T'ung Kuan's strategic incompetence, which impelled him to commit what remained of his armies to an impossible mission. Plotting to eradicate the Tangut menace once and for all, T'ung forced an unwilling Liu Fa to lead an invasion of Shuo-fang, at the core of the Hsi Hsia empire.[256] Leading two hundred thousand troops into what quickly became a suicide mission, Liu was attacked by a massive contingent of Tangut forces outside the walled city of T'ung-an.[257] Walking into a deadly trap with no escape route and short of food and water, Liu's armies were encircled by three hundred thousand Hsi Hsia infantry and cavalry, commanded by the Hsi Hsia prince Ch'a-ko. A hundred thousand Sung troops survived, fleeing some twenty miles under the cloak of night, only to be pursued and ambushed the next day, when Liu was beheaded. Soon thereafter, Ch'a-ko's forces besieged the Sung cliffside fortress at Chen-wu, and Liu Chung-wu and his remaining garrison were decimated. As with prior defeats, T'ung Kuan covered up these massacres, preventing the news from reaching Hui-tsung; as late as 1119 he was claiming continued victories in his reports to the throne.[258]

After these bloodbaths, whose casualty count exceeded that of the Yung-lo ch'eng debacle of 1082, T'ung Kuan had no choice but to concede defeat. When T'ung suggested a cease-fire to the Tangut command, the Hsi Hsia extracted an apology from Hui-tsung, who promulgated an edict that abolished the military command structure in the six northwestern military circuits. In its

[253] SS 486, p. 14020. The *Sung shih* authors have apparently misattributed these events to Wang Hou, for all other sources (including his *Sung shih* biography, SS 328, pp. 10582–4) suggest that Wang died around 1106.

[254] Jen-to-ch'üan roughly corresponds to the seat of modern Men-yüan county in Tsinghai province.

[255] SS 486, p. 14020. Aside from this single mention in the *Sung shih*, the fortress of Ching-hsia was not referred to elsewhere. While it was likely located in Ching-yüan circuit, its present-day coordinates are unknown. See Li, *Sung Hsia kuan-hsi shih*, p. 247.

[256] SS 468, p. 13659. Shuo-fang corresponds to modern Ling-wu in Ningsia province.

[257] SS 486, p. 14021. The exact location of T'ung-an is now unknown.

[258] SS 468, p. 13659; 22, p. 404.

final and most brutish phase, the Sung-Tangut war had proven a huge waste of financial resources and human life. Sacrificing hundreds of thousands of soldiers to briefly recapture a barren stretch of land, T'ung Kuan had miscalculated the strength of the Hsi Hsia military. Following the conclusion of the Sung-Tangut peace agreement, Hui-tsung's court shifted its attentions from the northwest to the northeastern frontier. In the early 1120s, the empire was shaken by popular uprisings in the southeast, which forced the court to divert military resources to quell domestic unrest. The massacres at T'ung-an and Chen-wu foreshadowed the carnage in years to come, when the emperor and his ministers embroiled the Sung in a near-fatal conflict with the Jurchen. In retrospect, the sacrifice of imperial troops in the Shuo-fang offensive was rendered meaningless by the Chin conquest of 1127, after which the truncated Southern Sung empire would no longer even adjoin Tangut territory. Judging from their abject failure to subdue an adversary of lesser strength, the Sung armed forces would never stand a chance against the Jurchen, who were swallowing everything in their path, as they stormed to dominance over the territories on both sides of the Great Wall. As with the Tangut conflict, the ignominious Sung defeat in the next series of border wars did not result from any quantitative disadvantage, but from strategic, tactical, and diplomatic ineptitude.

Immiseration and insurrection: Popular uprisings, 1119–1121

As the court became embroiled in armed conflict with border states, it was simultaneously placed on the defensive by internal rebellion. Immiserated and dispossessed by confiscatory taxation and extraordinary levies, bands of commoners took up arms, and the empire convulsed with large-scale popular uprisings. In 1119 and 1120, the rebellion of Fang La ravaged entire circuits, until it was extinguished by a massive deployment of imperial troops. Diverting armed forces and military resources from the border to the interior, these uprisings also destabilized border relations with the Jurchen Chin at an extremely vulnerable moment. On the home front, after the damage was done, the economy of one of the empire's most productive regions was crippled, and the legitimacy of the Sung court was threatened.

The most highly commercialized area of the Sung empire, the rice-producing Liang-che circuit was an unlikely crucible for a full-blown popular uprising.[259] But during the Hui-tsung reign, the region's economy was sapped by the imperial court's fiscal parasitism. Its inhabitants suffered disproportionately from the confiscatory exactions imposed by the "flower and rock

---

[259] For an expanded treatment of the Fang La uprising, see Kao Yu-kung, "A study of the Fang La rebellion," *Harvard Journal of Asiatic Studies* 24 (1962–3), pp. 17–63.

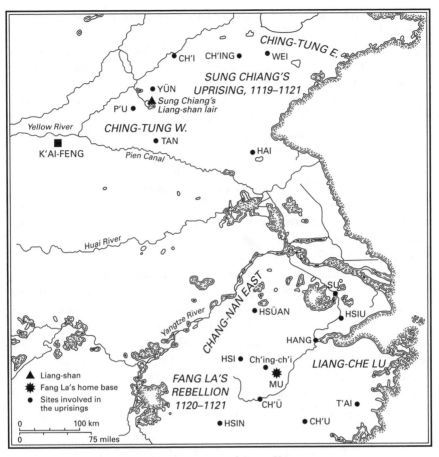

Map 19. Uprisings of Fang La and Sung Chiang, 1119–1121.

network," whose tentacles penetrated into the circuit's remote areas as well as its major cities.[260] With an untapped reservoir of dispossessed commoners, Liang-che became a breeding ground for the popular uprising of Fang La. In three short months in 1120–1, Feng's small band of backcountry brigands swelled into a formidable guerrilla army. The epicenter of Fang's rebellion was Mu-chou, a ruggedly mountainous and densely wooded hinterland on the circuit's western border, an area of tea, lumber, and lacquer production. Many local tea-growing households had been bankrupted by the court's tea certificate

---

[260] According to Ts'ai T'ao's historical narrative, the "flower and rock network" affected Liang-che the most directly: "From Lake Tai, there were numinous jades; from Tz'u-hsi and Wu-k'ang there were various rocks. From Liang-che, there were flowers, bamboo, assorted trees, and sea delicacies." See *CPPM* 128, p. 3884.

policy. The prefecture's forests had been felled to fill Hui-tsung's gardens and to build his palaces.

Fang La experienced the depredations of the "flower and rock network" firsthand, and his economic grievances impelled him to organize a guerrilla resistance in Mu-chou. Fang's family had once owned a lacquer plantation in Ch'ing-ch'i county, which had been forcibly seized by Chu Mien's Imperial Provisioning Bureau.[261] Swearing vengeance upon the emperor's "Six Felons," Fang La assembled a bandit gang. While the vicissitudes of political economy provided the impetus for rebellion, a millenarian ideology united Fang's followers into a congregation of religious believers. Syncretizing aspects of Manichaeanism, Buddhism, and Taoism, Fang preached to his believers that the path to salvation would be cleansed with the blood of imperial officials and soldiers. In the tenth month of 1120, Fang and his sect arose in open revolt, first murdering a large landowner in the county seat of Ch'ing-ch'i.[262] Fleeing west, he and his fellow brigands hid out in a vast network of caves, a base from which they staged ever-larger raids and attracted increasing numbers of adherents. The next month, Fang issued a direct challenge to imperial hegemony by displaying the symbols of sectarian rebellion and manifesting imperial pretensions. Proclaiming himself a "Sagely Lord" (sheng-kung) with the reign title of Yung-lo (Everlasting Joy), he ordered his followers to don red turbans, an old symbol of millenarian rebels.[263] On the last day of the eleventh month, he and several thousand followers captured Ch'ing-ch'i county. A few days later, his force of twenty thousand men was strong enough to subdue a garrison of a thousand government troops and to conquer the prefectural seat of Mu-chou.[264]

Incorporating followers from smaller opportunistic uprisings, the ranks of Fang's armed forces swelled. Seizing the opportunity to renew the world, several outlying sectarian communities were subsumed under Fang's banner, as well. Partitioned into three separate marches, rebel forces occupied Liang-che circuit and most of neighboring Chiang-nan East circuit. Garrisons of imperial troops offered scant resistance, and local administrators fled in panic, abandoning county after county to the rebels. By the first month of 1121, the boundaries of Fang La's kingdom stretched north to the Yangtze River and south to the seacoast. From Mu-chou, one division of the rebel army advanced west to penetrate into the neighboring circuit of Chiang-nan East, killing a

---

[261] Ch'en et al., Sung-shih chi-shih pen-mo (1977) 54, p. 555. Ch'ing-hsi county corresponds to modern Tun-an county in Chekiang province.

[262] CPPM 141, pp. 4273–4.

[263] SS 468, p. 13659.

[264] CPPM 141, p. 4274.

contingent of government troops in Hsi-chou (in 1121 renamed Hui-chou).[265] Another force split off to the southeast, conquering Ch'u-chou and T'ai-chou with little resistance, and subsequently seizing Ch'ü-chou and Hsin-chou2. At the same time the main rebel force, led by Fang La himself, headed east from Mu-chou to conquer the regional metropolis of Hang-chou. When they sacked the emptied city, the home base of the Imperial Provisioning Bureau, the rebels chanted the slogan "Kill Chu Mien!"[266] One anecdotal source alleged that Fang even dispatched his followers to desecrate the graves of Ts'ai Ching's ancestors, in a potent illustration of their extreme hatred of the emperor's ministry of "Six Felons."[267]

By the time the imperial court took decisive countermeasures against the uprising, Fang La's kingdom had succeeded in engulfing nearly the entire circuit of Liang-che in the span of two months. Meanwhile, Hui-tsung's ministers and generals were distracted by their plans for the expedition to attack the Liao Southern Capital. There is some evidence that a cover-up occurred at the highest levels of the Council of State. Wang Fu, the current chief councilor and another of the "Six Felons," prevented the circuit intendants' reports from Liang-che from reaching the emperor.[268] Finally, the situation forced the court to act in the first month of 1121. T'ung Kuan was appointed pacification commissioner (hsüan-fu shih) of several southeastern circuits and entrusted with the mission of exterminating the rebels.[269] Hui-tsung apparently granted T'ung Kuan's request to abolish the "flower and rock network," which had in all likelihood sparked the rebellion in the first place.[270] Some one hundred and fifty thousand crack troops intended for the northern front were hastily rerouted south to Liang-che circuit. This massive diversion of troops came at an inopportune juncture, postponing the Sung attack on the Liao capital and jeopardizing the fragile Sung-Chin alliance.

While imperial forces never succeeded in conquering the Liao, they did move expeditiously to crush the Fang La rebellion before it could spread any further. In recent years, Sung armed forces had been outmatched by the Hsi Hsia, but poorly armed and armored rebels proved relatively easy opponents for the soldiers under T'ung Kuan's command. Their victory was assured when Fang La committed a grave tactical error. Instead of occupying the south bank

---

[265] CPPM 141, pp. 4274–5.

[266] SS 470, p. 13686.

[267] Tseng Min-hsing, Tu-hsing tsa-chih [Ts'ung-shu chi-ch'eng ch'u-pien 1935–7 ed.] (c. 1175; Peking, 1985), p. 7.

[268] SS 470, p. 13682.

[269] T'ung Kuan was granted command of imperial forces in the southeastern circuits of Liang-che, Chiang-nan, and Huai-nan. See CPPM 141, p. 4276.

[270] CPPM 128, pp. 3886–7.

of the Yangtze, and employing the river as a natural defensive boundary, he concentrated his forces to besiege the city of Hsiu-chou (modern Chia-hsing), where they were caught and defeated by a pincer movement of converging imperial troops.[271] Retreating south in the second and third months of 1121, what remained of the main rebel contingents were routed at Hsüan-chou and Hang-chou.[272] In the fourth month, Fang La and a small rebel remnant were surrounded in the caves west of Ch'ing-ch'i, where their uprising had originated. Other rebel offshoots continued to move through Liang-che and Chiang-nan East circuits, where mopping up the remnants of the uprising occupied another year. The Sung court did not declare final victory over the rebels until the third month of 1122, seven months after the execution of Fang La.

In the last analysis, the rebellion and its aftermath had devastated Liang-che, laying waste to six prefectures and fifty-two counties, and resulting in the deaths of one or two million civilians.[273] Commoners were massacred indiscriminately by the guerrilla forces as well as by imperial troops. It is likely that counterinsurgency units beheaded innocent civilians in order to fulfill imposed quotas.[274] To compound the tragedy, Wang Fu revived the flower and rock network in the first month of 1121, before the insurrection had even been quelled. Concealing the extent of popular discontent from Hui-tsung, Wang informed the emperor that the sole cause of the uprising had been the salt and tea monopolies. Wang overrode the objections of T'ung Kuan, who urged the monarch to cease the extraction of resources from war-torn Liang-che.[275] Until the end of Hui-tsung's reign, booty was shipped to K'ai-feng by reestablished Imperial Provisioning Bureaus, supervised by a rehabilitated Chu Mien.[276] Clearly, the imperial court had learned no lessons from the Fang La rebellion, as Wang Fu still monopolized executive power and the state continued to extract resources from a restive society.

While the Fang La rebellion was devastating Liang-che circuit, smaller-scale popular uprisings raged elsewhere in the empire. The most historically significant of these was the uprising of Sung Chiang, a Robin Hood of popular memory who would be celebrated in the Ming dynasty novel *The water margin* (*Shui-hu chuan*). Surrounded by a ring of mountains, the marshes surrounding Liang-shan Lake in Yün-chou (Ching-tung West circuit) had long been a bandit stronghold.[277] As with the Fang La rebellion, the penetration of the

---

[271] *CPPM* 141, pp. 4277–8.

[272] *CPPM* 141, p. 4279.

[273] This casualty count is extremely unreliable and was most likely inflated. *SS* 468, p. 13660.

[274] Tseng, *Tu-hsing tsa-chih*, p. 7.

[275] *CPPM* 128, pp. 3886–7.

[276] *SS* 470, p. 13686.

[277] The area corresponds to the Tung-ping marshes in western Shantung. During the Shen-tsung reign, P'u Tsung-meng, who had served as prefect of Yün-chou, employed such brutal methods to subdue

state into the rural economy ignited another popular uprising. When their farms were seized as "public lands" (*kung-t'ien*) by the court in the mid-1110s, local peasants in Ching-tung were forced to remit extortionate rent payments to the imperial treasury. The connection between economic oppression and the emergence of the rebellion is unclear, since no extant document explains when, why, or how Sung Chiang's insurrection arose.

The paper trail begins after the rebels had become a sufficiently potent force for their existence to be acknowledged in court documents. Toward the end of 1119, Hui-tsung ordered the arrest and conviction of the "Ching-tung rebel" Sung Chiang.[278] Government troops did not confront this small bandit gang, which ranged freely across the countryside, spreading through four prefectures (P'u-chou, Tan-chou, Ch'i-chou, and Ch'ing-chou) in the Ching-tung circuits by the end of 1120.[279] The court made half-hearted efforts to order local administrators to apprehend Sung, but he and his growing band repeatedly evaded capture. When the rebels reached the coastal prefecture of Hai-chou in the winter of 1121, Prefect Chang Shu-yeh received imperial orders to suppress the rebellion once and for all. Infiltrating the bandits' lair with spies, Chang learned that the rebels controlled a fleet of boats, the nucleus of a pirate navy.[280] Imperial troops surrounded the bandits on the beaches, and forced Sung Chiang's surrender. But back on the shores of Liang-shan Lake, bands of commoners continued to rebel against the seizure of "public lands," a government initiative that was supervised by the eunuch Li Yen, another of the "Six Felons." Hui-tsung's ministers obtusely refused to learn any lessons from the Fang La and Sung Chiang rebellions. Even as their fiscal policies provided tinder to be sparked into armed uprisings, which were quashed at great human and financial cost, the central government continued to extort revenues and resources from the countryside.

Using barbarians to control barbarians: Concluding the Sung-Chin alliance,
1115–1123

Since the founding of the Sung, its monarchs had desired to complete their reunification of the empire by reclaiming the so-called Sixteen Prefectures from the Liao, but bitter experience had shown that these lost territories could not be reconquered unless the Sung court found an ally to counterbalance

---

a popular uprising that he received a censorial impeachment. According to P'u's *Sung shih* biography, "bandits had been numerous" in the Liang-shan area. See *SS* 328, pp. 10571–2.

[278] Li, *Huang Sung shih-ch'ao kang-yao* (1995) 18, p. 10b.

[279] Sung Chiang occupied these four prefectures in succession. One contemporary observer claimed that Sung Chiang's gang numbered thirty-six men. See Hou Meng's memorial in *SS* 351, p. 11114.

[280] *SS* 353, p. 11141.

Khitan military power. When the Jurchen, a vassal tribe of the Liao, rebelled against Khitan hegemony and founded the Chin dynasty in 1115, the Sung court saw its chance to recover the Sixteen Prefectures. Commanded by the chieftain Wan-yen A-ku-ta, who was enthroned as Emperor Ch'in T'ai-tsu (r. 1115–23), Jurchen forces stormed across the eastern fringes of the Liao empire, in present-day Manchuria. After decisively defeating more than one hundred thousand Liao troops in battle, A-ku-ta's troops went from strength to strength, conquering the Liao Eastern Capital of Liao-yang in 1116.[281] Seriously threatening Khitan dominance, the Chin appeared to be the ally the Sung court required, if it was ever to fulfill dynastic aspirations to regain the Yen-Yün region. In the parlance of the times, the Sung would be "using barbarians to control barbarians" (*i-i chih-i*).

The Sung-Chin alliance underwent a lengthy and painful gestation, stalled by halting negotiations between the two parties, as well as by simultaneous Liao-Chin diplomatic efforts.[282] First reports of the Chin rebellion began to trickle into K'ai-feng in 1115, when Ma Chih, a Liao subject from Yen, defected to the Sung. Granted the imperial surname and renamed Chao Liang-ssu by court decree, he informed Hui-tsung and his ministers that Chin incursions had rendered the Liao vulnerable to attack. Chao's reports of Liao weakness rekindled hopes of reconquering the Sixteen Prefectures, and the chief councilors Ts'ai Ching and Wang Fu persuaded Hui-tsung to open diplomatic channels with the Jurchen.[283] Even while he was mired in a losing war of attrition with the Tanguts in 1118, T'ung Kuan formulated plans for an invasion of the Sixteen Prefectures, indicating that the court had begun to heed Chao Liang-ssu's advice.[284] After an abortive embassy of 1117 never even reached the Jurchen homeland, a secret mission of 1118 was welcomed by the Chin court. Since ambassadors could not cross Liao territory, Sung-Chin diplomacy was conducted by diplomats who sailed across the Po-hai Gulf from the Shantung peninsula into Jurchen territory. Broaching the possibility of a military alliance, the Sung ambassadors were accompanied back to K'ai-feng by Jurchen envoys.[285] When they were received at the Sung court, the Jurchen

[281] T'o-t'o, ed., *Chin shih* (1344; Peking, 1975) 2, p. 29. The Chin conquest of the Liao is depicted on map 8 of Denis C. Twitchett and Klaus-Peter Tietze, "The Liao," in *The Cambridge history of China*, volume 6: *Alien regimes and border states, 907–1368*, ed. Herbert Franke and Denis C. Twitchett (New York, 1994), p. 145.

[282] This section draws heavily upon Tao Jing-shen (T'ao Chin-sheng), *Two sons of heaven: Studies in Sung-Liao relations* (Tucson, Ariz.,1988), pp. 87–97. Also see Wu Ching-hung, "Sung-Chin kung Liao chih wai-chiao," in *Sung-shih yen-chiu chi: ti shih-erh chi*, ed. Sung-shih tso-t'an-hui (Taipei, 1978), pp. 169–83. For Chao Liang-ssu's biography, see *SS* 472, pp. 13733–5.

[283] Wu, "Sung-Chin kung Liao chih wai-chiao," pp. 169–74.

[284] Hsü Meng-hsin, *San-ch'ao pei-meng hui-pien* (1196; Shanghai, 1987) 2, p. 11a.

[285] Hsü, *San-ch'ao pei-meng hui-pien* (1987) 2, pp. 11a–13b; T'o-t'o, *Chin shih* 2, p. 30.

ambassadors declared that if a joint invasion was launched against the Liao, the victors would divide the spoils, taking whatever territories they conquered.[286]

Such 'vague diplomatic pronouncements emboldened Hui-tsung and his ministers in their bid to recover the Sixteen Prefectures, but the collapse of the Liao was not yet imminent. In 1119, Sung-Chin negotiations were forestalled by abortive Chin-Liao peace talks, which broke down when A-ku-ta refused to accept inferior diplomatic status as a vassal king of the declining Liao.[287] After the Jurchen rejected an alliance with the Khitan, a Sung-Chin alliance became a possibility. In the spring of 1120, leading a Sung embassy to the Chin court, Chao Liang-ssu sought to formalize the terms of the deal and petitioned for the return of the Sixteen Prefectures after victory in a joint assault on the Liao.[288] A-ku-ta orally assented to the Sung-Jurchen alliance, but he demanded that the Sung court transfer its tribute payments from the Liao to the Chin to help defray his military expenditures.[289] Jurchen envoys returned to K'ai-feng with Chao's embassy in the fall and presented a formal declaration that promised the cession of the Yen-ching region to the Sung.[290] In the eleventh month of 1120, Sung ambassadors to Chin agreed to divert annual tribute payments of two hundred thousand taels of silver and three hundred thousand bolts of silk from the Liao to the Chin. For the Sung court, switching one disadvantageous diplomatic relationship for another was considered a necessary evil, if the Sixteen Prefectures could be recovered in the end. Making annual payments to the Jurchen seemed eminently reasonable, considering that they were shouldering the brunt of the military burden against the Liao.

Since the Chin court was negotiating from a position of strength, having conquered the Liao Supreme Capital of Lin-huang in mid-1120, the terms of alliance became ever more disadvantageous for the Sung.[291] A-ku-ta refused to allow the return of all Sixteen Prefectures to the Sung, reserving three eastern coastal prefectures (P'ing-chou, Lüan-chou, and Ying-chou6), along with the Liao Western Capital of Ta-t'ung, for himself.[292] In the first month of the following year, a Chin embassy announced that the Sung would not be permitted to reclaim Ta-t'ung unless they committed their forces to conquer the city.[293] Hui-tsung and his ministers could not simply recover the Yen-Yün

---

[286] T'o-t'o, *Chin shih* 2, p. 30.

[287] T'o-t'o, *Chin shih* 2, p. 33.

[288] Hsü, *San-ch'ao pei-meng hui-pien* (1987) 4, pp. 3a–b; T'o-t'o, *Chin shih* 2, p. 33.

[289] Hsü, *San-ch'ao pei-meng hui-pien* (1987) 4, pp. 3b–7b.

[290] Hsü, *San-ch'ao pei-meng hui-pien* (1987) 4, pp. 7b–8b.

[291] T'o-t'o, *Chin shih* 2, p. 34.

[292] Hsü, *San-ch'ao pei-meng hui-pien* (1987) 4, pp. 12a–b. These three prefectures correspond to modern Hu-lung, Lüan, and Ch'ang-li counties in Hopei province.

[293] Hsü, *San-ch'ao pei-meng hui-pien* (1987) 4, pp. 16a–b.

region in return for transferring their annual tribute payments to the Chin. The
Sung-Chin alliance would have to be backed up with a military commitment,
and the Sixteen Prefectures would have to be paid for with a concerted assault
on the walled city of Ta-t'ung.

However, the Sung court's hands were tied, even as the Chin launched a
war on all fronts, conquering the remnants of the Liao empire. For instead
of assaulting the Liao Western Capital, the key to recovering the Sixteen
Prefectures, one hundred and fifty thousand crack imperial troops under T'ung
Kuan's command had been diverted from the Liao border south to Liang-che
to suppress the Fang La rebellion. By the time the Sung court could commit
itself to military action against the Khitan, the Chin had already defeated the
main Liao army in battle, capturing the Liao Central Capital of Ta-ting in
the first month of 1122.[294] The surviving Khitan forces were scattered and
fragmented. Emperor Liao T'ien-tso, the last of the Liao imperial clan, fled
to safety in the Western Capital, and a splinter regime, the Northern Liao,
was established in the Southern Capital of Yen-ching. Although the Sung and
Chin had agreed to a diplomatic and military alliance against the Liao, no
formal treaty had yet been signed. By conquering the Liao empire on its own,
the Jurchen managed to gain the spoils of war before diplomatic negotiations
began, and before the Sung court could claim the disputed Liao territories for
itself.[295]

Seeing their chance to regain the Sixteen Prefectures slip away, Hui-tsung
and his ministers mobilized an assault upon the remaining Liao strongholds.
No longer squandering its resources upon crushing popular uprisings, the Sung
court could now shift the focus of its military efforts to the northern border.
In the fourth month of 1122, T'ung Kuan commanded one hundred thousand
imperial troops in an assault upon the Liao Southern Capital of Yen-ching, from
whence the Liao nobleman Yeh-lü Ch'ün ruled the rump state of Northern
Liao.[296] Apparently, the Sung court intended to compel Yeh-lü to submit as
a vassal; if his expeditionary forces could not capture Yen-ching, T'ung was
instructed to retreat. But imperial troops proved incapable of fulfilling any of
these mission objectives, and were soundly defeated by Yeh-lü Ch'ün's army
the following month.[297] Even after the Northern Liao had pledged its fealty
as a Sung vassal, a second assault was launched in the fall of 1122, which failed
to conquer the city yet again.[298] These strategic and tactical debacles ensured

---

[294] T'o-t'o, *Chin shih* 2, p. 36.

[295] Jing-shen Tao suggests that the "Jurchen were trying to capture as much Liao territory as possible
before sitting down at the negotiating table with the Chinese." See Tao, *Two sons of heaven*, p. 90.

[296] Hsü, *San-ch'ao pei-meng hui-pien* (1987) 5, pp. 8b–10b.

[297] Hsü, *San-ch'ao pei-meng hui-pien* (1987) 7, pp. 4b–6b.

[298] Hsü, *San-ch'ao pei-meng hui-pien* (1987) 10, pp. 1a–4a; 11, pp. 1a–6a.

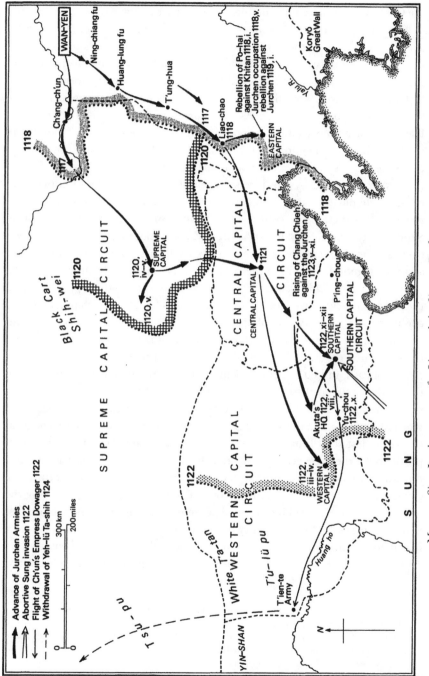

Map 20. Sino-Jurchen contest for Liao and the Sixteen Prefectures, 1117–1124.

that the Sung court would henceforth conduct diplomatic negotiations with the Chin on even more unfavorable terms. After the first defeat at Yen-ching, A-ku-ta changed the terms of the proposed alliance, promising only Yen-ching and six prefectures to the Sung, and dismissing Sung demands to receive Ta-t'ung and three coastal prefectures.[299] No match for even the Northern Liao, the Sung court had displayed its military weaknesses to a far superior ally.

Further indignities awaited the Sung court and its commanders. In the twelfth month of 1122, when A-ku-ta's army reached Yen-ching, the city's Han Chinese administrators unconditionally surrendered to the Chin before the battle had even begun.[300] Having failed to uphold its part of the bargain, the Sung court's continued demands for the cession of the Sixteen Prefectures were perceived by the Jurchen leadership as laughable. Occupying an unassailable position after conquering four of the five Liao capitals, A-ku-ta proceeded to dictate the terms of the formal Sung-Chin treaty of alliance. Sung negotiation tactics led to acrimony, and talks frequently broke down over territorial boundaries and indemnity payments. Concluded in the third and fourth months of 1123, the pact was decidedly disadvantageous to the Sung court. The Chin ceded Yen-ching and six surrounding prefectures to the Sung (Cho-chou, I-chou, T'an-chou2, Shun-chou, Ching-chou3, and Chi-chou) and their twenty-six subordinate counties. In return, the Sung would provide annual tribute payments of two hundred thousand taels of silver and three hundred thousand bolts of silk, and a one-time payment of one million strings of cash, in lieu of tax payments from the Yen region.[301] Furthermore, the border between the two states was decreed to be impermeable, and both sides were forbidden to harbor defectors, a provision that the Sung court soon violated. In the fourth month of 1123 Sung troops led by T'ung Kuan and Ts'ai Ching's eldest son, Ts'ai Yu (1077–1126), triumphantly entered Yen-ching, proclaiming the recovery of a city that had been under Khitan rule for two centuries. Two months later, the retired councilor Ts'ai Ching submitted a congratulatory memorial to Hui-tsung, praising the emperor for realizing the glorious martial legacy of his imperial progenitors by ensuring the extension of Sung hegemony.[302] But the reality beneath this overheated rhetoric was sobering. Before ceding the city, the Jurchen had looted its wealth and enslaved its citizens, rendering this so-called victory both literally and figuratively hollow.

[299] Hsü, San-ch'ao pei-meng hui-pien (1987) 11, pp. 6b–12a; 12, pp. 1b–3b.
[300] Hsü, San-ch'ao pei-meng hui-pien (1987) 12, pp. 4b–6a.
[301] For the Chin version of the treaty, see Hsü, San-ch'ao pei-meng hui-pien (1987) 15, pp. 11b–12b. For an English translation of the document, see Herbert Franke, "Treaties between Sung and Chin," in Études Song: In memoriam Étienne Balazs, ed. Françoise Aubin (Paris, 1970), pp. 60–4.
[302] Hsü, San-ch'ao pei-meng hui-pien (1987) 17, pp. 5a–6b.

Incapable of conquering the Sixteen Prefectures on its own, the Sung army had contributed little to the defeat of the Liao. Resigning themselves to the Jurchens' engulfing the greater part of the Liao empire, Hui-tsung and his ministers were fortunate to have recovered a mere six of the Sixteen Prefectures. By buying peace with the Chin and playing a minor role in the conquest of the Liao, the Sung concluded a Faustian bargain with an ally they could not defeat, let alone control. In their failed assault upon the Liao, the Sung revealed its feeble military capabilities to a potential adversary that had stormed across the steppe in a matter of years, and was still consolidating and expanding its dominion. And instead of ensuring peace along the northern border and stable diplomatic relations between the two empires, the Sung-Chin alliance quickly foundered.

Playing with fire: The first Sung-Chin war, 1123–1126

After the conclusion of the treaty of 1123, the Sung court soon provoked a renewed war with the Jurchen. Before the detailed terms of the pact could be implemented, the Sung apparently violated the spirit and the letter of the agreement. The Sixteen Prefectures were a politically unstable region, where spheres of influence were still undefined, and the loyalties of local administrators were uncertain. In the fifth month of 1123, Chang Chüeh, the onetime Liao military governor of P'ing-chou, assassinated the Chin regional commander and rebelled against Jurchen domination.[303] Commanding a formidable army, Chang transferred his allegiance to the Sung empire, which subsequently reappointed him to his former position.[304] Under their new monarch Wu-ch'i-mai (1075–1135), who succeeded his brother A-ku-ta and ascended the throne as Emperor Chin T'ai-tsung in 1123, the Chin dispatched a punitive expedition to P'ing-chou, defeating Chang's rebel army.[305] When Jurchen forces reconquered the renegade territories in the eleventh month of 1123, Chang Chüeh fled to Yen-ching, where he sought asylum. Deeming Chang a rebel and a traitor, Wu-ch'i-mai demanded his execution, and the Sung complied by sending his severed head to the Chin court. However, it was already too late to appease the Chin emperor; by harboring this defector, the Sung had broken its peace agreement with the Jurchen leadership, which exploited the unstable border situation to reassert direct control over the occupied territories. Two years later, Chang Chüeh's defection would provide Wu-ch'i-mai with a pretext for invading the Sung empire.

[303] *CPPM* 144, pp. 4349–51.
[304] *CPPM* 144, pp. 4352–5.
[305] *CPPM* 144, p. 4355.

In the meantime, Hui-tsung's courtiers were conducting border diplomacy with an arrogance above their station. The final status of the Yen-Yün region remained disputed and unsettled. In early 1124, with boldness that belied its military capabilities and diplomatic status, the Sung court demanded the cession of nine prefectures just north of the Liao border with Ho-tung circuit (modern Shansi). Dissent raged within the Jurchen inner circle over how to respond to these Sung demands. Wu-ch'i-mai favored ceding at least some of these disputed territories to the Sung, as he believed A-ku-ta might have done.[306] The Jurchen warrior princes Wan-yen Tsung-han and Wan-yen Tsung-wang vehemently opposed their new ruler's intentions, arguing that the Sung deserved no such reward.[307] Unwilling to divide his forces, which were committed to defeating Emperor Liao T'ien-tso, Wu-ch'i-mai granted two prefectures, Wu-chou3 and Shuo-chou (Shansi), to the Sung.[308] But this diplomatic feint represented the Chin court's final territorial concession to Hui-tsung and his ministers. Enraged by persistent Sung demands for more of the Sixteen Prefectures, the Jurchen leadership embraced military solutions in order to teach Hui-tsung and his ministers a lesson in humility.

Before it engaged the Sung in total war, the Jurchen commanders eliminated the remaining independent forces. To free their southwestern flank, the Chin court imposed a peace treaty upon the Hsi Hsia in the spring of 1124. In the northeast, Jurchen troops chased Emperor Liao T'ien-tso and his small personal army to Ying-chou6, where he was captured early the next year, thereby extinguishing the Liao dynasty. In the tenth month of 1125, Wu-ch'i-mai announced that the time had finally arrived to mobilize for a massive assault upon the Sung empire.[309] In his declaration of war, the Chin emperor announced his intention to punish the Sung court for its violation of the treaty of 1123. He chastised Hui-tsung and his ministers not only for harboring the fugitive rebel Chang Chüeh but also for falling behind in tribute payments and for failing to repatriate Chin refugees. Endangering a fragile alliance, the Sung court had been playing with fire, and the insolence of Sung diplomacy and the weakness of its military impelled the Jurchen to invade the Yellow River valley.

Chin forces stormed the northern fringes of the Sung empire, swiftly bringing the imperial court to its knees. In the eleventh month of 1125, Chin forces began a two-pronged southward assault, dividing into two marches.

---

[306] T'o-t'o, *Chin shih* 3, p. 49.

[307] T'o-t'o, *Chin shih* 74, p. 1695.

[308] Wu-chou3 and Shuo-chou correspond to modern Shen-chih and Shuo counties, respectively, in Shansi province.

[309] T'o-t'o, *Chin shih* 3, p. 53; 74, p. 1704.

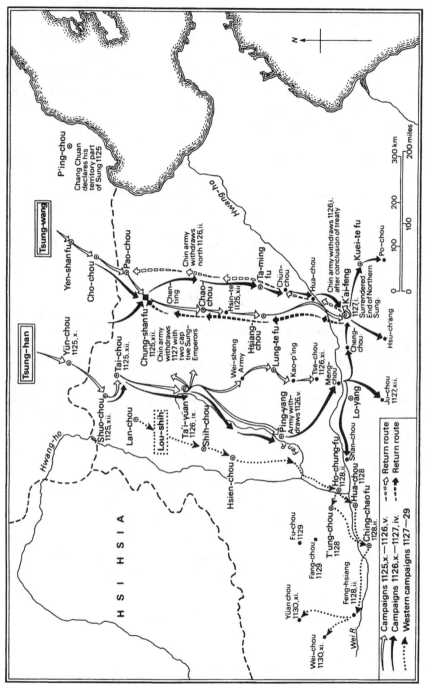

Map 21. The Chin invasions of Northern Sung.

The western army, under Wan-yen Tsung-han, swept south toward T'ai-yüan and Lo-yang, while the eastern army, under Wan-yen Tsung-wang, targeted Yen-ching and K'ai-feng. Without the Sixteen Prefectures to protect it, the entire North China Plain presented few obstacles to invasion from the north. By the end of 1125, Sung border garrisons in Ho-tung had fallen in quick succession to Tsung-han's forces.[310] When the western march laid siege to the Sung Northern Capital of T'ai-yüan, an alarmed T'ung Kuan deserted his post and fled back to the capital. In his absence, defenders under the general Wang Ping offered staunch resistance, and the strategic garrison valiantly held out until the ninth month of 1126, preventing the western march of Chin forces from reaching the Western Capital of Lo-yang.[311] Meanwhile, Tsung-wang and his eastern march met with little resistance in their lightning offensive. At Yen-ching, the former Liao general Kuo Yao-shih betrayed the Sung when he surrendered and defected to the Chin.[312] Using Kuo's inside information, the eastern march conquered the plains of Ho-pei unopposed, capturing the strategic garrisons of Chung-shan and Chen-ting by the end of 1125.[313] In the first days of the new year, the Jurchen army approached the banks of the Yellow River, reaching within striking distance of K'ai-feng.

As disaster reports arrived from both fronts, the Sung court was thrown into panic and turmoil, and Hui-tsung made belated and half-hearted efforts to manage the crisis.[314] In a bid to regain the loyalty of his disgruntled subjects, he assented to the abolition of the flower and rock network, which had been revived right after the quelling of the Fang La rebellion. Foreseeing certain disaster, the state councilor Yü-wen Hsü-chung convinced the emperor to assume personal responsibility for the dire military situation. In a self-incriminatory edict issued at the end of the year, Hui-tsung voiced his profound regret for failing to preserve the legacy of his imperial progenitors, and summoned a loyalist citizen army to the rescue of the dynasty.[315] But the time for noble and empty words had passed, as Jurchen forces threatened K'ai-feng, only a week's march away. Scared witless by these events beyond his control, Hui-tsung informed his councilors that he desired to vacate the capital and flee to safety in the south. Led by Wu Min and Li Kang, the emperor's inner circle of ministers persuaded him that such a course was tantamount to surrender, and asserted that his only alternative was to abdicate the throne in favor of the heir apparent. Departing

[310] T'o-t'o, *Chin shih* 3, p. 54; Hsü, *San-ch'ao pei-meng hui-pien* (1987) 23, pp. 10a–11b.

[311] T'o-t'o, *Chin shih* 3, pp. 54–5; Hsü, *San-ch'ao pei-meng hui-pien* (1987) 53, pp. 1a–3a.

[312] *SS* 472, p. 13739.

[313] T'o-t'o, *Chin shih* 3, p. 54.

[314] For an English-language treatment of the "tragedy of Ching-k'ang," see John Winthrop Haeger, "1126–27: Political crisis and the integrity of culture," in *Crisis and prosperity in Sung China*, ed. John Winthrop Haeger (Tucson, Ariz., 1975), pp. 143–61.

[315] *CPPM* 146, pp. 4416–9.

K'ai-feng with his retinue to establish a separate court in the relative safety of the Southern Capital of Ying-t'ien-fu, Hui-tsung retained the title Emperor Emeritus (*t'ai-shang huang-ti*), with ritual authority but no political power. On the twenty-third day of the twelfth month of 1125, his eldest son, Chao Huan (1100–61), assumed the throne as the last monarch of the Northern Sung, and would be known to history as Emperor Sung Ch'in-tsung (r. 1126–7).[316] An unprecedented event in Sung imperial ritual, Hui-tsung's abdication (*nei-ch'an*) apparently elicited little criticism from the Council of State, who rationalized that an abdicated ruler was eminently preferable to a defunct dynasty.

While he was a more activist monarch than his father, Ch'in-tsung was not the determined ruler the dynasty required, and he proved to be overly impressionable. Easily swayed by the counsel of an ever-changing cast of ministers, Ch'in-tsung vacillated between appeasing the Jurchen and provoking them. However, not even a resolute sovereign could have saved the dynasty at this juncture. With a vastly superior enemy approaching the capital, the symbolic revitalization of the monarchy and the installation of Ch'in-tsung could not extricate the Sung from its disastrous entanglement with the Jurchen.

When Jurchen forces crossed the Yellow River early in the new year, the first year of the Ching-k'ang era, the court was sharply divided between hawks and doves. Opposing the appeasers Pai Shih-chung and Li Pang-yen, Li Kang convinced the timorous Ch'in-tsung to mount a resolute defense of K'ai-feng. Li and his allies gained the emperor's trust for the time being, and an imperial edict of the seventh day of the first month of 1126 admonished K'ai-feng's soldiers and citizens to prepare siege defenses.[317] That evening, when the vanguard of Jurchen troops approached the walls of K'ai-feng, Li Kang led a small contingent to repel them, forcing the invaders to momentarily withdraw.[318] But when an entire Chin army encircled the capital, the divided Sung court desperately decided to pursue diplomacy instead. Ch'in-tsung dismissed Li Kang from court and authorized his ministers to begin peace negotiations with the Chin commanders. Hesitant to incur huge casualties during a protracted siege, the Jurchen commanders made Sung envoys an offer they could not refuse. During the negotiations, Ch'in-tsung's younger brother Prince K'ang (the future Emperor Kao-tsung) and the accommodationist minister Chang Pang-ch'ang were held as hostages. With reinforcements far from the capital and the enemy at the gates, the Sung court was caught in a painfully vulnerable position. The withdrawal of the Jurchen army would come at an astronomically high price: cession of the three strategic prefectures of T'ai-yüan, Chung-shan, and Ho-chien, which lay directly south of the Sixteen Prefectures and constituted

---

[316] *CPPM* 146, pp. 4423–8; *SS* 23, p. 421.
[317] Hsü, *San-ch'ao pei-meng hui-pien* (1987) 28, pp. 5a–6a.
[318] Hsü, *San-ch'ao pei-meng hui-pien* (1987) 28, pp. 7b–9a.

the Sung empire's northeastern defensive perimeter. Further exacerbating the situation, annual tribute payments to the Chin court would be substantially increased to three hundred thousand taels of silver, three hundred thousand bolts of silk, and one million strings of cash.

Debate raged at court over whether Ch'in-tsung should accept the terms of this dictated peace. Pai Shih-chung and Li Pang-yen deemed these sacrifices necessary to save the dynasty. To Li Kang and other intransigents like him, this hard bargain appeared extortionate, a violation of the territorial and moral integrity of the empire. As the bulk of Sung forces reached the capital from the northwestern border at the end of the first month of 1126, recalcitrant elements gained the upper hand at court. In an audience before the throne held on the twenty-seventh day of the first month of 1126, Li Kang advocated the deployment of crack troops against the Chin forces, who remained encamped outside the city walls. Li convinced the emperor that since Sung forces outnumbered the adversary three to one, they would be assured victory.[319] Recently returned from the northwestern front, the general Ch'ung Shih-tao concurred with Li Kang's prognosis. Ch'ung articulated a plan to stubbornly defend K'ai-feng until the Chin troops were fatigued and their provisions were exhausted, after which Sung forces would intercept the withdrawing Jurchen army. His colleague Yao P'ing-chung suggested a nighttime ambush on the Chin encampments, but when it was carried out the mission was a complete fiasco, further enraging Prince Tsung-wang.[320] Under duress to apologize to the Jurchen, Ch'in-tsung dismissed Li, Ch'ung, and Yao from their posts, and reappointed the appeasers Chang Pang-ch'ang and Li Pang-yen to his Council of State.

This forced concession precipitated a popular outcry among the residents of K'ai-feng, led by the Imperial University student Ch'en Tung, who has been lionized by traditional historiography as a loyalist hero and martyr.[321] Ch'en repeatedly memorialized the throne to demand the execution of Hui-tsung's ministers Ts'ai Ching, T'ung Kuan, Wang Fu, Liang Shih-ch'eng, Li Yen, and Chu Mien, whom he condemned as the "Six Felons" (*liu tsei*).[322] He alleged that the corrupt and sinister regime of these "treacherous ministers" had enervated the empire from within while recklessly opening rifts with neighboring

---

[319] Hsü, *San-ch'ao pei-meng hui-pien* (1987) 32, pp. 3b–4a. Sung troops numbered two hundred thousand, while approximately seventy thousand Chin troops were encamped at K'ai-feng.

[320] Hsü, *San-ch'ao pei-meng hui-pien* (1987) 33, pp. 1a–2b.

[321] For Ch'en Tung's official biography as an exemplar of "loyalty and righteousness" (*i-chung*), see SS 455, pp. 13359–62. For a brief English-language biography of Ch'en Tung, see Edward H. Kaplan, "Ch'en Tung," in *Sung biographies*, ed. Herbert Franke (Wiesbaden, 1976), vol. 1, pp. 124–32. Also see Richard L. Davis, *Wind against the mountain: The crisis of politics and culture in thirteenth-century China* (Cambridge, Mass., 1996), pp. 126–7.

[322] *Ching-k'ang yao-lu* [*Ts'ung-shu chi-ch'eng ch'u-pien* 1935–7 ed.] (c. 1165; Peking, 1985) 2, pp. 24–8.

states. In later memorials, Ch'en implored the emperor to replace the current proappeasement ministers with Li Kang, whom he deemed a suitably intransigent candidate for the councilorship. On the fifth day of the second month of 1126, Ch'en Tung led a massive political demonstration that turned into a near-revolt, when irate commoners stormed the palace gates on a rampage, slaughtering dozens of eunuchs. The murderous crowd dispersed after the court announced that Ch'en's demands would be met.

Succumbing to popular pressure, the emperor ordered the execution of these "treacherous ministers" who had brought the empire to the brink of destruction. Now elderly and blind, Ts'ai Ching was banished from court in the second month of 1126, dying under house arrest in T'an-chou (modern Ch'ang-sha) five months later; his sons and grandsons were either executed or exiled to the fringes of the empire.[323] After escaping with the abdicating Hui-tsung, T'ung Kuan was dismissed from service, banished, and ultimately decapitated, signaling the end of eunuch domination of the inner court. Punished as scapegoats for the Chin invasion, the remaining "Six Felons" were also sentenced to death the same year. After monopolizing power for twenty-five years, Hui-tsung's "treacherous ministers" did not live to see the dynasty fall, but would be subject to the everlasting condemnation of history.

With a restive city still under siege, Ch'in-tsung finally decided to accommodate the invaders rather than his protesting subjects. Some of their demands had been met: the "Six Felons" were punished, but Li Kang was not reinstated. The appeasers who dominated the Council of State persuaded the emperor to avoid any further provocation by signing the dictated peace agreement and authorizing the cession of the three garrisons to the Chin. When the emperor officially apologized, and his councilors voiced their commitment to uphold the treaty, the Chin army withdrew from the capital on the tenth day of the second month of 1126. Returning Prince K'ang and Chang Pang-ch'ang to the Sung court, Tsung-wang's eastern march proceeded north with the Prince of Hsiao, the emperor's younger brother, as its hostage. The Jurchen had been appeased with territory, and if a lasting peace had not been achieved, at least disaster had been staved off and time had been bought.

The tragedy of Ching-k'ang: The second Sung-Chin war and its aftermath, 1126–1127

After the Jurchen lifted their siege of K'ai-feng and returned north, Ch'in-tsung rehabilitated the prowar faction and committed himself to a policy of armed resistance. But by shifting again from accommodation to provocation,

---

[323] *SS* 472, pp. 13727–8; *CPPM* 131, pp. 4007–8.

the emperor incited a second war with the Jurchen. For most of the next eight months, the Council of State and command structure were dominated by ministers and generals who rejected the recently concluded Sung-Chin treaty. On the twenty-fifth day of the second month of 1126, the appeasers Li Pang-yen and Chang Pang-ch'ang were ousted from court, to be replaced by Li Kang and Wu Min.[324] Ch'ung Shih-tao was also reappointed to the emperor's war cabinet, commanding imperial troops to resist Jurchen domination of Ho-pei and Ho-tung circuits. Before Prince Tsung-wang's eastern march reclaimed Chung-shan and Ho-chien, they met with staunch resistance from Sung defenders.

With both sides unaware of the peace agreement, the conflict raged on in the valleys of mountainous Ho-tung circuit (Shansi), where the western march of the Chin armed forces continued on the warpath, butchering the defenders of Lung-te, who had dared to resist the invaders.[325] When Tsung-han's main force withdrew north to Ta-t'ung in the third month of 1126, he left a smaller force behind to continue besieging T'ai-yüan. Between the second and seventh months of 1126, several Sung forces were dispatched to Ho-tung to rescue the city. Time and again, these relief divisions were isolated and defeated by the Chin before they could reach T'ai-yüan. Ch'in-tsung's court did not completely lack glimmers of hope, but scattered Sung victories at Shou-yang and Yü-tz'u in mid-1126 merely postponed the inevitable.

Not surprisingly, the Jurchen leadership interpreted the resolute Sung defense of the three ceded prefectures as a violation of the recently signed armistice. In the eighth month of 1126, Wan-yen Tsung-han and Tsung-wang committed themselves to a punitive assault on the Sung empire, again dividing their troops into eastern and western marches.[326] Tsung-han's forces proceeded south to mount a ferocious attack upon T'ai-yüan. Stubbornly holding out for more than two hundred fifty days, its defenders exhausted all their provisions, and approximately ninety percent of the city's residents died of starvation or disease.[327] On the third day of the ninth month of 1126, the last pockets of Sung resistance were eliminated, when the intransigent general Wang Ping died in battle and the defeated city's prefect surrendered to the Jurchen.[328] Not only had Sung troops failed to lift the siege, but the remaining crack divisions had been annihilated in the process, rendering K'ai-feng indefensible in the face of the oncoming Jurchen onslaught.

[324] *SS* 23, p. 425.

[325] *SS* 23, p. 425; T'o-t'o, *Chin shih* 3, p. 54. Lung-te *fu* corresponds to modern Ch'ang-chih city, Shansi province.

[326] T'o-t'o, *Chin shih* 3, p. 55.

[327] Hsü, *San-ch'ao pei-meng hui-pien* (1987) 53, pp. 6a–8b.

[328] *SS* 23, p. 430; T'o-t'o, *Chin shih* 3, p. 55.

All of the north was now theirs for the taking. After pacifying T'ai-yüan, Tsung-wang's western march swept southward, conquering the major garrisons of southern Shansi in the eleventh month of 1126. Soundly defeating a contingent of Sung forces at the Yellow River crossing, they proceeded to force the surrender of the Western Capital of Lo-yang and then marched east to K'ai-feng. Under Tsung-han's command, the eastern wing of the Chin army also conquered everything in its path, meeting with minimal opposition from beleaguered Sung reserve forces. By the end of the eleventh month, they recaptured the key Ho-pei cities of Chen-ting and Ta-ming, crossed the Yellow River, and reached the walls of the capital.[329] Early in the following intercalary month, imperial troops emerged from the threatened capital to engage the Jurchen in a disastrous battle. A few days later, the two marches of the Chin army were reunited outside the gates of K'ai-feng, which they encircled for the second time that year.

In the intervening months, Ch'in-tsung's court had undergone yet another change of ministerial regimes. The fall of T'ai-yüan was the turning point of the Sung–Chin wars, revealing the futility of continued resistance and resulting in the fall of the war faction. Led by T'ang K'o and Keng Nan-chung, advocates of appeasement regained the emperor's ear. Panicked peace overtures to the Jurchen commanders resumed in the tenth month of 1126 and continued for another month. A series of envoys, which included the emperor's brother Chao Kou, Prince K'ang, opened diplomatic channels with the Jurchen commanders in a desperate attempt to save the dynasty from certain collapse. As they had twice before, the Sung negotiators offered land for peace, but the return of the three previously ceded prefectures of T'ai-yüan, Chung-shan, and Ho-chien was by the Chin high command rejected as a mere token gesture.[330]

By the beginning of the eleventh month, the Chin marches crossed the Yellow River and closed in on K'ai-feng, making the conclusion of peace at any price an urgent matter for Ch'in-tsung and his councilors. But because the Sung court had (from the Chin perspective) repeatedly negotiated in bad faith and its armed forces were all but powerless, the Jurchen were in a position to demand staggering territorial sacrifices. To prevent the imminent Jurchen conquest, the Sung court would have to authorize the cession of all territories north of the Yellow River, which would be demarcated as the new interstate boundary.[331] To help seal the pact, an imperial edict of the seventh day of the eleventh month of 1126 ordered the millions of imperial subjects in

---

[329] T'o-t'o, *Chin shih* 3, p. 56. Chen-ting and Ta-ming correspond to modern Pao-ting and Ta-ming in Hopei province.

[330] Hsü, *San-ch'ao pei-meng hui-pien* (1987) 58, pp. 6a–7a.

[331] Hsü, *San-ch'ao pei-meng hui-pien* (1987) 63, pp. 13b–14b.

Ho-pei and Ho-tung to open their gates to the invaders and surrender without a fight.[332] The next day, the cession of territory was intensely debated at court, but the emperor overrode opposition from the war faction to resume peace talks.[333] While the court remained divided between advocates of surrender and resistance, the negotiations continued, even after the battle for the capital had begun.

Toward the end of the year, the two Jurchen armies began their siege of K'ai-feng, meeting with heavy resistance for more than twenty days, with severe casualties on both sides.[334] But before long the capital's defenders were virtually annihilated and its inner defenses severely compromised. The first wave of Chin troops broke through the walls under the cover of a snowstorm.[335] Ch'in-tsung emerged from the defeated city to discuss terms with the princes Wan-yen Tsung-han and Wan-yen Tsung-wang at their encampment, and his official declaration of unconditional surrender was issued on the second day of the last month of 1126.[336] Four days later, representatives of the imperial court officially ceded Ho-tung and Ho-pei circuits in their entirety to the Chin; an imperial edict ordered Sung subjects in these territories to surrender to their new masters. In celebration of their momentous victory, Jurchen soldiers looted K'ai-feng. In the first days of the new year, Ch'in-tsung and his councilors were summoned to the Chin field headquarters and held hostage while the city was plundered, yielding massive quantities of gold, silver, and silk.

In the final tragic act of the "Calamity of Ching-k'ang," the physical and living symbols of the dynasty and monarchy were captured and stripped of their potency. Raiding the palace precincts, the Jurchen emptied the palace treasure houses of imperial seals, jewels, antiquities, rare books, art objects, and ritual implements, and captured hundreds of members of the imperial retinue.[337] Chin forces also captured Emperor Hui-tsung, interrupting his flight to safety in the south, and delivered him as a prisoner to the Jurchen commanders at K'ai-feng. On the sixth day of the second month of 1127, the Chin court issued an edict that symbolically decapitated the dynasty by stripping both Ch'in-tsung and Hui-tsung of imperial status.[338] With these brushstrokes, embodied by its monarchs, the Northern Sung government effectively ceased to exist. Its demise had been hastened by negligent and vacillating monarchs, whose irredentist ministers and generals had dragged the empire into two wars

---

[332] Hsü, *San-ch'ao pei-meng hui-pien* (1987) 62, pp. 8b–10a.
[333] Hsü, *San-ch'ao pei-meng hui-pien* (1987) 62, pp. 10b–13a.
[334] *SS* 23, pp. 433–4.
[335] Hsü, *San-ch'ao pei-meng hui-pien* (1987) 69, pp. 1a–6b.
[336] Hsü, *San-ch'ao pei-meng hui-pien* (1987) 71, pp. 3b–5a.
[337] Hsü, *San-ch'ao pei-meng hui-pien* (1987) 77, pp. 12b–14a.
[338] Hsü, *San-ch'ao pei-meng hui-pien* (1987) 78, pp. 9a–11b; T'o-t'o, *Chin shih* 3, p. 56.

with the Jurchen. With duplicitous diplomacy and strategic negligence, the courts of Hui-tsung and Ch'in-tsung had squandered their resources in border entanglements.

When the Jurchen commanders triumphantly returned north to the Jurchen homeland, they were trailed by a caravan filled with treasures from the imperial palace. Humiliated by the sack of K'ai-feng, the two former Sung emperors and an entourage of three thousand followed behind as captives. Their number included almost the entire imperial clan, comprising consorts, princes, and princesses, as well as eunuchs, entertainers, artisans, and servants. After a long and arduous journey, Hui-tsung and Ch'in-tsung spent the rest of their lives as prisoners in the alien forests of modern Heilungkiang, their retinue enslaved. In 1135, Hui-tsung passed away at the age of fifty-four; his son and successor Ch'in-tsung would spend more than half of his life in captivity, before dying in 1161.[339]

After the fall of K'ai-feng and the capture of the two emperors, the Sung dynasty's fate dangled by a slender thread. Across their occupied territories in Ho-pei and Ho-tung, the Jurchen conquerors faced widespread noncompliance from armed Sung loyalists. Instead of immediately incorporating them into the Chin empire, the Chin leaders relinquished former Sung territories north of the Yellow River to a puppet regime headed by the former chief councilor Chang Pang-ch'ang, who was enthroned as emperor of the newly created state of Ta Ch'u in the third month of 1127.[340] Alone among Hui-tsung's progeny, Chao Kou, Prince K'ang, had escaped the siege of K'ai-feng and was able to to command resistance efforts in Ho-pei. In the fifth month of 1127, Chang Pang-ch'ang was persuaded to relinquish his throne to Chao Kou, who was proclaimed emperor of the Sung at its Southern Capital of Ying-t'ien-fu. Under the rule of Kao-tsung, the Sung polity was restored in the south as a rump state with its temporary capital at Lin-an (present-day Hang-chou). After its refounding, the Sung court's armed forces waged a protracted war against the Chin empire until a peace was negotiated in 1142. But in the immediate aftermath of the "Calamity of Ch'ing-k'ang," it remained to be seen whether Kao-tsung's resuscitated imperial regime could rescue the empire from the brink of ruin.

---

[339] SS 22, p. 417; 23, p. 436.

[340] Hsü, San-ch'ao pei-meng hui-pien (1987) 84, pp. 5a–6a; SS 475, pp. 13790–1; T'o-t'o, Chin shih 3, p. 56.

CHAPTER 8

THE MOVE TO THE SOUTH AND THE REIGN OF KAO-TSUNG (1127–1162)

Tao Jing-shen

Chao Kou (1107–87), known by his posthumous temple name as Kao-tsung (r. 1127–62), was the ninth son of Emperor Hui-tsung (r. 1100–26) and a younger brother of Emperor Ch'in-tsung (r. 1126–7). Kao-tsung was the emperor who led the restoration of the Sung dynasty and inaugurated what is known as the Southern Sung dynasty (1127–1279). Resisting the Chin dynasty's attempts at further conquest, the Southern Sung dynasty lasted more than one hundred and fifty years and enjoyed decades of economic and cultural prosperity. In traditional Chinese historiography the Southern Sung is considered a weak dynasty, humiliated as a vassal state by the Chin (Jurchen) dynasty (1115–1234). Kao-tsung is criticized for being a weak ruler unable to avenge Sung's humiliation at the hands of Chin and unable to recover the Sung's former northern territory. Kao-tsung is also criticized because he and his vilified chief councilor, Ch'in Kuei (1090–1155), were responsible for the death of general Yüeh Fei (1103–41), who, because of his efforts in resisting Chin, came to be regarded as a "national hero." Despite these criticisms, Kao-tsung is perhaps better to be remembered as the young emperor who reigned through a period of disastrous military defeats and near-terminal political crises as the Sung dynasty faced oblivion, and yet later oversaw two decades of resistance, stability, and recovery.

THE ESTABLISHMENT OF KAO-TSUNG'S RULE

In the winter of 1125, the Chin sent two armies to attack the Sung. The Chin accused the Sung of not observing the treaty of 1123, which had specified the terms of the alliance between the two states against the now vanquished Liao. The western Chin army, under the command of Wan-yen Nien-han (also known as Wan-yen Tsung-han, 1079–1136), laid siege to the important northern fortress city of T'ai-yüan (Shansi). The eastern Chin army, under the command of Wan-yen Wo-li-pu (or Tsung-wan, d. 1127), met little resistance as it advanced from the former Liao Southern Capital (modern Peking) toward the Central Plains. In early 1126, Wo-li-pu's army crossed the Yellow River and laid siege to the Sung capital, K'ai-feng. The Sung emperor, Hui-tsung, after hastily abdicating the throne to his son Ch'in-tsung, had already fled south. Many officials now encouraged Ch'in-tsung also to escape, but Li Kang (1083–1140), vice-minister of war, who along with others had urged Hui-tsung to abdicate, convinced the new emperor to remain and resist the Chin invasion.

Ch'in-tsung relied heavily on Li Kang to organize the capital's defenses, and Li sent officers to summon reinforcements from other Sung armies.[1] The Sung court also sent a diplomatic mission to negotiate with the Jurchen leadership. The Sung proposed a peace treaty stipulating that the Sung would send vastly increased annual payments to Chin as they had done with Liao, and the Sung would cede three strategic frontier prefectures, Chung-shan and Ho-chien in Ho-pei, and T'ai-yüan in Ho-tung, possession of which would permit Chin to dominate the northeastern regions of Ho-pei and Shansi. The Sung government dispatched a royal prince as a hostage to accompany the Chin army on its return to the north, and also a chief councilor to see that the three Sung prefectures were duly handed over.[2] Ch'in-tsung's younger brother, Chao Kou, who then held the title Prince K'ang, volunteered to go to the Chin camp to negotiate. However, soon after he and Chief Councilor Chang Pang-ch'ang (1081–1127) arrived at the Jurchen headquarters, Yao P'ing-chung (b. 1099), a Sung military officer, launched an unauthorized surprise attack on the Jurchen encampment in an abortive attempt to capture Wan-yen Wo-li-pu and free Prince K'ang. The attack enraged Wo-li-pu, but he nevertheless concluded the treaty. The Sung court in K'ai-feng held Li Kang responsible for the military fiasco and had him dismissed. Disgusted with this decision by the government, students of the Imperial University (*T'ai-hsüeh*), led by Ch'en Tung, staged a demonstration in front of the imperial palaces in K'ai-feng, where they were

[1] For the siege of K'ai-feng and the role of Li Kang, see John W. Haeger, "1126–27: Political crisis and the integrity of culture," in *Crisis and prosperity in Sung China*, ed. John W. Haeger (Tucson, Ariz., 1975), pp. 143–61. See also the preceding chapter.

[2] The principal historical source for Kao-tsung's reign is the *Chien-yen i-lai hsi-nien yao-lu* [hereafter *CYYL* (1936)] [*Shih hsüeh ts'ung shu* 1899–1902 ed.] (1253–8; Shanghai, 1936) by the Szechwanese historian Li Hsin-ch'uan (1166–1243). The three most useful overviews of Kao-tsung's reign are Liu Tzu-chien (James T. C. Liu), *China turning inward: Intellectual-political changes in the early twelfth century* (Cambridge, Mass., 1988); Teraji Jun, *Nan-Sō shoki seijishi kenkyū* (Hiroshima, 1988), translated into Chinese as *Nan Sung ch'u-ch'i cheng-chih-shih yen-chiu*, trans. Liu Ching-chen and Li Chin-yun (Taipei, 1995); and Ho Chung-li and Hsü Chi-chün, *Nan Sung shih-kao: Cheng-chih, chün-shih, wen-hua* (Hang-chou, 1999), pp. 3–197. The clearest account of the Chin conquest in English is Herbert Franke, "The Chin dynasty," in *The Cambridge history of China*, volume 6: *Alien regimes and border states, 907–1368*, ed. Herbert Franke and Denis C. Twitchett (New York, 1994), pp. 215–320. For a discussion of the treaty between the Sung and the Chin, see Herbert Franke, "Treaties between Sung and Chin," in *Études Song: In memoriam Étienne Balazs*, ed. Françoise Aubin (Paris, 1970), pp. 54–84.

joined by more than one hundred thousand citizens. A riot ensued in which several eunuchs were killed. To appease the protestors, the new emperor, Ch'in-tsung, restored Li Kang's official title and gave him the additional position of grand commissioner of defense (*shou-yü shih*).

In the spring of 1126, Chin forces raised their siege of K'ai-feng and their armies returned north. The abdicated emperor, Hui-tsung, returned to K'ai-feng in the fourth month of 1126. Everything seemed to return to normal. Li Kang was again dismissed. His defense plans were laid aside, and the government canceled all the orders he had issued summoning reinforcements to bolster the defenses of K'ai-feng. But the Sung court also refused to give up the three strategic prefectures to Chin as had been agreed. In the autumn of 1126, charging that the Sung court had breached the treaty, the Jurchen generals renewed their attacks. T'ai-yüan fell in the ninth month of 1126, and the western and eastern Jurchen armies advanced, converging on K'ai-feng. On the ninth of January 1127, the capital fell after weeks of heavy fighting. The city was plundered by the Chin army. The Jurchen captured the two emperors, Hui-tsung and his son Ch'in-tsung, and in May 1127 removed them to the north together with many members of the imperial clan and their entourage of palace ladies, eunuchs, musicians, artisans, and officials, and the palace treasures. This tragic incident has become known as the Calamity of Ching-k'ang (*Ching-k'ang chih-nan*), Ching-k'ang being Ch'in-tsung's reign title.[3]

At this stage of the invasion it seemed that the Jurchen were not considering the conquest of the whole of the Sung empire. Jurchen forces, although formidable in battle, were comparatively small in numbers, and were still engaged in establishing firm control over the extensive former territories of Liao that they had just acquired. They, therefore, decided to establish a buffer state under their own control to rule over the conquered Sung territory, and employed a policy of what was called "using Chinese to control the Chinese." Before Chin forces left K'ai-feng to return north, they set up the new puppet regime called Ta Ch'u (Great Ch'u) to rule over most of the occupied territories, with the former Sung chief councilor, Chang Pang-ch'ang, enthroned as its emperor. They then withdrew most of their forces north from the K'ai-feng region.

Chang Pang-ch'ang, while enticed by the prospect of being an emperor, did not dare to assume full Sung imperial regalia or to exercise full powers. Only when he had to meet his Jurchen masters would he put on an emperor's yellow

---

[3] For a discussion of some of the historiographical implications of the fall of the Northern Sung, see Chao Hsiang-en (Samuel H. Chao), "The day Northern Sung fell," *Chung-yüan hsüeh-pao* No. 8 (1979), pp. 144–57, and Charles Hartman, "The reluctant historian: Sun Ti, Chu Hsi, and the fall of Northern Sung," *T'oung Pao* 89 Nos. 1–3 (2003), pp. 100–48.

robes. To give some legitimacy and stability to his new regime, he enlisted the support of Dowager Empress Yüan-yu (1077–1135), whom he entitled the Dowager Empress of Sung. The former wife of Emperor Che-tsung (r. 1085–1100), the dowager empress had escaped capture by the Chin army with the rest of the imperial family only because in 1096 Che-tsung had demoted her from her rank as empress, and in 1126 she was residing outside the palace in a private mansion.[4]

Survival

When Chin forces had first besieged K'ai-feng in 1125–6, Prince K'ang (the future Kao-tsung) volunteered to serve as a hostage, but Sung leaders instead sent his more tractable older brother, Prince Su (Hui-tsung's third son, d. 1129). When Chin attacked the capital for the second time in 1126, Prince K'ang was again sent by the Sung court to negotiate with the invaders. But the prince never reached his destination. On the way north, he was detained by the people of Tz'u-chou (modern Tz'u county, Hopei), who were enraged about the situation. From the besieged city of K'ai-feng, Emperor Ch'in-tsung sent an order appointing Prince K'ang as the overall commander of the armed forces in Ho-pei. Prince K'ang was the only imperial prince not in K'ai-feng when the city came under siege and thereby escaped capture by the Chin army when they finally took the capital at the end of 1126.

After the Jurchen armies withdrew, the remaining Sung officials persuaded the Ta Ch'u "emperor," Chang Pang-ch'ang, to relinquish his throne in favor of Prince K'ang, who had not returned to K'ai-feng during or after the siege and did not arrive in Ying-t'ien fu (at Kuei-te, the present Shang-ch'iu in Honan), the site of the Sung's provisional Southern Capital, until the twenty-fourth of the fourth month 1127. Chang Pang-ch'ang offered no objections, and on the first of the fifth month of 1127 at Ying-t'ien fu Dowager Empress Yüan-yu proclaimed Prince K'ang as the new Sung emperor. The state of Ta Ch'u had lasted for barely one month. The proclamation of the succession observed: "After nine generations the house of Han met with misfortune; then there came Han Kuang-wu-ti's restoration [in 25 C.E.]. Among the nine sons of Duke Hsien [of the state of Chin during the Spring and Autumn period], Chung-erh alone survived. This was ordained by Heaven, and was not the work of human beings."[5]

The enthronement of Prince K'ang was thus compared to the restoration of the Liu family with the enthronement of Emperor Han Kuang-wu-ti (r. 25–56)

---

[4] T'o-t'o et al., eds., *Sung shih* [hereafter *SS*] (1345; Peking, 1977) 243, pp. 8633–5.
[5] *CYYL* (1936) 4, p. 107.

of the Eastern Han dynasty (25–220). Moreover, the number "nine" was used by the new regime to show cosmic symmetry between Prince K'ang and the Sung dynastic line, as there had been nine previous emperors in what would be known as the Northern Sung, and Chao Kou, Prince K'ang, was the ninth son of Hui-tsung.

Now Chao Kou unexpectedly found himself on the throne facing the enormous responsibilities of saving and rebuilding the dynasty. He was only twenty-one years old. There had been little or no prospect of Chao Kou's ever becoming emperor, and he had never been trained for the exercise of power as heir apparent, although he was well educated and a fine calligrapher. Over the previous year and a half he had already experienced many hardships, and had twice narrowly escaped death. During his brief diplomatic mission with Chin generals in 1126, he had conducted himself with courage and dignity. When Yao P'ing-chung launched his surprise attack on the Chin army encampment, while Chao Kou was hostage there, the Jurchen general, Wan-yen Wo-li-pu, was furious at Prince K'ang and Chang Pang-ch'ang for the disruption of the negotiations, but he spared their lives and released them. Chao Kou was reported to have been "very alarmed."[6] It must have been a terrifying experience, especially when Chao Kou realized that the Jurchen could have held him forever. Again, when Chao Kou was on the second diplomatic mission, had he not been detained by the people in Tz'u-chou but proceeded to the Jurchen camp to negotiate as planned, he might never have been released by the Chin forces.

As the new emperor, Kao-tsung appointed Li Kang as his first chief councilor, and also created the new office of commissioner of the imperial encampment (*yü-ying shih*) for him. Without a large imperial army readily available, Li Kang suggested that the new court immediately concentrate on strengthening the defenses in the north. Li appointed Chang So and Fu Liang to manage military affairs in Ho-pei and Ho-tung, respectively, and recommended that the elderly Tsung Tse (1059–1128) be placed in charge of defending the capital, K'ai-feng, and of planning a northern counteroffensive against Chin. However, the new emperor at this point had no intention of returning with his court to K'ai-feng, which was vulnerable to renewed Chin attacks. Instead, he was in favor of retreating to the southeast, a policy quite contrary to Li Kang's idea, which was to move west to Teng-chou2 (Nan-yang) or still farther west to

---

6 According to Hsü Meng-hsin, *San-ch'ao pei-meng hui-pien* (1196; Taipei, 1962) 33, pp. 8a–10, "the Prince was very alarmed." However, SS 24, pp. 439–40, indicates that Chang Pang-ch'ang was frightened, whereas Prince K'ang was not, and that this was why Wo-li-pu asked for his replacement with the more tractable Prince Su. This version of events is supported by Li Kang's personal memoir of the Ching-k'ang reign.

the key strategic stronghold of Hsiang-yang. Moreover, Li Kang took a hard line that opposed negotiating with the Chin, and he also insisted that Chang Pang-ch'ang be punished as a usurper and traitor.[7] Eventually Kao-tsung gave in, and the unfortunate Chang Pang-ch'ang was executed.

Although he gave in to Li Kang on this issue, Kao-tsung came to put more confidence in Huang Ch'ien-shan (d. 1129) and Wang Po-yen, who were among the first officials to join him when he was raising an army of resistance.[8] Huang and Wang were said to have treated Kao-tsung "like nursemaids protecting a baby." Kao-tsung especially liked Huang, and years later the emperor praised him for his great contributions to the establishment of the new regime at a time when Kao-tsung himself admitted that he had not had the slightest idea what to do.

Kao-tsung soon showed the independent and decisive side of his character, however, when after only seventy-five days in office Chief Councilor Li Kang was dismissed and Kao-tsung formally replaced him with Huang Ch'ien-shan and Wang Po-yen. Both men shared the emperor's reluctance to return to K'ai-feng and advised him to plan instead to move his court farther south. On their advice he also decided to execute Ch'en Tung and Ou-yang Ch'e, two student leaders who had organized the antigovernment demonstration in K'ai-feng in 1126. After Kao-tsung's enthronement, the two student leaders had criticized the emperor's appointment of Huang Ch'ien-shan and Wang Po-yen and the dismissal of Li Kang, and had even gone so far as to question the legitimacy of Kao-tsung's succession. They claimed that the emperor should not have ascended the throne but should have waited for the return of Ch'in-tsung from captivity in the north. Enraged, Kao-tsung accepted Huang and Wang's suggestion that the student leaders should be executed, an act he later came to regret, remorsefully admitting that this severe punishment was a result of his own youthful intemperance.[9]

The Chin regime, realizing that the Sung was reneging on the terms of the treaty with the abolition of their puppet regime of Ta Ch'u and the execution of its "emperor," Chang Pang-ch'ang, prepared to launch a renewed attack on Sung. The Sung general, Tsung Tse, had hastily strengthened the defenses around K'ai-feng, and had established a frontline network of defenses along the Yellow River by organizing local militia forces as well as bandit groups. Together with Chang So, he enlisted capable young officers such as Yüeh Fei

---

[7] For the Chang Pang-ch'ang regime, see Chu Hsi-tsu, *Wei Ch'u lu chi-pu* (Taipei, 1955).

[8] Hu Yin, *Fei-jan chi* [*Ssu-k'u ch'üan-shu, Wen-yüan ko* 1779 ed.] (12th c.; Shanghai, 1934–5) 16, p. 3b; *CYYL* (1936) 99, p. 1633. For a discussion of Kao-tsung's personality, see Tao Jing-shen (T'ao Chin-sheng), "The personality of Sung Kao-tsung (r: 1127–1162)," in *Ryū Shiken hakuse shōju kinen: Sō-shi kenkyū ronshū*, ed. Kinugawa Tsuyoshi (Kyoto, 1989), pp. 531–43.

[9] *CYYL* (1936) 112, p. 1812.

and Wang Yen2 (1090–1139) to assist in organizing the resistance. Tsung submitted a stream of more than twenty memorials to Kao-tsung, desperately urging the emperor to return to K'ai-feng and head the defense effort, but to no avail. The emperor had set his mind on removing his court to the south. In the ninth month of 1128, Kao-tsung sent orders to the governor of Yang-chou to repair the defenses of the city in preparation for his arrival, and to begin the training of the naval forces on the Huai and Yangtze rivers. On the first of the tenth month, Kao-tsung left Ying-t'ien fu and set off in a great flotilla of barges down the Grand Canal. Passing through Ssu-chou and Ch'u-chou, he arrived in Yang-chou on the twenty-seventh day.

In the following months the Chin gradually regained control of most of the Ho-pei circuits and the Central Plains, as Jurchen forces overran much of the north. Denied the reinforcements he so desperately needed, Tsung Tse organized the best defense he could but he died, frustrated, late in 1128 after heavy fighting. He was succeeded in K'ai-feng by a lackluster commander, Tu Ch'ung.

Legitimacy and the establishment of authority

The legitimacy of Kao-tsung's regime was precarious despite Dowager Empress Yüan-yu's declaration in his favor. In those chaotic years from 1126 to 1132, there was criticism of his enthronement and several rival claimants to the throne emerged.[10] Moreover, the new regime's military and administrative capabilities were in disarray as it tried to consolidate power and resources.

Kao-tsung had left Kuei-te in the tenth month of 1127 to move south, and in early 1129 he was still in Yang-chou, preparing to cross the Yangtze River to move even farther south. Chin armies were making inroads into the Huai River valley, and another Chin force was poised to fight its way south down the Grand Canal to Ssu-chou and Ch'u-chou. The speed of their advance surprised Kao-tsung. A Jurchen vanguard detachment reached the outskirts of Yang-chou and attacked the imperial entourage. In the ensuing confusion, the emperor escaped on horseback, accompanied by only a few officials. He was able to cross the river in a small boat and made his way south to Hang-chou.[11]

The emperor had barely settled at Hang-chou when he faced an uprising. In the third month of 1129, Miao Fu and Liu Cheng-yen, two officers of the Imperial Guard who were disgruntled over Kao-tsung's appointment of

---

[10] CYYL (1936) 112, p. 1812.
[11] An account of this escape is given in Frederick W. Mote, Imperial China: 900–1800 (Cambridge, Mass., 1999), pp. 292–6.

Wang Yüan as their commanding officer and fearful of the pursuing Jurchen army, mutinied. Miao and Liu killed Wang Yüan and many of the eunuchs, including K'ang Lü, Kao-tsung's favorite. The mutineers demanded that the court negotiate a peace settlement with the Chin, and they declared that Kao-tsung should never have been made emperor. If the rightful emperor, Ch'in-tsung, were to return from captivity, they asked, what would Kao-tsung do about him? The question echoed the criticism that had been voiced by the student leader Ch'en Tung. Probably wishing to be rid of the new Sung emperor in order to work out their own peace settlement with the Chin, the officers forced Kao-tsung to abdicate in favor of his infant son. They installed Dowager Empress Yüan-yu to rule "behind the screen" as regent, and the reign title was changed to Ming-shou.

In the ensuing confusion, the recently appointed chief councilor, Chu Sheng-fei (1082–1144), who had earlier played an important part in Kao-tsung's enthronement in Ying-t'ien fu, was the key figure at the court. He appeased the two officers, Miao and Liu, and persuaded them to accede to Kao-tsung's return to the throne. Meanwhile, Lü I-hao (1091–1139), pacification commissioner of Chiang-tung (an-fu chih-chih shih) and governor of Chiang-ning (also known as Chien-k'ang, modern Nanking), and Chang Chün2 (1086–1154), an official in the office of the commissioner of the imperial encampment, called on the powerful generals Han Shih-chung (1089–1151) and Chang Chün (1097–1164) to move their troops to Hang-chou. Without much fighting, the generals arrested the rebel leaders and summarily executed them.[12] Although the mutiny was suppressed within a month, the fact that the two officers had deposed Kao-tsung and endangered his life must have had a profound impact on him, and apparently strengthened his determination to develop policies to centralize power, especially military power, in his own hands. This determination manifested itself in the frequent changes of chief councilors during the first decade of his reign, as he sought chief executives with aims and policies congruent with his own.[13]

During the crisis, the deposed emperor's title had been reduced to that of grand marshal (ta yüan-shuai), and after Kao-tsung's restoration, he was apparently embarrassed to continue Chu Sheng-fei's appointment as chief councilor because Chu had temporarily been his peer. Chu Sheng-fei was therefore allowed to retire and given a prestigious regional appointment; he was replaced

---

[12] For the Miao-Liu mutiny, see Hsü Ping-yü, "Sung Kao-tsung chih tui Chin cheng-ts'e" (M.A. thesis, Kuo-li T'ai-wan ta-hsüeh, 1984), pp. 58–60. Also her "Yu Miao-Liu chih pien k'an Nan-Sung ch'u-ch'i ti chün-ch'üan," Shih-huo yüeh-k'an 16 Nos. 11–12 (1988), pp. 446–59.

[13] On Kao-tsung's relationships with his chief councilors, see the analysis in Liu, China turning inward, pp. 81–101.

by Lü I-hao. Chang Chün, a native of Szechwan, emerged as an important military figure, serving as deputy commissioner of military affairs.

The consolidation of the new regime

Soon after Kao-tsung was restored to his throne in 1129 after the Miao-Liu mutiny, several measures were carried out to reestablish his credibility as monarch. First, the regnal title Chien-yen was restored, and as was customary at the beginning of a new reign a general amnesty was declared. Second, a prohibition was announced forbidding eunuchs to meddle in court affairs, and any eunuch disobeying this order was to be punished under military law. This prohibition reinforced the strong actions taken against the eunuchs under Ch'in-tsung that had culminated in the execution of the baleful eunuch and senior military commander, T'ung Kuan (1054–1126).[14] Third, Kao-tsung moved from Hang-chou northwest to Chiang-ning as a gesture of defiance toward the Chin. His cortège left Hang-chou on the twentieth of the fourth month of 1129 and, after stopping at Ch'ang-chou and Chen-chiang, arrived in Chiang-ning on the eighth of the fifth month. The city was renamed Chien-k'ang, its name when it had been the capital of the southern dynasties in the fifth and sixth centuries. It was a more central base for government and military operations than Hang-chou had been, and an excellent communications center, well placed on the Southern Sung's main artery, the Yangtze River. Accommodations for the emperor and his court and government had to be hurriedly improvised, and Kao-tsung moved into his "temporary palace" (hsing-kung) on the twenty-seventh of the fifth month of 1129.

Most important to consolidating the new regime, a beginning was made in reorganizing the new government structure to remedy its military and administrative weaknesses. In the fourth month of 1129, a reform of the bureaucratic structure of the Sung central government was carried out. This reform, proposed by the chief councilor, Lü I-hao, simplified the structure of the bureaucracy in order to better cope with emergencies. The traditional three departments, the Secretariat (Chung-shu sheng), the Chancellery (Men-hsia sheng), and the Department of State Affairs (Shang-shu sheng), were merged into a single organization, still called the Department of State Affairs (Shang-shu sheng). It was headed by two chief councilors serving the emperor directly, whose titles were chief councilor of the left vice-director of the Department of State Affairs (Shang-shu tso-p'u-yeh t'ung chung-shu men-hsia p'ing-chang-shih) and chief councilor of the right vice-director of the Department of State Affairs

---

[14] See the previous chapter, and Brian E. McKnight, "T'ung Kuan," in Sung Biographies, ed. Herbert Franke (Wiesbaden, 1976), vol. 3, pp. 1090–7.

(*Shang-shu yu-p'u-yeh t'ung chung-shu men-hsia p'ing-chang-shih*). The chief councilor of the left also concurrently held the position of commissioner of the imperial encampment, which gave him control of the imperial army.[15] This measure greatly broadened the power of the chief councilors, who for most of the Northern Sung period had not participated in military decisions.

Lü I-hao was responsible for another important administrative change, when in 1131 Kao-tsung ordered him to restore the central government's authority over the fragmented local administration in financial matters and the appointment of officials. Although this change was not widely accepted, it established the emperor's determination to restore central authority and to consolidate his own power.

Another event that would have long-term repercussions was the death, on the eleventh day of the seventh month of 1129, of Kao-tsung's three-year-old and only son, his heir apparent Chao Fu.[16] The emperor's own succession was already questionable and the appointment of a potential successor was thus a matter of urgency for his dynasty's continued stability and survival, but Kao-tsung at first refused even to consider the matter. The first official who raised the issue was promptly exiled to his native place. Later, however, in 1130, the emperor ordered that a number of young sons within the imperial clan be selected and raised in the palace. In the same year, however, Lou Yin-liang, a county magistrate, memorialized suggesting that a number of the young descendants of Emperors T'ai-tsu and T'ai-tsung should be selected to be brought up under the care of the government. His proposal was accepted by the emperor. Dowager Empress Yüan-yu and Chief Councilor Fan Tsung-yin made similar suggestions. As a result, some ten boys of Emperor T'ai-tsu's lineage were found and raised by ladies in the palace.[17]

A further series of administrative changes affected the circuit bureaucracy and especially the role of the military. We shall discuss them later. But in general the new emperor was still only beginning gradually to get a grasp on the institutions through which he would have to govern and establish order in the territories he still ruled.

Chin troops cross the Yangtze

The Sung's military situation meanwhile was deteriorating. Although the Sung still occupied K'ai-feng, Tsung Tse's death in mid-1128 had seriously

---

[15] *CYYL* (1936) 32, pp. 631, 645; 34, p. 658.

[16] Pi Yüan, *Hsü Tzu-chih t'ung-chien* [*Te-yü-t'ang tsang-pan* 1801 ed.] (1792; Peking, 1957) 105, p. 2776.

[17] See Lau Nap-yin, "The absolutist reign of Sung Hsiao-tsung (r. 1163–1189)" (diss., Princeton University, 1986), p. 10; Tao, "The personality of Sung Kao-tsung," p. 539.

weakened the defense of the Central Plains. In the late summer of 1129 Chin forces were preparing for a decisive assault against the south, and in the sixth month Tsung Tse's mediocre successor, Tu Ch'ung, decided to withdraw from the former capital, K'ai-feng, despite the protests of his generals, especially Yüeh Fei, who believed with some reason that the Central Plains could be successfully defended. As a result, having been in Chien-k'ang for only three months the emperor decided to return to Hang-chou for safety. Leaving Chien-k'ang in the hands of Tu Ch'ung, placing Han Shih-chung in charge of the delta area at Chen-chiang, and giving Liu Kuang-shih command of the area upstream from Chien-k'ang, Kao-tsung left Chien-k'ang on the twenty-sixth of the eighth month. After staying in Chen-chiang for six weeks he traveled on to Hang-chou (which had been renamed Lin-an on the fourteenth of the seventh month), where he arrived on the eighth of the tenth month. The dowager empress had been dispatched for safety to Hung-chou (in Kiangsi), and she eventually retreated to the south of the region. Kao-tsung himself still felt vulnerable, and after staying in Lin-an for only seven days, on the seventeenth of the tenth month, he crossed the Che River and proceeded south to Yüeh-chou (renamed Shao-hsing three days later), and then to Ming-chou (modern Ning-po) where he arrived on the second of the twelfth month. He had left in the nick of time.

In the eleventh month of 1129, the crisis became acute. The Chin army and its Chinese detachments invaded Huai-nan in two columns, one of which, under general Wan-yen Wu-chu (d. 1148), rapidly advanced through Ho-chou3 and Huang-chou and forced a crossing of the Yangtze at Ma-chia-tu, upriver west of Chien-k'ang, inflicting a smashing blow to the defending forces.[18] Although Yüeh Fei fought a desperate rearguard action to halt the Chin advance on the city, Tu Ch'ung decided to abandon Chien-k'ang, and surrendered to the Chin, whose army occupied the city. At the same time another column made a crossing at Chiang-chou, still farther upstream, and struck south into Kiangsi, where the dowager empress had been sent for safety. They took the major city of Hung-chou on the fourteenth of the eleventh month and continued to move south down the Kan River valley.

The main Chin army set out from Chien-k'ang in pursuit of Kao-tsung. The Jurchen cavalry advanced at great speed, meeting no opposition to speak of. They forced Han Shih-chung to retreat from his base at Chen-chiang to Chiang-yin in the Yangtze delta, and took Ch'ang-chou on the seventh of the

---

[18] James Liu notes, "The Jurchen were the first steppe or pastoral-nomadic nationality in Chinese history to cross the Yangtze." See Liu Tzu-chien (James T. C. Liu), "The Jurchen-Sung confrontation: Some overlooked points," in *China under Jurchen rule: Essays on Chin intellectual and cultural history*, ed. Hoyt C. Tillman and Stephen H. West (Albany, N.Y., 1995), p. 39.

twelfth month; only four days later, the garrison in Lin-an abandoned the city to the enemy. On the twenty-fourth the Chin took Shao-hsing. They pressed on until they were finally held back by General Chang Chün2 in the battle of Ming-chou (modern Ning-po), allowing Kao-tsung time to board ship and escape by sea just one day ahead of his pursuers. He sailed south to safety in T'ai-chou and then to Wen-chou. Wan-yen Wu-chu commandeered ships and pursued Kao-tsung by sea for over a hundred miles before abandoning the chase.[19]

Wan-yen Wu-chu had advanced too far and too fast, making scant attempt either to occupy territory or to secure his line of retreat. Only when he decided to abandon the chase and turn his forces back north did he meet serious resistance. On the third of the second month his army left Ming-chou. Ten days later they pillaged and abandoned Lin-an; on the twenty-fifth they took the rich city of P'ing-chiang (Su-chou), which suffered the same fate. On the first of the third month they left P'ing-chiang and were challenged near Lake T'ai by an army under Ch'en Ssu-kung (dates unknown). The Chin were now being harried by various Sung forces, including those of Yüeh Fei. On the tenth, the retreating army entered Ch'ang-chou, which had been reoccupied by Sung troops. Pressing on toward Chen-chiang, they encountered Han Shih-chung's main army and suffered a heavy defeat. Wan-yen Wu-chu, however, persevered in his attempt to force a crossing of the Yangtze River at Huang-t'ien-tang, near Chen-chiang on the lower Yangtze. To prevent the Chin forces from crossing to safety, Han Shih-chung had assembled a fleet of sea-going ships handled by seasoned troops, and he deployed them at anchor across the river. Wan-yen Wu-chu was at first frustrated by this stratagem but finally defeated Han Shih-chung by using archers firing incendiary arrows to attack Han's vastly superior ships, setting fire to their sails and thus immobilizing them. Wan-yen Wu-chu's army was then able to cross the Yangtze in their small boats. The Chin forces regrouped at Liu-ho in Huai-nan, opposite Chien-k'ang.

Early in the fifth month, Wan-yen Wu-chu unexpectedly recrossed the Yangtze farther upstream, apparently to retrieve the plunder that had been left behind in Chien-k'ang. The Sung had left the city undefended, and the Chin invaders looted Chien-k'ang and its environs before crossing back and successfully retiring to the north. But Sung naval strength and mobility had so surprised the Chin forces that Wan-yen Wu-chu never again ventured to cross the Yangtze.

[19] As both James Liu and F. W. Mote note, this was the first time a Chinese ruler had fled to the open sea to avoid capture. See Liu, "The Jurchen–Sung confrontation," p. 40; Mote, *Imperial China* (Cambridge, Mass., 1999), p. 297.

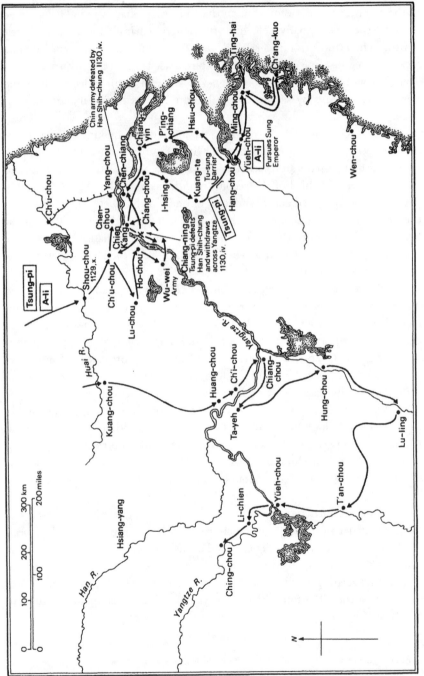

Map 22. Chin raids south of the Yangtze, 1129–1130.

At about the same time, Chin's western invasion forces penetrated the Kiangsi region as far south as Lu-ling. They then swept west into the area of northern Hunan, where at the beginning of the second month of 1130 they took T'an-chou (modern Ch'ang-sha), the administrative seat of the Ching-hu South circuit, sacked the city and massacred its population, who had put up a strong defense. The army then turned north to take Yüeh-chou2 (modern Yüeh-yang) before crossing the Yangtze River to attack Ching-chou2 (modern Chiang-ling). Meanwhile, Jurchen raiding parties penetrated the region of southern Hunan as far as the silver-mining center of Ch'en-chou2, and other Chin troops raided the area south of the Tung-t'ing Lake, taking Ting-chou2 and Li-chou4. At the end of the fourth month this invading force was also ordered to withdraw north to Chin territory after creating widespread havoc and a breakdown of authority in the central Yangtze region.

Chin armies north of the Yangtze River had meanwhile not been idle. On the thirteenth day of the second month of 1130 they finally took K'ai-feng. The Sung provisional governor, Shang-kuan Wu, took flight and was killed by bandits. Under the leadership of Wan-yen Ta-lan, Chin troops also began to drive southward down the Grand Canal from Ssu-chou. In early 1131 they attacked Ch'u-chou, which was staunchly defended by its prefect, Chao Li, and eventually relieved by Liu Kuang-shih. Bypassing the city, the Chin continued to advance toward Yang-chou, taking Ch'eng-chou2 (Kao-yu), and then moving into the coastal area north of the Yangtze mouth, attacking T'ai-chou2 and T'ung-chou2. In T'ai-chou2, Wan-yen Ta-lan's forces came up against a well-organized bandit army led by Chang Jung, who defeated them. The Sung court rewarded Chang by appointing him prefect of T'ai-chou2.[20]

The establishment of Ta Ch'i

The most powerful Chin generals were Wan-yen Tsung-han in the Shansi region and Wan-yen Ta-lan in the Shantung and Ho-pei regions. Wan-yen Ta-lan had found a promising collaborator in Liu Yü (1073–1143), the former Sung prefect of Chi-nan in Shantung who had defected to Chin in 1128 and won the personal favor of its emperor, Chin T'ai-tsung (r. 1123–35) Wan-yen Wu-chi-mai. Chin was still determined to rule most of the conquered Sung territory through surrogates, and established a second puppet regime. Liu Yü secured Wan-yen Tsung-han's backing and, at the end of 1129, the Chin emperor's permission to set up another puppet state in 1130, called Ta Ch'i (Great Ch'i), with Liu Yü as its emperor. The Ta Ch'i capital was first established at Ta-ming (in Ho-pei) but was later moved to Tung-p'ing (in

---

[20] CYYL (1936) 43, p. 781.

Shantung). In 1131, Liu Yü was also given control of the Shensi region, and in 1132 he transferred his capital to K'ai-feng. Ta Ch'i's domain covered present-day Hopei, Shantung, Honan, and Shensi, and all the land between the Yellow River and the Huai River. Ta Ch'i, unlike Ta Ch'u, had all the trappings of an independent state, with its own reign title, Fu-ch'ang; a bureaucracy with its own Department of State Affairs and Six Ministries; its own armies; a new tax system; new laws; and its own coinage and paper currency. But it was created as a vassal state of Chin, and the Chin emperor and Liu Yü had a fictive "father-son" relationship. Chin generals made all decisions for Liu Yü, and Chin troops were sent to garrison some key posts and keep an eye on him. Chin used the puppet regime both to restore order and as a frontline Chinese force to continue fighting against the Southern Sung.[21]

The area Liu Yü nominally ruled as Chin's surrogate was very large, but this territory was in a state of military and political chaos, with many isolated Sung army units still in place. There also were bandit forces, some of considerable size, and some of them self-proclaimed Sung loyalists, conducting guerilla warfare everywhere and especially in the Shantung region. Liu Yü spent much of his effort trying to restore some degree of civil order in the war-ravaged Central Plains and in the Shantung region, but he was also expected to mobilize his armies to fight whenever needed as auxiliaries of Chin. These armies of Ta Ch'i carried the burden of much of the fighting from 1130 to 1138.

In the south, Kao-tsung and his ministers realized that they could not restore control of the north by conquest in the near future. Instead, they decided to rely on diplomacy. From 1127 to 1129, thirteen missions were sent to Chin to request the return of Hui-tsung and Kao-tsung's mother, and to explore the possibility of a peace settlement. But no reply to these missions was given.[22] Having survived the Chin invasions in 1129–30, the southern regime devoted most of its strength to stabilizing its authority in the southeast. The establishment of the state of Ta Ch'i in the north somewhat reduced direct Chin pressure on the Sung, and for some time the Southern Sung treated Ta Ch'i as an equal in order to buy time for its own political, financial, and military reorganization. In the early 1130s the Southern Sung was able to pacify many local rebels and bandits who had grown stronger during the turmoil in their own territory with a carrot-and-stick approach that first lured the rebels and bandits to surrender, and then organized their followers into government military units.[23] Some of these groups fled to the north, where most of them

---

[21] For the Liu Yü regime, see Chu Hsi-tsu, *Wei Ch'i lu chiao-pu* (Chung-ching, 1944).

[22] See Hsü, "Sung Kao-tsung chih tui Chin cheng-ts'e," pp. 179–80.

[23] The metaphor of stick and carrot is also used by James Liu. See Liu, "The Jurchen-Sung confrontation," p. 43.

were eventually incorporated into the Ta Ch'i army. The rest were wiped out by the Sung generals Chang Chün2, Han Shih-chung, and Yüeh Fei.

The western campaign

In early 1129, Kao-tsung appointed Chang Chün as pacification commissioner of the Shensi region and his native Szechwan. He was given this post because Chang had emphasized that the eventual task of restoration should begin in the west. The strategic objective was clear and remained an important element in Sung defense policy for the remainder of the dynasty. Not only was Szechwan a rich and prosperous region whose loss the dynasty could ill afford, but if the Chin seized the southern Shensi and Szechwan regions, it would be extremely difficult to defend the southeast against an enemy invading downstream along the Yangtze River. At the beginning of the dynasty Sung T'ai-tsu (r. 960–76) had begun his conquest of the south by first conquering the Szechwan kingdom of Shu, and later in the thirteenth century the Mongols would employ the same grand strategy against the Southern Sung. Retaining military control of this region was all important. Chang Chün was a loyal official who had emerged as the leader of the war faction at the Sung court, but he was apparently an idealist without much experience in military affairs and inept at handling subordinates. He took a dislike to Ch'ü Tuan, one of his most able generals, and paid no heed to the advice of the other generals or the civil officials under his command.

As early as 1128, the Sung had sent an envoy, Hsieh Liang, to the Hsi Hsia state in the northwest to attempt to forge an alliance with the Tanguts to contain the power of the Chin. But having already submitted to the Chin as a vassal state in 1124, the Hsi Hsia leadership had taken advantage of the Sung-Chin conflict to occupy a few of the remaining Sung border prefectures in the northwest. The Hsi Hsia had then become disillusioned with their situation because Chin had promised to give them part of the newly acquired Sung territories but had reneged on the agreement. After Chang Chün took charge in 1129 in Szechwan, he sent Hsieh Liang once again to the Hsi Hsia to exploit this disillusionment and attempt to negotiate an alliance, but once more the talks failed.

When, in the autumn of 1130, Chin forces invaded the northern Kiangsu region, they overcame fierce resistance by the prefect Chao Li, who died at the siege of Ch'u-chou. The attacking forces took the city and drove south, threatening to cross the Yangtze River near Yang-chou. The Sung court was shocked by the swift advance of the Chin troops and made preparations to escape by sea. Earlier the court had urged Chang Chün to launch an attack on Chin in the west to relieve pressure in the east. In the ninth month of 1130, Chang Chün assembled a huge army, said to number four hundred thousand men, against Chin, but it was defeated by Wan-yen Wu-chu at Fu-p'ing (northeast of modern Hsi-an). Chang Chün had his subordinate general Ch'ü Tuan executed for disobeying orders, and submitted himself to Kao-tsung for punishment for the defeat. But Kao-tsung was unable to find anyone to replace Chang and retained him in overall command of the troops in the Szechwan region.

Chin forces continued to advance in the northwest, penetrating to Chieh-chou (modern Wu-tu, Kansu), near the border of Szechwan. When the Chin forces finally ceased their military operations, they occupied the regions of Shensi and a large part of eastern Kansu. The Sung retained control of only five prefectures in the southern Kansu region: Chieh-chou, Ch'eng-chou (T'ung-ku), Min-chou (Min county), Feng-chou (Liang-ch'uan), and T'ao-chou (Lin-t'an), and the two strategic areas of Ho-shan yüan in Feng-chou and Fang-shan yüan in Lung-chou (Lung county, Shensi). But Szechwan remained safe.

In 1131–2, the main military operations between the Sung and the Chin continued in the western theater, where Chin's southwestward advances were checked by Sung generals Wu Chieh, Wu Lin, and Liu Tzu-yü (1097–1146). In the fifth and tenth months of 1131, Wu Chieh defeated Chin forces at Ho-shan yüan. Unable to penetrate into Szechwan, Wan-yen Wu-chu himself returned to his headquarters in Yen-ching (modern Peking).

Early in the following year, 1132, Chin forces invaded the northwest Hupei and southern Shensi regions, capturing Chin-chou2 (An-k'ang, Shensi) and the Jao-feng Pass (near Chen-fu county in Shensi east of Yang county). Wu Chieh and Wang Yen2 retreated with their armies to Szechwan. Although Wang Yen2 recovered Chin-chou2 in the fifth month of 1133, the Chin general Wan-yen Wu-chu captured Ho-shan yüan later in the year. The following spring, in the third month of 1134, Wu-chu advanced from Pao-chi, trying to cross the Ch'in-ling Mountains and enter Szechwan. However, he was stopped by Wu Chieh and Wu Lin at the Hsien-jen Pass. After this battle, stalemate resulted in the west, and the Chin leaders launched no further large-scale attacks there during the remaining years of the 1130s.

Kao-tsung returns to Lin-an

In the east, following the withdrawal north by the Chin invasion forces, Kao-tsung remained in his provisional capital Shao-hsing until the beginning of 1131 when, after celebrating the new year, and leading the court in making obeisance in absentia to the two captive Sung emperors in Chin hands, he changed the regnal title to Shao-hsing, and issued a grand act of grace offering the remission of outstanding taxes, the restoration of the examinations for office, and pardons for any rebels who willingly submitted. In the first month of 1132 he and his court returned to Lin-an. He still apparently regarded the city as his "temporary capital" (*hsing-tsai*), even though during the early years of the Southern Sung most officials favored moving permanently to Chien-k'ang (Nanking).[24]

The choice of a permanent seat of government was crucial. Security ruled out any city (such as Yang-chou) north of the Yangtze. The lower Yangtze River and the delta region contained several great cities: Chen-chiang at the junction between the southern section of the Grand Canal and the Yangtze River, the administrative center of Che-hsi in the late T'ang dynasty (618–907); the flourishing cities of Su-chou and Ch'ang-chou in the rich agricultural basin around Lake T'ai; Chien-k'ang (Nanking), farther upstream on the Yangtze and with excellent communication links; and Lin-an (Hang-chou) on the coast at the southern edge of the delta region. Chien-k'ang had an ancient aura of political authority. It had been capital of the Eastern Chin and the succeeding southern dynasties from 317 to 589, a period when it was the undisputed center of Chinese high culture, and more recently, from 937 to 975, it had been the capital of the Southern T'ang dynasty, the only southern state of the Five Dynasties period with imperial pretensions. Chien-k'ang also had an extensive city site. Hang-chou was probably the richest of all these cities as a result of its having been from 907 to 978 the capital of the Wu-Yüeh state, the longest lasting, most successful, and wealthiest of the Ten Kingdoms, ruling over the area of modern Chekiang. Hang-chou was well defended, surrounded by triple walls, but compared with Chien-k'ang it had the disadvantage of being a cramped site, between the coastal estuary of the Che River and the famous Western Lake, which put strict limits on its development and physical expansion, and meant the city was always congested. This space limitation became more pressing in the 1130s when the city became packed with refugees from the north and Huai-nan. Hang-chou's location was also less central both for communications and for strategic command.[25] But Hang-chou was famous for its natural beauty, and it had the attraction of being on the coast with the possibility of escape by sea in case of an invasion, as Kao-tsung had already discovered in 1130.[26] Hang-chou was clearly Kao-tsung's personal preference,

---

[24] Making Chien-k'ang the permanent capital was suggested in 1131 by Liao Kang, *CYYL* (1936) 48, p. 861; in 1132 by Hu An-kuo, *CYYL* (1936) 53, pp. 934–5; in 1136 by Chang Chün, *CYYL* (1936) 102, p. 1668; in 1138 by Chang Shou (1084–1145), *CYYL* (1936) 116, p. 1898; and in 1139 by Chang Hsing-ch'eng, *CYYL* (1936) 128, p. 2079. In each case the opinion was ignored.

[25] For a discussion of Hang-chou's site and its suitability as a dynastic capital, see Chye Kiang Heng, *Cities of aristocrats and bureaucrats: The development of medieval Chinese cityscapes* (Honolulu, 1999), pp. 139–50, and the map on p. 142.

[26] Shortly after the move a detailed registration of all sea-going ships in the coastal ports was ordered, in part with this in mind.

but it was not designated as the capital of the Southern Sung until 1138, and even after that it was still known as the "temporary capital." Kao-tsung never traveled west of Chien-k'ang in his entire reign.

Hang-chou's large prefectural official residence, once the Wu-Yüeh royal palace, was adapted and expanded as the royal palace, and some further building works were undertaken piecemeal in the 1130s and 1140s. Various ministries and other offices were established in the larger monasteries and great mansions of the city, but the palace and government buildings were always inadequate compared with those of Northern Sung K'ai-feng, with many of the buildings being used for more than one function, under different names.

BANDITRY, THE SUPPRESSION OF LOCAL DISORDER, AND THE POWER OF THE GENERALS

Aside from the need to defend Southern Sung territory against Chin invasions, the government also relied upon the military to pacify and suppress the numerous rebel and bandit groups that had arisen during the collapse of Northern Sung military and civil authority in the crisis of 1126–7. This collapse resulted in complete chaos, with units of Sung troops left scattered all over former Sung territory in the north. Some of these troops were organized by their officers or by local strongmen into self-defense units; others became roving bands of warriors, sometimes allied with the regular local government, living as predators in one locality after another; still others became simple bandits. Following the Chin invasion of the south in 1130, banditry by army deserters mushroomed in the Huai-nan region and south of the Yangtze River. Banditry emerged often as the result of the ravages of war and the burden of heavy taxation that was imposed to finance the establishment of the Southern regime, which were aggravated by the depredations of government troops now forced to live off the land. Many local people joined the bandits out of desperation when they found that it was difficult or impossible for them to make a normal living. The constant flood of refugees from the north and from war zones further destabilized the safety and security of local populations.

Army mutinies were widespread, and bands of wandering unpaid soldiers (*i-ping*) roamed the border regions, living off the land. For example, when Kao-tsung took refuge in Wen-chou, the nearby Fu-chien prefecture of Chien-chou was in the throes of such an uprising. At the same time, during the invasion of the south, Dowager Empress Lung-yu (the new title given to Dowager Empress Yüan-yu), who had been sent to Chi-chou3 (modern Chi-an, Kiangsi) for safety, barely escaped with her life when the Sung troops escorting her mutinied and deserted. Her treasury was looted, and one hundred and sixty of her attendant palace women were abducted.[27]

Co-option of bandits and the organization of "righteous" armies

The Southern Sung policy of appeasing different bandit groups resulted in the organization of bandits into regular military units. Fan Ch'iung, a recalcitrant general who was executed during the Miao-Liu mutiny in 1129, had claimed that he had recruited one hundred and ninety thousand soldiers from various groups of bandits in this way.[28] The standard policy for the Sung was to separate large bodies of surrendered bandits into several manageable groups and attach these to different armies.

In the process of suppressing and pacifying the bandits, the Sung government also revived efforts to organize irregular *i-chün* ("righteous" armies) as loyalist troops along the borders and even inside Chin territory. As early as 1127, Tsung Tse and Li Kang had begun to organize local self-defense forces and bandits into military units to act as insurgent forces inside Chin territory. For a while some of these units were active far behind enemy lines. Wang Yen2's *pa-tzu chün* (Army of Eight Characters) (the eight characters being *ch'ih-hsin pao-kuo, shih-sha Chin tsei*, "serve the country with passion; swear to kill the Chin bandits") was active in the T'ai-hang Mountains of Shansi. In another instance, Ma K'uo met with Prince Hsin (d. 1140), who had escaped from the Chin army on its way north to the Chin heartland (Manchuria). Together they established a stronghold in the Wu-ma Mountains near Chen-ting (northern Ho-pei) and held out for several months in 1128 until, as they were far beyond the reach of any assistance or reinforcement from Sung, Chin troops eventually were able to wipe them out and recapture Prince Hsin.

In the battle for K'ai-feng in the sixth month of 1128, Tsung Tse died, and was succeeded by the inept Tu Ch'ung (d. 1140), who was unable to rally the support of the righteous armies. These insurgent groups began to disintegrate, and many of their members fell into simple banditry.

In time, however, the new Sung regime realized that the so-called "righteous" armies operating in Chin-held territory, particularly in the Shantung and Honan regions, could be useful, and began again to support and subsidize their activities. One advantage in supplying them with funds was that this enabled their organizations to provide intelligence and help the operations of the Sung regular army. In addition, their mountain fortresses and river

---

[27] *CYYL* (1936) 29, p. 577.
[28] *CYYL* (1936) 25, p. 509.

hideouts could be very effective bases for conducting guerilla warfare, since the Chin cavalry was at a disadvantage operating in mountainous terrain and their water forces were not as good as those of the Sung. By far the most impressive of the insurgent operations was that led by Chai Hsing (1073–1133) and his son Chai Ts'ung (dates unknown). Using a mountain fortress in I-yang (in southwestern Honan) as their base, they once even briefly captured Lo-yang. They were able to hold out in their mountain stronghold until 1133.[29]

Banditry and rebels in the south

Some of the more powerful and well-organized bandit groups were located along the Huai River frontier and the coastal area east of Yang-chou, and in the central basin of the Yangtze River (modern Hunan and Hupei). In 1129, numerous small groups of bandits were reported in Huai-nan, each comprising a few thousand men, and also larger groups numbering in the tens of thousands.[30] Among their leaders, Hsüeh Ch'ing and Chang Jung were especially powerful. As we have seen, in 1131 Chang Jung established a river base near T'ai-chou2 (modern T'ai county, Kiangsu) where he was able to defeat Chin forces under the command of Wan-yen Ta-lan, and was rewarded by the Sung court with the appointment of prefect of T'ai-chou2.

In 1130 it was again reported that bandits were rampant in the Huai-nan, Hunan, and Hupei regions. Powerless to suppress them by force, the Sung court continued its policy of appeasement, enticing some bandits with offers of government positions. The great Southern Sung chronicler Li Hsin-ch'uan describes the situation as follows:

At that time, more bandits rose in the circuits north of the Yangtze, and in Ching-hu (Hunan and Hupei). Large groups among them had several tens of thousands of men each, and occupied many prefectures. The court was powerless to control them. In places where there were no bandits, powerful local men, scattered military officers, or acting officials were appointed to take charge. The government only exercised loose control (*chi-mi*) over them.[31]

It was mainly on account of the court's inability to control banditry that Fan Tsung-yin proposed appointing some of their leaders to regional military posts. As a result, in the northern Hupei region in late 1130, Sang Chung, a rebel with more than one hundred thousand men under his command, was appointed prefect of the strategic city of Hsiang-yang.[32] In Fu-chien another

[29] Huang K'uan-ch'ung, *Nan Sung shih-tai k'ang Chin ti i-chün* (Taipei, 1988), pp. 1–101.
[30] *CYYL* (1936) 25, p. 508.
[31] *CYYL* (1936) 33, pp. 639–40.
[32] For Sang Chung's appointment, see *CYYL* (1936) 36, p. 698.

bandit leader, Fan Ju-wei, was also given an official title before he proved recalcitrant and caused further trouble. Eventually he was killed by Han Shih-chung in 1132.

The most important and dangerous uprising centered on a rebel leader in the Hunan-Hupei region. In 1131, after the Chin invasion of the south, it was reported that throughout the region from Kiangsu to Hunan, Chin invaders and regional bandits had continued to devastate towns and countryside. Around the rivers and marshes surrounding Tung-t'ing (northern Hunan), a charismatic local sectarian leader called Chung Hsiang had built up a large following and dominated large tracts of countryside since the early 1120s. The area had been ravaged by the Chin invasion of 1129–30, and the regional capital T'an-chou (modern Ch'ang-sha) had been sacked and its inhabitants slaughtered. Most of the local officials were killed, and the apparatus of local government was destroyed. The area had then been pillaged by various roving groups of soldiers and deserters. In this atmosphere of lawlessness, Chung Hsiang finally rebelled in 1130, calling himself Great Heavenly Sage and King of Ch'u, and announced his own regnal title as a further symbol of independence. His followers wrecked the prefectural city of Ting-chou2, killing officials, members of the educated elite, and rich merchants. Although after a "reign" of only thirty-five days he was captured and subsequently killed by K'ung Yen-chou (1107–61), himself a surrendered bandit leading a small personal army, Chung's followers, led by Yang Yao, escaped to occupy the waterworld of marshes and rivers around Tung-t'ing Lake. They built a number of stockades and a fleet of large boats with paddlewheels, which were escorted by smaller and more mobile boats ("sea eels"). Yang Yao and his men raided far and wide, preying upon the shipping on the major rivers that discharged into the lake.[33] Nineteen counties were affected. Because the seat of regional government lay in ruins and communications in the area had broken down, word of the rebellion took several weeks to reach the Sung court. Several serious government attempts to deal with Yang Yao's group failed, and, as will be discussed later, they were not suppressed until their defeat by Yüeh Fei in 1135.[34]

Also at this time, north of the Yangtze River in Huai-nan another powerful rebel, Li Ch'eng, a former military officer who had mutinied once before in 1128 and was later given amnesty, had taken advantage of the chaos following the Chin invasion in 1130 to occupy six or seven prefectures in Huai-nan

---

[33] *CYYL* (1936) 41, p. 759; 59, p. 1026.

[34] See Edward H. Kaplan, "Yüeh Fei and the founding of the Southern Sung" (diss., University of Iowa, 1970), p. 621; John W. Haeger, "Between north and south: The lake rebellion in Hunan, 1130–1135," *Journal of Asian Studies* 28 No. 3 (1969), pp. 469–88.

West. In 1131, Li Ch'eng crossed the Yangtze River and captured Chiang-chou (modern Chiu-chiang in Kiangsi). Another bandit leader, Ts'ao Ch'eng, also moved into the Kiangsi region at this time. As a result, the whole area from Hunan to Hsiang-yang in eastern Hupei had become ungovernable. Generals Chang Chün2, Yüeh Fei, and Yang Ch'i-chung (1102–66) attacked and pursued Li Ch'eng to Hupei, where Li was defeated and fled to surrender to the Ta Ch'i regime, under which he became an important general.[35]

The bandit leader Ts'ao Ch'eng then moved south. The Sung court appointed the former chief councilor Li Kang as commissioner of the regions of Hunan and Kwangtung, and Li Kang, with the help of generals Han Shih-chung and Yüeh Fei, quashed Ts'ao Ch'eng and his bandit forces. Yüeh Fei routed Ts'ao Ch'eng in the far south in Ho-chou (modern Ho county, Kwangsi) and chased him back to Hunan, where he was eventually subdued when Li Kang successfully lured him to surrender with the offer of an official title in 1132.[36]

The Ta Ch'i regime, for its part, eagerly continued to subvert Sung military officers with lavish rewards and offers of high official positions. In the summer of 1132, the Sung general, K'ung Yen-chou, whose own depredations had helped produce administrative collapse in the Tung-t'ing area, became another such defector, taking his troops over with him. In the next year, Hsü Wen2, a naval officer, also joined the Ta Ch'i regime.[37]

GOVERNMENT REORGANIZATION

From 1127 until 1130 the Southern Sung regime had only one objective, sur-vival, and it was touch and go whether they would achieve it. Government was largely a matter of ad hoc decisions. Ministries lacked trained staff, per-manent premises, records, and information from outlying regions. Many local government posts were vacant. The same was true of the military. Generals led what mostly amounted to private armies. There was no strong formal chain of command and no organized logistical support for the individual forces, whose troops lived off the country and were constantly left unpaid.[38]

In 1130 the position of commissioner of the imperial encampment was abol-ished, and the chief councilor began to hold the concurrent position of com-missioner of military affairs. In an emergency, the chief councilor sometimes

---

[35] *CYYL* (1936) 41, pp. 755–7, 760; 44, p. 806.

[36] *CYYL* (1936) 51, p. 903; 60, p. 1037.

[37] *CYYL* (1936) 55, p. 970; 64, p. 1097.

[38] James Liu claims that the defeat of the Northern Sung was brought about by conscious neglect of the military by Sung emperors because of their "fear of an internal coup." See Liu, *China turning inward*, p. 55.

even became a military commander. For example, in 1132, when Lü I-hao was planning a northern expedition, he was given the position of commander in chief (*Tu-tu*) of all army units on the lower Yangtze River. The Office for Emergencies (*Chi-su fang*) also handled important and urgent matters and was empowered to ignore or even to override many established procedures and protocols.[39] Kao-tsung together with the chief councilors made decisions and formulated policies without paying due attention to the checks and balances that had existed during the Northern Sung. In these years of emergency, the lines of authority were confused. On the one hand, this way of governing gave the chief councilors more centralized political and military authority; on the other, the emergency delegation of authority to generals and regional officials promoted decentralization.

Control of the military

During the early years of the new regime, the government struggled not only against the unpredictable military pressure and incursions from Chin forces but also against widespread internal disturbances and rampant lawlessness caused by its own instability. As early as 1127, just after Kao-tsung ascended the throne, Li Kang suggested that the court establish a number of military governors, patterned after those in the late T'ang dynasty, to control the most vulnerable regions of Ho-pei and Shansi, and to deploy a series of powerful army units along the Yellow, Huai, and Yangtze rivers, with military commanders stationed at strategic posts. Although Kao-tsung agreed to this plan in principle, it was difficult to implement because of a lack of trained troops and limited financial resources.[40]

After the new Sung regime moved south, the Chin threat and widespread banditry and lawlessness continued to beset the dynasty for some years. In 1130, the emperor adopted a proposal by Fan Tsung-yin (1098–1136) similar to Li Kang's earlier suggestion to establish a system of so-called military governors (*chieh-tu shih*), which delegated power to a number of regional officials who could enjoy long tenure in their posts and full authority within their respective domains.[41] The plan was to be implemented only on the northern frontier, where these posts and their armies would serve as a first defensive line. Accordingly, the Sung court appointed a few top-ranking civilian officials and military officers as pacification commissioners (*hsüan-fu shih*) to control larger

---

[39] *CYYL* (1936) 68, p. 1157; 74, p. 1223.

[40] See the "Memorial on national affairs" in Li Kang, *Liang-hsi hsien-sheng ch'üan-chi* (Taipei, 1970) 58, pp. 3a–4b.

[41] *CYYL* (1936) 33, p. 640. See also Hsü, "Sung Kao-tsung chih tui Chin cheng-ts'e," pp. 64–6.

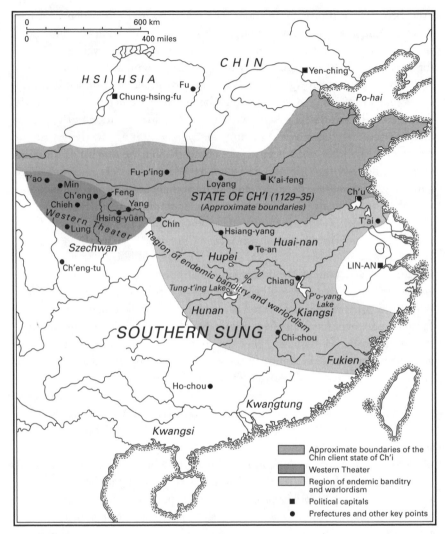

Map 23. The embattled Southern Sung, c. 1130.

key areas.[42] These measures ran counter to the Northern Sung policy of centralizing military authority. In Northern Sung times, to protect against the emergence of overly powerful military commanders, the government had not permitted generals to have their own armies or to exercise full authority over the areas under their command.[43]

---

[42] Li Hsin-ch'uan, *Chien-yen i-lai ch'ao-yeh tsa-chi* (c. 1202 *chia* volume, 1216 *i* volume; Shanghai, 1935–7) *chia* 11, pp. 3139–40.
[43] See Chapter 3 of this volume.

During this initial phase of the Southern Sung period, a chief councilor would sometimes be given the title of commander in chief (*tu-tu*) and would function as a military commander.[44] The implementation of Fan Tsung-yin's plan for military reorganization in 1130 was so important that Fan was made chief councilor of the right at the age of thirty-two. As a result of the military reorganization, a number of local officials and military officers, as well as some former bandit leaders, lured by offers of government largesse, received appointments as military commissioners (*chen-fu shih*) to defend important prefectures. Between 1130 and 1135, thirty-nine such posts were established in the northern border areas.[45] In 1130 a second, similar rank at the circuit level was created with the title of pacification commissioner in chief (*an-fu ta-shih*).[46]

Although the position of military commissioner was abolished in 1135, the larger strategic areas under the control of the pacification commissioners evolved into the famous "four garrisons" of the early Southern Sung. These were the four regional posts commanding the main strategic sectors of the frontier that were assigned to generals Chang Chün2, Han Shih-chung, Liu Kuang-shih, and Yüeh Fei. In theory, these garrison forces were under the control of the central government and they were named as if they were units of the central army, but in practice they all enjoyed a large degree of autonomy and their troops operated over broad areas as needed.

In addition, the regions of Szechwan and the southern part of Shensi in the west, which were too far from Hang-chou for the central government to exercise effective direct control, were also placed under the authority of a pacification commissioner. The armies there, first under the command of Wu Chieh (1093–1139), and later of his brother Wu Lin (1102–67), enjoyed the same autonomy as the four garrisons in the northeast.

The commanders of these garrisons grew so powerful that members of the court suggested ways to keep them under control, for the matter was of pressing concern for Kao-tsung and the civil officials. As early as 1130, when Fan Tsung-yin proposed the establishment of military governors, many officials opposed this reversal of a basic policy of the Northern Sung period. In the next year, Wang Tsao (1079–1154), a Han-lin academician, proposed several ways to control the generals, who should be strictly disciplined and not permitted to

---

[44] For the reorganization of this institution, see *CYYL* (1936) 22, p. 474. For their control over military affairs, see Li, *Chien-yen i-lai ch'ao-yeh tsa-chi* (1935–7) *chia* 10, pp. 290–1. The post of *tu-tu* was abolished in 1134. See *CYYL* (1936) 73, p. 1213; 74, p. 1223.

[45] Huang K'uan-ch'ung, "Nan-Sung tui ti-fang wu-li ti li-yung ho k'ung-chih: i chen-fu shih wei-li," in *Chung-yang yen-chiu-yüan ti erh chieh kuo-chi Han-hsüeh hui-i lun-wen-chi: Ch'ing-chu Chung-yang yen-chiu-yüan yüan-ch'ing liu-shih chou-nien*, ed. Chung-yang yen-chiu-yüan pien-yin (Taipei, 1986), pp. 1047–80.

[46] *CYYL* (1936) 34, p. 666.

take part in policy making. He also urged the government to control corrupt practices in the military, such as the generals' inflating the numbers of soldiers under their command (so as to increase payments from the government), and the pilfering of local government funds. In addition, Wang suggested that the emperor should not grant further autonomous powers to the generals because autonomy was easy to confer but difficult to take back. Wang's most important suggestion was that instead of having just a handful of overpowerful generals, there should be many of them so that no single general would have too many soldiers under his command and enjoy too much autonomy. The generals resented Wang's criticisms and wrote a rebuttal, claiming that the civil officials alone bore the responsibility for the collapse of the Northern Sung and for the deplorable situation now facing the new regime.[47]

In 1131, Liao Kang (1071–1143), an official in the Ministry of Personnel, proposed strengthening Kao-tsung's Imperial Guard, arguing that it was the tradition of the dynasty to have a strong central army, and that the court should try to adhere to the Sung tradition of "strengthening the trunk and weakening the branches" (ch'iang-kan jo-chih).[48]

Much later, in 1137, when Chang Chün was chief councilor (1135–7), the problem of overly powerful generals persisted, and Chang tried to replace the military commanders with civil officials. Although his own disastrous attempt at reorganizing the military command structure would lead to the defection of the general Li Ch'iung and his army of forty thousand to the Ta Ch'i and frustrate Kao-tsung's grand plan for a counteroffensive against Chin, Chang's failure did not change the mind of the emperor, who became even more convinced that the most urgent task was to achieve more central and civilian control of the military. In 1138, on the eve of the return of K'ai-feng by Chin, Chang Chieh2 (chin-shih 1124) suggested that a number of lesser officers be appointed to take command of portions of the troops of the great generals, thereby subdividing their forces.[49] Even the warlike Wang Shu2 (d. 1142), deputy commissioner of military affairs, who was against peace negotiations, realized the danger of generals' having too much autonomy and made efforts to reestablish the authority of central command.[50]

During the first decade of Kao-tsung's reign, one policy to deal with the dilemma of generals with too much autonomy was to assign civilian officials to supervise them. To defend against the Chin, Kao-tsung needed the strongest armies and generals he could muster, but at some point a general's strength

[47] CYYL (1936) 42, pp. 771–3.
[48] CYYL (1936) 46, p. 838.
[49] CYYL (1936) 119, p. 1124.
[50] CYYL (1936) 118, pp. 1910–11.

could become so great that the general could be a threat to the vulnerable emperor. This tension was dynamic. As the Chin threat waxed and waned so did Kao-tsung's need for strong generals, but the speed with which the Chin threat could increase meant that Kao-tsung had to err on the side of granting the generals more power than they would need at a given moment so that the Sung could respond quickly. This command structure kept the situation highly unstable for Kao-tsung. The generals with great power and mobility were potential rivals to the throne, as well as great prizes to be lured away by the Chin. It is not surprising that Kao-tsung was interested in a peace settlement as one of the few ways he could regain internal political control of his empire. The protracted war weakened Kao-tsung's control of his realm. The assignment of chief councilors as commanders in chief was done exactly for the purpose of bolstering the emperor's control. Another way for Kao-tsung to retain control was for him to appoint trusted and loyal generals in areas close to the capital, and to strengthen the Imperial Guard so as to guarantee that he always had at his disposal a powerful fighting force of proven loyalty close at hand. Among the generals in whom Kao-tsung especially put his trust were Chang Chün2 and Han Shih-chung, who had suppressed the Miao-Liu mutiny in Hang-chou in 1129 at the beginning of his reign.

A more drastic solution was simply to strip the generals of their personal armies and sweeping military powers. This measure, however, could be taken only when there was no longer the need to maintain strong regional military forces. This was exactly what Ch'in Kuei and Kao-tsung did in 1141, after the peace treaty with Chin was concluded. Acting on an earlier suggestion by Fan T'ang (1097–1134), the emperor and Chin Kuei stripped the three most powerful autonomous generals of their field commands and promoted the generals to be commissioners of military affairs and thus part of the central command. Command of the generals' field armies was given to their former seconds in command.[51] Kao-tsung often worried more about his recalcitrant generals than about Chin. In 1136, when the report of a major victory over the Ta Ch'i puppet regime reached the court, Kao-tsung remarked that he was less gratified by the reported victory than by learning of the loyalty of his generals.[52] After peace had been concluded with the Chin, Kao-tsung was pleased that he could now change the generals' appointments at will, just as he could with civil officials.[53] In 1146 he commented that he was at last able to exercise full control over his generals.[54]

[51] *CYYL* (1936) 140, p. 2247.
[52] *CYYL* (1936) 106, p. 1731.
[53] *CYYL* (1936) 147, p. 2372.
[54] *CYYL* (1936) 155, p. 2515.

Kao-tsung and his councilors

Kao-tsung was not only suspicious of his generals. At first he was also very careful to prevent his councilors and ministers from gaining too much power. Kao-tsung was even worried about Lü I-hao, who had helped him to take up his duties as emperor in 1129, and who had suggested that Kao-tsung escape by sea when Chin troops attacked Lin-an and Ming-chou. Lü I-hao served as chief councilor twice, but the first time he had been dismissed for aggressively monopolizing political and military power. The second time he was granted retirement on the grounds that he had failed to report natural calamities to the throne, a rather minor yet fungible offense that could be used as a reason for dismissal. Similarly, Fan Tsung-yin, entrusted with the task of reorganizing the military, was later accused of forming a clique and dismissed.[55]

During the early years of his reign, Kao-tsung frequently changed his chief councilors.[56] He had the largest number of chief councilors in Sung history, but he eventually came to put all his trust in Ch'in Kuei, who was chief councilor for eighteen years, second only to Shih Mi-yüan's (1164–1233) tenure of twenty-three years, the longest serving chief councilor of the Sung period. However, before Ch'in Kuei helped Kao-tsung make peace in 1141, the emperor was constantly looking for someone he could trust, and even Ch'in's first appointment as chief councilor (1131–2) lasted for less than two years.

WAR AND DIPLOMACY 1131–1141

Although Chin inflicted major defeats against the Sung, it was unable to destroy the regime. If the Chin could not terminate the Sung, and the Sung was powerless to dislodge the Chin, the political alternative of peaceful coexistence seemed possible. At this juncture a new figure emerged at the Sung court who was to be pivotal in the clash between the unrealistic aggressive revanchists and those seeking a peaceful accommodation with the Chin. This was Ch'in Kuei (1090–1155). A *chin-shih* graduate of 1115, Ch'in was from the region of modern Nanking and was married to a granddaughter of Wang Kuei, an associate of Wang An-shih. Ch'in Kuei had passed the advanced placement examination in 1123 and was made an instructor at the Imperial University, and later a censor. During the siege of K'ai-feng he was promoted to head

---

[55] For a biography of Fan Tsung-yin, see SS 362, pp. 11325–6, and Satake Yasuhiko, "Fan Tsung-yin," in *Sung biographies*, ed. Herbert Franke (Wiesbaden, 1976), vol. 1, pp. 345–7. For the biography of Lü I-hao, see SS 362, pp. 11319–24. See CYYL (1936) 47, pp. 850–1, for Shen Yü-ch'iu's attack on Fan's "twenty crimes."

[56] See Liu, *China turning inward*, pp. 81–115.

the Censorate. When K'ai-feng fell in 1127 and much of the Sung imperial family was captured by the Chin army, many Sung officials protested against the occupying Chin forces. A few officials were killed, and numerous others were detained. Among the latter group was Ch'in Kuei, who after his capture acted as secretary to the deposed emperor Ch'in-tsung. He also won the favor of the Chin general Wan-yen Ta-lan, a younger brother of the Chin emperor, who retained him in his army. In the tenth month of 1130, Ch'in Kuei and his wife escaped under suspicious circumstances from the Chin army in Kiangsu, and fled to the Sung court, where Ch'in Kuei gained the attention and favor of Kao-tsung by making his first proposal for peace. No details of this proposal survive, except for Ch'in Kuei's famous statement suggesting a peaceful coexistence of the northern and southern regimes: "If it is desirable that there will be no more conflicts under Heaven, it is necessary for the southerners to stay in the south and the northerners in the north."[57]

Kao-tsung did not follow Ch'in Kuei's advice immediately, but Ch'in was appointed minister of rites, and within a year was promoted to assistant councilor. In the second month of 1131, he replaced Fan Tsung-yin, an old friend who had vouched for him when he escaped from Chin, as chief councilor of the right. At that time, however, Ch'in Kuei's influence at court was overshadowed by that of Lü I-hao, who became chief councilor of the left in the ninth month. It may be that Ch'in Kuei had antagonized the emperor, who is reported to have angrily snapped, "Ch'in Kuei advocates a policy of sending the northerners back to the north. I am a northerner. Where should I go?"[58] It is also possible that Ch'in Kuei was removed because of his disruptive rivalry with Lü I-hao, who accused him of forming a faction.[59] In any case, in the eighth month of 1132, Ch'in Kuei was dismissed and appointed to a sinecure. He was replaced by Chu Sheng-fei.

Also in 1132, the Chin court returned to the south a captive Sung envoy, Wang Lun (1084–1144), who had been detained since 1127. Wang Lun carried a Chin message of peace that requested the sending of ambassadors to Chin. The Sung court dispatched two missions in 1133, conveying diplomatic messages couched in language humble enough to indicate Kao-tsung's willingness to

---

[57] CYYL (1936) 38, pp. 718–21; 57, pp. 999–1000. Li Hsin-ch'uan suspects, with good reason, that Ch'in had been deliberately released by Wan-yen Ta-lan. Ch'in's proposal is in CYYL (1936) 29, pp. 733–4. For a review of Ch'in Kuei's influence, see Liu Tzu-chien (James T. C. Liu), "Ch'in Kuei ti ch'in-yu," Shih-huo yüeh-k'an 14 No. 7–8 (1984), pp. 310–23. See also his Liang Sung shih yen-chiu hui-pien (Taipei, 1987), pp. 143–71. The most important English-language study of Ch'in Kuei is Charles Hartman, "The making of a villain: Ch'in Kuei and Tao-hsüeh," Harvard Journal of Asiatic Studies 58 No. 1 (1998), pp. 59–146.

[58] CYYL (1936) 57, pp. 999–1000.

[59] See Hartman, "The making of a villain," p. 63.

submit as a vassal to the Chin emperor, Chin T'ai-tsung. When the second mission returned to Lin-an, it was accompanied by two Chin envoys. Nothing was achieved by these peace overtures, however, because of Chin's demand that the Yangtze River constitute the border between Sung and the puppet state of Ta Ch'i.

In the tenth month of 1133 the Ta Ch'i ruler Liu Yü ordered the newly defected Sung general Li Ch'eng to lead an army to invade Sung. In the tenth month Li succeeded in capturing the strategically vital fortress city of Hsiang-yang on the Han River (northeastern Hupei) and the surrounding prefectures of T'ang-chou, Sui-chou2, and Yang-chou, and he began to set a civil administration in place. This victory, by opening the main route for an advance into the middle Yangtze River valley, threatened to cut the Southern Sung territory in half, giving the Chin armies easy access to the Han River valley and to the central circuits of Ching-hu (modern Hunan and Hupei). In response, in the fifth month of 1134, the Sung court ordered General Yüeh Fei to recover Hsiang-yang and to prevent Li Ch'eng from establishing ties with powerful bandits led by Yang Yao, who was based around Tung-t'ing Lake (northern Hunan). Yüeh Fei drove back Li Ch'eng's Ta Ch'i army in a pitched battle to recapture Hsiang-yang, forcing Li to withdraw his troops north into the region of Honan. Yüeh Fei also recovered the neighboring prefectures of T'ang-chou, Sui-chou2, and Teng-chou2, giving Hsiang-yang defense in depth. This greatly strengthened the Sung's strategic position and freed the central Yangtze region from the immediate threat of invasion. Yüeh Fei was emerging as one of the best and most successful Sung generals, and he won the emperor's approbation.

But in the ninth month of 1134, Chin and Ta Ch'i forces followed up their unsuccessful initial assault on Hsiang-yang with a major invasion farther to the east into the Huai River valley. Although it was suggested in Lin-an that the armies should withdraw to the Yangtze and that Kao-tsung should take flight once again, Chief Councilor Chao Ting (1085–1147) persuaded the emperor to face down the threat and move to Chien-k'ang (Nanking) instead. Kao-tsung's edict showed courage by announcing that he would lead the armies in person to attack the puppet Ta Ch'i regime. This edict, promulgated in 1134, was the first time that he had publicly denounced Ta Ch'i and Liu Yü as a rebel traitor. Acting on Chao Ting's proposal, Kao-tsung traveled west toward Chien-k'ang as far as P'ing-chiang (modern Su-chou) on the twenty-third day of the tenth month, and remained there until the second month of 1135. At one point, Kao-tsung wanted to cross the Yangtze River to fight a decisive battle with the Chin forces himself, but was dissuaded by Chao Ting. Again accepting Chao's recommendation, Kao-tsung appointed Chang Chün as commissioner of military affairs.

In the ensuing conflict, the Chin and Ta Ch'i invading forces at first advanced down the Grand Canal almost to Yang-chou and took several major cities in the Huai valley, but the tide turned against them. They were defeated by the armies of Han Shih-chung at Ta-i (to the northwest of Yang-chou), and also the forces of Yüeh Fei at Lu-chou2 (modern Ho-fei). Then, at the end of 1134, the emperor Chin T'ai-tsung died suddenly and the Jurchen generals were obliged to return to the capital to elect a successor. Their armies and the Ta Ch'i forces fell back to the north of the Huai River.

These military conflicts did not stop diplomacy. When Ta Ch'i and Chin had begun military operations in the ninth month of 1134, Sung envoys were still being dispatched to the Chin court. Kao-tsung's instructions were clear. He was not opposed to sending annual tribute to Chin. His main objective was to negotiate a settlement under which his parents could be returned to the south. Having crossed the battlefield near Yang-chou, the Sung envoys were received by Wan-yen Ta-lan, who said that it was possible to negotiate, pointing out that Ch'in Kuei understood the Chin position well. The Sung mission returned in the twelfth month, but nothing was accomplished because the Chin made no promises to return Kao-tsung's parents. In addition, the Chin leaders again insisted on the unacceptable condition that the Yangtze River constitute the border between the two states. In any case, Chao Ting was, at the time, opposed to making peace.[60]

With the Chin and Ta Ch'i threat temporarily at an end, in 1135 Kao-tsung decided to eliminate the Tung-t'ing rebels. Chang Chün, who had just been made a chief councilor, was sent to take charge of the war zone. He arranged the surrender of many of the rebel leaders while Yueh Fei prepared the ground for a meticulously planned strike that he executed in the sixth month, crushing the last rebel strongholds in only eight days.[61] Yueh Fei then supervised the restoration of civil order and made plans to remove the causes of the rebellion. In many regions peace and internal security were steadily strengthening the Sung state, civil administration was becoming firmly reestablished, and revenue was coming in. These military successes also strengthened Kao-tsung's hand in negotiations. However, the existence of the Ta Ch'i state seemed to be an obstacle to peace. In early 1135, Kao-tsung appointed Chao Ting and Chang Chün as joint chief councilors, ordering them to plan for a more positive defense strategy. Chao Ting, a northerner whose teacher Shao Po-wen (1057–1134) had been a follower of the teachings of the Ch'eng brothers, had served Kao-tsung since the beginning of the Southern Sung, and had recommended Chang Chün

[60] CYYL (1936) 80, pp. 1311, 1315; 81, p. 1340; 82, p. 1357; 83, p. 1359. For details, see Hsü, *San-ch'ao pei-meng hui-pien*, pp. 161–3. See also Liu, *China turning inward*, pp. 114–18.

[61] CYYL (1936) 89, p. 198; 90, p. 199.

to handle military affairs. Chang, who had succeeded in bringing Szechwan under some measure of central control and in stopping the westward expansion of Chin military forces, continued to hold the position of commissioner of military affairs as well.

In the autumn of 1136, Ta Ch'i renewed its attacks on the Sung in Huai-nan, but in the tenth month its main army was defeated by Yang Ch'i-chung in the battle of Ou-t'ang (northwest of Ch'u county, Anhwei). Based on this success, Chang Chün suggested that the government adopt a more aggressive stance against Ta Ch'i. With this in view, Kao-tsung left Lin-an for Chien-k'ang in the ninth month of 1136, stopping at P'ing-chiang. Eventually, in the third month of 1137, he made it to Chien-k'ang, where the city's fortifications were repaired. Kao-tsung and Chang Chün began to prepare a counteroffensive and assemble an army to launch a northern expedition. Earlier in 1136, Chao Ting, who was more cautious and had opposed Chang's aggressive strategy, had been dismissed. Chao had suggested that rather than launch an offensive, the court should order Yang Ch'i-chung, Liu Kuang-shih, and others to prepare strong defenses against the enemy along the Yangtze. Once Chao Ting was out of office, Chang Chün was left with full authority to carry out his more aggressive plans. One of his first measures was to replace Liu Kuang-shih, whom he felt was too timid, with Wang Te (1087–1154), one of Liu's own subordinates, while Lu Chih, a civilian official, was appointed to command the army units of Liu Kuang-shih and to oversee the transition of command. However, these arrangements proved ill-considered. Wang Te and another of Liu's officers, Li Ch'iung, were bitter enemies, and when Li heard that the court had chosen to replace Liu with Wang, he murdered his civilian superior, Lu Chih, and in the eighth month defected to Ta Ch'i with his forty thousand soldiers.[62] The northern expedition was canceled even before it had begun.

This disastrous incident marked a turning point in Kao-tsung's attitude toward the Chin. Frustrated, Kao-tsung canceled the planned counteroffensive and decided to return to Lin-an. There, in the ninth month of 1137, he replaced Chang Chün, who was exiled to Yung-chou in Hunan, with the more cautious former chief councilor, Chao Ting. Chao was teamed with Ch'in Kuei, who was recalled to the capital. Chang was exiled to a remote area of southern Hunan and was left permanently in retirement. From 1137 on, Kao-tsung paid more attention to controlling his own generals than to fighting Chin.

---

[62] *CYYL* (1936) 113, pp. 1826–7. Appraising the career of the Szechwanese scholar and military organizer Chang Chün, historians in general have not paid enough attention to his efforts to centralize
military power. An example is Yang Te-ch'uan, "Chang Chün shih-chi shu-p'ing," in *Sung-shih yen-chiu
lun-wen-chi: 1982 nien nien-hui pien-k'an*, ed. Teng Kuang-ming and Li Chia-chü (Cheng-chou, 1984),
pp. 563–92.

At this time, the Chin government again began to make peace overtures. When the Chin emperor T'ai-tsung died in the first month of 1135, he was succeeded by a young grandson of A-ku-ta who would reign as the emperor Chin Hsi-tsung from 1135 to 1150. Hsi-tsung was suspicious of Liu Yü, whom he suspected of secretly negotiating with Yüeh Fei. Despite Li Ch'iung's defection to Ta Ch'i with his large army, some Chin ministers and generals, with Wan-yen Ta-lan as their leader, had been disappointed at the poor results of Liu Yü's military adventures, and instead favored establishing peaceful coexistence with the Sung. These reassessments were reflected in the change in Chin foreign policy.

In early 1137, Ho Hsien, a Sung envoy who had been detained at the Chin court for more than a year, was released and returned south to Lin-an, carrying with him the official news of the deaths of Emperor Hui-tsung and his empress. (Hui-tsung had died two years earlier, in 1135.) The Sung court immediately responded by sending Wang Lun to Chin, asking for the return of Hui-tsung's coffin. In his talks with Wan-yen Ta-lan and Wan-yen Wu-chu, Wang Lun was able to drive a wedge between the Chin generals and Liu Yü, convincing the generals that in order to end the conflict it would be necessary to abolish Liu Yü's Ta Ch'i regime. To the complete surprise of many Sung officials, in late 1137 Chin abolished Ta Ch'i, removed Liu Yü from his throne, confiscated the enormous wealth he had accumulated, and sent him into comfortable exile in the region of Inner Mongolia. The Chin government then renewed negotiations with the Sung. The Chin tentatively agreed to return the coffin of Hui-tsung and to hand back to the Sung their captured territory south of the Yellow River, including K'ai-feng.[63]

THE PEACE PROCESS, 1138–1142

In the next year, 1138, Kao-tsung reappointed Ch'in Kuei, who had been prefect of Wen-chou in Fu-chien, as chief councilor of the right, and made him responsible for negotiating with Chin. His fellow councilor Chao Ting, who insisted that Kao-tsung reject the Chin demand that Kao-tsung become a tributary king subject to the Chin emperor, resigned in the twelfth month of 1138 and was appointed to a sinecure. In his last audience with Kao-tsung, Chao Ting warned that after his dismissal some might try to persuade the emperor to seek peace on grounds of filial piety, in other words, suggest that the emperor might try to hasten the return of his father's remains and of his mother regardless of the cost to the Sung regime. Wang Shu2, the deputy

---

[63] For Chin policy toward Sung, see Tao Jing-shen (T'ao Chin-sheng), *The Jurchen in twelfth-century China* (Seattle, Wash., 1976), p. 35.

commissioner of military affairs, who was also opposed to peace negotiations, proposed that no more envoys should be sent to Chin, and that the court should concentrate on military preparations. Wang even offered his resignation, saying that his duty was to fight against the enemy, not to participate in any scheme to sue for peace. General Han Shih-tsung also submitted several memorials warning the court about the unreliability of the Chin offer, and the general worried that entering into peace talks would damage the morale of the military.

Despite these cautionary admonitions, and having heard that the Chin peace mission had crossed the border, Kao-tsung announced that he would be willing to submit to the Chin if this would alleviate the suffering of his people caused by the war. He issued an edict in the eleventh month of 1138 announcing his intention to submit to the Chin in exchange for the return of Hui-tsung's coffin and of his own mother (Wei Kuei-fei). Kao-tsung asked officials and censors to express their opinions on the best way to proceed. A heated debate ensued. In response to the edict, a large group of officials opposed the opening of negotiations.[64] In their arguments they pointed out that the Jurchen had inflicted a great insult on the Sung and that there was no reason whatsoever for negotiations.[65] Several officials cited the passage from *Li-chi* (*Book of rites*) that "one could not bear to live under the same sky with an enemy who had inflicted insults on one's parents" – the standard canonical justification for vengeance and retribution. The emperor should not submit to the Jurchen and thus invite even more humiliation and insults both for himself and for his subjects. Even if peace were restored, the Chin might make further demands and might fail to return Hui-tsung's coffin, Kao-tsung's mother, or other imperial family members. They emphasized that the court should never trust an enemy's proposals, and that there were many reasons to distrust the Chin leadership in particular. Since ancient times, they contended, barbarians had never wanted peaceful coexistence with the Chinese except when the empire was powerful, and the Sung was certainly not powerful enough to force the Chin to negotiate. In their view, the Chin were using the peace talks simply as a tactic to frustrate the Sung, and to diminish the Sung martial spirit, so that in the future the Chin could again invade the south.

The officials further pointed out that the argument that Kao-tsung should submit on the grounds of his own filial obligations to his parents was fallacious. Filial piety, they claimed, was a virtue that could be practiced by a sovereign

---

[64] These included Chang T'ao (1092–1166), Yen Tun-fu (1071–1145), Hu Ch'üan (1102–80), Tseng K'ai (*chin-shih* 1103), Fan Ju-kuei (1102–60), Li Kang, Li Mi-hsun (1089–1153), Wei Chiang (*chin-shih* 1121), Chu Sung (1097–1143), Ling Ching-hsia (d. 1175), Hu Ch'eng (*chin-shih* 1121), Ch'ang T'ung (1090–1149), Liang Ju-chia (1096–1154), and Chang Shen.

[65] *CYYL* (1936) 123, p. 1989; 124, pp. 2018–20, 2015–16. For these arguments, see *CYYL* (1936) 122–4; Hsü, *San-ch'ao pei-meng hui-pien*, pp. 183–90.

only in times of peace. In times of war, however, the emperor should give priority to the security of the dynasty and of the people over his duties to his own family. Also, he should listen to the opinions of the people, his generals, and the soldiers. This last point was put forward because the generals Han Shih-chung and Yüeh Fei were strongly opposed to a peace settlement and public opinion agreed with them. If the emperor ignored this opinion and went ahead with the humiliating peace plan, he would lose the support of the people, and invite unpredictable disorders. The officials advised the emperor to be patient and to wait for a better time to avenge Chin insults.

Finally, officials tried to convince Kao-tsung that he should not naively believe in the efficacy of demilitarization. They stressed that the conclusion of a peace treaty would not necessarily lead to disarmament, because without military force the Sung would be unable to maintain peace. Even if a settlement were reached, the Sung would still have to be ready to take military action against the Chin in the future if and when the Chin made any unreasonable demands.

By far the strongest of the arguments against a peace settlement came from Hu Ch'üan, a former local militia leader and current Bureau of Military Affairs functionary who criticized the court's willingness to accept the Chin's terms both as adding further insult to the injury the Chin had already inflicted on the imperial ancestors and as submitting to a barbarian culture. Insult should be avenged, Hu stressed, and advocates of peace such as Wang Lun, Ch'in Kuei, and the assistant councilor Sun Chin (*chin-shih* 1103) should be executed. Hu's memorial was widely copied and even printed among the people in the capital. Hu became very popular, but the emperor continued to place his trust in Ch'in Kuei.

In contrast, those who favored peace talks were few, and included Mo Chiang (*chin-shih* 1138), Kou-lung Ju-yüan (1093–1154), and Feng Chi (d. 1152). They argued that submission for the sake of the emperor's parents and brother, and for the recovery of the temples and cemeteries of the imperial ancestors, was motivated by the emperor's kindness and filial piety, and that there had been many historical precedents for expedient submission to buy time for later revenge. Once peace was restored, territories might be recovered without fighting. On a more practical level, despite the recent Sung victories, it seemed impossible to conquer the enemy, and finally achieving peace would enable the government to deal with its pressing financial problems, and to bring prosperity to the people.

In the midst of the debate, Wang Shu2, who had submitted seven memorials and had had six audiences with the emperor arguing against peace negotiations, was transferred away from the capital and appointed to a prefectural post. Kao-tsung criticized the hawks for their "irresponsible" comments on his conduct, which he claimed represented a "corruption of customs." Sun Chin suggested using the threat of severe punishments to deter them. To counter the opposition, Ch'in Kuei had his supporter Kou-lung Ju-yüan appointed as vice–censor in chief (*yü-shih chung-ch'eng*) and another supporter, Shih T'ing-ch'en (*chin-shih* 1121), as investigating censor (*chien-ch'a yü-shih*), and employed them to denounce all those who opposed his policies.

Ch'in Kuei's control of the Censorate was the key to his establishment of personal dominance at court. He had briefly held the highest office in the Censorate under Ch'in-tsung in 1126, and his failure to control the censors during his first short term as chancellor in 1131–2 had made it possible for Lü I-hao to engineer his dismissal on charges of forming a faction. Chang Chün had also misused a packed Censorate as a political weapon in 1136–7.[66] Ch'in Kuei used the Censorate now to enable him to denounce, impeach, or arrange the demotion of any official who crossed him, and he was to exploit this technique to the full. One of the first victims was Hu Ch'üan, who was banished.

After this purge Kao-tsung said that he had never wanted to be emperor, and his sole objective in making peace had only been to serve his mother. But he remained in control in the background without objecting as Ch'in Kuei forced through the policies and personnel changes of which the emperor approved. But severe criticism of Kao-tsung continued, and he then issued an edict banning slander by the court. Chao Ting, the most influential of the opponents of peace, had already been posted away from K'ai-feng, having been appointed governor of Shao-hsing earlier in 1138. Forced to seek retirement after 1138, Chao Ting was subjected to a series of false charges, demotions, and finally exile, first to Ch'ao-chou in 1140, and finally to Chi-yang chün (modern Yai-chou, on Hainan Island) in 1144. He was kept under rigorous surveillance by Ch'in Kuei's agents; nobody dared to communicate with him, and in 1147 he starved himself to death, fearing that his family would also be persecuted.[67] Other purges quickly followed. Later in 1138, Tseng K'ai and Wang Shu2 were forced to retire.[68] In their place, Ch'in Kuei, initially against Kao-tsung's advice, recommended Li Kuang (1077–1155) as an assistant councilor. A leading scholar-official from the south, Li Kuang's main concerns were the serious financial situation of the goverment, the rural impoverishment resulting from wartime destruction, and the heavy tax burden caused by military expenses. Li's

---

[66] See *CYYL* (1936) 115, p. 1860. Ironically, at the time of Chang Chün's fall his successor, Chao Ting, had asked to remove and replace Chang's tame censors, but he was refused by the emperor because allowing every new councilor to make such changes would lead to factionalism. See Hartman, "The making of a villain," p. 137 n. 165.

[67] *CYYL* (1936) 155, p. 2537. Also Liu, *China turning inward*, pp. 114–27.

[68] *CYYL* (1936) 123, pp. 1997–8.

appointment seemed to reflect the aspirations of people from the south, who were in general less enthusiastic than those people who had been displaced from the north about continuing the war. However, Li proved to be an unsuitable choice. He unexpectedly opposed the peace policy and lost his position as assistant councilor after only one year, in 1138, for criticizing Cheng I-nien, a relative of Ch'in Kuei who had served under the Ta Ch'i puppet regime. In banishment, Li Kuang was trapped into writing verse critical of Ch'in Kuei, and he too was exiled to faraway Hainan Island. He wrote a *hsiao shih* (little history), breaking the ban on private histories, and was ordered never to be pardoned and reemployed. In 1150 his son was banished, and his friends were demoted.[69] These cases exemplify Ch'in Kuei's relentless vindictiveness toward those he believed were a threat to him.

When Ch'in Kuei had Shih T'ing-ch'en promoted to the rank of attendant censor (*shih yü-shih*), many in the bureaucracy became seriously alarmed. Two staunch peace opponents, Chang T'ao (1091–1165) and Yen Tun-fu (1071–1144), requested that the emperor punish Kou-lung Ju-yüan and Shih T'ing-ch'en, but their requests went unheeded. Later, when peace was about to be restored, the emperor bitterly complained to Kou-lung Ju-yüan and Li I (*chin-shih* 1124) that the scholar-officials cared only about themselves, and that even if he, the emperor, had kowtowed a hundred times to the enemy when the Jurchen were attacking Ming-chou (in 1130), these officials would not have cared. Ch'in Kuei told Tseng K'ai that all the critics wanted was great fame for themselves, whereas all he wanted was to resolve the problems of the dynasty.[70]

Despite the protests from those opposed to peace, Kao-tsung ordered that peace negotiations proceed. But among the issues to be resolved was the difficult matter of protocol. The head of the Chin mission was entitled to an investiture envoy (*chao-yü shih*), since Kao-tsung had expressed himself as willing to be invested to serve the Chin emperor as a subject. Kao-tsung was therefore now required to perform a ceremony formally accepting investiture by the Chin emperor. This humiliation caused deep concern at court and unrest in the capital, Lin-an. One court official, Lou Chao (1088–1160), suggested that the emperor could avoid taking part in the investiture ceremony by using the excuse that when in mourning for his father a man should not speak to anyone. The emperor followed this suggestion, and thus it was Ch'in Kuei who accepted the Chin investiture on Kao-tsung's behalf.[71]

[69] *CYYL* (1936) 160, p. 2599; 161, pp. 2604, 2607–8; 168, p. 2747. See also Teraji, *Nan-Sō shoki seijishi kenkyū*, pp. 177–90, 301–2, 315–16; Teraji Jun, *Nan-Sō seiken kakuritsu katei kenkyū oboegaki: Sō-Kin wagi, heiken kaishū, keikaihō no seijishiteki kōsatsu* (Hiroshima, 1982), pp. 8–51; Hartman, "The making of a villain," pp. 99–101.

[70] *CYYL* (1936) 124, p. 2024. For the biography of Tseng K'ai, see *SS* 382, pp. 11769–71.

[71] *CYYL* (1936) 124, pp. 2024–5, 2027–8.

To the surprise of those opposed to peace, and in a large measure due to the temporary domination of the Chin court by its own peace faction, the two states concluded their peace treaty in the tenth month of 1138. The treaty stipulated that Kao-tsung would style himself as a "subject" (*ch'en*) of the Chin emperor, and that the new border between the two states was to be the latest course of the Yellow River. The Sung authorized Wang Lun to take over the territory controlled by the Chin, and Wang was appointed governor of K'ai-feng. However, there were strong objections to the settlement on both sides, which quickly undermined the treaty's promise of a lasting peace.

In a power struggle at the Chin court in 1139, Wan-yen Ta-lan, the chief architect of the peace settlement on the Chin side, was ousted and executed, along with several of his propeace colleagues, by Wan-yen Wu-chu in the name of the sixteen-year-old Chin emperor Hsi-tsung. In 1140, Wan-yen Wu-chu broke the peace treaty. Renewed attacks on Sung penetrated into the Honan region and recaptured K'ai-feng. Fierce fighting broke out again. Wan-yen Wu-chu was defeated in a decisive battle at Shun-ch'ang (modern Fo-ch'ang, in Anhwei) by the Sung general Liu Ch'i2, whose infantry employed a new tactic to counter the formidable Jurchen cavalry by using long pikes like scythes to hack at their horses' legs. Further Chin advances were held in check by Yüeh Fei, who won battles at Yen-ch'eng and Ying-ch'ang (present-day Hsü-ch'ang in Honan). Liu Ch'i2 then took the initiative and, despite repeated calls from the emperor to abandon his advance and withdraw, drove deep into enemy-held territory to recapture Lo-yang and reach the outskirts of K'ai-feng. However, without the government's support, and denied the reinforcements he required to capitalize on his victories, Yüeh Fei was overextended, and he was finally forced to withdraw, as had his fellow generals. In early 1141, Yang Ch'i-chung defeated Chin forces at Che-kao (east of modern Ho-fei), but Wan-yen Wu-chu regrouped and captured Hao-chou (Feng-yang, in Anhwei). The fighting now reached a stalemate, and Wang-yen Wu-chu was ready to negotiate. He took the initiative by sending diplomatic letters and returning detained Sung envoys. Ch'in Kuei again convinced Kao-tsung to write humble letters begging for the restoration of peace.

Probably as a gesture to show the Chin that the Sung court was sincere in seeking peace, in mid-1141 Kao-tsung suddenly ordered his chief generals Han Shih-chung, Chang Chün2, and Yüeh Fei to attend an audience at the court to receive rewards for their victories. Han and Chang were promoted to be commissioners of military affairs, and Yüeh was made a deputy commissioner of military affairs. But the generals, now safely seconded to the central government establishment, were stripped of their personal commands, which were divided up and assigned to civil officials. With the three great generals stripped of their personal military power, the peace negotiations proceeded

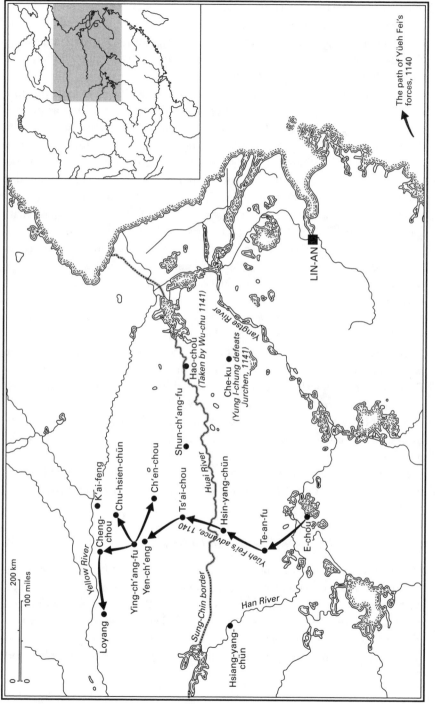

Map 24. Yüeh Fei's incursions into Chin territory, 1140.

smoothly. Unlike the situation in 1138, in 1141 the majority of the court officials remained silent about the negotiations. Most of the opponents of Ch'in
Kuei had been ousted, and the few who remained dared not speak out against
Kao-tsung and Ch'in Kuei. Only Han Shih-chung openly opposed the peace
plan, and he was allowed to retire from public life.

In the winter of 1141, a new treaty was concluded between the Sung and
the Chin. The treaty declared the Sung a vassal state of the Chin as before,
with Kao-tsung referring to the Chin as *shang-kuo* (superior state), and his own
dynasty as *pi-i* (insignificant fiefdom). In state letters to the Chin, Kao-tsung
referred to himself as "subject" and he was not recognized as "emperor" by the
Chin government. The Sung was committed to sending the Chin an annual
tribute (*kung2*) of a quarter million taels of silver and a quarter million bolts
of silk. The border between the two states was to follow the Huai River in
the east and to run south of the prefectures of T'ang-chou and Teng-chou2
in the west. This new border was considerably south of the one negotiated in
1138, and left K'ai-feng and the Honan region in Chin hands. The two states
would exchange envoys regularly to celebrate the New Year and the birthdays
of their respective emperors. Kao-tsung eventually accepted this humiliating
investiture document on 11 October 1142, and the imperial coffins and Kao-
tsung's mother were duly returned to Lin-an.[72]

Soon after the Sung acceptance of the treaty in 1142, the two states, Sung
and Chin, established a number of border markets to revive mutual trade.
Exports from the south included tea, spices, drugs, silk, cotton, coins, cattle,
and rice. The export of the last three items was forbidden by the Sung government, but large quantities of these commodities were smuggled north. Imports
from Chin to Sung included hides, pearls, ginseng, silk, and horses. The Chin
government banned the export of horses, but smuggling went on regardless. In this trade the Sung government enjoyed an export surplus and consequently gained an influx of silver that more than compensated for the tribute
payments.

The execution of Yüeh Fei

During the treaty negotiations, in the seventh month 1141, Yüeh Fei was
indicted by the censors under the control of Ch'in Kuei, arrested, and charged
with treason. His trial at the Court of Judicial Review (*Ta-li ssu*) dragged
on inconclusively for weeks; neither the president of the court nor his two
vice-presidents thought Yüeh Fei was guilty. But Ch'in Kuei was determined
to rid himself of his adversary. The blunt Yüeh Fei had been outspoken and

---

[72] On these events, see Franke, "Treaties between Sung and Chin," pp. 76–81.

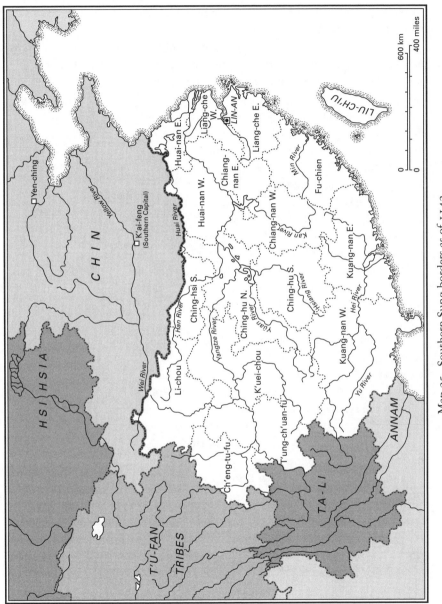

Map 25. Southern Sung borders as of 1142.

undiplomatic, and evidence was either fabricated or misinterpreted to uphold the charges. Before the treaty was concluded, on the last day of the twelfth month of 1141, Yüeh Fei was either executed or forced to commit suicide in prison by order of Ch'in Kuei. It is disputed whether Kao-tsung himself was involved in the decision.

This flagrant act of injustice, the execution of Sung's most successful commander and a national hero in order to achieve a humiliating peace, became the "defining act" of Kao-tsung's reign, and has provoked violently partisan controversy in the ensuing centuries. Yüeh Fei became a folk hero, eventually canonized as one of the gods of war, together with his own hero, Kuan Yü, making it doubly difficult for a historian to make a dispassionate judgment of his case. In contrast, Ch'in Kuei was vilified after his death to such an extent that it is difficult to assess the politics of his long period of political dominance that followed these events.

Ever since Yüeh Fei's death, historians have argued that Yüeh Fei was framed and deliberately killed by Ch'in Kuei in order to remove the most prominent and outspoken obstacle to peace negotiations. Some have gone further and suspected that Ch'in Kuei had Yüeh Fei eliminated at the request of the Chin commander, Wan-yen Wu-chu, who wished to be permanently rid of his most dangerous military adversary. There is no doubt that Yüeh Fei was a victim of Kao-tsung's policy to restore the central government's control of its overly powerful generals, and that he was also a principal obstacle to the peace settlement for which both Kao-tsung and Ch'in Kuei were obsessively striving. Yüeh Fei had the misfortune to fall victim to the process of centralizing military power just when, ironically, he and the other generals had obtained a military stalemate against Chin forces. His execution, which followed the removal of himself and his fellow generals from their commands, was a stark warning to other military men that they were no longer an irreplaceable pivotal force in the survival of the Sung state.[73] Yüeh Fei was not the only great commander with whom Ch'in Kuei was at odds; Ch'in Kuei was also on difficult terms with Kao-tsung's most trusted general, Han Shih-chung.

The argument that Ch'in Kuei was an agent acting for the Chin lacks all credibility and was probably an unfounded attempt to blacken Ch'in Kuei's

---

[73] For appraisals of Yüeh Fei, see Hellmut Wilhelm, "From myth to myth: The case of Yüeh Fei's biography," in *Confucian personalities*, ed. Arthur F. Wright and Denis C. Twitchett (Stanford, Calif., 1962), pp. 146–61; Liu Tzu-chien (James T. C. Liu), "Yüeh Fei (1103–1141) and China's heritage of loyalty," *Journal of Asian Studies* 31 No. 2 (1972), pp. 291–7. See also "Yüeh Fei" in his *Liang Sung shih yen-chiu hui-pien*, pp. 185–207. Liu, *China turning inward*, pp. 98–105. See the critical appraisal in Hartman, "The making of a villain," pp. 59–146.

reputation. Although Ch'in Kuei has been accused by many historians of being a traitor, there is no substantial evidence to prove that he ever actively collaborated with the Chin. He had relatives who had served in the Ta Ch'i puppet regime, and through them he might have obtained important information about the political and military situation in the north. But this hardly constitutes treason.

Kao-tsung too has been severely criticized by some historians as cowardly for not openly challenging the demands of the Chin and for selfishly wanting to preserve his throne at all costs. These historians point out that the Chin not only threatened to conquer the Southern Sung but also used their captive, the former emperor Ch'in-tsung, as political leverage against the younger brother, Kao-tsung. If the Chin had chosen to return Ch'in-tsung to the Southern Sung, it would have created political confusion since Kao-tsung's legitimacy would have been seriously compromised. Ch'in-tsung's return also would have threatened Ch'in Kuei's dominance. There is no record that Kao-tsung ever asked for the return either of Ch'in-tsung, or of his own wife, Empress Hsing (who died in 1138), either before or after 1141. Thus these historians conclude that neither Kao-tsung nor Ch'in Kuei really wanted Ch'in-tsung back, and that this was a major reason for Kao-tsung's failure to take an aggressive stand against the Chin. However, when Kao-tsung's mother, the Dowager Empress Hsien-jen, was returned to the south in 1142, she carried a message from Ch'in-tsung, who asked only to be allowed to live in retirement if he was released from captivity.[74] Again Ch'in Kuei seems to have been closely involved with this matter. In 1143, Chang Shao (1096–1156), a Sung envoy, reported to Ch'in Kuei that the Chin seemed to be willing to return Ch'in-tsung, and suggested sending a special ambassador to request Ch'in-tsung's release. Ch'in Kuei became angry and demoted Chang.[75] Clearly, Ch'in Kuei considered

[74] See *Ch'ao-yeh i-chi* (13th c.; Taipei, 1964), vol. 1, p. 1199. For critical views of Kao-tsung and Ch'in Kuei, see "Kao-tsung" in Wang Fu-chih, *Sung lun* (c. 1690–2; Peking, 1964) 10, pp. 167–202; Miao Feng-lin, "Sung Kao-tsung yü Nu-chen i-ho lun," *Kuo-feng pan-yüeh-k'an* 8 No. 2 (1936), pp. 39–44; Chu Hsieh, "Sung Chin i-ho chih hsin fen-hsi," *Tung-fang tsa-chih* 33 No. 10 (1936), pp. 65–74; Miyazaki Ichisada, "Nan-Sō seijishi gaisetsu," in *Ajia-shi kenkyū dai ni*, Miyazaki Ichisada (Kyoto, 1959), pp. 174–7; and Teng Kuang-ming, "Nan Sung tui Chin tou-cheng chung ti chi-ko wen-t'i," *Li-shih yen-chiu* No. 2 (1963), pp. 21–32; also Teng Kuang-ming, *Yüeh Fei chuan*, rev. ed. (Peking, 1983); Tseng Ch'iung-pi, *Ch'ien-ku tsui-jen Ch'in Kuei* (Cheng-chou, 1984). For revisionist views, see Chao I, *Nien-erh shih cha-chi* (1799; Taipei, 1968) 26, and Ch'en Teng-yüan, "Ch'in Kuei p'ing," *Chin-ling hsüeh-pao* 1 No. 1 (1931), pp. 27–46. Other traditional views are cited in Kuan Lü-ch'üan, *Liang Sung shih-lun* (Cheng-chou, 1983), p. 250. For Southern Sung patriotism, see Hoyt C. Tillman, "Proto-nationalism in twelfth-century China? The case of Ch'en Liang," *Harvard Journal of Asiatic Studies* 39 No. 2 (1979), pp. 403–28.

[75] *CYYL* (1936) 150, p. 2410.

the return of Ch'in-tsung, conveniently for the emperor and himself, a dead issue.

In fairness to Kao-tsung, his policies toward the Chin during the early years of his reign were not simply those of passive appeasement, even though envoys were constantly sent to the Chin court requesting the return of Emperor Hui-tsung and Kao-tsung's mother, the dowager empress Hsien-jen (d. 1159). When Ch'in Kuei first became chief councilor in 1131, he proposed peaceful coexistence with the Chin, but Kao-tsung had not yet come either to accept the situation or to trust Ch'in Kuei completely. Thus when Lü I-hao wished to have Ch'in Kuei replaced with Chu Sheng-fei as chief councilor, Lü attacked Ch'in Kuei on the grounds that by advocating peace with the enemy he was blocking plans for recovering the lost territories. Lü also charged that Ch'in Kuei had formed a clique and was attempting to monopolize political power. Kao-tsung gave in and dismissed Ch'in Kuei. In those early years, however, Ch'in Kuei was by no means alone in promoting peace, and five years later, in 1136, even Chao Ting was in favor of peace.[76]

The turning point from a proactive, aggressive military policy to a passive, defensive one was Kao-tsung's abortive attempt to carry out a northern expedition in 1137. The defection to Ta Ch'i of one of Kao-tsung's key generals with his powerful army dealt the war faction a serious blow. From that time on, Ch'in Kuei gradually won the complete trust of Kao-tsung, serving as chief councilor from 1138, and concluding a peace settlement with Chin. After the final treaty was concluded in 1142, Ch'in Kuei was granted the august title of senior preceptor (*t'ai-shih*), and became the dominant figure in government. He was regarded by some as a sage chief minister (*sheng-hsiang*), by others as a tyrant.

It was apparently Kao-tsung's own determination that led him to put such unquestioning confidence in Ch'in Kuei. There is an anecdote about how Ch'in Kuei secured Kao-tsung's trust in 1138. When Kao-tsung was inclined to accept a peace settlement, Ch'in asked him to consider the issue for three days, and after three days, he asked the emperor to consider it for three more days. After that he asked Kao-tsung to give him full authority to go ahead with the peace plan, free of interference from any other minister.[77] Years later, in 1148, Kao-tsung recalled Ch'in Kuei's first proposal for peace (in 1131), saying that even at that time Ch'in had already made up his mind to make peace. But when Kao-tsung attributed the achievement of peace to Ch'in Kuei, Ch'in replied: "The decision to make peace was entirely Your Majesty's.

---

[76] *CYYL* (1936) 106, p. 1727.
[77] Hsü, *San-ch'ao pei-meng hui-pien* 184, pp. 5b–6b.

Your servant only carried it out; what achievement was there in this for me?"[78]

CH'IN KUEI'S DOMINANCE, 1141–1155

Kao-tsung was a serious and diligent ruler who wanted to make all important decisions on state affairs by himself. He was committed to a strict daily routine. Kao-tsung met with his officials in the morning, and spent much of the afternoon and evening reading. He was fond of the *Shih-chi* (*Records of the historian*), the *Shu-ching* (*Book of documents*), the *Ch'un-ch'iu* (*Spring and Autumn annals*), and especially the *Tso-chuan* (*Tso tradition*), which he would go through every twenty-four days. It seems that Kao-tsung's interest in the *Spring and Autumn annals* was as a political tool. He not only studied it diligently himself but also encouraged his ministers to do the same, aiming to enhance his authority by association with the kingly and sagely tone of the work. In addition to reading, he practiced archery and calligraphy, and attended to memorials in the evening.

The driving objective of Kao-tsung's early years on the throne was the restoration of strong central control of the different branches of government, centering on the control of the military. He was ruling a society that had been militarized at every level after nearly twenty years of conflict. This objective continued, but the style of his rule changed somewhat after 1141. Before 1141 he had admired Emperor Han Kuang-wu-ti (r. 25–57) of the Later Han dynasty, who had restored the Han dynasty after it had been overthrown. He contrasted Han Kuang-wu-ti's reign with that of the T'ang dynasty emperor T'ang T'ai-tsung (r. 626–49), saying that T'ang T'ai-tsung had loved fame too much and was not as direct and honest as Han Kuang-wu-ti had been. After 1141, however, Kao-tsung began to admire the Han dynasty emperor Wen-ti (r. 180–157 B.C.E.), who had attempted to adhere to the principle of nonaction (*wu wei*) to attain peace and prosperity, and to establish the primacy of civil government over the military and the use of force. While the apparent reason for Kao-tsung's attempt to emulate Wen-ti's style of governing was to preserve the peace concluded between the Sung and the Chin, a consistent new theme emerged in his discussions with his ministers. Kao-tsung said that he preferred a "soft" (*jou*) approach to politics, and that he liked Emperor Han Kuang-wu-ti's "soft" policies and admired the Sung emperor Jen-tsung's (r. 1022–63) benevolent rule. Kao-tsung cited the peace that had been made with the Liao as a good precedent and one that, if followed, would benefit the

[78] *CYYL* (1936) 158, p. 2564.

people. Kao-tsung once said that the emperors in the Northern Sung period had never wanted war and that like them he employed the "way of softness" (*jou-tao*) to "control" (*yü*) the Jurchen Chin.[79]

Ch'in Kuei's monopoly of power

When he allowed his chief minister, Ch'in Kuei, freedom to direct state affairs after 1141, Kao-tsung was emulating the emperor Han Wen-ti. However, Ch'in Kuei, who may have been an advocate of peace, could hardly be called an exponent of "soft government." Having already purged most of the war party from central government, he systematically replaced his political enemies with his own relatives and trusted followers. Born in the south, Ch'in Kuei did not come from a great clan, but his wife was from a famous branch of the Wang lineage, which originally came from Szechwan. They had settled in K'ai-feng when her grandfather Wang Kuei (1019–85) had become an important minister and eventually chief councilor in the 1070s and 1080s. Ch'in's father-in-law, Wang Chung-shan, and Wang's younger brother, Wang Chung-i, were sons of Wang Kuei, and both had surrendered in 1129 to the Chin army during its invasion. When Ch'in Kuei became chief councilor, the Wang brothers as well as Cheng I-nien, a cousin of Ch'in Kuei's wife who had served the short-lived Ta Ch'u regime of Chang Pang-ch'ang in the north, were all pardoned and given official appointments in the Sung administration. Wang Huan2 and Wang Hui, Ch'in's brothers-in-law, were also made officials of the middle rank. Through these personal connections and through envoys like Wang Lun, Ch'in Kuei may have gained important and detailed information about the political and military situations in the north. Ch'in Kuei also established close relationships with Chang Ch'u-wei, a eunuch, and with Wang Chi-hsien (1098–1181), Kao-tsung's favorite physician, who was also a "sworn brother" of Ch'in's wife. Through them, Ch'in Kuei and his adopted son, Ch'in Hsi (d. 1161), obtained inside personal information about Kao-tsung and his opinions.[80]

During Ch'in Kuei's period in control of the state Chin Kuei remained the only chief councilor. A large number of assistant councilors were appointed, usually with some specific policy in mind, but most of them enjoyed tenures of a year or less, after which they were either posted far from the capital where

---

[79] Tao, *The Jurchen in twelfth-century China*, pp. 192–3, 195.

[80] See Liu, "Ch'in Kuei ti ch'in-yu," pp. 310–23, and Teraji, *Nan-Sō shoki seijishi kenkyū*, pp. 348–67. For a valuable study of the creation of Ch'in Kuei's historical image, see Hartman, "The making of a villain," pp. 59–146.

they could have little influence on policy, or they were simply impeached by the censors at Ch'in Kuei's bidding.[81]

Ch'in Kuei's tampering with the dynastic record

Ch'in Kuei was concerned that the historical record show in the most favorable light his role in the controversial events of Kao-tsung's reign. The early Sung emperors established arrangements for an official from the History Office to compile what would become a *Veritable record* (*Shih-lu*) of each reign, garnered first from the *Court diary of activity and repose* (*Ch'i-chü chu*), and then from the *Daily calendar* (*jih-li*). The compilation for a reign's *Veritable record* had been modified in Hui-tsung's time, when the History Office was left unstaffed and the collection of the record entrusted to the editorial secretaries of the Palace Library (*Pi-shu sheng*). The *Veritable record* of Shen-tsung's reign (r. 1067–85) had been revised repeatedly in later reigns because of the contemporary political implications of the policies of Shen-tsung's chief councilor, Wang An-shih (1021–68). The *Veritable record* for Shen-tsung was revised in 1135 and again in 1138 under the chief councilors Chang Chün and Chao Ting. Under Ch'in Kuei, the History Office was abolished in 1140. All of its projects were entrusted to staff in the Palace Library who had been specially assigned by the chief councilor, the official who was effectively in complete control of the compilation of the dynastic record. After 1143 no court diarists were appointed, and the compilation of the *Court diary of activity and repose* was in abeyance. This left the collection and preservation of the other relevant archival materials on state policy in the hands of the chief councilor, that is to say, in the hands of Ch'in Kuei himself. In 1142, Ch'in Kuei had Ch'in Hsi, who had just earned a *chin-shih* degree, appointed to the Palace Library; subsequently Ch'in Hsi was made the library's vice-director. In 1144, Ch'in Hsi was given a newly created post as supervisor of all the library's business, a position he held until Ch'in Kuei's death in 1155, shortly before which a grandson was also appointed to a library office.

Ch'in Hsi and two colleagues began by completing retroactively a new *Daily calendar* of the years since the Chien-yen reign period to replace the existing *Daily calendars* for 1127–42. They gave Ch'in Kuei's version of events in place of the contemporary accounts of the court diarists. They also compiled a *Sung lun*, a general discussion of the events leading to the peace of 1142. Moreover, Ch'in Kuei had altered or suppressed much of the archival material about his first

---

[81] For a list, see Gung Wei Ai, "The role of censorial officials in the power struggle during Southern Sung China, 1127–1278" (M.A. thesis, University of Malaya, 1971), pp. 308–12.

tenure as a councilor in 1131–2. After his death these distortions were further confounded by later, mostly "Learning of the Way" (*Tao-hsüeh*), historians, anxious to reverse Ch'in Kuei's version of events and to present a negative view of him and his policies. These distortions piled upon distortions have left the historiography of Kao-tsung's reign a minefield for later historians, who have been trying gallantly since the twelfth century to sort out the obfuscations.[82] This problem was further complicated by the imposition of a ban on the private writing of histories and by the institution of what amounted to state control over books and publication.

When the Palace Library was opened in grand new premises in 1144, Kao-tsung remarked on the small size of its collection. The original Sung palace libraries had been lost when the Chin captured K'ai-feng, and a great effort was made to locate and solicit the gift of works to fill the lacunae. In 1143 standard rates to be paid for copies of missing works were set, and when this failed to persuade owners to meet the library's needs, all local jurisdictions were ordered to appoint officials to take copies of rare works in the hands of local scholars. To encourage officials to take this task seriously, an order was issued in 1146 that the local authorities were to be paid rewards as well as the owners.

At the same time, private publishing of all sorts continued to grow, especially in Fu-chien and Szechwan. By law, depository copies of all newly printed books, printed on special yellow paper, were required to be sent to the Palace Library. Local authorities were empowered to prevent the printing of and destroy the printing blocks for any works deemed not "beneficial to learning." This escalated into an attempt to impose strict censorship, and it was applied with great severity to all unofficial writing of histories and political memoirs, though at first the ban was widely disregarded. Apprehension about the draconian way these standards were applied by local petty officials caused the loss or voluntary destruction of the writings of many scholars and the scattering of important collections. There is no doubt that Ch'in Kuei envisaged these rules as a form of heavy censorship – even thought control.[83]

The worst aspect of this control on books, printing, and open discourse was that people were encouraged to send in denunciations (*kao-chieh*) of others for antigovernment views expressed in their private papers, correspondence, or even conversation. Such denunciations, coupled with Ch'in Kuei's systematic use of the Censorate as a mechanism to purge officialdom of all his opponents, poisoned the atmosphere of politics, which became more oppressive

---

[82] See the account in Hartman, "The making of a villain," pp. 68–80.
[83] The term "thought control" is used in Liu, *China turning inward*, p. 100. Liu's use is quoted in Hartman, "The making of a villain," p. 61.

and sharply polarized. Ch'in Kuei saw signs of dissent everywhere, and became increasingly suspicious and vindictive as the years passed. To suppress dissident opinions, especially any criticism of the treaty with the Chin, ever more stringent measures of censorship, the banning and burning of literature, and the encouragement of personal impeachment and denunciations were imposed, leading to a reign of terror in which many officials and scholars who had been critical of Ch'in Kuei or his policies were branded members of hostile cliques, banished, and even killed. Their followers and associates were also demoted or banished. Just before his death in 1155, Ch'in Kuei arranged for the mass treason trial of fifty-three suspect literati, who escaped death only because Ch'in Kuei died before he could sign their death warrants. The list of Ch'in Kuei's victims is impressive, but the greatest victim was the atmosphere of collegial trust among the court officials.

Ch'in Kuei and the "Learning of the Way"

Peace and economic development not withstanding, the political atmosphere under Ch'in Kuei was repressive. A vindictive politician, he practiced nepotism on a wide scale, and hounded opponents remorselessly. But these persecutions were not purely acts of personal vengeance. There was also an ideological issue involved in many of Ch'in Kuei's attacks on his opponents. Since the establishment of the Southern Sung, the reputation of Wang An-shih and his followers had been under attack as part of blaming the debacle of 1126–7 on the revival of Wang's New Policies (*hsin-fa*) under Hui-tsung's powerful chief councilor, Ts'ai Ching (1046–1127). Ch'eng I (1033–1107), one of the founders of *Tao-hsüeh* learning and an opponent of Wang An-shih's reforms, had been granted posthumous honors by Hui-tsung. However, Ch'in Kuei and his followers disliked the use of *Tao-hsüeh* learning to criticize Kao-tsung, Ch'in himself, or the peace treaty of 1141. Sporadic attacks on the founders of *Tao-hsüeh* learning from a generation earlier, Ch'eng I and his followers, began throughout the 1130s and expanded in the 1140s, when Ch'in Kuei denounced Ch'eng I's "specialist learning" (*chuan-men hsüeh*). Chao Ting, the former chief councilor and Ch'in Kuei's bitter political rival, was an advocate of Ch'eng I's teachings, which were tainted when Chao was forced out of the government.[84] Another friend of *Tao-hsüeh* learning, Li Kuang, was forced from office in 1138 and also sent to Hainan Island. In 1155, Ssu-ma Kuang's famous notebook, *Su-shui chi-wen* (*Record by the Su River*), was banned at the

---

[84] Conrad Schirokauer, "Neo-Confucians under attack: The condemnation of *wei-hsüeh*," in *Crisis and prosperity in Sung China*, ed. John W. Haeger (Tucson, Ariz., 1975), pp. 163–98. These themes are also addressed in detail in Hartman, "The making of a villain," pp. 117–46.

request of his own great grandson for fear of possible political persecution.[85] After Ch'in Kuei's death in 1155, Kao-tsung reversed many of the orders that had persecuted Ch'in Kuei's political enemies and their families. Some of the men, even such controversial figures as Chao Ting and Yüeh Fei, were posthumously rehabilitated.

STABILIZING CIVILIAN GOVERNMENT

The stress placed by Kao-tsung and Ch'in Kuei on civilian control of the government and the military was accompanied by a general increase in state support for education. In 1134, Kao-tsung had been pleased that the Imperial University was reestablished, but he commented sadly that only after the restoration of peace would the people be able to begin turning again to the pursuit of learning.[86] Ch'in Kuei himself was a distinguished *chin-shih* graduate, and his first post was as an instructor at the university in K'ai-feng during the last years of Hui-tsung's reign, from 1123 to 1126. When Ch'in Kuei came to power as chief councilor he decided to promote education and culture. In an act that had political implications, the university was granted a new site in what had been Yüeh Fei's great mansion in Lin-an, and new premises were built and gradually expanded.

The school system also benefited. After Kao-tsung visited the new site of the Imperial University in 1144, he told Ch'in Kuei that had it not been for Ch'in's efforts to make peace, it would have been impossible to improve the schools.[87] Subsequently, it was required that every newly appointed local official should visit the local Confucian temple, where the school was normally located, before taking up any government administrative matters.[88] Twice in Northern Sung times, all prefectures and counties had been ordered to build schools, but these orders had not been followed everywhere and many places still did not have schools in early Southern Sung times. Moreover, quite a few existing schools had been destroyed during the war years, and it took some time to rebuild them. Schools were continuously being built during the Southern Sung, using local government funds, income from school land worked by tenant-farmers, donations from the rich, and labor from the poor.

The "school land" (*hsüeh-t'ien*) system had been an innovation in Northern Sung times. Under this system, the government granted an endowment of land to a prefecture or county, the income from which was to be used either to build a new school or to support an existing one. The first "school land"

---

[85] *CYYL* (1936) 154, p. 2477.
[86] *CYYL* (1936) 149, p. 2403.
[87] *CYYL* (1936) 151, p. 2429.
[88] *CYYL* (1936) 152, p. 2454.

was established in Yen-chou (modern Yen county, Shantung) in 1022. The same arrangement was followed in many prefectures, with the school property ranging from several tens of *mou* to over a thousand *mou*. The maintenance and expansion of *hsüeh-t'ien* in a prefecture required long-term efforts by local officials with local support. For example, under the Northern Sung the "school land" endowment in Yün-chou (modern Tung-p'ing county, Shantung) had been established by Fan Chung-yen (989–1052). Later, T'eng Yüan-fa (1020–90) obtained 2,500 *mou* of land for the prefectural school, which yielded an annual income of one million cash. In the south, the *hsüeh-t'ien* endowment of the Wu-hsing school began with 500 *mou* of land, which was increased by the prefect Pao K'o to 1,200 *mou*, bringing in an income sufficient to support one hundred students. The Chien-k'ang prefectural school started with a government land grant of 10 *ch'ing* (1,000 *mou*) in 1029. This was increased to 38 *ch'ing* and 57 *mou* (3,857 *mou*), including three wineries, and by the early 1130s it still had a total of 1,915 *mou*. In 1158, the school acquired 1,890 *mou*, and in the 1260s it had a total of 9,380 *mou*. In Ch'ih-ch'eng (modern Lin-hai, Chekiang), the six prefectural and county schools possessed 2,814.2 *mou* of arable land in Southern Sung times. The establishment of schools in every prefecture and county definitely helped to promote Confucian education widely, even in remote border areas.[89] A weakness of the public schools was that they trained students almost exclusively for the civil service examinations. In Southern Sung times private schools and academies also proliferated. In many of these, *Tao-hsüeh* (Learning of the Way) masters taught disciples who were not primarily interested in official civil service careers.[90] As part of the effort to promote schools and control school curricula, by the end of Kao-tsung's reign the government had published complete sets of the classics and the standard histories.[91]

As in the Northern Sung, the Southern Sung government relied on the civil service examinations for bureaucratic recruitment. These examinations were held every three years and produced a large number of *chin-shih* degree holders. In Northern Sung times, the pass rate for candidates for the *chin-shih* degree varied between one in ten and one in fifteen. During the early years of the Southern Sung, the success rate was one in eight. This disparity reflected the urgent need to replace the many officials lost with the Chin conquest of the north and from the destruction of war. During Kao-tsung's reign, the government could recruit potential officials only from the south, and

---

[89] See Tao Jing-shen (T'ao Chin-sheng), "Sung Chin miao-hsüeh yü ju-chia ssu-hsiang ti ch'uan-pu," in *Kuo-chi K'ung-hsüeh hui-i lun-wen-chi*, ed. Chung-hua min-kuo K'ung-Meng hsüeh-hui et al. (Taipei, 1988), pp. 536–7.

[90] See Thomas H. C. Lee, *Government education and examinations in Sung China* (New York, 1985); Linda A. Walton, *Academies and society in Southern Sung China* (Honolulu, 1999).

[91] Li, *Chien-yen i-lai ch'ao-yeh tsa-chi* (1935–7) *chia* 4, pp. 63–4.

enlisted an average of 336 *chin-shih* per triennial examination, which compares favorably with the averages of the first four reigns in the Northern Sung. The average number of *chin-shih* per examination during the later reign of Hsiao-tsung (1162–89) was 429.5, surpassing the average of 400 during Shen-tsung's reign (1067–85). One characteristic of the early Southern Sung civil service examinations was that the majority of *chin-shih* recruits came from nonofficial families, on the evidence of the extant list of *chin-shih* of 1148. Another feature was that the *chin-shih* were selected by local government authorities in the early years of Kao-tsung's reign. Later this form of local selection continued to be practiced in Szechwan, because it was very difficult for the Szechwanese candidates to travel to Lin-an.[92]

Kao-tsung's realization that the restoration of control over the north was temporarily unattainable can also be seen in his decision to make Hang-chou rather than Chien-k'ang (Nanking) the capital. In T'ang times Hang-chou had been a major regional city, important as the southern terminus of the Grand Canal. At the end of the T'ang it was the capital of the richest, most stable and enduring, regional state of the Five Dynasties, Wu-Yüeh. Situated on the northern bank of the Che River a few miles before it reaches Hang-chou Bay, the city had been heavily fortified, with a triple line of walls, and the narrowing terrain was also favorable for defense. Other possible choices in the lower Yangtze region to be a temporary capital were Su-chou, the center of the burgeoning rice-producing plain around Lake T'ai, and Chien-k'ang, once the capital of the southern dynasties, which had the advantage of being more central, and a more convenient place to exercise military command over the upper Yangtze valley. During the Chin invasion in 1130 it had been Kao-tsung's first choice as the temporary capital, but Hang-chou was close to the sea, and Kao-tsung had fled by sea in early 1130 when Wan-yen Wu-chu tried to capture him. Although Kao-tsung never announced that Hang-chou (after 1133, renamed Lin-an) was his permanent capital, from 1133 the construction there of the imperial ancestral temple and a *ming-tang* (Hall of Enlightenment) clearly revealed his long-term intentions. In 1135, when he was more confident about his ability to fight the Chin, he commented: "If the enemy dare come, I will personally lead the armies to meet the challenge and destroy them, and then we would be able to recover the Central Plain. If we again consider the policy of escaping by sea, how would we be able to maintain the nation?"[93]

---

[92] Edward A. Kracke, Jr., "Family vs. merit in the civil service examinations during the empire," *Harvard Journal of Asiatic Studies* 10 No. 2 (1947), pp. 105–23; Araki Toshikazu, *Sōdai kakyo seido kenkyū* (Kyoto, 1969), pp. 224, 450–9; Chapter 5 of John W. Chaffee, *The thorny gates of learning in Sung China: A social history of examinations* (Cambridge, 1985).

[93] *CYYL* (1936) 84, p. 1378.

From 1130 to 1137 the court was constantly on the move between Lin-an and Chien-k'ang. When the Sung were taking the initiative Chien-k'ang was the better command center. When the Sung were hard-pressed by the Chin and T'a Ch'i, Lin-an offered a safer refuge. Suggestions to make Chien-k'ang the permanent capital had been made by Wang T'ao2 (1074–1137) in 1135, by Chang Chün in 1136, by Chang Shou in 1138, and by Chang Hsing-ch'eng in 1139. All were ignored.[94] In 1161, when the ambitious Chin emperor Wan-yen Liang (r. 1149–61; known also as Prince Hai-ling) began his military campaign against the Sung, Kao-tsung again planned to escape by sea, although this proved unnecessary. During his reign, Kao-tsung never traveled west of Chien-k'ang.

Kao-tsung sponsored efforts to restore and improve court ceremony. When the Southern Sung was established, the imperial ceremonial implements were transported south from K'ai-feng but were lost or burned when Kao-tsung fled Yang-chou in 1129. Not much was done with respect to ritual and court ceremonies before 1141, although the Imperial Bureau of Music (*Chiao-fang*) had been restored in 1134, employing 416 musicians, with eunuchs in charge.[95] After the 1141 treaty with the Chin, the Sung gradually restored imperial ceremonies and ritual practices, and a school for imperial family members was also reestablished. Many instruments necessary for ritual were made in 1146. A "great audience" ceremony was finally performed for the first time in the Southern Sung period on New Year's Day 1155.[96] The next year, the requisite new ceremonial implements and regalia were ready for use, including the *pa-pao* ("the eight treasures," or "the eight imperial seals"). In 1157, the Imperial Ancestral Temple (*T'ai-miao*) was built in Lin-an. On this occasion Kao-tsung personally wrote out the *Hsiao-ching* (*Book of filial piety*), which was then copied and inscribed on steles in many prefectures.[97]

THE ECONOMY AND FINANCIAL POLICIES

The financial administration of the early Southern Sung differed from its northern predecessor in two fundamental ways. First, the emergencies caused by the war required a substantial part of the tax revenue from many areas to be retained by local fiscal intendants to fund military units there. This was especially true in Szechwan, where the central government's control was limited, and the

---

[94] Liao Kang had suggested in 1131 that Chien-k'ang be made the capital; see *CYYL* (1936) 48, p. 861. Other Chien-k'ang proponents were Hu An-kuo in 1132, *CYYL* (1936) 53, pp. 934–5; Chang Chün, *CYYL* (1936) 102, p. 1668; Chang Shou, *CYYL* (1936) 118, p. 1898; and Chang Hsing-ch'eng, *CYYL* (1936) 128, p. 2079.

[95] *CYYL* (1936) 151, p. 2426; Li, *Chien-yen i-lai ch'ao-yeh tsa-chi* (1935–7) *chia* 3, pp. 52–3.

[96] *CYYL* (1936) 153, p. 2461; Li, *Chien-yen i-lai ch'ao-yeh tsa-chi* (1935–7) *chia* 3, p. 47.

[97] *CYYL* (1936) 155, p. 2517. Li, *Chien-yen i-lai ch'ao-yeh tsa-chi* (1935–7) *chia* 3, p. 46.

region was almost completely financially independent. Szechwan was too far away to risk sending its tax revenues across ungoverned or enemy-controlled stretches to the central government in Lin-an. The same trend toward decentralization that was apparent in military and political administration was also dominant in the field of finance. Second, the Southern Sung was in severe financial difficulties in its early years, which forced the introduction of new taxes. By the end of Kao-tsung's reign, however, the government seems to have managed to achieve financial stability. From the estimates of government revenues it seems that the regime was fairly rich. For most of the early Southern Sung the government relied mainly upon the wealth of the southeast and of Szechwan. The bulk of government revenues came from taxes on salt, tea, liquor, and silk, in addition to the new taxes created in the early years for supporting the military. Government income around 1130, generated largely in the southeast, reached the figure of almost 30 million mixed units (one "unit" of copper cash was equivalent to one thousand cash).[98] This figure surpassed the 16 million units of the early years of the Northern Sung, when taxes were collected over the whole of the empire. Although in the first five years of Kao-tsung's reign the regime suffered from a severe shortage of financial resources to meet its military needs, by the end of the 1130s the situation had improved as more effective government control was reestablished over a larger part of the regions south of the Yangtze River. These regions had provided the bulk of state revenue in late Northern Sung times. By the early 1160s, the government's annual income had surged to 80 million units. Successful financial policies and administration played a great part helping prevent further Chin invasions. Kao-tsung's financial policies contributed to the success of the restoration.

The Southern Sung government continued the policy of imposing salt and tea monopolies. In Northern Sung, income from such monopolies constituted a significant part of total state revenues. In the early years of the Southern Sung, there was a reform of the monopolies in Szechwan, an important area of both salt and tea production. Chao K'ai (1066–1141), who proposed the reform, was sent to Szechwan to administer it. The local government began to sell salt and tea certificates to merchants who purchased salt and tea directly from the producers and resold it elsewhere. The government sought to control the trade more firmly and curtail smuggling more effectively. Tea was essential

---

[98] "Mixed units" refers to the strange convention used in finance of lumping together bushels of grain, lengths of silk, strings of cash, and ounces of silver to give one number. Some people call these "units of account" or "mixed accounting units." For discussion, see Peter J. Golas, "The Sung financial administration," in *The Cambridge history of China*, volume 5: *The Sung dynasty and its precursors, 907–1279, part 2*, ed. John W. Chaffee and Denis C. Twitchett (New York, forthcoming).

to procure horses from nomadic tribesmen in the western frontier and foreign states. The government therefore needed to secure a constant supply of tea to send to the western frontier. To do this, the government had to maintain more stringent control of the tea trade.[99]

During the war years of the 1120s and 1130s, many regions of Huai-nan, Hupei, and areas south of the Yangtze River were devastated by the conflict. Death, disease, famine, and lawlessness led to a massive migration of people from north to south. In particular, the populations of the war zones in Huai-nan and Hupei were greatly reduced, and agricultural production and thus tax revenues there did not recover for many decades. As late as 1159 the central government received no tax rice from the Huai-nan region. Nevertheless, government spending on defense was such that eighty percent of government revenue was needed to maintain armies equal in size to those fielded during the Northern Sung. Even after the peace of 1141, the number of troops continued to increase, and during the reign of Hsiao-tsung (r. 1162–89) it reached 418,000, double the figure of 1141.[100]

To generate more tax revenue, the government made efforts to increase arable land and redistribute uncultivated land. As an incentive to encourage people to resume farming, agricultural taxes were temporarily exempted. Land was distributed in three major ways. First, as a measure to encourage people who had fled from their home district to return, the government accepted applications from returning refugees for outright grants of land. In other cases, people rented land from the government in the expectation that ownership would be transferred to them after a specified period of time. Refugees from Chin-held territory and veterans were also granted land by the government. In many cases, the government lent (or with the veterans and northern refugees, simply gave) the farmers and tenant-farmers capital, seeds, tools, and even oxen at low or no interest. However, the government sometimes had difficulty finding land to assign for the huge numbers of refugees. Second, the government itself employed tenant-farmers to engage in agricultural production on state land. A system called *ying-t'ien* (land management) was implemented, under which the government contracted with the tenants to farm the land on favorable terms. These tenant-farmers were often organized to work in groups. Third, the military organized soldiers to work on state-run farms (*t'un-t'ien*) in the border areas during lulls in military activity. Government land was also sold to raise emergency funds. Sources of government land included land in border areas that had been abandoned by people fleeing south during wartime

---

[99] See Paul J. Smith, *Taxing heaven's storehouse: Horses, bureaucrats and the destruction of the Sichuan tea industry, 1074–1224* (Cambridge, Mass., 1991).

[100] Liang Keng-yao, *Nan Sung ti nung-ti li yung cheng-ts'e* (Taipei, 1977), pp. 66–7.

and land that the government had forcibly purchased or confiscated. Both the tenant farms of the civil government and the military-operated farms were well organized, and eventually the land was sold or given to individuals.

By the end of Kao-tsung's reign in the 1160s, government efforts to increase revenues through land distribution were generally successful. Taking advantage of the favorable terms offered by the government, large numbers of people had returned to their native places. Many others migrated from the more densely populated southeast regions inland to Hunan and Hupei. Consequently, from the last years of Kao-tsung's reign through the reign of Hsiao-tsung, the population in these two regions grew rapidly. Agriculture in these newly resettled regions recovered and not only produced enough food for the local population but also began to contribute grain as tax revenue to the central government by the end of the late 1180s.[101]

These new measures also had a downside. Throughout the early years of the Southern Sung, influential men increased their landholdings through the process called engrossment (chien-ping). Local strongmen and men with official status, some making use of their connections with local officials, took advantage of the government's resettlement plans to obtain large parcels of land for themselves or simply seized land. Many of them were able to avoid paying taxes, which resulted in the loss of tax revenues for the government. During this time, several officials complained that half of the land south of the Yangtze was owned by big landlords, many of them connected in some way to the government. Buddhist and Taoist temples also owned large estates, worked by tenants, that were second in size only to the lands owned by imperial relatives. From 1142 to 1149, the government tried to equalize taxes by investigating ownership of cultivated land and assessing proper taxes, but the efforts had only limited success.[102]

The total amount of property owned by government schools was dwarfed by the landholdings of Buddhist temples. For example, in contrast to the school property in Ch'ih-ch'eng, the local Pao-en Temple there had twice as much, more than sixty-five hundred mou. It is recorded that in 1143 there were two hundred thousand monks and nuns in Southern Sung territory. In Fu-chien, Buddhist temples not only were the largest owners of land, they possessed the best land. In addition to donations from laymen, members of the imperial family donated land to the temples. The temples also acquired

[101] Liang, Nan Sung ti nung-ti li yung cheng-ts'e, pp. 69–102.
[102] Liang Keng-yao, Nan Sung ti nung-ts'un ching-chi (Taipei, 1984), pp. 116–19. Ch'i Hsia, Sung-tai ching-chi shih (Shanghai, 1987–8), chapter 6, discusses estate formation during both the Northern and the Southern Sung.

land from farmers, and purchased and developed land. In southern Fu-chien the temples owned an average of one hundred and fifty *ch'ing* of land, whereas a rich landlord only had five to ten *ch'ing*.[103]

In the field of state finance, an important policy was implemented in 1142 at the suggestion of Li Ch'un-nien (d. 1159). Li pointed out ten problems in collecting land tax. Among these, the most serious was that powerful landlords paid less in taxes than did free farmers, which overburdened the peasantry and deprived local governments of needed revenue. Under the newly initiated "land survey measure" (*ching-chieh fa*), every three years local governments were to survey and register all cultivated land and assess tax appropriately. The measure aimed at increasing government income, and a bureau carried out the work until 1149.[104]

Southern Sung cities benefited from peace. The Chin invasion sent massive waves of refugees from the north and the Central Plains into Southern Sung territory, especially to the southeast. Officials, soldiers, and rich families began to settle in Hang-chou, Su-chou, Chien-k'ang, and Chen-chiang areas, stimulating commerce. The growth of trade brought merchants and artisans to urban areas, generating additional commercial taxes that were collected by the government in local, regional, and central market towns. Income from commercial taxes in Lan-ch'i county (near modern Chin-hua, Chekiang), which had been little more than 8,342 units of account in 1077, increased to 13,819 units during the reign of Kao-tsung. Government income from commercial taxes in Yen-chou4 increased from 35,316 units in 1139 to 38,275 units during the Ch'un-hsi era (1174–89) of Hsiao-tsung. Available data from local gazetteers show a spectacular growth of commercial tax revenue from the Northern Sung to the Southern Sung period. Commercial tax revenue from foreign trade along the southern coast also increased, from 1,101,000 units in the last decades of the Northern Sung to 2,000,000 units near the end of Kao-tsung's reign. These figures indicate a rapid recovery in commercial activity during Kao-tsung's reign. This increase in commercial activity was related to the growth of urban populations,[105] which are exemplified by the figures in Table 6 for the capital city of Hang-chou (Lin-an).[106]

---

[103] Huang Min-chih, *Sung-tai fo-chiao she-hui ching-chi shih lun-chi* (Taipei, 1989), pp. 19–89, 119–27, 352.

[104] Teraji, *Nan-Sō seiken kakuritsu katei kenkyū oboegaki*, pp. 78–108. See also his *Nan-Sō shoki seijishi kenkyū*, pp. 343–5, 392–416. For early Southern Sung finance and this measure, see Ch'i, *Sung-tai ching-chi shih*, pp. 422–50.

[105] Liang Keng-yao, "Nan Sung ch'eng-shih ti fa-chan (shang)," *Shih-huo yüeh-k'an* 10 No. 10 (1981), pp. 420–6.

[106] Sogabe Shizuo, *Sōdai zaiseishi* (1941; Tokyo, 1966), pp. 45–6. Also Liang, "Nan Sung ch'eng-shih ti fa-chan (shang)," pp. 434–5. Ch'i, *Sung-tai ching-chi shih*, pp. 1009–10.

Table 6. *Households and population of Hang-chou (Lin-an)*

Period	No. of Households	Population
Early Sung	70,465	–
Mid–Northern Sung	202,816	–
Early Southern Sung	205,369	–
1165–1173	261,692	552,607
1241–1252	381,335	767,739
1265–1274	391,259	1,240,760

Table 7. *Sung population growth of four Southern cities*

City	1078–1085	1165–1173	Percentage increase
Fu-chou	211,546	321,284	52
Hui-chou	105,984	122,014	13
Kuang-chou	143,259	185,713[a]	23
Wen-chou	121,916	170,035	34

[a] For 1174–89.

Aside from Hang-chou, there were three other cities in the Southern Sung that had 50,000 to 100,000 households: O-chou (Wu-ch'ang, Hupei), Ch'eng-tu (Szechwan), and Ch'üan-chou (Fu-chien). Twelve cities had from 5,000 to 50,000 households, and there were many towns with 1,000 to 5,000 households. Table 7 gives rates of population growth for four cities.[107]

A good example of the growth of small towns is T'ing-chou (modern Ch'ang-t'ing, Fukien). The walls of T'ing-chou were built in the mid-eleventh century with a circumference of slightly over five *li*. By Southern Sung times, only three of its wards (*fang2*) were inside the old city walls and no fewer than twenty-three were outside them. T'ing-chou also expanded to include a satellite town five *li* outside the walls. At the same time,[108] T'ing-chou's urban population grew from 5,285 households in the Northern Sung to 73,140 households in the 1250s. In the prefecture as a whole, the number of registered households increased from 81,456 in the period 1078–85 to 218,750 by 1190, an increase of 168 percent in a little over a century.[109]

[107] Liang, "Nan Sung ch'eng-shih ti fa-chan (shang)," pp. 424–6.

[108] Shiba Yoshinobu, *Commerce and society in Sung China*, trans. Mark Elvin (Ann Arbor, Mich., 1970), pp. 136–7. Also Shiba Yoshinobu, *Sōdai shōgyōshi kenkyū* (Tokyo, 1968), p. 310.

[109] Liang, "Nan Sung ch'eng-shih ti fa-chan (shang)," pp. 433, 437. These figures show urban growth and imply that the increase in rural population had its limits.

This robust population growth was replicated throughout the new Southern Sung domain during Kao-tsung's reign. But despite the concerns of some in government, the destabilizing process of land engrossment (*chien-ping*) and estate formation continued in the Southern Sung.[110] Powerful officials either received land from the imperial court as a reward, or used their influence to acquire it. For example, the court granted nine hundred and sixty *ch'ing* of land to Ch'in Kuei. Wang Chi-hsien, Kao-tsung's physician, seized several hundred houses and built mansions in Lin-an. The great generals also had large estates. Some, like General Chang Chün2, had them in several prefectures. He and his family members also engaged in overseas trade.[111]

THE END OF THE CH'IN KUEI ERA

On the twenty-first of the tenth month of 1155, Kao-tsung went to Ch'in Kuei's residence to make a sick visit. That same night Ch'in Kuei died. A new political alignment quickly emerged at the Sung court. Kao-tsung reversed Ch'in Kuei's practice of persecuting political enemies and their families. Some of Chin's victims, notably Chao Ting and Yüeh Fei, were posthumously rehabilitated, and many of Ch'in's relatives and partisans were sent into exile. Kao-tsung declined to make use of Ch'in's son, Ch'in Hsi, who had served as commissioner for military affairs, and when Ch'in Hsi maneuvered to try to succeed his father as chief councilor he was dismissed.[112]

But the peace policy continued. After the death of Ch'in Kuei, Kao-tsung commented that Ch'in Kuei had advocated peace and had emphasized that the peace settlement should be faithfully observed.[113] In 1156, when a report about the possibility of a Chin invasion reached the court, Kao-tsung did not believe it. He issued an edict to the effect that he alone had decided to conclude the peace with Chin. Reiterating that the late chief councilor Ch'in Kuei had only assisted him in carrying out that policy, he forbade the spreading of rumors about a Chin breach of the treaty and reaffirmed his continued belief in the settlement with Chin.[114] Kao-tsung's main consideration was security. He was able to obtain external security by concluding a peace settlement with Chin, and he achieved internal security by exercising complete control over the military.[115]

---

[110] Li, *Chien-yen i-lai ch'ao-yeh tsa-chi* (1935–7) *chia* 17, p. 257.
[111] Ch'i, *Sung-tai ching-chi shih*, pp. 259–62.
[112] *CYYL* (1936) 173, p. 2847.
[113] *CYYL* (1936) 170, p. 2794.
[114] *CYYL* (1936) 172, p. 2827.
[115] See Liu, *China turning inward*, p. 99.

The peace established in 1141 lasted for twenty years. Not only had Kao-tsung pursued a policy of coexistence, his contemporary, the emperor of Chin (Hsi-tsung, r. 1135–50), was a weak ruler, unbalanced, and preoccupied by relations with the emerging power of his northern neighbors, the Mongols. The peace was finally broken by the Chin ruler Wan-yen Liang (r. 1150–61), better known as Prince Hai-ling, who ruled for twelve years but was denied a temple name by his successors.[116] His ambition was to establish a unified Chinese-style dynasty that also controlled the south. Prince Hai-ling seized power in 1149, leading a coup in which his cousin the emperor Hsi-tsung was assassinated. Prince Hai-ling carried out purges of those who either opposed him or advocated continuing the policy of coexistence with the Sung. In 1152 he began to reconstruct the former Sung capital K'ai-feng, which became his own Southern Capital. In 1161 he moved the Chin capital there from Yen-ching. Despite opposition from the Jurchen tribal nobility and from their recently conquered Khitan subjects, who rebelled in 1161, he pressed ahead with his grandiose plans to conquer the Sung, recruiting a huge, mainly Chinese, army and building a navy. In the fifth month of 1161, the Chin court sent a diplomatic mission to the south, charging the Sung with breaking the treaty by accommodating refugees from the north and by smuggling horses from Chin territories. Chin also maintained that the Huai River was not a proper border, and demanded that the Sung court dispatch its chief councilors to negotiate a new settlement. The Sung tried to relax the tension by sending an envoy to congratulate Prince Hai-ling on moving the Chin capital to K'ai-feng, but the Chin emperor refused to receive him.

The battle of Ts'ai-shih and the treaty of 1165

Many in the south suspected for some years that war was coming. Reports by Sung envoys called the attention of the Sung court to the developments in the north, and persuaded it to make defensive preparations in 1160. Because of Kao-tsung's hesitation, however, only three military garrisons along the Yangtze River were hastily set up in 1161 to strengthen defenses.

In the autumn of 1162, Chin mobilized four armies, reportedly comprising a million men in all, to destroy the Sung. Three armies were dispatched to invade the present regions of Kiangsu, Anhwei, northern Hupei, and Shensi. In addition, a naval force was sent down the coast to make sure that this time Kao-tsung could not escape by sea. Commanding the central army in person, Prince Hai-ling invaded the Anhwei region. His armies crossed the Huai

---

[116] On Prince Hai-ling, see Franke, "The Chin dynasty," pp. 239–43.

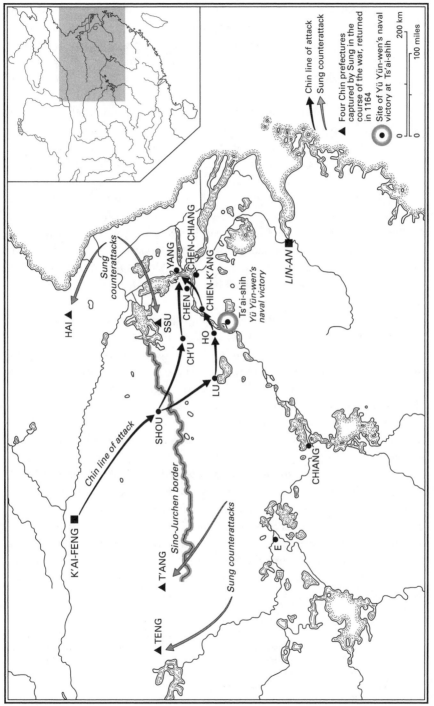

Map 26. Chin invasion of the Southern Sung, 1161–1162.

River on 28 October 1161. He did not meet any significant resistance, and Chin troops reached Ho-chou3 on the northern bank of the Yangtze River. On 26–27 November, they attempted to force a crossing of the Yangtze at Ts'ai-shih (south of modern Ma-an Shan). But Hai-ling's fleet of barges and small boats, carrying hundreds of soldiers trying to cross the river, were routed by the Southern Sung commander, Yü Yün-wen's, superior naval force, which included paddle wheel warships. Yü Yün-wen was a civilian official sent to supervise the army, which at that crucial moment had no single overall commander. After the river battle, Hai-ling moved his army east toward Yang-chou, planning to launch another attack there to cross the Yangtze River. But on 15 December near Yang-chou, Prince Hai-ling was assassinated in a mutiny by his own officers. They supposedly were fearful of the Sung navy that had annihilated the Chin fleet on the Yangtze at Ts'ai-shih. Hai-ling's fate was sealed in any case. After he had left K'ai-feng with his army on 15 October, and just prior to his launching his attack on the Southern Sung, Hai-ling's cousin, Wan-yen Wu-lu (Emperor Chin Shih-tsung, r. 1161–89) had taken control of Chin and enthroned himself on 27 October as the new Chin emperor.

The battle of Ts'ai-shih was mostly fought on the Yangtze River, and the small number of Chin soldiers who managed to land on the southern shore were either killed or captured. While Chin records indicate that their losses were minimal, Sung historians exaggerated Chin casualties. The *Chin dynastic history* (*Chin shih*) recorded Chin casualties as ranging from one *meng-an* (unit of 1,000 men) and 100 soldiers to two *meng-an* and 200 soldiers.[117] In sharp contrast, a Sung source indicates that "24,000 Chin warriors perished in the engagement. The Sung army captured five *meng-an* and 500 soldiers." A more reasonable contemporary account gives the following figures: twenty Chin boats with a total of 500 soldiers reached the south bank of the Yangtze River, and the soldiers were either killed or captured by Sung forces.[118]

The pivotal battle of Ts'ai-shih appears to have been fought on a surprisingly small scale. The reasons were twofold. First, Prince Hai-ling apparently underestimated the strength of the Sung army and the landing operation was not well planned. Although the Sung troops at Ts'ai-shih were dispersed, Yü Yün-wen was able to organize the soldiers and naval units into an army

---

[117] On the *meng-an* system of military organization, see Franke, "The Chin dynasty," pp. 275–6.

[118] The biographies of Li T'ung and Wu-yen P'u-lu-hu in T'o-t'o, ed., *Chin shih* [*Po-na-pen* 1930–7 ed.] (1344; Peking, 1975), pp. 129 and 80, indicate that only two military officers and 100 to 200 men were lost. Sung sources record Chin casualties from several hundred to half a million. I follow the most conservative Sung figure because Chin boats were small and after the Jurchen lost in the initial encounter, Hai-ling stopped military operations. See Tao Jing-shen (T'ao Chin-sheng), *Chin Hai-ling-ti ti fa Sung yü Ts'ai-shih chan-i ti k'ao-shih* (Taipei, 1963), pp. 150–67.

of eighteen thousand and used rewards to inspire his forces to fight bravely against the invaders. Had Yü Yün-wen not shown up at that critical moment, Hai-ling would have succeeded in crossing the river. Second, the small and poorly constructed boats limited the number of Jurchen soldiers that could take part in the operation. One source has it that Hai-ling ordered the building of the boats by using materials from razed houses, and that his army hastily made them within seven days. Contrasting these poor boats to the professional Sung navy, there is little reason to doubt the eyewitness description that Sung warships sank or smashed many Chin boats.

The battle of Ts'ai-shih stopped the large-scale Chin invasion, gave new confidence to the Sung armies, and stabilized the southern dynasty. It also ensured the continued coexistence of the two rival states. The battle taught Chin leaders that it was difficult for their cavalry to maneuver in the Sung's southeastern territory, where the terrain was full of rivers and lakes. The Chin never again made any serious attempt to cross the Yangtze. Early in 1162, Shih-tsung ordered the Chin armies to withdraw from the Yangtze front and sent envoys to request the resumption of normal relations. But fighting went on in both Huai-nan and Szechwan until a peace treaty was negotiated in 1165.

ABDICATION

The latest peace treaty between the Sung and the Chin was not made by Kao-tsung. Nine months after the Sung victory at Ts'ai-shih, Kao-tsung unexpect-edly abdicated the throne in favor of his adopted son and heir apparent, Chao Yüan (originally named Chao Po-ts'ung). After the death of Kao-tsung's infant son in 1129, the emperor did not have any more children. Rumors concerning the imperial childlessness swirled throughout the empire. One source claims that in order to improve the emperor's virility, his physician Wang Chi-hsien gave him an overdose of drugs that actually aggravated the problem. A more popular story has it that a rather bizarre incident occurred in 1129 at Yang-chou, where Kao-tsung was so shocked by hearing of a Chin surprise attack while indulging in intercourse that he lost his sexual potency.[119] Whatever the cause, it is a fact that Kao-tsung paid much attention to medicine. He trusted Wang Chi-hsien to such an extent that the doctor continued to meddle in state affairs until 1161. Soon after Wang's dismissal in that year, Kao-tsung abdicated the throne, apparently convinced of the hopelessness of his fathering another son.

---

[119] Li, *Chien-yen i-lai ch'ao-yeh tsa-chi* (1935–7) *i* 1, p. 688; Lau, "The absolutist reign of Sung Hsiao-tsung," pp. 9–10. See also Liu, *Liang Sung shih yen-chiu hui-pien*, pp. 162–6.

In 1129, not long after the death of Kao-tsung's son, a memorial had been submitted suggesting the establishment of an "acting" heir apparent.[120] Pressure to secure an heir was intensified because in the rival state of Ch'i, an official, Lo Yu, proposed that Ch'i launch a military expedition to destroy the southern dynasty. One of the reasons why the Sung could be conquered, according to Lo, was that the Sung ruler did not have an heir, and thus his regime was unstable.[121]

In 1135, when Kao-tsung was twenty-nine years old, one of these children, Chao Po-ts'ung (1127–94), was promoted to the rank of *kuo-kung* (Duke of State), and began receiving a formal education to prepare him to rule. There were subsequently several requests for the designation of Po-ts'ung as heir apparent. Among these, by far the most famous was made by Yüeh Fei. This request probably enraged Kao-tsung, as military men were not supposed to interfere in such matters. In 1142, Po-ts'ung (or Yüan, the personal name given him by Kao-tsung) was given the title of Prince P'u-an. Much later, in 1153, Ch'in Kuei also urged Kao-tsung to confirm the designation of Po-ts'ung as heir apparent (*t'ai-tzu*). However, the final decision to appoint Po-ts'ung heir apparent was delayed until 1160, several years after Ch'in Kuei's death. Probably Kao-tsung did not want Ch'in Kuei to have anything to do with the settlement of the succession problem. Two years later, Kao-tsung abdicated in favor of the heir apparent, and on 24 July 1162 Chao Po-ts'ung, known as Emperor Hsiao-tsung, succeeded Kao-tsung. Po-ts'ung's succession had for some time been complicated by the claims of another candidate, Chao Po-chiu, a young boy adopted by a consort and favored by Kao-tsung's mother, the dowager empress Hsien-jen, until her death in 1159.[122] In addition to this competition, Kao-tsung's delay in making his final decision seems to have been the result of his hope of producing another son.

In Kao-tsung's official statements establishing Chao Po-ts'ung as heir and then abdicating in his favor, he observed that now that the frontier was at peace, he could finally retire after thirty-six years of hard work as emperor. After the ceremony of abdication was completed, Kao-tsung said that he was old. He was sick and had long yearned for retirement. He was in fact in his mid-fifties and would live for another twenty-seven years.[123] Aside from these personal feelings, there seem to have been two major political reasons for Kao-tsung's act of abdication (*shan-jang*). First, Kao-tsung appears to have lost credibility

---

[120] For the death of Kao-tsung's only son, see Lau, "The absolutist reign of Sung Hsiao-tsung," p. 10; Tao, "The personality of Sung Kao-tsung," p. 539.

[121] *CYYL* (1936) 78, p. 1286.

[122] *CYYL* (1936) 183, p. 3065; 184, pp. 3079–80. See also Lau, "The absolutist reign of Sung Hsiao-tsung," p. 10.

[123] *CYYL* (1936) 200, pp. 3382–4.

in 1161 when he chose to continue to believe in the peace with Chin, despite reliable reports of an impending invasion. Second, when Kao-tsung finally realized that the Chin invasion was not just a rumor, he found himself ill-prepared for war, and reportedly was so frightened that he contemplated a last-ditch plan to escape from Lin-an by sea. After the Chin army was defeated in the battle of Ts'ai-shih in 1161, and the Chin ruler, Hai-ling, assassinated in a mutiny, Kao-tsung may have thought that the moment marked the end of an era.

Choosing Chao Po-ts'ung as heir apparent marked an important change in the dynastic line of succession. Instead of selecting a successor from among the descendants of Emperor T'ai-tsung (the second Sung emperor), Kao-tsung decided to switch back to the imperial line of Emperor T'ai-tsu, the founder of the Sung dynasty and elder brother of T'ai-tsung. Kao-tsung and his ministers involved in the decision praised Emperor T'ai-tsu's designation of his brother T'ai-tsung (Kao-tsung's ancestor) as heir, rather than one of his own sons. They compared the new emperor's succession with the case of Shun's succession to the ancient sage-king Yao – Yao, eschewing his own sons, had abdicated in favor of Shun.[124] Instead of clinging to the throne until death, Kao-tsung chose to abdicate, perhaps hoping that he would go down in history as a virtuous ruler comparable to those ancient sage-kings Yao and Shun. His honorific title included the term *kuang Yao*, or "Glorifying the tradition of Yao."[125]

[124] Li, *Chien-yen i-lai ch'ao-yeh tsa-chi* (1935–7) *i* 1, p. 690.
[125] Li, *Chien-yen i-lai ch'ao-yeh tsa-chi* (1935–7) *chia* 3, pp. 149–50.

CHAPTER 9

THE REIGN OF HSIAO-TSUNG (1162–1189)

Gong Wei Ai

INTRODUCTION

Relative to the entire Southern Sung period, Hsiao-tsung's reign (1162–89) stands out as the most tranquil and prosperous. Inheriting the throne in 1162 at the mature age of thirty-five, Hsiao-tsung proved himself a worthy descendant of T'ai-tsu, the founding Sung emperor. As an able and responsible ruler, Hsiao-tsung consolidated the Southern Sung regime on the foundations laid by his adoptive father, Kao-tsung. Politically, the reign was free from the upheavals and intense power struggles that had characterized his father's reign. Militarily, the empire became stronger than it had been for some time. After the 1165 treaty was concluded, Hsiao-tsung's administration maintained peace with Chin in the north. Peace fostered economic recuperation and general prosperity while Hsiao-tsung's policy of frugal government spending added further to the wealth of his state. As a consequence of his strict administrative control over both central and regional governments, general order and stability prevailed in domestic policies. The period was a time of great intellectual development, noted for the emergence of a large number of learned men in the fields of philosophy, poetry, and classical studies. For these reasons Hsiao-tsung is often singled out as the best of the Southern Sung monarchs,[1] and his reign is depicted as the "golden age" of the Southern Sung dynasty.[2]

Hsiao-tsung's accomplishments were built to some degree on foundations laid by Kao-tsung, but there were important differences between the reigns of these two emperors. Kao-tsung's reign had been, for the most part, an unstable period filled with external threats and internal political struggles, whereas overall Hsiao-tsung's reign was peaceful and orderly. Kao-tsung's reputation as a good Confucian monarch had been impaired by his excessive reliance on his

[1] See the annals of Hsiao-tsung in T'o-t'o et al., eds., *Sung shih* [hereafter SS] (1345; Peking, 1977) 35, p. 692. For a detailed study of Hsiao-tsung's reign, see Lau Nap-yin, "The absolutist reign of Sung Hsiao-tsung (r. 1163–89)" (diss., Princeton University, 1986).

[2] Wang Te-i, "Sung Hsiao-tsung chi ch'i shih-tai," *Kuo-li pien-i-kuan kuan-k'an* 2 No. 1 (1973), p. 4.

long-term chief councilor, Ch'in Kuei, who had been heavily criticized for his policies of appeasement, especially for ratifying the treaty of 1141, which had granted Chin concessions some saw as humiliating to the Sung.[3] In contrast, Hsiao-tsung appointed no such ill-famed councilor that tarnished his imperial image. The reign of Hsiao-tsung was the only period in Southern Sung history not marked by the presence of an all-powerful and notorious chief councilor. Enhancement of imperial authority was the notable feature of court policies during Hsiao-tsung's reign. Imperial control seems to have spread to all levels of the administration and imperial influence to every corner of Sung territory.

During his twenty-seven years on the throne, Hsiao-tsung assumed, as his personal responsibility, the three major tasks involved in dynasty building: founding it (ch'uang-yeh), reviving it (chung-hsing), and preserving it (shou-ch'eng).[4] Though the task of founding the Southern Sung dynasty had largely been accomplished by Kao-tsung, Hsiao-tsung considered it necessary to further the work of his father. The task of restoration, or reviving a dynasty after a major disaster, which had been carried out by Kao-tsung, was similarly continued by Hsiao-tsung. Hsiao-tsung's most outstanding contribution, however, was in the realm of consolidation, or imperial retrenchment, as the means to perpetuate the dynasty's social, economic, military, and cultural strength.

To consolidate the gains made during his father's reign, Hsiao-tsung seems to have had as his primary objective to strengthen and stabilize his regime by enhancing his own imperial authority. This objective was his overriding consideration in formulating policies and implementing reforms. Hsiao-tsung sought to preserve previous gains and to strengthen the Sung by concentrating political, military, and financial powers not just under the control of central government but into his own hands. As a result, the imperial authority he wielded rose to new heights compared to that of previous Sung emperors. Such a concentration of power in the hands of a strong and capable monarch like Hsiao-tsung was an effective means of rule. It had the positive consequence of stabilizing the regime and bringing about general order throughout the administration. But although the enhancement of imperial authority during Hsiao-tsung's reign contributed to his own success in solidifying the empire's security and strength, under less capable or more irresponsible successors this new level of imperial absolutism inevitably led to a power vacuum at the highest levels of government, and to serious consequent abuses.

---

[3] The great Ch'ing commentator on Sung history, Wang Fu-chih, besides criticizing Kao-tsung for his policy of appeasement, also censured the emperor for his "reliance on evil men." See Wang Fu-chih, Sung lun (c. 1690–2; Peking, 1964) 10, p. 200.

[4] For Hsiao-tsung's reference to these three mammoth tasks of founding, reviving, and preserving a dynasty, see Liu Cheng et al., Huang Sung chung-hsing liang-ch'ao sheng-cheng [Hsüan-yin wan-wei pieh-ts'ang 1935 ed.] (c. 1200; Taipei, 1967) 50, pp.15b–16a.

Hsiao-tsung's autocratic powers were limited in one important respect, however. Kao-tsung, though abdicated, retained the position of Supreme Emperor. Hsiao-tsung visited him at his palace four times a month, treating him with the utmost respect, and discussed all important decisions and appointments with him. Kao-tsung continued to press for peaceful relations with Chin and made it all but impossible for Hsiao-tsung to adopt any aggressive policy. He also lived in luxury far exceeding Hsiao-tsung's own simple lifestyle, and his palace and court were a huge expense. It is clear that this relationship affected Hsiao-tsung's policies well into the 1170s.[5]

Hsiao-tsung's personal character played a decisive role in making him a major architect of the Southern Sung empire. He was a conscientious, practical, and efficient administrator. He worked tirelessly day and night, carrying a heavy workload attending court, reading memorials, interviewing officials, and even holding discussions with his ministers in the evenings after normal court sessions. He kept everything under his own supervision and was reluctant to delegate authority to his assistants. His assertive and autocratic attitude characterized his style of governing.

During the later part of the Southern Sung the political climate became increasingly conservative in its outlook. This trend can already be seen during Hsiao-tsung's reign by comparing his earlier Ch'ien-tao (1165–73) reign period with his later Ch'un-hsi period (1174–89). The vigor and optimism prevailing at court during the Ch'ien-tao period gave way to a less healthy political atmosphere marked by a spirit of acceptance, conservatism, and pessimism in the Ch'un-hsi period. This change in political climate owed a great deal to the emperor's increasingly autocratic approach to governing, which tended to suppress political criticism and induce conformity. Although high-ranking officials and political elites felt a justifiable pride in the domestic achievements, this was accompanied by a sense of frustration and inadequacy regarding foreign relations, which served to entrench conservative attitudes.

This growing conservatism led to an eventual political stagnation effectively slowing the rate of societal change during the last century of the Southern Sung. Ironically, the stagnation of Chinese society after the thirteenth century can be traced to some extent to the political consolidation of the empire and to the stability attained during Hsiao-tsung's reign.[6] In this regard, Hsiao-tsung's

---

[5] Lau, "The absolutist reign of Sung Hsiao-tsung," pp. 36–55.

[6] Although the stability brought about by Hsiao-tsung's consolidation greatly strengthened the Southern Sung empire and enabled it to withstand both internal strains and external threats for almost another century, it should nevertheless be recognized that "it was a stability that suffered from a political standstill, even creeping deterioration." For the preceding quotation, see Liu Tzu-chien (James T. C. Liu), "Sung roots of Chinese conservatism: The administrative problems," *Journal of Asian Studies* 26 No. 3 (1967), p. 457.

reign was a crucial phase, not only for Sung history, but for Chinese history in general.

THE PEACE SETTLEMENT OF 1164–1165

When Hsiao-tsung ascended the throne in the sixth month of 1162, the Sung and Chin states were still at war. After the Chin defeat at Ts'ai-shih and the death of the Chin emperor, Wan-yen Liang (Prince Hai-ling), in late 1161, the Sung army had rapidly recovered the territories that had recently fallen into enemy hands. As fighting continued, the Sung troops were even able to recapture some of the prefectures and counties that had come under Chin control after the treaty of 1141. These included the four prefectures of Hai-chou (modern Tung-hai county, in Kiangsu), Ssu-chou (southeast of modern Ssu county, in Anhwei), T'ang-chou (T'ang-ho, Honan), and Teng-chou2 (modern Teng county, in Honan) in the Huai and Hsiang regions. Also, just before Hsiao-tsung ascended the throne, the pacification commissioner of Szechwan, Wu Lin (1102–67), had recovered a number of prefectures along the northwestern frontier.[7] Chin was unhappy with these developments, and these territories would become an important source of contention between the two states.

Following Wan-yen Liang's death, envoys went back and forth between the Sung and Chin courts to negotiate peace. Initial negotiations failed. The Sung refused to accede to Chin demands to restore the terms of the 1141 treaty. Hsiao-tsung initially hoped for an advantageous peace settlement; he was a more aggressive negotiator than his predecessor, Kao-tsung, and did not give in easily. One of his first acts as emperor was to summon to court the renowned war advocate from Szechwan, Chang Chün (1097–1164). This appointment signaled Hsiao-tsung's determination to keep the newly recovered territories. Hsiao-tsung expressed great confidence in Chang by granting him the honorary titles of Duke of National Guardians (*wei kuo-kung*) and court mentor (*shao-fu*), and by appointing him pacification commissioner of the Yangtze and Huai regions.[8] Besides Chang, Hsiao-tsung also summoned back to court another well-known war advocate, Hu Ch'üan, who had suffered persecution under Ch'in Kuei.[9] Hsiao-tsung further declared his position on the peace issue by granting posthumous honors to the most prominent victim of Ch'in Kuei's

---

[7] See Shen Ch'i-wei, *Sung Chin chan-cheng shih-lüeh* (Wu-han, 1958), p. 152.

[8] Li Hsin-ch'uan, *Chien-yen i-lai hsi-nien yao-lu* [hereafter CYYL (1956)] (1253–8; Peking, 1956) 200, p. 3391. For the imperial audience granted to Chang Chün in 1162, see the *hsing-chuang* (biographical account) of Chang Chün in Chu Hsi, *Hui-an hsien-sheng Chu Wen kung wen-chi* [Ming Chia-ching 1522–66 ed.] (1245; Shanghai, 1929) 95 *hsia*, p. 1696.

[9] Hu Ch'üan's biography appears in SS 374, p. 11583.

administration, Yüeh Fei – a repudiation of the pacifist Ch'in that signaled an endorsement of aggressive policies.[10]

Hsiao-tsung appears to have been impressed by Chang Chün. During their first interview, seeing that the emperor was inclined to favor war advocates, Chang seized the opportunity to encourage him to adopt a more aggressive foreign policy. Despite his personal inclinations, however, Hsiao-tsung was cautious in dealing with the Chin state. Undoubtably he was to some extent influenced in this direction by Shih Hao (1106–94), his powerful former tutor, who had played a large part in preparing him for the throne and had been promoted to assistant councilor soon after Hsiao-tsung's accession. Shih was to become Chang Chün's chief opponent in a number of subsequent controversies at court.[11]

One clash between the two men concerned the question of defense. Shih Hao was in favor of fortifying Kua-chou and Ts'ai-shih, located on the Yangtze River, but Chang Chün opposed this on the grounds that it would reveal Sung weakness. As an alternative, Chang proposed fortifying Ssu-chou, farther north.[12] The pacifists at court were, on the whole, in favor of consolidating the Sung position along the Yangtze, while those in favor of retaking formerly held territory in the north were more ambitious and insisted that defenses should be built up along the Huai River. The question of where to concentrate Sung defenses – on the Yangtze or farther north on the Huai River – was to become a matter of intense debate during the next few years of war against Chin.

The Sung court was confronted with two other major foreign relations problems. In the autumn of 1162, responding to Chin demands for peace, Hsiao-tsung had called upon his ministers to discuss two urgent matters. They were to discuss whether to submit to Chin demands for restoration of the territory agreed to under the treaty of 1141 or whether to refuse and keep on fighting. Next, they were to discuss the problem of the many refugees (*kuei-ching jen*) who were fleeing into Sung territory from the north. These refugees placed the Sung in a dilemma: to accept them would impose a heavy financial burden upon the Sung state; to refuse them would risk the loyalty of the people of the Central Plains (*chung-yüan*) living under Chin rule.[13] In the discussions at court, most officials appear to have been in favor of accepting the refugees. Most officials were also opposed to giving up control over the four recently recovered prefectures of Hai-chou, Ssu-chou, T'ang-chou, and Teng-chou2 that

---

[10] *CYYL* (1956) 200, p. 3392.

[11] For a discussion of Shih Hao, see Richard L. Davis, *Court and family in Sung China, 960–1279: Bureaucratic success and kinship fortunes for the Shih of Ming-chou* (Durham, N.C., 1986), pp. 54–67.

[12] For Chang Chün's memorial regarding the importance of defending Ssu-chou, see Fu Tseng-hsiang, comp., *Sung-tai Shu-wen chi-ts'un* (1943; Hong Kong, 1971) 43, pp. 6a–b.

[13] Li Hsin-ch'uan, *Chien-yen i-lai ch'ao-yeh tsa-chi* [*Shih-yüan ts'ung-shu* 1914 ed.] (c. 1202 *chia* volume; 1216 *i* volume; Taipei, 1967) *chia* 20, p. 6a.

Chin demanded. However, a note of caution was sounded by Shih Hao: "To first prepare ourselves for defense is the best strategy. Whether to have war or peace does not depend on us but on the enemy.... We should fortify the walls to defend against the enemy onslaught and await for an opportune time to carry out a campaign of reconquest."[14] Shih went on to accuse his opponents of irresponsibly advocating aggressive action, saying that much misery would be caused if their proactive policies were implemented.

Shih Hao's view on the refugee question also differed from that of most officials at court. After the military campaigns of 1161, a great number of refugees had crossed into Sung territory from the north. Sung policy toward them had been lenient, and the Sung authorities treated them well. Humanitarian considerations aside, some officials argued that acceptance of these refugees ensured the loyalty of former Sung subjects still living in enemy territory. Shih Hao, however, regarded the refugees with great suspicion and opposed accepting them because of the burden that their resettlement placed on the local populations.[15] Shih further argued that, since the Sung were not ready to launch an offensive that could succeed against Chin, it was useless to recruit the refugees as a means of ensuring the loyalty of the people of the Central Plains. Nevertheless, the war advocates believed that retaking the lost territory was imminent and that for reconquest to succeed it was essential to obtain the cooperation of Sung loyalists in the north.

During the first few months of his reign, Hsiao-tsung seemed undecided about this aspect of foreign policy. While putting his trust in Chang Chün to prepare for military action, he did not regard the counsel of Shih Hao lightly. Early in 1163, he promoted Shih to the position of chief councilor of the right, while Chang was appointed commissioner of the Bureau of Military Affairs and general superintendent of the armies in the Yangtze and Huai regions. Hsiao-tsung apparently intended their simultaneous appointments to these important posts as a means of maintaining balance between war and peace advocates during this time of indecision. Although the two chief councilors, Ch'en K'ang-po (1097–1165) and Shih Hao, were both opposed to war, the court increasingly became dominated by a group of outspoken militants who were ardent supporters of Chang Chün.

The abortive campaign of 1163 and the treaty of 1165

In 1161, during the first year of his reign, the Chin emperor Chin Shih-tsung had been troubled by uprisings in various parts of his own territory. However,

---

[14] Shih Hao, *Mou-feng chen-yin man-lu* [*Ssu-k'u ch'üan-shu, Wen-yüan ko* 1779 ed.] (c. 1181; Taipei, 1971) 8, p. 1b.

[15] See Shih Hao's memorial in his *Mou-feng chen-yin man-lu* 7, pp. 8b–11a.

by the autumn of 1162, having secured his own power and suppressed the rebels, the Chin emperor turned his attention to the Sung. Over the next few months, Chin began to mobilize troops in preparation for a southern expedition against the Sung. In the spring of 1163, the assistant commander of the Chin army, Ho-shih-lieh Chih-ning, sent Chang Chün a letter demanding the return of the prefectures that had fallen into Sung hands after 1161. He further insisted that former borders and all terms of the 1141 treaty be observed. Though Ho-shih-lieh threatened war if these demands were not met, Chang refused to submit to the pressure.[16]

While these diplomatic exchanges were occurring, Chin troops were being deployed in Hung county (modern Ssu county) and Ling-pi in northern Anhwei. Chang Chün, who felt that Sung forces were ready for war, decided it was time for them to begin a preemptive attack against Chin. In the summer of 1163, Chang Chün was summoned to court where he presented his proposal for a northern campaign against Chin. Chang's plan was vigorously opposed by Shih Hao, who tried to dissuade Hsiao-tsung from undertaking the campaign. In his memorial, Shih declared that although he fully understood the desire of the emperor to avenge the wrongs done by Chin, the fact had to be faced that the Sung state was simply not prepared for such a large-scale military campaign. He proposed instead building up the defenses of the country and attempting a campaign against Chin in another ten years' time.[17]

Shih Hao stressed the need to develop the nation's internal strength rather than seek to expand its dominions. Unfortunately, his advice was not adopted. Chang Chün is said to have told the emperor that Shih was too stubborn and that a golden opportunity might be lost on account of Shih's inflexibility. Chang Chün also stressed that Chin would certainly attack that autumn and that the Sung should surprise them by launching a preemptive offensive.[18] Despite his father's previous warnings not to heed Chang Chün,[19] Hsiao-tsung decided to launch the northern expedition. Because both chief councilors, Shih Hao and Ch'en K'ang-po, opposed the decision, Hsiao-tsung proceeded without going through the regular channels of the Three Departments and the Bureau of Military Affairs. Instead, secret orders were issued to Chang Chün to oversee mobilization of Sung troops in the Huai valley in preparation for the northern offensive. The campaign was launched in the summer of 1163 when

---

[16] Pi Yüan, *Hsü Tzu-chih t'ung-chien* [hereafter *HTC* (1957)] [*Te-yü-t'ang tsang-pan* 1801 ed.] (1792; Peking, 1957) 138, pp. 3661–2.

[17] For Shih Hao's memorial against the northern campaign, see his *Mou-feng chen-yin man-lu* 7, pp. 13b–14b.

[18] Ch'en Pang-chan et al., *Sung-shih chi-shih pen-mo* (1605; Peking, 1977) 77, p. 811.

[19] It is said that when the retired Kao-tsung heard of the intended campaign he asked Hsiao-tsung to ignore Chang Chün, whom he felt would bring more harm than good to the empire. See Chou Mi, *Ch'i-tung yeh-yü* (late 13th c.; Shanghai, 1922) 2, p. 14a.

Chang Chün ordered his two generals, Li Hsien-chung and Shao Hung-yüan, to attack Ling-pi and Hung-hsien, respectively.[20]

This attack was the first offensive that the Sung had mounted since the beginning of Sung-Chin hostilities nearly two years before, and they had considerable initial success. Less than ten days after the campaign was launched, Sung forces captured Ling-pi and Hung-hsien from the enemy. In another week's time they also succeeded in dislodging Chin troops from Su-chou2, north of the Huai River in northern Anhwei. Hsiao-tsung was overjoyed when he heard about these victories. In the meantime, however, Shih Hao had indignantly submitted his resignation in protest against the emperor's decision to launch the campaign without his knowledge. Despite his high regard for Shih, Hsiao-tsung accepted his resignation since Shih's uncompromising attitude would obstruct rather than help the emperor's aggressive foreign policy, which at that moment appeared successful. The subject of severe denunciation by prowar censors, Shih Hao spent the next several years away from court in retirement.[21] He nevertheless remained on good terms with Hsiao-tsung.

The triumph of the hawkish elements at court was short-lived. Less than a month after the offensive began, Sung forces suffered a disastrous defeat at Su-chou2. The rapidity of the Chin counterattack in response,[22] combined with the jealousy and lack of cooperation between the two principal Sung generals, Li Hsien-chung and Shao Hung-yüan, contributed to the Sung defeat. The animosity between the two commanders affected the morale of troops who were already unhappy with the paltry rewards they had received for recapturing Su-chou2.[23] Given this unease in the ranks, it is not surprising that demoralized officers in both Li's and Shao's commands fled with their troops at the approach of Chin reinforcements. Li was able to withstand the enemy assault for a while, but, because he received no assistance or support from Shao, he eventually had no choice but to flee as well. Consequently, Chin forces under Ho-shih-lieh Chih-ning retook Su-chou2, and went in pursuit of the retreating Sung armies. Sung forces were trapped at nearby Fu-li and suffered heavy losses. Many soldiers were killed, captured, or executed, and others drowned in the Huai River while attempting to escape.[24] Chin troops had scored a decisive victory

---

[20] Ch'en et al., *Sung-shih chi-shih pen-mo* (1977) 77, p. 811.

[21] On this episode, see Davis, *Court and family in Sung China*, pp. 53–67.

[22] It is said that after their defeat at Su-chou2, the Chin sent a select army of one hundred thousand men to fight the Sung forces at Su-chou2; in addition, a cavalry force of one hundred thousand men was dispatched from K'ai-feng for the counterattack. See *HTC* (1957) 138, p. 3668.

[23] The dissatisfaction of the Sung troops was regarded as the chief cause for the Sung defeat. See the tomb inscription for Chou K'uei in Chou Pi-ta, *Wen-chung chi* [*Ssu-k'u ch'üan-shu, Wen-yüan ko* 1779 ed.] (c. 1206; Taipei, 1971) 63, p. 9b.

[24] *HTC* (1957) 138, p. 3669. During the disaster at Fu-li, besides the countless number of soldiers who were drowned, the Chin decapitated more than four thousand men and confiscated thirty thousand sets of armor.

after their initial losses, which were minor compared with those inflicted on the Sung at Fu-li. Chin forces, however, did not follow up their victory at Su-chou2 and Fu-li with a sustained offensive against the Sung. Rather, a lull in the fighting ensued.

The Sung defeat must have been a shock and humiliation for Chang Chün and for the emperor. Chang submitted his resignation but was persuaded by the emperor to stay on and fortify the Sung defenses in the Huai region. Even though Hsiao-tsung put a brave face on the matter, the abortive attempt to recover lost territory was a great setback. Hsiao-tsung's subsequent actions showed that he was beginning to waver in his determination to continue the war. He soon appeared anxious to begin peace negotiations. The following month, Chang Chün was demoted from his post as general superintendent back to his former post of pacification commissioner in the Yangtze and Huai regions.[25] Chang's demotion was followed by the resignation from court of a number of prominent officials protesting the change in government policy from favoring war to favoring peace.

Though the proponents of peace carried more weight at court after the abortive campaign, their ascendancy was not total. In the autumn of 1163 Hsiao-tsung reinstalled Chang Chün as general superintendent of the Chiang-Huai armies.[26] While anxious to achieve peace, the emperor was nevertheless determined to negotiate with Chin from a position of strength and to strike a good bargain. If those negotiations failed, he felt he would still be able to rely on Chang Chün to carry on the war.

Soon after Chang's reinstatement, the Chin commander, Ho-shih-lieh Chih-ning, once again sent a letter to the Sung government demanding the return of the four prefectures of Hai-chou, Ssu-chou, T'ang-chou, and Teng-chou2; a resumption of annual payments; the submission of the Sung as a vassal state to Chin; and the return of refugees who had fled the Chin-held Central Plains. Ho-shih-lieh threatened to continue the war if these conditions were not met. Though Chang Chün opposed submitting to the demands, the court's general opinion favored pursuing negotiations with Chin, as it was believed that peace would enable the Sung state to put its own house in order before undertaking further military action.[27]

Over the next year and a half, several missions were sent to Chin in an attempt to arrive at mutually acceptable conditions for peace. After much bargaining and several breakdowns in negotiations, peace efforts began to gather momentum after Chang Chün's final dismissal in the summer of 1164

[25] HTC (1957) 138, p. 3670.
[26] Chu, Hui-an hsien-sheng Chu Wen kung wen-chi (1929) 95, p. 1700.
[27] Ch'en, Sung-shih chi-shih pen-mo (1977) 77, p. 814.

and his death that autumn. An agreement was reached between the two states in the winter of 1164. The Sung agreed to return the prefectures demanded by Chin. They also agreed to return Chin captives, but not those who had renounced Chin on their own initiative, a group that included the refugees. On the question of relative diplomatic status, both states agreed to adopt a pseudofamily relationship of "younger uncle and nephew" (*shu-chih*) instead of the former lord-vassal relationship. The 'uncle' in this equation was the retired emperor Kao-tsung, the nephew, the Chin emperor Shih-tsung. Chin, for its part, granted the Sung request that the annual payments of silver and silk be reduced by fifty thousand units each, and that the humiliating term "annual tribute" (*sui-kung*) for these levies be changed to "annual payments" (*sui-pi*).[28]

Early in 1165, a Sung diplomatic mission under the junior lord of imperial sacrifices, Wei Ch'i, was sent to the Chin court with a cordial letter from Hsiao-tsung confirming the treaty provisions. Meanwhile, an official announcement was made within the Sung empire that the peace negotiations had succeeded. The imperial proclamation stated: "As a result of the negotiations, the status of the Sung emperor is rectified with the establishment of the 'uncle-nephew' relation, the annual payments are reduced by 100,000 units, and the borders remain the same as before. . . . Because of humanitarian reasons, it is also decided not to deport the fugitive rebels on both sides."[29] The proclamation marked the conclusion of the peace settlement, although it was only in the following month that Wei Ch'i arrived in Chin and presented Hsiao-tsung's letter to the emperor, Shih-tsung, who then agreed to the terms of the treaty and declared that the war was over.[30]

The conditions imposed on the Sung by the peace settlement of 1165 were an improvement on those of the treaty of 1141. The humiliation of being a Chin vassal, as had been the Sung's status for the previous twenty years, was removed although the Sung still had to acknowledge the superior status of Chin. The reduction in the annual payments from 250,000 to 200,000 taels of silver and bolts of silk and the Chin agreement on the refugee question represented sizable concessions. However, the fact that the former borders of the 1141 treaty were reinstated meant that not a single inch of territory had been recovered by the Sung despite the costly efforts of the previous three years. Indeed, it seems Shih Hao and the other peace advocates had been right on this point. For the time being, Hsiao-tsung had to be content with maintaining

[28] *HTC* (1957) 138, p. 3670.
[29] Ch'en, *Sung-shih chi-shih pen-mo* (1977) 77, p. 823. This proclamation, however, represented a much shortened version of the original text of the treaty, which has not been preserved in any of the sources. See Herbert Franke, "Treaties between Sung and Chin," in *Études Song: In memoriam Étienne Balazs*, ed. Françoise Aubin (Paris, 1970), p. 81.
[30] Ch'en, *Sung-shih chi-shih pen-mo* (1977) 77, p. 823.

the status quo and putting his own state in order while awaiting another opportunity to pursue his life-long ambition of restoring former territories to the empire.

THE CH'IEN-TAO PERIOD (1165–1173): YEARS OF RECONSTRUCTION

After the peace settlement in 1165 was concluded, the Southern Sung dynasty experienced four decades of military stalemate and a continued uneasy coexistence with Chin. With the immediate threat of Chin invasion removed, the friction between the war and the peace advocates, which had dominated court politics over the previous two years, was largely terminated. The year 1165 saw not only the end of the war but also the beginning of a new era in domestic politics. Hsiao-tsung marked the occasion by changing the reign title from Lung-hsing (Eminent Ascendancy, 1163–4) to Ch'ien-tao (Supernal Way, 1165–73), the latter title being adopted at the beginning of 1165 and lasting for the next eight years. During the Ch'ien-tao period, the emperor and his ministers embarked on new tasks aimed at rebuilding the empire by strengthening defenses, improving the standards of central and local administrations, developing economic resources, and tending to the livelihood of the people. It was the court's objective to put the empire in order (*tzu-chih*) before actively considering any ambitious scheme or military campaign to reconquer territory. Although the long-term objective of recovery of lost territory (*hui-fu*) was constantly in the minds of the emperor and his officials, the court generally refrained from bellicose gestures after the disastrous campaign of 1163. Shih Hao was showered with royal gifts and regularly granted high-ranking sinecures, and he continued to recommend promising young candidates for office and to communicate with Hsiao-tsung.

During these years of reconstruction, major tasks that the court faced included administrative reforms and issues of finance, defense, and foreign policy. How the emperor and his officials dealt with these matters provides a picture of court politics and indicates that concern for internal development often emerged in the formulation of domestic and foreign policies. An examination of the relations between Hsiao-tsung and his ministers on the one hand and between him and his inner court favorites on the other affords insight into his character, his continued personal ambition to recover lost territory, and his desire to concentrate power into his own hands. His ability to concentrate power contributed to the growth of imperial absolutism in the Sung, especially during the latter part of his reign.

Historians have generally regarded Hsiao-tsung as a wise and responsible monarch embodying the Confucian virtues of filial piety, frugality, diligence, and willingness to seek the advice of his ministers on matters related to government and administration. Nevertheless, beneath the apparent peace and tranquility of the period, Hsiao-tsung's court was not free from tensions, strains, and even outright conflict between Hsiao-tsung and his ministers, among the ministers themselves, and between outer court bureaucrats and inner court attendants. Disagreements occasionally arose over some issue or policy, but despite these disputes, Hsiao-tsung was generally broad-minded enough not to hold a grudge against ministers who openly criticized him. Throughout his reign, despite these disagreements, the court remained largely free from truly divisive bureaucratic factionalism. It is to Hsiao-tsung's credit that he managed to keep everything under control and at the same time hold political tensions to an acceptable level.

Hsiao-tsung and his ministers

Hsiao-tsung's reign was one of the few during the Southern Sung that was not dominated by powerful councilors. The emperor's power held supreme and unchallenged. Hsiao-tsung was a demanding emperor who dismissed his ministers without hesitation if they failed to meet his expectations. The frequent dismissals of councilors and other officials led to much criticism of the emperor's personnel policy. In 1166 the lesser lord of agricultural supervision, Mo Chi, said to the emperor:

The way of government depends on the appointment of [the right] personnel, while the appointment of personnel depends on the fulfilling of responsibilities [by the personnel concerned]. If we appoint the officials but do not keep them in office for a sufficiently long period, we will not be able to judge the excellence of the good and the capable, while on the other hand, the evil and unworthy officials manage to go unpunished.[31]

Mo Chi criticized the emperor for dismissing councilors and other officials after they had served only a few months. Although Hsiao-tsung commended Mo for his criticism, he carried on as before. In addition to being dissatisfied with individual performances, it could well be that having personally witnessed the great power wielded by the chief councilor, Ch'in Kuei, during his father's reign, Hsiao-tsung was especially careful that no minister achieve such dominance during his own reign. A convenient way to restrict the growth of ministerial power was to limit the ministers' tenure of office, so that great ministers would be denied the opportunity to build a power base at court that could threaten the emperor's power.

Besides frequently removing councilors, Hsiao-tsung also sought to control them by curtailing their due authority. Early in 1167, the emperor had finally

---

[31] Liu et al., *Huang Sung chung-hsing liang-ch'ao sheng-cheng* 29, p. 5b.

filled every vacancy in the Council of State by appointing chief councilors of the left and right and two assistant councilors. The bureaucracy was generally pleased with the appointments of these key officials, but the remarks of the vice-minister for war, Ch'en Yen-hsiao, reveal a certain skepticism: "Your Majesty's recent appointments of the left and right chief councilors and the assistant councilors have led to much jubilation among the officials, who rejoice that the right men have been found to lead the government. However, in my opinion, the councilors should be given more power so that they can exercise the responsibility of governing the empire."[32] Clearly some officials were already concerned about the lack of authority granted to councilors. Although Hsiao-tsung is said to have heard Ch'en out, he never put Ch'en's advice into practice. Throughout Hsiso-tsung's reign, a chief complaint among the officials remained his tendency to impinge on their authority.

Hsiao-tsung appears to have realized the importance of placating his councilors by treating them with dignity and giving them full executive authority in principle, if not in practice. Ironically, during Hsiao-tsung's reign the councilors nominally were given widespread powers, but Hsiao-tsung's participation in all major decisions greatly limited their authority. Early in 1163, the chief councilors were appointed to the concurrent positions of commissioners of military affairs, by which appointment military authority was also formally assigned to them.[33] A few years later, in early 1167, the chief councilors were further granted financial authority when given the concurrent title of controller of national finance (*chih kuo-yung shih*).[34] This concentration of civil, military, and financial power into the hands of the chief councilors was to become an important factor in the rise of powerful councilors later in the Southern Sung, perhaps because of their long periods of tenure.[35] However, this was not the case during Hsiao-tsung's reign.

Hsiao-tsung intended that his ministers exercise their powers in ordinary administrative affairs, but the emperor was in the habit of jealously guarding

---

[32] Liu et al., *Huang Sung chung-hsing liang-ch'ao sheng-cheng* 29, pp. 12a–b.

[33] During the Northern Sung there were a few occasions, during times of emergency, when the chief councilors were appointed to concurrent positions in the Bureau of Military Affairs, but it was not until 1130 that they were appointed on a regular basis. However, after the death of Ch'in Kuei in 1155, the concurrent appointment of chief councilors to the post of commissioner of military affairs was again discontinued. The title was restored to the chief councilors after the accession of Hsiao-tsung. See Ma Tuan-lin, *Wen-hsien t'ung-k'ao* (c. 1308; Shanghai, 1936) 58, p. 528.

[34] Hsü Tzu-ming, *Sung tsai-fu pien-nien lu* [*Ching-hsiang-lou ts'ung-shu* 1929 ed.] (early 13th c.; Taipei, 1967) 17, p. 1545. For an account of the office of controller of national finance, see Li, *Chien-yen i-lai ch'ao-yeh tsa-chi* (1967) *chia* 10, pp. 3b–4a.

[35] See Lin T'ien-wei, "Sung-tai ch'üan-hsiang hsing-ch'eng chih fen-hsi," *Ssu yü yen* 10 No. 5 (1973), pp. 30–40; see also Liang T'ien-hsi, "Lun Sung tsai-fu hu-chien chih-tu," in *Sung-shih yen-chiu chi: Ti ssu chi*, ed. Sung-shih tso-t'an-hui (Taipei, 1969), p. 294.

his overriding imperial prerogatives and frequently exercised them, especially in military matters. Hung Mai (1123–1202), the Secretariat imperial recorder, remarked in 1167 that imperial orders issued to the Bureau of Military Affairs frequently went straight to the Imperial Chancellery, bypassing the Imperial Secretariat. This meant that the orders were issued without the knowledge or approval of the councilors, who were the heads of the Secretariat. Hung Mai requested that henceforth all orders issued to the Bureau of Military Affairs should go through the proper channels.[36] Though Hsiao-tsung promised to rectify this, orders on matters of great urgency still were dispatched directly to the Chancellery without going through the Secretariat. These were referred to as "confidential orders" (mi-pai).[37] Besides the use of "confidential orders," Hsiao-tsung employed similar methods to enhance his power in other areas. Notable among these were the use of "palace orders" (nei-p'i) and "imperial decrees" (yü-pi), which were issued directly from the palace without prior consultation with the councilors.[38]

The emperor's disregard for routine procedure caused great concern among the officials. Ch'en Chün-ch'ing (1113–86), one of Hsiao-tsung's former tutors, was also one of his most outspoken ministers and frequently confronted Hsiao-tsung over issues regarding national policies and the emperor's personal conduct. Ch'en was noted for his vigilant opposition to any infringement of bureaucratic powers by the emperor. On the eve of his appointment as chief councilor in 1168, Ch'en had a serious disagreement with Hsiao-tsung over the matter of secret orders directly issued to the army without going through the regular channels of the ministers at court. Ch'en and his colleagues in the Council of State presented a request that all departments, upon receiving imperial orders issued directly from the palace, should first memorialize the court for verification before implementing them. Hsiao-tsung initially agreed to this, but two days later changed his mind, much to his ministers' frustration. The emperor, unwilling to give up imperial prerogatives, tried to evade the issue by remarking that, "Doing this would mean that even when the palace wishes to get a drink or some food, it would have to obtain court verification. Now, would that not be overrestraining!" Ch'en Chün-ch'ing countered that the ministers were concerned with much more important matters, such as requesting that the Bureau of Military Affairs be notified on military matters, and that on financial matters the Three Departments be informed. Ch'en

---

[36] Liu et al., Huang Sung chung-hsing liang-ch'ao sheng-cheng 29, pp. 11b–12a.

[37] Liu et al., Huang Sung chung-hsing liang-ch'ao sheng-cheng 29, pp. 11b–12a.

[38] Both nei-p'i and yü-pi were imperial orders issued directly from the palace. These direct orders were traditionally known as nei-p'i, but the latter term yü-pi had been used since the time of Hui-tsung. These orders were not necessarily written by the emperor himself and were therefore different from "personally written decrees" (ch'in-pi). See Li, Chien-yen i-lai ch'ao-yeh tsa-chi (1967) i 11, p. 1a.

argued that, after all, the court belonged to the emperor, and the ministers were merely carrying out the emperor's orders, and that therefore, court verification of all matters meant that ultimate decisions still lay in the hands of the emperor. Finally, Ch'en expressed his fear that the emperor had changed his mind after being influenced by elements within the palace.[39] Such strongly worded criticism angered Hsiao-tsung, but Ch'en was unwilling to yield.

Subsequently, Ch'en Chün-ch'ing submitted a self-impeaching memorial for having offended the emperor, but Hsiao-tsung refused to accept his resignation. Though frequently offended by Ch'en's criticism, the emperor recognized Ch'en to be a righteous and responsible minister. A few days after this exchange, Ch'en was promoted to chief councilor of the right. In so doing, Hsiao-tsung indicated that though he was not completely indifferent to criticism, he could reward ministers for their loyalty even though what they said sometimes displeased him.

Despite his autocratic tendencies, Hsiao-tsung tried to project the image of an enlightened and open-minded monarch. He often encouraged his officials to speak their minds and even invited criticism of himself. In 1166, the Chancellery imperial recorder, Chiang Fei, who was a newly appointed drafting official of the Secretariat on probation, told Hsiao-tsung apologetically that, as a drafting official who had veto power, he was afraid he might occasionally offend the emperor in the course of his official duties. Hsiao-tsung replied that this was exactly what he expected from the drafting official, and that Chiang should not confine himself to commenting on political matters and appointments but could also criticize the ruler if the latter had committed any faults.[40] But although Hsiao-tsung tried to be receptive to criticism, he did not always live up to this ideal.

Hsiao-tsung made it a point to keep in close touch with his ministers. In the summer of 1165, he expressed his regrets to the councilors that he could not afford more time with them during morning court sessions and proposed inviting them to the palace in the evenings to discuss the "way of government" (chih-tao).[41] Hsiao-tsung and his ministers frequently held policy discussions in the Hsüan-te Hall in the palace.[42] Relations between the emperor and his ministers were especially cordial during the period of Yü Yün-wen's (1110–74) tenure as chief councilor, from 1169 to 1172. On one occasion in 1171, Hsiao-tsung said to the councilors: "During the time of the founding ancestors,

---

[39] For an account of this episode, see the hsing-chuang of Ch'en Chün-ch'ing in Chu, Hui-an hsien-sheng Chu Wen kung wen-chi (1929) 96, pp. 1716–17.

[40] Sung-shih ch'üan-wen Hsü Tzu-chih t'ung-chien (early 14th c.; Taipei, 1969) 24, p. 1911.

[41] Sung-shih ch'üan-wen Hsü Tzu-chih t'ung-chien 24, p. 1902.

[42] See "Hsüan-te-tien chi," in Chou, Wen-chung chi 104, p. 10b.

the councilors had frequently been invited to join in various leisure activities by the emperor.... On the days when I am free, I would like to invite you over for an archery match and to wine and dine together." When Yü and his colleagues praised Hsiao-tsung for his willingness to spend time with them, the emperor replied that it was important for the ruler and the ministers to be close and thus able to communicate with one another. He again emphasized that since the morning court sessions were too short for detailed discussion of government, he wished to spend more time with his ministers so that they could carry on their discussions in a relaxed manner.[43]

In an attempt to streamline the administration and bring about more effective government, Hsiao-tsung initiated a number of political reforms in 1172. In the spring of that year, the titles of the chief councilors were changed from left and right executives of the Department of Ministries (*shang-shu tso-yu p'u-yeh*) to left and right chief councilors (*tso-yu ch'eng-hsiang*).[44] The emperor's ostensible reason for this change was that he was unhappy with the ancient term *p'u-yeh*. Hsiao-tsung's objection to this term was that although it was originally a minor office during the Ch'in dynasty (221–206 B.C.E.), and did not carry much responsibility, after the Eastern Han dynasty (25–220) and into the T'ang, it had became increasingly important, but the holders of this post had not been heads of the bureaucracy.[45] Hsiao-tsung felt that, as heads of the bureaucracy, the chief councilors should be properly addressed, and the term *ch'eng-hsiang* (which is a close equivalent to the term "prime minister") seemed more appropriate and respectful. Thereafter, the designation *ch'eng-hsiang* remained in use for the duration of the Southern Sung dynasty. In addition, Hsiao-tsung reorganized the civil administration by eliminating the top administrative posts in the Three Departments and delegating their former responsibilities to the chief councilor, or sometimes jointly to both chief councilors. This proved to be a more important structural change than the renaming of the chief councilor's title.[46]

Though in principle these reforms expanded the authority of the councilors, in practice Hsiao-tsung exerted such rigorous control over the councilors that most were reduced to virtual sycophants. Councilors with strong views such as Shih Hao and Ch'en Chün-ch'ing soon left office and were replaced by others more amenable to the emperor's wishes. With the top offices occupied by men easily manipulated by the throne, Hsiao-tsung managed to maintain effective personal command over the entire bureaucratic machine.

[43] *Sung-shih ch'üan-wen Hsü Tzu-chih t'ung-chien* 25, p. 1980.
[44] Liu et al., *Huang Sung chung-hsing liang-ch'ao sheng-cheng* 51, p. 3b.
[45] For the evolution of the office of *p'u-yeh*, see Ma, *Wen-hsien t'ung-k'ao* (1936) 51, pp. 470–1.
[46] Liu et al., *Huang Sung chung-hsing liang-ch'ao sheng-cheng* 51, p. 4a.

Hsiao-tsung and the inner court

Another method that Hsiao-tsung employed to enhance his personal power was to use inner court personnel as a counterweight to the regular bureaucracy. Because of their proximity to the throne and the tendency of the emperor to regard them as his confidants, palace attendants were a constant source of anxiety for the ministers of the outer court. Hsiao-tsung showed great favor to certain members of the inner court and occasionally used them to bypass the normal operations of the bureaucracy. It is therefore not surprising that imperial favors given the so-called close attendants (*chin-hsi*) in the inner court frequently led to protests from the officials.

During Hsiao-tsung's reign there were several occasions when outer court officials quarreled with inner court attendants. Soon after his ascension in 1162, Hsiao-tsung appointed Lung Ta-yüan and Tseng Ti, two of his favorite palace attendants, to important positions in the Bureau of Military Affairs. Both Lung and Tseng had won Hsiao-tsung's confidence while he was still crown prince, but they were extremely unpopular among the regular bureaucrats, who regarded them as petty men and sycophants. As a result of censorial impeachments in 1163, Hsiao-tsung decided to appoint them instead as audience commandants in the Office of Audience Ceremonies (*Ko-men ssu*), a position lower in rank but nonetheless important as it gave them easy access to the emperor and the opportunity to influence imperial decisions. This appointment immediately led to further protests from the officials in the outer court. Among those opposed to the appointments of Lung and Tseng were censors, drafting officials, and an assistant councilor. Hsiao-tsung, angered by this combined attack on his favorites, commented to Chief Councilor Shih Hao that the officials would not have dared do such a thing during the reign of Kao-tsung.[47] Suspecting the officials of factionalism, he had them dismissed one by one. Although Hsiao-tsung temporarily withdrew the appointments of Lung and Tseng, two months later he appointed them as audience commandants, and they remained in these posts for the next few years despite frequent criticism against them.

Among outer court ministers, Ch'en Chün-ch'ing in particular was noted for his opposition to the emperor's favorites. In 1167, just two months after becoming associate administrator in the Bureau of Military Affairs, Ch'en had his first confrontation with the emperor over this issue. The incident was sparked when Ch'en heard that Lung Ta-yüan and Tseng Ti had leaked information regarding official appointments. Ch'en immediately informed his colleagues in the Council of State of this disclosure of confidential matters

---

[47] Li, *Chien-yen i-lai ch'ao-yeh tsa-chi* (1967) *i* 6, pp. 1a–2b.

by Lung and Tseng, whereupon all the councilors agreed that they should bring this matter before the throne. Still unable to contain his indignation, Ch'en personally questioned Hsiao-tsung, who denied that he had ever consulted Lung and Tseng regarding official appointments. The emperor further commended Ch'en for his loyalty and promised that he would have the two attendants dismissed. Consequently, Lung and Tseng were both given prefectural appointments away from court, much to the joy of the officials.[48] On this occasion at least, the councilors had scored a victory against the emperor's favorites. Hsiao-tsung probably considered it unwise to go against the wishes of the ministers, since they had obtained evidence against his favorites. He might also have felt that the palace attendants had gone too far in abusing their power and decided to teach them a lesson.

Despite demoting Lung and Tseng, Hsiao-tsung still had a soft spot for them. After Lung's death in 1168, Hsiao-tsung took pity on Tseng and considered summoning him back to court. He was admonished against doing so by both the assistant councilor Ch'en Chün-ch'ing and the associate administrator of the Bureau of Military Affairs, Liu Kung (1122–78), who shared Ch'en's intense dislike and distrust of the inner court favorites.[49] Faced with this opposition from his ministers, Hsiao-tsung decided not to summon Tseng. However, soon after Ch'en Chün-ch'ing left office in 1170, Tseng was reappointed to court, and no one dared to speak against his reappointment. Tseng once again rose in power, as the emperor bestowed numerous favors and honorary titles on him over the next decade.

In addition to opposing Tseng Ti, Ch'en Chün-ch'ing was also vigilant in his opposition to inner court personnel gaining undue power by other means. He was especially concerned about palace attendants coming into contact with generals. In 1167, the commander of the Chen-chiang army, Ch'i Fang, was dismissed for oppressing his soldiers by employing them for forced labor services. Ch'en Chün-ch'ing brought to the emperor's notice that certain members of the inner court had close connections with Ch'i Fang. Subsequently, two of the inner court attendants were charged with having received bribes from Ch'i and were demoted and exiled. An edict that threatened severe punishment for future offenders was then issued prohibiting military officials from befriending inner court attendants.[50]

Besides Tseng Ti and Lung Ta-yüan, another prominent palace favorite of Hsiao-tsung was Chang Yüeh, who was the husband of the dowager empress's

---

[48] For an account of this incident, see Li, *Chien-yen i-lai ch'ao-yeh tsa-chi* (1967) *i* 6, pp. 5a–b.

[49] For Liu's protest, see Chu, *Hui-an hsien-sheng Chu Wen kung wen-chi* (1929) 97, p. 1929, and for Ch'en Chün-ch'ing's admonition, see 96, p. 1716.

[50] *Sung-shih ch'üan-wen Hsü Tzu-chih t'ung-chien* 24, p. 1934.

younger sister. In 1171, Chang Yüeh was promoted from audience commandant to notary official at the Bureau of Military Affairs. The appointment of
a minor palace official to such a high-ranking office led to great controversy
at court. The imperial lecturer, Chang Shih (1133–80), submitted a memorial admonishing Hsiao-tsung. At the same time, Chang reproached Chief
Councilor Yu Yün-wen for allowing this to happen.[51] The drafting official at
the Secretariat, Fan Ch'eng-ta (1126–93), also opposed the appointment and
refused to endorse it.[52] The emperor was obliged to compromise by giving
Chang Yüeh a sinecure and the honorary title of military governor (*chieh-tu
shih*).

In the following year, another attempt was made to appoint Chang Yüeh
as notary official at the Bureau of Military Affairs. By this time both Chang
Shih and Fan Ch'eng-ta had left court and were holding prefectural positions.
Although Hsiao-tsung may have believed that there would not be any strong
opposition to the appointment, this was not the case. When Chang's appointment was announced, it was again opposed by various censorial and drafting
officials.[53] The emperor was undeterred by their opposition, however, and the
officials were either dismissed or demoted for their defiance. Throughout the
incident Chief Councilor Yü Yün-wen remained noncommittal, and his tolerance of the emperor's favorites and support for the emperor's policies must
have been noted by Hsiao-tsung as Yü served for a longer period than most of
his colleagues.

Owing to the strong opposition to the undue influence of palace personnel
by ministers such as Ch'en Chün-ch'ing and Liu Kung, during the eight years
of the Ch'ien-tao period Hsiao-tsung was, on the whole, more restrained than
he later would be in bestowing favors on personal attendants. However, toward
the end of his reign, palace favorites became more influential as they faced less
opposition from top civil officials in the government.

Financial policy

In addition to the consolidation of the emperor's hold over the court, the Ch'ien-
tao period also witnessed consolidation in other fields. Like his predecessor,
Kao-tsung, Hsiao-tsung realized the importance of finance in strengthening

---

[51] *HTC* (1957) 142, p. 3795. Chang is said to have told Yü Yün-wen, "The appointment of eunuchs to
councilor positions started with Ts'ai Ching and Wang Fu (bad last ministers of Northern Sung), while
the appointment of close attendants to councilor positions began with you, sir!"

[52] Tomb inscription for Fan Ch'eng-ta in Chou, *Wen-chung chi* 61, pp. 18b–19a; *HTC* (1957) 142,
p. 3796.

[53] *HTC* (1957) 143, p. 3811.

the Southern Sung regime. One of his first acts after his ascension to the throne was to examine the accounts of the Ministry of Finance.[54] His thorough investigation of the ministry's income and expenditures led to a protest by its vice-minister, Chou K'uei, in 1163. Chou, in his memorial, referred to the emperor's queries into the "minor details" of financial matters and suggested that the imperial inquiry was instigated by "petty elements" at court (an obvious attack on Lung Ta-yüan and Tseng Ti).[55] Besides worrying about the influence these imperial favorites were having on the emperor, Chou K'uei and other officials, in opposing Hsiao-tsung's interest in the details of financial administration, implied that the emperor should concern himself with more important tasks than examining mundane financial records. This was clearly a difference of opinion between the emperor and scholar-officials on the significance of administrative details. Hsiao-tsung was unhappy with the general indifference shown by the scholar-officials toward financial administration and criticized them for their attitude. In 1167, the emperor voiced his concern about the ignorance of scholar-officials, trained in the Confucian textual tradition, in financial and agricultural matters, and expressed his wish that they should devote more attention to specific aspects of these areas.[56] Again, in 1171, Hsiao-tsung severely criticized the scholar-officials for not discussing finance and agriculture, even though these formed the basis of the well-being of the state.[57]

Strongly endorsing the view that agriculture was the foundation of the state, Hsiao-tsung on numerous occasions admonished prefectural officials to play a more active role in promoting farming. In the autumn of 1164 he ordered the administrators of various prefectures in the Yangtze and Chekiang regions to look into the irrigation and farming conditions of their respective territories with a view to increasing farm productivity.[58] Irrigation projects were subsequently initiated in prefectures in the region. Hsiao-tsung also expressed his personal interest in agriculture by following Kao-tsung's example of practicing ritual grain cultivation and sericulture within the palace compound.[59] On many occasions he genuinely expressed joy over good harvests and anxiety when adverse weather conditions threatened his crops.

---

[54] Hsiao-tsung frequently summoned finance officials to the palace and carefully examined the finances and revenues of the government. He also personally checked the accounts books of the various treasuries. See Li, *Chien-yen i-lai ch'ao-yeh tsa-chi* (1967) *i* 3, p. 6a.

[55] *HTC* (1957) 138, p. 3689.

[56] Liu et al., *Huang Sung chung-hsing liang-ch'ao sheng-cheng* 46, p. 1a.

[57] Liu et al., *Huang Sung chung-hsing liang-ch'ao sheng-cheng* 50, pp. 17a–b.

[58] Hsü Sung et al., *Sung hui-yao chi-kao* [hereafter *SHY* (1997)] (1809, 1936, 1957; Peking, 1997) *shih-huo* 61, p. 116; *HTC* (1957) 138, p. 3689.

[59] Liu et al., *Huang Sung chung-hsing liang-ch'ao sheng-cheng* 59, p. 13a.

In addition to promoting agriculture, Hsiao-tsung sought to strengthen the empire's economy through a series of financial reforms, some of which were aimed at achieving more effective control of the central government's expenditures. In 1167, in response to an earlier proposal by a remonstrance official, Ch'en Liang-yu, that national expenditures should be properly controlled, the emperor appointed the chief councilor and assistant councilor respectively to concurrent positions of controller and co-controller of national finance.[60] By so doing, Hsiao-tsung intended that his councilors play a more effective role in financial administration, but he also intended to impose a more centralized control on national finance by placing it under the supervision of the chief ministers of state. Another measure to control government expenditures was introduced in the spring of 1167, when the emperor ordered all officials, whether civil or military and whether in the inner or outer court, to submit on the fifth day of every month to the Bureau of State Expenditure (*Kuo-yung fang*) statements of their official spending. This regulation did not apply only to officials in the capital. Government personnel in all prefectures were required to submit these monthly accounts.[61] The purpose of the measure was to enforce more careful spending by government personnel and to reduce the misappropriation of funds. An additional reform to strictly control state finance was introduced in 1168, when in accord with a proposal by the supervisor of public revenue, Chao Pu-ti, a centralized Register of Public Revenue (*Tu-chih tu-chi*) was established. The purpose of this register was to easily verify the accounts, as well as to prevent abuses by corrupt clerks.[62]

In addition to emphasizing stricter fiscal control, Hsiao-tsung also sought to reduce expenditures. The theme of frugality often emerged in policy discussions, and calls for retrenchment were repeatedly promulgated during the early years of the Ch'ien-tao period. In an imperial decree issued in 1163, Hsiao-tsung ordered the Ministry of Finance and the censorial officials to discuss ways to cut excessive spending.[63] This was followed by a decree in 1164 announcing the emperor's decision to reduce expenses in the performance of religious ceremonies.[64] Besides reducing unnecessary or excessive expenses in ritual matters, Hsiao-tsung and his court also sought to decrease military expenditures, which constituted the largest item in the state budget.[65] The

---

[60] *Sung-shih ch'üan-wen Hsü Tzu-chih t'ung-chien* 24, p. 1923; *SHY* (1997) *chih-kuan* 6, pp. 20–1.

[61] *Sung-shih ch'üan-wen Hsü Tzu-chih t'ung-chien* 24, p. 1926.

[62] Liu et al., *Huang Sung chung-hsing liang-ch'ao sheng-cheng* 47, pp. 3a–b; *SHY* (1997) *shih-huo* 51 p. 46.

[63] *HTC* (1957) 138, p. 3665.

[64] *HTC* (1957) 138, p. 3679.

[65] The termination of war with the Chin did not mean the relaxation of national defense, and eighty percent of the empire's income continued to be allotted to the army. See Chou Pi-ta's tomb inscription in Lou Yüeh [Yao], *Kung-k'uei chi* [*Wu-ying tien* 1736–95 ed.] (c. early 13th c.; Shanghai, 1929) 93, p. 887.

large number of soldiers enlisted during the Ch'ien-tao period, estimated at no fewer than four hundred thousand men,[66] prompted various proposals for military reform to reduce costs and improve troop quality.

Hsiao-tsung's frugality has often been commended as one of his greatest virtues. The emperor himself claimed he had never spent a single cash extravagantly.[67] In 1170 he discussed his frugality publicly in a conversation with Hsiao Kuo-liang, the collator of the Palace Library. Hsiao was reiterating a long-held criticism of Han Wu-ti (r. 141–87 B.C.E.), an expansionist emperor during the Han dynasty (206 B.C.E.–220 C.E.) whose extravagance had irreparably weakened the dynasty. To this, Hsiao-tsung responded: "It was not only Han Wu-ti. Since antiquity rulers have always observed frugality during times of difficulties, but after the establishment of peace few have not become extravagant. I have no other accomplishment apart from frugality."[68] Frugal himself, the emperor disapproved of the extravagant practices of the populace, especially those of the more well-to-do farmers. In the autumn of 1172, he criticized the people for lavish spending during times of good harvests and advised them to save for times of emergency.[69]

Despite all his attempts to reduce expenditures, Hsiao-tsung found that he had to continue to impose heavy taxes. During his reign, supplementary and commercial taxes previously introduced by Kao-tsung continued to contribute greatly to state income.[70] The heavy tax burden borne by the people led to numerous criticisms against oppressive taxation by prefectural authorities, whose chief concern was to meet the tax quotas imposed by the central government. Though Hsiao-tsung was troubled by the problem of heavy taxation and frequently expressed his desire to abolish all the irregular and supplementary taxes, he found that he could not do away with them because of the regime's extremely heavy military expenses. However, Hsiao-tsung did attempt to lessen the burden on taxpayers through such measures as tax remission and the prohibition of oppressive taxes. While his predecessor, Kao-tsung, had sought to increase state income by introducing many new taxes, Hsiao-tsung stressed instead the importance of systematically reducing expenditures as the means to balancing the government's budget and strengthening its finances.

[66] See Li, *Chien-yen i-lai ch'ao-yeh tsa-chi* (1967) *chia* 18, pp. 4b–5a.

[67] Hsiao-tsung made this claim in 1168, in response to an official's request that taxes should be reduced to lessen the people's burden. See Liu et al., *Huang Sung chung-hsing liang-ch'ao sheng-cheng* 47, p. 5a.

[68] Liu et al., *Huang Sung chung-hsing liang-ch'ao sheng-cheng* 48, p. 6a.

[69] *Sung-shih ch'üan-wen Hsü Tzu-chih t'ung-chien* 25, p. 2003.

[70] Li, *Chien-yen i-lai ch'ao-yeh tsa-chi* (1967) *chia* 15, pp. 4b–5a. Government income from commercial tax amounted to 14.4 million strings (*min*) of cash, which represented about twenty percent of its annual revenue from the southeastern region.

Defense and foreign policy

Despite the conclusion of the peace settlement with the Chin in the north, military and defense preparations constituted a major item in Hsiao-tsung's reconstruction program. Military recruitment was a matter of primary importance. In 1165, Wang Chi-chung2, the Secretariat's imperial recorder, raised the issue by pointing out that descendants of military officials appeared ashamed to keep up the military tradition of their families. He added that although the country was at the moment free of disturbances, it was a good time to recruit military personnel so that the Sung would not be caught unprepared in the event of war. Wang Chi-chung2 proposed selecting from among the families of former generals those men capable of a military career, and encouraging them to continue the family's military tradition by awarding them special honors.[71] Hsiao-tsung agreed with both the proposal and that this should be the urgent task of the day. Thus, the peace settlement did not result in slackened Sung efforts at defense.

Military preparation also involved building and fortifying walls in strategic locations. Wall repairs were carried out in Chien-k'ang (Nanking) after the war in 1165.[72] Particular attention was paid to the defenses of the region north of the Yangtze in 1167 and 1168. Wall repair projects were also implemented in Hsiang-yang and in the Huai region in 1169 and 1170. These fortification projects were opposed by some officials on the grounds that such defense measures might arouse Chin suspicion and provoke renewed hostilities. Hsiao-tsung, though, felt safe in carrying out these defense preparations and complained that some officials were being inflexible.[73]

Apart from their fear of provoking Chin, officials may also have opposed some defense projects because of financial considerations. Since the bulk of governmental expenditures were on defense, Hsiao-tsung and his ministers often debated how best to strengthen the empire without overtaxing the people. Though he was obliged to reduce the number of soldiers in certain areas in order to curtail military expenditures, Hsiao-tsung did not neglect the need for defensive preparedness in either the Yangtze or the Huai regions. The government also gave high priority to defending the northwestern frontier. After the famous Sung general Wu Lin died in 1167, the administrator of the Bureau of Military Affairs, Yü Yün-wen, was sent to take his place as pacification commissioner of Szechwan. Yü began building up defenses in the Szechwan and Shensi regions. He personally recruited new generals, and he improved

---

[71] *Sung-shih ch'üan-wen Hsü Tzu-chih t'ung-chien* 24, p. 1899.

[72] *SHY* (1997) *fang-yü* 9, p. 13.

[73] *Sung-shih ch'üan-wen Hsü Tzu-chih t'ung-chien* 24, p. 1930.

the army's efficiency by discharging unfit and overage soldiers.[74] One of Yü Yün-wen's outstanding contributions to northwestern frontier defense was the reorganization of the local defense corps known as *i-shih* (loyalist soldiers). A kind of militia, these loyalist soldiers were meant to defend their own localities without incurring heavy costs to the imperial treasury. Instead of maintaining a regular army, Yü advocated the use of these *i-shih*, who could be trained during the slack winter seasons of the farming year in preparation for an emergency. In the 1130s, the *i-shih* had been a considerable force, numbering around seventy thousand, but by 1161 it had dwindled to a mere six thousand. After Yü's recruitment efforts in 1167, the number of *i-shih* in the northwestern prefectures came to around twenty-four thousand men.[75] These *i-shih* were given regular military training and contributed in no small way to local defense.

The *i-shih* system was now extended to other parts of the empire. Militia recruitment and training also took place in the Huai and Yangtze regions and in Hupei and Hunan. Rewards were given as incentives to outstanding men among the trainees.[76] In order not to impose too heavy a burden upon the farmers, the court's policy was to assemble the militia for a training period of only one month per year in late autumn or in winter, during which time their needs were provided for by the state.[77]

Besides the use of local militia, the establishment of military farms, self-supporting military settlements sometimes called colonies (*t'un-t'ien*), was also a policy designed to strengthen defenses and save costs. Under this military colony system, farms were to be worked by soldiers and militia stationed at the colony. Although normally they farmed, these men were also regularly trained and kept in readiness to take up arms at short notice during times of emergency.[78] This system was seen as an inexpensive way of defending the borders, since the soldiers were to be self-supporting. However, these farm colony projects were not always successful owing either to poor management or to other factors such as regional depopulation. In 1165, various generals, military commanders, and circuit attendants were assigned responsibility for the military farms in different parts of the empire.[79] Subsequently, the scheme was abandoned in those areas where the colonies ran at a loss, with the land allotted for military farms either leased to members of the public or used to resettle refugees.

---

[74] See Yü's memorials in Fu, *Sung-tai Shu-wen chi-ts'un* (1971) 57, pp. 9a–10a, 13a–b.

[75] Fu, *Sung-tai Shu-wen chi-ts'un* (1971) 58, pp. 18b–19a.

[76] SHY (1997) *ping* 1, p. 33.

[77] SHY (1997) *ping* 1, p. 36.

[78] For an account of the *t'un-t'ien* of Southern Sung, see Li, *Chien-yen i-lai ch'ao-yeh tsa-chi* (1967) *chia* 16, pp. 1b–3a.

[79] HTC (1957) 139, p. 3698.

Hsiao-tsung's concern about national defense also found expression in his interest in the practice of warfare. He personally took part in five major military maneuvers. Three of these were carried out during the Ch'ien-tao period, in 1166, 1168, and 1170. On each occasion, he donned armor and directed the maneuvers. It was a grand spectacle, and all participants were richly rewarded.[80] The emperor also regularly practiced horsemanship and archery. His enthusiasm for the military arts and the tactical aspects of war was not, however, shared by his ministers, who feared he might injure himself and who also doubted that his interest in practical warfare would contribute much to the dynasty's long-range preparations for the reconquest of its lost northern territories. In 1169, after Hsiao-tsung injured an eye while practicing archery, he was admonished by Chief Councilor Ch'en Chün-ch'ing that his top priority was to govern the country well, and that it was unnecessary for him to engage in personally fighting an enemy.[81] Ch'en believed that to achieve the goal of retaking the lost territories long-term planning was far more important than the war games and martial training so esteemed by the emperor.

The emperor found himself restrained by his ever-cautious ministers not only in his participation in the military arts and physical sports but in the broader area of foreign policy as well. He was constantly being reminded not to act rashly. During the early years of the Ch'ien-tao period, the court's policy was to maintain an unaggressive posture in relations with Chin. In 1167, in a court debate on reconquest, the associate administrator of the Bureau of Military Affairs, Liu Kung, said that though revenge against Chin should be the major objective, he believed that the Sung should make no rash move until internal reforms had been undertaken for ten years.[82] Liu Kung's views reflected the general opinion at court, since most officials also favored a period of internal reconstruction and development before embarking on an aggressive foreign policy against Chin.

Nevertheless, long before the end of the ten-year period advocated by Liu Kung, Hsiao-tsung began to show signs of impatience with the court's cautious attitude. During the summer of 1167, when the chief remonstrance official, Ch'en Liang-yu, told Hsiao-tsung that the officials did not regard the recent repairs to the walls in Yang-chou as beneficial, the emperor rejoined, "How can defense preparations not be beneficial?" Ch'en replied: "Supposing the enemy were to attack us and we failed to defend the city [of Yang-chou],

---

[80] For an account of the five military inspections carried out by Hsiao-tsung, see Li, *Chien-yen i-lai ch'ao-yeh tsa-chi* (1967) i 4, pp. 12a–14b.

[81] *Sung-shih ch'üan-wen Hsü Tzu-chih t'ung-chien* 25, p. 1950.

[82] Liu et al., *Huang Sung chung-hsing liang-ch'ao sheng-cheng* 46, pp. 15a–b.

we would have fortified the city for them. Now that we have sent twenty to thirty thousand men across the Yangtze [for wall-repairs and defense of Yang-chou], fresh hostilities might break out if the enemy came to know about it." Unconvinced, Hsiao-tsung commented, "Such measures should indeed not be carried out [even farther north] in the Huai region, but what is the harm of doing so in an internal area?" Ch'en still insisted that the emperor be cautious. He concluded his objection by referring to the empire's need for further internal strengthening, emphasizing that the essential requirements for defense were to select military personnel, accumulate resources, see to the people's well-being, and provide for the soldiers.[83]

The emperor at this point appeared to possess more zeal than his ministers in matters of defense and foreign policy. He occasionally adopted a more militant attitude in foreign relations. This became especially noticeable in the later years of the Ch'ien-tao period, during which he found a great supporter in Yü Yün-wen, who also favored a more aggressive foreign policy. On becoming chief councilor of the right in 1169, Yü suggested sending envoys to Chin to request retrocession of territory that included the Sung imperial tombs in Honan. The chief councilor of the left, Ch'en Chün-ch'ing, strongly opposed this action on grounds that it might put the Chin on alert or even provoke them into attacking the Sung, who were far from ready to fight.[84] Because of Ch'en's opposition, Hsiao-tsung postponed sending envoys that year (1169), but he adopted Yü's proposal and sent them the following year.

In the summer of 1170, at Yü Yün-wen's recommendation, the Chancellery imperial recorder, Fan Ch'eng-ta, was appointed envoy to Chin. While Fan Ch'eng-ta's major assignment was to request the return of the territory containing the Sung imperial tombs, he was given the additional duty of requesting an alteration in the rites with which the Sung emperor received Chin letters of state. The 1141 treaty had required the Sung emperor to descend from his elevated throne when receiving letters of state from the Chin envoy. The same procedure was required under the 1165 treaty. Hsiao-tsung felt that this practice was degrading, and for some time he had wanted to change the ceremony, but he had been discouraged from trying to do so by Ch'en Chün-ch'ing. Fearing that this request might provoke Chin, Hsiao-tsung omitted it from the state letter, and instead verbally instructed Fan Ch'eng-ta to raise the matter.[85]

In the autumn of 1170, Fan Ch'eng-ta returned from Chin. Although the request to alter the rites had not been included in the Sung state letter, Fan had managed to submit a memorial on the issue to the Chin emperor. Chin

[83] *Sung-shih ch'üan-wen Hsü Tzu-chih t'ung-chien* 24, p. 1931.

[84] Chu, *Hui-an hsien-sheng Chu Wen kung wen-chi* (1929) 96, p. 1718.

[85] See the biography of Fan Ch'eng-ta in *SS* 386, p. 11868.

rejected the requests both to return territory and to alter the rites, but the initiative shown by Fan in negotiating the Sung case was deeply appreciated by Hsiao-tsung.[86] Despite the failure of Fan's mission, Hsiao-tsung did not give up trying to persuade Chin to grant the two requests. During the winter of 1170, when Chao Hsiung, the drafting official at the Secretariat, was sent on an official mission to greet the Chin emperor on his birthday, he carried a letter that again asked to alter the rites for receiving Chin state letters.[87] The Chin court rejected this appeal as well.

Hsiao-tsung's ambition to reincorporate former territory became more apparent during the last years of the Ch'ien-tao period. Following Fan Ch'eng-ta's mission, many opportunists presented plans for how the reconquest might be achieved. More than ten men were rewarded with official positions for having impressed the emperor with their proposals.[88] During the ninth month of 1172 the emperor decided to send Yü Yün-wen (who had resigned his position as chief councilor) once again to Szechwan as its pacification commissioner. The grand farewell given Yü indicates the importance Hsiao-tsung attached to Yü's assignment.[89] It is said that before Yü left for Szechwan, the emperor discussed with him a plan to attack the Central Plains by having Yü move the Szechwan army eastward from Szechwan while the emperor led the imperial army northward from the Yangtze valley. He even ordered Yü to set a time for such a joint military action to invade Honan.[90] Hsiao-tsung's parting instructions to Yü indicated his intention to play a personal role in the military campaign. It was Hsiao-tsung's cherished dream to personally lead his army to victory.

During this second appointment as pacification commissioner of Szechwan, Yü Yün-wen further strengthened Szechwan's defensive capability by selecting able generals, raising the soldiers' morale with higher pay, increasing the supply of horses, and reorganizing the troops for better coordination in the event of war.[91] Hsiao-tsung, however, became dissatisfied because Yü, after having been in Szechwan for more than a year, still had not set a date for the joint attack. Becoming impatient, the emperor sent confidential messages to Yü urging him

[86] *HTC* (1957) 142, p. 3785.

[87] *HTC* (1957) 142, p. 3789.

[88] Chou, *Wen-chung chi* 61, p. 18b.

[89] Yü Yün-wen was allowed to leave with great honor. Hsiao-tsung presented him with valuable gifts consisting of sacrificial vessels from the imperial temple and personally wrote Yü a poem. It is said that the grand treatment given to Yü was unprecedented in the farewell given to any of the chief councilors since the beginning of the Southern Sung. See Li, *Chien-yen i-lai ch'ao-yeh tsa-chi* (1967) *i* 12, pp. 5a–b.

[90] *HTC* (1957) 143, p. 3821.

[91] See the tomb inscription for Yü Yün-wen in Yang Wan-li, *Ch'eng-chai chi* (c. 1208; Shanghai, 1929) 120, pp. 1072–3.

to get on with the plans for reconquest of the north. When Yü replied that the army was not yet ready for an offensive campaign, Hsiao-tsung was displeased. When Yü died the following year, it is said that the emperor refused to grant him any posthumous honors. However, Hsiao-tsung's disappointment with Yü's efforts vanished upon seeing the high quality of the Szechwan troops in a subsequent military exercise. Hsiao-tsung then gave Yü posthumous honors, as due credit for his painstaking efforts in selecting and training the soldiers.[92]

In addition to his growing optimism regarding reconquest, Hsiao-tsung became more persistent in bargaining for a more equal diplomatic relationship with Chin. The fact that he felt confident enough to adopt a more aggressive foreign policy by the end of the Ch'ien-tao period in 1173 indicates that after a decade of reconstruction, the Southern Sung had rebuilt its military and could face Chin with greater confidence.

THE CH'UN-HSI PERIOD (1174–1189): THE GROWTH OF ABSOLUTISM

At the beginning of 1174, Hsiao-tsung changed his reign title from Ch'ien-tao to Ch'un-hsi (Pure Serenity, 1174–89). Although the Ch'ien-tao period had been one of revival and restoration after the 1161–4 war, the emperor did not appear satisfied with his accomplishments. He was troubled that the Sung was still militarily far weaker than the Han and T'ang dynasties had been at their peaks. One of his greatest regrets was his inability, during the Ch'ien-tao period, to reconquer lands in the north formerly held by the Sung. By the end of 1173, however, given his increasingly aggressive stance in foreign relations, the emperor appears to have intended to create a militarily glorious reign in the ensuing years.

The Ch'un-hsi reign period lasted sixteen years, until Hsiao-tsung's abdication in 1189. During this time, in foreign policy, the Sung government sought to improve its status with Chin. Domestically, the Sung empire enjoyed political stability and economic prosperity. The years of reconstruction of the previous period had borne fruit. The populace lived more comfortably and even enjoyed some luxury. As a result of Hsiao-tsung's frugality, the imperial treasuries were filled to the brim. Politically, the emperor was the unchallenged apex of power, and he exercised this power in an assertive manner. Prompted by his success in domestic politics and ever more confident in himself, Hsiao-tsung, who had already shown autocratic tendencies during his early years on the throne, manifested them more distinctly after 1174. As his grip over the bureaucracy tightened, officials became more submissive to his authority. Most of the chief councilors who served during the Ch'un-hsi period were men

---

[92] HTC (1957) 143, p. 3821.

whose political views seldom differed from the emperor's and who were more
compliant about imperial conduct and court policy. Court politics became less
marked by the tensions and in-fighting that had occasionally occurred during
the preceding reign period. In these ways, the Ch'un-hsi period witnessed a
growth in the emperor's absolute power. This absolutism was not necessarily
a negative development. It appears to have brought a further period of order
to the Southern Sung.

FOREIGN RELATIONS AFTER 1174

During the last years of the Ch'ien-tao period, Hsiao-tsung became more
persistent in negotiating to improve the Sung's status in diplomatic relations.
At the beginning of 1174, Hsiao-tsung adopted his most aggressive posture
on relations with Chin. The Chin envoy Wan-yen Chang, who delivered New
Year's greetings to the Sung court, was initially prevented from seeing the
emperor because of a disagreement over the protocol for receiving Chin letters
of state. Hsiao-tsung, who had always been unhappy about having to descend
from his throne to receive the state letters from Chin, again attempted to alter
the ceremonies stipulated by the 1165 treaty. The envoy was given an imperial
audience after the retired emperor, Kao-tsung, intervened, persuading Hsiao-
tsung to observe the required ceremonies for the time being.[93] However,
on his return to Chin in the second month of 1174, Wan-yen Chang was
severely punished for having brought dishonor to the Chin government during
his mission.[94] Though the Sung records are silent about the incident, the
indignation of Chin suggests that the proper ceremonies had not been observed
during Wan-yen Chang's embassy. Hsiao-tsung's apparent lack of concern over
the possible consequences of his action probably demonstrated his confidence
in Sung ability to confront Chin.

Following Wan-yen Chang's punishment, rumors arose among Chin officials
that hostilities between the two states might be renewed. Nothing happened,
however, as neither the Chin nor the Sung were eager to go to war. Nevertheless,
Chin sent a special mission to the Sung in the spring of 1174 inquiring about
the Sung failure to adhere to the stipulated ceremonies during the previous
embassy. When the Chin envoy arrived at the Sung court, Hsiao-tsung saw
how offended Chin was, and decided to comply with its wishes by rising from
his throne to receive the letter of state.[95] Hsiao-tsung seems to have avoided

---

[93] *HTC* (1957) 143, p. 3836.

[94] Wan-yen Chang was accused of allowing the Chin state letter to be taken from him in an improper
manner and of succumbing to bribery by the Sung. See T'o-t'o, ed., *Chin shih* [Po-na-pen 1930–7 ed.]
(1344; Peking, 1975) 61, p. 1453; *HTC* (1957) 144, p. 3838.

[95] See the biography of Liang Su in T'o-t'o, *Chin shih* 86, pp. 1983–4.

war by doing so. Another factor that might have influenced the emperor to back down from his aggressive stance was Yü Yün-wen's death in the second month of 1174. The loss at this crucial moment of his strongest foreign policy supporter must have disheartened Hsiao-tsung and might have prompted him to placate Chin. This setback did not mean he was willing to drop the issue, for he made several more attempts to have the ceremonies changed. During the fourth month of 1174, the minister of works, Chang Tzu-yen, was sent to Chin to respond to the Chin inquiry and, at the same time, to formally request again an alteration in the ceremony for receiving Chin state letters. The request was once again denied by the Chin emperor, who insisted that the Sung continue to observe the established protocol.[96]

Apart from the issue of protocol, the fact that the Sung imperial tombs remained in Chin hands continued to disturb Hsiao-tsung. Despite the failure of Fan Ch'eng-ta's mission in 1170 to negotiate the return of the territory containing the imperial tombs, Hsiao-tsung refused to give up hope. Five years later in the autumn of 1175, he sent the remonstrance official T'ang Pang-yen on a similar mission to Chin. The boldness of T'ang, a protégé of Yü Yün-wen, in voicing criticism had initially impressed the emperor. However, T'ang turned out to be a great disappointment to Hsiao-tsung. While at the Chin court, T'ang, so trusted by the emperor, failed to utter a single word advocating the Sung cause.[97] When T'ang returned south in the spring of 1176, the angry emperor ordered him exiled for failing to preserve Sung honor. From then on, Hsiao-tsung dropped the issue of the imperial tombs and sent no more envoys on such futile missions.

The emperor also continued to try to improve the Sung's diplomatic status by attempting to weaken the provisions of previous treaties with Chin. Early in 1182, the Chin envoy on a New Year's greetings mission to the Sung was involved in yet another controversy over the ceremonies for receiving the Chin state letter. Hsiao-tsung once again insisted that he would remain seated on his throne when the letter was handed over to him. He sent Wang Pien, a trusted inner court attendant and the chief recipient of edicts at the Bureau of Military Affairs, to speak to the Chin envoy in an attempt to influence the latter to agree to the alteration in the ceremony. Wang, however, failed in his task and instead gave in to Chin demands by consenting that the protocol be followed.[98] The emperor was displeased and had Wang dismissed the following month. This was the last occasion on which the issue of the receipt of state letters was raised.

[96] HTC (1957) 144, p. 3842.
[97] Liu et al., Huang Sung chung-hsing liang-ch'ao sheng-cheng 54, p. 16a.
[98] Liu et al., Huang Sung chung-hsing liang-ch'ao sheng-cheng 56, p. 9a; HTC (1957) 148, p. 3954.

Because Hsiao-tsung's many attempts to upgrade the diplomatic status of the Sung with Chin did not achieve the changes he wanted, it is understandable that he felt frustrated in the area of foreign diplomacy and frequently expressed his regret over the Sung's military weakness. In 1176, when he was praised by his ministers for his financial frugality in the palace, Hsiao-tsung replied, "The domestic laws in our dynasty are far superior to those of Han and T'ang; the only thing in which we lag behind is military achievement."[99] In 1184, in a conversation with his chief councilor, Wang Huai (1127–90), Hsiao-tsung again commented that the Sung's military power was less than that of the Han and T'ang dynasties, and he attributed Sung victories in certain battles to Heaven's help. Wang agreed, replying supportively that the benevolence of the Sung rulers would lead to victories not through force, but through moral justice. The emperor then consoled himself by recalling Han Wu-ti's failure: "During the reign of Han Wu-ti the military power of the empire caused awe and trembling thousands of miles away, but what had it accomplished? Instead, the losses incurred were much too great!"[100] Hsiao-tsung's comments in these conversations underscore the contention that although he was unhappy over his lack of military success, he was undoubtedly proud of his achievements in domestic affairs.

Despite Hsiao-tsung's personal disappointment, under his reign the Sung gained a stronger diplomatic position with Chin than it had enjoyed before. This was a result of the consolidation of military power and the constant defensive preparations initiated by the emperor and his court. During the Ch'un-hsi period two large-scale military exercises were held, in 1177 and 1185. Military training of archers was frequently held in the palace, and archery contests also took place in conjunction with palace feasts.[101] To encourage scholar-officials to cultivate an interest in the military arts, Imperial University students and successful *chin-shih* candidates were required to take part in archery contests and were rewarded according to their skills.[102]

Despite the various efforts made during the Ch'ien-tao period to reduce military expenditures, the number of soldiers in the imperial army remained at about four hundred thousand and their maintenance alone cost eighty million strings of cash annually.[103] Training militia, procuring and tending calvary horses, and the management of military colonies further increased governmental expenses. These heavy military expenditures imposed a great drain on the taxpayers.

---

[99] Liu et al., *Huang Sung chung-hsing liang-ch'ao sheng-cheng* 54, p. 23b.

[100] Liu et al., *Huang Sung chung-hsing liang-ch'ao sheng-cheng* 61, p. 7a; *HTC* (1957) 149, p. 3988.

[101] Liu et al., *Huang Sung chung-hsing liang-ch'ao sheng-cheng* 53, pp. 2b, 13a.

[102] Liu et al., *Huang Sung chung-hsing liang-ch'ao sheng-cheng* 59, p. 19b; Ma, *Wen-hsien t'ung-k'ao* (1936) 32, p. 301.

[103] Li, *Chien-yen i-lai ch'ao-yeh tsa-chi* (1967) *chia* 18, pp. 4b–5a.

As a consequence of Hsiao-tsung's vigilance in matters of defense, it was said that the Chin feared that the Sung might one day launch an attack against them.[104] Hsiao-tsung's attempts to upgrade Sung's diplomatic position were not in vain, since they had the effect of keeping Chin on their guard and prolonging the diplomatic tension. Although Hsiao-tsung never achieved his lifelong ambition of retaking former Sung territory in the north, he was able to provide resistance against Chin that kept the peace through stalemate.

The absolute monarch

In the early years of the Ch'un-hsi period Hsiao-tsung had behaved autocratically toward his ministers. Ruling without the assistance of a chief councilor, he administered the bureaucracy largely by himself. From 1175 until 1178, Hsiao-tsung left the position of chief councilor vacant and functioned both as head of state and as chief administrator of his empire. These conditions greatly enhanced his personal authority.

The dismissal of Assistant Councilor Kung Mao-liang in 1177 and its aftermath illustrates the development of imperial absolutism during this period. An efficient administrator, zealous in performing his duties, Kung was not afraid to offend other officials or inner court personnel, some of whom were imperial favorites. This may have been one of the reasons the emperor was reluctant to promote him to the position of chief councilor. In any event, Kung's refusal to ingratiate himself with inner court officials led to a quarrel with Tseng Ti, who brought about Kung's dismissal. After Tseng Ti had returned to court in 1170, he enjoyed seemingly boundless imperial favor and became increasingly powerful.[105] In the fourth month of 1177, confident of the emperor's support, and in disregard of the civil service regulations on appointments, Tseng intended to ask that his descendants be permitted to hold civil (instead of military) ranks. But his request was circumvented by Kung, who insisted that civil and military officials were allowed to have their descendants sponsored only into that service to which they themselves had belonged.[106] Soon after that, an angry Tseng Ti sought revenge. At Tseng's instigation, officers under him behaved disrespectfully toward Kung by deliberately blocking his way while he was leaving court. When ordered by a street patrol to move aside, the officers defiantly rejoined, "How much longer can the assistant councilor remain in his position?" Kung reported the incident to the emperor, stating that although the insult did not matter to him personally he was afraid the honor of the entire court was at stake. Hsiao-tsung then attempted to reconcile

---

[104] SS 35, p. 692.

[105] For the numerous honors awarded to Tseng Ti, see his biography in SS 470, p. 13690.

[106] HTC (1957) 145, p. 3882; biography of Kung Mao-liang in SS 144, p. 11845.

them by asking Tseng to apologize to Kung Mao-liang. Tseng did so, but Kung rebuffed the apology with the terse reminder, "An assistant councilor is a councilor of the court." Seeing that Kung was still indignant, the emperor warned him not to act rashly. Kung Mao-liang, however, proceeded further. He issued an order for the officers involved to be flogged and dismissed. Hsiao-tsung was displeased that Kung had disregarded his warning and faulted him for being too quick to punish the officers concerned.[107]

Kung Mao-liang soon suffered the consequences of his action. Hsiao-tsung apparently did not want to create the impression that he was taking sides in this quarrel so he resorted to using the censors against Kung. A month after the incident, Hsieh Kuo-jan, a friend of Tseng Ti, was appointed palace censor on a direct order by the palace. Immediately upon taking office in the Censorate, Hsieh impeached Kung, accusing him of feigning an imperial order in sentencing the officers under Tseng Ti.[108] Kung Mao-liang was obliged to resign with a plea of illness, and he was dismissed as assistant councilor. He was then appointed administrator of Chien-k'ang. Hsieh Kuo-jan, however, refused to leave him alone, and Kung was removed from his new post after being accused of usurping authority and cultivating factions at court. In the seventh month of 1177, as a result of further accusations by Hsieh, Kung was exiled to Ying-chou5, where he died the following year. Such severe punishment of a high-ranking official was very rare during Hsiao-tsung's reign. Nonetheless, though Kung Mao-liang's downfall has generally been attributed to Tseng Ti's machinations, had Kung not displeased the emperor it is unlikely that he would have suffered such a tragic fate. Kung's quarrel with Tseng Ti would not have annoyed Hsiao-tsung to the extent that it did had Kung not rejected the emperor's advice. To an absolutist emperor like Hsiao-tsung, such an offense was unforgivable.

Hsiao-tsung's reaction to the incident extended beyond Kung's dismissal. An imperial edict issued in the sixth month of 1177, immediately after Kung's removal, required the Three Departments and the Bureau of Military Affairs to resubmit imperial orders (chih2) that they had received after court assembly for final confirmation by the emperor before they could be permitted to implement them.[109] This edict was a direct response to Kung Mao-liang's having issued an imperial order that the emperor disapproved of. The edict made doubly sure that all imperial orders were genuine and that no future councilor could act on his own authority to issue imperial orders. By insisting on imperial verification of all matters, Hsiao-tsung sought to insure that there would be no loopholes bureaucrats could manipulate.

---

[107] HTC (1957) 145, p. 3883.
[108] HTC (1957) 145, p. 3884.
[109] Chou, Wen-chung chi 181, p. 4a.

In 1177, Hsiao-tsung seems to have decided to end his attempt to rule without a chief councilor. After an absence of more than thirteen years, in 1177 the emperor's former tutor and chief councilor, Shih Hao, now seventy-one years old, was summoned back to court and appointed reader-in-waiting; the next year, he was again appointed chief councilor of the right. But as before, Shih Hao's upright and unyielding character made it difficult for him to serve under Hsiao-tsung, who was equally strong willed and uncompromising. It was not long before they fell into a serious disagreement.

The rift between Hsiao-tsung and Shih Hao arose from Shih Hao's dissatisfaction with the way the emperor had dealt with a legal case involving a fight between civilians and palace guardsmen. During the tenth month of 1178, Wang Pien, the chief recipient of edicts at the Bureau of Military Affairs, asked permission to impress six thousand men to fill vacancies in military units in the capital. To accomplish this, a commander of the Palace Guard used force to press men into service. This caused a great commotion in the capital, and some potential conscripts mutilated themselves to avoid being drafted. Resisters were intimidated, with unruly soldiers even seizing some civilians' property. Riots erupted and many were arrested. At the ensuing trial death sentences were imposed on one of the soldiers and on one civilian accused of inciting the riot. Other rioters were released.[110]

Shih Hao argued that the sentences were ill advised. While agreeing that the soldier deserved capital punishment, Shih advised against imposing the same sentence on the civilian on the grounds that the latter had acted in self-defense. Shih now raised the political stakes by criticizing the emperor for an error of judgment in trying to placate the military by diluting responsibility for the violence. Shih warned the emperor that the consequences of allowing the military to run rough-shod over citizens were serious, and he alluded to the story of two peasants, Ch'en She and Wu Kuang, who in 209 B.C.E. precipitated the overthrow of the Ch'in dynasty because they were unable to report on time for conscript labor service, an offense punishable by death under Ch'in law.[111] The implied criticism infuriated Hsiao-tsung, who accused Shih Hao of comparing him to the second Ch'in dynasty emperor, Ch'in Erh-shih huang-ti (r. 210–207 B.C.E.). Shih Hao remained adamant, even in the face of the civilian's execution, and in the eleventh month of 1178 tendered his resignation. The emperor later remarked that he "regretted the circumstances

---

[110] For an account of this incident, see the biography of Shih Hao in *SS* 396, pp. 12067–8; Lou, *Kung-k'uei chi* (1929) 93, p. 880.

[111] For the allusion, see Ssu-ma Ch'ien, *Shih chi* [*Po-na-pen* 1930–7 ed.] (c. 90 B.C.E.; Peking, 1972) 48, pp. 1949–50, and Michael Loewe, "The Former Han dynasty," in *The Cambridge history of China*, volume 1: *The Ch'in and Han empires, 221 B.C.–A.D. 220*, ed. Denis C. Twitchett and Michael Loewe (Cambridge, 1986), pp. 112–13. This passage of the *SS* is also discussed in Davis, *Court and family in Sung China*, p. 70.

under which Shih left."[112] Despite their disagreement, the emperor showered
Shih Hao with gifts and treated him with the utmost respect by appointing him
to various sinecures and ranks of nobility and by making him junior mentor
and, for a while, keeping him as reader-in-waiting. Now in his seventies,
however, Shih Hao retired to his home in Ming-chou, but he continued to
exert influence at court by sponsoring a group of brilliant and able younger
men.

This affair highlights Hsiao-tsung's complex behavior as a monarch and
also his indulgence of the military. Hsiao-tsung seems to have adopted a more
favorable attitude toward the military than Kao-tsung. In the selection of
prefectural administrators, an office generally held only by civilian officials,
Hsiao-tsung held that, as long as candidates from the military were capable,
they too could be appointed regardless of their status as military officials.[113]
Furthermore, Hsiao-tsung, in keeping with his autocratic style, held the armies
under his direct command by appointing the generals himself, in consultation
with his close attendants. He sent confidential orders to the army by employing
palace attendants as his messengers. This direct control over military personnel was an imperial prerogative that Hsiao-tsung guarded jealously against
all encroachment.[114] Nevertheless, for the most part he treated his generals
liberally.[115]

The emperor augmented the trend toward absolutism by relying on his
palace favorites, most of whom had military links, to offset bureaucratic power.
As a result, Hsiao-tsung's ministers frequently criticized both his favoritism
toward the military and his indulgence of inner court personnel. Strangely
enough, just before his appointment as councilor Shih Hao had memorialized protesting about this. Hsiao-tsung's inclination toward holding absolute
power was even more noticeable during the Ch'un-hsi period, as the "close
attendants" of the emperor became more powerful through his support and as
opposition from high-ranking ministers at court diminished.

Among the most notorious palace attendants were Tseng Ti, Wang Pien,
and Kan Pien. Hsiao-tsung's employment of and favoritism toward Tseng
Ti and Wang Pien, men rapidly advanced from lowly military backgrounds,
has already been described. The third attendant was a eunuch, Kan Pien,
who had been recommended by Kao-tsung, and was already influential in the
capital during the Ch'ien-tao period.[116] During the late 1170s and early 1180s

---

[112] SS 396, p. 12068.
[113] This was stated in an imperial decree issued in the eleventh month of 1176. See Liu et al., *Huang Sung
chung-hsing liang-ch'ao sheng-cheng* 54, p. 26b.
[114] See the tomb inscription for Chou Pi-ta in Lou, *Kung-k'uei chi* (1929) 93, p. 887.
[115] Li, *Chien-yen i-lai ch'ao-yeh tsa-chi* (1967) i 2, p. 10a.
[116] See the biography of Kan Pien in SS 469, pp. 13672–3.

this trio is said to have collaborated with one another in exercising control. Their increasing power encouraged some ambitious officials unconcerned with bureaucratic protocol and integrity to seek their collaboration.[117]

The activities of the three favorites led to protests by outer court officials. One of the severest criticisms came from the renowned scholar-official Chu Hsi (1130–1200).[118] In 1180, while serving as administrator of Nan-k'ang (Nan-ch'ang, in modern Kiangsi), Chu Hsi responded to an imperial proclamation by submitting a sealed memorial in which he criticized Hsiao-tsung for relying on his personal associates. Chu Hsi alleged that the emperor did not allow his ministers to exercise their proper authority but instead discussed matters only with one or two of his close personal associates. According to Chu Hsi, these few vicious men were guilty of misleading the emperor, manipulating appointments, and robbing the emperor of his wealth. Chu Hsi even claimed that the emperor's authority was being usurped by these unscrupulous sycophants:

As these people establish their power and influence, the whole nation bows before them. As a result, Your Majesty's decrees and orders, promotions and demotions are no longer issued from the court but from the residences of these one or two persons. The so-called personal decisions of Your Majesty are in fact the doing of this handful of men who secretly exercise your power of control.[119]

Hsiao-tsung was enraged by this memorial but was persuaded by Chief Councilor Chao Hsiung to ignore it, and Chu Hsi was allowed to remain in his post.

This criticism and the many other protests against inner court favorites expressed the anger felt by officials at the emperor's placing his trust in close attendants rather than in ministers of the regular bureaucracy. Having obtained their positions through the civil service examinations, the scholar-officials regarded themselves as representatives of long-held administrative traditions. In their opinion, palace attendants lacked both credentials and moral authority because they had not been vetted by the regular civil service system. The officials were extremely concerned that the emperor was allowing his authority to be usurped by these favorites and sycophants. However, although Hsiao-tsung was indulgent toward his favorites, he never allowed them to get out of control. Contrary to the officials' objections, Hsiao-tsung made use of these palace personnel to achieve his own purposes and did not simply

---

[117] Liu et al., *Huang Sung chung-hsing liang-ch'ao sheng-cheng* 56, p. 8b.

[118] For an account of the political career of Chu Hsi, see Conrad Schirokauer, "Chu Hsi's political career: A study in ambivalence," in *Confucian personalities*, ed. Arthur F. Wright and Denis C. Twitchett (Stanford, Calif., 1962), pp. 162–88.

[119] Chu, *Hui-an hsien-sheng Chu Wen kung wen-chi* (1929) 11, pp. 167–8.

comply with their plans. Inner court functionaries would carry out Hsiao-tsung's wishes without question, whereas ministers might oppose and obstruct the emperor if they disagreed with his policies or decisions. Since the advice of the scholar-officials was frequently unpalatable to him, it is understandable that an autocrat like Hsiao-tsung would prefer to consult his attendants rather than seek his ministers' opinions.

At the heart of Chu Hsi's memorial was the concern that the emperor did not trust his ministers and would not let them fulfill their proper responsibilities. In another memorial addressed to the throne in 1181, Chu Hsi stated that while Hsiao-tsung had once made an effort to appoint capable officials to serve in government, because of his dissatisfaction with the results and an abiding fear of ministerial usurpation of power, he had given up looking for good and virtuous men and was content to appoint men he could more easily control. For Chu Hsi, the emperor's actions were directly responsible for the declining authority of the chief councilors,[120] a weakness that accompanied the expansion of imperial power during the Ch'un-hsi reign period. Apart from Shih Hao, who lasted just over a year in the highest office, the chief councilors appointed after him during this period were generally more passive and conforming, and less noted for opposing the emperor in matters of policy.[121] This passivity may explain why the chief councilors during this period were able to serve comparatively longer terms than their more troublesome counterparts of the Ch'ien-tao period.[122]

Hsiao-tsung's autocratic approach to his ministers also elicited an admonition from Yang Wan-li (1127–1206), the division chief in the Ministry of Personnel. In 1185, in response to an imperial proclamation requesting memorials commenting on public policies after the occurrence of an earthquake, Yang memorialized that "a ruler should refrain from exercising all the responsibilities himself. . . . By assuming authority in all matters, the ruler is depriving the ministers of their functions."[123] As Yang saw it, the emperor was making decisions on all matters by himself and using the councilors merely to carry out his orders.[124] Chu Hsi reiterated this theme in 1188. He argued that because of the emperor's policy of appointing timid and submissive men as councilors and then refusing to entrust them with important responsibilities,

---

[120] Chu, *Hui-an hsien-sheng Chu Wen kung wen-chi* (1929) 11, pp. 167–8.

[121] A good example of this category of ministers is Chao Hsiung. For his official biography, see *SS* 396, pp. 12073–5.

[122] The chief councilor who served the longest term during Hsiao-tsung's reign was Wang Huai. His tenure in office lasted for almost seven years, from 1181 to 1188. For an account of his career, see his *hsing-chuang* in Lou, *Kung-k'uei chi* (1929) 87, pp. 800–10; *SS* 391, pp. 12069–72.

[123] For Yang Wan-li's memorial, see his *Ch'eng-chai chi* 62, pp. 500–4.

[124] *HTC* (1957) 150, p. 4003.

the so-called chief ministers were reduced to the status of functionaries expected to obey imperial orders without question.[125] Although the ministers considered such autocratic behavior an obvious violation of traditional standards, Hsiao-tsung certainly thought otherwise. From his viewpoint, his policies ensured the orderly conduct of government, with the emperor controlling the bureaucracy as he should. He therefore did not heed Yang's or Chu's advice.

Administrative and financial control

The emperor's ability to eliminate factions from court contributed to achieving political order in the central government. Hsiao-tsung took pride in the fact that factions never became a problem during his reign. In a conversation with Chief Councilor Shih Hao in 1178, he commented that chief councilors should refrain from forming factions, but that the ruler should also refrain from charging his ministers with factionalism because such accusations would, in effect, force them to enter into factions. He stated that his policy was to dismiss bad officials and appoint good ones, even if the good ones had been recommended by ministers who were later disgraced. He went on to attribute the prevalence of factionalism in previous dynasties to the ruler's lack of discernment.[126] Hsiao-tsung's resulting personnel policy and his astute administrative practices freed the court from a major problem that had plagued the dynasty during late Northern Sung and during Kao-tsung's reign.

A further benefit of the absence of factionalism was that censors did not participate in power struggles at court. Unlike their counterparts during other periods of the Southern Sung, censors dutifully performed their tasks as the "ears and eyes" of the emperor, but did not actively engage in any political infighting at court. But their comparatively quiet role during Hsiao-tsung's reign may also have been because the office of the chief official of the Censorate was left vacant during the fourteen years from 1169 to 1183.[127] An obvious implication of this unusual circumstance is that the emperor did not want the Censorate to become too influential and took the preventive measure of not providing it with a chief executive who could act as its spokesperson. This tactic was similar to the approach he used to control the chief councilors. Moreover, Hsiao-tsung chose to appoint quiet and upright officials to the other censorial positions – a policy that also contributed to tranquility at court.[128]

[125] Chu, *Hui-an hsien-sheng Chu Wen kung wen-chi* (1929) 11, p. 173.

[126] For their discussion on factions, see Shih, *Mou-feng chen-yin man-lu* 10, p. 1b.

[127] Liu et al., *Huang Sung chung-hsing liang-ch'ao sheng-cheng* 60, p. 1b.

[128] See the tomb inscription for Hsieh O in Chou, *Wen-chung chi* 68, p. 15b.

In addition to imposing order on the central bureaucracy, Hsiao-tsung also successfully extended imperial control to the circuits and prefectures of the empire. He was concerned about proper administration at the prefectural level and personally selected circuit intendants (*chien-ssu*) and prefectural administrators (*chün-shou*). He made it a point to interview all new appointees before they took up their posts in the prefectures. As Kao-tsung had done before him, Hsiao-tsung had a screen set up in his palace on which was listed the names of all the circuit intendants and prefectural administrators for the entire realm.[129] The screen enabled him to keep check on the officials assigned to the different administrative units of the empire and signaled to the administrative officials that their names were known to the emperor. Hsiao-tsung also sought to keep circuit and prefectural administrations under the close supervision of the central government. Administrators at the circuit (*lu*) level, namely, the military intendants (*shuai-ch'en*) and circuit intendants, were required regularly to assess the performance of the prefectural administrators under their jurisdiction and to submit reports to the central government.[130] The system of merit evaluation of prefectural administrators was strictly enforced during the mid-Ch'un-hsi period. In 1181, an imperial decree was issued ordering circuit intendants and military intendants to submit annual evaluation reports on the prefectural administrators under their supervision. These circuit authorities were required to investigate subordinates' performance carefully before submitting their reports. Those who failed to give unbiased reports on their subordinates were to be impeached by the censors.[131] In 1183, several prefectural officials were promoted or dismissed on the basis of the reports made by their administrative superiors. Two years later, two circuit intendants were demoted for submitting their evaluation reports late. Though the merit-evaluation system was not completely free of abuses,[132] its successful implementation during the Ch'un-hsi period resulted in an efficient system of administration away from the capital that enabled the central government to exercise unprecedented control over the imperial domain.

In financial matters Hsiao-tsung stressed proper control and careful management of the state's economy. His monetary policy was prudent and included strict control over the circulation of paper money. The main paper currency of

---

[129] Chou, *Wen-chung chi* 104, p. 10b; Chu Hsi, *Chu-tzu yü-lei* [1473 ed.] (1270; Taipei, 1962) 127, p. 4962.

[130] Hsiao-tsung issued this edict in late 1162, but it was not implemented then because of war. See Li, *Chien-yen i-lai ch'ao-yeh tsa-chi* (1967) *chia* 5, p. 11b.

[131] Liu et al., *Huang Sung chung-hsing liang-ch'ao sheng-cheng* 59, pp. 4b–5a; Li, *Chien-yen i-lai ch'ao-yeh tsa-chi* (1967) *chia* 5, p. 11b.

[132] Although the system of merit evaluation resulted in a less corrupt administration, circuit authorities could still be bribed into giving favorable reports on their subordinates. The evaluation system was abolished in 1199 during the reign of Ning-tsung. See Li, *Chien-yen i-lai ch'ao-yeh tsa-chi* (1967) *chia* 6, pp. 4a–b.

the Southern Sung, known as *hui-tzu*, had first been issued by the government in 1160 during Kao-tsung's reign.[133] Its convenience was widely recognized, but, in a few years time, its unit value began to drop because of overissue. In 1167, in an attempt to remedy the situation, Hsiao-tsung released two million taels of silver from the imperial treasury to be exchanged in the markets for *hui-tzu* notes that were then destroyed.[134] This strict control of the amount of paper currency issued and the money's popularity, especially among the merchant community, led to a shortage of notes in the Liang-Huai region (modern Kiangsu-Anhwei) in 1175, and more notes had to be issued to meet the demand. In 1175, a half million strings worth of *hui-tzu* was designated for circulation in the Huai region in exchange for copper coins.[135] The emperor continued to manage paper currency with extreme care. In 1183, on seeing the number of notes that had been newly issued, Hsiao-tsung expressed concern that the increase might lead to a drop in value. In 1185 he reiterated his policy that the paper money should not be issued in large numbers and that its circulation should be curtailed once military expenses were reduced.[136] Hsiao-tsung sought to check the devaluation of the *hui-tzu* by guarding strictly against overissuing paper money, a policy that contributed to stability in the Southern Sung economy.

One of Hsiao-tsung's greatest satisfactions was that, through his frugality, he was able to increase greatly the wealth in his own palace treasuries. But some of the government's regular treasuries were meagerly stocked. The emperor's policy was to channel easily collected sources of revenue into treasuries serving as his privy purse while leaving the state treasuries to collect more difficult items, even though as a result the State Treasury might suffer frequent deficits.[137] This policy appears to have been motivated not only by selfish interest but by Hsiao-tsung's pragmatism. Seeing the scholar-officials' reluctance to contemplate recovery of the lost territories, Hsiao-tsung probably realized that if he were ever to attain this goal he would have to build up

---

[133] For an account of the *hui-tzu* and other paper currencies of the Sung period, see Yang Lien-sheng, *Money and credit in China: A short history* (Cambridge, Mass., 1952), pp. 51–61. The Sung financial administration is discussed in greater detail in Peter J. Golas, "The Sung financial administration," in *The Cambridge history of China*, volume 5: *The Sung dynasty and its precursors, 907–1279, part 2*, ed. John W. Chaffee and Denis C. Twitchett (New York, forthcoming).

[134] See *Jung-chai san-pi* 14, pp. 584–5, in Hung Mai, *Jung-chai sui-pi* (Taipei, 1981).

[135] See Liu et al., *Huang Sung chung-hsing liang-ch'ao sheng-cheng* 54, pp. 1b–2a.

[136] Liu et al., *Huang Sung chung-hsing liang-ch'ao sheng-cheng* 60, p. 1b; 62, p. 8a.

[137] This asymmetry was pointed out by Chu Hsi, who alleged that while the palace treasuries obtained their revenue from easily collected, well-recorded items, the state treasuries were left trying to obtain income from items that were more difficult to collect or that might exist only on paper. See Chu, *Chu-tzu yü-lei* 111, p. 6b; see also Chu Hsi's sealed memorial of early 1189 in Chu, *Hui-an hsien-sheng Chu Wen kung wen-chi* (1929) 11, p. 175.

his own personal resources so he could be ready to launch a military campaign against the north when the right moment arrived. This policy of diverting revenues into treasuries under his personal control was first implemented when Yü Yün-wen was chief councilor.[138] Yü shared the emperor's vision of reconquest of the north and thus did not oppose this policy of building up financial reserves controlled by the emperor to prepare for such future contingencies. But while Hsiao-tsung's intention in increasing the store of privately controlled funds was closely linked to his ambition to retake territory, his gaining personal management and control of the empire's treasuries is yet another aspect of the deliberate increase in the emperor's absolute power at the expense of the central administration during the Ch'un-hsi period.

There were two major types of treasuries during the Sung dynasty: the State Treasury (*Tso-tsang k'u*) controlled by the Ministry of Finance (*Hu-pu*), and the Palace Treasury (*Nei-tsang k'u*) located in the inner court, which served as the emperor's private treasury. The Palace Treasury became increasingly important during the Sung, for it not only functioned as the emperor's privy purse, but since Hui-tsung's time it had also played a significant role in government finances under the new political system that Hui-tsung had initiated.[139] The Palace Treasury was a source of the emperor's personal power, for, though part of the empire's public wealth was stored in it, the details of its contents were kept confidential and dispersals were made by the emperor. By the time of the Southern Sung, the Palace Treasury had acquired still greater significance, for by then half the government's revenues were channeled into it.[140] Whereas the State Treasury was responsible for handling most of the state's regular recurrent expenditures, such as providing salaries for civil and military personnel, funds from the Palace Treasury were withdrawn only occasionally, for specific military expenses and for emergencies such as relief measures necessitated by natural calamities.

Besides the Palace and the State treasuries, a third type of treasury also developed during the Sung to meet the need to spend unusually large amounts of money on military expenses and on maintaining an enlarged bureaucracy. To meet these heavy expenses, funds had sometimes been withdrawn from the palace treasuries as a temporary measure to relieve the government of its financial difficulties. As such borrowing became more frequent, a separate office was set up to keep track of these funds that were being constantly withdrawn, and a new type of treasury was designated to store them. From this, the empire's

---

[138] Chu, *Hui-an hsien-sheng Chu Wen kung wen-chi* (1929) 11, p. 175.

[139] For two studies of the treasuries of the Sung dynasty, see Umehara Kaoru, "Sōdai no naizō to sazō," *Tōhō gakuhō (Kyoto)* 42 (1971), pp. 127–75, and Robert M. Hartwell, "The imperial treasuries: Finance and power in Song China," *Bulletin of Sung-Yüan Studies* 20 (1988), pp. 18–89.

[140] *CYYL* (1956) 193, p. 3420.

original two-level treasury system evolved into three levels.[141] This new third kind of treasury became important during the reign of Hsiao-tsung, who was responsible for establishing both the Southern Storehouse of the State Treasury (*Tso-tsang nan-k'u*) and the Sealed Treasury (also known as the Storehouse for Reserves of the State Treasury [*Tso-tsang feng-chuang k'u*]). Though their names suggest they were subordinate sections of the state treasury (*Tso-tsang k'u*), they were different from the state treasuries under the direct control of the Ministry of Finance. They fell under the emperor's control and were thus similar to the palace treasuries in function, although they were located and administered by the outer court, not the palace.

The Southern Storehouse was a special treasury set up for the payment of military expenses. It had been established in 1162 by transferring one of the palace treasuries, the Imperial Treasury of Awards (*yü-ch'ien chuang-kuan chi-shang k'u*), to the State Treasury. Although it was attached in theory to the State Treasury, in practice it remained a palace treasury. It continued to be used to meet military expenses, and its revenues came directly from the court (*ch'ao-t'ing*) rather than through the Ministry of Finance.[142] During the Ch'ien-tao period, the Southern Storehouse was considered one of the richest treasuries of the empire. On occasion, it provided loans to the State Treasury when the latter was in serious financial difficulty.[143] During the Ch'un-hsi period, however, another treasury, the Sealed Treasury (*Feng-chuang k'u*), began to overshadow the Southern Storehouse in importance and to assume a more significant role than the Southern Storehouse by serving as the emperor's privy purse.

Hsiao-tsung established the Sealed Treasury in 1170 with the specific proviso that no funds should be withdrawn from it except those used to pay military expenses and the sizable allowances of the retired emperor and dowager empress.[144] After its establishment, Hsiao-tsung made it a repository for the state's reserves. The date of its creation is significant. During 1170, with the support and encouragement of Chief Councilor Yü Yün-wen, the emperor began pursuing a more aggressive policy in foreign affairs. The attention given the Sealed Treasury indicates the importance Hsiao-tsung attached to his twin objectives of reconquest and filial devotion. In a reform implemented in early 1176, a main section of the Southern Storehouse was incorporated into the Sealed Treasury.[145] As a result, the holdings of the Southern Storehouse were drastically reduced and those of the Sealed Treasury rapidly increased. The

[141] See Umehara, "Sōdai no naizō to sazō," p. 142.

[142] Li, *Chien-yen i-lai ch'ao-yeh tsa-chi* (1967) *chia* 17, p. 4a.

[143] For example, in 1171 Hsiao-tsung inquired about the four million strings (*min*) of cash borrowed by the Ministry of Finance from the Southern Storehouse of the State Teasury. See Liu et al., *Huang Sung chung-hsing liang-ch'ao sheng-cheng* 50, pp. 9a–b.

[144] Wang Ying-lin, *Yü-hai* [1337 ed.] (1266; Taipei, 1964) 183, pp. 26a–b.

[145] Liu et al., *Huang Sung chung-hsing liang-ch'ao sheng-cheng* 54, p. 13b.

Sealed Treasury became so rich that in 1179 it was even reported (in the words of a Han dynasty cliché) that the strings used for tying cash were rotting after having been kept there for so many years.[146] In 1183 the total value of goods and cash stored in the Sealed Treasury was said to amount to over thirty million strings of cash.[147] This was no small sum, as it represented half the annual revenue received from the wealthiest region of the empire – the lower Yangtze valley – and was equivalent to more than a third of the annual military budget.[148]

In 1183, Hsiao-tsung decided to transfer the less important Southern Storehouse back to the State Treasury, claiming this would save him the trouble of overseeing the treasury himself.[149] It soon became apparent that there were other reasons why the emperor decided to yield control of the Southern Storehouse. The minister of finance, Wang Tso, pointed out that because of the deficits incurred by the Southern Storehouse, transfer of control to the ministry of finance would bring more harm than good to the ministry.[150] Wang proposed instead that the Southern Storehouse be incorporated into the Sealed Treasury, but Hsiao-tsung found this proposal unacceptable. He obviously attached great importance to the Sealed Treasury, which functioned as his personal treasure-house for the rest of his reign. Although it was supposed to store reserves for use in emergencies, during the final years of the Ch'un-hsi period, funds from the Sealed Treasury were frequently transferred to the palace treasuries for the manufacture of military equipment or under the pretext of rewarding the troops,[151] and the Ministry of Finance was unable to do anything about it. By the end of Hsiao-tsung's reign, the Sealed Treasury had evolved into an important organ that augmented the throne's power, bypassing the supervision of the Ministry of Finance.

Hsiao-tsung's abdication

A crucial moment in Hsiao-tsung's political career came when his adoptive father, Kao-tsung, died, in the tenth month of 1187. Having served the retired emperor to the full extent of his filial responsibilities for the previous twenty-five years,[152] Hsiao-tsung was left grief stricken by Kao-tsung's death. Despite

---

[146] Liu et al., *Huang Sung chung-hsing liang-ch'ao sheng-cheng* 57, p. 6a.

[147] Liu et al., *Huang Sung chung-hsing liang-ch'ao sheng-cheng* 60, p. 11a.

[148] By the end of the Ch'un-hsi period, the annual revenue from the southeast is said to have been around 65.3 million strings (*min*) of cash. See Li, *Chien-yen i-lai ch'ao-yeh tsa-chi* (1967) *chia* 14, p. 1a.

[149] Liu et al., *Huang Sung chung-hsing liang-ch'ao sheng-cheng* 60, p. 10a.

[150] Wang, *Yü-hai* 183, p. 26a. According to the calculation made by Wang Tso, the deficit came to a total of 440,000 strings (*min*) of cash. See Li, *Chien-yen i-lai ch'ao-yeh tsa-chi* (1967) *chia* 14, p. 1a.

[151] Li, *Chien-yen i-lai ch'ao-yeh tsa-chi* (1967) *chia* 17, p. 4b; Wang, *Yü-hai* 183, p. 26b.

[152] Hsiao-tsung's extraordinary devotion to the retired emperor was a significant feature of his behavior within the imperial family and in court politics. For his entire reign he played the dual role of emperor

the counsel of his ministers, he insisted on observing the mourning rites for the full three years.[153] Though he may have considered abdicating immediately, as a responsible emperor he found it necessary to provide the forty-two-year-old heir apparent, Chao Tun, with a period of intensive training to prepare him for the throne.

In the month after Kao-tsung died, Hsiao-tsung issued a decree authorizing the heir apparent to participate in the empire's administration. He told the councilors that, from then on, the heir apparent would discuss state matters with them. The emperor's decision caused consternation among the officials, who feared this action might promote political instability since it implied having two rulers at the same time.[154] The heir apparent himself was fearful and declined to take up his newly assigned responsibilities. Hsiao-tsung, however, had already made up his mind to familiarize his son with governmental matters and rejected his son's refusal. In fact, he accelerated Chao Tun's training. Early in 1188, a new office called the Policy Deliberation Hall (*I-shih t'ang*) was established in the palace. There the heir apparent met the councilors on alternate days to discuss state matters.[155] Almost immediately, the emperor announced to his ministers that, having participated in policy discussions, the heir apparent was becoming well acquainted with affairs of the empire. Hsiao-tsung also declared his intention that the heir would attend future sessions of court.[156]

Hsiao-tsung was grooming Chao Tun to take over the throne as soon as possible. His decision to grant more and more responsibility to the heir apparent made his ministers more anxious. They repeatedly submitted requests that the emperor return to his duties at court. Hsiao-tsung, however, had decided to fulfill the three-year mourning period for his father and would not change his mind. He made it clear in an order issued in the spring of 1188 that he would have no peace of mind if he failed to carry out the mourning rites fully. He ordered the officials not to present any more requests on the matter.[157]

Meanwhile, Hsiao-tsung continued to educate his son about important affairs of state and the administration of the empire. From the advice he gave, it is evident that even until the last days of his reign, finance and defense remained Hsiao-tsung's main concerns. Before stepping down, Hsiao-tsung's

and filial son, and occasionally he compromised his own ideals for the sake of filial obligation. For example, although frugal himself, he submitted to the requests of his extravagant father, whose monthly stipends amounted to forty thousand strings of cash. See Chou, *Wen-chung chi* 164, pp. 1a–b, 2b.

[153] Liu et al., *Huang Sung chung-hsing liang-ch'ao sheng-cheng* 63, p. 15b.

[154] See, for example, Yang Wan-li's memorial in his *Ch'eng-chai chi* 62, pp. 509–11.

[155] *Sung-shih ch'üan-wen Hsü Tzu-chih t'ung-chien* 27, p. 2199.

[156] *Sung-shih ch'üan-wen Hsü Tzu-chih t'ung-chien* 27, p. 2200.

[157] Liu et al., *Huang Sung chung-hsing liang-ch'ao sheng-cheng* 64, p. 5a.

last important act was to fill the top positions of the bureaucracy with dependable men who could assist his son in running the government. In the first month of 1189, he appointed Chou Pi-ta (1126–1204) chief councilor of the left and Liu Cheng (1129–1206) chief councilor of the right, and assigned the blunt-spoken Wang Lin (?–1201) the position of assistant councilor.[158] Hsiao-tsung felt that he could retire in peace only after everything was put in good order. Before the end of the month, Kao-tsung's former residence, the Te-shou Palace, was renamed the Ch'ung-hua Palace and prepared for Hsiao-tsung's occupation in retirement. In the second month of 1189, in an abdication ceremony similar to Kao-tsung's in 1162, Hsiao-tsung left his throne after having reigned for twenty-seven years.

Hsiao-tsung's belief that he had left everything in government in good order was to prove an illusion. Hsiao-tsung's style of governance demanded a powerful and immensely committed emperor. Chao Tun, for all his father's training, had such serious character defects that he made a disastrous ruler, and very soon he withdrew from public life and broke off all relations with his father. The court passed from an autocratic rulership to total lack of leadership. Within five years, Hsiao-tsung had died and soon after the high officials and courtiers forced Kuang-tsung to abdicate.

Both during Kao-tsung's lifetime and after his death, Hsiao-tsung demonstrated the filial devotion that earned him his posthumous title Hsiao-tsung – the "Filial Ancestor." His filial devotion was one of his most-praised virtues, and greatly impressed historians. But the most important achievement of his administration, his development of the Southern Sung dynasty's economic and military strength, is sometimes overlooked.

Wang Fu-chih (1619–92), the Ch'ing dynasty (1644–1911) author of the *Discourse on the Sung* (*Sung lun*), criticized Hsiao-tsung for his inability to reconquer lost territory and for his lack of fighting spirit after the Sung defeat at Fu-li in 1163.[159] Wang Fu-chih saw Hsiao-tsung as a frustrated emperor who had accomplished little for his empire after failing in his first attempt to recover the northern territories. Similarly, the late Ming dynasty (1368–1644) commentator on the *Sung-shih chi-shih pen-mo*, Chang P'u, stated that at the beginning of Hsiao-tsung's career there were ample opportunities to reconquer the lost territories, but the emperor had failed to make good use of them.[160] Even the Yüan period compilers of the Sung dynastic history, *Sung*

---

[158] *Sung-shih ch'üan-wen Hsü Tzu-chih t'ung-chien* 27, p. 2219.

[159] Wang, *Sung lun* (1964) 11, pp. 179–81.

[160] Ch'en Pang-chan et al., *Sung-shih chi-shih pen mo* (1605; Taipei, 1963) 78, p. 172. (The text used for this note is that published by San-min shu-chü, Taipei, 1963, as the Peking edition cited in the other notes does not contain the comments of Chang P'u.)

shih, while recognizing Hsiao-tsung as the best of the Southern Sung rulers and commending him for bringing about improvements in Sung foreign relations, seem apologetic for Hsiao-tsung's failure to recapture the north, commenting that it was the will of Heaven that the northern territories had not been recovered.[161]

These historians, all writing under foreign domination in their own day, so concentrated their attention on the issue of reconquest of the north that they overlooked the outstanding contributions Hsiao-tsung made to his empire's economic, military, and cultural strength. Moreover, Wang Fu-chih's criticism is not accurate, as the defeat at Fu-li did not dampen the emperor's enthusiasm for reconquest. After the abortive campaign of 1163, the consolidation of the empire's cultural, military, and economic strength began. The dynastic goal of reconquest continued to spur Hsiao-tsung and his court to greater efforts to reconstruct and strengthen their empire to the point where reconquest might have become possible. Hsiao-tsung admittedly had faults. His management of personnel was often overindulgent, he manipulated his ministers, and he governed his empire autocratically. Yet by building up the Southern Sung's strength, Hsiao-tsung succeeded in protecting the war-shaken regime he had inherited from his father. He also gave the regime a stronger political order, a robust economy, and defenses sufficiently solid to enable the dynasty to last another ninety years under increasingly difficult circumstances.

[161] *SS* 35, p. 692.

CHAPTER 10

THE REIGNS OF KUANG-TSUNG (1189–1194) AND NING-TSUNG (1194–1224)

Richard L. Davis

Southern Sung prosperity struck turbulent waters in the late twelfth century. During his twenty-six-year reign, Hsiao-tsung (r. 1162–89) was a conscientious and strong ruler, yet when his adopted father, the retired emperor Kao-tsung, died in 1187, Hsiao-tsung had a very difficult time coping with the loss. Although suspending court was normal under the circumstances, when Hsiao-tsung did not resume audiences for over a month, pressure on him from officials mounted. Hsiao-tsung returned, but reportedly was able to walk only with the aid of a cane, a sign of his physical and emotional frailty. Once the epitome of political activism, Hsiao-tsung now turned to the heir apparent to assist him in managing state affairs.[1]

The heir, Chao Tun (1147–1200), found himself cast in the role of auxiliary emperor. Chief ministers were instructed to consult Chao Tun every two days, and his presence was expected at court audiences. This arrangement troubled officials from the outset. Reader-in-waiting Yang Wan-li (1127–1206) took the arrangement to imply the existence of two rulers and warned of potential instability. Ignoring the warning, Hsiao-tsung spurned Chao Tun's own offer to take a diminished role at court.[2] Hsiao-tsung also insisted on performing to their fullest mourning rites for Kao-tsung. Most previous Sung emperors had accepted a less rigorous mourning regime, and officials proposed as much for Hsiao-tsung. The emperor would hear nothing of it, and ordered audiences to be held in the inner palace. Hsiao-tsung never seemed to appreciate the officials' dilemma of seeking to serve two political authorities without the

---

[1] On the last years of Hsiao-tsung, see chapter 9 of this volume. Also see Miyazaki Ichisada, "Hsiao-tsung," in *Sung biographies*, ed. Herbert Franke (Wiesbaden, 1976), pp. 400–1; Liu Li-yen (Lau Nap-yin), "Nan Sung cheng-chih ch'u-t'an: Kao-tsung yin-ying hsia ti Hsiao-tsung," in *Sung-shih yen-chiu chi* (Taipei, 1989) 19, pp. 203–56; see *chüan* 35–6 in T'o-t'o et al., eds., *Sung shih* [hereafter *SS*] (1345; Peking, 1977); Pi Yüan, *Hsü Tzu-chih t'ung-chien* [hereafter *HTC* (1958)] [*Te-yü-t'ang tsang-pan* 1801 ed.] (1792; Peking, 1958), *chüan* 151; *Sung-shih ch'üan-wen Hsü Tzu-chih t'ung-chien* (early 14th c.; Taipei, 1969), *chüan* 27–8.

[2] *HTC* (1958) 151, p. 4030.

certainty as to which authority was more important, the seated emperor or the already influential heir apparent.

In the late 1180s, the bureaucracy was headed by Chou Pi-ta (1126–1204) and Liu Cheng (1129–1206). Chou was born to a family from the north, but raised in Lu-ling, Chiang-nan West. The son of an erudite at the Imperial University, he earned his *chin-shih* degree in 1151 and the prestigious "erudite literatus" (*po-hsüeh hung-tz'u*) credentials six years later. Chou Pi-ta had served Hsiao-tsung in various capacities, including that of Han-lin academician, before becoming assistant councilor in 1180 and chief councilor of the right in 1187.[3] Hsiao-tsung appears to have held him in high esteem, as did his colleagues in the bureaucracy, for the sixty-one-year-old Chou Pi-ta stood as a successful official with sound scholarly credentials. Liu Cheng was of comparable stature and influence. A native of Ch'üan-chou, Fu-chien, he was descended from Liu Ts'ung-hsiao, an official who had made a name for himself two centuries earlier at the court of Sung T'ai-tsu, the dynasty's founder. Liu Cheng received his *chin-shih* in 1160, the last examination held under Kao-tsung.[4] In addition to his extensive service away from the capital, Liu Cheng accumulated metropolitan experience as master of remonstrance, vice-minister of war, minister of personnel, and assistant councilor. Like Chou Pi-ta, Liu Cheng commanded the respect of colleagues and the confidence of the throne. The two also shared a common sense of urgency in resolving the current political crisis.

In late 1188, Chou Pi-ta had spoken with Hsiao-tsung about abdication. The idea reportedly won the endorsement of Kao-tsung's widow, Dowager Empress Wu (1115–97), and it may have been under her influence that Hsiao-tsung signaled his approval to Chou Pi-ta.[5] In the interim, Hsiao-tsung elevated Chou Pi-ta to councilor of the left and Liu Cheng to councilor of the right. On 18 February 1189, less than a month after Chang-tsung had become emperor of Chin in the north, Chao Tun ascended the throne as the future Kuang-tsung (r. 1189–94). Hsiao-tsung, now retired, moved into his father's former residence, renamed the Ch'ung-hua Palace. There Hsiao-tsung secluded himself for the remaining five years of his life.

[3] On Chou Pi-ta, see Kinugawa Tsuyoshi, "Chou Pi-ta," in *Sung Biographies*, ed. Herbert Franke (Wiesbaden, 1976), vol. 2, pp. 675–7; *SS* 391, pp. 11965–72; Huang Tsung-hsi et al., *Sung Yüan hsüeh-an* (1838; Taipei, 1973) 35, p. 702; Chou Pi-ta, *Chou I-kuo Wen-chung kung chi nien-p'u* (n.p., 1848), p. 26a; Lou Yüeh [Yao], *Kung-k'uei chi* [*Ssu-pu ts'ung-k'an ch'u-pien* 1929 ed.] (c. early 13th c.; Taipei, 1979) 93, pp. 19b–32a; 94, pp. 1a–24b; Fu Tseng-hsiang, comp., *Sung-tai Shu-wen chi-ts'un* (1943; Taipei, 1974) 75, pp. 14a–27b.

[4] On Liu Cheng, see Conrad Schirokauer, "Liu Cheng," in *Sung biographies*, ed. Herbert Franke (Wiesbaden, 1976), pp. 624–8; *SS* 391, pp. 11972–7; Huang et al., *Sung Yüan hsüeh-an* 97, pp. 1816–17.

[5] Chou, *Chou I-kuo Wen-chung kung chi nien-p'u*, p. 26a; *SS* 243, pp. 9646–8; *HTC* (1958) 151, p. 4051; *Sung-shih ch'üan-wen Hsü Tzu-chih t'ung-chien* 27, pp. 51a–b.

THE REIGN OF KUANG-TSUNG (1189–1194)

A court in turmoil

Chao Tun was the third but only surviving son of Hsiao-tsung and his first wife, Empress Kuo2 (1126–56), who had died when he was a child of nine. Hsiao-tsung is said to have loved the empress deeply, which may explain his attention to the child despite the boy's secondary position in the line of succession.[6] Hsiao-tsung's eldest son and original heir apparent had died in 1167, but Hsiao-tsung did not rush to name a replacement. Perhaps he feared that too early a selection might leave the candidate arrogant and complacent; more likely, his hesitancy reflected doubts about Chao K'ai2 (1146–80), his second son and next in line of succession. Only under mounting bureaucratic pressure did Hsiao-tsung overcome these concerns, and bypass Chao K'ai2 to designate the reputedly more precocious Chao Tun as heir in 1171. Approaching twenty-four years of age at the time, Chao Tun would be forty-one before taking the throne in 1189.

Prior to the accession, many had considered Chao Tun ideal as a prospective ruler. Hsiao-tsung regarded him as most "exquisite" in character and took a personal interest in his education. The Confucian luminary Chu Hsi (1130–1200), attributed to Chao Tun the gifts of intelligence and wisdom, the virtues of filial devotion and quiet reverence, the temperament of extensive humaneness and universal love, and the majesty of the supernaturally martial without violence. Palace lecturer P'eng Kuei-nien (1142–1206) characterized him as pure and dedicated.[7] When Kuang-tsung became emperor, he initially discharged his responsibilities with the same conscientiousness as his predecessor. He held regular audiences and seriously weighed ministerial advice. But beneath the facade of composure lay an intensely distressed personality, and it did not take long for his troubles to surface and affect the functioning of the court.

Kuang-tsung, like most imperial sons, had lived secluded within the palace. The ideal in previous dynasties had been to appoint imperial sons to some regional post while they were in their teens, which provided them with administrative experience and removed the young men from the secure walls of the

---

[6] SS 36, pp. 693–4; 243, pp. 8650–1; 246, pp. 8732–4. For detailed overviews of the reign, see *Liang-ch'ao kang-mu pei-yao* [*Ssu-k'u ch'üan-shu, Wen-yüan ko* 1779 ed.] (1228–33; Taipei, 1970), *chüan* 1–3; Liu Shih-chü, *Hsü Sung chung-hsing pien-nien tzu-chih t'ung-chien* [1522–66 ed.] (13th–14th c.; Shanghai, 1927), *chüan* 11.

[7] SS 36, p. 694; Chu Hsi, *Hui-an hsien-sheng Chu Wen kung wen-chi* [Ming *Chia-ching* 1522–66 ed.; *Ssu-pu ts'ung-k'an ch'u-pien* 1929 ed.] (1245; Taipei, 1979) 12, p. 1a; P'eng Kuei-nien, *Chih-t'ang chi* [*Ssu-k'u ch'üan-shu, Wen-yüan ko* 1779 ed.] (12th c.; Taipei, 1975) 4, p. 12a.

palace, thereby freeing them from the grip of powerful palace personalities and exposing them to life outside the capital. With the exception of the first three emperors, this opportunity was never afforded to Sung emperors. In the case of Chao Tun, his administrative experience was confined to the capital as nominal vice-prefect and then prefect of Lin-an.[8] His father once contemplated giving him a regional appointment farther away from court, but for unnamed reasons did not order it. Throughout his life, Chao Tun remained deeply dependent on the old palace friends among whom he had grown up.

These personalities around him intensified his insecurity. His father was a stern, intimidating character with strong opinions and an intolerant streak, and during his adolescence Chao Tun lacked a maternal figure. After his mother, Empress Kuo2, died when he was nine, his father delayed taking a second wife until Chao Tun was sixteen. There is no mention of Chao Tun having had close ties to his paternal grandfather, the retired Kao-tsung, either, despite the physical proximity of their palaces. The young prince was under the constant influence of palace attendants and, beginning in his teens, his wife.

The future Empress Li2 (1145–1200) was the daughter of Li Tao, an accomplished military figure of the early Southern Sung.[9] Betrothed to Chao Tun during the last years of Kao-tsung's reign, when the two were still teenagers, she gave birth in 1168 to his second son and heir, Prince Chia. By then, Chao Tun was already in his twenty-second year. Kao-tsung and Empress Wu were probably responsible for the match, but they lived to regret it. Even as a princess Lady Li2 proved politically insensitive and selfishly indulgent, insufferably arrogant and violently jealous. Hsiao-tsung was at one point so piqued by her that he threatened her with deposition. This would have been an extreme act, especially for a princess who had already given birth to a male heir. Hsiao-tsung nevertheless approved her installation as empress in 1189, no doubt reluctantly. Yet Hsiao-tsung's threat of deposition had incurred the undying enmity of his daughter-in-law, who proceeded to poison the relationship between father and son. Meanwhile, she drove her weak husband to virtual insanity.

Kuang-tsung was never an altogether healthy man. Even before his accession, he received medication on a regular basis. The exact nature of his infirmity is uncertain; historical records simply allude to some malady of the heart. Conceivably, this may have been a physical disorder. Contemporary documents clearly imply the problem was largely a reaction to a domineering wife. There are numerous incidents of her overbearing and ruthless personality. Toward the

---

[8] *SS* 36, pp. 693–4; Chu, *Hui-an hsien-sheng* (1979) 12, p. 1a.

[9] *SS* 36, p. 706; 243, pp. 8653–5; 391, p. 11974; 398, p. 12114; *HTC* (1958) 151, p. 4053; 152, p. 4079; 152, p. 4090.

close of 1191, Kuang-tsung was reportedly washing his hands in the palace and noticed the delicate hands of a palace lady. He commented, casually, on their attractiveness. Presently, while sitting down to a meal he opened a container of food and found the two hands inside, a reminder from a jealous wife that she would tolerate no infidelity. Prior to this, Kuang-tsung had coped with his overbearing wife through the company of consorts. Kao-tsung had reportedly been concerned about the youth's noticeable lack of sexual diversion. Consort Huang, a gift to Kuang-tsung from his grandfather, had met a sudden death. The emperor's favor was apparently her undoing.[10] It was alleged to have been the handiwork of Empress Li2, and the death of this favorite forced Kuang-tsung to avoid other women. After 1191, his mental condition took a turn for the worse and he withdrew within the palace. There he took to drinking heavily, adding to his many other problems. He rarely held court and refused to undertake all but a few imperial responsibilities.[11]

Kuang-tsung's emotional isolation and domestic unhappiness were aggravated by growing tension between him and his retired father. In part, this stemmed from the influence of Empress Li2. Her embitterment had several apparent sources. First, there were Hsiao-tsung's earlier threats to divest her of her rank as princess. Second, even after his son Kuang-tsung's accession, Hsiao-tsung refused to endorse the nomination of Empress Li2's son, Prince Chia (Chao K'uo, r. as Ning-tsung 1194–1224), as his heir apparent. This refusal could be interpreted as an act of spite, and perhaps even as a veiled threat to deny the prince his inheritance. Finally, when Kuang-tsung became bedridden in 1191, his father and stepmother paid him a courtesy call. Attendants blamed Empress Li2 for Kuang-tsung's emotional problems, and at hearing this, Hsiao-tsung harshly reprimanded her.[12] In doing this, Hsiao-tsung compounded private threats with public insults. To protect the position of the vulnerable Prince Chia, and also to avenge such indignities, Empress Li2 provoked tension between the two emperors.

Before the ascendency of his wife, Kuang-tsung as a prince had been subject to the influence of palace eunuchs and attendants. Hsiao-tsung was himself known to favor certain dutiful attendants, but Hsiao-tsung's strength of character precluded dominance by any one favorite. Not so for Kuang-tsung, who was often blindly loyal and recklessly indulgent to palace friends. Eunuch Ch'en Yüan, for example, was favored by Kao-tsung and Hsiao-tsung for

[10] SS 36, p. 701; HTC (1958) 152, p. 4079.

[11] On the emperor's problem, see Conrad Schirokauer, "Neo-Confucians under attack: The condemnation of wei-hsüeh," in Crisis and prosperity in Sung China, ed. John W. Haeger (Tucson, Ariz.,1975), pp. 163–98, especially p. 175; P'eng, Chih-t'ang chi 1, p. 20a; SS 393, p. 12008; HTC (1958) 151, p. 4053.

[12] Fu, Sung-tai Shu-wen chi-ts'un (1974) 71, p. 1b; HTC (1958) 152, p. 4079.

many years. Yet, when remonstrance official Chao Ju-yü (1140–96) exposed the eunuch's illicit intrusion into military affairs, Hsiao-tsung banished Ch'en Yüan to the far south.[13] Kuang-tsung, apparently on close personal terms with Ch'en Yüan since boyhood, brooded over the decision and upon taking the throne, ordered the eunuch's return. Once back in Lin-an, Ch'en Yüan came to be suspected of intentionally planting the seeds of distrust between the two emperors as revenge for Hsiao-tsung's earlier treatment of him. Although the veracity of the suspicion cannot be determined, many court officials believed it to be true, and this prompted their demands for the eunuch's dismissal. Kuang-tsung chose instead to promote him. Drafting secretary Ch'en Fu-liang (1137–1203), a representative of bureaucratic opinion, refused to compose the promotion edict. His protest had no effect. Ch'en Yüan remained a palace fixture for the rest of Kuang-tsung's reign.

Dominated, voluntarily or involuntarily, by a vengeful Ch'en Yüan and by Empress Li2, Kuang-tsung's relationship with his father deteriorated rapidly. Early in his reign, Kuang-tsung reduced audience visits to Hsiao-tsung's Ch'ung-hua Palace from six per month to four and then to one. Within a year, formal audiences were downgraded to official visits, and their frequency diminished. After two years, visits became so infrequent and tensions so apparent that officials began to denounce inner court influence. In spring 1191, the capital was hit by strong winds, followed immediately by snow, then sunlight, and more snow. To officials, such irregularities signaled Heaven's angry response to an imbalance on the earth, with the implication of imperial misconduct. Officials such as Assistant in the Palace Library Huang Shang (1146–94), Investigating Censor Lin Ta-chung (1131–1208), and Imperial Diarist P'eng Kuei-nien were but a few of the critics who related changes in weather to the ascendancy of *yin* over *yang*.[14] *Yin*, representing petty men and women, was usurping the dominant position of *yang*, the emperor. If *yang* was not restored to its normal supremacy, if the emperor did not assert control over the palace, the outcome, it was believed, could be disastrous. With such warnings came remonstrances that Kuang-tsung curtail his indulgence in feasts and alcohol. But nothing changed. The controversial eunuch Ch'en Yüan remained. Empress Li2's appetite for self-indulgence grew. Toward the close of 1192, the empress arranged for three recent generations of her own ancestors to be enfeoffed as princes, and, on the occasion of her visiting her family's elaborate ancestral temple, special imperial favors were extended to 26 of her relatives,

---

[13] On Ch'en Yüan, see *SS* 393, p. 11996; 469, p. 13672; *HTC* (1958) 151, p. 4055; 152, pp. 4089–90; 153, p. 4097; P'eng, *Chih-t'ang chi* 4, p. 18a.

[14] *SS* 393, p. 12013; *HTC* (1958) 152, pp. 4071–2; P'eng, *Chih-t'ang chi* 1, pp. 7a–21a; Lou, *Kung-k'uei chi* (1979) 99, p. 7b.

and official rank was conferred on another 172. This extravagance of imperial favor infuriated the bureaucracy. Vice-Minister of Rites Ni Ssu (1147–1220) would later portray Empress Li2 as a threat to Sung stability comparable to Empress Lü of the Han dynasty and Empress Wu Tse-t'ien of the T'ang, the most vilified women in Chinese history.[15]

BUREAUCRATIC LEADERSHIP

During the final years of Kuang-tsung's brief reign, the chief councilor, Liu Cheng, began to be eclipsed by two other men, initially collaborators but later rivals. The first of these, Han T'o-chou (1152–1207), while identified as a native of Hsiang-chou2, near K'ai-feng, was born and raised in the south.[16] His great grandfather Han Ch'i (1008–75) had served nobly as chief councilor under both Jen-tsung and Ying-tsung. His father, Han Ch'eng, had an undistinguished political career but an enviable set of marriage relations. Himself a maternal grandson of Shen-tsung, Han Ch'eng was married to the younger sister of the influential Dowager Empress Wu, wife of Kao-tsung. Han T'o-chou was married to a niece of the same empress, a union cut short by the woman's premature death, but one that served its purpose nonetheless as a confirmation of imperial favor.[17] Further cementing the ties of Han T'o-chou's family to the palace was the betrothal of the daughter of Han T'o-chou's nephew to Chao K'uo, heir to Kuang-tsung's throne, a marriage arranged by Dowager Empress Wu. In this way, men of the Han clan had been linked by marriage with the royal family for more than a century, yet at no time did those links yield as much political power as during the late twelfth century.

Dowager Empress Wu, the lifelong spouse of Kao-tsung, wielded considerable power in her own discreet way even after her husband's abdication. It was out of deference to her that Hsiao-tsung had appointed her two brothers, Wu I (1124–71) and Wu Kai (1125–66), to high-level bureaucratic posts and had conferred on them various honorific titles, culminating in their enfeoffment as princes. Wu I's son and nephew of the empress, Wu Chü, had similarly received numerous coveted posts under Hsiao-tsung and Kuang-tsung, among them prefectural vice-administrator of Lin-an and

---

[15] SS 243, p. 8654; 398, p. 12114; HTC (1958) 152, p. 4090.

[16] On Han T'o-chou, see Herbert Franke, "Han T'o-chou," in Sung biographies, ed. Herbert Franke (Wiesbaden, 1976), pp. 376–84; Richard L. Davis, Court and family in Sung China, 960–1279: Bureaucratic success and kinship fortunes for the Shih of Ming-chou (Durham, N.C., 1986), pp. 84–92; SS 474, pp. 13771–8; Ch'en Teng-yüan, "Han P'ing-yüan p'ing," Chin-ling hsüeh-pao 4 No. 1 (1934), pp. 89–149; Chiba Hiroshi, "Kan Takuchū – Sōdai kanshinden sono ni," in Yamazaki sensei taikan kinen Tōyō shigaku ronsō, ed. Yamazaki Sensei Taikan Kinenkai (Tokyo, 1967), pp. 279–89.

[17] Liang-ch'ao kang-mu pei-yao 10, p. 28b.

prefect of Ming-chou. For a non–degree holder, these were significant achievements.[18] The Empress Wu's extraordinary network of family contacts, combined with her status as grand dowager empress since her husband's death, virtually ensured that court officials would turn to her during the major crisis for the imperial family when Kuang-tsung became emotionally debilitated. This crisis also placed her nephew Han T'o-chou in a highly opportune position.

Despite a prestigious family background and impressive array of palace contacts, Han T'o-chou held no great promise as a civil servant. For him, no less than for his father, the lack of examination credentials meant that access to the bureaucracy came through the hereditary privilege accorded to kinsmen of great officials or from favor derived through marriage ties with palace women. Except for brief stints as regional sheriff and keeper of the imperial insignia and seals, Han T'o-chou's own bureaucratic experience was confined to the Office of Audience Ceremonies (*Ko-men ssu*), where under Hsiao-tsung he had served as audience usher, attendant, and commandant. He had also served twice as an emissary to the Chin, first in 1189, shortly after Kuang-tsung took the throne, and again in 1195, following Ning-tsung's accession.[19]

It was common practice in Southern Sung times to send two chief envoys, one a ranking civilian official and another representing the military. Ceremony officials such as Han T'o-chou were responsible for the access through the doors of the palace and for announcing visitors; they had security duties and were thus attached to the military bureaucracy, although in function they lay somewhere between the civilian and military services, with neither the literary skills of credentialed scholars nor the martial skills of ordinary guardsmen.[20]

The Office of Audience Ceremonies also included men such as Wu Chieh (1093–1139), brother of Szechwan military magnate Wu Lin, who became audience attendant in recognition of his distinguished military record, and Chiang T'e-li, Han T'o-chou's predecessor as audience commandant, who had received the assignment by recommendation after successfully suppressing pirates off the coast.[21] These assignments were often a reward for martial valor, yet the ceremonies office also contained many individuals with no record of military service. Often the assignment was a special act of imperial favor. Wang Pien (d. 1184), for example, had become audience commandant under Hsiao-tsung as reward for negotiating a favorable treaty with the Jurchen. A doctor of Kuang-tsung had been assigned to the office in 1190 due to his effective

---

[18] *SS* 465, pp. 13591–2.
[19] T'o-t'o, *Chin shih* (1344; Peking, 1975) 61, p. 1450; 62, p. 1464.
[20] Lou, *Kung-k'uei chi* (1979) 29, p. 9a; 30, p. 12a.
[21] *SS* 366, p. 11414; 470, p. 13695.

medical treatment.[22] Many others made their way to the office through ties with influential palace women, most often empresses. The appointment of Chang Yüeh (d. 1180) had stemmed from his marriage to Dowager Empress Wu's younger sister. Yang Tz'u-shan (1139–1219), brother of Ning-tsung's empress, had become commandant following the installation of his sister as imperial concubine; subsequently, his son inherited the same post. Han Ch'eng, son of Emperor Shen-tsung's daughter, and Han T'o-chou, closely related to two different empresses, similarly owed their appointments to prominent women.[23] There are so many cases of audience officials being linked to palace women that the office may well have been dominated by the maternal side of the ruling family, not professional military men. A comment by Chou Pi-ta in 1189 is quite revealing in this regard. When approached by Chiang T'e-li, the quasi-military figure with no known blood or marriage ties to palace consorts, for information about Hsiao-tsung's forthcoming abdication, Chou Pi-ta responded, "This is not something the maternal side should dare to learn."[24] The statement suggests that Chiang T'e-li, merely by serving in the Office of Audience Ceremonies, was automatically identified with the interests and power of palace women. The reasons for entrusting consort relatives with control over palace doors are not entirely clear, although one could speculate that a brother would guard his sister differently than a stranger might, but the preference for relatives, as a matter of policy, is undeniable. It was precisely this policy that facilitated the rise of Han T'o-chou.

Another emerging figure of the Liu Cheng era who would later eclipse Han T'o-chou was the imperial clansman Chao Ju-yü. A descendant seven generations removed from Emperor T'ai-tsung's eldest son Chao Yüan-tso, he was born and raised in Jao-chou, Chiang-nan East.[25] Like many distant members of the dynasty's massive imperial clan, and especially those who had migrated south in the chaos of the Jurchen takeover, Chao Ju-yü was no stranger to adversity. His father and grandfather had both held posts of local, but not national, importance.[26] This humble condition made him a man of simple needs, who was devoted to his family. Chao Ju-yü was filial to a fault. At the death of his mother, contemporaries report, he wept so bitterly as to cough blood and later became emaciated by mourning. The account may be somewhat exaggerated, but it illustrates a widespread perception of

[22] SS 470, pp. 13693–4; HTC (1958) 152, pp. 4065–6.

[23] SS 392, p. 11982; 465, pp. 13595–6; 474, p. 13771.

[24] HTC (1958) 151, pp. 4050–1.

[25] On Chao Ju-yü, see Herbert Franke, "Chao Ju-yü," in Sung biographies, ed. Herbert Franke (Wiesbaden, 1976), pp. 59–63; SS 392, pp. 11981–90; Fu, Sung-tai Shu-wen chi-ts'un (1974) 71, pp. 1a–15b.

[26] John W. Chaffee, Branches of heaven: A history of the imperial clan of Sung China (Cambridge, Mass., 1999), p. 189.

Chao Ju-yü as an exemplar of Confucian virtue. He was no less committed to classical studies. Passing civil service qualifying examinations with distinction, he had placed first in the *chin-shih* examination of 1165. Court policy denied this honor to imperial clansmen, however, and he was demoted to second place. A poet in his own right, his literary interests included more than poetry. He collected books on a wide range of topics, boasting a personal library of fifty thousand *chüan*.

Chao Ju-yü was an imposing presence at the court of Hsiao-tsung. Colleagues in the Palace Library knew him as a man of exceptional integrity who refused to flatter the influential merely to advance his own career. He confirmed this in 1171 when the audience commandant Chang Yüeh was named notary official at the Bureau of Military Affairs. Advancement from the disesteemed Ceremonies Office to the second highest rung of the military bureaucracy was highly irregular. To Chao Ju-yü and many others, Chang Yüeh was undeserving. Fully aware of Chang Yüeh's close relationship with the emperor and cognizant of Chang's potential value as a political ally, Chao Ju-yü nevertheless insulted him by refusing to offer traditional courtesies. Later, Chao Ju-yü even joined others in the campaign against Chang Yüeh that culminated in Chang's dismissal. Another audience official denounced by Chao Ju-yü was Wang Pien. As vice-minister of personnel, Chao charged Wang Pien with exploiting political divisions to enhance his own standing. No less critical of Hsiao-tsung's appointment of the eunuch Ch'en Yüan to a high-level military post, Chao warned of the danger of entrusting eunuchs with such power.[27] More than any other prominent official of the late twelfth century, Chao Ju-yü persistently denounced the special privileges and influence of palace eunuchs and audience officials – always aware that his candor might well offend their patron, the emperor. Yet the risks to Chao's career never dampened his commitment to high bureaucratic standards.

Chao Ju-yü held regional posts during Hsiao-tsung's last decade in power in the 1180s, and also served in the capital as lecturer-in-waiting and chief advisor to the heir apparent, the future Kuang-tsung. These posts gave him considerable exposure to Chao Tun, who in 1191 summoned him from Fu-chou to head the Ministry of Personnel. In light of Chao Ju-yü's well-established reputation as a critic of the inner court, the appointment must have easily won the endorsement of, if it was not originally initiated by, Chief Councilor Liu Cheng. In office, Chao Ju-yü denounced petty men in high places, and challenged the emperor's personal conduct. At the request of colleagues, he discussed privately with Kuang-tsung the crisis created by the estrangement of

---

[27] On these incidents, see *SS* 392, p. 11982; 469, p. 13672; 470, p. 13692, p. 13694; *HTC* (1958) 142, pp. 3795–6; 148, pp. 3942, 3955–6; Fu, *Sung-tai Shu-wen chi-ts'un* (1974) 71, p. 9a.

the two palaces. As a member of the imperial clan, his intercession carried special weight and contributed to temporarily improved relations between father
and son.[28] Kuang-tsung's visits to his father in early 1193 are attributed chiefly
to Chao Ju-yü's mediation. The ultimate failure of that effort at reconciliation
was a personal setback for Chao Ju-yü.

Adding to the intensity of the court crisis during the 1190s was the untimely
death of a notary official at the Bureau of Military Affairs, Hu Chin-ch'en (d.
1193). Hu was a close confidant of Liu Cheng, and his death coincided with
Liu's 140-day "political strike," which created a serious leadership vacuum.[29]
The secondary chief councilor at the time, Ko Pi, proved timid and was virtually paralyzed by the court tensions. Soon after Liu Cheng returned, Ko's
ten-month tenure came to an end.[30] In the interim, Chao Ju-yü had risen to
second spot at the Bureau of Military Affairs, a position from which he would
ultimately overshadow an increasingly demoralized Liu Cheng.

ROYALTY AT ODDS

Officials were ineffective at swaying the emperor, a situation that may have
been exacerbated by Kuang-tsung's viewing them as annoying extensions of
his retired father's influence. After all, Chou Pi-ta and Liu Cheng had each been
named councilors under Hsiao-tsung. Only a few months into Kuang-tsung's
reign Chou Pi-ta fell victim to an indictment by Ho Tan, a remonstrance officer,
who allegedly acted against Chou Pi-ta out of personal spite. Given that Ho
Tan had been sponsored for office by Liu Cheng, the possibility of collusion is
great. Chou Pi-ta did not resist, having been repeatedly frustrated by the dual
demands of the palace and the bureaucracy.[31] Chou's departure enabled Liu
Cheng to emerge as sole councilor and chief decision maker, a role he retained
for much of Kuang-tsung's reign. Like Chou Pi-ta, Liu Cheng had once served
as an advisor to the prince before his accession. This gave Liu Cheng personal
access to the emperor, but the two were hardly close. Liu Cheng had spent
much of the 1180s, the decade directly preceding Kuang-tsung's accession,
away from the capital. Liu Cheng's retention of the chief councilorship after
the departure of Chou Pi-ta reflects not so much the emperor's special favor
as his reservations about alternative candidates. This ambivalence would not
augur well for the Liu Cheng administration.

[28] *SS* 392, p. 11983; *HTC* (1958) 152, pp. 4089–90.
[29] *HTC* (1958) 153, p. 4096; *SS* 391, p. 11978.
[30] *SS* 385, pp. 11827–9.
[31] *SS* 391, p. 11971; 394, p. 12025; Fu, *Sung-tai Shu-wen chi-ts'un* (1974) 75, p. 25b.

Chief Councilor Liu Cheng's difficulties are best illustrated by Liu's inability to resolve two troubling political crises: the timely nomination of Prince Chia as heir apparent, and the mending of relations between the two imperial palaces. Officials had good reason to press for the speedy designation of an heir. The education of the heir apparent was very important, and an early appointment gave tutors valuable time to mold the future emperor's personality and inculcate him with Confucian attitudes toward governance and personal conduct. Early appointment of the heir apparent also enabled officials to supervise the transfer of power with minimal input from palace eunuchs and consorts, avoiding the aggressive political power plays that accompanied an uncertain succession. From the outset of his councilorship, Liu Cheng pressed for Prince Chia's installation as heir. As the emperor's eldest surviving son and the child of his primary wife, Prince Chia held a very strong claim to the succession. Postponement of his appointment seemed senseless. Empress Li2 also lobbied on her son's behalf. But it was Hsiao-tsung, not Kuang-tsung, who opposed the appointment. The former emperor was apparently on good terms with his grandson, and historical documents do not allude to an alternative heir backed by Hsiao-tsung. There is no indication that Hsiao-tsung genuinely intended to deny Prince Chia this privilege. Rather, Hsiao-tsung probably held out merely to frustrate his ill-tempered daughter-in-law, by retaining some leverage to use against her. In any case, Kuang-tsung did not force the issue, which meant that Liu Cheng could not achieve this major objective of training an heir apparent during Hsiao-tsung's lifetime.

Liu Cheng faced an even greater challenge in trying to convince Kuang-tsung to make amends with his father. Beginning in 1193 and continuing through the next year, Liu Cheng and many other officials repeatedly requested, indeed begged, Kuang-tsung to visit the Ch'ung-hua Palace, only a few buildings away. But Kuang-tsung paid official visits only four times in 1193, once in the company of his empress. Three of the four visits occurred in the first three months of the year, when the influence of court officials enjoyed a brief rally. In the fall, when the emperor seemed to be capitulating to official prodding, Empress Li2 interceded and had the visit canceled. A visit planned a month later was similarly canceled, with Kuang-tsung professing illness. Liu Cheng, his patience stretched to the limit and his resignation having been refused, abruptly fled the capital in protest. He would stay away a hundred and forty days, returning only after he had obtained Kuang-tsung's promise to visit Hsiao-tsung, which occurred before year's end, followed by another visit on the first day of the 1194 lunar new year. This would be their last meeting. In midspring, Hsiao-tsung fell ill, and Liu Cheng, joined by countless others, pleaded for a visit of compassion. Imperial Diarist P'eng Kuei-nien, having recently memorialized the throne on three separate occasions, appeared at court. He hit his forehead against the floor while performing an unending series of kowtows, until his blood covered the tiles. He won the emperor's attention, but no change of heart.[32] To court observers, Kuang-tsung's persistent refusal to visit his dying father showed a total disregard for filial piety, which reflected poorly upon him as a ruler. The emperor's failure to resolve this affair eroded confidence in Liu Cheng's authority and statesmanship.

The crisis peaked in June 1194, as Hsiao-tsung's condition deteriorated and his death approached. Censors intensified their attacks on petty men who tried to provoke rifts between the two palaces. Liu Cheng, in the company of other high officials, assembled at the palace to plead with Kuang-tsung. Attendants shut the door in their faces as they wept outside. Prince Chia, who was in regular contact with his dying grandfather throughout this difficult time, is reported similarly to have shed tears as he tried, in vain, to reunite his family. The rift between the two emperors had irreparably widened, seemingly the result of Kuang-tsung's sensitivity to his father's meddling and exacerbated by court officials, eunuchs, and family members who exploited the rift for personal gain. When death came to him on 28 June 1194, Hsiao-tsung had not seen his son for six months. Worse yet, Kuang-tsung adamantly refused to perform the funeral rites for his father. Prince Chia and his great grandmother, Dowager Empress Wu, were obliged to preside over the wake in Kuang-tsung's place.[33]

Even before the death of Hsiao-tsung, Liu Cheng's success as councilor was undermined by precisely the influential palace personalities he was committed to uprooting. Prominent among these was Chiang T'e-li, a non–degree holder whose entry into the civil service had come through hereditary privilege (*yin2*).[34] Chao Ju-yü, who had lauded Chiang T'e-li's suppression of pirates along coastal Fu-chien, recommended his promotion to the capital. Once there, Chiang T'e-li had served Hsiao-tsung as audience attendant and herald of the heir apparent's palace. Hsiao-tsung even employed him in 1187 as Sung emissary to the Chin court. The posts themselves carried only modest prestige, but Chiang T'e-li had exploited these offices to establish powerful political connections. One such connection included Hsiao-tsung's heir apparent, and soon after his accession in 1189 Kuang-tsung promoted Chiang to commandant of the Office of Audience Ceremonies.

[32] *SS* 393, p. 11997; *HTC* (1958) 153, p. 4105. Also see *SS* 393, pp. 1195–6; Lou, *Kung-k'uei chi* (1979) 96, pp. 1a–14b.

[33] See Chaffee, *Branches of heaven*, p. 192, for a description of the funeral. *HTC* (1958) 153, p. 4108.

[34] Additional information is available in *SS* 470, pp. 13695–6; T'o-t'o, *Chin shih* 61, p. 1447; *HTC* (1958) 151, pp. 4050–1; 151, p. 4055; 153, pp. 4096–7; 153, p. 4101; 156, p. 4190.

Chiang T'e-li, however, was not so favored among the high officials. Chou Pi-ta complained of his attempted interference in the abdication of 1189, a serious breach of etiquette for a petty palace attendant. Liu Cheng criticized Chiang's excessive influence over Kuang-tsung. Only days after Chou Pi-ta resigned, an increasingly confident Liu Cheng demanded the dismissal of Chiang T'e-li, whom he charged with coveting political power and accepting bribes. Kuang-tsung reluctantly consented but insisted on a respectable reassignment for Chiang T'e-li to a post nearby and a provision of traveling money for him totaling two thousand strings of cash. In the summer of 1193 the emperor reversed his decision and ordered Chiang T'e-li's recall. In protest against this reversal, and against Kuang-tsung's stubborn refusal to visit his father, Liu Cheng staged his dramatic 140-day absence from the capital. Kuang-tsung acquiesced by ordering a second reassignment for Chiang T'e-li. This was only a modest victory for the chief councilor. Under crisis conditions, he could wring out of Kuang-tsung a few face-saving concessions, but could never thwart in any lasting way the excessive privileges that Kuang-tsung granted palace favorites. Chiang T'e-li subsequently received further promotions.

Liu Cheng led an unrelenting, often solitary, struggle against the emperor's granting unwarranted appointments in the palace and his disregard for imperial obligations, and this difficult task earned Liu the sympathy of some. However, these two issues of unwarranted appointments and dereliction of imperial duty became the foci of an expanding polarization at court, brought about by a campaign by moralistic statesmen to curtail the ascendancy of the inner court over the outer court, and of palace favorites over civil officials. The intensity of the conflict resulted largely from the dramatic rise in stature of the intellectual movement called "Learning of the Way" (*Tao-hsüeh*). Under Kuang-tsung, a growing number of its adherents, and their sympathizers came to hold high offices, from which they influenced court politics in Lin-an as never before.

Leading the late-twelfth-century ascent of *Tao-hsüeh* was Chu Hsi, a native of Kiangsi. His bureaucratic record may have been unimpressive and his political exposure limited, but his scholarship and teaching earned him an unmatched reputation. His fame was so widespread that a Sung emissary on an official visit to Chin in 1193, in token deference, had been asked about the health of Master Chu.[35] Chou Pi-ta held Chu Hsi in particularly high esteem and had sought his appointment to a metropolitan post in 1188. Bureaucratic opposition to

---

[35] *HTC* (1958) 153, p. 4103. Also see Conrad Schirokauer, "Chu Hsi's political career: A study in ambivalence," in *Confucian personalities*, ed. Arthur F. Wright and Denis C. Twitchett (Stanford, Calif., 1962), pp. 162–88; Brian E. McKnight, "Chu Hsi and his world," in *Chu Hsi and Neo-Confucianism*, ed. Wing-tsit Chan (Honolulu, 1986), pp. 408–36; Hoyt C. Tillman, *Confucian discourse and Chu Hsi's ascendancy* (Honolulu, 1992), pp. 133 and throughout.

the appointment had forced a retreat, and Liu Cheng chose not to press the issue, but he demonstrated his goodwill toward the *Tao-hsüeh* movement by appointing to high office individuals who, if not personally identified with the movement, at least were sympathetic toward it. These included, to name but a few of the more prominent members, P'eng Kuei-nien, who rose from executive aide at the Directorate of Education to imperial diarist; Lou Yüeh (1137–1213), who was advanced from vice-director of education to drafter in the Secretariat; Ch'en Fu-liang (1137–1203), the judicial commissioner of Che-hsi, who joined the Secretariat in a similar capacity; Yeh Shih (1150–1223), a Palace Library executive who moved on to the Ministry of Personnel; and Chao Ju-yü, the former prefect of Fu-chou who became minister of personnel and eventually chief councilor.[36] Through such men, the *Tao-hsüeh* movement developed an influential presence at court. Liu Cheng facilitated the movement's political prominence, and also came under its influence.

Despite the growing stature of Chu Hsi and the generous patronage of Liu Cheng, the *Tao-hsüeh* movement with its stress on personal conduct held unique appeal in the early 1190s due to the combustible political climate. The emperor's excessive drinking, emotional frailty, disregard for filial devotion, and irresponsibility toward his imperial duties, compounded by his indulgence of a brutish spouse and shameless palace attendants, all contributed to the politicization of personal conduct, especially imperial conduct, at the court and among intellectual elites. Within this milieu Liu Cheng struck an alliance with the *Tao-hsüeh* proponents and their sympathizers against the emperor and his favorites. Liu Cheng does not seem to have been intentionally promoting factionalism, for the court critics that he allied himself with represented a community whose boundaries were never clearly defined and whose objectives, apart from enlightening the throne, were otherwise ambiguous. Liu Cheng brought together concerned scholars of varied intellectual pedigrees to rally around a common cause in the hopes of bringing official and moral pressure to bear upon a recalcitrant ruler.

As Hsiao-tsung's health deteriorated in early 1194, over a hundred officials threatened to resign en masse unless the emperor met his filial obligations. Liu Cheng and Chao Ju-yü applied additional pressure by abruptly leaving the capital. They were soon summoned to return. Yet the catalyst for decisive action came on the ninth day of the sixth month with the death of Hsiao-tsung. Previously, officials had hoped that Kuang-tsung would somehow overcome the evil influences surrounding him and regain his senses. His shockingly unfilial response to his father's death proved that this hope was in vain. Court

---

[36] On the intellectual background of Chou Pi-ta and Liu Cheng, see Huang et al., *Sung Yüan hsüeh-an* 35, p. 702; 97, pp. 1816–17.

officials felt that Kuang-tsung had gone completely insane and was unfit to govern. They began to entertain seriously the need for Kuang-tsung's abdication. Both Liu Cheng and Chao Ju-yü, to varying degrees, supported the move, as did a growing number of their colleagues.[37]

Abdication in this instance, compared to Hsiao-tsung's abdication in 1188–9, was far more complex. Most important, this time there was no heir apparent. Chao K'uo had yet to be installed. Hsiao-tsung's death in the summer of 1194 had removed the only serious obstacle to Chao K'uo's nomination and freed high officials to act independently. But they were in no position to do so on their own authority. The palace had to be involved, and Kuang-tsung's instability forced them to involve the leading palace women. Dowager Empress Wu was reportedly reluctant to become involved in so sensitive an affair, especially when other powerful palace women, such as Empress Hsieh, Kao-tsung's stepmother, might be drawn into a bitter conflict over the issue. Only after lengthy exchanges and much prodding from Liu Cheng and Chao Ju-yü did she agree.[38] But a serious rift had developed between the two leading bureaucrats. The cautious Liu Cheng would have been satisfied with simply elevating Chao K'uo to heir apparent, for Liu's immediate concern lay in removing uncertainty about the succession. The less patient and more pessimistic Chao Ju-yü insisted that Chao K'uo be named heir *and* appointed emperor in a single stroke; Chao had no delusions about Kuang-tsung's prospects for recovery.

No official, in advancing a prince to the throne, needed to act with greater circumspection than Chao Ju-yü. Denying imperial clansmen any significant role in matters of succession was a hallowed Sung tradition, which sought to avoid the contention among clansmen so common under other dynasties. Imperial kin, living away from the capital and without autonomous armies, were intended to be powerless to challenge court policies and actions. Further weakening royal kin, the Southern Sung government had denied them, as a matter of policy, access to councilor-level posts, in an attempt to preclude the manipulation of the succession using the civil service. In 1193, Kuang-tsung had made an exception with Chao Ju-yü's appointment, reflecting perhaps Chao's extraordinary credentials and the high esteem accorded him by many of his civil service colleagues. This appointment placed the clansman Chao Ju-yü, as a proponent of abdication, in an exceedingly sensitive position, and it explains the special care he took to muster support from eminent colleagues

[37] SS 434, pp. 12890–1; HTC (1958) 153, pp. 4108–11; Lin Jui-han, Sung-tai cheng-chih shih (Taipei, 1989), pp. 353–7; Harold L. Kahn, Monarchy in the emperor's eyes: Image and reality in the Ch'ien-lung reign (Cambridge, Mass., 1971), pp. 220–5; Chaffee, Branches of heaven, pp. 190–5.

[38] Liang-ch'ao kang-mu pei-yao 3, pp. 5a–7b; SS 243, p. 8648; 391, pp. 11975–6; 392, p. 11984; 465, p. 13592; HTC (1958) 153, pp. 4108–11.

and senior palace women, despite the rules of meticulous seclusion that left palace women highly inaccessible.

The complexities of the succession crisis, however, presented a singular opportunity for Han T'o-chou. Related by marriage to Dowager Empress Wu, and uncle to Empress Li2's daughter-in-law, he stood in a unique position to influence the two women whose cooperation was most critical in the plan to replace Kuang-tsung as emperor. As audience commandant, Han T'o-chou controlled the palace doors and gates. Communication between court officials and palace women required his assistance. At the same time, noncastrated men, which included Han T'o-chou, were expressly prohibited from direct dealings with consorts. Eunuchsm, who often had special influence over consorts, being their only male companions,[39] had to assist as intermediaries. By enlisting the services of the eunuch Kuan Li, Han T'o-chou was able to win the support of a reluctant Dowager Empress Wu. Although Kuan Li had done most to persuade her, Han T'o-chou took most of the credit. After Chao Ju-yü had won Dowager Empress Wu's support, Liu Cheng again left the capital, Lin-an, intending by this move to disassociate himself from the potentially controversial actions of his military commissioner.[40] With Dowager Empress Wu personally affixing the imperial seal to the documents naming Chao K'uo emperor, Kuang-tsung, powerless to reject the pressure to abdicate, passively stepped down and retired.

This political coup had swiftly resolved an intolerable situation and came as a triumph for all involved. Han T'o-chou had proven himself a valuable link between the inner palace and the outer court, considerably enhancing his reputation and political power. A day after the accession, and at the recommendation of Dowager Empress Wu, Han T'o-chou's grandniece became empress to the new emperor. With the accession, Kuang-tsung's wife, Empress Li2, must have sighed in relief, the old cloud of uncertainty gone and her son's inheritance secured. Court officials must have taken quiet delight at witnessing the end of a reign that, with all the tension and emotion it generated, proved the least productive in Sung history. Even greater consolation derived from the retirement of Empress Li2, whose crude antics had created endless embarrassment.

The succession proceeded smoothly and without challenge for two reasons. First, it resulted from the close cooperation of the inner and outer courts. Liu Cheng and Chao Ju-yü insisted on the involvement of the empresses, an important source of dynastic legitimacy, and kept their own colleagues well informed of developments. They publicized the emperor's private communications, in which he reportedly affirmed his willingness to abdicate, thereby forestalling

---

[39] *SS* 469, pp. 13674–5; *HTC* (1958) 153, pp. 4109–10.
[40] *HTC* (1958) 153, pp. 4108–9.

charges of acting without imperial consent or of overriding proper authority. In addition, members on the paternal and maternal sides of the ruling house joined in supporting the initiative. Historically, these two camps were more often at odds, with officialdom preferring to deal with neither. Overcoming these animosities and conflicting suspicions was no mean accomplishment and was successful largely owing to the contributions of Han T'o-chou and Chao Ju-yü. Despite their vastly different backgrounds and motives, the two had a single objective in resolving the succession crisis, and they maintained a degree of cordiality. The cooperation established during the succession crisis would not, however, last.

AUTOCRACY UNDER NING-TSUNG (1194–1224)

Chao K'uo (1168–1224), posthumously known as Ning-tsung (r. 1194–1224), the second and only surviving son of Kuang-tsung, was scarcely a man of the world.[41] A pampered child, he had remained at home even after coming of age, the royal family being unwilling to part with him.[42] He had held no bureaucratic posts and had no experience of official responsibilities. A life spent in the palace had denied him exposure to the outside world, and tensions within his family must have made for a stressful youth. His great grandfather, Kao-tsung, who had lived to see Chao K'uo reach eighteen years, had spent many hours with him. His grandfather, Hsiao-tsung, saw him reach twenty-five; they, too, were close. Yet both emperors represented authority figures who expected filial submission from Chao K'uo. In light of Hsiao-tsung's aggressive and stern character, he must have been especially exacting on the grandson. Kuang-tsung was surely too preoccupied with his own personal problems to scrutinize his son's behavior, but where he proved slack, his overbearing empress compensated by keeping a tight rein on the young man. Chao K'uo's anguish, additionally, in being caught in the crossfire between his mother and grandparents can well be imagined. Dowager Empress Wu, more compassionate than Empress Li2, was no less meddlesome: the marriage of Chao K'uo, her great grandson, to Lady Han was her handiwork, proof that she had not lost her knack for managing the personal lives of family men. Navigating such tempestuous waters would strain even the strongest of characters, but Chao K'uo was noticeably short on fortitude and emerged from the experience deficient in both self-confidence and emotional stability. Passivity, his primary

---

[41] SS 37, p. 713, cites Ning-tsung as the second son; Chaffee, *Branches of heaven*, p. 192, cites genealogical sources that place him as a third son.

[42] SS 39, p. 713; 391, p. 11974; Chao Hsi-nien, *Chao-shih tsu-p'u* [Academia Sinica, Fu Ssu-nien Library, rare edition] (Hong Kong, 1937) 1, pp. 65b–66b.

means of coping with a conflict-riddled family, became his greatest single fault once he was on the throne.

Chao K'uo possessed few of the character traits of a great ruler, but his personal inadequacies were aggravated by the actions of a thoughtless family. Prominent personalities acted on his behalf, frequently without bothering to consult or even inform him, as though he were a mere pawn in a complex play for power that needed no explanation. Dowager Empress Wu's decision to endorse his elevation to the throne reached his ears only as the ceremony began. His imperial robes were ordered without his knowledge; the accession ceremony was kept secret. Chao Ju-yü had expected, according to official sources, that the timid prince would not countenance any effort to deprive his father of the throne. Chao Ju-yü had no time to persuade him, and so at the appointed hour, Chao Ju-yü lured the prince to the palace and announced, before the coffin of Hsiao-tsung, the impending accession. The prince declined on the grounds of filial devotion, but the imperial robe was suddenly thrust upon his shoulders. Civil officials then rushed in to do obeisance as the new emperor wept in fear and disbelief. Such an account, so incredibly melodramatic, may well have been embellished by later historians seeking to vindicate Ning-tsung of complicity in his father's abdication; it would not be the first time that the sensitive circumstances surrounding a succession were contorted in the interest of image building. Yet this particular portrayal probably contains more than a kernel of truth. Sources other than the official history confirm that Chao K'uo never coveted the throne.[43] After coming to power, he was aloof and easily manipulated by those around him, appearing almost timid and frightened, and he deferred decision making to others. Reluctance to make decisions was a trait he shared with his father. In the case of Kuang-tsung, it resulted from serious physical and emotional problems. With Ning-tsung it grew out of a frail, feeble personality.

Politically aloof perhaps, Chao K'uo could also be a highly sensitive individual, one who developed a genuinely personal commitment to those he worked closely with. He so revered his former tutor Huang Shang that a high-level appointment was planned for him soon after the accession. But, Huang Shang died before the emperor could act. This coincided in 1194 with the death of another respected tutor, Lo Tien, only recently appointed notary official at the Bureau of Military Affairs. Ning-tsung's attachment to the two men was remarkably personal, for he later spoke quite emotionally about mourning their loss.[44] Their untimely deaths had a significant political impact. Being

---

[43] *HTC* (1958) 153, p. 4115.

[44] Chen Te-hsiu, *Hsi-shan hsien-sheng Chen Wen-chung kung wen-chi* [Ming *Cheng-te* 1506–21 ed.; *Ssu-pu ts'ung-k'an ch'u-pien* 1929 ed.] (13th c.; Taipei, 1979) 43, p. 12a.

irreplaceable as the emperor's most trusted advisors, their departure signaled the decline of the outer court and Ning-tsung's increased reliance upon palace figures. His relationship with aides could be close at least on a personal level, yet this made a poor basis for administrative policy. Ning-tsung did not inherit the unique balance that Hsiao-tsung struck between reverence for talented advisors and autonomy in decision making. Ning-tsung could not separate political from personal judgments. His humane side became a liability when it blinded him to the faults of those he trusted and cared for. Consequently, his ties to the two men he came to trust most, Han T'o-chou and Shih Mi-yüan, were severed only by death.

HAN T'O-CHOU AGAINST THE BUREAUCRACY

Immediately after Ning-tsung's accession, the emperor summoned Liu Cheng to resume responsibilities as councilor of the left. The recall reportedly came at the recommendation of Chao Ju-yü, who apparently held no grudge over Liu Cheng's untimely desertion. Still, Liu Cheng returned to Lin-an with a severely impaired reputation.[45] In his ten-day absence, a new emperor had been enthroned and, perhaps more unsettling, a junior colleague had now come to eclipse him. As a reward for resolving a difficult crisis, Ning-tsung was fully prepared to name Chao Ju-yü as councilor of the right. However, fear of bureaucratic resistance to an imperial clansman's appointment to the post, combined with Chao's concern that his motives for interceding in the accession should not appear selfish, forced Chao to decline. Instead, he accepted the top position at the Bureau of Military Affairs, rising from associate administrator to administrator. Chao Ju-yü's new appointment and the eroded stature of Liu Cheng gave rise to the eventual tensions between the two men, despite their once cordial ties. The catalyst for their hostility was the selection of the burial site for Hsiao-tsung.[46]

Controversy over the emperor's burial originated with a recommendation by the eminent Confucian scholar and *Tao-hsüeh* proponent, Chu Hsi. Sponsored by Chao Ju-yü, Chu Hsi had been summoned recently to Lin-an to serve as academician and expositor-in-waiting. Chu Hsi apparently visited the proposed grave site in the suburbs of K'uai-chi (modern Shao-hsing). Because of the shallowness of the soil, which sat on a bed of waterlogged gravel, Chu

[45] SS 37, p. 715; 391, p. 11976; 392, p. 11987; HTC (1958) 153, pp. 4111–12.

[46] On the controversy, see SS 392, p. 11987; 397, p. 12100; 429, pp. 12763–5; HTC (1958) 153, p. 4115; Wing-tsit Chan, *Chu Hsi: New Studies* (Honolulu, 1989), p. 120. For Chu Hsi's broader interest in divination, see the chapter "Chu Hsi and Divination," in Kidder Smith, Jr., et al., *Sung dynasty uses of the I Ching* (Princeton, N.J., 1990), pp. 169–205.

concluded that the location was geomantically undesirable and requested a new divination. Chao Ju-yü concurred, but not the chief councilor, Liu Cheng. Perhaps not so meticulous about matters of ritual, Liu Cheng considered relocation unnecessary, and he had the support of many colleagues. This created a deep rift in the bureaucracy, and Ning-tsung, preoccupied with mourning and funeral-related rites, allowed the divisions to deepen.

A compromise could have been reached relatively easily if indeed the sole issue had been Hsiao-tsung's grave site. But much more was at stake. The dispute illustrated the enhanced standing at court of *Tao-hsüeh* proponents such as Chu Hsi, individuals profoundly sensitive to matters of ritual and increasingly identified with Chao Ju-yü. The group had no personal vendetta against Liu Cheng, who had long been on cordial terms with them, but Liu's willingness to sacrifice ritual probity for political expedience was, in this instance, intolerable to them. This dispute was cleverly exploited by the audience officer Han T'o-chou, who hoped to magnify differences between the two factions to weaken the outer court. Han harbored a special enmity for Liu Cheng, so rumor has it, stemming from the councilor's long-standing campaign against palace favorites, and took delight in the recent challenges to Liu's authority. Eventually, the burial controversy lost steam, and the emperor was buried as planned, but the political contest ended in a short-term victory for those who wanted to move the burial site. Only a month after his recall, Liu Cheng was dismissed and Chao Ju-yü became chief councilor of the right. But this dispute within the bureaucracy was to prove less threatening to Chao Ju-yü and his supporters than the political fissure developing between the bureaucracy and the inner court.

With Liu Cheng's departure, Chao Ju-yü lost a potent ally in the increasing struggle against the inner court, a loss made all the more acute by Chao's special vulnerability as an imperial clansman. His appointment to the Bureau of Military Affairs in 1193 had already attracted censorial attention, the court being reminded of the long-standing exclusionary policy toward clansmen.[47] Kuang-tsung had ignored the remonstrance, probably out of deference to Liu Cheng, and Ning-tsung out of gratitude for securing his accession, but not everyone in the capital shared their indifference to precedent. The scrutiny Chao Ju-yü received made his attempt to consolidate power exceedingly difficult. For example, although he utterly despised Han T'o-chou, his own political insecurity precluded direct confrontation with the well-connected audience officer. Chao opted to minimize differences and cooperate.[48] He had been warned, even before becoming councilor, of the need to rein in Han T'o-chou

---

[47] SS 36, p. 705; 392, p. 11983, 393, p. 12002; *HTC* (1958) 153, p. 4094.
[48] SS 392, p. 11987; *HTC* (1958) 153, pp. 4113–14.

and remove his foothold in the palace. However, political expediency forced Chao to involve Han T'o-chou in the succession talks, even though Chao knew that such involvement might have undesirable repercussions. Moreover, Chao Ju-yü erred in refusing to reward Han T'o-chou for assisting in the succession. In light of Chao's own promotion to chief councilor, an esteemed if only nominal promotion for Han T'o-chou was doubtlessly expected. When it did not come, the audience officer was left understandably bitter. He had been outmaneuvered.

With methodical caution, Chao Ju-yü sought to undermine Han T'o-chou. By promoting to top offices individuals who shared his high standard of political conduct, Chao hoped eventually to create the political will necessary to subdue the inner court. For example, Chu Hsi was already in place as Han-lin expositor-in-waiting, a post that gave him a platform from which to influence the throne. Chao Ju-yü, with the help of Liu Cheng, had won a substantial increase in the number of Han-lin expositors and readers. Heading the list of recent appointees were Ch'en Fu-liang, Huang Shang, and P'eng Kuei-nien. Lin Ta-chung had been recalled from regional service to become drafter at the Secretariat. Lou Yüeh, whose elegant prose had graced Kuang-tsung's abdication rescript, was promoted from the Secretariat to master of remonstrance. Liu Kuang-tsu (1142–1222), summoned from the distant southwest, filled vacancies in the Censorate and the Imperial Diary Office. Yüan Hsieh (1144–1224) and Huang Tu (1138–1213) also moved from regional to metropolitan posts, the former as instructor at the Imperial University and the latter as policy monitor.[49] Despite their widely disparate regional and intellectual backgrounds, they all shared two common traits. At some point, each had asserted the prerogative of the outer court to guide and direct governmental decision making, thereby challenging the influence of Han T'o-chou and other prominent members of the inner court. And each had also shown strong convictions about how the emperor should conduct himself. These men figured prominently among those who had criticized the antics of Empress Li2 and had beseeched Kuang-tsung to visit his dying father.

After five years of imperial dereliction during Kuang-tsung's reign, Chao Ju-yü sought to revitalize a demoralized political climate by promoting Confucian standards, especially those promulgated by *Tao-hsüeh* proponents. Han T'o-chou recognized the impending threat and responded by extending his

---

[49] On these various movements, see *SS* 393, pp. 11998, 12004, 12010, 12014; 395, pp. 12046–7; 397, p. 12100; 400, p. 12146; 429, p. 12763; *HTC* (1958) 153, pp. 4121–2; 154, pp. 4124–7; Lou, *Kung-k'uei chi* (1979) 30, pp. 11a–13a; 96, p. 2a; 98, pp. 6a–7a; Yeh Shih, *Shui-hsin hsien-sheng wen-chi* [Ming *Chia-ching* 1522–66 ed.; *Ssu-pu ts'ung-k'an* 1929 ed.] (13th c.; Taipei, 1979) 16, pp. 4a–7a; Yüan Hsieh, *Chieh-chai chi* [*Ssu-k'u ch'üan-shu, Wen-yüan ko* 1779 ed.] (c. 12th c.; Taipei, 1975) 11, pp. 17a–20b.

influence from the palace to the Censorate. Exploiting ties in the bureaucracy, he won appointment to surveillance agencies for Liu Te-hsiu and Hsü Chi-chih (d. 1201). The sudden rise of both men from minor to major posts left them permanently indebted to Han T'o-chou, and they were not alone. One contemporary insists that already by the end of 1194, Han T'o-chou held the censorial agencies firmly in his grip.[50] This was possible only because Han had astutely garnered the support of more than minor lackeys; neutral elements turned to him as well. Ho Tan (*chin-shih* 1166), who owed his early advancement to Liu Cheng, subsequently had differences with Liu's supporters and, as censor, became a severe critic of them. Ching T'ang (1138–1200), a respected statesman who replaced Lo Tien as notary official at the Bureau of Military Affairs, similarly joined the Han T'o-chou camp after having a falling-out with Chao Ju-yü. Perhaps most surprising was Han T'o-chou's successful courting of Hsieh Shen-fu (*chin-shih* 1166), an individual once highly critical of eunuch power and positively disposed toward Chu Hsi.[51] The conversion of neutral elements did not reflect a newfound loyalty to the inner court or affection for Han T'o-chou; rather, it reflected their contempt for Liu Cheng's ideological supporters, who were in the ascendant. Han's faction was a marriage of convenience, one powerful enough to enable him to secure the dismissal of Chao Ju-yü's supporters and thereby pave the way for Han's own court dominance.

Han T'o-chou had not initially been regarded favorably by the emperor in 1194. Directly following the accession, Ning-tsung honored Chao Ju-yü and others with highly esteemed posts and titles, while offering Han T'o-chou only a minor post in the Bureau of Military Affairs. This slight is attributed to Chao Ju-yü, who insisted that kin of the ruling house deserved no special reward for assisting their family in time of need.[52] Nevertheless, by year's end, a radical change had occurred. According to the expositor-in-waiting P'eng Kuei-nien, the court began to make wide-ranging decisions on the advice of Han T'o-chou without consulting the chief councilor. Worse yet, an otherwise critical bureaucracy had been effectively silenced through intimidation.[53] P'eng Kuei-nien, warning of the threat to dynastic stability posed by inner court influence, demanded Han T'o-chou's dismissal, to which Ning-tsung responded: "I trust T'o-chou with the utmost sincerity. There is confidence and no doubt."[54]

Clearly, Han T'o-chou's standing had improved dramatically during the first crucial months of the Ning-tsung reign, enabling him quickly to overshadow

---

[50] *SS* 392, p. 11988; 394, p. 12042; 474, p. 13772; Lou, *Kung-k'uei chi* (1979) 96, p. 12a.

[51] On such neutral figures, see *SS* 394, pp. 12024–6, 12036–8, 12038–41; *HTC* (1958) 153, pp. 4116–17.

[52] *SS* 474, p. 13772; *HTC* (1958) 153, p. 4112.

[53] See Lou, *Kung-k'uei chi* (1979) 96, pp. 1a–14b, especially p. 12a; P'eng, *Chih-t'ang chi* 5, pp. 16b–20b, especially pp. 18a and 19a.

[54] *SS* 393, p. 11998; *HTC* (1958) 153, p. 4121.

Chao Ju-yü. This meteoric rise, coinciding with one of the largest assaults on palace influence in Southern Sung history, seems paradoxical. Perhaps the new Empress Han exploited her intimacy with Ning-tsung to win favor for her uncle. Yet the character of the empress suggests otherwise. In contrast to the notorious Empress Li2, she was a woman of considerable reserve who meticulously shunned political involvement. Her mere presence must have enhanced the stature of her uncle, but there is no indication that she aggressively advanced his interests. A more likely reason for Han T'o-chou's ascent is Ning-tsung's changing attitude toward Chao Ju-yü and his supporters, whose demands on his conduct the emperor found unreasonably burdensome. The new emperor lacked Hsiao-tsung's admiration of self-discipline and personal standards. Ning-tsung was skeptical about moralistic judgments and probably suspicious of the motives of those who made them. Before the accession, instructor P'eng Kuei-nien had advised Ning-tsung to shun petty men. He responded: "But in the end, how are we to know? Superior men consider petty men to be petty men, petty men similarly consider superior men to be petty men. I fear they will be indistinguishable from each other."[55] Prone to such skepticism, Ning-tsung probably rejected as utter chicanery Chao Ju-yü and his cohort's denigration of Han T'o-chou as a petty man. Indeed, the more they pressed this seemingly senseless issue, the greater became the emperor's disaffection.

Chao Ju-yü's limited exposure to Ning-tsung prior to the accession was another decisive factor in his ultimate political defeat. Before Kuang-tsung had ascended the throne Chao had served him as expositor-in-waiting and chief secretary. In the process, Chao had earned Kuang-tsung's respect and confidence. As emperor, Kuang-tsung had bypassed tradition and appointed his clansman to a councilor-level post. Unfortunately, Chao Ju-yü had never served Ning-tsung in an official capacity before his accession. Ning-tsung had named him chief councilor not out of close personal ties, but in recognition of his role in the succession. This lack of familiarity denied Chao Ju-yü the additional leverage he needed to displace Han T'o-chou. The only members of the outer court who could have wielded sufficient personal influence, Huang Shang and Lo Tien, had both died in 1194. At their deaths, Chao Ju-yü commented: "The misfortune of these two officials is the misfortune of the entire realm."[56] It was an astonishingly prescient assessment.

In late 1194 and early 1195, Chao's faction launched a bitter assault against the inner court, hoping to reverse fortunes that had declined steadily over the past half year. Triggering the assault was the dismissal of the policy monitor

---

[55] Lou, *Kung-k'uei chi* (1979) 96, pp. 6b–7a.
[56] *SS* 393, p. 12009; *HTC* (1958) 153, p. 4115.

Huang Tu, a prominent critic of Han T'o-chou.[57] An imperial edict, allegedly forged by Han, ordered Huang Tu's transfer to a regional post. An incensed Chu Hsi denounced the arbitrariness of the dismissal and cautioned against trusting individuals who seek to encroach upon the imperial sway and jeopardize the empire's security. The allusion to Han T'o-chou was unmistakable. In retribution Chu Hsi was then also reassigned to a regional post. Chao Ju-yü pleaded for recision of the order and threatened to resign. Ning-tsung rejected both his resignation and his advice. Secretariat official Ch'en Fu-liang and Imperial Diarist Liu Kuang-tsu, among others, similarly protested Chu Hsi's reassignment. They too were demoted. P'eng Kuei-nien, an old foe of Han T'o-chou, who was also disinclined to sacrifice candor for diplomacy, soon joined the defense of Chu Hsi, a close friend. P'eng predicted imminent disaster should Han T'o-chou be retained. When he too received a transfer, Policy Monitor Lin Ta-chung and Secretariat official Lou Yüeh joined the fray, defending P'eng Kuei-nien's integrity and genuineness of heart. They proposed either the recall of P'eng Kuei-nien to the capital or the reassignment of Han T'o-chou to regional service. The compromise was rejected. A succession of remonstrances and ultimatums followed, gambits intended to pressure the throne. Few could have imagined that they would backfire and that the emperor would sacrifice a galaxy of prestigious officials simply to retain one favorite. Han T'o-chou was commonly equated with the vilified eunuch Ch'en Yüan, prominent during the reigns of Kao-tsung and Hsiao-tsung; politically, he proved far more indestructible.[58]

As the campaign against Han T'o-chou progressed, the court grew ever more polarized. In theory, this should have united the outer court against the palace favorites. Regardless of political allegiance, civil officials shared a common concern for the regular functioning of the bureaucratic machinery of government, and Han T'o-chou presented a grave threat to its integrity. The recent rash of dismissals, for example, was highly irregular. The chief councilor had not approved them, as was customary, and the Secretariat had not drafted the necessary rescripts. The dismissal notices were special palace orders that had never passed through regular bureaucratic channels. Even more curious, Ning-tsung had spent much of late 1194 away from court at the former palace of Hsiao-tsung, apparently performing funeral rites. This absence raised serious questions about the origin of the rescripts. In Sung times, bypassing the bureaucracy to conduct government business by imperial

---

[57] SS 393, pp. 11998, 12010–11, 12015; 395, p. 12047; 429, p. 12766; 434, p. 12888; HTC (1958) 153; Lou, Kung-k'uei chi (1979) 30, pp. 11a–13a; 96, pp. 1a–14b; 98, pp. 6b–7a; Yüan, Chieh-chai chi 11, p. 20b.
[58] SS 40, p. 781.

favorites was unusual; when done with any regularity, it generally presaged the emergence of autocratic leadership by the emperor or, more commonly, by some imperial favorite. *Tao-hsüeh* proponents in the bureaucracy, fearing an institutional crisis, supported Chao Ju-yü. Most notably, even Ch'en K'uei (1128–1203), an executive at the Bureau of Military Affairs, who so hated Chao Ju-yü that the two refused to attend the same audience, defended the councilor's close ally P'eng Kuei-nien in the crisis and was himself banished. However, other bureaucrats proved less courageous. Censor Hsieh Shen-fu, Assistant Councilor Ching T'ang, and Bureau of Military Affairs executive Yü Tuan-li (1135–1201) were among those who abandoned the *Tao-hsüeh* proponents.[59] The anticipated consensus against Han T'o-chou never materialized. Not all bureaucrats could agree on the seriousness of Han T'o-chou's political threat, nor were all sympathizers with the *Tao-hsüeh* movement willing to sacrifice their short-term personal interests for the long-term welfare of bureaucratic governance.

Soon after the accession of Ning-tsung, Chao Ju-yü was reportedly advised by Yeh Shih and Chu Hsi to reward Han T'o-chou but keep him at a safe distance, on the assumption that a petty man can readily be bought but never trusted. Chao allegedly gave little thought to the advice, confident in his own ability to prevail.[60] But Chao seriously underestimated the wiles of his political opponent. By January 1195, the most ideological of Chao's supporters had been removed from posts of power. For Chao Ju-yü, demoralized at having to fight a lone battle and frustrated by Han T'o-chou's circumvention of bureaucratic authority, dismissal must have come as a relief. Li Mu, a policy monitor and political crony of Han T'o-chou, again brought forward the issue of the long-standing policy that imperial clansmen were to be excluded from high office and the throne used this as a pretext for Chao's dismissal. This dismissal confirmed again the emperor's confidence in Han T'o-chou. Yang Chien (1140–1226), a professor at the Directorate of Education, and Lü Tsu-chien (d. 1196), an executive aide at the Court of Imperial Treasury, each denounced the decision and were banished for their audacity. Students at the Imperial University in Lin-an staged a sizable demonstration of protest. The court, clearly annoyed at the students' political action, made an example of six instigators. Rounded up by the prefect of Lin-an, they were exiled to the remote south.[61] Dozens of others suffered similar punishment for defending Chao Ju-yü and his associates. The final sweep against the critics of Han T'o-chou came as an anticlimax. By this time, most of their energy had been spent.

---

[59] *SS*, 394, pp.12036–8, 12038–41; 398, pp. 12103–6; *HTC* (1958) 153, pp. 4121–2.

[60] *SS* 392, p. 11987; 434, p. 12871; *HTC* (1958) 153, p. 4112.

[61] *SS* 407, pp. 12289–92; 455, pp. 13368–71, 13373–5; 474, pp. 13772–3; *HTC* (1958) 154, pp. 4126–29.

With the departure of Chao Ju-yü from government in the early part of
1195, Han T'o-chou moved quickly to realign the bureaucracy. The new councilor of the right was Yü Tuan-li, who would serve for only a year, followed by
Ching T'ang, who held the post from 1196 until his death in 1200. Both men
were established scholars and competent officials. The two have fared poorly at
the hands of later historians, who despised them for their cooperation with Han
T'o-chou; but they were more than mere sycophants. As for Han T'o-chou,
honors came in steady succession. Within two years, he rose from regional
surveillance commissioner (*kuan-ch'a shih*, 5a) with titular honors to regional
commissioner (*chieh-tu shih*, 2b) and then to supreme commandant (*k'ai-fu i-
t'ung san-ssu*, 1b), the highest rank of sinecure posts. Subsequent honorific titles
were granted him, including junior mentor, junior preceptor, grand mentor,
and grand preceptor, and, finally, he received his ennoblement as a prince.
Han's father, whose career had hardly extended beyond the Office of Audience
Ceremonies, was posthumously honored with the title "loyal and fixed," a title
normally reserved for only the most accomplished of officials. The emperor
spared little when it came to honors and accolades, yet the highest civil service
post initially given to Han T'o-chou was assistant recipient of edicts in the
Bureau of Military Affairs. This makes him the only statesman in Southern
Sung times to control the bureaucracy, indeed the empire, without holding an
executive post to legitimize that control.

Ning-tsung hesitated to advance Han T'o-chou to a councilor-level post for
the same reason that the outer court resented Han's intrusion into decision making – he lacked civil service credentials. Han T'o chou held no official degree
and had passed no recruitment examination. His bureaucratic experience was
very limited. Men of military background who distinguished themselves at
war were often rewarded with prestigious office, yet the hostilities witnessed by
Han T'o-chou never extended beyond those at the court. He had entered government service through family privilege and had risen through marriage ties.
Prior to the accession of Ning-tsung, his administrative talent was untested.
During the high degree of cooperation between inner and outer courts that
culminated in the 1194 abdication, he had served as liaison, conveying messages from Chao Ju-yü, through the eunuch Kuan Li, to Dowager Empress
Wu. He had provided a vital link in communication, but his own input
appears to have been negligible. Han T'o-chou lacked intellectual achievements as well. He was identified with no major thinker or school of thought,
save for having received childhood instruction from Ch'en Tzu-ch'iang, an
obscure individual who later became a professor at the Imperial University.[62]
Neither steeped in classical literature nor immersed in traditional values,

---

[62] *SS* 394, p. 12034; 474, p. 13774; *HTC* (1958) 155, p. 4166; 155, p. 4181.

Han T'o-chou represents the exact antithesis of the Sung civil servant ideal. For the quintessential scholar and bureaucrat Chao Ju-yü, who had faced great obstacles in his own rise to power, the astonishing success of this mediocre audience officer must have been galling. *Chin-shih* credentials had come to be expected of those holding councilor-level posts. Despite the emperor's high regard for Han T'o-chou and special favor for his niece, the Empress Han, Ning-tsung did not violate bureaucratic precedent and give Han a councilor-level post. This left Han T'o-chou's position highly irregular. His policies were often shaped by a curious combination of arrogance and insecurity, the arrogance being a function of pedigree, and the insecurity a product of powers that lacked the authority of office.

THE BAN ON TAO-HSÜEH

After eliminating all serious opposition in the capital and procuring for himself an impressive string of court titles, Han T'o-chou sought to justify the dismissal of his opponents on more substantial grounds, such as disloyalty to the throne or breach of official conduct. Beyond bolstering his own status as the individual who rid the empire of a grave menace, this move would additionally discredit the opposition so as to make their political revival next to impossible. Han T'o-chou also longed to undertake some courageous exploit, an opportunity to prove his worth and perhaps justify his appointment as chief councilor.

In pursuit of the first set of objectives – to discredit the opposition – Han began a political campaign so disastrous that he would be compelled, in the end, to undo his own deed. Writing in late 1194, P'eng Kuei-nien, quoting Ou-yang Hsiu, noted: "Since antiquity, petty men who wish to empty the empire of [talented] men have always resorted to talk about factions and parties."[63] It was a forecast of the line of attack that would be chosen by Han T'o-chou to pummel and humiliate his already weakened critics. His impatient ambition far exceeding his political craft, Han T'o-chou would not settle for denunciation of individual critics as factionalists. For him, the *Tao-hsüeh* movement seemed somehow conspiratorial. With Chu Hsi such a popular figure within that group, it seemed only logical to identify the movement he represented as the source of factional strife. Han T'o-chou declared war on the movement.

But the history of the *Tao-hsüeh* movement was complex. Even a hundred years earlier, by the mid-eleventh century, a discernible schism had developed between traditional Confucianism (*Ju-hsüeh*) and the Learning of the Way

---

[63] P'eng, *Chih-t'ang chi* 4, p. 18a. For the original citation, see Ou-yang Hsiu, *Historical records of the Five Dynasties*, trans. Richard L. Davis (New York, 2004), p. 294.

(*Tao-hsüeh*) (often referred to as Neo-Confucianism). Both groups aspired to revive antiquity and restore the simplistic beauty of ancient literary styles long displaced by abstruse new forms; resuscitate ancient rites and institutions long debased by vulgar conventions; and celebrate proper human relationships in the face of competition from the otherworldliness of Buddhism. Traditional Confucianism stressed the spirit or essence of antiquity, while the *Tao-hsüeh* movement took a more literal approach to the imitation of the old. As James T. C. Liu has noted, this new Confucian movement insisted on strict adherence to the rituals and lifestyle of the past, an attitude widely criticized by contemporaries as pretentious and unrealistic.[64]

In the twelfth century, *Tao-hsüeh* practices continued to irritate fellow bureaucrats and, increasingly, the throne. The sanctimonious frugality of *Tao-hsüeh* adherents could often appear excessive. At one point, Palace Library executive Hu Hung paid a social call upon Chu Hsi at Fu-chou. He received memorably wretched meals, about which he later commented with indignation, "There's not that much shortage in the mountains!"[65] His miserly host, Hu concluded, lacked decorum in treating friends. In a similar vein, Chu Hsi was once accused of feeding coarse food even to his mother, an accusation that implied great filial impiety. Such complaints may seem petty minded, but they reveal in Chu Hsi a distinctive set of values that many contemporaries did not appreciate and indeed found personally offensive. The liberties taken by Chu Hsi in criticizing others, and his apparent lack of restraint, also came at great cost to his career. As a regional official, he denounced corrupt and negligent bureaucrats with uncommon frequency. His scrutiny often extended beyond subordinates to include their superiors. This was highly irregular conduct for a noncensorial official and raised questions about his motives – were they professional or political? Later historians may have drawn inspiration from his dedication to bureaucratic integrity and his moral courage, but his contemporaries commonly regarded Chu Hsi as self-righteous and excessively contentious.[66] Memorializing the throne in 1180, he astonished all by openly criticizing the emperor's unhealthy reliance on a small coterie of men, and predicting imminent calamity. Quite understandably, an infuriated Hsiao-tsung

---

[64] Liu Tzu-chien (James T. C. Liu), "How did a Neo-Confucian school become the state orthodoxy?" *Philosophy East and West* 23 No. 4 (1973), pp. 483–505, especially p. 497; Ch'en, "Han P'ing-yüan p'ing," pp. 123–8.

[65] *SS* 394, p. 12023; Li Hsin-ch'uan, *Tao ming lu* (1239; Shanghai, 1937), pp. 58–9, 67–9. For related information on Chu Hsi's eccentric lifestyle, see Chan, *Chu Hsi*, pp. 44–89, and Julia Ching, "Chu Hsi on personal cultivation," in *Chu Hsi and Neo-Confucianism*, ed. Wing-tsit Chan (Honolulu, 1986), pp. 273–91.

[66] Sung Hsi, "Chu Hsi ti cheng-chih lun," in *Sung-shih yen-chiu chi: Ti shih chi*, ed. Sung-shih tso-t'an-hui (Taipei, 1978), pp. 355–69.

took this as an evil wish, not constructive advice, and withdrew his former sympathies for Chu Hsi.[67] Chu Hsi also came under fire for ostentatiously declining public office, especially metropolitan posts, despite repeated offers. To many, Chu Hsi's refusals reflected patent arrogance, a ploy to enhance his reputation by appearing unavailable even to the throne.[68] Liu Kuang-tsu, an imperial diarist and a man sympathetic to *Tao-hsüeh*, summarized the reasons for the unpopularity of the movement stating: "The superior men of today do not comprehend the Great Way. They regard themselves too highly while castigating others as too base."[69]

At court, exaggerated stress on moral purity wore thin the welcome for *Tao-hsüeh* proponents, for their criticism extended even to the emperor. Worse yet, their criticism often appeared totally unjustified. *Tao-hsüeh* proponents idealized an austere lifestyle and impugned indulgence in wine or women, especially by the Son of Heaven, as he should personify the noblest of human virtues. The *Tao-hsüeh* movement's animosity toward Han T'o-chou grew in part out of his indifference to moral standards. Ignoring the custom of taking only one primary wife, he reportedly had a total of four, all of whom he insisted on calling "Madame" (*fu-jen*). In addition, he kept ten secondary wives – a small harem – plus many other women.[70] Alcohol and frivolity inevitably accompanied female entertainment, and Han T'o-chou was notorious for drinking late into the night. When Kuang-tsung had developed similar habits, palace favorites, perhaps eunuchs, were presumed responsible. When Ning-tsung now fell into the same vices, the influence of Han T'o-chou seemed undeniable.

Both Kuang-tsung and Ning-tsung were negatively predisposed against *Tao-hsüeh*, resenting its intrusion into their personal lives, especially the heavy ceremonial obligations of filial devotion. Kuang-tsung hated his father with intense passion, and moralist pressure to visit Hsiao-tsung in the Ch'ung-hua Palace only incited Kuang-tsung further. Ning-tsung had still greater reason to be bitter. By the end of 1194, having performed, on his father's behalf, the stressful funeral rituals for Hsiao-tsung, the emperor prepared to observe a shortened and less rigorous period of mourning. The heavy demands of governing made this a perfectly proper decision; indeed, the same had been proposed for Hsiao-tsung's mourning of Kao-tsung, and the father-son relationship was more formalized than that of grandfather-grandson. Nevertheless, Chu Hsi pressed for strict adherence to ritual. Given Hsiao-tsung's precedent of compliance to the requirements of these rituals, as new emperor Ning-tsung

[67] SS 429, p. 12754; Chu, *Hui-an hsien-sheng* (1979) 11, pp. 11a–18a.

[68] SS 394, p. 12031; Li, *Tao ming lu*, pp. 47–8.

[69] Chen, *Hsi-shan hsien-sheng Chen Wen-chung kung wen-chi* 43, p. 8a.

[70] SS 474, p. 13777; Ting Ch'uan-ching, *Sung-jen i-shih hui-pien* (1935; Taipei, 1982) 17, p. 886.

could hardly do otherwise without drawing heavy criticism.[71] The death of the eighty-three-year-old Dowager Empress Wu in 1197 raised the issue of Ning-tsung and mourning rites once again. Han T'o-chou is said to have proposed that funeral rites be simplified and expenses reduced. This incensed Liu Kuang-tsu. Memorializing the throne from a regional post, he charged Han T'o-chou with treating the emperor's great-grandmother as a petty woman.[72] Ning-tsung consented to a full year's mourning, having only recently concluded observances for his grandfather. In the year 1200, as a cruel fate would have it, both his mother and father died. There was no question that formal and full-length observances were in order. In this way, Ning-tsung devoted much of a decade to the rigors of mourning. The strict demands dictated by *Tao-hsüeh* proponents made the emperor's mourning unduly protracted, and he appears never to have forgotten, or forgiven, them.

Against this background, Han T'o-chou's proposal to proscribe *Tao-hsüeh* adherents drew no noticeable objection from the emperor. The idea was hardly original. Earlier in the century, under Hui-tsung, a ban had been imposed on antireformists of the Yüan-yu era (1086–93). Implemented in 1102 under Chief Councilor Ts'ai Ching (1047–1126), the ban had sought to discredit anti–Wang An-shih elements at court. The names of alleged partisans, initially ninety-eight, but later over three hundred in number, were inscribed in stone. In punishment, offenders and their descendants were excluded from metropolitan posts and prohibited from entering the capital; their literary productions were proscribed, and, in certain cases, printing blocks of their works were reduced to ashes.[73] A second ban had occurred under Councilor Ch'in Kuei. Beginning in 1136 as an injunction against using the classical exegesis of Ch'eng I for civil service examinations, the ban was broadened eight years later to include any "specialized and obscure learning" (*chuan-men ch'ü-hsüeh*).[74] Ch'in Kuei's proscription of the 1140s was in many ways similar to Ts'ai Ching's, but it differed in one important respect: it focused on intellectual, not just political, associations. Ts'ai Ching had directed his ban against political opponents, including men of vastly different intellectual backgrounds. Ch'in Kuei, by identifying and attacking his political opponents on the basis of their intellectual association, had established the model that Han T'o-chou would use sixty years later.

---

[71] *SS* 429, p. 12766; *HTC* (1958) 153, p. 4120.

[72] *SS* 397, p. 12101; *HTC* (1958) 154, p. 4153.

[73] On the ban, see Chapter 7 of this volume; *SS* 472, pp. 13721–8; *HTC* (1958) 88, pp. 2244–5; 88, p. 2252; Li, *Tao ming lu*, pp. 15–9; and references to it in Huang et al., *Sung Yüan hsüeh-an, chüan* 96.

[74] *SS* 473, p. 13760; Huang et al., *Sung Yüan hsüeh-an, chüan* 96; Li, *Tao ming lu*, pp. 37–9; also see Huang K'uan-ch'ung, "Ch'in Kuei yü wen-tzu yü," in *Sung-shih ts'ung-lun*, Huang K'uan-ch'ung (Taipei, 1974), pp. 41–72.

The political influence of the *Tao-hsüeh* adherents had been, for most of the early twelfth century, appreciated little under Hsiao-tsung. Hsiao-tsung's assertive leadership curtailed special favor being given to any one group. In addition, Hsiao-tsung's highly eclectic attitude toward ideas, and his belief in the Three Teachings (Confucianism, Taoism, and Buddhism) as being complementary and deserving of equal attention, alienated the more adamant *Tao-hsüeh* proponents.[75] Only under Kuang-tsung did the *Tao-hsüeh* movement's fortunes improve markedly, a development in which not everyone took delight.

Competitive examinations were the cornerstone of the Sung civil service, and a candidate's understanding and interpretation of the classics affected his success. Intellectual associations profoundly influenced careers and livelihoods. Hermeneutics, the interpretation of texts, and one's intellectual disposition were not just an academic issue in this competitive environment, and this partly explains the controversy triggered by the advancement of *Tao-hsüeh* adherents under Chou Pi-ta, Liu Cheng, and Chao Ju-yü. The balance sought by Hsiao-tsung, where no single teaching was to achieve preeminence, had begun to shift. This emerging realignment was closely followed by those who had been taught and supported different intellectual traditions.

Being outside the civil service mainstream, Han T'o-chou would have been disconnected from the academic dispute, but in this case his political interests coincided with the political and academic concerns of others. Most likely at his prompting, censors began, in 1195, to attack *Tao-hsüeh* partisans and denounce *Tao-hsüeh* ideas as "spurious teachings" (*wei-hsüeh*). Indictments against Chu Hsi himself and many others soon followed. Had it not been for the intervention of Dowager Empress Wu, the court may well have imposed a general proscription from the outset. As the oldest living member of the royal family, she probably remembered better than others the lasting ill effects of such intolerance in the past. The alleged partisans were initially excluded only from the metropolitan bureaucracy.[76] After her death in 1197, with no powerful sponsor to oppose them, the sanctions were extended and formalized. Officially imposed in 1198, the ban, called the *Tao-hsüeh chin*, directly affected fifty-nine individuals.[77]

In scope and severity, the ban of 1198 scarcely compared to the Yüan-yu ban of Ts'ai Ching a hundred and ten years earlier. Apart from affecting far

---

[75] Li Hsin-ch'uan, *Chien-yen i-lai ch'ao-yeh tsa-chi* [*Shih-yüan ts'ung-shu* 1914 ed.] (c. 1202 *chia* volume, 1216 *i* volume; Taipei, 1967) *i* 3, pp. 8a–b; Chen, *Hsi-shan hsien-sheng Chen Wen-chung kung wen-chi* 11, pp. 37b–38a.

[76] *HTC* (1958) 154, p. 4140.

[77] *SS* 394, p. 12033.

fewer people, the ban was also far less drastic. Proscribed scholars found it
difficult to publish their scholarship, yet the government appears not to have
burned books or printing blocks. In fact, this limited and short-lived attempt
at political revenge may have deserved no more than a historian's footnote
were it not for the eminence of its targets. Three former chief councilors, Chou
Pi-ta, Liu Cheng, and Chao Ju-yü, headed the list. Also stigmatized were
the philosopher Chu Hsi, the renowned essayist Lou Yüeh, the outspoken
professor Ts'ai Yu-hsüeh (1154–1217), the accomplished classicist Yeh Shih,
the nonpartisan censor Liu Kuang-tsu, and *Tao-hsüeh* luminaries such as Ch'en
Fu-liang, Lin Ta-chung, Lü Tsu-chien, Liu Yüeh2 (1144–1216), Yang Chien,
and Yüan Hsieh.[78]

Those who supported the ban denounced all fifty-nine proscribed scholars
as *Tao-hsüeh* adherents who advanced strictly partisan interests to the detriment of the government. The charge was preposterous. Some of those banned,
including Lou Yüeh, Yang Chien, and Yüan Hsieh, held close ties to Lu Chiu-
yüan, a leading rival of Chu Hsi's. Others, Ch'en Fu-liang, Ts'ai Yu-hsüeh,
and Yeh Shih, identified themselves with the Yung-chia School centered at
Wen-chou.[79] Chou Pi-ta, Liu Cheng, and Chao Ju-yü had no discernible ties
to *Tao-hsüeh* partisans either, even though they may have sympathized with
the views of individual adherents. The persecuted were from several regions
of the empire, and there are no indications of their having a regional association. The only common ground appears to have been their concern for strict
ethical standards and conduct in government; their only consensus on practical policy appears to have been on the need to bring palace favorites under
control. The entire suppression effort would seem to have been intellectually
baseless.

The ad hoc political nature of the *Tao-hsüeh* ban is further illustrated by
its poorly defined ideological objectives. Suppression began two years after
the purge and death of Chao Ju-yü, by which time *Tao-hsüeh* proponents no
longer posed a serious threat. The ban had lost its political utility. Were ideological conformity its objective, one would expect some effort to destroy the
writings of proponents, as under the Yüan-yu ban. This did not occur. Nor
did Han T'o-chou promote some rival school, which would have been another
means of ideologically undermining *Tao-hsüeh*. Even simple revenge cannot
fully explain the ban. The proscription was far from comprehensive, affecting

[78] A complete listing is to be found in Huang et al., *Sung Yüan hsüeh-an, chüan* 97; *HTC* (1958) 154,
pp. 4153–4; Li, *Tao ming lu*, pp. 81–3; see also Schirokauer, "Neo-Confucians under attack."

[79] See Schirokauer, "Neo-Confucians under attack," and Lo Wen (Winston W. Lo), *The life and thought of
Yeh Shih* (Gainsesville, Fla., 1974). For a thorough study of the Yung-chia School and its influence on
the examination curriculum, see Hilde de Weerdt, *Competition over content: Negotiating standards for the
civil service examinations in imperial China (1127–1279)* (Cambridge, Mass., 2007).

only prominent critics, not their many teachers, disciples, and associates. Neither was the ban strictly enforced. Most men remained free to travel; they retained bureaucratic status and salary; they continued to teach; their writings continued to be read; and as one historian has demonstrated, they continued to pass the civil service examinations.[80] That Han T'o-chou did not resort to violent intimidation similarly implies a restrained malice. The chief impetus behind the ban, it appears, was an anti-intellectualism that went along with a desire to silence the most moralizing of court critics. Both Ning-tsung and Han T'o-chou held no special reverence for intellectuals, and the hounding they received from the *Tao-hsüeh* supporters over the issue of mourning rites may have spurred them to react, however clumsily.

The entire effort at imposing a ban ended in embarrassing failure. A poorly defined target group made the ban appear ill considered and irresponsible.[81] Guided by emotion and personal animosity, it was neither comprehensive nor strictly enforced. The restrained support of the bureaucracy, especially Ching T'ang and Hsieh Shen-fu, also undermined its effect.[82] By the end of 1199, less than two years after the ban's imposition, it was relaxed at the recommendation of Chief Councilor Ching T'ang. Rumor had it that even Han T'o-chou had come to regret the action. When Chu Hsi died a few months later, his well-attended funeral vividly illustrated that the proscription had neither discredited the teacher nor intimidated his students.[83] On the contrary, by victimizing so many well-respected men, the ban had legitimized the objectives of *Tao-hsüeh*, winning it a new respectability and a broader spectrum of sympathetic support.

RAPPROCHEMENT AND THE K'AI-HSI WAR (1205–1207)

With the decision to relax the 1198 ban, the court gradually restored offices and titles to the once-disgraced officials. Liu Cheng, the first to be honored, became junior guardian. Other restorations were delayed because of the indiscretion of Lü Tsu-t'ai, a disciple of Chu Hsi, who in late autumn 1200 presented a memorial to the throne that viciously denounced Han T'o-chou and demanded his execution.[84] Lü Tsu-t'ai was a first cousin of Lü Tsu-chien, also a critic of Han T'o-chou, who had suffered banishment in 1195 and had died a year later. In 1200 there had been a string of deaths of notable persons involved in

---

[80] Schirokauer, "Neo-Confucians under attack," p. 193.

[81] Chiba, "Kan Takuchū," pp. 283–4.

[82] See *SS* 394, pp. 12036–8; 394, pp. 12038–41; *HTC* (1958) 154, p. 4144; 155, p. 4172.

[83] *SS* 429, p. 12768; *HTC* (1958) 155, p. 4176.

[84] *SS* 455, pp. 13371–2; *HTC* (1958) 155, pp. 4181–2.

the incident: Chu Hsi in the spring; Chief Councilor Ching T'ang, Emperor Kuang-tsung, and Empress Li2 in the summer; and Empress Han in early winter. Lü Tsu-t'ai may have reasoned, erroneously it turns out, that these events had weakened Han T'o-chou's political influence, but censors loyal to Han T'o-chou turned against Lü and called for his execution. The court decided on flogging with a hundred blows of a heavy stick – an unusually cruel punishment by Sung standards – and exile to the remote southwest. The court also chose to suspend the rehabilitation of other officials proscribed in the Ch'ing-yüan ban.

However, rapprochement began in earnest in 1202. Chu Hsi was posthumously restored as academician-in-waiting, Chao Ju-yü was made an academician of the Tzu-cheng Hall, and the seventy-six-year-old Chou Pi-ta was reinstated as grand academician of the Kuan-wen Hall. Preproscription rank was also restored to Liu Kuang-tsu, Ch'en Fu-liang, Yeh Shih, and Ts'ai Yu-hsüeh, among others. A year later, P'eng Kuei-nien was reinstated in the civil service, and the exiled Lü Tsu-t'ai was given a special pardon.[85]

Still, the hostilities between Han T'o-chou and the opposition were not easily forgotten. Most of those who had their rank restored never resumed office. Chou Pi-ta and Liu Cheng, both elderly at this point, formally retired. P'eng Kuei-nien, Lou Yüeh, and Lü Tsu-t'ai accepted rank but not office. Ch'en Fu-liang and Liu Kuang-tsu were offered regional appointments but opted for sinecures instead. The only prominent critics to accept metropolitan assignments were Ts'ai Yu-hsüeh, who became drafting official at the Secretariat, and Yeh Shih, subsequently vice-director at the Ministry of War, the Ministry of Works, and the Ministry of Personnel. Most critics preferred to boycott the administration. Han T'o-chou's rapprochement was no more successful than the ban had been. By drawing men of integrity back into participation in the regime he still controlled, he hoped to restore and enhance his own political reputation. But he failed, and his critics remained too powerful to ignore. Unsuccessful in this attempt to bolster his power by ideological restrictions, he turned to foreign policy as an alternative arena in which to demonstrate his effectiveness as a political leader.

Sung and Chin had been at peace since the early 1160s and relations were cordial. In the north, the Chin emperor Chin Shih-tsung (r. 1161–89), known by admirers as a "second Yao or Shun," was the most humane of Jurchen rulers. Much of the same held for the Sung emperor Hsiao-tsung in the south, whose reign (1162–89) has been dubbed the golden age of the Southern Sung. While both publicly laid claim to parts of the other's territory, neither ruler

---

[85] *HTC* (1958) 156, pp. 4198, 4203, 4205, 4213; Lou, *Kung-k'uei chi* (1979) 96, p. 12b.

dared risk what they currently controlled in costly and uncertain military adventures. Hsiao-tsung had expressed a firm commitment to restoration of the north, whereas Kuang-tsung and Ning-tsung appeared indifferent. Thus, when Ning-tsung chose to resume hostilities against the Chin, responsibility for this plan was inevitably attributed to the wiles of Han T'o-chou.

Signs of an impending shift in foreign policy had already appeared by the turn of the century. In the summer of 1201, a minor official had recommended the elevation of Han T'o-chou to manager of national security (*p'ing-chang chün-kuo shih*), an ad hoc post generally awarded only in times of war that had been conferred upon a total of four men in the dynasty's past, all during the Northern Sung. It gave sweeping authority over the civilian, military, and fiscal bureaucracies. Understandably, appointees had to be impeccably trustworthy. All previous nominees had been distinguished chief councilors.[86] The 1201 recommendation to revive the post must have been prompted by Han T'o-chou himself; no minor official acting on his own initiative would have dared to be so bold, especially in a time of peace. Han T'o-chou declined, but the mere proposal was an indicator that a military venture was in the making. There were other indicators. In 1202 the court named Su Shih-tan (d. 1207), a crony of Han T'o-chou, as chief recipient of edicts at the Bureau of Military Affairs. This appointment put control of all military communications into Han's hands. In the same year the Szechwan military magnate Wu Hsi became prefect for strategic Hsing-chou3, in the heart of the northwestern Li-chou circuit, strengthening the leadership in the west for a possible attack from that direction. These appointments were soon followed by Han T'o-chou's titular promotion to grand preceptor.

That these military-related moves coincided with Han T'o-chou's rapprochement with his court critics was no accident. Given the revanchist orientation of *Tao-hsüeh* thinkers and sympathizers, a militant foreign policy, if not successful at winning their favor, might at least succeed in stealing their thunder. It also made good sense from a military standpoint. As early as 1200, the Chin court, worried about the growing Mongol menace, had begun to reinforce military installations along their northern border.[87] For the first time since its seizure of power in 1115, Chin strategic concerns had shifted from south to north. Worse yet, in Chin the new Mongol pressure and increased military expenditures had coincided with a period of repeated large-scale natural disasters and a dramatic decline in state revenues. The destitute took to banditry, and the Chin government faced the dual threats of domestic insurrection and

[86] See, Lin T'ien-wei, "Sung-tai ch'üan-hsiang hsing-ch'eng chih fen-hsi," in *Sung-shih yen-chiu chi: Ti pa chi*, ed. Sung-shih tso-t'an-hui (Taipei, 1976), pp. 141–70, especially pp. 154–9.

[87] *HTC* (1958) 155, p. 4180.

foreign invasion. In 1203, as Sung ambassador Teng Yu-lung was making his way to the Chin capital, he observed the impoverished state of the countryside and held clandestine meetings with informants. In his report to the court on his return to Lin-an, he portrayed the north as more vulnerable than ever before. Two years later in 1205, envoy Li Pi (1159–1222), vice-minister of rites, filed a similar report. Support for aggression also came from Hsin Ch'i-chi (1140–1207), the renowned poet serving as military commissioner in Che-tung. Hsin predicted an imminent demise for Jurchen rule.[88] Many concurred with this assessment of Chin's new vulnerability. There was less of a consensus, however, about Sung military strength.

As early as 1203, the Chin began reinforcing their defenses along the Sung border. The objective was probably to contain bandits and to prevent refugees from seeking sanctuary in the south, as commonly happened in times of internal disorder. These border reinforcements were not primarily directed against the Sung. In 1203, Wan-yen A-lu-tai, the Chin envoy to the Sung, traveling to Lin-an through the lower Huai and Yangtze regions, observed military drills being conducted regularly and an abnormally high demand for horses, both unmistakable signs of preparations for an impending war. When he informed the Chin court of this on his return, he was flogged because his comments were considered inflammatory.[89] Again, when a Sung spy was captured in 1205 and informed the Chin of troop movements in Sung territory, his captors were staggered in disbelief.[90] The Chin emperor, Chang-tsung (r. 1189–1208), continued to react with caution, hoping to avert conflict. Natural disasters, infrequent in the first decade of his reign, had become endemic in the second. Shantung was especially hard-pressed and had required massive relief.[91] There was also serious domestic unrest in the face of widespread poverty. In this context, Chang-tsung decided to respond to the potential Sung threat by further strengthening his own border defenses and by using diplomacy to dissuade the Sung leaders from attacking. In all previous conflicts with the Sung, hostilities had been initiated by the Chin. A reversal of roles must have required Chin to rethink its strategic goals and reassess its defensive tactics.

Apart from troop movements in the Huai region, heightened Sung military activity took place in the strategic Ching-hsi circuit centered in the northwest corner of modern Hupei. Military commands were also restructured throughout the Sung domain. The Sung court entrusted command of the Huai-nan

---

[88] For these various views, see SS 398, p. 12106; HTC (1958) 156, pp. 4214, 4216–17. Also see Ch'en, "Han P'ing-yüan p'ing" p. 108; Kinugawa Tsuyoshi, "Kaiki Yōhei o megutte," Tōyōshi kenkyū 36 No. 3 (1977), pp. 128–51.

[89] T'o-t'o, Chin shih 11, p. 261; HTC (1958) 156, p. 4214.

[90] T'o-t'o, Chin shih 12, p. 271; 62, p. 1475; HTC (1958) 157, p. 4227.

[91] T'o-t'o, Chin shih 12, p. 272.

East circuit to Assistant Councilor Chang Yen, command of the Huai-nan West circuit to Bureau of Military Affairs executive Ch'eng Sung, and command of Liang-che East circuit to Chief Minister of Justice Hsin Ch'i-chi. Ministry of Works executive Ch'iu Ch'ung (1135–1208) became custodial prefect of the strategic port city of Ming-chou.[92] Clearly, by 1203 at the latest, the Sung court had begun to lay the foundation for a major offensive. The court deliberately chose to staff its military commands with prominent civilian officials, thereby ensuring central government control over regional armies, especially in the east.

Extensive preparations and precautions notwithstanding, the Sung court was slow to undertake war. Han T'o-chou was determined first to strengthen his hand at home. To appease his former critics, he arranged high honors for the recently deceased Chou Pi-ta, another posthumous advancement for one-time critic Chao Ju-yü, and dismissal for Liu Te-hsiu, the censor who had been directly responsible for the purge of *Tao-hsüeh* partisans, and who now became a scapegoat for Han T'o-chou. There were posthumous honors for Yüeh Fei, an icon of irredentism in the Kao-tsung reign, and demotion for his nemesis, the reviled pacifist Ch'in Kuei. The court also ordered the compilation of several historical works on earlier Sung reigns. These publication projects were designed to legitimize aggression and encourage revanchist zeal, and all bore the name of Han T'o-chou as project director.[93] Meanwhile, it was essential, assuming that he would direct the war effort, for Han T'o-chou to hold a post of appropriate overall authority. This came in 1205 with his appointment as manager of national security. Even with his new appointment, Han T'o-chou proved exceedingly cautious. Deciding first to probe enemy strength, he sponsored bandit raids in which Sung agents harassed towns and villages along the border to gather information on the size, disposition, and readiness of enemy forces.[94] The Sung court also began underwriting loyalist groups in Chin territory, mostly northern brigands who declared nominal fealty to the Sung in exchange for provisions and occasional refuge. Such groups were most active in Shantung, where a weak government presence and marginal living conditions resulting from years of natural calamities had badly affected the region. The Sung risked little by supporting such nominally "loyalist" armies operating almost entirely within Chin territory. Moreover, the difficulties the Chin faced in suppressing the rebels provided the Sung with some measure of its enemy's military effectiveness. Chin efforts at suppression were feeble, and the Sung drew the appropriate conclusions but did not act.

[92] *HTC* (1958) 156, p. 4214.
[93] *SS* 38, pp. 735, 738–9; Liu, *Hsü Sung chung-hsing pien-nien tzu-chih t'ung-chien* 13, pp. 4b, 6a.
[94] T'o-t'o, *Chin shih* 12, pp. 272–3.

The policy of aggression aroused substantial criticism. Vice-Minister of Public Works Yeh Shih, among the most prominent proponents of aggression at this time, nevertheless concluded that the vulnerability of Sung border defenses made conflict highly risky. Another staunch irredentist, Liu Kuang-tsu, drew the same conclusion, prompting him to resign from his high-level post in Li-chou circuit. Both men, despite persecution under the Ch'ing-yüan ban, had subsequently cooperated with the Han T'o-chou administration. Mere partisanship cannot explain their newfound caution. Similarly, Ch'iu Ch'ung, custodial prefect of Ming-chou, another recent recruit once known for his strident militancy, now voiced his opposition to war against the Chin. For one enraged student at the Military Academy (*Wu-hsüeh*), the war policy was so fraught with potential peril that Han T'o-chou, its witless architect, deserved death; for his temerity, the student was banished. In spring 1206, the greatest political setback to the plans to attack Chin came when Assistant Councilor Ch'ien Hsiang-tsu was compelled to resign because of his differences with Han T'o-chou over border management.[95] It seems that throughout the bureaucracy many questions remained both about Han T'o-chou's motives and about his competence to direct the war effort. Once hostilities erupted, these questions would multiply.

Despite the objections and resignations, in May 1206 the Sung offensive began in earnest. The commander Pi Tsai-yü was especially impressive in battle. He quickly captured the Chin prefecture of Ssu-chou, just north of the Huai River in modern Anhwei province. Soon, Sung forces took several counties in the southern part of Chin's Nan-ching circuit, in modern Honan. Although neither of these attacks had received official sanction by the court, which still sought to fully test enemy strength before committing Sung armies, the aggressive commanders had clearly been urged on by the court. Events to the west unfolded less impressively for the Sung. An offensive centered on Ts'ai-chou (Honan), ended in resounding defeat, as did another in Szechwan led by the pacification commissioner Ch'eng Sung. This somewhat weak initial showing did not dampen the enthusiasm of Han T'o-chou, and an official declaration of war soon followed within weeks. Already, the bureaucracy began to resist the war policy. Academician Yeh Shih, given the dubious honor of drafting the declaration of war, refused. This came as a considerable political embarrassment, but no more so than the military developments along the border. Following the brief capture of Ssu-chou in the east, the Sung scored only one other notable victory in 1206: local militia in the west seized control

---

[95] For these several opinions, see *SS* 243, p. 8657; 398, p. 12111; 434, pp. 12892–3; Huang et al., *Sung Yüan hsüeh-an* 54, pp. 985–8; *HTC* (1958) 157, pp. 4228, 4231–2, 4236, 4239; Chen, *Hsi-shan hsien-sheng Chen Wen-chung kung wen-chi* 43, p. 14b; Yeh, *Shui-hsin hsien-sheng wen-chi* 1, pp. 19b–21a.

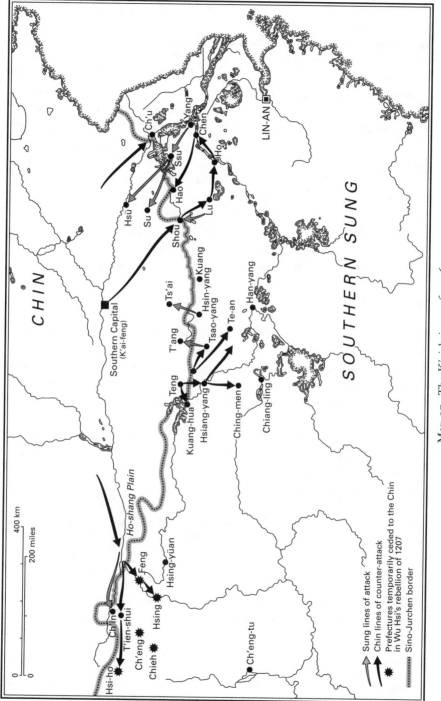

Map 27. The K'ai-hsi war of 1206.

of the Ho-shang Plain, a hotly contested area in the Li-chou circuit. Offensives against Su-chou2 and Hsü-chou in the east, and T'ang-chou, Shou-chou, and Ts'ai-chou in the central border region, all ended in defeat. The Sung drive lasted a mere three months, the time required for Chin forces to launch a counterattack.

Not only did the Chin succeed in promptly repulsing Sung armies, by late fall it was responding with an offensive of its own. A reputed seventy thousand Chin troops led by Ho-she-li Chih-chung (d. 1213) descended on the border town of Ch'u-chou, in modern Anhwei province. Chin troops outnumbered Sung defenders ten to one and were staved off only through the extraordinary resourcefulness of Pi Tsai-yü, now prefect of nearby Hsü-i. Apart from delivering desperately needed reinforcements to Ch'u-chou, Pi also cleverly managed, under the guise of darkness, to penetrate enemy lines and set fire to the Chin's provisions. The mere presence of Pi Tsai-yü, who was known for his ferocity in battle, did much to strengthen the resolve of Sung troops. The siege of Ch'u-chou continued for three months before the weary Chin forces retreated.[96] The encirclement of Ch'u-chou was only one leg of a massive nine-pronged Chin offensive that reputedly involved hundreds of thousands of troops and affected most of the twelve hundred–mile border separating the two empires. In addition to the campaign to the east, which resulted in penetrations deep into the eastern and western Huai-nan circuits, Chin forces also attacked commanderies along the central border. The Chin military leader Wan-yen K'uang led assaults on Tsao-yang, Kuang-hua, Te-an, and Hsiang-yang. The first two of these commanderies readily knuckled under, but Te-an and Hsiang-yang doggedly resisted massive three-month encirclements before the Chin forces withdrew.[97] To the west, Chin armies commanded by Fu-ch'a-chen delivered a severe blow to Sung defenders at T'ien-shui, Hsi-ho-chou, Mien-chou, and the Ho-shang Plain, all in northwest Li-chou circuit. Within less than a half year, Chin forces, by seizing the initiative, had managed to expose Sung vulnerability. The speed with which the tide had turned demonstrated that the Sung effort had been based on a serious underestimation of Chin capability. By year's end, the Sung court was prepared to try to restore peace.

INSURRECTION IN SZECHWAN

In its war with Chin, Sung setbacks in the east were overshadowed by the calamity that struck the Sung forces in their defeats in Szechwan in 1207.

---

[96] SS 402, pp. 12186–7; HTC (1958) 157, p. 4247.

[97] See HTC (1958), chüan 157–8; Herbert Franke, "Siege and defense of towns in medieval China," in Chinese ways in warfare, ed. Frank A. Kierman, Jr., and John K. Fairbank (Cambridge, Mass., 1974), especially pp. 179–88.

The Sung battle plan seems to have rested upon two major simultaneous offensives, an eastern thrust from Huai-nan East circuit into Shantung and a western thrust from Li-chou circuit into Ching-chao and Feng-hsiang in the Wei valley. A strong showing in the west could have pressured the Chin into transferring troops currently fighting in the east to the western front. This transfer was imperative if the Sung were to defend the Huai region successfully. Unfortunately, the Sung offensive in the west relied too heavily on a single commander.

That commander, Wu Hsi (d. 1207), hailed from a long line of eminent military leaders. Two generations earlier, the orphaned brothers Wu Chieh (1093–1139) and Wu Lin (1102–67), natives of Te-hsün, modern Kansu, had served in the armies of the late Northern Sung at the height of the Tangut and Jurchen invasions. With the loss of the northern part of the Sung empire the brothers had fled south. Wu Chieh became pacification commissioner of Szechwan and eventually military governor of Li-chou circuit. The younger brother, Wu Lin, had inherited that post, and groomed his own son, Wu T'ing (d. 1193), as his successor. Wu Lin and Wu T'ing were not altogether undeserving of the rewards they had been given. During the Chin invasion of 1161, father and son had performed impressively in frustrating the enemy's sixty-day siege of the Ta-san Pass, winning for Wu T'ing the military commissionership for western Li-chou circuit.[98]

Sung control over the military establishment in the west had always been tenuous. Maintaining long-distance control of the western regions by the Sung government in Lin-an had entailed a careful distribution of military authority to prevent any one commander in Szechwan from becoming too powerful. Regular transfers, a hallmark of the civilian bureaucracy, were less common in the military, so regional political autonomy was held in check by summoning commanders to the capital for regular audiences and by assigning civilian commissioners to supervise their activities at home. Additionally, the Sung sometimes housed a commander's family in the capital, the equivalent to holding them as hostages. In this way, the younger son of Wu T'ing, Wu Hsi, had spent much of his youth in Lin-an.[99]

By the late twelfth century, Wu Hsi had held an array of military titles; he had even served, in 1186, as an ambassador to the Chin. He had held posts with important responsibilities, including militia commander for Hao-chou

---

[98] On the Wu family, see SS 366, pp. 11408–14, 11421–4; 475, pp. 13811–14; Ihara Hiroshi, "Nan-Sō Shisen ni okeru Go Shi no seiryoku – Go Ki no ran zenshi," in *Aoyama Hakushi koki kinen Sōdai shi ronsō*, ed. Aoyama Hakushi Koki Kinen Sōdai-shi Ronsō Kankokai (Tokyo, 1974), pp. 1–33; Yamauchi Seibaku, "Nan-Sō no Shisen ni okeru Chō Shun to Go Kai – sono seiryoku kōtai no katei o chūshin to shite," *Shirin* 44 No. 1 (1961), pp. 98–124.

[99] HTC (1958) 156, p. 4192.

and commander of Chien-k'ang. It is no coincidence that both these assignments were in the east. Even in the later years of Hsiao-tsung's reign, officials
had expressed concern about the Wu family's growing might in Szechwan and
urged the court to assert itself. Chao Ju-yü had warned that continued tolerance
of such autonomy threatened to undermine the dynasty. Hsiao-tsung apparently had shared this apprehension, despite his usual inclination to indulge
the military, and named Chao Ju-yü military commissioner in chief of Szechwan and prefect of the circuit capital, Ch'eng-tu. Similarly, Vice-Minister of
Finance Ch'iu Ch'ung, a man with extensive experience in the region, had later
cautioned Kuang-tsung against permitting the sons of Wu T'ing to inherit
their father's military machine. Investigating Censor Huang Tu also argued
that further indulgence of the Wu family would spell imminent disaster.
These reservations were reiterated by Liu Cheng, who had preceded Chao Ju-
yü as commissioner in chief of Szechwan. "Of the three generals of the west,"
he noted, "only the Wu house has inherited power for generations. Theirs is
known as the 'Army of the Wu House' and they are oblivious to the commands
of the court."[100] When Wu T'ing died in 1193, Liu Cheng intentionally named
an outsider as military commissioner for Li-chou. As Wu Hsi assumed his own
post at a distant Hao-chou in Huai-nan, the prospect of his returning to his
home region must have seemed dim.

Later historians, with the advantage of hindsight, are quick to portray
Wu Hsi as a typical renegade, arrogant and insubordinate from the outset.
The views of contemporaries were initially not so damning. Sung officials,
in warning the government against tolerating one-family military dominance
in Szechwan, were not accusing a particular Wu kinsman, Wu T'ing or Wu
Hsi, of treasonous intent. They were concerned with preventing hereditary
control over regional armies, a practice that ran against the Sung tradition
of centralized, civilian control. Strong personal links between generals and
their armies undermined the authority of the central government, and regional
control weakened the empire's ideal of fiscal interdependence. In the vicinity of
Ta-san Pass, half of the revenues generated by government-leased landholdings
(*ying-t'ien*) were siphoned off by Wu T'ing and Kuo Kao (d. 1200), the two
leading military magnates in the region. Their economic clout was backed
by their broad popular support. The people of Szechwan, finding security
in continuity of leadership, reportedly "looked with necks outstretched" at
learning of Wu Hsi's imminent return.[101] Chao Ju-yü and Liu Cheng were
sensitive to the problem of Szechwan regionalism owing to their many years of

---

[100] On these views, see *SS* 391, pp. 11974–5; 392, pp. 11982–3; 383, p. 12010; 398, pp. 12110–11; *HTC*
    (1958) 152, p. 4083; Fu, *Sung-tai Shu-wen chi-ts'un* (1974) 71, p. 10a.
[101] *HTC* (1958) 155, pp. 4186–7; 156, p. 4193.

experience in the west. Lack of such experience partly explains why Han T'o-chou in mobilizing men and matériel for a major military initiative took the risk in the summer of 1201 of naming Wu Hsi prefect and general commander of the strategically important Hsing-chou2.[102] Some of Han's closest associates criticized the decision, including executives at the Bureau of Military Affairs. Official historians suggest that Wu Hsi received the appointment only by bribing high-level bureaucrats, but this may well be malicious gossip, without merit.[103]

Wu Hsi's vanity and ambition, if not previously apparent, became so upon his return to Szechwan. He immediately constructed a temple in honor of his grandfather, Wu Lin, spending a hundred thousand strings of cash on the main hall alone, probably using government funds. He then engineered the dismissal of Wang Ta-chieh, second in command at Hsing-chou2, whose considerable influence threatened his own autonomy.[104] The Sung court responded in 1205 by transferring Ch'eng Sung from Huai-nan West to Szechwan as military commissioner in chief, and thus Wu Hsi's superior. The presence of a trusted leader from the outside was to provide an important check on Wu Hsi, but unfamiliarity with the region placed Ch'eng Sung at a serious disadvantage. Troop levels presented an even greater problem. As assistant pacification commissioner for Szechwan, Wu Hsi directed an army of roughly sixty thousand; Ch'eng Sung commanded only half that number.[105] This disparity left the Sung court with little leverage to use against the Szechwan general. Much rested on simple good faith and mutual benefit.

In their 145,000-man counterattack in the winter of 1206, the Chin assigned over 100,000 troops for the campaign in the east and central border regions, committing only a small force to the western front. The Sung court worked from an opposite strategy. Its armies at Ch'u-chou, Te-an, and Hsiang-yang often contained no more than 10,000 men, and were sometimes outnumbered by the enemy ten to one, whereas in the west Ch'eng Sung and Wu Hsi commanded over 90,000 trained soldiers plus countless militia. The decision to invest troop strength heavily in Szechwan was strategically justifiable. By confining early combat to faraway Szechwan, the Sung court minimized the chance of retaliatory threats to its political and economic center in the east. And with Chin forces concentrated in the east, the center of previous wars, Chin's western flank was potentially vulnerable. But war had broken out in the Huai region, where the fighting had not

---

[102] *HTC* (1958) 156, pp. 4192–3.
[103] *SS* 394, pp. 12026, 12035; *HTC* (1958) 156, p. 4192.
[104] *SS* 475, p. 13812; *HTC* (1958) 156, pp. 4192–3.
[105] *HTC* (1958) 157, p. 4236.

gone well for the Sung. This prompted Han T'o-chou to embrace new battle plans.

Despite their considerable military forces in the west, the Sung scored no notable victories there. A sizable offensive commanded by Wu Hsi, his only offensive, was launched in the summer of 1206. It was an ill-timed assault on the Yen-ch'uan garrison, and Wu's forces were ultimately routed by Wan-yen Wang-hsi. After regrouping, Wu Hsi led fifty thousand men against the strategically vital Ch'in-chou (on the south bank of the Wei River, about 150 miles west of Chin-held Ch'ang-an [Hsi-an]). Although the Chin were probably outnumbered, the Sung forces made a poor showing and were forced to retreat.[106] Later that summer, the Sung commissioner Ch'eng Sung personally directed an offensive to capture the Fang-shan Plain, a hotly contested area subordinate to Feng-hsiang. Chin forces prevailed here too, and they followed up their victory by capturing the Ho-shang Plain. This Chin victory opened the Sung's western flank to enemy attack; before long, the prefecture of Hsi-ho-chou, scarcely sixty miles from Wu Hsi's base at Hsing-chou2, was being attacked. The Sung response was inexplicably weak. Even the Chin strike against T'ung-ch'ing, a scant thirty miles from Hsing-chou2, did not provoke a counterattack. By fall 1206, Wu Hsi had clearly withdrawn active support for the war effort and meticulously tried to avoid any serious engagement with the enemy, allowing Chin forces to overrun much of Li-chou circuit. Wu's reluctance to fight, in turn, immobilized his superior, Ch'eng Sung, who relied heavily upon him to provide both manpower and arms.

The reason for Wu Hsi's reluctance to fight the Chin cannot be easily assessed; official accounts are uniformly unsympathetic to him. Yet to assume, as do traditional historians, that he had always harbored seditious aims ignores his contribution to the midsummer offensive. The investment of fifty thousand men, the backbone of his army, in one assault at Ch'in-chou can hardly be dismissed as a token gesture, even if it was repulsed. At some point during or before the war, circumstances had forced Wu Hsi to reassess his role in the geopolitical struggle between the Sung and the Chin. Perhaps, after initially engaging Chin armies, he simply realized that he could not defeat them. Perhaps he wanted to avoid high-risk conflict and preserve his army and his command by taking a low-risk defensive posture in the mountainous terrain of northern Szechwan. Maybe tensions emerged between him and either his local superior, Ch'eng Sung, or the remote Sung court, leaving Wu Hsi disillusioned.

By the end of 1206, Chin forces had defeated Sung armies from Ch'in-chou in the west to Ch'u-chou in the east. The greatest blow to the Sung came on

---

[106] T'o-t'o, *Chin shih* 12, pp. 276–7.

the lunar new year in 1207, when Wu Hsi renounced his fealty to the Sung and accepted Chin ennoblement as Prince of Shu. He adopted his own reign title and elevated his palace at Hsing-chou2 to an imperial residence. According to Chin records, the astonishing coup was brought about through simple bribery.[107] Yet Wu Hsi may have switched sides to stem the further advance of Chin forces into his area of control. The Chin had already seized Ho-shang Pass and were beginning assaults on Ch'eng-chou to the northwest of Hsing-chou2 and Feng-chou to the northeast. Chin forces had also begun to besiege Chieh-chou, Hsi-ho-chou, T'ung-ch'ing, and Feng-chou. These prefectures, surrendered to the Chin by Wu Hsi, provided an important foothold in Sung territory in the northwest. Chin control over these four prefectures also formed a convenient cluster around Hsing-chou2 and made it easy for Chin to contain Wu Hsi, should he, through inflated ambition or recklessness, choose to turn on his new patrons. The Chin had good reason for concern about the ambitions of Szechwan's overlord. Soon after betraying the Sung, Wu Hsi had promised to join forces with the Chin in a major offensive against the Sung, one that would focus on the strategically important Hsiang-yang (in Hupei) on the Han River.[108] Already under siege for over a month and vastly outnumbered by the enemy, Hsiang-yang looked certain to crumble under such heavy pressure. Fortunately for the Sung, the crisis caused by Wu Hsi's defection and the loss of the court's control over Szechwan would soon be resolved by further regional political upheavals in Szechwan, which would result in new pressures on Chin in the west.

Wu Hsi's extended absence from Szechwan prior to 1201 had limited his ability to quickly create strong bonds with subordinates and keep these men in line. During the crisis, Wu Hsi had to contend with several regional military leaders, including An Ping (d. 1221), a former protégé of Wu T'ing and the military intendant of Ta-an commandery, about thirty miles south of Hsing-chou2. After his break with the Sung, Wu Hsi invited An Ping to serve as his senior chief councilor. Whether An Ping accepted is not known. The reward of office does not seem to have swayed him, and he was to prove thoroughly duplicitous in his later dealings both with Wu Hsi and with the Sung court.[109] Another potential foe whom Wu Hsi needed to win over was his erstwhile superior Ch'eng Sung. Wu Hsi had betrayed him at the close of 1206 by reneging on a promise to join in the defense of Feng-chou. Nevertheless, Ch'eng Sung had accepted a post under Wu Hsi in his new Szechwan regime, but he did so only under duress, trapped between the Jurchen to the north and

[107] T'o-t'o, *Chin shih* 12, p. 279.
[108] *SS* 475, p. 13813; *HTC* (1958) 158, p. 4257.
[109] *SS* 38, p. 744; 402, pp. 12189, 12195, 12198.

Wu Hsi to the south. He was a prisoner, unable to flee to Sung-held territory. Wu Hsi could not be sure of Ch'eng's loyalty, especially in light of Ch'eng's close ties to the Sung court as one-time executive at the Bureau of Military Affairs. Wu Hsi's arrangement with Ch'eng did not endure, and he impatiently ordered Ch'eng Sung's assassination. Unwittingly, Wu Hsi's actions triggered a coup that would lead to his own death.[110]

Before the order to kill Ch'eng Sung had been given, a conspiracy against Wu Hsi had been hatched by two men, Yang Chü-yüan (d. 1207), a minor inspector of military supplies at Hsing-chou2, and Li Hao-i (d. 1207), a commander there. It seems that both were motivated by loyalty to the Sung, but Wu Hsi's stinginess in sharing the spoils may also have alienated them.[111] Whatever their motives, Yang Chü-yüan and Li Hao-i moved quickly to mobilize military support. They established a liaison with the intended assassin of Ch'eng Sung, Li Kuei, from early on. Having additionally won the assent of An Ping, the two mutineers led a small contingent of seventy men under the cover of darkness to Wu Hsi's "imperial residence" at Hsing-chou2. A thousand guards were reportedly assigned to the palace, but they were neutralized by instructions from An Ping. Trapped in his bedchamber, Wu Hsi was seized and decapitated; as a further humiliation his corpse was cut in half at the waist. Only forty-one days after its official inauguration, the "Shu government" ceased to exist. Upon learning of Wu Hsi's death, the people of Hsing-chou2 are said to have rejoiced to the point of "shaking Heaven and Earth." The head of Wu Hsi was hung in the marketplace as a grim reminder of the risks of duplicity. Wu Hsi's wife, close relatives, and supporters were all put to the sword.

The assassination of Wu Hsi was planned and carried out by members of the military establishment in northern Szechwan, apparently without any involvement by the Sung court. In fact, Han T'o-chou had only recently written to Wu Hsi with offers of Sung ennoblement, in an effort to outbid the Chin for Wu's loyalty.[112] Yet Wu's attempt to gain full autonomy and his subsequent assassination underscored, if nothing else, the inability of the Sung court to control men and events in distant Szechwan. Over the next months, the Sung court would handle the Szechwan situation with extreme care, seeking to strengthen its own hand without inciting the regional power brokers who could easily undo everything. The court dismissed Ch'eng Sung for failing to control Wu Hsi and replaced him with Yang Fu, the prefect of Ch'eng-tu. Yang

---

[110] On the coup against Wu Hsi, see SS 402, pp. 12189, 12194–6, 12198–9; 475, pp. 13813–14; HTC (1958) 158, pp. 4260–1.

[111] SS 402, p. 12194.

[112] SS 402, p. 12189; 475, p. 13813; Liu, Hsü Sung chung-hsing pien-nien tzu-chih t'ung-chien 13, p. 10b; Liang-ch'ao kang-mu pei-yao 10, pp. 4b–5b.

Fu had years of service in the west and possessed an uncompromised loyalty to the Sung court. He seemed the ideal choice as pacification commissioner.[113] For additional control, the court named a special imperial commissioner for Szechwan and appointed the impeccably credentialed Hsü I (1170–1219). Hsü, first in the *chin-shih* list of 1199, was also, by no coincidence, a native of Chien-chou2, near Ch'eng-tu. More than a reliable civilian official, he was familiar with the region and commanded local respect as a distinguished degree holder.[114] After dismissing Ch'eng Sung, the court might have moved against another prominent Szechwan leader, An Ping. Instead, the court promoted him from military intendant to assistant pacification commissioner of Szechwan. An Ping had been given Wu Hsi's old post. This controversial decision may well have been in reward for An Ping's collaboration in Wu Hsi's overthrow. It seems the Sung court had very few options. Having inherited much of Wu Hsi's military machine, An Ping was too powerful to challenge outright.

An Ping's elevation to assistant pacification commissioner was no guarantee of his loyalty; neither would the appointments of Yang Fu and Hsü I provide fail-proof checks. Developments after the coup only underscored how dangerously autonomous the west had become. In April 1207, Li Hao-i, a former conspirator in the overthrow of Wu Hsi, retook Hsi-ho-chou, followed by Ch'eng-chou, Chieh-chou, Feng-chou, and the Ta-san Pass. All territory ceded to the Chin by Wu Hsi had been regained and was now nominally controlled by the Sung. Chin forces, caught off guard, retreated north with unexpected haste. The success so intoxicated Szechwan leaders that Li Hao-i went on the offensive, attacking Ch'in-chou, the Chin border town that Wu Hsi had attacked the previous summer in 1206. The campaign helped to invigorate Sung armies and won Li Hao-i an appointment as assistant commandant of Hsing-chou2 and later as prefect of Hsi-ho-chou. Yet at the moment of these successes, the military leaders in Szechwan began to turn on one another.

Within months, mutiny erupted. Coalitions formed within the Hsing-chou2 military establishment following the demise of Wu Hsi began to break apart. After the overthrow of Wu Hsi, some factions within the Szechwan leadership had acquiesced to a tenuous cooperation under An Ping, but Li Hao-i's prominent role in the overthrow, and his recent military victories, fostered dangerous rivalries. Commanders Wang Hsi and Liu Ch'ang-kuo turned against the increasingly powerful Li Hao-i. Wang Hsi had never been on good terms with Li Hao-i, and the enmity between them was now so strong that Wang Hsi had Li Hao-i poisoned by Liu Ch'ang-kuo. To the Sung court this revenge killing was a senseless act, depriving them of a prized

---

[113] *HTC* (1958) 158, pp. 4258–9, 4262.
[114] *SS* 406, pp. 12267–71; *HTC* (1958) 158, p. 4262.

commander at a difficult time. The execution of Wang Hsi would have been appropriate punishment; instead, the Sung court only transferred Wang Hsi to be commandant for eastern Ching-hu North.[115] Apparently too intimidated by Wang's military power to act more decisively, the court had to be content with simply removing him from Szechwan.

Within two weeks of Li Hao-i's death, another prominent commander met a violent end. Yang Chü-yüan, as a minor supplies inspector, had masterminded and carried out the coup against Wu Hsi, yet court honors seem not to have adequately recognized his contributions. While An Ping, Li Hao-i, and even the treacherous Wang Hsi had won prestigious appointments, Yang Chü-yüan was only promoted to military consultant to the pacification commissioner, a paltry reward for a leading rebel suppressor. Yang Chü-yüan may well have attributed such parsimony to An Ping, for tensions between the two had heightened soon after Wu Hsi's assassination, prompting An Ping to question Yang's loyalty. In a clever move to discredit Yang Chü-yüan, An Ping secretly ordered him to execute a disfavored commander charged with cowardice in the defense of the Ta-san Pass. This order seemed to be a test of Yang Chü-yüan's loyalty and Yang had to act, yet in so doing his reputation suffered. Yang's dissatisfaction with Szechwan's military leadership was well known, and his participation in a second notable execution gave an impression of uncontrolled ambition. An Ping quickly had Yang Chü-yüan arrested and then informed the Sung court of Yang's suicide. Despite An Ping's efforts to cast the dead man as a rebel, Commissioner in Chief Yang Fu and others were not easily deceived.[116] The Sung court was warned by Yang Fu and others against further indulging An Ping's lawlessness, but Han T'o-chou turned a deaf ear. He could not risk the dangerous vacuum certain to accompany any further significant restructuring of the Szechwan leadership. Instead, An Ping was promoted to grand military commissioner in chief.

Admittedly, An Ping had played a critical role in eliminating Wu Hsi and restoring Sung authority in the west. Although he never betrayed the court's trust, he still acted out of arrogance and self-interest. Many died at his hands or those of his agents. Yang Chü-yüan was the victim of his superior's jealousy and suspicion; like Li Hao-i, a rival to An Ping, Yang was too successful for his own good. His elimination served An Ping's personal interests, and perhaps even the short-term interests of a distant Sung court concerned with survival and stability, rather than with the long-term interests of the dynasty. Loyalist soldiers in Szechwan reportedly broke into tears at learning of the death of Yang Chü-yüan. His and Li Hao-i's valor had inspired countless

[115] SS 402, pp. 12200–1; HTC (1958) 158, pp. 4264–6.
[116] SS 402, pp. 12190, 12196–8; HTC (1958) 158, pp. 4264–5.

troops. The intrigue and turmoil surrounding their deaths must have taken its toll on morale. The consolidation of military power under An Ping did not strengthen the western front, as might be expected, for the emerging atmosphere of suspicion, treachery, intimidation, and alienation left Szechwan divided within and vulnerable from outside.

THE COUP IN LIN-AN

Within a month of its official launch in the summer of 1206, the Sung offensive against the Chin in the east had degenerated into a humiliating retreat. The Chin had begun their own advance in late autumn, in some places pushing ninety miles into Sung territory. Still, the Chin were unable to establish a firm foothold in the south. Sung armies, under the command of Pi Tsai-yü along the coast and Commissioner Chao Fang (d. 1221) in the central border regions, defended their territory with a dogged determination absent earlier when they had fought on unfamiliar terrain. In the west, Chin forces all too easily surrendered territory acquired through the Wu Hsi defection. Having unwisely committed up to three hundred thousand men in the protracted sieges of Ch'u-chou, Hsiang-yang, and Te-an, the Chin had precious few reserves for deployment in the west, and Wu Hsi was assassinated before the Chin could consolidate their new holdings in northern Szechwan.[117] At the same time, Sung-affiliated armies in Szechwan, aggressive in recovering lost territory, seemed powerless to expand their limited defensive success into a more general offensive. Sung and Chin forces continued to clash throughout much of 1207, yet neither side could claim the upper hand. Fighting gave way to negotiation.

Already in late 1206, the Sung court had initiated peace overtures, authorizing the general commander for the eastern flank, Ch'iu Ch'ung, to approach Pu-sa K'uei (var. P'u-san K'uei, d. 1207), Chin commander for the central Huai region.[118] The proposed Chin terms were harsh: reducing the diplomatic status of Sung to vassal state of Chin, increasing the annual tribute paid to Chin, and surrendering the culprit responsible for starting the fighting.[119] The Chin were negotiating from a position of strength, and their initial demands were excessive. The Sung broke off negotiations. Toward year's end, with Wu Hsi's defection to the Chin already certain, Pu-sa K'uei had dispatched his own envoy, Han Yüan-ching, to the camp of Ch'iu Ch'ung. The envoy, reputedly a descendant of Han Ch'i and thus a distant younger cousin of Han T'o-chou,

[117] HTC (1958) 158, p. 4261.
[118] T'o-t'o, Chin shih 12, p. 278. Only Chin shih attributes the initiative to the Sung court.
[119] HTC (1958) 157, p. 4249.

pleaded for a peace pact with the Sung on the personal grounds that the current conflict had made protection of their common Han family ancestral tombs at Hsiang-chou2 exceedingly difficult.[120] Han Yüan-ching never met his cousin in person, but the Sung court ordered Ch'iu Ch'ung to conduct negotiations at the border. These efforts proved inconclusive. The Chin were insistent upon imposing some sort of punitive ransom, and the Sung were adamant in refusing.

Negotiations resumed in late spring 1207, when the Sung dispatched Fang Hsin-ju (1177–1222) to K'ai-feng, where he met with Councilor of the Left Wan-yen Ch'ung-ho (d. 1207). The Chin, sensing that the Sung court was desperate for a pact, toughened their demands: new territorial concessions and an unacceptably large increase in annual tribute. They also demanded, for the first time quite specifically, the head of Han T'o-chou. In summer and early fall, Fang Hsin-ju made three trips north. Ch'iu Ch'ung had, by this time, been replaced as chief commander of the eastern flank by Chang Yen, a concurrent assistant councilor and Bureau of Military Affairs executive.[121] It was Chang Yen who advised Fang Hsin-ju, and the two appear intentionally to have kept Han T'o-chou uninformed about specific Chin demands. These were divulged to Han T'o-chou only when Fang Hsin-ju returned in defeat to Lin-an, in late September. A furious Han T'o-chou not only dismissed the envoy but also had Chang Yen removed from his border command.

By this time, Han T'o-chou had become isolated at court. This isolation had its roots in dismissals made in summer 1206, when he had begun impulsively to replace military leaders who had failed to achieve victories. Teng Yu-lung (*chin-shih* 1172), a former censor serving as special commissioner for the Huai region, was dismissed after only three months, his defeats being too numerous. A similar reason had been given for the dismissal of the chief commander of Chien-k'ang, Li Shuang, and the assistant commander for the Ching-hsi North circuit, Huang-fu Pin. The records show that both had fought valiantly and won praise from their fellow commanders, but Han T'o-chou it seems was more concerned with the final outcome than with the special circumstances of particular battles.[122] Wang Ta-chieh's offensive against Ts'ai-chou (also in Ching-hsi North) had also been courageously fought, yet defeat resulted in his banishment to Ling-nan (in modern Kwangtung province), on the southern fringes of Sung civilization. For the same reason, Li Ju-i, chief commander for Huai-nan West, was also banished. Thus, early on in the war, Han T'o-chou had

---

[120] SS 398, p. 12112; T'o-t'o, *Chin shih* 93, pp. 2067–71; HTC (1958) 157, p. 4253.

[121] On these negotiations, see SS 395, pp. 12059–62; T'o-t'o, *Chin shih* 93, pp. 2072–80; HTC (1958) 158, pp. 4262, 4266–9.

[122] HTC (1958) 157, pp. 4251–64.

brought about a sweeping reorganization of military commands. By abruptly entrusting military leadership to inexperienced officials, Han T'o-chou came to appear impulsive and unpredictable.

Han T'o-chou's increasing isolation also resulted from his calculated removal of once trusted supporters. He had assisted Su Shih-tan, a longtime associate, in rising to the post of general recipient of edicts at the Bureau of Military Affairs in 1201 and subsequently an audience commandant.[123] Yet the protégé was not popular within the bureaucracy, and he was denounced as blatantly corrupt. As war fortunes began to dip, Han T'o-chou distanced himself from Su Shih-tan and appeared to be blaming the entire policy on Su, a once vocal advocate of aggression. To appease critics while absolving himself of responsibility, Han T'o-chou permitted Su Shih-tan to be stripped of official status, banished to distant Shao-chou2, and further humiliated by official confiscation of his family property.[124] Such scapegoating must have left other of his associates apprehensive. Equally unsettling was Fang Hsin-ju's return to Lin-an. The emissary to Chin had been unsuccessful in negotiations, and speculation arose that an angry Han T'o-chou planned to break the diplomatic impasse by escalating the fighting. This brought one-time supporters and neutral elements at court into an alliance that spelled doom for Han T'o-chou. Central to this alliance was Shih Mi-yüan (1164–1233).

A native of Ming-chou, modern Ning-po, Shih Mi-yüan was the third son of Shih Hao, Hsiao-tsung's trusted tutor and chief minister.[125] During Han T'o-chou's twelve years of dominance, Shih Mi-yüan had risen from legal examiner at the High Court of Justice to vice-minister of rites. His ascent to power, uncommonly smooth for the time, stems partly from the goodwill of Chief Councilor Ching T'ang; yet Ching's death in 1200 had no noticeable effect upon Shih Mi-yüan's further advancement. Shih was apparently quite skillful at avoiding confrontation by steering a clear path through politically troubled waters. His attitude toward the *Tao-hsüeh* movement, much like his father's, was conveniently ambiguous, and this probably explains his political survival during the purges of the early Ning-tsung era. In 1205, by which time he was already well entrenched in the bureaucracy, he offered his first known criticism of Han T'o-chou.[126] In a carefully worded memorial, he labeled the war policy venturesome. Shih Mi-yüan stressed the importance of defending

---

[123] On Su Shih-tan, see *SS* 38, p. 741; 398, pp. 12107–8, 12115; 474, pp. 13774–7; *HTC* (1958) 156, pp. 4197, 4210; 157, pp. 4229, 4243–4; 158, p. 4271.

[124] *SS* 398, p. 12107–8.

[125] On Shih Mi-yüan, see Davis, *Court and family in Sung China*, pp. 81–117; *SS* 414, pp. 12415–18; Yüan Chüeh, *Yen-yu Ssu-ming chih* (1320; Taipei, 1978) 5, pp. 10b–12a; Tai Mei et al., *Hsin-hsiu Yin-hsien chih* [Academia Sinica, Fu Ssu-nien ed.] (n.p., 1877) 14, pp. 26b–34a.

[126] Yang Shih-ch'i, *Li-tai ming-ch'en tsou-i* (1416; Taipei, 1964) 235, p. 6a.

the south and protecting the lives of its tens of millions. He never mentioned Han T'o-chou by name, never exploited this policy difference to denounce the chief policy maker, and never protested government actions by withdrawing from office. Han T'o-chou apparently appreciated the courtesy, for Shih Mi-yüan was subsequently enfeoffed as Baron of Yin county. Policy differences notwithstanding, there is no evidence of personal animosity or political tension between Shih Mi-yüan and Han T'o-chou. The former typified the neutral element at court, namely, individuals who had long cooperated with Han's administration, but now, under new and unbearable pressures, felt compelled to act against its leader.

In 1206, Assistant Councilor Ch'ien Hsiang-tsu resigned. He had never been enthusiastic about the war policy and resigned as the policy's disastrous outcome became increasingly apparent. Resuming responsibilities in spring 1207, Ch'ien did so with no confidence in Han T'o-chou. Li Pi, a fellow assistant councilor, had from the outset proposed inciting the Chin to war and responding in full force instead of initiating hostilities on foreign soil, as the court planned. This would have lent greater legitimacy to the Sung court's cause and augmented popular support.[127] Li's counsel was rejected; nevertheless, he supported the war cause, until Han T'o-chou threatened an escalation of the fighting.

Action by the disaffected officials came on the morning of the twenty-fourth day of the eleventh month in 1207. En route to court and reportedly frazzled after a long night of drink and merriment, Han T'o-chou was intercepted at the Sixth Platoon Bridge, within the walls of the imperial city and near an audience chamber. Palace Guard commander Hsia Chen, in the company of several hundred elite guardsmen, informed him of an imperial rescript ordering his dismissal. Permitting no more than a brief curse from their victim, Hsia Chen's men dragged Han T'o-chou outside the wall of the imperial city to the Yü-chin Garden, where they bludgeoned him to death.[128] The assassination was unprecedented. Civility had been the hallmark of Sung politics, and contemporaries took pride in the unique Sung tradition of venerating scholar-officials. Chief ministers might suffer banishment for improper conduct or misguided policies, but never had a chief minister been assassinated while in office. Worse yet, enacting this brutal scenario in the emperor's own precincts suggested complicity at the highest levels.

[127] On their views, see SS 398, pp. 12107–8; HTC (1958) 157, p. 4236.

[128] For a more thorough treatment, see Davis, *Court and family in Sung China*, pp. 84–92. Also see Liu, *Hsü Sung chung-hsing pien-nien tzu-chih t'ung-chien* 13, pp. 11a–12a; Li, *Chien-yen i-lai ch'ao-yeh tsa-chi* (1967) i 10, pp. 6b–10a; Chou Mi, *Ch'i-tung yeh-yü* (1291; Peking, 1983) 3, pp. 45–52; SS 243, pp. 8656–7; HTC (1958) 158, pp. 4269–71.

It is difficult given the plethora of contradictory sources to understand the major events surrounding Han T'o-chou's assassination. Shih Mi-yüan undeniably played an important role in the conspiracy, and he certainly reaped great political benefit from Han T'o-chou's demise. Many sources have portrayed him as chief conspirator.[129] But these sources ignore the issue of motive. Shih Mi-yüan's only grievance against Han T'o-chou related to war policy. In the absence of evidence to suggest personal or even professional conflict between the two, it is doubtful that he was powerful enough to inspire such a dangerous act. A far more likely suspect is Empress Yang2 (Yang Mei-tzu, 1162–1232).

Tensions between Han T'o-chou and Ning-tsung's second empress can be traced to Empress Yang2's installation. Han T'o-chou's niece, Empress Han, had died in 1200, three years after the death of his influential aunt, Dowager Empress Wu. These deaths must have gravely troubled Han T'o-chou, for so much of his own influence had rested upon the standing of these two women within the palace. The only empress still alive by late 1200 was Hsiao-tsung's third wife, Dowager Empress Hsieh2, an exceedingly servile and politically detached personality. In the absence of a strong dowager empress to arrange a marriage, Ning-tsung had the rare privilege of personally selecting a new spouse. This opportunity did not augur well for Han T'o-chou. Ning-tsung, at the time, had become enamored with Consort Yang, a woman of humble birth but many talents, and he elevated her to imperial concubine shortly before the death of Empress Han. Han T'o-chou must have appreciated that the native intelligence and self-assertiveness of this commoner-turned-consort could jeopardize his own dominance, and this prompted him to recommend a more pliant woman, Lady Ts'ao, to succeed his niece. Two full years passed before the emperor acted, suggesting tensions over the nomination, but he ultimately installed his favorite, Empress Yang2, in 1203. Empress Yang2 is said never to have forgiven Han T'o-chou for his interference. Relations between the two had started off poorly and never improved.[130]

The *Sung dynastic history* (*Sung shih*), while not altogether consistent, does at times identify Empress Yang2 as a prime mover in the assassination conspiracy. Empress Yang2 had prompted her twelve-year-old stepson, Chao Hsün (1192–1220), to appeal to the emperor to end the war. In the summer of 1207 she offered her own criticisms, a vituperative assessment of court policy and a personal excoriation of Han T'o-chou.[131] She exploited the occasion, so rumor

---

[129] SS 394, p. 12035; 398, p. 12108; 474, pp. 13776–7; Liu, *Hsü Sung chung-hsing pien-nien tzu-chih t'ung-chien* 16, pp. 6b–7a; *Liang-ch'ao kang-mu pei-yao* 10, p. 28b; Yüan, *Yen-yu Ssu-ming chih* 5, pp. 10b–11a.

[130] On conflict between the two, see SS 243, pp. 8656–7; Chou, *Ch'i-tung yeh-yü* (1983) 3, p. 47; HTC (1958) 156, p. 4204.

[131] Shih Mi-yüan may have prodded the child as well, see SS 246, pp. 8734–5.

has it, to rally bureaucratic support. Through her adopted brother, Yang Tz'u-shan, she established links with sympathetic officials that drew Shih Mi-yüan and others into the conspiracy. The imperial rescript ordering dismissal for Han T'o-chou is considered by some to have been her handiwork.[132] Later, Empress Yang2 ordered the public flogging of one of Han T'o-chou's four widows, undeniable proof of a deep animosity and of the empress's contempt for Han T'o-chou.[133]

However, other sections of the *Sung dynastic history* ascribe to the empress a passive role in the conspiracy and portray Shih Mi-yüan as the chief villain. This conflicting emphasis probably reflects the bias of Yüan historians, the compilers of the *Sung shih*, who had no great esteem for Shih Mi-yüan. Yet Shih Mi-yüan had neither sufficient motive nor the political clout to carry out this shocking coup alone. Empress Yang2 would continue to prove herself the most politically astute empress of the Southern Sung, more daring than most men around her. She would also be remembered as a great patron of the arts and an accomplished calligrapher.[134] Active involvement by an empress in affairs of state ordinarily evoked official censure, but in this case it did not, perhaps because she camouflaged her actions with consummate skill and allowed praise and blame to fall on the men who did her bidding.

A still thornier issue in Han T'o-chou's assassination is Ning-tsung's role. By some accounts, Empress Yang2 and Shih Mi-yüan, whether alone or together, acted entirely on their own and presented an astonished Ning-tsung with a fait accompli. By other accounts, the emperor ordered the dismissal of Han T'o-chou, but was uninvolved in his murder. A third position charges that the emperor issued a secret directive ordering the execution of Han T'o-chou. All three versions appear in different sections of the *Sung dynastic history*,[135] implying that historians in the Yüan dynasty with access to a wide range of court documents were unable or unwilling to discern the emperor's role in the coup. Near contemporaries of the event tended also to be inconsistent. Historian Li Hsin-ch'uan (1167–1244) places responsibility for the assassination squarely upon the shoulders of Ning-tsung. Anecdotist Chou Mi (1232–1308) insists that the emperor learned of the coup only after the fact.[136] But most writers agree on one point: Ning-tsung, not an original party to the conspiracy, was taken into confidence only when it was in the process of being carried out.

---

[132] Ting, *Sung-jen i-shih hui-pien* (1982) 17, p. 876.

[133] Ting, *Sung-jen i-shih hui-pien* (1982) 17, p. 877.

[134] Wen C. Fong, *Beyond representation: Chinese painting and calligraphy, 8th–14th century* (New York, 1992), pp. 234–7.

[135] Compare accounts in *SS* 38, p. 746; 243, p. 8657; 414, p. 12416; 474, pp. 13776–7; also see Davis, *Court and family in Sung China*, pp. 89–92.

[136] Li, *Chien-yen i-lai ch'ao-yeh tsa-chi* (1967) *i* 10, pp. 6b–10a; Chou, *Ch'i-tung yeh-yü* (1983) 3, pp. 45–52.

Being kept in the dark, if Ning-tsung was, appears not to have troubled the emperor, for he immediately responded with a generous round of promotions. Assistant councilor Ch'ien Hsiang-tsu was promoted at the Bureau of Military Affairs and eventually named chief councilor of the right; Li Pi was advanced at the same bureau; Vice-Minister of Rites Shih Mi-yüan became minister of rites; Yang Tz'u-shan, advanced from grand marshal to junior guardian, was enfeoffed as a prince; even the emperor's adopted son, Chao Hsün, was rewarded for his precocious advice with installation as heir apparent. Conversely, those who had been closely associated with Han T'o-chou's irredentist policies were uniformly punished. Heading the list was Han's former instructor, the reviled Ch'en Tzu-ch'iang, who was exiled to Kuang-chou (Canton). Dismissals also awaited many lesser officials, but only one other official shared with Han T'o-chou the ultimate humiliation. Su Shih-tan, a crony who was under banishment in Kuang-chou, was executed at court order. As for the family of Han T'o-chou, the court banished his son Han Kung to a distant offshore island.

With new political leadership, the Sung court revived the deadlocked peace talks with Chin. Their chief envoy was a scholar at the Directorate of Education, Wang Nan (1158–1213), grandson of Wang Lun (1084–1144), a former emissary killed sixty-three years earlier on a mission for Kao-tsung.[137] Wang Nan had initially been dispatched by Han T'o-chou, and the new administration ordered a second envoy to join him, no doubt with new instructions. The second envoy was Hsü I, commissioner for Szechwan. Under pressure to strike a speedy accord, Wang Nan made concessions that his predecessor Fang Hsin-ju had rejected outright. Wang agreed to increase the Sung court's annual subsidy from 250,000 to 300,000 units of account calculated in ounces of silver and bolts of silk, an unhealthy precedent according to Fang Hsin-ju.[138] Wang Nan and Hsü I also offered the heads of Han T'o-chou and Su Shih-tan, whom the Chin had previously alleged were the Sung court's chief instigators of war.[139] The Chin dropped their demand for territorial concessions and adjustments in diplomatic status, but the Sung still had to endure the indignity of the corpse of its high minister being publicly defiled by the "foreign occupiers" of their lost northern lands.

The unusual demand for the heads of Han and Su by the Chin seems to have been less intended to humiliate the Sung than to obtain retribution for humiliation the Chin themselves had suffered when, following the mutiny by pro-Sung elements in Szechwan, the head of the Chin confederate Wu Hsi had been hung on display in the marketplaces of Hsing-chou2 and Lin-an.

---

[137] SS 395, p. 12062; HTC (1958) 158, pp. 4268, 4275–8.
[138] SS 395, p. 12061.
[139] SS 395, p. 12062; HTC (1958) 158, p. 4275.

The Chin had taken this as a personal insult, and Sung officials interpreted the Chin request as a matter of injured pride. Before complying, however, the Sung court ordered the bodies of Han T'o-chou and Su Shih-tan exhumed and their heads placed on public display. Thoroughly repudiating them at home would presumably diminish the symbolic impact of shipping their remains north. Many endorsed the concession. Minister of Personnel Lou Yüeh represented perhaps the majority at court in stating, "The peace negotiations represent an important matter which awaits only this to be resolved. Why should the already putrefied heads of treacherous traitors merit our concern?" But others demurred. Responding to Lou Yüeh, the envoy, Wang Nan, retorted, "The head of Han T'o-chou may not be worthy of our concern, but the empire's status is of concern!"[140] Minister of War Ni Ssu decried the act for similar reasons. Vice-Minister of Imperial Sacrifices Huang Tu portrayed the accommodation as tantamount to insulting the Sung state. Chen Te-hsiu (1178–1235), a professor at the Imperial University, was joined by students in denouncing the concession as an unprecedented shame.[141] Interestingly, Huang Tu and Chen Te-hsiu, although they had been persecuted under the *Tao-hsüeh* ban, opposed the posthumous humiliation of their persecutor. They did so in defense of the empire's dignity, not on humanitarian grounds nor out of compassion for the dead individual.

SHIH MI-YÜAN IN POWER

Compromise and conflict

Although the new peace treaty was crafted by Wang Nan and other on-site negotiators, responsibility for accepting its controversial terms lay with two men: Ch'ien Hsiang-tsu, chief councilor and concurrent head of the Bureau of Military Affairs, and his counterpart as administrator at the Bureau of Military Affairs, Shih Mi-yüan. Whatever their personal feelings about the agreement, the two wasted no time before implementing it. Three months after exhuming the bodies of Han T'o-chou and Su Shih-tan, they forwarded the two heads to the Chin under the escort of Wang Nan. By some accounts, the remains were hung in a public thoroughfare, then embalmed and stored in a military warehouse. Others allege that the Chin, considering Han T'o-chou to have been a loyal official, provided an honorable burial alongside his ancestor Han

---

[140] *SS* 395, pp. 12047, 12062; *HTC* (1958) 158, p. 4275.
[141] On their views, see Ting, *Sung-jen i-shih hui-pien* (1982) 17, p. 878; *SS* 398, p. 12115; 393, p. 12011; 437, pp. 12957–8; *HTC* (1958) 158, p. 4281.

Ch'i.[142] Control over Ta-san Pass in the west and Hao-chou in the east, two areas still in Chin hands in mid-1208, was restored to the Sung.

A new era in Southern Sung politics

The end of war also marked the beginning of a distinctive era in Southern Sung politics. Under Kuang-tsung, statesmen with ties to the *Tao-hsüeh* movement and access to influential posts had touched off an impassioned campaign to promote their political agenda in government, a campaign that ultimately backfired and facilitated the ascendency of the inner court. The inner court, led by Han T'o-chou, subsequently launched its own campaigns: first, the inner court tried to cow *Tao-hsüeh* proponents through proscription and intimidation, and when this failed, they tried to win glory through an ambitious recovery of the north. Various defeats awaited the more extremist elements of both groups, for some of the *Tao-hsüeh* supporters were too dogmatic, and some of the inner palace group too self-serving to create lasting coalitions. With the restoration of peace in 1208, philosophical hauteur and political bravado gave way to moderation and compromise as new leaders emerged to reconcile political divisions.

Ch'ien Hsiang-tsu remained chief councilor through 1208, yet his time in favor was on the wane. The emperor increasingly placed his confidence in Shih Mi-yüan. This transfer owed something to the special relationship Shih had developed with Empress Yang2. The coup against Han T'o-chou had demonstrated the effectiveness of their collaboration. In time, Shih Mi-yüan proved sufficiently assertive to keep the forces of hostile opinion in line, yet he was sufficiently diplomatic to avoid dangerous confrontation. Such a balance, a very difficult one to achieve, had completely eluded Han T'o-chou. Also unlike Han, Shih Mi-yüan did not take Empress Yang2's political astuteness as a personal threat. She on her side deferred daily administration to him. In this way, under Shih Mi-yüan's leadership the combination of a weak emperor and a strong inner court did not create the sort of political tension that had been so pronounced in the two preceding decades. Further enhancing Shih Mi-yüan's political stature was his close relationship with the heir apparent. In his capacities as instructor and, later, as lecturer at the several schools for imperial princes, Shih Mi-yüan came to know Chao Hsün when Chou was a small child. Upon Chao Hsün's nomination as heir apparent in 1208, Shih Mi-yüan became his chief advisor and the general supervisor of his household.

---

[142] T'o-t'o, *Chin shih* 12, p. 284; *HTC* (1958) 158, p. 4278; Chou, *Ch'i-tung yeh-yü* (1983) 3, pp. 45–52; Li, *Chien-yen i-lai ch'ao-yeh tsa-chi* (1967) *i* 7, p. 10a.

The throne also honored Shih Mi-yüan as junior mentor to the heir, additional confirmation of its confidence in him. With Ning-tsung long accustomed to relying heavily upon Han T'o-chou and lesser palace favorites, Shih Mi-yüan's close ties with the two most powerful palace personalities served him well.

In summer 1208, Shih Mi-yüan rose to be assistant councilor and soon became chief councilor of the right with concurrent authority over the Bureau of Military Affairs. Ch'ien Hsiang-tsu served briefly as councilor of the left, but was dismissed by year's end. Reasons were not given, but the dismissal appears to have been part of a much broader policy of eliminating holdovers from the Han T'o-chou administration. Li Pi, another holdover, had already been dismissed the previous year in 1207. The military commissioner in chief Yeh Shih similarly was demoted, his irredentist views being fundamentally at odds with current pacifist policies. Within a year's time, the purge that began with Han T'o-chou's death ended in the elimination of all serious rivals to Shih Mi-yüan, who emerged as the key link between the throne and the bureaucracy. However, Shih was sufficiently astute not to rely exclusively on imperial favor. He aggressively courted *Tao-hsüeh* proponents in and away from the capital, men who had been alienated under the preceding administration, in the hope of enhancing his image and support within the civil service.

Lin Ta-chung, a former censor persecuted under the Ch'ing-yüan ban, was restored to metropolitan service in 1208 as notary official at the Bureau of Military Affairs. Another persecuted censor, Liu Kuang-tsu, returned to Lin-an as court compiler, his first metropolitan post since 1194. Lü Tsu-t'ai, another alleged partisan, ended his exile with a prestigious sinecure. Lü unfortunately soon after died of pneumonia, and an image-conscious Shih Mi-yüan commissioned the distinguished envoy Wang Nan to accompany the coffin to its burial place. Two others also persecuted under the old ban, Lou Yüeh and Yang Chien, accepted metropolitan assignments for the first time in a decade. Yang Chien became vice-minister of war and Lou Yüeh assistant councilor. Posthumous honors were given to many of the deceased. P'eng Kuei-nien, Chu Hsi, and Chao Ju-yü, only partially rehabilitated under Han T'o-chou's limited amnesty, received full honors under the new councilor.[143]

In his long career, Shih Mi-yüan's father, Shih Hao, had recommended many men for office who later appeared on the list of banned *Tao-hsüeh* partisans, including Chu Hsi, Yeh Shih, Yang Chien, and Yüan Hsieh. Although Shih Hao had shown respect for *Tao-hsüeh* thinkers and sympathizers, he was not himself involved in the movement. Shih Mi-yüan had inherited from his father

---

[143] On these actions, see *SS* 393, p. 12016; Chen, *Hsi-shan hsien-sheng Chen Wen-chung kung wen-chi* 43, p. 15a; *SS* 455, p. 13372; 395, p. 12047; 407, p. 12290; *HTC* (1958) 158, p. 4277; *SS* 429, p. 12758; 392, pp. 11989–90, respectively.

a political tradition of nonpartisanship, although the younger Shih had also developed his own brand of political skills. Shih Mi-yüan had matured during the time when the Confucian teachings of Lu Chiu-yüan (1139–93) (also known as Lu Hsiang-shan), Chu Hsi's most compelling rival, had dominated the intellectual landscape of Shih's native Ming-chou. Differences between the two sets of teachings, which originally had seemed uncontentious, became so sharply articulated and tendentious that the loose, accommodating stance of Shih Hao and others during the Hsiao-tsung era was not easily sustained in succeeding reigns. The intellectual pedigree of Shih Mi-yüan himself may be difficult to establish, but it is common knowledge that he and his kinsmen frequently associated with proponents of Lu Chiu-yüan's teachings.[144] Although he lacked any identifiable links to *Tao-hsüeh*, his extension of court honors to these proponents was apparently intended to create a reputation for himself as a sponsor of talent, no less than his father, and to symbolically break with the parochialism and intolerance of the recent past. Shih also appointed men from his native Ming-chou to several important posts: Lou Yüeh, Lin Ta-chung, Yang Chien, and Yüan Hsieh. These men were not simply fellow provincials sharing common interests, but were also respected thinkers sympathetic to, but strictly speaking not adherents of, *Tao-hsüeh*. They were men who enhanced the intellectual diversity of the metropolitan bureaucracy and helped Shih deny any one group unchallenged supremacy. Shih Mi-yüan's refusal, in the face of considerable pressure, to officially endorse Chu Hsi's commentaries on the Four Books (*Analects*, *Mencius*, *Chung-yung*, and *Ta-hsüeh*) or to honor the founders of the *Tao-hsüeh* movement in the Temple of Confucius, demonstrates his initial commitment to maintaining intellectual diversity.[145]

Restoration of peace and the veneration of learning, the hallmarks of Shih Mi-yüan's early years in power, rapidly earned him the confidence of the throne. When Shih's mother died within a month of his elevation to councilor, this event should have entailed Shih's resignation from office and three years of mourning. Yet although Shih did return home, he stayed for only five months before the emperor interceded, in early 1209, waiving the mourning obligation and recalling Shih Mi-yüan to office.[146] In his absence, Ning-tsung had refused to appoint an interim councilor and probably relied heavily upon Assistant Councilor Lou Yüeh, a man with close ties to Shih Mi-yüan. Upon returning to Lin-an, Shih received a handsome official residence, a sign that the emperor intended him to stay awhile. Shih Mi-yüan held onto the councilorship for nearly twenty-five years, the longest uninterrupted tenure in Sung history.

---

[144] Huang et al., *Sung Yüan hsüeh-an* 74.
[145] *HTC* (1958) 159, p. 4309.
[146] *HTC* (1958) 158, p. 4288.

Although he began as a popular executive, Shih Mi-yüan quickly acquired a growing chorus of critics. Minister of War Ni Ssu was among the more acrid of these early detractors. A precocious scholar who had gained the *chin-shih* when he was only nineteen and the prestigious Erudite Literatus degree at thirty-two, Ni Ssu was a prolific writer and one-time professor at the Imperial University. Dismissed during Han T'o-chou's administration for his criticism of policies, Ni Ssu had returned to the capital after Han's death only to find the one-man dominance he had denounced was now revived under a new favorite, Shih Mi-yüan. Ni Ssu was alarmed at Shih Mi-yüan's growing authority; even before Shih's advancement to chief councilor, Shih would replace key officials without consulting or even informing the senior councilor, Ch'ien Hsiang-tsu – a tactic formerly employed by Han T'o-chou to undermine the bureaucratic chain of command. Signs of nepotism by Shih in appointing close associates or relatives to prominent posts all pointed to political realignment and consolidation, and provided yet another bone of contention.[147] Ni Ssu also complained about the government's humiliating concessions to Chin. Differences between the two men were so great that Ni Ssu requested a reassignment away from the capital. Ni Ssu's conflicts with bureaucratic chiefs dated back to Chou Pi-ta and Chao Ju-yü, reflecting his unusually testy character. Were he alone in casting aspersions on Shih Mi-yüan, he might have been dismissed as pugnacious and eccentric. He was not alone.

Less acidic but equally ruffled by Shih Mi-yüan were Wei Liao-weng and Chen Te-hsiu. Wei and Chen, who had both passed the *chin-shih* examination of 1199 at the height of Han T'o-chou's persecution of *Tao-hsüeh* partisans, served together as editors at the Palace Library, subordinates of the then vice-director Shih Mi-yüan. The two had differed sharply with Han T'o-chou over policy, but nevertheless at first served under him. Wei Liao-weng, a native of Szech-wan, appears to have been more negatively disposed toward Shih Mi-yüan, which prompted him to decline metropolitan appointments for some seventeen years.[148] Chen Te-hsiu tended to be more accommodating, although he was no less disillusioned with Shih Mi-yüan, especially regarding foreign policy. The peace concessions of 1208, in Chen's view, had only increased the possibility of future conflict, since implicit signs of Sung weakness would invite more enemy exploitation. Chen Te-hsiu also opposed the emerging trend of military retrenchment, which undermined the empire's preparedness for war. Over-all, Chen believed that Shih Mi-yüan's foreign policy was excessively naive, and that in handling civil officials, Shih was disrespectful and manipulative

---

[147] *SS* 398, pp. 12113–16; *HTC* (1958) 158, pp. 4274–5, 4280–1; Wei Liao-weng, *Ho-shan hsien-sheng ta ch'üan-chi* [*Ssu-pu ts'ung-k'an ch'u-pien* 1929 ed.] (1249; Taipei, 1979) 85, pp. 1a–12b.

[148] *SS* 437, pp. 12965–71.

by controlling bureaucrats through strict apportionment of their rank and salary.[149] This manipulation implied political intolerance, and an unwillingness to acknowledge the contributions of his colleagues. More personally, Chen Te-hsiu and Wei Liao-weng, both *Tao-hsüeh* sympathizers, resented Shih Mi-yüan's resistance to officially endorsing the movement's teachings. These fundamentally different views of governing prompted Chen Te-hsiu from time to time to withdraw from metropolitan service, yet he generally stayed on, optimistically hoping to have some influence, however modest, on border policy and other decision making.

Other prominent statesmen who expressed similar concerns left the capital voluntarily or involuntarily. Hsü I, who had assisted Wang Nan in negotiating the recent peace treaty with Chin, criticized the emperor's special treatment toward Yang Tz'u-shan and Shih Mi-yüan, a protest that resulted in Hsü's reassignment away from the capital. Regional transfer also awaited Ts'ai Yu-hsüeh, a once-persecuted *Tao-hsüeh* proponent whose reservations about the new administration closely resembled those of Chen Te-hsiu and Wei Liao-weng. Yüan Hsieh presents a parallel case: a victim of the *Tao-hsüeh* ban and politically rehabilitated under Shih Mi-yüan, he subsequently was pressured to leave the capital. He too had denounced the controversial peace pact.[150] Some such critics were demoted or retired by censorial indictment, and others left of their own volition. Most officials, however, were like Chen Te-hsiu, who remained in Lin-an, despite the challenges of swaying someone who often seemed indifferent. For his part, Shih Mi-yüan was for most of his tenure tolerant of his critics, not vindictive or arbitrary like Han T'o-chou. Although there were some important resignations, no mass exodus from government service occurred. By monopolizing imperial favor and administrative authority, Shih did not silence so much as frustrate his critics, ushering in an era characterized by administrative efficiency yet lacking innovation and adaptability.

Foreign policy

The extraordinary duration of Shih Mi-yüan's tenure does not imply uneventful tranquility. On the contrary, these years from 1208 to 1233 represent some of the most tumultuous of the Southern Sung, a time of profound political, economic, and social change. Nowhere is this upheaval more apparent than in foreign affairs. Previously, the only menace to the Sung had come from the

---

[149] SS 437, pp. 12957–65; HTC (1958) 158, p. 4281; Chen, *Hsi-shan hsien-sheng Chen Wen-chung kung wen-chi* 2, pp. 1a–7b.
[150] On these criticisms, see SS 406, p. 12269; HTC (1958) 158, p. 4276; Wei, *Ho-shan hsien-sheng ta ch'üan-chi* 69, p. 14b.

Jurchen Chin. The Tangut–Hsi Hsia kingdom in the northwest shared no common border with the Southern Sung and had not engaged Chin armies in over eighty years. As for the Chin, it maintained friendly tributary relations with the Hsi Hsia and with Koryŏ. Although Chin occasionally came into conflict with the Sung, their two recent wars had lasted scarcely two years and had no significant effect upon the balance of power. For several generations, the two sides had known mostly peace, a situation that did little to enhance the preparedness of their armies. With no one state able to impose its military will upon the others, the three states came to accept the political division while enjoying general stability. This accommodation, revived somewhat after the Sung-Chin conflict in 1208, was now shattered by the Mongols. Sweeping across central and northern Asia, they began pillaging the Hsi Hsia border in spring 1209. Hsi Hsia, a Chin tributary state, turned to the Jurchen for assistance. The Chin refused, fearing Mongol retaliation, but in the process incited the embittered Hsi Hsia to open hostilities against Chin, a war that benefited no one more than the Mongols.

The Chin, having already provoked Chinggis khan (Temüjin) by supporting rival tribes in Mongolia against him, desperately sought neutrality in the expanding Tangut-Mongol contest. They had only recently concluded war with the Sung, and Emperor Chang-tsung, who died at the close of 1208, bequeathed his throne to the half-witted seventh son of Shih-tsung, Prince Wei (r. 1208–13). Bandits in Shantung continued to make mischief with local authorities, while severe drought and continued famine in 1210 strained the resources of the government. The Chin simply could not risk war with the Mongols. Yet if they considered neutrality a means of preserving peace, they were tragically mistaken. The Mongols moved with unanticipated speed and, within a year, began raiding the northern Chin border. With the formal commencement of hostilities in 1211, the Chin found themselves fending off two enemies, the Tanguts and the Mongols. Over the next two years, the Mongol inroads into Chin territory were such that the Mongols were able to lay siege to the Chin capital at Chung-tu (modern Peking), a grave political as well as economic challenge. The initial Mongol thrust had concentrated on the Chin Western Capital Hsi-ching (Ta-t'ung, in northern Shansi province), and it soon extended east as far as central Pei-ching circuit (Peking) and south into Ho-tung North (central Shansi) and Ho-pei West (central Hopei province).[151] Chin armies, despite their numerical superiority, were outmatched. In addition

---

[151] On these developments, see T'o-t'o, *Chin shih* 13; *SS* 39; *HTC* (1958) 159; Hu Chao-hsi et al., *Sung Meng (Yüan) kuan-hsi shih* (Ch'eng-tu, 1992), pp. 1–17; H. Desmond Martin, *The rise of Chingis Khan and his conquest of north China* (Baltimore, 1950), pp. 113–54; Thomas J. Barfield, *The perilous frontier: Nomadic empires and China* (Cambridge, Mass., 1989), pp. 197–202.

to the extraordinary martial prowess of their horsemen, the Mongols had an unbeatable strategy. In wars against the Sung, the Chin armies had proven most effective when they overwhelmed the Sung with massive attacks against a few strategic areas, creating a shock that often paralyzed the defenders. In contrast, the Mongols preferred to scatter their armies and conduct a large number of smaller campaigns. This diminished the risk of large, decisive battles, while helping to identify and exploit the enemy's vulnerable points. The Chin could not develop a suitable defense.

The defeats inflicted by invading cavalry were made more painful by the increasing instability of Chin internal politics. Incompetent as he was unpopular, the Chin ruler Prince Wei, Wei Chao Wang (r. 1209–13), responded to the ever closer Mongol assaults with self-imposed isolation, which in turn sparked mass hysteria in the capital. In the summer of 1213, Prince Wei was assassinated in a coup led by a highly decorated veteran of the K'ai-hsi war and now assistant supreme commander, Ho-she-li Chih-chung. Ho-she-li installed the elder brother of Chang-tsung as the emperor, Chin Hsüan-tsung (r. 1213–23). Many military and civilian leaders resented the domination of Ho-she-li Chih-chung, and some even suspected him of conspiring to usurp the throne himself; within months, Ho-she-li Chih-chung was assassinated. This assassination coincided precisely with the Mongol encirclement of Chung-tu. The summer assault on Chung-tu was so frightful that to forestall a mass exodus the Chin government prohibited all males from leaving the city. A Sung embassy within thirty miles of the capital was ordered to return south, without delivering its precious tribute. The siege lasted three months and effectively made Chin Hsüan-tsung a prisoner in his own capital. When the Mongols withdrew at the beginning of 1214, the Chin paid them with offerings of servants, horses, gold, and silk.[152] This withdrawal gave Chin Hsüan-tsung an opportunity to flee his vulnerable capital. When he did this in the summer of 1214, he angered the Mongols, who resumed hostilities. Chung-tu fell to them the next spring.

Developments in the north moved with such astounding speed that the Sung court and Shih Mi-yüan in particular were unable to develop a coherent response. Despite widespread chaos in the north, the Sung remained unrelentingly loyal to its commitment to pay biannual tribute to Chin. No mission had reached its destination since 1210–11, yet Shih Mi-yüan chose not to risk war by interrupting the tribute payments, so embassies set out punctually for the next three years only to be turned back before reaching Chung-tu in the north. Shih Mi-yüan was insistent that tribute items be kept in storage, rather than

[152] T'o-t'o, *Chin shih* 14, p. 304; *HTC* (1958) 160, p. 4334.

returned to the government exchequer for government use. This implied that
the tribute payments would be resumed later. The image of timidity that this
unseemly accommodation presented disturbed no small number of Sung officials. As with this diplomatic crisis, Shih Mi-yüan's response to the impending
military crisis was frustratingly indecisive. He ordered the reinforcement of
border defense installations, but no general mobilization for war. As early as
1211, Chen Te-hsiu, the most articulate and perhaps best-informed critic of
court policy, a former ambassador with firsthand knowledge of conditions in
the north, predicted the imminent demise of the Chin and urged his government to prepare for an inevitable showdown with the Mongols.[153] After
the Chin court had moved its capital to K'ai-feng in 1214, it demanded the
immediate delivery of the three years of outstanding peace payments. Chen
Te-hsiu pleaded for the tribute's formal termination. Convinced that the Sung
would at some point be drawn into the conflict between the Chin and the Mongols, Chen thought it senseless to cling to an outdated policy of restraint and
maintain the illusion of cordial relations. Chen Te-hsiu's stand on the tribute
controversy was pragmatic, for a large sum of back payments was involved, but
it was also emotional. Now that the Chin court had moved to K'ai-feng, the
Sung envoys would have to present themselves before alien rulers in the palace
where earlier Sung emperors had once sat enthroned. This was a deep humiliation for them, and an unpardonable indignity to the dynasty's illustrious
ancestors.[154]

Many others shared Chen Te-hsiu's views. Yüan Hsieh, a somewhat militant
statesman from Ming-chou, joined in calling for the termination of the peace
payments.[155] The much less militant Liu Kuang-tsu, prefect of T'ung-ch'uan,
agreed. In addition to the issue of the Chin court's receiving Sung envoys in
former Sung palaces, Liu was livid at the short-sightedness of current policies.
Writing in 1215, he stated: "We and the Jurchen have an enmity that cannot
permit coexistence under Heaven. Heaven [wishes to] eliminate these bandits
and has sent them to die at Pien-liang [K'ai-feng]. Your Majesty, although
Son of Heaven, does not comprehend the plan which it has devised. Not
to take what Heaven offers is known as abandoning Heaven. Never can one
abandon Heaven without Heaven becoming angry."[156] Coinciding as it did
with widespread natural disasters, Liu's warning packed a powerful punch.
Liu Kuang-tsu, like Chen Te-hsiu, hoped to accelerate the demise of the Chin,

[153] SS 437, p. 12959; Chen, Hsi-shan hsien-sheng Chen Wen-chung kung wen-chi 2, pp. 19b–22a; Wei, Ho-shan
hsien-sheng ta ch'üan-chi 69, p. 14a.
[154] SS 437, p. 12959; HTC (1958) 160, pp. 4338–9; Chen, Hsi-shan hsien-sheng Chen Wen-chung kung wen-chi
3, p. 17b.
[155] Chen, Hsi-shan hsien-sheng Chen Wen-chung kung wen-chi 47, p. 13a.
[156] Chen, Hsi-shan hsien-sheng Chen Wen-chung kung wen-chi 43, p. 16b; SS 397, p. 12101.

and terminating the peace payments was an important first step. One of the few opposing views on record came from Ch'iao Hsing-chien (1156–1241), an official with extensive regional experience then serving as fiscal overseer in Huai-nan West. Ch'iao preferred deferring any policy response until the outcome of the conflict in the north was more certain. He urged Shih Mi-yüan to resume the gift offerings, thereby assisting the Chin in their fight against the far greater threat to stability in the region, the Mongols. The proposal, novel for the time and eminently pragmatic, was so poorly received in Lin-an that irate students at the Imperial University demanded Ch'iao Hsing-chien's execution.[157]

Shih Mi-yüan, although sensitive to official opinion, was too cautious to abandon the current policies and provoke the Chin. Twice in 1214 the Chin, desperately in need of funds, sent missions to Lin-an to expedite the delivery of peace payments. They even recalled an envoy to protest against the Sung's procrastination.[158] To ignore the Chin protest would have threatened to escalate into a military response. Our sources make no mention of payment being made, but the exchange of envoys was resumed by year's end, which suggests that Shih Mi-yüan may have quietly done so. By ignoring the opinion of influential colleagues and trying to maintain normal diplomatic relations with the Chin by appeasement, Shih Mi-yüan was endangering his support at home. The Sung was the only major power of the time to maintain its tributary relations with the beleaguered Chin. The Hsi Hsia and Koryŏ (Korea) had both severed their tributary ties with the Chin over the preceding five years.

The peace payment controversy was not the only source of dissatisfaction with Shih Mi-yüan's foreign policy. As early as 1214, the Hsi Hsia had approached the Sung to discuss a possible alliance against the Chin. A cautious Shih Mi-yüan ignored the overtures and lost, in consequence, a unique opportunity to expand his empire's influence in the northwest. A year later in 1215, the Sung requested a reduction in its tribute offering. The Chin court in Pien-liang (K'ai-feng) balked, and the Sung court gave in. In 1216, when an army of reportedly a hundred thousand Ch'in-chou "loyalists" from the west of Chin sought asylum in Sung territory, they were turned away, the Sung being still unwilling to jeopardize relations with the Chin.[159] Ironically, such extraordinary accommodations coincided with the further decline of Chin power. The Mongols, having seized Chung-tu in spring 1215, led their armies to within seven miles of K'ai-feng. The Chin were demoralized, beset with defections throughout the north and conspiracies directed at the throne. But

[157] SS 417, p. 12489; HTC (1958) 160, pp. 4339, 4341.
[158] SS 39, p. 760; HTC (1958) 160, pp. 4333, 4339.
[159] See SS 39, p. 760; T'o-t'o, Chin shih 62, p. 1483; SS 39, p. 763.

although the situation within Chin had deteriorated, Shih Mi-yüan remained committed to neutrality. Ultimately, only a hostile initiative from the Chin would force a change in policy.

In the spring of 1217, the Chin declared war against the Sung. Chin assaults on targets in the central border region – Kuang-chou2, Tsao-yang, Kuang-hua, and Hsin-yang – were accompanied by a sizable drive in the west against Ta-san Pass, Hsi-ho-chou, Chieh-chou, and Ch'eng-chou. Ostensibly, the Chin attacks were in response to the Sung's alleged incitement of bandit activity along the Huai River border in the east. The charge was not entirely baseless. The Sung-Chin border had witnessed various incidents of provocation for some time, responsibility for which partly lay with the Sung. In early 1214, a small force of irregulars from Szechwan had crossed the border and attacked Ch'in-chou, spurred on by the military commissioner An Ping.[160] The action, perhaps a test of Chin strength, had not been sanctioned by the Sung court, and when the band returned south, its members were rounded up and executed by the Sung commander at Hsing-chou2. An Ping was then summoned to the capital and named associate commissioner at the Bureau of Military Affairs, in effect, being reprimanded with a promotion. Subsequent regional assignments in the central or southwest part of the empire, away from northern Szechwan, further demonstrated Shih Mi-yüan's disavowal of the venture at Ch'in-chou. The Chin certainly understood this, for they took no immediate retaliation. On the eastern front, however, where the Sung court theoretically exercised far better control, frequent skirmishes along the border and the proliferation of bandit groups were much more suspect. Instability in Chin territory gave rise to banditry and insurrection. Many of the insurgents, by identifying themselves culturally with Han Chinese rule in the south, appeared to be agents of the Sung, even if many, perhaps most, had no such backing. At other times, Sung border officials had surreptitiously aided rebels and refugees, violating court policy and treaty commitments. The Sung court never condoned the practice, and occasionally as an act of good faith it punished officials found guilty, but the Chin held the Sung accountable all the same.

More important than Sung provocation, the motive for the Chin attacks against the south was their need to prepare an escape from further defeat by the Mongols in the north. Since 1215, the emperor, Chin Hsüan-tsung, had come under the influence of Chu-ho-lo Kuo-le-ch'i (d. 1219), the privy councilor and later chief minister.[161] Chu-ho-lo, with every justification, feared the Mongols, and desired a twofold strategy for dealing with them. First, he proposed the

---

[160] SS 402, pp. 12191–2; *Sung-shih ch'üan-wen Hsü Tzu-chih t'ung-chien* 30, p. 16a; *HTC* (1958) 160, p. 4332.

[161] *HTC* (1958) 160, pp. 4345, 4350–1, 4356–7, 4359–61; 161, pp. 4378, 4383–4.

concentrated defense of strategic cities, lest scarce military resources be spread too thin. This left lesser cities to fend for themselves. Second, rather than risk direct, probably suicidal, confrontation, he preferred to protect the court through higher and stronger walls and, of course, distance. By attacking the Sung, the Chin could avoid confrontation with the Mongols while expanding its influence south of the Huai in preparation for further retreat. The insecure Chin Hsüan-tsung initially rejected this counsel. It appeared foolhardy to open another front, in light of declining revenues and the current heavy fighting in the north.[162] A brief rally against the Mongols in 1216, combined with considerable pressure from Chu-ho-lo, finally swayed Chin Hsüan-tsung.

The Sung response to the Chin attacks was intentionally weak. Hoping to contain the conflict, the Sung court instructed border officials to confine themselves to defensive actions. Shih Mi-yüan waited two months to declare war. He did so then only after much prodding by Chao Fang, the distinguished military commissioner of Ching-hu.[163] Shih's indecision hardly endeared him to military commanders, but they had further reason to be irritated. Unlike Han T'o-chou, and perhaps learning from his negative example, Shih Mi-yüan had permitted individual commanders to exercise substantial independence in conducting the war effort in their respective theaters. Interference from Lin-an was minimal. The approach certainly had its merits: commanders in the field were better able to assess a region's strengths and mobilize its resources rapidly in response to attack than were officials in the distant capital. By delegating greater discretionary authority to regional leaders, Shih Mi-yüan could relieve himself of personal responsibility for the outcome of any specific battle or campaign.

LOYALISTS OF SHANTUNG

Another telling sign of Shih Mi-yüan's inadequacies as a decision maker is his treatment of "loyalist armies." In many parts of Chin territory ever since the Chin conquest of the north, rebels, often claiming loyalty to the Sung, had attempted to overthrow the Jurchen. In some cases, these insurrections had coalesced around a desire on the part of Han Chinese to restore Sung rule as an expression of their cultural self-awareness and their wish for political self-determination. In other cases, rebels sought to advance their personal interests, and swore allegiance to the Sung simply to attract material support from Lin-an or to lend a veneer of legitimacy to what otherwise was simple banditry. Commonly known in the south as "loyal and righteous armies" (*chung-i-chün*),

---

[162] Lin Jui-han, "Wan Chin kuo-ch'ing chih yen-chiu," *Ta-lu tsa-chih* 16 No. 7 (1958), pp. 22–6.
[163] SS 403, pp. 12203–7; HTC (1958) 160, p. 4362.

such bands were most active in the Shantung circuits.[164] Geographically isolated, impoverished, and with a long tradition of insurgency, the region had
suffered heavily from frequent natural disasters, the most common stimulus for
outbreaks of banditry. These loyalists – or rebels, from the Chin perspective –
were most active and threatening to authorities in times of military conflict.
Treaty commitments prohibited the Sung court from supporting such groups,
but in wartime there were no such restrictions. If these domestic upheavals
did not win the Sung a foothold in the north, at least they forced the Chin to
divert some attention from their external to their internal enemy. Moreover,
the Sung risked little by supporting loyalists, for loyalist armies lived and
operated almost entirely in Chin territory.

Among the more prominent of Shantung loyalists had been Yang An-erh
(var. Yang An-kuo, d. 1214), a former saddle maker from I-tu, the capital
of Shantung East circuit. During the K'ai-hsi war of 1206 to 1208 he had
joined other marauders in pillaging the countryside, where they acquired the
sobriquet "Red-jacket bandits" (*Hung-ao tsei*). Chin authorities were unable to
suppress the rebels by force, and after the war they had offered titular posts
to Yang An-erh and his confederates in exchange for their promises of fealty.
However, once the Mongols had begun their invasion, the Red-jackets returned
to brigandry. About fifty miles east of I-tu, at Wei-chou5, there emerged
another brigand leader, Li Ch'üan (d. 1231).[165] Of peasant stock, he and his
brother reportedly turned to banditry after their mother and eldest brother
were killed by Mongol invaders.[166] The war had led to increased taxation, and
natural disasters had so strained the regional economy that Li Ch'üan had little
problem attracting recruits; his band soon grew to be several thousand strong.
Yang An-erh had died in 1214, killed by greedy boatmen who sought the
bounty of one thousand ounces of gold that the Chin government had offered
for his head. His younger sister, Yang Miao-chen, herself a skilled rider and
archer, assumed command of the rebel remnants. Before long, she married Li
Ch'üan, and their two bands merged to create a force of some fifteen thousand
to twenty thousand.

During the K'ai-hsi era (1205–7), Yang An-erh had assisted the Sung in
temporarily controlling parts of Shantung, but his own dynastic ambitions

[164] See Huang K'uan-ch'ung's series of two articles, "Lüeh-lun Nan Sung shih-tai ti kuei-cheng-jen
(shang)," *Shih-huo yüeh-k'an* 7 No. 3 (1977), pp. 111–20; and "Lüeh-lun Nan Sung shih-tai ti kuei-
cheng-jen (hsia)," *Shih-huo yüeh-k'an* 7 No. 4 (1977), pp. 172–83, and Huang's *Nan Sung shih-tai k'ang
Chin ti i-chün* (Taipei, 1988), pp. 1–30, 171–223.

[165] *SS* 476–7; *HTC* (1958) 159, p. 4307; 160, pp. 4336–7, 4341, 4343; 161, pp. 4364–5; also see the
chapter "Nan Sung Chin Yüan chien ti Shan-tung chung-i-chün yü Li Ch'üan," in Sun K'o-k'uan,
Meng-ku Han-chün chi Han wen-hua yen-chiu (Taipei, 1958), pp. 11–43.

[166] *SS* 476, p. 13817; *HTC* (1958) 160, p. 4336.

later proved far stronger than any professed fealty to the Sung. Li Ch'üan, in contrast, apparently began with few personal ambitions and maintained close ties to the south. When the Chin attacked the Sung in 1217, Li's increased stature in Shantung and his commitment to the Sung cause made him attractive to border officials, who saw Li's disruptive activities as a valuable counter to Chin influence in the Huai region. Ying Ch'un-chih, the prefect of Ch'u-chou, was one such optimist. He believed that with the Chin pressed by the Mongols to the north, a thrust from the east by Shantung loyalists might lead to Sung recovery of the entire north. Another border official, Chia She (d. 1223), evinced similar enthusiasm and helped Ying Ch'un-chih in supporting and organizing loyalist armies in Chin territory. The insightful Chen Te-hsiu worded his support for these plans somewhat differently. He thought assistance to such groups was morally obligatory and, should the Sung court fail to provide aid, the consequent ill will might ultimately end in disaster, and provoke anti-Sung hostility.[167] Shih Mi-yüan shared neither the optimism of regional officers nor the sense of obligation to the loyalist rebels of Chen Te-hsiu, but he did not entirely ignore bureaucratic opinion. When Sung-Chin hostilities resumed, Ying Ch'un-chih extended massive aid to Shantung, apparently without court authorization, but without its opposition either. Shih Mi-yüan later approved the action, but only in secret correspondence, thereby distancing himself from what must have seemed a risky venture.[168]

In the absence of an empirewide policy toward loyalist armies, regional civilian and military leaders formulated their own. Support for insurrections had been relatively modest in central and western regions of Chin-held territory, where northern rebels were less organized and Sung border officials more cautious in backing them. In the east, not only did rebel bands have strong, competent leadership, but the Sung regional officials who dealt with the rebels wielded more influence at court and came, in time, to affect its attitude. Toward the close of 1217 and with substantial assistance from the south, Li Ch'üan and his brother Li Fu2 laid claim to Chü-chou and I-tu, two strategic prefectures in the central and northern parts of the Shan-tung circuits. For the first time, Shih Mi-yüan publicly acknowledged his endorsement of loyalist activity by honoring Li Ch'üan with the title commander in chief of Shantung.

In the coming years, Li Ch'üan became a valued Sung ally. In addition to gradually acquiring additional territory in Shantung, he occasionally assisted Sung regular armies in campaigns in central China. He also helped recruit other rebels to the Sung cause. The 1219 defection of the Chin commander

---

[167] On their views, see HTC (1958) 161, p. 4364; SS 403, pp. 12207–10; Chen, Hsi-shan hsien-sheng Chen Wen-chung kung wen-chi 34, pp. 18a–20a, respectively.

[168] SS 403, pp. 12207; HTC (1958) 161, pp. 4363–4.

Chang Lin2 is a prominent example; with this one stroke, the Chin lost twelve prefectures.[169] Defections and defeats in the Shantung region were so pervasive that by 1221 Chin authority was confined to only a few pockets. The Sung court subsequently committed itself to strengthening ties with loyalists in the hope of annexing the entire region. To Shih Mi-yüan, cautious and suspicious of loyalists' motives, the goodwill and loyal service that were so critical to the plan's success could best be won through generously conferring official rank and material wealth on the successful loyalist leaders, essentially the same policy he applied at court in Lin-an to harness the bureaucracy. Shih named Li Ch'üan first as regional supervisor and then regional commander, two sinecures of considerable prestige, and by 1224 Sung subsidies for this single Shantung army rose to three hundred thousand strings of cash.[170]

Officials, many of whom had once criticized Shih Mi-yüan for inadequate support for "loyalists," found his new enthusiasm for Li Ch'üan even more unsettling. Greater status and wealth, they feared, might turn the head of the loyalist leader by stoking his personal ambitions. Chia She reportedly commented in 1222: "The court knows only that office and rank can be used to obtain one's heart. Does it not also know that arrogant commanders, in the end, cannot be controlled?" Chia later resigned in frustration over Li Ch'üan's insubordinate arrogance. Chia She's replacement as prefect of Ch'u-chou, Hsü Kuo (d. 1225), quickly became even more incensed, and accused Li of seditious intentions.[171] There was good reason for their suspicions. To tighten his grip on the Shantung region, Li Ch'üan had begun as early as 1220 to conspire against rival leaders, a move that alienated both fellow loyalists and Sung border officials. Among Li Ch'üan's first notable victims was an assistant commander for militias in southern Shantung, the influential Chi Hsien (d. 1220). A jealous Li Ch'üan convinced Chia She of Chi Hsien's duplicity and brought about Chi's execution in the summer of 1220. Later that year, Li engineered the purge of Chi Hsien's court-appointed successor, Shih Kuei (d. 1220), another individual whose popularity among rival leaders presented a personal threat to Li. Similarly charged with duplicity, Shih was assassinated.[172] Li Ch'üan also bore indirect responsibility for the 1221 defection to the Mongols of Chang Lin2 whom he had himself won over to the Sung side only two years earlier. Chang Lin2 publicly indicted Li Ch'üan for forcing his defection to the Mongols. But he was most likely motivated by opportunism, since he returned

[169] SS 476, p. 13820; HTC (1958) 161, p. 4382.
[170] HTC (1958) 162, p. 4421.
[171] SS 403, p. 12209; HTC (1958) 162, pp. 4412, 4418.
[172] SS 476, pp. 13821–2; HTC (1958) 161, pp. 4386–7, 4391.

to the Sung cause only a year later.[173] The incident confirmed the wisdom of Chia She's counsel and the injudiciousness of Shih Mi-yüan's indulgence of Shantung rebel agents. But once the policy had been set, Shih Mi-yüan refused to acknowledge his mistake and continued to indulge Li Ch'üan until Li himself forced a change.

SUNG-CHIN CONFLICT

However hesitant decision making at the Sung court may have appeared, the Sung military leadership at the border offered a clear contrast. In the first year of the war, 1217, the Chin twice attempted to capture strategic Tsao-yang and Sui-chou2, access to which would expose Hsiang-yang, the capital of Ching-hsi2 circuit, to a westward attack. Hsiang-yang was the strategic pivot of Sung defenses in its central territory, and Chin forces had to be stopped. Under the general direction of Chao Fang, commanders Meng Tsung-cheng and Hu Tsai-hsing inflicted heavy casualties upon the advancing Chin, forcing their retreat from both Tsao-yang and Sui-chou2. The second Chin campaign in early 1218, chiefly targeting Sui-chou2, involved an estimated one hundred thousand Chin troops and represented a crucial test of strength for the two powers. Some seventy battles and three months later, the encirclement of Sui-chou2 had been broken and the Chin troops again withdrew. Undaunted, Chin forces resumed their attack a year later. This time the blockade lasted eighty days and cost the north thirty thousand men.[174]

The Chin also did not make significant inroads farther east, in the Huai River region. Chin offensives in 1219 were launched against Ch'u-chou, Hao-chou, and Kuang-chou2, where again they committed a huge force, said to number one hundred thousand troops; each offensive failed to yield a lasting foothold in Sung territory. During these attacks, loyalist armies had been deployed by Chia She with remarkable success. The Shantung loyalists Chi Hsien, Shih Kuei, Li Ch'üan, and Li Fu2 all cooperated in defense operations and proved that loyalists could be deployed on the Huai frontier as well as in the interior of Shantung.[175] In the west, the Chin managed to temporarily capture the Ta-san Pass and Hsi-ho-chou, but these were their only noteworthy victories.

The performance of the Sung troops decidedly outclassed and frightened the Chin. Not only did the Sung succeed in repulsing repeated massive

---

[173] SS 476, pp. 13823–4; HTC (1958) 162, pp. 4401–2, 4415.
[174] SS 403, pp. 12205, 12210, 12211–12; HTC (1958) 160, p. 4361; 161, pp. 4369, 4375, 4380–1.
[175] SS 403, p. 12208; 476, pp. 13819–20; HTC (1958) 161, pp. 4376–7.

enemy invasions, but they launched some retaliatory strikes that permanently shattered the old myth of Jurchen invincibility. Outside the Shantung theater, southern armies joined by loyalists attacked the strategically vital Ssu-chou, just north of the Huai River, in the spring of 1218. Another Sung offensive followed three years later. Neither ended in lasting success, but Sung casualties appear to have been modest. In the central border region of the Sung, where they faced heavy and sustained Chin onslaughts, Sung armies still mustered the strength to turn from defense to mounting a counteroffensive. In the summer of 1219, troops directed by Chao Fang crossed the border to raid T'ang-chou and Teng-chou2 in modern Honan, subsequently turning back to attack from the rear Chin encampments threatening Hsiang-yang and Tsao-yang. Having masterfully executed the campaign, Chao Fang felt sufficiently confident to order another assault on T'ang-chou and Teng-chou2 toward year's end, this time reputedly employing sixty thousand men. Chin losses, again heavy, were compounded by the deaths of several valued commanders. The Sung had no intention of holding the two cities, merely to destroy stores of provisions and exert pressure on the Chin. Having achieved these objectives, Sung forces withdrew from T'ang-chou and Teng-chou2.

In the west, Sung armies fought with similar confidence and determination. An Ping had probed enemy strength at Ch'in-chou as early as 1214 and paid for this unauthorized initiative with losing his command and reassignment in the east. He subsequently returned to Szechwan in an unofficial capacity, forming a secret liaison in 1218 with the Hsi Hsia for a joint campaign against the Chin. The bold plan fell through, however, when Tangut armies failed to reach the target cities of Ch'in-chou and Kung-chou2. The Sung invaders, unable to hold out on their own, lost tens of thousands in the retreat. A few months later, the Sung conducted another offensive against Ch'in-chou, employing an estimated one hundred thousand men, both regulars and loyalists. Ta-san Pass, then in Chin hands, was retaken en route to Ch'in-chou, but the campaign was aborted on instructions from the capital. Sung casualties again mounted as troops retreated under enemy pressure. In both offensives, optimistic Sung generals considered victory had been within their grasp and many blamed the failure to back them up on Tung Chü-i, the military commissioner for Szechwan since An Ping's dismissal in 1214. In consequence, back at the Sung court a movement developed to restore An Ping to leadership of the western front, a move that was supported by impartial statesmen such as Wei Liao-weng, a Szechwan native, and Chao Fang, a commander with experience in the region. Both of these men viewed An Ping as the only leader capable of harnessing the forces in the west. But given An Ping's checkered past, it may have been the need to quell the growing problems of rebellion in Szechwan, rather than the need for a more offensive-minded commander, that led to An

Ping's return and appointment as pacification commissioner of Szechwan. In the end, regional problems, specifically rebellion, prevented An Ping from reviving the offensive, but at a time of acute vulnerability he succeeded in stabilizing the Sung position and frustrating enemy advances.[176]

These Sung victories do not mean that the Chin had suddenly become an inept fighting force. Their initial attacks in the west may have foundered disastrously, yet they launched an awesome second western offensive in late 1217. This enabled them to capture, if only temporarily, several strategic outposts and towns south of the border, including Ta-san Pass. Repeated raids in the west in late 1217 and early 1218 reportedly furnished the Chin with ninety thousand bushels of grain, tens of millions in strings of cash, and unknown quantities of military supplies.[177] Clearly, plunder was the chief motive for the aggression here. But this appears not to have been the case with the raids in the spring of 1219, which culminated in victories as far south as Ta-an commandery, in the heart of Li-chou circuit ninety miles from the border. Northern armies also overwhelmed Sung defenders at nearby Hsi-ho-chou, Hsing-yüan, and Yang-chou2. Fortunately for the Sung, these enemy gains were not permanent. Moreover, Chin's victories in the west were largely offset by its defeats to the east.

The third and final Chin offensive during Ning-tsung's reign occurred in the spring of 1221. Focusing on the central border region, the Chin shocked the Sung by penetrating over one hundred and twenty miles into its heartland and overcoming the defenders of Ch'i-chou2, north of the Yangtze, in Huai-nan West. The Sung, through the daring leadership of Hu Tsai-hsing and Li Ch'üan, nonetheless battled back and repelled them.

The overall failure of the Chin military campaign stemmed, in part, from an exceptional Sung defense. Perhaps more crucial, however, was the diminishment of Chin morale. From the outset, the Chin emperor had opposed the plan to take the offensive against the Sung. Only under mounting pressure did Chin Hsüan-tsung reluctantly agree, and the tally after a year's effort proved it to have been a disastrous decision. At the close of 1218, Chin Hsüan-tsung dispatched a peace envoy to the south. Public opinion in Lin-an, however, was now vehemently opposed to an accommodation with the Chin. Indeed, one minister was cruelly humiliated by angry students at the Imperial University for airing what the students considered pacifist views.[178] Public sentiment was unmistakable; Shih Mi-yüan unceremoniously rebuffed the Chin envoy.

---

[176] See SS 40; 402, pp. 12192–4; 403, pp. 12204–13, 12207; 476, p. 13818; T'o-t'o, Chin shih 15; HTC (1958), chüan 160–2.

[177] T'o-t'o, Chin shih 15, p. 336; HTC (1958) 161, p. 4370.

[178] HTC (1958) 161, pp. 4378.

Defeated in their initiatives at war and at peace, the Chin were beset with other problems, including court intrigue and defections abroad.

In 1218 in northern Shantung, Assistant Fiscal Supervisor Ch'eng Chien planned to defect to the Sung, but did not succeed. However, the plans of commanders Chang T'ien-i and Chang Lin2 went ahead a year later. Slightly to the west, regional leader Yen Shih and others defected in 1220, giving the Sung nominal control over a cluster of prefectures north and east of the Chin capital, K'ai-feng. Leaders in Ta-ming fu renounced the Chin in 1224. These are but a few of many such incidents. Defections to the Mongols were even more numerous. There were also plots and high-level intrigues at the capital. Chin's chief councilor Kao Ch'i (d. 1220) was imprisoned in 1219 and subsequently executed, the victim of intrigue. Military affairs executive Pu-sa An-chen (d. 1221) suffered a similar fate, charged with rebellious intentions by political rivals. The loss of distinguished statesmen and the political infighting behind it signaled and exacerbated the rapid weakening of the Chin dynasty.

DOMESTIC CONCERNS

As a whole, the Sung period commonly inspires images of extraordinary material wealth and domestic tranquility, images that reflect some measure of the historical record, even though the dynasty was hardly immune to natural disasters and human crises. Scholar-official discontent with political leadership notwithstanding, the Kuang-tsung and early Ning-tsung years represent the last era of genuine prosperity during the Southern Sung; natural disasters were comparatively infrequent, and domestic order largely prevailed. With the rise of Shih Mi-yüan, and to the fault of no one individual or policy, the prolonged good fortune of the dynasty began to languish.

One major area of concern for officials was the economy. In the aftermath of the K'ai-hsi war, rampant inflation had reduced many affluent families to bankruptcy, prompting the court to take responsibility in compensating for losses incurred.[179] At the same time, natural disasters impeded the restoration of economic stability. The Che-hsi and Che-tung circuits were especially hard-hit. Severe droughts had parched that area in 1208, 1214, and 1215; floodwaters had hit in 1210, 1212, 1213, and 1217; invasions by plagues of locusts had come in 1208, 1209, 1210, and 1215; and massive fires had erupted in the crowded Sung capital in 1208, 1211, and 1220, destroying tens of thousands of private homes and large sections of the imperial city. In

---

[179] HTC (1958) 158, p . 4286. Also see Ch'üan Han-sheng, "Sung-mo ti t'ung-huo p'eng-chang chi ch'i tui-yü wu-chia ti ying-hsiang," in Sung-shih yen-chiu chi: Ti erh chi, ed. Sung-shih tso-t'an-hui (Taipei, 1964), pp. 283–325.

the west, earthquakes had struck Szechwan in early, middle, and late 1216. The tremors, extending from the eastern to western extremities of the region, must have inflicted much human suffering, not to mention material loss. Luckily, the worst of these natural disturbances occurred before the Chin resumed hostilities.

The Kuang-tsung and early Ning-tsung years also were largely free of insurrection, except for two insignificant and readily suppressed army mutinies and a few minor raids on the southwest border by neighboring tribes. However, the first major outbreak had begun in 1208 in Ch'en-chou2, an important mining center in southern Ching-hu South circuit. The insurgency was led by Lo Shih-ch'uan (d. 1211),[180] a man of Yao2 extraction, who was probably reacting to long-standing tensions between an expanding Han Chinese population and local ethnic groups who were being displaced. Suppression of Lo's forces did not take long. The insurgents were few in number and poorly organized. Armies from northern Ching-hu South and neighboring Chiang-nan West, commanded in part by Shih Mi-chien (1164–1232), the prefect of T'an-chou (modern Ch'ang-sha) and brother of the chief councilor, pressed Lo Shih-ch'uan to capitulate in exchange for government stipends and provisions.

Another insurgent, Li Yüan-li (d. 1210), who had perhaps been encouraged by the precedent of compromise and unsteady government resolve, led an uprising in the same region in early 1210. This uprising was far more serious than that of Lo Shih-ch'uan. The outlaws numbered several tens of thousands and raided east into Chiang-nan West. Whether Li represented a specific group is not clear, but the discontent that Li Yüan-li tapped into extended beyond ethnic tensions as the uprising took on rebellious dimensions. In response, Sung reinforcements from as far north as Ch'ih-chou, in central Chiang-nan East, were ordered to assist in the suppression. Still, the outlaws multiplied with unexpected speed and dealt some devastating blows to government forces. The Sung proved incapable of halting the eastern thrust of Li Yüan-li, and its great fear was an alliance between Li and Lo Shih-ch'uan. This never materialized, their differences being too numerous. Meanwhile, the Sung court had appointed Wang Chü-an (*chin-shih* 1187), prefect of Lung-hsing2, to lead the suppression. By recruiting local militia, a resourceful Wang Chü-an managed to stem the tide. He was also successful at undermining the enemy through intrigue. Wang had carefully planted the seeds of mistrust among the rebels, which culminated in the execution of Li Yüan-li by Lo Shih-ch'uan toward the close of 1210. This intensive feuding eliminated the government's most

---

[180] On these rebellions, see *SS* 405, pp. 12253–4; 493, pp. 14195–6; *HTC* (1958) 158, pp. 4275, 4289–90; 159, pp. 4296–4300, 4304; Li Jung-ts'un, "Hei-feng-tung pien-luan shih-mo," *Chung-yang yen-chiu-yüan li-shih yü-yen yen-chiu-so chi-k'an* 41 No. 3 (1969), pp. 497–533.

serious threat, Li Yüan-li. Shih Mi-yüan then intervened, extending to Lo
Shih-ch'uan various titles and ranks in a bid for his loyalty, but Lo Shih-ch'uan
himself fell victim to an assassin in 1211, most probably also at the instigation
of Wang Chü-an. Still, Councilor Shih insisted on having the last word: the
rank awarded to Lo Shih-ch'uan would pass to his assassin.

The mutiny in 1219 led by Chang Fu (d. 1219) and Mo Chien (d. 1219) was
smaller in scope and duration. Chang Fu and Mo Chien, both military men
from Hsing-yüan prefecture, northern Szechwan, commanded supposedly over
ten thousand men in a self-proclaimed Red Turban (*Hung-chin*) uprising.[181]
Although it lasted only from spring to summer, this rebellion presented a far
greater challenge to the Sung court than those in the southwest nine years
earlier. Erupting during wartime, the proximity of the rebels to the Chin
border must have heightened fears of a possible alliance with the north, in
effect, a repeat of the Wu Hsi fiasco twelve years earlier. The insurgents moved
with astounding speed and precision. They appear not to have captured Hsing-
yüan, the capital of Li-chou circuit, but the prefecture Li-chou2 did fall, forcing
a hasty retreat by the military commissioner of Szechwan. Rebels executed
Szechwan's fiscal supervisor and pillaged Lang-chou and Kao-chou. Within
a month they had advanced a hundred and eighty miles from Hsing-yüan.
The shock reverberated throughout Szechwan, reportedly exceeding in impact
the earlier Wu Hsi defection, and prompted the Sung court to reappoint An
Ping as pacification commissioner. Chang Fu soon captured Sui-ning and, after
destroying much of the city, moved on to P'u-chou2, in the central part of
T'ung-ch'uan circuit. Surrounded there by Sung forces led by An Ping, the
rebels, Chang Fu, Mo Chien, and over a thousand confederates were captured
and put to death. An Ping emerged from the suppression a hero, his reputation
restored after having been severely tarnished by his unauthorized raids against
the north in 1214. He was appointed prefect of Hsing-yüan and regional
commander. Although army mutinies and bandit activities continued to erupt
at intervals, most were confined to Szechwan and speedily suppressed.

Other signs of instability, less imposing in scale perhaps, nonetheless proved
unsettling, for they directly threatened Shih Mi-yüan. In 1209 a commander
of loyalist armies who had been closely associated with Han T'o-chou, Lo
Jih-yüan (d. 1209), hatched an elaborate conspiracy against Shih Mi-yüan,
apparently out of dissatisfaction with the harsh terms of amnesty granted him
following Han T'o-chou's death.[182] Lo's plan involved the assassination of
Shih Mi-yüan and his retinue of high officials during their procession toward

---

[181] *SS* 40, pp. 772–3; 402, pp. 12192–3; 403, p. 12215; *HTC* (1958) 161, pp. 4376–80.
[182] *SS* 39, p. 752; *HTC* (1958) 158, p. 4288.

Lin-an in the sixth month of 1209, and the seizure of power at court, no doubt to purge it of remaining Shih Mi-yüan elements. Shih was returning to the capital after briefly mourning his mother's death, and Ning-tsung, as a sign of special favor, had arranged an elaborate ceremony to welcome him. The occasion probably drew most government notables, with the crowds and festivities providing a convenient cover for the perpetrators. However, the wildly ambitious plan was never put into action. A fellow conspirator had turned government informer, and Lo Jih-yüan was executed. Another attempt against Shih Mi-yüan was reported soon thereafter, this time concocted by a self-righteous, if not insane, student at Lin-an's military academy. It too was exposed and the man executed.[183] This was the last known conspiracy against the controversial councilor.

Not so easy to suppress was the uprising of the Man ethnic groups. Living in the region of southwest Szechwan, the Man had raided Li-chou3 in 1195 and Ya-chou in 1206, but the uprising led by Hsü Pu in 1208 easily dwarfed the others. The inaccessibility of the southern part of the Li-chou circuit inhibited the deployment of government troops from the north, which left the court dependent on informal local militia to restore order. In practice, when a militia failed to do its job, political and monetary concessions often provided the right incentive for the insurgents to disband. The first strategy, coercion, had failed disastrously in the case of Hsü Pu, whose lawlessness continued sporadically for the next six years, but in the end he surrendered in exchange for a handsome government stipend. While he was active, Hsü Pu's defiance encouraged others in the region to rebel. An uprising in 1211 had struck nearby Hsü-chou, and another had hit Chia-ting in 1213, and there were outbreaks at Ya-chou in 1217 and 1220.[184] The relatively small scale and geographic remoteness of Man and Yao2 insurgencies limited their impact on the political fortunes of Shih Mi-yüan, yet when viewed within the broader contexts of Sung domestic instability and foreign invasion, they were surely interpreted as signs of Heaven's dissatisfaction with the court at Lin-an.

AN UNCERTAIN SUCCESSION

After a decade in power, Shih Mi-yüan had alienated many inside and outside the capital. His prominent role in controversial court decisions, his

---

[183] Wang Chien-ch'iu, "Sung-tai t'ai-hsüeh yü t'ai-hsüeh-sheng" (M.A. thesis, Fu-jen T'a-hsüeh, 1965), p. 305.

[184] On these various outbreaks, see SS 37–40; 494, pp. 14195–6; HTC (1958) 154, p. 4124; 157, p. 4236; 158, pp. 4285, 4290–1; 159, pp. 4304, 4311–12; 160, p. 4329.

manipulative approach to dealing with colleagues, his caution in conducting foreign affairs all detracted from his original appeal and left him increasingly isolated from the bureaucracy. Still, the emperor maintained an unwavering confidence in him. The chief councilor's policies, although widely assailed, were hardly unsound. They maintained a high level of order while holding at bay the empire's various enemies, domestic and foreign, in difficult circumstances. Moreover, those bureaucrats who disapproved of Shih Mi-yüan had no single issue around which to rally, that is, until the emperor's death.

Before assuming the throne in 1194, Ning-tsung had fathered two sons, both of whom died young. At least seven other sons would follow, but they too would all die within months of birth. The emperor's sole daughter suffered a similar fate. In none of these cases is the maternity recorded, for all the mothers were apparently lesser consorts. No reasons for their deaths are given, and there is no suggestion of foul play. Lacking an heir, in 1197 the emperor adopted the four-year-old Chao Hsün (1193–1220), a descendant of Sung founder T'ai-tsu's second son, Chao Te-chao.[185] The youth became heir apparent at sixteen and spent the next decade in training for the throne. As a mark of his favor, the emperor permitted Chao Hsün occasionally to join in court audiences. The heir was no less favored by Empress Yang2 and Shih Mi-yüan, especially the latter, who served the prince in various capacities, including lecturer and chief advisor. When the twenty-eight-year-old Chao Hsün died in the early autumn of 1220, the loss to Shih Mi-yüan was personal no less than political. The death raised the difficult problem of the succession. Three generations earlier, an heirless Kao-tsung had adopted two sons from the imperial clan and eventually selected the more promising one as heir. Ning-tsung did not follow this farsighted precedent. By adopting only one child in 1197, he had no alternative heir when Chao Hsün died in 1220, and the highly charged process of identifying a suitable candidate had to begin anew. At fifty-two, the emperor's age seemed to preclude adoption of a young child, although this was the normal ideal, to avoid the succession of a child emperor and a regency after his own death. The nominee also had to be closely related to the royal family. In the context of such limitations, Ning-tsung selected Chao Hung

---

[185] On the succession, see Richard L. Davis, "Evolution of an historical stereotype for the Southern Sung – the case against Shih Mi-yüan," in Ryū Shiken hakuse shōju kinen: Sō-shi kenkyū ronshū, ed. Kinugawa Tsuyoshi (Kyoto, 1989), pp. 357–86; Chaffee, Branches of heaven, pp. 202–5; SS 41, pp. 783–4; 243, pp. 8656–7; 246, pp. 8733–8; 419, pp. 12551–2; 465, p. 13596; Sung-shih ch'üan-wen Hsü Tzu-chih t'ung-chien 31, pp. 1a–2a; HTC (1958) 158, pp. 4269, 4271; 161, p. 4387; 162, pp. 4395–7, 4399, 4406–7, 4422–4; Liu K'o-chuang, Hou-ts'un hsien-sheng ta ch'üan-chi [Ssu-yen t'ang 1304 ed.; Ssu-pu ts'ung-k'an ch'u-pien 1929 ed.] (1270; Taipei, 1979) 170, p. 2b; Chao I, Nien-erh shih cha-chi, ed. and ann. Tu Wei-yün (1799; Taipei, 1975) 23, pp. 496–7.

(d. 1225), the adopted son of the deceased Chao Kai,[186] himself the son of Chao K'ai2 (1146–80), at one time heir to Hsiao-tsung.[187]

In view of his preeminence at court, Shih Mi-yüan certainly played some role in choosing Chao Hung, yet problems emerged from early on. The selection required nearly a year's consideration, suggesting both the complexity of the process and the existence of serious reservations about the candidate. Moreover, Chao Hung proved, as prince, to be exceedingly abrasive and rebellious. Making no secret of his enmity for Shih Mi-yüan, he threatened him with future banishment to the remote south. The councilor is said to have learned of Chao Hung's animosity through a young beauty surreptitiously planted in the palace, but Shih hardly needed an informant, for Chao Hung was not in the least discreet and his feelings became common knowledge in the capital. Empress Yang2 found the youth equally offensive. Having arranged his marriage to Princess Wu, her grand-niece, she was allegedly infuriated by the prince's neglect of his wife and devotion to several favored concubines, and concluded that he was undeserving of the throne.[188] The alienation of both the empress and chief councilor is evidenced by Chen Te-hsiu's admonition to the prince in the summer of 1222, which warned him: "If Your Highness, the emperor's son, can be filial to Your beneficent mother and reverent to high officials, then Heaven's mandate will be vested in You. If not, You can imagine the serious consequences!"[189] The force of the statement, the warning about "serious consequences," suggests a conflict of considerable intensity soon after Chao Hung's adoption. Chen Te-hsiu's admonition also alludes to the prince's association with persons of ill-repute and the notoriety of various unnamed indiscretions.[190] Understandably, the emperor did not rush to install him as heir apparent.

[186] Chao Hung's birth father was Chao Hsi-ch'ü. See SS 246, p. 8735.

[187] It is noteworthy that Chao Hsün and Chao Hung both descended from the line of Chao Te-chao, second son of T'ai-tsu. All Northern Sung emperors descended from T'ai-tsung, brother of T'ai-tsu, as did Kao-tsung of the Southern Sung. But the next three emperors – Hsiao-tsung, Kuang-tsung, and Ning-tsung – descended from T'ai-tsu's fourth son, Chao Te-fang, effectively restoring the throne to the line of T'ai-tsu, the dynasty's founder. Chao Hsün and all subsequent heirs to the Sung throne descended from the same line, but, as just noted, from a different son, the second son of T'ai-tsu, not the fourth. Reasons for the shift are obscure, owing as much to adoption patterns established two generations earlier as to contemporary policy. Still, the decision would prove politically sensitive in time. See Chao, Chao-shih tsu-p'u 1, pp. 41a, 66a–67b; Chaffee, Branches of heaven, pp. 25–30.

[188] Chou Mi, Kuei-hsin tsa-chih [Hsüeh-chin t'ao-yüan 1806 ed.; 1922 ed.] (c. 1298; Taipei, 1965) hou, pp. 28b–29a.

[189] HTC (1958) 162, p. 4406.

[190] Chen, Hsi-shan hsien-sheng Chen Wen-chung kung wen-chi 37, pp. 6a–12a.

Only months after the adoption, Ning-tsung had named Chao Yün (1205–64), an obscure scion of the imperial clan, who like Chao Hung was a descendant of T'ai-tsu's second son Chao Te-chao, to replace Chao Hung as heir to the line of Chao Te-chao. Chao Yün was a native of Shao-hsing. The youth reportedly came at the recommendation of Yü T'ien-hsi, a one-time teacher of Shih Mi-yüan who considered Chao Yün promising.[191] The nomination was significant, for the line of Chao Te-chao had already produced one heir to the throne and might be called upon for a second, should the need arise. The nomination also gave Chao Yün exposure to influential court and palace figures. He struck a handsome image, it is said. He was regarded as a serious youth of few words, pure and refined, fond of learning. He immediately appealed to Shih Mi-yüan, whose disappointment with Chao Hung had already prompted thought of a switch. In the interim, the education of Chao Yün was entrusted to Cheng Ch'ing-chih (1176–1251), Shih's protégé and fellow Ming-chou provincial. For the next three years, the court took no further action concerning any change in succession.

Ning-tsung fell ill in the summer of 1224, and died on 17 September at age fifty-six. An edict, dated only days before, elevated Chao Yün to imperial son, a status equal to that of Chao Hung. On the night of the death, in accordance with the emperor's will, Chao Yün succeeded as heir to the throne. At the last minute, Chao Hung had been passed over. Both the final edict and the dying testament of Ning-tsung were drafted by Shih Mi-yüan, as was standard practice in Sung times, yet whether the change represented the dying wish of the emperor or was the illicit deed of his councilor is controversial. By official accounts, Empress Yang2 learned of the impending switch only upon her husband's death and initially demurred; only under Shih Mi-yüan's sustained pressure did she consent. Shih Mi-yüan then summoned Chao Yün to the palace late that night and supervised, under heavy guard, the nineteen-year-old's accession as the new emperor. With assistance from the Palace Guard commander Hsia Chen, who had been the assassin of Han T'o-chou seventeen years earlier, Shih Mi-yüan disarmed Chao Hung's guards and read out the imperial testament (i-shu) that disinherited Chao. Shih Mi-yüan then made Chao Hung make obeisance to the new emperor. There was no violence, and no resistance from the empress or from the divested prince, who was immediately exiled to Hu-chou, some sixty miles from the capital. Shih Mi-yüan's tight grip on the court had precluded open confrontation.

Shih Mi-yüan has been widely assailed for Chao Hung's last-minute disinheritance. Many contemporaries and later historians charge that Shih Mi-yüan

---

[191] HTC (1958) 162, pp. 4396.

had imposed his will upon the emperor and empress – in effect usurping imperial authority.[192] However, the charge is not supported by substantial evidence, and it disregards the special position of Empress Yang2 at court, including her involvement in the earlier conspiracy against Han T'o-chou, her consequent close ties with Shih Mi-yüan, and her continued prominence over the next seventeen years of Li-tsung's reign. She was hardly one to be easily cowed, and the chief councilor, knowing her better than most, surely recognized her importance as arbiter of palace matters involving the imperial family. She must have been at least consulted, if indeed she did not join Shih Mi-yüan in initiating the switch. That she should be called upon, after the accession, to govern from "behind the bamboo screen" as regent confirms her political stature at the time, although it was an honor she declined. In addition, Shih Mi-yüan had built his reputation upon caution and prudence, and this did not change after Ning-tsung's death.

Had the succession's legitimacy been seriously questioned, the Sung bureaucratic leadership would certainly have inundated the court with memorials of protest, vehemently attacking Shih Mi-yüan for his arrogation of authority. This did not occur in the months directly following the incident. It seems most likely that all concerned knew that Chao Hung would be a disaster as emperor and willingly accepted the fait accompli. It is noteworthy that Chao Hung's highly regarded tutor, Chen Te-hsiu, returned to Lin-an soon after the accession and was appointed as vice-minister of rites. In light of his history of tension with Shih Mi-yüan and his close association with Chao Hung, he would never have accepted the post had the succession of Chao Yün appeared to him in any way improper. However, the transition of power, which went so smoothly at first, would create difficulties with lasting consequence for Shih Mi-yüan, and for the dynastic line.

During the thirty-five years of Kuang-tsung's and Ning-tsung's reigns the Southern Sung was confronted with some of its greatest challenges. The Sung endured periods of intense factionalism at court and two major border wars with the Chin. It suffered through a succession of natural disasters and contended with several large uprisings. It endured imperial leadership that was at best inattentive and at worst mentally incompetent. Although people of the time may have looked back nostalgically to the reign of Hsiao-tsung, the possibility of the imminent demise of the Chin presented unforeseen and unpredictable opportunities. These included regaining territory lost a century before, the possible termination of peace payments, and a prospective end to

---

[192] For a fuller analysis, see Davis, "Evolution of an historical stereotype," and Davis, *Court and family in Sung China*, pp. 95–105.

the diplomacy of humiliation. The Mongols, at this point, were openly determined to annihilate the Chin, and they seemed to have had no quarrel with
the Sung. Decisions made over the next few years would profoundly affect
whether the Mongols and the Sung emerged after the elimination of Chin as
friends or foes.

CHAPTER 11

THE REIGN OF LI-TSUNG (1224–1264)

Richard L. Davis

SHIH MI-YÜAN IN ISOLATION

The sudden elevation of Chao Yün (1205–64) to imperial son only five days before the death of Emperor Ning-tsung and the replacing of Chao Hung as heir to the throne might have turned the Sung court into a battlefield of warring factions. Instead, this irregular transfer of power took place initially without incident. No mutiny erupted among the guards assigned to protect Chao Hung. The guards were forcibly detained outside the palace on the night of Ning-tsung's death and thereby denied any opportunity to interrupt the accession. Imperial clansmen living away from Lin-an raised no armies to lead against the capital with a pledge to restore the throne to its rightful occupant. The bureaucracy was also muted in its response. No one attempted to assassinate the chief councilor, Shih Mi-yüan, for his leading role in the controversial succession. There was no repeat of the Han T'o-chou incident. Students at the Imperial University proved uncharacteristically quiet. No indictments were submitted against powerful ministers exceeding their authority. The political elite, if not regarding the succession as legitimate, found it expedient to confine its suspicions and gossip to private quarters. Even the hot-tempered Chao Hung seems to have passively accepted his fate. He made no attempt to turn the bureaucracy against Shih Mi-yüan, its increasingly unpopular chief. The new emperor, known to history as Li-tsung, opted against a distant exile for his adoptive brother. Chao Hung was quickly moved to the quiet, scenic fishing town of Hu-chou, where he probably enjoyed considerable freedom of movement. His noble status was elevated from duke to prince. The indecorous succession proceeded with face-saving civility, or so seemed the intent of the parties involved.

The fate of Chao Hung

The nineteen-year-old Li-tsung, acceding to the throne on 17 September 1224, occupied himself for the next five months with routine matters of state, as Chao Hung settled into his new home away from the capital. The northern border, in uncommon placidity, seemed to be mirroring the climate at court. Then suddenly, and apparently without the slightest warning or provocation, an incident that threatened rebellion occurred at Hu-chou.[1] In the second month of 1225 three local men – P'an Jen, his brother P'an Ping, and a cousin, P'an Fu – led a motley band of fishermen and local militia to the prefectural government offices, enumerated the crimes of the chief councilor, and demanded Chao Hung's prompt installation as emperor. Claiming the allegiance of some two hundred thousand crack troops and the support of the prominent Shantung loyalist Li Ch'üan, they threatened to march on the capital if their demands were not met. Whether the P'an threesome were themselves fishermen is not clear. Reports of their attempting, sometime before the outbreak, to contact Li Ch'üan suggests some familiarity with the complex array of power among Lin-an, K'ai-feng, and Shantung and their determination to exploit it. Such astuteness can hardly be expected of ordinary commoners, yet their amateur effort implies that the rebels were neither realistic nor experienced in high-stakes political affairs. With a relatively small force and a remote hope for assistance from a far-off dissident, the three men dared to challenge the awesome might of an imperial government only sixty or so miles away.

Contemporary documents and later histories absolve Chao Hung of complicity in the affair, although his presence at Hu-chou may have inspired the action. When the rebels came searching for him, it is rumored that he hid himself in a drainage ditch. When captured and forced to don the yellow robes of the throne, he consented only after soliciting promises to harm neither the empress nor "officials," an apparent allusion to Shih Mi-yüan. Subsequently, the prince allegedly accepted the entire effort as doomed and voluntarily led prefectural troops in suppressing the outbreak, and killing P'an Ping and P'an

[1] On the uprising, see T'o-t'o et al., eds., *Sung shih* [hereafter *SS*] (1345; Peking, 1977) 246, pp. 8735–8; 476, pp. 13826, 13829; Pi Yüan, *Hsü Tzu-chih t'ung-chien* [hereafter *HTC* (1958)] [*Te-yü-t'ang tsang-pan* 1801 ed.] (1792; Peking, 1958) 163, pp. 4426–7; Chou Mi, *Ch'i-tung yeh-yü* (1291; Peking, 1983) 14, pp. 252–9; Chou Mi, *Kuei-hsin tsa-chih* [*Hsüeh-chin t'ao-yüan* 1806 ed.; 1922 ed.] (c. 1298; Taipei, 1965) *pieh-chi*, pp. 38b–39a; Richard L. Davis, *Court and family in Sung China, 960–1279: Bureaucratic success and kinship fortunes for the Shih of Ming-chou* (Durham, N.C.,1986), pp. 95–105; John W. Chaffee, *Branches of heaven: A history of the imperial clan of Sung China* (Cambridge, Mass., 1999), pp. 202–4; Charles A. Peterson, "Old illusions and new realities: Sung foreign policy, 1217–1234," in *China among equals: The Middle Kingdom and its neighbors, 10th–14th centuries*, ed. Morris Rossabi (Berkeley, Calif.,1983), pp. 204–39. For an interesting but questionable account, see *Sung-chi san-ch'ao cheng-yao* [*Shou-shan ko ts'ung-shu* n.d. ed.] (Taipei, 1968) 1, pp. 1a–b.

Fu. He promptly informed the court of the affair. Shih Mi-yüan, however, had already dispatched the Palace Guard to Hu-chou with specific instructions, so it is alleged, to execute Chao Hung. Chao Hung was captured and died by strangulation. From beginning to end, the incident scarcely lasted two weeks.

Virtually all extant source materials are highly biased against Shih Mi-yüan. Most writers, especially those from the Ming dynasty, denounced Shih as an assassin and go to great lengths to extol the moral virtues of Chao Hung.[2] These writers, pointing to the spontaneous character and small scale of the rebellion, as well as noting the duress involved in Chao Hung's initial submission to the rebels and his voluntary role in their suppression, present Shih Mi-yüan's drastic response as savagely inhumane and unjustified. But these critics emphasize only one side of the story. There is also evidence implicating Chao Hung. First, although responsibility for the outbreak is placed solely with the P'an cousins, once imperial robes were thrust upon Chao Hung, the prefect of Hu-chou reportedly led a sizable entourage of official colleagues to the prefectural office to submit their congratulations to the would-be emperor. By their conduct, they too became implicated in the rebellion. If they had believed the incident was truly hatched by a tiny band of politically insignificant actors who lacked the enthusiastic support of the prince, such high-level endorsement would have been inconceivable. Second, the outbreak is portrayed as spontaneous, but the rebels by their own admission were in contact with Li Ch'üan some three hundred to four hundred miles away in central Shantung. Such distant communication also involved crossing the Sung-Chin border at a time of war, so the rebels must have established a link with Li Ch'üan long before the incident.

If the rebels were in contact with Li Ch'üan, then the spontaneity claimed in later accounts is not credible. Nor is support from an eminent Li Ch'üan a reasonable expectation for illiterate fishermen without some advance encouragement from Chao Hung. The prince must have given the rebels at least tacit support from early on. However, Chao Hung is presented as a moderating force among the rebels, one whose concern for the well-being of Empress Yang2 and Shih Mi-yüan is remarkably noble, especially in the context of their having aggressively intervened to deny him the throne only a few months earlier. Such magnanimity completely contradicts Chao Hung's character prior to this. As noted in the preceding chapter, his uncontrollable temper and lack of discretion as imperial son, which included threats to banish Shih Mi-yüan and conflicts with Empress Yang2, had made influential enemies for him. Neither

---

[2] On Ming and Ch'ing dynasty interpretations of the succession controversy, see Richard L. Davis, "Evolution of an historical stereotype for the Southern Sung – the case against Shih Mi-yüan," in *Ryū Shiken hakuse shōju kinen: Sō-shi kenkyū ronshū*, ed. Kinugawa Tsuyoshi (Kyoto, 1989), pp. 357–86.

moderate nor forgiving, Chao Hung had despised the chief councilor, whose intervention in the accession could only have deepened Chao Hung's enmity toward him. To be sure, a glaring contradiction exists between depictions of Chao Hung's extreme personality prior to 1225 and accounts of his "moderate" role in the rebellion.

In effect, Chao Hung in death appears far nobler than he did in life. For the first time, he won sympathy from many men who had said nothing in his defense five months earlier, when his royal inheritance was snatched away. Differing accounts of the incident in Hu-chou rushed through the capital like floodwaters. Memorials of protest inundated the court. One rumor blamed Chao Hung's death on a retainer of Shih Mi-yüan, someone specifically instructed by the councilor to assassinate the prince.[3] One youthfully intemperate scholar, Teng Jo-shui (chin-shih 1220), submitted an impassioned memorial accusing the councilor of outright sedition and demanded his execution. Not incidentally, Teng also charged Shih Mi-yüan with forging Ningtsung's testament (i-shu) on the eve of the emperor's death.[4] This was an issue no other official dared to raise, let alone publicize, owing to its implications concerning the legitimacy of Li-tsung himself.

Most official protests, while less offensively worded, were nonetheless scathingly critical. The complaints of Wei Liao-weng, a Tao-hsüeh proponent with a long history of conflict with Shih Mi-yüan, focused not on the legitimacy of the succession itself, but on the moral and political implications of the conflict in Hu-chou. Wei stressed that events at Hu-chou reflected a much larger problem, the political instability resulting from Shih Mi-yüan's dominance and seemingly interminable tenure as chief councilor.[5] For those who agreed with Wei Liao-weng, Shih Mi-yüan had become more than a political liability for the court – he was a bad moral influence on the impressionable new emperor. But perhaps the most incisive criticism came from Chen Te-hsiu, then vice-minister of rites, an individual known for cooperating with Shih Mi-yüan despite policy differences. Sharing with Wei Liao-weng a firm moralistic outlook, Chen Te-hsiu was troubled by Li-tsung's cold indifference toward his stepbrother in refusing to appoint an heir for Chao Hung following the death of Chao's only son so that Chao Hung's lineage would not be extinguished and ritual sacrifices to the dead prince could be performed. Chen felt that this refusal betrayed an alarming deficiency in the fraternal affection that was a cardinal virtue of Confucian morality.[6] This theme of fraternal devotion, and

---

[3] Chou, Ch'i-tung yeh-yü (1983) 14, p. 253; HTC (1958) 163, p. 4427.
[4] SS 455, pp. 13378–81; HTC (1958) 163, pp. 4435–6.
[5] SS 437, pp. 12967–8.
[6] SS 437, pp. 12961–2; HTC (1958) 163, pp. 4427–8, 4439–41.

the role of the emperor as paragon of that virtue, runs through many other memorials, and overshadows all concern for the rebellion at Hu-chou or even for the death of Chao Hung. Clearly, this issue had been seized upon by opponents of Shih Mi-yüan and politicized to implicate the new emperor as well. Chen Te-hsiu had pressed for an open investigation of the Hu-chou incident. His request was firmly denied.

Rather than placate the critics, Li-tsung aggravated them. On first learning of Chao Hung's death, he suspended court for a day and considered posthumous honors. Yet within months, not only was Chao Hung posthumously demoted to duke, his old titular status, but he was buried without honors on a straw mat. Chao Hung's demotion coincided with the elevation of Shih Mi-yüan to grand preceptor. Li-tsung, no doubt, intended the latter move to demonstrate his continued confidence in the councilor. In the view of Shih Mi-yüan critics, however, to demote Chao Hung, a perceived innocent victim of circumstance, while bestowing high honors upon his executioner, appeared morally unacceptable. Shih Mi-yüan declined the tribute, but this did not appease those in the outer court, who continued their denunciations. Two memorials from Hu Meng-yü (1185–1226), then a minor executive at the Ministry of Personnel, drew much sympathy.[7] In justifying his appeal for compassion, Hu compared the court's treatment of Chao Hung to the treatment afforded another ill-fated Sung prince, Chao T'ing-mei (947–84), brother of T'ai-tsu and T'ai-tsung. Chao T'ing-mei had been suspected of sedition, exiled to Fang-chou, and demoted in rank from prince to duke. When news of Chao T'ing-mei's death reached the capital, T'ai-tsung was moved to restore his princely status. Reflecting on this early precedent of magnanimity, Hu Meng-yü's memorials, without the malice of many other petitions, made a strong plea for compassion.

Despite such appeals, the court's response was rigid. Shih Mi-yüan had always been a man of compromise, not inclined to confrontation, so this new firmness may reflect the emperor's wishes. With the now twenty-year-old Li-tsung attempting to prove his worth, compromise with the forces of opinion was untimely: the emperor could not afford to appear weak lest the bureaucracy become unmanageable. In consequence, the court used the Censorate to silence the critics. By the end of 1225, Teng Jo-shui, Wei Liao-weng, and Chen Te-hsiu were all censured and demoted. The forty-one-year-old Hu Meng-yü, stripped of official status, was exiled to a distant Kwangsi, where he died the next year of dysentery. His death was widely thought unjust within the civil service and cost Shih Mi-yüan many supporters. Ch'iao Hsing-chien, for

---

[7] Hu Meng-yü and Hu Chih-jou, *Hsiang-t'ai shou-mo* (1225; Taipei, 1965–70); SS 244, pp. 8666–70.

example, had served under Shih in various capacities prior to 1225 and the two were apparently quite cordial, yet Ch'iao Hsing-chien joined those in the outer court protesting the posthumous humiliation of Chao Hung. Members of Shih Mi-yüan's own kin group similarly voiced their opposition. A cousin, Shih Mi-kung, demanded that the spirit of Chao Hung be given rest through proper burial and adoption of a male heir.[8] In effect, the Chao Hung incident provided moralists long opposed to Shih Mi-yüan with precisely the issue they needed to mobilize official opinion against him. The incident had in turn shattered the broad alliance established by Shih Mi-yüan following the death of Han T'o-chou, an alliance of politicians and *Tao-hsüeh* proponents that had weakened over the years but had still been alive. Relying on only a handful of close friends, Shih Mi-yüan became "isolated on high."

In the end, dissidents could not be silenced by demotion and exile. They would soon be emboldened by other events. The early years of the Li-tsung reign were visited by natural disasters of every variety: floods in Huai-nan and Che-hsi, devastating fires at Ch'u-chou and Ch'i-chou2, an earthquake not far from Lin-an, and massive flooding in Szechwan following the rupture of a mountain. The heavens proved equally disquieted. Falling stars were frequently reported, and the path of Venus (*chin-hsing*) was described as inconstant. Many officials, making the traditional assumption that disruptions in nature reflect disharmony among humans, were quick to suggest a connection between the natural events and Chao Hung's posthumous treatment. According to Yeh Wei-tao (*chin-shih* 1220), later named a professor at the Imperial University, Chao Hung's *ch'i* (life force) had not dispersed, owing to Chao's improper burial and the absence of an heir to conduct ritual sacrifices to him, and this *ch'i* was wreaking havoc throughout the empire. Others concurred and pleaded for appropriate atonement.[9] The court refused, at least for Shih Mi-yüan's remaining eight years, and the controversy continued to smolder. Such inflexibility may appear petty minded, but there was more at stake. The naming of an heir for Chao Hung could lead to a future crisis if the adopted son proved politically ambitious and coveted the throne denied his adopted father. The cautious Shih Mi-yüan could not bring himself to take that risk. For the sake of the young emperor, if not for his own political security, he made a decision that cost his reputation dearly. He would go down in history as the councilor whose main accomplishment was the murder and humiliation of a royal prince. Shih Mi-yüan's reputation might well have been salvaged by an imaginative, successful border policy, but Sung's foreign enemies proved unaccommodating.

---

[8] *SS* 417, pp. 12489–92; 423, p. 12637.
[9] *SS* 438, pp. 12986–7; 434, p. 12900; *HTC* (1958) 163, p. 4434.

The loyalist outbreak

Border hostilities had subsided somewhat when Li-tsung took the throne. The Chin braced themselves for a final showdown with the Mongols after striking a peace agreement with the Hsi Hsia in late 1224 that ended their foolhardy war. The Mongols had withdrawn briefly from the region, but were again in full force at Hsi Hsia borders by early 1226 to begin their final assault on that empire. With Temüjin (Chinggis khan) in personal command of Mongol armies, the Hsi Hsia capital fell within a year.[10] The concentration of Mongol energies on the Hsi Hsia gave the Chin a respite of sorts. The death of Temüjin in the summer of 1227 in the midst of the Hsi Hsia campaign must also have come as welcome news. Beyond a lull in fighting, it brought the prospect of a succession dispute that might set contending Mongol camps against one another. The Chin made new peace overtures, and the Mongols, by ignoring them, implied an inevitable resumption of hostilities. For the Sung, which in the mid-1220s had squandered valuable energy on domestic issues, recent developments were ominous. Mongol acquisition of the Hsi Hsia domain placed them in proximity to northern Szechwan. Worse yet, any hiatus in fighting to the north might free the Chin to resume hostilities against the south. Conflict with either the Chin or Mongols was seen as inevitable by many Sung statesmen, but Shih Mi-yüan, clinging to his old ambivalence in foreign affairs, simply chose to reinforce border defenses while denying that there was a serious military challenge.

The beleaguered Chin posed only a modest threat to the south by this time, but Sung China had other menaces to confront. In the preceding chapter, mention was made of the preponderance of rebel bands in Shantung, some claiming allegiance with Sung, and others asserting their autonomy from the Chin in the aftermath of Mongol incursions. With the Chin seemingly on the verge of extinction, the Sung could not but reassess its policies toward these loyalists in Shantung. To exclude the Mongols from the northeast and perhaps even reclaim the territory for itself, the Sung court needed an early foothold in the region and loyalists could provide the means.

Shantung activists, anxious to procure material assistance from the south and to legitimate their own activities, were happy to acquiesce to the Sung court, and the court had much to gain from the arrangement. Apart from providing

---

[10] For details, see H. Desmond Martin, "The Mongol wars with Hsi Hsia (1205–1227)," *Journal of the Royal Asiatic Society of Great Britain and Ireland* Nos. 3–4 (1942), pp. 195–228; Li Tse-fen, *Yüan-shih hsin-chiang* (Taipei, 1978), vol. 1, pp. 491–510; and Ruth W. Dunnell, "The Hsi Hsia," in *The Cambridge history of China*, volume 6: *Alien regimes and border states, 907–1368*, ed. Herbert Franke and Denis C. Twitchett (New York, 1994), pp. 205–14.

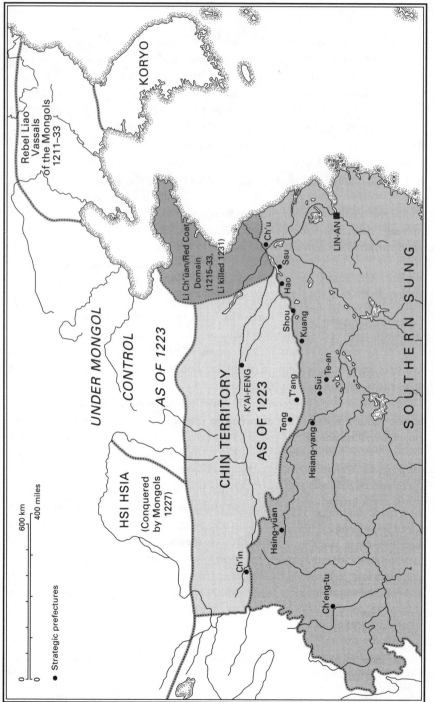

Map 28. Border situation as of Li-tsung's succession, c. 1224.

nominal Sung authority over the Shantung region, the arrangement enabled the Sung to deploy loyalists in the south, as in the case of Li Ch'üan, to assist in defending the Sung-Chin border. Although Shih Mi-yüan showed little interest in venturesome military undertakings and extended aid only under pressure from border officials, the limited assistance would steadily expand. By the late 1220s, conferral of handsome subsidies and lofty titles on loyalists in the north became established policy. The court honored Li Ch'üan, whose territory now stretched from I-tu in a southeasterly direction along the coast, as regional commandant, and P'eng I-pin (d. 1225) became military director, with control centering on western Shantung and extending toward Ta-ming. The total cost of loyalist subsidies is uncertain, yet official records indicate that in 1224, as court support began to increase, the armies of Li Ch'üan and P'eng I-pin drew subsidies of some three hundred thousand strings of cash.[11] In exchange for its largesse, the Sung court expected loyalists to defer to the authority of Sung border commanders, a demand that irritated some loyalists.

For the Sung court, the most difficult loyalist was Li Ch'üan.[12] Under Ning-tsung, through a clever combination of conquest and alliance, Li Ch'üan had proven himself a valued asset to the south, but his own ambitions had undermined his usefulness to the Sung. As early as 1222, he began trying to eliminate neighboring loyalists in the northeast, which forced some would-be loyalists into the arms of the Mongols. Li also proceeded to harass Sung border authorities. Among the numerous military supervisors from the region of the eastern Huai River, Chia She had achieved greater success than most at coordinating loyalists and subordinating them to Sung command. Chia She was realistic about the loyalties of such groups. He once complained of Shih Mi-yüan's excessive generosity toward Li Ch'üan, and in this way implied that loyalists in general, but especially Li Ch'üan, were scarcely better than brigands, of potential value to be sure, but also a potentially dangerous source of future trouble.[13] Chia She's death in 1223 curtailed the Sung's limited success with the loyalist movements. Succeeding supervisors were sometimes contentious and at other times ingratiating toward loyalists, in either event weakening the hand of the Sung court. Hsü Kuo (d. 1225) who had been a minor officer before becoming a military supervisor, lacked Chia She's extensive experience in negotiations, and his hostility toward Li Ch'üan was a matter of

---

[11] *HTC* (1958) 162, p. 4421.

[12] Davis, *Court and family in Sung China*, pp. 107–10; the chapter "Nan Sung Chin Yüan chien ti Shan-tung chung-i-chün yü Li Ch'üan," in Sun K'o-k'uan, *Meng-ku Han-chün chi Han wen-hua yen-chiu* (Taipei, 1958), pp. 11–43; Sun K'o-k'uan, *Yüan-tai Han wen-hua chih huo-tung* (Taipei, 1968), pp. 65–83; *SS* 476–7; Chou, *Ch'i-tung yeh-yü* (1983) 9, pp. 157–64; Ch'ien Shih-sheng, *Nan Sung shu* (c. 1590; n.p., 1792) 44, pp. 1a–10b; 54, pp. 3b–4a.

[13] *SS* 403, p. 12209.

public record. Chia She had perceived the Shantung activist as arrogant and
unruly, but not altogether disloyal; Hsü Kuo, however, considered Li Ch'üan
totally self-serving and treacherous. Shih Mi-yüan seems to have reasoned that
the forceful personality Hsü Kuo commanded at the border might intimidate
and perhaps humble Li Ch'üan, which would explain his appointment of Hsü
Kuo. If this was the case, Shih was gravely mistaken. As tension between Hsü
and Li increased, Li Ch'üan instigated a mutiny in the border town of Ch'u-
chou, and Hsü Kuo died in flight. This challenge to Sung authority on Sung
territory occurred in early spring of 1225, only a month after the uprising of
the deposed Chao Hung at Hu-chou.[14]

Even before the Ch'u-chou mutiny, the Li Ch'üan threat must have been
apparent. The rebels at Hu-chou, in turning to Shantung for assistance against
the Sung court, had demonstrated that the possibility of Li Ch'üan's duplicity
was common knowledge. Several months after the Hu-chou uprising, one of
its leaders, rebel P'an Jen, surfaced at Ch'u-chou, apparently en route to Shantung. His cover exposed, he was captured and sent to Lin-an for execution. The
linkage between Li Ch'üan and the Hu-chou insurgents increased pressures in
Lin-an to act against the Shantung leader. Chao K'uei (1186–1266) and Chao
Fan, sons of the eminent commander Chao Fang, had boldly advocated a northern expedition even before 1225. Ch'en Hsün, nephew of Shih Mi-yüan and
erudite of ceremonials, now similarly demanded firm action. Even the ordinarily moderate Ch'iao Hsing-chien took a militant stand in this case, recognizing
that further indulgence of Li Ch'üan might undermine Sung authority on a
much larger scale. Finally, the military director of the main insurgent group
in western Shantung, P'eng I-pin, outraged at Li Ch'üan's duplicity, joined
Sung authorities in conspiring against his neighbor, Li Ch'üan. But, the conspiracy ended with P'eng I-pin's untimely death later in the year 1225.[15] As
had occurred with Wu Hsi's uprising of 1207 in Szechwan, Shih Mi-yüan may
have hoped that P'eng I-pin would succeed in resolving the loyalist threat
internally, which would have spared Shih the risks of direct intervention.
When Peng's death ruled this out, Shih Mi-yüan settled for an unseemly but
convenient appeasement. He appointed accommodating commanders to the
strategic post at Ch'u-chou and continued to provision the armies of Li Ch'üan.

However, Li Ch'üan's position in the region was not stable. In the spring
of 1226, the Mongols trapped Li Ch'üan at I-tu, his base in central Shantung.
The encirclement, lasting over a year, permitted the Sung court to strengthen

---

[14] *SS* 476, pp. 13825–7; *HTC* (1958) 162, p. 4418; 163, pp. 4430–2.

[15] References are in *SS* 417, pp. 12499–500, 12505–6; 423, p. 12639; 417, p. 12492; 476, p. 13828; *HTC*
(1958) 163, pp. 4436–7; Sun K'o-k'uan, *Meng-ku ch'u-ch'i chih chün-lüeh yü Chin chih peng-k'uei* (Taipei,
1955), pp. 65–81; Hu Chao-hsi et al., *Sung Meng (Yüan) kuan-hsi shih,* (Ch'eng-tu, 1992), pp. 36–41.

its hand in southern Shantung, where the remnants of Li Ch'üan's army had taken refuge. The time seemed right for confrontation. Halting provisions to Li Ch'üan from the south, the new prefect of Ch'u-chou, Liu Cho (d. 1227), moved quickly to mobilize opponents of Li Ch'üan against Li's remnant forces. The ploy failed because of the resourcefulness of Yang Miao-chen, the wife of Li Ch'üan, who had temporarily taken command of Li's armies and who outmaneuvered Liu Cho and forced him to flee Ch'u-chou under cover of night. His garrison went over to the rebels. Meanwhile, the year-long siege of Li Ch'üan at I-tu had reduced the city's population to a fraction of its original several hundred thousand, yet cleverly Li Ch'üan was spared imminent defeat by striking a deal with the Mongols. In exchange for formally relinquishing the city, he received appointment as regional administrator (*hsing-t'ai shang-shu sheng*) of Shantung. Shih Mi-yüan in response named Yao Ch'ung (d. 1227) to be prefect of Ch'u-chou. Rather than attack, Yao tried to ingratiate himself with Li Ch'üan. The gesture did not appease Yang Miao-chen or Li Fu2, brother of Li Ch'üan. Within six months, Yao Ch'ung was driven out of Ch'u-chou, fleeing an assassination plot hatched by Yang Miao-chen and Li Fu2. In effect, the rebels had overrun a vital city on the Sung border and they posed a growing menace to the lower Huai region and especially to the strategically vital Yang-chou, less than sixty miles to the south.

The mutiny at Ch'u-chou could not be sustained by Yang Miao-chen and Li Fu2. A son and a concubine of Li Ch'üan had been killed in the fighting, and when Li Ch'üan returned to retake the city in the early autumn of 1227, he wore Mongol vestments as symbols of his new allegiance. The abortive Ch'u-chou mutiny had been led by Shih Ch'ing (d. 1227), a former Li Ch'üan subordinate, with the aid of a local Sung commander. Li Ch'üan quickly won back the city, ending its month-long autonomy, and Shih Ch'ing died at his hands. The overconfident Li Ch'üan now began to assemble a naval force in preparation for war against the Sung. For the next two years, Shih Mi-yüan tried to use lofty titles and royal stipends to appease the Shantung leader; he continued to ignore the appeals of colleagues to take up arms against Li Ch'üan. For his part, Li Ch'üan rejected the Sung court's offers, showing that he was fixed in his commitment to the Mongols. The inability of the Sung court to control Li Ch'üan's ambitions was most glaringly apparent in the early 1230s, as Li Ch'üan expanded his territory in the direction of Yang-chou, and Shih Mi-yüan still did not abandon the policy of provisioning him.[16]

By late 1230, Li Ch'üan began a siege of T'ai-chou, sixty miles into Sung territory and only twelve miles east of Yang-chou. The sixty-six-year-old

---

[16] *SS* 477, pp. 13842–3; *HTC* (1958) 165, pp. 4492–3, 4496.

Shih Mi-yüan still did not declare war himself, but deferred the honor to Cheng Ch'ing-chih, his close confidant and assisting executive at the Bureau of Military Affairs. Once the decision to act was made, the court moved swiftly, entrusting the brothers Chao K'uei and Chao Fan with general command of the punitive campaign. The showdown occurred at Yang-chou, where the rebels reportedly numbered several hundred thousand. Even assuming the induction of nearby residents into military service, this is not a believable estimate; the armies of Li Ch'üan appear never to have exceeded thirty thousand men. Even so, a force of thirty thousand was not to be taken lightly, and the Chao brothers, no doubt with a force of equal if not greater size, broke the rebel blockade and destroyed much of Li's army. Defeat for Li Ch'üan was resounding. He died on 18 February 1231. Sung armies moved north, recapturing border towns such as Ch'u-chou and Huai-an and purging them of Li Ch'üan partisans. The remnants of the Shantung army returned north, and were never again a serious threat.

The speed with which Sung armies eradicated the Li Ch'üan menace reflected poorly on the judgment of Shih Mi-yüan by making his earlier reluctance to act appear unwarranted. Some might conclude that the military folly of Han T'o-chou a generation earlier had left Shih Mi-yüan a prisoner of historical precedent, unable to grasp the differences of past and present and to act accordingly. But the issues confronting Shih Mi-yüan went far beyond the old choices of aggressive intervention or passive neglect.

Beyond the Chin response to Sung actions in Shantung, the Sung had to consider Mongol reactions as well. Early on in their conquest of Chin, the Mongols held territory along the western border of Shantung and aggressively encouraged the activities of local rebels to undermine Chin authority. By 1221 the Mongols had won the favor of Chang Lin2, a rebel lured by Li Ch'üan into the Sung camp two years earlier, who abruptly abandoned the Sung when personal rivalry divided the two men. Chang Lin2's base of operations centered on northwest Shantung and extended into Ho-pei East circuit. In 1223, however, Chang Lin2 abandoned the Mongols and submitted once more to the Sung. The Sung court could hardly turn him away, although entering into a bidding war with the Mongols in Shantung could have costly repercussions. Sung relations with another loyalist, P'eng I-pin, proved even more sensitive. With a base south of Chang Lin2's, P'eng I-pin repeatedly engaged Mongol armies as he expanded his territory north into Ta-ming. Holding Sung rank and firmly committed to the Sung court, he could only be viewed by the Mongols as a Sung agent. Chang Lin2 and P'eng I-pin may have brought the Sung into indirect conflict with the Mongols, but the use of Sung regular troops in the suppression of Li Ch'üan risked, for the first time, direct conflict between the Mongols and the Sung. In this context, Shih Mi-yüan had good reason to act with caution, for the Sung could ill-afford to incur another powerful enemy and trigger yet another war.

However defensible, Shih Mi-yüan's caution may have forced Li Ch'üan into the waiting arms of the Mongols. The Yüan dynasty (1260–1368) compilers of the *Sung dynastic history (Sung shih)* have no high regard for Li Ch'üan. An uncommonly long biography, subsumed under "treasonous officials," portrays Li Ch'üan as a self-serving traitor from the outset. The modern historian Sun K'o-k'uan has challenged this view, demonstrating rather convincingly that official chroniclers were biased against loyalist groups in general. They even denied a biography to the one Shantung activist who remained loyal to the Sung court until the end, P'eng I-pin, seeking to exclude any loyalist who failed to fit their Li Ch'üan stereotype of duplicity. Sun K'o-k'uan and others characterize Shantung loyalists as more than just opportunists; they see them as patriots imbued with "ethnic consciousness" and seeking to restore majority rule to China. The failure of the loyalist mission may relate, in part, to the destructive tensions among rivals in Shantung, but the transformation of Sung loyalists into traitors is blamed largely upon Shih Mi-yüan.[17] More committed to securing the south than regaining the north, and distrustful of armies not directly responsible to him, Shih Mi-yüan sought simply to harness loyalist armies for the Sung's advantage. Li Ch'üan, quite simply, found the terms unacceptable.

Notwithstanding the need to reassess the loyalist question independent of court historians, Sun K'o-k'uan's view appears as yet another extreme. Li Ch'üan may have begun as a source of loyalist unity, but after 1221 his preoccupation with his own territorial expansion and dominance of the Shantung region made him the principal source of division. Ambition of this sort cannot be easily blamed on the Sung court. Moreover, Li Ch'üan's submission to the Mongols and his war against the Sung are curious moves for an "ethnically conscious" individual. Autonomy, after all, was not altogether unfeasible in an area as isolated as Shantung. Yüan historians may have treated Li Ch'üan harshly because of the duplicity of his adopted son, Li T'an, several decades later, rather than judging Li Ch'üan on his own merits. It would also be equally erroneous to portray Li Ch'üan as a tragic hero. Better suited for that role is perhaps P'eng I-pin, the hapless loyalist who, in the face of many hardships, died while trying to oust the Mongols from Ho-pei West. Trapped between Li Ch'üan to the east, the Chin to the west, the Mongols to the northwest, and the Mongol puppets Yen Shih and Chang Lin2 to the north, P'eng's position was far more tenuous, yet never once did he abandon the Sung, even in the face

[17] Sun, *Meng-ku ch'u-ch'i chih chün-lüeh yü Chin chih peng-k'uei*, pp. 65–81; Huang K'uan-ch'ung, *Nan Sung shih-tai k'ang Chin ti i-chün* (Taipei, 1988), pp. 224–33.

of the Sung's annoyingly short-sighted policies. Li Ch'üan, a totally different character, was ruined by his own uncontrolled arrogance and ambition.

FOREIGN POLICY

The strategic see-saw

During the Ning-tsung era, Sung-Mongol relations were characterized more by ambivalence than by relations between friend or foe. Despite long-standing Sung-Chin tensions, few Sung officials promoted an alliance with the Mongols against the Jurchen. A forceful performance in the brief K'ai-hsi war that had been concluded only a few years before, in 1208, had clearly demonstrated that Chin military power was far from spent. The expectation that the Chin could arrest the Mongol advance was not totally fanciful. Few in the Sung capital had seriously entertained the ominous prediction of Chen Te-hsiu in 1214, who warned that the Mongol menace would likely become the future Sung peril. Shih Mi-yüan had not departed from his long-standing policy of noninvolvement. Even the reopening of hostilities along the Sung-Chin border did not substantially affect Sung-Mongol relations. The Mongols had initiated overtures to the Sung as early as 1214, although it was not until 1221 that the Sung court conducted its first successful mission to their encampments. Coinciding with a massive Chin offensive against the Sung, the mission was intended to remind the Chin of the risks of fighting on two fronts. The next serious effort at dialogue occurred in 1225, in the midst of a major Mongol drive against Li Ch'üan.[18] Outside of this, the Sung made, at most, only half-hearted efforts to expand its dialogue with the Mongols and put pressure on the Jurchen. However, in 1231, when a Mongol envoy arrived at the Sung border to negotiate the passage of their armies through Huai-nan en route to the Chin capital K'ai-feng, he was killed by Sung patrols.[19] The action, while probably not sanctioned by the court, represented a provocation requiring military retaliation. An ambivalent Sung court, it appears, did not bother with an apology.

The retaliation that followed was not the first time that Mongol and Sung armies had clashed.[20] In their conquest of the Hsi Hsia in the summer of 1227, the Mongols had attacked the Chin empire's western flank at strategically vital Feng-hsiang and Shang-chou, only miles from the Sung border. Nearby

---

[18] Sung Lien et al., *Yüan shih* [*Po-na-pen* 1930–7 ed.] (1370; Peking, 1976) 1, pp. 21, 23; Hu et al., *Sung Meng (Yüan) kuan-hsi shih*, pp. 17–26; Peterson, "Old illusions and new realities," pp. 218–19.

[19] Sung et al., *Yüan shih* 2, p. 31; *HTC* (1958) 165, pp. 4501–2.

[20] Li T'ien-ming, *Sung Yüan chan-shih* (Taipei, 1988), pp. 38–45, 75–86.

Sung prefectures of Feng-chou, Hsi-ho-chou, and Chieh-chou were also hit. No rationale was given for entering Sung territory. On his deathbed, Temüjin reportedly acknowledged that speedy annihilation of the Chin required attacking K'ai-feng from the south, because the swift, wide Yellow River protecting the Chin capital on the north made a direct north-to-south frontal assault unmanageable for his cavalry forces.[21] Temüjin's lieutenants may have forced their way through Sung lands for lack of time or patience to win a negotiated passage, but this cannot explain their attacks as far south as Chieh-chou and Mien-chou, some sixty miles into the Sung domain. Perhaps the Mongols, having depopulated and destroyed most of the Tangut empire, merely came for booty. Whatever their motives, they soon returned home to battle over the succession to Temüjin.

Ögödei (r. 1229–41), Temüjin's successor, has been portrayed as a man of sound judgment and impressive administrative talent, more committed to political consolidation than his father the warrior had been.[22] Despite the execution of Li Ch'üan by Sung armies, Ögödei chose not to resume hostilities against the Sung. In the summer of 1231, just months after Li Ch'üan's death, Ögödei dispatched an emissary to Lin-an to negotiate the passage of Mongol troops through Sung territory. That the mission ended in failure was bad enough, but during the return trip home the envoy was killed by an assassin, allegedly a Sung commander at Mien-chou. In response, Mongol armies overran Szechwan and penetrated as far south as Lang-chou, some one hundred and eighty miles into the interior of Sung territory. The rapid strike, which cost the Sung countless civilian lives, lasted no more than a month and appears to have been largely a show of force, perhaps even a forage for booty, but certainly not a serious effort at conquest. This is implied by the commissioning of a second Mongol envoy who specifically sought provisions. The Mongols must have assumed that the Sung would relent only under duress. What is most perplexing about these developments in 1231 is Shih Mi-yüan's intransigence. For a councilor who favored accommodation over confrontation, he seems hardly the type to forgo an opportunity to patch up differences. Anti-Mongol sentiment in the south may have been a factor: Shih Mi-yüan had always been more responsive to critics at home than to enemies abroad. With popular passions running high against the Mongols in the aftermath of the Li Ch'üan affair, the time was not right for a rapprochement.

Mounting tensions along the border and the emotional pressures they created left the aging Shih Mi-yüan, according to some contemporary accounts, so depressed that he attempted suicide.[23] Court gossip of this sort should always be viewed with skepticism, but it is known that the emperor, in January 1231, had reduced court attendance for Shih Mi-yüan to once every ten days, an unmistakable sign of diminished vigor. Li-tsung also restored rank and salary to prominent critics Chen Te-hsiu and Wei Liao-weng, men who had been demoted six years earlier for challenging the posthumous treatment of Chao Hung. It seemed to many that Shih Mi-yüan had begun to fall from grace and that the emperor was on the verge of asserting himself. But it was not so. Although politically revived, the critics received no appointments in the capital. Nor did Li-tsung appoint a second councilor to share power with Shih Mi-yüan. Routine administrative chores fell increasingly upon the shoulders of Cheng Ch'ing-chih, assistant councilor since January 1231. As the chief councilor's protégé and handpicked successor, Cheng represents largely an extension of Shih Mi-yüan's influence. Only death, which came in the autumn of 1233, would end Shih's marathon tenure as chief councilor.

Shih Mi-yüan's legacy engendered hostility, not deference, from many of his contemporaries, and malicious denunciation from later historians. Policy failures aside, Shih Mi-yüan's extraordinary tenure made unpopularity virtually inevitable. In 1231 a collator at the Palace Library wrote:

[Your Majesty] has held the throne eight years now, but one never hears of things being done [by You]. In the promotion and demotion of talent, initiation and renunciation of political matters, all in the realm say, "This is the chief councilor's will.".... You may be the Son of Heaven, lord of the people, yet starting with the court and extending throughout the realm, all speak of the councilor and do not speak of the ruler.[24]

The memorialist does not attack specific policies, merely the dominance that Shih Mi-yüan represented, overshadowing the throne. This theme figures prominently in the criticisms of others as well. Wei Liao-weng, soon after the councilor's death, composed an emotional excoriation of Shih Mi-yüan's "eight failures." The memorial, focusing principally on the recent trend toward all-powerful ministers, concludes by advocating a division of bureaucratic powers.[25] Scant attention is paid to the councilor's foreign policy or to his role in the 1224 succession of Li-tsung; such issues are more compelling to critics of the Ming and Ch'ing periods. Observers, contemporary and modern, rarely credit Shih Mi-yüan with maintaining an enduring stability along the Sung-Chin border and rarely commend him for successfully evading a premature

[23] On Shih Mi-yüan's last years, see Davis, *Court and family in Sung of China*, pp. 110–17.

[24] *HTC* (1958) 165, pp. 4504–5.

[25] Wei Liao-weng, *Ho-shan hsien-sheng ta ch'üan-chi* [*Ssu-pu ts'ung-k'an ch'u-pien* 1929 ed.] (1249; Taipei, 1979) 19, pp. 1a–18a.

clash with Mongol armies.[26] As neighboring empires crumbled around it, the Sung retained a semblance of order and this owes much to the policies of Shih Mi-yüan. He introduced no significant reforms to address the chronic military and fiscal problems besetting the empire. He lacked either the imagination or courage to do so. Reflecting his preoccupation with security and predictability, the times were characterized by moderation, not by progress. A moderate Shih Mi-yüan left no dramatic political legacy, yet his policies would affect the dynasty for many years to come.

An unpropitious alliance

Mongol entreaties to the Sung to cooperate in exterminating the Jurchen regime may have appealed to some in the south. But the alliance of a century earlier between the Sung and the Jurchen against the Khitan had cost the Sung the northern part of its empire. Mongol incursions into the south in 1227 and 1231, not to mention their devastation of Hsi Hsia and much of the north, inhibited an entente, yet the Mongols wanted Sung cooperation and threatened to use military action, if necessary, to coerce an otherwise recalcitrant Sung court into an alliance.[27] In the early months of 1232, having conquered the Chin-controlled city of T'ang-chou, the Mongols advanced north to K'ai-feng and encircled the Chin capital. The siege lasted nearly a year. High casualties and cannibalism caused by famine were enough to undermine Chin resolve, but the siege also produced an epidemic of massive proportions, allegedly claiming over a million lives. Victory must have seemed imminent to the Mongols, yet the Chin valiantly held on. K'ai-feng would eventually fall two years later, but to accelerate their conquest the Mongols approached the Sung court at the close of 1232 with a view to collaboration.

In anticipation of hostilities in the central border region, the Sung had reorganized their military commands. The accomplished Meng Kung, a native of Tsao-yang, became supreme commander of Ching-hsi circuit, and Shih Sung-chih (1189–1257), a nephew of Councilor Shih Mi-yüan, became military commissioner in chief for the Ching-hsi and Ching-hu circuits. Shih Sung-chih's views on border security closely resembled those of his uncle: a preoccupation with stability that precluded adventurist intervention in the north. His appointment at this critical juncture suggests the Sung court's reaffirmation of the essentially defensive policies of his uncle. Still, in late 1232,

---

[26] The exception among modern historians is Li T'ien-ming; see his *Sung Yüan chan-shih*, pp. 203–4.

[27] Hu Chao-hsi, "Lüeh-lun Nan Sung mo-nien Ssu-ch'uan chün-min k'ang-chi Meng-ku kuei-tsu ti tou-cheng," in *Sung-shih yen-chiu lun-wen-chi: Chung-hua wen-shih lun-ts'ung tseng-k'an*, ed. Teng Kuang-ming and Ch'eng Ying-liu (Shanghai, 1982), pp. 374–409, especially p. 376.

the Sung court authorized talks between its border officials and the envoy
Wang Chi, a Chinese literatus in the service of the Mongols. Shih Sung-chih
and Meng Kung directed the exchange near Hsiang-yang. The talks inspired
lots of fanfare and superficial goodwill but no agreement resulted. The details
are shrouded in secrecy, but in all likelihood the talks failed because of Sung
tactics of delay and evasion. In the interim, the Chin court had abandoned a
besieged K'ai-feng, and took refuge by late summer 1233 at Ts'ai-chou, a mere
forty miles from the Sung border. For Mongol decision makers, the move made
assistance from the south all the more pressing, if only to block the further
retreat of the Chin ruler (Ai-tsung, r. 1223–34). Negotiations intensified and
resulted in an informal agreement.[28] The Mongols received some three hundred thousand piculs of rice, twenty thousand fresh soldiers, and the Sung's
commitment to join in the assault on Ts'ai-chou. In exchange, the Sung court
received vague promises of restoration of some territory in southern Honan. It
was a lopsided agreement, the Sung receiving nothing more for their valued
men and supplies than indefinite promises about the future.[29]

Sung and Chin armies clashed in late summer 1233 after nearly a decade of
relative inactivity along the border, and initial exchanges reflected well upon
Sung preparedness. Rumor had it that the Chin regional secretariat, Wu Hsien
(d. 1234), planned to open a southwesterly path to Szechwan as an escape
route for Emperor Ai-tsung. Wu crossed the Sung border near Teng-chou2
and attacked the nearby Kuang-hua commandery, a foray handily repulsed by
Meng Kung. In the interim, Shih Sung-chih led an offensive against T'ang-
chou, effectively isolating remaining Chin forces at Ts'ai-chou from reserves
at Teng-chou2. Inadequate men and provisions precluded a sustained Chin
resistance, and T'ang-chou collapsed. Shou-chou, to the east, fell to Sung
armies in late summer, giving the Sung a solid foothold in Honan. The Chin,
now trapped, were also denied the option of a negotiated settlement. Chin
envoys sent to discuss a possible truce with the Sung were turned back at
the border, an emphatic demonstration of the Sung court's confidence in its
newfound strength.

The Sung campaign against Ts'ai-chou, launched in early November, was
commanded by Meng Kung.[30] Mongol armies had attacked Ts'ai-chou in

---

[28] On the negotiations, see Sung et al., *Yüan shih* 2, p. 32; 153, p. 3613; *SS* 412, pp. 12370–3; *HTC*
(1958) 166, p. 4528; 167, pp. 4546–7; Peterson, "Old illusions and new realities," pp. 218–25; Hu,
"Lüeh-lun Nan Sung mo-nien," p. 376; Hu et al., *Sung Meng (Yüan) kuan-hsi shih*, pp. 48–55; Li, *Sung
Yüan chan-shih*, pp. 129–42, 162–4.

[29] See Peterson, "Old illusions and new realities," pp. 222–4, concerning the problems in the historical
record and attempts to understand Sung reasons for forming the alliance.

[30] On the Ts'ai-chou conflict, see T'o-t'o, ed., *Chin shih* [*Po-na-pen* 1930–7 ed.] (1344; Peking, 1975)
18, pp. 400–3; *SS* 412, pp. 12369–80; Li Yü-t'ang, *Chin-shih chi-shih pen-mo* (1893; Peking, 1980),
pp. 787–97; Huang K'uan-ch'ung, "Meng Kung nien-p'u," *Shih yüan* 4 (1973), pp. 79–135, especially
pp. 95–104; Li, *Yüan-shih hsin-chiang*, vol. 1, pp. 558–70.

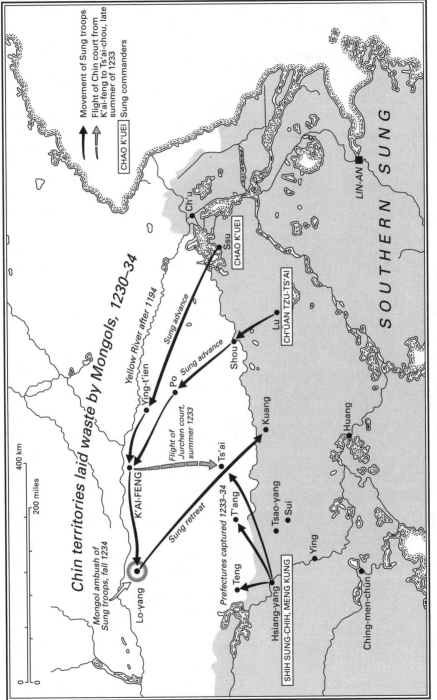

Map 29. Abortive Sung intervention in Honan, 1234.

October, but heavy casualties forced them to wait for the arrival of reinforcements from the Sung. Ts'ai-chou, only half the size of K'ai-feng, contained precious few human and material resources, making protracted resistance impossible. Within three months of its arrival there and only weeks after the Mongol
siege began, the Chin court had depleted their provisions and the population
was reduced to cannibalism. After filling a lake near the city walls with bundles
of sticks and reeds, invaders stormed Ts'ai-chou in full force. Mass desertions
followed, and the city fell on 9 February 1234. Emperor Ai-tsung committed
suicide, while the loyal few made their last stand in the city's streets and alleys.
Meng Kung retrieved the Chin imperial seals and part of Ai-tsung's charred
corpse, testaments to his victory, which he turned over to Shih Sung-chih. The
Sung quickly established military garrisons at T'ang-chou and Teng-chou2.
With the exception of Shou-chou, this was the only Chin territory acquired
by the south.

Before the Chin demise at Ts'ai-chou, and even before conclusion of the
Sung-Mongol alliance, an ambitious few in Lin-an had begun to speculate
about the limits of their government's involvement in the north. In September 1233 and a few weeks before Shih Mi-yüan's death, the court received a
memorial from Wu Yung (*chin-shih* 1208), a Szechwan native with midlevel
metropolitan experience under Shih Mi-yüan. The narrative leaves little doubt
that some considered an alliance with the Mongols as merely the first step in
a general reconquest of the northern territory. Wu Yung, who dismissed the
notion as foolhardy, compared it to "squandering what our empire has stored
away to acquire land of no use."[31]

In the aftermath of the Ts'ai-chou victory, the speculations of a few flared
into heated debate over the wisdom of further expansion. The source of the
proposal cannot be determined, but by early 1234 the Sung court began to seriously entertain the notion, preposterous though it may seem, of dispatching
troops to capture the three former capitals of the Northern Sung, K'ai-feng,
Ying-t'ien, and Lo-yang.[32] If implemented, this plan would represent a dramatic departure from the cautious foreign policy of the past. The inclination
to intervene reflects, to some historians, Li-tsung's misguided effort to assert
himself after nearly a decade of domination by his excessively pragmatic councilor Shih Mi-yüan. Others consider intervention to reflect the fundamentally
incompatible views of Shih Mi-yüan and Cheng Ch'ing-chih, the latter being
less preoccupied with political entrenchment and more committed to the irredentist cause. Neither explanation is wholly convincing. With the legitimacy
of his succession in question, Li-tsung may have seen in the move a grand

---

[31] Wu Yung, *Ho-lin chi* [*Ssu-k'u ch'üan-shu*, *Wen-yüan ko* 1779 ed.] (early 13th c.; Taipei, 1969) 18,
pp. 8a–12a, especially p. 10b; 19, pp. 12b–20a.
[32] Hu et al., *Sung Meng (Yüan) kuan-hsi shih*, pp. 87–91; Li, *Sung Yüan chan-shih*, pp. 170–81.

opportunity to prove himself deserving of the throne, but there is not the slightest shred of historical evidence to suggest that the emperor genuinely cared to assert himself. For the duration of his reign, Li-tsung delegated most decision making to chief ministers, essentially sanctioning whatever policies they recommended. As for Cheng Ch'ing-chih, his differences with Shih Mi-yüan should not be exaggerated. There is nothing to document serious rifts between the two over border policy. Admittedly, it may have been politically expedient to distance himself from his highly unpopular predecessor, and a more ambitious foreign policy might provide a convenient vehicle for so doing, but Cheng Ch'ing-chih could have devised some less risky action to accomplish the same objective. There is yet another reason to suspect that the emperor and his new councilor, although perhaps tantalized by revanchist aspirations, did not originally favor military intervention. Returning south immediately after the Chin defeat, the troops of Meng Kung made little effort to retain a military presence in southern Honan. Only a half year later, though, the Sung court ordered troops north once again. A stunning reversal of court policy had occurred.

Later chroniclers, with the advantage of historical hindsight, are intentionally generous in recording the views of moderates while neglecting the proponents of aggression. Even after accounting for historical bias of this sort, we must still conclude that the vast majority of officialdom, and especially court officials, opposed aggression.[33] Assistant Councilors Ch'iao Hsing-chien, Tseng Ts'ung-lung (*chin-shih* 1199), and Ch'en Kuei-i (1183–1234), all of whom held concurrent appointments at the Bureau of Military Affairs, were in complete agreement about the injudiciousness of sending troops north. Ch'en Kuei-i, realizing that his council would go unheeded, resigned in protest. Joining those who objected was Investigating Censor Li Tsung-mien (*chin-shih* 1205), who pointed to the tactical difficulty of provisioning troops in the north where local supplies of food, strained by years of war, were almost nonexistent. In candor, he exclaimed that "at this time it is impossible even to defend [the south]. How is it possible to attempt invasion [of the north]?"[34] His fellow censor Tu Fan (1182–1245) concurred. Fiscal Overseer for Huai-nan West, Wu Ch'ien (*chin-shih* 1217), commented, "Seizing [the north] may be easy, but defending it will prove difficult."[35] A succession of other memorialists reminded the court of the vulnerability of Sung forces, the uselessness

[33] On the abortive campaign, see SS 405, p. 12234; 412, pp. 12374, 12381; 417, pp. 12492–4; 418, pp. 12516–17; Chou Mi, *Ch'i-tung yeh-yü* (1983) 5, pp. 77–80; Ch'en Pang-chan et al., *Sung-shih chi-shih pen-mo* (1605; Peking, 1977) 92, pp. 1037–42; Huang Tsung-hsi et al., *Sung Yüan hsüeh-an* (1838; Taipei, 1973) 73, p. 1278; Ch'ien, *Nan Sung shu* 53, pp. 3b, 6b; Peterson, "Old illusions and new realities," pp. 225–30; Li, *Sung Yüan chan-shih*, pp. 181–8; Li, *Yüan-shih hsin-chiang*, vol. 2, pp. 176–82.

[34] SS 405, p. 12234.

[35] SS 418, p. 12516.

of gaining barren land and depopulated cities, and perhaps most important, the need to retain cordial relations with an unpredictable new northern neighbor, the Mongols. Many of these memorialists possessed extensive experience, as well as personal ties to the new councilor Cheng Ch'ing-chih, and their arguments were well reasoned. Why then did the court support the minority position in favor of an offensive and, in the process, annoy a sensitive bureaucracy at home and provoke a dangerous ally abroad? The change in policy apparently stemmed from a rift between metropolitan advisors and regional administrators.

Among advocates of aggression, the most vocal appears to have been Chao K'uei, a commander of the army that had triumphed over Li Ch'üan in 1231. In addition to an illustrious family background and distinguished record of military service, Chao had personal credibility with Cheng Ch'ing-chih, his one-time teacher. Chao K'uei was on equally good terms, it appears, with Chao Shan-hsiang (*chin-shih* 1196), a highly decorated military leader whose status as imperial clansman with affinal ties to the house of Shih Mi-yüan provided an unusually wide array of contacts.

Chao K'uei advocated a firm, even aggressive, border policy. Long before Li Ch'üan had presented a serious menace, Chao had urged the Sung court to use force against the Shantung leader. Subsequently, Chao K'uei came to exemplify the opinion of many within the military establishment, and especially among commanders in the eastern part of the Yangtze River basin, where Chao had gained his experience. Ch'üan Tzu-ts'ai, another prominent military figure who had extensive experience in the northeast, also endorsed the interventionist position.[36] The *Sung dynastic history* identifies Tu Kao, prefect of the border commandery of An-feng, as the only regional official who dared to oppose Chao K'uei's adventurism.[37] Although the group typified by Chao K'uei were unlike their colleagues in the capital in supporting a less timid and more aggressive border policy, they were not all in agreement. Meng Kung, a commander in the central part of Sung territory, refused to endorse the change in policy. Even Chao Fan, elder brother of Chao K'uei, disassociated himself from the aggressive proposal and later criticized his brother for having endangered the empire.[38] Thus neither a united military establishment nor a solid block of

---

[36] The eminent Ch'ing historian Ch'ien Ta-hsin (1728–1804) insists that Chao K'uei and Ch'üan Tzu-ts'ai were scapegoats for Cheng Ch'ing-chih, their political standing having been too modest to effect a redirection of court policy. However, this ignores, first, the special influence derived from Chao K'uei's personal ties with the councilor, and, second, the important role of regional officials and commanders as policy consultants for the court. See Ch'ien Ta-hsin, *Nien-erh shih k'ao-i* (1806; Ch'ang-sha, 1884) 80, p. 10b.

[37] *SS* 412, p. 12382.

[38] *SS* 41, p. 803; 417, p. 12502; *HTC* (1958) 167, p. 4567.

regional officials supported Chao K'uei and Ch'üan Tzu-ts'ai; the support they did have apparently came from outside the capital, not from the court, and largely from the eastern Yangtze region, not from central and western parts of Sung territory. This is hardly coincidental.

Armies of the eastern Yangtze, in particular those of Chao K'uei and Chao Fan, were probably not involved in the final campaign against the Chin at Ts'ai-chou; they had no personal exposure to conditions in the region. Furthermore, with the Mongol military presence weakest in the east, precisely where Sung strength was greatest, Chao K'uei may have underestimated Mongol ability to counter Sung aggression. Chao seems also to have reasoned that troops from the south, once they moved north, would receive generous assistance from the local Chinese populace, much as in Shantung. Perceptions such as these may have inspired revanchists to press for a northern expedition. The euphoria accompanying victory at Ts'ai-chou in early 1234 must have helped their case as well.

Decision makers at the Sung court were confronted with new opportunities suddenly available to them. In the eighth lunar month, the Sung sent a delegation to offer sacrifices at the Eight Tombs, the burial place of Northern Sung emperors in a remote spot northeast of Lo-yang. Having conducted no ritual sacrifices there for over a century, the Sung court did not know the condition of the tombs. Upon returning south, the delegates informed the court that the tombs were in serious disrepair and that water inundated the surrounding land. As Li-tsung listened, so chroniclers say, he heaved a deep sigh and fought back tears.[39] In this emotionally charged context, the court, surrendering to sentiment, decided to dispatch armies north to recover the three capitals. The decision was not calculated; it reflected in some measure the naive optimism that the ancestral spirits would intervene on the side of humanity. Just two months before the campaign, the emperor restored titular honors to his step-brother, Chao Hung, and authorized sacrifices at his grave site. He honored the widow of Chao Hung, living incognito as a nun in Shao-hsing, with an esteemed title and, for good measure, a generous monthly stipend. Clearly, Li-tsung wanted all the spirits, including the spirit of his disgraced brother, to support this sacred mission.

In the summer of 1234, either in the sixth or eighth lunar month, the Sung unleashed its armies.[40] Ch'üan Tzu-ts'ai led a reported ten thousand men from Lu-chou2 to K'ai-feng, encountering no significant resistance. En

---

[39] SS 41, p. 803.

[40] SS 41, p. 803, gives the eighth month of 1234 as the date of troop deployment; Chou Mi in *Ch'i-tung yeh-yü* (1983) 5, p. 77, gives the sixth month, as does *Sung-shih ch'üan-wen Hsü Tzu-chih t'ung-chien* (early 14th c.; Taipei, 1969) 32, pp. 14a–b.

route, he passed through Shou-chou and Hao-chou, where he found once-flourishing cities reduced to a few hundred inhabitants and the surrounding countryside rendered a wasteland, the outcome of more than two decades of war. In K'ai-feng, where six hundred to seven hundred local militia were on hand to greet the Sung army, surviving inhabitants numbered only a thousand households. Sword and lance were not the sole causes of the depopulation. A year earlier, Mongol invaders had breached several dikes on the Yellow River, inundating K'ai-feng and flooding lands as far south as Shou-chou, near the Sung border.[41] Communities in the north, a fraction of their former size, could scarcely feed themselves, leaving Ch'üan Tzu-ts'ai with no local supplies of food to requisition. After a two-week, two-hundred-fifty-mile-trek, his forces urgently awaited provisions from the south. Chao K'uei soon arrived with a reported fifty thousand additional men. The original plan had envisioned combining the two armies, adding available conscripts in the north, and then proceeding to Lo-yang. With provisions so scarce, troops were disinclined to move on. Roughly one-fourth did, but hunger-induced exhaustion rendered them useless. In the interim, a smaller Sung force had already taken Lo-yang, birthplace of the Sung founder. Here as well, most of the population was either dead or scattered when reinforcements arrived from the east. Lo-yang had expected provisions from K'ai-feng and when the only arrivals were hungry soldiers the men started eating their horses. Worse yet, by one account, Mongol armies had learned of Sung designs well in advance and had laid a lethal trap. They lured southern troops into seemingly undefended northern cities and launched surprise strikes from the suburbs.[42] The rout was decisive and Sung armies retreating from Lo-yang lost eighty to ninety percent of their men to injury or death. Forces at K'ai-feng withdrew at virtually the same time, aborting the month-long campaign.

Returning south, Ch'üan Tzu-ts'ai blamed Shih Sung-chih for the reversal. As commissioner in chief for the central border region, Shih had allegedly withheld supplies in order to undermine intentionally an operation he opposed. Regardless of the merit of the allegation, the delay in provisioning Sung armies was not the decisive factor in their defeat. As Chao Fan later admitted, the heavy losses related also to the confusion accompanying the retreat, with Sung troops exhibiting poor discipline. Even more critical, it would seem, was the glaring lack of planning by the campaign's proponents. Earlier visitors to the north had reported, often in grim detail, the widespread devastation and

---

[41] Chou, *Ch'i-tung yeh-yü* (1983) 5, p. 78. The *Sung dynastic history (Sung shih)*, compiled in 1345 under Mongol auspices, attributes flooding to the natural collapse of dikes along the Pien River; see SS 417, p. 12502.

[42] Hu et al., *Sung Meng (Yüan) kuan-hsi shih*, p. 92.

starvation in the region. With this intelligence, dispatching a force of sixty thousand men on a major campaign with no more than two week's provisions was wildly irresponsible. It was naive, moreover, to expect them to prevail without encountering significant resistance, either from the Mongols or their surrogates. The small contingent initially sent to Lo-yang – fewer than ten thousand men – suggests precisely this naive assumption. With most of the men and supplies for the Lo-yang campaign expected to come from K'ai-feng, progress in one area was entirely dependent upon success in another. There is no mention of contingency plans. Owing to poor planning, the Sung leadership dispatched too few soldiers to Lo-yang, where the enemy was strong, and too many to K'ai-feng, where it was weak. Curiously, even with the advantage of numbers of troops at both cities, the Sung still suffered defeat. The hasty retreat suggests that the Sung armies were unenthusiastic about the venture, which mirrored divisions within the command. The campaign, over by late summer in 1234, reflected poorly upon leadership in Lin-an.

Protracted confrontation

Up to one hundred thousand soldiers and civilians, according to the *Sung dynastic history*, were lost in the occupation effort during the summer of 1234.[43] This is an unlikely number for so limited a venture, but the war that was triggered by this campaign lasted nearly forty-five years and claimed innumerable lives. The Mongol leadership was initially slow in responding to the Sung invasion, although it knew of Sung intentions well in advance.[44] Ögödei, then convening with commanders in the Altai Mountains, over nine hundred miles away, had matters beyond the Sung to deliberate. Not until year's end did he dispatch Wang Chi, the envoy who had negotiated the 1233 alliance, to reprimand the Sung. In turn, the Sung court sent several envoys of its own, which signaled a desire to avoid a dangerous confrontation. The court's entreaties fell upon deaf ears, for Sung transgressions did not go unpunished. With Ögödei personally committed to conquest of the regions of what was to become eastern Russia, he entrusted the punitive expedition against the Sung to his sons Köten and Köchü.[45]

Relative to earlier assaults on Koryŏ (Korea) in 1231 and the current campaign pushing eastward past the Volga River, the operation against the Sung

---

[43] *SS* 407, p. 12281.

[44] *SS* 412, p. 12374; Luc Kwanten, *Imperial nomads: A history of Central Asia, 500–1500* (Philadelphia, 1979), p. 133.

[45] For a discussion of this campaign, see Thomas T. Allsen, "The rise of the Mongolian empire and Mongolian rule in north China," in *The Cambridge history of China*, volume 6: *Alien regimes and border states, 907–1368*, ed. Herbert Franke and Denis C. Twitchett (New York, 1994), pp. 368–72.

seemed to have received low priority. But in the summer of 1235, Mongol armies struck with a force that suggested otherwise. Focusing on central Sung territory, they first expelled occupying forces commanded by Ch'üan Tzu-ts'ai from T'ang-chou, territory seized by the Sung a year earlier. Crossing the Sung border, they then raided Tsao-yang and Ying-chou3 in late autumn. When they chose to withdraw, the Mongols carted off all that their horse transport could carry. Köchü supervised activity in the east and the center of Sung territory, while Köten moved against Szechwan with an assault on Mien-chou, in the center of Li-chou circuit. With only a small defense force, and relying on the natural barrier of mountains for protection, the unwalled prefecture fell quickly. Ts'ao Yu-wen (*chin-shih* 1226) directed a spirited sortie launched from T'ien-shui and succeeded in expelling the invaders. The Mongols, content at this point with harassing the Sung and pillaging when circumstances permitted, likely did not consider their retreat a defeat.

The Mongols returned to menace the Sung the next spring, in 1236.[46] Köchü, now with reinforcements, lashed out at Sui-chou2, and Ying-chou3, both in Ching-hsi circuit. Crossing the Han River, he advanced against Ching-men commandery, nearly one hundred and twenty miles into the Sung interior. This attack coincided with the eruption of a mutiny at Hsiang-yang, creating chaotic conditions in this strategically vital prefecture before a successful suppression. The Mongols resumed hostilities along the central Sung border in late summer, but this was overshadowed by developments in the west. Commanding a half million men – Mongol, Tangut, Jurchen, and Uighur – Köten initiated a formidable offensive against Ta-an commandery, south of Mien-chou and deep in Szechwan. These numbers were certainly exaggerated, but the force was still large enough to overwhelm Sung armies. Within weeks Ta-an capitulated. The Sung commander, Ts'ao Yu-wen, and his brother perished in Ta-an's defense. The Mongol forces subsequently moved against Chieh-chou and Wen-chou2 on the western fringes of Li-chou circuit. Sung troops and subjects died by the tens of thousands. Even Ch'eng-tu, some three hundred miles south of the border, temporarily fell into hostile hands. In November at this critical moment in the campaign fate intervened. Köchü, the designated heir to Ögödei, died suddenly, which prompted Köten to withdraw in the west.

The southern offensive continued during the close of 1236 without Köten. Focus now shifted to the central Huai region, placing the Mongols closer to the Sung empire's political center. Interruption of hostilities out west and reassignment of troops from that theater to reinforce their armies in the Huai

---

[46] *HTC* (1958) 168, pp. 4585–94; Li, *Sung Yüan chan-shih*, pp. 301–20.

region may explain the Mongols' initial success against the Sung in the two Huai-nan circuits. At the battle of Chen-chou2, Mongol combatants reportedly outnumbered Sung troops ten to one and in the end claimed a hundred thousand Chinese lives, military and civilian.[47] However, a sound strategy of defense by Shih Sung-chih, Meng Kung, and Ch'iu Yüeh enabled the Sung to recoup most of its territorial losses, including a devastated Chen-chou2.[48] After the fighting subsided and the Mongol forces left, only Hsiang-yang remained in hostile hands. A half year later, in the autumn of 1237, the Mongols reapplied pressure against the central Huai region, harassing Kuang-chou2 and Shou-ch'un. For a while, they even seized Fu-chou3, some one hundred and twenty miles into Sung territory. The loss of Fu-chou3 seriously threatened Chiang-ling, the capital of the Ching-hu North circuit. The Sung successfully counterattacked, with Meng Kung again contributing the most to pushing the northern intruders out of the region.

By early 1238, the Mongols had withdrawn from much of Sung territory, and they approached the Sung court about a truce. The annual tribute of silver and silk that they demanded was no more than what had been given to Chin, and seemed acceptable under the circumstances.[49] The Mongols had exposed a weakness in the Sung's ability to defend its borders, but they had also learned a lesson about Sung tenacity. Sung territory was easier to seize than to retain because the Sung had been able to regroup after each setback. In a larger context, the Mongol empire was also in the midst of an intense struggle in the region of eastern Russia, having recently taken Moscow and Vladimir, and this may have made material goods momentarily more valuable to the needs of their campaigns than additional territory. Unfortunately for both sides, no agreement was reached. In response to Mongol overtures, the Sung court dispatched a mission of its own. They apparently refused peace payments but sought to improve relations. Official opinion on the Sung side left negotiators with little latitude. A high-level executive at the Bureau of Military Affairs and future chief councilor, Li Tsung-mien, opposed even modest concessions. Beyond the issue of implicit humiliation, he feared that an initially small sum might well grow, to become an enormous burden. Commander Meng Kung similarly rejected peace proposals, as did Chief Councilor Ts'ui Yü-chih (1158–1239). For the latter, an abrupt change in policy might undermine the morale of border troops, which would leave the Sung vulnerable should fighting resume.[50] Others questioned whether Mongols could be trusted when

---

[47] Hu, "Lüeh-lun Nan Sung mo-nien," p. 378.
[48] *HTC* (1958) 168, p. 4596.
[49] *HTC* (1958) 169, p. 4611.
[50] On these views, see *SS* 405, p. 12237; 406, p. 12263; 412, p. 12374; *HTC* (1958) 169, p. 4611.

their deeds suggested a brutal indifference to their own promises. The court's chief advisor for the Huai region, Shih Sung-chih, is portrayed in primary sources as the only prominent proponent of negotiated settlement. He did not prevail.

In the summer of 1238, Sung forces recovered some lost territory, most crucially Hsiang-yang, where a defection in the Mongol camp played into Sung hands. Late 1238 and early 1239 brought two major confrontations. The first was a large Mongol offensive against Lu-chou2, in the east. The second was an assault in the west on K'uei-chou.[51] In both instances, the invading forces consisted of some eight hundred thousand men. Even a large fraction of that number would have overwhelmingly outnumbered defenders at Lu-chou2, a city of less than a half million residents. Defenses must have been strong, for the enemy voluntarily withdrew. Mongol incursions into the K'uei-chou region proved equally fruitless. Indeed, the significance of the maneuvers of 1238–9 lies not so much in the territory gained as in the arms invested. The Mongols, clearly offended by Sung resistance to their peace offer, deployed vast numbers of men to attack the Sung. Some of these men were no doubt deflected from the campaign in Koryŏ, where the Mongol conquest was winding down; others represented recent Chinese and Central Asian conscripts, for the Mongols enforced mandatory military service and every household in its territories had to surrender at least one male. Their ability to conscript manpower from a seemingly inexhaustible pool made the Mongols more formidable than any alien menace before them.

For the Sung, the only source of additional troops was North China's refugee population. This left southern armies at a numerical disadvantage.[52] Even more alarming was the Mongols' adaptability. Early campaigns against the Chin had been largely confined to cooler months, for the winter-hardened Mongols did not perform well in the heat of summer. By the 1230s, partly because of their now more ethnically diverse armies, their movements became far less predictable. A brief assault in mid-1239 on Ch'ung-ch'ing, a city infamous for its dreadfully humid summers, must have caught Sung defenders off guard as the historic pattern for Mongol armies was to retreat northward at the peak of summer. In the face of the enemy's growing strength and adaptability, continued Sung success at repulsing Mongol attacks suggests that Sung forces, regarded even at home as no match for the Mongols, were not so weak after all. Moreover, maintaining their superior command of rivers and tributaries to the east, the Sung were able to move troops and provisions with relative speed along efficient lines of communication. Mongols would require decades

---

[51] Li, *Sung Yüan chan-shih*, pp. 345–54, 363–70.
[52] Li, *Sung Yüan chan-shih*, pp. 363–5, 368–70.

to make this additional adaptation. Finally, to avoid suicidal confrontations, the Sung commonly took recourse to tactical retreat and regrouping, thereby saving precious lives. Unfortunately, because of unrelenting enemy pressure the Sung court was never able to seize the military initiative, and this left it reacting to intrusions rather than initiating counterattacks.

Despite their campaigns against the Sung, the Mongols did not abandon peace negotiations. Envoy Wang Chi conducted five missions on their behalf between 1233 and his death in 1240.[53] Even as late as 1241, the Mongols did not appear committed to conquest of the south. The assaults against Ch'eng-tu and Han-chou, toward the close of 1241, did not end in the acquisition of territory or great wealth. When Han-chou fell after prolonged siege, the attackers carried out a general massacre and then unexpectedly withdrew. With this awesome show of force, the Mongols accomplished little militarily, save for humiliating the Sung. At the outset of 1242, months after the death of Ögödei and the Szechwan offensive, the Mongols dispatched a large delegation of seventy for Lin-an to reopen talks. Approaching from the west, the chief envoy, and perhaps the entire delegation, was jailed at Ch'ang-sha by a Sung regional commander, ostensibly angered by the envoy's arrogance. The Sung court apparently offered no formal apology for the incident, and the envoys advanced no farther. Nothing developed from the northern initiative. The extent of Sung intransigence is difficult to understand. The chief councilor at the time, Shih Sung-chih, held Li-tsung's complete confidence and acted, infamously so, as the most articulate spokesperson for peaceful coexistence between the Sung and the Mongols. A possible explanation is intransigence at the Sung court. Sung leadership may have misread the struggle over the Mongol succession following Ögödei's death, which was so intense as to threaten a deadly civil war. Instability in the Mongol leadership contrasted sharply with Sung accomplishments in the south, where the two-year lull in fighting had enabled the Sung to replenish their armies and recover a good measure of lost territory. Some credit for this southern rally belongs to Shih Sung-chih, but it may have left him overconfident.

For the next ten years, fighting continued sporadically.[54] In the west, the Mongols raided cities deep inside Szechwan: Sui-ning (1242), Tzu-chou2 (1243), and Shu-chou (1242), all in T'ung-ch'uan circuit. Along the central Sung border, the Mongols raided targets in Huai-nan West in 1244 and again in 1246. For the first time it appears, the Mongols struck against targets

---

[53] Ch'en Kao-hua, "Wang Chi shih Sung shih-shih k'ao-lüeh," in *Ryū Shiken hakuse shōju kinen: Sō-shi kenkyū ronshū*, ed. Kinugawa Tsuyoshi (Kyoto, 1989), pp. 103–11; Hu et al., *Sung Meng (Yüan) kuan-hsi shih*, pp. 119–21, 142–5.
[54] On these, see Li, *Sung Yüan chan-shih*, pp. 406–502; Li, *Yüan-shih hsin-chiang*, vol. 2, pp. 183–219.

along the eastern Sung border, for example, T'ung-chou2 in 1242, a city located near the mouth of the Yangtze River and within easy reach by sea of the Sung capital. Still, peace more than conflict characterized the decade, as the Mongol leadership was plagued by persistent squabbling. Ögödei had died in 1241, but opposition to the accession of his infant grandson, the heir apparent, delayed for five years the crowning of Güyük (r. 1246–8), Ögödei's younger son. Almost immediately Güyük found himself at war with the politically ambitious Batu, a descendant of Chinggis khan. In 1248, Güyük died in the vicinity of Samarkand, in his war against Batu. This gave the Mongols another succession to fight over, a contest requiring three years to resolve. In the interim, North China suffered a severe drought that destroyed vegetation and depleted the horse and cattle population by ninety percent. Nor were the people spared, leaving Mongol forces short on men no less than horses. For the decade following Ögödei's death, little diplomatic contact is recorded, save for half-hearted overtures in 1247, when both sides spurned envoys owing to mutual distrust.[55]

Having ruled out peaceful coexistence, the Sung government took advantage of this respite to strengthen its military defenses, especially in the west, where years of war had taken a heavy toll. A major shift of military commands came in 1242, when the Sung court transferred its prized general, Meng Kung, from the central border region to Szechwan, to become military commissioner in chief and prefect of K'uei-chou2. Joining Meng Kung as Szechwan commissioner was the former overlord of Huai-nan East, Yü Chieh (d. 1253), who served concurrently as prefect of Ch'ung-ch'ing. The Sung also managed in some places to strengthen border fortifications by organizing informal regional militia. At the same time, the relative tranquility of the decade allowed the disbanding of some border militia that were perceived as a threat to local order.[56] The number of government regulars declined as well. In better times, Szechwan had been defended by up to eighty thousand men. This number fell to less than fifty thousand by the 1240s.[57] The quality of military leadership in Szechwan may have been enhanced, but the quantity of material resources invested by the Sung court was minimal. Commissioner Yü Chieh, for all the court's goodwill, had to rely largely on local capital and initiative to strengthen defenses, and Szechwan was abjectly short of both. In effect, Li-tsung recognized the strategic importance of the west, but undermined its security by his excessive parsimony in the allocation of the empire's wealth.

The Sung did not enjoy the respite from Mongol attacks for long. By 1251, the Mongols had a new ruler, Möngke (r. 1251–9), a shrewd and disciplined

[55] Hu et al., *Sung Meng (Yüan) kuan-hsi shih*, pp. 166–7, 182–3, 193–4.
[56] *HTC* (1958) 173, p. 4725.
[57] *SS* 411, p. 12357.

man now resolved to conquer the Sung. He entrusted supervision of the China theater to his younger brother Khubilai. Möngke devoted his own energies to the invasion of Persia. The earlier raids of the 1230s and 1240s may have sought to weaken and demoralize the Sung, but after 1253, Mongol objectives in East Asia became focused on long-term conquest.[58] Khubilai first eliminated the Ta-li empire, in modern Yunnan, and within three years he had reduced all of the autonomous groups of the distant southwest to vassal status. He initially launched no major campaign against the Sung heartland, and border flare-ups remained minor. Instead, the agenda of the early 1250s entailed a calculated encirclement of the southern Sung empire by developing the southwest, a region long neglected by the Sung, as a base of operations. The same maneuver used to destroy the Chin was being used for the Sung: secure neighboring lands to the north and south in preparation for the lethal squeeze from all sides. The battle plan was not lost on the Sung court, which transferred a reputed one hundred thousand troops from the northeast to Szechwan in early 1257. These reinforcements had scarcely arrived when the Mongols, in full force, lunged into the area.

Ch'eng-tu, with a population of nearly one million and the cultural center of Szechwan, fell to the Mongols in early 1258 after offering a spirited resistance. A half-dozen nearby prefectures capitulated swiftly. Before long, the Mongols' forces held much of the Ch'eng-tu Plain, from which they moved north into Li-chou and west into T'ung-ch'uan circuits. Complementing the western thrust were lesser raids on targets in eastern and central Sung territory, providing just enough pressure to inhibit the Sung court from transferring troops from the east to Szechwan. Möngke personally joined in the Szechwan campaign toward the close of 1258. From Khara Khorum he moved directly south with an army reported to be forty thousand strong. Skirting Li-chou, the circuit closest to the Mongol border, he joined his men at Han-chou, central Szechwan, where he helped consolidate existing holdings before moving against Li-chou. Ya-chou and Lung-chou2 in the far southwest, along with Li-chou and P'eng-chou in the heart of Szechwan, are but a few of about ten prefectures to come under Mongol control, all within a month or two. The Szechwan campaign proceeded with the ease that the Mongols confidently had expected and that the Sung woefully had feared, that is, until the battle at Ho-chou4.[59]

---

[58] Hu et al., *Sung Meng (Yüan) kuan-hsi shih*, pp. 208–17; Li, *Sung Yüan chan-shih*, pp. 583–703, 713–97; Li, *Yüan-shih hsin-chiang*, vol. 2, pp. 192–3.

[59] Hu et al., *Sung Meng (Yüan) kuan-hsi shih*, pp. 217–33; Li, *Sung Yüan chan-shih*, pp. 723–6; Wang I-ch'eng, *Wang Chien shih-chi k'ao* (Hsin-ying, 1983); Yao Ts'ung-wu, "Sung Meng Tiao-yü-ch'eng chan-i chung Hsiung-erh fu-jen chia shih chi Wang Li yü Ho-chou huo-te pao-ch'üan k'ao," in *Sung-shih yen-chiu chi: Ti erh chi*, ed. Sung-shih tso-t'an-hui (Taipei, 1964), pp. 123–40.

In March 1259, Möngke laid siege to Ho-chou4 (modern Ho-ch'uan, in central Szechwan), a city of roughly one hundred and fifty thousand in the heart of the T'ung-ch'uan circuit. Defense of the city was led by Wang Chien2 (d. 1259), an individual whose resolve would not be shaken despite a siege that went on for five months. Apart from a committed populace, Wang Chien2 was also assisted by nature. Heavy rains during the early months of the siege seriously sapped the morale of Mongol besiegers housed in tents. At the same time, an epidemic broke out among the Mongol ranks. Apparently, this disease claimed the life of Möngke, who died outside Ho-chou4 on 11 August. Khubilai, disbanding his army, hastened to Khara Khorum for the upcoming elective assembly *khuriltai*, which took place on 5 May 1260.[60] The offensive against the Sung was postponed indefinitely.

Again, the Sung was afforded a reprieve despite meager investment in the southwest. The loss of two prized commanders, Meng Kung in 1246 and Yü Chieh in 1253, had heightened the Sung sense of vulnerability, and Sung morale was further weakened by intense court factionalism. Nonetheless, the battle at Ho-chou4 vividly demonstrated the hardened resistance that the Mongols could expect if they proceeded east toward the Sung capital. The mountains and the Yangtze gorges in the west and the rivers in central Sung territory presented formidable obstacles to the Mongols. Perhaps their recognition of these obstacles explains why the Mongols dispatched, just prior to the 1260 installation of Khubilai as khaghan, a new peace envoy, followed soon by two more. The Sung court rebuffed all such initiatives, apparently unconvinced of its adversary's genuine intent.

Mongol demands probably included only the payment of annual tribute in exchange for peace, yet in 1260 the Sung court seemed intentionally set on provoking the Mongols when they imprisoned the northern envoy, Hao Ching. It is not altogether clear why the Sung, keenly interested in peace talks in the 1240s, became unresponsive by 1260. By some accounts, the Sung court considered Hao Ching to be a spy. By others, the chief councilor, Chia Ssu-tao, had personally ordered the envoy's incarceration to conceal unseemly promises that Chia had made to Hao Ching a year earlier when the threat of Mongol invasion was imminent.[61] Nevertheless, the arrest had signaled the Sung's unwillingness to placate the Mongols. At this point in the negotiations it seemed as if the two powers were speaking at cross-purposes. The Sung saw peace as the simple absence of belligerency. The Mongols saw peace as an

---

[60] Morris Rossabi, "The reign of Khubilai khan," in *The Cambridge history of China*, volume 6: *Alien regimes and border states, 907–1368*, ed. Herbert Franke and Denis C. Twitchett (New York, 1994) p. 423.

[61] *SS* 474, p. 13782; Sung et al., *Yüan shih* 157, pp. 3708–9; *HTC* (1958) 176, p. 4802.

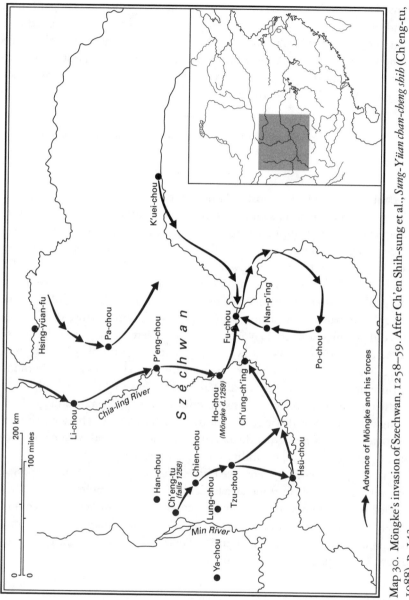

Map 30. Möngke's invasion of Szechwan, 1258–59. After Ch'en Shih-sung et al., *Sung-Yüan chan-cheng shih* (Ch'eng-tu, 1988), p. 143.

alliance between the two.[62] The Sung court also may have hoped that conflicts over succession would preoccupy the Mongols and buy the Sung more time. This was not total fancy, for soon after his accession in 1260, Khubilai found himself engaged in a three-year war for the throne against his younger brother Arigh Böke.[63] These events coincided with a rebellion in Shantung led by Li T'an, adopted son of Li Ch'üan, whose defection to the Sung gravely threatened Mongol authority in the northeast.[64] Further, economic devastation in the wartorn northeastern region brought on by locusts and drought must have made the Mongol position there even more tenuous.

BUREAUCRATIC LEADERSHIP AND THE FORCES OF OPINION

The besieged emperor

Li-tsung may well be the most unfathomable of the Southern Sung emperors. The paucity of late Sung source material is part of the problem, but so is the complexity of the man. Few emperors match his compassion and charity, as evidenced by his unprecedented establishment of the Child Benevolence Service (Tz'u-yu chü) to care for unwanted children in the capital and a medical service (Yao chü) to distribute medicine to the needy.[65] He was compassionate and had an unalterable loyalty to trusted officials, regardless of political pressures. More than once, Li-tsung was compelled to dismiss a trusted official, but this did not affect imperial favor and such men were never made scapegoats to exonerate the throne. Malicious campaigns against Shih Mi-yüan, for example, did not prompt the emperor to placate influential critics by posthumously humiliating him. Nor did Li-tsung respond to an ill-conceived, ultimately disastrous, foreign policy by punishing its architect, Cheng Ch'ing-chih. Li-tsung's steadfastness distinguished him from Kao-tsung, whose posthumous mistreatment of Ch'in Kuei displayed a reluctance to deal with court critics and accept personal responsibility for the actions of surrogates.

Li-tsung was generally sensitive to the forces of opinion. When opposition to a certain policy or bureaucratic leader threatened the political stability, he tended to compromise rather than risk confrontation. Moreover, he could be magnanimous in the face of censure, as revealed in his response to the acrimony of one overly zealous remonstrator: "[The official's] words are exceedingly direct. How could I ever be angered by direct words?"[66] Valuing candor over

[62] Hu et al., *Sung Meng (Yüan) kuan-hsi shih*, pp. 119–21, 166–7, 181–2, 193–4.

[63] See Rossabi, "The reign of Khubilai khan," p. 422.

[64] Kwanten, *Imperial nomads*, pp. 146–7; Sung et al., *Yüan shih* 206, pp. 4591–6; Li, *Yüan-shih hsin-chiang*, vol. 2, pp. 267–9.

[65] *SS* 43, p. 840.

[66] *SS* 421, p. 12593.

obsequiousness, Li-tsung often advanced his most vocal critics to prominent posts. Trusting the judgment of leading advisors, he refused to challenge or overturn their policy decisions. Such tolerance and support distinguished him from Hsiao-tsung, whose frequent rejection of ministerial advice left an indelibly autocratic imprint on an otherwise estimable reign.

Li-tsung also managed the imperial household better than most Sung emperors. His empress, Hsieh Ch'iao (1210–83), although attuned to the politics of the day, maintained a low profile for the duration of her husband's reign. She was not Li-tsung's first choice as empress nor his favored companion, but this emotional distance generated no perceptible tensions within the royal family. She gave no public display of indignation at his intemperance, sexual and otherwise. Domestic discipline is also evinced in the rearing of his adopted son and eventual successor, Tu-tsung, from whom Li-tsung expected serious attention toward his studies and submissiveness toward authority. Such circumspection within the royal family offers a sharp contrast to the chaos of the Kuang-tsung years.

Li-tsung had few scholarly pretenses, unlike Hsiao-tsung, yet he presents an image of thoughtfulness, even wit, certainly not characteristic of his better-regarded predecessor Hsiao-tsung. Li-tsung often responded, when he *chose* to respond, with meticulous care and cogency to the remonstrance of officials. In deliberation and articulation, he easily surpassed Ning-tsung, the "tranquil," whose unopinionated silence seemed almost depersonalized.

As emperor, Li-tsung combined his native intelligence with the two Confucian ideals of compassion for the ordinary people and respect for scholar-officials. Never was he so smug as to tire of improving himself, nor so vain as to deny his personal shortcomings. A man of immense potential, Li-tsung might have ushered in a golden age for the southern empire. He did not, and the fault was not entirely his.

From the outset of his reign in 1224, the nineteen-year-old emperor faced the perennial threat of war. The conflict with Chin he inherited, but he triggered the Mongol war. He was censured by later writers for starting a war that his empire stood no chance of winning. The assessment seems unduly harsh. Mongol and Sung armies had clashed long before 1234. Had the Sung remained a submissive ally, it would have been only a matter of time before the Mongols turned a covetous eye toward it. Recognizing this threat, the advocates of war at the Sung court sought to seize the initiative by acting before the Mongols could consolidate power and mobilize resources in the north. Once unleashed, war imposed an immense strain on already overextended military and economic systems. Li-tsung and his ministers never developed a satisfactory means of financing the protracted conflict, nor did they ever develop a coherent long-term strategy to win it. But the reproach of later historians does not rest exclusively on Li-tsung's failures in foreign policy.

Li-tsung also had to engage with the political forces of prominent intellectual movements. Li-tsung was the first emperor to endorse parts of the tenets
of the *Tao-hsüeh* movement articulated by Chu Hsi. Li-tsung also was not one
to slight traditional rituals. Within two months of assuming the throne, he
performed the elaborate Ming-t'ang (Hall of Brilliance) rituals, and continued
this tradition once every three years for nearly the duration of his reign. He
may have inherited this habit from his predecessor, for Ning-tsung was even
more meticulous about performing this and other sacrifices. Recurring natural
disasters and the traditional assumption that these reflected the dissatisfaction
of Heaven may also explain Li-tsung's special concern with mollifying the
spirits. The high cost of new temples to imperial ancestors and the elaborate
feasts accompanying ritual sacrifices irritated many critics, with some concluding that the sacrifices served merely as pretexts for merriment. "In praying to
Heaven one employs sincerity, not excess," warned one official, who viewed
imperial extravagance as inappropriate at a time of national adversity.[67] But
historians' reproof of Li-tsung does not rest upon his excessive dedication to
ritual, either.

The emperor's one shortcoming that most irritated contemporary and later
observers was the immodesty of his amorous indulgences.[68] Some blame Shih
Mi-yüan, insisting that he had intentionally "poisoned" the emperor's mind
through an abundance of female companions intended to preoccupy him within
the palace. The placing of responsibility with Shih Mi-yüan is questionable,
but Li-tsung's inclination toward sexual intemperance appears undeniable, and
it persisted for the duration of his reign. Consort Chia (d. 1247), daughter of
Commissioner Chia She, became imperial consort in 1232 after winning the
emperor's affections. Li-tsung so doted on her that one disapproving official
compared this to the infamous affair of Emperor T'ang Hsüan-tsung and Yang
Kuei-fei, a romance that nearly toppled the T'ang dynasty in the 750s. After
Chia's death, Li-tsung took to another consort, née Yen (d. 1260). Neither
woman cared much for politics, and so official concern would have been moderate had the emperor confined his energies to such liaisons with his recognized
consorts. He did not. In his middle years, he took to entertaining Taoist nuns
in his palace. Their comings and goings were repeatedly criticized in official memorials and sparked unending innuendo and scandal. Li-tsung drew
even more criticism in 1255, by summoning common street prostitutes to the
palace for his new year's entertainment. Officials were quick to condemn such

[67] SS 44, p. 852; 405, p. 12247; 411, p. 12358; 418, p. 12521; 438, p. 12985.

[68] On Li-tsung's personal life, see SS 44, p. 854; 243, pp. 8658–60; 407, pp. 12279–89; 418, p. 12515;
    421, pp. 12586, 12588; 438, p. 12985; 474, p. 13780; Ting Ch'uan-ching, *Sung-jen i-shih hui-pien*
    (1935; Taipei, 1982) 18, p. 915.

conduct but were generally not interested in understanding the factors contributing to it.

Contemporaries portrayed Li-tsung, prior to his accession, as mild-mannered, serious, and stable, with greater promise than the irascible Chao Hung. His youth was spent in a secluded area of Shao-hsing. He moved to the capital, Lin-an, only two years before becoming emperor. He never received the extensive training and political exposure commonly afforded candidates for the throne. Then, literally overnight, he became imperial son and emperor, all arranged by the chief councilor, Shih Mi-yüan, and Dowager Empress Wu. Becoming emperor seems to have changed him. Although never hopelessly indolent like most stereotypical last rulers in the Chinese historiographic tradition, Li-tsung was criticized early on for holding court irregularly. His withdrawal, and his cynicism about the conduct of government, grew more acute with time. During Li-tsung's first eight years in power, Shih Mi-yüan was on hand to advise the youth on political matters and Dowager Empress Yang2 to supervise his personal life. By their mere presence, these two discouraged the emperor from asserting himself, rendering him deferentially detached. Li-tsung never overcame this detachment, even after the deaths of the empress in 1232 and Shih in 1233 and the "era of change" (keng-hua) that he proclaimed in their wake. Imperial indifference, it would seem, related also to pressures from the bureaucracy. The question of the posthumous status of Chao Hung, for example, appeared and reappeared in official memorials for decades. Officials seemed indifferent to Li-tsung's insecurity as an upstart and to the possibility that their persistent criticisms might drive the emperor from the court at a time when the empire most needed a strong, unified leadership.

The sway of Ming-chou favorites

Although Ch'in Kuei and Han T'o-chou each held power for a significant period of time and were able to cow the civil service into submission, eventually their unpopularity overwhelmed them and their deaths brought retaliation from opposition groups. Loss of posthumous honors, persecution of kin, and confiscation of family property were their long-term reward. Shih Mi-yüan, while considerably more powerful and controversial than either Ch'in Kuei or Han T'o-chou, did not suffer similar humiliation. The emperor was steadfast in his favor. Two decades after Shih Mi-yüan's death, Li-tsung composed a tomb inscription in his memory. Those opposed to Shih's policies tirelessly attempted to undermine that favor, but failed. Nor could they uproot the dead councilor's influence, a result related in part to the emperor's character but also to the shrewd political maneuvering of Shih Mi-yüan himself. Not content merely with his own personal entrenchment, Shih Mi-yüan had built up a younger generation of talent and had helped place them in key bureaucratic posts. His associates held impeccable scholarly credentials and occasionally voiced critical opinions of him. They were not mere lackeys. Some, like Shih Mi-yüan himself, came from Ming-chou (modern Ning-po, also referred to as Ch'ing-yüan in some Sung texts), but not all. Their appointments did not rest exclusively on provincial ties. Interestingly, none was Shih's relative, despite the proliferation of credentialed officials among his kin. Shih Mi-yüan cultivated patronage, not nepotism. His protégés were well qualified and well connected, and their continued presence at court long after his death helped moderate any political backlash toward Shih and his policies.

The most notable of these protégés was Cheng Ch'ing-chih.[69] A Ming-chou native who had studied at the Imperial University beginning in 1202, Cheng later held various teaching posts in and away from the capital before returning to the university as a professor. Cheng was appointed personal tutor to the future Li-tsung nearly two years before Li-tsung's accession, and Cheng Ch'ing-chih may have assisted Shih Mi-yüan in arranging Chao Yün's controversial installation as son and then successor. Named assistant councilor in 1230, Cheng became chief councilor just days before Shih Mi-yüan's death, a position Cheng held for the next three years.

Cheng Ch'ing-chih owed much to Shih Mi-yüan's patronage, yet his willingness to speak out on the Li Ch'üan affair, urging the use of force, and the subsequent success of the 1230 suppression contributed significantly to his own independent political capital. Official acquiescence in Cheng Ch'ing-chih's rise to power relates also to his support for the *Tao-hsüeh* proponents, Wei Liao-weng and Chen Te-hsiu. Restoration of rank and salary to the two, occurring in Shih Mi-yüan's last years, was attributed to Cheng's influence. As the new councilor in 1233, Cheng promoted these once-alienated intellectuals to high-level metropolitan posts. Chen Te-hsiu was made an assistant councilor and Wei Liao-weng an executive at the military bureau. Cheng Ch'ing-chih also restored to office other one-time opponents of Shih Mi-yüan, while removing some of the less esteemed partisans. Already holding the confidence of the throne, Cheng apparently made such moves to generate goodwill outside the palace and thereby consolidate his influence within the civil service.

The Cheng Ch'ing-chih years were characterized by reconciliation within the bureaucracy. Apart from politically reviving the careers of many *Tao-hsüeh* proponents, the court approved a modest elevation in the posthumous status of Chao Hung, a continuing cause célèbre for critics of Shih Mi-yüan's

---

[69] SS 414, pp. 12419–23; Richard W. Bodman and Charles A. Peterson, "Cheng Ch'ing-chih," in *Sung biographies*, ed. Herbert Franke (Wiesbaden, 1976), vol. 1, pp. 156–63.

legacy. Another bid for support from *Tao-hsüeh* proponents came from Ch'iao Hsing-chien, a close associate of Cheng serving as an executive at the Bureau of Military Affairs. Ch'iao proposed offering state sacrifices at the imperial Confucian temple to the five *Tao-hsüeh* masters (Chu Hsi, Chou Tun-i, Ch'eng Hao, Ch'eng I, and Chang Tsai). A shrine to Chao Ju-yü, a popular figure among contemporary thirteenth-century *Tao-hsüeh* proponents, was proposed for the temple of Ning-tsung. For the first time, the ideas and instructions of the Learning of the Way (*Tao-hsüeh*), officially persecuted less than four decades earlier, were granted government approval, and became in stages the cornerstone of the curriculum at the Imperial University and hence throughout the empire. To the modern researcher, such changes in the ideological direction of the bureaucracy may appear as scarcely more than window dressing, changes in form, not substance. The test of innovation on the part of the administration under Li-tsung was whether it could substantially alter the widely assailed tradition and practices of one-man dominance that had been reinforced by the twenty-five-year tenure of Shih Mi-yüan.

During Hsiao-tsung's reign, the government had moved toward a two-councilor system. The councilor of the right, although the junior position, was where power rested. The position of councilor of the left tended to be reserved for elder statesmen, who often lacked the vitality to actively engage in decision making. However, after the death of Han T'o-chou in 1207, there was only one councilor. Ning-tsung never bothered to name a second councilor, and Shih Mi-yüan did not insist that another councilor serve with him. Within a week of Shih Mi-yüan's death in 1233, Wei Liao-weng requested restoration of the dual councilorship and that bureaucratic authority be divided in such a way as to forestall the emergence of future autocrats.[70] Li-tsung responded, albeit a year and a half later, by naming Ch'iao Hsing-chien councilor of the right and elevating Cheng Ch'ing-chih to be senior councilor. The move did not imply Li-tsung's confidence in such a division of power, however. No sooner had Li-tsung appointed Ch'iao Hsing-chien than he commented: "I employ Ch'ing-chih quite exclusively, but owing to the many affairs of the realm being too much for one councilor to manage, Hsing-chien is named assistant."[71] The dual councilorship persisted for five years, yet there occurred no reorganization of the metropolitan bureaucracy along the lines recommended by Wei Liao-weng and others. Perhaps sweeping institutional change appeared too dangerous in a time of war; but even an extended peace might not have changed things. In 1236, when the prefect of Lin-an raised the issue of lengthy terms of office, a less than subtle allusion to Shih Mi-yüan's marathon tenure, Li-tsung responded:

---

[70] *SS* 437, p. 12968; *HTC* (1958) 167, pp. 4550–1; Wei, *Ho-shan hsien-sheng ta ch'üan-chi* 19, pp. 1a–18a.
[71] *HTC* (1958) 168, p. 4577.

"In utilizing men, it is unnecessary to change them frequently."[72] Maintaining a high turnover, especially in the bureaucracy's upper echelons, was precisely the method employed by Hsiao-tsung to prevent his executives from becoming too powerful. Li-tsung took an antithetical approach to governing. He was never convinced that domination by one man was destabilizing, that lifelong tenures were politically unsound, or that powerful ministers were a threat to the imperial sway. To him, good government rested upon employing the right men, not a complex array of institutional controls.

The tenure of Cheng Ch'ing-chih lasted three years and ended in autumn 1236, but not because the emperor sought to infuse new blood into the bureaucracy. Nor was imperial confidence shaken by charges of grossly unethical conduct, including charges that Cheng had accepted bribes and allowed his status to be exploited by his son for their personal profit.[73] The most vocal critic of Cheng Ch'ing-chih was Tu Fan, an eloquent *Tao-hsüeh* proponent then serving as attending censor. Although the *Tao-hsüeh* intellectuals had won initial appointment to such high metropolitan posts through the councilor's patronage, they were the first to criticize him. When the Mongols launched their massive assault on Hsiang-yang in 1236, Cheng Ch'ing-chih almost by necessity submitted his resignation, which was often intended as a ceremonious gesture; the emperor unceremoniously accepted it.

The departure of Cheng Ch'ing-chih, however, had a negligible effect on court policy. Ch'iao Hsing-chien replaced him as councilor of the left, and Ts'ui Yü-chih was appointed councilor of the right. Both men supported the previous administration's rapprochement with the *Tao-hsüeh* proponents, even though they had no close personal links to those involved in the movement. Both men embraced a conciliatory policy toward Mongol aggression in the aftermath of the Sung's failed attempt to recapture K'ai-feng two years earlier in the summer of 1234. They preferred peace while preparing for war. According to Ts'ui Yü-chih, peace was feasible only "if in negotiating a peace, we can also have security."[74] The new councilors shared with Cheng Ch'ing-chih the experience of serving under Shih Mi-yüan during his last turbulent decade. All three were on cordial terms, despite differences on the specifics of foreign policy, and they followed, in some measure, Shih's tactic of moderation. At least in domestic policies, the late 1230s were years of continuity.

Such continuity helps explain the rise of yet another Shih kinsman from Ming-chou to prominence in the capital. Shih Mi-yüan hailed from an

---

[72] *HTC* (1958) 168, p. 4587.

[73] On these charges, see *SS* 407, p. 12282; 409, p. 12333; 415, p. 12458; 424, pp. 12659–60; 437, p. 12964; 438, p. 12987; *HTC* (1958) 168, p. 4595; Ch'ien, *Nan Sung shu* 53, p. 7a.

[74] *SS* 406, p. 12263.

exceedingly accomplished kin group, with some sixty nephews and cousins holding civil service rank in the thirteenth century. He probably did not know most of them well, having spent the bulk of his adult years in Lin-an, but his influence affected the careers of some. Shih Sung-chih, for example, a collateral nephew who received his *chin-shih* degree in 1220, won appointment to a number of influential military-related posts through his uncle's intervention.[75] He earned recognition as an innovative administrator in his own right. By streamlining and making self-sufficient the military organizations in strategically vital Hsiang-yang and Tsao-yang, for example, Shih Sung-chih helped prepare these two prefectures for the deadly conflict ahead. Later, he served as prefect of Hsiang-yang and military commissioner in chief for the Ching-hsi and Ching-hu circuits of central Sung territory, which made him the most influential military figure in the empire. Shih Sung-chih also supervised the talks that culminated in the anti-Chin alliance with the Mongols of 1233. He commanded the offensive against T'ang-chou, directed the final assault against Ts'ai-chou, and forwarded to Lin-an the Chin imperial paraphernalia that he retrieved from the defeated Chin emperor.[76] A grateful court rewarded him with appointment as minister of war.

Shih Sung-chih had vehemently opposed Cheng Ch'ing-chih's ill-fated military offensive to retake K'ai-feng. He had denounced the 1234 action much as Shih Mi-yüan had denounced the initiatives of Han T'o-chou. By then commissioner for the central Huai River region and with fifteen years of military experience there, Shih Sung-chih noted that recent floods and crop failures had left the region too impoverished to support an offensive. "People with no home to return to will join together as bandits; soldiers suffering from hunger and starvation will be defeated even before combat."[77] His warnings, however prophetic, were ignored. The outcome of the campaign in the north was that with their provisions exhausted, Sung troops returned south having accomplished nothing, save inciting the Mongols. Revanchists charged Shih Sung-chih with intentionally withholding provisions to ensure the Sung defeat. Shih Sung-chih may have boycotted the effort in the north for fear of endangering his own troops or simply in response to pressures from other commanders, Chao Yen-na for example, who also boycotted the campaign.[78] Such acts of insubordination were not isolated, but the censure of Shih Sung-chih was the most strident. He responded by surrendering his war ministership, a largely nominal post in Sung times.

[75] On his career, see Davis, *Court and family in Sung China*, pp. 142–57.
[76] Li, *Sung Yüan chan-shih*, pp. 162–6.
[77] SS 414, p. 12424.
[78] SS 413, p. 12400.

In the mid-1230s, Shih Sung-chih continued to receive high-level regional appointments, a clear sign of imperial favor, despite perceptible tensions between him and Cheng Ch'ing-chih. Although he never resided in Lin-an, his input on border policy was assured through memorials on various topics, from troop morale to fiscal management. Shih Sung-chih's credibility was further enhanced by his success in routing major Mongol assaults on Kuang-chou2 and Huang-chou in 1237, which led to a reduction in fighting and new peace overtures from the north. A grateful court responded by naming him assistant councilor in 1238 and, a year later, chief councilor of the right. This made him the third chief councilor to emanate from his Ming-chou clan, Shih Hao and Shih Mi-yüan having preceded him.

Shih Sung-chih initially shared power with Li Tsung-mien, councilor of the left, and Ch'iao Hsing-chien, distinguished military councilor (p'ing-chang chün-kuo chung-shih). It seemed an odd threesome. The new councilor was a prominent proponent of peace, and his elevation to the high post, coinciding with the arrival of a Mongol emissary, appeared to represent the emperor's official endorsement of propeace advocates and policies. Advancement of Yü T'ien-hsi (chin-shih 1223), another Ming-chou native closely identified with Shih Mi-yüan, to assistant councilor suggests the same. Yet Li Tsung-mien and Ch'iao Hsing-chien shared none of Shih Sung-chih's commitment to peace. They opposed on principle all significant concessions. Perhaps this was still a time of indecision for Li-tsung, or maybe he was unwilling to sacrifice an older generation of trusted officials to accommodate the new. Whatever the emperor's motives, this contradictory set of appointments ensured no abrupt change in policy. The deaths of both Li Tsung-mien and Ch'iao Hsing-chien in early 1241, however, left Shih Sung-chih with undisputed authority at court. For the next four years, he remained the only chief councilor, effectively reviving, for better or worse, one-man dominance.

Shih Sung-chih was never popular among his colleagues. As early as 1234, Investigating Censor Wang Sui2 (chin-shih 1202) accused him of imperiling the empire to advance his personal reputation. Wang Yeh (chin-shih 1220), a minor official at the Bureau of Military Affairs, charged that Shih's propeace sentiments undermined the empire's defense effort. Attendant Censors Hsieh Fang-shu (chin-shih 1223) and Wang Wan (chin-shih 1223) questioned Shih Sung-chih's overall competence and advised against his further advancement.[79] The charges, made while Shih Sung-chih was assistant councilor, reveal not just disesteem, but outright contempt. These feelings seem especially curious for a man whose advice on border policy and conduct of the war proved, in the

---

[79] On early criticisms, see SS 41, p. 801; 415, p. 12461; 416, pp. 12984–5; 417, p. 12510; 420, p. 12575.

long run, to be sound. Justified or not, critics continued their reproofs after he became councilor. Countering them was not easy.

As chief councilor, Shih Sung-chih retained general command of the Huai, Ching-hu, and Szechwan armies. It was a privilege enjoyed by few councilors of the Southern Sung, not even the powerful Shih Mi-yüan. The prestige of the dual appointments notwithstanding, the responsibilities were too much for one man. Shih Sung-chih spent his first year as chief councilor monitoring the volatile border in the west, and returned to Lin-an in the spring of 1240. In his absence, the capital was hit with a famine so severe that ordinary citizens disappeared in broad daylight as the marketplace traded daily in human flesh. Never in Li-tsung's long reign, before or after, did calamity hit so close to home. Shih Sung-chih's presence in Lin-an could hardly have forestalled natural disaster or alleviated the human suffering, but his conspicuous absence implied an indifference that antagonized many.

Subsequently, Shih Sung-chih spent more time in the capital. The border situation had largely stabilized after 1241, but the empire's domestic problems seemed as intractable as ever. Tu Fan twice memorialized the throne in 1240 about crises of unprecedented proportions.[80] Natural disasters extended from the lower Huai to Fu-chien, bringing with them and exacerbating soaring prices, bandit outbreaks, alien invasions, empty granaries, and widespread vagrancy. There was disorder in the heavens and turbulence on earth. Despite these upheavals, Shih Sung-chih's defensive achievements were numerous. Beyond denying the Mongols a foothold in Sung territory, he presided over the restoration of territory that had been regained. He also devised a highly imaginative scheme of regional defense by providing refugees with land to till with guaranteed low rents, while organizing them into militia reserve units for use in times of emergency.[81] Reminiscent of Wang An-shih's *pao-chia* system, its objective was to curtail military expenditures while strengthening regional defense. However, Shih Sung-chih's record contained no notable accomplishments beyond military policy. He had not managed to reach a peace accord with the Mongols, a failure that ensured prolonged instability and hardship along the empire's border. Nor had he developed a coherent economic policy in the face of spiraling defense costs and declining revenues. Finally, he never developed a close working relationship with the civil service as a whole, never acquired the political adeptness needed to manipulate groups and individuals who held differing views, and never built a solid base of support within the bureaucracy. Focused on regional service, his career had not given him exposure

[80] SS 407, pp. 12282–6; Tu Fan, *Ch'ing-hsien chi* [*Ssu-k'u ch'üan-shu, Wen-yüan ko* 1779 ed.] (Taipei, 1971) 9, pp. 2b–11a; Davis, *Court and family in Sung of China*, pp. 131–2.
[81] SS 176, p. 4275.

to the management of the metropolitan bureaucracy. Critics often referred to him with contempt, as a "powerful councilor," yet his career left him more vulnerable within the government than other powerful men of Southern Sung.

Shih Sung-chih was rarely so rash or so secure as to dismiss or demote critics outright. In the case of Tu Fan, for example, he reportedly "gave an outer expression of forbearance while detesting him inside."[82] Shih made no apparent effort to block Tu Fan's appointment to an executive post at the Bureau of Military Affairs, where he also had a seat. The nomination may well have been initiated by him in the hope of mollifying critics, a tactic in the tradition of Shih Mi-yüan. Cooperation between Shih Sung-chih and Tu Fan nonetheless proved impossible. Tu Fan, following his 1244 promotion to second spot in the military bureaucracy, threatened to resign if Li Ming-fu (chin-shih 1209), an assistant councilor with close ties to Shih Sung-chih, was not dismissed. Challenging one superior and insulting another, the demand betrayed a profound arrogance. Students at the Imperial University, no doubt prompted by professors sympathetic to Tu Fan, joined in attacking Li Ming-fu and ultimately the chief councilor himself. Realizing that Tu Fan would accept nothing short of his own resignation, Shih Sung-chih orchestrated the dismissals of both Tu Fan and Li Ming-fu. The emperor, detesting the unseemliness of confrontation, supported Shih's decision. The dismissal of Tu Fan roused others to speak out, including Huang Shih-yung (chin-shih 1226) and Liu Ying-ch'i, to name but two. The dismissals also served to polarize much of the bureaucracy against Shih Sung-chih, which set the stage for another conflict.

In the autumn of 1244, tensions between Shih Sung-chih and the prominent forces of opinion finally exploded into political battle. The death of Shih's father led the opposition to believe that Shih Sung-chih would step down and observe the traditional three years of mourning expected of a son. However, Li-tsung intervened, waiving the customary mourning obligation and retaining Shih in office. There were abundant precedents for the emperor's action. Ning-tsung had waived mourning for commanders Chao Fan and Chao K'uei following the death of their father in 1222, and that of their mother in 1230. The two waivers for the Chao brothers went virtually unnoticed. Shih Sung-chih's uncle had received a similar waiver in 1209, while Shih's own unique qualifications as civil and military leader offered similarly compelling reasons to forego ritual and retain his services. The reaction by many officials to this simple restoration directive was unusually strident. Memorials of protest flooded the court, the most notable coming from the metropolitan student population. Signing petitions were 144 students at the Imperial University, 67 at the Military Academy, 94 at the Lin-an Academy, and 34 at the Imperial Clan

---

[82] SS 407, p. 12286.

Academy (*Tsung-hsüeh*). The most widely publicized of these petitions came from the Imperial University, where students refused to conceal their contempt for Shih Sung-chih. They attacked him on moral grounds. By orchestrating his own recall, they charged, he was being shamelessly unfilial. He was accused of bribing his way to the councilorship and then exploiting the privileges of the office for personal profit. Apart from issues of personal morality and political ethics, students warned that three consecutive generations of councilors from one family posed a grave threat to dynastic stability. "Since antiquity, when high officials [from families] which, for as many as three generations, monopolized imperial favor and exploited the power [vested in them], they were inevitably [responsible for] the collapse of their empires.... Alas, the Shih house has held onto power now for three generations!"[83]

The opposition's large numbers and cogent arguments did not easily shake the emperor's resolve. Within a month of his father's death, Shih Sung-chih was ordered to hasten his return to Lin-an. He delayed, perhaps out of frustration, and this only strengthened the hand of the opposition. In the interim, the throne summoned Tu Fan to the capital, ostensibly for consultation. The emperor appointed Liu Han-pi (d. 1244), a vocal critic of Shih Sung-chih, as censor, and named two other prominent men of *Tao-hsüeh* convictions, Li Hsin-ch'uan (1167–1244) and Ch'en Hua (*chin-shih* 1205), to executive posts in the bureaucracy.[84] These moves are commonly interpreted as signs of the emperor's coming to his senses about his unworthy councilor, an interpretation totally unjustified, for the councilor's seat remained vacant. Li-tsung's gesture, it appears, had the limited objective of silencing the opposition without sacrificing his favorite. However, Shih Sung-chih's narrow political base continued to erode and, after three months of relentless pressure, his resignation was accepted by the emperor.

Shih's resignation was not enough for his opponents; only a permanent discrediting of Shih Sung-chih could guarantee no future revival. The throne restored the dual councilorship. The senior position went to Fan Chung (*chin-shih* 1208), a former chancellor at the Imperial University and a professor at the Military Academy. This was certainly a concession to students. Succeeding Shih Sung-chih as councilor of the right was Tu Fan, which was another victory for *Tao-hsüeh* proponents. With a more favorable bureaucratic leadership, the opponents of Shih pushed their assault. The summer of 1245 brought the sudden death of Hsü Yüan-chieh (*chin-shih* 1232), a one-time chancellor at

[83] On the dismissal of Shih Sung-chih, see Davis, *Court and family in Sung China*, pp. 150–4; Wang Chien-ch'iu, "Sung-tai t'ai-hsüeh yü t'ai-hsüeh-sheng" (M.A. thesis, Fu-jen Ta-hsüeh, 1965), pp. 306–7.

[84] *SS* 406, pp. 12275–7; 419, pp. 12560–4; 438, pp. 12984–6; *HTC* (1958) 171, pp. 4660–1.

the university whose opposition to Shih Sung-chih was well known. Hsü had dined the night before he died with Fan Chung, a man close to Shih Sung-chih, and many suspected foul play. Two other critics of Shih Sung-chih, the censor Liu Han-pi and Shih's own nephew Shih Ching-ch'ing, died under similarly suspicious circumstances.[85] Tu Fan had died earlier in 1245 of natural causes, but the rash of deaths among prominent critics appeared more than coincidental. Seventy-three students at the Imperial University, exercising their new political might, seized on such rumors and demanded an open investigation. The emperor graciously granted the demand. He even offered an unusual reward of one hundred thousand strings of cash for information pertaining to the cases. No evidence was ever found to support the assassination theory or to implicate Shih Sung-chih, but the damage to his reputation had been done. When Li-tsung considered reappointing him in 1246, resistance from Shih's opponents forced the emperor's retreat. Shih Sung-chih never returned to public life.

The fall of Shih Sung-chih did not, however, end the dominance of Ming-chou favorites. The former chief councilor, Cheng Ch'ing-chih, returned from retirement in 1245 as palace lecturer. In the spring of 1247, Councilors Fan Chung and Yu Ssu (*chin-shih* 1220) retired. The emperor promptly replaced them with Cheng Ch'ing-chih. Cheng remained in power for the next four and a half years, sharing it, albeit only briefly, with Commander Chao K'uei. The potentially controversial decision to restore Cheng Ch'ing-chih, already in his seventies, to power encountered surprisingly little resistance, which suggests that Cheng enjoyed some measure of respect among court critics despite his former failures. The late 1240s were generally tranquil years, the border and the bureaucracy relatively free of conflict, except for the occasional opposition to some of the councilor's high-level appointments.

One of Cheng's rising favorites was Shih Chai-chih (1205–49), the son of Shih Mi-yüan. Shih Chai-chih appears to have been on especially good terms with the emperor, the two being roughly the same age and frequently in one another's company. On the eve of his father's death in 1233, Shih Chai-chih had received honorary *chin-shih* status and a high-level sinecure. Having never passed the examinations on his own, these extraordinary acts symbolized the emperor's enduring goodwill toward that branch of the Shih clan. As early as 1240, Li-tsung had sought to have Shih Chai-chih return to the capital. The opportunity finally came in 1248, and Shih Chai-chih emerged as minister of personnel and subsequently associate chief at the Bureau of Military Affairs. Whether the promotion was initiated by the emperor or by his chief councilor,

---

[85] On the incident, see *SS* 414, pp. 12426–7; 415, pp. 12454–9; 424, pp. 12660–2; *HTC* (1958) 171, pp. 4656–9; Chou Mi, *Kuei-hsin tsa-chih*, vol. 6 *pieh-chi*, pp. 18a–20a.

Cheng Ch'ing-chih, we do not know. In the light of old debts to Shih Mi-yüan, no doubt both men endorsed the move despite the younger Shih's unpopularity among court critics. With such support, Shih Chai-chih may well have risen even higher, but he died prematurely the next year.

Another Ming-chou native advanced to high office under Cheng Ch'ing-chih was Ying Yao (*chin-shih* 1223), a former professor at the Imperial University. His sound official record and good overall reputation may explain why his advancement to assistant councilor in 1249 encountered no notable opposition, despite overtones of regional favoritism. Not so readily accepted, however, was the nomination of Pieh Chih-chieh (d. 1253) to assistant councilor in the summer of 1247. An individual closely identified with the administration of Shih Sung-chih, Pieh was forced to resign within a year. Cheng Ts'ai (d. 1249), named to an executive post at the Bureau of Military Affairs, encountered similar opposition and for the same reason: he had been a partisan of Shih Sung-chih. He was dismissed. Such selections suggest that Cheng Ch'ing-chih, in choosing high-level subordinates, gave clear preference to Ming-chou provincials or to individuals identified with the Shih Sung-chih administration. The opposition to Cheng's appointments contrasts significantly with the success of Shih Mi-yüan, who commonly employed fellow provincials, but did so less blatantly and rarely made objectionable appointments. The resistance encountered by Cheng Ch'ing-chih implies that the lengthy dominance of Ming-chou scholars at court, having made too many enemies on all sides, was nearing its end.

Cheng Ch'ing-chih's greatest shortcoming was not regional favoritism, but his indulgence of family members. His wife and son were notorious for their political deal making and profiteering.[86] Already seventy when recalled to office, Cheng should have been provided by the emperor with a second councilor to assist in routine administration. The lack of a second man created a vacuum. During his long tenure in power, Shih Mi-yüan had consciously nurtured a younger generation of talent capable of winning the emperor's trust and the bureaucracy's respect. Cheng Ch'ing-chih did not do so, perhaps because he had been out of power for a decade, or perhaps because he lacked foresight, or perhaps because border problems and constant bickering with a vexatious bureaucracy sapped too much of his energy. He left no well-placed protégés to whom the throne could turn. As an older generation of statesmen died off, the political vacuum became more serious. From 1248 to 1251, Cheng Ch'ing-chih petitioned at least five times asking to retire, but each time his request was denied. With few reliable associates, the aging councilor looked to his family to assist him in routine matters. The combination of nepotism and

---

[86] *SS* 414, p. 12423.

graft stemming from this arrangement discredited not only him personally, but the entire Ming-chou group.

The death of Cheng Ch'ing-chih in 1251 marked the end of an era in Sung history. By a combination of sheer coincidence and clever orchestration, Ming-chou natives had been an influential political force for nearly a half century, surviving Shih Mi-yüan by nearly two decades. Never before had the region known such political stature, and it never would again. Until the end of the dynasty, Ming-chou provincials continued to produce great numbers of metropolitan and regional officials, but they no longer dominated the court. Responsibility for this lies squarely with Shih Sung-chih and Cheng Ch'ing-chih. Shih Mi-yüan may have been censured for encroaching upon the privileges of the emperor, but he had never been known for corruption or graft. He may have indulged in political favoritism, but he did not give his wife and children a free run of the court. His successors from Ming-chou proved far less scrupulous, which gave public opinion grounds to denounce them and make future advancement difficult for others from Ming-chou.

Filling the vacuum

When Cheng Ch'ing-chih died in 1251, the emperor reportedly contemplated recalling Shih Sung-chih.[87] Either in response to or in anticipation of widespread opposition, he instead selected Hsieh Fang-shu as councilor of the left and Wu Ch'ien as councilor of the right.[88] A native of western Szechwan's Wei-chou6, Hsieh Fang-shu had received Shih Sung-chih's initial recommendation for office, but Hsieh had tended to be critical of his sponsor and sympathetic toward the moralist opposition. His relations with Cheng Ch'ing-chih had been more cordial, which enabled him to rise to assistant councilor, and placed him in a position to be made Cheng's successor. Wu Ch'ien, a native of Ning-kuo (in modern Anhwei province) and the top-ranked *chin-shih* in 1217, had also served under Cheng Ch'ing-chih as assistant councilor. Although he had opposed the military offensive of 1234, this did not preclude his collaboration with Cheng Ch'ing-chih in the late 1240s.

That Cheng Ch'ing-chih's successors were to be his own handpicked subordinates may partly reflect imperial confidence in the senior statesman's good judgment; Cheng had been the emperor's tutor, after all. The selection of Hsieh Fang-shu and Wu Ch'ien also reflects the emperor's desire to maintain administrative continuity at a time of military and economic upheaval. The empire might have fared better, however, with discontinuity, for the old policies were neither insightful nor flexible. In border affairs, even ten years after

[87] *HTC* (1958) 173, p. 4718.
[88] *SS* 417, pp. 12510–12; Wu Ch'ien's biography is in *SS* 418, pp. 12515–20.

the initial Mongol victories, the Sung was no closer to security with peace or preparedness for war. Although the court lavished retrospective honors on the *Tao-hsüeh* masters of the eleventh and twelfth centuries, the moral message these intellectuals had advocated had no noticeable impact upon the personal lives of the emperor or of his trusted ministers. As Wu Ch'ien lectured Li-tsung on curbing his sensual indulgences and reining in palace favorites who encroached upon the imperial authority, his colleague Hsieh Fang-shu had sabotaged the effort by routinely permitting members of his own family to intrude into political matters. Under censorial indictment, Wu Ch'ien fell from power after scarcely a year in office. The emperor's patience was no doubt worn thin by Wu's annoying diligence in scrutinizing affairs within the palace. Hsieh Fang-shu dominated the bureaucracy for the next three years. His personal influence over the throne, however, was never significant, and he fell, uneventfully after censorial indictment, in the summer of 1255. Both councilors had failed in their commitment to deliver Li-tsung from the grip of well-entrenched and resourceful eunuchs serving in the inner palace.

To the outer court, the eunuchs Tung Sung-ch'en and Lu Yün-sheng were the palace figures most responsible for the throne's indifference to the details of governance.[89] The most hated eunuch of the thirteenth century, Tung enjoyed the emperor's favor for the last two decades of the reign. Court officials accused Tung Sung-ch'en of accepting bribes for political favors, arranging choice appointments for relatives of palace women, and encouraging the emperor in his theatrical amusements and carnal indulgences, including the notorious summoning of local prostitutes to the palace in 1255. In times of severe economic hardship, Tung allegedly confiscated privately owned lands to erect pleasure pavilions for the emperor. Tung even dared, according to critics, to participate in ceremonies at the Imperial Ancestral Temple (*T'ai-miao*), a profound insult to royal ancestors that implied treacherous ambitions.[90] Such charges were probably exaggerated if not altogether fabricated and may only reflect later historians' condemnation of eunuch power. Nonetheless, they signal an ascendency of the inner court over the outer court. By this stage of both Li-tsung's reign eunuchs and consorts, two groups more frequently political competitors than collaborators, had learned to cooperate, an inauspicious development from the perspective of outer court officials. This was the first time in Li-tsung's reign that he placed his trust not in bureaucratic executives but in eunuchs. Most of the political infighting in the 1250s centered on the contest between eunuch power and bureaucratic authority.

---

[89] *SS* 469, pp. 13675–6; Chou Mi, *Ch'i-tung yeh-yü* (1983) 7, pp. 120–5.

[90] On these charges, see *SS* 411, p. 12358; 474, p. 13782; *HTC* (1958) 174, p. 4748; 174, pp. 4750–63; Hsü Ching-sun, *Chü-shan ts'un-kao* [*Ssu-k'u ch'üan-shu*, Wen-yüan ko 1779 ed.] (13th c.; Taipei, 1976) 1, pp. 27a–31b.

Wu Ch'ien had cautioned the court against the influence of inner court staff, but to no avail. In 1255, Censor Hung T'ien-hsi (*chin-shih* 1226) denounced eunuch power as well, and resigned when the emperor was unresponsive. Students at the Imperial University and prominent officials rushed to the censor's defense, which further polarized the court. Hsieh Fang-shu maintained a low profile during the controversy, and this led to accusations, unsubstantiated but also difficult to refute, that he had formed some secret liaison with eunuchs. His credibility shattered, Hsieh stepped down. The conflict between bureaucratic professionals and imperial favorites festered.

The emperor appointed Tung Huai (*chin-shih* 1213), a native of the border city of Hao-chou, to be Hsieh's successor. Like some earlier councilors, Tung Huai had close ties to the *Tao-hsüeh* movement; unlike most, his lengthy career had been devoted largely to regional office, with his first appointment in the capital coming only six years before his elevation to the councilorship. This proved a serious handicap. Probably close to seventy, Tung Huai's candid yet tactful approach to counseling the throne earned him the emperor's respect but not necessarily his confidence. The problem of eunuch power persisted, compounded by imperial indulgence of various other favorites. Male relatives of the empress, favored consorts, even Taoist nuns received special conferrals of bureaucratic rank and office. One *Tao-hsüeh* proponent at the Ministry of Works, Mou Tzu-ts'ai (*chin-shih* 1223), resigned in outrage at such improprieties. His departure and that of Hung T'ien-hsi, which roughly coincided, left Tung Huai alone in the struggle against palace favorites. Unfortunately, his enemies were not confined to the inner court.

The one figure in the outer court who incurred the wrath of the civil service more than did the palace favorites was the knavish Ting Ta-ch'üan (*chin-shih* 1238). A native of Chen-chiang (near the Yangtze River in Kiangsu), Ting held various regional posts prior to entering the metropolitan bureaucracy in the early 1250s. According to traditional accounts, Ting's advancement to policy monitor and palace censor derived directly from the relationships he cultivated with the imperial concubine Yen and the eunuchs Tung Sung-ch'en and Lu Yün-sheng. However, Ting Ta-ch'üan possessed examination credentials and had a long record of regional service. He was not altogether unqualified to participate in government. His association with palace favorites appears undeniable, but whether the liaisons occurred before or after his political ascent is unknown.

Ting's undisguised ambition and political maneuverings were widely criticized, and no bureaucrat was more incensed by them than the chief councilor Tung Huai. From early on, Tung admonished the throne to advance talented men and curb the influence of relatives, and by implication their confederates. Ting Ta-ch'üan allegedly made friendly overtures, but Tung Huai responded in mid-1256 by denouncing him as vile and threatening to resign if the censor remained in his post. Li-tsung preferred inaction, but not Censor Ting, who in an unprecedented display of arrogance led a hundred palace guardsmen to the councilor's home. Under the cover of darkness, Tung Huai was dragged off to the law enforcement office, no doubt threatened with torture, and then crudely deposited outside the city walls. More than just a humiliating insult to an elder statesman, this also represented an outrageous affront to bureaucratic authority. The emperor officially ordered the councilor's dismissal a day later, in effect justifying after the fact Censor Ting's excess. This was no consolation for Tung Huai's many sympathizers, who launched a major political campaign against Ting. At its forefront were students at the Imperial University, who demanded exile for the insubordinate censor. The emperor, ordinarily inclined to compromise, must have been unusually piqued. He ordered eight students at the university and seven at the Imperial Clan Academy, the alleged provocateurs, to be rounded up and banished to the far south. He also instructed university officials to restore order to the campus and curb political activism there.[91] These actions by the emperor represented a major political setback for Tung Huai's supporters and a reassertion of the imperial will.

The successor of Tung Huai was Ch'eng Yüan-feng (chin-shih 1228), a Hui-chou (Anhwei) native with professorial status at both the Imperial University and the Imperial Clan Academy.[92] Having applied the stick, the emperor may have used Ch'eng's appointment as a carrot to appease the disaffected. When Ch'eng Yüan-feng had been an investigating censor, he was critical of the moribund Cheng Ch'ing-chih administration and the political decadence it tolerated. Such views ensured Ch'eng's support by Tao-hsüeh proponents. Yet Ch'eng Yüan-feng clearly anticipated stormy waters, for he declined the councilorship several times before submitting to imperial pressure.

Beginning in the summer of 1256 and for nearly two years after, Ch'eng remained the court's sole councilor; yet as long as Ting Ta-ch'üan held Li-tsung's confidence, Ch'eng would never function as chief policy maker. The decision to banish university students, coinciding with the fourth month of Ch'eng Yüan-feng's term, must have come as a personal, not just a political, setback. As a former professor and current chief councilor he was unable to shield defenseless students from intimidation by his subordinates. This inability to act constituted an embarrassing image of political impotence. Conditions along the border inspired no optimism either. Under Ch'eng Yüan-feng, Sung and Mongol armies clashed with greater frequency and intensity, as Möngke prepared for a renewed Mongol offensive. The Mongol assault on Szechwan that began in 1258, and lasted nearly two years, represented by far the most

---

[91] On the incident, see SS 44, p. 857; 405, p. 12242; 414, p. 12432; 474, pp. 13778–9; HTC (1958) 174, pp. 4761–2, 4764.
[92] SS 418, pp. 12520–3.

intense fighting in two decades. From the outset of his tenure in 1256, Councilor Ch'eng had aggressively promoted the strengthening of border defenses,
no doubt having anticipated an escalation of fighting. Yet his only notable
achievement was augmenting the standing army by a hundred thousand men.
He devised no imaginative scheme for financing an expanding war, no new
strategy to counter the Mongol initiative in Szechwan, and no peace alternative should the fortunes of war turn unfavorable. Immersed in petty court
squabbles, he lost sight of these far more pressing issues.

Only a few months into the new conflict, in the spring of 1258, Ch'eng
Yüan-feng stepped down. His replacement was Ting Ta-ch'üan, an unfortunate
choice. Despite the Mongol offensive in the west, which grew progressively
more ferocious during the Ting Ta-ch'üan years, Ting is charged by traditional
historians with being oblivious to the crisis. Initially refuting his predecessor's
warning about inadequate defenses, he later imposed a ban on all discussion
of the border situation.[93] The effort to silence the war debate, whether it was
motivated by political intolerance or by concern over troop morale and popular
support, proved unproductive and unenforceable, another blemish on Ting's
already tarnished reputation. Even allowing for historical bias, Ting Ta-ch'üan
was the most imprudent of Li-tsung's fifteen councilor appointees. He had
negligible exposure to military affairs, inexperience that an empire at war
could ill afford. Ting's appointment was unwise for another reason. His crude
insolence in the ouster of Tung Hai and unseemly ties to the inner court ensured
that Ting Ta-ch'üan, as councilor, was perpetually at odds with moralist critics.
The Sung court faced new internal conflicts that were additional drains on
valuable resources. Unfortunately, the arrogant use of power and disinclination
to tolerate criticism influenced Li-tsung as well. After decades of conflict within
the intellectual and political communities, a weary Li-tsung lost his former
political tolerance.

THE RISE OF CHIA SSU-TAO

The emperor finally dismissed and abandoned Ting Ta-ch'üan in November of 1259. Censorial indictments provided the pretext, and serious military setbacks in Szechwan the occasion. The elderly Wu Ch'ien returned to
Lin-an as councilor of the left, but he held the post for only a half year. Court
attention instead focused on the new councilor of the right, Chia Ssu-tao
(1213–75).[94] A native of T'ai-chou, in coastal Chekiang, he was the son of

---

[93] SS 438, p. 12988; 474, pp. 13778–9; HTC (1958) 175, pp. 4776–7.
[94] Biographical information can be found in Herbert Franke, "Chia Ssu-tao (1213–1275): A 'bad last
   minister'?" in Confucian personalities, ed. Arthur F. Wright and Denis C. Twitchett (Stanford, Calif.,

Shantung commissioner Chia She and the brother of Li-tsung's once favored Consort Chia. Even though he lacked *chin-shih* credentials, by all indications he had held the high regional posts of prefect, pacification commissioner, and fiscal overseer, all while still in his thirties. These promotions were rare even for degree holders, and Chia Ssu-tao's meteoric rise can be explained only by his natural talent, backed by family privilege, most probably the favor enjoyed by Consort Chia. But he was an unusually experienced official. Most of his early career was spent in regional offices, but his extensive exposure to military matters resulted in an appointment as associate administrator at the Bureau of Military Affairs in 1254, his first executive post in the capital. The timing was more than coincidental.

From early on, Li-tsung had apparently been on close personal terms with Chia Ssu-tao, who was eight years his junior. In the mid-1230s, when both men were in their twenties, the emperor had commented, with envy, on Chia Ssu-tao's amorous escapades. Rumor had it that they subsequently caroused together.[95] Following the death of Cheng Ch'ing-chih in 1251, the emperor's only notable close acquaintance from his early years still alive and politically active was Chia Ssu-tao. Employing him in high office must have seemed only natural to an emperor known for his loyalty to old friends.

In assessing the reasons for Chia Ssu-tao's advancement, it would be unfair, as Herbert Franke demonstrates, to focus exclusively on Chia's personal ties and ignore his official record. In the decade preceding his appointment to the Bureau of Military Affairs, Chia Ssu-tao served as commissioner for Chiang-nan West, Ching-hu, and the Yangtze region – all strategically vital areas that gave Chia valuable professional experience. Increasingly, Chia Ssu-tao identified himself with the military bureaucracy. This may reflect the influence of his father, who similarly lacked examination credentials and exploited military service to win quasi-military posts ordinarily beyond the reach of those without the *chin-shih* degree. Yet the appointment had plenty of recent precedents. Shih Sung-chih and Chao K'uei had both acquired councilorships through their distinction as military leaders, although Shih had obtained examination degrees as well. Because of the military crisis at hand, Li-tsung needed to place an unusually high premium on military expertise, in some ways countering the Sung dynasty's practice of disdaining martial skills. This may be also seen in Li-tsung's frequent advancement of military men to eminent civilian posts, and in the temporary revival of the special military councilorship in the 1230s. Moreover, Li-tsung's high regard for Chia Ssu-tao appears to have been shared and reinforced by others. Shih Yen-chih (fl. 1217–60), prefect of Lin-an and brother of Shih Sung-chih, had once remarked to the throne, "Although Ssu-tao has the habits of youth [in being so carefree], his talents are capable of extensive use."[96] At the time, Chia Ssu-tao was still in his early twenties and already marked for advancement.

There was never a political honeymoon for the new councilor. Many bureaucrats, considering him an extension of inner court influence in the tradition of Ting Ta-ch'üan, held Chia Ssu-tao in profound contempt from the outset. But his favored sister, the Consort Chia, had died in 1247 over a decade before his nomination as councilor, and the emperor had since taken up with other consorts. Chia's great civil service attainments cannot be explained simply with reference to her influence. Nor is there evidence to document Chia Ssu-tao's alliance with any specific court faction. His appointment to the Bureau of Military Affairs occurred under Hsieh Fang-shu, and to assistant councilor under Tung Huai and Ch'eng Yüan-feng. These were all men highly regarded for their professional integrity. If not personally responsible for his advancement, at least the three did nothing to block it. Eight months into the tenure of Ting Ta-ch'üan, Chia Ssu-tao was appointed as supreme commander for the Huai region. His return to regional military service may reflect heightened concern over the worsening border situation, yet it may also imply an unharmonious relationship with Ting Ta-ch'üan. Upon becoming councilor, Chia Ssu-tao moved to eliminate the political cronies of Ting Ta-ch'üan and Tung Sung-ch'en,[97] and he intentionally distanced himself from earlier favorites and their policies. For example, contemporary critics allege that when Tung Sung-ch'en had proposed, in the wake of a threatening enemy offensive in 1259, that the capital be moved to Ming-chou, an action that Councilor Wu Ch'ien endorsed,[98] Chia Ssu-tao reportedly rejected such defeatism and insisted on a firm stand at the border, to project an image of fortitude and resolve. Still, his bold determination did not dispel the shadow of official criticism or the rumors of spineless pacifism.

Fiscal crisis and land policy

The empire under Li-tsung was beset with difficult problems, but none more intractable than the economy. Accumulation of land by the wealthy, commonly

---

[96] SS 474, p. 13780.

[97] HTC (1958) 175, p. 4788; 176, p. 4798.

[98] Huang Kan, Mien-chai chi [Ssu-k'u ch'üan-shu, Wen-yüan ko 1779 ed.] (Taipei, 1971) 38, p. 29a; SS 173, pp. 4179–80.

designated as "monopolists" (*chien-ping chih chia*), had plagued Sung society since the early eleventh century, a problem frequently mentioned but never resolved. Land accumulation inevitably affected government revenues, for influential landowners, legally or otherwise, could claim exemptions and evade taxation more effectively than could simple peasants. In the thirteenth century, new strains on the economy created new pressures for government intervention. Early in the tenure of Shih Mi-yüan, Li Tao-ch'uan (*chin-shih* 1196), brother of famed historian Li Hsin-ch'uan and a professor at the Imperial University, had demanded the imposition of strict limits on landholding. Hsieh Fang-shu had also made a similar recommendation in 1246, a few years before becoming councilor.[99] The devastation imposed by natural disasters and the revenues consumed by prolonged war left the court with few alternatives besides coercive action. After several years of deliberation, Chia Ssu-tao's first move was to conduct a massive land survey (probably in 1262). By correcting tax registers that no longer reflected the rural landholding, Chia hoped to identify tax evaders and increase revenues. This was followed, in 1263, by the public fields (*kung-t'ien*) measure.

Public fields was a policy that had been put forward during the last years of the Northern Sung and originally was devised to defray military expenditures. It had the same basic function in the 1260s.[100] Chia Ssu-tao also abolished the old Harmonious Grain (*ho-ti*) levy, which compelled farmers to sell grain to the government at artificially low prices for use as army provisions. Abolition of the practice, a source of considerable discontent, must have been welcome, but Chia Ssu-tao did not act out of charity. Large landholdings in the hands of powerful landlords able to claim exemptions made even ordinary land taxes formidably difficult to collect and must also have radically reduced procurement of supplementary taxes such as the Harmonious Grain levy. The government seemed to have only two options: redistribute land among poor, tax-paying peasants, an administratively onerous task, or seize private lands for the state. Chia Ssu-tao took the second path. He restricted the landholdings of tax-exempt officials and mandated that the state purchase one-third of all holdings in excess of two hundred *mu* (approximately thirty acres). Initially, this program was implemented near the capital; later, it was extended to most of the southeast. It was applied first to official households and then was expanded

---

[99] *SS* 417, pp. 12510–11; 425, pp. 12670–1.

[100] On land tenure and reform for the era, see Franke, "Chia Ssu-tao (1213–1275)," pp. 229–31; Chao Ya-shu, "Sung-tai ti t'ien-fu chih-tu yü t'ien-fu shou-ju chuang k'uang" (M.A. thesis, Kuo-li T'ai-wan ta-hsüeh, 1969), pp. 85–94; Chang Yin-lin, "Nan Sung wang-kuo shih pu," in *Sung-shih yen-chiu chi: Ti erh chi*, ed. Sung-shih tso-t'an-hui (Taipei, 1964), pp. 105–22, especially pp. 117–22; Ch'en Teng-yüan, *Chung-kuo t'u-ti chih-tu* (Shanghai, 1932), pp. 195–200; Liang Keng-yao, *Nan Sung ti nung-ts'un ching-chi* (Taipei, 1984), pp. 83–150; *SS* 173, pp. 4194–5; *HTC* (1958) 177, p. 4837; Chou, *Ch'i-tung yeh-yü* (1983) 17, pp. 313–17; Hsü, *Chü-shan ts'un-kao* 3, pp. 15a–17a.

to cover all landowners. Moreover, the two hundred *mu* exemption was soon cut in half. Because the government lacked the financial resources to offer adequate compensation, some landowners received as little as five percent of their land's market value. There were other inequities as well. Payment for larger holdings was generally made not in cash, but in progressively larger quantities of inflated paper currency, tax remission certificates, or worse yet, certificates conferring official status. This policy made the state the largest landowner in the empire. For example, the government claimed a reported twenty percent of all arable land in Che-hsi circuit.[101] Although many officials appreciated the seriousness of the financial crisis facing the Sung, few endorsed Chia Ssu-tao's overhaul of the entire landowning system. Such objections by officials may have reflected their self-interest, for officials constituted a significant share of the landowning population, but genuine policy differences were also at work.

The most difficult aspect of the public fields initiative was implementation. Local officials, pressured by the Sung court, often confiscated more land than stipulated while compensating the owners with less than the regulations obliged. In their misguided enthusiasm, some local officials went so far as to threaten noncomplying landowners with mutilation and other illegal punishments. Critics charged that the program "disturbed the people" (*jao-min*).[102] By "people," they seemed to have meant rich landlords and officials, those with the most wealth to lose. When the government confiscated up to twenty percent of a region's arable land, when it attempted to manage vast state holdings without substantially augmenting its civil service, when it flagrantly undercut the interests of precisely the group responsible for implementing its measures, during a time of military conflict, political disruption of some sort was inevitable. Had Chia Ssu-tao redistributed land among poor peasants rather than claiming everything for the state, the program may have won greater acceptance. Instead, he strengthened the state at the expense of the people, alienating rich landlords and landless peasants alike. Moreover, as the Sung court lacked the resources to supervise state lands, mismanagement and neglect were unavoidable. The public fields program lasted, at least nominally, for twelve years, an exceedingly long life for such a contentious and ill-conceived policy.

Success or failure of the public fields policy aside, Chia Ssu-tao faced an old and difficult problem of revenue shortfall that less courageous predecessors had evaded. He also showed courage in curtailing the privileges of the ruling elite and landowning class to which he himself belonged, scholar-officialdom. Later writers often compared Chia Ssu-tao to Wang Mang, a minister and then

---

[101] Franke, "Chia Ssu-tao (1213–1275)," p. 230.
[102] Ch'en et al., *Sung-shih chi-shih pen-mo* (1977) 98, p. 1087.

emperor (r. 9–23) who ended the Western Han dynasty (206 B.C.E.–8 C.E.). Wang Mang undertook drastic land reform and impoverished the wealthy.[103] However, this comparison is exaggerated.[104] The Sung government confiscated only one-third of *excess* holdings and offered compensation, however modest. It also provided tax relief through the abolition of the Harmonious Grain system. All this suggests intentional moderation on Chia's part. However, Chia Ssu-tao and Li-tsung were viewed as hypocrites for demanding sacrifice from others while spending lavishly on themselves. In 1262, a year before the public fields measure, the emperor had built, at state expense, a private home and ancestral temple for Chia Ssu-tao. Costing a million strings of cash, the buildings probably rivaled even imperial structures in their sumptuousness.[105] This extravagance, compounded with the emperor's lavish expenditures within his own palace, must have left many dispossessed landowners embittered, certain that revenues earned from their former lands would only be squandered on imperial frivolities.

Bureaucratic discontent was also directed toward Chia Ssu-tao's conduct of foreign policy. As noted earlier, the armies of Khubilai had largely withdrawn from the south following Möngke's death in 1259. At that point, they decided to test the diplomatic waters, sending a peace envoy, Hao Ching, to the Sung in the spring of 1260. Sixty miles into Sung territory, at Chen-chou2, a border official arrested him. This arrest was allegedly made on orders from the chief councilor without the emperor's knowledge.[106] In light of the acute vulnerability of its southwest, the Sung could scarcely afford to offer such provocation to the enemy. Moreover, with the Sung having apparently made peace overtures to the Mongols only a year earlier, the sudden change in attitude is rather baffling. Hao Ching was suspected, by some reports, to be a spy. If true, a more responsible court would have simply turned him away at the border, rather than further provoke the Mongols by incarcerating their envoy. Other reports allude to some secret understanding between the councilor and the Mongols, concluded during the pressures of the 1259 offensive, which had offered what in retrospect represented politically awkward concessions. For fear of these concessions being made public, Chia Ssu-tao isolated Hao

---

[103] See Hans Bielenstein, "Wang Mang, the restoration of the Han dynasty, and Later Han," in *The Cambridge history of China*, volume 1: *The Ch'in and Han empires, 221 B.C.–A.D. 220*, ed. Denis C. Twitchett and Michael Loewe (Cambridge, 1986), pp. 232–51.

[104] Franke, "Chia Ssu-tao," p. 231 n. 61.

[105] Ting, *Sung-jen i-shih hui-pien* 18, p. 924; SS 45, p. 880. See also Richard L. Davis, *Wind against the mountain: The crisis of politics and culture in thirteenth-century China* (Cambridge, Mass., 1996), pp. 42–6.

[106] Sung et al., *Yüan shih* 206, pp. 4591–4; HTC (1958) 176, p. 4802; Franke, "Chia Ssu-tao (1213–1275)," pp. 226–9; Morris Rossabi, *Khubilai Khan: His life and times* (Berkeley, Calif., 1988), pp. 56, 81; Hu et al., *Sung Meng (Yüan) kuan-hsi shih*, pp. 260–9; Li, *Yüan-shih hsin-chiang*, vol. 2, pp. 266–7.

Ching. As demonstrated by Herbert Franke, documents given to the envoy contain no reference to tribute payment or to any previous concessions.[107] The only feasible explanation for Sung intransigence in this case is the weight of revanchist bureaucratic opinion.

For much of the thirteenth century, the Sung bureaucracy had favored arms over negotiation, activism over passivism, and had taken a dim view of appeasement: Shih Mi-yüan had been criticized by Chia She for using wealth and office to buy the loyalties of Li Ch'üan, Shih Sung-chih had been denounced for compromising revanchist idealism in the base pursuit of peace, Ting Ta-ch'üan had been criticized for doing too little to strengthen border defenses, and Tung Sung-ch'en had come under fire for proposing a tactical retreat by relocating the capital farther southeast. In this general atmosphere of militancy, Chia Ssu-tao, as a councilor still new to the office, could not afford to incur the bureaucracy's wrath. His apparent indifference to the threat posed by the Mongols may also relate to his doubts about Mongol intentions. Having rebuffed Sung overtures a year earlier, the Mongols' sudden interest in talks would naturally have aroused suspicion.

In the early part of 1261, Chia Ssu-tao faced a new challenge caused by the loyalists of Shantung. Thirty years before, in 1231, Sung armies had killed Li Ch'üan, following his abortive invasion of the south. Li Ch'üan's wife, Yang Miao-chen, had then led her remnant armies in retreat to the northeast, never again to threaten the south. Li T'an, the adopted son of the two, had inherited their base at I-tu (near modern Ch'ing-chou, in central Shantung). The Mongols subsequently entrusted Li T'an with control over much of Shantung, hoping eventually to unleash the Shantung armies upon the Sung. With expanded aid from Khubilai, Li T'an began to harass the Sung border in 1261. His intention, however, must have been to obtain, by coercion if necessary, support from the Sung, for in March 1262, in the most stunning defection of the Li-tsung reign, Li T'an turned on the Mongols and declared fealty to the Sung.[108] The move was perhaps inspired by greed, as Li had been disappointed with Mongol aid, or perhaps by opportunism, with Li seeking to exploit Mongol preoccupations in the west to assert his control in the east, or perhaps by fear, with Li apprehensive about his place in the long-term Mongol plans for Shantung. Whatever his motives, the decision to ally himself with the Sung, the government responsible for his father's death, rather than declare

---

[107] Franke, "Chia Ssu-tao (1213–1275)," pp. 226–9.

[108] On the Li T'an affair, see Sung et al., *Yüan shih* 206, pp. 4591–6; *HTC* (1958) 176, pp. 4819–24; Li, *Sung Yüan chan-shih*, pp. 863–74; Li, *Yüan-shih hsin-chiang*, vol. 2, pp. 267–73; Otagi Matsuo, "Ri Tan no hanran to sono seijiteki igi – Mōkōchō chika ni okeru Kanchi no hōkensei to sono shūkensei e no tenkai," *Tōyōshi kenkyū* 6 No. 4 (1941), pp. 1–26.

independence from both the Mongols and the Sung, suggests that Li T'an had been given a substantial incentive. The Sung court must have made an irresistible bid for his loyalty. As bureaucratic chief, Chia Ssu-tao would deserve some credit for this. But the risks in this venture turned out to be too great for Chia Ssu-tao.

In contrast to his father, Li T'an commanded an unimpressive army of roughly twenty thousand men, which posed no serious military challenge to Khubilai. For Li to become a serious challenger, the Sung would have had to commit to Shantung, on short notice, a very large army of reinforcements, weakening their defenses elsewhere. Chia Ssu-tao had no manpower to do this, even if he wished to do so, and refused to take advantage of Li T'an's offer. Consequently, the Li T'an uprising lasted scarcely a month. The Sung accomplished nothing in the venture, save for further provoking the new Mongol ruler. Only one year earlier, a prominent commander at Lu-chou3, Liu Cheng, had defected to the Mongols, thereby strengthening their hand in the west in Szechwan. The rebellion of Li T'an, by forcing the Mongols to assert their authority in the Shantung region, brought new pressure against the Southern Sung on another front.

Tao-hsüeh *and the Imperial University*

Perceiving failures in Sung political leadership and the increased foreign military threat, the students at the Imperial University (*T'ai-hsüeh*) emerged in Li-tsung's reign as a potent political influence. In the last years of the Northern Sung, students had been vocal critics of government policy, but their activism erupted in a brief and violent episode that held no prospect of sustaining itself. Activism in the Southern Sung dated from the early Ning-tsung years, when students had protested the dismissals in 1195 of Li Hsiang (*chin-shih* 1163) and Yang Chien (1140–1226), men identified with Chao Ju-yü and openly hostile toward Han T'o-chou. Li Hsiang, then chancellor (*chi-chiu*) of the Directorate of Education (*Kuo-tzu chien*), held professorships at both the Imperial University and the Directorate. No less distinguished was Yang Chien, a professor at the university and an eminent philosopher. The 1195 protest had helped polarize officialdom when Han T'o-chou responded by banishing the student ringleader to distant Ling-nan. Eight years later, when one brazen youth at the Military Academy had verbally accosted Han T'o-chou, his temerity was rewarded with arrest and exile.[109] These arrests had hardly endeared Han

---

[109] On these incidents, see *SS* 407, pp. 12289–90; 455, pp. 13369, 13372–8; Wang, "Sung-tai t'ai-hsüeh yü t'ai-hsüeh-sheng," pp. 260–1, 298–306; Thomas H. C. Lee, *Government education and examinations in Sung China* (New York, 1985), pp. 186–96.

T'o-chou to students, but the coercion had succeeded in keeping university campuses relatively quiet.

Shih Mi-yüan's approach to handling student critics was entirely different. Avoiding confrontation, he courted men popular at the university, especially *Tao-hsüeh* proponents. He appointed, for example, Chen Te-hsiu, an individual with impeccable moralist credentials, as university professor. There was always an element of tension between the pacifist councilor and the revanchist university leaders, but such tension never escalated into confrontation. Despite his long and controversial tenure, Shih Mi-yüan drew no more than minor criticism from students.[110]

Compromises made by Shih Mi-yüan should not cloud the fact that he was a clever manipulator who apparently controlled students through their professors. With roughly sixteen hundred students and only three professors, not counting many more lecturers, at the university, such manipulation was feasible. University appointments required special examination credentials, yet approval of appointments rested with the chief councilor, and Shih Mi-yüan exploited this prerogative.[111] In this way, Cheng Ch'ing-chih, the chief councilor's closest confidant, received appointments to the Imperial University, the Directorate of Education, and the Imperial Clan Academy. As a university official at the time of Li-tsung's controversial succession, Cheng's presence, more than any other single factor, explains the lack of student criticism of the affair. Other Ming-chou natives or close associates of the councilor also received teaching or administrative assignments at the university, including Ying Yao, Hsüan Tseng, Yüan Hsieh, Ch'iao Hsing-chien, and many of Shih Mi-yüan's own kinsmen. At least eight of Shih Mi-yüan's collateral nephews were identified with the university in or around the time of his councilorship.[112] Not all these kinsmen approved of their uncle, and some even criticized him publicly, but as a whole they probably had a generally moderating effect on student opinion.

The successors of Shih Mi-yüan, lacking his skills in political manipulation, were often humbled by pressures from the university. The first major clash of the Li-tsung reign between the bureaucratic leadership and university students occurred during the years of Shih Sung-chih's dominance, from 1241 to 1245. The younger Shih's elevation to chief councilor in 1239 was poorly received at

[110] *SS* 419, pp. 12555–6; 420, pp. 12572–4; 423, p. 12629; Ch'en Teng-yüan, *Kuo-shih chiu-wen* (Peking, 1958) 35, p. 378.

[111] *SS* 246, p. 8736; 400, pp. 12146–7; 419, p. 12543; 420, p. 12571; Huang et al., *Sung Yüan hsüeh-an* 73, pp. 1278, 1388.

[112] *SS* 423, pp. 12637–8; Lou Yüeh [Yao], *Kung-k'uei chi* [*Ssu-pu ts'ung-k'an ch'u-pien* 1929 ed.] (c. early 13th c.; Taipei, 1979) 105, p. 11b; Tai Mei et al., *Hsin-hsiu Yin-hsien chih* (1877) 20, p. 35a; *Hsiao-shan Shih-shih tsung-p'u* [Columbia University copy] (n.p., 1892) 5, pp. 31b, 32b, 41a, 45a.

the university, and complaints arose early on. Students later criticized Shih's pacifist inclinations and found fault with the Shih family's domination at court.[113] These issues did not suddenly emerge under Shih Sung-chih; it is merely that students had won, for the first time in three or four decades, the courage to address their political concerns in a public, confrontational manner. Their courage stemmed from the new councilor's background. For virtually his entire career, Shih Sung-chih had served away from the court. Even as chief councilor, various military responsibilities often took him away from Lin-an. Unlike his uncle, Shih Sung-chih did not have the extensive network of contacts within the metropolitan bureaucracy and the university necessary to manipulate or influence political opinion in the capital. Shih Sung-chih had also struck an unseemly image of a professional bureaucrat, an unscholarly official with scant interest in the ethical concerns of philosophers and students. Never bothering to court *Tao-hsüeh* proponents as his uncle had done, he probably underestimated the group's importance in shaping political opinion.

Nothing incensed students more about Shih Sung-chih than his apparent pacifism, for irredentism had an extraordinary appeal at the university. This tradition drew some inspiration from the late Northern Sung, but it was strengthened by the distinctive conditions of the diminished southern empire. *Tao-hsüeh* ideas fueled such idealism. The leading Southern Sung thinker, Chu Hsi, was a vocal proponent of an aggressive policy against the north. In his 1163 memorial to Hsiao-tsung, for example, he had endorsed the revanchist policies of Councilor Chang Chün. Despite the councilor's ultimate defeat in battle, Chu Hsi appears not to have changed his position, as evidenced by the militancy of his later writings.[114] Other statesmen and scholars, such as Yeh Shih, Hsin Ch'i-chi, Ch'en Liang, and Chang Shih2, although coming from quite different intellectual traditions, shared a radical militancy with *Tao-hsüeh* proponents. Quite unlike the intellectuals, wielders of political power tended toward pragmatic moderation, if not pacifism, in foreign policy, which caused the two groups to clash often at court. For *Tao-hsüeh* proponents, these differences went beyond policy convictions. Having achieved unparalleled supremacy in the realm of thought, they felt they had consistently been denied a share of political power commensurate with their intellectual standing.

[113] Huang Hsien-fan, *Sung-tai t'ai-hsüeh-sheng chiu-kuo yün-tung* (Shanghai, 1936), pp. 73–8.
[114] Chu Hsi, *Hui-an hsien-sheng Chu Wen kung wen-chi* [Ming *Chia-ching* 1522–66 ed.; *Ssu-pu ts'ung-k'an ch'u-pien* 1929 ed.] (1245; Taipei, 1979) 11, pp. 1a–40b; 13, pp. 1a–8a. Also see Conrad Schirokauer, "Chu Hsi's political career: A study in ambivalence," in *Confucian personalities*, ed. Arthur F. Wright and Denis C. Twitchett (Stanford, Calif., 1962), pp. 162–88; Brian E. McKnight, "Chu Hsi and his world," in *Chu Hsi and Neo-Confucianism*, ed. Wing-tsit Chan (Honolulu, 1986), pp. 408–36, especially pp. 422–5; Lo Wen (Winston W. Lo), *The life and thought of Yeh Shih* (Gainsesville, Fla., 1974), pp. 57–74; *SS* 429, pp. 12751–70; Ch'en, *Kuo-shih chiu-wen*, pp. 374–9.

But with the thirteenth-century court dominated by entrenched councilors and their cliques, the prospects for effecting change, compared with the eleventh and twelfth centuries, were diminished. To be sure, conflicting views on war and peace often fell along outer and inner court lines, but militancy among *Tao-hsüeh* proponents and their sympathizers also resulted from the group's profound sensitivity to the Sung dynasty's crisis of legitimacy.

The Sung loss of its northern territories, including the Central Plains in 1126, to the Chin conquerors had dealt a severe blow to the Sung ruling house. Descent from the Chao lineage offered Southern Sung rulers some legitimacy, yet the raison d'être of any government-in-exile is the promise of eventual return to full powers and restoration of lost lands. The harsh realities of Chin strength and Sung weakness, however, left Sung statesmen and intellectuals alike scrambling to address legitimacy issues, often using scholarship to serve their political agenda. The compilation, *Outline and details of the comprehensive mirror (Tzu-chih t'ung-chien kang-mu)*, written under the auspices of Chu Hsi's students and published in 1172, offers a prime example.[115] In their digest of Ssu-ma Kuang's massive history *The comprehensive mirror for aid in government (Tzu-chih t'ung-chien)*, the authors devoted much space to assessing the legitimacy of past dynasties. Their objective was to develop rules of legitimacy that would firmly place the Southern Sung in a more favorable light than the Chin.[116] In addition to employing historical arguments, those using scholarship to serve their political agenda also exploited philosophical legacies to augment the Sung dynasty's political status. Southern Sung *Tao-hsüeh* proponents, because of their close intellectual links with the distinctive Northern Sung tradition of Chou Tun-i and the Ch'eng brothers, boldly declared a connection between political succession and "Succession to the Way" (*tao-t'ung*), reasoning that where philosophical orthodoxy lies, so does political legitimacy.[117] This ideological commitment to defending the dynasty came with a political agenda of incessant pressure to recover the north. These revanchists often argued for the restoration of the Sung's former boundaries, but they had a scant appreciation of the practical limits to state power. To a throne obsessed with its own legitimacy, *Tao-hsüeh* proponents may have had irresistible appeal, but each emperor who was temporarily won over to support their militancy – Hsiao-tsung, Ning-tsung, and Li-tsung in turn – paid dearly for those sympathies.

[115] Conrad Schirokauer, "Chu Hsi's sense of history," in *Ordering the world: Approaches to state and society in Sung dynasty China*, ed. Robert P. Hymes and Conrad Schirokauer (Berkeley, Calif., 1993), p. 200.

[116] Schirokauer, "Chu Hsi's sense of history," pp. 195–206; Jao Tsung-i, *Chung-kuo shih-hsüeh-shang chih cheng-t'ung lun: Chung-kuo shih-hsüeh kuan-nien t'an-t'ao chih i* (Hong Kong, 1977), pp. 35–7; Ch'en Ch'ing-ch'üan et al., *Chung-kuo shih-hsüeh-chia p'ing-chuan* (Cheng-chou, 1985), vol. 2, pp. 600–21.

[117] Wing-tsit Chan, *Chu Hsi: New studies* (Honolulu, 1989), pp. 320–5; Richard L. Davis, "Historiography as politics in Yang Wei-chen's 'Polemic on legitimate succession,'" *T'oung Pao* 69 Nos. 1–3 (1983), pp. 33–72, especially pp. 40–2, 48, 69–70.

In the end, moderates generally prevailed, but to do so the court had to sacrifice the abstract enhancement of the legitimacy that the revanchists offered it for the tangible maintenance of peace.

During the Sung, the influence of the Learning of the Way (*Tao-hsüeh*) at the Imperial University fluctuated immensely. On the rise in late Northern Sung, it entered a dramatic decline in the early Southern Sung due to the hostility of power brokers at court such as Ch'in Kuei. Its fortunes improved modestly under Hsiao-tsung, one of few emperors whose personal lifestyle came close to the high moral standards set by the movement, but then declined again under Ning-tsung. Of the most notable disciples of Chu Hsi listed in the *Sung dynastic history* (*Sung shih*), only two can be identified with the university system. Most of them apparently preferred to teach at state or privately run regional academies, where they cultivated a growing body of followers.[118] Initially underrepresented at metropolitan institutions, and short on influential court officers and university professors, the *Tao-hsüeh* movement figured prominently in regional education; it was unmatched in the zeal with which it propagated its ideas at the local level.[119] By the early thirteenth century, the school's influence, once concentrated in the Fu-chien region, had spread throughout the south. Men originally independent of the movement – Chen Te-hsiu and Wei Liao-weng, to name two illustrious examples – came to sympathize with its persecuted leaders and their moral message.[120] *Tao-hsüeh* values were also favorably received by some powerful bureaucrats, such as Cheng Ch'ing-chih and Tung Huai, natives of Liang-che whose intellectual pedigrees differed radically from those of the Fu-chien school. The movement's influence on education ensured that it would eventually alter, however indirectly, the empire's leading educational institution, the Imperial University. This expanded influence also came about owing to a generally sympathetic leadership at court beginning with Shih Mi-yüan.

The growing stature of the *Tao-hsüeh* at the Imperial University was related to the curriculum. During the Northern Sung, the university had tended to stress poetry. In the Southern Sung, it stressed the classics.[121] The effect of

---

[118] *SS* 429–30.

[119] Hoyt C. Tillman, *Confucian discourse and Chu Hsi's ascendancy* (Honolulu, 1992), pp. 37–42, 133–44, 231–4; Linda A. Walton, "The institutional context of Neo-Confucianism: Scholars, schools, and *shu-yüan* in Sung-Yüan China," in *Neo-Confucian education: The formative stage*, ed. Wm. Theodore de Bary and John W. Chaffee (Berkeley, Calif., 1989), pp. 457–92.

[120] Liu Tzu-chien (James T. C. Liu), "Wei Liao-weng's thwarted statecraft," in *Ordering the world: Approaches to state and society in Sung dynasty China*, ed. Robert P. Hymes and Conrad Schirokauer (Berkeley, Calif., 1993), pp. 336–48; Wm. Theodore de Bary, "Chen Te-hsiu and statecraft," in *Ordering the world: Approaches to state and society in Sung dynasty China*, ed. Robert P. Hymes and Conrad Schirokauer (Berkeley, Calif., 1993), pp. 349–79.

[121] Chao T'ieh-han, "Sung-tai ti t'ai-hsüeh," in *Sung-shih yen-chiu chi: Ti i chi*, ed. Sung-shih yen-chiu-hui (Taipei, 1958), pp. 317–56.

this difference in emphasis is unmistakable. Since the *Tao-hsüeh* movement produced the most prolific classicists of the thirteenth century, candidates preparing for civil service examinations, including university students, were almost certain to come under its influence. At the end of 1212 the university formally adopted Chu Hsi's commentaries on the *Analects* and the *Mencius* as canonical, officially confirming the preeminence of *Tao-hsüeh* scholarship as an intellectual force and also as the key to examination success.

The transfer of *Tao-hsüeh* ideas into political action owes something to the emperor. Li-tsung bestowed court honors on leaders of the *Tao-hsüeh* movement with extraordinary generosity. In 1227, Chu Hsi's compilation of commentary on the Four Books (*Analects*, *Mencius*, *Chung-yung*, and *Ta-hsüeh*) received imperial sanction. In 1230 a descendant of Confucius was favored with a government post. In 1241 the posthumous ranks of Chou Tun-i, Chang Tsai, the Ch'eng brothers, and Chu Hsi were all elevated and tablets for them placed in the Temple of Confucius. Their teachings in effect were sanctioned as state orthodoxy. But as demonstrated by James T. C. Liu, imperial goodwill was hardly divorced from pragmatic politics.[122] With his own succession shrouded in controversy and with a new military power menacing the northern border, Li-tsung exploited rapidly evolving intellectual and ideological traditions of the Confucian canon to enhance the image of himself and his administration. At the same time, he continued to indulge his material and sensual impulses in flagrant violation of the high moral expectations of the *Tao-hsüeh* movement. His hypocrisy angered many, Tu Fan being the most notable critic, yet most aspiring officials could ill afford such candor. Unable to risk indicting the emperor personally, they focused on his chief advisors instead, blaming them for everything from enemy victories along the border, to irregularities in the heavens, and even to the emperor's sexual appetites.

Shih Sung-chih rose to the councilorship in the early 1240s, an exceedingly troubled time. Natural disasters reduced hungry residents of the capital to cannibalism; heavenly portents foretold a grim future for the ruler and the ruled; the Mongol offensive, though largely arrested, left a vast trail of devastation and human suffering; and scandalous rumors about the emperor's personal life circulated widely. The spreading conviction that dynastic fortunes were taking a turn for the worse, combined with Shih Sung-chih's generally low standing at the Imperial University, emboldened the students. The thrust of their indictments was that Shih Sung-chih, by orchestrating his own recall following his father's death, had exhibited a lack of the important Confucian virtue of filial piety. Being disloyal to his own father, how could he be loyal to his ruler?

---

[122] Liu Tzu-chien (James T. C. Liu), "How did a Neo-Confucian school become the state orthodoxy?" *Philosophy East and West* 23 No. 4 (1973), pp. 483–505.

It was a moral indictment, and may well have been orchestrated by moralist teachers or their associates in the capital. Certain university chancellors and professors at the time were indirectly linked to the *Tao-hsüeh* movement, and contemporary documents occasionally refer to students being encouraged in their attacks by their teachers.[123] Students and teachers in Lin-an interacted freely, contravening the rules restricting such interaction in force during the Northern Sung. At the same time, moralist elements had hardly overrun the university. The most prominent chancellor under Shih Sung-chih, Chin Yüan (*chin-shih* 1214), had no known ties to *Tao-hsüeh*.[124] In all likelihood, students were influenced by individual professors and administrators, but they were more than mere pawns in a power struggle between bureaucratic insiders and outsiders. On the contrary, once stirred by political events in the capital, they quickly seized the initiative and became a vigorously independent force.

The confrontation between Shih Sung-chih and the Imperial University students added a new dimension to Southern Sung politics. For the preceding century, student outbursts had been infrequent and largely unfruitful. But as the university grew in the early Southern Sung from a few hundred students to over sixteen hundred by the early thirteenth century, numbers that were augmented by the formation of the Military Academy and the Lin-an Academy in the late twelfth century, so did the students' potential to have an influence.[125] Reflecting in part the confidence that comes with greater numbers, and by sheer persistence, they won the resignation of Assistant Councilor Li Ming-fu, a close associate of Shih Sung-chih, in early 1244.[126] This victory, more than any other factor, explains the students' belligerence later in the year, when controversy erupted over the recall from mourning of Shih Sung-chih. Rather than act as individuals, as in the past, they acted as a group. One hundred and forty students at the Imperial University, almost ten percent of the student body, petitioned for Shih's dismissal. With support from the other metropolitan academies and from many officials in the civil service, they immobilized the throne. Li-tsung yielded to their demands after three intense months, and replaced Shih Sung-chih with Tu Fan, a favorite among the critics. Student pressure had, almost on its own, destroyed a chief councilor, a victory that legitimized student opinion while enhancing the university's status. It also, more importantly, exposed the chief councilor, and even the emperor, as vulnerable to the forces of opinion. Li-tsung's decision in 1245 to investigate the questionable deaths of several of the critics of Shih Sung-chih, again a

[123] *SS* 409, p. 12323; 418, p. 12529; 419, pp. 12553–5; 422, pp. 12614–15.
[124] *SS* 419, pp. 12558–9.
[125] *SS* 157, pp. 3685–6.
[126] Ch'ien, *Nan Sung shu* 53, pp. 8a–b.

concession to student demands, only confirmed this. No longer, it seemed, would the university be cowed by bureaucratic chiefs, bought off by petty favors, or humbled by the imperial will.

Students played little part in politics for the next decade, however. The calm at the university related to the recall in 1247 of Cheng Ch'ing-chih to serve as councilor. Cheng Ch'ing-chih fared better than most owing to his close association with *Tao-hsüeh* proponents and his many years of service at the various university campuses, where he seems to have made many allies. The late 1240s had more than its share of political problems, but students did not attempt to intervene. They offered no resistance to the nomination of Shih Chai-chih, son of Shih Mi-yüan, as minister of personnel and later as executive at the Bureau of Military Affairs, despite his reputation for corruption and mediocrity. Students held their silence about Cheng Ch'ing-chih's blatant indulgence of a politically manipulative wife and a criminally larcenous son. Even when they came out in support of Ch'eng Kuang-hsü (*chin-shih* 1211), a drafter at the Secretariat whom the councilor wished to dismiss, students carefully avoided offending Cheng Ch'ing-chih personally.[127] Such unusual pliability owed something to the strong ties of Councilor Cheng to the university, but also to his skill at steering opinion. For example, when making the potentially controversial nomination of Shih Chai-chih to the Bureau of Military Affairs, he appointed Ying Yao, a former university professor, as the younger Shih's superior and subsequently as assistant councilor. Similarly, the elevation of the experienced frontier commander Chao K'uei first to assistant councilor and then to chief councilor would placate irredentist students inclined to challenge the appointment of Shih Chai-chih. The strategy proved exceedingly successful.

The death of Cheng Ch'ing-chih in 1251 and the dismissal of Wu Ch'ien in 1252 compounded by the ascendancy of royal favorites and eunuchs at court and the impotence of the succeeding councilors to curb their excesses, prompted a new generation of students to take the offensive again. They were apparently inspired to do so by Investigating Censor Hung T'ien-hsi. Allegations that the eunuch Tung Sung-ch'en had illegally confiscated private property, which coincided with the promotion of the notoriously unscrupulous Ting Ta-ch'üan to a censorial post, so incensed Hung T'ien-hsi that he resigned in protest. His resignation generated widespread censure of the chief councilor, Hsieh Fang-shu, whose failure to defend his respected colleague implied his support for the inner court. University students demanded Hsieh's resignation. In response, the eunuch Tung Sung-ch'en resorted to bribing a student at the university to dispute the other students' criticism. The ploy failed and the student, denounced by his peers, was dismissed from the university, while

---

[127] *SS* 415, p. 12459.

Hsieh Fang-shu resigned.[128] The students failed to win the recall of Hung T'ien-hsi, but they had succeeded in having a second councilor driven from office and in reasserting their political influence, a feat made easier by Tung Sung-ch'en's misguided effort to bribe one of their own.

This new victory added fire to the student movement. When the notorious Ting Ta-ch'üan, in liaison with prominent eunuchs and consorts, forced Chief Councilor Tung Huai out of the capital, a group of students led by Liu Fu (b. 1217) and Ch'en I-chung (chin-shih 1262) protested. Ignoring imperial instructions to refrain from criticizing court policy, they agitated for the dismissal of Ting Ta-ch'üan, and sustained their pressure for most of 1256. The result was far from favorable for the students. Fifteen activists at the Imperial University and the Imperial Clan Academy were rounded up, expelled from the schools, and banished to the south to live under surveillance.[129] The university's vice-chancellor responded by organizing a massive demonstration, in the hope of forcing a compromise. But Li-tsung not only refused to reverse his decision, he ordered a stone tablet to be erected on the campus inscribed with a permanent injunction against the "irresponsible discussion of state affairs" by students. Additionally, Li-tsung instructed university officials to scrutinize all student memorials before releasing them, a futile attempt at reviving the censorship tactics that had been used by Han T'o-chou. School officials demurred, for the most part, so the directive was chiefly ignored. Imperial pressure, meanwhile, did not halt the student campaign of protest against Ting Ta-ch'üan, which ended in his removal three years later.

After 1259, university influence improved only modestly. With Wu Ch'ien as councilor of the left, the banished students were permitted to return to the capital, and in a gesture of goodwill, the throne even exempted them from departmental examinations in qualifying for chin-shih status. In this way, Ch'en I-chung, a figure destined for later prominence, gained second place in the palace examination of 1262. Calm returned to the campus for the next several years, despite the emperor's continued support for the eunuch Tung Sung-ch'en and the nomination of Chia Ssu-tao as councilor. Much of the credit for this stability belongs to Chia Ssu-tao. Through increased student stipends, larger university enrollments, and special gifts to lesser school officials, he garnered university support.[130] In other circles, Chia was increasingly despised and assailed, but not at the university. In the early 1260s several audacious students criticized Chia Ssu-tao's tight control of the court. Chia instructed the prefect of Lin-an to round up the agitating students and tattoo them like

[128] SS 417, pp. 12511–12; 424, pp. 12655–6; HTC (1958) 174, pp. 4752–3; Ch'ien, Nan Sung shu 53, pp. 10a–b.
[129] SS 474, p. 13778; HTC (1958) 175, p. 4764.
[130] Wang, "Sung-tai t'ai-hsüeh yü t'ai-hsüeh-sheng," p. 206.

common criminals.[131] Chia's severe order did not provoke the usual stir at the university. Not until the councilor's final years, in the early 1270s, did students reassert themselves.

In explaining the heightened student activism in the Li-tsung era, modern Chinese scholars often relate it to the "nationalism" or "national consciousness" that emerged as a spontaneous emotional response to developments, largely but not exclusively in foreign relations, that threatened the Sung dynasty. Student activism during the Northern Sung had been most pronounced under Hui-tsung and in the Southern Sung under Li-tsung, both periods characterized by a faction-riddled court, an exploitative government, and the ravages of border warfare. Yet student censure was by no means confined to issues of foreign policy. Students at the Imperial University may have resented Shih Sung-chih's perceived pacifism, but their 1244 indictment had focused specifically on his personal ethics and, to a lesser extent, on the dangers associated with one-family political dominance. Student criticisms of Tung Sung-ch'en and Ting Ta-ch'üan during the early 1250s had addressed the threat to political stability posed by eunuchs and families of the inner court; deteriorating conditions along the border were of secondary importance. To portray the external threat of foreign invasion as the essential stimulus to student activism ignores the unique character of thought and politics in late Sung. It implies that had either the Chin or Mongol armies not menaced the south, students at the Imperial University would have remained tranquil despite the presence, at various times, of eunuch power, consort influence, and imperial laxity. This scenario underestimates the role of *Tao-hsüeh* teachings in inspiring student idealism, the role of political tolerance in encouraging dissent, and the distinct character of individual decision makers who, at different times, inspired, incited, patronized, and pressured different centers of power within the capital and throughout the empire.

Domestic concerns

During Li-tsung's reign, criticism of imperial conduct and government policies was heightened by an onslaught of natural disasters. In Li-tsung's long reign, official records report seven major droughts in 1239, 1240, 1241, 1245, 1246, 1247, and 1254, and seven years of serious floods in 1229, 1236, 1242, 1251, 1252, 1255, and 1259; most of these occurred in central Sung territory. The magnitude of these disasters was enormous. The floods of 1259 reportedly took the lives of millions in Che-hsi circuit.[132] Other disasters had human causes. Major fires struck Lin-an in 1231, 1235, 1237, 1252, 1257, 1263, and 1264.

---

[131] *SS* 474, p. 13782.
[132] *SS* 409, pp. 12326–7.

The overcrowded, urban living conditions of the capital, the narrowness of the city's streets, and the incendiary quality of building materials all made fires difficult to prevent and easy to spread. They often continued for days and caused incalculable loss.[133] A sizable part of the Imperial City was ravaged by fire in 1231; in 1237 fires affected vast numbers of buildings spread through most of the capital. Severe earthquakes were reported in the west in 1240 and 1255, devastating invasions of locusts in the east in 1240 and 1242, and scattered epidemic outbreaks in 1251. These disasters in turn caused famine and death on a massive scale. Mongol-held territory in the north was not spared these types of natural disasters either, and many northerners, receiving no meaningful relief from their Mongol occupiers, chose to flee south. In 1239, the numbers of refugees swelled to over a hundred thousand.[134] Such calamities, coinciding with military confrontations that dragged on for decades, further strained the resources of a hard-pressed government.

As illustrated by Sogabe Shizuo, the Southern Sung empire still produced an unprecedented level of wealth. With only half the territorial expanse, the total government revenues during the late twelfth century roughly equaled those of the Northern Sung at its height.[135] Revenues from the salt and wine monopolies were not negatively affected by the loss of territory either. This phenomenon owes something to continuing population growth during the Southern Sung period and to increased productivity in a generally prosperous southern environment, but no less important to government revenues were the proportionately higher tax rates and the imposition of a wide array of new imposts and surcharges. Sung taxes may well have exceeded those imposed during the Han and T'ang dynasties by *ten* times, and the Southern Sung taxes were most often justified on the grounds of military preparedness.[136] Military expenditures notwithstanding, the Sung empire's exchequer had boasted sizable surpluses for most of the twelfth century. Such good fortune did not persist under Kuang-tsung and Ning-tsung. Years of border conflict claimed a growing share of the empire's budget as tax revenues began to decline. From a height of sixty-five million strings of cash under Hsiao-tsung, revenues plummeted to roughly thirty-five million by Ning-tsung's reign. The plunge is often attributed to the corruption of local clerks, under whom a progressively larger share of taxes failed to reach the capital.[137] Another factor was the growing

---

[133] Jacques Gernet, *Daily life in China on the eve of the Mongol invasion, 1250–1276*, trans. H. M. Wright (Stanford, Calif., 1962), pp. 34–8.

[134] SS 414, p. 12429. Northern refugees were joined by a growing stream of migrants fleeing Mongol assaults on Szechwan. See Paul J. Smith, "Family, landsmann, and status-group affinity in refugee mobility strategies: The Mongol invasions and the diaspora of Sichuanese elites, 1230–1330," *Harvard Journal of Asiatic Studies* 52 No. 2 (1992), pp. 665–708.

[135] Sogabe Shizuo, *Sōdai zaiseishi* (Tokyo, 1941), pp. 37–75.

[136] Ch'en, *Chung-kuo t'u-ti chih-tu*, pp. 168–200, especially p. 191.

[137] SS 41, p. 791; 42, pp. 815–16.

tendency of regional governments to retain local tax revenues to cover the escalating costs of regional defense. In effect, unbridled defense expenditures fostered the decentralization of Sung fiscal authority.

By Li-tsung's time, the fiscal pinch had become an acute crisis. The Mongol invasion depopulated and left a wide expanse of border territory agriculturally unproductive, causing a mammoth forty-five-year drain on revenues. In scale and intensity, the new war easily dwarfed earlier Sung conflicts with the Tangut and Jurchen. Szechwan, the center of many Mongol offensives, reportedly sent no revenues to Lin-an after 1234; in better days it had annually provided as much as twenty to thirty million strings of cash.[138] The empire's vast storehouse of reserves shrank to a fraction of their former size. Intensification of Mongol military activity in the 1250s only added more economic pressure. At the height of the 1259–60 conflict, the Sung court disbursed an extra one hundred and sixty-five million strings of cash, largely in the form of paper currency, to pay for extraordinary military expenses. Efforts made to control the spiraling military budget, such as forcing soldiers to till nearby fields and adopting the local community defense system (*pao-chia*), appear to have netted little savings for the government.[139] Military expenditures, clerical corruption, and disaster relief were not the only strains on the imperial exchequer. More intrusive government policies had to be enforced, and this required more and more officials to supervise each scheme. And the increasing population added to the pressure. The Sung government was succumbing to the weight of its own bureaucracy. As one censor observed in the 1250s, the Northern Sung government had required only ten thousand officials to administer its 320-odd administrative counties. The late Southern Sung empire, reduced to only 100 counties, employed in excess of twenty-four thousand officials.[140]

Rising expenditures and declining revenues left the Sung court little alternative to issuing massive amounts of paper money. According to Ch'üan Han-sheng, the printing of paper currency began under Ning-tsung to subsidize the K'ai-hsi war in 1206. From a circulation of paper notes with a total nominal value of 24 million strings of copper cash in the late twelfth century, the issue had increased to 140 million by 1207. Issues subsequently grew to 230 million strings in 1224, 320 million strings in 1234, and by 1247 to an astonishing 650 million strings.[141] Within a half century, the annual amounts of paper currency issued had increased by a factor of twenty-five. No

---

[138] *SS* 422, p. 12614; *HTC* (1958) 171, p. 4649.

[139] *SS* 44–5.

[140] *SS* 44, p. 858.

[141] Ch'üan Han-sheng, "Sung-mo ti t'ung-huo p'eng-chang chi ch'i tui-yü wu-chia ti ying-hsiang," in *Sung-shih yen-chiu chi: Ti erh chi*, ed. Sung-shih tso-t'an-hui (Taipei, 1964), pp. 263–325, especially pp. 286–7; *SS* 423, pp. 12634–6.

statistics exist for the 1250s, but in light of the government's extraordinary expenditures, a circulation of paper notes nominally worth in excess of a billion strings of copper cash is quite likely. There was rampant inflation. The Sung court apparently spent much of its stock of precious metals, which supposedly had been set aside to back the paper currency. In 1259–60 the government released over 150,000 ounces of silver, in addition to vast quantities of silk and other valuables, to subsidize defense costs.[142] Some of this may have come from the emperor's private treasury, which still contained sizable reserves, but most apparently did not.

High taxes and soaring prices were enough to enrage bureaucrats living on fixed salaries, city dwellers victimized by an unstable money supply, and peasants unable to afford marketplace essentials. The high-handedness of a hard-pressed government only compounded the problem. In 1238 under Shih Sung-chih, for example, the Sung court printed a new issue currency and required an unwilling populace to exchange five of the old for one of the new notes. Shih Mi-yüan had done much the same nearly thirty years before, but at a less onerous two-to-one exchange rate.[143] Even more unsettling for ordinary people was the collection of taxes years in advance, a practice introduced early in Li-tsung's reign. One censor writing in 1248 noted that taxes had already been collected for 1254, six years in advance.[144] In subsequent decades, as dynastic fortunes continued to decline, such abuses grew worse.

It is easy to denounce Li-tsung's court for its fiscal irresponsibility and insensitivity to the plight of an overtaxed population. If Li-tsung had been more conscientious as a ruler, more frugal in his personal use of dwindling resources, and more insightful in his selection of chief ministers, could things have turned out differently? The first economic crisis for the Southern Sung had stemmed from military expenditures, and the subsequent deterioration of the economy was related also to war. Perhaps the K'ai-hsi war of 1206 could have been averted and confrontation with border military threats could have been delayed, yet the Sung court had, in the final analysis, no means of predicting Mongol actions in the north nor Mongol designs on the south. Restraint in the printing of unbacked paper notes would have been more fiscally responsible, but a government in desperation rarely practices such rational restraint. The Sung was the first dynasty to experiment with paper currency, and having little experience to draw upon, it had scant appreciation of the long-term economic impact of its politically expedient measures. The curbing of local bureaucratic

---

[142] SS 44, pp. 867–8.
[143] Ch'üan, "Sung-mo ti t'ung-huo p'eng-chang chi ch'i tui-yü wu-chia ti ying-hsiang," pp. 297, 308; SS 42, p. 816.
[144] SS 174, p. 4221.

corruption would probably have offered some fiscal relief, yet the problem of local bureaucratic misconduct was as old as the dynasty itself, and years of experimentation had yielded no easy solutions. Corruption was probably the rationale behind substantially increasing the size of the sub-bureaucracy, but more clerks did not necessarily produce better administration, and whatever graft the government, through additional clerks, managed to curtail, the extra income derived was ultimately spent on the salaries of an enlarged bureaucracy. Action to reduce tax evasion and land accumulation, if introduced early on, probably would have eased the pinch, yet sweeping reforms were certain to meet bureaucratic resistance. Most inhibiting with regard to efforts to save the dynasty was the conviction by *Tao-hsüeh* proponents that the emperor's moral example was more critical than were legal reforms and pragmatic institutional changes. A political climate that stressed ethics at the expense of methods became an administrative impediment. When political reform finally came in the 1260s, it was too late.

The combination of rampant inflation, bureaucratic corruption, inequitable landownership, incessant war, and a long succession of natural disasters had under past dynasties brought about widespread domestic unrest. The Southern Sung was hardly immune to the consequences of such conditions. Excluding Li Ch'üan and his confederates, who were banished and operated largely beyond the Sung border, the first noteworthy outbreak of banditry under Li-tsung had occurred in 1229–30. For years prior to this, small marauding bands had pillaged the countryside; an edict in the spring of 1230 alludes to scattered banditry throughout the Chiang-nan West, Ching-hu South, and Fu-chien circuits, extending into Kuang-nan. The most ominous threat came initially from coastal Fu-chien.[145] These outbreaks must have been serious, for the Sung court offered a general amnesty to all bandits who agreed to lay down their arms. It also promised official rank to locals who contributed substantially to any suppression efforts and granted tax exemption to the affected areas. The government dispatched a small contingent of the Palace Guard and the imperial navy to assist in the suppression, apparently fearing local forces would be insufficient. Scarcely two months later, in the late spring of 1230, regional armies at Chang-chou suffered a humiliating defeat at the hands of bandits. At the urgent request of Shih Mi-chung, a minor supervisor in Fu-chien and the father of the future councilor Shih Sung-chih, the Sung court appointed Ch'en Hua prefect of Nan-chien-chou and chief director of the suppression effort. A

---

[145] On these outbreaks, see *SS* 419, pp. 12553–4, 12561–4; 420, pp. 12575–6; 437, p. 12963; 449, p. 13227; 453, p. 13337; *HTC* (1958) 164, p. 4473; 165, pp. 4488–9, 4499; Hua Shan, "Nan Sung Shao-ting, Tuan-p'ing chien ti Chiang, Min, Kuang nung-min ta ch'i-i," *Wen shih che* No. 43 (1956), pp. 41–8.

disciple of Yeh Shih, Ch'en Hua was a native of Fu-chien whose familiarity with local topography and customs the court hoped to exploit. Ch'en's mission was not easy. Having been neglected for years, the region's bandits allegedly numbered in the tens of thousands. T'ing-chou, Shao-wu, and the wealthy part of Ch'üan-chou all were centers of bandit activities, as indeed was most of Fu-chien, from its coastal ports to its western inland frontier.[146]

In mid-1230, a major confrontation between government forces and insurgents occurred at T'ing-chou, the inland refuge in southwestern Fu-chien for weary bandits from coastal Chang-chou and Ch'üan-chou. Order was restored by year's end in large part by local defenders organized by the redoubtable widow of a magistrate. Confrontations the next year occurred to the north, in the vicinity of Shao-wu (in northwest Fukien province). In his efforts at suppression, Ch'en Hua journeyed as far south as Ch'ü-chou, in western Che-tung, which is some indication of the difficulty he experienced containing the outbreak. Another front in southern Fu-chien was commanded by Hsü Ying-lung (chin-shih 1208), formerly a distinguished professor at the Imperial University and another Fu-chien native. Named prefect of Ch'ao-chou (Kuang-nan East near Fu-chien circuit), Hsü Ying-lung challenged the forces of "Three-Spear" Ch'en (Ch'en san-ch'iang), a bandit operating out of Kan-chou (southern Kiangsi province) who supposedly butchered people over a wide area. With assistance from Ch'en Hua, now prefect of Lung-hsing2, and armies from western Fu-chien, Hsü Ying-lung launched a devastating three-pronged offensive. Three-Spear Ch'en and his confederates were pursued into Hsing-ning county, northern Kuang-nan East, captured there, and returned to Lung-hsing2 for execution in 1234. This marked the end of major bandit activity in the southeast. A grateful court later awarded Ch'en Hua with an appointment as assistant councilor.

The suppression of banditry involved mobilization of thousands of crack troops and tens of thousands of militia, plus over four years of fighting. To prevail, the Sung government implemented a variety of unpopular measures, including revival of the local community defense system (pao-chia) and conscription for local militias. The desperation of Sung tactics and the duration of the suppression effort suggest an imposing bandit force, but the outlaws generally appear to have lacked organization and competent leadership. Had the Sung not been at war with Chin, and had the bulk of its army not been tied down along the northern border, such motley bands would probably have been eliminated more quickly. Contemporaries attributed the bandit activity of the era chiefly to bureaucratic corruption, excessive taxation, and pirate activity

---

[146] See HTC (1958) 165, p. 4499.

along the coast.[147] The insurrections remained diffused and weak, and without higher political aims to record.

Despite the deteriorating fiscal health of the Sung empire, only two bandit outbreaks are recorded after 1234.[148] Despite repeated military setbacks, only three notable army mutinies erupted and these were easily quelled.[149] Despite uninspiring political leadership, no bureaucratic challenge to the throne emerged in the form of a coup. Indeed, more bandit outbreaks and army mutinies are recorded for Ning-tsung's twenty-five years, a time of greater relative stability, than in Li-tsung's tumultuous forty years.

Li-tsung's death was sudden and unexpected. On 14 November 1264 he was too sick to attend court. Two days later he was dead. His formal testamentary edict appointed his nephew and adoptive heir, Chao Ch'i (Tu-tsung, r. 1264–74), as his successor, and the succession passed without incident. Chia Ssu-tao remained firmly in control at court, enjoying a sumptuous lifestyle and accumulating lavish treasures, and firmly supported by the new young emperor.

For the moment the Mongol pressure on the empire was eased. In 1259 the death of Möngke had led to Mongol civil conflict, and Khubilai, who was responsible for the eastern Mongol domains, was temporarily preoccupied with developments in Inner Asia. But Khubilai's position remained strong. In 1254 he had carried out a campaign to outflank the Sung by driving down the mountains on the western border of Szechwan to conquer the Ta-li realm in Yunnan, and to subjugate northern Vietnam. He had overrun much of Szechwan, and although the Sung had restored control over much of it, the Mongols were still in a powerful position along the Sung western and northern borders. The Sung military had not been overwhelmed, even though the Mongols always held the initiative. In the east, Sung forces had maintained control of the Huai frontier, and they tenaciously held on to the two vital strategic fortresses of Ho-chou3, the key to an eastern advance down the Yangtze River, and Hsiang-yang, which defended against advances from the north into the Hupei region and down the Han River valley.

---

[147] SS 437, p. 12963.

[148] SS 421, p. 12591; HTC (1958) 173, pp. 4725–6. One writer attributes the infrequency of rebel activity to poor documentation for the last half century of Sung rule. However, the Veritable records (shih-lu) for the Li-tsung reign, compiled in 1268, were certainly available to historians compiling the Sung dynastic history; therefore, poor documentation alone cannot explain the dearth of references in official sources to popular rebellions after 1230; see Li Jung-ts'un, "Sung-tai Hu-pei lu liang-chiang ti-ch'ü ti man-luan," Pien-cheng yen-chiu-so nien-pao 9 (1978), pp. 131–81.

[149] SS 417, p. 12508; 454, p. 13346.

CHAPTER 12

THE REIGN OF TU-TSUNG (1264–1274) AND HIS SUCCESSORS TO 1279

Richard L. Davis

DYNASTY BESIEGED

As it approached its end, the Southern Sung dynasty had been weakened by spendthrift emperors, disabled by squabbling bureaucrats, and stretched to the brink of bankruptcy by the costs of wars that had lingered for six decades. By the 1260s a certain disillusionment and fatalism hung over Lin-an. The emperor, Li-tsung (r. 1224–64), seemed to be evading despair by escaping into lechery. His high officials evaded responsibility for their failures by engaging in political vendettas. Attempts at reviving economic prosperity through government initiatives had lost their appeal after several disastrous failures. The active pursuit of peace was similarly abandoned. Adding to this malaise was the inability of the Chao imperial line to provide suitable heirs on a regular basis.

Three of the six Southern Sung emperors before 1275 did not produce a son who survived him, and this lack of patrilineal succession necessitated the adoption of sons from less prestigious branches of the imperial clan. Kao-tsung, Ning-tsung, and Li-tsung all had lengthy reigns that began in early adulthood and continued for three decades or more, yet they all died without sons to succeed them. Hsiao-tsung, Kuang-tsung, and Tu-tsung (r. 1264–74) were succeeded by infant sons who were ineffectual rulers. Historical records provide few clues as to why sons were in short supply. What is known is that the absence of a proper heir, namely the son of the emperor's primary wife, created political instability at the time of succession.

Li-tsung was infamous for his unruly passions. His special favor toward con-sorts Chia and Yen may have been, for court observers, pardonable excesses. His indiscretions such as cavorting with common street prostitutes and entertaining Buddhist nuns in the palace were not. These liaisons reflected an obsession with the opposite sex and compromised the majesty of the throne. The obsession did not yield its usual fruit, an abundance of sons who would have been potential heirs. No children were born to him and Empress Hsieh. Lesser consorts gave birth to four boys, but they all died relatively young.[1] Li-tsung had a daughter, born to his favored Consort Chia, whom he reportedly loved immensely, but the daughter died at age twenty-one.

In the 1240s, roughly twenty years into the reign and as Li-tsung approached his forties, pressure emerged from the bureaucracy for Li-tsung to adopt one or several imperial clansmen in preparation for the eventual nomination of an heir. The emperor had agreed to bring selected young clansmen into the palace for special instruction. He would go no further. Apparently still in good health, he probably felt no compelling reason for haste. In 1253, as he approached fifty, the pressure for an heir intensified. He elevated one of those youths, the only one known to have entered the palace in the 1240s, to the status of imperial son (*huang-tzu*). The nomination generated tension at court. The nominee, Chao Ch'i (b. 1240), was the emperor's nephew, born to his younger brother, Chao Yü-jui. Li-tsung and Chao Yü-jui shared a common set of parents, so the blood ties between Li-tsung and Chao Ch'i were close. The adoption of nephews was common within the Chao imperial family, and there was precedent for the action. Yet questions about the legitimacy of Chao Ch'i detracted from his desirability as a candidate.

Chao Ch'i was probably born to one of Chao Yü-jui's secondary wives, and adopted by another, no doubt Chao Yü-jui's primary wife.[2] With concubines generally of lower social standing, their offspring tended to have a diminished status. Genealogy also posed problems in that Chao Ch'i descended from the line of Chao Te-chao, the Sung founder T'ai-tsu's second son, like Li-tsung himself and in contrast to the preceding three rulers, who had descended from Chao Te-fang, T'ai-tsu's fourth son. Some at court may have preferred, to the extent that adoption was necessary anyway, for the emperor to revert back to the line of earlier emperors, which in effect would undo the intervention by Shih Mi-yüan in 1224. This would require the emperor to abandon his own nephew in favor of more distant kin descended from earlier emperors. Li-tsung did not do this. There also were other more sinister concerns. The Sung dynasty had experienced several cases of familial struggles over the throne, either between father and son or between brothers. With Chao Yü-jui still living in nearby Shao-hsing, there was the potential threat of conflict should he develop greater political ambitions and seek to overthrow his son Chao Ch'i.

---

[1] On the succession affair, see T'o-t'o et al., eds., *Sung shih* [hereafter *SS*] (1345; Peking, 1977) 42, pp. 817, 820; 43, p. 847; 248, pp. 8789–90; Chao Hsi-nien, *Chao-shih tsu-p'u* [Academia Sinica, Fu Ssu-nien Library, rare edition] (Hong Kong, 1937) 1, pp. 41a, 69a; John W. Chaffee, *Branches of heaven: A history of the imperial clan of Sung China* (Cambridge, Mass., 1999), pp. 216, 243.

[2] K'o Wei-ch'i, *Sung-shih hsin-pien* (1557; Shanghai, 1936) 14, p. 52b; Ch'ien Shih-sheng, *Nan Sung shu* (c. 1590; n.p., 1792) 6, p. 1a. Most sources intentionally avoid discussion of the emperor's maternity; see *SS* 46, p. 891; Chao, *Chao-shih tsu-p'u* 1, p. 69b; Pi Yüan, *Hsü Tzu-chih t'ung-chien* [hereafter *HTC* (1958)] [*Te-yü-t'ang tsang-pan* 1801 ed.] (1792; Peking, 1958) 178, p. 4853.

Some officials had suggested that adopting the son of a dead clansman would be a safer choice. Li-tsung dismissed the idea that Chao Yü-jui posed a threat, no doubt concluding that he understood his brother's character better than the bureaucrats. With historical hindsight, we know his faith to be justified, for Chao Yü-jui never developed imperial ambitions.

The bureaucracy was also concerned about the abilities and training of the next emperor. Chief Councilor Wu Ch'ien, with reference to the succession, is reported to have said: "I lack the talent of Shih Mi-yüan and Prince Chung [Chao Ch'i] lacks the good fortune of Your Majesty."[3] The statement, made while the now adopted son, Chao Ch'i, had yet to be installed as heir apparent, came without explanation. But we can see that Wu Ch'ien had created a complex reference that compares his own humility with respect to the long-deceased Shih Mi-yüan, still highly regarded by Li-tsung, and the expectation that Chao Ch'i would be ill equipped, either by nature or by circumstances, to confront the difficulties of succession in a way that Li-tsung was not. However it was interpreted at court, the quote leaves little doubt that Wu Ch'ien anticipated an uneasy transfer of power following Li-tsung's death. Four decades earlier, on the eve of Ning-tsung's death in 1224, Chief Councilor Shih Mi-yüan had engineered, reportedly at the emperor's instructions, the last-minute replacement of Ning-tsung's adopted son, Chao Hung, and elevated Ning-tsung's nephew, the future Li-tsung, to the throne. The switch might have precipitated a civil war had Shih Mi-yüan not acted with consummate political skill, inasmuch as the emperor was not around to verify the decision. Traditional historians have interpreted Wu Ch'ien's statement a generation later to imply that he opposed the elevation of Chao Ch'i. This would be rather curious. Wu Ch'ien had pressed Li-tsung to name an heir at a time when the only available candidate was Chao Ch'i. The same Wu Ch'ien, by disassociating himself from Shih Mi-yüan's activism, was showing he had no interest in tampering with the line of succession. In this context, Wu Ch'ien may have regarded Li-tsung's procrastination in installing an heir as a threat to the succession of Chao Ch'i, just as decades earlier Ning-tsung's procrastination in the elevation of Chao Hung left him vulnerable to the possible overreach of Shih Mi-yüan. Wu Ch'ien may have wanted to preclude interference in an orderly succession, whether of Chao Ch'i or anyone else.

Chao Ch'i was finally appointed heir apparent (*t'ai-tzu*) in the sixth month of 1260, and his training seems to have been very strict.[4] The councilor of the right, Chia Ssu-tao, is portrayed as fully supportive of the Chao Ch'i nomination, even to the point of personally imploring Li-tsung to act. For

---

[3] On the statement and its significance, see *SS* 418, pp. 12517–19; 45, p. 873; 425, p. 12669; 474, p. 13781; Ch'ien, *Nan Sung shu* 43, p. 12a; 56, p. 2b.

[4] *HTC* (1958) 176, p. 4801.

the eminently practical Chia Ssu-tao, nothing mattered more than a smooth transfer of power. Chao Ch'i, whom Chia had served as tutor, had proven himself both deferential and submissive. By aggressively supporting the young man's advancement, Chia Ssu-tao sought to win his lasting favor, just as Shih Mi-yüan's 1224 intervention won him the enduring goodwill of Li-tsung. Li-tsung suddenly died on 16 November 1264 after only two days of illness, just shy of sixty years old. His throne passed without incident to the twenty-four-year-old Chao Ch'i, known to history as Tu-tsung.

Chao Ch'i is described by authors of the *Sung dynastic history* (*Sung shih*), as being bright, perceptive, and earnest in his studies. These traits had convinced Li-tsung of Chao Ch'i's worthiness to inherit the throne.[5] Such assertions may be little more than perfunctory, a reflection of later historians' unquestioning commitment to defending the imperial institution, a commitment that often entailed compromises in the interest of image building. Nothing in Tu-tsung's later conduct suggested the total absence of such traits, so we may grant some kernel of truth to the description. Nonetheless, much like Li-tsung before him, Tu-tsung's conduct took a bad turn soon after he assumed the reins of power. The once-disciplined Tu-tsung was subsequently accused, among other things, of unconscionable extravagance.[6] He regularly held court feasts on an elaborate scale, paid for increasingly with public funds rather than from his private treasury. Equally alarming was his indiscriminate advancement of meritless kinsmen, his own and those of his empress, to honored titular posts. Such advancements sometimes involved over a hundred individuals at once. Tu-tsung held the elaborate Ming-t'ang (Hall of Brilliance) ceremonies at least twice during his ten-year reign. The cost of the ceremonies, though consider-able, was dwarfed by the cost of the great feasts and generous round of civil service promotions that invariably accompanied the events. Such extravagance implied irresponsibility, an emperor out of touch with the times, insensitive to the plight of his overtaxed and war-weary people.

Tu-tsung also drew censure from later historians and contemporaries for his dependence on Chia Ssu-tao. Chia was a holdover from the previous reign. As councilor of the right since 1259 and the sole councilor after 1260, he was well entrenched before the Tu-tsung accession. Even allowing for any political debt associated with Chia's supporting his 1260 nomination as heir, Tu-tsung's attachment to his councilor seemed excessive. In the case of Li-tsung, favor for Chia Ssu-tao seems to have grown out of his affection for a favorite consort, who was Chia Ssu-tao's elder sister. The two men, being of comparable age

---

[5] *SS* 46, pp. 891–2.

[6] *SS* 46, pp. 895, 897, 898, 900, 903, 904, 918–19; Ch'ien, *Nan Sung shu* 6, p. 5b; *HTC* (1958) 179, p. 4893; 180, pp. 4926–7.

and sharing the same passion for sensual indulgence, had become fast friends. Circumstances surrounding Tu-tsung's favor shown to Chia were entirely different. Twenty-seven years Tu-tsung's senior, Chia Ssu-tao had served him as grand preceptor for four years prior to the 1264 accession. Lacking examination credentials, Chia Ssu-tao had struck most of officialdom as deserving of neither the position nor the respect shown by his imperial student. Tu-tsung, however, attached no importance to Chia's lack of credentials. He had set the entire court on edge by referring to Chia Ssu-tao as teacher, not servant, by rising when Chia Ssu-tao made court appearances, and by kneeling in tears to beseech him to remain in office.[7] This gave Tu-tsung, and indeed the throne itself, an image of subservience. So complete was Tu-tsung's confidence and reliance on Chia Ssu-tao that in 1267 he promoted Chia to esteemed special military councilor (*p'ing-chang chün-kuo chung-shih*), a post Chia retained for the duration of the reign.

Extravagance and dependence aside, perhaps Tu-tsung's most unfortunate shortcoming, by traditional historical accounts, was his overall ambivalence toward the ever-present Mongol threat.[8] The cost of ambivalence was high. Compared with the previous decade, the Tu-tsung years (1264–74) were tranquil. Border hostilities persisted, but on a smaller scale. Natural disasters occurred, but with less damage. Expenditures for war and extravagances undermined the economy, but without completely exhausting imperial treasuries. If Tu-tsung, by making the most of these tranquil times, had made significant progress toward either defeating the Mongols or striking a peace accord with them, or had he solicited and applied solutions to the Sung empire's mounting pile of persistent problems, then his decade-long reign may have renewed confidence in the dynasty and stimulated loyalty among its officials. This is the view of traditional critics, but the reality is that war, peace, conservation, and reform had all been attempted only a few years earlier. The results had been unimpressive at best, and at times were disastrous. Perhaps the conflict and divisiveness of the recent past, more than the emperor's timid personality, explain why Tu-tsung chose to do nothing dramatic in seeking to reverse the situation. These were largely years of maintenance, not years entirely wasted.[9]

Military confrontation: Setting the stage

The overriding concern of the era, for the emperor and officials alike, was border stability. Tu-tsung's decision to retain the services of Chia Ssu-tao may

---

[7] *SS* 418, p. 12524; 474, pp. 13783–4; *HTC* (1958) 178, p. 4879; 179, p. 4897.

[8] *SS* 46, p. 918; K'o, *Sung-shih hsin-pien* 14, p. 54a.

[9] Hu Chao-hsi et al., *Sung Meng (Yüan) kuan-hsi shih* (Ch'eng-tu, 1992), pp. 281–96.

partly have been due to Chia's extensive military experience. The son of a distinguished commander, Chia Ssu-tao himself had emerged late in the Li-tsung reign as civil and military commissioner in the central Sung territories. He had led armies there against the Mongols. His promotion to chief councilor in 1260 was, in theory, a reward for directing the successful defense of Hsiang-yang. Chia Ssu-tao's critics, past and present, have dismissed him as a fraud, someone who exaggerated or misrepresented military feats merely to enhance his political status when, in fact, he cared little for the empire's defense.[10] In this way, an empire that should have been preparing for war was allowed to drift. This charge is similar to the one leveled against Shih Sung-chih a generation earlier, and it is equally groundless.

The Chia Ssu-tao administration invested substantially in the defense of strategic areas. The "Basic Annals" section of the *Sung dynastic history* reports that under Tu-tsung some fourteen million strings of cash were allocated for defense of the Ching-hu region (mostly for Hsiang-yang), another ten million strings for Szechwan (largely its eastern regions, which were still administered by the Sung), and another four million strings for the Huai border area to the east.[11] Concentrated between 1269 and 1273 and apparently intended as a supplement to regional defense allocations, these appropriations were ear-marked for either compensating soldiers or fortifying cities. The court also made a special effort, according to the "Basic Annals," to provide extraordi-nary commendations and material rewards for meritorious service along the border, to heighten the morale of troops. As for military installations, regional governments, often at directives from the Sung court, prepared for war at a frenzied pace.

In the west, administrators at Ho-chou4 were determined to increase agri-cultural productivity and directed soldiers to till the land. They reinforced city walls to reduce vulnerability and built palisades along the Chia-ling River to defend Ho-chou4 against boats approaching from the north. At Ching-chou2 (modern Chiang-ling, Hupei) storehouses were filled with provisions and the able-bodied men recruited for military training. At nearby Ying-chou3, where a new city had been built on the southern side of the Han River, walls were heavily fortified and the riverbanks planted with trees to make access to the shore difficult. The court ordered new walls to be built around Lin-an to

---

[10] *SS* 474, pp. 13780–1; Herbert Franke, "Chia Ssu-tao (1213–1275): A 'bad last minister'?" in *Confucian personalities*, ed. Arthur F. Wright and Denis C. Twitchett (Stanford, Calif., 1962), pp. 217–34, especially pp. 224–5; Richard L. Davis, *Wind against the mountain: The crisis of politics and culture in thirteenth-century China* (Cambridge, Mass., 1996), pp. 42–9.

[11] *SS* 46; Hu et al., *Sung Meng (Yüan) kuan-hsi shih*, pp. 320, 331–7.

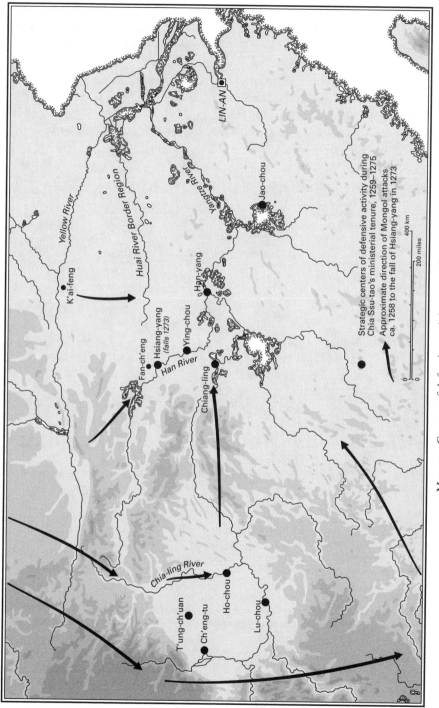

Map 31. Centers of defensive activity, c. 1258–1273.

Strategic centers of defensive activity during Chia Ssu-tao's ministerial tenure, 1259–1275

Approximate direction of Mongol attacks ca. 1258 to the fall of Hsiang-yang in 1273

400 km

200 miles

LIN-AN

Jao-chou

Yellow River

Huai River Border Region

K'ai-feng

Yangtze River

Han-yang

Fan-ch'eng

Hsiang-yang (falls 1273)

Ying-chou

Han River

Chiang-ling

Chia-ling River

T'ung-ch'uan

Ch'eng-tu

Ho-chou

Lu-chou

enhance the security of the emperor and court.[12] The Sung did not stand idly by as the Mongols began to tighten their hold on already conquered territory or heavily besieged border towns. The Mongols' encirclement of Hsiang-yang was maintained for five years, yet the Sung managed repeatedly to penetrate Mongol lines to deliver desperately needed provisions to defenders. In the west, again at Ho-chou4, the Sung frustrated Mongol efforts to build a nearby wall designed to protect its armies from Sung counterattacks.[13] Sung defensive measures were complemented by offensives attempting to regain lost territories. Their counteroffensives against Mongol-held Ch'eng-tu, Lu-chou3, and T'ung-ch'uan in the west of Szechwan, and Jao-chou (in Kiangsi) yielded some gains.[14] These activities reveal not only the Sung court's anticipation of military conflict but also its commitment to doing everything possible to defeat the Mongols. As special military councilor and chief decision maker at court, Chia Ssu-tao deserves some credit for this.

The Sung's problem lay not so much with a lack of preparation as with an inability to keep pace with the preparations being made by a resourceful enemy. The Mongol military machine was formidable, especially under the direction of its shrewd new ruler. Prior to the 1260 accession of Khubilai, the Mongol court, recognizing that its strength lay in cavalry, had attempted a conquest of the Sung from the west, by overrunning Szechwan. This bold strategy had seemed sound, yet conquering the mountainous southwest proved far more exacting than had been envisioned, a struggle underscored by the long and fruitless siege of Ho-chou4, where the previous Mongol ruler, Möngke, had died in 1259. Upon accession, Khubilai initiated a major policy change. The Mongols now focused their resources on central Sung territory and exploited the waterways there to menace Lin-an at closer range.[15] Khubilai chose largely to ignore the Szechwan theater. Indispensable to this new strategy was building a sizable naval force, a somewhat novel idea for the horse-loving Mongols, but an excellent tactic nonetheless. The *Yüan dynastic history* (*Yüan shih*) reports that by the late 1260s the Mongols had begun to train a navy of their own. Recruiting some seventy thousand men from its territory along the Yangtze River, the Mongols built a sizable arsenal of ships and weapons, and collected

---

[12] SS 451, pp. 13280–3; Ch'ien, *Nan Sung shu* 59, p. 14b; 60, p. 3a; Sung Lien et al., *Yüan shih* [Po-na-pen 1930–7 ed.] (1370; Peking, 1976) 127, p. 3100; *HTC* (1958) 179, p. 4895; Hu Chao-hsi et al., *Sung-mo Ssu-ch'uan chan-cheng shih-liao hsüan-pien* (Ch'eng-tu, 1984), p. 156; Li T'ien-ming, *Sung Yüan chan-shih* (Taipei, 1988), pp. 945–52, 965–7.

[13] *HTC* (1958) 179, pp. 4886, 4895; 180, pp. 4915, 4921.

[14] Hu et al., *Sung-mo Ssu-ch'uan*, pp. 138, 547; Li, *Sung Yüan chan-shih*, pp. 1040–2; SS 451, p. 13272; *HTC* (1958) 178, p. 4862.

[15] Hu et al., *Sung Meng (Yüan) kuan-hsi shih*, pp. 313–17; Li, *Sung Yüan chan-shih*, pp. 925–30; Sung et al., *Yüan shih* 128, p. 3125; *HTC* (1958) 178, pp. 4875–6.

provisions from as far as K'ai-feng to store along the central border region.[16] Allocation of more men and matériel followed. To meet the growing need for manpower, Mongol commanders had no hesitation about pillaging. Mongol armies repeatedly descended the Han River and attacked cities and counties in the vicinity of Hsiang-yang, taking in each foray as many as fifty thousand prisoners and hundreds of ships, all, of course, later to be used against the Sung.[17] Men were also snatched up in Szechwan, probably with the same objective.[18] The Mongols acknowledged their own inexperience in naval warfare by incorporating more and more Chinese into their armed forces. Drawing increasingly upon the vast numbers and technical knowledge of the Han Chinese majority, the Mongols waged campaigns in which the Han Chinese in their armies outnumbered Mongols five to one.[19]

Forced assimilation into the Mongol military presented an agonizing challenge to the Sung court. As Mongols carted off a growing number of Han Chinese from the south, the Sung found itself short of prospective soldiers and taxpayers, a problem that undermined the empire's military and economic viability. The immediate military threat proved easier to address than the economic crisis, but the Sung response was desperate. In the case of Hsiang-yang, large numbers of children, probably teenagers, were inducted into regional armies.[20] In Lin-an and its vicinity, all males fifteen and older were pressed into service.[21] Armies contained large numbers of older men as well, as the Sung was forced to delay retirement of soldiers. According to the prefect of Chiang-ling, at least twenty percent of the Sung army was either too young or too old.[22] This is, in all likelihood, a conservative estimate. Another short-term solution to the shortage of men was to shift responsibility for regional defense to informally recruited militias (*min-ping*) or, as was common farther south, to draw upon the large pool of non–Han Chinese groups.[23] The resort to popular militias occurred largely in the early 1270s, toward the close of the dynasty, by which time government fears about controlling such armies were overcome by its desperate need to survive. In its last years, the court of Tu-tsung moved to pardon rather than reprimand deserters. It offered high office and generous rewards in the hope of winning back some of the martial

---

[16] Sung et al., *Yüan shih* 7, pp. 128, 131, 133; 128, p. 3120; *HTC* (1958) 178, pp. 4879–80; 179, p. 4894; 180, p. 4917.

[17] Sung et al., *Yüan shih* 6, pp. 115, 121; 128, p. 3119; *HTC* (1958) 178, p. 4873; 179, pp. 4885, 4902.

[18] Sung et al., *Yüan shih* 7, p. 129.

[19] Sung et al., *Yüan shih* 8, p. 160; *HTC* (1958) 178, pp. 4879–80.

[20] *SS* 422, p. 12619; *HTC* (1958) 180, p. 4920.

[21] *SS* 418, p. 12531.

[22] Ch'ien, *Nan Sung shu* 59, p. 7b.

[23] *SS* 47, p. 935; 418, p. 12534; Ch'ien, *Nan Sung shu* 60, p. 4b; 61, p. 7b; K'o, *Sung-shih hsin-pien* 175, pp. 8b–9a.

talent lost to the enemy.[24] Nothing worked. A practical solution would have involved adoption of enemy tactics by harassing the northern border region, carting off provisions, and snatching up young men for induction into the armed services. The Sung did not do this.

For virtually the entire Tu-tsung reign, both Sung and Mongol military efforts centered on controlling the area surrounding Hsiang-yang, along the central border. The reason was simple. If the Mongols captured the cities along the Han River, the one hundred and eighty–mile stretch from Hsiang-yang to Han-yang, then they could easily gain access to the Yangtze River. Command of the Yangtze would in turn leave Lin-an vulnerable to assault from the west. With the dynasty's fate so closely tied to the fate of Hsiang-yang, the Sung invested heavily in reinforcing cities along the Han River. The Mongols responded with an increasingly unbreakable encirclement of Hsiang-yang in 1268 that continued for another five years.[25] Sung tactics consisted largely of building stronger walls and sabotaging Mongol efforts to navigate the Han River. However, the Mongols were more aggressive and innovative. In addition to a major expansion of naval power that yielded an additional seventy thousand men and five thousand boats, the Mongols built observation towers in the riverbed and forts along the shores, isolating the city from outside information and supplies.

Directing the Mongol offensive was A-chu (Aju, 1234–87), a commander destined to rise to great heights after his stunning successes against the Sung. Fully surrounding Hsiang-yang posed immense obstacles, for the heavily defended city sat on the southern bank of the Han River and, when cut off by land from the south, could often turn for assistance to Fan-ch'eng, a town directly opposite on the Han River's northern bank. The Mongols began a blockade of Fan-ch'eng in 1268 by building more walled barriers and settlements. The Sung responded with more men, and assigned to the defensive campaign three of its most esteemed commanders, Chang Shih-chieh (d. 1279), Hsia Chen, and Li T'ing-chih (d. 1276). It even dispatched, at one point, the assistant commander of the Palace Guard, Fan Wen-hu, to join in the defense. Investments on both sides reached the extent that in 1271 the Sung deployed over a hundred thousand men for a single naval maneuver. Despite investments

[24] SS 46, p. 913.
[25] On the Hsiang-yang conflict, see SS 450, pp. 13248–9; 451, p. 13272; Sung et al., Yüan shih 128, pp. 3119–20; HTC (1958) 178, pp. 4875–6, 4881; 179, pp. 4883, 4886, 4888, 4890, 4898–4909; 180, pp. 4911–17; Fang Chen-hua, "Chia Ssu-tao yü Hsiang Fan chih chan," Ta-lu tsa-chih 21 No. 90.4 (1995), pp. 31–7; Hu et al., Sung Meng (Yüan) kuan-hsi shih, pp. 317–30; Li, Sung Yüan chan-shih, pp. 945–1133; Li Chen et al., Chung-kuo li-tai chan-cheng shih (Taipei, 1968), vol. 11, pp. 416–22; Morris Rossabi, Khubilai khan: His life and times (Berkeley, Calif., 1988), pp. 82–6; Davis, Wind against the mountain, pp. 48–59.

of this magnitude, most battles in the region were won by the northern armies. In late 1272, the Mongols intensified their assaults on Fan-ch'eng while diligently patrolling Han waters to stop the flow of reinforcements from the south. Early in 1273 Fan-ch'eng was overrun and its inhabitants slaughtered. In the third month, Hsiang-yang escaped the same fate when its governor surrendered. With these victories, the Mongols gained their long sought-after objective of gaining easier access to the Hupei region and the south. This loss triggered panic among officials in Lin-an.

Changing political currents at court

The chief councilor, Chia Ssu-tao, dominates most narratives of late Southern Sung history. He was the strongest single political figure at Tu-tsung's court; however, other prominent men were emerging at the time who, disillusioned with Chia Ssu-tao, joined ranks and attempted to terminate his fifteen-year grip on power. Of the elder statesmen who worked to remove Chia from power, Chiang Wan-li (1188–1275), Wang Yüeh (d. 1276), and Wang Ying-lin (1223–96) are the most noteworthy.[26] All three men had held metropolitan posts under Li-tsung, which had given them valuable experience and political exposure. Chiang Wan-li, a graduate of the Imperial University, served at various censorial organizations before returning to the university to become its chancellor. Tu-tsung promoted Chiang to assistant councilor in early 1265, and he rose, in 1269, to serve for roughly a year as chief councilor. For the most part, Chiang Wan-li cooperated with Chia Ssu-tao, rather than boycotting Chia's administration as many others did, but there were tensions between the two men. When Chia Ssu-tao tendered his resignation in 1269, it was perceived as a political ploy designed to enhance his status in the capital. As the weeping emperor began to kneel down to beg him to stay, an astounded and angry Chiang Wan-li forcibly propped up Tu-tsung and spoke harshly to Chia Ssu-tao. Chiang also differed with the special military councilor over Chia's defense plans for Hsiang-yang, which to Chiang contained too much caution and too little commitment. Few in the capital presented as great a political threat to Chia Ssu-tao as Chiang Wan-li. His high-level association with the Imperial University placed Chiang Wan-li in a position to mobilize the influential institution against Chia Ssu-tao, should the need arise.

---

[26] On their careers, see SS 418, pp. 12523–5, 12525–8; 438, pp. 12987–91; HTC (1958) 179, p. 4893; Davis, *Wind against the mountain*, pp. 83–92; Jennifer W. Jay, *A change in dynasties: Loyalism in thirteenth-century China* (Bellingham, Wash., 1991), pp. 13–60; chapters 3 and 4 of Charles B. Langley, "Wang Yinglin (1223–96): A study in the political and intellectual history of the demise of Song" (diss., Indiana University, 1980).

Wang Yüeh, who had received his *chin-shih* in 1219, possessed even better bureaucratic credentials than Chiang Wan-li, having served in several regional as well as metropolitan posts. Wang enjoyed the esteem that came with service to three consecutive emperors over the course of sixty years. A one-time advisor to Tu-tsung before his accession, Wang Yüeh quickly rose after the accession to assistant councilor. Historical records reveal nothing about his relationship with Chia Ssu-tao, but in light of the respect Wang later enjoyed among Chia Ssu-tao's detractors, it is safe to assume that the two were not close political allies.

The third in this group of elder statesmen, Wang Ying-lin, was the most imposing. Having earned his *chin-shih* degree in 1241 and obtained the distinction of passing the "erudite literatus" (*po-hsüeh hung-tz'u*) examination in 1256, he had served as managing officer at the Directorate of Education (*Kuo-tzu chien*), as professor at the Military Academy, and as tutor to the heir apparent, during Li-tsung's reign. Aside from a political career that included distinguished secretarial appointments, he also was one of the most prolific scholars of late Sung times. He was an accomplished lexicographer, classicist, and historian. Like Chiang Wan-li, Wang Ying-lin's dissatisfaction with Chia Ssu-tao stemmed chiefly from the councilor's perceived indifference to the military crisis unfolding at Hsiang-yang.

The presence at court of these highly independent and eminently qualified and experienced officials denied Chia Ssu-tao the political monopoly that his critics often associate with his tenure. But although Tu-tsung always had alternative sources of advice, in the end he gave greatest credence to the counsel of the individual who was least qualified academically. Yet after 1268, Chia Ssu-tao, the man most trusted by the emperor, was in semiretirement, and was required to attend court only once every six days and only once every ten days after 1270. Given this arrangement, it is easy to see how the court gave the appearance of being indifferent to the military menace in the north. Such perceptions may have tormented the elder statesman, but they incited great passions among the younger generation of aspiring officials. In many cases, these passionate officials were men born and raised under conditions of war, men who, after nearly forty-five years, still saw no end in sight.

Among the more prominent, and eventually most controversial, within this younger group was Ch'en I-chung (*chin-shih* 1262).[27] Ch'en, whose father was a clerk, was born in humble circumstances in modern Wen-chou. He studied at the Imperial University until 1256, when he was banished from the capital for having joined five other students in publicly denouncing the authoritarian

---

[27] *SS* 418, pp. 12529–32; *HTC* (1958) 175, p. 4764; Davis, *Wind against the mountain*, pp. 63–94.

Ting Ta-ch'üan. Permitted to return during Chia Ssu-tao's administration, Ch'en I-chung then placed second in the palace examination of 1262, and was conferred *chin-shih* status. He served for most of Tu-tsung's reign away from the capital, but as a once-persecuted critic of an unpopular autocrat, Ch'en enjoyed a considerable reputation in Lin-an and played a leading role in political affairs in the last five years of the Sung dynasty.

Also commanding a considerable measure of respect among officials in the capital was Ch'en Wen-lung (1232–77).[28] A Fu-chou native who had studied for a time at the Imperial University, Ch'en Wen-lung had taken top honors among the *chin-shih* graduates of 1269. Serving as a censor under Chia Ssu-tao, he maintained a good measure of independence thanks to the deference accorded to him for his high ranking in the examinations. After the fall of Hsiang-yang in early 1273, tensions among high-ranking officials mushroomed into confrontation. Ch'en Wen-lung, as censor, questioned the chief councilor's judgment in appointing inexperienced men to important military posts and in pardoning cowardly commanders who had recently abandoned their posts under enemy pressure. When Chia Ssu-tao had Ch'en banished in the summer of 1273, Ch'en departed Lin-an with the sympathy of many colleagues, for he had dared to express precisely the lack of confidence in Chia Ssu-tao's leadership that many felt.

Also among this list of passionate officials was Wen T'ien-hsiang (1236–83), a native of Chi-chou3 (modern Chi-an in Kiangsi).[29] Wen had earned his *chin-shih* credentials, also with top honors, in 1256, and had impressed Chief Examiner Wang Ying-lin with his stunning sense of history and civic duty. Wen was imbued with idealism and a zeal to revitalize the dynasty, but from the outset of his career he was on a collision course with the men who dominated the court. In Wen's view, these men were pragmatists prone to compromise. In 1259, when the eunuch Tung Sung-ch'en proposed that the capital be moved to a safer location along the coast, a furious Wen T'ien-hsiang demanded Tung's immediate execution. Wen T'ien-hsiang resented the favored standing of Chia Ssu-tao at court. New tensions surfaced in the 1260s, and Wen T'ien-hsiang, under censorial indictment, was relieved of his

[28] SS 451, pp. 13278–80; Ch'ien, *Nan Sung shu* 59, pp. 5a–6a; *HTC* (1958) 180, p. 4919; *Chao chung lu* [Shou-shan ko ts'ung-shu 1922 ed.] (c. 1290; Taipei, 1968), pp. 31a–32a.

[29] For biographical information, see SS 418, pp. 12533–40; *Chao chung lu*, pp. 17a–22b; *HTC* (1958) 175, p. 4789; 179, pp. 4895–6; Wen T'ien-hsiang, *Wen T'ien-hsiang ch'üan-chi*, ed. Lo Hung-hsien, (1560; Shanghai, 1936) 17, pp. 443–68; William A. Brown, *Wen T'ien-hsiang: A biographical study of a Sung patriot* (San Francisco, 1986), pp. 95–225; chapter 5 of Davis, *Wind against the mountain*; Horst Huber, "Wen T'ien-hsiang, 1236–1283: Vorstufen zum Verständnis seines Lebens" (diss., Universität zu München, 1983), summarized in Horst Huber, "Wen T'ien-hsiang," in *Sung biographies*, ed. Herbert Franke (Wiesbaden, 1976), vol. 3, pp. 1187–201.

metropolitan responsibilities and for most of Tu-tsung's reign served in various regional posts. His reputation for no compromise in domestic politics and no capitulation in foreign affairs made him a popular figure among Chia Ssu-tao's critics.

All six men, each eminently qualified for high office, were respected within Lin-an's growing cohort of disgruntled officials, and especially within the Imperial University. The younger three tended to be more vociferous. Throughout their careers, Ch'en I-chung and Wen T'ien-hsiang petitioned for the execution of officials who, in their estimation, had betrayed the throne through their ill-conceived advice. Execution was not in Sung times the usual punishment for poor political counsel, the precedent of Han T'o-chou's overthrow notwithstanding. That radical views of this sort gained greater currency in these last years of Tu-tsung's reign reflects the desperation that prevailed. There was a growing conviction among the idealists that, after years of toying with grave problems, only radical measures could save the dynasty. Under these conditions, Chia Ssu-tao became an easy scapegoat. Defeats on the borders were blamed on ministerial neglect, not on the superiority of the enemy forces and tactics. Defections of military and civilian officers in outlying regions were blamed on ministerial misuse of rewards and punishments, not on fatigue following decades of fighting. The emperor's inclination toward licentiousness was blamed on his councilor's evil influence, not on the predilections of the emperor himself.

This is not to say that this dissatisfaction was unjustified. Chia Ssu-tao may not have set out to destroy the dynasty, but certain of his actions had precisely that effect and can be explained only in terms of gross lack of judgment. For example, the peace envoy Hao Ching, dispatched south by Khubilai soon after his accession as khaghan in 1260, was taken captive at the border and remained in captivity for over fifteen years. The act is viewed by traditional historians as having been a ploy by Chia Ssu-tao to conceal the terms of a secret agreement containing embarrassing concessions he is alleged to have struck with the Mongols at the height of their 1259 campaign against the Sung. The charge is hard to credit and has been refuted by modern scholarship.[30] Since imprisoning an envoy for fifteen years only draws attention to the prisoner and the circumstances surrounding his detention, it would have been far easier simply to refuse him entry at the border on technical grounds, such as the use of improper documents or incorrect protocol. Other reasons for imprisonment were available as well. Sources suggest that Hao Ching had assisted northern

[30] Sung et al., *Yüan shih* 157, p. 3708; *HTC* (1958) 176, pp. 4796, 4802; Franke, "Chia Ssu-tao (1213–1275)," pp. 226–9; Hu et al., *Sung Meng (Yüan) kuan-hsi shih*, pp. 260–5; Davis, *Wind against the mountain*, pp. 30, 104–5.

rulers in drafting maps of the south for use by military strategists, so the Sung could have held him as a spy. Although Khubilai inquired repeatedly about Hao Ching's whereabouts, he did not press aggressively for his return. His formal declaration of war against the Sung in 1274 alluded to the envoy's capture, but the two actions were separated by fifteen years and Mongol designs on the Sung did not require a provocation. The detention of Hao Ching in effect served to impede further peace talks. Chia Ssu-tao's motive may have been the naive hope that Hao Ching would be a bargaining chip in some future negotiations between the two sides, but by initiating no new negotiations, he gained nothing with the envoy's prolonged detention. All the while, Chia's standing at home declined, for the action appeared senseless to contemporaries as well.[31]

Although Chia Ssu-tao is portrayed by later writers as abjectly interested in peace, under his leadership diplomatic activity was at its lowest since war with the Mongols began in the 1230s. The two sides, locked in conflict, concentrated instead on building up their arsenals. Khubilai was generally uninterested in peace, although he proclaimed to Sung residents in the summer of 1269 that he desired to avoid further warfare.[32] This proclamation coincided, however, with increasing pressure applied by his armies to the Han River valley and the declaration was most likely used as a ploy to undermine Sung resolve. Khubilai was consciously enhancing his political image by appearing less martial, as evidenced by his elaborate renovations of Confucian temples at Ch'ü-fu (in Shantung) and Shang-tu (in Ch'ang-an), so his overtures of peace may have grown out of efforts to present himself as transcending his warrior origins. At the end of 1272, when the military commissioner for the Ching-hu circuit, Li T'ing-chih, dispatched his own emissary to Mongol territory, the envoy was politely but promptly returned. Yüan sources allude to negotiations about border trade, but these did not abate the heightened level of hostilities.[33] During the prolonged siege of Hsiang-yang, a negotiated settlement of some sort to maintain the autonomy of the south may have been on the Sung agenda, but it held no appeal to Khubilai.

Failure either to repulse the Mongols at Hsiang-yang or to entice them into a peace treaty could have been enough to topple Chia Ssu-tao's administration, but Tu-tsung's confidence in Chia seemed unshakable. However, in 1274 the convergence of several disasters finally toppled Chia Ssu-tao. The first of these setbacks was the escalation of Mongol attacks. Early in the year, Khubilai had approved the mobilization of an additional one hundred thousand men for a

[31] *HTC* (1958) 180, pp. 4927–8.

[32] *HTC* (1958) 179, p. 4868.

[33] Sung et al., *Yüan shih* 7, pp. 143, 144; Hu et al., *Sung Meng (Yüan) kuan-hsi shih*, pp. 266–9.

new campaign against the Sung. Once his forces had captured Hsiang-yang, he decided to exploit the Sung's vulnerability.[34] A planned campaign against Japan was postponed, and this freed more resources for the southern offensive against the Sung. The declaration of full-scale war came in the sixth lunar month, and the principal thrust of the attacks, initiated three months later, was down the Han River valley. A-chu and Bayan of the Barin tribe, Khubilai's chief commanders, led the campaign.[35] Their first target was Ying-chou3, a sizable city roughly sixty miles down the Han River from Hsiang-yang. Sung military investment in the area had been substantial, and the Mongol armies faced formidable resistance. The old city, north of the river, had walls made of stone and the new city, on the southern bank, was heavily fortified.[36] Mongol armies attacked Ying-chou3 from the north by water and from the south by land. Chang Shih-chieh, one of the three prized commanders sent to defend the region, offered stiff resistance, forcing Mongol troops to move farther down the Han River to storm Hsin-ch'eng, Fu-chou3, the sister cities Han-k'ou and Han-yang, and then O-chou (modern Wu-ch'ang). All five cities fell by the end of the lunar year, early 1275, followed soon thereafter by Huang-chou and Ch'i-chou2. This victory gave the Mongols their long-awaited access to the Yangtze. Their horses were now able to cross the river by boat, and they were positioned to move east toward the Sung capital, only some three hundred and fifty miles away. Unfortunately for the Sung, the advancing Mongol army was not its only problem.

A second crisis had struck in the summer of 1274, scarcely a month after Khubilai announced his new campaign. The thirty-four-year-old Tu-tsung fell victim to a chronic infection and died. Historical records reveal nothing about the nature of his illness, nor is there any indication of a recent decline in health. It apparently caught everyone by surprise. The immediate banishment of his doctor under a cloud of controversy suggests that the malady grew out of control only because of ill-advised medical care.[37] Tu-tsung's second son, Chao Hsien, the only male born to him and Empress Ch'üan, succeeded him on the ninth day of the seventh lunar month in 1274. The new emperor was not yet four years old, prompting requests that Dowager Empress Hsieh, the widow of Li-tsung, assist in governing from behind the bamboo screen. Only once during the Northern Sung, under Che-tsung (r. 1085–1100), had a

[34] Sung et al., *Yüan shih* 8, p. 153; 128, pp. 3120–1.

[35] For a brief explanation of the Barin tribe, see Hsiao Ch'i-ch'ing, "Bayan," in *In the service of the Khan: Eminent personalities of the early Mongol-Yüan period (1200–1300)*, ed. Igor de Rachewiltz et al. (Wiesbaden, 1993), p. 584.

[36] Sung et al., *Yüan shih* 127, p. 3100; *HTC* (1958) 180, pp. 4929–35; Li et al., *Sung Yüan chan-shih*, pp. 1135–63; Li, *Chung-kuo li-tai chan-cheng shih* (1968), vol. 11, pp. 426–9.

[37] *SS* 46, p. 918; K'o, *Sung-shih hsin-pien* 14, pp. 3a–b.

young child inherited the throne. The power vacuum this created had proved highly destabilizing even then, at a time of relative peace. This time, with the Southern Sung dynasty facing a major invasion from the west, the succession of a powerless child had graver consequences. If Tu-tsung either had been childless or had his sickness lasted longer, he and his advisors could have selected a more competent heir through adoption, but this did not happen. Political instability at the apex of Sung power was certain to undermine an already weak decision-making process and exacerbate lethal tensions among rival civil servants, men who did not, in the end, rise above their own partisan interests for the sake of the empire.

A DYNASTY IN RETREAT

The reign of Chao Hsien (1274–1276)

Tu-tsung was survived by three infant sons: Chao Shih (1269–78), born to Consort Yang (1244–79); Chao Hsien (1271–unknown), born to Empress Ch'üan (1241–1309); and Chao Ping (1272–9), born to Consort Yü.[38] Prior to Tu-tsung's death, the emperor had not formally installed any one of them as heir. According to the *Sung dynastic history*, the middle son succeeded "in accordance with Tu-tsung's last testament." Secondary sources from the Ming and Ch'ing dynasties generally insist that the accession of Chao Hsien was fixed only after the death of Tu-tsung and that most court officials preferred the older son, Chao Shih. But Chia Ssu-tao supported Chao Hsien, and Chia's candidate prevailed.[39] The imperial testament (*i-chao*) was, in all likelihood, drafted by both Grand Dowager Empress Hsieh and Empress Ch'üan in consultation with chief councilors, including Chia Ssu-tao, soon after the emperor's unexpected death. The elevation of Chao Hsien was all but inevitable as he was the only son born to the emperor's primary wife, Empress Ch'üan. To vilify Chia Ssu-tao, as traditional historians do, for favoring the second son merely to ensure his own continued dominance, borders on the absurd. Chia could have just as easily dominated Tu-tsung's eldest son, Chao Shih, who was only five years old at the time. This is not to say that Chia Ssu-tao acted altogether selflessly, for support for Chao Hsien could have been used as a means to consolidate his relationship with the young Dowager Empress Ch'üan. The senior dowager

---

[38] *SS* 243, pp. 8658–62; Ch'ien, *Nan Sung shu* 7, pp. 6b–8b; Chao, *Chao shih tsu-p'u* 1, pp. 69a–70a. According to *SS* 46, p. 901, Tu-tsung had two other sons, both born in 1268, and both of whom apparently died early. A genealogy for the Chao clan (*Chao shih tsu-p'u*) makes no reference to them, and the naming pattern for the two is inconsistent with that for the other sons.

[39] *SS* 417, p. 921; Ch'ien, *Nan Sung shu* 6, p. 12a; K'o, *Sung shih hsin-pien* 14, p. 7a; *HTC* (1958) 180, pp. 4926–7.

empress, Hsieh Ch'iao, being nearly seventy and in ill health, could not be expected to hold onto her regency for long and the now Dowager Empress Ch'üan was her inevitable successor. A timely alliance with Dowager Empress Ch'üan certainly had its political utility, and the sixty-one-year-old Chia Ssu-tao, with his long history of close ties to palace women, probably understood this better than most court officials.

Dowager Empress Hsieh (1210–83), the empress of Li-tsung since 1230, was daughter of Hsieh Shen-fu, a chief councilor during the early reign of Ning-tsung.[40] Despite a forty-year marriage, she had the misfortune, like many Sung empresses before her, of never enjoying her husband's affection. Li-tsung had initially favored Consort Chia, and later Consort Yen, and had partaken in many less orthodox affairs. Li-tsung appears largely to have neglected his primary wife, whose betrothal had been arranged by his adoptive mother, Dowager Empress Yang2. Dowager Empress Hsieh, although from an accomplished scholar-official family, had meticulously avoided involvement in political matters during her husband's long reign, with the notable exception of voicing opposition to the 1259 proposal to relocate the capital along the coast. Tu-tsung's death and the accession of Chao Hsien had thrust her, as senior dowager empress, into the political arena, although she reportedly accepted her new prominence with great reluctance. Over the last few years of the dynasty, Grand Dowager Empress Hsieh became a moderating force at court. Far more responsible than either her husband or son, she cooperated with the civil service and shunned extreme political positions. Assertive when the need arose, she accepted counsel only after critical assessment, without alienating officials through arbitrary decisions. Not given to political vendettas, she could even be, much like her husband, magnanimous. For example, Chia Ssu-tao was the brother of the woman whose favor had denied the dowager empress Li-tsung's affections, but Dowager Empress Hsieh bore him no grudge. On the contrary, as regent she chose to retain Chia Ssu-tao and often proved his most loyal supporter before critics. Her chief concern was continuity and stability, and she showed little interest in replacing councilor-level officers.

Changes in bureaucratic leadership were nonetheless underway in 1274, even before Dowager Empress Hsieh's regency. The rising star of the era was Ch'en I-chung, the one-time university student with a reputation for uninhibited candor. From vice-minister of personnel, he rose to Bureau of Military Affairs executive in 1273. Late that year he became assistant councilor with concurrent authority over the Bureau of Military Affairs. Writers of the

[40] SS 243, pp. 8658–60; Chao, *Chao shih tsu-p'u* 1, p. 69a. For greater detail on the dowager empress's regency, see Davis, *Wind against the mountain*, pp. 32–42.

Sung dynastic history tried to portray Ch'en as a secret ally of Chia Ssu-tao and, despite Ch'en's militant rhetoric, as an utterly spineless character.[41] This characterization seems far-fetched. In 1273, while still with the Ministry of Personnel, Ch'en I-chung challenged the wisdom of Chia Ssu-tao's pardon of Fan Wen-hu, the commander who deserted at Hsiang-yang, and demanded Fan's execution.[42] Ch'en's actions, both then and later, confirmed that Ch'en I-chung considered the empire's inability to repel Mongol forces to be related to the inadequate discipline of commanders, a problem that Chen blamed on Chia Ssu-tao's tendency to compromise. Ch'en I-chung may have been unable to live up to the high standard he set for others, he may have lacked the courage to be the militant that he aspired to be, but this hardly makes him a Chia Ssu-tao partisan. Not only did Ch'en I-chung believe his own rhetoric, contemporaries apparently did as well. Wang Yüeh, for example, who had risen in late 1274 to become chief councilor of the left, generally sympathized with Ch'en I-chung despite their personal differences. The new councilor of the right, Chang Chien2, was more nondescript in character. A former subordinate of Wang Yüeh at the military bureau, he probably owed his promotion to Wang Yüeh's ascent.[43] Such promotions, made by the empress but probably with input from Chia Ssu-tao, suggest that the court, despite the handicaps of a heldover special councilor and a boy emperor, continued to attract politically diverse talent. Grand Dowager Empress Hsieh was at least as successful as her stepson, Tu-tsung, at diversifying the civil service at the top, and instilling in politically alienated officials some hope for change. This was no mean accomplishment in such difficult times.

Dowager Empress Hsieh, while recognizing the dynasty's great needs, saw no reason to abandon Chia Ssu-tao. Her support left only one person capable of bringing down the special councilor, the special councilor himself. The catalyst for this event was a succession of military setbacks in 1274–5. As military coordinator, Chia Ssu-tao's judgment had come into question some years earlier when he had reassigned his brother-in-law Fan Wen-hu, a commander for the lower Huai, to the Ching-hu region to bolster the forces at Hsiang-yang.[44] Leading an army of reportedly a hundred thousand men, Fan had been defeated by the Mongol commander A-chu in the summer of 1271. Hsiang-yang held out, but eventually fell in 1273. Most of Fan's soldiers had perished, and he came perilously close to meeting the same fate himself. The Sung court decided,

[41] *SS* 418, p. 12530.
[42] *HTC* (1958) 180, p. 4919.
[43] *SS* 418, pp. 12528–9.
[44] *HTC* (1958) 179, p. 4903; Li et al., *Sung Yüan chan-shih*, pp. 986–8, 1179–82; Li et al., *Chung-kuo li-tai chan-cheng shih* (1968), vol. 11, p. 419.

despite the magnitude of the defeat, on a demotion of only one rank, and Fan
was reassigned as prefect of An-ch'ing, a strategic city east of Hsiang-yang
on the Yangtze River. The lax discipline and the implicit nepotism in Chia's
handling of Fan's dismissal enraged Ch'en I-chung and others. Chia Ssu-tao's
credibility suffered further in early 1275 when the same Fan Wen-hu, offering
no resistance, surrendered An-ch'ing to the Mongols.[45] Less than two weeks
later came the most paralyzing defeat of the entire Southern Sung.

The military setbacks of late 1274 had so undermined morale in the south
that something dramatic needed to be done to stem the enemy's tide of victory,
and to restore confidence in the dynasty and its armies. Chia Ssu-tao, despite
his sixty-one years, decided to direct personally a vast and desperate campaign
aimed at driving the Mongols back across the Yangtze and Han rivers.[46]
Chia chose to focus his main counterattack on Chiang-chou, a city along the
northwestern tip of P'o-yang Lake that had recently fallen to the Mongols.
Clearly designed as a show of Sung strength, the plan involved spending some
100,000 ounces of gold, 500,000 ounces of silver, and 10 million strings of cash
on the counteroffensive. To further intimidate the Mongol troops, the court
reportedly placed under the general command of Chia Ssu-tao a million men,
mostly naval forces. Intimidation of the enemy entailed some exaggeration
of troop levels, so the boast of a million men cannot be taken at face value.
Other sources inform us that the entire Sung army contained no more than
700,000 regulars, and surely the Sung court did not commit its whole army in
a single campaign. Yüan sources suggest the Sung invested 130,000 men in
the battle, probably a more accurate estimate.[47] Even so, 130,000 represented
nearly one-fifth of the Sung army, an indication of the importance attached
to this particular campaign. Most of the troops were placed under the direct
command of Sun Hu-ch'en (d. 1276), who quickly came under attack from the
combined forces of Bayan and A-chu along the Yangtze River near Ting-chia-
chou downstream from Ch'ih-chou (modern Kuei-ch'ih, in Anhwei). Sun's men
bore the brunt of the Mongol counterattack, and when they were defeated the
entire campaign was doomed. Chia Ssu-tao, himself only twenty-five miles to
the east of Wu-hu on the Yangtze River, responded by fleeing downstream
to Yang-chou. With the defeat so decisive, Chia Ssu-tao was more than just
personally humiliated; the prospect of Mongol armies pressing east toward
the Sung capital seemed imminent. Chia proposed, apparently in an urgent

[45] HTC (1958) 181, p. 4939. Davis, Wind against the mountain, pp. 53–4, 76–7.

[46] On the campaign, see Sung et al., Yüan shih 8, p. 162; 127, pp. 3104–5; 128, p. 3122; HTC (1958)
    180, pp. 4934–5; 181, pp. 4942–3; Liu Min-chung, P'ing Sung lu [Shou-shan ko ts'ung-shu 1922 ed.]
    (1304; Taipei, 1968) 1, pp. 8b–9a; Hu et al., Sung Meng (Yüan) kuan-hsi shih, pp. 368–74; Li, Sung Yüan
    chan-shih, pp. 1182–9; Li, Chung-kuo li-tai chan-cheng shih (1968), vol. 11, pp. 429–31.

[47] Ch'ien, Nan Sung shu 59, p. 7b; Sung et al., Yüan shih 127, p. 3104.

letter sent from Yang-chou, that the court be moved to some more defensible location.[48]

The option of relocating the capital had already been considered intermittently for many years, indeed since the outset of the Southern Sung period. A coastal location such as Ming-chou (modern Ning-po) seemed preferable to many because it was farther east and afforded easy access to the ocean, should flight become necessary. With the Mongols now having invaded the Chiangnan East circuit, they were within striking distance of Lin-an via Wu-hu. Chia Ssu-tao's proposal sparked heated debate. Chief Councilor Wang Yüeh offered his vigorous opposition, but Assistant Councilor Ch'en I-chung was so outraged that he demanded death for Chia Ssu-tao,[49] who appears not yet to have returned to Lin-an. Dowager Empress Hsieh did not endorse relocation of the capital for fear of "disturbing the people." With Chia Ssu-tao not on hand to make his case, the idea went no further. A forgiving dowager empress firmly rejected calls for Chia's execution. Noting his years of meritorious service, she ordered his dismissal in the second lunar month of 1275. The purge of an unpopular Chia Ssu-tao was hardly sufficient to restore the civil service's confidence in the dynasty.

In the early months of 1275 the important Yangtze cities of O-chou, Huang-chou, Ch'i-chou2, Chiang-chou, and An-ch'ing had been captured by the Mongols. A few months after this, the defeat of Chia Ssu-tao's forces at Wu-hu touched off the surrenders of over a dozen more major prefectures in central and eastern Sung territory.[50] These included Jao-chou, Lung-hsing2, Lin-chiang, Wu-wei, T'an-chou, and most of the important cities along the lower reaches of the Huai River and the stretch of the Yangtze River around P'o-yang Lake. The Mongols concentrated on capturing larger cities, and by late spring, they began to seize strategically vital cities in the east as well, including Ch'u-chou, Chien-k'ang (Nan-ching), Chen-chiang, Ch'ang-chou, Wu-hsi, and P'ing-chiang (Su-chou). The Sung also suffered defeats at the Ning-kuo and Kuang-te commanderies, roughly sixty miles northwest of Lin-an. Most of these cities fell without offering any significant resistance. They were relinquished by civilian or military officers who, when not surrendering to the Mongols, had simply fled their posts. Desertion was not confined to the regional level; it infected the capital as well.

Earlier in 1275, when defeat at O-chou had posed a direct threat to the capital, the government issued a crisis call to regional officials and military commanders. The call to "rally on behalf the emperor" (ch'in-wang) drew responses

[48] SS 47, p. 926; 474, p. 13786; Ch'ien, Nan Sung shu 6, p. 7a.
[49] SS 474, p. 13786; HTC (1958) 181, pp. 4944, 4946; chapter 3 of Davis, Wind against the mountain.
[50] Li, Sung Yüan chan-shih, pp. 1178–80, 1189–96.

from only a few, among them Wen T'ien-hsiang, then prefect of Kan-chou (in southern Kiangsi); Li T'ing-chih, commissioner for the Huai region; and Chang Shih-chieh, a leading commander for the Ching-hu North frontier.[51] The court's agonizing sense of abandonment grew all the more acute a few months later, when leading metropolitan officials began to flee. Councilor of the Right Chang Chien2, nervous about the Mongol advance and nettled by persistent squabbles between Wang Yüeh and Ch'en I-chung, abandoned his office and fled the capital. Following his lead were three high-level executives at the Bureau of Military Affairs, a ranking censorial official, and numerous circuit-level chief administrators.[52]

These internal and external pressures aggravated tensions at court. Once again a call to relocate the capital was made, this time by Han Chen2, chief commander of the Palace Guard and an alleged ally of Chia Ssu-tao. An irascible, seemingly crazed Ch'en I-chung responded by secretly ordering Han Chen2's death by bludgeoning.[53] Later it was charged that Han Chen2 had intended to press the relocation issue by force of arms, in effect, making the court the hostage of its generals. This charge against Han Chen2 was apparently intended to justify the actions of Ch'en I-chung, who was new to power and zealous at guarding it. Ch'en I-chung may have intended to put an end to defeatism at the capital, but his methods invited more instability. Apart from aggravating an already ill-humored Wang Yüeh, the incident touched off a nighttime mutiny in the Palace Guard. Furious subordinates of Han Chen2 marched in protest on the southern gate of the imperial city and pelted the palaces inside the walls with incendiary devices. The mutiny was quelled by the next morning, but at the cost of a sizable number of guardsmen who defected to the Mongols.

Dowager Empress Hsieh's frustration was captured rather succinctly in a palace notice posted on her orders. It read: "Our dynasty for over three hundred years has treated scholar-officials with propriety (*li3*). While the new successor [Chao Hsien] and I have met with assorted family hardships, you subjects both high and low have offered no proposals whatsoever for saving the empire. Within [the capital], officials forsake their commissions and vacate posts. Away [from the capital], responsible officers relinquish their seals and abandon cities. Censorial officers are incapable of investigating and indicting for me, and the two or three at the councilor level cannot lead and direct the

---

[51] *SS* 47, p. 924; 418, p. 12534; 421, p. 12601; 451, p. 13272; Li, *Sung Yüan chan-shih*, pp. 1222–3; chapter 3 of Davis, *Wind against the mountain*.

[52] *SS* 47, p. 928.

[53] *SS* 47, pp. 927, 931; 418, p. 12530; Sung et al., *Yüan shih* 8, p. 163; *HTC* (1958) 181, p. 4947; Davis, *Wind against the mountain*, pp. 72–5.

efforts of the whole. Superficially, they cooperate [with me], but one after the other they flee by night."[54] Her biting rebuke reads as a sad commentary on the breakdown between the beleaguered regent and child-emperor and his court officials.

Desperately trying to restore order in the capital, Dowager Empress Hsieh moved quickly to fill the vacancies created by recent desertions. Chang Chien2, who had fled Lin-an shortly after Chia Ssu-tao's dismissal and who had refused repeated orders to return, fell under the indictment of Censor Wang Ying-lin. Ch'en I-chung replaced him as councilor of the right. The special post of military councilor, formerly held by Chia Ssu-tao, was not for the moment revived. The dowager empress had decided instead to entrust direction of the armed forces to her two chief councilors, Ch'en I-chung and Wang Yüeh. But, Ch'en I-chung had already emerged as the dowager empress's premier court advisor, if only by default. Wang Yüeh may have been the senior statesman, but he had long sought to retire, ostensibly for reasons of health. The court was adamant in refusing the request, in part because it desperately needed continuity at the top of the bureaucracy, and in part because of the negative effect on morale that another executive's departure would have. Only by quietly leaving the capital for his native Shao-hsing did Wang manage, in spring 1275, to negotiate his reassignment as distinguished pacification and bandit-suppressing commissioner for Che-hsi and Chiang-nan East, the metropolitan circuit.[55] Wang's departure, at the height of Lin-an's military crisis, created a political vacuum that was filled by Ch'en I-chung. Wang Yüeh did not disappear altogether, however. In summer 1275, he served briefly as councilor of the left and special military councilor in succession to Chia Ssu-tao. But he and Ch'en I-chung seemed perennially at odds, often belaboring the most trivial of matters, prompting the dowager empress, in July, to dismiss them both. By November, she had recalled Ch'en I-chung as chief councilor. Wang Yüeh died early the next year.

Perhaps under other leadership, the life-or-death struggle might have united Sung officials against the Mongol invasion. But morale continued to sink as Sung officials turned on one another. Ch'en I-chung, in assassinating Han Chen2, had contributed much to the vindictive and murderous climate of the day.[56] Ch'en I-chung had expressed the desire of many in the capital in demanding Chia Ssu-tao's execution, following his fall from power. Wang Ying-lin and Wang Yüeh made similar pleas, and were soon joined by students at Lin-an's three universities, very likely at Wang Yüeh's inspiration.

---

[54] *HTC* (1958) 181, p. 4950; Davis, *Wind against the mountain*, p. 75.
[55] *SS* 418, p. 12527.
[56] *SS* 474, pp. 13786–7; *HTC* (1958) 181, pp. 4945–6, 4948, 4958–9; 182, pp. 4964, 4970.

The court wasted much valuable time and energy debating Chia Ssu-tao's fate. In principle, Dowager Empress Hsieh opposed punishment of any sort, but under mounting pressure she acceded to progressively more severe forms of banishment and the confiscation of Chia family property. Despite her preference for leniency, Chia Ssu-tao was assassinated in October 1275 at Chang-chou (Fu-chien) by the court-designated sheriff charged with his custody. Responsibility for the order remains unclear, although explicit palace authorization for it appears unlikely. The murder contravened Dowager Empress Hsieh's earlier amnesty, and the two councilors who most despised Chia Ssu-tao, Wang Yüeh and Ch'en I-chung, were both temporarily out of office. Later, the court ordered the arrest and imprisonment of the sheriff responsible for the death. The arrest was made personally by Ch'en I-chung, who happened to be visiting the region. Writers of the *Sung dynastic history* implicate Tu-tsung's father, Chao Yü-jui, in Chia's assassination because he had held Chia Ssu-tao personally responsible for his son's poor medical care and untimely death and had decided to exact revenge.[57] Unauthorized and unwarranted, perhaps, but the assassination of Chia Ssu-tao disturbed few bureaucrats. Like Han T'o-chou seven decades earlier, Chia Ssu-tao had become a convenient scapegoat for a time without hope.

More agonizing and potentially destructive than this preoccupation with vendetta, was the inability of Dowager Empress Hsieh's executive officials to cooperate with each other. One possible solution open to the dowager empress was to replace the councilors, but the times were ill suited for overhauling the bureaucracy and the pool of candidates diminished daily as official ranks thinned out. She had ultimately decided to sacrifice the aged Wang Yüeh, at which point Ch'en I-chung was summoned to return to the capital. Ch'en's whereabouts for most of that summer of 1275 are uncertain, as are his motives for staying away. A student at the Metropolitan Academy, purportedly at Wang Yüeh's prompting, launched a caustic assault on Ch'en I-chung's official record, accusing him of being no better than Chia Ssu-tao. In support of Ch'en I-chung, the dowager empress ordered the student arrested.[58] Ch'en's period of withdrawal may have afforded him an opportunity to brood, while demonstrating his value to the empire. Ch'en I-chung lingered in his native Wen-chou and then was in Fu-chou, perhaps working unofficially with coastal defense forces. He returned to Lin-an in the tenth lunar month as councilor of the right. In his absence, Liu Meng-yen had served as chief councilor, but allegations of nepotism drew the censure of Wang Ying-lin and forced Liu into retirement.[59] This left Wang Ying-lin, whose previous indictments of Councilors

[57] *SS* 474, p. 13787; Chaffee, *Branches of heaven*, p. 243.
[58] *HTC* (1958) 181, pp. 4960–1.
[59] *SS* 438, p. 12991.

Chia Ssu-tao, Chang Chien2, and Wang Yüeh had drawn much court attention, as a rising star in Lin-an. Nothing could have pleased Ch'en I-chung
more, for Wang Ying-lin had supported him earlier over the controversial
execution of Han Chen2, and it appeared that Wang and Ch'en shared many
other views. Ch'en I-chung must have also taken heart in the advancement
to assistant councilor of another articulate critic of Chia Ssu-tao's leadership,
Ch'en Wen-lung. Ch'en I-chung thus returned to the capital with a generally supportive body of subordinates and the full confidence of the dowager
empress.

The fall of Lin-an

The summer months of 1275 had brought something of a respite to the Sung
court. Mongol armies, unaccustomed to the humid summers of the south and
taking stock of their recent victories, withdrew from many of the cities recently
conquered in the Sung interior. In early summer, Khubilai had summoned
Bayan north for consultations to Peking and later to Shang-tu. This respite
enabled the Sung to stage something of a rally.

In the strategically vital region of the lower Yangtze River, the Sung recaptured, in whole or in part, Yang-chou, Ch'ang-chou, P'ing-chiang, and Kuang-
te. In central Sung territory, they recovered Jao-chou, O-chou, and many
subprefectures near heavily contested cities.[60] Mongol control in the south
was still firm and extensive, especially in central Sung territory, but Sung
defenders did not remain inactive while the Mongol forces consolidated their
positions. Initially, the Sung court offered a general amnesty to high-level
regional officials who had recently deserted their posts, but when this was
ordered in April and May, the policy yielded unimpressive results. The court
subsequently threatened capital punishment for all deserters,[61] but this proved
equally futile. Having failed to substantially reclaim lost men and territory,
the court decided to cling to what territory remained and stave off the Mongol
armies when they attempted to drive east. Crucial to this strategy was the
city of Yang-chou, sitting to the north of the Yangtze River opposite Chen-
chiang. The Sung assigned its two prized commanders, Chang Shih-chieh and
Li T'ing-chih, to the defense of Yang-chou, which had fallen briefly to Mongol
armies in the spring but was recovered soon after.

A further disaster occurred on the Yangtze in the seventh lunar month of
1275. Sung forces under Chang Shih-chieh attempted to blockade the river at
Chiao-shan below Chen-chiang to deny the Mongol naval forces access to the
sea. The Sung moored a huge fleet of big ships across the river, anchored and

[60] Li, *Sung Yüan chan-shih*, pp. 1210–7.
[61] *SS* 47, pp. 927–8, 930.

chained together, and heavily protected. From their shore base at Chiao-shan the much smaller Mongol fleet attacked them with fire ships and incendiary arrows. Many of the immobilized ships burned, and at the same time Mongol land forces attacked the shore installations. The Mongols won an overwhelming victory, and captured seven hundred seagoing ships, which they could now deploy on the open sea. The Sung lost sixteen thousand men, and as many were taken captive.[62]

The Mongols pressed Yang-chou for much of the summer, and launched an all-out campaign in the autumn of 1275, all to no avail. Yang-chou would, in the end, hold out even after the capital Lin-an had fallen.[63] The same was true for neighboring Chen-chou2, which resisted repeated assaults. The Sung also hoped to strengthen defenses in the lower Yangtze River that autumn by appointing the increasingly prominent Wen T'ien-hsiang as prefect of P'ing-chiang (Su-chou), which had only recently been recaptured. A former minister of war, Wen T'ien-hsiang had gained notable success in recruiting local men for regional armies in other parts of the empire. He seemed to possess the organizational skills and the strength of character needed to keep the enemy at bay, a mission vital to the security of the capital. But despite such positive actions by the Sung court, previous Mongol attacks had already decimated too many units and left too many gaps in defenses for the efforts of one summer to restore Sung military effectiveness.

During the summer, Bayan, now chief minister, met with Khubilai to formulate their strategy to finish the campaign against the Sung. They decided to press ahead with a devastating three-pronged assault originating from Chien-k'ang (Nanking), on the south bank of the Yangtze River and ultimately directed against Lin-an.[64] Upon returning to the Yangtze front in December 1275, Bayan personally joined the siege of Ch'ang-chou, while A-chu augmented Mongol forces attacking Yang-chou. A-tz'u-han led the advance from west of Lin-an with an assault on Kuang-te commandery. Ch'ang-chou fell late in the year, following many months of stiff resistance, and Bayan ordered a general massacre of its populace. It was a tactic employed by the Mongols to intimidate neighboring cities by threatening the same for any other hold-outs. News of the massacre created a serious rift between Sung commanders determined to resist and city dwellers desperate to survive. As the campaign continued in the Yangtze delta, Chiang-yin commandery, about a hundred miles northeast of Lin-an, surrendered to the armies of Tung Wen-ping. The

[62] HTC (1958) 181, p. 4958; Davis, Wind against the mountain, pp. 80–2.
[63] Li, Sung Yüan chan-shih, pp. 1294–1305; Davis, Wind against the mountain, pp. 101–3.
[64] Sung et al., Yüan shih 8, p. 169; Li, Sung Yüan chan-shih, pp. 1240–53; Li et al., Chung-kuo li-tai chan-cheng shih (1968), vol. 11, pp. 435–9, 449–50.

main force advanced along the line of the Grand Canal; Wu-hsi and P'ing-chiang (Su-chou) fell to Bayan after the Sung court had summoned Wen T'ien-hsiang back to the capital. The city of Hu-chou and Tu-sung Pass, the strategic pass roughly forty miles west of the capital, fell to the armies of A-tz'u-han. These gains were strategically invaluable to the Mongols. Chiang-yin lay at the mouth of the Yangtze, and its capitulation gave the Mongols unobstructed access to the Yellow Sea and Hang-chou Bay. The Mongols, their fleet increased by the seven hundred ships captured at Chiao-shan, could now approach the Sung capital by sea. The capture of P'ing-chiang and Hu-chou consolidated the Mongol hold on the area around Lake T'ai, north of the capital. Control of Tu-sung Pass secured the Mongol western flank. As the year (1275) came to an end, the enemy converged on Lin-an. The remaining Sung leadership in Lin-an had to decide whether to retreat farther south or to stand firm. With a minimum of from thirty thousand to forty thousand troops available and irregulars numbering several times that, defeat was far from inevitable.[65] The alternative was to negotiate by making some irrefusably generous offer and stall for time.

It was only during Chia Ssu-tao's last month in power in early 1275, follow-ing his defeat at Wu-hu, that a peace envoy, Sung Ching, was dispatched to the camp of Bayan.[66] On the eve of Chia Ssu-tao's formal dismissal from office, the northern envoy Hao Ching, whom the Sung had continued to hold captive, was released and allowed to return home. The commissioning of Sung Ching is portrayed in the *Sung dynastic history* as the work of Chia Ssu-tao, and the release of Hao Ching as an independent gesture by the court. In fact, both acts took place during Chia Ssu-tao's absence from the capital, which leaves Wang Yüeh and Ch'en I-chung as the likely initiators of peace overtures. Unfortu-nately, their timidity doomed the mission. Despite the fact that Bayan's armies had by then already reached Ch'ih-chou, some one hundred and sixty miles from Lin-an, the Sung offered only a modest payment of tribute in exchange for unconditional withdrawal. The Mongols rejected the offer, but Khubilai appears to have dispatched an envoy a month later. The message he carried will never be known, for Sung officers assassinated him at the border. The Sung court, apologizing for the unauthorized act, approached Bayan in May with new peace proposals, but Bayan's return envoy was also assassinated. The Sung apparently made no special effort to protect emissaries from the north, having concluded that the Mongols were not acting in good faith. As a rule, the Sung court turned to negotiation only under severe military pressure from

---

[65] *HTC* (1958) 182, p. 4969.

[66] On peace talks, see *SS* 47, pp. 926, 936–7; Sung et al., *Yüan shih* 8, pp. 161, 165, 171; 9, pp. 175–6; 126, p. 3097; 127, pp. 3104–9; *HTC* (1958) 181, pp. 4944, 4953–4; 182, pp. 4970, 4975–6.

the Mongols, and then only as a delaying tactic. The militant Ch'en I-chung
and Wang Ying-lin could scarcely countenance the kind of compromises that a
peace treaty, negotiated from a position of weakness, would have entailed. The
Sung court delayed reopening talks until year's end, when Bayan's campaign
directed against Lin-an was already underway. In the twelfth lunar month (early
1276) there was a great flurry of diplomatic activity. The Mongols demanded
outright surrender. The Sung made concessions on issues of protocol but little else. With the Mongols having a clear military advantage and the Sung
attempting to preserve whatever autonomy it could, diplomacy did not work.

The position of the Sung empire deteriorated rapidly in early 1276.[67] In a
three-pronged attack, Bayan's troops closed in on the capital with the conquests
of Chia-hsing, An-chi (Wu-hsing), and Ch'ang-an Garrison (Lin-an's northern
suburbs), while the enemy troops of Tung Wen-ping made an amphibious
landing on the coast north of Lin-an, and approached the capital from the
northeast via Hang-chou Bay. On the third prong, A-tz'u-han's troops closed
in from the west. By the middle of the first lunar month, all three armies
converged at Kao-t'ing Mountain in the suburbs of Lin-an. Sung forces had
meanwhile suffered setbacks in the heart of modern Hunan and in northern
Kwangsi province. Defeat at T'an-chou (Ch'ang-sha), a city that had fought off
attacking armies for five months and endured tremendous losses, was quickly
followed by the fall of Yung-chou2, Ch'üan-chou2, and Kuei-yang (Kuei-lin),
and other cities in central and southern Sung territory. Mongol armies now
had secured control of the Yangtze valley, and were positioned for the final
assault on Lin-an.

News of the recent defeats touched off a new wave of desertions by leading
civil servants at the Sung court.[68] Chief Councilor of the Left Liu Meng-yen and
Minister of Rites Wang Ying-lin fled at the close of 1275. Their resignations
having been rejected, they did not respond to court messengers appealing for
their return. Less than two months later, after the fall of Chia-hsing, Assistant
Councilors Ch'en Wen-lung and Ch'ang Mao (d. 1282), Bureau of Military
Affairs officers Huang Yung and Hsia Shih-lin, various censorial officials, and
many others joined the long list of high-ranking deserters. The situation
became so acute that by early February court attendance had fallen to fewer
than ten civilian officials. There were also military desertions in and around
the capital. News of Mongol atrocities at nearby Ch'ang-chou panicked Lin-
an's scholar-officials. Anticipating a protracted battle over the capital, some
fled because they wished to be spared the pain of either violent death or

[67] HTC (1958) 182, pp. 4962–75; Hu et al., Sung Meng (Yüan) kuan-hsi shih, pp. 404–9; Li, Sung Yüan
chan-shih, pp. 1247–53.
[68] SS 47, pp. 935–7; K'o, Sung-shih hsin-pien 175, p. 8b.

humiliating captivity. Others left out of frustration with the leadership of Ch'en I-chung, and his inability to devise an effective military response to the Mongol advance and refusal to devise a strategy for retreat should Sung armies be unable to hold Lin-an. Wen T'ien-hsiang and Chang Shih-chieh, the court's leading commanders by early 1276, proposed that the royal family prepare to board ships in anticipation of a tactical retreat.[69] Ch'en I-chung opposed the move, purportedly because he still hoped a negotiated settlement could be worked out, but perhaps because he could not accept the notion of retreat. Even at the very end, Ch'en could only think of offering the Mongols meager concessions. Only after Lu Hsiu-fu (1238–79), vice-minister at the Court of the Imperial Clan, headed what turned out to be the final mission to the camp of Bayan, producing no tangible results for a settlement, did Ch'en I-chung finally endorse the withdrawal from Lin-an. Dowager Empress Hsieh at first rejected the idea, as she had previously, but after a day's reconsideration she agreed. The night before, on 4 February, Ch'en I-chung had fled to his native Wen-chou. The envoy, Lu Hsiu-fu, had already arranged a personal meeting the next day between the chief councilor Ch'en and Bayan at Ch'ang-an Garrison to discuss terms of surrender. The mission must have terrified Ch'en I-chung, and understandably so in light of the high mortality among recent envoys. Ch'en's departure forced the court to nominate someone else for this dangerous task.

Having lost most of her civil service, Dowager Empress Hsieh had no great pool of candidates from which to select a new chief councilor and head negotiator. Among the more accomplished of those available was Wen T'ien-hsiang. He became chief councilor and general commander of Sung armies on 5 February 1276. A day later, Wu Chien, councilor of the left since mid-January, and Chia Yü-ch'ing (d. 1276), the recently named prefect of Lin-an, accompanied Wen T'ien-hsiang to meet Bayan at his camp just north of Lin-an.[70] At this point, the Mongols had largely cut off Lin-an from the remaining Sung empire and were ready to take the city, yet the Sung mediators offered nothing new and were clearly only stalling for time. Bayan promptly sent the delegation home. He chose to retain Wen T'ien-hsiang, after having had a verbal confrontation with him that left Bayan angered and suspicious. Wen remained his captive for over a month. In the interim, on 22 February, the Sung court recommissioned the former envoys, Chia Yü-ch'ing, who now replaced Wen T'ien-hsiang as councilor of the right, and Wu Chien, to negotiate surrender. With Mongol armies already positioned along the Ch'ien-t'ang River, facing

[69] SS 451, p. 13273; HTC (1958) 182, p. 4976.
[70] On the mission, see HTC (1958) 182, p. 4977; Wen, Wen T'ien-hsiang ch'üan-chi 17, pp. 453–4; 19, pp. 498–9; Li, Sung Yüan chan-shih, pp. 1257–60.

the capital, nothing but unconditional surrender was acceptable. On 22 March, the twelfth day of the third lunar month, Bayan himself entered Lin-an to direct the occupation. The million or so inhabitants of the Sung capital had been spared a violent and destructive assault.[71]

The campaign against Lin-an was among the most carefully devised and least violent conquests in Mongol history. Not only did Bayan coordinate the movements of the three separate armies to ensure their convergence on the Kao-t'ing Mountains, he enforced a high degree of discipline on those armies.[72] On 5 February, he had issued orders strictly forbidding soldiers from entering Lin-an and threatening severe punishment for all transgressors. Twelve days later, after the Sung court issued its surrender decree, Bayan dispatched commanders of two lesser armies, Meng-ku-tai and Fan Wen-hu, a Mongol and a Sung deserter, to enter the capital and prepare for an orderly transition of power. He intentionally kept back the more powerful generals A-tz'u-han and Tung Wen-ping. In another week and a half, Sung eunuchs were instructed to begin collecting palace valuables and imperial paraphernalia. On the 28th of March, nearly two months after his arrival in the city's suburbs, Bayan paraded through the gates of Lin-an as conqueror of the once great Sung dynasty. Such restraint may not have been expected of a warrior famed for depopulating entire cities, but the circumstances of the occupation of the Sung capital made it expedient. There are reports that mass killings had taken place in the vicinity of Lin-an as the Mongol armies closed in. Bayan may have sought to forestall more violence, by delaying the takeover.[73] In addition, some sources suggest that as troops approached Lin-an they began to quarrel over the spoils that awaited them. Bayan may have acted to stem further problems within his own ranks while protecting the palaces from pillaging. Palace valuables were important to him, for he collected the treasures and dutifully forwarded them all to Khubilai. The valuables were later distributed among Mongol princes like any other booty.

At their Shang-tu meeting in the summer of 1276, Bayan and Khubilai had apparently decided on the fate of the Chao imperial family. The position had been articulated early on in the negotiations of 1275–6. In exchange for the Sung surrender, there would be no destruction of the state altars – "gods of soil and grain" (*she-chi*). The Chao ancestor cult would not be destroyed, and the imperial family would be spared in accordance with Chinese tradition to enable imperial descendants to continue offering sacrifices to the ancestral emperors.

---

[71] For details about the surrender, occupation, and treatment of conquered Sung adherents, see Hsiao, "Bayan," pp. 595–6.

[72] Sung et al., *Yüan shih* 127, p. 3109; *HTC* (1958) 182, pp. 4975–81.

[73] Sung et al., *Yüan shih* 9, p. 177; *HTC* (1958) 182, p. 4977.

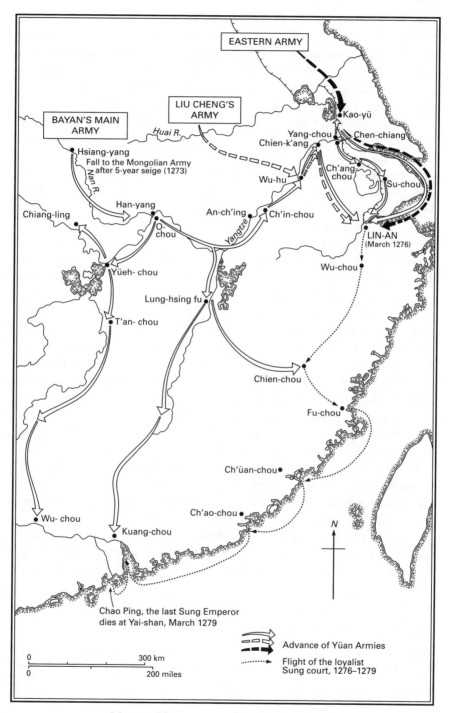

Map 32. The conquest of the Southern Sung.

To a child-emperor and an aging dowager empress, for whom political power mattered little anyway, this must have been an important factor in the decision to submit without resistance. Not all palace residents took consolation in such promises. Reportedly a hundred palace women, in fear of being raped and enslaved, committed suicide on the eve of Bayan's triumphal entry into Lin-an.[74] The incident may also be related to their learning that exile to the north was the fate awaiting them and other palace residents. All the eunuchs were roped together and placed under armed guard, so that they could ensure the safety of the women during the journey of over six hundred miles from Lin-an to Peking and beyond. Many palace women chose suicide en route. Other palace women committed suicide after they arrived in Peking out of fidelity to spouses long deceased. Most palace attendants accepted Mongol bondage, and Bayan spared members of the imperial family the humiliation of chains as they journeyed north.[75]

Forced removal of palace residents had previously occurred when a new dynasty came to power. To ward off a political or military challenge, new rulers had uprooted the elderly and powerful from their former political base and sent them to isolated places where they could be monitored.[76] In earlier times, forced migration had sometimes involved hundreds of thousands of persons. The Mongol action, which involved no more than a thousand captives, is noteworthy in one regard. Up to a hundred students at the three universities – only a fraction of the total student population, which stood at three thousand to four thousand – accompanied the imperial entourage on its trek north.[77] Their trip was voluntary for some, involuntary for others, but in the face of wholesale abandonment of the court by its most eminent officials, students seemed intent on making a strong statement of their com-mitment to the principle of loyalty. They likely drew inspiration from the chancellor of the university system, Yang Wen-chung (*chin-shih* 1253), and a former university official, Kao Ying-sun, two of only a handful of officials still in attendance at court during its last days.[78] Most of the students, like most lesser palace consorts and female servants, were eventually permitted to return south, while the prominent individuals were encouraged to remain in the north. Kao Ying-sun was not be among the returnees; he committed suicide

[74] K'o, *Sung-shih hsin-pien* 14, p. 6b; Ch'ien, *Nan Sung shu* 7, p. 6b; *HTC* (1958) 183, p. 4985; Davis, *Wind against the mountain*, pp. 115–19.

[75] Ch'ien, *Nan Sung shu* 59, p. 2a.

[76] Richard L. Davis, *Court and family in Sung China, 960–1279: Bureaucratic success and kinship fortunes for the Shih of Ming-chou* (Durham, N.C., 1986), pp. 2–3; Ou-yang Hsiu, *Historical records of the Five Dynasties*, trans. Richard L. Davis (New York, 2004), pp. 165–7.

[77] *SS* 421, p. 12598; 451, p. 13277; K'o, *Sung shih hsin-pien* 175, pp. 8b–9a; Sung et al., *Yüan shih* 9, pp. 180, 182.

[78] *SS* 425, p. 12687; 454, p. 13347; *HTC* (1958) 183, p. 4985.

by starvation soon after securing safe passage north for the imperial entourage. Many suicides that went unreported occurred both in Lin-an and in the north. At least one university student, Hsü Ying-piao, refused to join the move to Peking; he and his family committed suicide in Lin-an. A minor metropolitan official, Ko T'ien-ssu, opted to strangle himself rather than submit to the conquerors. Kung Chi, an executive of the agricultural bureau who accompanied the imperial entourage north, starved himself before reaching Peking.[79] The list of martyrs is far longer than existing documentation suggests, particularly documentation pertaining to events in the capital during the weeks directly preceding and following the Yüan occupation.

The lives of members of the Sung imperial family in the north passed without serious incident.[80] Chao Hsien, referred to in the official history as Ying-kuo kung, which was the Yüan court's official designation for him, and by Sung loyalists in the south as Kung-ti or Kung-tsung, stayed in Peking and Shang-tu only briefly. Later, he took up residence at a Buddhist monastery somewhere in the vicinity of Tun-huang, where he raised a family prior to becoming a monk. The sources suggest that his years as a former emperor were passed in relative comfort. Exiled to the north along with Chao Hsien was his great uncle, Chao Yü-jui, the father of Tu-tsung. At the time of Lin-an's surrender, he had voluntarily returned to the capital upon receiving an urgent summons from Dowager Empress Hsieh, presumably acting on instructions from Bayan. The subsequent fate of this senior member of the imperial family, a man probably in his sixties or seventies, is not known. The seventy-year-old dowager empress, seriously ill at the time of Bayan's occupation, was permitted to delay the trek north for five months. Sent to Peking that summer under special escort, she passed her final years in solitude at a nunnery in the area, before dying in 1283. Dowager Empress Ch'üan, the empress of Tu-tsung and Chao Hsien's mother, may have been in her mid-thirties during the conquest, but she was now the senior palace figure in the entourage that headed north in late March, stopping briefly in Peking, and arriving at Shang-tu in mid-June. She reportedly became absorbed in Buddhism in later years, perhaps explaining her son's subsequent devotion to the religion. When death came in 1309, she was buried somewhere near Peking alongside Dowager Empress Hsieh. She was survived by her son and apparently a grandson. Khubilai had kept his promise to cause them no harm.

[79] On these individuals, see SS 451, p. 13276; Sung et al., Yüan shih 9, p. 180; Feng Kuei-fen and Li Ming-wan, Su-chou fu-chih (1883; Taipei, 1970) 71, p. 19a; Li Jung et al., Hang-chou fu-chih (1888; Taipei, 1974) 130, pp. 9a–b; Davis, Wind against the mountain, pp. 124–6.

[80] On the whereabouts of the royal family, see SS 418, p. 12539; K'o, Sung-shih hsin-pien 14, p. 6b; Ch'ien, Nan Sung shu 6, p. 12a; 7, pp. 6b, 8b; Chao, Chao shih tsu-p'u 1, pp. 69a–70a, 71b; Davis, Wind against the mountain, pp. 120–1.

THE FUGITIVE COURT

Chao Shih (Tuan-tsung, r. 1276–1278)

The Mongol occupation of Lin-an sealed off the city, and most of the Sung imperial family were now captive, but a few prominent members had managed to escape and establish a court in exile in the far south. This government-in-exile still represented a challenge to the legitimacy of the Yüan dynasty. The court in exile gave Sung loyalists a symbol to rally around and a means of pressing their opposition to Mongol rule. Their victories in the lower Yangtze River notwithstanding, the Mongols required several more years to consolidate their control over all of the Southern Sung domain.

Dowager Empress Hsieh and Ch'en I-chung had initially rejected proposals to abandon Lin-an in search of safety farther south. They reasoned that the court's composure and confidence would strengthen the resolve of troops defending the city, should a confrontation occur. In time, Ch'en I-chung himself fled and by early February 1276, following the loss of Chia-hsing and Lu Hsiu-fu's abortive peace mission, the Sung court quietly appointed Tu-tsung's two remaining sons, Chao Shih and Chao Ping, to regional posts in the far south.[81] The decision was allegedly reached at the recommendation of Wen T'ien-hsiang and under pressure from members of the imperial clan, who were increasingly concerned about the safety of the emperor's two brothers, possible heirs to the throne. The two children departed Lin-an around 8 February, and in the nick of time, for within a matter of days the Mongol armies sealed off the city. Dowager Empress Hsieh may have authorized the boys' assignments to regional posts, but she clearly had not authorized their departure, for she dispatched messengers demanding the convoy's return. In all probability, the move was carried out by an alliance between prominent members of the imperial clan and operatives in the palace. At any rate, the two boys apparently left Lin-an under the cover of darkness and in the company of their mothers, a few close relatives, and a Palace Guard contingent.[82]

Leading the group was Yang Chen, sheriff of Lin-an and father of Tu-tsung's consort Yang. Mongol armies already controlled the northern portion of the Ch'ien-t'ang River leading to Hang-chou Bay and the ocean. The Mongols were determined to seal off the chief escape route – the ocean – and prevent repetition of a mistake made four decades earlier, when valuable energies were

---

[81] SS 47, p. 939; HTC (1958) 182, pp. 4975–6, 4980; Wen, Wen T'ien-hsiang ch'üan-chi 17, p. 453; Li, Sung Yüan chan-shih, pp. 1255–7; Chaffee, Branches of heaven, pp. 244–6.

[82] Chien Yu-wen, Sung-mo erh-ti nan-ch'ien nien-lu k'ao (Hong Kong, 1957), pp. 5–8; Davis, Wind against the mountain, pp. 113, 123, 166–7.

squandered in the prolonged pursuit of Chin rulers who, through Mongol carelessness, were allowed to flee their besieged capitals and continue resistance to the Mongol conquest. The Mongol position still left the Sung convoy with an alternative route to safety, sailing up the Ch'ien-t'ang River to Wu-chou4 (modern Chin-hua) and then traveling by land to sanctuary. It was a hazardous escape, and Mongol pursuit forced the fugitives into the mountains for a week, but their evasive tactics succeeded and they reached the coastal city of Wen-chou in southern Chekiang province. There, the group rested, replenished their military and naval forces, and set sail for Fu-chou. Mongol pursuers came perilously close to overtaking the convoy, and the messengers of Dowager Empress Hsieh did not convince them to return to the capital.

A frenzy of activity followed as the guardians of the two imperial princes tried to rally support among civilian and military officials. Former peace envoy Lu Hsiu-fu was enlisted early on, followed by commander Chang Shih-chieh. Also joining the group at Wen-chou was Wen T'ien-hsiang. The former councilor had been forcibly detained since early February by Bayan, who saw that Wen's strident loyalism was too great a threat to the current negotiations. Following the fall of Lin-an, Bayan prepared to have Wen T'ien-hsiang incarcerated in the north along with two other former councilors who had been peace envoys, Wu Chien and Chia Yü-ch'ing. The guards took too few precautions while transporting the men to Peking, with the result that Wen T'ien-hsiang managed to escape in the vicinity of Chen-chiang, recross the Yangtze, and flee to Chen-chou2. No sooner was he free than he found himself in mid-March the object of a murder conspiracy.[83] Military commissioner Li T'ing-chih, incensed by the uncontested surrender of Lin-an in the face of his own marathon defense of Yang-chou, blamed the surrender on the defeatist envoys who negotiated the truce. Presuming Wen T'ien-hsiang to have been party to the treachery, Li planned Wen's assassination as retribution. It was impossible for Li to know that the former councilor, held prisoner during the second round of negotiations, had voiced strong opposition to concessions. Wen T'ien-hsiang proved resourceful enough to convince the would-be assassins of his genuine loyalty to the Sung cause. His life was spared. His spirits buoyed by news of the imperial fugitives, he headed south to join them at Fu-chou, arriving in mid-May.

News of the presence of Tu-tsung's two surviving sons in the south, out of reach of the Mongols, inspired other acts of Sung loyalism. An attempt was made to rescue the imperial entourage, including deposed emperor Kung-ti,

<hr />

[83] SS 421, p. 12602; Wen, *Wen T'ien-hsiang ch'üan-chi* 17, pp. 453–5; K'o, *Sung shih hsin-pien* 175, p. 5a; HTC (1958) 183, p. 4982.

as they passed along the Grand Canal en route to Peking.[84] The incident in
April at Kua-chou (on the Yangtze River halfway between Chen-chou2 and
Yang-chou) was yet another trap sprung by Commissioner Li T'ing-chih, aided
by a reputed forty thousand men. But Dowager Empress Ch'üan refused to
support the loyalists, and their rescue effort failed after a brief encounter with
Yüan guards. Such a chilly response to rallying Sung loyalists was not universal.
Quite the contrary, popular uprisings erupted in support of the Sung, especially
in Fu-chien and Kuang-nan. Regional commanders and officials, once prepared
to surrender to the Mongols, now renewed their resolve to stand fast.[85] Mongol
strategists must have counted on the collapse of Sung resistance after Lin-an's
surrender, and had not prepared a detailed plan for a major drive against the
south comparable to their recent Yangtze campaign. They had not succeeded
in sealing off Lin-an from the south as well as the north.

Meanwhile, Sung loyalists in the south moved to consolidate their position.
Seven-year-old Chao Shih, eldest son of Tu-tsung and born to Consort Yang,
had been elevated to emperor on the first day of the fifth lunar month, 14
June 1276. The fugitive court, then safely in Fu-chou, occupied the offices
of the prefectural government and began appointing officials. Ch'en I-chung
had resurfaced from his Wen-chou home to join Sung supporters at Fu-chou,
where he was given the post of councilor of the left and quickly asserted his
dominance. Li T'ing-chih, in recognition of his sacrifices at Yang-chou, became
councilor of the right in absentia. He never took up his post or wielded any
political power, for the Mongols captured and executed him later that summer.
Another nominal councilor, appointed to the post in early summer, was Wen
T'ien-hsiang. Conflicts with Ch'en I-chung prompted Wen to resign. He went
home and devoted his energies to military mobilization in his native Kiangsi.
Chang Shih-chieh, a critical figure in the installation of Chao Shih, became
assisting executive in the Bureau of Military Affairs. He spent considerable
time away from Fu-chou, leading armies in battle. So did Fu-chou native
Ch'en Wen-lung, formerly an assistant councilor in Lin-an who had been
reappointed to that post in early summer. Ch'en Wen-lung concentrated on
solidifying Sung control over Fu-chien. The only individual to share power
with Ch'en I-chung over a significant span of time was Lu Hsiu-fu, a peace
emissary with extensive military experience. He became signatory official at
the Bureau of Military Affairs.

It seems curious that the court of Chao Shih should choose to retain the
services of Ch'en I-chung. He had already been exposed as incompetent at

---

[84] SS 421, p. 12602; 451, p. 13268; K'o, Sung shih hsin-pien 175, p. 2b; Ch'ien, Nan Sung shu 59,
pp. 4a–6b; HTC (1958) 182, p. 4982; Li, Sung Yüan chan-shih, pp. 1299–1300.

[85] Sung et al., Yüan shih 128, p. 3128; Wen, Wen T'ien-hsiang ch'üan-chi 17, p. 456; Yang Te-en, Wen
T'ien-hsiang nien-p'u, 2nd ed. (1937; Shanghai, 1947), pp. 247–8.

managing the Mongol menace, which revealed his political inflexibility, his ineffectiveness at managing the bureaucracy, and his cowardliness, having fled Lin-an and the Sung court at its time of greatest need. Ch'en I-chung may have argued, as did others who fled the besieged capital, that his sudden departure was motivated by the decision, in the face of overwhelming odds, to retreat strategically farther south and organize new armies. Even if extenuating circumstances explain his departure in terms other than of cowardice, he was still the least desirable candidate for chief councilor relative to others. Perhaps the insecure court, with Dowager Consort Yang serving as regent, considered that it enhanced its legitimacy by retaining the services of the last major councilor from the former capital. Perhaps Ch'en I-chung, as bureaucratic chief in Lin-an, had established a special liaison with Consort Yang's father, a one-time metropolitan sheriff, who must have wielded a large measure of influence at the Fu-chou court-in-exile because of his daughter. But the court seems to have had few alternatives to former deserters, for it also reappointed Ch'en Wen-lung to high office despite his earlier desertion. Whatever the reasons for the retention of Ch'en I-chung, this decision, more than any other made on the behalf of the child-emperor, weakened the loyalist cause from the outset.

There were other reasons why the Sung horizon of 1276 looked bleak. Under the direction of Chang Shih-chieh and Wen T'ien-hsiang, Sung armies had scored modest gains. In Che-tung, they had regained all or parts of Ch'ü-chou, Wu-chou4, and Ming-chou. They had recovered a significant part of central Kiangsi province. The battles for Fu-chien and Kuang-nan had been ferocious, with the Sung making significant gains, including the recovery of Shao-chou2 and Kuang-chou (Canton). Yet most of these recoveries were only temporary, and late summer brought bad news. Yang-chou and Chen-chou2, the strategic cites giving control of the mouth of the Yangtze River and also the two major Sung holdouts north of Lin-an, had finally collapsed after nearly a year of relentless siege. Captured during the takeover was Commissioner Li T'ing-chih, who attempted suicide and when this failed was executed. Having reconsolidated their control of the lower Yangtze, the Mongols pressured the south with a large autumn offensive. The armies of A-tz'u-han and Tung Wen-ping moved directly from the north, in a combined land and sea operation originating at Chen-chiang, while Lü Shih-k'uei and Li Heng advanced further west through Kiangsi, squeezing the Sung from two directions. When these armies converged on Chien-ning, northern Fu-chien, late in the year, the Sung court decided to abandon Fu-chou for safety still farther south. Protected by an army of reportedly a half million, a doubtfully large number, the court boarded ships headed for Ch'üan-chou, Fu-chien, and subsequently moved south to Ch'ao-chou, Hui-chou2, and then the greater Kuang-chou area, all in Kuang-nan East. Fu-chou fell to the Mongol advance at the end of the year, early in 1277. One-time Assistant Councilor Ch'en Wen-lung was taken captive there and sent north. Before reaching Lin-an, he starved himself to death.

More reversals for the Sung came in 1277, and the search for a safe haven continued to elude the fugitive court. Unlike the half year's respite at Fu-chou, which afforded Sung strategists precious time to regroup and reassess, subsequent lodgments proved brief. For a year and a half, from early 1277 to mid-1278, the ship-bound court meandered off the coast of Kuang-nan, disembarking at countless towns and outposts in the vicinity of Kuang-chou. Under constant enemy pressure, it spent no more than a month or two at each stop. For all their effort, the Sung forces rarely held onto territory recovered from the Mongols. Even in the coastal cities of the far south, the Sung hold was never firm. Kuang-chou changed hands at least five times before being permanently secured by the Mongols in late 1278. But by mooring for so long off the Kuang-nan coast the Sung emperor and his armies demonstrated a commitment to holding the area. Kuang-chou was, after all, the most economically prosperous and culturally developed city along the empire's southern rim, the indispensable base for any viable restoration movement. The Mongols understood this and directed their forces appropriately against Kuang-chou. Apart from the contest over Kuang-chou, the Mongols' attention also turned to the interior. Mongol military commander Li Heng continued his attack into Kiangsi, where he captured most of Wen T'ien-hsiang's family. From the heart of Kiangsi, Li Heng advanced into northern Kuang-nan. In late 1277 and early 1278, Li used the terror tactic of ordering a general massacre of Sung holdouts in Hsing-hua, Fu-chien, and in Ch'ao-chou, Kuang-nan East. This tactic further inhibited regional support for the Sung, as did local conditions and conflicts.

The Sung armies had not always tried to appease local populations. In late 1276, at the great port city of Ch'üan-chou, for example, Chang Shih-chieh had needlessly created a major incident by commandeering available ships and provisions.[86] This so incensed the powerful local trade and military commissioner, P'u Shou-keng, that prior to his surrender to the Mongols he responded by indiscriminately executing Chao imperial clansmen, many of whom resided in the area; Sung officials; and loyalist troops from the Yangtze region. During

---

[86] On these various incidents, see *SS* 47, p. 942; *HTC* (1958) 183, pp. 4995, 5000; Wen, *Wen T'ien-hsiang ch'üan-chi* 17, pp. 456–7; Li An, *Sung Wen ch'eng-hsiang T'ien-hsiang nien-p'u* (Taipei, 1980), pp. 72–81; Li, *Sung Yüan chan-shih*, pp. 1390–4; Brown, *Wen T'ien-hsiang*, pp. 212–14; Huber, "Wen T'ien-hsiang, 1236–1283," pp. 192–212; Jay, *A change in dynasties*, pp. 49–55; Davis, *Wind against the mountain*, pp. 168–9.

this unsettled time other regional contenders for power were emerging. There is record of an execution in Fu-chou in mid-1277 by Wen T'ien-hsiang of a bogus imperial claimant from T'ing-chou. The suspect, Huang Ts'ung, was apparently involved in a popular uprising in the interior of Fu-chien directed against the Sung government. Documents allude to an administrator at T'ing-chou having "seditious designs" of some sort, the details of which are now lost. Such incidents serve to demonstrate that Sung armies, while enjoying popular support in certain quarters, were not necessarily welcomed throughout the southeast, a situation that benefited no one more than the Mongol conquerors.

Tensions generated by a seemingly hopeless military conflict eventually took its toll on Sung loyalists. Lu Hsiu-fu reportedly suffered from such acute depression that while standing in place at court, he could frequently be seen in tears, having apparently recognized the futility of the cause.[87] Defeatism afflicted others as well. In late 1277, after an epidemic killed vast numbers of soldiers, Kuang-chou reverted once again to Mongol control, and in the eleventh lunar month the Sung court fled still farther south to Ching-ao, an island near modern Macao. This was its eighth stop in less than a year.[88] At that point, Ch'en I-chung must have come into conflict with others and, as usual for him in such tense settings, took flight. Sailing beyond Hainan Island, he sought sanctuary in modern Vietnam and later in Laos. References to the court's awaiting his return suggests that he had not been formally relieved of his duties. A palace guardsman was even dispatched to fetch him, which suggests that he had deserted, and was not lost at sea, as some have concluded. The court considered taking refuge in Vietnam, possibly at Ch'en I-chung's counsel. The decision against the move reflected the waxing influence of a more realistic and courageous Lu Hsiu-fu.[89] To make matters worse, child-emperor Chao Shih nearly died when his ship sank near Ching-ao. The incident occurred only a month after Ch'en I-chung's desertion and coincided with fresh Mongol advances. The imperial entourage had little alternative but to seek refuge still farther west. A new island sanctuary, Kang-chou, was near the southern tip of Kuang-nan West, not far from Hainan Island.[90] The emperor, though snatched from the sinking ship and spared a violent death, never recovered from the illness that followed the incident. He died on 9 May 1278, not yet ten years old, at the mountainous Kang-chou hideout. Given the temple name of

---

[87] SS 451, p. 13276.

[88] On the route taken, see Ch'eng Kuang-yü et al., *Chung-kuo li-shih ti-t'u* (Taipei, 1984), vol 2, p. 107.

[89] SS 418, p. 12532; Ch'ien, *Nan Sung shu* 6, p. 15a; 61, p. 7b; Li et al., *Chung-kuo li-tai chan-cheng shih* (1968), vol. 11, pp. 422–43.

[90] Some discrepancy exists about the location of Kang-chou; see Chien, *Sung-mo erh-ti nan-ch'ien*, pp. 77–89; Li *Sung Yüan chan-shih*, p. 1439; Li et al., *Chung-kuo li-tai chan-cheng shih* (1968), vol. 11, p. 442.

Tuan-tsung, he was eventually interred at the court's final sanctuary, an island known as Yai-shan.

Chao Ping (r. 1278–1279)

The third surviving son of Tu-tsung, Chao Ping, was not yet six years old when his half-brother died.[91] He had accompanied the court of Tuan-tsung throughout its hazardous trek from Lin-an to Kang-chou, attended by Consort Yü, his mother, plus his grandfather and close relatives. The regents of Tuan-tsung had never officially designated Chao Ping as heir, the transfer of power between brothers being generally thought undesirable. The seated emperor being young and of sound health, to name an heir for him would have appeared inauspicious. Consequently, when Tuan-tsung died, many officials considered disbanding the court. Under the influence of Lu Hsiu-fu, the resilient chief councilor, they endorsed elevation of Chao Ping to the throne. The prospect of the throne passing to yet another child must have been disheartening, but attrition had thinned the ranks of civilian officers, and this may explain Lu Hsiu-fu's ability to prevail. Military support for the action was crucial, and Chang Shih-chieh was predictably enthusiastic. Two days after his brother's death, Chao Ping became emperor. He reigned for the next year and a half at a court dominated by Lu Hsiu-fu as councilor, Chang Shih-chieh as assistant chief of the military bureau, and the child's stepmother, Dowager Consort Yang, whose two-year regency continued. No mention is made of Chao Ping's mother, Consort Yü, who if alive would certainly have played some role under the new regime. Wen T'ien-hsiang continued his military campaign on the mainland east of Kuang-chou, the metropolis north of the island capital, but he was isolated from court politics at Yai-shan. After the death of Ch'en Wen-lung and the desertion of Ch'en I-chung, Wen T'ien-hsiang may have been the most highly qualified civilian officer still serving the fugitive court, yet rarely, if ever, was he summoned to the island retreat for consultation.

Yai-shan was to be the Sung dynasty's last stand. The remaining leadership appears to have assumed from early on that the aimless itinerancy needed to end. The island, located just off the coast about twenty-five miles west of modern Macao, was part of Hsin-hui county and about sixty miles south of Kuang-chou (Canton).[92] Largely mountainous, Yai-shan contained a stretch of relatively flat or moderately hilly land. It was protected to the east and west by large

---

[91] SS 47, pp. 994–6; K'o, Sung-shih hsin-pien 15, pp. 7a–9b; Ch'ien, Nan Sung shu 6, pp. 15a–17a; Chao, Chao-shih tsu-p'u 1, pp. 74b–75a.

[92] Photographs contained in Chao, Chao-shih tsu-p'u 1, p. 74b; Chien Yu-wen, ed., Sung huang-t'ai chi-nien-chi (Hong Kong, 1960), pp. 1–22; Davis, Wind against the mountain, pp. 172–4.

precipitous islands, from which the name Yai-shan "Cliff Hills" derives. These tiny islets served as surveillance posts and obstructed passage for intruding vessels, while shallow waters inhibited any large-scale amphibious approach from the north. Another strategic advantage was the island's proximity to the coast, which facilitated immediate communication between the court and its remnant armies on the mainland.

Perhaps more telling in terms of dynastic intentions is the size of the Yai-shan stronghold. Sources vary somewhat, but the consensus appears to be that Sung settlers, importing craftsmen from coastal Kuang-nan, rapidly built some thirty palaces and three thousand other units to house the remaining two hundred thousand soldiers who had been compelled to live on ships for the past two years.[93] The Sung imperial entourage, even at this late stage, must have been larger than the small group that fled Lin-an two years earlier, even though the boast of two hundred thousand militia contradicts references to an army of "several tens of thousands," attributed to Lu Hsiu-fu shortly before the flight to Yai-shan.[94] Having suffered defeats on the mainland and repeated retreats along the coast, the fugitive Sung court is unlikely to have retained command of several hundred thousand men, however diligent it may have been in recruiting militia from the larger Kuang-nan region. The community on Yai-shan may have been only one-fourth its reported size, but a force approaching even fifty thousand represented a threat to Mongol hegemony.

The geographic scope of Sung resistance shrank substantially in 1278, just as the court was entrenching itself at Yai-shan in anticipation of a protracted war. The Szechwan region, if sufficiently free of enemy occupation, might have offered future sanctuary for imperial fugitives. Previously in 1258, the Mongols had gained a foothold in Szechwan when they captured Ch'eng-tu, neighboring cities, and counties to the north. The Sung had regained much of the territory lost that year, but not the strategically vital city of Ch'eng-tu, which except for a brief spell in early 1273, had remained firmly in Mongol hands and later became an administrative center for their western front. For most of Tu-tsung's reign, the Sung and Mongol armies had concentrated their attentions and resources on Hsiang-yang and central Sung territory. This strategy did not entirely neglect the Szechwan theater, and the Sung had made at least two unsuccessful attempts to regain Ch'eng-tu, in 1270, and in 1273.

Sung forces had more success in Ch'ung-ch'ing, the riverine hub that was critical to holding the western stretches of the Yangtze River. The city had come under repeated assault by Mongol forces between 1270 and 1272, but

[93] Chien, *Sung-mo erh-ti nan-ch'ien*, p. 90; Ch'ien, *Nan Sung shu* 6, p. 15b; *HTC* (1958) 184, p. 5015; Chao, *Chao-shih tsu-p'u* 1, p. 74b.

[94] *HTC* (1958) 183, p. 5012.

it had held its ground. Another important city on the upper Yangtze River, Lu-chou3, southwest of Ch'ung-ch'ing, had fallen to the Mongols twice in the early 1260s, but had been recovered both times and had remained part of Sung territory for the duration of the Tu-tsung reign. Ho-chou4 was an impenetrable Sung enclave located about sixty miles north of Ch'ung-ch'ing, where the Fu, Chia-ling, and Ch'ü rivers all converge as they turn south toward Ch'ung-ch'ing. Ho-chou4 is famed as the place where Möngke, the Mongol ruler, had died during a lengthy assault on the city in 1259. Frequently harassed by the enemy in the early 1270s, Ho-chou4 had remained firmly in Sung hands.[95] Sung control over these areas, by denying the Mongols access to the Yangtze River from the west, prevented the Mongols from using the river to launch large-scale naval offensives against cities downstream in eastern Szechwan and western Hupei. Over two-thirds of Szechwan had already been conquered by the Mongols by the Tu-tsung era. The Sung leadership and their agents in the west appear to have invested in the defense of major cities of Szechwan at the expense of smaller towns. This tactic preserved a facade of control but a vulnerable facade that mitigated against dynastic interests in the long term.

Khubilai had adopted an east-first strategy for conquering the Sung, and the fall of Lin-an enabled his armies to turn their attention once more to conquering Szechwan. In 1277 there were major assaults against Ch'ung-ch'ing, Ho-chou4, and Fu-chou6, all major centers in the western Sung empire. Results from these attacks were initially unimpressive, perhaps because conflict in the east prevented the Mongols from committing more than ten thousand or twenty thousand men in any one western campaign. However, perseverance by the Mongols paid off in 1278. Ch'ung-ch'ing and Lu-chou3 in the west fell early in the year, roughly coinciding with Mongol acquisition of Nan-p'ing, Po-chou2, and Shih-chou2, south of the Yangtze, and to the north, K'uei-chou2, capital of K'uei-chou circuit, and Wan-chou in the Yangtze gorges. This campaign completed Mongol command of the Yangtze River from the western fringes of Szechwan to the ocean. Among the last Szechwan cities to hold out was Ho-chou4. With a population of roughly eighty thousand households and no contact with the outside for several years, it staved off the enemy until early 1279. The reasons for prolonged resistance in the west, in some cases three years after the dynasty's formal surrender at Lin-an, are not easy to discern. Many Szechwan cities capitulated only in the aftermath of extended periods of drought and famine, which made further defense virtually impossible. The holdouts must have heard that the Sung court was in the far south following

---

95 On the conflict in these areas, see Hu et al., *Sung-mo Ssu-ch'uan*, pp. 138, 168, 259, 514–18, 547–51; Li, *Sung Yüan chan-shih*, pp. 1318–26.

the fall of Lin-an, but in the absence of official communications from the Sung court, and there had been none since its loss of Lin-an, they continued to defend Szechwan in the dynasty's name.[96] In contrast to the massive desertions in the east, the stubborn resistance in Szechwan could only have heartened the Sung court-in-exile. When the Mongols finally took Szechwan in 1278–9, the Sung court had very few outposts remaining of its once great empire.

With most of Hunan, Kwangsi, and Szechwan in hostile hands, the only hope for Sung resisters lay in retaining control of the southern Kiangsi and northern Kuang-nan regions where Wen T'ien-hsiang was currently fighting, and his prospects were bleak. Khubilai had reaffirmed his determination to conquer all of the Southern Sung realm with a new series of campaigns. In addition to a Kwangsi offensive launched in 1277 and a Yunnan offensive begun in the spring of 1278, Khubilai inaugurated a third and final sweep of the southeast coastal region in mid-1278.[97] Li Heng, a Tangut in the service of the Yüan, had already seized much of Kiangsi during the previous year, forcing Wen T'ien-hsiang to retreat from the interior to coastal Kuang-nan. The Mongol coastal offensive of 1278, intended to complement Li Heng's efforts, was amphibious. Deploying some twenty thousand men, the Mongols sought to consolidate control over the long-contested coastal cities of Fu-chien and Kuang-nan. Chang Hung-fan (d. 1280) was commissioned to supervise the naval force. This was a noteworthy selection because Chang Hung-fan was a Chinese commander and had blood ties to Chang Shih-chieh, his nephew serving the Sung as their general commander. The assignment underscored the increased isolation of the Southern Sung loyalists and the extent to which they had sacrificed home and family by refusing to submit. By the end of 1278, loyalist armies had lost the coastal prefectures of Chang-chou, Ch'ao-chou, and Hui-chou2, in effect, all of the remaining Sung holdings in coastal Fu-chien and Kuang-nan East. This left Wen T'ien-hsiang trapped inland at Wu-p'o-ling, a mountain range roughly fifty miles east of Hui-chou2 at Hai-feng in central Kuang-nan East. He and his army were overrun there on 2 February 1279 by a surprise attack led by Chang Hung-fan.[98] Attempting suicide, Wen was taken captive. Chang Hung-fan then joined forces with Li Heng at Kuang-chou, a city only recently retaken by Mongol armies. There they prepared for a naval assault on Yai-shan.

As the Mongol fleet made their approach to the Sung citadel at the end of February 1279, Chang Shih-chieh had already learned, no doubt from

[96] Hu et al., *Sung-mo Ssu-ch'uan*, p. 475.
[97] Sung et al., *Yüan shih* 129, pp. 3157–8; *HTC* (1958) 184, pp. 5016, 5020–1; Wen, *Wen T'ien-hsiang ch'üan-chi* 17, pp. 458–64.
[98] Davis, *Wind against the mountain*, p. 174.

informants, of their movements and was preparing for the attack.[99] Reports claim that in the harbor opening to Yai-shan, he formed a line of a thousand oceangoing boats and ships. Once they were anchored, maneuvered by his crack troops, and protected against arrows and incendiary missiles by matting along their sides, the Sung emperor and his court went on board a large vessel in the center of the line. The imperial presence was intended to strengthen the resolve of war-weary and homesick soldiers, but it may also have been designed to facilitate the court's swift flight should the need arise. Anticipating this, the Mongols first moved to seal off escape routes to the north and west, and then began harassing the Sung flotilla from the south. Chang Hung-fan pressed Wen T'ien-hsiang, held captive on board a Mongol ship, to plead with Chang Shih-chieh to surrender. Wen T'ien-hsiang adamantly refused, perhaps confident in the superiority of Sung naval strength. Chang Hung-fan then tried to set fire to the Sung ships, using incendiary rafts as had been done on the Yangtze at Chiao-shan. This also failed. Mongol forces appeared leery of risking an all-out assault, so they blockaded the Sung fleet, and maintained their pressure for over a half month.

The tension accompanying this confrontation with the Mongols weakened Sung patience and resolve, but other problems also took their toll. Although the Sung fleet had prepared for a battle, they were not ready for what amounted to a siege. Their supplies of fresh water were depleted, and some of those aboard the Sung ships drank seawater and became sick. Weapons too were in short supply, and probably food as well. On 19 March 1279 the Mongols exploited the changing tides to attack the anchored Sung ships from both north and south. The Sung losses were staggering. The next morning brought rain and dense fog, but this did not veil from Chang Shih-chieh and Lu Hsiu-fu the sad truth: they had lost the bulk of their navy, and this time there was no escape. Wishing to spare the six-year-old emperor the humiliation of captivity, Councilor Lu Hsiu-fu firmly clutched the child, dressed in his imperial robes and carrying the imperial seals, and plunged into the sea. Only a hundred or so military and civilian officers chose to surrender. According to most sources, including both the Sung and Yüan dynastic histories (*Sung shih* and *Yüan shih*), some one hundred thousand soldiers followed the emperor in suicidal drowning.[100] Chang Shih-chieh managed to escape with a dozen or so smaller ships. He returned before long to assess the situation and came upon Dowager Consort Yang, who was still within the Yai-shan stronghold. Mongol leaders

99 On the Yai-shan debacle, see Chiang I-hsüeh, *Lu Hsiu-fu nien-p'u* (Taipei, 1977), pp. 23–7; *HTC* (1958) 184, pp. 5024–8; Li, *Sung Yüan chan-shih*, pp. 1477–82; Li et al., *Chung-kuo li-tai chan-cheng shih* (1968), vol. 11, pp. 442–5; Davis, *Wind against the mountain*, pp. 1–5; Jay, *A change of dynasties*, pp. 56–9.

100 *SS* 47, p. 945; Sung et al., *Yüan shih* 129, p. 3158; Ch'ien, *Nan Sung shu* 6, p. 16b; 7, p. 7a; 61, p. 7b; *HTC* (1958) 184, p. 5027; Li et al., *Chung-kuo li-tai chan-cheng shih* (1968), vol. 11, pp. 444–5; Davis, *Wind against the mountain*, pp. 1–5.

apparently decided, after their sea victory, not to bother with occupation of the island. On learning of her stepson's death, the dowager threw herself into the sea. She was buried on the beach by Chang Shih-chieh, who then himself died by drowning, whether by accident or suicide is not known. His navy, reduced to about ten ships, disbanded.

Accounts of the last months of the Sung dynasty at Yai-shan must be viewed skeptically. Eyewitness accounts of the affair are few. Lu Hsiu-fu's personal diary, intended as a history of those crucial years, was lost. Mongol records, based most likely upon reports from military officers, are terse.[101] The only Sung survivor to bear personal witness to the Yai-shan defeat and commit it to written record was Wen T'ien-hsiang, a man too politically passionate to be wholly credible as a historical source, and the number of people he reports as dying at Yai-shan is clearly exaggerated. It is hardly credible that the Sung court during its last desperate days possessed either a thousand warships or a hundred thousand soldiers. The many thousands of bodies found floating on the sea may represent war casualties, not suicide victims. Combat into the late night and dense fog at the next dawn were also sources of confusion. However, the Mongol delay in attacking at Yai-shan until Sung forces were beset with shortages of food and water suggests that the Sung navy was far from small. The Mongol forces apparently stood at roughly thirty thousand to forty thousand, so a Sung force of fifty thousand or sixty thousand men is not unwarranted. As for mass suicide, while the numbers may be inflated, the incident undeniably occurred. Substantial documentation exists for other cases of mass suicide among Sung loyalists shortly before or after capitulation to the enemy. Perhaps the most notable was at T'an-chou (Ch'ang-sha) in 1275, where thousands took their own lives.[102] The question to be asked, therefore, is not whether tens of thousands committed suicide at Yai-shan, for the numbers are not as pertinent as the issue of *why*.

The siege of Lin-an had induced a cowardly response, with civilian and military officials deserting on a massive scale. The contrast with Yai-shan, just three years later, is confounding. Among traditional historians, a common explanation holds that the earlier ambivalence was a response to inept political leadership, which alienated many of those who were conscientious and loyal. Certainly, child-emperors occupied the throne in both Lin-an and Yai-shan, and the councilor Ch'en I-chung offered the same lackluster leadership at both courts. It may be that Dowager Empress Hsieh's decision, at Ch'en I-chung's prompting, to surrender Lin-an without a fight effectively demoralized court supporters and undermined much loyalist sentiment. The decision by Chang Shih-chieh and Lu Hsiu-fu to stand firm at Yai-shan was in

[101] *SS* 451, pp. 13276–7.
[102] *SS* 450, pp. 13253–6; Davis, *Wind against the mountain*, p. 110–12.

striking contrast. If standing firm was critical, then Dowager Empress Hsieh's initial decision to confront the enemy without moving the capital should have similarly inspired loyalists to resist militarily, if not to attack Lin-an to break the enemy encirclement, but this did not happen.

Another explanation of the contrast between 1276 and 1279 lies in the composition of the court. Those who followed the court all the way to Yai-shan were a small select group, more cohesive and steadfast in their loyalist convictions than the diverse body of officials serving in Lin-an. But there were some men, such as Ch'en Wen-lung, who fled Lin-an in 1276, but chose suicide over submission to the enemy in 1279. A factor that cannot be overlooked in the defeat at Yai-shan is sheer desperation. When the Mongols descended upon Lin-an, the Sung court could still claim control over a good deal of the far south, roughly half of the domain. For loyalists hoping to revive the dynasty, other places remained as alternative locations to carry on the resistance, while surrendering the city would avoid the slaughter of its million people. Yai-shan, on the contrary, represented the edge of the Sung world, and its collapse was the end of the Sung cause. There was no refuge left. Perhaps holdouts there, having learned of the brutal Mongol slaughter at Ch'ao-chou only a year earlier, assumed that a similar fate awaited them and chose suicide over execution.

Circumstantial factors aside, I suspect that the spirit of loyalism did not suddenly materialize at Yai-shan. It was always present, a product of the Sung dynasty's unique cultural traditions and a testimony to the government's effectiveness in using education to mold culture. Whatever the motives of the men and women at Yai-shan, the Sung court, and especially in the final weeks when confronted with the grim prospect of Mongol domination, was able to generate a high degree of loyalist fervor. To the Sung dynasty's great misfortune, the sense of common purpose that unified tens of thousands at Yai-shan did not surface sooner, during the 1250s and 1260s for example, when the Mongol pressure was relieved by their own civil warfare but most Sung civil servants allowed partisan interests to prevail at the expense of a shared commitment to the dynasty.

Legacy under assault

After the fall of Yai-shan, the body of Chao Ping, the child-emperor, was reportedly retrieved from the ocean and buried in the vicinity of modern Hong Kong, and a small temple was erected on the site.[103] Dowager Consort Yang and Lu Hsiu-fu were both buried, in unfitting simplicity, near Yai-shan. In the late fifteenth century, during Ming-dynasty China, a series of temples,

---

[103] *HTC* (1958) 184, p. 5026; Chao, *Chao-shih tsu-p'u* 1, p. 75a.

some of them impressive in grandeur, were built at Yai-shan in honor of those who perished there.[104] As for members of the imperial family who died in captivity, they were afforded honorable burials in the north.

With the exception of the last three child-emperors, most Southern Sung rulers and their empresses were buried in the western suburbs of Shao-hsing, not far from the eastern stretches of Hsiao-shan county about sixty miles east of Lin-an. The site was then known as Pao-shan, "Precious Mountain." Endowed with an abundance of level land relieved by rolling hills, the spot reflected the majesty of its imperial residents, yet it was sufficiently isolated to provide the dead with a relatively secure sanctuary. The Sung imperial tombs were scattered over a large area. Kao-tsung and Hsiao-tsung, along with their spouses, had been interred not far from one another, but a handsome distance separated Kuang-tsung and Ning-tsung from preceding emperors and from one another. The Li-tsung and Tu-tsung graves, probably reasonably close to each other, were similarly distanced from the others. Precious Mountain also contained the graves of the Northern Sung emperors Hui-tsung and Ch'in-tsung, who had died in Jurchen captivity. The bodies of Hui-tsung and his empress Wei had been transported south and interred at Precious Mountain, but Ch'in-tsung had been buried near Peking, probably alongside his wife, so his "tomb" at Precious Mountain was more a memorial shrine than an actual grave.

In light of Khubilai's beneficence toward the Chao imperial clan held captive by him, there was little reason to think that the Yüan would set out to desecrate the Sung imperial tombs. Yet sometime in early January 1279, as the Sung court-in-exile prepared for its final showdown at a distant Yai-shan, the Sung tombs at Precious Mountain were being unearthed and pillaged.[105] The chief instigator was Yang-lien Chen-chia, a Tangut monk prominent in the Yangtze region and politically well connected. His alleged motive was retribution for the Sung's one-time desecration of Buddhist temples. In constructing both the Ning-tsung tomb at Precious Mountain and a ritual altar by the Ch'ien-t'ang River in Lin-an, the Sung government had destroyed several well-known Buddhist temples. These actions apparently appeared to many, and especially to an angry Buddhist clergy, as an imperial assault on religious institutions that should not go unpunished. Yet the pillaging of precious funerary relics leaves little doubt that religious retribution was less an objective than simple theft. Without Khubilai's approval, Yang-lien Chen-chia chased away custodial guards and unearthed, first, the massive tombs of

---

[104] Chao, *Chao-shih tsu-p'u* 1, p. 80b.
[105] On the incident, see Wan Ssu-t'ung, comp., *Nan Sung liu-ling i-shih* [1821–50 ed.] (Taipei, 1968), pp. 1a–13b; *HTC* (1958) 184, pp. 5021–4; Chao, *Chao-shih tsu-p'u* 1, pp. 78b–80a; Ting Ch'uan-ching, *Sung-jen i-shih hui-pien* (Shanghai, 1935) I, pp. 98–101; Rossabi, *Khubilai khan*, pp. 195–9.

Ning-tsung and Ning-tsung's empress Yang2, then the magnificently appointed tombs of Li-tsung and Tu-tsung, followed before long by the crypts of other former emperors and empresses. In the process of plundering, the intruders crudely tore burial garments from bodies only partly decomposed. The head of Li-tsung, ripped from the body, was played with like a toy. The looters left corpses strewn about as well, with no apparent concern for either etiquette or hygiene, while destroying a sizable portion, if not all, of the magnificent funeral statuary surrounding the graves. Yang-lien Chen-chia's plan was to devote some of the wealth to building a Buddhist pagoda on the banks of Hang-chou's Ch'ien-t'ang River – indeed, on the very grounds of the Sung imperial palaces – while burying the bones of Sung emperors underneath, thereby achieving the dual insult of desecrating the former residences of these Sung emperors and forcing them to bear posthumous witness to it all.

Precisely what happened to the exhumed imperial bodies is the source of some debate. The consensus among later writers is that two heroic locals, T'ang Yü and Lin Te-yang, learned in advance of the intended unearthing and removed nearly all of the bodies beforehand. They subsequently reburied the remains elsewhere, some being interred as far away as Chia-hsing. Only the body of Li-tsung appears genuinely to have fallen into the looters' hands. This contradicts significantly the earliest known account of the incident, written by the eminent late Sung anecdotist Chou Mi (1239–98), who insisted that the graves had all, in fact, been desecrated by pillagers. Later writers dismiss this as erroneous. With tombs being so scattered, they note, disentombment would have demanded several months of effort, so the removal of bodies beforehand might have occurred. Advance removal is the only explanation for Chou Mi's reported astonishment at learning that the vaults of Hui-tsung, Kao-tsung, and Hsiao-tsung were totally empty, free even of bones.[106] This revisionist interpretation has its flaws. How did T'ang Yü and Lin Te-yang evade guards responsible for protecting Precious Mountain, guards whom Yang-lien Chen-chia overcame only with considerable force? How could two men, with no more than the help of a few friends, complete a massive unearthing and reburial on short order when tombs were large, well sealed, and scattered over an extensive area? I suspect both interpretations are partially correct. Disentombment by northern pillagers probably did occur, although they may well not have completed things before encountering some local reaction, namely, the intervention of our two heroes. In the case of Hui-tsung, Kao-tsung, and Hsiao-tsung, where pillaging occurred last, there may have been time for locals to remove the bodies in advance; otherwise, T'ang Yü and friends merely retrieved bodies already exhumed and abandoned near the vaults. In any event, the sprawling

---

[106] Wan, *Nan Sung liu-ling i-shih*, pp. 12b–13b.

burial preserve at Precious Mountain was gutted.[107] Palaces at Lin-an were not spared either. Some were demolished by Yang-lien Chen-chia to build his White Tower pagoda, while others were converted into monasteries.

According to contemporaries, Yang-lien Chen-chia confiscated precious objects from over a hundred tombs in the lower Yangtze and seized countless parcels of land.[108] Admittedly, the Yüan court did not authorize these actions and eventually intervened to stop them, yet vengeful malice of this sort should not be attributed to the eccentricity of a few religious fanatics. Mongol conquerors, by stripping Sung palaces of valuables and then distributing these among various princes, had set a precedent of cultural desecration that others with privilege learned to exploit aggressively.

Malice and greed are understandable, but the desecration helped reinforce loyalist sentiment among Han Chinese. Wen T'ien-hsiang was the most eminent personification of that spirit. The one-time Sung councilor, taken captive in Kuang-nan, remained in captivity in Peking for four years, 1279–83. Khubilai reportedly admired his fortitude and hoped to win him over. Wen T'ien-hsiang could not be swayed, and his execution in early 1283 further reinforced anti-Mongol sentiment in the south. This sentiment went along with the trend among a majority of educated men of the early Yüan, particularly southerners, to boycott the regime's civil service as they pursued other professional alternatives, even at economic and political sacrifice.[109]

The death in 1279 of the last established Sung emperor, and the loss of his imperial regalia, prompted a self-serving observation by the great Mongol military leader, Bayan. Alluding to Sung T'ai-tsu's dethronement in 959 of the six-year-old emperor Chou Kung-ti (r. 959), the last emperor of the Later Chou dynasty (951–9), Bayan observed that T'ai-tsu had taken the empire over from a child, and that the last of the Sung emperors was also a child.

---

[107] Ann Paludan notes: "For the second half of the Song dynasty, there were no spirit roads. Determined to regain the northern half of the country the Southern Song regarded their sojourn in Hangzhou as temporary. Burials were provisional, awaiting return to the dynastic graveyard at Gongxian. Their tombs were given the official name 'temporary sepulchres' (cuan gong) rather than mausoleum (ling), [and] the scale was very small, tumuli being only two metres high and a bare five metres in circumference"; see Ann Paludan, The Chinese spirit road: The classical tradition of stone tomb statuary (New Haven, Conn., 1991), p. 148.

[108] Wan, Nan Sung liu-ling i-shih, pp. 6a–b.

[109] Frederick W. Mote, "Confucian eremitism in the Yüan period," in The Confucian persuasion, ed. Arthur F. Wright (Stanford, Calif., 1960), pp. 202–43; Davis, Court and family in Sung China, pp. 164–5, 180–1. For contrasting views of the extent and significance of eremitism in the early Yüan, see Jay, A change in dynasties, and Paul J. Smith, "Fear of gynarchy in an age of chaos: Kong Qi's reflections on life in south China under Mongol rule," Journal of Economic and Social History of the Orient 41 No. 1 (1998), pp. 1–95.

BIBLIOGRAPHY

Adshead, S. A. M. *China in world history*. New York: St. Martin's Press, 1988.

Akisada Jitsuzō [Tamura Jitsuzō] 秋貞実造 「田村実造」. "Sen-en no meiyaku to sono shiteki igi (jō)" 澶淵の盟約と其の史的意義(上). *Shirin* 史林 20 No. 1 (1935), pp. 1–36.

Akisada Jitsuzō [Tamura Jitsuzō] 秋貞実造 「田村実造」. "Sen-en no meiyaku to sono shiteki igi (ge)" 澶淵の盟約と其の史的意義(下). *Shirin* 史林 20 No. 4 (1935), pp. 175–205.

Allsen, Thomas T. *Mongol imperialism: The policies of the Grand Qan Möngke in China, Russia, and the Islamic lands, 1251–1259*. Berkeley: University of California Press, 1987.

Allsen, Thomas T. "The rise of the Mongolian empire and Mongolian rule in north China." In *The Cambridge history of China*. Volume 6: *Alien regimes and border states, 907–1368*, ed. Herbert Franke and Denis C. Twitchett. New York: Cambridge University Press, 1994, pp. 321–413.

Anderson, James A. *The rebel den of Nùng Trí Cao: Eleventh-century rebellion and response along the Sino-Vietnamese frontier*. Seattle: University of Washington Press, 2006.

Anderson, James A. "Treacherous factions: Shifting frontier alliances in the breakdown of Sino-Vietnamese relations on the eve of the 1075 border war." In *Battlefronts real and imagined: War, border, and identity in the Chinese middle period*, ed. Donald J. Wyatt. New York: Palgrave Macmillan, 2008.

Ang, Melvin Thlick-Len. "Sung-Liao diplomacy in eleventh- and twelfth-century China: A study of the social and political determinants of foreign policy." Diss., University of Pennsylvania, 1983.

Aoyama Sadao 青山定雄. "The newly-risen bureaucrats in Fukien at the Five Dynasty-Sung period, with special reference to their genealogies." *Memoirs of the Research Department of the Tōyō Bunko* 21 (1962), pp. 1–48.

Araki Toshikazu 荒木敏一. "Nung Chih-kao and the k'o-ch'ü examinations." *Acta Asiatica* 50 (1986), pp. 73–94.

Araki Toshikazu 荒木敏一. "Sō Taiso sakekuse kō" 宋太祖酒癖考. *Shirin* 史林 38 No. 5 (1955), pp. 41–55.

Araki Toshikazu 荒木敏一. *Sōdai kakyo seido kenkyū* 宋代科舉制度研究. Tōyōshi kenkyū sōkan 東洋史研究叢刊 22. Kyoto: Tōyōshi Kenkyūkai, 1969.

Barfield, Thomas J. *The perilous frontier: Nomadic empires and China.* Studies in Social Discontinuity. Cambridge, Mass.: Basil Blackwell, 1989.

Bickford, Maggie. "Emperor Huizong and the aesthetic of agency." *Archives of Asian Art* 53 (2002–3), pp. 71–104.

Bielenstein, Hans. "Wang Mang, the restoration of the Han dynasty, and Later Han." In *The Cambridge history of China.* Volume 1: *The Ch'in and Han empires, 221 B.C.–A.D. 220,* ed. Denis C. Twitchett and Michael Loewe. Cambridge: Cambridge University Press, 1986, pp. 223–90.

Birch, Cyril, ed. *Anthology of Chinese literature.* 1965. Harmondsworth, U.K.: Penguin, 1967.

Birge, Bettine. "Women and Confucianism from Song to Ming: The institutionalization of patrilineality." In *The Song-Yuan-Ming transition in Chinese history,* ed. Paul J. Smith and Richard von Glahn. Harvard East Asian Monographs 221. Cambridge, Mass.: Harvard University Asia Center, 2003, pp. 212–40.

Bodman, Richard W., and Charles A. Peterson. "Cheng Ch'ing-chih." In *Sung biographies,* ed. Herbert Franke. 4 vols. Münchener Ostasiatische Studien 16, 1–3; 17, 4. Vol. 1. Wiesbaden: Franz Steiner Verlag, 1976, pp. 156–63.

Bol, Peter K. "Emperors can claim antiquity too – emperorship and autocracy under the New Policies." In *Emperor Huizong and late Northern Song China: The politics of culture and the culture of politics,* ed. Patricia B. Ebrey and Maggie Bickford. Cambridge, Mass.: Harvard University Asia Center, 2006, pp. 173–205.

Bol, Peter K. "Examinations and orthodoxies: 1070 and 1313 compared." In *Culture and state in Chinese history: Conventions, accommodations, and critiques,* ed. Theodore B. Huters et al. Stanford, Calif.: Stanford University Press, 1997, pp. 29–57.

Bol, Peter K. "Government, society, and state: On the political visions of Ssu-ma Kuang and Wang An-shih." In *Ordering the world: Approaches to state and society in Sung dynasty China,* ed. Robert P. Hymes and Conrad Schirokauer. Studies on China 16. Berkeley: University of California Press, 1993, pp. 128–92.

Bol, Peter K. "Neo-Confucianism and local society, twelfth to sixteenth century: A case study." In *The Song-Yuan-Ming transition in Chinese history,* ed. Paul J. Smith and Richard von Glahn. Harvard East Asian Monographs 221. Cambridge, Mass.: Harvard University Asia Center, 2003, pp. 241–83.

Bol, Peter K. "The Sung examination system and the *Shih.*" Review of *The thorny gates of learning in Sung China: A social history of examinations,* by John W. Chaffee. *Asia Major,* 3rd series, 3 No. 2 (1990), pp. 149–71.

Bol, Peter K. *"This culture of ours": Intellectual transition in T'ang and Sung China.* Stanford, Calif.: Stanford University Press, 1992.

Bol, Peter K. "Whither the emperor? Emperor Huizong, the New Policies, and the Tang-Song transition." *Journal of Sung-Yuan Studies* 31 (2001), pp. 103–34.

Boltz, Judith M. *A survey of Taoist literature: Tenth to seventeenth centuries.* China Research Monograph 32. Berkeley, Calif.: Institute of East Asian Studies, 1987.

Bossler, Beverly J. *Powerful relations: Kinship, status, and the state in Sung China (960–1279).* Harvard-Yenching Institute Mongraph Series 43. Cambridge, Mass.: Council on East Asian Studies, Harvard University, 1998.

Brown, William A. *Wen T'ien-hsiang: A biographical study of a Sung patriot.* Asian Library Series 25. San Francisco: Chinese Materials Center, 1986.

Cahill, Suzanne E. "Taoism at the Sung court: The Heavenly Text affair of 1008." *Bulletin of Sung-Yüan Studies* 16 (1981), pp. 23–44.

Chaffee, John C. "Two Sung imperial clan genealogies: Preliminary findings and questions." *Journal of Sung-Yuan Studies* 23 (1993), pp. 99–109.

Chaffee, John W. *Branches of heaven: A history of the imperial clan of Sung China.* Harvard East Asian Monographs 183. Cambridge, Mass.: Harvard University Asia Center, 1999.

Chaffee, John W. "From capital to countryside: Changing residency patterns of the Sung imperial clan." *Chinese Culture* 30 No. 1 (1989), pp. 21–34.

Chaffee, John W. "Huizong, Cai Jing, and the politics of reform." In *Emperor Huizong and late Northern Song China: The politics of culture and the culture of politics*, ed. Patricia B. Ebrey and Maggie Bickford. Cambridge, Mass.: Harvard University Asia Center, 2006, pp. 31–77.

Chaffee, John W. "The marriage of Sung imperial classwomen." In *Marriage and inequality in Chinese society*, ed. Rubie S. Watson and Patricia B. Ebrey. Studies on China 12. Berkeley: University of California Press, 1991, pp. 133–69.

Chaffee, John W. "The rise and regency of Empress Liu (969–1033)." *Journal of Sung-Yuan Studies* 31 (2001), pp. 1–26.

Chaffee, John W. *The thorny gates of learning in Sung China: A social history of examinations.* Cambridge: Cambridge University Press, 1985.

Chaffee, John W. *The thorny gates of learning in Sung China: A social history of examinations.* 1985. New ed. Albany: State University of New York Press, 1995.

Ch'ai Te-keng 柴德賡. "Sung huan-kuan ts'an-yü chün shih k'ao" 宋宦官參預軍事考. *Fu-jen hsüeh-chih* 輔仁學誌 10 No. 1–2 (1941), pp. 187–225.

Chan Chieh 詹玠. *I-shih chi-wen* 遺史記聞. In *Shuo-fu 120 chuan* 說郛120卷. Shanghai: Shang-wu yin-shu-kuan, 1927.

Chan Hok-lam. *Legitimation in imperial China: Discussions under the Jürchen-Chin dynasty (1115–1234).* Seattle: University of Washington Press, 1984.

Chan, Wing-tsit. *Chu Hsi: New studies.* Honolulu: University of Hawaii Press, 1989.

Chang Ch'i-fan 張其凡. "Sung T'ai-tsung lun" 宋太宗論. *Li-shih yen-chiu* 歷史研究 2 (1987), pp. 96–109.

Chang Ch'i-fan 張其凡. "Wu-tai cheng-ch'üan ti-shan chih k'ao-ch'a – chien-p'ing Chou Shih-tsung ti cheng chün" 五代政權遞嬗之考察——兼評周世宗的整軍. *Hua-nan shih-fan ta-hsüeh hsüeh-pao: She-hui k'o-hsüeh pan* 華南師范大學學報：社會科學版 1 (1985), pp. 22–30.

Chang Ch'i-fan 張其凡. *Wu-tai chin-chün ch'u-t'an* 五代禁軍初探. Hang-chou: Chi-nan ta-hsüeh ch'u-pan-she, 1993.

Chang Chia-chü 張家駒. *Chao K'uang-yin chuan* 趙匡胤傳. Nanking: Chiang-su jen-min ch'u-pan-she, 1959.

Chang Chia-chü 張家駒. *Liang Sung ching-chi chung-hsin ti nan-i* 兩宋經濟重心的南移. Wu-han: Hu-pei jen-min ch'u-pan-she, 1957.

Chang Fang-p'ing 張方平. *Le-ch'üan chi* 樂全集. c. 1100. [*Ssu-k'u ch'üan-shu* 四庫全書, *Wen-yüan ko* 文淵閣 1779 ed.]. In *Ssu-k'u ch'üan-shu chen-pen ch'u-chi* 四庫全書珍本初集. 1934–5. Vols. 252–5. Taipei: T'ai-wan shang-wu yin-shu-kuan, 1969.

Chang Fu-hua 張復華. *Pei Sung chung-ch'i i-hou chih kuan-chih kai-ko* 北宋中期以後之官制改革. Wen-shih che-hsüeh chi-ch'eng 文史哲學集成 246. Taipei: Wen-shih-che ch'u-pan-she, 1991.

Chang Hsi-wei 張熙惟. "Sung-tai che-pien-chih t'an-hsi" 宋代折變制探析. *Chung-kuo shih yen-chiu* 中國史研究 No. 1 (1992), pp. 26–33.

Chang Ming-fu 張明福. "Shih-lun Pei Sung Ch'ing-li nien-chien ti ping-pien" 試論北宋慶曆年間的兵變. *Shan-tung Shih-fan hsüeh-yüan hsüeh pao* 山東師範學院學報 2 (1980), pp. 49–54.

Chang T'ang-ying 張唐英. *Shu t'ao-wu* 蜀檮杌. 11th c. [*I-hai chu-ch'en* 藝海珠塵 c. 1800 ed.; 1850]. In *Pai-pu ts'ung-shu chi-ch'eng* 百部叢書集成. 1965–70. Vol. 35. Taipei: I-wen yin-shu-kuan, 1968.

Chang Tse-hsien 張澤咸. *T'ang Wu-tai nung-min chan-cheng shih-liao hui-pien* 唐五代農民戰爭史料彙編. 2 vols. Peking: Chung-hua shu-chü, 1979.

Chang Yin-lin 張蔭麟. "Nan Sung wang-kuo shih pu" 南宋亡國史補. In *Sung-shih yen-chiu chi: ti erh chi* 宋史研究集：第二輯, ed. Sung-shih tso-t'an-hui 宋史座談會. Chung-hua ts'ung-shu 中華叢書. Taipei: Chung-hua ts'ung-shu pien-shen wei-yüan-hui, 1964, pp. 105–22.

Chang Yin-lin 張蔭麟. "Sung T'ai-tsu shih-pei chi cheng-shih-t'ang k'o-shih k'ao" 宋太祖誓碑及政事堂刻石考. *Wen-shih tsa-chih* 文史雜誌 1 No. 7 (1940), pp. 15–18.

Chang Yin-lin 張蔭麟. "Sung T'ai-tsung chi-t'ung k'ao-shih" 宋太宗繼統考實. *Wen-shih tsa-chih* 文史雜誌 1 No. 8 (1941), pp. 26–31.

Ch'ang Pi-te 昌彼得 et al., eds. *Sung-jen chuan-chi tzu-liao so-yin* 宋人傳記資料索引. 6 vols. So-yin hui-k'an 索引彙刊. Taipei: Ting-wen shu-chü, 1974–76.

Chang, Curtis Chung. "Inheritance problems in the first two reigns of the Sung dynasty." *Chinese Culture* 9 No. 4 (1968), pp. 10–44.

Chao-chung lu 昭忠錄. c. 1290. [Shou-shan ko ts'ung-shu 守山閣叢書 1922 ed.]. In *Pai-pu ts'ung-shu chi-ch'eng* 百部叢書集成. 1965–70. Taipei: I-wen yin-shu-kuan, 1968.

Chao Hsi-nien 趙錫年. *Chao-shih tsu-p'u* 趙氏族譜. [Academia Sinica, Fu Ssu-nien 傅斯年 Library, rare edition]. Hong Kong: n.p., 1937.

Chao Hsiang-en (Samuel H. Chao) 趙享恩. "The day Northern Sung fell." *Chung-yüan hsüeh-pao* 中原學報 No. 8 (1979), pp. 144–57.

Chao I 趙翼. *Nien-erh shih cha-chi* 廿二史劄記. 1799, ed. and ann. Tu Wei-yün 杜維運. Taipei: Ting-wen shu-chü, 1975.

Chao I 趙翼. *Nien-erh shih cha-chi* 廿二史劄記. 1799, ed. and ann. Tu Wei-yün 杜維運. Taipei: Hua-shih ch'u-pan-she, 1977.

Chao I 趙翼. *Nien-erh shih cha-chi* 廿二史劄記. 1799. 3 vols. In *Ssu-pu pei-yao* 四部備要. 1920–33. Chung-hua shu-chü. Taipei: T'ai-wan chung-hua shu-chü, 1968.

Chao Ju-yü 趙汝愚. *Chu-ch'en tsou-i* 諸臣奏議. 1186. Sung-shih tzu-liao ts'ui-pien ti i chi 宋史資料萃編第一輯 Vols. 9–18. Taipei: Wen-hai ch'u-pan-she, 1970.

Chao Ju-yü 趙汝愚. *Sung-ch'ao chu-ch'en tsou-i* 宋朝諸臣奏議. 1186. 2 vols. Shanghai: Shang-hai ku-chi ch'u-pan-she, 1999.

Chao Kuang-yüan 趙光遠. "Lüeh-lun Ch'i-tan chün-tui tsai Chung-yüan 'Ta ts'ao-ku'" 略論契丹軍隊在中原「打草谷」. *Chung-kuo she-hui k'o-hsüeh-yüan yen-chiu-sheng-yüan hsüeh-pao* 中國社會科學院研究生院學報 6 (1986), pp. 67–71.

Chao Shin-yi. "Huizong and the Divine Empyrean palace temple network." In *Emperor Huizong and late Northern Song China: The politics of culture and the culture of politics*, ed. Patricia B. Ebrey and Maggie Bickford. Cambridge, Mass.: Harvard University Asia Center, 2006, pp. 324–58.

Chao Ti-hsien 趙滌賢. "Shih-lun Pei Sung pien-fa-p'ai chün-shih kai-ko ti ch'eng-kung" 試論北宋變法派軍事改革的成. *Li-shih yen-chiu* 歷史研究 250 (1997), pp. 143–60.

Chao T'ieh-han 趙鐵寒. "Sung-tai ti t'ai-hsüeh" 宋代的太學. In *Sung-shih yen-chiu chi: Ti i chi* 宋史研究集：第一輯, ed. Sung-shih yen-chiu-hui 宋史研究會. Chung-hua ts'ung-shu 中華叢書. Taipei: Chung-hua ts'ung-shu wei-yüan-hui, 1958, pp. 317–56.

Chao T'ieh-han 趙鐵寒. "Yen–Yün shih-liu chou ti ti-li fen-hsi (shang)" 燕雲十六州的地理分析 (上). *Ta-lu tsa-chih* 大陸雜誌 17 No. 11 (1958), pp. 3–7.

Chao T'ieh-han 趙鐵寒. "Yen–Yün shih-liu chou ti ti-li fen-hsi (hsia)" 燕雲十六州的地理分析(下). *Ta-lu tsa-chih* 大陸雜誌 17 No. 12 (1958), pp. 18–22.

Chao Ya-shu 趙雅書. "Sung-tai ti t'ien-fu chih-tu yü t'ien-fu shou-ju chuang k'uang" 宋代的田賦制度與天賦收入狀況. M.A. thesis, Kuo-li T'ai-wan ta-hsüeh 國立臺灣大學, 1969.

Chao Yü-yüeh 趙雨樂. *T'ang Sung pien-ko-ch'i chün-cheng chih-tu shih yen-chiu (1) – san-pan kuan-chih chih yen-pien* 唐宋變革期軍政制度史研究(一) – 三班官制之演變. Taipei: Wen-shih-che ch'u-pan-she, 1993.

Ch'ao-yeh i-chi 朝野遺記. 13th c. Hsüeh-hai lei-pien 學海類編. Taipei: Wen-hai ch'u-pan-she, 1964.

Chaves, Jonathan. *Mei Yao-ch'en and the development of early Sung poetry*. Studies in Oriental Culture 13. New York: Columbia University Press, 1976.

Chen Te-hsiu 真德秀. *Hsi-shan hsien-sheng Chen Wen-chung kung wen-chi* 西山先生真文忠公文集. 13th c. [Ming Cheng-te 正德 1506–21 ed.; *Ssu-pu ts'ung-k'an ch'u-pien* 四部叢刊初編 1929 ed.]. In *Ssu-pu ts'ung-k'an cheng-pien* 四部叢刊正編. Vol. 61. Taipei: T'ai-wan shang-wu yin-shu-kuan, 1979.

Ch'en Ch'ing-ch'üan 陳清泉 et al. *Chung-kuo shih-hsüeh-chia p'ing-chuan* 中國史學家評傳. 3 vols. Cheng-chou: Chung-chou ku-chi ch'u-pan-she, 1985.

Ch'en Fu-liang 陳傅良. *Chih-chai hsien-sheng wen-chi* 止齋先生文集. In *Ssu-pu ts'ung-k'an ch'u-pien* 四部叢刊初編. 1919–22. Shang-wu yin-shu-kuan. Taipei: T'ai-wan shang-wu yin-shu-kuan, 1979.

Ch'en I-yen 陳義彥. *Pei Sung t'ung-chih chieh-ts'eng she-hui liu-tung chih yen-chiu* 北宋統治階層社會流動之研究. Chia-hsin shui-ni kung-ssu wen-hua chi-chin-hui ts'ung-shu 嘉新水泥公司文化基金會叢書 226. Taipei: Chia-hsin shui-ni kung-ssu wen-hua chi-chin-hui, 1977.

Ch'en Kao-hua 陳高華. "Wang Chi shih Sung shih-shih k'ao-lüeh" 王偁使宋事實考略. In *Ryū Shiken hakuse shōju kinen: Sō-shi kenkū ronshū* 劉子健博士頌壽紀念：宋史研究論集, ed. Kinugawa Tsuyoshi 衣川強. Kyoto: Dōhōsha, 1989, pp. 103–11.

Ch'en Le-su 陳樂素. "Kuei-lin shih-k'o 'Yüan-yu tang-chi'" 桂林石刻《〈元祐黨籍〉》. *Hsüeh-shu yen-chiu* 學術研究 61 No. 6 (1983), pp. 63–71.

Ch'en Le-su 陳樂素. "Pei Sung kuo-chia ti ku-chi cheng-li yin-hsing shih-yeh chi ch'i li-shih i-i" 北宋國家的古籍整理印行事業及其歷史意義. In *Sung Yüan wen-shih yen-chiu* 宋元文史研究, ed. Ch'en Le-su 陳樂素. Kuang-chou: Kuang-tung jen-min ch'u-pan-she, 1988, pp. 65–90.

Ch'en Pang-chan 陳邦瞻 et al. *Sung-shih chi-shih pen mo* 宋史紀事本末. 1605. 2 vols. Taipei: San-min shu-chü, 1963.

Ch'en Pang-chan 陳邦瞻 et al. *Sung-shih chi-shih pen-mo* 宋史紀事本末. 1605. 3 vols. Peking: Chung-hua shu-chü, 1977.

Ch'en Shih-sung 陳世松 et al. *Sung-Yüan chan-cheng shih* 宋元戰爭史. Ch'eng-tu: Ssu-ch'uan-sheng she-hui ch'u-pan she, 1988.

Ch'en Teng-yüan 陳登原. "Ch'in Kuei p'ing" 秦檜評. *Chin-ling hsüeh-pao* 金陵學報 1 No. 1 (1931), pp. 27–46.

Ch'en Teng-yüan 陳登原. *Chung-kuo t'u-ti chih-tu* 中國土地制度. Shanghai: Shang-wu yin-shu-kuan, 1932.

Ch'en Teng-yüan 陳登原. "Han P'ing-yüan p'ing" 韓平原評. *Chin-ling hsüeh-pao* 金陵學報 4 No. 1 (1934), pp. 89–149.

Ch'en Teng-yüan 陳登原. *Kuo-shih chiu-wen* 國史舊聞. 2 vols. Peking: Chung-hua shu-chü, 1958–62.

Ch'en Teng-yüan 陳登原. *Kuo-shih chiu-wen* 國史舊聞. Peking: Sheng-huo, tu-shu, hsin-chih san-lien shu-tien, 1958.

Chen, Kenneth K. S. *Buddhism in China: A historical survey*. Princeton, N.J.: Princeton University Press, 1964.

Cheng Hsia 鄭俠. *Hsi-t'ang chi* 西塘集. [*Ssu-k'u ch'üan-shu* 四庫全書, *Wen-yüan ko* 文淵閣 1779 ed.]. In *Ssu-k'u ch'üan-shu chen-pen ssu-chi* 四庫全書珍本四集. 1973. Vols. 251–2. Taipei: T'ai-wan shang-wu yin-shu-kuan, 1973.

Cheng Hsüeh-meng 鄭學檬. "Kuan-yü Shih Ching-t'ang p'ing-chia ti chi-ko wen-t'i" 關於石敬瑭評價的幾個問題. *Hsia-men ta-hsüeh hsüeh-pao* 廈門大學學報 1 (1983), pp. 57–63.

Cheng Hsüeh-meng 鄭學檬. "Wu-tai shih-ch'i Ch'ang-chiang liu-yü chi Chiang-nan ti-ch'ü ti nung-yeh ching-chi" 五代時期長江流域及江南地區的農業經濟. *Li-shih yen-chiu* 歷史研究 4 (1985), pp. 32–44.

Cheng Shih-kang 鄭世剛. "Pei Sung ti chuan-yün-shih" 北宋的轉運使. In *Sung-shih yen-chiu lun-wen-chi: 1982 nien nien-hui pien-k'an* 宋史研究論文集：一九八二年會編刊, ed. Teng Kuang-ming 鄧廣銘 and Li Chia-chü 酈家駒. Cheng-chou: Ho-nan jen-min ch'u-pan-she, 1984, pp. 319–45.

Ch'eng Hao 程顥 and Ch'eng I 程頤. *Erh Ch'eng chi* 二程集, ed. Wang Hsiao-yü 王孝魚. 4 vols. Peking: Chung-hua shu-chü, 1981.

Ch'eng Kuang-yü 程光裕. "Shan-yüan chih-meng yü t'ien-shu (shang)" 澶淵之盟與天書(上). *Ta-lu tsa-chih* 大陸雜誌 22 No. 6 (1961), pp. 11–17.

Ch'eng Kuang-yü 程光裕. "Shan-yüan chih-meng yü t'ien-shu (hsia)" 澶淵之盟與天書(下). *Ta-lu tsa-chih* 大陸雜誌 22 No. 7 (1961), pp. 21–8.

Ch'eng Kuang-yü 程光裕. *Sung T'ai-tsung tui Liao chan-cheng k'ao* 宋太宗對遼戰爭考. Jen-jen wen-k'u 人人文庫 224. Taipei: T'ai-wan shang-wu yin-shu-kuan, 1972.

Ch'eng Kuang-yü 程光裕 et al. *Chung-kuo li-shih ti-t'u* 中國歷史地圖. 2 vols. Taipei: Chung-kuo wen-hua ta-hsüeh ch'u-pan-pu, 1984.

Ch'eng Min-sheng 程民生. "Lun Pei Sung ts'ai-cheng ti t'e-tien yü chi-pin ti chia-hsiang" 論北宋財政的特點與積貧的假象. *Chung-kuo shih yen-chiu* 中國史研究 3 (1984), pp. 27–40.

Ch'eng Min-sheng 程民生. "Pei Sung t'an-shih chi-kou – huang-ch'eng-ssu" 北宋探事機構 – 皇城司. *Ho-nan ta-hsüeh hsüeh-pao: Che-she pan* 河南大學學報：哲社版 4 (1984), pp. 37–41.

Chi Ch'ao-ting. *Key economic areas in Chinese history – As revealed in the development of public works for water-control*. London: George Allen and Unwin, 1936.

Chi Tzu-ya (Ch'i Hsia) 季子涯(漆俠). "Chao K'uang-yin ho Chao Sung chuan-chih chu-i chung-yang chi-chüan chih-tu ti fa-chan" 趙匡胤和趙宋專制主義中央集權制度的發展. *Li-shih chiao-hsüeh* 歷史教學 12 (1954), pp. 13–18.

Ch'i Hsia 漆俠. *Sung-tai ching-chi shih* 宋代經濟史. 2 vols. Chung-kuo ku-tai ching-chi-shih tuan-tai yen-chiu 中國古代經濟史斷代研究 5. Shanghai: Shang-hai jen-min ch'u-pan-she, 1987–8.

Ch'i Hsia 漆俠. *Wang An-shih pien-fa* 王安石變法. 2nd ed. Shanghai: Shang-hai jen-min ch'u-pan-she, 1979.

Chia Ta-ch'üan 賈大泉. "Lun Pei Sung ti ping-pien" 論北宋的兵變. In *Sung-shih yen-chiu lun-wen-chi: Chung-hua wen-shih lun-ts'ung tseng-k'an* 宋史研究論文集：中華文史論叢增刊, ed. Teng Kuang-ming 鄧廣銘 and Ch'eng Ying-liu 程應鏐. Chung-hua wen-shih lun-ts'ung tseng-k'an 中華文史論叢增刊. Shanghai: Shang-hai ku-chi ch'u-pan-she, 1982, pp. 453–65.

Chia Yü-ying 賈玉英. *Sung-tai chien-ch'a chih-tu* 宋代監察制度. Sung-tai yen-chiu ts'ung-shu 宋代研究叢書. K'ai-feng: Ho-nan ta-hsüeh ch'u-pan-she, 1996.

Chiang Fu-ts'ung 蔣復璁. "Sung Chen-tsung yü Shan-yüan chih-meng (shang)" 宋真宗與澶淵之盟(上). *Ta-lu tsa-chih* 大陸雜誌 22 No. 8 (1961), pp. 26–30.

Chiang Fu-ts'ung 蔣復璁. "Sung Chen-tsung yü Shan-yüan chih-meng (hsü)" 宋真宗與澶淵之盟(續). *Ta-lu tsa-chih* 大陸雜誌 22 No. 9 (1961), pp. 27–34.

Chiang Fu-ts'ung 蔣復璁. "Sung Chen-tsung yü Shan-yüan chih-meng (mo)" 宋真宗與澶淵之盟(末). *Ta-lu tsa-chih* 大陸雜誌 22 No. 10 (1961), pp. 32–6.

Chiang Fu-ts'ung 蔣復璁. "Sung-tai i-ko kuo-ts'e ti chien-t'ao" 宋代一個國策的檢討. *Ta-lu tsa-chih* 大陸雜誌 9 No. 7 (1954), pp. 21–36.

Chiang Fu-ts'ung 蔣復璁. "Sung T'ai-tsu chih peng pu yü-nien erh kai-yüan k'ao" 宋太祖之崩不逾年而改元考. In *Ch'ing-chu Chu Chia-hua hsien-sheng ch'i-shih-sui lun-wen-chi* 慶祝朱家驊先生七十歲論文集, ed. Ch'ing-chu Chu Chia-hua hsien-sheng ch'i-shih-sui lun-wen-chi bien-chi wei-yüan-hui 慶祝朱家驊先生七十歲論文集編輯委員會. Ta-lu tsa-chih t'e k'an 大陸雜誌特刊 2. Taipei: Ta-lu tsa-chih-she, 1962, pp. 457–60.

Chiang Fu-ts'ung 蔣復璁. "Sung T'ai-tsu shih T'ai-tsung yü Chao P'u ti cheng-cheng" 宋太祖時太宗與趙普的政爭. *Shih-hsüeh hui-k'an* 史學彙刊 5 (1973), pp. 1–14.

Chiang Fu-ts'ung 蔣復璁. "Sung T'ai-tsung Chin-ti mu-fu k'ao" 宋太宗晉邸幕府考. *Ta-lu tsa-chih* 大陸雜誌 30 No. 3 (1965), pp. 15–23.

Chiang Fu-ts'ung 蔣復璁. "Sung T'ai-tsung shih-lu tsuan-hsiu k'ao" 宋太祖實錄纂修考. In *Sung-shih hsin-t'an, Chiang Fu-ts'ung pien-chu* 宋史新探, 蔣復璁編著, ed. Chiang Fu-ts'ung 蔣復璁. Taipei: Cheng-chung shu-chü, 1966, pp. 61–72.

Chiang I-hsüeh 蔣逸雪. *Lu Hsiu-fu nien-p'u* 陸秀夫年譜. Jen-jen wen-k'u 人人文庫 2323. Taipei: T'ai-wan shang-wu yin-shu-kuan, 1977.

Chiba Hiroshi 千葉熙. "Kan Takuchū – Sōdai kanshinden sono ni" 韓侂胄——宋代姦臣傳その二. In *Yamazaki sensei taikan kinen Tōyō shigaku ronsō* 山崎先生退官記念東洋史學論叢, ed. Yamazaki Sensei Taikan Kinenkai 山崎先生退官記念会. Tokyo: Yamazaki Sensei Taikan Kinenkai, 1967, pp. 279–89.

Chiba Hiroshi 千葉熙. "Sōdai no kōhi – Taiso, Taisō, Shinsō, Jinsō shichō" 宋代の后妃——太祖、太宗、真宗、仁宗四朝. In *Aoyama Hakushi koki kinen Sōdai shi ronsō* 青山博士古稀紀念宋代史論叢, ed. Aoyama Hakushi Koki Kinen Sōdai-shi Ronsō Kankōkai 青山博士古稀紀念宋代史論叢刊行会. Tokyo: Seishin Shobō, 1974, pp. 209–38.

Chien Po-tsan 翦伯贊. *Chung-kuo shih kang-yao* 中國史綱要. 1962. 4 vols. Peking: Jen-min ch'u-pan-she, 1979.

Chien Yu-wen 簡又文, ed. *Sung huang-t'ai chi-nien-chi* 宋皇臺紀念集. Hong Kong: Hsiang-kang Chao tsu tsung ch'in tsung hui, 1960.

Chien Yu-wen 簡又文. *Sung-mo erh-ti nan-ch'ien nien-lu k'ao* 宋末二帝南遷輦路考. Meng-chin shu-wu ts'ung-shu 猛進書屋叢書. Hong Kong: Hsiang-kang Chao tsu tsung ch'in tsung hui, 1957.

Ch'ien Shih-sheng 錢士升. *Nan Sung shu* 南宋書. c. 1590. [Sung–Liao–Chin–Yüan ssu-shih 宋遼金元四史 ed.]. N.p.: n.p., 1792.

Ch'ien Ta-hsin 錢大昕. *Nien-erh shih k'ao-i* 廿二史考異. 1806. In *Chia-ting Ch'ien-shih Ch'ien-yen-t'ang ch'üan-shu* 嘉定錢氏潛研堂全書. 1884. Ch'ang-sha: Lung-shih chia-shu ch'ung-k'an, 1884.

Chin Chung-shu 金中樞. "Sung-tai san-sheng chang-kuan fei-chih ti yen-chiu" 宋代三省長官廢置的研究. *Hsin-ya hsüeh-pao* 新亞學報 11 No. 1 (1974), pp. 89–147.

Chin Yü-fu 金毓黻. *Sung Liao Chin shih* 宋遼金史. 1936. Shanghai: Shang-wu yin-shu-kuan, 1946.

Ch'in Hsiang-yeh 秦緗業 and Huang I-chou 黃以周. *Hsü tzu-chih t'ung-chien ch'ang-pien shih-pu* 續資治通鑑長編拾補. 1881. Taipei: Shih-chieh shu-chü, 1964.

Ching-k'ang yao-lu 靖康要錄. c. 1165. [Ts'ung-shu chi-ch'eng ch'u-pien 叢書集成初編 1935–7 ed.]. Peking: Chung-hua shu-chü, 1985.

Ching, Julia. "Chu Hsi on personal cultivation." In *Chu Hsi and Neo-Confucianism*, ed. Wing-tsit Chan. Honolulu: University of Hawaii Press, 1986, pp. 273–91.

Chou Chin-sheng 周金聲. *An economic history of China*, ed. and trans. Edward H. Kaplan. Western Washington State College, Program in East Asian Studies Occasional Papers 7. Bellingham: Western Washington State College, 1974.

Chou Mi 周密. *Ch'i-tung yeh-yü* 齊東野語. Late 13th c. Chin-tai mi-shu 津逮秘書. Shanghai: Po-ku-chai, 1922.

Chou Mi 周密. *Ch'i-tung yeh-yü* 齊東野語. 1291. T'ang Sung shih-liao pi-chi ts'ung-k'an 唐宋史料筆記叢刊. Peking: Chung-hua shu-chü, 1983.

Chou Mi 周密. *Kuei-hsin tsa-chih* 癸辛雜識. c. 1298. [*Hsüeh-chin t'ao-yüan* 學津討原 1806 ed.; 1922 ed.]. In *Pai-pu ts'ung-shu chi-ch'eng* 百部叢書集成. 1965–70. 46. Taipei: I-wen yin-shu-kuan, 1965.

Chou Pao-chu 周寶珠. "Lüeh-lun Lü Hui-ch'ing" 略論呂惠卿. In *Sung-shih yen-chiu lun-wen-chi: Chung-hua wen-shih lun-ts'ung tseng-k'an* 宋史研究論文集：中華文史論叢增刊, ed. Teng Kuang-ming 鄧廣銘 and Ch'eng Ying-liu 程應鏐. Chung-hua wen-shih lun-ts'ung tseng-k'an 中華文史論叢增刊. Shanghai: Shang-hai ku-chi ch'u-pan-she, 1982, pp. 335–49.

Chou Pi-ta 周必大. *Chou I-kuo Wen-chung kung chi* 周益國文忠公集. N.p.: Lu-ling Ou-yang shih Ying-t'ang pieh-shu ch'ung k'an, 1848.

Chou Pi-ta 周必大. *Wen-chung chi* 文忠集. c. 1206. [*Ssu-k'u ch'üan-shu* 四庫全書, *Wen-yüan ko* 文淵閣 1779 ed.]. In *Ssu-k'u ch'üan-shu chen-pen erh-chi* 四庫全書珍本二集. 1971. Vols. 274–93. Taipei: T'ai-wan shang-wu yin-shu-kuan, 1971.

Chou Tao-chi 周道濟. "Sung-tai tsai-hsiang ming-ch'eng yü ch'i shih-ch'üan chih yen-chiu" 宋代宰相名稱與其實權之研究. *Ta-lu tsa-chih* 大陸雜誌 17 No. 12 (1958), pp. 10–17.

Chou Yü-ch'ung 周羽翀. *San Ch'u hsin-lu* 三楚新錄. [*Hsüeh-hai lei-pien* 學海類編 1831 ed.; 1920]. In *Pai-pu ts'ung-shu chi-ch'eng* 百部叢書集成. 1965–70. Vol. 24. Taipei: I-wen yin-shu-kuan, 1967.

Chu Ch'ang-wen 朱長文. *Wu-chün t'u-ching hsü-chi* 吳郡圖經續記. 1084. In *Sung Yüan fang-chih ts'ung-k'an* 宋元方誌叢刊. Vol. 1, pp. 639–91. Peking: Chung-hua shu-chü, 1990.

Chu Hsi 朱熹. *Chu-tzu yü-lei* 朱子語類. 1270. [1473 ed.]. 8 vols. Taipei: Cheng-chung shu-chü, 1962.

Chu Hsi 朱熹. *Hui-an hsien-sheng Chu Wen kung wen-chi* 晦庵先生朱文公文集. 1245. [Ming *Chia-ching* 嘉靖 1522–66 ed.]. In *Ssu-pu ts'ung-k'an ch'u-pien* 四部叢刊初編. 1919–22. Shang-wu yin-shu-kuan. Vols. 58–9. Shanghai: Shang-wu yin-shu-kuan, 1929.

Chu Hsi 朱熹. *Hui-an hsien-sheng Chu Wen kung wen-chi* 晦庵先生朱文公文集. 1245. [Ming *Chia-ching* 嘉靖 1522–66 ed.; *Ssu-pu ts'ung-k'an ch'u-pien* 四部叢刊初編 1929 ed.]. In *Ssu-pu ts'ung-k'an cheng-pien* 四部叢刊正編. Vols. 52–3. Taipei: T'ai-wan shang-wu yin-shu-kuan, 1979.

Chu Hsi-tsu 朱希祖. *Wei Ch'i lu chiao-pu* 偽齊錄校補. Chung-ching: Tu-li ch'u-pan-she, 1944.

Chu Hsi-tsu 朱希祖. *Wei Ch'u lu chi-pu* 偽楚錄輯補. Taipei: Cheng-chung shu-chü, 1955.

Chu Hsieh 朱偰. "Sung Chin i-ho chih hsin fen-hsi" 宋金議和之新分析. *Tung-fang tsa-chih* 東方雜誌 33 No. 10 (1936), pp. 65–74.

Chü Ch'ing-yüan 鞠清遠. "T'ang-Sung shih-tai Ssu-ch'uan ti ts'an-shih" 唐宋時代四川的蠶市. *Shih-huo pan yüeh k'an* 食貨半月刊 3 No. 6 (1936), pp. 28–34.

Ch'üan Han-sheng 全漢昇. "Sung-mo ti t'ung-huo p'eng-chang chi ch'i tui-yü wu-chia ti ying-hsiang" 宋末的通貨膨脹及其對於物價的影響. In *Sung-shih yen-chiu chi: Ti erh chi* 宋史研究集：第二輯, ed. Sung-shih tso-t'an-hui 宋史座談會. Chung-hua ts'ung-shu 中華叢書. Taipei: Chung-hua ts'ung-shu pien-shen wei-yüan-hui, 1964, pp. 283–325.

Ch'üan Han-sheng 全漢昇. *T'ang Sung ti-kuo yün-ho* 唐宋帝國與運河. Kuo-li chung-yang yen-chiu-yüan li-shih yü-yen yen-chiu-so chuan-k'an 國立中央研究院歷史語言研究所傳刊 1. Chung-ching: Shang-wu yin-shu-kuan, 1944.

Chung Wei-min 仲偉民. *Sung Shen-tsung* 宋神宗. Sung-ti lieh-chuan 宋帝列傳. Ch'ang-ch'un: Chi-lin wen-shih ch'u-pan-she, 1997.

Chung, Priscilla Ching. "Political power and social prestige of palace women in the Northern Sung (960–1126)." Diss., University of Pennsylvania, 1977.

Ch'üeh Hao-tseng 闕鎬曾. "Sung Hsia kuan-hsi chih yen-chiu" 宋夏關係之研究. *Kuo-li Cheng-chih ta-hsüeh hsüeh-pao* 國立政治大學學報 9 (1964), pp. 267–317.

Clark, Hugh R. *Community, trade, and networks: Southern Fujian province from the third to the thirteenth century*. Cambridge: Cambridge University Press, 1991.

Clark, Hugh R. "Consolidation of the south China frontier: The development of Ch'üan-chou, 699–1126." Diss., University of Pennsylvania, 1981.

Clark, Hugh R. "An inquiry into the Xianyou Cai: Cai Xiang, Cai Que, Cai Jing, and the politics of kinship." *Journal of Sung-Yuan Studies* 31 (2001), pp. 67–101.

Clark, Hugh R. "Quanzhou (Fujian) during the Tang-Song interregnum 879–978." *T'oung Pao* 68 No. 1–3 (1982), pp. 132–49.

Dardess, John W. "Did the Mongols matter? Territory, power, and the intelligentsia in China from the Northern Song to the early Ming." In *The Song-Yuan-Ming transition in Chinese history*, ed. Paul J. Smith and Richard von Glahn. Harvard East Asian Monographs 221. Cambridge, Mass.: Harvard University Asia Center, 2003, pp. 111–34.

Davis, R. H. C. *King Stephen, 1135–1154*. London: Longman, 1967.

Davis, Richard L. *Court and family in Sung China, 960–1279: Bureaucratic success and kinship fortunes for the Shih of Ming-chou*. Durham, N.C.: Duke University Press, 1986.

Davis, Richard L. "Evolution of an historical stereotype for the Southern Sung – the case against Shih Mi-yüan." In *Ryū Shiken hakuse shōju kinen: Sō-shi kenkyū ronshū* 劉子健博士頌壽紀念 : 宋史研究論集, ed. Kinugawa Tsuyoshi 衣川強. Kyoto: Dōhōsha, 1989, pp. 357–86.

Davis, Richard L. "Historiography as politics in Yang Wei-chen's 'Polemic on legitimate succession'." *T'oung Pao* 69 No. 1–3 (1983), pp. 33–72.

Davis, Richard L. *Wind against the mountain: The crisis of politics and culture in thirteenth-century China*. Harvard-Yenching Institute Monograph Series 42. Cambridge, Mass.: Council on East Asian Studies, Harvard University, 1996.

de Bary, Wm. Theodore et al., eds. *Sources of Chinese tradition*. Introduction to Oriental Civilizations. New York: Columbia University Press, 1960.

de Bary, Wm. Theodore. "Chen Te-hsiu and statecraft." In *Ordering the world: Approaches to state and society in Sung dynasty China*, ed. Robert P. Hymes and Conrad Schirokauer. Studies on China 16. Berkeley: University of California Press, 1993, pp. 349–79.

De Weerdt, Hilde. *Competition over content: Negotiating Standards for the civil service examinations in imperial China (1127–1279)*. Cambridge, Mass.: Harvard University Asia Center, 2007.

des Rotours, Robert. "La révolte de P'ang Hiun, 868–869. "*T'oung Pao* 56 (1970), pp. 229–40.

Di Cosmo, Nicola. "State formation and periodization in Inner Asian history." *Journal of World History* 10 No. 1 (1999), pp. 1–40.

Dunnell, Ruth W. "The Hsi Hsia." In *The Cambridge history of China*, Volume 6: *Alien regimes and border states, 907–1368*, ed. Herbert Franke and Denis C. Twitchett. New York: Cambridge University Press, 1994, pp. 154–214.

Dunnell, Ruth W. "Tanguts and the Tangut state of Ta Hsia." Diss., Princeton University, 1983.

Dunstheimer, Guillaume. "Some religious aspects of secret societies." In *Popular movements and secret societies in China, 1840–1950*, ed. Jean Chesneaux. Stanford, Calif.: Stanford University Press, 1972, pp. 23–8.

Eberhard, Wolfram. *Conquerors and rulers: Social forces in medieval China*. 2nd ed. Leiden: E. J. Brill, 1965.

Eberhard, Wolfram. "Die Beziehungender Staaten der T'o-pa und der Sha-t'o zum Ausland." *Annales de l'Université d'Ankara* 2 (1948), pp. 141–213.

Eberhard, Wolfram. "Remarks on the bureaucracy in north China during the tenth century." *Oriens* 4 (1951), pp. 280–99.

Ebrey, Patricia B. "Taoism and art at the court of Song Huizong." In *Taoism and the arts of China*, ed. Stephen Little and Shawn Eichman. Chicago: Art Institute of Chicago, 2000, pp. 94–111.

Ebrey, Patricia B. "Women, money, and class: Ssu-ma Kuang and Sung Neo-Confucian views on women." In *Chung-kuo chin-shih she-hui wen-hua-shih lun-wen-chi* 中國近世社會文化史論文集, ed. Chung-yang yen-chiu-yüan li-shih yü-yen yen-chiu-so ch'u-pan-p'in pien-chi wei-yüan-hui 中央研究院歷史語言研究所出版品編輯委員會. Taipei: Chung-yang yen-chiu-yüan li-shih yü-yen yen-chiu-so, 1992, pp. 613–69.

Egan, Ronald C. *Word, image, and deed in the life of Su Shi*. Harvard-Yenching Institute Mongraph Series 39. Cambridge, Mass.: Council on East Asian Studies, Harvard University, 1994.

Enoki Kazuo 榎一雄. "Ō Sei no Kasei keiryaku ni tsuite" 王韶の熙河經略について. *Mōko gakuhō* 蒙古学報 1 (1940), pp. 87–168.

Fan Ch'eng-ta 范成大. *Wu-chün chih* 吳郡志. 1192. In *Sung Yüan fang-chih ts'ung-k'an* 宋元方誌叢刊. Vol. 1, pp. 693–1049. Peking: Chung-hua shu-chü, 1990.

Fan Chiung 范坰 and Lin Yü 林禹. *Wu-Yüeh pei-shih* 吳越備史. 11th c. In *Ssu-pu ts'ung-k'an hsü-pien* 四部叢刊續編. 1934. Taipei: T'ai-wan shang-wu yin-shu-kuan, 1966.

Fan Chung-yen 范仲淹. *Fan Wen-cheng kung cheng-fu tsou-i* 范文正公政府奏議. 1053. In *Ssu-pu ts'ung-k'an ch'u-pien so-pen* 四部叢刊初編縮本. Vol. 45. Taipei: T'ai-wan shang-wu yin-shu-kuan, 1967.

Fang Chen-hua 方震華. "Chia Ssu-tao yü Hsiang Fan chih chan" 賈似道與襄樊之戰. *Ta-lu tsa-chih* 大陸雜誌 21 No. 90.4 (1995), pp. 31–7.

Fang Chen-hua 方震華. "Wan Sung cheng-cheng tui pien-fang ti ying-hsiang" 晚宋政爭對邊防的影響. *Ta-lu tsa-chih* 大陸雜誌 88 No. 5 (1994), pp. 19–31.

Fei Kun 費袞. *Liang-hsi man-chih* 梁谿漫志. 1192. [*Ts'ung-shu chi-ch'eng ch'u-pien* 叢書集成初編 1935–7 ed.]. Peking: Chung-hua shu-chü, 1991.

Feng Kuei-fen 馮桂芬 and Li Ming-wan 李銘晥. *Su-chou fu-chih* 蘇州府志. 1883. 6 vols. Chung-kuo fang-chih ts'ung-shu Hua-chung ti-fang 中國方志叢書華中地方 5. Taipei: Ch'eng-wen ch'u-pan-she, 1970.

Feng Tung-li 馮東禮 and Mao Yüan-yu 毛元佑. *Pei Sung Liao Hsia chün-shih shih* 北宋遼夏軍事史. Chung-kuo chün-shih t'ung-shih 中國軍事通史 12. Peking: Chün-shih k'o-hsüeh chu-pan-she, 1998.

Fichtenau, Heinrich. *Living in the tenth century: Mentalities and social orders*, trans. Patrick J. Geary. Chicago: University of Chicago Press, 1991.

Fisher, Carney T. "The ritual dispute of Sung Ying-tsung." *Papers on Far Eastern History* 36 (1987), pp. 109–38.

Flessel, Klaus. *Der Huang-ho und die historische Hydrotechnik in China: Unter besonderer Berücksichtigung der Nödlichen-Sung-Zeit und mit einem Ausblick auf den vergleichbaren Wasserbau in Europa*. Tübingen: Eigenverlag Klaus Flessel, 1974.

Flessel, Klaus. "Early Chinese newspapers (tenth to thirteenth centuries)." In *Collected papers of the XXIXth Congress of Chinese Studies, 10th–15th September 1984, University of Tübingen*, ed. Tilemann Grimm et al. Tübingen: Tübingen University Press, 1988, pp. 61–71.

Fong, Wen C. *Beyond representation: Chinese painting and calligraphy, 8th–14th century*. Princeton Monographs in Art and Archaeology 48. New York: Metropolitan Museum of Art, 1992.

Forage, Paul C. "Science, technology, and war in Song China: Reflections in the Brush talks from the Dream Creek by Shen Kuo, 1031–1095." Diss., University of Toronto, 1991.

Franke, Herbert. "Chao Ju-yü." In *Sung biographies*, ed. Herbert Franke. 4 vols. Münchener Ostasiatische Studien 16, 1–3; 17, 4. Wiesbaden: Franz Steiner Verlag, 1976, pp. 59–63.

Franke, Herbert. "Chia Ssu-tao." In *Sung biographies*, ed. Herbert Franke. 4 vols. Münchener Ostasiatische Studien 16, 1–3; 17, 4. Vol. 1. Wiesbaden: Franz Steiner Verlag, 1976, pp. 203–7.

Franke, Herbert. "Chia Ssu-tao (1213–1275): A 'bad last minister'?" In *Confucian personalities*, ed. Arthur F. Wright and Denis C. Twitchett. Stanford Studies in the Civilizations of Eastern Asia. Stanford, Calif.: Stanford University Press, 1962, pp. 217–34.

Franke, Herbert. "The Chin dynasty." In *The Cambridge history of China*. Volume 6: *Alien regimes and border states, 907–1368*, ed. Herbert Franke and Denis C. Twitchett. New York: Cambridge University Press, 1994, pp. 215–320.

Franke, Herbert. *Diplomatic missions of the Sung state, 960–1276*. Canberra: Australian National University Press, 1981.

Franke, Herbert. "Han T'o-chou." In *Sung biographies*, ed. Herbert Franke. 4 vols. Münchener Ostasiatische Studien 16, 1–3; 17, 4. Wiesbaden: Franz Steiner Verlag, 1976, pp. 376–84.

Franke, Herbert. "Siege and defense of towns in medieval China." In *Chinese ways in warfare*, ed. Frank A. Kierman, Jr., and John K. Fairbank. Harvard East Asian Series 74. Cambridge, Mass.: Harvard University Press, 1974, pp. 151–201.

Franke, Herbert. "Sung embassies: Some general observations." In *China among equals: The Middle Kingdom and its neighbors, 10th–14th centuries,* ed. Morris Rossabi. Berkeley: University of California Press, 1983, pp. 116–48.

Franke, Herbert. "Treaties between Sung and Chin." In *Études Song: In memoriam Étienne Balazs,* ed. Françoise Aubin. Série I, Histoire et Institutions 1. Paris: Mouton & Co., 1970, pp. 54–84.

Franke, Herbert, and Denis C. Twitchett, eds. *The Cambridge history of China.* Volume 6: *Alien regimes and border states, 907–1368.* New York: Cambridge University Press, 1994.

Franke, Herbert, and Denis C. Twitchett. "Introduction." In *The Cambridge history of China.* Volume 6: *Alien regimes and border states, 907–1368,* ed. Herbert Franke and Denis C. Twitchett. New York: Cambridge University Press, 1994, pp. 1–42.

Franke, Wolfgang. "Historical precedent or accidental repetition of events? K'ou Chun in 1004 and Yu Ch'ien in 1449." In *Études Song: In memoriam Étienne Balazs,* ed. Françoise Aubin. Série I, Histoire et Institutions 3. Paris: Mouton & Co., 1976, pp. 199–206.

Freeman, Michael D. "Lo-yang and the opposition to Wang An-shih: The rise of Confucian conservatism, 1068–1086." Diss., Yale University, 1973.

Freeman, Michael D. "Lü Kung-chu." In *Sung biographies,* ed. Herbert Franke. 4 vols. Münchener Ostasiatische Studien 16, 1–3; 17, 4. Wiesbaden: Franz Steiner Verlag, 1976, pp. 719–22.

Freeman, Michael D., and Chikusa Masaaki. "Fan Shun-jen." In *Sung biographies,* ed. Herbert Franke. 4 vols. Münchener Ostasiatische Studien 16, 1–3; 17, 4. Wiesbaden: Franz Steiner Verlag, 1976, pp. 334–7.

Freeman, Michael D., and Chikusa Masaaki. "Liu Chih." In *Sung biographies,* ed. Herbert Franke. 4 vols. Münchener Ostasiatische Studien 16, 1–3; 17, 4. Wiesbaden: Franz Steiner Verlag, 1976, pp. 634–6.

Freeman, Michael D., and Chikusa Masaaki. "Lü Ta-fang." In *Sung biographies,* ed. Herbert Franke. 4 vols. Münchener Ostasiatische Studien 16, 1–3; 17, 4. Wiesbaden: Franz Steiner Verlag, 1976, pp. 735–8.

Fu Tseng-hsiang 傅增湘, comp. *Sung-tai Shu-wen chi-ts'un* 宋代蜀文輯存. 1943. 2 vols. Hong Kong: Lung-men shu-tien, 1971.

Fu Tseng-hsiang 傅增湘, comp. *Sung-tai Shu-wen chi-ts'un* 宋代蜀文輯存. 1943. 2 vols. Taipei: Hsin-wen-feng ch'u-pan kung-ssu, 1974.

Fujita Toyohachi 藤田豐八. "Nan-Kan Ryū-shi no sosen ni tsuite" 南漢劉氏の祖先について. *Tōyō gakuhō* 東洋學報 6 No. 2 (1916), pp. 247–57.

Fujita Toyohachi 藤田豐八. "Sōdai shihakushi oyobi shihaku jōrei" 宋代市舶司及び市舶條例. *Tōyō gakuhō* 東洋學報 7 No. 2 (1917), pp. 159–246.

Furugaki Kōichi 古垣光一. "Sōchō kenkokuki no kenkyū sono ichi: Sōho no setsudoshi o chūshin to shite" 宋朝建國期の研究其の一:宋初の節度使を中心として. *Chūō Daigaku Daigakuin ronkyū* 中央大学大学院論究 4 No. 1 (1972), pp. 27–44.

Furugaki Kōichi 古垣光一. "Sōdai no kanryō sū ni tsuite" 宋代の官僚數について. In *Sōdai no shakai to shūkyō* 宋代の社会と宗教, ed. Sōdai-shi Kenkyūkai 宋代史研究会. Tokyo: Kyūko Shoin, 1985, pp. 121–58.

Gernet, Jacques. *Buddhism in Chinese society: An economic history from the fifth to the tenth centuries*, trans. Franciscus Verellen. New York: Columbia University Press, 1995.

Gernet, Jacques. *Daily life in China on the eve of the Mongol invasion, 1250–1276*, trans. H. M. Wright. Stanford, Calif.: Stanford University Press, 1962.

Golas, Peter J. "A copper production breakthrough in the Song: The copper precipitation process." *Journal of Sung-Yuan Studies* 25 (1995), pp. 153–68.

Golas, Peter J. "Rural China in the Song." *Journal of Asian Studies* 39 No. 2 (1980), pp. 291–325.

Golas, Peter J. "The Sung financial administration." In *The Cambridge history of China*. Volume 5: *The Sung dynasty and its precursors, 907–1279, part 2*, ed. John W. Chaffee and Denis C. Twitchett. New York: Cambridge University Press, forthcoming.

Goldschmidt, Asaf. "Huizong's impact on medicine and on public health." In *Emperor Huizong and late Northern Song China: The politics of culture and the culture of politics*, ed. Patricia B. Ebrey and Maggie Bickford. Cambridge, Mass.: Harvard University Asia Center, 2006, pp. 275–323.

Graff, David. *Medieval Chinese warfare, 300–900*. London: Routledge, 2002.

Gray, Basil. *Sung porcelain and stoneware*. London: Faber and Faber, 1984.

Gung Wei Ai. "The participation of censorial officials in politics during the Northern Sung dynasty (960–1126 A.D.)." *Chinese Culture* 5 No. 2 (1974), pp. 30–41.

Gung Wei Ai. "Prevalence of powerful chief ministers in Southern Sung China, 1127–1279 A.D." *Chinese Culture* 40 No. 2 (1999), pp. 103–14.

Gung Wei Ai. "The role of censorial officials in the power struggle during Southern Sung China, 1127–1278." M.A. thesis, University of Malaya, 1971.

Gung Wei Ai. "The usurpation of power by Ch'in Kuei through the censorial organ (1138–1155 A.D.)." *Chinese Culture* 15 No. 3 (1974), pp. 25–42.

Haeger, John W. "1126–27: Political crisis and the integrity of culture." In *Crisis and prosperity in Sung China*, ed. John W. Haeger. Tucson: University of Arizona Press, 1975, pp. 143–61.

Haeger, John W. "Between north and south: The Lake rebellion in Hunan, 1130–1135." *Journal of Asian Studies* 28 No. 3 (1969), pp. 469–88.

Haeger, John W. "The significance of confusion: The origin of the T'ai-p'ing yü-lan." *Journal of the American Oriental Society* 88 No. 3 (1968), pp. 401–10.

Hai Jui 海瑞. *Yüan-yu tang-chi pei-k'ao* 元祐黨籍碑考. c. 1570. [*Ts'ung-shu chi-ch'eng ch'u-pien* 叢書集成初編 1935–7 ed.]. Peking: Chung-hua shu-chü, 1985.

Han Kuo-p'an 韓國磐. *Ch'ai Jung* 柴榮. Shanghai: Shang-hai ku-chi ch'u-pan-she, 1956.

Han Kuo-p'an 韓國磐. "T'ang-mo Wu-tai ti fan-chen ko-chü" 唐末五代的藩鎮割据. In *Sui T'ang Wu-tai shih lun-chi* 隋唐五代史論集. 1958. Han Kuo-p'an 韓國磐. Peking: Sheng-huo, tu-shu, hsin-chih san-lien shu-tien, 1979, pp. 308–20.

Hargett, James M. "A chronology of the reigns and reign-periods of the Song dynasty (960–1279)." *Bulletin of Sung-Yüan Studies* 19 (1987), pp. 26–34.

Hargett, James M. "Huizong's magic Marchmount: The Genyue Pleasure Park of Kaifeng." *Monumenta Serica* 38 (1989), pp. 1–48.

Hartman, Charles. "The making of a villain: Ch'in Kuei and Tao-hsüeh." *Harvard Journal of Asiatic Studies* 58 No. 1 (1998), pp. 59–146.

Hartman, Charles. "The reluctant historian: Sun Ti, Chu Hsi, and the fall of Northern Sung." *T'oung Pao* 89 No. 1–3 (2003), pp. 100–48.

Hartman, Charles. "A textual history of Cai Jing's biography in the *Song shi*." In *Emperor Huizong and late Northern Song China: The politics of culture and the culture of politics*, ed. Patricia B. Ebrey and Maggie Bickford. Cambridge, Mass.: Harvard University Asia Center, 2006, pp. 517–64.

Hartwell, Robert M. "A cycle of economic change in imperial China: Coal and iron in northeast China, 750–1350." *Journal of the Economic and Social History of the Orient* 10 No. 1 (1967), pp. 102–59.

Hartwell, Robert M. "Demographic, political, and social transformations of China, 750–1550." *Harvard Journal of Asiatic Studies* 42 No. 2 (1982), pp. 365–442.

Hartwell, Robert M. "The evolution of the early Northern Sung monetary system, A.D. 960–1025." *Journal of the American Oriental Society* 87 No. 3 (1967), pp. 280–9.

Hartwell, Robert M. "Financial expertise, examinations, and the formation of economic policy in Northern Sung China." *Journal of Asian Studies* 30 No. 2 (1971), pp. 281–314.

Hartwell, Robert M. "Historical analogism, public policy, and social science in eleventh- and twelfth-century China." *American Historical Review* 76 No. 3 (1971), pp. 690–727.

Hartwell, Robert M. "The imperial treasuries: Finance and power in Song China." *Bulletin of Sung-Yüan Studies* 20 (1988), pp. 18–89.

Hartwell, Robert M. "Markets, technology, and structure of enterprise in development of 11th-century Chinese iron and steel industry." *Journal of Economic History* 26 No. 1 (1966), pp. 29–58.

Hatch, George C. "Su Hsün." In *Sung biographies*, ed. Herbert Franke. 4 vols. Münchener Ostasiatische Studien 16, 1–3; 17, 4. Vols. 2–3. Wiesbaden: Franz Steiner Verlag, 1976, pp. 885–968.

Heng, Chye Kiang. *Cities of aristocrats and bureaucrats: The development of medieval Chinese cityscapes*. Honolulu: University of Hawaii Press, 1999.

Hervouet, Yves, ed. *A Sung bibliography (Bibliographie des Sung)*. Hong Kong: Chinese University Press, 1978.

Higashi Ichio 東一夫. *Ō Anseki jiten* 王安石事典. Tokyo: Kokusho Kankōkai, 1980.

Higashi Ichio 東一夫. *Ō Anseki shinpō no kenkyū* 王安石新法の研究. Tokyo: Kazama Shobō, 1970.

Hino Kaisaburō 日野開三郎. "Godai Binkoku to taichūgen chōkō to bōeki (jō)" 五代閩國と對中原朝貢と貿易(上). *Shien* 史淵 26 (1941), pp. 1–50.

Hino Kaisaburō 日野開三郎. "Godai Binkoku to taichūgen chōkō to bōeki (ge)" 五代閩國と對中原朝貢と貿易(下). *Shien* 史淵 27 (1942), pp. 1–41.

Hino Kaisaburō 日野開三郎. "Godai chinshō kō" 五代鎮將考. *Tōyō gakuhō* 東洋學報 25 (1938), pp. 54–85.

Hino Kaisaburō 日野開三郎. "Godai jidai ni okeru Kittan to Shina to no kaijōbōeki (jō)" 五代時代に於ける契丹と支那との海上貿易(上). *Shigaku zasshi* 史學雜誌 52 No. 7 (1941), pp. 1–47.

Hino Kaisaburō 日野開三郎. "Godai jidai ni okeru Kittan to Shina to no kaijōbōeki chū" 五代時代に於ける契丹と支那との海上貿易(中). *Shigaku zasshi* 史學雜誌 52 No. 8 (1941), pp. 60–85.

Hino Kaisaburō 日野開三郎. "Godai jidai ni okeru Kittan to Shina to no kaijōbōeki (ge)" 五代時代に於ける契丹と支那との海上貿易(下). *Shigaku zasshi* 史學雜誌 52 No. 9 (1941), pp. 55–82.

Hino Kaisaburō 日野開三郎. "Godai nanboku Shina rikujō kōtsūro ni tsuite" 五代南北支那陸上交通路について. *Rekishigaku kenkyū* 歷史學研究 11 No. 6 (1941), pp. 2–32.

Hino Kaisaburō 日野開三郎. "So no Ma In to tsūka seisaku to Godai jidai no kinyū gyōsha (jō)" 楚の馬殷通貨政策と五代時代の金融業者(上). *Tōyō gakuhō* 東洋學報 54 No. 2 (1971), pp. 1–49.

Hino Kaisaburō 日野開三郎. "So no Ma In to tsūka seisaku to Godai jidai no kinyū gyōsha (ge)" 楚の馬殷通貨政策と五代時代の金融業者(下). *Tōyō gakuhō* 東洋學報 54 No. 3 (1971), pp. 57–89.

Hino Kaisaburō 日野開三郎. "Tōdai hanchin no bakko to chinshō (ichi)" 唐代藩鎮の跋扈と鎮將(一). *Tōyō gakuhō* 東洋學報 26 No. 4 (1939), pp. 1–37.

Hino Kaisaburō 日野開三郎. "Tōdai hanchin no bakko to chinshō (ni)" 唐代藩鎮の跋扈と鎮將(二). *Tōyō gakuhō* 東洋學報 27 No. 1 (1939), pp. 1–62.

Hino Kaisaburō 日野開三郎. "Tōdai hanchin no bakko to chinshō (san)" 唐代藩鎮の跋扈と鎮將(三). *Tōyō gakuhō* 東洋學報 27 No. 2 (1940), pp. 1–60.

Hino Kaisaburō 日野開三郎. "Tōdai hanchin no bakko to chinshō (shi)" 唐代藩鎮の跋扈と鎮將(四). *Tōyō gakuhō* 東洋學報 27 No. 3 (1940), pp. 1–40.

Hino Kaisaburō 日野開三郎. *Zoku Tōdai teiten no kenkyū* 續唐代邸店の研究. Fukuoka: Kyūshū Daigaku Bungakubu Tōyōshi Kenkyūshitsu, 1970.

Ho Chung-li 何忠禮 and Hsü Chi-chün 徐吉軍. *Nan Sung shih-kao: Cheng-chih, chün-shih, wen-hua* 南宋史稿：政治軍事文化. Hang-chou: Hang-chou Ta-hsüeh ch'u-pan-she, 1999.

Ho Kuang-yüan 何光遠. *Chien-chieh lu* 鑒誡錄. [*Hsüeh-chin t'ao-yüan* 學津討原 1805 ed.; 1922]. In *Pai-pu ts'ung-shu chi-ch'eng* 百部叢書集成. 1965–70. Vol. 46. Taipei: I-wen yin-shu-kuan, 1965.

Ho Man-tzu 何滿子. "Yüan-yu Shu-Lo tang-cheng ho Su Shih ti fan Tao-hsüeh tou-cheng (shang)" 元祐蜀洛黨爭和蘇軾的反道學鬥爭(上). *Sung-liao hsüeh-pao: She-hui k'o-hsüeh pan* 松遼學報：社會科學版 2 (1984), pp. 1–7.

Ho T'ien-ming 何天明. "Lun Liao cheng-ch'üan chieh-kuan Yen–Yün ti pi-jan-hsing chi li-shih tso-yung" 論遼政權接管燕雲的必然性及歷史作用. In *Liao Chin shih lun-chi* 遼金史論集, ed. Ch'en Shu 陳述. Vol. 4. Peking: Shu-mu wen-hsien ch'u-pan-she, 1989, pp. 100–15.

Ho T'ien-ming 何天明. "Shih-lun Liao-ch'ao chieh-kuan Yen-Yün ti-ch'ü" 試論遼朝接管燕雲地區. *Liao Chin Ch'i-tan Nü-chen shih yen-chiu tung-t'ai* 遼金契丹女真史研究動態 2 (1986), pp. 14–18.

Ho Yu-sen 何佑森. "Liang Sung hsüeh-feng ti ti-li fan-pu" 兩宋學風的地理分佈. *Hsin-ya hsüeh-pao* 新亞學報 1 No. 1 (1955), pp. 331–79.

Holmgren, Jennifer. "Imperial marriage in the native Chinese and non-Han state, Han to Ming." In *Marriage and inequality in Chinese society*, ed. Rubie S. Watson and Patricia B. Ebrey. Studies on China 12. Berkeley: University of California Press, 1991, pp. 58–96.

Hori Toshikazu 堀敏一. "Gi–Haku Tenyū gun no rekishi – Tō Godai bujin seiryoku no ichi keitai" 魏博天雄軍の歷史━━唐五代武人勢力の一形態. *Rekishi kyōiku* 歷史教育 6 No. 6 (1958), pp. 65–72.

Hori Toshikazu 堀敏一. "Shu Zenchū no chōshito" 朱全忠の廳子都. In *Wada Hakushi koki kinen Tōyōshi ronsō: Shōwa 35-nen 11-gatsu* 和田博士古稀紀念東洋史論叢：昭和35年 11月, ed. Wada Hakushi Koki Kinen Tōyōshi Ronsō Hensan Iinkai 和田博士古稀紀念東洋史論叢編纂委員會. Tokyo: Kōdansha, 1961, pp. 819–31.

Hsiao Ch'i-ch'ing. "Bayan." In *In the service of the khan: Eminent personalities of the early Mongol-Yüan period (1200–1300)*, ed. Igor de Rachewiltz et al. Asiatische Forschungen Band 121. Wiesbaden: Harrassowitz Verlag, 1993, pp. 584–607.

Hsiao-shan Shih-shih tsung-p'u 蕭山史氏宗譜. [Columbia University copy]. N.p.: Pa-hsing t'ang, 1892.

Hsing I-t'ien 邢義田. "Ch'i-tan yü Wu-tai cheng-ch'üan keng-tieh chih kuan-hsi" 契丹與五代政權更迭之關係. *Shih-huo yüeh-k'an* 食貨月刊 1 No. 6 (1971), pp. 296–307.

Hsü Ching-sun 徐經孫. *Chü-shan ts'un-kao* 矩山存稿. 13th c. [*Ssu-k'u ch'üan-shu* 四庫全書, *Wen-yüan ko* 文淵閣 1779 ed.]. In *Ssu-k'u ch'üan-shu chen-pen liu-chi* 四庫全書珍本六集. 1976. Taipei: T'ai-wan shang-wu yin-shu-kuan, 1976.

Hsü Hsüan 徐鉉. *Chi-shen lu* 稽神錄. Late 10th c. [*Hsüeh-chin t'ao-yüan* 學津討原 1805 ed.; 1922]. In *Pai-pu ts'ung-shu chi-ch'eng* 百部叢書集成. 1965–70. Taipei: I-wen yin-shu-kuan, 1965.

Hsü Huai-lin 許懷林. "Pei Sung chuan-yün-shih chih-tu lüeh-lun" 北宋轉運使制度略論. In *Sung-shih yen-chiu lun-wen-chi: 1982 nien nien-hui pien-k'an* 宋史研究論文集：一九八二年年會編刊, ed. Teng Kuang-ming 鄧廣銘 and Li Chia-chü 酈家駒. Cheng-chou: Ho-nan jen-min ch'u-pan-she, 1984, pp. 287–318.

Hsü Kuei 徐規. "Sung T'ai-tsu shih-yüeh pien-hsi" 宋太祖誓約辨析. *Li-shih yen-chiu* 歷史研究 4 (1986), pp. 190–2.

Hsü Meng-hsin 徐夢莘. *San-ch'ao pei-meng hui-pien* 三朝北盟會編. 1196. 4 vols. Taipei: Wen-hai ch'u-pan-she, 1962.

Hsü Meng-hsin 徐夢莘. *San-ch'ao pei-meng hui-pien* 三朝北盟會編. 1196. 2 vols. Sung-shih yao-chi hui-pien 宋史要籍彙編. Shanghai: Shang-hai ku-chi ch'u-pan-she, 1987.

Hsü Ping-yü 徐秉愉. "Sung Kao-tsung chih tui Chin cheng-ts'e" 宋高宗之對金政策. M.A. thesis, Kuo-li T'ai-wan ta-hsüeh 國立臺灣大學, 1984.

Hsü Ping-yü 徐秉愉. "Yu Miao-Liu chih pien k'an Nan-Sung ch'u-ch'i ti chün-ch'üan" 由苗劉之變看南宋初期的君權. *Shih-huo yüeh-k'an* 食貨月刊 16 Nos. 11–12 (1988), pp. 446–59.

Hsü Sung 徐松 et al., comps. *Sung hui-yao chi-kao* 宋會要輯稿. 1809, 1936. Taipei: Shih-chieh shu-chü, 1964.

Hsü Sung 徐松 et al., comps. *Sung hui-yao chi-kao* 宋會要輯稿. 1809, 1957. 8 vols. Peking: Chung-hua shu-chü, 1997.

Hsü Sung 徐松 et al., comps. *Sung hui-yao chi-pen* 宋會要輯本. 1809, 1936. 16 vols. Taipei: Shih-chieh shu-chü, 1964.

Hsü Tzu-ming 徐自明. *Sung tsai-fu pien-nien lu* 宋宰輔編年錄. Early 13th c. [*Ching-hsiang-lou ts'ung-shu* 敬鄉樓叢書 1929 ed.]. Sung-shih tzu-liao ts'ui-pien ti erh-chi 宋史資料萃編第二輯. Vols. 37–9. Taipei: Wen-hai ch'u-pan-she, 1967.

Hsü Tzu-ming 徐自明. *Sung tsai-fu pien-nien lu* 宋宰輔編年錄. Early 13th c. Peking: Chung-hua shu-chü, 1986.

Hsü Tzu-ming 徐自明. *Sung tsai-fu pien-nien lu chiao-pu* 宋宰輔編年錄校補. c. 1220, ed. Wang Jui-lai 王瑞來. 4 vols. Peking: Chung-hua shu-chü, 1986.

Hsüeh Chü-cheng 薛居正 et al., eds. *Chiu Wu-tai shih* 舊五代史. 974. 6 vols. Erh-shih-ssu shih 二十四史 18. Peking: Chung-hua shu-chü, 1976.

Hu Chao-hsi 胡昭曦. "Lüeh-lun Nan Sung mo-nien Ssu-ch'uan chün-min k'ang-chi Meng-ku kuei-tsu ti tou-cheng" 略論南宋末年四川軍民抗擊蒙古貴族的鬥爭. In *Sung-shih yen-chiu lun-wen-chi: Chung-hua wen-shih lun-ts'ung tseng-k'an* 宋史研究論文集：中華文史論叢增刊, ed. Teng Kuang-ming 鄧廣銘 and Ch'eng Ying-liu 程應鏐. Chung-hua wen-shih lun-ts'ung tseng-k'an 中華文史論叢增刊. Shanghai: Shang-hai ku-chi ch'u-pan-she, 1982, pp. 374–409.

Hu Chao-hsi 胡昭曦 et al. *Sung-mo Ssu-ch'uan chan-cheng shih-liao hsüan-pien* 宋末四川戰爭史料選編. Ch'eng-tu: Ssu-ch'uan jen-min ch'u-pan-she, 1984.

Hu Chao-hsi 胡昭曦 et al. *Sung Meng (Yüan) kuan-hsi shih* 宋蒙(元)關系史. Ch'eng-tu: Ssu-ch'uan ta-hsüeh ch'u-pan-she, 1992.

Hu Meng-yü 胡夢昱 and Hu Chih-jou 胡知柔. *Hsiang-t'ai shou-mo* 象台首末. 1225. In *Pai-pu ts'ung-shu chi-ch'eng* 百部叢書集成. 1965–70. 54. Taipei: I-wen yin-shu-kuan, 1965–70.

Hu Yin 胡寅. *Fei-jan chi* 斐然集. 12th c. [*Ssu-k'u ch'üan-shu* 四庫全書, *Wen-yüan ko* 文淵閣 1779 ed.]. In *Ssu-k'u ch'üan-shu chen-pen ch'u-chi* 四庫全書珍本初集. 1934–5. Shanghai: Shang-wu ch'u-pan-she, 1934–5.

Hua Shan 華山. "Nan Sung Shao-ting, Tuan-p'ing chien ti Chiang, Min, Kuang nung-min ta ch'i-i" 南宋紹定、端平間的江、閩、廣農民大起義. *Wen shih che* 文史哲 No. 43 (1956), pp. 41–8.

Hua Shan 華山. *Sung-shih lun-chi* 宋史論集. Chi-nan: Ch'i Lu shu-shih, 1982.

Huang Ch'i-chiang 黃啓江. "Wu-tai shih-ch'i nan-fang chu-kuo ti ching-ying" 五代時期南方諸國的經營. M.A. thesis, Kuo-li T'ai-wan ta-hsüeh 國立臺灣大學, 1976.

Huang Hsien-fan 黃現璠. *Sung-tai t'ai-hsüeh-sheng chiu-kuo yün-tung* 宋代太學生救國運動. Shih-ti hsiao ts'ung-shu 史地小叢書. Shanghai: Shang-wu yin-shu-kuan, 1936.

Huang Hsiu-fu 黃休復. *Mao-t'ing k'o-hua* 茅亭客話. Early 11th c. [*Lin-lang pi-shih ts'ung-shu* 琳琅祕室叢書 1853 ed.; 1887, 1888]. In *Pai-pu ts'ung-shu chi-ch'eng* 百部叢書集成. 1965–70. Taipei: I-wen yin-shu-kuan, 1967.

Huang Kan. 黃榦 *Mien-chai chi* 勉齋集. [*Ssu-k'u ch'üan-shu* 四庫全書, *Wen-yüan ko* 文淵閣 1779 ed.]. In *Ssu-k'u ch'üan-shu chen-pen erh-chi* 四庫全書珍本二集. 1971. Vols. 296–300. Taipei: T'ai-wan shang-wu yin-shu-kuan, 1971.

Huang K'uan-ch'ung 黃寬重. "Ch'in Kuei yü wen-tzu yü" 秦檜與文字獄. In *Sung-shih ts'ung-lun* 宋史叢論. Huang K'uan-ch'ung 黃寬重. Taipei: Hsin-wen-feng ch'u-pan kung-ssu, 1974, pp. 41–72.

Huang K'uan-ch'ung 黃寬重. "Lüeh-lun Nan Sung shih-tai ti kuei-cheng-jen (shang)" 略論南宋時代的歸正人(上). *Shih-huo yüeh-k'an* 食貨月刊 7 No. 3 (1977), pp. 111–20.

Huang K'uan-ch'ung 黃寬重. "Lüeh-lun Nan Sung shih-tai ti kuei-cheng-jen (hsia)" 略論南宋時代的歸正人(下). *Shih-huo yüeh-k'an* 食貨月刊 7 No. 4 (1977), pp. 172–83.

Huang K'uan-ch'ung 黃寬重. "Meng Kung nien-p'u" 孟珙年譜. *Shih yüan* 史原 4 (1973), pp. 79–135.

Huang K'uan-ch'ung 黃寬重. *Nan Sung shih-tai k'ang Chin ti i-chün* 南宋時代抗金的義軍. Taipei: Lien-ching ch'u-pan shih-yeh kung-ssu, 1988.

Huang K'uan-ch'ung 黃寬重. "Nan-Sung tui ti-fang wu-li ti li-yung ho k'ung-chih: i chen-fu shih wei-li" 南宋對地方武力的利用和控制：以鎮撫使為例. In *Chung-yang yen-chiu-yüan ti erh chieh kuo-chi Han-hsüeh hui-i lun-wen-chi: Ch'ing-chu Chung-yang yen-chiu-yüan yüan-ch'ing liu-shih chou-nien* 中央研究院第二屆國際漢學會議論文集：慶祝中央研究院院慶六十週年, ed. Chung-yang yen-chiu-yüan pien-yin 中央研究院編印. 10 vols. Taipei: Chung-yang yen-chiu-yüan, 1986, pp. 1047–80.

Huang Min-chih 黃敏枝. *Sung-tai fo-chiao she-hui ching-chi shih lun-chi* 宋代佛教社會經濟史論集. Shih-hsüeh ts'ung-shu 史學叢書 12. Taipei: T'ai-wan hsüeh-sheng shu-chü, 1989.

Huang Tsung-hsi 黃宗羲 et al. *Sung Yüan hsüeh-an* 宋元學案. 1838. 3 vols. Taipei: Shih-chieh shu-chü, 1973.

Huber, Horst. "Wen T'ien-hsiang." In *Sung biographies*, ed. Herbert Franke. 4 vols. Münchener Ostasiatische Studien 16, 1–3; 17, 4. Vol. 3. Wiesbaden: Franz Steiner Verlag, 1976, pp. 1187–1201.

Huber, Horst. "Wen T'ien-hsiang, 1236–1283: Vorstufen zum Verständnis seines Lebens." Diss., Universität zu München, 1983.

Hucker, Charles O. *A dictionary of official titles in imperial China.* Stanford, Calif.: Stanford University Press, 1985.

Hung Mai 洪邁. *Jung-chai sui-pi* 容齋隨筆. 1180–1202. Shanghai: Shang-hai ku-chi ch'u-pan-she, 1978.

Hung Mai 洪邁. *Jung-chai sui-pi* 容齋隨筆. 1180–1202. 2 vols. Taipei: Ta-li ch'u-pan-she, 1981.

Hung Mai 洪邁. *Jung-chai sui-pi* 容齋隨筆. 1180–1202. Shanghai: Shang-hai ku-chi ch'u-pan-she, 1996.

Hymes, Robert P. *Statesmen and gentlemen: The elite of Fu-chou, Chiang-hsi, in Northern and Southern Sung.* Cambridge Studies in Chinese History, Literature, and Institutions. Cambridge: Cambridge University Press, 1986.

Hymes, Robert P. *Way and byway: Taoism, local religion, and models of divinity in Sung and modern China.* Berkeley: University of California Press, 2002.

Ihara Hiroshi 伊原弘. "Nan-Sō Shisen ni okeru Go Shi no seiryoku – Go Ki no ran zenshi" 南宋四川における呉氏の勢力─呉曦の乱前史. In *Aoyama Hakushi koki kinen Sōdai shi ronsō* 青山博士古稀紀念宋代史論叢, ed. Aoyama Hakushi Koki Kinen Sōdai-shi Ronsō Kankōkai 青山博士古稀紀念宋代史論叢刊行会. Tokyo: Seishin Shobō, 1974, pp. 1–33.

Iwasaki Tsutomu. "A study of Ho-hsi Tibetans during the Northern Sung dynasty." *Memoirs of the Research Department of the Tōyō Bunko* 44 (1986), pp. 57–132.

Jao Tsung-i 饒宗頤. *Chung-kuo shih-hsüeh-shang chih cheng-t'ung lun: Chung-kuo shih-hsüeh kuan-nien t'an-t'ao chih i* 中國史學上之正統論：中國史學觀念探討之一. Hong Kong: Lung-men shu-tien, 1977.

Jay, Jennifer W. *A change in dynasties: Loyalism in thirteenth-century China*. Studies on East Asia 18. Bellingham: Western Washington University Press, 1991.

Jen Ch'ung-yüeh 任崇岳. "Ch'i-tan yü Wu-tai Shan-hsi ko-chü cheng-ch'üan" 契丹与五代山西割据政權. In *Ch'i-tan shih-lun chu hui-pien* 契丹史論著匯編, ed. Sun Chin-chi 孫進己 et al. 2 vols. Pei-fang shih-ti tzu-liao 北方史地資料 4. Vol. 1. Shen-yang: N.p., 1988, pp. 384–8.

Jen Ch'ung-yüeh 任崇岳. *Sung Hui-tsung Sung Ch'in-tsung* 宋徽宗宋欽宗. Sung-ti lieh-chuan 宋帝列傳. Ch'ang-ch'un: Chi-lin wen-shih ch'u-pan-she, 1996.

Ji Xiaobin 冀小斌. "Conservatism and court politics in Northern Song China: The thought and career of Ssu-ma Kuang (1019–1086)." Diss., Princeton University, 1998.

Ji Xiaobin 冀小斌. "Pei Sung chi-p'in hsin-chieh – shih-lun 'kuo-yung pu-tsu' yü Wang An-shih hsin-fa chih cheng" 北宋積貧新解 – 試論「國用不足」與王安石新法之爭. In *Kuo-shih fu-hai k'ai-hsin-lu: Yü Ying-shih chiao-shou jung-t'ui lun-wen-chi* 國史浮海開新錄：余英時教授榮退論文集, ed. Chou Chih-p'ing 周質平 and Willard J. Peterson. Taipei: Lien-ching ch'u-pan shih-yeh kung-ssu, 2002, pp. 283–300.

Johnson, David G. "The last years of a great clan: The Li family of Chao Chün in late T'ang and early Sung." *Harvard Journal of Asiatic Studies* 37 No. 1 (1977), pp. 5–102.

Kahn, Harold L. *Monarchy in the emperor's eyes: Image and reality in the Ch'ien-lung reign*. Harvard East Asian Series 18. Cambridge, Mass.: Harvard University Press, 1971.

Kao Yu-kung. "A study of the Fang La rebellion." *Harvard Journal of Asiatic Studies* 24 (1962–3), pp. 17–63.

Kaplan, Edward H. "Ch'en Tung." In *Sung biographies*, ed. Herbert Franke. 4 vols. Münchener Ostasiatische Studien 16, 1–3; 17, 4. Vol. 1. Wiesbaden: Franz Steiner Verlag, 1976, pp. 124–32.

Kaplan, Edward H. "Yüeh Fei and the founding of the Southern Sung." Diss., University of Iowa, 1970.

Kawahara Masahiro 河原正博. *Kan minzoku Kanan hattenshi kenkyū* 漢民族華南發展史研究. Tokyo: Yoshigawa Kōbunkan, 1984.

Kawahara Yoshirō 河原由郎. *Hoku-Sō ki tochi shoyū no mondai to shōgyō shihon* 北宋期土地所有の問題と商業資本. Fukuoka: Nishi Nihon Gakujitsu Shuppansha, 1964.

Kinugawa Tsuyoshi 衣川強. "Chou Pi-ta." In *Sung biographies*, ed. Herbert Franke. 4 vols. Münchener Ostasiatische Studien 16, 1–3; 17, 4. Vol. 2. Wiesbaden: Franz Steiner Verlag, 1976, pp. 675–7.

Kinugawa Tsuyoshi 衣川強. "Kaiki Yōhei o megutte" 開禧用兵をめぐって. *Tōyōshi kenkyū* 東洋史研究 36 No. 3 (1977), pp. 128–51.

Ko Chao-kuang 葛兆光. "Lo-yang yü Pien-liang: Wen-hua chung-hsin yü cheng-chih chung-hsin ti fen-li – kuan-yü shih-i shih-chi pa-shih nien-tai li-hsüeh li-shih yü ssu-hsiang ti k'ao-ch'a" 洛陽與汴梁：文化重心與政治重心的分離 – 關於 I I 世紀80年代理學曆史與 思想的考察. *Li-shih yen-chiu* 歷史研究 267 (2000), pp. 24–37.

Ko Shao-ou 葛紹歐. "Pei Sung chih san-ssu-shih" 北宋之三司使. *Shih-huo yüeh-k'an* 食貨月刊 8 No. 2 (1978), pp. 113–35.

K'o Wei-ch'i 柯維騏. *Sung-shih hsin-pien* 宋史新編. 1557. Shanghai: Ta-kuang shu-chü, 1936.

Koiwai Hiromitsu 小岩井弘光. *Sōdai heiseishi no kenkyū* 宋代兵制史の研究. Kyūko sōsho 汲古叢書 15. Tokyo: Kyko Shoin, 1998.

Kondo Kazunari 近藤一成. "Ō Anseki no kakyo kaikaku o megutte" 王安石の科學改革をめぐって. *Tōyōshi kenkyū* 東洋史研究 46 No. 3 (1987), pp. 21–46.

Kondo Kazunari 近藤一成. "Sai Kei no kakyō – gakkō seisoku" 蔡京の科舉一学校政策. *Tōyōshi kenkyū* 東洋史研究 53 No. 1 (1994), pp. 25–49.

Kracke, Edward A., Jr. *Civil service in early Sung China, 960–1067; with particular emphasis on the development of controlled sponsorship to foster administrative responsibility*. Harvard-Yenching Institute Mongraph Series 13. Cambridge, Mass.: Harvard University Press, 1953.

Kracke, Edward A., Jr. "Family vs. merit in the civil service examinations during the empire." *Harvard Journal of Asiatic Studies* 10 No. 2 (1947), pp. 105–23.

Krompart, Robert. "The southern restoration of T'ang: Counsel, policy and parahistory in the stabilization of the Chiang-Huai region, 887–943." Diss., University of California at Berkeley, 1973.

Ku Chi-kuang 谷霽光. "Fan-lun T'ang-mo Wu-tai ti ssu-chün ho ch'in-chün, i-erh" 汎論唐末五代的私兵和親軍、義兒. *Li-shih yen-chiu* 歷史研究 2 (1984), pp. 21–34.

Ku Chi-kuang 谷霽光. "Sung-tai chi-ch'eng wen-t'i shang-ch'üeh" 宋代繼承問題商榷. *Ch'ing-hua hsüeh-pao* 清華學報 13 No. 1 (1941), pp. 87–113.

Kuan Lü-ch'üan 關履權. *Liang Sung shih-lun* 兩宋史論. Sung-shih yen-chiu ts'ung-shu 宋史研究叢書. Cheng-chou: Chung-chou shu-hua-she, 1983.

Kumamoto Takashi 熊本崇. "Chūshoken seikan – Ō Anseki seiken no ninaitetachi" 中書檢正官一王安石政權闗 のにないてかた. *Tōyōshi kenkyū* 東洋史研究 47 No. 1 (1988), pp. 54–80.

Kung Yen-ming 龔延明. "Pei Sung Yüan-feng kuan-chih kai-ko lun" 北宋元豐官制改革論. *Chung-kuo shih yen-chiu* 中國史研究 No. 1 (1990), pp. 132–43.

Kuo Fei 郭棐 et al. *(Wan-li) Kuang-tung t'ung-chih* 萬歷廣東通志. 1602. [Naikaku Bunko collection]. N.p.: n.p., n.d.

Kuo Po-kung 郭伯恭. *Sung ssu-ta-shu k'ao* 宋四大書考. Jen-jen wen-k'u 人人文庫 427. Taipei: T'ai-wan shang-wu yin-shu-kuan, 1967.

Kuo Yün-tao 郭允蹈. *Shu chien* 蜀鑒. 13th c. [*Shou-shan-ko ts'ung-shu* 守山閣叢書 1844 ed.; 1922]. In *Pai-pu ts'ung-shu chi-ch'eng* 百部叢書集成. 1965–70. Vol. 52. Taipei: I-wen yin-shu-kuan, 1968.

Kurihara Masuo 栗原益男. *Godai Sōsho hanchin nenpyō* 五代宋初藩鎮年表. Tokyo: Tōkyōdō Shuppan, 1988.

Kurihara Masuo 栗原益男. *Ransei no kōtei – "Kō-Shū" no Seisō to sono jidai* 亂世の皇帝——「後周」の世宗とその時代. Tōgen sensho 桃源選書 30. Tokyo: Tōgensha, 1968.

Kurihara Masuo 栗原益男. "Tō-Godai no kafushiteki ketsugō no seikaku" 唐五代の假父子的結合の性格. *Shigaku zasshi* 史學雜誌 62 No. 6 (1953), pp. 1–30.

Kurihara Masuo 栗原益男. "Tōmatsu Godai no kafushiteki ketsugō ni okeru seimei to nenrei" 唐末五代の假父子的結合における姓名と年齢. *Tōyō gakuhō* 東洋學報 38 No. 4 (1956), pp. 61–88.

Kurz, Johannes L. "The politics of collecting knowledge: Song Taizong's compilations project." *T'oung Pao* 87 Nos. 4–5 (2001), pp. 289–316.

Kurz, Johannes L. "Survey of the historical sources for the Five Dynasties and Ten States in Song times." *Journal of Sung-Yuan Studies* 33 (2003), pp. 187–224.

Kuwabara Jitsuzō. "On P'u Shou-keng, part 1." *Memoirs of the Research Department of the Tōyō Bunko* 2 (1928), pp. 1–82.

Kwanten, Luc. *Imperial nomads: A history of Central Asia, 500–1500*. Philadelphia: University of Pennsylvania Press, 1979.

Labadie, John R. "Rulers and soldiers: Perception and management of the military in Northern Sung China (960–1060)." Diss., University of Washington, 1981.

Lam, Joseph S. M. "Huizong's dashengyue: A musical performance of emperorship and officialdom." In *Emperor Huizong and late Northern Song China: The politics of culture and the culture of politics*, ed. Patricia B. Ebrey and Maggie Bickford. Cambridge, Mass.: Harvard University Asia Center, 2006, pp. 395–452.

Lamouroux, Christian. "Crise politique et developpement rizicole en Chine: la region du Jiang-Huai (VIIIe-Xe siècle)." *Bulletin de l'École Française d'Extrême-Orient* 82 (1995), pp. 145–83.

Langley, Charles B. "Wang Yinglin (1223–96): A study in the political and intellectual history of the demise of Song." Diss., Indiana University, 1980.

Lau Nap-yin. "The absolutist reign of Sung Hsiao-tsung (r. 1163–1189)." Diss., Princeton University, 1986.

Lau Nap-yin. "Waging war for peace? The peace accord between the Song and the Liao in AD 1005." In *Warfare in Chinese history*, ed. Hans J. van de Ven. Sinica Leidensia 47. Leiden: Brill, 2000, pp. 180–221.

Lee, Thomas H. C. *Government education and examinations in Sung China*. New York: St. Martin's Press, 1985.

Lei Fei-lung 雷飛龍. "Pei Sung hsin-chiu tang-cheng yü ch'i hsüeh-shu cheng-ts'e chih kuan-hsi" 北宋新舊黨爭與其學術政策之關係. *Kuo-li Cheng-chih ta-hsüeh hsüeh-pao* 國立政治大學學報 11 (1965), pp. 201–44.

Levenson, Joseph R. *Confucian China and its modern fate*. 3 vols. Berkeley: University of California Press, 1965.

Levine, Ari D. "A house in darkness: The politics of history and the language of politics in the late Northern Song, 1066–1126." Diss., Columbia University, 2002.

Levine, Ari D. "Terms of estrangement: Factional discourse in the early Huizong reign." In *Emperor Huizong and late Northern Song China: The politics of culture and the culture of politics*, ed. Patricia B. Ebrey and Maggie Bickford. Cambridge, Mass.: Harvard University Asia Center, 2006, pp. 131–70.

Leyser, Karl. *Rule and conflict in an early medieval society*. Oxford: Blackwell, 1979.

Li An 李安. *Sung Wen ch'eng-hsiang T'ien-hsiang nien-p'u* 宋文丞相天祥年譜. Hsin-pien Chung-kuo ming-jen nien-p'u chi-ch'eng 新編中國名人年譜集成 10. Taipei: T'ai-wan shang-wu yin-shu-kuan, 1980.

Li Chen 李震 and Ch'en T'ing-yüan 陳廷元. *Chung-kuo li-tai chan-cheng shih* 中國歷代戰爭史. Taipei: Li-ming wen-hua shih-yeh ku-fen yu-hsien kung-ssu, 1976.

Li Chen 李震 et al. *Chung-kuo li-tai chan-cheng shih* 中國歷代戰爭史. 16 vols. Taipei: San-chün lien-ho ts'an-mou ta-hsüeh, 1968.

Li Chih 李直. *Huang Sung shih-ch'ao kang-yao* 皇宋十朝綱要. c. 1213. Sung-shih tzu-liao ts'ui-pien ti i chi 宋史資料萃編第一輯. Vol. 3. Taipei: Wen-hai ch'u-pan-she, 1980.

Li Chih 李直. *Huang Sung shih-ch'ao kang-yao* 皇宋十朝綱要. c. 1213. Hsü-hsiu ssu-k'u ch'üan-shu 續修四庫全書. Shanghai: Shang-hai ku-chi ch'u-pan-she, 1995.

Li Chün 李俊. *Chung-kuo tsai-hsiang chih-tu* 中國宰相制度. Taipei: T'ai-wan shang-wu yin-shu-kuan, 1966.

Li Han 李涵. "Ts'ung Tseng Pu ken-chiu shih-i wei-fa-t'iao ti fen-cheng k'an hsin-tang nei-pu ti mao-tun yü wen-t'i" 從曾布根究市易違法案的紛爭看新黨內部的矛盾與問題. In *Sung-shih yen-chiu lun-wen-chi: 1984 nien nien-hui pien-k'an* 宋史研究論文集：一九八四年年會編刊, ed. Teng Kuang-ming 鄧廣銘 et al. Hang-chou: Che-chiang jen-min ch'u-pan-she, 1987, pp. 267–81.

Li Hsin-ch'uan 李心傳. *Chien-yen i-lai ch'ao-yeh tsa-chi* 建炎以來朝野雜記. c. 1202 *chia* volume, 1216 *i* volume. In *Ts'ung-shu chi-ch'eng ch'u-pien* 叢書集成初編. 1935–7. Shanghai: Shang-wu ch'u-pan-she, 1935–7.

Li Hsin-ch'uan 李心傳. *Chien-yen i-lai ch'ao-yeh tsa-chi* 建炎以來朝野雜記. c. 1202 *chia* volume, 1216 *i* volume. [*Shih-yüan ts'ung-shu* 適園叢書 1914 ed.]. Sung-shih tzu-liao ts'ui-pien ti i chi 宋史資料萃編第一輯. Vols. 21–2. Taipei: Wen-hai ch'u-pan-she, 1967.

Li Hsin-ch'uan 李心傳. *Chien-yen i-lai hsi-nien yao-lu* 建炎以來繫年要錄. 1253–8. [*Shih hsüeh ts'ung shu* 史學叢書 1899–1902 ed.]. In *Ts'ung-shu chi-ch'eng ch'u-pien* 叢書集成初編. 1935–7. Vols. 3861–78. Shanghai: Shang-wu yin-shu-kuan, 1936.

Li Hsin-ch'uan 李心傳. *Chien-yen i-lai hsi-nien yao-lu* 建炎以來繫年要錄. 1253–8. 4 vols. Kuo-hsüeh chi-pen ts'ung-shu 國學基本叢書. Peking: Chung-hua shu-chü, 1956.

Li Hsin-ch'uan 李心傳. *Tao ming lu* 道命錄. 1239. 2 vols. In *Ts'ung-shu chi-ch'eng ch'u-pien* 叢書集成初編. 1935–7. Shanghai: Shang-wu yin-shu-kuan, 1937.

Li Hua-jui 李華瑞. *Sung Hsia kuan-hsi shih* 宋夏關系史. Shih-chia-chuang: Ho-pei jen-min ch'u-pan-she, 1998.

Li Jung 李榕 et al. *Hang-chou fu-chih* 杭州府志. 1888. Chung-kuo fang-chih ts'ung-shu Hua-chung ti-fang 中國方志叢書華中地方 199. Taipei: Ch'eng-wen ch'u-pan-she, 1974.

Li Jung-ts'un 李榮村. "Hei-feng-tung pien-luan shih-mo" 黑鳳峒變亂始末. *Chung-yang yen-chiu-yüan li-shih yü-yen yen-chiu-so chi-k'an* 中央研究院歷史語言研究所集刊 41 No. 3 (1969), pp. 497–533.

Li Jung-ts'un 李榮村. "Sung-tai Hu-pei lu liang-chiang ti-ch'ü ti man-luan" 宋代湖北路兩江地區的蠻亂. *Pien-cheng yen-chiu-so nien-pao* 邊政研究所年報 9 (1978), pp. 131–81.

Li Kang 李綱. *Liang-hsi hsien-sheng ch'üan-chi* 梁谿先生全集. 10 vols. Sung-ming-chia chi hui-k'an 宋名家集彙刊. Taipei: Han-hua wen-hua shih-yeh ku-fen yü-hsien kung-ssu, 1970.

Li Lin-fu 李林甫 et al., comps. *Ta T'ang liu-tien* 大唐六典. 738. [1515 ed.]. Taipei: Wen-hai ch'u-pan-she, 1974.

Li T'ao 李燾. *Hsü Tzu-chih t'ung-chien ch'ang-pien* 續資治通鑑長編. 1183. [*Che-chiang shu-chü* 浙江書局 1881 ed.]. 15 vols. Taipei: Shih-chieh shu-chü, 1961–4.

Li T'ao 李燾. *Hsü tzu-chih t'ung-chien ch'ang-pien* 續資治通鑑長編. 1183. 34 vols. Peking: Chung-hua shu-chü, 1979–95.

Li T'ao 李燾. *Hsü Tzu-chih t'ung-chien ch'ang-pien* 續資治通鑑長編. 1183. [*Che-chiang shu-chü* 浙江書局 1881 ed.]. 5 vols. Shanghai: Shang-hai ku-chi ch'u-pan-she, 1986.

Li T'ien-ming 李天鳴. *Sung Yüan chan-shih* 宋元戰史. 4 vols. Taipei: Shih-huo ch'u-pan-she, 1988.

Li Tse-fen 李則芬. *Yüan-shih hsin-chiang* 元史新講. 5 vols. Taipei: Chung-hua shu-chü, 1978.

Li Tung-hua 李東華. *Ch'üan-chou yü wo-kuo chung-ku ti hai-shang chiao-t'ung: Chiu shih-chi mo – shih-wu shih-chi ch'u* 泉州與我國中古的海上交通：九世紀末 – 十 五世紀初. Shih-hsüeh ts'ung-shu 史學叢書. Taipei: T'ai-wan hsüeh-sheng shu-chü, 1986.

Li Wei-kuo 李偉國. "Lun Sung-tai nei-k'u ti ti-wei ho tso-yung" 論宋代內庫的地位和作用. *Sung Liao Chin shih lun-ts'ung* 宋遼金史論叢 1 (1985), pp. 192–215.

Li Yü-t'ang 李育棠. *Chin-shih chi-shih pen-mo* 金史紀事本末. 1893. 3 vols. Peking: Chung-hua shu-chü, 1980.

Liang Keng-yao 梁庚堯. "Nan Sung ch'eng-shih ti fa-chan (shang)" 南宋城市的發展(上). *Shih-huo yüeh-k'an* 食貨月刊 10 No. 10 (1981), pp. 420–43.

Liang Keng-yao 梁庚堯. *Nan Sung ti nung-ti li yung cheng-ts'e* 南宋的農地利用政策. Kuo-li T'ai-wan ta-hsüeh wen-shih ts'ung-k'an 國立臺灣大學文史叢刊 46. Taipei: Kuo-li T'ai-wan ta-hsüeh wen-hsüeh-yüan, 1977.

Liang Keng-yao 梁庚堯. *Nan Sung ti nung-ts'un ching-chi* 南宋的農村經濟. Taipei: Lien-ching ch'u-pan shih-yeh kung-ssu, 1984.

Liang Keng-yao 梁庚堯. "Shih-i fa shu" 市易法述. *Kuo-li T'ai-wan ta-hsüeh li-shih hsüeh-hsi hsüeh-pao* 國立臺灣大學歷史學系學報 Nos. 10–11 (1984), pp. 171–242.

Liang Keng-yao 梁庚堯. "Shih-i fa shu" 市易法述. In *Sung-tai she-hui ching-chi shih lun-chi* 宋代社會經濟史論集, ed. Liang Keng-yao 梁庚堯. 2 vols. Yün-ch'en ts'ung-k'an 允晨叢刊 68–9. Taipei: Yün-ch'en wen-hua shih-yeh ku-fen yu-hsien kung-ssu, 1997, pp. 104–260.

Liang K'o-chia 梁克家. *Ch'un-hsi San-shan chih* 淳熙三山志. 1182. In *Sung Yüan fang-chih ts'ung-k'an* 宋元方誌叢刊. Vol. 8, pp. 7781–8267. Peking: Chung-hua shu-chü, 1990.

Liang K'o-chia 梁克家. *Ch'un-hsi San-shan chih* 淳熙三山志. 1182. In *Sung Yüan ti-fang-chih ts'ung-shu* 宋元地方志叢書. Vol. 12. Taipei: Ta-hua shu-chü, 1980.

Liang T'ien-hsi 梁天錫. "Lun Sung tsai-fu hu-chien chih-tu" 論宋宰輔互兼制度. In *Sung-shih yen-chiu chi: Ti ssu chi* 宋史研究集：第四輯, ed. Sung-shih tso-t'an-hui 宋史座談會.

Chung-hua ts'ung-shu 中華叢書. Taipei: Chung-hua ts'ung-shu pien-shen wei-yüan-hui, 1969, pp. 275–308.

Liang T'ien-hsi 梁天錫. *Sung shu-mi-yüan chih-tu* 宋樞密院制度. 2 vols. Taipei: Li-ming wen-hua shih-yeh ku-fen yu-hsien kung-ssu, 1981.

Liang T'ien-hsi 梁天錫. "Ts'ung Tsun-yao-lu k'an Sung-ch'u ssu-ch'ao chih chün-shih yü cheng-chih" 從遵堯錄看宋初四朝之軍事與政治. *Ta-lu tsa-chih* 大陸雜誌 31 No. 6 (1965), pp. 24–9.

Liang-ch'ao kang-mu pei-yao 兩朝綱目備要. 1228–33. [*Ssu-k'u ch'üan-shu* 四庫全書, *Wen-yüan ko* 文淵閣 1779 ed.]. In *Ssu-k'u ch'üan-shu chen-pen ch'u-chi* 四庫全書珍本初集. 1934–5. 105–6. Taipei: Shang-wu yin-shu-kuan, 1970.

Liao Lung-sheng 廖隆盛. "Sung Hsia kuan-hsi chung ti ch'ing-pai yen wen-t'i" 宋夏關係中的青白鹽問題. *Shih-huo yüeh-k'an* 食貨月刊 5 No. 10 (1976), pp. 14–21.

Lin Jui-han 林瑞翰. *Sung-tai cheng-chih shih* 宋代政治史. Taipei: Chung-cheng shu-chü, 1989.

Lin Jui-han 林瑞翰. "Wan Chin kuo-ch'ing chih yen-chiu" 晚金國情之研究. *Ta-lu tsa-chih* 大陸雜誌 16 No. 7 (1958), pp. 22–6.

Lin T'ien-wei 林天蔚. "Sung-tai ch'üan-hsiang hsing-ch'eng chih fen-hsi" 宋代權相形成之分析. *Ssu yü yen* 思與言 10 No. 5 (1973), pp. 30–40.

Lin T'ien-wei 林天蔚. "Sung-tai ch'üan-hsiang hsing-ch'eng chih fen-hsi" 宋代權相形成之分析. In *Sung-shih yen-chiu chi: Ti pa chi* 宋史研究集：第八輯, ed. Sung-shih tso-t'an-hui 宋史座談會. Chung-hua ts'ung-shu 中華叢書. Taipei: Chung-hua ts'ung-shu pien-shen wei-yüan-hui, 1976, pp. 141–70.

Lin T'ien-wei 林天蔚. "Ts'ai Ching yü chiang-i ssu" 蔡京與講議司. *Shih-huo yüeh-k'an* 食貨月刊 6 No. 4 (1971), pp. 137–43.

Liu Cheng 留正 et al. *Huang Sung chung-hsing liang-ch'ao sheng-cheng* 皇宋中興兩朝聖政. c. 1200. [*Hsüan-yin wan-wei pieh-ts'ang* 選印宛委別藏 1935 ed.]. Sung-shih tzu-liao ts'ui-pien ti i chi 宋史資料萃編第一輯 Vols. 4–6. Taipei: Wen-hai ch'u-pan-she, 1967.

Liu Ching-chen 劉靜貞. "Pei Sung ch'ien-ch'i huang-ch'üan fa-chan chih yen-chiu – huang-ti cheng-chih chiao-se ti fen-hsi" 北宋前期皇權發展之研究 —皇帝政治角色的分析. Diss., Kuo-li T'ai-wan ta-hsüeh 國立臺灣大學, 1987.

Liu Ching-chen 劉靜貞. *Pei Sung ch'ien-ch'i huang-ti ho t'a-men ti ch'üan-li* 北宋前期皇帝和他們的權力. Taipei: Tao-hsiang ch'u-pan-she, 1996.

Liu Ching-chen 劉靜貞. "Ts'ung huang-hou kan-cheng tao t'ai-hou she-cheng – Pei Sung Chen-Jen chih chi nü-chu cheng-chih ch'üan-li shih-t'an" 從皇后干政到太后攝政 — 北宋真仁之際女主政治權力試探. In *Kuo-chi Sung-shih yen-t'ao-hui lun-wen-chi* 國際宋史研討會論文集, ed. Kuo-chi Sung-shih yen-t'ao-hui 國際宋史研討會. Taipei: Chung-kuo wen-hua ta-hsüeh shih-hsüeh yen-chiu-so shih-hsüeh-hsi, 1988, pp. 579–606.

Liu Hsü 劉昫 et al., eds. *Chiu T'ang-shu* 舊唐書. 945. 16 vols. Erh-shih-ssu shih 二十四史. Peking: Chung-hua shu-chü, 1975.

Liu K'o-chuang 劉克莊. *Hou-ts'un hsien-sheng ta ch'üan-chi* 後村先生大全集. 1270. [*Ssu-yen t'ang* 賜硯堂 1304 ed.; *Ssu-pu ts'ung-k'an ch'u-pien* 四部叢刊初編 1929 ed.]. In *Ssu-pu ts'ung-k'an cheng-pien* 四部叢刊正編. Vols. 62–3. Taipei: T'ai-wan shang-wu yin-shu-kuan, 1979.

Liu K'un-t'ai 劉坤太. "Wang An-shih kai-ko li-chih ti she-hsiang yü shih-chien" 王安石改革吏治的設想與實踐. In *Sung-shih yen-chiu lun-wen-chi: 1984 nien nien-hui pien-k'an* 宋史研究論文集：一九八四年年會編刊, ed. Teng Kuang-ming 鄧廣銘 et al. Hang-chou: Che-chiang jen-min ch'u-pan-she, 1987, pp. 282–96.

Liu Li-yen 柳立言. "Nan Sung cheng-chih ch'u-t'an: Kao-tsung yin-ying hsia ti Hsiao-tsung" 南宋政治初探：高宗陰影下的孝宗. In *Sung-shih yen-chiu chi: Ti shih-chiu chi* 宋史研究集：第十九輯. Sung-shih tso-t'an-hui 宋史座談會. Chung-hua ts'ung-shu 中華叢書. Taipei: Kuo-li pien-i-kuan, 1989, pp. 203–56.

Liu Min-chung 劉敏中. *P'ing Sung lu* 平宋錄. 1304. [Shou-shan ko ts'ung-shu 守山閣叢書 1922 ed.]. In *Pai-pu ts'ung-shu chi-ch'eng* 百部叢書集成. 1965–70. Taipei: I-wen yin-shu-kuan, 1968.

Liu Po-chi 劉伯驥. "Yüan-yu tang-cheng chih yen-pien yü liu-tu" 元祐黨爭之演變與流毒. In *Shih-hsüeh lun-chi* 史學論集, ed. Chung-hua hsüeh-shu yüan 中華學術院. Chung-hua hsüeh-shu yü hsien-tai wen-hua ts'ung-shu 中華學術與現代文化叢書 3. Taipei: Hua-kang ch'u-pan yu-hsien kung-ssu, 1977, pp. 240–66.

Liu Shih-chü 劉時舉. *Hsü Sung chung-hsing pien-nien tzu-chih t'ung-chien* 續宋中興編年資治通鑑. 13th–14th c. [1522–66 ed.]. Shanghai: Tung-fang hsüeh-hui, 1927.

Liu Ting-chih 劉定之. *Tai-chai ts'un-kao* 呆齋存稿. 15th c. [1506–21 ed; Kuo-li Pei-ching t'u-shu-kuan 國立北京圖書館 microfilm ed.; Fu Ssu-nien tu-shu-kuan 傅斯年圖書館]. 6 vols. Taipei: 20th c.

Liu Tzu-chien (James T. C. Liu) 劉子健. "An administrative cycle in Chinese history: The case of Northern Sung emperors." *Journal of Asian Studies* 21 No. 2 (1962), pp. 137–52.

Liu Tzu-chien (James T. C. Liu) 劉子健. "Ch'in Kuei ti ch'in-yu" 秦檜的親友. *Shih-huo yüeh-k'an* 食貨月刊 14 Nos. 7–8 (1984), pp. 310–23.

Liu Tzu-chien (James T. C. Liu) 劉子健. *China turning inward: Intellectual-political changes in the early twelfth century*. Harvard East Asian Monographs 132. Cambridge, Mass.: Council on East Asian Studies, Harvard University, 1988.

Liu Tzu-chien (James T. C. Liu) 劉子健. "An early Sung reformer: Fan Chung-yen." In *Chinese thought and institutions*, ed. John K. Fairbank. Comparative Studies of Cultures and Civilizations. Chicago: University of Chicago Press, 1957, pp. 105–31.

Liu Tzu-chien (James T. C. Liu) 劉子健. "Fan Chung-yen." In *Sung biographies*, ed. Herbert Franke. 4 vols. Münchener Ostasiatische Studien 16, 1–3; 17, 4. Vol. 1. Wiesbaden: Franz Steiner Verlag, 1976, pp. 321–30.

Liu Tzu-chien (James T. C. Liu) 劉子健. "How did a Neo-Confucian school become the state orthodoxy?" *Philosophy East and West* 23 No. 4 (1973), pp. 483–505.

Liu Tzu-chien (James T. C. Liu) 劉子健. "The Jurchen-Sung confrontation: Some overlooked points." In *China under Jurchen rule: Essays on Chin intellectual and cultural history*, ed. Hoyt C. Tillman and Stephen H. West. SUNY Series in Chinese Philosophy and Culture. Albany: State University of New York Press, 1995, pp. 39–49.

Liu Tzu-chien (James T. C. Liu) 劉子健. *Liang Sung shih yen-chiu hui-pien* 兩宋史研究彙編. Taipei: Lien-ching ch'u-pan shih-yeh kung-ssu, 1987.

Liu Tzu-chien (James T. C. Liu) 劉子健. "Lü I-chien." In *Sung biographies*, ed. Herbert Franke. 4 vols. Münchener Ostasiatische Studien 16, 1–3; 17, 4. Vol. 2. Wiesbaden: Franz Steiner Verlag, 1976, pp. 713–19.

Liu Tzu-chien (James T. C. Liu) 劉子健. *Ou-yang Hsiu: An eleventh century Neo-Confucianist*. Stanford, Calif.: Stanford University Press, 1967.

Liu Tzu-chien (James T. C. Liu) 劉子健. *Reform in Sung China: Wang An-shih (1021–1086) and his New Policies*. Harvard East Asian Series 3. Cambridge, Mass.: Harvard University Press, 1959.

Liu Tzu-chien (James T. C. Liu) 劉子健. "Sung roots of Chinese conservatism: The administrative problems." *Journal of Asian Studies* 26 No. 3 (1967), pp. 457–63.

Liu Tzu-chien (James T. C. Liu) 劉子健. "Sung T'ai-tsung yü Sung-ch'u liang-tz'u ts'uan-wei" 宋太宗與宋初兩次篡位. *Shih-huo yüeh-k'an* 食貨月刊 17 Nos. 3–4 (1988), pp. 1–5.

Liu Tzu-chien (James T. C. Liu) 劉子健. "Wei Liao-weng's thwarted statecraft." In *Ordering the world: Approaches to state and society in Sung dynasty China*, ed. Robert P. Hymes and Conrad Schirokauer. Studies on China 16. Berkeley: University of California Press, 1993, pp. 336–48.

Liu Tzu-chien (James T. C. Liu) 劉子健. "Yüeh Fei (1103–1141) and China's heritage of loyalty." *Journal of Asian Studies* 31 No. 2 (1972), pp. 291–7.

Lo Chia-hsiang 羅家祥. *Pei Sung tang-cheng yen-chiu* 北宋黨爭研究. Ta-lu ti-ch'ü po-shih lun-wen ts'ung-k'an 大陸地區博士論文叢刊. Taipei: Wen-chin ch'u-pan-she, 1993.

Lo Chia-hsiang 羅家祥. *P'eng-tang chih cheng yü Pei Sung cheng-chih* 朋黨之爭與北宋政治. Hua-tung shih-fan ta-hsüeh ch'u-pan chi-chin ts'ung-shu. Hsüeh-shu chu-tso hsi-lieh 華東師範大學出版基金叢書學術著作系列. Wu-han: Hua-tung shih-fan ta-hsüeh ch'u-pan-shih, 2002.

Lo Ch'iu-ch'ing 羅球慶. "Pei Sung ping-chih yen-chiu" 北宋兵制研究. *Hsin-ya hsüeh-pao* 新亞學報 3 No. 1 (1957), pp. 169–270.

Lo Ch'iu-ch'ing 羅球慶. "Sung Hsia chan-cheng-chung-te fan-pu yü pao-chai" 宋夏戰爭中的蕃部與堡寨. *Ch'ung-chi hsüeh-pao* 崇基學報 6 No. 2 (1967), pp. 223–43.

Lo Jung-pang. "The emergence of China as a sea power during the late Sung and early Yüan periods." *Far Eastern Quarterly* 14 (1954–5), pp. 489–503.

Lo Jung-pang. "Maritime commerce and its relation to the Sung navy." *Journal of Economic and Social History of the Orient* 22 No. 1 (1969), pp. 57–101.

Lo Wen (Winston W. Lo) 羅文. "Circuits and circuit intendants in the territorial administration of Sung China." *Monumenta Serica* 31 (1974–5), pp. 39–107.

Lo Wen (Winston W. Lo) 羅文. *An introduction to the civil service of Sung China: With emphasis on its personnel administration*. Honolulu: University of Hawaii Press, 1987.

Lo Wen (Winston W. Lo) 羅文. *The life and thought of Yeh Shih*. Gainsesville: University Presses of Florida, 1974.

Lo Wen (Winston W. Lo) 羅文. "Provincial government in Sung China." *Chinese Culture* 19 No. 4 (1978), pp. 19–45.

Lo Wen (Winston W. Lo) 羅文. *Szechwan in Sung China: A case study in the political integration of the Chinese empire*. Taipei: The University of Chinese Culture Press, 1982.

Loewe, Michael. "The Former Han dynasty." In *The Cambridge history of China*. Volume 1: *The Ch'in and Han empires, 221 B.C.–A.D. 220*, ed. Denis C. Twitchett and Michael Loewe. Cambridge: Cambridge University Press, 1986, pp. 103–222.

Lorge, Peter. "The entrance and exit of the Song founders." *Journal of Sung-Yuan Studies* 29 (1999), pp. 43–62.

Lorge, Peter. "War and the creation of the Northern Song." Diss., University of Pennsylvania, 1996.

Lou Yüeh [Yao] 樓鑰. *Kung-k'uei chi* 攻媿集. c. early 13th c. [*Wu-ying tien* 武英殿 1736–95 ed.]. In *Ssu-pu ts'ung-k'an ch'u-pien* 四部叢刊初編. 1919–22. Shang-wu yin-shu-kuan. Vols. 61–2. Shanghai: Shang-wu yin-shu-kuan, 1929.

Lou Yüeh [Yao] 樓鑰. *Kung-k'uei chi* 攻媿集. c. early 13th c. [*Ssu-pu ts'ung-k'an ch'u-pien* 四部叢刊初編 1929 ed.]. In *Ssu-pu ts'ung-k'an cheng-pien* 四部叢刊正編. Vol. 55. Taipei: T'ai-wan shang-wu yin-shu-kuan, 1979.

Lu Chen 路振. *Chiu-kuo chih* 九國志. c. 1000. [*Shou-shan-ko ts'ung-shu* 守山閣叢書 1844 ed.; 1922]. In *Pai-pu ts'ung-shu chi-ch'eng* 百部叢書集成. 1965–70. Vol. 52. Taipei: I-wen yin-shu-kuan, 1968.

Lu Yu 陸游. *Lu-shih Nan T'ang shu* 陸氏南唐書. 12th c. [*Ch'ien Shu-pao* 錢叔寶 handwritten Ming dynasty ed.]. In *Ssu-pu ts'ung-k'an hsü-pien* 四部叢刊續編. 1934. Shanghai: Shang-wu yin-shu-kuan, 1934.

Lü Chung 呂中. *Sung ta-shih-chi chiang-i* 宋大事記講義. [*Ssu-k'u ch'üan-shu* 四庫全書, Wen-yüan ko 文淵閣 1779 ed.]. Ying-yin Wen-yüan-ko Ssu-k'u ch'üan-shu 景印文淵閣四庫全書 686. Taipei: T'ai-wan shang-wu yin-shu-kuan, 1983.

Lü Ssu-mien 呂思勉. *Sui T'ang Wu-tai shih* 隋唐五代史. 1959. Shanghai: Shang-hai ku-chi ch'u-pan-she, 1984.

Lü T'ao 呂陶. *Ching-te chi* 淨德集. c. 1100. In *Wu-ying tien chü-chen pan-shu* 武英殿聚珍版書. 1899. N.p.: Kuang-ya shu-chü, 1899.

Ma Ling 馬令. *Ma-shih Nan T'ang shu* 馬氏南唐書. 1105. In *Ssu-pu ts'ung-k'an hsü-pien* 四部叢刊續編. 1934. Shanghai: Shang-wu yin-shu-kuan, 1934.

Ma Tuan-lin 馬端臨. *Wen-hsien t'ung-k'ao* 文獻通考. c. 1308. In *Shih-t'ung* 十通. Vols. 13–15. Shanghai: Shang-wu yin-shu-kuan, 1936.

Ma Tuan-lin 馬端臨. *Wen-hsien t'ung-k'ao* 文獻通考. c. 1308. [*Shang-wu yin-shu-kuan* 商務印書館 1935–7 ed.]. In *Shih-t'ung* 十通. Vols. 13–15. Kuo-hsüeh chi-pen ts'ung-shu 國學基本叢書. Taipei: Hsin-hsing shu-chü, 1965.

Mao Han-kuang 毛漢光. "T'ang-mo Wu-tai cheng-chih she-hui chih yen-chiu – Wei–Po erh-pai-nien shih-lun" 唐末五代政治社會之研究–魏博二百年史論. *Li-shih yü-yen yen-chiu-so chi-k'an* 歷史語言研究所集刊 50 (1979), pp. 301–60.

Martin, H. Desmond. "The Mongol wars with Hsi Hsia (1205–1227)." *Journal of the Royal Asiatic Society of Great Britain and Ireland* Nos. 3–4 (1942), pp. 195–228.

Martin, H. Desmond. *The rise of Chingis Khan and his conquest of north China*. Baltimore: Johns Hopkins University Press, 1950.

Matsui Shūichi 松井秀一. "Roryō hanchin kō" 盧龍藩鎮攷. *Shigaku zasshi* 史學雜誌 68 (1959), pp. 1397–1432.

Matsui Shūichi 松井秀一. "Tōdai kōhanki no Kō-Wai ni tsuite – kōzoku oyobi Kō Zen-tai, Kyū Ho no hanran o chūshin to shite" 唐代後半期の江淮について—江賊及び康全泰,

裘甫の叛亂を中心として. *Shigaku zasshi* 史學雜誌 66 No. 2 (1957), pp. 1–29.

Matsui Shūichi 松井秀一. "Tōdai kōhanki no Shisen – kanryō shihai to dogōsō no shutsugen o chūshin to shite" 唐代後半期の四川――官僚支配と士豪層の出現を中心として. *Shigaku zasshi* 史學雜誌 73 No. 10 (1964), pp. 46–88.

Matsui Shūichi 松井秀一. "Tōmatsu no minshū hanran to Godai no keisei" 唐末の民衆叛亂と五代の形勢. In *Iwanami Kōza Sekai rekishi 6 – Kodai 6* 岩波講座世界歷史ア6――古代ア6. Tokyo: Iwanami Shoten, 1971, pp. 237–78.

McGrath, Michael C. "Military and regional administration in Northern Sung China (960–1126)." Diss., Princeton University, 1982.

McKnight, Brian E. "Chu Hsi and his world." In *Chu Hsi and Neo-Confucianism*, ed. Wing-tsit Chan. Honolulu: University of Hawaii Press, 1986, pp. 408–36.

McKnight, Brian E. "Fiscal privileges and social order in Sung China." In *Crisis and prosperity in Sung China*, ed. John W. Haeger. Tucson: University of Arizona Press, 1975, pp. 79–100.

McKnight, Brian E. *Law and order in Sung China*. Cambridge: Cambridge University Press, 1992.

McKnight, Brian E. "T'ung Kuan." In *Sung biographies*, ed. Herbert Franke. 4 vols. Münchener Ostasiatische Studien 16, 1–3; 17, 4. Vol. 3. Wiesbaden: Franz Steiner Verlag, 1976, pp. 1090–7.

McKnight, Brian E. *Village and bureaucracy in Southern Sung China*. Chicago: University of Chicago Press, 1971.

Miao Feng-lin 繆鳳林. "Sung Kao-tsung yü Nu-chen i-ho lun" 宋高宗與女真議和論. *Kuo-feng pan-yüeh-k'an* 國風半月刊 8 No. 2 (1936), pp. 39–44.

Mihelich, Mira A. "Polders and the politics of land reclamation in southeast China during the Northern Sung dynasty (960–1126)." Diss., Cornell University, 1979.

Miyakawa Hisayuki 宮川尚志. "Rin Reiso to Sō no Kisō" 林靈素と宋の徽宗. *Tōkai Daigaku kiyō: Bungaku bu* 東海大學紀要：文学部 24 (1975), pp. 1–8.

Miyazaki Ichisada 宮崎市定. "Ō Anseki no rishi gōitsu saku – sōhō o chūshin to shite" 王安石の吏士合――策――倉法を中心として. In *Ajia-shi kenkyū* アジア史研究. Miyazaki Ichisada 宮崎市定. Tōyōshi kenkyū sōkan 東洋史研究叢刊. Vol. 4, Part 2. Kyoto: Tōyōshi Kenkyūkai, 1959, pp. 311–64.

Miyazaki Ichisada 宮崎市定. *Godai Sōsho no tsūka mondai* 五代宋初の通貨問題. Kyoto: Hoshino Shoten, 1943.

Miyazaki Ichisada 宮崎市定. "Godai Sōsho no tsūka mondai kōgai" 五代宋初の通貨問題梗概. In *Ajia-shi kenkyū dai ni* アジア史研究第二. Miyazaki Ichisada 宮崎市定. Tōyōshi kenkyū sōkan 東洋史研究叢刊 4. Kyoto: Tōyōshi Kenkyūkai, 1959, pp. 130–9.

Miyazaki Ichisada 宮崎市定. "Hsiao-tsung." In *Sung biographies*, ed. Herbert Franke. 4 vols. Münchener Ostasiatische Studien 16, 1–3; 17, 4. Vol. 2. Wiesbaden: Franz Steiner Verlag, 1976, pp. 400–1.

Miyazaki Ichisada 宮崎市定. "Ko Jidō ryakuden" 賈似道略傳. *Tōyōshi kenkyū* 東洋史研究 6 No. 3 (1941), pp. 54–73.

Miyazaki Ichisada 宮崎市定. "Nan-Sō seijishi gaisetsu" 南宋政治史概説. In *Ajia-shi kenkyū dai ni* アジア史研究第二. Miyazaki Ichisada 宮崎市定. Tōyōshi kenkyū sōkan 東洋史研究叢刊 4. Kyoto: Tōyōshi Kenkyūkai, 1959, pp. 158–92.

Miyazaki Ichisada 宮崎市定. "Sō no Taiso hishū setsu ni tsuite" 宋の太祖被弑説について. *Tōyōshi kenkyū* 東洋史研究 9 No. 4 (1945), pp. 1–16.

Miyazaki Ichisada 宮崎市定. "Sōdai kansei josetsu – Sō-shi shokkanshi o ika ni yomubeki ka" 宋代官制序説——宋史職官志を如何に読ジむべき. In *Sō-shi shokkanshi sakuin* 宋史職官志索引. Saeki Tomi 佐伯富. Dai 2-han. Tōyōshi kenkyū sōkan 東洋史研究叢刊 II. Kyoto: Dōhōsha, 1974, pp. 1–57.

Miyazaki Ichisada 宮崎市定. "Ying-Tsung." In *Sung biographies*, ed. Herbert Franke. 4 vols. Münchener Ostasiatische Studien 16, 1–3; 17, 4. Vol. 3. Wiesbaden: Franz Steiner Verlag, 1976, pp. 1257–8.

Miyazawa Tomoyuki 宮澤知之. "Hoku-Sō no zaisei to kahei keizai" 北宋の財政と貨幣經濟. In *Chūgoku sensei kokka to shakai tōgō* 中國專制國家と社會統合, ed. Chūgokushi Kenkyūkai 中國史研究会. Kyoto: Bunrikaku, 1990, pp. 281–332.

Miyazawa Tomoyuki 宮澤知之. "Sōdai no toshi shōgyō to kokka – shiekihō shinkō" 宋代の都市商業と國家——市易法新考. In *Chūgoku kinsei no toshi to bunka* 中國近世の都市と文化, ed. Umehara Kaoru 梅原郁. Kyoto: Kyōto Daigaku Jinbun Kagaku Kenkyūjo, 1984, pp. 321–58.

Mote, Frederick W. "Confucian eremitism in the Yüan period." In *The Confucian persuasion*, ed. Arthur F. Wright. Stanford Studies in the Civilizations of Eastern Asia. Stanford, Calif.: Stanford University Press, 1960, pp. 202–40.

Mote, Frederick W. *Imperial China: 900–1800*. Cambridge, Mass.: Harvard University Press, 1999.

Moule, Arthur C. *The rulers of China, 221 B.C.–A.D. 1949; chronological tables. With an introductory section on the earlier rulers c. 2100–249 B.C.* by W. Perceval Yetts. Books that Matter. New York: Frederick A. Praeger, 1957.

Murck, Alfreda. *Poetry and painting in Song China: The subtle art of dissent*. Harvard-Yenching Institute Mongraph Series. Cambridge, Mass.: Harvard University Council on East Asian Studies, 2000.

Nieh Ch'ung-ch'i 聶崇歧. "Lun Sung T'ai-tsu shou ping-ch'üan" 論宋太祖收兵權. *Yenching hsüeh-pao* 燕京學報 34 (1948), pp. 85–106.

Nieh Ch'ung-ch'i 聶崇歧. "Sung i-fa shu" 宋役法述. In *Sung-shih ts'ung-k'ao* 宋史叢考. Nieh Ch'ung-ch'i 聶崇歧. 2 vols. Vol. 1. Peking: Chung-hua shu-chü, 1980, pp. 1–70.

Nishikawa Masao 西川正夫. "Go, Nan-Tō ryō ōchō no kokka kenryoku no seikaku: Sōdai kokuseishi kenkyū josetsu no tame ni, sono ichi" 呉、南唐兩王朝の國家權力の性格：宋代國制史研究序説のかめに、其の一. *Hōseishi kenkyū* 法制史研究 9 (1958), pp. 95–171.

Novey, Janet McCracken. "Yü Ching, a Northern Sung statesman, and his treatise on the Ch'i-tan bureaucracy." Diss., Indiana University, 1983.

Okada Kōji 岡田宏二. "Godai So ōkoku no 'Keishū dōchū' ni tsuite" 五代楚王國の「溪州銅柱」について. *Daitō Bunka Daigaku kiyō (Jinbun kagaku)* 大東文化大学紀要(人文科学) 22 (1984), pp. 123–43.

Okada Kōji 岡田宏二. "Godai So ōkoku no kenkoku seido" 五代楚王國の建國制度. *Daitō Bunka Daigaku kiyō (Jinbun kagaku)* 大東文化大学紀要(人文科学) 19 (1981), pp. 73–89.

Okada Kōji 岡田宏二. "Godai So ōkoku no seikaku" 五代楚王國の性格. In *Nakajima Satoshi Sensei koki kinen ronshū* 中島敏先生古稀記念論集, ed. Nakajima Satoshi Sensei Koki Kinen Jigyōkai 中島敏先生古稀記念事業會. 2 vols. Vol. 2. Tokyo: Nakajima Satoshi Sensei Koki Kinen Jigyōkai, 1980–1, pp. 67–95.

Okada Kōji 岡田宏二. "Tōmatsu Godai Sōsho Konan chiiki no minzoku mondai – toku ni Hō-shi no keifu to Tōcha-zoku to no kankei o chūshin to shite" 唐末五代宋初湖南地域の民族間 —とくに彭氏の系譜と土家 族との関係を中心として. *Tōyō kenkyū* 東洋研究 71 (1984), pp. 87–132.

Okazaki Seirō 岡崎精郎. "Kō-Tō no Minsō ni kyūshū (jō)" 後唐の明宗に舊習(上). *Tōyōshi kenkyū* 東洋史研究 9 No. 4 (1945), pp. 50–62.

Okazaki Seirō 岡崎精郎. "Kō-Tō no Minsō ni kyūshū (ge)" 後唐の明宗に舊習(下). *Tōyōshi kenkyū* 東洋史研究 10 No. 2 (1948), pp. 29–40.

Olsson, Karl F. "The structure of power under the third emperor of Sung China: The shifting balance after the peace of Shan-yüan." Diss., University of Chicago, 1974.

Otagi Matsuo 愛宕松男. "Ri Tan no hanran to sono seijiteki igi – Mōkōchō chika ni okeru Kanchi no hōkensei to sono shūkensei e no tenkai" 李璮の叛亂と其の政治的意義——蒙古朝治下に於ける漢地の封建制とそ の州縣制の展開. *Tōyōshi kenkyū* 東洋史研究 6 No. 4 (1941), pp. 1–26.

Ou-yang Hsiu 歐陽修. *Historical records of the Five Dynasties*, trans. Richard L. Davis. New York: Columbia University Press, 2004.

Ou-yang Hsiu 歐陽修. *Hsin T'ang shu* 新唐書. 1060. 20 vols. Peking: Chung-hua shu-chü, 1975.

Ou-yang Hsiu 歐陽修. *Hsin Wu-tai shih* 新五代史. 1073. 3 vols. Erh-shih-ssu shih 二十四史. Peking: Chung-hua shu-chü, 1974.

Ou-yang Hsiu 歐陽修. *Kuei-t'ien lu* 歸田錄. 1067. T'ang Sung shih-liao pi-chi ts'ung-k'an 唐宋史料筆記叢刊. Peking: Chung-hua shu-chü, 1981.

Paludan, Ann. *The Chinese spirit road: The classical tradition of stone tomb statuary*. New Haven, Conn.: Yale University Press, 1991.

P'eng Chiu-sung 彭久松. "Pei Sung 'Shen-tsung shih-lu' ssu hsiu k'ao" 北宋《〈神宗實錄〉》四修考. *Wen-shih* 文史 24 (1985), pp. 179–88.

P'eng Kuei-nien 彭龜年. *Chih-t'ang chi* 止堂集. 12th c. [*Ssu-k'u ch'üan-shu* 四庫全書, Wen-yüan ko 文淵閣 1779 ed.]. In *Ssu-k'u ch'üan-shu chen-pen pieh-chi* 四庫全書珍本別集. Vols. 339–40. Taipei: T'ai-wan shang-wu yin-shu-kuan, 1975.

P'eng Pai-ch'uan 彭百川. *T'ai-p'ing chih-chi t'ung-lei* 太平治蹟統類. c. 13th c. 3 vols. Taipei: Ch'eng-wen ch'u-pan-she, 1966.

Peterson, Charles A. "The autonomy of the northeastern provinces in the period following the An Lu-shan rebellion." Diss., University of Washington, 1966.

Peterson, Charles A. "Court and province in mid- and late T'ang." In *The Cambridge history of China*. Volume 3: *Sui and T'ang China, 589–906, Part 1*, ed. Denis C. Twitchett. Cambridge: Cambridge University Press, 1979, pp. 464–560.

Peterson, Charles A. "First Sung reactions to the Mongol invasion of the north, 1211–17." In *Crisis and prosperity in Sung China*, ed. John W. Haeger. Tucson: University of Arizona Press, 1975, pp. 215–52.

Peterson, Charles A. "Old illusions and new realities: Sung foreign policy, 1217–1234." In *China among equals: The Middle Kingdom and its neighbors, 10th–14th centuries*, ed. Morris Rossabi. Berkeley: University of California Press, 1983, pp. 204–39.

Peterson, Charles A. "The restoration completed: Emperor Hsian-tsung and the provinces." In *Perspectives on the T'ang*, ed. Arthur F. Wright and Denis C. Twitchett. New Haven, Conn.: Yale University Press, 1973, pp. 151–92.

Pi Chung-yu 畢仲游. *Hsi-t'ai chi* 西臺集. c. 1117. In *Ts'ung-shu chi-ch'eng hsin-pien* 叢書集成新編. Taipei: Hsin-wen-feng ch'u-pan kung-ssu, 1986.

Pi Yüan 畢沅. *Hsü Tzu-chih t'ung-chien* 續資治通鑑. 1792. [*Te-yü-t'ang tsang-pan* 德裕堂藏板 1801 ed.]. 12 vols. Peking: Chung-hua shu-chü, 1957.

Pi Yüan 畢沅. *Hsü Tzu-chih t'ung-chien* 續資治通鑑. 1792. [*Te-yü-t'ang tsang-pan* 德裕堂藏板 1801 ed.]. 12 vols. Peking: Ku-chi ch'u-pan-she, 1957.

Pi Yüan 畢沅. *Hsü Tzu-chih t'ung-chien* 續資治通鑑. 1792. [*Te-yü-t'ang tsang-pan* 德裕堂藏板 1801 ed.]. 4 vols. Peking: Ku-chi ch'u-pan-she, 1958.

Pi Yüan 畢沅. *Hsü tzu-chih t'ung-chien* 續資治通鑑. c. 1880. [*Shih-chieh shu-chü* 世界書局 1935 ed.]. Shanghai: Shang-hai ku-chi ch'u-pan-she, 1987.

Pien Hsiao-hsüan 卞孝宣 and Cheng Hsüeh-meng 鄭學檬. *Wu-tai shih-hua* 五代史話. Peking: Pei-ching ch'u-pan-she, 1985.

Pines, Yuri. "Friends or foes: Changing concepts of ruler-minister relations and the notion of loyalty in pre-imperial China." *Monumenta Serica* 50 (2002), pp. 35–74.

Po-yang 柏楊. *Chung-kuo ti-wang huang-hou ch'in-wang kung-chu shih-hsi lu* 中國帝王皇后親王公主世系錄. 2 vols. Taipei: Hsing-kuang ch'u-pan-she, 1977.

Robinet, Isabelle. *Taoism: Growth of a religion*, trans. Phyllis Brooks. Stanford, Calif.: Stanford University Press, 1997.

Rossabi, Morris, ed. *China among equals: The Middle Kingdom and its neighbors, 10th–14th centuries*. Berkeley: University of California Press, 1983.

Rossabi, Morris. *Khubilai khan: His life and times*. Berkeley: University of California Press, 1988.

Rossabi, Morris. "The reign of Khubilai khan." In *The Cambridge history of China*. Volume 6: *Alien regimes and border states, 907–1368*, ed. Herbert Franke and Denis C. Twitchett. New York: Cambridge University Press, 1994, pp. 414–89.

Saeki Tomi 佐伯富. "Ō Anseki" 王安石. In *Chūgoku-shi kenkyū* 中國史研究. Saeki Tomi 佐伯富. 3 vols. Tōyōshi kenkyū sōkan 東洋史研究叢刊 21. Kyoto: Dōhōsha, 1969, pp. 329–464.

Saeki Tomi 佐伯富. "Godai ni okeru sūmitsushi ni tsuite" 五代における枢密使について. *Shisō* 史窓 46 (1989), pp. 1–19.

Saeki Tomi 佐伯富. *Sō-shi shokkanshi sakuin* 宋史職官志索引. Dai 2-han. Tōyōshi kenkyū sōkan 東洋史研究叢刊 II. Kyoto: Dōhōsha, 1974.

Saeki Tomi 佐伯富. "Sōdai ni okeru jūhō chibun ni tsuite" 宋代における重法地分について. In *Chūgoku-shi kenkyū* 中國史研究. Saeki Tomi 佐伯富. 3 vols. Tōyōshi kenkyū sōkan 東洋史研究叢刊 21. Kyoto: Dōhōsha, 1969, pp. 458–87.

Saeki Tomi 佐伯富. "Sōdai no kōjōshi ni tsuite – kunshu dokusaiken kenkyū no hitokoma" 宋代の皇城司に就いて――君主獨裁權研究の一齣. *Tōhō gakuhō (Kyoto)* 東方学報京都 9 (1938), pp. 158–96.

Saeki Tomi 佐伯富. "Sōdai Yūshū ni okeru kanshōchi ryōyuchi ni tsuite" 宋代雄州に於ける緩衝地兩輸地に就いて. *Tōa jinbun gakuhō* 東亜人文学報 1 No. 2 (1941), pp. 127–56.

Saeki Tomi 佐伯富. "Sōsho ni okeru cha no senbai seido" 宋初における茶の專賣制度. In *Chūgoku-shi kenkyū* 中國史研究. Saeki Tomi 佐伯富. 3 vols. Tōyōshi kenkyū sōkan 東洋史研究叢刊 21. Kyoto: Dōhōsha, 1969, pp. 377–408.

Sakurai Haruko 桜井ハ子. "Godai Jikkoku no Go-Etsu ni tsuite" 五代渚曹呉越について. *Nara shien* 寧樂史苑 15 (1967), pp. 11–24.

San-men-hsia-shih wen-wu kung-tso tui 三門峡市文物工作隊, comp. *Pei Sung Shan-chou lou-tse-yüan* 北宋陝州漏澤園. Peking: Wen-wu ch'u-pan-she, 1999.

Sariti, Anthony W. "Monarchy, bureaucracy, and absolutism in the political thought of Ssu-ma Kuang." *Journal of Asian Studies* 32 No. 1 (1972), pp. 53–76.

Satake Yasuhiko 佐竹靖彦. "Fan Tsung-yin." In *Sung biographies*, ed. Herbert Franke. 4 vols. Münchener Ostasiatische Studien 16, 1–3; 17, 4. Vol. 1. Wiesbaden: Franz Steiner Verlag, 1976, pp. 345–7.

Satake Yasuhiko 佐竹靖彦. "Ō-Shoku seiken seiritsu no zentei ni tsuite" 王蜀政權成立の前提について. *Tōyō Bunka Kenkyūjo kiyō* 東洋文化研究所紀要 99 (1986), pp. 21–69.

Schafer, Edward H. *The empire of Min.* Rutland, Vt.: Tuttle, 1954.

Schafer, Edward H. "The history of the empire of Southern Han, according to chapter 65 of the *Wu-tai shih* of Ou-yang Hsiu." In *Sōritsu nijūgo shūnen kinen ronbunshū {The silver jubilee volume of the Zinbun Kagaku Kenkyusyo, Kyoto University}* 創立二曙周年記念論文集, ed. Kyōtō Daigaku Jinbun Kagaku Kenkyūjo 京都大学人文科学研究所. 2 vols. Kyoto: Jinbun kagaku kenkyūjō, 1954, pp. 339–69.

Schirokauer, Conrad. "Chu Hsi's political career: A study in ambivalence." In *Confucian personalities*, ed. Arthur F. Wright and Denis C. Twitchett. Stanford Studies in the Civilizations of Eastern Asia. Stanford, Calif.: Stanford University Press, 1962, pp. 162–88.

Schirokauer, Conrad. "Chu Hsi's sense of history." In *Ordering the world: Approaches to state and society in Sung dynasty China*, ed. Robert P. Hymes and Conrad Schirokauer. Studies on China 16. Berkeley: University of California Press, 1993, pp. 193–220.

Schirokauer, Conrad. "Liu Cheng." In *Sung biographies*, ed. Herbert Franke. 4 vols. Münchener Ostasiatische Studien 16, 1–3; 17, 4. Wiesbaden: Franz Steiner Verlag, 1976, pp. 624–8.

Schirokauer, Conrad. "Neo-Confucians under attack: The condemnation of *wei-hsüeh*." In *Crisis and prosperity in Sung China*, ed. John W. Haeger. Tucson: University of Arizona Press, 1975, pp. 163–98.

Scogin, Hugh. "Poor relief in Northern Sung China." *Oriens extremus* 25 No. 1 (1978), pp. 30–46.

Searle, Eleanor. *Predatory kingship and the creation of Norman power.* Berkeley: University of California Press, 1988.

Sen Tansen. *Buddhism, diplomacy, and trade: The realignment of Sino-Indian relations, 600–1400*. Asian Interactions and Comparisons. Honolulu: Association for Asian Studies, 2003.

Shao Po 邵博. *Shao-shih wen-chien hou-lu* 邵氏聞見後錄. 1157, ed. Liu Te-ch'üan 劉德權 and Li Chien-hsiung 李劍雄. T'ang Sung shih-liao pi-chi ts'ung-k'an 唐宋史料筆記叢刊. Peking: Chung-hua shu-chü, 1983.

Shao Po-wen 邵伯溫. *Shao-shih wen-chien lu* 邵氏聞見錄. 1151. T'ang Sung shih-liao pi-chi ts'ung-k'an 唐宋史料筆記叢刊. Peking: Chung-hua shu-chü, 1983.

Shen Ch'i-wei 沈起煒. *Sung Chin chan-cheng shih-lüeh* 宋金戰爭史略. Wu-han: Hu-pei jen-min ch'u-pan-she, 1958.

Shen Sung-ch'in 沈松勤. "Pei Sung t'ai-chien chih-tu yü tang-cheng" 北宋臺諫制度與黨爭. *Li-shih yen-chiu* 歷史研究 254 (1998), pp. 27–44.

Shiba Yoshinobu 斯波義信. *Commerce and society in Sung China*, trans. Mark Elvin. Michigan Abstracts of Chinese and Japanese Works on Chinese History 2. Ann Arbor: Center for Chinese Studies, University of Michigan, 1970.

Shiba Yoshinobu 斯波義信. *Sōdai kōnan keizaishi no kenkyū* 宋代江南経済史の研究. Tōkyō Daigaku Tōyō Bunka Kenkyūjo hōkoku 東京大学東洋文化研究所報告. Tokyo: Tōkyō Daigaku Tōyō Bunka kenkyūjo, 1988.

Shiba Yoshinobu 斯波義信. "Sōdai shiteki seido no enkaku" 宋代市糴制度の沿革. In *Aoyama Hakushi koki kinen Sōdai shi ronsō* 青山博士古稀紀念宋代史論叢, ed. Aoyama Hakushi Koki Kinen Sōdai-shi Ronsō Kankōkai 青山博士古稀紀念宋代史論叢刊行会. Tokyo: Seishin Shobō, 1974, pp. 123–59.

Shiba Yoshinobu 斯波義信. *Sōdai shōgyōshi kenkyū* 宋代商業史研究. Tokyo: Kazama Shobō, 1968.

Shiba Yoshinobu 斯波義信. "Sung foreign trade: Its scope and organization." In *China among equals: The Middle Kingdom and its neighbors, 10th–14th centuries*, ed. Morris Rossabi. Berkeley: University of California Press, 1983, pp. 89–115.

Shiba Yoshinobu 斯波義信. "Wang Kuei." In *Sung biographies*, ed. Herbert Franke. 4 vols. Münchener Ostasiatische Studien 16, 1–3; 17, 4. Wiesbaden: Franz Steiner Verlag, 1976, vol. 4, pp. 1115–17.

Shih Hao 史浩. *Mou-feng chen-yin man-lu* 鄮峰真隱漫錄. c. 1181. [*Ssu-k'u ch'üan-shu* 四庫全書, *Wen-yüan ko* 文淵閣 1779 ed.]. In *Ssu-k'u ch'üan-shu chen-pen erh-chi* 四庫全書珍本二集. 1971. Vols. 259–62. Taipei: T'ai-wan shang-wu yin-shu-kuan, 1971.

Shih Su 施宿 et al. *Chia-t'ai Kuei-chi chih* 嘉泰會稽志. 1201. In *Sung Yüan fang-chih ts'ung-k'an* 宋元方誌叢刊. Vol. 7. pp. 6711–7090. Peking: Chung-hua shu-chü, 1990.

Shimasue Kazuyasu 島居一康. "Sōdai shinteizei no shokeitō" 宋代身丁税の諸系統. *Tōyōshi kenkyū* 東洋史研究 45 No. 3 (1986), pp. 119–44.

Shui-li-pu Huang-ho shui-li wei-yüan-hui "Huang-ho shui-li-shih shu-yao" pien-hsieh-tsu 水利部黄河水利委員會〈〈黃河水利史述要〉〉編寫組. *Huang-ho shui-li-shih shu-yao* 黃河水利史述要. Peking: Shui-li ch'u-pan-she, 1982.

Smith, Kidder, Jr., et al. *Sung dynasty uses of the I Ching*. Princeton, N.J.: Princeton University Press, 1990.

Smith, Paul J. "Commerce, agriculture, and core formation in the upper Yangzi, 2 A.D. to 1948." *Late Imperial China* 9 No. 1 (1988), pp. 1–78.

Smith, Paul J. "Family, landsmann, and status-group affinity in refugee mobility strategies: The Mongol invasions and the diaspora of Sichuanese elites, 1230–1330."*Harvard Journal of Asiatic Studies* 52 No. 2 (1992), pp. 665–708.

Smith, Paul J. "Fear of gynarchy in an age of chaos: Kong Qi's reflections on life in south China under Mongol rule."*Journal of Economic and Social History of the Orient* 41 No. 1 (1998), pp. 1–95.

Smith, Paul J. "Introduction: Problematizing the Song-Yuan-Ming transition." In *The Song-Yuan-Ming transition in Chinese history*, ed. Paul J. Smith and Richard von Glahn. Harvard East Asian Monographs 221. Cambridge, Mass.: Harvard University Asia Center, 2003, pp. 1–34.

Smith, Paul J. "Irredentism as political capital: The New Policies and the annexation of Tibetan domains in Hehuang (the Qinghai-Gansu highlands) under Shenzong and his sons, 1068–1108." In *Emperor Huizong and late Northern Song China: The politics of culture and the culture of politics*, ed. Patricia B. Ebrey and Maggie Bickford. Cambridge, Mass.: Harvard University Asia Center, 2006, pp. 78–130.

Smith, Paul J. "State power and economic activism during the New Policies, 1068–1085: The tea and horse trade and the 'Green Sprouts' loan policy." In *Ordering the world: Approaches to state and society in Sung dynasty China*, ed. Robert P. Hymes and Conrad Schirokauer. Studies on China 16. Berkeley: University of California Press, 1993, pp. 76–127.

Smith, Paul J. *Taxing heaven's storehouse: Horses, bureaucrats and the destruction of the Sichuan tea industry, 1074–1224*. Harvard-Yenching Institute Mongraph Series 32. Cambridge, Mass.: Council on East Asian Studies, Harvard University, 1991.

Smith, Paul J., and Richard von Glahn, eds. *The Song-Yuan-Ming transition in Chinese history*. Harvard East Asian Monographs 221. Cambridge, Mass.: Harvard University Asia Center, 2003.

Sogabe Shizuo 曾我部静雄. "Ō Anseki no boyakuhō" 王安石の募役法. In *Sōdai zaiseishi* 宋代財政史. 1941. Sogabe Shizuo 曾我部静雄. Chūgoku gakujutsu kenkyū sōsho 中国学術研究双書 1. Tokyo: Daian, 1966, pp. 143–98.

Sogabe Shizuo 曾我部静雄. "Ō Anseki no hokōhō" 王安石の保甲法. In *Sōdai seikeishi no kenkyū* 宋代政經史の研究. Sogabe Shizuo 曾我部静雄. Tokyo: Yoshikawa Kōbunkan, 1974, pp. 1–63.

Sogabe Shizuo 曾我部静雄. *Sōdai zaiseishi* 宋代財政史. Tokyo: Seikatsusha, 1941.

Sogabe Shizuo 曾我部静雄. *Sōdai zaiseishi* 宋代財政史. 1941. Chūgoku gakujutsu kenkyū sōsho 中国学術研究双書 1. Tokyo: Daian, 1966.

Somers, Robert. "Banditry, militarization and state formation in late T'ang: The origins of Sung China." Seattle. 31 May 1979.

Somers, Robert. "The end of T'ang." In *The Cambridge history of China*. Volume 3: *Sui and T'ang China, 589–906, Part 1*, ed. Denis C. Twitchett. Cambridge: Cambridge University Press, 1979, pp. 682–789.

Ssu-ch'uan ta-hsüeh li-shih-hsi "Wang Hsiao-p'o Li Shun ch'i-i" tiao-ch'a tsu-pien 四川大學歷史系〈〈王小波李順起義〉〉調查組編. *Wang Hsiao-p'o Li Shun ch'i-i tzu-liao hui-pien* 王小波李順起義資料匯編. Ch'eng-tu: Ssu-ch'uan jen-min ch'u-pan-she, 1978.

Ssu-ma Ch'ien 司馬遷. *Shih chi* 史記. c. 90 B.C.E. [*Po-na-pen* 百衲本 1930–7 ed.]. Peking: Chung-hua shu-chü, 1972.

Ssu-ma Kuang 司馬光. *Ssu-ma Kuang tsou-i* 司馬光奏議, ed. Wang Ken-lin 王根林. San Chin ku-chi ts'ung-shu 三晉古籍叢書. T'ai-yüan: Shan-hsi jen-min ch'u-pan-she, 1986.

Ssu-ma Kuang 司馬光. *Ssu-ma Wen-cheng kung ch'uan-chia chi* 司馬文正公傳家集. Mid-12th c. In *Kuo-hsüeh chi-pen ts'ung-shu* 國學基本叢書. Shanghai: Shang-wu yin-shu-kuan, 1937.

Ssu-ma Kuang 司馬光. *Su-shui chi-wen* 涑水記聞. c. 1180. Tseng-ting Chung-kuo hsüeh-shu ming-chu 增訂中國學術名著 1. Taipei: Shih-chieh shu-chü, 1962.

Ssu-ma Kuang 司馬光. *Tzu-chih t'ung-chien* 資治通鑑. 1086. 20 vols. Peking: Chung-hua shu-chü, 1956.

Standen, Naomi. "Frontier crossings from north China to Liao, c. 900–1005." Diss., University of Durham, 1994.

Standen, Naomi. *Unbounded loyalty: Frontier crossings in Liao China.* Honolulu: University of Hawaii Press, 2007.

Standen, Naomi. "Raiding and frontier society in the Five Dynasties." In *Political frontiers, ethnic boundaries, and human geographies in Chinese history*, ed. Nicola Di Cosmo and Donald J. Wyatt. London: Routledge Curzon, 2003, pp. 160–91.

Standen, Naomi. "What nomads want: Raids, invasions, and the Liao conquest of 947." In *Mongols, Turks, and others: Eurasian nomads and the sedentary world*, ed. Reuven Amitai and Michal Biran. Brill's Inner Asian Library 11. Leiden: Brill, 2005, pp. 129–74.

Strickmann, Michel. "The longest Taoist scripture." *History of Religions* 17 Nos. 3–4 (1978), pp. 331–54.

Sturman, Peter C. "Cranes above Kaifeng: The auspicious image in the court of Huizong." *Ars Orientalis* 20 (1990), pp. 33–68.

Su Ch'e 蘇轍. *Luan-ch'eng chi* 欒城集. 1541. 4 vols. In *Ssu-pu pei-yao* 四部備要. 1920–33. Chung-hua shu-chü. Taipei: T'ai-wan chung-hua shu-chü, 1965–6.

Su Ch'e 蘇轍. *Su Ch'e chi* 蘇轍記, ed. Ch'en Hung-t'ien 陳宏天 and Kao Hsiu-fang 高秀芳. 4 vols. Chung-kuo ku-tien wen-hsüeh chi-pen ts'ung-shu 中國古典文學基本叢書. Peking: Chung-hua shu-chü, 1990.

Su Chi-lang 蘇基朗. "Wu-tai ti shu-mi-yüan" 五代的樞密院. *Shih-huo yüeh-k'an* 食貨月刊 10 Nos. 1–2 (1980), pp. 3–19.

Su Shih 蘇軾. *Ching-chin Tung-po wen-chi shih-lüeh* 經進東坡文集事略. c. 1173. In *Ssu-pu ts'ung-k'an ch'u-pien so-pen* 四部叢刊初編縮本. Vol. 52. Taipei: T'ai-wan shang-wu yin-shu-kuan, 1967.

Su Shih 蘇軾. *Su Shih wen-chi* 蘇軾文記, ed. K'ung Fan-li 孔凡禮. 6 vols. Chung-kuo ku-tien wen-hsüeh chi-pen ts'ung-shu 中國古典文學基本叢書. Peking: Chung-hua shu-chü, 1986.

Sudō Yoshiyuki 周藤吉之. "Godai setsudoshi no gagun ni kansuru ichi kōsatsu – bukyoku to no kanren ni oite" 五代節度使の牙軍關する一考察 – 部との關聯において. *Tōyō Bunka Kenkyūjo kiyō* 東洋文化研究所紀要 2 (1951), pp. 3–72.

Sudō Yoshiyuki 周藤吉之. "Godai setsudoshi no shihai taisei" 五代節度使の支配體制. *Shigaku zasshi* 史學雜誌 61 (1952), pp. 289–329, 521–39.

Sudō Yoshiyuki 周藤吉之. "Nan-Sō no Ri Tō to *Zoku Shichi tsugan chōhen* no seiritsu" 南宋李燾と「續資治通鑑長編」の成立. In *Sōdai-shi kenkyū* 宋代史研究. Sudō Yoshiyuki 周藤吉之. Tōyō bunko ronsō 東洋文庫論叢 50. Tokyo: Tōyō Bunko, 1969, pp. 469–512.

Sudō Yoshiyuki 周藤吉之. "Ō Anseki no boyakusen chōshū no sho mondai" 王安石の免役錢徴收の諸問題. In *Sōdai-shi kenkyū* 宋代史研究. Sudō Yoshiyuki 周藤吉之. Tōyō bunko ronsō 東洋文庫論叢 50. Tokyo: Tōyō Bunko, 1969, pp. 189–259.

Sudō Yoshiyuki 周藤吉之. "Ō Anseki no seibyoho no shiko katei" 王安石の青苗法の施行過程. *Tōyō Daigaku Daigakuin kiyo* 東洋大学大学院紀要 8 (1972), pp. 172–4.

Sudō Yoshiyuki 周藤吉之. "Ō Anseki no shinpō to sono shiteki igi – nōmin seisaku o chushin to shite" 王安石の新法とその史的意義——農民政策を中心として. In *Sōdai-shi kenkyū* 宋代史研究. Sudō Yoshiyuki 周藤吉之. Tōyō bunko ronsō 東洋文庫論叢 50. Tokyo: Tōyō Bunko, 1969, pp. 1–25.

Sudō Yoshiyuki 周藤吉之. "Sōdai gōsonsei no hensen katei" 宋代郷村制の變遷過程. In *Tō-Sō shakai keizaishi kenkyū* 唐宋社會經濟史. Sudō Yoshiyuki 周藤吉之. Tokyo: Tōkyō Daigaku Shuppankai, 1965, pp. 561–644.

Sudō Yoshiyuki 周藤吉之. "Sōdai shuken no shokuyaku to shuri no hatten" 宋代州縣の職役と胥吏の發展. In *Sōdai keizaishi kenkyū* 宋代經濟史研究. Sudō Yoshiyuki 周藤吉之. Tokyo: Tōkyō Daigaku Shuppankai, 1962, pp. 655–816.

Sudō Yoshiyuki 周藤吉之. "Tōmatsu Godai no shōensei" 唐末五代の莊園制. In *Chūgoku tochi seidoshi kenkyū* 中國土地制度史研究. Sudō Yoshiyuki 周藤吉之. Tokyo: Tōkyō Daigaku Shuppankai, 1954, pp. 7–64.

Sun K'o-k'uan 孫克寬. *Meng-ku ch'u-ch'i chih chün-lüeh yü Chin chih peng-k'uei* 蒙古初期之軍略與金之崩潰. Pien-chiang ts'ung-shu 邊疆叢書. Taipei: Chung-yang wen-wu kung-ying-she, 1955.

Sun K'o-k'uan 孫克寬. *Meng-ku Han-chün chi Han wen-hua yen-chiu* 蒙古漢軍及漢文化研究. Taipei: Wen-hsing shu-tien, 1958.

Sun K'o-k'uan 孫克寬. *Sung-Yüan tao-chiao chih fa-chan* 宋元道教之發展. Tung-hai ta-hsüeh yen-chiu ts'ung-shu 東海大學叢書. Tai-chung: Tung-hai ta-hsüeh, 1965.

Sun K'o-k'uan 孫克寬. *Yüan-tai Han wen-hua chih huo-tung* 元代漢文化之活動. Taipei: T'ai-wan chung-hua shu-chü, 1968.

Sun Kuang-hsien 孫光憲. *Pei-meng so-yen* 北夢所言. 10th c. [*Ya-yü t'ang ts'ang-shu* 雅雨堂藏書 1756 ed.]. In *Pai-pu ts'ung-shu chi-ch'eng* 百部叢書集成. 1965–70. Vol. 36. Taipei: I-wen yin-shu-kuan, 1966.

Sun Kuo-tung 孫國棟. "Sung-tai kuan-chih wen-luan tsai T'ang-chih ti ken-yüan – Sung-shih chih-kuan-chih shu Sung-tai luan chih ken-yüan pien" 宋代官制紊亂在唐制的根源 – 宋史職官志述宋代亂制根源辨. *Chung-kuo hsüeh-jen* 中國學人 1 (1970), pp. 41–54.

Sun Kuo-tung 孫國棟. "T'ang Sung chih chi she-hui men-ti chih hsiao-jung" 唐宋之際社會門第之消融. *Hsin-ya hsüeh-pao* 新亞學報 4 No. 1 (1959), pp. 211–304.

Sung Ch'ang-lien 宋常廉. "Kao-liang-ho chan-i k'ao-shih" 高梁河戰役考實. *Ta-lu tsa-chih* 大陸雜誌 39 No. 10 (1969), pp. 26–36.

Sung Hsi 宋晞. "Chu Hsi ti cheng-chih lun" 朱熹的政治論. In *Sung-shih yen-chiu chi: ti shih chi* 宋史研究集：第十輯, ed. Sung-shih tso-t'an-hui 宋史座談會. Chung-hua ts'ung-shu 中華叢書. Taipei: Kuo-li pien-i-kuan Chung-hua ts'ung-shu pien-shen wei-yüan-hui, 1978, pp. 355–69.

Sung Lien 宋濂 et al. *Yüan shih* 元史. 1370. [*Po-na-pen* 百衲本 1930–7 ed.]. 15 vols. Peking: Chung-hua shu-chü, 1976.

Sung Min-ch'iu 宋敏求. *Ch'un-ming t'ui-ch'ao lu* 春明退朝錄. c. 1070. Peking: Chung-hua shu-chü, 1980.

Sung-chi san-ch'ao cheng-yao 宋季三朝政要. [*Shou-shan ko ts'ung-shu* 守山閣叢書 n.d, ed.]. In *Pai-pu ts'ung-shu chi-ch'eng* 百部叢書集成. 1965–70. Vol. 54. Taipei: I-wen yin-shu-kuan, 1968.

Sung-shih chüan pien-tsuan wei-yüan-hui 宋史卷編纂委員會. *Chung-kuo li-shih ta tz'u-tien: Sung-shih chüan* 中國歷史大辭典：宋史卷. Shanghai: Shang-hai tz'u-shu ch'u-pan-she, 1984.

Sung-shih ch'üan-wen Hsü Tzu-chih t'ung-chien 宋史全文續資治通鑑. Early 14th c. Sung-shih tzu-liao ts'ui-pien ti erh-chi 宋史資料萃編第二輯. Vols. 4–8. Taipei: Wen-hai ch'u-pan-she, 1969.

Tai I-hsüan 戴裔煊. *Sung-tai ch'ao-yen chih-tu yen-chiu* 宋代鈔鹽制度鹽究. Shanghai: Shang-wu yin-shu-kuan, 1957.

Tai I-hsüan 戴裔煊. *Sung-tai ch'ao-yen chih-tu yen-chiu* 宋代鈔鹽制度鹽究. 1957. Taipei: Hua-shih ch'u-pan-she, 1982.

Tai Mei 戴枚 et al. *Hsin-hsiu Yin-hsien chih* 新修鄞縣志. [Academia Sinica, Fu Ssu-nien 傅斯年 ed.]. N.p.: n.p., 1877.

T'an Ch'i-hsiang 譚其驤, ed. *Chung-kuo li-shih ti-t'u chi* 中國歷史地圖集. 8 vols. Shanghai: T'i-t'u ch'u-pan-she, 1982.

Tanaka Seiji 田中整治. "Go-Etsu to Bin to no kankei" 呉越と閩との關係. *Tōyōshi kenkyū* 東洋史研究 28 No. 1 (1969), pp. 28–51.

Tanaka Seiji 田中整治. "So to Nan-Kan to no kankei" 楚と南漢との關係. In *Tamura hakushi shōju Tōyōshi ronsō* 田村博士頌壽東洋史論叢, ed. Tamura Hakushi Taikan Kinen Jigyōkai 田村博士退官記念事業會. Kyoto: Tamura Hakushi Taikan Kinen Jigyōkai, 1968, pp. 359–74.

Tanigawa Michio 谷川道雄. "Tōdai no hanchin ni tsuite – Setsusei no baai" 唐代の藩鎮について──浙西の場合. *Shirin* 史林 35 No. 3 (1952), pp. 280–99.

Tanigawa Michio 谷川道雄 and Mori Masao 森正夫, eds. *Chūgoku minshū hanranshi* 中國民衆叛乱史. 4 vols. Tōyō bunko 東洋文庫 336, 351, 408, 409. Tokyo: Heibonsha, 1978–83.

Tao Jing-shen (T'ao Chin-sheng) 陶晉生. "Barbarians or northerners: Northern Sung images of the Khitans." In *China among equals: The Middle Kingdom and its neighbors, 10th–14th centuries*, ed. Morris Rossabi. Berkeley: University of California Press, 1983, pp. 66–86.

Tao Jing-shen (T'ao Chin-sheng) 陶晉生. *Chin Hai-ling-ti ti fa Sung yü Ts'ai-shih chan-i ti k'ao-shih* 金海陵帝的伐宋與采石戰役的考實. Kuo-li T'ai-wan ta-hsüeh wen-shih ts'ung-k'an 國立臺灣大學文史叢刊. Taipei: Kuo-li T'ai-wan ta-hsüeh wen-hsüeh-yüan, 1963.

Tao Jing-shen (T'ao Chin-sheng) 陶晉生. *The Jurchen in twelfth-century China*. Publications on Asia of the Institute for Comparative and Foreign Area Studies 29. Seattle: University of Washington Press, 1976.

Tao Jing-shen (T'ao Chin-sheng) 陶晉生. "The personality of Sung Kao-tsung (r: 1127–1162)." In *Ryū Shiken hakuse shōju kinen: Sō-shi kenkyū ronshū* 劉子健博士頌壽紀念：宋史研究論集, ed. Kinugawa Tsuyoshi 衣川強. Kyoto: Dōhōsha, 1989, pp. 531–43.

Tao Jing-shen (T'ao Chin-sheng) 陶晉生. "Sung Chin miao-hsüeh yü ju-chia ssu-hsiang ti ch'uan-pu" 宋金廟學與儒家思想的傳布. In *Kuo-chi K'ung-hsüeh hui-i lun-wen-chi* 國際孔學會議論文集, ed. Chung-hua min-kuo K'ung-Meng hsüeh-hui et al. Taipei: Kuo-chi K'ung-hsüeh hui-i ta-hui mi-shu-ch'u, 1988, pp. 536–7.

Tao Jing-shen (T'ao Chin-sheng) 陶晉生. *Two sons of heaven: Studies in Sung-Liao relations*. Tucson: University of Arizona Press, 1988.

Tao Jing-shen (T'ao Chin-sheng) 陶晉生. "Yü Ching and Sung policies towards Liao and Hsia, 1042–1044." *Journal of Asian History* 6 No. 2 (1972), pp. 114–22.

Tao Jing-shen (T'ao Chin-sheng) 陶晉生 and Wang Min-hsin 王民信, eds. *Li T'ao Hsü Tzu-chih t'ung-chien ch'ang-p'ien Sung Liao kuan-hsi shih-liao chi-lu* 李燾續資治通鑑長編宋遼關係史料輯錄. 3 vols. Shih-liao ts'ung-shu 史料叢書. Taipei: Chung-yang yen-chiu-yüan li-shih yü-yen yen-chiu-so, 1974.

T'ao Ku 陶穀. *Ch'ing-i lu* 清異錄. c. 960–70. [*Pao-yen t'ang pi-chi* 寶顏堂祕笈 1606 ed.]. In *Pai-pu ts'ung-shu chi-ch'eng* 百部叢書集成. 1965–70. Vol. 18. Taipei: I-wen yin-shu-kuan, 1965.

T'ao Mao-ping 陶懋炳. *Wu-tai shih-lüeh* 五代史略. Peking: Jen-min ch'u-pan-she, 1985.

T'ao Yüeh 陶岳. *Wu-tai shih-pu* 五代史補. 1012. In *Yü-chang ts'ung-shu* 豫章叢書. Nan-ch'ang: Yü-chang ts'ung-shu pien-ko chü, 1915.

Taylor, Keith W. *The birth of Vietnam*. Berkeley: University of California Press, 1983.

Teng Kuang-ming 鄧廣銘. "Ch'en-ch'iao ping-pien huang-p'ao chia-shen ku-shih k'ao-shih" 陳橋兵變黃袍加身故事考釋. *Chen-li tsa-chih* 真理雜誌 1 No. 1 (1944), pp. 61–8.

Teng Kuang-ming 鄧廣銘. "Nan Sung tui Chin tou-cheng chung ti chi-ko wen-t'i" 南宋對金鬥爭中的幾個問題. *Li-shih yen-chiu* 歷史研究 No. 2 (1963), pp. 21–32.

Teng Kuang-ming 鄧廣銘. "Pei Sung ti mu-ping chih-tu chi ch'i yü tang-shih chi-jo chi-p'an ho nung-yeh sheng-ch'an ti kuan-hsi" 北宋的募兵制度及其與當時積弱積貧和農業生產的關係. *Chung-kuo shih yen-chiu* 中國史研究 4 (1980), pp. 61–77.

Teng Kuang-ming 鄧廣銘. "Sung T'ai-tsu T'ai-tsung shou-shou pien" 宋太祖太宗授受辨. *Chen-li tsa-chih* 真理雜誌 1 No. 2 (1944), pp. 177–92.

Teng Kuang-ming 鄧廣銘. *Wang An-shih: Chung-kuo shih-i shih-chi ti kai-ko-chia* 王安石中國十一世紀的改革家. Rev. ed. Peking: Jen-min ch'u-pan-she, 1975.

Teng Kuang-ming 鄧廣銘. "Wang An-shih tui Pei Sung ping-chih ti kai-ko ts'o-shih chi ch'i she-hsiang" 王安石對北宋兵制的改革措施及設想. In *Sung-shih yen-chiu lun-wen-chi: Chung-hua wen-shih lun-ts'ung tseng-k'an* 宋史研究論文集：中華文史論叢增刊, ed. Teng Kuang-ming 鄧廣銘 and Ch'eng Ying-liu 程應鏐. Chung-hua wen-shih lun-ts'ung tseng-k'an 中華文史論叢增刊. Shanghai: Shang-hai ku-chi ch'u-pan-she, 1982, pp. 318–20.

Teng Kuang-ming 鄧廣銘. *Yüeh Fei chuan* 岳飛傳. Rev. ed. Peking: Jen-min ch'u-pan-she, 1983.

Teng, Ssu-yu 鄧嗣禹, and Knight Biggerstaff. *An annotated bibliography of selected Chinese reference works.* 3rd ed. Harvard-Yenching Institute Studies 2. Cambridge, Mass.: Harvard University Press, 1971.

Teraji Jun 寺地遵. *Nan Sung ch'u-ch'i cheng-chih-shih yen-chiu* 南宋初期政治史研究, trans. Liu Ching-chen 劉靜貞 and Li Chin-yun 李今芸. Shih-hsüeh ts'ung-shu hsi-lieh 史學叢書系列. Taipei: Tao-ho ch'u-pan-she, 1995.

Teraji Jun 寺地遵. *Nan-Sō seiken kakuritsu katei kenkyū oboegaki: Sō-Kin wagi, heiken kaishū, keikaihō no seijishiteki kōsatsu* 南宋政權確立過程研究覺書：宋金和議、兵權回收、経界法の政治史 的考察. Hiroshima Daigaku Bungakubu kiyō 広島大學文學部紀要 42. Hiroshima: Hiroshima Daigaku Bungakubu, 1982.

Teraji Jun 寺地遵. *Nan-Sō shoki seijishi kenkyū* 南宋初期政治史研究. Hiroshima: Keisuisha, 1988.

Tiao Chung-min 刁忠民. "Lun Sung Che-tsung chih Kao-tsung shih-ch'i chih t'ai-chien chih-tu" 論宋哲宗至高宗時期之台諫制度. *Ssu-ch'uan ta-hsüeh hsüeh-pao* 四川大學學報 105 (1999), pp. 61–9.

Tietze, Klaus-Peter. *Ssuch'uan vom 7. bis 10. Jahrhundert: Untersuchungen zur frühen Geschichte einer chinesischen Provinz.* Münchener Ostasiatische Studien Bd. 23. Wiesbaden: Franz Steiner Verlag, 1980.

Tillman, Hoyt C. *Confucian discourse and Chu Hsi's ascendancy.* Honolulu: University of Hawaii Press, 1992.

Tillman, Hoyt C. "Proto-nationalism in twelfth-century China? The case of Ch'en Liang." *Harvard Journal of Asiatic Studies* 39 No. 2 (1979), pp. 403–28.

Ting Ch'uan-ching 丁傳靖. *A compilation of anecdotes of Sung personalities*, ed. and trans. Chu Djang 鞠清遠 and Jane C. Djang. Taipei: St. John's University Press, 1989.

Ting Ch'uan-ching 丁傳靖. *Sung-jen i-shih hui-pien* 宋人軼事彙編. 1935. 3 vols. Peking: Chung-hua shu-chü, 1981.

Ting Ch'uan-ching 丁傳靖. *Sung-jen i-shih hui-pien* 宋人軼事彙編. 1935. 2 vols. Taipei: T'ai-wan shang-wu yin-shu-kuan, 1982.

T'o-t'o 脫脫, ed. *Chin shih* 金史. 1344. [*Po-na-pen* 百衲本 1930–7 ed.]. 8 vols. Peking: Chung-hua shu-chü, 1975.

T'o-t'o 脫脫 et al., eds. *Liao shih* 遼史. 1344. 5 vols. Erh-shih-ssu shih 二十四史 21. Peking: Chung-hua shu-chü, 1974.

T'o-t'o 脫脫 et al., eds. *Sung shih* 宋史. 1345. 40 vols. Erh-shih-ssu shih 二十四史 20. Peking: Chung-hua shu-chü, 1977.

Tonami Mamoru 礪波護. "Chang Chih-po." In *Sung biographies*, ed. Herbert Franke. 4 vols. Münchener Ostasiatische Studien 16, 1–3; 17, 4. Vol. 1. Wiesbaden: Franz Steiner Verlag, 1976, pp. 10–11.

Tonami Mamoru 礪波護. *FuDō* 馮道. Tokyo: Jinbutsu ōraisha, 1966.

Tonami Mamoru 礪波護. "Wang Tseng." In *Sung biographies*, ed. Herbert Franke. 4 vols. Münchener Ostasiatische Studien 16, 1–3; 17, 4. Vol. 3. Wiesbaden: Franz Steiner Verlag, 1976, pp. 1159–61.

Ts'ai Ch'ung-pang 蔡崇榜. *Sung-tai hsiu-shih chih-tu yen-chiu* 宋代修史制度研究. Ta-lu ti-ch'ü po-shih lun-wen ts'ung-k'an 大陸地區博士論文叢刊. Taipei: Wen-chin ch'u-pan-she, 1991.

Ts'ai Mei-piao 蔡美彪 et al. *Chung-kuo t'ung-shih: Ti wu ts'e* 中國通史：第五冊. 5th ed. Peking: Jen-min ch'u-pan-she, 1978.

Ts'ai Shang-hsiang 蔡上翔. *Wang Ching kung nien-p'u k'ao-lüeh* 王荊公年譜考略. 1804. Shanghai: Jen-min ch'u-pan-she, 1974.

Ts'ai T'ao 蔡絛. *T'ieh-wei shan ts'ung-t'an* 鐵圍山叢談. c. 1130, ed. Feng Hui-min 馮惠民 and Shen Hsi-lin 沈錫麟. T'ang Sung shih-liao pi-chi ts'ung-k'an 唐宋史料筆記叢刊. Peking: Chung-hua shu-chü, 1983.

Tsang Jung 臧嶸. "Lun Wu-tai ch'u-ch'i ti Pien-Chin cheng-heng" 論五代初期的汴晉爭衡. *Shih-hsüeh yüeh-k'an* 史學月刊 3 (1984), pp. 34–40.

Tseng Ch'iung-pi 曾瓊碧. *Ch'ien-ku tsui-jen Ch'in Kuei* 千古罪人秦檜. Cheng-chou: Ho-nan jen-min ch'u-pan-she, 1984.

Tseng Kung 曾鞏. *Tseng Kung chi* 曾鞏集. 1078–83. 2 vols. Chung-kuo ku-tien wen-hsüeh chi-pen ts'ung-shu 中國古典文學基本叢書. Peking: Chung-hua shu-chü, 1984.

Tseng Kung 曾鞏. *Yüan-feng lei-kao* 元豐類稿. c. 1038. Kuo-hsüeh chi-pen ts'ung-shu ssu-pai chung 國學基本叢書四百種 292. Taipei: T'ai-wan shang-wu yin-shu-kuan, 1968.

Tseng Min-hsing 曾敏行. *Tu-hsing tsa-chih* 獨醒雜志. c. 1175. [*Ts'ung-shu chi-ch'eng ch'u-pien* 叢書集成初編 1935–7 ed.]. Peking: Chung-hua shu-chü, 1985.

Tu Fan 杜範. *Ch'ing-hsien chi* 清獻集. [*Ssu-k'u ch'üan-shu* 四庫全書, *Wen-yüan ko* 文淵閣 1779 ed.]. In *Ssu-k'u ch'üan-shu chen-pen erh-chi* 四庫全書珍本二集. 1971. Vols. 302–3. Taipei: T'ai-wan shang-wu yin-shu-kuan, 1971.

Tu Wen-yü 杜文玉. "Lun Wu-tai shu-mi-shih" 論五代樞密使. *Chung-kuo shih yen-chiu* 中國史研究 1 (1988), pp. 63–73.

Twitchett, Denis C., ed. *The Cambridge history of China*. Volume 3: *Sui and T'ang China, 589–906, Part 1*. Cambridge: Cambridge University Press, 1979.

Twitchett, Denis C. "The Fan clan's charitable estate, 1050–1760." In *Confucianism in action*, ed. David S. Nivison and Arthur F. Wright. Stanford Studies in the Civilizations of Eastern Asia. Stanford, Calif.: Stanford University Press, 1959, pp. 97–133.

Twitchett, Denis C. *Financial administration under the T'ang dynasty*. 2nd ed. Cambridge: Cambridge University Press, 1970.

Twitchett, Denis C. "Varied patterns of provincial autonomy in the T'ang dynasty." In *Essays on T'ang society: The interplay of social, political and economic forces*, ed. John Curtis Perry and Bardwell L. Smith. Leiden: E. J. Brill, 1976, pp. 90–109.

Twitchett, Denis C., and Klaus-Peter Tietze. "The Liao." In *The Cambridge history of China*. Volume 6: *Alien regimes and border states, 907–1368*, ed. Herbert Franke and Denis C. Twitchett. New York: Cambridge University Press, 1994, pp. 43–153.

Umehara Kaoru 梅原郁. *Sōdai kanryō seido kenkyū* 宋代官僚制度研究. Tōyōshi kenkyū sōkan 東洋史研究叢刊 37. Kyoto: Dōhōsha, 1985.

Umehara Kaoru 梅原郁. "Sōdai no naizō to sazō" 宋代の内藏と左藏. *Tōhō gakuhō (Kyoto)* 東方学報京都 42 (1971), pp. 127–75.

Verellen, Franciscus. "A forgotten T'ang restoration: The Taoist dispensation after Huang Ch'ao." *Asia Major*, 3rd series, 7 No. 1 (1994), pp. 107–53.

Vierhaus, Rudolf. "Absolutism, History of." In *International encyclopedia of the social and behavioral sciences*, ed. Neil J. Smelser and Paul B. Baltes. 26 vols. Vol. 1. Amsterdam: Elsevier, 2001, pp. 5–9.

Vittinghoff, Helmolt. *Proskription und Intrige gegen Yüan-yu-Parteigänger: Ein Beitrag zu den zur Kontroversen nach den Reformen des Wang An-shih, dargestellt an den Biographien des Lu Tien (1042–1102) und des Ch'en Kuan (1057–1124)*. Würzburger Sino-Japonica 5. Bern: Herbert Lang, 1975.

von Glahn, Richard. *The country of streams and grottoes: Expansion, settlement, and the civilizing of the Sichuan frontier in Song times*. Harvard East Asian Monographs 123. Cambridge, Mass.: Council on East Asian Studies, Harvard University, 1987.

von Glahn, Richard. "The country of streams and grottoes: Geography, settlement, and the civilizing of China's southwestern frontier, 1000–1250." Diss., Yale University, 1983.

Wada Hisanori 和田久徳. "Tōdai ni okeru shihakushi no shōchi" 唐代における市舶司の創置. In *Wada Hakushi koki kinen Tōyōshi ronsō: Shōwa 35-nen 11-gatsu* 和田博士古稀紀念東洋史論叢：昭和35年11月, ed. Wada Hakushi Koki Kinen Tōyōshi Ronsō Hensan Iinkai 和田博士古稀紀念東洋史論叢編纂委員會. Tokyo: Kōdansha, 1961, pp. 1051–62.

Walton, Linda A. *Academies and society in Southern Sung China*. Honolulu: University of Hawaii Press, 1999.

Walton, Linda A. "The institutional context of Neo-Confucianism: Scholars, schools, and *shu-yüan* in Sung-Yüan China." In *Neo-Confucian education: The formative stage*, ed. Wm. Theodore de Bary and John W. Chaffee. Studies on China 9. Berkeley: University of California Press, 1989, pp. 457–92.

Wan Ssu-t'ung 萬斯同, comp. *Nan Sung liu-ling i-shih* 南宋六陵遺事. [1821–50 ed.]. Chao-tai ts'ung-shu 昭代叢書. Taipei: Kuang-wen shu-chü, 1968.

Wang An-li 王安理. *Wang Wei kung chi* 王魏公集. In *Yü-chang ts'ung-shu* 豫章叢書. Vols. 106–8. Nan-ch'ang: Te-lu, 1915–20.

Wang An-shih 王安石. *Wang Lin-ch'uan ch'üan-chi* 王臨川全集. c. 1100. 2nd ed. Taipei: Shih-chieh shu-chü, 1966.

Wang Ch'eng 王稱. *Tōto jiryaku* 東都事略. 1186, ed. and ann. Nagasawa Kikuya 長澤規矩也. [*Shinshūkan* 1849 ed.]. Wakokubon seishi 和刻本正史 1. Tokyo: Koten Kenkyūkai, 1973.

Wang Ch'eng 王稱. *Tung-tu shih-lüeh* 東都史略. 1186. Sung-shih tzu-liao ts'ui-pien ti i chi 宋史資料萃編第一輯 Vols. 11–14. Taipei: Wen-hai ch'u-pan-she, 1967.

Wang Chien-ch'iu 王建秋. "Sung-tai t'ai-hsüeh yü t'ai-hsüeh-sheng" 宋代太學與太學生. M.A. thesis, Fu-jen Ta-hsüeh 輔仁大學, 1965.

Wang Fu-chih 王夫之. *Sung lun* 宋論. c. 1690–2. Peking: Chung-hua shu-chü, 1964.

Wang Gungwu. "*The Chiu Wu-tai shih* and history-writing during the Five Dynasties." *Asia Major*, new series, 6 No. 1 (1958), pp. 1–22.

Wang Gungwu. "Feng Tao: An essay on Confucian loyalty." In *Confucian personalities*, ed. Arthur F. Wright and Denis C. Twitchett. Stanford Studies in the Civilizations of Eastern Asia. Stanford, Calif.: Stanford University Press, 1962, pp. 123–45.

Wang Gungwu. "The middle Yangtse in T'ang politics." In *Perspectives on the T'ang*, ed. Arthur F. Wright and Denis C. Twitchett. New Haven, Conn.: Yale University Press, 1973, pp. 193–235.

Wang Gungwu. "The rhetoric of a lesser empire: Early Sung relations with its neighbors." In *China among equals: The Middle Kingdom and its neighbors, 10th–14th centuries*, ed. Morris Rossabi. Berkeley: University of California Press, 1983, pp. 47–65.

Wang Gungwu. *The structure of power in north China during the Five Dynasties*. Kuala Lumpur: University of Malaya Press, 1963.

Wang Han 汪函. *Sung Che-tsung* 宋哲宗. Sung-ti lieh-chuan 宋帝列傳. Ch'ang-ch'un: Chi-lin wen-shih ch'u-pan-she, 1997.

Wang Huai-ling 汪槐齡. "Lun Sung T'ai-tsung" 論宋太宗. *Hsüeh-shu yüeh-k'an* 學術月刊 3 (1986), pp. 61–8.

Wang I-ch'eng 王以成. *Wang Chien shih-chi k'ao* 王堅史蹟考. Hsin-ying: Wang I-ch'eng, 1983.

Wang Jui-lai 王瑞來. "Lun Sung-tai hsiang-ch'üan" 論宋代相權. *Li-shih yen-chiu* 歷史研究 2 (1985), pp. 106–20.

Wang Min-hsin 王民信. "Liao Sung Shan-yüan meng-yüeh ti-chieh ti pei-ching (shang)" 遼宋澶淵盟約締結的背景(上). *Chung-kuo shu-mu chi-k'an* 中國書目季刊 9 No. 2 (1975), pp. 35–49.

Wang Min-hsin 王民信. "Liao Sung Shan-yüan meng-yüeh ti-chieh ti pei-ching (chung)" 遼宋澶淵盟約締結的背景(中). *Chung-kuo shu-mu chi-k'an* 中國書目季刊 9 No. 3 (1975), pp. 45–56.

Wang Min-hsin 王民信. "Liao Sung Shan-yüan meng-yüeh ti-chieh ti pei-ching (hsia)" 遼宋澶淵盟約締結的背景下(). *Chung-kuo shu-mu chi-k'an* 中國書目季刊 9 No. 4 (1975), pp. 53–64.

Wang Min-hsin 王民信. "Shan-yüan ti-meng chih chien-t'ao" 澶淵締盟之檢討. *Shih-huo yüeh-k'an* 食貨月刊 5 No. 3 (1975), pp. 1–12.

Wang Ming-ch'ing 王明清. *Hui-chu lu* 揮麈錄. 1194. Sung-tai shih-liao pi-chi tsung-k'an 宋代史料筆記叢刊. Peking: Chung-hua shu-chü, 1961.

Wang Po-ch'in 汪伯琴. "Sung ch'u erh-ti ch'üan-wei wen-t'i ti p'ou-hsi" 宋初二帝傳位問題的剖析. *Ta-lu tsa-chih* 大陸雜誌 32 No. 10 (1966), pp. 15–22.

Wang P'u 王溥. *Wu-tai hui-yao* 五代會要. 961. Shanghai: Shang-hai ku-chi ch'u-pan-she, 1978.

Wang Shou-nan 王壽南. "Lun wan T'ang Ch'iu Fu chih luan" 論晚唐裘甫之亂. *Kuo-li Cheng-chih ta-hsüeh hsüeh-pao* 國立政治大學學報 19 (1969), pp. 283–308.

Wang Te-i 王德毅. "Sung Hsiao-tsung chi ch'i shih-tai" 宋孝宗及其時代. *Kuo-li pien-i-kuan kuan-k'an* 國立編譯館館刊 2 No. 1 (1973), pp. 1–28.

Wang Tseng-yü 王曾瑜. "Lo, Shu, Shuo tang-cheng pien" 洛, 蜀, 朔黨爭辨. In *Chin-hsin-chi: Chang Cheng-lang hsien-sheng pa-shih ch'ing-shou lun-wen-chi* 盡心集：張政烺先生八十慶壽論文集, ed. Wu Jung-tseng 吳榮曾. Peking: Chung-kuo she-hui k'o-hsüeh ch'u-pan-she, 1996, pp. 351–69.

Wang Tseng-yü 王曾瑜. "Pei Sung ti Ssu-nung-ssu" 北宋的司農寺. In *Sung-shih yen-chiu lun-wen-chi: 1987 nien nien-hui pien-k'an* 宋史研究論文集：一九八七年年會編刊, ed. Teng Kuang-ming 鄧廣銘 et al. Shih-chia-chuang: Ho-pei chiao-yu ch'u-pan-she, 1989, pp. 8–35.

Wang Tseng-yü 王曾瑜. "Pei Sung wan-ch'i cheng-chih chien-lun" 北宋晚期政治簡論. *Chung-kuo shih yen-chiu* 中國史研究 4 (1994), pp. 82–7.

Wang Tseng-yü 王曾瑜. *Sung-ch'ao ping-chih ch'u-t'an* 宋朝兵制初探. Chung-hua li-shih ts'ung-shu 中華歷史叢書. Peking: Chung-hua shu-chü, 1983.

Wang Tseng-yü 王曾瑜. "Sung ya-ch'ien tsa-lun (1)" 宋衙前雜論(一). *Pei-ching shih-yüan hsüeh-pao* 北京師院學報 No. 3 (1986), pp. 76–82.

Wang Tseng-yü 王曾瑜. "Sung ya-ch'ien tsa-lun (2)" 宋衙前雜論(二). *Pei-ching shih-yüan hsüeh-pao* 北京師院學報 No. 1 (1987), pp. 49–57.

Wang Tseng-yü 王曾瑜. "Wang An-shih pien-fa chien-lun" 王安石變法簡論. *Chung-kuo she-hui k'o-hsüeh* 中國社會科學 3 (1980), pp. 131–54.

Wang Ts'un 王存. *Yüan-feng chiu-yü-chih* 元豐九域志. 1089. 2 vols. Chung-kuo ku-tai ti-li tsung-chih ts'ung-k'an 中國古代地理總志叢刊. Peking: Chung-hua shu-chü, 1984.

Wang Ying-lin 王應麟. *Yü-hai* 玉海. 1266. [1337 ed.]. 8 vols. Taipei: Hua-lien ch'u-pan-she, 1964.

Wang Yü-chi 王育濟. "Lun mu-ping chih-tu tui Pei Sung she-hui ti ying-hsiang" 論募兵制度對北宋社會的影響. *Chung-kuo che-hsüeh-shih yen-chiu* 中國哲學史研究 1 (1987), pp. 81–91.

Wang Yung 王庸. *Yen-i i-mou lu* 燕翼詒謀錄. c. 1227. Peking: Chung-hua shu-chü, 1981.

Wechsler, Howard J. *Offerings of jade and silk: Ritual and symbol in the legitimation of the T'ang dynasty*. New Haven, Conn.: Yale University Press, 1985.

Wei Liang-t'ao 魏良弢. "I-erh, erh-huang-ti" 義兒、兒皇帝. *Li-shih yen-chiu* 歷史研究 1 (1991), pp. 164–7.

Wei Liao-weng 魏了翁. *Ho-shan hsien-sheng ta ch'üan-chi* 鶴山先生大全集. 1249. [*Ssu-pu ts'ung-k'an ch'u-pien* 四部叢刊初編 1929 ed.]. In *Ssu-pu ts'ung-k'an cheng-pien* 四部叢刊正編. Vol. 60. Taipei: T'ai-wan shang-wu yin-shu-kuan, 1979.

Wen T'ien-hsiang 文天祥. *Wen T'ien-hsiang ch'üan-chi* 文天祥全集. 1560, ed. Lo Hung-hsien 羅洪先. Shanghai: Shih-chieh shu-chü, 1936.

Wen-ying 文瑩. *Hsiang-shan yeh-lu* 湘山野錄. c. 1073. Peking: Chung-hua shu-chü, 1984.

Wilhelm, Hellmut. "From myth to myth: The case of Yüeh Fei's biography." In *Confucian personalities*, ed. Arthur F. Wright and Denis C. Twitchett. Stanford Studies in the Civilizations of Eastern Asia. Stanford, Calif.: Stanford University Press, 1962, pp. 146–61.

Wilhelm, Richard. *The I Ching or Book of Changes*. 1950. Trans. Cary F. Baynes. 3rd ed. Bollingen Series 19. Princeton: Princeton University Press, 1977.

Williamson, Henry R. *Wang An Shih, a Chinese statesman and educationalist of the Sung dynasty*. 2 vols. Probsthain's Oriental Series 21–2. London: Arthur Probsthain, 1935–7.

Winkelman, John H. *The imperial library in Southern Sung China, 1127–1279: A study of the organization and operation of the scholarly agencies of the central government*. Transactions of the American Philosophical Society. Vol. 64, Part 8. Philadelphia: American Philosophical Society, 1974.

Wittfogel, Karl A., and Feng Chia-sheng. *History of Chinese society, Liao (907–1125)*. Transactions of the American Philosophical Society Vol. 36. Philadelphia: American Philosophical Society, 1949.

Wong Hon-chiu. "Government expenditures in Northern Sung China (960–1127)." Diss., University of Pennsylvania, 1975.

Worthy, Edmund H., Jr. "Diplomacy for survival: Domestic and foreign relations of Wu Yüeh, 907–978." In *China among equals: The Middle Kingdom and its neighbors, 10th–14th centuries*, ed. Morris Rossabi. Berkeley: University of California Press, 1983, pp. 17–44.

Worthy, Edmund H., Jr. "The founding of Sung China, 950–1000: Integrative changes in military and political institutions." Diss., Princeton University, 1976.

Worthy, Edmund H., Jr. "Regional control in the Southern Sung salt administration." In *Crisis and prosperity in Sung China*, ed. John W. Haeger. Tucson: University of Arizona Press, 1975, pp. 101–41.

Wu Chih-hao 吳之皥 et al. *(Wan-li) Ch'ung-hsiu Ssu-ch'uan tsung-chih* 萬歷重修四川總志. [National Diet Library Collection]. N.p.: n.p., 1619.

Wu Ching-hung 吳景宏. "Sung-Chin kung Liao chih wai-chiao" 宋金攻遼之外交. In *Sung-shih yen-chiu chi: Ti shih-erh chi* 宋史研究集：第十二輯, ed. Sung-shih tso-t'an-hui 宋史座談會. Chung-hua ts'ung-shu 中華叢書. Taipei: Kuo-li pien-i-kuan Chung-hua ts'ung-shu pien-shen wei-yüan-hui, 1980, pp. 169–83.

Wu Jen-ch'en 吳任臣. *Shih-kuo ch'un-ch'iu* 十國春秋. 1669. 4 vols. Peking: Chung-hua shu-chü, 1983.

Wu-kuo ku-shih 五國故事. c. 11th c. In *Chih-pu-tsu chai ts'ung-shu* 知不足齋叢書. Shanghai: Ku-shu liu-t'ung-ch'u, 1921.

Wu T'ien-ch'ih 吳天墀. *Hsi Hsia shih-kao* 西夏史稿. Ch'eng-tu: Ssu-ch'uan jen-min ch'u-pan-she, 1981.

Wu T'ien-ch'ih 吳天墀. *Hsin Hsi Hsia shih* 新西夏史. Taipei: Ta-tien ch'u-pan-she, 1987.

Wu Yung 吳泳. *Ho-lin chi* 鶴林集. Early 13th c. [*Ssu-k'u ch'üan-shu* 四庫全書, *Wen-yüan ko* 文淵閣 1779 ed.]. In *Ssu-k'u ch'üan-shu chen-pen ch'u-chi* 四庫全書珍本初集. 1934–5. Vols. 312–14. Taipei: T'ai-wan shang-wu yin-shu-kuan, 1969.

Yamauchi Masahiro. "Wang Ch'in-jo." In *Sung biographies*, ed. Herbert Franke. 4 vols. Münchener Ostasiatische Studien 16, 1–3; 17, 4. Vol. 3. Wiesbaden: Franz Steiner Verlag, 1976, pp. 1105–9.

Yamauchi Seibaku 山内正博. "Nan-Sō no Shisen ni okeru Chō Shun to Go Kai – sono seiryoku kōtai no katei o chūshi to shite" 南宋の四川における張浚と吳玠. *Shirin* 史林 44 No. 1 (1961), pp. 98–124.

Yanagida Setsuko 柳田節子. "Sōdai no teizei" 宋代の丁税. In *Sō-Gen gōsonsei no kenkyū* 宋元鄉村制の研究. Yanagida Setsuko 柳田節子. Tokyo: Sōbunsha, 1986, pp. 324–50.

Yang Chung-liang 楊仲良. *Tzu-chih t'ung-chien ch'ang-pien chi-shih pen-mo* 資治通鑑長編紀事本末. 1253. Sung-shih tzu-liao ts'ui-pien ti erh-chi 宋史資料萃編第二輯 Vols. 21–6. Taipei: Wen-hai ch'u-pan-she, 1967.

Yang Lien-sheng. "Female rulers in imperial China." *Harvard Journal of Asiatic Studies* 23 (1960–61), pp. 47–61.

Yang Lien-sheng. "Hostages in Chinese history." In *Studies in Chinese institutional history*, ed. Yang Lien-sheng. Harvard-Yenching Institute Studies 20. Cambridge, Mass.: Harvard University Press, 1961, pp. 43–57.

Yang Lien-sheng. *Money and credit in China: A short history*. Harvard-Yenching Institute Mongraph Series 12. Cambridge, Mass.: Harvard University Press, 1952.

Yang Lien-sheng. "The organization of Chinese official historiography: Principles and methods of the standard histories from the T'ang through the Ming dynasty." In *Historians of China and Japan*, ed. William G. Beasley and Edwin G. Pulleyblank. Historical Writing on the Peoples of Asia. London: Oxford University Press, 1961, pp. 44–59.

Yang Lien-sheng. "A 'posthumous letter' from the Chin emperor to the Khitan emperor in 942." *Harvard Journal of Asiatic Studies* 10 Nos. 3–4 (1947), pp. 418–28.

Yang Shih-ch'i 楊時奇. *Li-tai ming-ch'en tsou-i* 歷代名臣奏議. 1416. 6 vols. In *Chung-kuo shih-hsüeh ts'ung-shu* 中國史學叢書. Taipei: T'ai-wan hsüeh-sheng shu-chü, 1964.

Yang Te-ch'üan 楊德泉. "Chang Chün shih-chi shu-p'ing" 張浚事蹟述評. In *Sung-shih yen-chiu lun-wen-chi: 1982 nien nien-hui pien-k'an* 宋史研究論文集：一九八二年年會編刊, ed. Teng Kuang-ming 鄧廣銘 and Li Chia-chü 酈家駒. Cheng-chou: Ho-nan jen-min ch'u-pan-she, 1984, pp. 563–92.

Yang Te-ch'üan 楊德泉 and Liu Tzu-chien (James T. C. Liu) 劉子健. "The image of scholar-generals and a case in the Southern Sung." *Saeculum* 37 No. 2 (1986), pp. 182–91.

Yang Te-en 楊德恩. *Wen T'ien-hsiang nien-p'u* 文天祥年譜. 1937. 2nd ed. Chung-kuo shih-hsüeh ts'ung-shu 中國史學叢書. Shanghai: Shang-wu yin-shu-kuan, 1947.

Yang Wan-li 楊萬里. *Ch'eng-chai chi* 誠齋集. c. 1208. In *Ssu-pu ts'ung-k'an ch'u-pien* 四部叢刊初編. 1919–22. Shang-wu yin-shu-kuan. Vols. 64–5. Shanghai: Shang-wu ch'u-pan-she, 1929.

Yang Wei-li 楊偉立. *Ch'ien Shu Hou Shu shih* 前蜀後蜀史. Ssu-chuan li-shih ts'ung-shu 四川歷史叢書. Ch'eng-tu: Ssu-ch'uan sheng she-hui k'o-hsüeh-yüan ch'u-pan-she, 1986.

Yang Yüan 楊遠. "Pei Sung tsai-fu jen-wu ti ti-li fen-pu" 北宋宰輔人物的地理分佈. *Hsiang-kang Chung-wen ta-hsüeh Chung-kuo wen-hua yen-chiu-so hsüeh-pao* 香港中文大學中國文化研究所學報 13 (1982), pp. 147–211.

Yao Ts'ung-wu 姚從吾. "A-pao-chi yü Hou T'ang shih-ch'en Yao K'un hui-chien t'an-hua chi-lu" 阿保機與後唐使臣姚坤會見談話集錄. *Wen-shih-che hsüeh-pao* 文史哲學報 5 (1953), pp. 91–112.

Yao Ts'ung-wu 姚從吾. "Sung Meng Tiao-yü-ch'eng chan-i chung Hsiung-erh fu-jen chia shih chi Wang Li yü Ho-chou huo-te pao-ch'üan k'ao" 宋蒙釣魚城戰役中熊耳夫人家世及王立與合州獲得保全考. In *Sung-shih yen-chiu chi: Ti erh chi* 宋史研究集：第二輯, ed. Sung-shih tso-t'an-hui 宋史座談會. Chung-hua ts'ung-shu 中華叢書. Taipei: Chung-hua ts'ung-shu pien-shen wei-yüan-hui, 1964, pp. 123–40.

Yao Ying-t'ing 姚瀛艇. "Lun T'ang Sung chih-chi ti t'ien-ming yü fan-tien-ming ssu-hsiang" 論唐宋之際的天命與反天命思想. In *Sung-shih yen-chiu lun-wen-chi: 1982 nien nien-hui pien-k'an* 宋史研究論文集：一九八二年年會編刊, ed. Teng Kuang-ming 鄧廣銘

and Li Chia-chü 酈家駒. Cheng-chou: Ho-nan jen-min ch'u-pan-she, 1984, pp. 370–84.

Yeh Meng-te 葉夢得. *Pi-shu lu-hua* 避暑錄話. 1135. [*Ts'ung-shu chi-ch'eng ch'u-pien* 叢書集成初編 1935–7 ed.]. Peking: Chung-hua shu-chü, 1985.

Yeh Shih 業適. *Shui-hsin hsien-sheng wen-chi* 水心先生文集. 13th c. [*Ming Chia-ching* 嘉靖 1522–66 ed.; *Ssu-pu ts'ung-k'an* 四部叢刊 1929 ed.]. In *Ssu-pu ts'ung-k'an cheng-pien* 四部叢刊正編. Vol. 59. Taipei: T'ai-wan shang-wu yin-shu-kuan, 1979.

Yeh T'an 葉坦. "Lun Pei Sung 'ch'ien-huang'" 論北宋「錢荒」. *Chung-kuo shih yen-chiu* 中國史研究 No. 2 (1991), pp. 20–30.

Yen Ch'in-heng 閻沁恆. "Pei Sung tui Liao t'ang-ti she-shih chih yen-chiu" 北宋對遼榷場設施之研究. *Kuo-li Cheng-chih ta-hsüeh hsüeh-pao* 國立政治大學學報 8 (1963), pp. 247–58.

Yen Ch'in-heng 閻沁恆. "Sung-tai tsou-ma ch'eng-shou kung-chih k'ao" 宋代走馬承受公事考. *Kuo-li Cheng-chih ta-hsüeh hsüeh-pao* 國立政治大學學報 9 (1964), pp. 319–37.

Yü Tsung-hsien 儉宗憲. "Lun Wang An-shih mien-i fa" 論王安石免役法. In *Sung-shih lun-chi* 宋史論集, ed. Chung-chou shu-hua-she 中州書畫社. Sung-shih yen-chiu ts'ung-shu 宋史研究叢書. Cheng-chou: Chung-chou shu-hua-she, 1983, pp. 107–23.

Yüan Chüeh 袁桷. *Yen-yu Ssu-ming chih* 延祐四明志. 1320. In *Sung Yüan ti-fang-chih ts'ung-shu* 宋元地方志叢書. 9. Taipei: Chung-kuo ti-chih yen-chiu-hui, 1978.

Yüan-feng kuan-chih 元豐官志. 1081. [Kyoto University photocopy of T'ai-pei kuo-li chung-yang t'u-shu-kuan holding]. N.p.: n.p., 1972.

Yüan Hsieh 袁燮. *Chieh-chai chi* 絜齋集. c. 12th c. [*Ssu-k'u ch'üan-shu* 四庫全書, *Wen-yüan ko* 文淵閣 1779 ed.]. In *Ssu-k'u ch'üan-shu chen-pen pieh-chi* 四庫全書珍本別集. Vols. 341–6. Taipei: T'ai-wan shang-wu yin-shu-kuan, 1975.

Yüan I-t'ang 袁一堂. "Pei Sung ch'ien-huang: ts'ung pi-chih tao liu-t'ung t'i-chih ti k'ao-ch'a" 北宋錢荒：從幣制到流通體制的考察. *Li-shih yen-chiu* 歷史研究 No. 4 (1991), pp. 129–40.

Yüeh Shih 樂史. *T'ai-p'ing huan-yü chi* 太平寰宇記. c. 980. [Edited by Ch'en Lan-sen 陳蘭森 1793 ed.]. 2 vols. Taipei: Wen-hai ch'u-pan-she, 1963.

Yüeh Shih 樂史. *Ying Sung-pen T'ai-p'ing Huan-yü-chi pu-ch'üeh* 影宋本太平寰宇記補闕. c. 980. [A supplement of the missing chapters of the *T'ai-p'ing huan-yü-chi* 1882–4 ed.]. Taipei: Wen-hai ch'u-pan-she, 1963.

Yung-le ta-tien 永樂大典. 1408. 202 vols. Peking: Chung-hua shu-chü, 1960.

GLOSSARY–INDEX